World Trade and Investment Law

Documents

World Trade and Investment Law

– Documents –

edited by

Professor Dr. Frank Emmert, LL.M., FCIArb

**the John S. Grimes Professor of Law
& Director of the Center for International and Comparative Law
at Indiana University Robert H. McKinney School of Law**

**and the President and CEO of
the International Smart Mediation and Arbitration Institute, Indianapolis**

1st ed. 2018

Published by
Council on International Law and Politics, LL.C.
55 East 70th Street
Indianapolis, IN 46220
http://www.cilpnet.com

Publications Coordinator: Salma Taman

Cover design: Salma Taman
Cover art: Frank Emmert, for more information see http://www.TheIMACGallery.com

Font Myriad Pro

Printed by CreateSpace

ISBN: 978-0-9858156-7-7

for Salma
always & forever

Part One: General Trade and Investment Law

I. General Principles Concerning the Rights and Duties of States
1. 1945 Charter of the United Nations (excerpts) 1
2. 1959 OECD Draft Convention on Investment Abroad
   (Abs-Shawcross Convention) 3
3. 1962 UN General Assembly Resolution on Permanent Sovereignty
   over Natural Resources 6
4. 1969 Vienna Convention on the Law of Treaties 9
5. 1974 UN General Assembly Resolution on the Establishment of
   a New International Economic Order 29
6. 1974 UN General Assembly Charter of Economic Rights and Duties of States 32
7. 2001 International Law Commission Draft Articles on Responsibility of States
   for Internationally Wrongful Acts 41

II. Early Examples of Trade and Investment Treaties: Turkish and Chinese Capitulations (1st
generation bilateral investment treaties (BITs))
1. 1661 Ottoman Capitulations [excerpts] 50
2. 1838 Treaty of Balta Liman Between the UK and the Ottoman Empire 57
3. 1842 Treaty of Nanjing 61
4. 1843 Treaty of the Bogue Between the UK and China 64

**III. More Modern and More Balanced Treaties of Friendship, Commerce and Navigation
(FCNs)** (2nd generation BITs)
1. 1853 U.S. - Argentina Treaty of Friendship, Commerce and Navigation 70
2. 1954 U.S. – Germany Treaty of Friendship, Commerce and Navigation 74

IV. 20th Century Bilateral Investment Treaties (BITs) (3rd generation BITs)
1. 1959 Germany – Pakistan Bilateral Investment Treaty 86
2. 2008 German Model BIT 91

V. 21st Century Bilateral Investment Treaties (BITs) (4th generation BITs)
1. 2007 Norway Model BIT..97
2. 2012 U.S. Model BIT 109

VI. Multilateral International Investment Treaties (IITs)
1. 1985 Multilateral Investment Guarantee Agency (MIGA) Convention 134
2. 1998 OECD Multilateral Agreement on Investment (MAI) (draft) 155

VII. Relevant International Labor Treaties and Conventions
1. 1998 ILO Declaration on Fundamental Principles and Rights at Work 193
2. 2008 ILO Declaration on Social Justice for a Fair Globalization 196
3. 1977 Tripartite Declaration of Principles Concerning Multinational
   Enterprises and Social Policy (as amended in 2017)... 201

VIII. Relevant International Environmental Treaties and Conventions
1. 1994 Energy Charter Treaty 211
2. 2015 International Energy Charter 240

IX. Dispute Settlement
1. 1958 UN Convention on the Recognition and Enforcement
   of Foreign Arbitral Awards (New York Convention) 248
2. 1965 Convention on the Settlement of Investment Disputes between States
   and Nationals of other States (ICSID) 252
3. ICSID Rules of Procedure for Conciliation and Arbitration Proceedings 265
4. 2013 UNCITRAL Rules on Transparency in Investor-State Arbitration 318

X. Other Relevant National and International Rules and Guidelines
1. 1976 OECD Guidelines for Multinational Enterprises 324
2. 1977 U.S. Foreign Corrupt Practices Act (excerpts) 333
3. 1999 OECD Principles of Corporate Governance 346
4. 1999 OECD Convention on Combating Bribery of Foreign Public
   Officials in International Business Transactions 375
5. 2000 UN Global Compact 380
6. 2005 UN Convention Against Corruption 382
7. 2011 UN Guiding Principles on Business and Human Rights 415
8. 2014 Norwegian Guidelines for Observation and Exclusion of Companies 435

XI. Examples of Regional Free Trade and Investment Agreements
1. 2003 U.S. – Chile Free Trade Agreement (excerpts) 439
2. 1992 NAFTA Agreement (excerpts) 462
3. 2009 ASEAN Comprehensive Investment Agreement 479

Part Two: GATT and WTO Law

XII. Main WTO Documents Resulting from the Uruguay Round
1. Marrakesh Declaration of 15 April 1994 500
2. Final Act Embodying the Results of the Uruguay Round
   of Multilateral Trade Negotiations 502
3. Marrakesh Agreement Establishing the World Trade Organization 503

XIII. Annexes
1. Annex 1A Multilateral Agreements on Trade in Goods 512
   General Agreement on Tariffs and Trade (GATT) 1994 512
   General Agreement on Tariffs and Trade (GATT) 1947 514
   Agreement on Agriculture 550
   Agreement on the Application of Sanitary and Phytosanitary (SPS)
       Measures 561
   Agreement on Technical Barriers to Trade (TBT) 571
   Agreement on Trade-Related Investment Measures (TRIMs) 587
   Agreement on Implementation of Article VI of the GATT 1947
       (Antidumping) 590
   Agreement on Implementation of Article VII of the GATT 1947
       (Valuation) 609
   Agreement on Preshipment Inspection 629
   Agreement on Rules of Origin 636
   Agreement on Import Licensing Procedures 644
   Agreement on Subsidies and Countervailing Measures 650
   Agreement on Safeguards 683
2. Annex 1B General Agreement on Trade in Services 690
3. Annex 1C Agreement on Trade-Related Aspects of Intellectual Property
   Rights (TRIPs) 715
4. Annex 2 Understanding on Rules and Procedures Governing
   the Settlement of Disputes 739
5. Annex 3 Trade Policy Review Mechanism ....[omitted]
6. Annex 4 Plurilateral Trade Agreements ....[omitted]

I. General Principles Concerning the Rights and Duties of States

I.1. 1945 CHARTER OF THE UNITED NATIONS (excerpts)
I UNTS XVI

Preamble

WE THE PEOPLES OF THE UNITED NATIONS

DETERMINED to save succeeding generations from the scourge of war, which twice in our life-time has brought untold sorrow to mankind, and

to reaffirm faith in fundamental human rights, in the dignity and worth of the human person, in the equal rights of men and women and of nations large and small, and

to establish conditions under which justice and respect for the obligations arising from treaties and other sources of international law can be maintained, and

to promote social progress and better standards of life in larger freedom,

AND FOR THESE ENDS

to practice tolerance and live together in peace with one another as good neighbours, and

to unite our strength to maintain international peace and security, and

to ensure, by the acceptance of principles and the institution of methods, that armed force shall not be used, save in the common interest, and

to employ international machinery for the promotion of the economic and social advancement of all peoples,

HAVE RESOLVED TO COMBINE OUR EFFORTS TO ACCOMPLISH THESE AIMS

Accordingly, our respective Governments, through representatives assembled in the city of San Francisco, who have exhibited their full powers found to be in good and due form, have agreed to the present Charter of the United Nations and do hereby establish an international organiza-tion to be known as the United Nations.

CHAPTER I: PURPOSES AND PRINCIPLES

Article 1

The Purposes of the United Nations are:

1) To maintain international peace and security, and to that end: to take effective collective measures for the prevention and removal of threats to the peace, and for the suppression of acts of aggression or other breaches of the peace, and to bring about by peaceful means, and in con-formity with the principles of justice and international law, adjustment or settlement of inter-national disputes or situations which might lead to a breach of the peace;

2) To develop friendly relations among nations based on respect for the principle of equal rights and self-determination of peoples, and to take other appropriate measures to strengthen universal peace;

3) To achieve international co-operation in solving international problems of an economic, social, cultural, or humanitarian character, and in promoting and encouraging respect for human rights and for fundamental freedoms for all without distinction as to race, sex, language, or religion; and

4) To be a centre for harmonizing the actions of nations in the attainment of these common ends.

Article 2

The Organization and its Members, in pursuit of the Purposes stated in Article 1, shall act in accordance with the following Principles.

1)   The Organization is based on the principle of the sovereign equality of all its Members.

2)   All Members, in order to ensure to all of them the rights and benefits resulting from membership, shall fulfill in good faith the obligations assumed by them in accordance with the present Charter.

3)   All Members shall settle their international disputes by peaceful means in such a manner that international peace and security, and justice, are not endangered.

4)   All Members shall refrain in their international relations from the threat or use of force against the territorial integrity or political independence of any state, or in any other manner inconsistent with the Purposes of the United Nations.

5)   All Members shall give the United Nations every assistance in any action it takes in accordance with the present Charter, and shall refrain from giving assistance to any state against which the United Nations is taking preventive or enforcement action.

6)   The Organization shall ensure that states which are not Members of the United Nations act in accordance with these Principles so far as may be necessary for the maintenance of international peace and security.

7)   Nothing contained in the present Charter shall authorize the United Nations to intervene in matters which are essentially within the domestic jurisdiction of any state or shall require the Members to submit such matters to settlement under the present Charter; but this principle shall not prejudice the application of enforcement measures under Chapter VII.

[...]

I.2. 1959 OECD DRAFT CONVENTION ON INVESTMENT ABROAD

(Abs–Shawcross Convention)

The High Contracting Parties:

Believing that peace, security, and progress in the world can only be attained and ensured by fruitful co-operation between all peoples on a basis of international law and mutual confidence;

Appreciating also the importance of encouraging commercial relations and promoting the flow of capital for economic activity and development; and considering the contribution which may be made towards these-ends by a restatement of principles of conduct relating to foreign investments;

Have resolved for this purpose to conclude the present Convention.

Article I

Each Party shall at all times ensure fair and equitable treatment to the property of the nationals of the other Parties. Such property shall be accorded the most constant protection and security within the territories shall not in any way be impaired by unreasonable or discriminatory measures.

Article II

Each Party shall at all times ensure the observance of any undertakings, which it may have given in relation to investments made by nationals of any other Party.

Article III

No Party shall take any measures against nationals of another Party to deprive them directly or indirectly of their property except under due process of law and provided that such measures are not discriminatory or contrary to undertakings given by that Party and are accompanied by the payment of just and effective compensation. Adequate provision shall have been made at or prior to the time of deprivation for the prompt determination and payment of such compensation, which shall represent the genuine value of the property affected, be made in transferable form, and be paid without undue delay.

Article IV

Any breach of this Convention shall entail the obligation to make full reparation. The Parties shall not recognise or enforce within their territories any measures conflicting with the principles of this Convention and affecting the property of nationals of any of the Parties until reparation is made or secured.

Article V

No Party may take measures derogating from the present Convention unless it is involved in war, hostilities, or other public emergency, which threatens its life; and such measures shall be limited in extent and duration to those strictly required by the exigencies of the situation. Nothing in this Article shall be construed as superseding the generally accepted laws of war.

Article VI

The provisions of this Convention shall not prejudice the application of any present or future treaty or municipal law under which more favourable treatment is accorded to nationals of any of the Parties.

Article VII

1.   Any dispute as to the interpretation or application of the present Convention may, with the consent of the interested Parties, be submitted to an Arbitral Tribunal set up in accordance with the provisions of the Annex to this Convention. Such consent may take the form of specific agreements or of unilateral declarations. In the absence of such consent or of agreement for settlement by other specific means, the dispute may be submitted by either Party to the International Court of Justice.

2.   A national of one of the Parties claiming that he has been injured by measures in breach of this Convention may institute proceedings against the Party responsible for such measures before the Arbitral Tribunal referred to in paragraph 1 of this Article, provided that the Party against which the claim is made has declared that it accepts the jurisdiction of the said Arbitral Tribunal in respect of claims by nationals of one or more Parties, including the Party concerned.

Article VIII

If a Party against which a judgement or award is given fails to comply with the terms thereof, the other Parties shall be entitled, individually or collectively, to take such measures as are strictly required to give effect to that judgement or award.

Article IX

For the purposes of this Convention,

a.   "nationals" in relation to a Party includes (i) companies which under the municipal law of that Party are considered national companies of that Party and (ii) companies in which nationals of that Party have directly or indirectly a controlling interest.

"Companies" includes both juridical persons recognised as such by the law of a Party and associations even if they do not possess legal personality.

b.   "property" includes all property, rights, and interests, whether held directly or indirectly. A member of a company shall be deemed to have an interest in the property of the company.

Article X

Final clauses relating to ratification, entry into force, accession, deposit, etc.

ANNEX RELATING TO THE ARBITRAL TRIBUNAL

1.   The Arbitral Tribunal referred to in Article VII of the Convention shall consist of three persons appointed as follows: one arbitrator shall be appointed by each of the parties to the arbitration proceedings; a third arbitrator (hereinafter sometimes called "the Umpire") shall be appointed by agreement of the parties or, if they shall not agree, by the President of the International Court of Justice, or failing appointment by him, by the Secretary-General of the United Nations. If either of the parties shall fail to appoint an arbitrator, such arbitrator shall be appointed by the Umpire. In case any arbitrator appointed in accordance with this Article shall resign, die, or become unable to act, a, successor arbitrator shall be appointed in the same manner as herein prescribed for the appointment of the original arbitrator and such successor shall have all the powers and duties of such original arbitrator.

2.   Arbitration proceedings may be instituted upon notice by the party instituting such proceedings (whether a Party to the Convention or a national of a Party to the Convention, as the case may be) to the other-party. Such notice shall contain a statement setting forth the nature of the relief sought, and the name of the arbitrator appointed by the party instituting such proceedings.

Within 30 days after the giving of such notice, the adverse party shall notify the party instituting proceedings of the name of the arbitrator appointed by such adverse party.

3.   If, within 60 days after the giving of such notice instituting the arbitration proceedings, the parties shall not have agreed upon an Umpire, either party may request the appointment of an Umpire as provided in, Article 1 of this Annex.

4.   The Arbitral Tribunal shall convene at such time and place as shall be fixed by the Umpire.

Thereafter, the Arbitral Tribunal shall determine where and when it shall sit.

5.   Subject to the provisions of this Annex and except as the parties shall otherwise agree, the Arbitral Tribunal, shall decide all questions relating to its competence and, shall determine its procedure and all questions relating to costs. All decisions of the Arbitral Tribunal shall be by majority vote.

6.   The Arbitral Tribunal shall afford to all parties a fair hearing and shall render its award in writing. Such award may be rendered by default. An award signed by the majority of the Arbitral Tribunal shall constitute the award of such Tribunal. A signed counterpart of the award shall be transmitted to each party. Any such award rendered in accordance with the provisions of this Annex shall be final and binding upon the parties and shall be published. Each party shall abide by and comply with any such award rendered by the Arbitral Tribunal.

I.3. PERMANENT SOVEREIGNTY OVER NATURAL RESOURCES

United Nations General Assembly Resolution 1803 (XVII) of 14 December 1962

The General Assembly,

Recalling its resolutions 523 (VI) of 12 January 1952 and 626 (VII) of 21 December 1952,

Bearing in mind its resolution 1314 (XIII) of 12 December 1958, by which it established the Commission on Permanent Sovereignty over Natural Resources and instructed it to conduct a full survey of the status of permanent sovereignty over natural wealth and resources as a basic constituent of the right to self-determination, with recommendations, where necessary, for its strengthening, and decided further that, in the conduct of the full survey of the status of the permanent sovereignty of peoples and nations over their natural wealth and resources, due regard should be paid to the rights and duties of States under international law and to the importance of encouraging international co-operation in the economic development of developing countries,

Bearing in mind its resolution 1515 (XV) of 15 December 1960, in which it recommended that the sovereign right of every State to dispose of its wealth and its natural resources should be respected,

Considering that any measure in this respect must be based on the recognition of the inalienable right of all States freely to dispose of their natural wealth and resources in accordance with their national interests, and on respect for the economic independence of States,

Considering that nothing in paragraph 4 below in any way prejudices the position of any Member State on any aspect of the question of the rights and obligations of successor States and Governments in respect of property acquired before the accession to complete sovereignty of countries formerly under colonial rule,

Noting that the subject of succession of States and Governments is being examined as a matter of priority by the International Law Commission,

Considering that it is desirable to promote international co-operation for the economic development of developing countries, and that economic and financial agreements between the developed and the developing countries must be based on the principles of equality and of the right of peoples and nations to self-determination,

Considering that the provision of economic and technical assistance, loans and increased foreign investment must not be subject to conditions which conflict with the interests of the recipient State,

Considering the benefits to be derived from exchanges of technical and scientific information likely to promote the development and use of such resources and wealth, and the important part which the United Nations and other international organizations are called upon to play in that connexion,

Attaching particular importance to the question of promoting the economic development of developing countries and securing their economic independence,

Noting that the creation and strengthening of the inalienable sovereignty of States over their natural wealth and resources reinforces their economic independence,

Desiring that there should be further consideration by the United Nations of the subject of permanent sovereignty over natural resources in the spirit of international co-operation in the field of economic development, particularly that of the developing countries,

I

Declares that:

1.   The right of peoples and nations to permanent sovereignty over their natural wealth and resources must be exercised in the interest of their national development and of the well-being of the people of the State concerned.

2.   The exploration, development and disposition of such resources, as well as the import of the foreign capital required for these purposes, should be in conformity with the rules and conditions which the peoples and nations freely consider to be necessary or desirable with regard to the authorization, restriction or prohibition of such activities.

3.   In cases where authorization is granted, the capital imported and the earnings on that capital shall be governed by the terms thereof, by the national legislation in force, and by international law. The profits derived must be shared in the proportions freely agreed upon, in each case, between the investors and the recipient State, due care being taken to ensure that there is no impairment, for any reason, of that State's sovereignty over its natural wealth and resources.

4.   Nationalization, expropriation or requisitioning shall be based on grounds or reasons of public utility, security or the national interest which are recognized as overriding purely individual or private interests, both domestic and foreign. In such cases the owner shall be paid appropriate compensation, in accordance with the rules in force in the State taking such measures in the exercise of its sovereignty and in accordance with international law. In any case where the question of compensation gives rise to a controversy, the national jurisdiction of the State taking such measures shall be exhausted. However, upon agreement by sovereign States and other parties concerned, settlement of the dispute should be made through arbitration or international adjudication.

5.   The free and beneficial exercise of the sovereignty of peoples and nations over their natural resources must be furthered by the mutual respect of States based on their sovereign equality.

6.   International co-operation for the economic development of developing countries, whether in the form of public or private capital investments, exchange of goods and services, technical assistance, or exchange of scientific information, shall be such as to further their independent national development and shall he based upon respect for their sovereignty over their natural wealth and resources.

7.   Violation of the rights of peoples and nations to sovereignty over their natural wealth and resources is contrary to the spirit and principles of the Charter of the United Nations and hinders the development of international cooperation and the maintenance of peace.

8.   Foreign investment agreements freely entered into by or between sovereign States shall be observed in good faith; States and international organizations shall strictly and conscientiously respect the sovereignty of peoples and nations over their natural wealth and resources in accordance with the Charter and the principles set forth in the present resolution.

II

Welcomes the decision of the International Law Commission to speed up its work on the codification of the topic of responsibility of States for the consideration of the General Assembly;

III

Requests the Secretary-General to continue the study of the various aspects of permanent sovereignty over natural resources, taking into account the desire of Member States to ensure the protection of their sovereign rights while encouraging international co-operation in the field of economic development, and to report to the Economic and Social Council and to the General Assembly, if possible at its eighteenth session.

1194th plenary meeting,
14 December 1962.

I.4. 1969 Vienna Convention on the Law of Treaties

done at Vienna, 23 May 1969; entered into force 27 January 1980; 1155 UNTS 331

The States Parties to the present Convention,

Considering the fundamental role of treaties in the history of international relations,

Recognizing the ever-increasing importance of treaties as a source of international law and as a means of developing peaceful cooperation among nations, whatever their constitutional and social systems,

Noting that the principles of free consent and of good faith and the *pacta sunt servanda* rule are universally recognized,

Affirming that disputes concerning treaties, like other international disputes, should be settled by peaceful means and in conformity with the principles of justice and international law,

Recalling the determination of the peoples of the United Nations to establish conditions under which justice and respect for the obligations arising from treaties can be maintained,

Having in mind the principles of international law embodied in the Charter of the United Nations, such as the principles of the equal rights and self-determination of peoples, of the sovereign equality and independence of all States, of non-interference in the domestic affairs of States, of the prohibition of the threat or use of force and of universal respect for, and observance of, human rights and fundamental freedoms for all,

Believing that the codification and progressive development of the law of treaties achieved in the present Convention will promote the purposes of the United Nations set forth in the Charter, namely, the maintenance of international peace and security, the development of friendly relations and the achievement of cooperation among nations,

Affirming that the rules of customary international law will continue to govern questions not regulated by the provisions of the present Convention,

Have agreed as follows:

Part I. Introduction

Article 1 Scope of the Present Convention

The present Convention applies to treaties between States.

Article 2 Use of Terms

1. For the purposes of the present Convention:

(a) 'treaty' means an international agreement concluded between States in written form and governed by international law, whether embodied in a single instrument or in two or more related instruments and whatever its particular designation;

(b) 'ratification', 'acceptance', 'approval' and 'accession' mean in each case the international act so named whereby a State establishes on the international plane its consent to be bound by a treaty;

(c) 'full powers' means a document emanating from the competent authority of a State designating a person or persons to represent the State for negotiating, adopting or authenticating the text of a treaty, for expressing the consent of the State to be bound by a treaty, or for accomplishing any other act with respect to a treaty;

(d) 'reservation' means a unilateral statement, however phrased or named, made by a State, when signing, ratifying, accepting, approving or acceding to a treaty, whereby it purports to exclude or to modify the legal effect of certain provisions of the treaty in their application to that State;

(e) 'negotiating State' means a State which took part in the drawing up and adoption of the text of the treaty;

(f) 'contracting State' means a State which has consented to be bound by the treaty, whether or not the treaty has entered into force;

(g) 'party' means a State which has consented to be bound by the treaty and for which the treaty is in force;

(h) 'third State' means a State not a party to the treaty;

(i) 'international organization' means an intergovernmental organization.

2.   The provisions of paragraph 1 regarding the use of terms in the present Convention are without prejudice to the use of those terms or to the meanings which may be given to them in the internal law of any State.

Article 3 International Agreements Not Within the Scope of the Present Convention

The fact that the present Convention does not apply to international agreements concluded between States and other subjects of international law or between such other subjects of international law, or to international agreements not in written form, shall not affect:

(a) the legal force of such agreements;

(b) the application to them of any of the rules set forth in the present Convention to which they would be subject under international law independently of the Convention;

(c) the application of the Convention to the relations of States as between themselves under international agreements to which other subjects of international law are also parties.

Article 4 Non-Retroactivity of the Present Convention

Without prejudice to the application of any rules set forth in the present Convention to which treaties would be subject under international law independently of the Convention, the Convention applies only to treaties which are concluded by States after the entry into force of the present Convention with regard to such States.

Article 5 Treaties Constituting International Organizations and Treaties Adopted Within an International Organization

The present Convention applies to any treaty which is the constituent instrument of an international organization and to any treaty adopted within an international organization without prejudice to any relevant rules of the organization.

Part II. Conclusion and Entry into Force of Treaties

SECTION 1. CONCLUSION OF TREATIES

Article 6 Capacity of States to Conclude Treaties

Every State possesses capacity to conclude treaties.

Article 7 Full Powers

1.   A person is considered as representing a State for the purpose of adopting or authenticating the text of a treaty or for the purpose of expressing the consent of the State to be bound by a treaty if:

(a)   he produces appropriate full powers; or

(b)   it appears from the practice of the States concerned or from other circumstances that their intention was to consider that person as representing the State for such purposes and to dispense with full powers.

2.   In virtue of their functions and without having to produce full powers, the following are considered as representing their State:

(a)   Heads of State, Heads of Government and Ministers for Foreign Affairs, for the purpose of performing all acts relating to the conclusion of a treaty;

(b)   heads of diplomatic missions, for the purpose of adopting the text of a treaty between the accrediting State and the State to which they are accredited;

(c)   representatives accredited by States to an international conference or to an international organization or one of its organs, for the purpose of adopting the text of a treaty in that conference, organization or organ.

Article 8 Subsequent Confirmation of an Act Performed Without Authorization

An act relating to the conclusion of a treaty performed by a person who cannot be considered under article 7 as authorized to represent a State for that purpose is without legal effect unless afterwards confirmed by that State.

Article 9 Adoption of the Text

1.   The adoption of the text of a treaty takes place by the consent of all the States participating in its drawing up except as provided in paragraph 2.

2.   The adoption of the text of a treaty at an international conference takes place by the vote of two-thirds of the States present and voting, unless by the same majority they shall decide to apply a different rule.

Article 10 Authentication of the Text

The text of a treaty is established as authentic and definitive:

(a)   by such procedure as may be provided for in the text or agreed upon by the States parti-cipating in its drawing up; or

(b)   failing such procedure, by the signature, signature ad referendum or initialling by the representatives of those States of the text of the treaty or of the Final Act of a conference incorporating the text.

Article 11 Means of Expressing Consent to Be Bound by a Treaty

The consent of a State to be bound by a treaty may be expressed by signature, exchange of instruments constituting a treaty, ratification, acceptance, approval or accession, or by any other means if so agreed.

Article 12 Consent to Be Bound by a Treaty Expressed by Signature

1.   The consent of a State to be bound by a treaty is expressed by the signature of its representative when:

(a)   the treaty provides that signature shall have that effect;

(b)   it is otherwise established that the negotiating States were agreed that signature should have that effect; or

(c)   the intention of the State to give that effect to the signature appears from the full powers of its representative or was expressed during the negotiation.

2.   For the purposes of paragraph 1:

(a)   the initialling of a text constitutes a signature of the treaty when it is established that the negotiating States so agreed;

(b)   the signature ad referendum of a treaty by a representative, if confirmed by his State, constitutes a full signature of the treaty.

Article 13 Consent to Be Bound by a Treaty Expressed by an Exchange of Instruments Constituting a Treaty

The consent of States to be bound by a treaty constituted by instruments exchanged between them is expressed by that exchange when:

(a)   the instruments provide that their exchange shall have that effect; or

(b)   it is otherwise established that those States were agreed that the exchange of instruments should have that effect.

Article 14 Consent to Be Bound by a Treaty Expressed by Ratification, Acceptance or Approval

1.   The consent of a State to be bound by a treaty is expressed by ratification when:

(a)   the treaty provides for such consent to be expressed by means of ratification;

(b)   it is otherwise established that the negotiating States were agreed that ratification should be required;

(c)   the representative of the State has signed the treaty subject to ratification; or

(d)   the intention of the State to sign the treaty subject to ratification appears from the full powers of its representative or was expressed during the negotiation.

2.   The consent of a State to be bound by a treaty is expressed by acceptance or approval under conditions similar to those which apply to ratification.

Article 15 Consent to Be Bound by a Treaty Expressed by Accession

The consent of a State to be bound by a treaty is expressed by accession when:

(a)   the treaty provides that such consent may be expressed by that State by means of accession;

(b)   it is otherwise established that the negotiating States were agreed that such consent may be expressed by that State by means of accession; or

(c)   all the parties have subsequently agreed that such consent may be expressed by that State by means of accession.

Article 16 Exchange or Deposit of Instruments of Ratification, Acceptance, Approval or Accession

Unless the treaty otherwise provides, instruments of ratification, acceptance, approval or accession establish the consent of a State to be bound by a treaty upon:

(a) their exchange between the contracting States;

(b) their deposit with the depositary; or

(c) their notification to the contracting States or to the depositary, if so agreed.

Article 17 Consent to Be Bound by Part of a Treaty and Choice of Differing Provisions

1. Without prejudice to articles 19 to 23, the consent of a State to be bound by part of a treaty is effective only if the treaty so permits or the other contracting States so agree.

2. The consent of a State to be bound by a treaty which permits a choice between differing provisions is effective only if it is made clear to which of the provisions the consent relates.

Article 18 Obligation Not to Defeat the Object and Purpose of a Treaty Prior to its Entry into Force

A State is obliged to refrain from acts which would defeat the object and purpose of a treaty when:

(a) it has signed the treaty or has exchanged instruments constituting the treaty subject to ratification, acceptance or approval, until it shall have made its intention clear not to become a party to the treaty; or

(b) it has expressed its consent to be bound by the treaty, pending the entry into force of the treaty and provided that such entry into force is not unduly delayed.

SECTION 2. RESERVATIONS

Article 19 Formulation of Reservations

A State may, when signing, ratifying, accepting, approving or acceding to a treaty, formulate a reservation unless:

(a) the reservation is prohibited by the treaty;

(b) the treaty provides that only specified reservations, which do not include the reservation in question, may be made; or

(c) in cases not falling under sub-paragraphs (a) and (b), the reservation is incompatible with the object and purpose of the treaty.

Article 20 Acceptance of and Objection to Reservations

1. A reservation expressly authorized by a treaty does not require any subsequent acceptance by the other contracting States unless the treaty so provides.

2. When it appears from the limited number of the negotiating States and the object and purpose of a treaty that the application of the treaty in its entirety between all the parties is an essential condition of the consent of each one to be bound by the treaty, a reservation requires acceptance by all the parties.

3. When a treaty is a constituent instrument of an international organization and unless it otherwise provides, a reservation requires the acceptance of the competent organ of that organization.

4.   In cases not falling under the preceding paragraphs and unless the treaty otherwise provides:

(a) acceptance by another contracting State of a reservation constitutes the reserving State a
     party to the treaty in relation to that other State if or when the treaty is in force for those
     States;

(b) an objection by another contracting State to a reservation does not preclude the entry into
     force of the treaty as between the objecting and reserving States unless a contrary intention
     is definitely expressed by the objecting State;

(c) an act expressing a State's consent to be bound by the treaty and containing a reservation is
     effective as soon as at least one other contracting State has accepted the reservation.

5.   For the purposes of paragraphs 2 and 4 and unless the treaty otherwise provides, a
reservation is considered to have been accepted by a State if it shall have raised no objection to
the reservation by the end of a period of twelve months after it was notified of the reservation or
by the date on which it expressed its consent to be bound by the treaty, whichever is later.

Article 21 Legal Effects of Reservations and of Objections to Reservations

1.   A reservation established with regard to another party in accordance with articles 19, 20 and
23:

(a) modifies for the reserving State in its relations with that other party the provisions of the
     treaty to which the reservation relates to the extent of the reservation; and

(b) modifies those provisions to the same extent for that other party in its relations with the
     reserving State.

2.   The reservation does not modify the provisions of the treaty for the other parties to the
treaty inter se.

3.   When a State objecting to a reservation has not opposed the entry into force of the treaty
between itself and the reserving State, the provisions to which the reservation relates do not
apply as between the two States to the extent of the reservation.

Article 22 Withdrawal of Reservations and of Objections to Reservations

1.   Unless the treaty otherwise provides, a reservation may be withdrawn at any time and the
consent of a State which has accepted the reservation is not required for its withdrawal.

2.   Unless the treaty otherwise provides, an objection to a reservation may be withdrawn at any
time.

3.   Unless the treaty otherwise provides, or it is otherwise agreed:

(a) the withdrawal of a reservation becomes operative in relation to another contracting State
     only when notice of it has been received by that State;

(b) the withdrawal of an objection to a reservation becomes operative only when notice of it
     has been received by the State which formulated the reservation.

Article 23 Procedure Regarding Reservations

1.   A reservation, an express acceptance of a reservation and an objection to a reservation must
be formulated in writing and communicated to the contracting States and other States entitled
to become parties to the treaty.

2.   If formulated when signing the treaty subject to ratification, acceptance or approval, a
reservation must be formally confirmed by the reserving State when expressing its consent to be
bound by the treaty. In such a case the reservation shall be considered as having been made on
the date of its confirmation.

3.   An express acceptance of, or an objection to, a reservation made previously to confirmation
of the reservation does not itself require confirmation.

4.   The withdrawal of a reservation or of an objection to a reservation must be formulated in writing.

SECTION 3. ENTRY INTO FORCE AND PROVISIONAL APPLICATION OF TREATIES

Article 24 Entry into Force

1.   A treaty enters into force in such manner and upon such date as it may provide or as the negotiating States may agree.

2.   Failing any such provision or agreement, a treaty enters into force as soon as consent to be bound by the treaty has been established for all the negotiating States.

3.   When the consent of a State to be bound by a treaty is established on a date after the treaty has come into force, the treaty enters into force for that State on that date, unless the treaty otherwise provides.

4.   The provisions of a treaty regulating the authentication of its text, the establishment of the consent of States to be bound by the treaty, the manner or date of its entry into force, reservations, the functions of the depositary and other matters arising necessarily before the entry into force of the treaty apply from the time of the adoption of its text.

Article 25 Provisional Application

1.   A treaty or a part of a treaty is applied provisionally pending its entry into force if:

(a)   the treaty itself so provides; or

(b)   the negotiating States have in some other manner so agreed.

2.   Unless the treaty otherwise provides or the negotiating States have otherwise agreed, the provisional application of a treaty or a part of a treaty with respect to a State shall be terminated if that State notifies the other States between which the treaty is being applied provisionally of its intention not to become a party to the treaty.

Part III. Observance, Application and Interpretation of Treaties

SECTION 1. OBSERVANCE OF TREATIES

Article 26 Pacta sunt servanda

Every treaty in force is binding upon the parties to it and must be performed by them in good faith.

Article 27 Internal Law and Observance of Treaties

A party may not invoke the provisions of its internal law as justification for its failure to perform a treaty. This rule is without prejudice to article 46.

SECTION 2. APPLICATION OF TREATIES

Article 28 Non-Retroactivity of Treaties

Unless a different intention appears from the treaty or is otherwise established, its provisions do not bind a party in relation to any act or fact which took place or any situation which ceased to exist before the date of the entry into force of the treaty with respect to that party.

Article 29 Territorial Scope of Treaties

Unless a different intention appears from the treaty or is otherwise established, a treaty is binding upon each party in respect of its entire territory.

Article 30 Application of Successive Treaties Relating to the Same Subject-Matter

1.   Subject to Article 103 of the Charter of the United Nations, the rights and obligations of States parties to successive treaties relating to the same subject-matter shall be determined in accordance with the following paragraphs.

2.   When a treaty specifies that it is subject to, or that it is not to be considered as incompatible with, an earlier or later treaty, the provisions of that other treaty prevail.

3.   When all the parties to the earlier treaty are parties also to the later treaty but the earlier treaty is not terminated or suspended in operation under article 59, the earlier treaty applies only to the extent that its provisions are compatible with those of the latter treaty.

4.   When the parties to the later treaty do not include all the parties to the earlier one:

(a)   as between States parties to both treaties the same rule applies as in paragraph 3;

(b)   as between a State party to both treaties and a State party to only one of the treaties, the treaty to which both States are parties governs their mutual rights and obligations.

5.   Paragraph 4 is without prejudice to article 41, or to any question of the termination or suspension of the operation of a treaty under article 60 or to any question of responsibility which may arise for a State from the conclusion or application of a treaty, the provisions of which are incompatible with its obligations towards another State under another treaty.

SECTION 3. INTERPRETATION OF TREATIES

Article 31 General Rule of Interpretation

1.   A treaty shall be interpreted in good faith in accordance with the ordinary meaning to be given to the terms of the treaty in their context and in the light of its object and purpose.

2.   The context for the purpose of the interpretation of a treaty shall comprise, in addition to the text, including its preamble and annexes:

(a)   any agreement relating to the treaty which was made between all the parties in connexion with the conclusion of the treaty;

(b)   any instrument which was made by one or more parties in connexion with the conclusion of the treaty and accepted by the other parties as an instrument related to the treaty.

3.   There shall be taken into account, together with the context:

(a)   any subsequent agreement between the parties regarding the interpretation of the treaty or the application of its provisions;

(b)   any subsequent practice in the application of the treaty which establishes the agreement of the parties regarding its interpretation;

(c)   any relevant rules of international law applicable in the relations between the parties.

4.   A special meaning shall be given to a term if it is established that the parties so intended.

Article 32 Supplementary Means of Interpretation

Recourse may be had to supplementary means of interpretation, including the preparatory work of the treaty and the circumstances of its conclusion, in order to confirm the meaning resulting from the application of article 31, or to determine the meaning when the interpretation according to article 31:

(a)   leaves the meaning ambiguous or obscure; or

(b)   leads to a result which is manifestly absurd or unreasonable.

Article 33 Interpretation of Treaties Authenticated in Two or More Languages

1.   When a treaty has been authenticated in two or more languages, the text is equally authoritative in each language, unless the treaty provides or the parties agree that, in case of divergence, a particular text shall prevail.

2.   A version of the treaty in a language other than one of those in which the text was authenticated shall be considered an authentic text only if the treaty so provides or the parties so agree.

3.   The terms of the treaty are presumed to have the same meaning in each authentic text.

4.   Except where a particular text prevails in accordance with paragraph 1, when a comparison of the authentic texts discloses a difference of meaning which the application of articles 31 and 32 does not remove, the meaning which best reconciles the texts, having regard to the object and purpose of the treaty, shall be adopted.

SECTION 4. TREATIES AND THIRD STATES

Article 34 General Rule Regarding Third States

A treaty does not create either obligations or rights for a third State without its consent.

Article 35 Treaties Providing for Obligations for Third States

An obligation arises for a third State from a provision of a treaty if the parties to the treaty intend the provision to be the means of establishing the obligation and the third State expressly accepts that obligation in writing.

Article 36 Treaties Providing for Rights for Third States

1.   A right arises for a third State from a provision of a treaty if the parties to the treaty intend the provision to accord that right either to the third State, or to a group of States to which it belongs, or to all States, and the third State assents thereto. Its assent shall be presumed so long as the contrary is not indicated, unless the treaty otherwise provides.

2.   A State exercising a right in accordance with paragraph 1 shall comply with the conditions for its exercise provided for in the treaty or established in conformity with the treaty.

Article 37 Revocation or Modification of Obligations or Rights of Third States

1.   When an obligation has arisen for a third State in conformity with article 35, the obligation may be revoked or modified only with the consent of the parties to the treaty and of the third State, unless it is established that they had otherwise agreed.

2.   When a right has arisen for a third State in conformity with article 36, the right may not be revoked or modified by the parties if it is established that the right was intended not to be revocable or subject to modification without the consent of the third State.

Article 38 Rules in a Treaty Becoming Binding on Third States
Through International Custom

Nothing in articles 34 to 37 precludes a rule set forth in a treaty from becoming binding upon a third State as a customary rule of international law, recognized as such.

Part IV. Amendment and Modification of Treaties

Article 39 General Rule Regarding the Amendment of Treaties

A treaty may be amended by agreement between the parties. The rules laid down in Part II apply to such an agreement except in so far as the treaty may otherwise provide.

Article 40 Amendment of Multilateral Treaties

1. Unless the treaty otherwise provides, the amendment of multilateral treaties shall be governed by the following paragraphs.

2. Any proposal to amend a multilateral treaty as between all the parties must be notified to all the contracting States, each one of which shall have the right to take part in:

(a) the decision as to the action to be taken in regard to such proposal;

(b) the negotiation and conclusion of any agreement for the amendment of the treaty.

3. Every State entitled to become a party to the treaty shall also be entitled to become a party to the treaty as amended.

4. The amending agreement does not bind any State already a party to the treaty which does not become a party to the amending agreement; article 30, paragraph 4(b), applies in relation to such State.

5. Any State which becomes a party to the treaty after the entry into force of the amending agreement shall, failing an expression of a different intention by that State:

(a) be considered as a party to the treaty as amended; and

(b) be considered as a party to the unamended treaty in relation to any party to the treaty not bound by the amending agreement.

Article 41 Agreements to Modify Multilateral Treaties
Between Certain of the Parties Only

1. Two or more of the parties to a multilateral treaty may conclude an agreement to modify the treaty as between themselves alone if:

(a) the possibility of such a modification is provided for by the treaty; or

(b) the modification in question is not prohibited by the treaty and:

  (i) does not affect the enjoyment by the other parties of their rights under the treaty or the performance of their obligations;

  (ii) does not relate to a provision, derogation from which is incompatible with the effective execution of the object and purpose of the treaty as a whole.

2. Unless in a case falling under paragraph 1(a) the treaty otherwise provides, the parties in question shall notify the other parties of their intention to conclude the agreement and of the modification to the treaty for which it provides.

Part V. Invalidity, Termination and Suspension of the Operation of Treaties

SECTION 1. GENERAL PROVISIONS

Article 42 Validity and Continuance in Force of Treaties

1.   The validity of a treaty or of the consent of a State to be bound by a treaty may be impeached only through the application of the present Convention.

2.   The termination of a treaty, its denunciation or the withdrawal of a party, may take place only as a result of the application of the provisions of the treaty or of the present Convention. The same rule applies to suspension of the operation of a treaty.

Article 43 Obligations Imposed by International Law Independently of a Treaty

The invalidity, termination or denunciation of a treaty, the withdrawal of a party from it, or the suspension of its operation, as a result of the application of the present Convention or of the provisions of the treaty, shall not in any way impair the duty of any State to fulfil any obligation embodied in the treaty to which it would be subject under international law independently of the treaty.

Article 44 Separability of Treaty Provisions

1.   A right of a party, provided for in a treaty or arising under article 56, to denounce, withdraw from or suspend the operation of the treaty may be exercised only with respect to the whole treaty unless the treaty otherwise provides or the parties otherwise agree.

2.   A ground for invalidating, terminating, withdrawing from or suspending the operation of a treaty recognized in the present Convention may be invoked only with respect to the whole treaty except as provided in the following paragraphs or in article 60.

3.   If the ground relates solely to particular clauses, it may be invoked only with respect to those clauses where:

(a)   the said clauses are separable from the remainder of the treaty with regard to their application;

(b)   it appears from the treaty or is otherwise established that acceptance of those clauses was not an essential basis of the consent of the other party or parties to be bound by the treaty as a whole; and

(c)   continued performance of the remainder of the treaty would not be unjust.

4.   In cases falling under articles 49 and 50 the State entitled to invoke the fraud or corruption may do so with respect either to the whole treaty or, subject to paragraph 3, to the particular clauses alone.

5.   In cases falling under articles 51, 52 and 53, no separation of the provisions of the treaty is permitted.

Article 45 Loss of a Right to Invoke a Ground for Invalidating, Terminating,
Withdrawing from or Suspending the Operation of a Treaty

A State may no longer invoke a ground for invalidating, terminating, withdrawing from or suspending the operation of a treaty under articles 46 to 50 or articles 60 and 62 if, after becoming aware of the facts:

(a)   it shall have expressly agreed that the treaty is valid or remains in force or continues in operation, as the case may be; or

(b)   it must by reason of its conduct be considered as having acquiesced in the validity of the treaty or in its maintenance in force or in operation, as the case may be.

SECTION 2. INVALIDITY OF TREATIES

Article 46 Provisions of Internal Law Regarding Competence to Conclude Treaties

1.   A State may not invoke the fact that its consent to be bound by a treaty has been expressed in violation of a provision of its internal law regarding competence to conclude treaties as invalidating its consent unless that violation was manifest and concerned a rule of its internal law of fundamental importance.

2.   A violation is manifest if it would be objectively evident to any State conducting itself in the matter in accordance with normal practice and in good faith.

Article 47 Specific Restrictions on Authority to Express the Consent of a State

If the authority of a representative to express the consent of a State to be bound by a particular treaty has been made subject to a specific restriction, his omission to observe that restriction may not be invoked as invalidating the consent expressed by him unless the restriction was notified to the other negotiating States prior to his expressing such consent.

Article 48 Error

1.   A State may invoke an error in a treaty as invalidating its consent to be bound by the treaty if the error relates to a fact or situation which was assumed by that State to exist at the time when the treaty was concluded and formed an essential basis of its consent to be bound by the treaty.

2.   Paragraph 1 shall not apply if the State in question contributed by its own conduct to the error or if the circumstances were such as to put that State on notice of a possible error.

3.   An error relating only to the wording of the text of a treaty does not affect its validity; article 79 then applies.

Article 49 Fraud

If a State has been induced to conclude a treaty by the fraudulent conduct of another nego-tiating State, the State may invoke the fraud as invalidating its consent to be bound by the treaty.

Article 50 Corruption of a Representative of a State

If the expression of a State's consent to be bound by a treaty has been procured through the corruption of its representative directly or indirectly by another negotiating State, the State may invoke such corruption as invalidating its consent to be bound by the treaty.

Article 51 Coercion of a Representative of a State

The expression of a State's consent to be bound by a treaty which has been procured by the coercion of its representative through acts or threats directed against him shall be without any legal effect.

Article 52 Coercion of a State by the Threat or Use of Force

A treaty is void if its conclusion has been procured by the threat or use of force in violation of the principles of international law embodied in the Charter of the United Nations.

Article 53 Treaties Conflicting with a Peremptory Norm of General International Law (jus cogens)

A treaty is void if, at the time of its conclusion, it conflicts with a peremptory norm of general international law. For the purposes of the present Convention, a peremptory norm of general international law is a norm accepted and recognized by the international community of States as a whole as a norm from which no derogation is permitted and which can be modified only by a subsequent norm of general international law having the same character.

SECTION 3. TERMINATION AND SUSPENSION OF THE OPERATION OF TREATIES

*Article 54 Termination of or Withdrawal from a Treaty under its Provisions
or by Consent of the Parties*

The termination of a treaty or the withdrawal of a party may take place:

(a)   in conformity with the provisions of the treaty; or

(b)   at any time by consent of all the parties after consultation with the other contracting States.

*Article 55 Reduction of the Parties to a Multilateral Treaty below the Number
Necessary for its Entry into Force*

Unless the treaty otherwise provides, a multilateral treaty does not terminate by reason only of the fact that the number of the parties falls below the number necessary for its entry into force.

*Article 56 Denunciation of or Withdrawal from a Treaty Containing No Provision Regarding
Termination, Denunciation or Withdrawal*

1.   A treaty which contains no provision regarding its termination and which does not provide for denunciation or withdrawal is not subject to denunciation or withdrawal unless:

(a)   it is established that the parties intended to admit the possibility of denunciation or withdrawal; or

(b)   a right of denunciation or withdrawal may be implied by the nature of the treaty.

2.   A party shall give not less than twelve months' notice of its intention to denounce or withdraw from a treaty under paragraph 1.

*Article 57 Suspension of the Operation of a Treaty under its Provisions
or by Consent of the Parties*

The operation of a treaty in regard to all the parties or to a particular party may be suspended:

(a)   in conformity with the provisions of the treaty; or

(b)   at any time by consent of all the parties after consultation with the other contracting States.

*Article 58 Suspension of the Operation of a Multilateral Treaty
by Agreement Between Certain of the Parties Only*

1.   Two or more parties to a multilateral treaty may conclude an agreement to suspend the operation of provisions of the treaty, temporarily and as between themselves alone, if:

(a)   the possibility of such a suspension is provided for by the treaty; or

(b)   the suspension in question is not prohibited by the treaty and:

   (i)   does not affect the enjoyment by the other parties of their rights under the treaty or the performance of their obligations;

   (ii)   is not incompatible with the object and purpose of the treaty.

2.   Unless in a case falling under paragraph 1(a) the treaty otherwise provides, the parties in question shall notify the other parties of their intention to conclude the agreement and of those provisions of the treaty the operation of which they intend to suspend.

Article 59 Termination or Suspension of the Operation of a Treaty
Implied by Conclusion of a Later Treaty

1.   A treaty shall be considered as terminated if all the parties to it conclude a later treaty relating to the same subject-matter and:

(a)   it appears from the later treaty or is otherwise established that the parties intended that the matter should be governed by that treaty; or

(b)   the provisions of the later treaty are so far incompatible with those of the earlier one that the two treaties are not capable of being applied at the same time.

2.   The earlier treaty shall be considered as only suspended in operation if it appears from the later treaty or is otherwise established that such was the intention of the parties.

Article 60 Termination or Suspension of the Operation of a Treaty
as a Consequence of its Breach

1.   A material breach of a bilateral treaty by one of the parties entitles the other to invoke the breach as a ground for terminating the treaty or suspending its operation in whole or in part.

2.   A material breach of a multilateral treaty by one of the parties entitles:

(a)   the other parties by unanimous agreement to suspend the operation of the treaty in whole or in part or to terminate it either:

(i)   in the relations between themselves and the defaulting State, or

(ii)   as between all the parties;

(b)   a party specially affected by the breach to invoke it as a ground for suspending the operation of the treaty in whole or in part in the relations between itself and the defaulting State;

(c)   any party other than the defaulting State to invoke the breach as a ground for suspending the operation of the treaty in whole or in part with respect to itself if the treaty is of such a character that a material breach of its provisions by one party radically changes the position of every party with respect to the further performance of its obligations under the treaty.

3.   A material breach of a treaty, for the purposes of this article, consists in:

(a)   a repudiation of the treaty not sanctioned by the present Convention; or

(b)   the violation of a provision essential to the accomplishment of the object or purpose of the treaty.

4.   The foregoing paragraphs are without prejudice to any provision in the treaty applicable in the event of a breach.

5.   Paragraphs 1 to 3 do not apply to provisions relating to the protection of the human person contained in treaties of a humanitarian character, in particular to provisions prohibiting any form of reprisals against persons protected by such treaties.

Article 61 Supervening Impossibility of Performance

1.   A party may invoke the impossibility of performing a treaty as a ground for terminating or withdrawing from it if the impossibility results from the permanent disappearance or destruction of an object indispensable for the execution of the treaty. If the impossibility is temporary, it may be invoked only as a ground for suspending the operation of the treaty.

2.   Impossibility of performance may not be invoked by a party as a ground for terminating, withdrawing from or suspending the operation of a treaty if the impossibility is the result of a breach by that party either of an obligation under the treaty or of any other international obligation owed to any other party to the treaty.

Article 62 Fundamental Change of Circumstances

1.   A fundamental change of circumstances which has occurred with regard to those existing at the time of the conclusion of a treaty, and which was not foreseen by the parties, may not be invoked as a ground for terminating or withdrawing from the treaty unless:

(a)   the existence of those circumstances constituted an essential basis of the consent of the parties to be bound by the treaty; and

(b)   the effect of the change is radically to transform the extent of obligations still to be performed under the treaty.

2.   A fundamental change of circumstances may not be invoked as a ground for terminating or withdrawing from a treaty:

(a)   if the treaty establishes a boundary; or

(b)   if the fundamental change is the result of a breach by the party invoking it either of an obligation under the treaty or of any other international obligation owed to any other party to the treaty.

3.   If, under the foregoing paragraphs, a party may invoke a fundamental change of circumstances as a ground for terminating or withdrawing from a treaty it may also invoke the change as a ground for suspending the operation of the treaty.

Article 63 Severance of Diplomatic or Consular Relations

The severance of diplomatic or consular relations between parties to a treaty does not affect the legal relations established between them by the treaty except in so far as the existence of diplomatic or consular relations is indispensable for the application of the treaty.

Article 64 Emergence of a New Peremptory Norm of General International Law
(ius cogens)

If a new peremptory norm of general international law emerges, any existing treaty which is in conflict with that norm becomes void and terminates.

SECTION 4. PROCEDURE

Article 65 Procedure to Be Followed with Respect to Invalidity, Termination, Withdrawal from or Suspension of the Operation of a Treaty

1.   A party which, under the provisions of the present Convention, invokes either a defect in its consent to be bound by a treaty or a ground for impeaching the validity of a treaty, terminating it, withdrawing from it or suspending its operation, must notify the other parties of its claim. The notification shall indicate the measure proposed to be taken with respect to the treaty and the reasons therefor.

2.   If, after the expiry of a period which, except in cases of special urgency, shall not be less than three months after the receipt of the notification, no party has raised any objection, the party making the notification may carry out in the manner provided in article 67 the measure which it has proposed.

3.   If, however, objection has been raised by any other party, the parties shall seek a solution through the means indicated in article 33 of the Charter of the United Nations.

4.   Nothing in the foregoing paragraphs shall affect the rights or obligations of the parties under any provisions in force binding the parties with regard to the settlement of disputes.

5.   Without prejudice to article 45, the fact that a State has not previously made the notification prescribed in paragraph 1 shall not prevent it from making such notification in answer to another party claiming performance of the treaty or alleging its violation.

Article 66 Procedures for Judicial Settlement, Arbitration and Conciliation

If, under paragraph 3 of article 65, no solution has been reached within a period of 12 months following the date on which the objection was raised, the following procedures shall be followed:

(a) any one of the parties to a dispute concerning the application or the interpretation of articles 53 or 64 may, by a written application, submit it to the International Court of Justice for a decision unless the parties by common consent agree to submit the dispute to arbitration;

(b) any one of the parties to a dispute concerning the application or the interpretation of any of the other articles in Part V of the present Convention may set in motion the procedure specified in the Annexe to the Convention by submitting a request to that effect to the Secretary-General of the United Nations.

Article 67 Instruments for Declaring Invalid, Terminating, Withdrawing from or Suspending the Operation of a Treaty

1. The notification provided for under article 65 paragraph 1 must be made in writing.

2. Any act declaring invalid, terminating, withdrawing from or suspending the operation of a treaty pursuant to the provisions of the treaty or of paragraphs 2 or 3 of article 65 shall be carried out through an instrument communicated to the other parties. If the instrument is not signed by the Head of State, Head of Government or Minister for Foreign Affairs, the representative of the State communicating it may be called upon to produce full powers.

Article 68 Revocation of Notifications and Instruments Provided for in Articles 65 and 67

A notification or instrument provided for in articles 65 or 67 may be revoked at any time before it takes effect.

SECTION 5. CONSEQUENCES OF THE INVALIDITY, TERMINATION OR SUSPENSION OF THE OPERATION OF A TREATY

Article 69 Consequences of the Invalidity of a Treaty

1. A treaty the invalidity of which is established under the present Convention is void. The provisions of a void treaty have no legal force.

2. If acts have nevertheless been performed in reliance on such a treaty:

(a) each party may require any other party to establish as far as possible in their mutual relations the position that would have existed if the acts had not been performed;

(b) acts performed in good faith before the invalidity was invoked are not rendered unlawful by reason only of the invalidity of the treaty.

3. In cases falling under articles 49, 50, 51 or 52, paragraph 2 does not apply with respect to the party to which the fraud, the act of corruption or the coercion is imputable.

4. In the case of the invalidity of a particular State's consent to be bound by a multilateral treaty, the foregoing rules apply in the relations between that State and the parties to the treaty.

Article 70 Consequences of the Termination of a Treaty

1. Unless the treaty otherwise provides or the parties otherwise agree, the termination of a treaty under its provisions or in accordance with the present Convention:

(a) releases the parties from any obligation further to perform the treaty;

(b) does not affect any right, obligation or legal situation of the parties created through the execution of the treaty prior to its termination.

2. If a State denounces or withdraws from a multilateral treaty, paragraph 1 applies in the relations between that State and each of the other parties to the treaty from the date when such denunciation or withdrawal takes effect.

Article 71 Consequences of the Invalidity of a Treaty Which Conflicts
with a Peremptory Norm of General International Law

1. In the case of a treaty which is void under article 53 the parties shall:

(a) eliminate as far as possible the consequences of any act performed in reliance on any provision which conflicts with the peremptory norm of general international law; and

(b) bring their mutual relations into conformity with the peremptory norm of general international law.

2. In the case of a treaty which becomes void and terminates under article 64, the termination of the treaty:

(a) releases the parties from any obligation further to perform the treaty;

(b) does not affect any right, obligation or legal situation of the parties created through the execution of the treaty prior to its termination; provided that those rights, obligations or situations may thereafter be maintained only to the extent that their maintenance is not in itself in conflict with the new peremptory norm of general international law.

Article 72 Consequences of the Suspension of the Operation of a Treaty

1. Unless the treaty otherwise provides or the parties otherwise agree, the suspension of the operation of a treaty under its provisions or in accordance with the present Convention:

(a) releases the parties between which the operation of the treaty is suspended from the obligation to perform the treaty in their mutual relations during the period of the suspension;

(b) does not otherwise affect the legal relations between the parties established by the treaty.

2. During the period of the suspension the parties shall refrain from acts tending to obstruct the resumption of the operation of the treaty.

Part VI. Miscellaneous Provisions

Article 73 Cases of State Succession, State Responsibility and Outbreak of Hostilities

The provisions of the present Convention shall not prejudge any question that may arise in regard to a treaty from a succession of States or from the international responsibility of a State or from the outbreak of hostilities between States.

Article 74 Diplomatic and Consular Relations and the Conclusion of Treaties

The severance or absence of diplomatic or consular relations between two or more States does not prevent the conclusion of treaties between those States. The conclusion of a treaty does not in itself affect the situation in regard to diplomatic or consular relations.

Article 75 Case of an Aggressor State

The provisions of the present Convention are without prejudice to any obligation in relation to a treaty which may arise for an aggressor State in consequence of measures taken in conformity with the Charter of the United Nations with reference to that State's aggression.

Part VII. Depositaries, Notifications, Corrections and Registration

Article 76 Depositaries of Treaties

1.   The designation of the depositary of a treaty may be made by the negotiating States, either in the treaty itself or in some other manner. The depositary may be one or more States, an international organization or the chief administrative officer of the organization.

2.   The functions of the depositary of a treaty are international in character and the depositary is under an obligation to act impartially in their performance. In particular, the fact that a treaty has not entered into force between certain of the parties or that a difference has appeared between a State and a depositary with regard to the performance of the latter's functions shall not affect that obligation.

Article 77 Functions of Depositaries

1.   The functions of a depositary, unless otherwise provided in the treaty or agreed by the contracting States, comprise in particular:

(a) keeping custody of the original text of the treaty and of any full powers delivered to the depositary;

(b) preparing certified copies of the original text and preparing any further text of the treaty in such additional languages as may be required by the treaty and transmitting them to the parties and to the States entitled to become parties to the treaty;

(c) receiving any signatures to the treaty and receiving and keeping custody of any instruments, notifications and communications relating to it;

(d) examining whether the signature or any instrument, notification or communication relating to the treaty is in due and proper form and, if need be, bringing the matter to the attention of the State in question;

(e) informing the parties and the States entitled to become parties to the treaty of acts, notifications and communications relating to the treaty;

(f)   informing the States entitled to become parties to the treaty when the number of signatures or of instruments of ratification, acceptance, approval or accession required for the entry into force of the treaty has been received or deposited;

(g) registering the treaty with the Secretariat of the United Nations;

(h) performing the functions specified in other provisions of the present Convention.

2.   In the event of any difference appearing between a State and the depositary as to the performance of the latter's functions, the depositary shall bring the question to the attention of the signatory States and the contracting States or, where appropriate, of the competent organ of the international organization concerned.

Article 78 Notifications and Communications

Except as the treaty or the present Convention otherwise provide, any notification or communication to be made by any State under the present Convention shall:

(a) if there is no depositary, be transmitted direct to the States for which it is intended, or if there is a depositary, to the latter;

(b) be considered as having been made by the State in question only upon its receipt by the State to which it was transmitted or, as the case may be, upon its receipt by the depositary;

(c) if transmitted to a depositary, be considered as received by the State for which it was intended only when the latter State has been informed by the depositary in accordance with article 77, paragraph 1(e).

Article 79 Correction of Errors in Texts or in Certified Copies of Treaties

1.   Where, after the authentication of the text of a treaty, the signatory States and the contracting States are agreed that it contains an error, the error shall, unless they decide upon some other means of correction, be corrected:

(a)   by having the appropriate correction made in the text and causing the correction to be initialled by duly authorized representatives;

(b)   by executing or exchanging an instrument or instruments setting out the correction which it has been agreed to make; or

(c)   by executing a corrected text of the whole treaty by the same procedure as in the case of the original text.

2.   Where the treaty is one for which there is a depositary, the latter shall notify the signatory States and the contracting States of the error and of the proposal to correct it and shall specify an appropriate time-limit within which objection to the proposed correction may be raised. If, on the expiry of the time-limit:

(a)   no objection has been raised, the depositary shall make and initial the correction in the text and shall execute a procès-verbal of the rectification of the text and communicate a copy of it to the parties and to the States entitled to become parties to the treaty;

(b)   an objection has been raised, the depositary shall communicate the objection to the signatory States and to the contracting States.

3.   The rules in paragraphs 1 and 2 apply also where the text has been authenticated in two or more languages and it appears that there is a lack of concordance which the signatory States and the contracting States agree should be corrected.

4.   The corrected text replaces the defective text ab initio, unless the signatory States and the contracting States otherwise decide.

5.   The correction of the text of a treaty that has been registered shall be notified to the Secretariat of the United Nations.

6.   Where an error is discovered in a certified copy of a treaty, the depositary shall execute a procès-verbal specifying the rectification and communicate a copy of it to the signatory States and to the contracting Slates.

Article 80 Registration and Publication of Treaties

1.   Treaties shall, after their entry into force, be transmitted to the Secretariat of the United Nations for registration or filing and recording, as the case may be, and for publication.

2.   The designation of a depositary shall constitute authorization for it to perform the acts specified in the preceding paragraph.

Part VIII. Final Provisions

Article 81 Signature

The present Convention shall be open for signature by all States Members of the United Nations or of any of the specialized agencies or of the International Atomic Energy Agency or parties to the Statute of the International Court of Justice, and by any other State invited by the General Assembly of the United Nations to become a party to the Convention, as follows: until 30 November 1969, at the Federal Ministry for Foreign Affairs of the Republic of Austria, and subsequently, until 30 April 1970, at United Nations Headquarters, New York.

Article 82 Ratification

The present Convention is subject to ratification. The instruments of ratification shall be deposited with the Secretary-General of the United Nations.

Article 83 Accession

The present Convention shall remain open for accession by any State belonging to any of the categories mentioned in article 81. The instruments of accession shall be deposited with the Secretary-General of the United Nations.

Article 84 Entry into Force

1.   The present Convention shall enter into force on the thirtieth day following the date of deposit of the thirty-fifth instrument of ratification or accession.

2.   For each State ratifying or acceding to the Convention after the deposit of the thirty-fifth instrument of ratification or accession, the Convention shall enter into force on the thirtieth day after deposit by such State of its instrument of ratification or accession.

Article 85 Authentic Texts

The original of the present Convention, of which the Chinese, English, French, Russian and Spanish texts are equally authentic, shall be deposited with the Secretary-General of the United Nations.

IN WITNESS WHEREOF the undersigned Plenipotentiaries, being duly authorized thereto by their respective Governments, have signed the present Convention.

DONE at Vienna, this twenty-third day of May, one thousand nine hundred and sixty-nine.

I.5. 1974 DECLARATION ON THE ESTABLISHMENT OF A NEW INTERNATIONAL ECONOMIC ORDER

UN General Assembly Resolution 3201 (S-VI), 1974

We, the Members of the United Nations,

Having convened a special session of the General Assembly to study for the first time the problems of raw materials and development, devoted to the consideration of the most important economic problems facing the world community,

Bearing in mind the spirit, purposes and principles of the *Charter of the United Nations* to promote the economic advancement and social progress of all peoples,

Solemnly proclaim our united determination to work urgently for the Establishment of a New International Economic Order based on equity, sovereign equality, interdependence, common interest and cooperation among all States, irrespective of their economic and social systems which shall correct inequalities and redress existing injustices, make it possible to eliminate the widening gap between the developed and the developing countries and ensure steadily accelerating economic and social development and peace and justice for present and future generations, and, to that end, declare:

1.   The greatest and most significant achievement during the last decades has been the independence from colonial and alien domination of a large number of peoples and nations which has enabled them to become members of the community of free peoples. Technological progress has also been made in all spheres of economic activities in the last three decades, thus providing a solid potential for improving the well-being of all peoples. However, the remaining vestiges of alien and colonial domination, foreign occupation, racial discrimination, apartheid and neo-colonialism in all its forms continue to be among the greatest obstacles to the full emancipation and progress of the developing countries and all the peoples involved. The benefits of technological progress are not shared equitably by all members of the international community. The developing countries, which constitute 70 per cent of the world's population, account for only 30 per cent of the worlds income. It has proved impossible to achieve an even and balanced development of the international community under the existing international economic order. The gap between the developed and the developing countries continues to widen in a system which was established at a time when most of the developing countries did not even exist as independent States and which perpetuates inequality.

2.   The present international economic order is in direct conflict with current developments in international political and economic relations. Since 1970 the world economy has experienced a series of grave crises which have had severe repercussions, especially on the developing countries because of their generally greater vulnerability to external economic impulses. The developing world has become a powerful factor that makes its influence felt in all fields of international activity. These irreversible changes in the relationship of forces in the world necessitate the active, full and equal participation of the developing countries in the formulation and application of all decisions that concern the international community.

3.   All these changes have thrust into prominence the reality of interdependence of all the members of the world community. Current events have brought into sharp focus the realization that the interests of the developed countries and those of the developing countries can no longer be isolated from each other, that there is a close interrelationship between the prosperity of the developed countries and the growth and development of the developing countries, and that the prosperity of the international community as a whole depends upon the prosperity of its constituent parts. International co-operation for development is the shared goal and common duty of all countries. Thus the political, economic and social well-being of present and future

generations depends more than ever on co-operation between all the members of the international community on the basis of sovereign equality and the removal of the disequilibrium that exists between them.

4.   The new international economic order should be founded on full respect for the following principles:

a.   Sovereign equality of States, self-determination of all peoples, inadmissibility of the acquisition of territories by force, territorial integrity and non-interference in the internal affairs of other States;

b.   The broadest co-operation of all the States members of the international community, based on equity, whereby the prevailing disparities in the world may be banished and prosperity secured for all;

c.   Full and effective participation on the basis of equality of all countries in the solving of world economic problems in the common interest of all countries, bearing in mind the necessity to ensure the accelerated development of all the developing countries, while devoting particular attention to the adoption of special measures in favour of the least developed landlocked and island developing countries as well as those developing countries most seriously affected by economic crises and natural calamities, without losing sight of the interests of other developing countries;

d.   The right of every country to adopt the economic and social system that it deems the most appropriate for its own development and not to be subjected to discrimination of any kind as a result;

e.   Full permanent sovereignty of every State over its natural resources and all economic activities. In order to safeguard these resources, each State is entitled to exercise effective control over them and their exploitation with means suitable to its own situation, including the right to nationalization or transfer of ownership to its nationals, this right being an expression of the full permanent sovereignty of the State. No State may be subjected to economic, political or any other type of coercion to prevent the free and full exercise of this inalienable right;

f.   The right of all States, territories and peoples under foreign occupation, alien and colonial domination or apartheid to restitution and full compensation for the exploitation arid depletion of, and damages to, the natural resources and all other resources of those States, territories and peoples;

g.   Regulation and supervision of the activities of transnational corporations by taking measures in the interest of the national economies of the countries where such transnational corporations operate on the basis of the full sovereignty of those countries;

h.   The right of the developing countries and the peoples of territories under colonial and racial domination and foreign occupation to achieve their liberation and to regain effective control over their natural resources and economic activities;

i.   The extending of assistance to developing countries, peoples and territories which are under colonial and alien domination, foreign occupation, racial discrimination or apartheid or are subjected to economic, political or any other type of coercive measures to obtain from them the subordination of the exercise of their sovereign rights and to secure from them advantages of any kind, and to neo colonialism in all its forms, and which have established or are endeavouring to establish effective control over their natural resources and economic activities that have been or are still under foreign control;

j.   Just and equitable relationship between the prices of raw materials, primary commodities, manufactured and semi-manufactured goods exported by developing countries and the prices of raw materials, primary commodities, manufactures, capital goods and equipment imported by them with the aim of bringing about sustained improvement in their un-satisfactory terms of trade and the expansion of the world economy;

k. Extension of active assistance to developing countries by the whole international com-munity, free of any political or military conditions;

l. Ensuring that one of the main aims of the reformed international monetary system shall be the promotion of the development of the developing countries and the adequate flow of real resources to them;

m. Improving the competitiveness of natural materials facing competition from synthetic substitutes;

n. Preferential and non-reciprocal treatment for developing countries, wherever feasible, in all fields of international economic co-operation whenever possible;

o. Securing favourable conditions for the transfer of financial resources to developing countries.

p. Giving to the developing countries access to the achievements of modern science and technology, and promoting the transfer of technology and the creation of indigenous technology for the benefit of the developing countries in forms and in accordance with procedures which are suited to their economies;

q. The need for all States to put an end to the waste of natural resources, including food products;

r. The need for developing countries to concentrate all their resources for the cause of deve-lopment;

s. The strengthening, through individual and collective actions, of mutual economic, trade, financial and technical co-operation among the developing countries, mainly on a preferential basis;

t. Facilitating the role which producers' associations may play within the framework of international co-operation and, in pursuance of their aims, inter alia assisting in the pro-motion of sustained growth of the world economy and accelerating the development of developing countries.

5. The unanimous adoption of the International Development Strategy for the Second United Nations Development Decade (Resolution 2626 (XXV)) was an important step in the promotion of international economic co-operation on a just and equitable basis. The accelerated implementation of obligations and commitments assumed by the international community within the framework of the Strategy, particularly those concerning imperative development needs of developing countries, would contribute significantly to the fulfilment of the aims and objectives of the present Declaration.

6. The United Nations as a universal organization should be capable of dealing with problems of international economic co-operation in a comprehensive manner and ensuring equally the interests of all countries. It must have an even greater role in the establishment of a new international economic order. The Charter of Economic Rights and Duties of States, for the preparation of which the present Declaration will provide an additional source of inspiration, will constitute a significant contribution in this respect. All the States Members of the United Nations are therefore called upon to exert maximum efforts with a view to securing the implementation of the present Declaration, which is one of the principal guarantees for the creation of better conditions for all peoples to reach a life worthy of human dignity.

7. The present Declaration on the Establishment of a New International Economic Order shall be one of the most important bases of economic relations between all peoples and all nations.

2229th plenary meeting, 1 May 1974

I.6. 1974 CHARTER OF ECONOMIC RIGHTS AND DUTIES OF STATES

UN General Assembly Resolution 3281 (XXIX), 1974

The General Assembly,

Recalling that the United Nations Conference on Trade and Development, in its resolution 45 (III) of 18 May 1972, stressed the urgency to establish generally accepted norms to govern international economic relations systematically and recognized that it is not feasible to establish a just order and a stable world as long as a charter to protect the rights of all countries, and in particular the developing States, is not formulated,

Recalling further that in the same resolution it was decided to establish a Working Group of governmental representatives to draw up a draft Charter of Economic Rights and Duties of States, which the General Assembly, in its resolution 3037 (XXVII) of 19 December 1972, decided should be composed of forty Member States,

Noting that, in its resolution 3082 (XXVIII) of 6 December 1973, it reaffirmed its conviction of the urgent need to establish or improve norms of universal application for the development of international economic relations on a just and equitable basis and urged the Working Group on the Charter of Economic Rights and Duties of States to complete, as the first step in the codification and development of the matter, the elaboration of a final draft Charter of Economic Rights and Duties of States, to be considered and approved by the General Assembly at its twenty-ninth session,

Bearing in mind the spirit and terms of its resolutions 3201 (S-VI) and 3202 (S-VI) of 1 May 1974, containing, respectively, the Declaration and the Programme of Action on the Establishment of a New International Economic Order, which underlined the vital importance of the Charter to be adopted by the General Assembly at its twenty-ninth session and stressed the fact that the Charter shall constitute an effective instrument towards the establishment of a new system of international economic relations based on equity, sovereign equality and interdependence of the interests of developed and developing countries,

Having examined the report of the Working Group on the Charter of Economic Rights and Duties of States on its fourth session,35 transmitted to the General Assembly by the Trade and Development Board at its fourteenth session,

Expressing its appreciation to the Working Group on the Charter of Economic Rights and Duties of States which, as a result of the task performed in its four sessions held between February 1973 and June 1974, assembled the elements required for the completion and adoption of the Charter of Economic Rights and Duties of States at the twenty-ninth session of the General Assembly, as previously recommended,

Adopts and solemnly proclaims the following Charter:

PREAMBLE

The General Assembly,

Reaffirming the fundamental purposes of the United Nations, in particular the maintenance of international peace and security, the development of friendly relations among nations and the achievement of international co-operation in solving international problems in the economic and social fields,

Affirming the need for strengthening international co-operation in these fields,

Reaffirming further the need for strengthening international co-operation for development,

Declaring that it is a fundamental purpose of the present Charter to promote the establishment of the new international economic order, based on equity, sovereign equality, interdependence, common interest and co-operation among all States, irrespective of their economic and social systems,

Desirous of contributing to the creation of conditions for:

(a) The attainment of wider prosperity among all countries and of higher standards of living for all peoples,

(b) The promotion by the entire international community of the economic and social progress of all countries, especially developing countries,

(c) The encouragement of co-operation, on the basis of mutual advantage and equitable benefits for all peace-loving States which are willing to carry out the provisions of the present Charter, in the economic, trade, scientific and technical fields, regardless of political, economic or social systems,

(d) The overcoming of main obstacles in the way of the economic development of the developing countries,

(e) The acceleration of the economic growth of developing countries with a view to bridging the economic gap between developing and developed countries,

(f) The protection, preservation and enhancement of the environment,

Mindful of the need to establish and maintain a just and equitable economic and social order through:

(a) The achievement of more rational and equitable international economic relations and the encouragement of structural changes in the world economy,

(b) The creation of conditions which permit the further expansion of trade and intensification of economic co-operation among all nations,

(c) The strengthening of the economic independence of developing countries,

(d) The establishment and promotion of international economic relations, taking into account the agreed differences in development of the developing countries and their specific needs,

Determined to promote collective economic security for development, in particular of the developing countries, with strict respect for the sovereign equality of each State and through the co-operation of the entire international community,

Considering that genuine co-operation among States, based on joint consideration of and concerted action regarding international economic problems, is essential for fulfilling the international community's common desire to achieve a just and rational development of all parts of the world,

Stressing the importance of ensuring appropriate conditions for the conduct of normal economic relations among all States, irrespective of differences in social and economic systems, and for the full respect of the rights of all peoples, as well as strengthening instruments of international economic co-operation as a means for the consolidation of peace for the benefit of all,

Convinced of the need to develop a system of international economic relations on the basis of sovereign equality, mutual and equitable benefit and the close interrelationship of the interests of all States,

Reiterating that the responsibility for the development of every country rests primarily upon itself but that concomitant and effective international cooperation is an essential factor for the full achievement of its own development goals,

Firmly convinced of the urgent need to evolve a substantially improved system of international economic relations,

Solemnly adopts the present Charter of Economic Rights and Duties of States.

CHAPTER I – FUNDAMENTALS OF INTERNATIONAL ECONOMIC RELATIONS

Economic as well as political and other relations among States shall be governed, inter alia, by the following principles:

(a) Sovereignty, territorial integrity and political independence of States;

(b) Sovereign equality of all States;

(c) Non-aggression;

(d) Non-intervention;

(e) Mutual and equitable benefit;

(f) Peaceful coexistence;

(g) Equal rights and self-determination of peoples;

(h) Peaceful settlement of disputes;

(i) Remedying of injustices which have been brought about by force and which deprive a nation of the natural means necessary for its normal development;

(j) Fulfilment in good faith of international obligations;

(k) Respect for human rights and fundamental freedoms;

(l) No attempt to seek hegemony and spheres of influence;

(m) Promotion of international social justice;

(n) International co-operation for development;

(o) Free access to and from the sea by landlocked countries within the framework of the above principles.

CHAPTER II – ECONOMIC RIGHTS AND DUTIES OF STATES

Article 1

Every State has the sovereign and inalienable right to choose its economic system as well as its political, social and cultural systems in accordance with the will of its people, without outside interference, coercion or threat in any form whatsoever.

Article 2

1. Every State has and shall freely exercise full permanent sovereignty, including possession, use and disposal, over all its wealth, natural resources and economic activities.

2. Each State has the right:

(a) To regulate and exercise authority over foreign investment within its national jurisdiction in accordance with its laws and regulations and in conformity with its national objectives and priorities. No State shall be compelled to grant preferential treatment to foreign investment;

(b) To regulate and supervise the activities of transnational corporations within its national jurisdiction and take measures to ensure that such activities comply with its laws, rules and regulations and conform with its economic and social policies. Transnational corporations shall not intervene in the internal affairs of a host State. Every State should, with full regard for its sovereign rights, co-operate with other States in the exercise of the right set forth in this subparagraph;

(c) To nationalize, expropriate or transfer ownership of foreign property, in which case appropriate compensation should be paid by the State adopting such measures, taking into account its relevant laws and regulations and all circumstances that the State considers pertinent. In any case where the question of compensation gives rise to a controversy, it shall be settled under the domestic law of the nationalizing State and by its tribunals, unless it is freely and mutually agreed by all States concerned that other peaceful means be sought on the basis of the sovereign equality of States and in accordance with the principle of free choice of means.

Article 3

In the exploitation of natural resources shared by two or more countries, each State must co-operate on the basis of a system of information and prior consultations in order to achieve optimum use of such resources without causing damage to the legitimate interest of others.

Article 4

Every State has the right to engage in international trade and other forms of economic co-operation irrespective of any differences in political, economic and social systems. No State shall be subjected to discrimination of any kind based solely on such differences. In the pursuit of international trade and other forms of economic co-operation, every State is free to choose the forms of organization of its foreign economic relations and to enter into bilateral and multilateral arrangements consistent with its international obligations and with the needs of international economic co-operation.

Article 5

All States have the right to associate in organizations of primary commodity producers in order to develop their national economies, to achieve stable financing for their development and, in pursuance of their aims, to assist in the promotion of sustained growth of the world economy, in particular accelerating the development of developing countries. Correspondingly, all States have the duty to respect that right by refraining from applying economic and political measures that would limit it.

Article 6

It is the duty of States to contribute to the development of international trade of goods, particularly by means of arrangements and by the conclusion of long-term multilateral commodity agreements, where appropriate, and taking into account the interests of producers and consumers. All States share the responsibility to promote the regular flow and access of all commercial goods traded at stable, remunerative and equitable prices, thus contributing to the equitable development of the world economy, taking into account, in particular, the interests of developing countries.

Article 7

Every State has the primary responsibility to promote the economic, social and cultural development of its people. To this end, each State has the right and the responsibility to choose its means and goals of development, fully to mobilize and use its resources, to implement progressive economic and social reforms and to ensure the full participation of its people in the process and benefits of development. All States have the duty, individually and collectively, to co-operate in eliminating obstacles that hinder such mobilization and use.

Article 8

States should co-operate in facilitating more rational and equitable international economic relations and in encouraging structural changes in the context of a balanced world economy in harmony with the needs and interests of all countries, especially developing countries, and should take appropriate measures to this end.

Article 9

All States have the responsibility to co-operate in the economic, social, cultural, scientific and technological fields for the promotion of economic and social progress throughout the world, especially that of the developing countries.

Article 10

All States are juridically equal and, as equal members of the international community, have the right to participate fully and effectively in the international decision-making process in the solution of world economic, financial and monetary problems, inter alia, through the appropriate international organizations in accordance with their existing and evolving rules, and to share equitably in the benefits resulting therefrom.

Article 11

All States should co-operate to strengthen and continuously improve the efficiency of international organizations in implementing measures to stimulate the general economic progress of all countries, particularly of developing countries, and therefore should co-operate to adapt them, when appropriate, to the changing needs of international economic co-operation.

Article 12

1.   States have the right, in agreement with the parties concerned, to participate in subregional, regional and interregional co-operation in the pursuit of their economic and social development. All States engaged in such co-operation have the duty to ensure that the policies of those groupings to which they belong correspond to the provisions of the present Charter and are outward-looking, consistent with their international obligations and with the needs of international economic co-operation, and have full regard for the legitimate interests of third countries, especially developing countries.

2.   In the case of groupings to which the States concerned have transferred or may transfer certain competences as regards matters that come within the scope of the present Charter, its provisions shall also apply to those groupings in regard to such matters, consistent with the responsibilities of such States as members of such groupings. Those States shall co-operate in the observance by the groupings of the provisions of this Charter.

Article 13

1.   Every State has the right to benefit from the advances and developments in science and technology for the acceleration of its economic and social development.

2.   All States should promote international scientific and technological co-operation and the transfer of technology, with proper regard for all legitimate interests including, inter alia, the rights and duties of holders, suppliers and recipients of technology. In particular, all States should facilitate the access of developing countries to the achievements of modern science and technology, the transfer of technology and the creation of indigenous technology for the benefit of the developing countries in forms and in accordance with procedures which are suited to their economies and their needs.

3.   Accordingly, developed countries should cooperate with the developing countries in the establishment, strengthening and development of their scientific and technological infrastructures and their scientific research and technological activities so as to help to expand and transform the economies of developing countries.

4.   All States should co-operate in research with a view to evolving further internationally accepted guidelines or regulations for the transfer of technology, taking fully into account the interests of developing countries.

Article 14

Every State has the duty to co-operate in promoting a steady and increasing expansion and liberalization of world trade and an improvement in the welfare and living standards of all peoples, in particular those of developing countries. Accordingly, all States should co-operate, inter alia, towards the progressive dismantling of obstacles to trade and the improvement of the international framework for the conduct of world trade and, to these ends, co-ordinated efforts shall be made to solve in an equitable way the trade problems of all countries, taking into account the specific trade problems of the developing countries. In this connexion, States shall take measures aimed at securing additional benefits for the international trade of developing countries so as to achieve a substantial increase in their foreign exchange earnings, the diversification of their exports, the acceleration of the rate of growth of their trade, taking into account their development needs, an improvement in the possibilities for these countries to participate in the expansion of world trade and a balance more favourable to developing countries in the sharing of the advantages resulting from this expansion, through, in the largest possible measure, a substantial improvement in the conditions of access for the products of interest to the developing countries and, wherever appropriate, measures designed to attain stable, equitable and remunerative prices for primary products.

Article 15

All States have the duty to promote the achievement of general and complete disarmament under effective international control and to utilize the resources released by effective disarmament measures for the economic and social development of countries, allocating a substantial portion of such resources as additional means for the development needs of developing countries.

Article 16

l.   It is the right and duty of all States, individually and collectively, to eliminate colonialism, apartheid, racial discrimination, neo-colonialism and all forms of foreign aggression, occupation and domination, and the economic and social consequences thereof, as a prerequisite for development. States which practise such coercive policies are economically responsible to the countries, territories and peoples affected for the restitution and full compensation for the exploitation and depletion of, and damages to, the natural and all other resources of those countries, territories and peoples. It is the duty of all States to extend assistance to them.

2.   No State has the right to promote or encourage investments that may constitute an obstacle to the liberation of a territory occupied by force.

Article 17

International co-operation for development is the shared goal and common duty of all States. Every State should co-operate with the efforts of developing countries to accelerate their economic and social development by providing favourable external conditions and by extending active assistance to them, consistent with their development needs and objectives, with strict respect for the sovereign equality of States and free of any conditions derogating from their sovereignty.

Article 18

Developed countries should extend, improve and enlarge the system of generalized non-reciprocal and non-discriminatory tariff preferences to the developing countries consistent with the relevant agreed conclusions and relevant decisions as adopted on this subject, in the framework of the competent international organizations. Developed countries should also give serious consideration to the adoption of other differential measures, in areas where this is feasible and appropriate and in ways which will provide special and more favourable treatment, in order to meet the trade and development needs of the developing countries. In the conduct of international economic relations the developed countries should endeavour to avoid measures having a negative effect on the development of the national economies of the developing countries, as promoted by generalized tariff preferences and other generally agreed differential measures in their favour.

Article 19

With a view to accelerating the economic growth of developing countries and bridging the economic gap between developed and developing countries, developed countries should grant generalized preferential, non-reciprocal and non-discriminatory treatment to developing countries in those fields of international economic co-operation where it may be feasible.

Article 20

Developing countries should, in their efforts to increase their over-all trade, give due attention to the possibility of expanding their trade with socialist countries, by granting to these countries conditions for trade not inferior to those granted normally to the developed market economy countries.

Article 21

Developing countries should endeavour to promote the expansion of their mutual trade and to this end may, in accordance with the existing and evolving provisions and procedures of international agreements where applicable, grant trade preferences to other developing countries without being obliged to extend such preferences to developed countries, provided these arrangements do not constitute an impediment to general trade liberalization and expansion.

Article 22

1.   All States should respond to the generally recognized or mutually agreed development needs and objectives of developing countries by promoting increased net flows of real resources to the developing countries from all sources, taking into account any obligations and commitments undertaken by the States concerned, in order to reinforce the efforts of developing countries to accelerate their economic and social development.

2.   In this context, consistent with the aims and objectives mentioned above and taking into account any obligations and commitments undertaken in this regard, it should be their endeavour to increase the net amount of financial flows from official sources to developing countries and to improve the terms and conditions thereof.

3.   The flow of development assistance resources should include economic and technical assistance.

Article 23

To enhance the effective mobilization of their own resources, the developing countries should strengthen their economic co-operation and expand their mutual trade so as to accelerate their economic and social development. All countries, especially developed countries, individually as well as through the competent international organizations of which they are members, should provide appropriate and effective support and co-operation.

Article 24

All States have the duty to conduct their mutual economic relations in a manner which takes into account the interests of other countries. In particular, all States should avoid prejudicing the interests of developing countries.

Article 25

In furtherance of world economic development, the international community, especially its developed members, shall pay special attention to the particular needs and problems of the least developed among the developing countries, of land-locked developing countries and also island developing countries, with a view to helping them to overcome their particular difficulties and thus contribute to their economic and social development.

Article 26

All States have the duty to coexist in tolerance and live together in peace, irrespective of differences in political, economic, social and cultural systems, and to facilitate trade between States having different economic and social systems. International trade should be conducted without prejudice to generalized non-discriminatory and non- reciprocal preferences in favour of developing countries, on the basis of mutual advantage, equitable benefits and the exchange of most-favoured-nation treatment.

Article 27

1.   Every State has the right to enjoy fully the benefits of world invisible trade and to engage in the expansion of such trade.

2.   World invisible trade, based on efficiency and mutual and equitable benefit, furthering the expansion of the world economy, is the common goal of all States. The role of developing countries in world invisible trade should be enhanced and strengthened consistent with the above objectives, particular attention being paid to the special needs of developing countries.

3.   All States should co-operate with developing countries in their endeavours to increase their capacity to earn foreign exchange from invisible transactions, in accordance with the potential and needs of each developing country and consistent with the objectives mentioned above.

Article 28

All States have the duty to co-operate in achieving adjustments in the prices of exports of developing countries in relation to prices of their imports so as to promote just and equitable terms of trade for them, in a manner which is remunerative for producers and equitable for producers and consumers.

CHAPTER III – COMMON RESPONSIBILITIES TOWARDS THE INTERNATIONAL COMMUNITY

Article 29

The sea-bed and ocean floor and the subsoil thereof, beyond the limits of national jurisdiction, as well as the resources of the area, are the common heritage of mankind. On the basis of the principles adopted by the General Assembly in resolution 2749 (XXV) of 17 December 1970, all States shall ensure that the exploration of the area and exploitation of its resources are carried out exclusively for peaceful purposes and that the benefits derived therefrom are shared equitably by all States, taking into account the particular interests and needs of developing countries; an international regime applying to the area and its resources and including appropriate international machinery to give effect to its provisions shall be established by an international treaty of a universal character, generally agreed upon.

Article 30

The protection, preservation and enhancement of the environment for the present and future generations is the responsibility of all States. All States shall endeavour to establish their own environmental and developmental policies in conformity with such responsibility. The environmental policies of all States should enhance and not adversely affect the present and future development potential of developing countries. All States have the responsibility to en-sure that activities within their jurisdiction or control do not cause damage to the environment of other States or of areas beyond the limits of national jurisdiction. All States should co-operate in evolving international norms and regulations in the field of the environment.

CHAPTER IV – FINAL PROVISIONS

Article 31

All States have the duty to contribute to the balanced expansion of the world economy, taking duly into account the close interrelationship between the well-being of the developed countries and the growth and development of the developing countries, and the fact that the prosperity of the international community as a whole depends upon the prosperity of its constituent parts.

Article 32

No State may use or encourage the use of economic, political or any other type of measures to coerce another State in order to obtain from it the subordination of the exercise of its sovereign rights.

Article 33

1.   Nothing in the present Charter shall be construed as impairing or derogating from the provisions of the Charter of the United Nations or actions taken in pursuance thereof.

2.   In their interpretation and application, the provisions of the present Charter are interrelated and each provision should be construed in the context of the other provisions.

Article 34

An item on the Charter of Economic Rights and Duties of States shall be included in the agenda of the General Assembly at its thirtieth session, and thereafter on the agenda of every fifth session. In this way a systematic and comprehensive consideration of the implementation of the Charter, covering both progress achieved and any improvements and additions which might become necessary, would be carried out and appropriate measures recommended. Such consideration should take into account the evolution of all the economic, social, legal and other factors related to the principles upon which the present Charter is based and on its purpose.

2315th plenary meeting

12 December 1974

I.7. DRAFT ARTICLES ON STATE RESPONSIBILITY

International Law Commission
Draft Articles on Responsibility of States for Internationally Wrongful Acts
as last amended in 2001[1]

Part One: The Internationally Wrongful Act of a State

Chapter I – GENERAL PRINCIPLES

Article 1. Responsibility of a State for its Internationally Wrongful Acts

Every internationally wrongful act of a State entails the international responsibility of that State.

Article 2. Elements of an Internationally Wrongful Act of a State

There is an internationally wrongful act of a State when conduct consisting of an action or omission:

(a)   is attributable to the State under international law; and

(b)   constitutes a breach of an international obligation of the State.

Article 3. Characterization of an Act of a State as Internationally Wrongful

The characterization of an act of a State as internationally wrongful is governed by international law.

Such characterization is not affected by the characterization of the same act as lawful by internal law.

Chapter II – ATTRIBUTION OF CONDUCT TO A STATE

Article 4. Conduct of Organs of a State

1.   The conduct of any State organ shall be considered an act of that State under international law, whether the organ exercises legislative, executive, judicial or any other functions, whatever position it holds in the organization of the State, and whatever its character as an organ of the central Government or of a territorial unit of the State.

2.   An organ includes any person or entity which has that status in accordance with the internal law of the State.

Article 5. Conduct of Persons or Entities Exercising Elements of Governmental Authority

The conduct of a person or entity which is not an organ of the State under article 4 but which is empowered by the law of that State to exercise elements of the governmental authority shall be considered an act of the State under international law, provided the person or entity is acting in that capacity in the particular instance.

Article 6. Conduct of Organs Placed at the Disposal of a State by Another State

The conduct of an organ placed at the disposal of a State by another State shall be considered an act of the former State under international law if the organ is acting in the exercise of elements of the governmental authority of the State at whose disposal it is placed.

---

1   The Draft Articles, together with extensive commentary, are available at
http://legal.un.org/ilc/texts/instruments/english/commentaries/9_6_2001.pdf.

Article 7. Excess of Authority or Contravention of Instructions

The conduct of an organ of a State or of a person or entity empowered to exercise elements of the governmental authority shall be considered an act of the State under international law if the organ, person or entity acts in that capacity, even if it exceeds its authority or contravenes instructions.

Article 8. Conduct Directed or Controlled by a State

The conduct of a person or group of persons shall be considered an act of a State under international law if the person or group of persons is in fact acting on the instructions of, or under the direction or control of, that State in carrying out the conduct.

Article 9. Conduct Carried out in the Absence or Default of the Official Authorities

The conduct of a person or group of persons shall be considered an act of a State under international law if the person or group of persons is in fact exercising elements of the governmental authority in the absence or default of the official authorities and in circumstances such as to call for the exercise of those elements of authority.

Article 10. Conduct of an Insurrectional or Other Movement

1.   The conduct of an insurrectional movement which becomes the new Government of a State shall be considered an act of that State under international law.

2.   The conduct of a movement, insurrectional or other, which succeeds in establishing a new State in part of the territory of a pre-existing State or in a territory under its administration shall be considered an act of the new State under international law.

3.   This article is without prejudice to the attribution to a State of any conduct, however related to that of the movement concerned, which is to be considered an act of that State by virtue of articles 4 to 9.

Article 11. Conduct Acknowledged and Adopted by a State as its Own

Conduct which is not attributable to a State under the preceding articles shall nevertheless be considered an act of that State under international law if and to the extent that the State acknowledges and adopts the conduct in question as its own.

Chapter III – BREACH OF AN INTERNATIONAL OBLIGATION

Article 12. Existence of a Breach of an International Obligation

There is a breach of an international obligation by a State when an act of that State is not in conformity with what is required of it by that obligation, regardless of its origin or character.

Article 13. International Obligation in Force for a State

An act of a State does not constitute a breach of an international obligation unless the State is bound by the obligation in question at the time the act occurs.

Article 14. Extension in Time of the Breach of an International Obligation

1.   The breach of an international obligation by an act of a State not having a continuing character occurs at the moment when the act is performed, even if its effects continue.

2.   The breach of an international obligation by an act of a State having a continuing character extends over the entire period during which the act continues and remains not in conformity with the international obligation.

3.   The breach of an international obligation requiring a State to prevent a given event occurs when the event occurs and extends over the entire period during which the event continues and remains not in conformity with that obligation.

Article 15. Breach Consisting of a Composite Act

1.   The breach of an international obligation by a State through a series of actions or omissions defined in aggregate as wrongful occurs when the action or omission occurs which, taken with the other actions or omissions, is sufficient to constitute the wrongful act.

2.   In such a case, the breach extends over the entire period starting with the first of the actions or omissions of the series and lasts for as long as these actions or omissions are repeated and remain not in conformity with the international obligation.

Chapter IV – RESPONSIBILITY OF A STATE IN CONNECTION WITH THE ACT OF ANOTHER STATE

Article 16. Aid or Assistance in the Commission of an Internationally Wrongful Act

A State which aids or assists another State in the commission of an internationally wrongful act by the latter is internationally responsible for doing so if:

(a)   that State does so with knowledge of the circumstances of the internationally wrongful act; and

(b)   the act would be internationally wrongful if committed by that State.

Article 17. Direction and Control Exercised over the Commission
of an Internationally Wrongful Act

A State which directs and controls another State in the commission of an internationally wrongful act by the latter is internationally responsible for that act if:

(a)   that State does so with knowledge of the circumstances of the internationally wrongful act; and

(b)   the act would be internationally wrongful if committed by that State.

Article 18. Coercion of Another State

A State which coerces another State to commit an act is internationally responsible for that act if:

(a)   the act would, but for the coercion, be an internationally wrongful act of the coerced State; and

(b)   the coercing State does so with knowledge of the circumstances of the act.

Article 19. Effect of this Chapter

This chapter is without prejudice to the international responsibility, under other provisions of these articles, of the State which commits the act in question, or of any other State.

Chapter V – CIRCUMSTANCES PRECLUDING WRONGFULNESS

Article 20. Consent

Valid consent by a State to the commission of a given act by another State precludes the wrongfulness of that act in relation to the former State to the extent that the act remains within the limits of that consent.

Article 21. Self-Defence

The wrongfulness of an act of a State is precluded if the act constitutes a lawful measure of self-defence taken in conformity with the Charter of the United Nations.

Article 22. Countermeasures in Respect of an Internationally Wrongful Act

The wrongfulness of an act of a State not in conformity with an international obligation towards another State is precluded if and to the extent that the act constitutes a countermeasure taken against the latter State in accordance with chapter II of Part Three.

Article 23. Force Majeure

1.   The wrongfulness of an act of a State not in conformity with an international obligation of that State is precluded if the act is due to force majeure, that is the occurrence of an irresistible force or of an unforeseen event, beyond the control of the State, making it materially impossible in the circumstances to perform the obligation.

2.   Paragraph 1 does not apply if:

(a)   the situation of force majeure is due, either alone or in combination with other factors, to the conduct of the State invoking it; or

(b)   the State has assumed the risk of that situation occurring.

Article 24. Distress

1.   The wrongfulness of an act of a State not in conformity with an international obligation of that State is precluded if the author of the act in question has no other reasonable way, in a situation of distress, of saving the author's life or the lives of other persons entrusted to the author's care.

2.   Paragraph 1 does not apply if:

(a)   the situation of distress is due, either alone or in combination with other factors, to the conduct of the State invoking it; or

(b)   the act in question is likely to create a comparable or greater peril.

Article 25. Necessity

1.   Necessity may not be invoked by a State as a ground for precluding the wrongfulness of an act not in conformity with an international obligation of that State unless the act:

(a)   is the only way for the State to safeguard an essential interest against a grave and imminent peril; and

(b)   does not seriously impair an essential interest of the State or States towards which the obligation exists, or of the international community as a whole.

2.   In any case, necessity may not be invoked by a State as a ground for precluding wrong-fulness if:

(a)   the international obligation in question excludes the possibility of invoking necessity; or

(b)   the State has contributed to the situation of necessity.

Article 26. Compliance with Peremptory Norms

Nothing in this chapter precludes the wrongfulness of any act of a State which is not in conformity with an obligation arising under a peremptory norm of general international law.

Article 27. Consequences of Invoking a Circumstance Precluding Wrongfulness

The invocation of a circumstance precluding wrongfulness in accordance with this chapter is without prejudice to:

(a)   compliance with the obligation in question, if and to the extent that the circumstance precluding wrongfulness no longer exists;

(b)   the question of compensation for any material loss caused by the act in question.

Part Two: Content of the International Responsibility of a State

Chapter I – GENERAL PRINCIPLES

Article 28. Legal Consequences of an Internationally Wrongful Act

The international responsibility of a State which is entailed by an internationally wrongful act in accordance with the provisions of Part One involves legal consequences as set out in this Part.

Article 29. Continued Duty of Performance

The legal consequences of an internationally wrongful act under this Part do not affect the continued duty of the responsible State to perform the obligation breached.

Article 30. Cessation and Non-Repetition

The State responsible for the internationally wrongful act is under an obligation:

(a)   to cease that act, if it is continuing;

(b)   to offer appropriate assurances and guarantees of non-repetition, if circumstances so require.

Article 31. Reparation

1.   The responsible State is under an obligation to make full reparation for the injury caused by the internationally wrongful act.

2.   Injury includes any damage, whether material or moral, caused by the internationally wrongful act of a State.

Article 32. Irrelevance of Internal Law

The responsible State may not rely on the provisions of its internal law as justification for failure to comply with its obligations under this Part.

Article 33. Scope of International Obligations Set out in this Part

1.   The obligations of the responsible State set out in this Part may be owed to another State, to several States, or to the international community as a whole, depending in particular on the character and content of the international obligation and on the circumstances of the breach.

2.   This Part is without prejudice to any right, arising from the international responsibility of a State, which may accrue directly to any person or entity other than a State.

Chapter II – REPARATION FOR INJURY

Article 34. Forms of Reparation

Full reparation for the injury caused by the internationally wrongful act shall take the form of restitution, compensation and satisfaction, either singly or in combination, in accordance with the provisions of this chapter.

Article 35. Restitution

A State responsible for an internationally wrongful act is under an obligation to make restitution, that is, to re-establish the situation which existed before the wrongful act was committed, provided and to the extent that restitution:

(a)   is not materially impossible;

(b)   does not involve a burden out of all proportion to the benefit deriving from restitution instead of compensation.

Article 36. Compensation

1.   The State responsible for an internationally wrongful act is under an obligation to compensate for the damage caused thereby, insofar as such damage is not made good by restitution.

2.   The compensation shall cover any financially assessable damage including loss of profits insofar as it is established.

Article 37. Satisfaction

1.   The State responsible for an internationally wrongful act is under an obligation to give satisfaction for the injury caused by that act insofar as it cannot be made good by restitution or compensation.

2.   Satisfaction may consist in an acknowledgement of the breach, an expression of regret, a formal apology or another appropriate modality.

3.   Satisfaction shall not be out of proportion to the injury and may not take a form humiliating to the responsible State.

Article 38. Interest

1.   Interest on any principal sum due under this chapter shall be payable when necessary in order to ensure full reparation. The interest rate and mode of calculation shall be set so as to achieve that result.

2.   Interest runs from the date when the principal sum should have been paid until the date the obligation to pay is fulfilled.

Article 39. Contribution to the Injury

In the determination of reparation, account shall be taken of the contribution to the injury by wilful or negligent action or omission of the injured State or any person or entity in relation to whom reparation is sought.

Chapter III – SERIOUS BREACHES OF OBLIGATIONS UNDER PEREMPTORY NORMS OF GENERAL INTERNATIONAL LAW

Article 40. Application of this Chapter

1.   This chapter applies to the international responsibility which is entailed by a serious breach by a State of an obligation arising under a peremptory norm of general international law.

2.   A breach of such an obligation is serious if it involves a gross or systematic failure by the responsible State to fulfil the obligation.

Article 41. Particular Consequences of a Serious Breach of an Obligation under this Chapter

1.   States shall cooperate to bring to an end through lawful means any serious breach within the meaning of article 40.

2.   No State shall recognize as lawful a situation created by a serious breach within the meaning of article 40, nor render aid or assistance in maintaining that situation.

3.   This article is without prejudice to the other consequences referred to in this Part and to such further consequences that a breach to which this chapter applies may entail under international law.

Part Three: The Implementation of the International Responsibility of a State

Chapter I – INVOCATION OF THE RESPONSIBILITY OF A STATE

Article 42. Invocation of Responsibility by an Injured State

A State is entitled as an injured State to invoke the responsibility of another State if the obligation breached is owed to:

(a) that State individually; or

(b) a group of States including that State, or the international community as a whole, and the breach of the obligation:

    (i) specially affects that State; or

    (ii) is of such a character as radically to change the position of all the other States to which the obligation is owed with respect to the further performance of the obligation.

Article 43. Notice of Claim by an Injured State

1. An injured State which invokes the responsibility of another State shall give notice of its claim to that State.

2. The injured State may specify in particular:

(a) the conduct that the responsible State should take in order to cease the wrongful act, if it is continuing;

(b) what form reparation should take in accordance with the provisions of Part Two.

Article 44. Admissibility of Claims

The responsibility of a State may not be invoked if:

(a) the claim is not brought in accordance with any applicable rule relating to the nationality of claims;

(b) the claim is one to which the rule of exhaustion of local remedies applies and any available and effective local remedy has not been exhausted.

Article 45. Loss of the Right to Invoke Responsibility

The responsibility of a State may not be invoked if:

(a) the injured State has validly waived the claim;

(b) the injured State is to be considered as having, by reason of its conduct, validly acquiesced in the lapse of the claim.

Article 46. Plurality of Injured States

Where several States are injured by the same internationally wrongful act, each injured State may separately invoke the responsibility of the State which has committed the internationally wrongful act.

Article 47. Plurality of Responsible States

1. Where several States are responsible for the same internationally wrongful act, the responsibility of each State may be invoked in relation to that act.

2. Paragraph 1:

(a) does not permit any injured State to recover, by way of compensation, more than the damage it has suffered;

(b) is without prejudice to any right of recourse against the other responsible States.

Article 48. Invocation of Responsibility by a State Other than an Injured State

1.   Any State other than an injured State is entitled to invoke the responsibility of another State in accordance with paragraph 2 if:

(a)   the obligation breached is owed to a group of States including that State, and is established for the protection of a collective interest of the group; or

(b)   the obligation breached is owed to the international community as a whole.

2.   Any State entitled to invoke responsibility under paragraph 1 may claim from the responsible State:

(a)   cessation of the internationally wrongful act, and assurances and guarantees of non-repetition in accordance with article 30; and

(b)   performance of the obligation of reparation in accordance with the preceding articles, in the interest of the injured State or of the beneficiaries of the obligation breached.

3.   The requirements for the invocation of responsibility by an injured State under articles 43, 44 and 45 apply to an invocation of responsibility by a State entitled to do so under paragraph 1.

Chapter II – COUNTERMEASURES

Article 49. Object and Limits of Countermeasures

1.   An injured State may only take countermeasures against a State which is responsible for an internationally wrongful act in order to induce that State to comply with its obligations under Part Two.

2.   Countermeasures are limited to the non-performance for the time being of international obligations of the State taking the measures towards the responsible State.

3.   Countermeasures shall, as far as possible, be taken in such a way as to permit the resumption of performance of the obligations in question.

Article 50. Obligations Not Affected by Countermeasures

1.   Countermeasures shall not affect:

(a)   the obligation to refrain from the threat or use of force as embodied in the Charter of the United Nations;

(b)   obligations for the protection of fundamental human rights;

(c)   obligations of a humanitarian character prohibiting reprisals;

(d)   other obligations under peremptory norms of general international law.

2.   A State taking countermeasures is not relieved from fulfilling its obligations:

(a)   under any dispute settlement procedure applicable between it and the responsible State;

(b)   to respect the inviolability of diplomatic or consular agents, premises, archives and documents.

Article 51. Proportionality

Countermeasures must be commensurate with the injury suffered, taking into account the gravity of the internationally wrongful act and the rights in question.

Article 52. Conditions Relating to Resort to Countermeasures

1.   Before taking countermeasures, an injured State shall:

(a)   call upon the responsible State, in accordance with article 43, to fulfil its obligations under Part Two;

(b)   notify the responsible State of any decision to take countermeasures and offer to negotiate with that State.

2.   Notwithstanding paragraph 1 (b), the injured State may take such urgent countermeasures as are necessary to preserve its rights.

3.   Countermeasures may not be taken, and if already taken must be suspended without undue delay if:

(a)   the internationally wrongful act has ceased; and

(b)   the dispute is pending before a court or tribunal which has the authority to make decisions binding on the parties.

4.   Paragraph 3 does not apply if the responsible State fails to implement the dispute settlement procedures in good faith.

Article 53. Termination of Countermeasures

Countermeasures shall be terminated as soon as the responsible State has complied with its obligations under Part Two in relation to the internationally wrongful act.

Article 54. Measures Taken by States Other than an Injured State

This chapter does not prejudice the right of any State, entitled under article 48, paragraph 1, to invoke the responsibility of another State, to take lawful measures against that State to ensure cessation of the breach and reparation in the interest of the injured State or of the beneficiaries of the obligation breached.

Part Four: General Provisions

Article 55. Lex Specialis

These articles do not apply where and to the extent that the conditions for the existence of an internationally wrongful act or the content or implementation of the international responsibility of a State are governed by special rules of international law.

Article 56. Questions of State Responsibility Not Regulated by These Articles

The applicable rules of international law continue to govern questions concerning the responsibility of a State for an internationally wrongful act to the extent that they are not regulated by these articles.

Article 57. Responsibility of an International Organization

These articles are without prejudice to any question of the responsibility under international law of an international organization, or of any State for the conduct of an international organization.

Article 58. Individual Responsibility

These articles are without prejudice to any question of the individual responsibility under international law of any person acting on behalf of a State.

Article 59. Charter of the United Nations

These articles are without prejudice to the Charter of the United Nations.

II. Early Examples of Trade and Investment Treaties

(1st Generation Bilateral Investment Treaties (BITs))

II.1. THE CAPITULATIONS AND ARTICLES OF PEACE BETWEEN THE MAJESTY OF THE KING OF ENGLAND, SCOTLAND, FRANCE & IRELAND &C. AND THE SULTAN OF THE OTTOMAN EMPIRE

Printed at Constantinople in the year of our Lord 1663 [excerpts]

as they have been augmented, & altered in the times of every Ambassador and as now lately in the City of Adrianople in the month of January 1661 they have been augmented, renewed, & amplified with diverse additional articles, & privileges, which serve towards the maintenance of a well grounded peace, & security of the trade, & traffic of his Majesties subjects in the Levant, by his Excellency Heneage Earle of Winchilsea Ambassador Extraordinary from his Majesty Charles the Second King of Great Britain, France, & Ireland to Sultan Mahomet Han the Most Puissant Prince, & Emperor of the Turkes.

According to My Imperial Command let it be observed, & let no Act be permitted contrary hereunto.   Mahomet

The command of this sublime, & lofty, & imperial signature preserved, & exalted by divine providence, whose triumph and glory is renowned through all the world:

By the favour of the nourisher of all things, & mercy & grace of the Merciful, I that am the powerful Lord of Lords of the whole world whose name is formidable upon earth, giver of all crownes of the universe, Sultan Mahomet Han, Son of Sultan Ibrahim Han, Son of Sultan Ahmet Han, [...].

To the glorious among the Great Princes of Jesus reverenced by the high Potentates of the people of the Messiah Sole Directour of the important affaires of the Nazarene Nation, Lord of the limits of decency, & honour of greatness, & fame, Charles the Second King of England, & Scotland, that is of Great Britain, France, & Ireland, whose end, & enterprises may the omnipotent God conclude with bliss, & favour with the illumination of his holy will.

In times past the Queen of the aforesaid Kingdoms sent diverse of her esteemed gentlemen & persons of quality, with letters & ships, to this Imperial High Port (the refuge of the princes of the world & the retreat of the kings of the whole universe) in the happy times of famous memory of my ancestors, now placed in paradise, whose souls be replenished with divine mercy, which gentlemen & presents were gratefully accepted, making declaration & offering in the name of the said Queen an entire good peace & pure friendship & demanding that their subjects might have leave to come from England into our ports. Our said ancestors of happy memory did then grant their Imperial license & gave into the hands of the English nation diverse special & Imperial commands, to the end that they might safely & securely come & go into these dominions & in coming or returning either by land, or sea, in their way & passage, that they should of no man be molested, or hindered. After which time in the days of our Grandfather Sultan Mahomet Han of famous memory (unto whose soul be granted divine absolution) it being anew desired that the subjects, merchants & their interpreters might freely & securely come, merchandise & negotiate through all the parts of this Imperial dominion & that such capitulations & other privileges & Imperial commands, as had been granted unto the nation of the Kings & Princes in peace & amity, with this High Port, as France, Venice, Poland & others, might also be granted to the subjects of the said Queen & all others coming under the English banner. In confirmation of which request, were given & confirmed by our ancestors of famous memory the Imperial Capitulations, & privileges, succeeding to say it is commanded &c.

I

First that the said Nation & the English merchants & any other nation, or merchants which are or shall come under the English banner & protection, with their ships small & great, merchandise, faculties & all other their goods, may always pass safely in our seas & freely & in all security may come & go into any part of the Imperial limits of our dominion in such sort that neither any of the nation, their goods & faculties shall receive any hindrance, or molestation from any person whatsoever.

II

The said nation shall & may in like manner freely & securely come & go by land through all the Imperial limits of our dominions, so that neither their persons, beasts, goods, or faculties, shall any trouble, or impediment be given, nor any injury be done unto them but they shall always at their own pleasures safely & securely traffic in all parts of our dominions.

III

And if it happens that any of the said nation coming into our dominions by land, or passing into any other country shall be stayed, or arrested by any of our ministers, such persons shall be set free & at liberty & afterwards shall receive no hindrance in his journey.

IV

All English ships, or vessels, small or great, shall & may at any time safely & securely come & harbour in any of the scales & ports of our dominions & likewise may from thence depart at their pleasure without the detention or hindrance of any man.

V

And if it shall happen that any English vessel, great or small, fall into any misfortune, danger of sea, or any other necessity, all the vessels, as well Imperial, as belonging to private men that shall be near, or present, as also others that inhabit the seas, shall give them help & succour & being come into our ports or scales they shall freely stay in them as long as they please & for their money provide them of all necessaries & provision & may take water without the let, or hindrance of any man.

VI

And if it shall happen that any of their ships shall have suffered shipwreck, or been broken, or in distress, shall be cast upon any coast of our dominions in which case all Beglarbeggs, Caddees, Governours, Ministers & other our slaves, shall give them all assistance, succour & help & whatever goods & faculties shall be saved, or recovered in the said ships shall be restored to the English & if they shall be informed that any part of their goods & faculties shall be stolen, or taken away, our said Ministers with all diligence shall make sufficient search & examination to find out & recover the goods & restore them to the English.

VII

The English merchants, interpreters, brokers & all other subjects of that nation, whether by sea or land, may freely & safely come & go in all the ports of our dominions, or returning into their own country, all our Beglerbeges, Ministers, Governours & other Officers, Captains by sea of ships & others whomsoever our slaves & subjects, we command, that none of them do, or shall lay hands upon their persons, of faculties, or upon any pretense shall do them any hindrance or injury.

VIII

If any English man, either for his own debt, or for surerie of ship shall absent himself, or make escape away, or shall be bankrupt, the creditor shall only pretend his debt upon his own debtor, not on any other English. And if the creditor have not authentic hoget or bill of suretyship made by an English man, he shall not pretend his debt of any other English man.

IX

In all causes & businesses & occasions which shall occur between the said nation, their merchants, interpreters & brokers, or servants & any other whatsoever, that is to say, in selling, or buying, in paying, or receiving, in giving, or taking security, or pledge, debt, or credit & all other such things which appertain to the ministers of the law & justice, they may always (if they please) in such occasions go to the Caddee, who is the Judge of the law & there make a hoget or public authentic act with witness & register the same & take a copy of the same to keep by them, to the end that if in the future any difference or pretense shall arise between the said parties, they may both have recourse to the said hoget & act. And when the pretense shall be conformable to the tenor of the hoget registered, then it shall be accordingly thereunto observed. And if the plaintiff has not in his hands any such authentic hoget, but only brings partial witness, which makes cavills, or pretenses, our Ministers shall not give to them, but observe the written authentic hoget.

X

And if any one within our dominions shall accuse any English man to have done him wrong & shall therefore raise any pretense upon him, by violent or partial witness, our Ministers shall not give care unto them, nor accept them, but the cause shall be advised to the Ambassador or Consul Resident of the English nation, to the end that the business may be decided with his knowledge & in his presence, that the English may always have recourse to their defense & protection.

XI

If any English man having committed an offense shall make his escape, or absent himself, no other Englishman not being pledge, shall be taken, or molested for him.

XII

All Englishmen, or subjects of England, which shall be found slaves in our state, or shall be demanded by the Ambassador, or Consul, the cause shall be duly examined & such persons as are found truly to be subjects of England, shall be set free & delivered to the Ambassador, or Consul.

XIII

All Englishmen & all other subjects of the crown of England which shall dwell, or reside in our dominions, whether they be married, or single, may buy, sell & traffic & of them shall no harach or head money be demanded.

XIV

The English Ambassador or Resident in Aleppo, Alexandria, Tripoli of Syria, or Tunis, Algier, Tripoli of Barbarie, in Smyrna, the ports of Cairo, or any other parts of our dominions, may at their pleasure establish their Consuls & in like manner remove them, or change & appoint others in their places & none of our Ministers shall oppose or refuse to accept them.

XV

In all causes concerning law & justice between the English nation & any other, in the absence of their interpreters, the judges, nor any other of our Ministers, shall not proceed to give sentence.

XVI

If there happens any controversy amongst themselves, the decision thereof shall be wholly left to their own Ambassador or Consul, according to their own right & laws & with no such causes our Ministers shall intermeddle.

XVII

Our Armada of gallies, ships, or any other vessels of our Empire, which at sea meet, or find any English ships, they shall not do them, nor suffer to be done to them, the least injury, or trouble, nor shall they stay them, demand, pretend, or take anything from them, but shall salute & show them good & mutual friendship, the one to the other, without offense.

XVIII

All these particular privileges & capitulations, which in former times have been granted to the French, Venetians, or any other Christian nation, whose King is in peace, or friendship with this Port, in like manner the same were granted & given to the said English nation, to the end that in time to come, the tenour of this our Imperial Capitulations may be always observed by all men & that none may in any manner upon any pretense presume to contradict, or violate it.

XIX

If the pirates or events who infest the seas with their fregates, shall be found to have taken any English vessel, or to have robbed, or spoiled their goods & faculties, also if it shall be found, that in any of our dominions, any shall have violently taken goods of any English man, our Ministers shall with all diligence seek out such offenders & severely punish them & cause that all such goods, ships, moneys & whatsoever has been taken away from the English nation, shall be presently, justly & absolutely restored to them.

XX

All our Beglerbeges, Beges, Captaines, Masters of Imperial ships & other private Judges, Governours, Customers, Farmers & all our Ministers, Subjects & Slaves shall always obey & keep the tenour of these our Capitulations & shall with all observance, respect the friendship & good correspondence established on both parties; every one in particular taking special care not to commit any act contrary thereunto. And as long as the said Queen of England, according to this present agreement of sincere friendship & good correspondence shall be herself & remain with us, in peace, friendship & league, firm, constant & sincere, we do promise also on our parts reciprocally that this peace, friendship, Articles of Capitulations & correspondence in the fore written form shall be forever maintained, observed & respected & of no man any part thereof shall be contradicted, or infringed all which abovementioned Articles of Peace & Friendship were concluded, signed & an Imperial Capitulation granted & confirmed by our ancestors of happy memory.

Since which time his Majesty of England James deceased in the time of our Grandfather of happy memory Sultan Achmet Han having sent unto our Imperial throne, its Ambassadors, letters & presents which were most acceptable. And desired that the already contracted peace & friendship & good correspondence made with our Grandfathers & the Capitulations, Articles, and privileges above written should be again ratified & the said peace & friendship renewed. Further requesting that certain articles very necessary should to the same Capitulations be added. The desire of his Majesty being declared in the Imperial presence of our said Grandfather Sultan Achmet Han was presently granted. And he gave express command, and ordered that the said peace & friendship should be renewed & fortified & the ancient Capitulations & privileges confirmed & that the renewed articles should be inserted & added to the Imperial Capitulations. Granting further to the English nation all those articles & further privileges which were given & written in any Capitulations with other nations, potentates or kings in peace & amity with this Imperial Port; & by this Imperial command he gave order that these his Imperial commands should be obeyed of all men & the tenour of them duly observed. The articles which then were granted & added to the Capitulations were the following.

XXI

That our Ministers shall not demand, or take of the said English nation any custom or other duties of all the dollars & chequeens, they or any under their banner, shall bring in, or transport from place to place, or carry out of our dominions & that neither Beglerbeges, Beyes, Caddees, Treasurers, Mint-Matters, or other, shall take, demand, either dollars, or chequeens from the said nation to change them into small aspres, nor shall give or do them any violance or trouble there upon.

XXII

The English nation & all those that come under their banner, their vessels small & great, shall & may navigate, traffic, buy, sell & abide in all parts of our dominions & excepting arms, gunpowder & other such prohibited commodities, they may load & carry away in their ships whatsoever of our merchandise at their own pleasure, without the impeachment or trouble of any man & their ships & vessels may come safely & securely to anchor at all times & traffic at all times in every part of our dominions & with their money buy virtuals & all other things without any contradiction, or hindrance of any man.

XXIII

And if any difference shall happen with any of the said English nation, by suite in law, or any other controversy, the Caddees, or any other Ministers of our justice, shall not hear, nor decide the cause, until the Ambassador, Consul, or Druggerman of the said nation shall be present.

XXIV

All difference, or suites of law depending with the said nation which shall exceed the value of 4000 aspers shall always be heard & decided at our Imperial port.

XXV

The English nation's Consul, or Resident, in any port of our dominions, being established by the Ambassador resident for the English nation, our Ministers shall have no power to imprison or examine, or seal up their houses, nor to dismiss or displace them from their charge & office, but in case of any difference, or suite with the Consul, there shall be made a certificate to the Imperial port, to that end that the Ambassador may protect & answer for them.

XXVI

When any Englishman, or other under their banner, shall die in our dominions, with their goods or faculties, or anything that belonged unto them, our Escheators, Caddees, or other Minister upon pretense they are goods of the dead, without any owner, shall not meddle, take, or seize any part thereof but they shall always be consigned & remaining to such other English, as the deceased shall by his testament assign & if he died intestate, then the English Consul shall take & receive his faculties & goods & if there be no Consul, the English Resident there shall take the possession & in case there be neither Consul, nor English, the said goods & faculties whatsoever shall be received into the custody of the Caddee of that place & having advised the English Ambassador thereof, the said Caddee shall resign all the said goods unto such persons as the Ambassador shall send with commission to receive them.

XXVII

All these privileges & other liberties granted to the English Nation & those who come under their protection by diverse Imperial commands, whether before or after the date of these Imperial Capitulations, shall be always obeyed & observed & shall always be understood & interpreted in favour of the English nation, according to the tenour & true contents thereof.

XXVIII

Neither the officer called the Caflam or gatherer of the Caddees duties in case of death, nor the Caddee shall pretend, or take of the English nation, any kind of tenths, or Casmetts or fee of division.

XXIX

The Ambassador of the King of England, or Consul residing in our dominions, shall & may take into their service, any ianizary or interpreter at their own charge & choice & no ianizarie nor other slaves shall put them dues or intermeddle with their service against their liking or content.

XXX

The Ambassador of his Majesty of England & Consul & the English nation residing in our Empire, for the use of their own person & families, making must or wine in their own houses, none of our Ministers, Caddees, or Ianizaries shall molest, or hinder them, or demand any duties, or money, or do them any violence, or impediment.

XXXI

In the Port of Constantinople, Aleppo, Alexandria, Scio, Smirna & in other parts of our dominions, the English merchants having paid the custom of their merchandise, according to the tenour of the Imperial Capitulations, no man shall molest, or trouble, or take from them anything more & whatsoever merchandise shall be loaded upon their ships & brought in our dominions & landed at any scale, they being desirous to load it again & to transport it to any other scale, or port, the same goods arriving in the second place & scale & being there unladen, neither the customer, nor farmers, nor any other our officers shall pretend, or take against any customs, or gabells of the said merchandise, that the said nation may always freely & securely trade & follow their business. [...]

XXXVI

The English merchants & all under their banner, shall & may safely throughout our dominion, trade, buy, sell, (except only commodities prohibited) all sorts of merchandise. Likewise, either by land, or sea, they may go & traffic, or by the way of the river Tanais [Don] in Moscovia or by Russia & from thence may bring their merchandise into our Empire, also to & from Persia, they may go & trade & through all that part newly by us conquered & through those confines, without the impediment, or molestation of any of our Ministers & they shall pay the customs & other duties of that country & nothing more.

XXXVII

The English merchants & all under their banner shall & may safely & freely trade & negotiate in Aleppo, Cairo, Scio, Smirna & in all parts of our dominions & according to our ancient customs of all their merchandise, they shall pay three in the hundred for customs & nothing more. [...]

XLI

And if it happens that any of the said English nation, or any under their banner, shall commit manslaughter, bloodshed, or any other like offense, or that there shall happen any cause appertaining to the law, or justice, until the Ambassador or Consul shall be present to examine the cause, the Judges, nor other Ministers, shall not decide nor give any sentence, but such controversy shall always be declared in the presence of the Ambassador, or Consul to the end, that no man be judged, or condemned contrary to the law & the Capitulations. [...]

XLIII

That English merchants which trade at Aleppo, & those under their banner of all the silk which they shall buy & load upon their ships, shall pay the customs & other duties, as the French & Venetian merchants do pay & not one asper, or farthing more. [...]

LXI

And the customs being once paid of any sort of merchandise not sold in that port, which is to be transported to another scale, entire credit shall be given to the Teschere & a second custom shall not be so much as farther pretended. [...]

Let all the forementioned Articles be punctually observed. And the said Ambassador desiring that these additions should be inserted in the Imperial Capitulations, his request was graciously received; & the Imperial Capitulations which were formerly given are renewed & conjoined with these present [articles]. And we command that whilst this present King of England Charles the Second, whose end terminate in bliss & happiness, does in the same manner, as in the times of my deceased progenitors confer the like friendly & faithful correspondence. I do accept &

promise to observe & according to my promise & oath, I swear & promise by that One God, Creator of Heaven & Earth & all of the creatures, that contrary to these present Capitulations, no breach, nor violence shall be offered either by me, or mine but shall be observed by all.

In the Imperial City of Adrianople

Written at the end of the Moone of Zamafiel Vlla in the year 1072

Which is in the month of January 1661

II.2. 1838 TREATY OF BALTA LIMAN

Convention of Commerce and Navigation Between Her Britannic Majesty and the Sultan of the Ottoman Empire

Convention Appended to the Capitulations Granted to Great Britain by the Ottoman Porte, Amending and Altering Certain Stipulations Therein Contained, as Regards the Commerce and Navigation of the Two Countries.

Preamble

During the friendly intercourse which has happily subsisted so long between the Sublime Porte and the Kings of Great Britain. Capitulations granted by the Porte, and Treaties concluded between the Two Powers, have regulated the rates of duties payable on merchandise exported from, and imported into, the Dominations of the Sublime Porte, and have established and declared the rights, privileges, immunities, and obligations of British merchants trading to, or residing in, the Imperial territories. But since the period when the above mentioned stipulations were last revised, changes of various kinds have happened in the internal administration of the Ottoman Empire, and in the external relations of that Empire with other Powers; and Her Majesty the Queen of the United Kingdom of Great Britain and Ireland, and His Highness the Sultan, have therefore agreed now to regulate again, by a special and additional Act, the commercial intercourse of their subjects, in order to increase the trade between their respective Dominions, and to render more easy the exchange of the produce of the one country for that of the other.

They have consequently named for their Plenipotentiaries for this purpose, [...], who after having communicated their respective Full Powers, found to be in due and proper form, have agreed upon and conducted the following Articles:

Article 1

All rights privileges, and immunities which have been conferred on the suspects or ships of Great Britain by the existing Capitulations and Treaties, are confirmed now and for ever, expect in as far as they may be specifically altered by the present Convention; and it is, moreover, expressly stipulated, that all rights, privileges, or immunities which the Sublime Porte now grants, or may here after grant, to the ships and subjects of any other Foreign Power, or which it may suffer the ships and subjects of any other Foreign Power to enjoy, shall be equally granted to, and exercised and enjoyed by, the subjects and ships of Great Britain.

Article 2

The subjects of Her Britannic Majesty, or their agents, shall be permitted to purchase at all places in the Ottoman Dominions (whether for the purposes of internal trade or exportation) all articles, without any exception whatsoever, the produce, growth, or manufacture of the said Dominions; and the Sublime Porte formally engages to abolish all monopolies of agricultural produce, or of any other articles whatsoever, as well as all permits from the local Governors, either for the purchase of any article, or for its removal from one place to another when purchased; and any attempt to compel the subjects of Her Britannic Majesty to receive such permits from the local Governors, shall be considered as an infraction of Treaties, and the Sublime Porte shall immediately punish with severity and Viziers and other Officers who shall have been guilty of such misconduct, and render full justice to British subjects for all injuries or losses which they may duly prove themselves to have suffered.

Article 3

If any article of Turkish produce, growth, or manufacture, be purchased by the British Merchant or his agent, for the purpose of selling the same for internal consumption in Turkey, the British merchant or his agent shall pay, at the purchase and sale of such articles, and in any manner of trade therein, the same duties that are paid, in similar circumstances, by the most favored class of Turkish subjects engaged in the internal trade of Turkey, whether Mussulmans or Rayas.

Article 4

If any article of Turkish produce, growth, or manufacture, be purchased for exportation, the same shall be conveyed by the British Merchant or his agent, free of any kind of charge or duty whatsoever, to a convenient place of shipment, on its entry into which it shall be liable to one fixed duty of nine per cent, ad valorem, in lieu of all other interior duties.

Subsequently, on exportation, the duty of three per cent, as established and existing at present, shall be paid. But all articles bought in the shipping ports for exportation, and which have already paid the interior duty at entering into the same, will only pay the three per cent, export duty.

Article 5

The regulations under which Firmans are issued to British merchant vessels for passing the Dardanelles and the Bosphorus, shall be so framed as to occasion to such vessels the least possible delay.

Article 6

It is agreed by the Turkish Government, that the regulations established in the present Convention, shall be general throughout the Turkish Empire, whether in Turkey in Europe or Turkey in Asia, in Egypt, or other African possessions belonging to the Sublime Porte, and shall be applicable to all the subjects, whatever their description, of the Ottoman Dominions; and the Turkish Government also agrees not to object to other Foreign Powers settling their trade upon the basis of this present Convention.

Article 7

It having been the custom of Great Britain and the Sublime Porte, with a view to prevent all difficulties and delay in estimating the value of articles imported into the Turkish Dominions, or exported therefrom, by British subjects, to appoint, at intervals of fourteen years, a Commission of men well acquainted with the traffic of both countries, who have fixed by a tariff the sum of money in the coin of the Grand Signior, which should be paid as duty on each article; and the term of fourteen years, during which the last adjustment of the said tariff was to remain in force, having expired, the High Contracting Parties have agreed to name conjointly fresh Commissioners to fix and determine the amount in money which is to be paid by British subjects, as the duty of three per cent, upon the value of all commodities imported and exported by them; and the said Commissioners shall establish an equitable arrangement for estimating the interior duties which, by the present Treaty, are established on Turkish goods to be exported, and shall also determine on the places of shipment where it may be most convenient that such duties should be levied.

The new tariff thus established, to be enforce seven years after it has been fixed, at the end of which time it shall be in the power of either of the parties to demand a revision of that tariff; but if no such demand be made on either side, within the six months after the end of the first seven years, then the tariff shall remain in force for seven years more, reckoned from the end of the preceding seven years , and so it shall be at the end of each successive period of seven years.

Article 8

The Present Convention shell be ratified, and the ratifications shall be exchanged at Constantinople within space of four months.

In witness where of, the respective Plenipotentiaries have signed the same, and have affixed their Seals thereunto.

Done at Balta-Liman, near Constantinople, on the 16th day of August, 1838.
(L.S.) MUSTAPHA RESCHID   (L.S.) PONONBY
(L.S) MUSTAPHA KIANEE
(L.S.) MEHMET NOURY

ADDITIONAL ARTICLES

Certain difficulties having arisen between the Ambassador of Her Britannic Majesty and the Plenipotentiaries of the Sublime Porte, in fixing the new conditions which should regulate the commerce in British goods imported into the Turkish Dominions, or passing through the same in transit, it is agreed between his Excellency the British Ambassador and the Plenipotentiaries of the Sublime Porte, that the Present Convention should receive their signatures, without the Articles which have reference to the abovementioned subjects forming part of the body of the said Convention.

But at the same time it is also agreed – the following Articles having been consented to by the Turkish Government – that they shall be submitted to the approbation of Her Majesty's Government, and should they be approved and accepted by her Majesty's Government, they shall then form an integral part of the Treaty now concluded.

The Articles in question are the following:

Article 1

All articles being the growth, produce, or manufacture of the United Kingdom of Great Britain and Ireland and its dependencies, and all merchandise of whatsoever description, embarked in British vessels, and being the property of British subjects, or being brought over land, or by sea, from other Countries by the same, shall be admitted, as heretofore, into all parts of the Ottoman Dominions, without exception, on the payment of three per cent duty, calculated upon the value of such articles.

And in lieu of all other and interior duties, whether levied on the purchaser or seller, to which these articles are at present subject, it is agreed that the importer, after receiving his goods, shall pay, if he sells them at the place of reception, or if he sends them hence to be sold elsewhere in the interior of the Turkish Empire, one fixed duty of two per cent; after which such goods may be sold and resold in the interior, or exported, without any further duty whatsoever being levied or demanded on them.

But all goods that have paid the three per cent import duty at one Port, shall be sent to another free of any further duty, and it is only when sold there or transmitted thence into the interior, that the second duty shall be paid.

It is always understood that Her Majesty's Government do not pretend, either by this Article or any other in the present Treaty, to stipulate for more than the plain and fair construction of the terms employed; nor to preclude, in any manner, the Ottoman Government from the exercise of its rights of internal administration, where the exercise of those rights does not evidently infringe upon the privileges accorded by ancient Treaties, or the present Treaty, to British merchandize or British subjects.

Article 2

All foreign goods brought into Turkey from the other Countries, shall be freely purchased and traded in, in any manner, by the subjects of Her Britannic Majesty, or the agents of the same, at any place in the Ottoman dominions; and if such foreign goods have paid no other duty than the duty paid on importation, then the British subject or his agent shall be able to purchase such foreign goods on paying the extra duty of two per cent, which he will have to pay on the sale of his own imported goods, or on their transmission for sale into the interior; and after that such foreign goods shall be resold in the interior, or exported without further duty; or should such foreign goods have already paid the amount of the two duties (i.e. the import duty and the one fixed interior duty), then they shall be purchased by the British subject or his agent, and afterwards resold or exported, without being ever submitted to any further duty.

Article 3

No charge whatsoever shall be made upon British goods – such being growth, produce, or manufacture of the United Kingdom or its Dependencies, or the growth, produce, or manufacture of any foreign Country, and charged in British vessels and belonging to British subjects – passing through the Straits of the Dardanelles, of the Bosphorus, and of the Black Sea, whether such goods shall pass through those straits in the ships that brought them, or are transshipped in those straits, or, destined to be sold elsewhere, are landed with a view to their being transferred to other vessels (and thus to proceed on their voyage) within a reasonable time.

All merchandise imported into Turkey for the purpose of being transmitted to the other Countries, or which, remaining in the hands of the importer, shall be transmitted by him for sale to other Countries, shall only pay the duty of three per cent paid on importation, and no other duty whatsoever.

Done at Balta-Liman, near Constantinople, the 16th day of August, in the year 1838.

II.3. 1842 TREATY OF NANKING [NANJING]

(Ratifications exchanged at Hongkong, 26 June 1843)

VICTORIA, by the Grace of God, Queen of the United Kingdom of Great Britain and Ireland, Defender of the Faith, etc., etc., etc. To All and Singular to whom these Presents shall come, Greeting! Whereas a Treaty between Us and Our Good Brother The Emperor of China, was concluded and signed, in the English and Chinese Languages, on board Our Ship the Cornwallis, at Nanking, on the Twenty-ninth day of August, in the Year of Our Lord One Thousand Eight Hundred and Forty-two, by the Plenipotentiaries of Us and Our said Good Brother, duly and respectively authorized for that purpose; which Treaty is hereunto annexed in Original:

TREATY

Her Majesty the Queen of the United Kingdom of Great Britain and Ireland, and His Majesty the Emperor of China, being desirous of putting an end to the misunderstandings and consequent hostilities which have arisen between the two Countries, have resolved to conclude a Treaty for that purpose, and have therefor named as their Plenipotentiaries, that is to say:—

Her Majesty the Queen of Great Britain and Ireland, SIR HENRY POTTINGER, Bart., a Major-General in the Service of the East India Company, etc., etc.;

And His Imperial Majesty the Emperor of China, the High Commissioners KEYING [...]

Who, after having communicated to each other their respective Full Powers and found them to be in good and due form, have agreed upon, and concluded, the following Articles:

ARTICLE I

There shall henceforward be Peace and Friendship between Her Majesty the Queen of the United Kingdom of Great Britain and Ireland, and His Majesty the Emperor of China, and between their respective Subjects, who shall enjoy full security and protection for their persons and property within the Dominions of the other.

ARTICLE II

His Majesty the Emperor of China agrees that British Subjects, with their families and establishments, shall be allowed to reside, for the purpose of carrying on their Mercantile pursuits, without molestation or restraint at the Cities and Towns of Canton, Amoy, Foochow-fu, Ningpo, and Shanghai, and Her Majesty the Queen of Great Britain, etc., will appoint Superintendents or Consular Officers, to reside at each of the above-named Cities or Towns, to be the medium of communication between the Chinese Authorities and the said Merchants, and to see that the just Duties and other Dues of the Chinese Government as hereafter provided for, are duly discharged by Her Britannic Majesty's Subjects.

ARTICLE III

It being obviously necessary and desirable, that British Subjects should have some Port whereat they may careen and refit their Ships, when required, and keep Stores for that purpose, His Majesty the Emperor of China cedes to Her Majesty the Queen of Great Britain, etc., the Island of Hongkong, to be possessed in perpetuity by Her Britannic Majesty, Her Heirs and Successors, and to be governed by such Laws and Regulations as Her Majesty the Queen of Great Britain, etc., shall see fit to direct.

ARTICLE IV

The Emperor of China agrees to pay the sum of Six Millions of dollars as the value of Opium which was delivered up at Canton in the month of March 1839, as a Ransom for the lives of Her Britannic Majesty's Superintendent and Subjects, who had been imprisoned and threatened with death by the Chinese High Officers.

ARTICLE V

The Government of China having compelled British Merchants at Canton to deal exclusively with certain Chinese Merchants called Hong Merchants (or Cohong) who had been licensed by the Chinese Government for that purpose, the Emperor of China agrees to abolish that practice in future at all Ports where British Merchants may reside, and to permit them to carry on their mercantile transactions with whatever persons they please, and His Imperial Majesty further agrees to pay to the British Government the sum of Three Millions of Dollars, on account of Debts due to British Subjects by some of the said Hong Merchants (or Cohong), who have become insolvent, and who owe very large sums of money to Subjects of Her Britannic Majesty.

ARTICLE VI

The Government of Her Britannic Majesty having been obliged to send out an Expedition to demand and obtain redress for the violent and unjust Proceedings of the Chinese High Authorities towards Her Britannic Majesty's Officer and Subjects, the Emperor of China agrees to pay the sum of Twelve Millions of Dollars on account of the Expenses incurred, and Her Britannic Majesty's Plenipotentiary voluntarily agrees, on behalf of Her Majesty, to deduct from the said amount of Twelve Millions of Dollars, any sums which may have been received by Her Majesty's combined Forces as Ransom for Cities and Towns in China, subsequent to the 1st day of August 1841.

ARTICLE VII

It is agreed that the Total amount of Twenty-one Millions of Dollars, described in the three preceding Articles, shall be paid as follows:—

Six Millions immediately.

Six Millions in 1843. That is:

> Three Millions on or before the 30th of the month of June, and Three Millions on or before the 31st of December.

Five Millions in 1844. That is:

> Two Millions and a Half on or before the 30th of June, and Two Millions and a Half on or before the 31st of December.

Four Millions in 1845. That is:

> Two Millions on or before the 30th of June, and Two Millions on or before the 31st of December;

and it is further stipulated, that Interest at the rate of 5 per cent. per annum, shall be paid by the Government of China on any portions of the above sums that are not punctually discharged at the periods fixed.

ARTICLE VIII

The Emperor of China agrees to release unconditionally all Subjects of Her Britannic Majesty (whether Natives of Europe or India) who may be in confinement at this moment, in any part of the Chinese Empire.

ARTICLE IX

The Emperor of China agrees to publish and promulgate, under His Imperial Sign Manual and Seal, a full and entire amnesty and act of indemnity, to all Subjects of China on account of their having resided under, or having had dealings and intercourse with, or having entered the Service of Her Britannic Majesty, or of Her Majesty's Officers, and His Imperial Majesty further engages to release all Chinese Subjects who may be at this moment in confinement for similar reasons.

ARTICLE X

His Majesty the Emperor of China agrees to establish at all the Ports which are by the 2nd Article of this Treaty to be thrown open for the resort of British Merchants, a fair and regular Tariff of Export and Import Customs and other Dues, which Tariff shall be publicly notified and promulgated for general information, and the Emperor further engages, that when British Merchandise shall have once paid at any of the said Ports the regulated Customs and Dues agreeable to the Tariff, to be hereafter affixed, such Merchandise may be conveyed by Chinese Merchants, to any Province or City in the interior of the Empire of China on paying a further amount as Transit Duties which shall not exceed [ ] per cent. on the tariff value of such goods.

ARTICLE XI

It is agreed that Her Britannic Majesty's Chief High Officer in China shall correspond with the Chinese High Officers, both at the Capital and in the Provinces, under the term "Communication". The Subordinate British Officers and Chinese High Officers in the Provinces under the terms "Statement" on the part of the former, and on the part of the latter "Declaration", and the Subordinates of both Countries on a footing of perfect equality. Merchants and others not holding official situations and, therefore, not included in the above, on both sides, to use the term "Representation" in all papers addressed to, or intended for the notice of the respective Governments.

ARTICLE XII

On the assent of the Emperor of China to this Treaty being received and the discharge of the first instalment of money, Her Britannic Majesty's Forces will retire from Nanking and the Grand Canal, and will no longer molest or stop the Trade of China. The Military Post at Chinhai will also be withdrawn, but the Islands of Koolangsoo and that of Chusan will continue to be held by Her Majesty's Forces until the money payments, and the arrangements for opening the Ports to British Merchants be completed.

ARTICLE XIII

The Ratification of this Treaty by Her Majesty the Queen of Great Britain, etc., and His Majesty the Emperor of China shall be exchanged as soon as the great distance which separates England from China will admit; but in the meantime counterpart copies of it, signed and sealed by the Plenipotentiaries on behalf of their respective Sovereigns, shall be mutually delivered, and all its provisions and arrangements shall take effect.

Done at Nanking and Signed and Sealed by the Plenipotentiaries on board Her Britannic Majesty's ship Cornwallis, this twenty-ninth day of August, 1842, corresponding with the Chinese date, twenty-fourth day of the seventh month in the twenty- second year of TAOU KWANG.

(L.S.) HENRY POTTINGER,

Her Majesty's Plenipotentiary   Chinese Signatures (3)

II.4. 1843 TREATY OF THE BOGUE

Supplementary Treaty Signed by Their Excellencies
Sir Henry Pottinger and Ki Ying Respectively,
on the Part of the Sovereigns of Great Britain and China,

at the Bogue, 8th October 1843

WHEREAS a Treaty of perpetual Peace and Friendship between Her Majesty the Queen of the United Kingdom of Great Britain and Ireland and His Majesty the Emperor of China was concluded at Nanking and signed on board Her said Majesty's ship Cornwallis on the 29th day of August A.D. 1842, corresponding with the Chinese date of the 24th day of the 7th month of the 22nd year of TAOU KWANG; of which said Treaty of perpetual Peace and Friendship the Ratifications, under the respective Seals and Signs Manual of the Queen of Great Britain, &c., and the Emperor of China, were duly exchanged at Hong Kong on the 26th day of June A.D. 1843 corresponding with the Chinese date, the 29th day of the Fifth month, in the 23rd year of TAOU KWANG; And WHEREAS in the said Treaty it was provided (amongst other things), that the five Ports of Canton, Fuchow-foo, Amoy, Ningpo and Shanghai should he thrown open for the resort and residence of British Merchants, and that a fair and regular Tariff of Export and Import Duties and other Dues should be established at such Ports; And WHEREAS various other matters of detail connected with, and hearing relation to, the said Treaty of perpetual Peace and Friendship have been since under the mutual discussion and consideration of the Plenipotentiary and accredited Commissioners of the High contracting Parties, and the said Tariff and Details having been now finally examined into, adjusted and agreed upon, it has been determined to arrange and record them in the form of a Supplementary Treaty of Articles, which Articles shall he held to be as binding, and of the same efficacy as though they had been inserted in the original Treaty of perpetual Peace and Friendship.

ARTICLE I

The Tariff of Export and Import Duties which is hereunto attached – under the Seals and Signatures of the respective Plenipotentiary and Commissioners – shall henceforward be in force at the five Ports of Canton, Fuchowfoo, Amoy, Ningpo, and Shanghai.

ARTICLE II

The General Regulations of Trade which are hereunto attached – under the Seals and Signatures of the respective Plenipotentiary and Commissioners – shall henceforward be in force at the five aforenamed Ports.

ARTICLE III

All penalties enforced or confiscations made under the III clause of the said General Regulations of Trade shall belong, and be appropriated, to the Public Service of the Government of China.

ARTICLE IV

After the Five Ports of Canton, Fuchow, Amoy, Ningpo and Shanghai shall be thrown open, English merchants shall be allowed to trade only at those Five Ports. Neither shall they repair to any other ports or places, nor will the Chinese people at any other ports or places, be permitted to trade with them. If English merchant vessels shall, in contravention of this Agreement, and of a proclamation to the same purport to be issued by the British Plenipotentiary, repair to any other ports or places, the Chinese Government Officers shall be at liberty to seize and confiscate both vessels and cargoes, and should Chinese people be discovered clandestinely dealing with English merchants at any other ports or places, they shall be punished by the Chinese Government in such manner as the Law may direct.

ARTICLE V

The IV clause of the General Regulations of Trade, on the subject of Commercial Dealings and Debts between English and Chinese merchants is to be clearly understood to be applicable to both Parties.

ARTICLE VI

It is agreed, that English merchants and others residing at or resorting to the Five Ports to be opened shall not go into the surrounding country beyond certain short distances to be named by the local authorities, in concert with the British Consul, and on no pretence for purposes of traffic. Seamen and persons belonging to the ships shall only be allowed to land under authority and rules which will be fixed by the Consul, in communication with the local officers and should any persons whatever infringe the stipulations of this Article and wander away into the country, they shall be seized and handed over to the British Consul for suitable punishment.

ARTICLE VII

The Treaty of perpetual Peace and Friendship provides for British Subjects and their families residing at the Cities and Towns of Canton, Fuchow, Amoy, Ningpo and Shanghai without moles-tation or restraint. It is accordingly determined, that ground and houses; the rent and price of which is to he fairly and equitably, arranged for, according to the rates prevailing amongst the people, without exaction on either side, shall be set apart by the local Officers, in communication with the Consul, and the number of houses built or rented, will be reported annually to the said local Officer by the Consul for the information of their respective Viceroys and Governors, but the number cannot be limited, seeing that it will be greater or less according to the resort of merchants.

ARTICLE VIII

The Emperor of China having been graciously pleased to grant, to all foreign Countries, whose Subjects, or Citizens, have hitherto traded at Canton the privilege of resorting for purposes of trade to the other four Ports of Fuchow, Amoy, Ningpo and Shanghai, on the same terms as the English, it is further agreed, that should the Emperor hereafter, from any cause whatever, be pleased to grant, additional privileges or immunities to any of the subjects or Citizens of such Foreign Countries, the same privileges and immunities will be extended to and enjoyed by British Subjects; but it is to be understood that demands or requests are not, on this plea, to be un-necessarily brought forward.

ARTICLE IX

If lawless natives of China, having committed crimes, or offences, against their own Government, shall flee to Hongkong or to the English Ships of War or English merchant ships for refuge; they shall, if discovered by the English Officers, be handed over once to the Chinese Officers for trial and punishment; or if, before such discovery be made by the English Officers, it should be ascertained, or suspected, by the Officers of the Government of China whither such criminals and offenders have fled, communication shall be made to the proper English Officer, in order that the said criminals and offenders may be rigidly searched for, seized, and, on proof or admission of their guilt, delivered up. In like manner, if any soldier or sailor or other person – whatever his caste or country – who is a Subject of the Crown of England, shall from any cause, or on any pretence, desert, fly, or escape into the Chinese Territory, such soldier, or sailor, or other person, shall be apprehended and confined by the Chinese Authorities, and sent to the nearest British Consular or other Government Officer. In neither case shall concealment or refuge be afforded.

ARTICLE X

At each of the five Ports to be opened to British Merchants one English Cruiser will be stationed to enforce good order and discipline amongst the crews of merchant shipping, and to support the necessary authority of the Consul over British Subjects. The crew of such Ship of War will be carefully restrained by the Officer commanding the Vessel, and they will be subject to all the rules regarding going on shore and straying into the country, that are already laid down for the crews of merchant vessels. Whenever it may be necessary to relieve such Ships of War by another, intimation of that intention will be communicated by the Consul, or by the British Super-intendent of Trade where circumstances will permit, to the local Chinese Authorities, lest the appearance of an additional ship should excite misgivings amongst the people; and the Chinese Cruisers are to offer no hindrance to such relieving ship, nor is she to be considered liable to any port charges or other rules laid down in the General Regulations of Trade, seeing that British Ships of War never trade in any shape.

ARTICLE XI

The Posts of Chusan and Koolangsoo will be withdrawn, as provided for in the Treaty of perpetual Peace and Friendship, the moment all the monies stipulated for in that Treaty shall be paid, and the British Plenipotentiary distinctly and voluntarily agrees that all dwelling houses, store houses, barracks, and other buildings that the British troops or people may have occupied or intermediately built, or repaired, shall be handed over, on the evacuation of the posts, exactly as they stand, to the Chinese Authorities, so as to prevent any pretence for delay, or the slightest occasion for discussion, or dispute, on those points.

ARTICLE XII

A fair and regular Tariff of Duties and other dues having now been established, it is to be hoped, that the system of smuggling which has heretofore been carried on between English and Chinese merchants – in many cases with the open connivance and collusion of the Chinese Custom House Officers – will entirely cease, and the most peremptory Proclamation to all English merchants has been already issued on this subject by the British Plenipotentiary, who will also instruct the different Consuls to strictly watch over and carefully scrutinize the conduct of all persons, using British Subjects, trading under his superintendence. If any positive instance of smuggling transactions coming to the Consul's knowledge he will instantly apprise the Chinese Authorities of the fact, and they will proceed to seize and confiscate all goods – whatever their value or nature – that may have been so smuggled, and will also be at liberty, if they see fit, to prohibit the ship from which the smuggled goods were landed from trading further, and to send her away as soon as her accounts are adjusted and paid. The Chinese Government Officers will, at the same time adopt whatever measures they may think fit with regard to the Chinese merchants and Custom House Officers who may be discovered to be concerned in smuggling.

ARTICLE XIII

All persons whether natives of China, or otherwise, who may wish to convey goods from anyone of the five Ports of Canton, Fuchowfoo, Amoy, Ningpo, and Shanghai to Hong Kong for sale or consumption, shall be at full and perfect liberty to do so on paying the duties on such goods and obtaining a Pass or Port Clearance from the Chinese Custom House at one of the said Ports. Should natives of China wish to repair to Hong Kong to purchase goods, they shall have free and full permission to do so, and should they require a Chinese vessel to carry away their purchases, they must obtain a Pass or Port Clearance, for her at the Custom House of the Port whence the vessel may sail for Hong Kong. It is further settled that in all cases these Passes are to be returned to the Officers of the Chinese Government, as soon as the trip for which they may he granted shall be completed.

ARTICLE XIV

An English Officer will be appointed at Hong Kong one part of whose duty will be to examine the registers and Passes of all Chinese vessels that may repair to that Port to buy or sell goods, and should such Officer at any time find that any Chinese merchant vessel has not a Pass or Register from one of the five Ports, she is to be considered as an unauthorised or smuggling vessel, and is not to be allowed to trade, whilst a report of the circumstance is to be made to the Chinese

Authorities. By this arrangement it is to be hoped, that piracy and illegal traffic will be effectually prevented.

ARTICLE XV

Should natives of China who may repair to Hong Kong to trade, incur debts there, the recovery of such debts must be arranged for, by the English Courts of Justice on the spot, but if the Chinese debtor shall abscond and be known to have property real or personal within the Chinese territory, the rule laid down in the IV Clause of the General Regulations for Trade shall be applied to the case, and it will be the duty of the Chinese Authorities, on application by, and in concert with, the British Consuls, to do their utmost to see justice done between the parties. On the same principle, should a British merchant incur debts at any of the five Ports and fly to Hong Kong, the British Authorities will, on receiving an application from the Chinese Government Officers accompanied by statements and full proofs of the debts, institute an investigation into the claims, and, when established, oblige the defaulter, or debtor, to settle them to the utmost of his means.

ARTICLE XVI

It is agreed, that the Custom House Officers at the five Ports shall make a monthly return to Canton of the Passes granted to vessels proceeding to Hong Kong, together with the nature of their cargoes, and a copy of these returns will be embodied in one return and communicated once a month to the proper English Officer at Hong Kong. The said English Officer will, on his part, make a similar return or communication to the Chinese Authorities at Canton showing the names of Chinese vessels arrived at Hong Kong or departed from that Port, with the nature of their cargoes, and the Canton Authorities will apprise the Custom Houses at the five Ports in order that by these arrangements and precautions all clandestine and illegal trade under the cover of Passes may be averted.

ARTICLE XVII – Additional Article Relating to British Small Craft [...]

A MOST IMPORTANT SUPPLEMENTARY TREATY

Signed and Sealed at Hoomun Chai on the Eighth day of October 1843, corresponding with the Chinese date of the Fifteenth day of the Eighth moon of the 23rd year of TAOU KWANG.

(Signed) HENRY POTTINGER

(Signed) KI YING (in Tartar)

I. PILOTS [...]

VI. IMPORT AND EXPORT DUTIES

Goods, whether imported into, or exported from, any one of the above-mentioned five ports, are henceforward to be taxed according to the Tariff as now fixed and agreed upon, and no further sums are to be levied beyond those which are specified in the Tariff. All duties incurred by an English merchant vessel, whether on goods imported or exported, or in the shape of tonnage dues, must first be paid up in full, which done, the Superintendent of Customs will grant a Port Clearance, and this being shown to the British Consul, he will thereupon return the ship's papers and permit the vessel to depart.

VII. EXAMINATION OF GOODS AT THE CUSTOM-HOUSE

Every English merchant having cargo to load or discharge, must give due intimation thereof and hand particulars of the same to the Consul, who will immediately dispatch a recognised linguist of his own establishment to communicate the particulars to the Superintendent of Customs, that the goods may be duly examined and neither party subjected to loss. The English merchant must also have a properly qualified person on the spot to attend to his interests, when his goods are being examined for duty; otherwise, should there be complaints, these cannot be attended to.

Regarding such goods as are subject by the Tariff to an ad valorem duty, if the English merchant cannot agree with the Chinese officer on fixing a value, the each party shall call two or three Merchants to look at the goods, and the highest price, at which any of these Merchants would be willing to purchase, shall be assumed as the value of the goods.

To fix the tare on any article, such as tea, if the English Merchant cannot agree with the Custom-house officer, then each party shall chose so many chests out of every hundred, which being first weighed in gross, shall afterwards be tared, and the average tare upon these chests shall be assumed as the tare upon the whole, and upon this principle shall the tare be fixed upon all other goods in packages.

If there should still, be any disputed points which cannot be settled, the English merchant may appeal to the Consul, who will communicate the particulars of the case to the Superintendent of the Customs, that it may be equitably arranged. But the appeal must be made on the same day, or it will not be regarded. While such points are still open, the Superintendent of Customs will delay to insert the same in his books, thus affording all opportunity that the merits of the case may be duly tried and sifted.

VIII. MANNER OF PAYING THE DUTIES.

It is hereinbefore provided that every English vessel that enters anyone of the five Ports shall pay all duties and tonnage dues before she be permitted to depart. The Superintendent of Customs will select certain shroffs, or banking establishments, of known stability, to whom he will give licences, authorising them to receive duties from the English merchants on behalf of Government, and the receipt of these shroffs for any moneys paid them shall be considered as a Government Voucher. In the paying of these duties different kinds of foreign money may be made use of, but as foreign money is not of equal purity with sycee silver, the English Consuls appointed to the different ports will, according to time, place, and circumstances, arrange with the Superintendent of Customs at each, what coins may be taken in payment, and what percentage may be necessary to make them equal to standard or pure silver.

IX. WEIGHTS AND MEASURES.

Sets of balance yards for the weighing of goods, of money weights, and of measures, prepared in exact conformity to those hitherto in use at the Custom House of Canton, and duly stamped and sealed in proof thereof, will be kept in possession of the Superintendent of Customs, and also at the British Consulate, at each of the five Ports, and these shall be the standards by which all duties shall be charged, and all sums paid to Government. In case or any dispute arising between British merchants and Chinese Officers of Customs regarding the weights or measures of goods, reference shall be made to these standards, and disputes decided accordingly.

X. LIGHTERS OR CARGOBOATS [...]

XI. TRANSHIPMENT OF GOODS

No English merchant ships may transship goods without special permission; should any urgent case happen where transhipment is necessary, the circumstances must first he submitted to the Consul, who will give a certificate to that effect, and the Superintendent of Customs will then send a Special Officer to be present at the transhipment. If anyone presumes to tranship without such permission being asked for and obtained, the whole of the goods so illicitly transhipped will be confiscated.

XII.SUBORDINATE CONSULAR OFFICERS [...]

XIII. DISPUTES BETWEEN BRITISH SUBJECTS AND CHINESE

Whenever a British subject has reason to complain of a Chinese, he must first proceed to the Consulate and state his grievance. The Consul will thereupon inquire into the merits of the case, and do his utmost to arrange it amicably. In like manner, if a Chinese have reason to complain of a British subject, he shall no less listen to his complaint and endeavour to settle it in a friendly manner. If an English merchant have occasion to address the Chinese authorities, he shall send such address through the Consul, who will see that the language is becoming; and if otherwise, will direct it to be changed, or will refuse to convey the address. If unfortunately any disputes take place of such a nature that the Consul cannot arrange them amicably, then he shall request the assistance of a Chinese officer that they may together examine into the merits of the case, and decide it equitably. Regarding the punishment of English criminals, the English Government will enact the laws necessary to attain that end, and the Consul will be empowered to put them in force; and regarding the punishment of Chinese criminals, these will be tried and punished by their own laws, in the way provided for by the correspondence which took place at Nanking after the concluding of the peace.

XIV. BRITISH GOVERNMENT CRUISERS ANCHORING WITHIN THE PORTS [...]

XV. ON THE SECURITY TO BE GIVEN FOR BRITISH MERCHANT VESSELS [...]

(Signed) HENRY POTTINGER

Signature of Chinese Plenipotentiary.

III. More Modern and More Balanced Treaties of Friendship, Commerce and Navigation (FCNs)

(2nd Generation BITs)

III.1. 1854 U.S. – ARGENTINA TREATY OF FRIENDSHIP, COMMERCE AND NAVIGATION

Concluded 27 July 1853, Ratifications Exchanged 20 December 1854,
Proclaimed 9 April 1855

Commercial intercourse having been for some time established between the United States and the Argentine Confederation, it seems good for the security as well as the encouragement of such commercial intercourse, and for the maintenance of good understanding between the two Governments, that the relations now subsisting between them should be regularly acknowledged and confirmed by the signing to a treaty of friendship, commerce and navigation; for this purpose they have nominated their respective Plenipotentiaries, [...]

Who, after having communicated to each other their full powers, found in good and due form, have agreed upon the following articles:

ARTICLE I [Perpetual Friendship]

There shall be perpetual amity between the United States and their citizens on the one part, and the Argentine Confederation and its citizens on the other part.

ARTICLE II [Freedom of Commerce]

There shall be between all the territories of the United States and all the territories of the Argentine Confederation a reciprocal freedom of commerce. The citizens of the two countries, respectively, shall have liberty, freely and securely, to come with their ships and cargoes to all places, ports and rivers in the territories of either, to which other foreigners, or the ships or cargoes of any other foreign nation or State, are, or may be, permitted to come; to enter into the same, and to remain and reside in any part thereof, respectively; to hire and occupy houses and warehouses, for the purposes of their residence and commerce; to trade in all kinds of produce, manufactures and merchandise of lawful commerce; and generally to enjoy, in all their business, the most complete protection and security, subject to the general laws and usages of the two countries respectively. In like manner, the respective ships of war, and post-office or passenger packets of the two countries, shall have liberty, freely and securely, to come to all harbors, rivers and places to which other foreign ships of war and packets are, or may be, permitted to come; to enter into the same to anchor and remain there and refit, subject always to the laws and usages of the two countries respectively.

ARTICLE III [General MFN]

The two high contracting parties agree that any favor, exemption, privilege or immunity what-ever, in matters of commerce or navigation, which either of them has actually granted, or may hereafter grant, to the citizens or subjects of any other government, nation or state, shall extend, in identity of cases and circumstances, to the citizens of the other contracting party, gratuitously, if the concession in favor of that other government, nation or state, shall have been gratuitous; or, in return for an equivalent compensation, if the concession shall have been conditional.

ARTICLE IV [MFN in Customs Duties]

No higher or other duties shall be imposed on the importation into the territories of either of the two contracting parties of any article of the growth, produce or manufacture of the territories of the other contracting party, than are, or shall be, payable on the like article of any other foreign country; nor shall any other or higher duties or charges be imposed in the territories of either of the contracting parties' on the exportation of any article to the territories of the other, than such as are, or shall be, payable on the exportation of the like article to any other foreign country; nor shall any prohibition be imposed upon the importation or exportation of any article of the growth, produce or manufacture of the territories of either of the contracting parties, to or from the territories of the other, which shall not equally extend to the like article of any other foreign country.

ARTICLE V [MFN in Charges Having Equivalent Effect]

No other or higher duties or charges, on account of tonnage, light or harbor dues, pilotage, salvage in case of average or shipwreck, or any other local charges, shall be imposed in the ports of the two contracting parties on the vessels of the other, than those payable in the same ports on its own vessels.

ARTICLE VI

The same duties shall be paid, and the same drawbacks and bounties allowed, upon the importation or exportation of any article into or from the territories of the United States, or into or from the territories of the Argentine Confederation, whether such importation or exportation be made in vessels of the United States or in vessels of the Argentine Confederation.

ARTICLE VII

The contracting parties agree to consider and treat as vessels of the United States and of the Argentine Confederation all those which, being furnished by the competent authority with a regular passport or sea-letter, shall, under the then existing laws and regulations of either of the two Governments, be recognized fully and bona fide as national vessels, by that country to which they respectively belong.

ARTICLE VIII [Limited National Treatment]

All merchants, commanders of ships and others, citizens of the United States, shall have full liberty, in all the territories of the Argentine Confederation, to manage their own affairs themselves, or to commit them to the management of whomsoever they please, as broker, factor, agent or interpreter; nor shall they be obliged to employ any other persons in those capacities than those employed by citizens of the Argentine Confederation, nor to pay them any other salary or remuneration than such as is paid in like cases by citizens of the Argentine Confederation. And absolute freedom shall be allowed in all cases to the buyer and seller to bargain and fix the price of any goods, wares or merchandise imported into, or exported from, the Argentine Confederation, as they shall see good, observing the laws and established customs of the country. The same rights and privileges, in all respects, shall be enjoyed in the territories of the United States, by the citizens of the Argentine Confederation. The citizens of the two contracting parties shall reciprocally receive and enjoy full and perfect protection for their persons and property, and shall have free and open access to the courts of justice in the said countries respectively, for the prosecution and defense of their just rights, and they shall be at liberty to employ in all cases such advocates, attorneys or agents as they may think proper; and they shall enjoy, in this respect, the same rights and privileges therein as native citizens.

ARTICLE IX

In whatever relates to the police of the ports, the lading and unlading of ships, the safety of the merchandise, goods and erects, and to the acquiring and disposing of property of every sort and denomination, either by sale, donation, exchange, testament or in any other manner whatsoever, as also to the administration of justice, the citizens of the two contracting parties shall reciprocally enjoy the same privileges, liberties and rights, as native citizens; and they shall not be charged, in any of those respects, with any higher imposts or duties than those which are paid, or may be paid, by native citizens, submitting, of course, to the local laws and regulations of each country respectively. If any citizen of either of the two contracting parties shall die without will or testament, in any of the territories of the other, the Consul-General or Consul of the nation to which the deceased belonged, or the representative of such Consul-General or Consul, in his absence, shall have the right to intervene in the possession, administration and judicial liquidation of the estate of the deceased, conformably with the laws of the country, for the benefit of the creditors and legal heirs.

ARTICLE X

The citizens of the United States residing in the Argentine Confederation, and the citizens of the Argentine Confederation residing in the United States, shall be exempted from all compulsory military service whatsoever, whether by sea or by land, and from all forced loans, requisitions or military exactions; and they shall not be compelled, under any pretext whatever, to pay any ordinary charges, requisitions or taxes, greater than those that are paid by native citizens of the contracting parties respectively.

ARTICLE XI

It shall be free for each of the two contracting parties to appoint Consuls, for the protection of trade, to reside in any of the territories of the other party; but, before any Consul shall act as such, he shall, in the usual form, be approved and admitted by the Government to which he is sent; and either of the contracting parties may except from the residence of Consuls such particular peaces as they judge fit to be excepted.

The archives and papers of the consulates of the respective Governments shall be respected inviolably, and under no pretext whatever shall any magistrate, or any of the local authorities, seize, or in any way interfere with them.

The Diplomatic Agents and Consuls of the Argentine Confederation shall enjoy, in the territories of the United States, whatever privileges, exemptions and immunities are, or shall be, granted to agents of the same rank, belonging to the most favored nation; and, in like manner, the Diplomatic Agents and Consuls of the United States, in the territories of the Argentine Confederation, shall enjoy, according to the strictest reciprocity, whatever privileges, exemptions and immunities are, or may be, granted in the Argentine Confederation to the Diplomatic Agents and Consuls of the most favored nation.

ARTICLE XII

For the better security of commerce between the United States and the Argentine Confederation, it is agreed that if, at any time, any interruption of friendly commercial intercourse, or any rupture, should unfortunately take place between the two contracting parties, the citizens of either of them, residing in the territories of the other, shall have the privilege of remaining and continuing their trade or occupation therein, without any manner of interruption, so long as they behave peaceably and commit no offense against the laws; and their edects and property, whether intrusted to individuals or to the State, shall not be liable to seizure or sequestration, or to any other demands than those which may be made upon the like effects or property belonging to the native inhabitants of the State in which such citizens may reside.

ARTICLE XIII

The citizens of the United States, and the citizens of the Argentine Confederation, respectively, residing in any of the territories of the other party, shall enjoy, in their houses, persons and properties, the full protection of the Government.

Then shall not be disturbed, molested nor annoyed in any manner, on account of their religious belief, nor in the proper exercise of their peculiar worship, either within their own houses or in their own churches or chapels, which they shall be at liberty to build and maintain, in convenient situations, to be approved of by the local Government, interfering in no way with, but respecting the religion and customs of the country in which they reside. Liberty shall also be granted to the citizens of either of the contracting parties to bury those who may die in the territories of the other, in burial places of their own, which, in the same manner, may be freely established and maintained.

ARTICLE XIV

The present treaty shall be ratified on the part of the Government of the United States within fifteen months from the date, and within three days by His Excellency the Provisional Director of the Argentine Confederation, who will also present it to the first Legislative Congress of the Confederation, for their approval.

The ratifications shall be exchanged at the seat of Government of the Argentine Confederation within the term of eighteen months.

In witness whereof, the respective Plenipotentiaries have signed this treaty, and affixed thereto their seals.

Done at San Jose, on the twenty-seventh day of July, in the year of our Lord one thousand eight hundred and fifty-three.

[SEAL.] ROB'T C. SCHENK

[SEAL.] JNO PENDLETON

[SEAL.] SALVADOR MA. Del CARRIL

[SEAL.] JOSE B. GOROSTIAGA

III.2. 1954 U.S. – Germany Treaty of Friendship, Commerce and Navigation

Signed at Washington 29 October 1954; Ratifications exchanged at Bonn 14 June 1956; Entered into force 14 July 1956

The United States of America and the Federal Republic of Germany,

desirous of strengthening the bonds of friendship existing between them and of encouraging closer economic and cultural relations between their peoples, and being cognizant of the contributions which may be made toward these ends by arrangements promoting mutually advantageous commercial intercourse, encouraging mutually beneficial investments, and establishing mutual rights and privileges,

have resolved to conclude a Treaty of Friendship, Commerce and Navigation, based in general upon the principles of national and of unconditional most-favored-nation treatment reciprocally accorded, [...]

ARTICLE I [General Principles]

1. Each Party shall at all times accord fair and equitable treatment to the nationals and companies of the other Party, and to their property, enterprises and other interests.

2. Between the territories of the two Parties there shall be, in accordance with the provisions of the present Treaty, freedom of commerce and navigation.

ARTICLE II

1. Nationals of either Party shall, subject to the laws relating to the entry and sojourn of aliens, be permitted to enter the territories of the other Party, to travel therein freely, and to reside at places of their choice. Nationals of either Party shall in particular be permitted to enter the territories of the other Party and to remain therein:

(a) for the purpose of carrying on trade between the territories of the two Parties and engaging in related commercial activities;

(b) for the purpose of developing and directing the operations of an enterprise in which they have invested, or in which they are actively in the process of investing, a substantial amount of capital.

2. Each Party undertakes to make available the best facilities practicable for travel by tourists and other visitors with respect to their entry, sojourn and departure, and for the distribution of information for tourists.

3. Nationals of either Party, within the territories of the other Party, shall enjoy freedom of conscience; and they shall be at liberty to hold religious services, both private and public, at suitable places of their choice.

4. Nationals of either Party shall be permitted, within the territories of the other Party, to gather information material for dissemination to the public, and shall enjoy freedom of transmission of such material to be used abroad for publication by the press, radio, television, motion pictures, and other means; and they shall be permitted to communicate freely with other persons inside and outside such territories by mail, telegraph and other means open to general public use.

5. The provisions of the present Article shall be subject to the right of either Party to apply measures that are necessary to maintain public order and protect the public health, morals and safety.

ARTICLE III

1. Nationals of either Party within the territories of the other Party shall be free from molestations of every kind, and shall receive the most constant protection and security. They shall be

accorded in like circumstances treatment no less favorable than that accorded nationals of such other Party for the protection and security of their persons and their rights. The treatment accorded in this respect shall in no case be less favorable than that accorded nationals of any third country or that required by international law.

2.   If, within the territories of either Party, a national of the other Party is taken into custody, the nearest consular representative of his country shall on the demand of such national be immediately notified and shall have the right to visit and communicate with such national. Such national shall:

(a)   receive reasonable and humane treatment;

(b)   be formally and immediately informed of the accusations against him;

(c)   be brought to trial as promptly as is consistent with the proper preparation of his defense; and

(d)   enjoy all means reasonably necessary to his defense, including the services of competent counsel of his choice.

ARTICLE IV

1.   Nationals of either Party shall be accorded national treatment in the application of laws and regulations within the territories of the other Party that establish a pecuniary compensation or other benefit or service, on account of disease, injury or death arising out of and in the course of employment or due to the nature of employment.

2.   Nationals of either Party shall furthermore be accorded national treatment with regard to the application of social security laws and regulations within the territories of the other Party under which benefits are provided without examination of financial need in the following cases:

(a)   sickness, including Temporary disability for work, and maternity;

(b)   old age, invalidity, or occupational disability;

(c)   death of the father, spouse, or any other person liable for maintenance;

(d)   unemployment.

ARTICLE V

1.   Property of nationals and companies of either Party shall receive the most constant protection and security within the territories of the other Party.

2.   The dwellings, offices, warehouses, factories and other premises of nationals and companies of either Party located within the territories of the other Party shall not be subject to molestation or to entry without just cause. Official searches and examinations of such premises and their contents, when necessary shall be made only according to law and with careful regard for the convenience of the occupants and the conduct of business.

3.   Neither Party shall take unreasonable or discriminatory measures that would impair the legally acquired rights or interests within its territories of nationals and companies of the other Party in the enterprises which they have established, in their capital, or in the skills, arts or technology which they have supplied.

4.   Property of nationals and companies of either Party shall not be taken within the territories of the other Party, except for the public benefit and in accordance with due process of law, nor shall it be taken without just compensation. Such compensation shall represent the equivalent of the property taken and shall be made in an effectively realizable form and without unnecessary delay. Adequate provision shall have been made at latest by the time of the taking for the determination and the giving of the compensation.

5.   Nationals and companies of either Party shall in no case be accorded, within the territories of the other Party, less than national treatment and most-favored-nation treatment with respect to

the matters set forth in paragraphs 2 and 4 of the present Article. Moreover, enterprises in which nationals or companies of either Party have a substantial interest shall be accorded, within the territories of the other Party, not less than national treatment and most-favored-nation treatment in all matters relating to the taking of privately owned enterprises into public ownership and to the placing of such enterprises under public control.

ARTICLE VI

1.   Nationals and companies of either Party shall be accorded national treatment with respect to access to the courts of justice and to administrative tribunals and agencies within the territories of the other Party, in all degrees of jurisdiction, both in pursuit and in defense of their rights. It is understood that companies of either Party not engaged in activities within the territories of the other Party shall enjoy such access therein without any requirement of registration or domestication.

2.   Contracts entered into between nationals or companies of either Party and nationals or companies of the other Party, that provide for the settlement by arbitration of controversies, shall not be deemed unenforceable within the territories of such other Party merely on the grounds that the place designated for the arbitration proceedings is outside such territories or that the nationality of one or more of the arbitrators is not that of such other Party. Awards duly rendered pursuant to any such contracts, which are final and enforceable under the laws of the place where rendered, shall be deemed conclusive in enforcement proceedings brought before the courts of competent jurisdiction of either Party, and shall be entitled to be declared enforceable by such courts, except where found contrary to public policy. When so declared, such awards shall be entitled to privileges and measures of enforcement appertaining to awards rendered locally. It is understood, however, that awards rendered outside the United States of America shall be entitled in any court in any State thereof only to the same measure of recognition as awards rendered in other States thereof.

ARTICLE VII

1.   Nationals and companies of either Party shall be accorded, within the territories of the other Party, national treatment with respect to engaging in all types of commercial, industrial, financial and other activity for gain, whether in a dependent or an independent capacity, and whether directly or by agent or through the medium of any form of lawful juridical entity. Accordingly, such nationals and companies shall be permitted within such territories:

(a) to establish and maintain branches, agencies, offices, factories and other establishments appropriate to the conduct of their business;

(b) to organize companies under the general company laws of such other Party, and to acquire majority interests in companies of such other Party; and

(c) to control and manage enterprises which they have established or acquired. Moreover, enterprises which they control, whether in the form of individual proprietorships, companies or otherwise, shall in all that relates to the conduct of the activities thereof, be accorded treatment no less favorable than that accorded like enterprises controlled by nationals or companies of such other Party.

2.   Each Party reserves the right to limit the extent to which aliens may establish, acquire interests in, or carry on enterprises engaged within its territories in communications, air or water transport, taking and administering trusts, banking involving depository functions, or the exploitation of land or other natural resources. However, new limitations imposed by either Party upon the extent to which aliens are accorded national treatment, with respect to carrying on such activities within its territories, shall not be applied as against enterprises which are engaged in such activities therein at the time such new limitations are adopted and which are owned or controlled by nationals or companies of the other Party. Moreover, neither Party shall deny to transportation, communications and banking companies of the other Party the right to maintain

branches and agencies, in conformity with the applicable laws and regulations, to perform functions necessary for essentially international operations in which they engage.

3.   The provisions of paragraph I of the present Article shall not prevent either Party from prescribing special formalities in connection with the establishment of alien controlled enterprises within its territories; but such formalities may not impair the substance of the rights set forth in said paragraph.

4.   Nationals and companies of either Party, as well as enterprises controlled by such nationals or companies, shall in any event be accorded most-favored-nation treatment with reference to the matters treated in the present Article.

ARTICLE VIII

1.   Nationals and companies of either Party shall be permitted to engage, within the territories of the other Party, accountants and other technical experts, executive personnel, attorneys, agents and other specialists of their choice. Moreover, such nationals and companies shall be permitted to engage accountants and other technical experts regardless of the extent to which they may have qualified for the practice of these professions within the territories of such other Party, for the particular purpose of making for internal purposes examinations, audits and technical investigations for, and rendering reports to, such nationals and companies in connection with the planning and operation of their enterprises, and enterprises in which they have a financial interest, within such territories.

2.   Nationals and companies of either Party shall be accorded, within the territories of the other Party, national treatment and most-favored-nation treatment with respect to engaging in scientific, educational, religious and philanthropic activities, and shall be accorded the right to form associations for that purpose under the laws of the country. Nothing in the present Treaty shall be deemed to grant or imply any right to engage in political activities.

ARTICLE IX

1.   Nationals and companies of either Party shall be accorded within the territories of the other Party:

(a)   national treatment with respect to leasing land, buildings and other real property appropriate to the conduct of activities in which they are permitted to engage pursuant to Articles VII and VIII and for residential purposes, and with respect to occupying and using such property; and

(b)   other rights in real property permitted by the applicable laws of such other Party.

2.   Nationals and companies of either Party shall be accorded, within the territories of the other Party, national treatment and most-favored-nation treatment with respect to acquiring, by purchase, lease, or otherwise, and with respect to owning and possessing, personal property of all kinds, both tangible and intangible. However, either Party may impose restrictions on alien ownership of materials dangerous from the standpoint of public safety and alien ownership of interests in enterprises carrying on the activities listed in the first sentence of paragraph 2 of Article VII, but only to the extent that this can be done without impairing the rights and privileges secured by Article VII or by other provisions of the present Treaty.

3.   Nationals and companies of either Party shall be or accorded national treatment, within the territories of the other Party, with respect to acquiring property of all kinds by testate or intestate succession or under judicial sale to satisfy valid claims. Should they because of their alienage be ineligible to continue to own any such property, they shall be allowed a period of at least five years in which to dispose of it.

4.   Nationals and companies of either Party shall be accorded, within the territories of the other Party, national treatment and most-favored-nation treatment with respect to disposing of property of all kinds.

ARTICLE X [National Treatment in IPRs]

1.   Nationals and companies of either Party shall be accorded, within the territories of the other Party, national treatment with respect to obtaining and maintaining patents of invention, and with respect to rights in trade-marks, trade names, trade-labels, and industrial property of every kind.

2.   The Parties undertake to cooperate in furthering to the interchange and use of scientific and technical knowledge, particularly in the interests of increasing productivity and improving standards of living within their respective territories.

ARTICLE XI [National Treatment in Taxation]

1.   Nationals of either Party residing within the territories of the other Party, and nationals and companies of either Party engaged in trade or other gainful pursuit or in scientific, educational, religious or philanthropic activities within the territories of the other Party, shall not be subject to the payment of taxes, fees or charges imposed upon or applied to income, capital, transactions, activities or any other object, or to requirements with respect to the levy and collection thereof, within the territories of such other Party, more burdensome than those borne in like situations by nationals and companies of such other Party.

2.   With respect to nationals of either Party who are neither resident nor engaged in trade or other gainful pursuit within the territories of the other Party, and with respect to companies of either Party which are not engaged in trade or other gainful pursuit within the territories of the other Party, it shall be the aim of such other Party to apply in general the principle set forth in paragraph 1 of the present Article.

3.   Nationals and companies of either Party shall in no case be subject, within the territories of the other Party, to the payment of taxes, fees or charges imposed upon or applied to income, capital, transactions, activities or any other object, or to requirements with respect to the levy and collection thereof, more burdensome than those borne in like situations by nationals, residents and companies of any third country.

4.   In the case of companies and of nonresident nationals of either Party engaged in trade or other gainful pursuit, within the territories of the other Party, such other Party, shall not impose or apply any tax, fee or charge upon any income, capital or other basis in excess of that reasonably allocable or apportionable to its territories, nor grant deductions and exemptions less than those reasonably allocable or apportionable to its territories. A comparable rule shall apply also in the case of companies organized and operated exclusively for scientific, educational, religious or philanthropic purposes.

5.   Each Party reserves the right to:

(a)   extend specific tax advantages on the basis of reciprocity;

(b)   accord special tax advantages by virtue of agreements for the avoidance of double taxation or the mutual protection of revenue; and

(c)   apply special provisions in allowing, to nonresidents, exemptions of a personal nature in connection with income and inheritance taxes.

ARTICLE XII [Free Movement of Capital]

1.   Nationals and companies of either Party shall be accorded national treatment and most-favored-nation treatment by the other Party with respect to the assumption of undertakings for, and the making of, payments, remittances, and transfers of moneys and financial instruments.

2.   It is agreed that no provision of the present Treaty shall be applied in such a manner as to alter arrangements applicable to either Party by virtue of its membership in the international Monetary Fund.

3.   Neither Party may, with respect to the other Party, in any manner impose exchange restrictions which are unnecessarily detrimental to or arbitrarily discriminate against the claims, investments, transportation, trade or other interests of nationals and companies of such other Party or their competitive position. Should either Party impose exchange restrictions with respect to the other Party, it will remove them as rapidly as it is able to do so considering its economic condition.

4.   The two Parties, recognizing that the international movement of investment capital and the returns thereon would be conducive to the full realization of the objectives of the present Treaty, are agreed that such movements shall not be unnecessarily hampered. In accordance with this mutually agreed principle, each Party undertakes to afford to nationals and companies of the other Party reasonable facilities for the withdrawal of funds earned by them as a result of making or maintaining capital investments as well as for the transfer of capital investments. The same principle applies with respect to the compensation referred to in Article V, paragraph 4.

5.   The term "exchange restrictions" as used in the present Article includes all restrictions, regu-lations, charges, taxes, fees, and other requirements imposed by either Party, which burden or interfere with the assumption of undertakings for, or the making of, payments, remittances, or transfers of moneys and financial instruments.

6.   All questions arising under the present Treaty concerning foreign exchange restrictions will be governed by the provisions of the present Article.

ARTICLE XIII

Nationals and companies of either Party engaged in business within the territories thereof may operate as commercial travelers either directly or by means of agents or employees within the territories of the other Party, in conformity with the applicable laws and regulations. Such commercial travelers shall, upon their entry into and departure from the territories of such other Party and during their sojourn therein, be accorded most-favored-nation treatment in respect of the customs and other matters, including subject to the exceptions in Article XI, paragraph 5, taxes and charges applicable to them, their samples, their advertising material and the taking of orders, and regulations governing the exercise of their functions.

ARTICLE XIV [MFN and National Treatment]

1.   Each Party shall accord most-favored-nation treatment to products of the other Party, from whatever place and by whatever type of carrier arriving, and to products destined for exportation to the territories of such other Party, by whatever route and by whatever type of carrier, with respect to customs duties and charges of any kind imposed on or in connection with importation or exportation or imposed on the international transfer of payments for imports or exports, and with respect to the method of levying such duties and charges, and with respect to all rules and formalities in connection with importation and exportation.

2.   Neither Party shall impose restrictions or prohibitions on the importation of any product of the other Party, or on the exportation of any product to the territories of the other Party, unless the importation of the like product of, or the exportation of the like product to, all third countries is similarly restricted or prohibited.

3.   Either Party may impose prohibitions or restrictions on sanitary or other customary grounds of a non-commercial nature, or in the interest of preventing deceptive or unfair practices, provided such prohibitions or restrictions do not arbitrarily discriminate against the commerce of the other Party.

4.   Nationals and companies of either Party shall be accorded national treatment and most-favored-nation treatment by the other Party with respect to all matters relating to importation and exportation.

5.   If at any time a question should arise concerning the application of paragraph 2 of the present Article, the two Parties shall consult with a view to determining the application thereof. If such consultation, or consultation pursuant to Article XXIV, paragraph 5, does not lead to a mutually satisfactory conclusion, either Party may give written notice of termination of the present Article; and, notwithstanding the provisions of Article XXIX, the present Article shall terminate three months following receipt of such notice by the other Party.

6.   The provisions of the present Article shall not apply to advantages accorded by either Party by virtue of a customs union or free-trade area of which it may become a member, so long as it informs the other Party of its plans and affords such other Party adequate opportunity for consultation.

ARTICLE XV

1.   Each Party shall promptly publish laws, regulations, and administrative rulings of general application pertaining to rates of duty, taxes or other charges, to the classification of articles for customs purposes, and to requirements or restrictions on imports and exports or the transfers of payments, therefor, or affecting their sale, distribution or use; and shall administer such laws, regulations and rulings in a uniform, impartial and reasonable manner. As a general practice, new or more burdensome administrative requirements affecting imports shall not be enforced until after public notice thereof.

2.   Each Party shall maintain an appeals procedure under which nationals and companies of the other Party, and importers of products of such other Party, shall be able to obtain prompt and impartial review, and correction when warranted, of administrative action relating to customs matters, including the imposition of fines and penalties, confiscations, and rulings on questions of customs classification and valuation by the administrative authorities. Penalties imposed for infractions of the customs and shipping laws and regulations concerning documentation shall be merely nominal in cases resulting from clerical errors or when good faith can be demonstrated.

3.   With reference to marking requirements applicable to imported products, each Party shall as a general practice:

(a)   allow required marks of origin to be affixed after importation;

(b)   not permit markings that result in misrepresenting the true origin of the products; and

(c)   not apply requirements that entail an expense which is economically prohibitive or that result in seriously damaging the product.

ARTICLE XVI

1.   Products of either Party shall be accorded, within the territories of the other Party, national treatment and most-favored-nation treatment in all matters affecting internal taxation, sale, distribution, storage and use.

2.   Articles produced by nationals and companies of either Party within the territories of the other Party or by companies of the latter Party controlled by such nationals and companies, shall be accorded therein treatment no lees favorable than that accorded to like articles of national origin by whatever person or company produced, in all matters affecting exportation, taxation, sale, distribution, storage and use.

ARTICLE XVII [Public Procurement]

1.   Each Party undertakes

(a)   that enterprises owned or controlled by its Government, and that monopolies or agencies granted exclusive or special privileges within its territories, shall make their purchases and sales involving either imports or exports affecting the commerce of the other Party solely in accordance with commercial considerations, including price, quality, availability, marketability, transportation and other conditions of purchase or sale; and

(b) that the nationals, companies and commerce of such other Party shall be afforded adequate opportunity, in accordance with customary business practice, to compete for participation in such purchases and sales.

2. Each Party shall accord to the nationals, companies and commerce of the other Party fair and equitable treatment, as compared with that accorded to the nationals, companies and commerce of any third country, with respect to:

(a) the governmental purchase of supplies;

(b) the awarding of concessions and other government contracts; and

(c) the sale of any service sold by the government or by any monopoly or agency granted exclusive or special privileges.

3. Neither Party shall impose any measure of a discriminatory nature that hinders or prevents the importer or exporter of products of either country from obtaining marine insurance on such products in companies of either Party.

ARTICLE XVIII

1. The two Parties agree that business practices which restrain competition, limit access to markets or foster monopolistic control, and which are engaged in or made effective by one or more private or public commercial enterprises or by combination, agreement or other arrangement among such enterprises, may have harmful effects upon commerce between their respective territories. Accordingly, each Government agrees upon the request of the other Government to consult with respect to any such practices and to take such measures, not precluded by its legislation, as it deems appropriate with a view to eliminating such harmful effect.

2. No enterprise of either Party, including corporations, associations, and government agencies and instrumentalities, which is publicly owned or controlled shall, if it engages in commercial, industrial, shipping or other business activities within the territories of the other Party, claim or enjoy, either for itself or for its property, immunity therein from taxation, suit, execution of judgment or other liability to which privately owned and controlled enterprises are subject therein.

ARTICLE XIX

1. Vessels under the flag of either Party, and carrying the papers required by its law in proof of nationality, shall be deemed to be vessels of that Party.

2. So long as both Parties follow systems of tonnage measurement which are substantially similar, tonnage certificates issued by either Party shall be accepted by the other Party, and vessels shall not be subject to new measurements in the ports of such other Party.

3. The term "vessels", as used in the present Treaty, means all types of vessels, whether privately owned or operated, or publicly owned or operated; but this term does not include vessels of war.

ARTICLE XX

1. Vessels of either Party shall have liberty, on equal terms with vessels of the other Party and on equal terms with vessels of any third country, to come with their cargoes to all ports, places and waters of such other Party open to foreign commerce and navigation. Such vessels and cargoes shall in the ports, places and waters of such other Party be accorded in all respects national treatment and most-favored nation treatment.

2. Vessels of either Party shall be accorded national treatment and most-favored-nation treatment with respect to the right to carry all cargo that may be carried by vessel to or from the territories of the other Party.

3. Goods carried by vessels under the flag of either Party to or from the territories of the other Party shall enjoy the same favors as when transported in vessels sailing under the flag of such

other Party. This applies especially with regard to customs duties and all other fees and charges, to bounties, drawbacks and other privileges of this nature, as well as to the administration of the customs and to transport to and from port by rail and other means of transportation.

4.   The coasting trade and inland navigation are excepted from the provisions of the present Article. However, the vessels of each Party shall be accorded by the other Party most favored-nation treatment with respect to the coasting trade and inland navigation. Moreover, it is understood that vessels of either Party shall be permitted to discharge portions of cargoes at any ports, places or waters of the other Party open to foreign commerce and navigation, and to proceed with the remaining portions of such cargoes to any other such ports, places or waters, and they shall be permitted to load in like manner in the same voyage outward, at the various ports, places and waters open to foreign commerce and navigation; but a right to engage in the coasting trade or inland navigation may not thereby be claimed.

5.   The provisions of the present Article shall not apply to fishing vessels.

ARTICLE XXI

If a vessel of either Party runs aground or is wrecked on the coasts of the other Party, or if it is in distress and must put into a port of the other Party, the latter Party shall extend to the vessel as well as to the crew, the passengers, the personal property of crew and passengers, and to the cargo of the vessel, the same protection and assistance as would have been extended to a vessel under its own flag in like circumstances; and shall permit the vessel after repairs to proceed with its voyage upon conformity with the laws applicable alike to vessels under its own flag. Articles salvaged from the vessel shall be exempt from all customs duties unless they pass into internal consumption; but articles not entered for consumption may be subject to measures for the protection of the revenue pending their exit from the country.

ARTICLE XXII

1.   In all ports of either Party the masters of all vessels under the flag of the other Party, whose crews have ceased to be fully constituted on account of illness or for any other cause, shall be permitted to engage such seamen as may be necessary for the continuation of the voyage.

2.   Nationals of either Party who are seamen may be sent to ports of the other Party to join national vessels, in care of consular officers, either individually or in groups on the basis of seamen's papers issued in lieu of passports. Likewise, nationals of either Party shall be permitted to travel through the territory of the other Party on their way to join vessels or to be repatriated on the basis of seamen's papers used in lieu of passports.

ARTICLE XXIII

1.   There shall be freedom of transit through the territories of each Party by the routes most convenient for international transit:

(a)   for nationals of the other Party, together with their baggage;

(b)   for other persons, together with their baggage, en route to or from the territories of such other Party; and

(c)   for products of any origin en route to or from the territories of such other Party, with or without trans-shipment, warehousing, breaking bulk or change in the mode of transport.

2.   The persons and things referred to in paragraph 1 of the present Article shall be exempt from customs duties, from duties imposed by reason of transit, and from unreasonable charges and requirements; and shall be free from unnecessary delays and restrictions.

3.   The provisions of the present Article shall be subject to the right of either Party to apply measures referred to in Article II, paragraph 5, and nondiscriminatory regulations necessary to prevent abuse of the transit privilege.

ARTICLE XXIV [Exceptions]

1.   The present Treaty shall not preclude the application by either Party of measures:

(a)   regulating the importation or exportation of gold, silver, platinum and the alloys thereof;

(b)   relating to fissionable materials, to radioactive by-products of the utilization or processing thereof, or to materials that are the source of fissionable materials;

(c)   regulating the production of or traffic in arms, ammunition and implements of war, or traffic in other materials carried on directly or indirectly for the purpose of supplying a military establishment;

(d)   necessary to fulfill its obligations for the maintenance or restoration of international peace and security, or necessary to protect Its essential security interests;

(e)   denying to any company in the ownership or direction of which nationals of any third country or countries have directly or indirectly the controlling interest, the advantages of the present Treaty, except with respect to recognition of juridical status and with respect to access to courts; and

(f)   reserving rights and privileges with respect to its national fisheries and marine hunting, and the landing in its ports of fish or fish products or the catch or products of marine hunting taken on board the transporting vessel at sea.

2.   The most-favored-nation provisions of the present Treaty relating to the treatment of goods shall not apply to advantages accorded by the United States of America or its Territories and possessions to one another, to the Republic of Cuba, to the Republic of the Philippines, to the Trust Territory of the Pacific Islands or to the Panama Canal Zone.

3.   The most-favored-nation treatment provisions of the present Treaty shall not apply to advantages accorded by either Party to adjacent countries in order to facilitate frontier traffic.

4.   The provisions of the present Treaty relating to the treatment of goods shall not preclude action by either Party which is required or permitted by the General Agreement on Tariffs and Trade during such time as such Party is a contracting party to the General Agreement. Similarly, the most-favored-nation provisions of the present Treaty shall not apply to special advantages accorded by virtue of the aforesaid Agreement.

5.   If at any time the arrangements provided in the first sentence of paragraph 4 of the present Article should cease to be applicable, the provisions of Article XIV, paragraph 2, shall not apply for a period of twelve months to restrictions in effect at that time. During this period the two Parties will, upon the request of either of them, consult with a view to determining whether, in the light of circumstances then prevailing, any further adjustment may be necessary.

6.   The present Treaty does not affect provisions of statute under which aliens may be permitted entry into the territories of a Party subject to express conditions regarding their engaging in gainful occupations therein.

ARTICLE XXV [Definitions]

1.   The term "national treatment" means treatment accorded within the territories of a Party upon terms no less favorable than the treatment accorded therein, in like situations, to nationals, companies, products, vessels or other objects, as the case may be, of such Party.

2.   National treatment is accorded by the Federal Republic of Germany in the provisions of the present Treaty in consideration of the national treatment accorded by the United States of America to the nationals, companies, products, vessels, or other objects, of the Federal Republic of Germany, with respect to the same subject matter.

3.   National treatment accorded under the provisions of the present Treaty to companies of the Federal Republic of Germany shall, in any State, Territory, or possession of the United States of

America, be the treatment accorded therein to companies created or organized in other States, Territories, and possessions of the United States of America.

4.   The term "most-favored-nation treatment" means treatment accorded within the territories of a Party upon terms no less favorable than the treatment accorded therein, in like situations, to nationals, companies, products, vessels or other objects, as the case may be, of any third country.

5.   As used in the present Treaty, the term "companies" means corporations, partnerships, companies and other associations, whether or not with limited liability and whether or not for pecuniary profit. Companies constituted under the applicable laws and regulations within the territories of either Party shall be deemed companies thereof and shall have their juridical status recognized within the territories of the other Party.

6.   Without prejudice to other methods of establishing nationality, a person in possession of a valid passport issued by the competent authorities of either Party, or a valid identity document named in the Protocol, shall be considered a national of that Party.

ARTICLE XXVI [Scope of Application]

1.   The territories to which the present Treaty extends shall comprise all areas of land and water under the sovereignty or authority of each Party, other than the Panama Canal Zone and the Trust Territory of the Pacific Islands.

2.   The present Treaty shall also apply from the date specified in Article XXIX, paragraph 2, to Land Berlin which for the purposes of the present Treat comprises those areas over which the Berlin Senate exercises jurisdiction.

3.   It is a condition to the application of the present Treaty to Land Berlin, in accordance with the preceding paragraph, that the Government of the Federal Republic of Germany shall previously have furnished to the Government of the United States of America a notification that all legal procedures in Berlin necessary for the application of the present Treaty therein have been complied with.

ARTICLE XXVII [Dispute Settlement]

1.   Each Party shall accord sympathetic consideration to, and shall afford adequate opportunity for consultation regarding, such representations as the other Party may make with respect to any matter affecting the operation of the present Treaty.

2.   Any dispute between the Parties as to the interpretation or the application of the present Treaty which the Parties do not satisfactorily adjust by diplomacy or some other agreed means shall be submitted to arbitration or, upon agreement of the Parties, to the international Court of Justice.

ARTICLE XXVIII

The present Treaty shall replace and terminate provisions in force in Articles I through V, VII through XVI, and XXIX through XXXII, of the treaty of friendship, commerce and consular rights between the United States of America and Germany, signed at Washington December 8, 1923, as amended by an exchange of notes dated March 19 and May 21, 1925 and the agreement signed at Washington June 3, 1835, and as applied by the agreement of June 3, 1953, Article VI having terminated on June 2, 1954. Articles XVII through XXVIII of the said treaty, as amended by Article II of the agreement of June 3, 1953, shall continue in force between the United States of America and the Federal Republic of Germany, with territorial application to the same extent as that provided in Article XXVI of the present Treaty, until replaced by a consular convention between the two Parties or until six months after either Party shall have given to the other Party a written notice of termination of the said Articles.

ARTICLE XXIX

1.   The present Treaty shall be ratified, and the ratifications thereof shall be exchanged at Bonn as soon as possible.

2.   The present Treaty shall enter into force one month after the day of exchange of ratifications. It shall remain in force for ten years and shall continue in force thereafter until terminated as provided herein.

3.   Either Party may, by giving one year's written notice to the other Party, terminate the present Treaty at the end of the initial ten-year period or at any time thereafter.

IN WITNESS WHEREOF the respective Plenipotentiaries have signed the present Treaty and have affixed hereunto their seals.

DONE in duplicate, in the English and German languages, both equally authentic, at Washington this twenty-ninth day of October, one thousand nine hundred fifty-four.

IV. 20th Century Bilateral Investment Treaties (BITs)

(3rd Generation BITs)

IV.1. 1959 GERMANY – PAKISTAN BILATERAL INVESTMENT TREATY

PAKISTAN

and

FEDERAL REPUBLIC OF GERMANY

Treaty for the Promotion and Protection of Investments

With Protocol and Exchange of Notes. Signed at Bonn, on 25 November 1959

The Federal Republic of Germany and Pakistan,

Desiring to intensify economic co-operation between the two States,

Intending to create favourable conditions for investments by nationals and companies of either State in the territory of the other State, and

Recognizing that an understanding reached between the two States is likely to promote investment, encourage private industrial and financial enterprise and to increase the prosperity of both the States,

Have agreed as follows :

Article 1

1.   Each contracting State hereafter called in this Treaty a Party will endeavour to admit in its territory, in accordance with its legislation and rules and regulations framed thereunder, the investing of capital by nationals or companies of the other Party and to promote such investments and will give sympathetic consideration to requests for the grant of necessary permissions. In the case of Pakistan such per missions shall be given with due regard also to their published plans and policies.

2.   Capital investments by nationals or companies of either Party in the territory of the other Party shall not be subjected to any discriminatory treatment on the ground that ownership of or influence upon it is vested in nationals or companies of the former Party, unless legislation and rules and regulations framed thereunder existing at the time of coming into force of this Treaty provide otherwise.

Article 2

Neither Party shall subject to discriminatory treatment any activities carried on in connection with investments including the effective management, use or enjoyment of such investments by the nationals or companies of either Party in the territory of the other Party unless specific stipulations are made in the documents of admission of an investment.

Article 3

1.   Investments by nationals or companies of either Party shall enjoy protection and security in the territory of the other Party.

2.   Nationals or companies of either Party shall not be subjected to expropriation of their investments in the territory of the other Party except for public benefit against compensation, which shall represent the equivalent of the investments affected. Such compensation shall be actually realizable and freely transferable in the currency of the other Party without undue delay. Adequate provision shall be made at or prior to the time of expropriation for the determination and the grant of such compensation. The legality of any such expropriation and the amount of compensation shall be subject to review by due process of law.

3.   Nationals or companies of either Party who owing to war or other armed conflict, revolution or revolt in the territory of the other Party suffer the loss of investments situated there, shall be accorded treatment no less favourable by such other Party than the treatment that Party accords to persons residing within its territory and to nationals or companies of a third party, as regards restitution, indemnification, compensation or other considerations. With respect to the transfer of such payments each Party shall accord to the requests of nationals or companies of the other Party treatment no less favourable than is accorded to comparable requests made by nationals or companies of a third party.

Article 4

Either Party shall in respect of all investments guarantee to nationals or companies of the other Party the transfer of the invested capital, of the returns therefrom and in the event of liquidation, the proceeds of such liquidation.

Article 5

If a claim arising out of a guarantee given for an investment is brought against a Party, the latter shall without prejudice to its rights under Article 11, be authorised, on the conditions stipulated by its predecessor in title, to exercise the rights having devolved on such Party by law or having been assigned to it by the predecessor in title (devolved interest). As regards the transfer of payments to be made by virtue of the devolved interest to the Party concerned, paragraphs (2) and (3) of Article 3 as well as Article 4 shall apply mutatis mutandis.

Article 6

1.   Transfers under paragraphs (2) or (3) of Article 3, under Article 4 or Article 5 shall be made without undue delay and at rates of exchange applicable to current transactions on the date the transfer is made.

2.   The rate applicable to current transactions shall be based on the par value agreed with the International Monetary Fund taking into account the provisions of Section 3 of Article 4 of the Articles of Agreement establishing the International Monetary Fund.

3.   In case no rate of exchange within the meaning of paragraph (2) above exists at the time of transfer the appropriate authorities of the Party in the territory of which the investment is situated shall admit a rate of exchange which is just and reasonable.

Article 7

If the legislation of either Party or international obligations existing at present or established hereafter between the Parties in addition to the present Treaty, result in a position entitling investments by nationals or companies of the other Party to treatment more favourable than is provided for by the present Treaty, such position shall not be affected by the present Treaty. Either Party shall observe any other obligation it may have entered into with regard to investments by nationals or companies of the other Party.

Article 8 [Definitions]

1.a) The term "investment" shall comprise capital brought into the territory of the other Party for investment in various forms in the shape of assets such as foreign exchange, goods, property rights, patents and technical knowledge. The term "investment" shall also include the returns derived from and ploughed back into such "investment".

b)   Any partnerships, companies or assets of similar kind, created by the utilisation of the above mentioned assets shall be regarded as "investment".

2.   The term "return" shall mean the amounts derived from investments as profits or interest for a specified period.

3.   The term "nationals" shall mean

a)   in respect of the Federal Republic of Germany, Germans within the meaning of the Basic Law for the Federal Republic of Germany;

b)   in respect of Pakistan, a person who is a citizen of Pakistan according to its laws.

4.   The term "companies" shall comprise

a)   in respect of the Federal Republic of Germany, any juridical person, any commercial company or any other company or association, with or without legal personality, having its seat in the territory of the Federal Republic of Germany and lawfully existing in accordance with its legislation, irrespective of whether the liability of its partners, associates or members is limited or unlimited and whether or not its activities are directed to pecuniary gain;

b)   in respect to Pakistan, any juridical person or any company or association, incorporated in the territory of Pakistan and lawfully existing in accordance with its legislation.

Article 9

The present Treaty shall also apply to approved investments made prior to its entry into force but not earlier than 1st September 1954, by nationals or companies of either Party in the territory of the other Party unless in any case it is specifically provided otherwise. This provision shall not affect the Agreement of 27th February 1953, on German External Debts.

Article 10

Each Party shall co-operate with the other in furthering the interchange and use of scientific and technical knowledge and development of training facilities particularly in the interest of increasing productivity and improving standards of living in their territories.

Article 11 [Dispute Settlement]

1.   In the event of disputes as to the interpretation or application of the present Treaty, the Parties shall enter into consultation for the purpose of finding a solution in a spirit of friendship.

2.   If no such solution is forthcoming, the dispute shall be submitted

a)   to the International Court of Justice if both Parties so agree or

b)   if they do not so agree to an arbitration tribunal upon the request of either Party.

3.a) The tribunal referred to in paragraph (2) (b) above shall be formed in respect of each specific case and it shall consist of three arbitrators. Each Party shall appoint one arbitrator and the two members so appointed shall appoint a chairman who shall be a national of a third country.

b)   Each Party shall appoint its arbitrator within two months after a request to this effect has been made by either Party. If either Party fails to comply with this obligation the arbitrator shall be appointed upon the request of the other Party by the President of the International Court of Justice.

c)   If within one month from the date of their appointment the arbitrators are unable to agree on the chairman of the arbitration tribunal such chairman shall upon the request of either Party be appointed by the President of the International Court of Justice.

d)   If the President of the International Court of Justice is prevented from acting upon a request under sub-paragraph (b) or sub-paragraph (c) of the present paragraph or if the President is a national of either Party the Vice-President shall make the appointment. If the Vice-President is prevented or if he is a national of either Party the appointment shall be made by the seniormost member of the International Court of Justice who is not a national of either Party.

e)   Unless the Parties otherwise decide, the arbitration tribunal shall determine its own rules of procedure.

f)   The arbitration tribunal shall take its decisions by a majority of votes. Such decisions shall be binding upon the Parties and shall be carried out by them.

Article 12

The provisions of the present Treaty shall remain in force also in the event of a conflict arising between the Parties without prejudice to the right of taking such temporary measures as are permitted under international law and are indispensable for assuring a supervision of invest- ments. Measures of this kind shall be repealed not later than the date of termination of the conflict, irrespective of whether or not diplomatic relations have been re-established.

Article 13

The present Treaty shall also apply to Land Berlin, provided that the Government of the Federal Republic of Germany has not made a contrary declaration to the Government of Pakistan within three months from the entry into force of the present Treaty.

Article 14

1.   The present Treaty shall be ratified and the instruments of ratification shall be exchanged as soon as possible.

2.   The present Treaty shall enter into force one month after the date of exchange of the instru- ments of ratification. It shall remain in force for a period of ten years and shall continue in force thereafter for an unlimited period unless notice of termination is given in writing by either Party one year before its expiry. After the expiry of the period of ten years, the present Treaty may be terminated at any time by either Party giving one year's notice.

3.   In respect of investments made prior to the date of expiry of the present Treaty, the pro- visions of Articles 1 to 13 shall continue to be effective for a further period of ten years from the date of expiry of the present Treaty.

DONE at Bonn on the twenty fifth day of November in the year nineteen hundred and fifty nine in duplicate, in the German and English languages, both texts being equally authentic.

For the Federal Republic of Germany: For Pakistan:

VON BRENTANO   S. A. HASNIE

PROTOCOL

On signing the Treaty for the Promotion and Protection of Investments concluded between the Federal Republic of Germany and Pakistan, the undersigned plenipotentiaries have, in addition, agreed to the following provisions which should be regarded as an integral part of the said Treaty :

1.   The Parties shall within one year after signing this Treaty enter into negotiations to conclude an establishment treaty which shall, inter alia, make provision for the following :

Immigration and emigration, temporary and permanent residence, protection from expulsion, taking up and carrying on business and professional activities on a basis of employment or self-employment, particularly in respect of managerial and technical staff, foundation of and participation in enterprises, protection and security of persons and property, free access to courts, freedom to contract, acquisition of real estate and other property and admission as arbitrator.

2.   The following shall in particular be deemed discrimination referred to in Article 2:

Restricting the purchase of raw or auxiliary materials, of power or fuel, or of means of production or operation of any kind, impeding the marketing of products within or outside the country, as well as any other measures not applied to the same extent either to persons residing within the country and to nationals of third states or to investments of such persons. Measures taken for reasons of public security and order, public health or morality shall not be deemed as discrimination within the meaning of Article 2.

3.   The term "expropriation" within the meaning of paragraph (2) of Article 3 shall also pertain to acts of sovereign power which are tantamount to expropriation, as well as measures of nationalization.

4.   With a view to ensuring an equitable share of cargo to their respective shipping either Party shall abstain from any discriminatory measures which, contrary to the principles of free competition are designed to eliminate or impair the participation of ships of the other Party in transporting the following goods:

a)   goods which represent an investment and are transported by sea-going vessels,

b)   goods which for the purpose of operating an enterprise in the territory of one Party are purchased by means of capital invested in the territory of that Party by nationals or companies of the other Party.

5.   Without prejudice to any other method of determining nationality, any person shall be deemed to be a national of a Party who is in possession of a national passport issued by the appropriate authority of the Party concerned or of a valid identity document of one of the following types: [...]

DONE at Bonn on the twenty fifth day of November in the year nineteen hundred and fifty nine in duplicate, in the German and English languages, both texts being equally authentic.

For the Federal Republic of Germany: For Pakistan:

VON BRENTANO   S. A. HASNIE

IV.2. 2008 GERMAN MODEL BIT

Treaty
between
the Federal Republic of Germany
and

....

concerning the Encouragement and Reciprocal Protection of Investments

The Federal Republic of Germany and

....

desiring to intensify economic co-operation between the two States,

intending to create favourable conditions for investments by investors of either State in the territory of the other State,

recognizing that the encouragement and contractual protection of such investments are apt to stimulate private business initiative and to increase the prosperity of both nations,

have agreed as follows:

Article 1 Definitions

Within the meaning of this Treaty,

1.   the term "investments" comprises every kind of asset which is directly or indirectly invested by investors of one Contracting State in the territory of the other Contracting State. The investments include in particular:

(a)   movable and immovable property as well as any other rights in rem, such as mortgages, liens and pledges;

(b)   shares of companies and other kinds of interest in companies;

(c)   claims to money which has been used to create an economic value or claims to any performance having an economic value;

(d)   intellectual property rights, in particular copyrights and related rights, patents, utility-model patents, industrial designs, trademarks, plant variety rights;

(e)   trade-names, trade and business secrets, technical processes, know-how, and goodwill;

(f)   business concessions under public law, including concessions to search for, extract or exploit natural resources;

any alteration of the form in which assets are invested shall not affect their classification as investment. In the case of indirect investments, in principle only those indirect investments shall be covered which the investor realizes via a company situated in the other Contracting State;

2.   the term "returns" means the amounts yielded by an investment for a definite period, such as profit, dividends, interest, royalties or fees;

3.   the term "investor" means

(a)   in respect of the Federal Republic of Germany:

–   any natural person who is a German within the meaning of the Basic Law of the Federal Republic of Germany or a national of a Member State of the European Union or of the European Economic Area who, within the context of freedom of establishment pursuant to Article 43 of the EC Treaty, is established in the Federal Republic of Germany;

- any juridical person and any commercial or other company or association with or without legal personality which is founded pursuant to the law of the Federal Republic of Germany or the law of a Member State of the European Union or the European Economic Area and is organized pursuant to the law of the Federal Republic of Germany, registered in a public register in the Federal Republic of Germany or enjoys freedom of establishment as an agency or permanent establishment in Germany pursuant to Articles 43 and 48 of the EC Treaty;

which in the context of entrepreneurial activity is the owner, possessor or shareholder of an investment in the territory of the other Contracting State, irrespective of whether or not the activity is directed at profit;

(b) in respect of ....:

    - ....

4. the term "territory" refers to the area of each Contracting State including the exclusive economic zone and the continental shelf insofar as international law allows the Contracting State concerned to exercise sovereign rights or jurisdiction in these areas.

Article 2 Admission and Protection of Investments

(1) Each Contracting State shall in its territory promote as far as possible investments by investors of the other Contracting State and admit such investments in accordance with its legislation.

(2) Each Contracting State shall in its territory in every case accord investments by investors of the other Contracting State fair and equitable treatment as well as full protection under this Treaty.

(3) Neither Contracting State shall in its territory impair by arbitrary or discriminatory measures the activity of investors of the other Contracting State with regard to investments, such as in particular the management, maintenance, use, enjoyment or disposal of such investments. This provision shall be without prejudice to Article 7 (3).

(4) Returns from an investment, as well as returns from reinvested returns, shall enjoy the same protection as the original investment.

Article 3 National and Most-Favoured-Nation Treatment

(1) Neither Contracting State shall in its territory subject investments owned or controlled by investors of the other Contracting State to treatment less favourable than it accords to investments of its own investors or to investments of investors of any third State.

(2) Neither Contracting State shall in its territory subject investors of the other Contracting State, as regards their activity in connection with investments, to treatment less favourable than it accords to its own investors or to investors of any third State. The following shall, in particular, be deemed treatment less favourable within the meaning of this Article:

1. different treatment in the event of restrictions on the procurement of raw or auxiliary materials, of energy and fuels, and of all types of means of production and operation;

2. different treatment in the event of impediments to the sale of products at home and abroad; and

3. other measures of similar effect.

Measures that have to be taken for reasons of public security and order shall not be deemed treatment less favourable within the meaning of this Article.

(3) Such treatment shall not relate to privileges which either Contracting State accords to investors of third States on account of its membership of, or association with, a customs or economic union, a common market or a free trade area.

(4) The treatment granted under this Article shall not relate to advantages which either Contracting State accords to investors of third States by virtue of an agreement for the avoidance of double taxation in the field of taxes on income and assets or other agreements regarding matters of taxation.

(5) This Article shall not oblige a Contracting State to extend to investors resident in the territory of the other Contracting State tax privileges, tax exemptions and tax reductions which according to its tax laws are granted only to investors resident in its territory.

(6) The Contracting States shall within the framework of their national legislation give sympathetic consideration to applications for the entry and sojourn of persons of either Contracting State who wish to enter the territory of the other Contracting State in connection with an investment; the same shall apply to employed persons of either Contracting State who in connection with an investment wish to enter the territory of the other Contracting State and sojourn there to take up employment. Where necessary, applications for work permits shall also be given sympathetic consideration.

(7) Notwithstanding any bilateral or multilateral agreements which are binding on both Contracting States, the investors of the Contracting States are free to select the means of transport for the international transportation of persons and of capital goods directly related to an investment within the meaning of this Treaty. Transport companies of the Contracting States shall not be discriminated against thereby.

Article 4 Compensation in Case of Expropriation

(1) Investments by investors of either Contracting State shall enjoy full protection and security in the territory of the other Contracting State.

(2) Investments by investors of either Contracting State may not directly or indirectly be expropriated, nationalized or subjected to any other measure the effects of which would be tantamount to expropriation or nationalization in the territory of the other Contracting State except for the public benefit and against compensation. Such compensation must be equivalent to the value of the expropriated investment immediately before the date on which the actual or threatened expropriation, nationalization or other measure became publicly known. The compensation must be paid without delay and shall carry the usual bank interest until the time of payment; it must be effectively realizable and freely transferable. Provision must have been made in an appropriate manner at or prior to the time of expropriation, nationalization or other measure for the determination and payment of such compensation. The legality of any such expropriation, nationalization or other measure and the amount of compensation must be subject to review by due process of law.

(3) Investors of either Contracting State whose investments suffer losses in the territory of the other Contracting State owing to war or other armed conflict, revolution, a state of national emergency, or revolt, shall be accorded treatment no less favourable by such other Contracting State than that State accords to its own investors as regards restitution, indemnification, compensation or other valuable consideration. Such payments must be freely transferable.

(4) Investors of either Contracting State shall enjoy most-favoured-nation treatment in the territory of the other Contracting State in respect of the matters provided for in the present Article.

Article 5 Free Transfer

(1) Each Contracting State shall guarantee to investors of the other Contracting State the free transfer of payments in connection with an investment, in particular

1. the principal and additional amounts to maintain or increase the investment;
2. the returns;
3. the repayment of loans;

4. the proceeds from the liquidation or the sale of the whole or any part of the investment;

5. the compensation provided for in Article 4.

(2) Transfers under Article 4 (2) or (3), under the present Article or Article 6, shall be made without delay at the market rate of exchange applicable on the day of the transfer. A transfer shall be deemed to have been made without delay if made within such period as is normally required for the completion of transfer formalities. The period shall commence with the submission of the corresponding application, where such an application is necessary, or the notification of the intended transfer, and must in no circumstances exceed two months.

(3) Should it not be possible to ascertain a market rate pursuant to paragraph (2), the cross rate obtained from those rates which would be applied by the International Monetary Fund on the date of payment for conversions of the currencies concerned into Special Drawing Rights shall apply.

Article 6 Subrogation

If either Contracting State makes payment to any of its investors under a guarantee it has assumed in respect of an investment in the territory of the other Contracting State, the latter Contracting State shall, without prejudice to the rights of the former Contracting State under Article 9, recognize the assignment, whether under a law or pursuant to a legal transaction, of any right or claim from such investors to the former Contracting State. Furthermore, the latter Contracting State shall recognize the subrogation of that Contracting State to any such right or claim (assigned claim), which that Contracting State shall be entitled to assert to the same extent as its predecessor in title. As regards the transfer of payments on the basis of such assignment, Article 4 (1) and (2) and Article 5 shall apply mutatis mutandis.

Article 7 Other Provisions

(1) If the legislation of either Contracting State or international obligations existing at present or established hereafter between the Contracting States in addition to this Treaty contain any provisions, whether general or specific, entitling investments by investors of the other Contracting State to a treatment more favourable than is provided for by this Treaty, such provisions shall prevail over this Treaty to the extent that they are more favourable.

(2) Each Contracting State shall fulfil any other obligations it may have entered into with regard to investments in its territory by investors of the other Contracting State.

(3) With regard to the treatment of income and assets for the purpose of taxation, precedence shall be given to the application of the agreements in force at the time between the Federal Republic of Germany and ... for the avoidance of double taxation in the field of taxes on income and assets.

Article 8 Scope of Application

This Treaty shall also apply to investments made prior to its entry into force by investors of either Contracting State in the territory of the other Contracting State consistent with the latter's legislation.

Article 9 Settlement of Disputes Between the Contracting States

(1) Disputes between the Contracting States concerning the interpretation or application of this Treaty should as far as possible be settled by the Governments of the two Contracting States.

(2) If a dispute cannot thus be settled, it shall upon the request of either Contracting State be submitted to an arbitral tribunal.

(3) The arbitral tribunal shall be constituted for each case as follows: each Contracting State shall appoint one member, and these two members shall agree upon a national of a third State as their chairman to be appointed by the Governments of the two Contracting States. The members shall be appointed within two months, and the chairman within three months, from the date on

which either Contracting State has informed the other Contracting State that it wants to submit the dispute to an arbitral tribunal.

(4) If the periods specified in paragraph (3) have not been observed, either Contracting State may, in the absence of any other relevant agreement, invite the President of the International Court of Justice to make the necessary appointments. If the President is a national of either Contracting State or if he is otherwise prevented from discharging the said function, the Vice-President should make the necessary appointments. If the Vice-President is a national of either Contracting State or if he, too, is prevented from discharging the said function, the Member of the Court next in seniority who is not a national of either Contracting State should make the necessary appointments.

(5) The arbitral tribunal shall reach its decisions by a majority of votes. Its decisions shall be binding. Each Contracting State shall bear the cost of its own member and of its representatives in the arbitration proceedings; the cost of the chairman and the remaining costs shall be borne in equal parts by the Contracting States. The arbitral tribunal may make a different regulation concerning costs. In all other respects, the arbitral tribunal shall determine its own procedure.

Article 10 Settlement of Disputes Between a Contracting State and an Investor of the Other Contracting State

(1) Disputes concerning investments between a Contracting State and an investor of the other Contracting State should as far as possible be settled amicably between the parties to the dispute. To help them reach an amicable settlement, the parties to the dispute also have the option of agreeing to institute conciliation proceedings under the Convention on the Settlement of Investment Disputes between States and Nationals of Other States of 18 March 1965 (ICSID).

(2) If the dispute cannot be settled within six months of the date on which it was raised by one of the parties to the dispute, it shall, at the request of the investor of the other Contracting State, be submitted to arbitration. The two Contracting States hereby declare that they unreservedly and bindingly consent to the dispute being submitted to one of the following dispute settlement mechanisms of the investor's choosing:

1. arbitration under the auspices of the International Centre for Settlement of Investment Disputes pursuant to the Convention on the Settlement of Investment Disputes between States and Nationals of Other States of 18 March 1965 (ICSID), provided both Contracting States are members of this Convention, or

2. arbitration under the auspices of the International Centre for Settlement of Investment Disputes pursuant to the Convention on the Settlement of Investment Disputes between States and Nationals of Other States of 18 March 1965 (ICSID) in accordance with the Rules on the Additional Facility for the Administration of Proceedings by the Secretariat of the Centre, where the personal or factual preconditions for proceedings pursuant to figure 1 do not apply, but at least one Contracting State is a member of the Convention referred to therein, or

3. an individual arbitrator or an ad-hoc arbitral tribunal which is established in accordance with the rules of the United Nations Commission on International Trade Law (UNCITRAL) as in force at the commencement of the proceedings, or

4. an arbitral tribunal which is established pursuant to the Dispute Resolution Rules of the International Chamber of Commerce (ICC), the London Court of International Arbitration (LCIA) or the Arbitration Institute of the Stockholm Chamber of Commerce, or

5. any other form of dispute settlement agreed by the parties to the dispute.

(3) The award shall be binding and shall not be subject to any appeal or remedy other than those provided for in the Convention or arbitral rules on which the arbitral proceedings chosen

by the investor are based. The award shall be enforced by the Contracting States as a final and absolute ruling under domestic law.

(4)   Arbitration proceedings pursuant to this Article shall take place at the request of one of the parties to the dispute in a State which is a Contracting Party to the United Nations Convention on the Recognition and Enforcement of Foreign Arbitral Awards of 10 June 1958.

(5)   During arbitration proceedings or the enforcement of an award, the Contracting State involved in the dispute shall not raise the objection that the investor of the other Contracting State has received compensation under an insurance contract in respect of all or part of the damage.

Article 11 Relations Between the Contracting States

This Treaty shall be in force irrespective of whether or not diplomatic or consular relations exist between the Contracting States.

Article 12 Registration Clause

Registration of this Treaty with the Secretariat of the United Nations, in accordance with Article 102 of the United Nations Charter, shall be initiated immediately following its entry into force by the Contracting State in which the signing took place. The other Contracting State shall be informed of registration, and of the UN registration number, as soon as this has been confirmed by the Secretariat of the United Nations.

Article 13 Entry into Force, Duration and Notice of Termination

(1)   This Treaty shall be subject to ratification; the instruments of ratification shall be exchanged as soon as possible.

(2)   This Treaty shall enter into force on the first day of the second month following the exchange of the instruments of ratification. It shall remain in force for a period of ten years and shall continue in force thereafter for an unlimited period unless denounced in writing through diplomatic channels by either Contracting State twelve months before its expiration. After the expiry of the period of ten years this Treaty may be denounced at any time by either Contracting State giving twelve months' notice.

(3)   In respect of investments made prior to the date of termination of this Treaty, the provisions of the above Articles shall continue to be effective for a further period of twenty years from the date of termination of this Treaty.

Done in on in duplicate in the German and .... languages, both texts being equally authentic.

For the Federal Republic of Germany _____

V. 21ˢᵗ Century Bilateral Investment Treaties (BITs)

(4ᵗʰ Generation BITs)

V.1. 2007 Norway Model BIT

AGREEMENT
BETWEEN
THE KINGDOM OF NORWAY
AND

....

FOR THE PROMOTION AND PROTECTION OF INVESTMENTS

The Kingdom of Norway and the................................., hereinafter referred to as the "Parties";

Desiring to develop the economic cooperation between the Parties;

Desiring to encourage, create and maintain stable, equitable, favourable and transparent conditions for investors of one Party and their investments in the territory of the other Party on the basis of equality and mutual benefit;

Desiring to achieve these objectives in a manner consistent with the protection of health, safety, and the environment, and the promotion of internationally recognized labour rights;

Desiring to contribute to a stable framework for investment in order to maximize effective and sustainable utilization of economic resources and improve living standards;

Conscious that the promotion and reciprocal protection of investments in accordance with this Agreement will stimulate the business initiative;

Emphasising the importance of corporate social responsibility;

Recognising that the development of economic and business ties can promote respect for internationally recognised labour rights;

Reaffirming their commitment to democracy, the rule of law, human rights and fundamental freedoms in accordance with their obligations under international law, including the principles set out in the United Nations Charter and the Universal Declaration of Human Rights;

Recognising that the promotion of sustainable investments is critical for the further development of national and global economies as well as for the pursuit of national and global objectives for sustainable development, and understanding that the promotion of such investments requires cooperative efforts of investors, host governments and home governments;

Recognising that the provisions of this agreement and provisions of international agreements relating to the environment shall be interpreted in a mutually supportive manner;

Determined to prevent and combat corruption, including bribery, in international trade and investment;

Recognising the basic principles of transparency, accountability and legitimacy for all participants in foreign investment processes;

Have agreed as follows:

SECTION I – SCOPE AND APPLICATION

Article 1 Scope

1.   This Agreement applies to measures adopted or maintained by a Party, after the entry into force of this Agreement, relating to investors of the other Party or to investments of investors of the other Party. The Section [Dispute Settlement Provisions] does not apply to disputes arising out of events that have occurred before the entry into force of this Agreement, cf. Article ["Non-Retroactive Application"].

2.   This Agreement applies to investments made prior to or after its entry into force.

3.   This Agreement shall apply to the land territory, internal waters, and the territorial sea of a Party, and the airspace above the territory in accordance with international law.

4.   This Agreement shall not apply to Svalbard, i.e. the land territory of the Archipelago, internal waters and the territorial sea of the Archipelago.

Article 2 Definitions

1.   "Investor" means:

i.   a natural person having the nationality of, or permanent residence in, a Party in accordance with its applicable law; or

ii.   any entity established in accordance with, and recognised as a legal person by the law of a Party, and engaged in substantive business operations in the territory of that Party, such as companies, firms, associations, development finance institutions, foundations or similar entities irrespective of whether their liabilities are limited and whether or not their activities are directed at profit.

2.   "Investment" means: Every kind of asset owned or controlled, directly or indirectly, by an investor of a Party, including, but not limited to:

i.   any entity established in accordance with, and recognised as a legal person by the law of a Party, whether or not their activities are directed at profit;

ii.   shares, stocks or other forms of equity participation in an enterprise, and rights derived therefrom;

iii. bonds, debentures, loans and other forms of debt, and rights derived therefrom;

iv.   rights under contracts, including turnkey, construction, management, production or revenue-sharing;

v.   contracts;

vi.   claims to money and claims to performance;

vii. intellectual property rights;

viii. rights conferred pursuant to law or contract such as concessions, licenses, authorisations, and permits;

ix.   any other tangible and intangible, movable and immovable property, and any related property rights, such as leases, mortgages, liens and pledges.

In order to qualify as an investment under this Agreement, an asset must have the characteristics of an investment, such as the commitment of capital or other resources, the expectation of gain or profit, or the assumption of risk.

SECTION 2 – TREATMENT AND PROTECTION OF INVESTORS AND INVESTMENTS

Article 3 National Treatment

1.   Each Party shall accord to investors of the other Party and to their investments, treatment no less favourable than the treatment it accords in like circumstances to its own investors and their

investments, in relation to the establishment, acquisition, expansion, management, conduct, operation and disposal of investments.

2.   National treatment shall not apply to the reservations set out in Annex [A].

Article 4 Most-Favoured-Nation Treatment

1.   Each Party shall accord to investors of the other Party and to their investments, treatment no less favourable than the treatment it accords in like circumstances to investors and their investments of any other State, subject to the country-specific reservations set out in Annex [B], in relation to the establishment, acquisition, expansion, management, conduct, operation and disposal of investments.

2.   If a Party accords more favourable treatment to investors of any other State or their invest-ments by virtue of a free trade agreement, customs union [or similar agreement that also provides for substantial liberalisation of investments] or by a labour market integration agree-ments, it shall not be obliged to accord such treatment to investors of the other Party or their investments. However, upon request from another Party, it shall afford adequate opportunity to negotiate the benefits granted therein.

3.   For greater certainty, treatment referred to in paragraph [1] does not encompass dispute resolution mechanisms provided for in this Agreement or other International Agreements.

Article 5 General Treatment and Protection

Each Party shall accord to investors of the other Party, and their investments treatment in accordance with customary international law, including fair and equitable treatment and full protection and security.

Article 6 Expropriation

1.   A Party shall not expropriate or nationalise an investment of an investor of the other Party except in the public interest and subject to the conditions provided for by law and by the general principles of international law.

2.   The preceding provision shall not, however, in any way impair the right of a Party to enforce such laws as it deems necessary to control the use of property in accordance with the general interest or to secure the payment of taxes or other contributions or penalties.

Article 7 Compensation for Losses

1.   Investors whose investments have suffered losses due to armed conflict or civil strife, shall benefit from treatment in accordance with Article [National treatment] and Article [MFN] as regards restitution, indemnification, compensation or any other settlement it adopts or maintains relating to such losses.

2.   Without prejudice to paragraph 1 of this Article, an investor of a Party who, in any of the situations referred to in that paragraph, suffers a loss in the area of another Party resulting from

i.   requisitioning of its investment or part thereof by the latter's forces or authorities, or

ii.   destruction of its investment or part thereof by the latter's forces or authorities,

which was not required by the necessity of the situation, shall be accorded restitution or com-pensation .

Article 8 Performance Requirements

1.   No Party may impose or enforce any of the following requirements, or enforce any com-mitment or undertaking in connection with the establishment, acquisition, expansion, manage-ment, conduct or operation of an investment of an investor of the other Party:

i.   [to export a given level or percentage of goods or services;]

ii.   [to achieve a given level or percentage of domestic content;]

iii. [to purchase, use or accord a preference to goods produced or services provided in its territory, or to purchase goods or services from persons in its territory;]

iv. [to relate in any way the volume or value of imports to the volume or value of exports or to the amount of foreign exchange inflows associated with such investment;]

v. [to restrict sales of goods or services in its territory that such investment produces or provides by relating such sales to the volume or value of its exports or foreign exchange earnings;]

vi. [to transfer technology, a production process or other proprietary knowledge to a natural or legal person in its territory, except when the requirement]

   (a) is imposed or the commitment or undertaking is enforced by a court, administrative tribunal or competition authority to remedy an alleged violation of competition laws, or

   (b) concerns the transfer of intellectual property and is undertaken in a manner not inconsistent with the TRIPS Agreement;]

vii. [to locate its headquarters for a specific region or the world market in the territory of that Party;]

viii. [to supply one or more of the goods that it produces or the services that it provides to a specific region or the world market exclusively from the territory of that Party;]

ix. [to achieve a given level or value of research and development in its territory;]

x. [to hire a given level of nationals;]

xi. [to achieve a minimum level of domestic equity participation other than nominal qualifying shares for directors or incorporators of corporations.]

2.   A measure that requires an investment to use a technology to meet generally applicable health, safety or environmental requirements shall not be construed to be inconsistent with paragraph 1.

3.   Performance requirements, other than those referred to in paragraph 1, shall only be applied in the public interest and shall be set forth in the national legislation of the Party imposing the requirement and published in the official gazette or otherwise be publicly available according to Article [Transparency] so that investors may become acquainted with them before the investment decision is made. All performance requirements shall be applied against all investors and their investments in a non-discriminatory, transparent and objective manner.

4.   A Party may not apply new performance requirements to existing investments, or amend existing performance requirements in a manner restricting the commercial freedom of the investor, except where such requirements are at the same time made applicable to all other investors in that Party.

Article 9 Transfer

1.   Each Party shall ensure that all payment relating to an investment of an investor of another Party may be freely transferred into and out of its territory without delay. Such transfers shall include, in particular, though not exclusively:

i.   the initial capital and additional amounts to maintain or increase an investment;

ii.   profits, interest, dividends, capital gains, royalties, fees and returns in kind;

iii.   payments made under a contract including a loan agreement;

iv.   proceeds from the sale or liquidation of all or any part of an investment;

v.   earnings and other remuneration of personnel engaged from abroad in connection with an investment.

2.   Each Party shall further ensure that such transfers may be made in a freely convertible currency. Freely convertible currency means a currency that is widely traded in international foreign exchange markets and widely used in international transactions. Transfers shall be made at the market rate of exchange prevailing on the date of transfer.

3.   It is understood that paragraphs 1 and 2 are without prejudice to the equitable, non-discriminatory and good faith application of measures:

i.   to protect the rights of creditors,

ii.   relating to or ensuring compliance with laws and regulations

(a) on the issuing, trading and dealing in securities, futures and derivatives,

(b) concerning reports or records of transfers,

(c) concerning the payment of contributions or penalties, or

(d) concerning financial security or any other equivalent regarding the prevention and remedying of environmental damage

iii. in connection with criminal offences and orders or judgments in administrative and adjudi-catory proceedings.

Article 10 Key Personnel

1.   Each Party shall, subject to its laws and regulations relating to the entry, stay and work of natural persons, grant natural persons of the other Party, and key personnel who are employed by natural or juridical persons of the other Party, temporary entry and stay in its territory in order to engage in activities connected with an investment, including the provision of advice or key technical services.

2.   Each Party shall, subject to its laws and regulations, permit natural or legal/juridical persons of another Party to employ, in connection with an investment, any key personnel of the natural or legal/juridical person's choice provided that such key personnel has been permitted to enter, stay and work in its territory and that the employment concerned conforms to the terms, conditions and time limits of the permission granted to such key personnel.

3.   The Parties shall, subject to their laws and regulations, grant temporary entry and stay and provide any necessary confirming documentation to the spouse and minor children of a natural person who has been granted temporary entry, stay and authorisation to work in accordance with paragraphs 1 and 2. The spouse and minor children shall be admitted for the period of the stay of that person.

Article 11 Not Lowering Standards

1.   The Parties recognize that it is inappropriate to encourage investment by relaxing domestic health, safety or environmental measures or core labour standards. Accordingly, a Party should not waive or otherwise derogate from, or offer to waive or otherwise derogate from, such measures as an encouragement for the establishment, acquisition, expansion or retention of an investment of an investor.

2.   If a Party considers that the other Party has offered such an encouragement, it may request consultations under Article [Joint Committee].

Article 12 Right to Regulate

Nothing in this Agreement shall be construed to prevent a Party from adopting, maintaining or enforcing any measure otherwise consistent with this Agreement that it considers appropriate to ensure that investment activity is undertaken in a manner sensitive to health, safety or environ-mental concerns.

SECTION 3 – DISPUTE SETTLEMENT PROVISIONS

Article 13 Non-Retroactive Application

This Section does not apply to disputes arising out of events that have occurred before the entry into force of this Agreement.

Article 14 Governing Law

1.   A Tribunal established under this Section shall make its award based on the provisions of this Agreement interpreted and applied in accordance with the rules of interpretation of international law.

2.   An interpretation by the Joint Committee of a provision of this Agreement shall be binding on a Tribunal established under this Section.

A. DISPUTES BETWEEN A PARTY AND AN INVESTOR OF THE OTHER PARTY

Article 15 Disputes Between a Party and an Investor of the Other Party

1.   This Article applies to legal disputes between a Party and an investor of the other Party arising directly out of an investment of the latter that falls under the jurisdiction of the former. The dispute must be based on a claim that the Party has breached an obligation under this Agreement and that the investor of the other Party has incurred loss or damage by that breach.

2.   Any dispute under this Article shall, if possible, be settled amicably. The Party and an investor of the other Party should initially seek to resolve the dispute through consultation.

3.   If any such dispute should arise and either

i.   agreement cannot be reached between the parties to this dispute within 36 months from its submission to a local court for the purpose of pursuing local remedies, after having exhausted any administrative remedies; or

ii.   there are no reasonably available local remedies to provide effective redress of this dispute, or the local remedies provide no reasonable possibility of such redress, [and,

iii.   the investor has provided a clear and unequivocal waiver of any right to pursue the matter before local courts,]

then each Party hereby consents to the submission of such dispute to arbitration under the Convention on the Settlement of Investment Disputes between States and Nationals of Other States opened for signature at Washington on 18 March 1965 (ICSID Convention) in accordance with the provisions of this Article. The consent and the submission of the dispute by an investor under this Article shall be considered to satisfy the requirements of Article 25 of the ICSID Convention [ICSID Additional Facility Rules, with the approval of the Agreement by the Secretary General to ICSID].

4.   [An investor may not submit a dispute for resolution according to paragraph [3] if more than ten years have elapsed from the date the investor first acquired knowledge of the events giving rise to the claim.]

5.   Each request for arbitration shall include information sufficient to present clearly the issues in dispute so as to allow the Parties and the public to become acquainted with them. All requests for arbitration shall be made publicly available by the Parties and by ICSID.

Article 16 Additional Procedural Issues

The Tribunal shall, as appropriate, take into account the principles of res judicata and lis pendens, in accordance with international law, to hinder abuse of rights under this agreement, as well as otherwise exercising sound judicial economy. If all parties to the dispute so agree, the Tribunal may consolidate claims.

Article 17 The Award

1.   Any arbitral award rendered pursuant to Article [Disputes between a Party and an Investor of the other Party], shall be final and binding on the Parties to the dispute.

2.   Where a Tribunal makes an award against a Party pursuant to Article [Disputes between a Party and an Investor of the other Party], the Tribunal may only award monetary damages, including applicable interest, as well as costs in accordance with the applicable arbitration rules.

3.   All awards and substantive decisions of the Tribunal shall be made publicly available.

4.   The costs of arbitration shall in principle be borne by the unsuccessful Party. However, the Tribunal may apportion such costs between the Parties if it determines that apportionment is reasonable, taking into account the circumstances of the case.

Article 18 Participation in the Proceedings

1.   The Party complained against shall, within 30 days after receiving a request for arbitration, notify the other Party in writing and transmit a copy of the request.

2.   The Tribunal shall give the other Party the opportunity to:

i.   be present at the substantive meetings of the Tribunal with the parties to the dispute preceding, except for portions of such meetings when confidential information designated as such by the Party that submitted it is discussed;

ii.   make a written submission prior to the first oral hearing; and

iii.   make an oral presentation to the Tribunal at the first oral hearing;

provided that it has informed the Tribunal no later than [30 days] after the establishment of the Tribunal of its desire to participate in the proceedings.

3.   The Tribunal shall have the authority to accept and consider written amicus curiae submissions from a person or entity that is not a disputing Party, provided that the Tribunal has determined that they are directly relevant to the factual and legal issues under consideration. The Tribunal shall ensure an opportunity for the parties to the dispute, and to the other Party, to submit comments on the written amicus curiae observations.

4.   The Tribunal shall reflect submissions from the other Party and from amicus curiae in its report.

Article 19 Transparency of Proceedings

1.   All documents submitted to, or issued by, the Tribunal shall immediately be made publicly available by the Tribunal.

2.   When submitting information to the Tribunal, a Party to the dispute may designate specific information as confidential if the information

i.   is not generally known or accessible to the public, and

ii.   if disclosed would cause or threaten to cause prejudice to an essential interest of any individual or entity, or to the interest of a Party.

Such information shall be treated as confidential and shall only be made available to the parties to the dispute and to the other Party.

3.   If another Party objects to the designation of information as confidential, the Tribunal shall decide if the designation meets the above mentioned criteria. If the Tribunal considers that the information does not meet the criteria, the Party submitting the information may

i.   withdraw the information, or

ii.   withdraw the designation of the information as confidential.

4.   The Tribunal shall conduct hearings open to the public and shall determine, in consultation with the disputing parties, the appropriate logistical arrangements.

B. Disputes Between the Parties

Article 20 Disputes Between the Parties

1.   Any dispute between the Parties concerning the interpretation or application of this Agreement shall, whenever possible, be settled amicably through consultations in the Joint Committee.

2.   If the Parties are unable to reach a mutually satisfactory resolution of a matter through consultations, they may have recourse to good offices or to mediation or conciliation under such rules and procedures as they may agree.

3.   A Party may not initiate arbitration against the other Party under paragraph 4 of this Article unless the former Party has requested consultations and has afforded the other Party a consultation period of no less than 60 days after the date of the receipt of the request.

4.   Either Party that has complied with the consultation requirement of paragraphs 2 and 3 of this Article, may submit a dispute between them as to whether one of them has acted in contravention of this Agreement to final and binding arbitration in accordance with the Permanent Court of Arbitration Optional Rules for Arbitrating Disputes between Two States, as in effect on the date of this Agreement.

5.   The place of the arbitration proceedings shall be The Hague, The Netherlands.

6.   The language to be used in the arbitral proceedings shall be English.

7.   The appointing authority shall be the Secretary General of the Permanent Court of Arbitration.

8.   Nothing in the present Article impairs the right of the Parties to agree at any time to settle a dispute between them concerning the interpretation or application of this Agreement by any peaceful means of their own choice.

Article 21 Transparency of Proceedings

1.   All documents submitted to, or issued by, the Tribunal shall be made publicly available by the International Bureau of the Permanent Court of Arbitrations, except for confidential information contained therein.

2.   The Tribunal shall conduct hearings open to the public and shall determine, in consultation with the disputing parties, the appropriate logistical arrangements. The arbitral tribunal, after hearing the parties, may decide to close the hearings wholly or partially.

3.   The Tribunal shall have the authority to accept and consider written amicus curiae submissions from a person or entity that is not a disputing Party, provided that the tribunal has determined that they are directly relevant to the factual and legal issues under consideration.

4.   When submitting information to the Tribunal, a Party may designate specific information as confidential if the information

i.   is not generally known or accessible to the public, and

ii.   if disclosed would cause or threaten to cause [serious] prejudice to an essential interest of any individual or entity [lawfully in control of the information].

Such information shall not be disclosed and be treated in accordance with procedures to be established by the Tribunal for each particular case.

5.   If another Party objects to the designation of information as confidential, the Tribunal shall decide if the designation meets the above mentioned criteria. If the Tribunal considers that the information does not meet the criteria, the Party submitting the information may

i.   withdraw the information, or

ii.   withdraw the designation of the information as confidential.

C. Subrogation

Article 22 Subrogation

1.   If the investments of an investor are insured against non-commercial risks, any subrogation of the claims of the investor pursuant to this Agreement, shall be recognized by the other Party.

2.   Disputes between a Party and an insurer shall be settled in accordance with the provisions of [Annex C] of this Agreement.

SECTION 4 - INSTITUTIONAL PROVISIONS

Article 23 The Joint Committee

1.   The Parties hereby establish a Joint Committee composed of representatives of the Parties.

2.   The Joint Committee shall meet whenever necessary. Each Party may request at any time, through a notice in writing to the other Party, that a meeting of the Joint Committee be held. The request shall provide sufficient information to understand the basis for the request, including, where relevant, identification of issues in dispute. Such a meeting shall take place within 60 days of receipt of the request, unless the Parties agree otherwise.

3.   The Joint Committee shall:

i.   supervise the implementation of this Agreement;

ii.   in accordance with Article [Disputes between the Parties], endeavour to resolve disputes that may arise regarding the interpretation or application of this Agreement;

iii.   review the possibility of further removal of barriers to investment;

iv.   where relevant, suggest to the Parties ways to enhance and promote investment action;

v.   review investments covered by this Agreement;

vi.   review case-law of investment arbitration tribunals relevant to the implementation of this Agreement;

vii.   oversee the further elaboration of this Agreement;

viii.   where relevant, discuss issues related to corporate social responsibility, the preservation of the environment, public health and safety, the goal of sustainable development, anti-corruption, employment and human rights, and

ix.   consider any other matter that may affect the operation of this Agreement.

4.   Where appropriate, the Joint Committee may:

i.   decide to amend the Agreement, as set forth in Article [Amendments]; and

ii.   interpret this Agreement, bearing in mind that this competence shall not be used to under-mine the amendment provisions of Article [Amendments]. The Joint Committee should refrain from adopting interpretations of provisions already submitted to a Tribunal in a dispute between a Party and an Investor of the other Party.

5.   The Joint Committee may take decisions as provided for in this Agreement. On other matters the Joint Committee may make recommendations. Decisions and recommendations shall be made by consensus.

6.   The Joint Committee shall establish its rules of procedure.

SECTION 5 – EXCEPTIONS

Article 24 General Exceptions

Subject to the requirement that such measures are not applied in a manner which would constitute a means of arbitrary or unjustifiable discrimination between investments or between investors, or a disguised restriction on international [trade or] investment, nothing in this Agreement shall be construed to prevent a Party from adopting or enforcing measures necessary[1]

i.   to protect public morals or to maintain public order;[2]

ii.   to protect human, animal or plant life or health;

iii.   to secure compliance with laws and regulations that are not inconsistent with the provisions of this Agreement;

iv.   for the protection of national treasures of artistic, historic or archaeological value; or

v.   for the protection of the environment.

Article 25 Prudential Regulation

Notwithstanding any other provisions of this Agreement, a Party shall not be prevented from taking measures for prudential reasons, including for the protection of investors, depositors, policy holders or persons to whom a fiduciary duty is owed by a financial service supplier, to ensure the integrity and stability of the financial system, or to enhance market competition, including ownership control and limitation.

Where such measures do not conform with the provisions of the Agreement, they shall not be used as a means of avoiding the Party's commitments or obligations under the Agreement.

Article 26 Security Exceptions

Nothing in this Agreement shall be construed:

i.   to require any Party to furnish any information, the disclosure of which it considers contrary to its essential security interests; or

ii.   to prevent any Party from taking any action which it considers necessary for the protection of its essential security interests:

   (a)   relating to investment in defence and security sector[s];

   (b)   relating to fissionable and fusionable materials or the materials from which they are derived;

   (c)   taken in time of war or other emergency in international relations; or

iii.   to prevent any Party from taking any action in pursuance of its obligations for the maintenance of international peace and security, including under the United Nations Charter.

Article 27 Cultural Exceptions

The provisions of this Agreement shall not apply to a Party's laws and measures specifically designed to preserve and promote linguistic and cultural diversity, cultural and audiovisual policy, as well as rights and obligations of the Parties under international agreements and national laws and measures relating to copyright and related rights.

Article 28 Taxation

1.   Nothing in this Agreement shall affect the imposition, enforcement or collection of direct or indirect taxes imposed by a Party.

2.   Nothing in this Agreement shall create any right to any benefit under an agreement for the avoidance of double taxation concluded by a Party.

3.   Any dispute as to whether paragraphs 1 and 2 apply, may only be brought before the Competent Tax Authorities of the Parties according to the procedure of Article [The Joint Committee]

---

1   For greater certainty, the concept of "necessity" in this Article shall include measures taken by a Party as provided for by the precautionary principle, including the principle of precautionary action.

2   The public order exception may be invoked only where a genuine and sufficiently serious threat is posed to one of the fundamental interests of society.

or the national courts or appeal organs of a Party, and shall not be covered by Section [Dispute Settlement Provisions] of this Agreement.

4.   If the Competent Tax Authority of one of the Parties, after the procedure of Article [The Joint Committee] has been completed, does not agree that paragraph 1 above apply, but takes the position that the case should be considered under Article [Expropriation], then the dispute shall be covered by [Section [Dispute Settlement Provisions] of this Agreement.]

SECTION 6 – FINAL PROVISIONS

Article 29 Relation to Other International Agreements

The provisions of this Agreement shall be without prejudice to the rights and obligations of the Parties under other international agreements.

Article 30 Regional and Local Government

Each Party is fully responsible for the observance of all obligations and commitments under this Agreement by its respective regional and local governments and authorities, and by non-governmental bodies in the exercise of governmental powers delegated to them by central, regional and local governments or authorities.

Article 31 Transparency

1.   The Parties shall publish their laws, or otherwise make publicly available their laws, regulations and administrative rulings and judicial decisions of general application as well as their respective international agreements that may affect the operation of this Agreement.

2.   The Parties shall promptly respond to specific questions and provide, upon request, information to each other on matters referred to in paragraph 1.

Article 32 Corporate Social Responsibility

The Parties agree to encourage investors to conduct their investment activities in compliance with the OECD Guidelines for Multinational Enterprises and to participate in the United Nations Global Compact.

Article 33 Amendments

1.   Amendments to this Agreement, decided by the Joint Committee in accordance with Article [Joint Committee], shall be subject to ratification, acceptance or approval by the Parties.

2.   Amendments shall enter into force on the first day of the third month following the date of receipt of the last notification by a Party informing the other Party that its internal constitutional requirements have been fulfilled.

Article 34 Entry into Force

1.   This Agreement is subject to ratification, acceptance or approval.

2.   This Agreement shall enter into force on the first day of the third month following the receipt of the last notification informing the other Party that the internal constitutional requirements have been fulfilled.

Article 35 Duration and Termination

1.   Each Party to this Agreement may, by means of a written notification to the other Party, terminate this Agreement. The termination shall take effect on the first day of the [X] month after the date on which the notification was received by the other Party.

2.   In respect of investments made prior to the date of termination of this Agreement, the provisions of this Agreement shall remain in force for a further period of fifteen years from that date.

IN WITNESS WHEREOF the undersigned, being duly authorised thereto, have signed this Agreement.

Done at ...., this .... of .... 200x in duplicate [in the English, Norwegian and [XXX] languages, all texts being equally authentic. In case of divergence of interpretation, the English text shall prevail.

For the For the Kingdom of Norway

ANNEX A
RESERVATIONS/EXCEPTIONS FROM NATIONAL TREATMENT

1.   A Party may, at any time, remove in whole or in part its reservations set out in this Annex by written notification to the other Party.

2.   A Party may, at any time, incorporate a new reservation into this Annex, or amend an existing reservation, provided that the Party has offered compensatory adjustments that maintain the overall level of commitments of that Party under this Agreement as it existed immediately prior to the modification:

i.   A Party shall notify its intent to modify its list of reservations to the other Party and at the same time suggest appropriate compensatory adjustments. The Joint Committee shall immediately be seized of the matter. Where the Joint Committee approves the modifications, they shall enter into force [3 months] after the decision by the Joint Committee.

ii.   Where the Joint Committee has not made a decision within [6 months] of receipt of the notification by the modifying Party, the modification shall take effect. In such circumstances, the other Party may withdraw concessions equivalent to the modification within [6 months] thereafter.

3.   A modification pursuant to this Article may not impose on an investor a requirement to sell or otherwise dispose of an investment in the territory of the Party.

ANNEX B
EXCEPTIONS/RESERVATIONS FROM MOST FAVOURED NATION TREATMENT

1.   Article [Most-Favoured-Nations] shall not apply to treatment accorded under bilateral agreements signed by Norway prior to 1997 nor to treatment accorded under the EFTA-Singapore Free Trade Agreement signed 26 June 2002.

[Procedures for amendments/modification must be prepared]

ANNEX C
DISPUTES BETWEEN A CONTRACTING PARTY AND AN INSURER IN ACCORDANCE WITH ARTICLE [SUBROGATION] OF THIS AGREEMENT

1.   This Annex applies to legal disputes between an insurer and a Contracting Party, based on Article [Subrogation] of this Agreement, provided that the insurer does not have legal standing under Article 25(1) of the ICSID Convention.

2.   Each Party hereby consents to the submission by an insurer of a dispute, in accordance with Article [Subrogation] of this Agreement and Paragraph 1 of this Annex, to international arbitration under the UNCITRAL Arbitration Rules ("UNCITRAL").

3.   The consent under Paragraph 2 and the submission of the dispute by an insurer shall be considered to satisfy the requirements of Article 1 of UNCITRAL.

4.   Any arbitral award rendered pursuant to this Annex, shall be final and binding on the parties to the dispute and will be recognised and enforced in accordance with the Convention on the Recognition and Enforcement of Foreign Arbitral Awards, done in New York on 10 June 1958.

5.   Articles [alle som gjelder for investor-stat-tvisteløsning] of this Agreement and the procedural rules of ICSID shall apply to disputes under this Annex mutatis mutandis.

V.2. 2012 U.S. Model BIT[1]

Treaty
Between the Government of the United States of America
And the Government of [Country]
Concerning the Encouragement
And Reciprocal Protection of Investment

The Government of the United States of America and the Government of [Country] (hereinafter the "Parties");

Desiring to promote greater economic cooperation between them with respect to investment by nationals and enterprises of one Party in the territory of the other Party;

Recognizing that agreement on the treatment to be accorded such investment will stimulate the flow of private capital and the economic development of the Parties;

Agreeing that a stable framework for investment will maximize effective utilization of economic resources and improve living standards;

Recognizing the importance of providing effective means of asserting claims and enforcing rights with respect to investment under national law as well as through international arbitration;

Desiring to achieve these objectives in a manner consistent with the protection of health, safety, and the environment, and the promotion of internationally recognized labor rights;

Having resolved to conclude a Treaty concerning the encouragement and reciprocal protection of investment;

Have agreed as follows:

SECTION A

Article 1: Definitions

For purposes of this Treaty:

"central level of government" means:

(a)   for the United States, the federal level of government; and

(b)   for [Country], [ ].

"Centre" means the International Centre for Settlement of Investment Disputes ("ICSID") established by the ICSID Convention.

"claimant" means an investor of a Party that is a party to an investment dispute with the other Party.

"covered investment" means, with respect to a Party, an investment in its territory of an investor of the other Party in existence as of the date of entry into force of this Treaty or established, acquired, or expanded thereafter.

"disputing parties" means the claimant and the respondent.

"disputing party" means either the claimant or the respondent.

"enterprise" means any entity constituted or organized under applicable law, whether or not for profit, and whether privately or governmentally owned or controlled, including a corporation, trust, partnership, sole proprietorship, joint venture, association, or similar organization; and a branch of an enterprise.

---

1   See https://www.state.gov/documents/organization/188371.pdf. Footnotes omitted.

"enterprise of a Party" means an enterprise constituted or organized under the law of a Party, and a branch located in the territory of a Party and carrying out business activities there.

"existing" means in effect on the date of entry into force of this Treaty.

"freely usable currency" means "freely usable currency" as determined by the International Monetary Fund under its Articles of Agreement.

"GATS" means the General Agreement on Trade in Services, contained in Annex 1B to the WTO Agreement.

"government procurement" means the process by which a government obtains the use of or acquires goods or services, or any combination thereof, for governmental purposes and not with a view to commercial sale or resale, or use in the production or supply of goods or services for commercial sale or resale.

"ICSID Additional Facility Rules" means the Rules Governing the Additional Facility for the Administration of Proceedings by the Secretariat of the International Centre for Settlement of Investment Disputes.

"ICSID Convention" means the Convention on the Settlement of Investment Disputes between States and Nationals of Other States, done at Washington, March 18, 1965.

["Inter-American Convention" means the Inter-American Convention on International Commercial Arbitration, done at Panama, January 30, 1975.]

"investment" means every asset that an investor owns or controls, directly or indirectly, that has the characteristics of an investment, including such characteristics as the commitment of capital or other resources, the expectation of gain or profit, or the assumption of risk. Forms that an investment may take include:

(a) an enterprise;

(b) shares, stock, and other forms of equity participation in an enterprise;

(c) bonds, debentures, other debt instruments, and loans;

(d) futures, options, and other derivatives;

(e) turnkey, construction, management, production, concession, revenue-sharing, and other similar contracts;

(f) intellectual property rights;

(g) licenses, authorizations, permits, and similar rights conferred pursuant to domestic law; and

(h) other tangible or intangible, movable or immovable property, and related property rights, such as leases, mortgages, liens, and pledges.

"investment agreement" means a written agreement between a national authority of a Party and a covered investment or an investor of the other Party, on which the covered investment or the investor relies in establishing or acquiring a covered investment other than the written agreement itself, that grants rights to the covered investment or investor:

(a) with respect to natural resources that a national authority controls, such as for their exploration, extraction, refining, transportation, distribution, or sale;

(b) to supply services to the public on behalf of the Party, such as power generation or distribution, water treatment or distribution, or telecommunications; or

(c) to undertake infrastructure projects, such as the construction of roads, bridges, canals, dams, or pipelines, that are not for the exclusive or predominant use and benefit of the government.

"investment authorization" means an authorization that the foreign investment authority of a Party grants to a covered investment or an investor of the other Party.

"investor of a non-Party" means, with respect to a Party, an investor that attempts to make, is making, or has made an investment in the territory of that Party, that is not an investor of either Party.

"investor of a Party" means a Party or state enterprise thereof, or a national or an enterprise of a Party, that attempts to make, is making, or has made an investment in the territory of the other Party; provided, however, that a natural person who is a dual national shall be deemed to be exclusively a national of the State of his or her dominant and effective nationality.

"measure" includes any law, regulation, procedure, requirement, or practice.

"national" means:

(a) for the United States, a natural person who is a national of the United States as defined in Title III of the Immigration and Nationality Act; and

(b) for [Country], [ ].

"New York Convention" means the United Nations Convention on the Recognition and Enforcement of Foreign Arbitral Awards, done at New York, June 10, 1958.

"non-disputing Party" means the Party that is not a party to an investment dispute.

"person" means a natural person or an enterprise.

"person of a Party" means a national or an enterprise of a Party.

"protected information" means confidential business information or information that is privileged or otherwise protected from disclosure under a Party's law.

"regional level of government" means:

(a) for the United States, a state of the United States, the District of Columbia, or Puerto Rico; and

(b) for [Country], [ ].

"respondent" means the Party that is a party to an investment dispute.

"Secretary-General" means the Secretary-General of ICSID.

"state enterprise" means an enterprise owned, or controlled through ownership interests, by a Party.

"territory" means:

(a) with respect to the United States,

   (i)   the customs territory of the United States, which includes the 50 states, the District of Columbia, and Puerto Rico;

   (ii) the foreign trade zones located in the United States and Puerto Rico.

(b) with respect to [Country,] [ ].

(c) with respect to each Party, the territorial sea and any area beyond the territorial sea of the Party within which, in accordance with customary international law as reflected in the United Nations Convention on the Law of the Sea, the Party may exercise sovereign rights or jurisdiction.

"TRIPS Agreement" means the Agreement on Trade-Related Aspects of Intellectual Property Rights, contained in Annex 1C to the WTO Agreement.

"UNCITRAL Arbitration Rules" means the arbitration rules of the United Nations Commission on International Trade Law.

"WTO Agreement" means the Marrakesh Agreement Establishing the World Trade Organization, done on April 15, 1994.

Article 2: Scope and Coverage

1.   This Treaty applies to measures adopted or maintained by a Party relating to:

(a)   investors of the other Party;

(b)   covered investments; and

(c)   with respect to Articles 8 [Performance Requirements], 12 [Investment and Environment], and 13 [Investment and Labor], all investments in the territory of the Party.

2.   A Party's obligations under Section A shall apply:

(a)   to a state enterprise or other person when it exercises any regulatory, administrative, or other governmental authority delegated to it by that Party; and

(b)   to the political subdivisions of that Party.

3.   For greater certainty, this Treaty does not bind either Party in relation to any act or fact that took place or any situation that ceased to exist before the date of entry into force of this Treaty.

Article 3: National Treatment

1.   Each Party shall accord to investors of the other Party treatment no less favorable than that it accords, in like circumstances, to its own investors with respect to the establishment, acquisition, expansion, management, conduct, operation, and sale or other disposition of investments in its territory.

2.   Each Party shall accord to covered investments treatment no less favorable than that it accords, in like circumstances, to investments in its territory of its own investors with respect to the establishment, acquisition, expansion, management, conduct, operation, and sale or other disposition of investments.

3.   The treatment to be accorded by a Party under paragraphs 1 and 2 means, with respect to a regional level of government, treatment no less favorable than the treatment accorded, in like circumstances, by that regional level of government to natural persons resident in and enterprises constituted under the laws of other regional levels of government of the Party of which it forms a part, and to their respective investments.

Article 4: Most-Favored-Nation Treatment

1.   Each Party shall accord to investors of the other Party treatment no less favorable than that it accords, in like circumstances, to investors of any non-Party with respect to the establishment, acquisition, expansion, management, conduct, operation, and sale or other disposition of investments in its territory.

2.   Each Party shall accord to covered investments treatment no less favorable than that it accords, in like circumstances, to investments in its territory of investors of any non-Party with respect to the establishment, acquisition, expansion, management, conduct, operation, and sale or other disposition of investments.

Article 5: Minimum Standard of Treatment

1.   Each Party shall accord to covered investments treatment in accordance with customary international law, including fair and equitable treatment and full protection and security.

2.   For greater certainty, paragraph 1 prescribes the customary international law minimum standard of treatment of aliens as the minimum standard of treatment to be afforded to covered investments. The concepts of "fair and equitable treatment" and "full protection and security" do not require treatment in addition to or beyond that which is required by that standard, and do not create additional substantive rights. The obligation in paragraph 1 to provide:

(a)   "fair and equitable treatment" includes the obligation not to deny justice in criminal, civil, or administrative adjudicatory proceedings in accordance with the principle of due process embodied in the principal legal systems of the world; and

(b) "full protection and security" requires each Party to provide the level of police protection required under customary international law.

3.   A determination that there has been a breach of another provision of this Treaty, or of a separate international agreement, does not establish that there has been a breach of this Article.

4.   Notwithstanding Article 14 [Non-Conforming Measures](5)(b) [subsidies and grants], each Party shall accord to investors of the other Party, and to covered investments, non-discriminatory treatment with respect to measures it adopts or maintains relating to losses suffered by investments in its territory owing to armed conflict or civil strife.

5.   Notwithstanding paragraph 4, if an investor of a Party, in the situations referred to in paragraph 4, suffers a loss in the territory of the other Party resulting from:

(a)   requisitioning of its covered investment or part thereof by the latter's forces or authorities; or

(b)   destruction of its covered investment or part thereof by the latter's forces or authorities, which was not required by the necessity of the situation,

the latter Party shall provide the investor restitution, compensation, or both, as appropriate, for such loss. Any compensation shall be prompt, adequate, and effective in accordance with Article 6 [Expropriation and Compensation](2) through (4), mutatis mutandis.

6.   Paragraph 4 does not apply to existing measures relating to subsidies or grants that would be inconsistent with Article 3 [National Treatment] but for Article 14 [Non-Conforming Measures](5)(b) [subsidies and grants].

Article 6: Expropriation and Compensation

1.   Neither Party may expropriate or nationalize a covered investment either directly or indirectly through measures equivalent to expropriation or nationalization ("expropriation"), except:

(a)   for a public purpose;

(b)   in a non-discriminatory manner;

(c)   on payment of prompt, adequate, and effective compensation; and

(d)   in accordance with due process of law and Article 5 [Minimum Standard of Treatment](1) through (3).

2.   The compensation referred to in paragraph 1(c) shall:

(a)   be paid without delay;

(b)   be equivalent to the fair market value of the expropriated investment immediately before the expropriation took place ("the date of expropriation");

(c)   not reflect any change in value occurring because the intended expropriation had become known earlier; and

(d)   be fully realizable and freely transferable.

3.   If the fair market value is denominated in a freely usable currency, the compensation referred to in paragraph 1(c) shall be no less than the fair market value on the date of expropriation, plus interest at a commercially reasonable rate for that currency, accrued from the date of expropriation until the date of payment.

4.   If the fair market value is denominated in a currency that is not freely usable, the compensation referred to in paragraph 1(c) – converted into the currency of payment at the market rate of exchange prevailing on the date of payment – shall be no less than:

(a)   the fair market value on the date of expropriation, converted into a freely usable currency at the market rate of exchange prevailing on that date, plus

(b)   interest, at a commercially reasonable rate for that freely usable currency, accrued from the date of expropriation until the date of payment.

5.   This Article does not apply to the issuance of compulsory licenses granted in relation to intellectual property rights in accordance with the TRIPS Agreement, or to the revocation, limitation, or creation of intellectual property rights, to the extent that such issuance, revocation, limitation, or creation is consistent with the TRIPS Agreement.

Article 7: Transfers

1.   Each Party shall permit all transfers relating to a covered investment to be made freely and without delay into and out of its territory. Such transfers include:

(a)   contributions to capital;

(b)   profits, dividends, capital gains, and proceeds from the sale of all or any part of the covered investment or from the partial or complete liquidation of the covered investment;

(c)   interest, royalty payments, management fees, and technical assistance and other fees;

(d)   payments made under a contract, including a loan agreement;

(e)   payments made pursuant to Article 5 [Minimum Standard of Treatment](4) and (5) and Article 6 [Expropriation and Compensation]; and

(f)   payments arising out of a dispute.

2.   Each Party shall permit transfers relating to a covered investment to be made in a freely usable currency at the market rate of exchange prevailing at the time of transfer.

3.   Each Party shall permit returns in kind relating to a covered investment to be made as authorized or specified in a written agreement between the Party and a covered investment or an investor of the other Party.

4.   Notwithstanding paragraphs 1 through 3, a Party may prevent a transfer through the equitable, non-discriminatory, and good faith application of its laws relating to:

(a)   bankruptcy, insolvency, or the protection of the rights of creditors;

(b)   issuing, trading, or dealing in securities, futures, options, or derivatives;

(c)   criminal or penal offenses;

(d)   financial reporting or record keeping of transfers when necessary to assist law enforcement or financial regulatory authorities; or

(e)   ensuring compliance with orders or judgments in judicial or administrative proceedings.

Article 8: Performance Requirements

1.   Neither Party may, in connection with the establishment, acquisition, expansion, management, conduct, operation, or sale or other disposition of an investment of an investor of a Party or of a non-Party in its territory, impose or enforce any requirement or enforce any commitment or undertaking:

(a)   to export a given level or percentage of goods or services;

(b)   to achieve a given level or percentage of domestic content;

(c)   to purchase, use, or accord a preference to goods produced in its territory, or to purchase goods from persons in its territory;

(d)   to relate in any way the volume or value of imports to the volume or value of exports or to the amount of foreign exchange inflows associated with such investment;

(e)   to restrict sales of goods or services in its territory that such investment produces or supplies by relating such sales in any way to the volume or value of its exports or foreign exchange earnings;

(f)   to transfer a particular technology, a production process, or other proprietary knowledge to a person in its territory;

(g) to supply exclusively from the territory of the Party the goods that such investment produces or the services that it supplies to a specific regional market or to the world market; or

(h) (i) to purchase, use, or accord a preference to, in its territory, technology of the Party or of
persons of the Party; or

(ii) that prevents the purchase or use of, or the according of a preference to, in its territory,
particular technology,

so as to afford protection on the basis of nationality to its own investors or investments or to
technology of the Party or of persons of the Party.

2.   Neither Party may condition the receipt or continued receipt of an advantage, in connection
with the establishment, acquisition, expansion, management, conduct, operation, or sale or other
disposition of an investment in its territory of an investor of a Party or of a non-Party, on compliance with any requirement:

(a) to achieve a given level or percentage of domestic content;

(b) to purchase, use, or accord a preference to goods produced in its territory, or to purchase
goods from persons in its territory;

(c) to relate in any way the volume or value of imports to the volume or value of exports or to
the amount of foreign exchange inflows associated with such investment; or

(d) to restrict sales of goods or services in its territory that such investment produces or supplies
by relating such sales in any way to the volume or value of its exports or foreign exchange
earnings.

3.a) Nothing in paragraph 2 shall be construed to prevent a Party from conditioning the receipt
or continued receipt of an advantage, in connection with an investment in its territory of an
investor of a Party or of a non-Party, on compliance with a requirement to locate production,
supply a service, train or employ workers, construct or expand particular facilities, or carry
out research and development, in its territory.

(b) Paragraphs 1(f) and (h) do not apply:

(i) when a Party authorizes use of an intellectual property right in accordance with Article
31 of the TRIPS Agreement, or to measures requiring the disclosure of proprietary
information that fall within the scope of, and are consistent with, Article 39 of the TRIPS
Agreement; or

(ii) when the requirement is imposed or the commitment or undertaking is enforced by a
court, administrative tribunal, or competition authority to remedy a practice determined after judicial or administrative process to be anticompetitive under the Party's
competition laws.

(c) Provided that such measures are not applied in an arbitrary or unjustifiable manner, and
provided that such measures do not constitute a disguised restriction on international trade
or investment, paragraphs 1(b), (c), (f), and (h), and 2(a) and (b), shall not be construed to
prevent a Party from adopting or maintaining measures, including environmental measures:

(i) necessary to secure compliance with laws and regulations that are not inconsistent with
this Treaty;

(ii) necessary to protect human, animal, or plant life or health; or

(iii) related to the conservation of living or non-living exhaustible natural resources.

(d) Paragraphs 1(a), (b), and (c), and 2(a) and (b), do not apply to qualification requirements for
goods or services with respect to export promotion and foreign aid programs.

(e) Paragraphs 1(b), (c), (f), (g), and (h), and 2(a) and (b), do not apply to government procurement.

(f) Paragraphs 2(a) and (b) do not apply to requirements imposed by an importing Party relating to the content of goods necessary to qualify for preferential tariffs or preferential quotas.

4.   For greater certainty, paragraphs 1 and 2 do not apply to any commitment, undertaking, or requirement other than those set out in those paragraphs.

5.   This Article does not preclude enforcement of any commitment, undertaking, or requirement between private parties, where a Party did not impose or require the commitment, undertaking, or requirement.

Article 9: Senior Management and Boards of Directors

1.   Neither Party may require that an enterprise of that Party that is a covered investment appoint to senior management positions natural persons of any particular nationality.

2.   A Party may require that a majority of the board of directors, or any committee thereof, of an enterprise of that Party that is a covered investment, be of a particular nationality, or resident in the territory of the Party, provided that the requirement does not materially impair the ability of the investor to exercise control over its investment.

Article 10: Publication of Laws and Decisions Respecting Investment

1.   Each Party shall ensure that its:

(a) laws, regulations, procedures, and administrative rulings of general application; and

(b) adjudicatory decisions

respecting any matter covered by this Treaty are promptly published or otherwise made publicly available.

2.   For purposes of this Article, "administrative ruling of general application" means an administrative ruling or interpretation that applies to all persons and fact situations that fall generally within its ambit and that establishes a norm of conduct but does not include:

(a) a determination or ruling made in an administrative or quasi-judicial proceeding that applies to a particular covered investment or investor of the other Party in a specific case; or

(b) a ruling that adjudicates with respect to a particular act or practice.

Article 11: Transparency

1.   The Parties agree to consult periodically on ways to improve the transparency practices set out in this Article, Article 10 and Article 29.

2.   Publication: To the extent possible, each Party shall:

(a) publish in advance any measure referred to in Article 10(1)(a) that it proposes to adopt; and

(b) provide interested persons and the other Party a reasonable opportunity to comment on such proposed measures.

3.   With respect to proposed regulations of general application of its central level of government respecting any matter covered by this Treaty that are published in accordance with paragraph 2(a), each Party:

(a) shall publish the proposed regulations in a single official journal of national circulation and shall encourage their distribution through additional outlets;

(b) should in most cases publish the proposed regulations not less than 60 days before the date public comments are due;

(c) shall include in the publication an explanation of the purpose of and rationale for the proposed regulations; and

(d) shall, at the time it adopts final regulations, address significant, substantive comments received during the comment period and explain substantive revisions that it made to the proposed regulations in its official journal or in a prominent location on a government Internet site.

4. With respect to regulations of general application that are adopted by its central level of government respecting any matter covered by this Treaty, each Party:

(a) shall publish the regulations in a single official journal of national circulation and shall encourage their distribution through additional outlets; and

(b) shall include in the publication an explanation of the purpose of and rationale for the regulations.

5. Provision of Information

(a) On request of the other Party, a Party shall promptly provide information and respond to questions pertaining to any actual or proposed measure that the requesting Party considers might materially affect the operation of this Treaty or otherwise substantially affect its interests under this Treaty.

(b) Any request or information under this paragraph shall be provided to the other Party through the relevant contact points.

(c) Any information provided under this paragraph shall be without prejudice as to whether the measure is consistent with this Treaty.

6. Administrative Proceedings

With a view to administering in a consistent, impartial, and reasonable manner all measures referred to in Article 10(1)(a), each Party shall ensure that in its administrative proceedings applying such measures to particular covered investments or investors of the other Party in specific cases:

(a) wherever possible, covered investments or investors of the other Party that are directly affected by a proceeding are provided reasonable notice, in accordance with domestic procedures, when a proceeding is initiated, including a description of the nature of the proceeding, a statement of the legal authority under which the proceeding is initiated, and a general description of any issues in controversy;

(b) such persons are afforded a reasonable opportunity to present facts and arguments in support of their positions prior to any final administrative action, when time, the nature of the proceeding, and the public interest permit; and

(c) its procedures are in accordance with domestic law.

7. Review and Appeal

(a) Each Party shall establish or maintain judicial, quasi-judicial, or administrative tribunals or procedures for the purpose of the prompt review and, where warranted, correction of final administrative actions regarding matters covered by this Treaty. Such tribunals shall be impartial and independent of the office or authority entrusted with administrative enforcement and shall not have any substantial interest in the outcome of the matter.

(b) Each Party shall ensure that, in any such tribunals or procedures, the parties to the proceeding are provided with the right to:

(i) a reasonable opportunity to support or defend their respective positions; and

(ii) a decision based on the evidence and submissions of record or, where required by domestic law, the record compiled by the administrative authority.

(c)   Each Party shall ensure, subject to appeal or further review as provided in its domestic law, that such decisions shall be implemented by, and shall govern the practice of, the offices or authorities with respect to the administrative action at issue.

8.   Standards-Setting

(a)   Each Party shall allow persons of the other Party to participate in the development of standards and technical regulations by its central government bodies. Each Party shall allow persons of the other Party to participate in the development of these measures, and the development of conformity assessment procedures by its central government bodies, on terms no less favorable than those it accords to its own persons.

(b)   Each Party shall recommend that non-governmental standardizing bodies in its territory allow persons of the other Party to participate in the development of standards by those bodies. Each Party shall recommend that non-governmental standardizing bodies in its territory allow persons of the other Party to participate in the development of these standards, and the development of conformity assessment procedures by those bodies, on terms no less favorable than those they accord to persons of the Party.

(c)   Subparagraphs 8(a) and 8(b) do not apply to:

   (i)   sanitary and phytosanitary measures as defined in Annex A of the World Trade Organi-zation (WTO) Agreement on the Application of Sanitary and Phytosanitary Measures; or

   (ii)   purchasing specifications prepared by a governmental body for its production or con-sumption requirements.

(d)   For purposes of subparagraphs 8(a) and 8(b), "central government body", "standards", "technical regulations" and "conformity assessment procedures" have the meanings assigned to those terms in Annex 1 of the WTO Agreement on Technical Barriers to Trade. Consistent with Annex 1, the three latter terms do not include standards, technical regulations or conformity assessment procedures for the supply of a service.

Article 12: Investment and Environment

1.   The Parties recognize that their respective environmental laws and policies, and multilateral environmental agreements to which they are both party, play an important role in protecting the environment.

2.   The Parties recognize that it is inappropriate to encourage investment by weakening or reducing the protections afforded in domestic environmental laws. Accordingly, each Party shall ensure that it does not waive or otherwise derogate from or offer to waive or otherwise derogate from its environmental laws in a manner that weakens or reduces the protections afforded in those laws, or fail to effectively enforce those laws through a sustained or recurring course of action or inaction, as an encouragement for the establishment, acquisition, expansion, or retention of an investment in its territory.

3.   The Parties recognize that each Party retains the right to exercise discretion with respect to regulatory, compliance, investigatory, and prosecutorial matters, and to make decisions regar-ding the allocation of resources to enforcement with respect to other environmental matters determined to have higher priorities. Accordingly, the Parties understand that a Party is in compliance with paragraph 2 where a course of action or inaction reflects a reasonable exercise of such discretion, or results from a bona fide decision regarding the allocation of resources.

4.   For purposes of this Article, "environmental law" means each Party's statutes or regulations, or provisions thereof, the primary purpose of which is the protection of the environment, or the prevention of a danger to human, animal, or plant life or health, through the:

(a)   prevention, abatement, or control of the release, discharge, or emission of pollutants or environmental contaminants;

(b)   control of environmentally hazardous or toxic chemicals, substances, materials, and wastes, and the dissemination of information related thereto; or

(c)   protection or conservation of wild flora or fauna, including endangered species, their habitat, and specially protected natural areas,

in the Party's territory, but does not include any statute or regulation, or provision thereof, directly related to worker safety or health.

5.   Nothing in this Treaty shall be construed to prevent a Party from adopting, maintaining, or enforcing any measure otherwise consistent with this Treaty that it considers appropriate to ensure that investment activity in its territory is undertaken in a manner sensitive to environmental concerns.

6.   A Party may make a written request for consultations with the other Party regarding any matter arising under this Article. The other Party shall respond to a request for consultations within thirty days of receipt of such request. Thereafter, the Parties shall consult and endeavor to reach a mutually satisfactory resolution.

7.   The Parties confirm that each Party may, as appropriate, provide opportunities for public participation regarding any matter arising under this Article.

Article 13: Investment and Labor

1.   The Parties reaffirm their respective obligations as members of the International Labor Organization ("ILO") and their commitments under the ILO Declaration on Fundamental Principles and Rights at Work and its Follow-Up.

2.   The Parties recognize that it is inappropriate to encourage investment by weakening or reducing the protections afforded in domestic labor laws. Accordingly, each Party shall ensure that it does not waive or otherwise derogate from or offer to waive or otherwise derogate from its labor laws where the waiver or derogation would be inconsistent with the labor rights referred to in subparagraphs (a) through (e) of paragraph 3, or fail to effectively enforce its labor laws through a sustained or recurring course of action or inaction, as an encouragement for the establishment, acquisition, expansion, or retention of an investment in its territory.

3.   For purposes of this Article, "labor laws" means each Party's statutes or regulations, or provisions thereof, that are directly related to the following:

(a)   freedom of association;

(b)   the effective recognition of the right to collective bargaining;

(c)   the elimination of all forms of forced or compulsory labor;

(d)   the effective abolition of child labor and a prohibition on the worst forms of child labor;

(e)   the elimination of discrimination in respect of employment and occupation; and

(f)   acceptable conditions of work with respect to minimum wages, hours of work, and occupational safety and health.

4.   A Party may make a written request for consultations with the other Party regarding any matter arising under this Article. The other Party shall respond to a request for consultations within thirty days of receipt of such request. Thereafter, the Parties shall consult and endeavor to reach a mutually satisfactory resolution.

5.   The Parties confirm that each Party may, as appropriate, provide opportunities for public participation regarding any matter arising under this Article.

Article 14: Non-Conforming Measures

1.   Articles 3 [National Treatment], 4 [Most-Favored-Nation Treatment], 8 [Performance Requirements], and 9 [Senior Management and Boards of Directors] do not apply to:

(a) any existing non-conforming measure that is maintained by a Party at:

   (i)   the central level of government, as set out by that Party in its Schedule to Annex I or Annex III,

   (ii) a regional level of government, as set out by that Party in its Schedule to Annex I or Annex III, or

   (iii) a local level of government;

(b) the continuation or prompt renewal of any non-conforming measure referred to in sub-paragraph (a); or

(c) an amendment to any non-conforming measure referred to in subparagraph (a) to the extent that the amendment does not decrease the conformity of the measure, as it existed immediately before the amendment, with Article 3 [National Treatment], 4 [Most-Favored-Nation Treatment], 8 [Performance Requirements], or 9 [Senior Management and Boards of Directors].

2.   Articles 3 [National Treatment], 4 [Most-Favored-Nation Treatment], 8 [Performance Require-ments], and 9 [Senior Management and Boards of Directors] do not apply to any measure that a Party adopts or maintains with respect to sectors, subsectors, or activities, as set out in its Schedule to Annex II.

3.   Neither Party may, under any measure adopted after the date of entry into force of this Treaty and covered by its Schedule to Annex II, require an investor of the other Party, by reason of its nationality, to sell or otherwise dispose of an investment existing at the time the measure becomes effective.

4.   Articles 3 [National Treatment] and 4 [Most-Favored-Nation Treatment] do not apply to any measure covered by an exception to, or derogation from, the obligations under Article 3 or 4 of the TRIPS Agreement, as specifically provided in those Articles and in Article 5 of the TRIPS Agree-ment.

5.   Articles 3 [National Treatment], 4 [Most-Favored-Nation Treatment], and 9 [Senior Manage-ment and Boards of Directors] do not apply to:

(a) government procurement; or

(b) subsidies or grants provided by a Party, including government-supported loans, guarantees, and insurance.

Article 15: Special Formalities and Information Requirements

1.   Nothing in Article 3 [National Treatment] shall be construed to prevent a Party from adop-ting or maintaining a measure that prescribes special formalities in connection with covered investments, such as a requirement that investors be residents of the Party or that covered investments be legally constituted under the laws or regulations of the Party, provided that such formalities do not materially impair the protections afforded by a Party to investors of the other Party and covered investments pursuant to this Treaty.

2.   Notwithstanding Articles 3 [National Treatment] and 4 [Most-Favored-Nation Treatment], a Party may require an investor of the other Party or its covered investment to provide information concerning that investment solely for informational or statistical purposes. The Party shall protect any confidential business information from any disclosure that would prejudice the competitive position of the investor or the covered investment. Nothing in this paragraph shall be construed to prevent a Party from otherwise obtaining or disclosing information in connection with the equitable and good faith application of its law.

Article 16: Non-Derogation

This Treaty shall not derogate from any of the following that entitle an investor of a Party or a covered investment to treatment more favorable than that accorded by this Treaty:

1.   laws or regulations, administrative practices or procedures, or administrative or adjudicatory decisions of a Party;

2.   international legal obligations of a Party; or

3.   obligations assumed by a Party, including those contained in an investment authorization or an investment agreement.

Article 17: Denial of Benefits

1.   A Party may deny the benefits of this Treaty to an investor of the other Party that is an enterprise of such other Party and to investments of that investor if persons of a non-Party own or control the enterprise and the denying Party:

(a)   does not maintain diplomatic relations with the non-Party; or

(b)   adopts or maintains measures with respect to the non-Party or a person of the non-Party that prohibit transactions with the enterprise or that would be violated or circumvented if the benefits of this Treaty were accorded to the enterprise or to its investments.

2.   A Party may deny the benefits of this Treaty to an investor of the other Party that is an enterprise of such other Party and to investments of that investor if the enterprise has no substantial business activities in the territory of the other Party and persons of a non-Party, or of the denying Party, own or control the enterprise.

Article 18: Essential Security

Nothing in this Treaty shall be construed:

1.   to require a Party to furnish or allow access to any information the disclosure of which it determines to be contrary to its essential security interests; or

2.   to preclude a Party from applying measures that it considers necessary for the fulfillment of its obligations with respect to the maintenance or restoration of international peace or security, or the protection of its own essential security interests.

Article 19: Disclosure of Information

Nothing in this Treaty shall be construed to require a Party to furnish or allow access to confidential information the disclosure of which would impede law enforcement or otherwise be contrary to the public interest, or which would prejudice the legitimate commercial interests of particular enterprises, public or private.

Article 20: Financial Services

1.   Notwithstanding any other provision of this Treaty, a Party shall not be prevented from adopting or maintaining measures relating to financial services for prudential reasons, including for the protection of investors, depositors, policy holders, or persons to whom a fiduciary duty is owed by a financial services supplier, or to ensure the integrity and stability of the financial system. Where such measures do not conform with the provisions of this Treaty, they shall not be used as a means of avoiding the Party's commitments or obligations under this Treaty.

2.a) Nothing in this Treaty applies to non-discriminatory measures of general application taken by any public entity in pursuit of monetary and related credit policies or exchange rate policies. This paragraph shall not affect a Party's obligations under Article 7 [Transfers] or Article 8 [Performance Requirements].

(b)   For purposes of this paragraph, "public entity" means a central bank or monetary authority of a Party.

3.   Where a claimant submits a claim to arbitration under Section B [Investor-State Dispute Settlement], and the respondent invokes paragraph 1 or 2 as a defense, the following provisions shall apply:

(a) The respondent shall, within 120 days of the date the claim is submitted to arbitration under Section B, submit in writing to the competent financial authorities of both Parties a request for a joint determination on the issue of whether and to what extent paragraph 1 or 2 is a valid defense to the claim. The respondent shall promptly provide the tribunal, if constituted, a copy of such request. The arbitration may proceed with respect to the claim only as provided in subparagraph (d).

(b) The competent financial authorities of both Parties shall make themselves available for consultations with each other and shall attempt in good faith to make a determination as described in subparagraph (a). Any such determination shall be transmitted promptly to the disputing parties and, if constituted, to the tribunal. The determination shall be binding on the tribunal.

(c) If the competent financial authorities of both Parties, within 120 days of the date by which they have both received the respondent's written request for a joint determination under subparagraph (a), have not made a determination as described in that subparagraph, the tribunal shall decide the issue or issues left unresolved by the competent financial authorities. The provisions of Section B shall apply, except as modified by this subparagraph.

   (i)   In the appointment of all arbitrators not yet appointed to the tribunal, each disputing party shall take appropriate steps to ensure that the tribunal has expertise or experience in financial services law or practice. The expertise of particular candidates with respect to the particular sector of financial services in which the dispute arises shall be taken into account in the appointment of the presiding arbitrator.

   (ii) If, before the respondent submits the request for a joint determination in conformance with subparagraph (a), the presiding arbitrator has been appointed pursuant to Article 27(3), such arbitrator shall be replaced on the request of either disputing party and the tribunal shall be reconstituted consistent with subparagraph (c)(i). If, within 30 days of the date the arbitration proceedings are resumed under subparagraph (d), the disputing parties have not agreed on the appointment of a new presiding arbitrator, the Secretary-General, on the request of a disputing party, shall appoint the presiding arbitrator consistent with subparagraph (c)(i).

   (iii) The tribunal shall draw no inference regarding the application of paragraph 1 or 2 from the fact that the competent financial authorities have not made a determination as described in subparagraph (a).

   (iv) The non-disputing Party may make oral and written submissions to the tribunal regarding the issue of whether and to what extent paragraph 1 or 2 is a valid defense to the claim. Unless it makes such a submission, the non-disputing Party shall be presumed, for purposes of the arbitration, to take a position on paragraph 1 or 2 not inconsistent with that of the respondent.

(d) The arbitration referred to in subparagraph (a) may proceed with respect to the claim:

   (i)   10 days after the date the competent financial authorities' joint determination has been received by both the disputing parties and, if constituted, the tribunal; or

   (ii) 10 days after the expiration of the 120-day period provided to the competent financial authorities in subparagraph (c).

(e) On the request of the respondent made within 30 days after the expiration of the 120-day period for a joint determination referred to in subparagraph (c), or, if the tribunal has not been constituted as of the expiration of the 120-day period, within 30 days after the tribunal is constituted, the tribunal shall address and decide the issue or issues left unresolved by the competent financial authorities as referred to in subparagraph (c) prior to deciding the merits of the claim for which paragraph 1 or 2 has been invoked by the respondent as a defense. Failure of the respondent to make such a request is without prejudice to the right of the respondent to invoke paragraph 1 or 2 as a defense at any appropriate phase of the arbitration.

4.   Where a dispute arises under Section C and the competent financial authorities of one Party provide written notice to the competent financial authorities of the other Party that the dispute involves financial services, Section C shall apply except as modified by this paragraph and paragraph 5.

(a) The competent financial authorities of both Parties shall make themselves available for consultations with each other regarding the dispute, and shall have 180 days from the date such notice is received to transmit a report on their consultations to the Parties. A Party may submit the dispute to arbitration under Section C only after the expiration of that 180-day period.

(b) Either Party may make any such report available to a tribunal constituted under Section C to decide the dispute referred to in this paragraph or a similar dispute, or to a tribunal cons-tituted under Section B to decide a claim arising out of the same events or circumstances that gave rise to the dispute under Section C.

5.   Where a Party submits a dispute involving financial services to arbitration under Section C in conformance with paragraph 4, and on the request of either Party within 30 days of the date the dispute is submitted to arbitration, each Party shall, in the appointment of all arbitrators not yet appointed, take appropriate steps to ensure that the tribunal has expertise or experience in financial services law or practice. The expertise of particular candidates with respect to financial services shall be taken into account in the appointment of the presiding arbitrator.

6.   Notwithstanding Article 11(2)-(4) [Transparency – Publication], each Party, to the extent practicable,

(a) shall publish in advance any regulations of general application relating to financial services that it proposes to adopt and the purpose of the regulation;

(b) shall provide interested persons and the other Party a reasonable opportunity to comment on such proposed regulations; and

(c) should at the time it adopts final regulations, address in writing significant substantive comments received from interested persons with respect to the proposed regulations.

7.   The terms "financial service" or "financial services" shall have the same meaning as in sub-paragraph 5(a) of the Annex on Financial Services of the GATS.

8.   For greater certainty, nothing in this Treaty shall be construed to prevent the adoption or enforcement by a party of measures relating to investors of the other Party, or covered invest-ments, in financial institutions that are necessary to secure compliance with laws or regulations that are not inconsistent with this Treaty, including those related to the prevention of deceptive and fraudulent practices or that deal with the effects of a default on financial services contracts, subject to the requirement that such measures are not applied in a manner which would cons-titute a means of arbitrary or unjustifiable discrimination between countries where like con-ditions prevail, or a disguised restriction on investment in financial institutions.

Article 21: Taxation

1.   Except as provided in this Article, nothing in Section A shall impose obligations with respect to taxation measures.

2.   Article 6 [Expropriation] shall apply to all taxation measures, except that a claimant that asserts that a taxation measure involves an expropriation may submit a claim to arbitration under Section B only if:

(a) the claimant has first referred to the competent tax authorities of both Parties in writing the issue of whether that taxation measure involves an expropriation; and

(b)   within 180 days after the date of such referral, the competent tax authorities of both Parties
      fail to agree that the taxation measure is not an expropriation.

3.   Subject to paragraph 4, Article 8 [Performance Requirements] (2) through (4) shall apply to
all taxation measures.

4.   Nothing in this Treaty shall affect the rights and obligations of either Party under any tax
convention. In the event of any inconsistency between this Treaty and any such convention, that
convention shall prevail to the extent of the inconsistency. In the case of a tax convention
between the Parties, the competent authorities under that convention shall have sole responsibility for determining whether any inconsistency exists between this Treaty and that convention.

Article 22: Entry into Force, Duration, and Termination

1. This Treaty shall enter into force thirty days after the date the Parties exchange instruments of
ratification. It shall remain in force for a period of ten years and shall continue in force thereafter
unless terminated in accordance with paragraph 2.

2.   A Party may terminate this Treaty at the end of the initial ten-year period or at any time
thereafter by giving one year's written notice to the other Party.

3.   For ten years from the date of termination, all other Articles shall continue to apply to
covered investments established or acquired prior to the date of termination, except insofar as
those Articles extend to the establishment or acquisition of covered investments.

SECTION B

Article 23: Consultation and Negotiation

In the event of an investment dispute, the claimant and the respondent should initially seek to
resolve the dispute through consultation and negotiation, which may include the use of
non-binding, third-party procedures.

Article 24: Submission of a Claim to Arbitration

1.   In the event that a disputing party considers that an investment dispute cannot be settled
by consultation and negotiation:

(a)   the claimant, on its own behalf, may submit to arbitration under this Section a claim

   (i)   that the respondent has breached

      (A)   an obligation under Articles 3 through 10,

      (B)   an investment authorization, or

      (C)   an investment agreement; and

   (ii)   that the claimant has incurred loss or damage by reason of, or arising out of, that
          breach; and

(b)   the claimant, on behalf of an enterprise of the respondent that is a juridical person that the
      claimant owns or controls directly or indirectly, may submit to arbitration under this Section
      a claim

   (i)   that the respondent has breached

      (A)   an obligation under Articles 3 through 10,

      (B)   an investment authorization, or

      (C)   an investment agreement; and

   (ii)   that the enterprise has incurred loss or damage by reason of, or arising out of, that
          breach,

provided that a claimant may submit pursuant to subparagraph (a)(i)(C) or (b)(i)(C) a claim for breach of an investment agreement only if the subject matter of the claim and the claimed damages directly relate to the covered investment that was established or acquired, or sought to be established or acquired, in reliance on the relevant investment agreement.

2.   At least 90 days before submitting any claim to arbitration under this Section, a claimant shall deliver to the respondent a written notice of its intention to submit the claim to arbitration ("notice of intent"). The notice shall specify:

(a)   the name and address of the claimant and, where a claim is submitted on behalf of an enterprise, the name, address, and place of incorporation of the enterprise;

(b)   for each claim, the provision of this Treaty, investment authorization, or investment agreement alleged to have been breached and any other relevant provisions;

(c)   the legal and factual basis for each claim; and

(d)   the relief sought and the approximate amount of damages claimed.

3.   Provided that six months have elapsed since the events giving rise to the claim, a claimant may submit a claim referred to in paragraph 1:

(a)   under the ICSID Convention and the ICSID Rules of Procedure for Arbitration Proceedings, provided that both the respondent and the non-disputing Party are parties to the ICSID Convention;

(b)   under the ICSID Additional Facility Rules, provided that either the respondent or the non-disputing Party is a party to the ICSID Convention;

(c)   under the UNCITRAL Arbitration Rules; or

(d)   if the claimant and respondent agree, to any other arbitration institution or under any other arbitration rules.

4.   A claim shall be deemed submitted to arbitration under this Section when the claimant's notice of or request for arbitration ("notice of arbitration"):

(a)   referred to in paragraph 1 of Article 36 of the ICSID Convention is received by the Secretary-General;

(b)   referred to in Article 2 of Schedule C of the ICSID Additional Facility Rules is received by the Secretary-General;

(c)   referred to in Article 3 of the UNCITRAL Arbitration Rules, together with the statement of claim referred to in Article 20 of the UNCITRAL Arbitration Rules, are received by the respondent; or

(d)   referred to under any arbitral institution or arbitral rules selected under paragraph 3(d) is received by the respondent.

A claim asserted by the claimant for the first time after such notice of arbitration is submitted shall be deemed submitted to arbitration under this Section on the date of its receipt under the applicable arbitral rules.

5.   The arbitration rules applicable under paragraph 3, and in effect on the date the claim or claims were submitted to arbitration under this Section, shall govern the arbitration except to the extent modified by this Treaty.

6.   The claimant shall provide with the notice of arbitration:

(a)   the name of the arbitrator that the claimant appoints; or

(b)   the claimant's written consent for the Secretary-General to appoint that arbitrator.

Article 25: Consent of Each Party to Arbitration

1.   Each Party consents to the submission of a claim to arbitration under this Section in accordance with this Treaty.

2.   The consent under paragraph 1 and the submission of a claim to arbitration under this Section shall satisfy the requirements of:

(a)   Chapter II of the ICSID Convention (Jurisdiction of the Centre) and the ICSID Additional Facility Rules for written consent of the parties to the dispute; [and]

(b)   Article II of the New York Convention for an "agreement in writing[."] [;" and

(c)   Article I of the Inter-American Convention for an "agreement."]

Article 26: Conditions and Limitations on Consent of Each Party

1.   No claim may be submitted to arbitration under this Section if more than three years have elapsed from the date on which the claimant first acquired, or should have first acquired, knowledge of the breach alleged under Article 24(1) and knowledge that the claimant (for claims brought under Article 24(1)(a)) or the enterprise (for claims brought under Article 24(1)(b)) has incurred loss or damage.

2.   No claim may be submitted to arbitration under this Section unless:

(a)   the claimant consents in writing to arbitration in accordance with the procedures set out in this Treaty; and

(b)   the notice of arbitration is accompanied,

(i)   for claims submitted to arbitration under Article 24(1)(a), by the claimant's written waiver, and

(ii)   for claims submitted to arbitration under Article 24(1)(b), by the claimant's and the enterprise's written waivers

of any right to initiate or continue before any administrative tribunal or court under the law of either Party, or other dispute settlement procedures, any proceeding with respect to any measure alleged to constitute a breach referred to in Article 24.

3.   Notwithstanding paragraph 2(b), the claimant (for claims brought under Article 24(1)(a)) and the claimant or the enterprise (for claims brought under Article 24(1)(b)) may initiate or continue an action that seeks interim injunctive relief and does not involve the payment of monetary damages before a judicial or administrative tribunal of the respondent, provided that the action is brought for the sole purpose of preserving the claimant's or the enterprise's rights and interests during the pendency of the arbitration.

Article 27: Selection of Arbitrators

1.   Unless the disputing parties otherwise agree, the tribunal shall comprise three arbitrators, one arbitrator appointed by each of the disputing parties and the third, who shall be the presiding arbitrator, appointed by agreement of the disputing parties.

2.   The Secretary-General shall serve as appointing authority for an arbitration under this Section.

3.   Subject to Article 20(3), if a tribunal has not been constituted within 75 days from the date that a claim is submitted to arbitration under this Section, the Secretary-General, on the request of a disputing party, shall appoint, in his or her discretion, the arbitrator or arbitrators not yet appointed.

4.   For purposes of Article 39 of the ICSID Convention and Article 7 of Schedule C to the ICSID Additional Facility Rules, and without prejudice to an objection to an arbitrator on a ground other than nationality:

(a) the respondent agrees to the appointment of each individual member of a tribunal established under the ICSID Convention or the ICSID Additional Facility Rules;

(b) a claimant referred to in Article 24(1)(a) may submit a claim to arbitration under this Section, or continue a claim, under the ICSID Convention or the ICSID Additional Facility Rules, only on condition that the claimant agrees in writing to the appointment of each individual member of the tribunal; and

(c) a claimant referred to in Article 24(1)(b) may submit a claim to arbitration under this Section, or continue a claim, under the ICSID Convention or the ICSID Additional Facility Rules, only on condition that the claimant and the enterprise agree in writing to the appointment of each individual member of the tribunal.

Article 28: Conduct of the Arbitration

1.   The disputing parties may agree on the legal place of any arbitration under the arbitral rules applicable under Article 24(3). If the disputing parties fail to reach agreement, the tribunal shall determine the place in accordance with the applicable arbitral rules, provided that the place shall be in the territory of a State that is a party to the New York Convention.

2.   The non-disputing Party may make oral and written submissions to the tribunal regarding the interpretation of this Treaty.

3.   The tribunal shall have the authority to accept and consider amicus curiae submissions from a person or entity that is not a disputing party.

4.   Without prejudice to a tribunal's authority to address other objections as a preliminary question, a tribunal shall address and decide as a preliminary question any objection by the respondent that, as a matter of law, a claim submitted is not a claim for which an award in favor of the claimant may be made under Article 34.

(a) Such objection shall be submitted to the tribunal as soon as possible after the tribunal is constituted, and in no event later than the date the tribunal fixes for the respondent to submit its counter-memorial (or, in the case of an amendment to the notice of arbitration, the date the tribunal fixes for the respondent to submit its response to the amendment).

(b) On receipt of an objection under this paragraph, the tribunal shall suspend any proceedings on the merits, establish a schedule for considering the objection consistent with any schedule it has established for considering any other preliminary question, and issue a decision or award on the objection, stating the grounds therefor.

(c) In deciding an objection under this paragraph, the tribunal shall assume to be true claimant's factual allegations in support of any claim in the notice of arbitration (or any amendment thereof) and, in disputes brought under the UNCITRAL Arbitration Rules, the statement of claim referred to in Article 20 of the UNCITRAL Arbitration Rules. The tribunal may also consider any relevant facts not in dispute.

(d) The respondent does not waive any objection as to competence or any argument on the merits merely because the respondent did or did not raise an objection under this paragraph or make use of the expedited procedure set out in paragraph 5.

5.   In the event that the respondent so requests within 45 days after the tribunal is constituted, the tribunal shall decide on an expedited basis an objection under paragraph 4 and any objection that the dispute is not within the tribunal's competence. The tribunal shall suspend any proceedings on the merits and issue a decision or award on the objection(s), stating the grounds therefor, no later than 150 days after the date of the request. However, if a disputing party requests a hearing, the tribunal may take an additional 30 days to issue the decision or award. Regardless of whether a hearing is requested, a tribunal may, on a showing of extraordinary cause, delay issuing its decision or award by an additional brief period, which may not exceed 30 days.

6.   When it decides a respondent's objection under paragraph 4 or 5, the tribunal may, if warranted, award to the prevailing disputing party reasonable costs and attorney's fees incurred in submitting or opposing the objection. In determining whether such an award is warranted, the tribunal shall consider whether either the claimant's claim or the respondent's objection was frivolous, and shall provide the disputing parties a reasonable opportunity to comment.

7.   A respondent may not assert as a defense, counterclaim, right of set-off, or for any other reason that the claimant has received or will receive indemnification or other compensation for all or part of the alleged damages pursuant to an insurance or guarantee contract.

8.   A tribunal may order an interim measure of protection to preserve the rights of a disputing party, or to ensure that the tribunal's jurisdiction is made fully effective, including an order to preserve evidence in the possession or control of a disputing party or to protect the tribunal's jurisdiction. A tribunal may not order attachment or enjoin the application of a measure alleged to constitute a breach referred to in Article 24. For purposes of this paragraph, an order includes a recommendation.

9.a) In any arbitration conducted under this Section, at the request of a disputing party, a tribunal shall, before issuing a decision or award on liability, transmit its proposed decision or award to the disputing parties and to the non-disputing Party. Within 60 days after the tribunal transmits its proposed decision or award, the disputing parties may submit written comments to the tribunal concerning any aspect of its proposed decision or award. The tribunal shall consider any such comments and issue its decision or award not later than 45 days after the expiration of the 60-day comment period.

(b) Subparagraph (a) shall not apply in any arbitration conducted pursuant to this Section for which an appeal has been made available pursuant to paragraph 10.

10. In the event that an appellate mechanism for reviewing awards rendered by investor-State dispute settlement tribunals is developed in the future under other institutional arrangements, the Parties shall consider whether awards rendered under Article 34 should be subject to that appellate mechanism. The Parties shall strive to ensure that any such appellate mechanism they consider adopting provides for transparency of proceedings similar to the transparency provisions established in Article 29.

Article 29: Transparency of Arbitral Proceedings

1.   Subject to paragraphs 2 and 4, the respondent shall, after receiving the following documents, promptly transmit them to the non-disputing Party and make them available to the public:

(a) the notice of intent;

(b) the notice of arbitration;

(c) pleadings, memorials, and briefs submitted to the tribunal by a disputing party and any written submissions submitted pursuant to Article 28(2) [Non-Disputing Party submissions] and (3) [Amicus Submissions] and Article 33 [Consolidation];

(d) minutes or transcripts of hearings of the tribunal, where available; and

(e) orders, awards, and decisions of the tribunal.

2.   The tribunal shall conduct hearings open to the public and shall determine, in consultation with the disputing parties, the appropriate logistical arrangements. However, any disputing party that intends to use information designated as protected information in a hearing shall so advise the tribunal. The tribunal shall make appropriate arrangements to protect the information from disclosure.

3.   Nothing in this Section requires a respondent to disclose protected information or to furnish or allow access to information that it may withhold in accordance with Article 18 [Essential Security Article] or Article 19 [Disclosure of Information Article].

4.   Any protected information that is submitted to the tribunal shall be protected from disclosure in accordance with the following procedures:

(a) Subject to subparagraph (d), neither the disputing parties nor the tribunal shall disclose to the non-disputing Party or to the public any protected information where the disputing party that provided the information clearly designates it in accordance with subparagraph (b);

(b) Any disputing party claiming that certain information constitutes protected information shall clearly designate the information at the time it is submitted to the tribunal;

(c) A disputing party shall, at the time it submits a document containing information claimed to be protected information, submit a redacted version of the document that does not contain the information. Only the redacted version shall be provided to the non-disputing Party and made public in accordance with paragraph 1; and

(d) The tribunal shall decide any objection regarding the designation of information claimed to be protected information. If the tribunal determines that such information was not properly designated, the disputing party that submitted the information may (i) withdraw all or part of its submission containing such information, or (ii) agree to resubmit complete and redacted documents with corrected designations in accordance with the tribunal's determination and subparagraph (c). In either case, the other disputing party shall, whenever necessary, resubmit complete and redacted documents which either remove the information withdrawn under (i) by the disputing party that first submitted the information or redesignate the information consistent with the designation under (ii) of the disputing party that first submitted the information.

5.   Nothing in this Section requires a respondent to withhold from the public information required to be disclosed by its laws.

Article 30: Governing Law

1.   Subject to paragraph 3, when a claim is submitted under Article 24(1)(a)(i)(A) or Article 24(1)(b)(i)(A), the tribunal shall decide the issues in dispute in accordance with this Treaty and applicable rules of international law.

2.   Subject to paragraph 3 and the other terms of this Section, when a claim is submitted under Article 24(1)(a)(i)(B) or (C), or Article 24(1)(b)(i)(B) or (C), the tribunal shall apply:

(a) the rules of law specified in the pertinent investment authorization or investment agreement, or as the disputing parties may otherwise agree; or

(b) if the rules of law have not been specified or otherwise agreed:

(i)   the law of the respondent, including its rules on the conflict of laws; and

(ii) such rules of international law as may be applicable.

3.   A joint decision of the Parties, each acting through its representative designated for purposes of this Article, declaring their interpretation of a provision of this Treaty shall be binding on a tribunal, and any decision or award issued by a tribunal must be consistent with that joint decision.

Article 31: Interpretation of Annexes

1.   Where a respondent asserts as a defense that the measure alleged to be a breach is within the scope of an entry set out in Annex I, II, or III, the tribunal shall, on request of the respondent, request the interpretation of the Parties on the issue. The Parties shall submit in writing any joint decision declaring their interpretation to the tribunal within 90 days of delivery of the request.

2.   A joint decision issued under paragraph 1 by the Parties, each acting through its representative designated for purposes of this Article, shall be binding on the tribunal, and any decision or award issued by the tribunal must be consistent with that joint decision. If the Parties fail to issue such a decision within 90 days, the tribunal shall decide the issue.

Article 32: Expert Reports

Without prejudice to the appointment of other kinds of experts where authorized by the applicable arbitration rules, a tribunal, at the request of a disputing party or, unless the disputing parties disapprove, on its own initiative, may appoint one or more experts to report to it in writing on any factual issue concerning environmental, health, safety, or other scientific matters raised by a disputing party in a proceeding, subject to such terms and conditions as the disputing parties may agree.

Article 33: Consolidation

1.   Where two or more claims have been submitted separately to arbitration under Article 24(1) and the claims have a question of law or fact in common and arise out of the same events or circumstances, any disputing party may seek a consolidation order in accordance with the agreement of all the disputing parties sought to be covered by the order or the terms of paragraphs 2 through 10.

2.   A disputing party that seeks a consolidation order under this Article shall deliver, in writing, a request to the Secretary-General and to all the disputing parties sought to be covered by the order and shall specify in the request:

(a)   the names and addresses of all the disputing parties sought to be covered by the order;

(b)   the nature of the order sought; and

(c)   the grounds on which the order is sought.

3.   Unless the Secretary-General finds within 30 days after receiving a request under paragraph 2 that the request is manifestly unfounded, a tribunal shall be established under this Article.

4.   Unless all the disputing parties sought to be covered by the order otherwise agree, a tribunal established under this Article shall comprise three arbitrators:

(a)   one arbitrator appointed by agreement of the claimants;

(b)   one arbitrator appointed by the respondent; and

(c)   the presiding arbitrator appointed by the Secretary-General, provided, however, that the presiding arbitrator shall not be a national of either Party.

5.   If, within 60 days after the Secretary-General receives a request made under paragraph 2, the respondent fails or the claimants fail to appoint an arbitrator in accordance with paragraph 4, the Secretary-General, on the request of any disputing party sought to be covered by the order, shall appoint the arbitrator or arbitrators not yet appointed. If the respondent fails to appoint an arbitrator, the Secretary-General shall appoint a national of the disputing Party, and if the claimants fail to appoint an arbitrator, the Secretary-General shall appoint a national of the non-disputing Party.

6.   Where a tribunal established under this Article is satisfied that two or more claims that have been submitted to arbitration under Article 24(1) have a question of law or fact in common, and arise out of the same events or circumstances, the tribunal may, in the interest of fair and efficient resolution of the claims, and after hearing the disputing parties, by order:

(a)   assume jurisdiction over, and hear and determine together, all or part of the claims;

(b)   assume jurisdiction over, and hear and determine one or more of the claims, the determination of which it believes would assist in the resolution of the others; or

(c)   instruct a tribunal previously established under Article 27 [Selection of Arbitrators] to assume jurisdiction over, and hear and determine together, all or part of the claims, provided that

(i)   that tribunal, at the request of any claimant not previously a disputing party before that tribunal, shall be reconstituted with its original members, except that the arbitrator for the claimants shall be appointed pursuant to paragraphs 4(a) and 5; and

(ii)   that tribunal shall decide whether any prior hearing shall be repeated.

7.   Where a tribunal has been established under this Article, a claimant that has submitted a claim to arbitration under Article 24(1) and that has not been named in a request made under paragraph 2 may make a written request to the tribunal that it be included in any order made under paragraph 6, and shall specify in the request:

(a)   the name and address of the claimant;

(b)   the nature of the order sought; and

(c)   the grounds on which the order is sought.

The claimant shall deliver a copy of its request to the Secretary-General.

8.   A tribunal established under this Article shall conduct its proceedings in accordance with the UNCITRAL Arbitration Rules, except as modified by this Section.

9.   A tribunal established under Article 27 [Selection of Arbitrators] shall not have jurisdiction to decide a claim, or a part of a claim, over which a tribunal established or instructed under this Article has assumed jurisdiction.

10. On application of a disputing party, a tribunal established under this Article, pending its decision under paragraph 6, may order that the proceedings of a tribunal established under Article 27 [Selection of Arbitrators] be stayed, unless the latter tribunal has already adjourned its proceedings.

Article 34: Awards

1.   Where a tribunal makes a final award against a respondent, the tribunal may award, separately or in combination, only:

(a)   monetary damages and any applicable interest; and

(b)   restitution of property, in which case the award shall provide that the respondent may pay monetary damages and any applicable interest in lieu of restitution.

A tribunal may also award costs and attorney's fees in accordance with this Treaty and the applicable arbitration rules.

2.   Subject to paragraph 1, where a claim is submitted to arbitration under Article 24(1)(b):

(a)   an award of restitution of property shall provide that restitution be made to the enterprise;

(b)   an award of monetary damages and any applicable interest shall provide that the sum be paid to the enterprise; and

(c)   the award shall provide that it is made without prejudice to any right that any person may have in the relief under applicable domestic law.

3.   A tribunal may not award punitive damages.

4.   An award made by a tribunal shall have no binding force except between the disputing parties and in respect of the particular case.

5.   Subject to paragraph 6 and the applicable review procedure for an interim award, a disputing party shall abide by and comply with an award without delay.

6.   A disputing party may not seek enforcement of a final award until:

(a)   in the case of a final award made under the ICSID Convention,

(i)   120 days have elapsed from the date the award was rendered and no disputing party has requested revision or annulment of the award; or

(ii)   revision or annulment proceedings have been completed; and

(b)   in the case of a final award under the ICSID Additional Facility Rules, the UNCITRAL Arbitration Rules, or the rules selected pursuant to Article 24(3)(d),

(i)   90 days have elapsed from the date the award was rendered and no disputing party has commenced a proceeding to revise, set aside, or annul the award; or

(ii) a court has dismissed or allowed an application to revise, set aside, or annul the award and there is no further appeal.

7.   Each Party shall provide for the enforcement of an award in its territory.

8.   If the respondent fails to abide by or comply with a final award, on delivery of a request by the non-disputing Party, a tribunal shall be established under Article 37 [State-State Dispute Settlement]. Without prejudice to other remedies available under applicable rules of international law, the requesting Party may seek in such proceedings:

(a)   a determination that the failure to abide by or comply with the final award is inconsistent with the obligations of this Treaty; and

(b)   a recommendation that the respondent abide by or comply with the final award.

9.   A disputing party may seek enforcement of an arbitration award under the ICSID Convention or the New York Convention [or the Inter-American Convention] regardless of whether proceedings have been taken under paragraph 8.

10.   A claim that is submitted to arbitration under this Section shall be considered to arise out of a commercial relationship or transaction for purposes of Article I of the New York Convention [and Article I of the Inter-American Convention].

Article 35: Annexes and Footnotes

The Annexes and footnotes shall form an integral part of this Treaty.

Article 36: Service of Documents

Delivery of notice and other documents on a Party shall be made to the place named for that Party in Annex C.

SECTION C

Article 37: State-State Dispute Settlement

1.   Subject to paragraph 5, any dispute between the Parties concerning the interpretation or application of this Treaty, that is not resolved through consultations or other diplomatic channels, shall be submitted on the request of either Party to arbitration for a binding decision or award by a tribunal in accordance with applicable rules of international law. In the absence of an agreement by the Parties to the contrary, the UNCITRAL Arbitration Rules shall govern, except as modified by the Parties or this Treaty.

2.   Unless the Parties otherwise agree, the tribunal shall comprise three arbitrators, one arbitrator appointed by each Party and the third, who shall be the presiding arbitrator, appointed by agreement of the Parties. If a tribunal has not been constituted within 75 days from the date that a claim is submitted to arbitration under this Section, the Secretary-General, on the request of either Party, shall appoint, in his or her discretion, the arbitrator or arbitrators not yet appointed.

3.   Expenses incurred by the arbitrators, and other costs of the proceedings, shall be paid for equally by the Parties. However, the tribunal may, in its discretion, direct that a higher proportion of the costs be paid by one of the Parties.

4.   Articles 28(3) [Amicus Curiae Submissions], 29 [Investor-State Transparency], 30(1) and (3) [Governing Law], and 31 [Interpretation of Annexes] shall apply mutatis mutandis to arbitrations under this Article.

5.   Paragraphs 1 through 4 shall not apply to a matter arising under Article 12 or Article 13.

IN WITNESS WHEREOF, the respective plenipotentiaries have signed this Treaty.

DONE in duplicate at [city] this [number] day of [month, year], in the English and [foreign] languages, each text being equally authentic.

FOR THE GOVERNMENT OF   FOR THE GOVERNMENT OF

THE UNITED STATES OF AMERICA: [Country]:

Annex A
Customary International Law

The Parties confirm their shared understanding that "customary international law" generally and as specifically referenced in Article 5 [Minimum Standard of Treatment] and Annex B [Expropriation] results from a general and consistent practice of States that they follow from a sense of legal obligation. With regard to Article 5 [Minimum Standard of Treatment], the customary international law minimum standard of treatment of aliens refers to all customary international law principles that protect the economic rights and interests of aliens.

Annex B
Expropriation

The Parties confirm their shared understanding that:

1.   Article 6 [Expropriation and Compensation](1) is intended to reflect customary international law concerning the obligation of States with respect to expropriation.

2.   An action or a series of actions by a Party cannot constitute an expropriation unless it interferes with a tangible or intangible property right or property interest in an investment.

3.   Article 6 [Expropriation and Compensation](1) addresses two situations. The first is direct expropriation, where an investment is nationalized or otherwise directly expropriated through formal transfer of title or outright seizure.

4.   The second situation addressed by Article 6 [Expropriation and Compensation](1) is indirect expropriation, where an action or series of actions by a Party has an effect equivalent to direct expropriation without formal transfer of title or outright seizure.

(a)   The determination of whether an action or series of actions by a Party, in a specific fact situation, constitutes an indirect expropriation, requires a case-by-case, fact-based inquiry that considers, among other factors:

(i)   the economic impact of the government action, although the fact that an action or series of actions by a Party has an adverse effect on the economic value of an investment, standing alone, does not establish that an indirect expropriation has occurred;

(ii)   the extent to which the government action interferes with distinct, reasonable investment-backed expectations; and

(iii) the character of the government action.

(b)   Except in rare circumstances, non-discriminatory regulatory actions by a Party that are designed and applied to protect legitimate public welfare objectives, such as public health, safety, and the environment, do not constitute indirect expropriations.

Annex C
Service of Documents on a Party

United States: Notices and other documents shall be served on the United States by delivery to:
Executive Director (L/EX), Office of the Legal Adviser

Department of State,   Washington, D.C. 20520 United States of America

[Country]: Notices and other documents shall be served on [Country] by delivery to:

[insert place of delivery of notices and other documents for [Country]

VI. Multilateral International Investment Treaties

VI.1. 1985 MULTILATERAL INVESTMENT GUARANTEE AGENCY CONVENTION[1]

Convention Establishing the Multilateral Investment Guarantee Agency (MIGA)

PREAMBLE

The Contracting States

Considering the need to strengthen international cooperation for economic development and to foster the contribution to such development of foreign investment in general and private foreign investment in particular;

Recognizing that the flow of foreign investment to developing countries would be facilitated and further encouraged by alleviating concerns related to non-commercial risks;

Desiring to enhance the flow to developing countries of capital and technology for productive purposes under conditions consistent with their development needs, policies and objectives, on the basis of fair and stable standards for the treatment of foreign investment;

Convinced that the Multilateral Investment Guarantee Agency can play an important role in the encouragement of foreign investment complementing national and regional investment guarantee programs and private insurers of non-commercial risk; and

Realizing that such Agency should, to the extent possible, meet its obligations without resort to its callable capital and that such an objective would be served by continued improvement in investment conditions,

Have agreed as follows:

CHAPTER I – ESTABLISHMENT, STATUS, PURPOSES AND DEFINITIONS

Article 1. Establishment and Status of the Agency

(a) There is hereby established the Multilateral Investment Guarantee Agency (hereinafter called the Agency).

(b) The Agency shall possess full juridical personality and, in particular, the capacity to:

   (i)   contract;

   (ii) acquire and dispose of movable and immovable property; and

   (iii) institute legal proceedings.

Article 2. Objective and Purposes

The objective of the Agency shall be to encourage the flow of investments for productive purposes among member countries, and in particular to developing member countries, thus supplementing the activities of the International Bank for Reconstruction and Development (hereinafter referred to as the Bank), the International Finance Corporation and other international development finance institutions.

To serve its objective, the Agency shall:

(a) issue guarantees, including coinsurance and reinsurance, against non-commercial risks in respect of investments in a member country which flow from other member countries;

(b) carry out appropriate complementary activities to promote the flow of investments to and among developing member countries; and

---

1   Adopted 11 October 1985; entered into force 12 April 1988; 1508 UNTS 99 (I-26012).

(c) exercise such other incidental powers as shall be necessary or desirable in the furtherance of its objective.

The Agency shall be guided in all its decisions by the provisions of this Article.

Article 3. Definitions

For the purposes of this Convention:

(a) "Member" means a State with respect to which this Convention has entered into force in accordance with Article 61.

(b) "Host country" or "host government" means a member, its government, or any public authority of a member in whose territories, as defined in Article 66, an investment which has been guaranteed or reinsured, or is considered for guarantee or reinsurance, by the Agency is to be located.

(c) A "developing member country" means a member which is listed as such in Schedule A hereto as this Schedule may be amended from time to time by the Council of Governors referred to in Article 30 (hereinafter called the Council).

(d) A "special majority" means an affirmative vote of not less than two-thirds of the total voting power representing not less than fifty-five percent of the subscribed shares of the capital stock of the Agency.

(e) A "freely usable currency" means (i) any currency designated as such by the International Monetary Fund from time to time and (ii) any other freely available and effectively usable currency which the Board of Directors referred to in Article 30 (hereinafter called the Board) may designate for the purposes of this Convention after consultation with the International Monetary Fund and with the approval of the country of such currency.

CHAPTER II – MEMBERSHIP AND CAPITAL

Article 4. Membership

(a) Membership in the Agency shall be open to all members of the Bank and to Switzerland.

(b) Original member shall be the States which are listed in Schedule A hereto and become parties to this Convention on or before October 30, 1987.

Article 5. Capital

(a) The authorized capital stock of the Agency shall be one billion Special Drawing Rights (SDR 1,000,000,000). The capital stock shall be divided into 100,000 shares having a par value of SDR 10,000 each, which shall be available for subscription by members. All payment obligations of members with respect to capital stock shall be settled on the basis of the average value of the SDR in terms of United States dollars for the period January 1, 1981 to June 30, 1985, such value being 1.082 United States dollars per SDR.

(b) The capital stock shall increase on the admission of a new member to the extent that the then authorized shares are insufficient to provide the shares to be subscribed by such member pursuant to Article 6.

(c) The Council, by special majority, may at any time increase the capital stock of the Agency.

Article 6. Subscription of Shares

Each original member of the Agency shall subscribe at par to the number of shares of capital stock set forth opposite its name in Schedule A hereto. Each other member shall subscribe to such number of shares of capital stock on such terms and conditions as may be determined by the Council, but in no event at an issue price of less than par. No member shall subscribe to less than fifty shares. The Council may prescribe rules by which members may subscribe to additional shares of the authorized capital stock.

Article 7. Division and Calls of Subscribed Capital

The initial subscription of each member shall be paid as follows:

(i)   Within ninety days from the date on which this Convention enters into force with respect to such member, ten percent of the price of each share shall be paid in cash as stipulated in Section (a) of Article 8 and an additional ten percent in the form of non-negotiable, non-interest-bearing promissory notes or similar obligations to be encashed pursuant to a decision of the Board in order to meet the Agency's obligations.

(ii)   The remainder shall be subject to call by the Agency when required to meet its obligations.

Article 8. Payment of Subscription of Shares

(a)   Payments of subscriptions shall be made in freely usable currencies except that payments by developing member countries may be made in their own currencies up to twenty-five percent of the paid-in cash portion of their subscriptions payable under Article 7(i).

(b)   Calls on any portion of unpaid subscriptions shall be uniform on all shares.

(c)   If the amount received by the Agency on a call shall be insufficient to meet the obligations which have necessitated the call, the Agency may make further successive calls on unpaid subscriptions until the aggregate amount received by it shall be sufficient to meet such obligations.

(d)   Liability on shares shall be limited to the unpaid portion of the issue price.

Article 9. Valuation of Currencies

Whenever it shall be necessary for the purposes of this Convention to determine the value of one currency in terms of another, such value shall be as reasonably determined by the Agency, after consultation with the International Monetary Fund.

Article 10. Refunds

(a)   The Agency shall, as soon as practicable, return to members amounts paid on calls on subscribed capital if and to the extent that:

(i)   the call shall have been made to pay a claim resulting from a guarantee or reinsurance contract and thereafter the Agency shall have recovered its payment, in whole or in part, in a freely usable currency; or

(ii)   the call shall have been made because of a default in payment by a member and thereafter such member shall have made good such default in whole or in part; or

(iii)   the Council, by special majority, determines that the financial position of the Agency permits all or part of such amounts to be returned out of the Agency's revenues.

(b)   Any refund effected under this Article to a member shall be made in freely usable currency in the proportion of the payments made by that member to the total amount paid pursuant to calls made prior to such refund.

(c)   The equivalent of amounts refunded under this Article to a member shall become part of the callable capital obligations of the member under Article 7(ii).

CHAPTER III – OPERATIONS

Article 11. Covered Risks

(a)   Subject to the provisions of Sections (b) and (c) below, the Agency may guarantee eligible investments against a loss resulting from one or more of the following types of risk:

(i)   Currency Transfer

        any introduction attributable to the host government of restrictions on the transfer outside the host country of its currency into a freely usable currency or another currency acceptable to the holder of the guarantee, including a failure of the host government to act within a reasonable period of time on an application by such holder for such transfer;

(ii) Expropriation and Similar Measures

any legislative action or administrative action or omission attributable to the host government which has the effect of depriving the holder of a guarantee of his owner-ship or control of, or a substantial benefit from, his investment, with the exception of non-discriminatory measures of general application which governments normally take for the purpose of regulating economic activity in their territories;

(iii) Breach of Contract

any repudiation or breach by the host government of a contract with the holder of a guarantee, when (a) the holder of a guarantee does not have recourse to a judicial or arbitral forum to determine the claim of repudiation or breach, or (b) a decision by such forum is not rendered within such reasonable period of time as shall be prescribed in the contracts of guarantee pursuant to the Agency's regulations, or (c) such a decision cannot be enforced; and

(iv) War and Civil Disturbance

any military action or civil disturbance in any territory of the host country to which this Convention shall be applicable as provided in Article 66.

(b) In addition, the Board, by special majority, may approve the extension of coverage under this Article to specific non-commercial risks other than those referred to in Section (a) above, but in no case to the risk of devaluation or depreciation of currency.

(c) Losses resulting from the following shall not be covered:

(i) any host government action or omission to which the holder of the guarantee has agreed or for which he has been responsible; and

(ii) any host government action or omission or any other event occurring before the con-clusion of the contract of guarantee.

Article 12. Eligible Investments

(a) Eligible investments shall include equity interests, including medium- or long-term loans made or guaranteed by holders of equity in the enterprise concerned, and such forms of direct investment as may be determined by the Board.

(b) Loans other than those mentioned in Section (a) above are eligible for coverage

(i) if they are made to finance or are otherwise related to a specific investment or project in which some other form of direct investment is present, whether or not guaranteed by the Agency and regardless of when such other investment was made, or

(ii) as may be otherwise approved by the Board by special majority.

(c) The Board, by special majority, may extend eligibility to any other medium- or long-term form of investment.

(d) Guarantees shall generally be restricted to investments the implementation of which begins subsequent to the registration of the application for the guarantee by the Agency or receipt by the Agency of other satisfactory evidence of investor intent to obtain guarantees from the Agency. Such investments may include:

(i) a transfer of foreign exchange made to modernize, expand, or develop an existing investment, in which case both the original investment and the additional investment may be considered eligible for coverage;

(ii) the use of earnings from existing investments which could otherwise be transferred outside the host country;

(iii) the acquisition of an existing investment by a new eligible investor;

(iv) existing investments where an eligible investor is seeking to insure a pool of existing and new investments;

(v) existing investments owned by an eligible investor where there is an improvement or enhancement of the underlying project or the investor otherwise demonstrates medium- or long-term commitment to the project, and the Agency is satisfied that the project continues to have a high developmental impact in the host country; and

(vi) such other investments as may be approved by the Board by special majority.

(e) In guaranteeing an investment, the Agency shall satisfy itself as to:

(i) the economic soundness of the investment and its contribution to the development of the host country;

(ii) compliance of the investment with the host country's laws and regulations;

(iii) consistency of the investment with the declared development objectives and priorities of the host country; and

(iv) the investment conditions in the host country, including the availability of fair and equitable treatment and legal protection for the investment.

Article 13. Eligible Investors

(a) Any natural person and any juridical person may be eligible to receive the Agency's guarantee provided that:

(i) such natural person is a national of a member other than the host country;

(ii) such juridical person is incorporated and has its principal place of business in a member or the majority of its capital is owned by a member or members or nationals thereof, provided that such member is not the host country in any of the above cases; and

(iii) such juridical person, whether or not it is privately owned, operates on a commercial basis.

(b) In case the investor has more than one nationality, for the purposes of Section (a) above the nationality of a member shall prevail over the nationality of a non-member, and the nationality of the host country shall prevail over the nationality of any other member.

(c) Upon the joint application of the investor and the host country, the Board, by special majority, may extend eligibility to a natural person who is a national of the host country or a juridical person which is incorporated in the host country or the majority of whose capital is owned by its nationals, provided that the assets invested are transferred from outside the host country.

Article 14. Eligible Host Countries

Investments shall be guaranteed under this Chapter only if they are to be made in the territory of a developing member country.

Article 15. Host Country Approval

The Agency shall not conclude any contract of guarantee before the host government has approved the issuance of the guarantee by the Agency against the risks designated for cover.

Article 16. Terms and Conditions

The terms and conditions of each contract of guarantee shall be determined by the Agency subject to such rules and regulations as the Board shall issue, provided that the Agency shall not cover the total loss of the guaranteed investment. Contracts of guarantee shall be approved by the President under the direction of the Board.

Article 17. Payment of Claims

The President under the direction of the Board shall decide on the payment of claims to a holder of a guarantee in accordance with the contract of guarantee and such policies as the Board may adopt. Contracts of guarantee shall require holders of guarantees to seek, before a payment is made by the Agency, such administrative remedies as may be appropriate under the circumstances, provided that they are readily available to them under the laws of the host country. Such contracts may require the lapse of certain reasonable periods between the occurrence of events giving rise to claims and payments of claims.

Article 18. Subrogation

(a)   Upon paying or agreeing to pay compensation to a holder of a guarantee, the Agency shall be subrogated to such rights or claims related to the guaranteed investment as the holder of a guarantee may have had against the host country and other obligors. The contract of guarantee shall provide the terms and conditions of such subrogation.

(b)   The rights of the Agency pursuant to Section (a) above shall be recognized by all members.

(c)   Amounts in the currency of the host country acquired by the Agency as subrogee pursuant to Section (a) above shall be accorded, with respect to use and conversion, treatment by the host country as favorable as the treatment to which such funds would be entitled in the hands of the holder of the guarantee. In any case, such amounts may be used by the Agency for the payment of its administrative expenditures and other costs. The Agency shall also seek to enter into arrangements with host countries on other uses of such currencies to the extent that they are not freely usable.

Article 19. Relationship to National and Regional Entities

The Agency shall cooperate with, and seek to complement the operations of, national entities of members and regional entities the majority of whose capital is owned by members, which carry out activities similar to those of the Agency, with a view to maximizing both the efficiency of their respective services and their contribution to increased flows of foreign investment. To this end, the Agency may enter into arrangements with such entities on the details of such cooperation, including in particular the modalities of reinsurance and coinsurance.

Article 20. Reinsurance of National and Regional Entities

(a)   The Agency may issue reinsurance in respect of a specific investment against a loss resulting from one or more of the non-commercial risks underwritten by a member or agency thereof or by a regional investment guarantee agency the majority of whose capital is owned by members. The Board, by special majority, shall from time to time prescribe maximum amounts of contingent liability which may be assumed by the Agency with respect to reinsurance contracts. In respect of specific investments which have been completed more than twelve months prior to receipt of the application for reinsurance by the Agency, the maximum amount shall initially be set at ten percent of the aggregate contingent liability of the Agency under this Chapter. The conditions of eligibility specified in Articles 11 to 14 shall apply to reinsurance operations, except that the reinsured investments need not be implemented subsequent to the application for reinsurance.

(b)   The mutual rights and obligations of the Agency and a reinsured member or agency shall be stated in contracts of reinsurance subject to such rules and regulations as the Board shall issue. The Board shall approve each contract for reinsurance covering an investment which has been made prior to receipt of the application for reinsurance by the Agency, with a view to minimizing risks, assuring that the Agency receives premiums commensurate with its risk, and assuring that the reinsured entity is appropriately committed toward promoting new investment in developing member countries.

(c)   The Agency shall, to the extent possible, assure that it or the reinsured entity shall have the rights of subrogation and arbitration equivalent to those the Agency would have if it were the primary guarantor. The terms and conditions of reinsurance shall require that administrative remedies are sought in accordance with Article 17 before a payment is made by the Agency. Subrogation shall be effective with respect to the host country concerned only after its approval of the reinsurance by the Agency. The Agency shall include in the contracts of reinsurance provisions requiring the reinsured to pursue with due diligence the rights or claims related to the reinsured investment.

Article 21. Cooperation with Private Insurers and with Reinsurers

(a)   The Agency may enter into arrangements with private insurers in member countries to enhance its own operations and encourage such insurers to provide coverage of noncommercial risks in developing member countries on conditions similar to those applied by the Agency. Such arrangements may include the provision of reinsurance by the Agency under the conditions and procedures specified in Article 20.

(b)   The Agency may reinsure with any appropriate reinsurance entity, in whole or in part, any guarantee or guarantees issued by it.

(c)   The Agency will in particular seek to guarantee investments for which comparable coverage on reasonable terms is not available from private insurers and reinsurers.

Article 22. Limits of Guarantee

(a)   Unless determined otherwise by the Council by special majority, the aggregate amount of contingent liabilities which may be assumed by the Agency under this Chapter shall not exceed one hundred and 50 percent of the amount of the Agency's unimpaired subscribed capital and its reserves plus such portion of its reinsurance cover as the Board may determine. The Board shall from time to time review the risk profile of the Agency's portfolio in the light of its experience with claims, degree of risk diversification, reinsurance cover and other relevant factors with a view to ascertaining whether changes in the maximum aggregate amount of contingent liabilities should be recommended to the Council. The maximum amount determined by the Council shall not under any circumstances exceed five times the amount of the Agency's unimpaired subscribed capital, its reserves and such portion of its reinsurance cover as may be deemed appropriate.

(b)   Without prejudice to the general limit of guarantee referred to in Section (a) above, the Board may prescribe:

(i)   maximum aggregate amounts of contingent liability which may be assumed by the Agency under this Chapter for all guarantees issued to investors of each individual member. In determining such maximum amounts, the Board shall give due consideration to the share of the respective member in the capital of the Agency and the need to apply more liberal limitations in respect of investments originating in developing member countries; and

(ii)   maximum aggregate amounts of contingent liability which may be assumed by the Agency with respect to such risk diversification factors as individual projects, individual host countries and types of investment or risk.

Article 23. Investment Promotion

(a)   The Agency shall carry out research, undertake activities to promote investment flows and disseminate information on investment opportunities in developing member countries, with a view to improving the environment for foreign investment flows to such countries. The Agency may, upon the request of a member, provide technical advice and assistance to improve the investment conditions in the territories of that member. In performing these activities, the Agency shall:

(i)   be guided by relevant investment agreements among member countries;

(ii)   seek to remove impediments, in both developed and developing member countries, to the flow of investment to developing member countries; and

(iii)   coordinate with other agencies concerned with the promotion of foreign investment, and in particular the International Finance Corporation.

(b) The Agency also shall:

(i)   encourage the amicable settlement of disputes between investors and host countries;

(ii)   endeavor to conclude agreements with developing member countries, and in particular with prospective host countries, which will assure that the Agency, with respect to investment guaranteed by it, has treatment at least as favorable as that agreed by the member concerned for the most favored investment guarantee agency or State in an agreement relating to investment, such agreements to be approved by special majority of the Board; and

(iii)   promote and facilitate the conclusion of agreements, among its members, on the promotion and protection of investments.

(c)   The Agency shall give particular attention in its promotional efforts to the importance of increasing the flow of investments among developing member countries.

Article 24. Guarantees of Sponsored Investments

In addition to the guarantee operations undertaken by the Agency under this Chapter, the Agency may guarantee investments under the sponsorship arrangements provided for in Annex I to this Convention.

CHAPTER IV – FINANCIAL PROVISIONS

Article 25. Financial Management

The Agency shall carry out its activities in accordance with sound business and prudent financial management practices with a view to maintaining under all circumstances its ability to meet its financial obligations.

Article 26. Premiums and Fees

The Agency shall establish and periodically review the rates of premiums, fees and other charges, if any applicable to each type of risk.

Article 27. Allocation of Net Income

(a)   Without prejudice to the provisions of Section (a)(iii) of Article 10, the Agency shall allocate net income to reserves until such reserves reach five times the subscribed capital of the Agency.

(b)   After the reserves of the Agency have reached the level prescribed in Section (a) above, the Council shall decide whether, and to what extent, the Agency's net income shall be allocated to reserves, be distributed to the Agency's members or be used otherwise. Any distribution of net income to the Agency's members shall be made in proportion to the share of each member in the capital of the Agency in accordance with a decision of the Council acting by special majority.

Article 28. Budget

The President shall prepare an annual budget of revenues and expenditures of the Agency for approval by the Board.

Article 29. Accounts

The Agency shall publish an Annual Report which shall include statements of its accounts and of the accounts of the Sponsorship Trust Fund referred to in Annex I to this Convention, as audited by independent auditors. The Agency shall circulate to members at appropriate intervals a summary statement of its financial position and a profit and loss statement showing the results of its operations.

CHAPTER V – ORGANIZATION AND MANAGEMENT

Article 30. Structure of the Agency

The Agency shall have a Council of Governors, a Board of Directors, a President and staff to perform such duties as the Agency may determine.

Article 31. The Council

(a)   All the powers of the Agency shall be vested in the Council, except such powers as are, by the terms of this Convention, specifically conferred upon another organ of the Agency. The Council may delegate to the Board the exercise of any of its powers, except the power to:

(i)   admit new members and determine the conditions of their admission;

(ii)   suspend a member;

(iii) decide on any increase or decrease in the capital;

(iv)   increase the limit of the aggregate amount of contingent liabilities pursuant to Section (a) of Article 22;

(v)   designate a member as a developing member country pursuant to Section (c) of Article 3;

(vi)   classify a new member as belonging to Category One or Category Two for voting purposes pursuant to Section (a) of Article 39 or reclassify an existing member for the same purposes;

(vii) determine the compensation of Directors and their Alternates;

(viii) cease operations and liquidate the Agency;

(ix)   distribute assets to members upon liquidation; and

(x)   amend this Convention, its Annexes and Schedules.

(b)   The Council shall be composed of one Governor and one Alternate appointed by each member in such manner as it may determine. No Alternate may vote except in the absence of his principal. The Council shall select one of the Governors as Chairman.

(c)   The Council shall hold an annual meeting and such other meetings as may be determined by the Council or called by the Board. The Board shall call a meeting of the Council whenever requested by five members or by members having 25 percent of the total voting power.

Article 32. The Board

(a)   The Board shall be responsible for the general operations of the Agency and shall take, in the fulfillment of this responsibility, any action required or permitted under this Convention.

(b)   The Board shall consist of not less than twelve Directors. The number of Directors may be adjusted by the Council to take into account changes in membership. Each Director may appoint an Alternate with full power to act for him in case of the Director's absence or inability to act. The President of the Bank shall be ex officio Chairman of the Board, but shall have no vote except a deciding vote in case of an equal division.

(c)   The Council shall determine the term of office of the Directors. The first Board shall be constituted by the Council at its inaugural meeting.

(d)   The Board shall meet at the call of its Chairman acting on his own initiative or upon request of three Directors.

(e)   Until such time as the Council may decide that the Agency shall have a resident Board which functions in continuous session, the Directors and Alternates shall receive compensation only for the cost of attendance at the meetings of the Board and the discharge of other official functions on behalf of the Agency. Upon the establishment of a Board in continuous session, the Directors and Alternates shall receive such remuneration as may be determined by the Council.

Article 33. President and Staff

(a)   The President shall, under the general control of the Board, conduct the ordinary business of the Agency. He shall be responsible for the organization, appointment and dismissal of the staff.

(b)   The President shall be appointed by the Board on the nomination of its Chairman. The Council shall determine the salary and terms of the contract of service of the President.

(c)   In the discharge of their offices, the President and the staff owe their duty entirely to the Agency and to no other authority. Each member of the Agency shall respect the international character of this duty and shall refrain from all attempts to influence the President or the staff in the discharge of their duties.

(d)   In appointing the staff, the President shall, subject to the paramount importance of securing the highest standards of efficiency and of technical competence, pay due regard to the importance of recruiting personnel on as wide a geographical basis as possible.

(e)   The President and staff shall maintain at all times the confidentiality of information obtained in carrying out the Agency's operations.

Article 34. Political Activity Prohibited

The Agency, its President and staff shall not interfere in the political affairs of any member. Without prejudice to the right of the Agency to take into account all the circumstances surrounding an investment, they shall not be influenced in their decisions by the political character of the member or members concerned. Considerations relevant to their decisions shall be weighed impartially in order to achieve the purposes states in Article 2.

Article 35. Relations with International Organizations

The Agency shall, within the terms of this Convention, cooperate with the United Nations and with other inter-governmental organizations having specialized responsibilities in related fields, including in particular the Bank and the International Finance Corporation.

Article 36. Location of Principal Office

(a)   The principal office of the Agency shall be located in Washington, D.C., unless the Council, by special majority, decides to establish it in another location.

(b)   The Agency may establish other offices as may be necessary for its work.

Article 37. Depositories for Assets

Each member shall designate its central bank as a depository in which the Agency may keep holdings of such member's currency or other assets of the Agency or, if it has no central bank, it shall designate for such purpose such other institution as may be acceptable to the Agency.

Article 38. Channel of Communication

(a)   Each member shall designate an appropriate authority with which the Agency may communicate in connections with any matter arising under this Convention. The Agency may rely on statements of such authority as being statements of the member. The Agency, upon the request of a member, shall consult with that member with respect to matters dealt with in Articles 19 to 21 and related to entities or insurers of that member.

(b)   Whenever the approval of any member is required before any act may be done by the Agency, approval shall be deemed to have been given unless the member presents an objection within such reasonable period as the Agency may fix in notifying the member of the proposed act.

CHAPTER VI – VOTING, ADJUSTMENTS OF SUBSCRIPTIONS AND REPRESENTATION

Article 39. Voting and Adjustments of Subscriptions

(a)   In order to provide for voting arrangements that reflect the equal interest in the Agency of the two Categories of States listed in Schedule A of this Convention, as well as the importance of each member's financial participation, each member shall have 177 membership votes plus one subscription vote for each share of stock held by that member.

(b)   If at any time within three years after the entry into force of this Convention the aggregate sum of membership and subscription votes of members which belong to either of the two Categories of States listed in Schedule A of this Convention is less than 40 percent of the total voting power, members from such a Category shall have such number of supplementary votes as shall be necessary for the aggregate voting power of the Category to equal such a percentage of the total power. Such supplementary votes shall be distributed among the members of such Category in the proportion that the subscription votes of each bears to the aggregate of subscription votes of the Category. Such supplementary votes shall be subject to automatic adjustment to ensure that such percentage is maintained and shall be canceled at the end of the abovementioned three-year period.

(c)   During the third year following the entry into force of this Convention, the Council shall review the allocation of shares and shall be guided in its decision by the following

principles:

  (i)   the votes of members shall reflect actual subscriptions to the Agency's capital and the membership votes as set out in Section (a) of this Article;

  (ii)   shares allocated to countries which shall not have signed the Convention shall be made available for reallocation to such members and in such manner as to make possible voting parity between the above-mentioned Categories; and

  (iii)   the Council will take measures that will facilitate members' ability to subscribe to share allocated to them.

(d)   Within the three-year period provided for in Section (b) of this Article, all decisions of the Council and Board shall be taken by special majority, except that decisions requiring a higher majority under this Convention shall be taken by such higher majority.

(e)   In case the capital stock of the Agency is increased pursuant to Section (c) of Article 5, each member which so requests shall be authorized to subscribe a proportion of the increase equivalent to the proportion which its stock theretofore subscribed bears to the total capital stock of the Agency, but no member shall be obligated to subscribe any part of the increased capital.

(f)   The Council shall issue regulations regarding the making of additional subscriptions under Section (e) of this Article. Such regulations shall prescribe reasonable time limits for the submission by members of requests to make such subscriptions.

Article 40. Voting in the Council

(a)   Each Governor shall be entitled to cast the votes of the member he represents. Except as otherwise specified in this Convention, decisions of the Council shall be taken by a majority of the votes cast.

(b)   A quorum for any meeting of the Council shall be constituted by a majority of the Governors exercising not less than two-thirds of the total voting power.

(c)   The Council may by regulation establish a procedure whereby the Board, when it deems such action to be in the best interests of the Agency, may request a decision of the Council on a specific question without calling a meeting of the Council.

Article 41. Election of Directors

(a)   Directors shall be elected in accordance with Schedule B.

(b)   Directors shall continue in office until their successors are elected. If the office of a Director becomes vacant more than ninety days before the end of his term, another Director shall be elected for the remainder of the term by the Governors who elected the former Director. A majority of the votes cast shall be required for election. While the office remains vacant, the Alternate of the Former Director shall exercise his powers, except that of appointing an Alternate.

Article 42. Voting in the Board

(a)   Each Director shall be entitled to cast the number of votes of the members whose votes counted towards his election. All the votes which a Director is entitled to cast shall be cast as a unit. Except as otherwise specified in this Convention, decisions of the Board shall be taken by a majority of the votes cast.

(b)   A quorum for a meeting of the Board shall be constituted by a majority of the Directors exercising not less than one-half of the total voting power.

(c)   The Board may by regulation establish a procedure whereby its Chairman, when he deems such action to be in the best interests of the Agency, may request a decision of the Board on a specific question without calling a meeting of the Board.

CHAPTER VII – PRIVILEGES AND IMMUNITIES

Article 43. Purposes of Chapter

To enable the Agency to fulfill its functions, the immunities and privileges set forth in this Chapter shall be accorded to the Agency in the territories of each member.

Article 44. Legal Process

Actions other than those within the scope of Articles 57 and 58 may be brought against the Agency only in a court of competent jurisdiction in the territories of a member in which the Agency has an office or has appointed an agent for the purpose of accepting service or notice of process. No such action against the Agency shall be brought:

   (i)   by members or persons acting for or deriving claims from members or

   (ii)   in respect of personnel matters.

The property and assets of the Agency shall, wherever located and by whomsoever held, be immune from all forms of seizure, attachment or execution before the delivery of the final judgment or award against the Agency.

Article 45. Assets

(a)   The property and assets of the Agency, wherever located and by whomsoever held, shall be immune from search, requisition, confiscation, expropriation or any other form of seizure by executive or legislative action.

(b)   To the extent necessary to carry out its operations under this Convention, all property and assets of the Agency shall be free from restrictions, regulations, controls and moratoria of any nature; provided that property and assets acquired by the Agency as successor to or subrogee of a holder of a guarantee, a reinsured entity or an investor insured by a reinsured entity shall be free from applicable foreign exchange restrictions, regulations and controls in force in the territories of the member concerned to the extent that the holder, entity or investor to whom the Agency was subrogated was entitled to such treatment.

(c)   For purposes of this Chapter, the term "assets" shall include the assets of the Sponsorship Trust Fund referred to in Annex I to this Convention and other assets administered by the Agency in furtherance of its objective.

Article 46. Archives and Communications

(a)   The archives of the Agency shall be inviolable, wherever they may be.

(b)   The official communications of the Agency shall be accorded by each member the same treatment that is accorded to the official communications of the Bank.

Article 47. Taxes

(a)   The Agency, its assets, property and income, and its operations and transactions authorized by this Convention, shall be immune from all taxes and customs duties. The Agency shall also be immune from liability for the collection or payment of any tax or duty.

(b)   Except in the case of local nationals, no tax shall be levied on or in respect of expense allowances paid by the Agency to Governors and their Alternates or on or in respect of salaries, expense allowances or other emoluments paid by the Agency to the Chairman of the Board, Directors, their Alternates, the President or staff of the Agency.

(c)   No taxation of any kind shall be levied on any investment guaranteed or reinsured by the Agency (including any earnings therefrom) or any insurance policies reinsured by the Agency (including any premiums and other revenues therefrom) by whomsoever held:

  (i)   which discriminates against such investment or insurance policy solely because it is guaranteed or reinsured by the Agency; or

  (ii)   if the sole jurisdictional basis for such taxation is the location of any office or place of business maintained by the Agency.

Article 48. Officials of the Agency

All Governors, Directors, Alternates, the President and staff of the Agency:

  (i)   shall be immune from legal process with respect to acts performed by them in their official capacity;

  (ii)   not being local nationals, shall be accorded the same immunities from immigration restrictions, alien registration requirements and national service obligations, and the same facilities as regards exchange restrictions as are accorded by the members concerned to the representatives, officials and employees of comparable rank of other members; and

  (iii) shall be granted the same treatment in respect of travelling facilities as is accorded by the members concerned to representatives, officials and employees of comparable rank of other members.

Article 49. Application of the Chapter

Each member shall take such action as is necessary in its own territories for the purpose of making effective in terms of its own law the principles set forth in this Chapter and shall inform the Agency of the detailed action which it has taken.

Article 50. Waiver

The immunities, exemptions and privileges provided in this Chapter are granted in the interest of the Agency and may be waived, to such extent and upon such conditions as the Agency may determine, in cases where such a waiver would not prejudice its interests. The Agency shall waive the immunity of any of its staff in cases where, in its opinion, the immunity would impede the course of justice and can be waived without prejudice to the interests of the Agency.

CHAPTER VIII – WITHDRAWAL, SUSPENSION OF MEMBERSHIP AND CESSATION OF OPERATIONS

Article 51. Withdrawal

Any member may, after the expiration of three years following the date upon which this Convention has entered into force with respect to such member, withdraw from the Agency at any time by giving notice in writing to the Agency at its principal office. The Agency shall notify the Bank, as depository of this Convention, of the receipt of such notice. Any withdrawal shall become effective ninety days following the date of the receipt of such notice by the Agency. A member may revoke such notice as long as it has not become effective.

Article 52. Suspension of Membership

(a)   If a member fails to fulfill any of its obligations under this Convention, the Council may, by a majority of its members exercising a majority of the total voting power, suspend its membership.

(b)   While under suspension a member shall have no rights under this Convention, except for the right of withdrawal and other rights provided in this Chapter and Chapter IX, but shall remain subject to all its obligations.

(c)   For purposes of determining eligibility for a guarantee or reinsurance to be issued under Chapter III or Annex I to this Convention, a suspended member shall not be treated as a member of the Agency.

(d)   The suspended member shall automatically cease to be a member one year from the date of its suspension unless the Council decides to extend the period of suspension or to restore the member to good standing.

Article 53. Rights and Duties of States Ceasing to be Members

(a)   When a State ceases to be a member, it shall remain liable for all its obligations, including its contingent obligations, under this Convention which shall have been in effect before the cessation of its membership.

(b)   Without prejudice to Section (a) above, the Agency shall enter into an arrangement with such State for the settlement of their respective claims and obligations. Any such arrangement shall be approved by the Board.

Article 54. Suspension of Operations

(a)   The Board may, whenever it deems it justified, suspend the issuance of new guarantees for a specified period.

(b)   In an emergency, the Board may suspend all activities of the Agency for a period not exceeding the duration of such emergency, provided that necessary arrangements shall be made for the protection of the interests of the Agency and of third parties.

(c)   The decision to suspend operations shall have no effect on the obligations of the members under this Convention or on the obligations of the Agency towards holders of a guarantee or reinsurance policy or towards third parties.

Article 55. Liquidation

(a)   The Council, by special majority, may decide to cease operations and to liquidate the Agency. Thereupon the Agency shall forthwith cease all activities, except those incident to the orderly realization, conservation and preservation of assets and settlement of obligations. Until final settlement and distribution of assets, the Agency shall remain in existence and all rights and obligations of members under this Convention shall continue unimpaired.

(b)   No distribution of assets shall be made to members until all liabilities to holders of guarantees and other creditors shall have been discharged or provided for and until the Council shall have decided to make such distribution.

(c)   Subject to the foregoing, the Agency shall distribute its remaining assets to members in proportion to each member's share in the subscribed capital. The Agency shall also distribute any remaining assets of the Sponsorship Trust Fund referred to in Annex I to this Convention to sponsoring members in the proportion which the investments sponsored by each bears to the total of sponsored investments. No member shall be entitled to its share in the assets of the Agency or the Sponsorship Trust Fund unless that member has settled all outstanding claims by the Agency against it. Every distribution of assets shall be made at such times as the Council shall determine and in such manner as it shall deem fair and equitable.

CHAPTER IX – SETTLEMENT OF DISPUTES

Article 56. Interpretation and Application of the Convention

(a)   Any question of interpretation or application of the provisions of this Convention arising between any member of the Agency and the Agency or among members of the Agency shall be submitted to the Board for its decision. Any member which is particularly affected by the question and which is not otherwise represented by a national in the Board may send a representative to attend any meeting of the Board at which such question is considered.

(b)   In any case where the Board has given a decision under Section (a) above, any member may require that the question be referred to the Council, whose decision shall be final. Pending the result of the referral to the Council, the Agency may, so far as it deems necessary, act on the basis of the decision of the Board.

Article 57. Disputes Between the Agency and Members

(a)   Without prejudice to the provisions of Article 56 and of Section (b) of this Article, any dispute between the Agency and a member or an agency thereof and any dispute between the Agency and a country (or agency thereof) which has ceased to be a member, shall be settled in accordance with the procedure set out in Annex II to this Convention.

(b)   Disputes concerning claims of the Agency acting as subrogee of an investor shall be settled in accordance with either:

    (i)   the procedure set out in Annex II to this Convention, or

    (ii)   an agreement to be entered into between the Agency and the member concerned on an alternative method or methods for the settlement of such disputes.

In the latter case, Annex II to this Convention shall serve as a basis for such an agreement which shall, in each case, be approved by the Board by special majority prior to the undertaking by the Agency of operations in the territories of the member concerned.

Article 58. Disputes Involving Holders of a Guarantee or Reinsurance

Any dispute arising under a contract of guarantee or reinsurance between the parties thereto shall be submitted to arbitration for final determination in accordance with such rules as shall be provided for or referred to in the contract of guarantee or reinsurance.

CHAPTER X – AMENDMENTS

Article 59. Amendment by Council

(a)   This Convention and its Annexes may be amended by vote of three-fifths of the Governors exercising four-fifths of the total voting power, provided that:

    (i)   any amendment modifying the right to withdraw from the Agency provided in Article 51 or the limitation on liability provided in Section (d) of Article 8 shall require the affirmative vote of all Governors; and

    (ii)   any amendment modifying the loss-sharing arrangement provided in Articles 1 and 3 of Annex I to this Convention which will result in an increase in any member's liability thereunder shall require the affirmative vote of the Governor of each such member.

(b)   Schedules A and B to this Convention may be amended by the Council by special majority.

(c)   If an amendment affects any provision of Annex I to this Convention, total votes shall include the additional votes allotted under Article 7 of such Annex to sponsoring members and countries hosting sponsored investments.

Article 60. Procedure

Any proposal to amend this Convention, whether emanating from a member or a Governor or a Director, shall be communicated to the Chairman of the Board who shall bring the proposal before the Board. If the proposed amendment is recommended by the Board, it shall be submitted to the Council for approval in accordance with Article 59. When an amendment has been duly approved by the Council, the Agency shall so certify by formal communication addressed to all members. Amendments shall enter into force for all members ninety days after the date of the formal communication unless the Council shall specify a different date.

CHAPTER XI – FINAL PROVISIONS

Article 61. Entry into Force

(a)   This Convention shall be open for signature on behalf of all members of the Bank and Switzerland and shall be subject to ratification, acceptance or approval by the signatory States in accordance with their constitutional procedures.

(b)   This Convention shall enter into force on the day when not less than five instruments of ratification, acceptance or approval shall have been deposited on behalf of signatory States in Category One, and not less than fifteen such instruments shall have been deposited on behalf of signatory States in Category Two; provided that total subscriptions of these States amount to not less than one-third of the authorized capital of the Agency as prescribed in Article 5.

(c)   For each State which deposits its instrument of ratification, acceptance or approval after this Convention shall have entered into force, this Convention shall enter into force on the date of such deposit.

(d)   If this Convention shall not have entered into force within two years after its opening for signature, the President of the Bank shall convene a conference of interested countries to determine the future course of action.

Article 62. Inaugural Meeting

Upon entry into force of this Convention, the President of the Bank shall call the inaugural meeting of the Council. This meeting shall be held at the principal office of the Agency within sixty days from the date on which this Convention has entered into force or as soon as practicable thereafter.

Article 63. Depository

Instruments of ratification, acceptance or approval of this Convention and amendments thereto shall be deposited with the Bank which shall act as the depository of this Convention. The depository shall transmit certified copies of this Convention to States members of the Bank and to Switzerland.

Article 64. Registration

The depository shall register this Convention with the Secretariat of the United Nations in accordance with Article 102 of the Charter of the United Nations and the Regulations thereunder adopted by the General Assembly.

Article 65. Notification

The depository shall notify all signatory States and, upon the entry into force of this Convention, the Agency of the following:

(a)   signatures of this Convention;

(b)   deposits of instruments of ratification, acceptance and approval in accordance with Article 63;

(c)   the date on which this Convention enters into force in accordance with Article 61;

(d)   exclusions from territorial application pursuant to Article 66; and

(e)   withdrawal of a member from the Agency pursuant to Article 51.

Article 66. Territorial Application

This Convention shall apply to all territories under the jurisdiction of a member including the territories for whose international relations a member is responsible, except those which are excluded by such member by written notice to the depository of this Convention either at the time of ratification, acceptance or approval or subsequently.

Article 67. Periodic Reviews

(a)   The Council shall periodically undertake comprehensive reviews of the activities of the Agency as well as the results achieved with a view to introducing any changes required to enhance the Agency's ability to serve its objectives.

(b)   The first such review shall take place five years after the entry into force of this Convention. The dates of subsequent reviews shall be determined by the Council.

DONE at Seoul, in a single copy which shall remain deposited in the archives of the International Bank for Reconstruction and Development, which has indicated by its signature below its agreement to fulfill the functions with which it is charged under this Convention.

ANNEX I – GUARANTEES OF SPONSORED INVESTMENTS UNDER ARTICLE 24

Article 1. Sponsorship

(a)   Any member may sponsor for guarantee an investment to be made by an investor of any nationality or by investors of any or several nationalities.

(b)   Subject to the provisions of Sections (b) and (c) of Article 3 of this Annex, each sponsoring member shall share with the other sponsoring members in losses under guarantees of sponsored investments, when and to the extent that such losses cannot be covered out of the Sponsorship Trust Fund referred to in Article 2 of this Annex, in the proportion which the amount of maximum contingent liability under the guarantees of investments sponsored by it bears to the total amount of maximum contingent liability under the guarantees of investments sponsored by all members.

(c)   In its decisions on the issuance of guarantees under this Annex, the Agency shall pay due regard to the prospects that the sponsoring member will be in a position to meet its obligations under this Annex and shall give priority to investments which are co-sponsored by the host countries concerned.

(d)   The Agency shall periodically consult with sponsoring members with respect to its operations under this Annex.

Article 2. Sponsorship Trust Fund

(a)   Premiums and other revenues attributable to guarantees of sponsored investments, including returns on the investment of such premiums and revenues, shall be held in a separate account which shall be called the Sponsorship Trust Fund.

(b)   All administrative expenses and payments on claims attributable to guarantees issued under this Annex shall be paid out of the Sponsorship Trust Fund.

(c) The assets of the Sponsorship Trust Fund shall be held and administered for the joint account of sponsoring members and shall be kept separate and apart from the assets of the Agency.

Article 3. Calls on Sponsoring Members

(a) To the extent that any amount is payable by the Agency on account of a loss under a sponsored guarantee and such amount cannot be paid out of assets of the Sponsorship Trust Fund, the Agency shall call on each sponsoring member to pay into such Fund its share of such amount as shall be determined in accordance with Section (b) of Article 1 of this Annex.

(b) No member shall be liable to pay any amount on a call pursuant to the provisions of this Article if as a result total payments made by that member will exceed the total amount of guarantees covering investments sponsored by it.

(c) Upon the expiry of any guarantee covering an investment sponsored by a member, the liability of that member shall be decreased by an amount equivalent to the amount of such guarantee; such liability shall also be decreased on a pro rata basis upon payment by the Agency of any claim related to a sponsored investment and shall otherwise continue in effect until the expiry of all guarantees of sponsored investments outstanding at the time of such payment.

(d) If any sponsoring member shall not be liable for an amount of a call pursuant to the provisions of this Article because of the limitation contained in Sections (b) and (c) above, or if any sponsoring member shall default in payment of an amount due in response to any such call, the liability for payment of such amount shall be shared *pro rata* by the other sponsoring members. Liability of members pursuant to this Section shall be subject to the limitation set forth in Sections (b) and (c) above.

(e) Any payment by a sponsoring member pursuant to a call in accordance with this Article shall be made promptly and in freely usable currency.

Article 4. Valuation of Currencies and Refunds

The provisions on valuation of currencies and refunds contained in this Convention with respect to capital subscriptions shall be applied mutatis mutandis to funds paid by members on account of sponsored investments.

Article 5. Reinsurance

(a) The Agency may, under the conditions set forth in Article 1 of this Annex, provide re-insurance to a member, an agency thereof, a regional agency as defined in Section (a) of Article 20 of this Convention or a private insurer in a member country. The provisions of this Annex concerning guarantees and of Article 20 and 21 of this Convention shall be applied mutatis mutandis to reinsurance provided under this Section.

(b) The Agency may obtain reinsurance for investments guaranteed by it under this Annex and shall meet the cost of such reinsurance out of the Sponsorship Trust Fund. The Board may decide whether and to what extent the loss-sharing obligation of sponsoring members referred to in Section (b) of Article 1 of this Annex may be reduced on account of the reinsurance cover obtained.

Article 6. Operational Principles

Without prejudice to the provisions of this Annex, the provisions with respect to guarantee operations under Chapter III of this Convention and to financial management under Chapter IV of this Convention shall be applied *mutatis mutandis* to guarantees of sponsored investments except that:

    (i)   such investments shall qualify for sponsorship if made in the territories of any member, and in particular of any developing member, by an investor or investors eligible under Section (a) of Article 1 of this Annex, and

(ii)   the Agency shall not be liable with respect to its own assets for any guarantee or reinsurance issued under this Annex and each contract of guarantee or reinsurance concluded pursuant to this Annex shall expressly so provide.

Article 7. Voting

For decisions relating to sponsored investments, each sponsoring member shall have one additional vote for each 10,000 Special Drawing Rights equivalent of the amount guaranteed or reinsured on the basis of its sponsorship, and each member hosting a sponsored investment shall have one additional vote for each 10,000 Special Drawing Rights equivalent of the amount guaranteed or reinsured with respect to any sponsored investment hosted by it. Such additional votes shall be cast only for decisions related to sponsored investments and shall otherwise be disregarded in determining the voting power of members.

ANNEX II – SETTLEMENT OF DISPUTES BETWEEN A MEMBER AND THE AGENCY UNDER ARTICLE 57

Article 1. Application of the Annex

All disputes within the scope of Article 57 of this Convention shall be settled in accordance with the procedure set out in this Annex, except in the cases where the Agency has entered into an agreement with a member pursuant to Section (b)(ii) of Article 57.

Article 2. Negotiation

The parties to a dispute within the scope of this Annex shall attempt to settle such dispute by negotiation before seeking conciliation or arbitration. Negotiations shall be deemed to have been exhausted if the parties fail to reach a settlement within a period of one hundred and twenty days from the date of the request to enter into negotiation.

Article 3. Conciliation

(a)   If the dispute is not resolved through negotiation, either party may submit the dispute to arbitration in accordance with the provisions of Article 4 of this Annex, unless the parties, by mutual consent, have decided to resort first to the conciliation procedure provided for in this Article.

(b)   The agreement for recourse to conciliation shall specify the matter in dispute, the claims of the parties in respect thereof and, if available, the name of the conciliator agreed upon by the parties. In the absence of agreement on the conciliator, the parties may jointly request either the Secretary-General of the International Centre of Settlement of Investment Disputes (hereinafter called ICSID) or the President of the International Court of Justice to appoint a conciliator. The conciliation procedure shall terminate if the conciliator has not been appointed within ninety days after the agreement for recourse to conciliation.

(c)   Unless otherwise provided in this Annex or agreed upon by the parties, the conciliator shall determine the rules governing the conciliation procedure and shall be guided in this regard by the conciliation rules adopted pursuant to the Convention on the Settlement of Investment Disputes between States and Nationals of Other States.

(d)   The parties shall cooperate in good faith with the conciliator and shall, in particular, provide him with all information and documentation which would assist him in the discharge of his functions; they shall give their most serious consideration to his recommendations.

(e)   Unless otherwise agreed upon by the parties, the conciliator shall, within a period not exceeding one hundred and eighty days from the date of his appointment, submit to the parties a report recording the results of his efforts and setting out the issues controversial between the parties and his proposals for their settlement.

(f)   Each party shall, within sixty days from the date of the receipt of the report, express in writing its views on the report to the other party.

(g)   Neither party to a conciliation proceeding shall be entitled to have recourse to arbitration unless:

   (i)   the conciliator shall have failed to submit his report within the period established in Section (e) above; or

   (ii)   the parties shall have failed to accept all of the proposals contained in the report within sixty days after its receipt; or

   (iii)   the parties, after an exchange of views on the report, shall have failed to agree on a settlement of all controversial issues within sixty days after receipt of the conciliator's report; or

   (iv)   a party shall have failed to express its views on the report as prescribed in Section (f) above.

(h)   Unless the parties agree otherwise, the fees of the conciliator shall be determined on the basis of the rates applicable to ICSID conciliation. These fees and the other costs of the conciliation proceedings shall be borne equally by the parties. Each party shall defray its own expenses.

Article 4. Arbitration

(a)   Arbitration proceedings shall be instituted by means of a notice by the party seeking arbitration (the claimant) addressed to the other party or parties to the dispute (the respondent). The notice shall specify the nature of the dispute, the relief sought and the name of the arbitrator appointed by the claimant. The respondent shall, within thirty days after the date of receipt of the notice, notify the claimant of the name of the arbitrator appointed by it. The two parties shall, within a period of thirty days from the date of appointment of the second arbitrator, select a third arbitrator, who shall act as President of the Arbitral Tribunal (the Tribunal).

(b)   If the Tribunal shall not have been constituted within sixty days from the date of the notice, the arbitrator not yet appointed or the President not yet selected shall be appointed, at the joint request of the parties, by the Secretary-General of ICSID. If there is not such joint request, of if the Secretary-General shall fail to make the appointment within thirty days of the request, either party may request the President of the International Court of Justice to make the appointment.

(c)   No party shall have the rights to change the arbitrator appointed by it once the hearing of the dispute has commenced. In case any arbitrator (including the President of the Tribunal) shall resign, die, or become incapacitated, a successor shall be appointed in the manner followed in the appointment of his predecessor and such successor shall have the same powers and duties of the arbitrator he succeeds.

(d)   The Tribunal shall convene first at such time and place as shall be determined by the President. Thereafter, the Tribunal shall determine the place and dates of its meetings.

(e)   Unless otherwise provided in this Annex or agreed upon by the parties, the Tribunal shall determine its procedure and shall be guided in this regard by the arbitration rules adopted pursuant to the Convention on the Settlement of Investment Disputes between States and Nationals of Other States.

(f)   The Tribunal shall be the judge of its own competence except that, if an objection is raised before the Tribunal to the effect that the dispute falls within the jurisdiction of the Board or the Council under Article 56 or within the jurisdiction of a judicial or arbitral body designated in an agreement under Article 1 of this Annex and the Tribunal is satisfied that the objection is genuine, the objection shall be referred by the Tribunal to the Board or the Council or the designated body, as the case may be, and the arbitration proceedings shall be stayed until a decision has been reached on the matter, which shall be binding upon the Tribunal.

(g) The Tribunal shall, in any dispute within the scope of this Annex, apply the provisions of this Convention, any relevant agreement between the parties to the dispute, the Agency's by-laws and regulations, the applicable rules of international law, the domestic law of the member concerned as well as the applicable provisions of the investment contract, if any. Without prejudice to the provisions of this Convention, the Tribunal may decide a dispute *ex aequo et bono* if the Agency and the member concerned so agree. The Tribunal may not bring a finding of *non liquet* on the ground of silence or obscurity of the law.

(h) The Tribunal shall afford a fair hearing to all the parties. All decisions of the Tribunal shall be taken by a majority vote and shall state the reasons on which they are based. The award of the Tribunal shall be in writing, and shall be signed by at least two arbitrators and a copy thereof shall be transmitted to each party. The award shall be final and binding upon the parties and shall not be subject to appeal, annulment or revision.

(i) If any dispute shall arise between the Parties as to the meaning or scope of an award, either party may, within sixty days after the award was rendered, request interpretation of the award by an application in writing to the President of the Tribunal which rendered the award. The President shall, if possible, submit the request to the Tribunal which rendered the award and shall convene such Tribunal within sixty days after receipt of the application. If this shall not be possible, a new Tribunal shall be constituted in accordance with the provisions of Sections (a) to (d) above. The Tribunal may stay enforcement of the award pending its decision on the requested interpretation.

(j) Each member shall recognize an award rendered pursuant to this Article as binding and enforceable within its territories as if it were a final judgment of a court in that member. Execution of the award shall be governed by the laws concerning the execution of judgments in force in the State in whose territories such execution is sought and shall not derogate from the law in force relating to immunity from execution.

(k) Unless the parties shall agree otherwise, the fees and remuneration payable to the arbitrators shall be determined on the basis of the rates applicable to ICSID arbitration. Each party shall defray its own costs associated with the arbitration proceedings. The costs of the Tribunal shall be borne by the parties in equal proportion unless the Tribunal decides otherwise. Any question concerning the division of the costs of the Tribunal or the procedure for payment of such costs shall be decided by the Tribunal.

Article 5. Service of Process

Service of any notice or process in connection with any proceeding under this Annex shall be made in writing. It shall be made by the Agency upon the authority designated by the member concerned pursuant to Article 38 of this Convention and by that member at the principal office of the Agency.

SCHEDULE A – MEMBERSHIP AND SUBSCRIPTIONS

(please visit https://finances.worldbank.org/Shareholder-Equity/MIGA-Sub-scriptions-and-Voting-Power-of-Member-Coun/8rpb-qxnj for current data)

SCHEDULE B – ELECTIONS OF DIRECTORS [...]

VI.2. 1998 OECD Draft Multilateral Agreement on Investment (MAI)[1]

I. General Provisions

Preamble

The Contracting Parties to this Agreement,

Desiring to strengthen their ties of friendship and to promote greater economic co-operation between them;

Considering that international investment has assumed great importance in the world economy and has considerably contributed to the development of their countries;

Recognising that agreement upon the treatment to be accorded to investors and their investments will contribute to the efficient utilisation of economic resources, the creation of employment opportunities and the improvement of living standards;

Emphasising that fair, transparent and predictable investment regimes complement and benefit the world trading system;

[Wishing that this Agreement enhances international co-operation with respect to investment and the development of world-wide rules on foreign direct investment in the framework of the world trading system as embodied in the World Trade Organization;]

Wishing to establish a broad multilateral framework for international investment with high standards for the liberalisation of investment regimes and investment protection and with effective dispute settlement procedures;

[Recognising that investment, as an engine of economic growth, can play a key role in ensuring that economic growth is sustainable, when accompanied by appropriate environmental policies to ensure it takes place in an environmentally sound manner] [Recognising that appropriate environmental policies can play a key role in ensuring that economic development, to which investment contributes, is sustainable], and resolving to [desiring to] implement this agreement [in accordance with international environmental law and] in a manner consistent with sustainable development, as reflected in the Rio Declaration on Environment and Development and Agenda 21, [including the protection and preservation of the environment and principles of the polluter pays and the precautionary approach];

Renewing their commitment to the Copenhagen Declaration of the World Summit on Social Development and to observance of internationally recognised core labour standards, i.e. freedom of association, the right to organise and bargain collectively, prohibition of forced labour, the elimination of exploitative forms of child labour, and non- discrimination in employment, and noting that the International Labour Organisation is the competent body to set and deal with core labour standards worldwide.

Affirming their decision to create a free-standing Agreement open to accession by all countries;

[Noting] [Affirming their support for] the OECD Guidelines for Multinational Enterprises and emphasising that implementation of the Guidelines, which are non-binding and which are observed on a voluntary basis, will promote mutual confidence between enterprises and host countries and contribute to a favourable climate for investment;

HAVE AGREED AS FOLLOWS:

---

1   This draft consolidated text is based on the version available on the website of the OECD, see
     http://www.oecd.org/daf/mai/pdf/ng/ng987r1e.pdf. Extensive commentary and footnotes were omitted.
     [Square brackets] are in the original and indicate different options or versions supported by different
     delegations and/or text that has not been finally agreed upon.

II. Scope and Application

DEFINITIONS

1.   Investor means:

(i)   a natural person having the nationality of, or who is permanently residing in, a Contracting Party in accordance with its applicable law; or

(ii)   a legal person or any other entity constituted or organised under the applicable law of a Contracting Party, whether or not for profit, and whether private or government owned or controlled, and includes a corporation, trust, partnership, sole proprietorship, joint venture, association or organisation.

2.   Investment means:

Every kind of asset owned or controlled, directly or indirectly, by an investor, including:

(i)   an enterprise (being a legal person or any other entity constituted or organised under the applicable law of the Contracting Party, whether or not for profit, and whether private or government owned or controlled, and includes a corporation, trust, partnership, sole proprietorship, branch, joint venture, association or organisation);

(ii)   shares, stocks or other forms of equity participation in an enterprise, and rights derived therefrom;

(iii) bonds, debentures, loans and other forms of debt, and rights derived therefrom;

(iv)   rights under contracts, including turnkey, construction, management, production or revenue-sharing contracts;

(v)   claims to money and claims to performance;

(vi)   intellectual property rights;

(vii) rights conferred pursuant to law or contract such as concessions, licenses, authorisations, and permits;

(viii) any other tangible and intangible, movable and immovable property, and any related property rights, such as leases, mortgages, liens and pledges.

GEOGRAPHICAL SCOPE OF APPLICATION

This Agreement shall apply in:

(a)   the land territory, internal waters, and the territorial sea of a Contracting Party, and, in the case of a Contracting Party which is an archipelagic state, its archipelagic waters; and

(b)   the maritime areas beyond the territorial sea with respect to which a Contracting Party exercises sovereign rights or jurisdiction in accordance with international law, as reflected particularly in the 1982 United Nations Convention on the Law of the Sea.

APPLICATION TO OVERSEAS TERRITORIES

1.   A State may at any time declare in writing to the Depositary that this Agreement shall apply to all or to one or more of the territories for the international relations of which it is responsible. Such declaration, made prior to or upon ratification, accession or acceptance, shall take effect upon entry into force of this Agreement for that State. A subsequent declaration shall take effect with respect to the territory or territories concerned on the ninetieth day following receipt of the declaration by the Depositary.

2.   A Party may at any time declare in writing to the Depositary, that this Agreement shall cease to apply to all or to one or more of the territories for the international relations of which it is responsible. Such declaration shall take effect upon the expiry of one year from the date of receipt of the declaration by the Depositary, with the same effect regarding existing investment as withdrawal of a Party.

III. Treatment of Investors and Investments

NATIONAL TREATMENT AND MOST FAVOURED NATION TREATMENT

1. Each Contracting Party shall accord to investors of another Contracting Party and to their investments, treatment no less favourable than the treatment it accords [in like circumstances] to its own investors and their investments with respect to the establishment, acquisition, expansion, operation, management, maintenance, use, enjoyment and sale or other disposition of investments.

2. Each Contracting Party shall accord to investors of another Contracting Party and to their investments, treatment no less favourable than the treatment it accords [in like circumstances] to investors of any other Contracting Party or of a non-Contracting Party, and to the investments of investors of any other Contracting Party or of a non-Contracting Party, with respect to the establishment, acquisition, expansion, operation, management, maintenance, use, enjoyment, and sale or other disposition of investments.

3. Each Contracting Party shall accord to investors of another Contracting Party and to their investments the better of the treatment required by Articles 1.1 and 1.2, whichever is the more favourable to those investors or investments.

TRANSPARENCY

1. Each Contracting Party shall promptly publish, or otherwise make publicly available, its laws, regulations, procedures and administrative rulings and judicial decisions of general application as well as international agreements which may affect the operation of the Agreement. Where a Contracting Party establishes policies which are not expressed in laws or regulations or by other means listed in this paragraph but which may affect the operation of the Agreement, that Contracting Party shall promptly publish them or otherwise make them publicly available.

2. Each Contracting Party shall promptly respond to specific questions and provide, upon request, information to other Contracting Parties on matters referred to in Article 2.1.

3. Nothing in this Agreement shall prevent a Contracting Party from requiring an investor of another Contracting Party, or its investment, to provide routine information concerning that investment solely for information or statistical purposes. Nothing in this Agreement requires a Contracting Party to furnish or allow access to:

a) information related to the financial affairs and accounts of individual customers of particular investors or investments, or

b) any confidential or proprietary information, including information concerning particular investors or investments, the disclosure of which would impede law enforcement or be contrary to its laws protecting confidentiality or prejudice legitimate commercial interests of particular enterprises.

TEMPORARY ENTRY, STAY AND WORK OF INVESTORS AND KEY PERSONNEL

1. Subject to the application of Contracting Parties' national laws, regulations and procedures affecting the entry, stay and work of natural persons:

(a) Each Contracting Party shall grant temporary entry, stay and authorisation to work and provide any necessary confirming documentation to a natural person of another Contracting Party who is:

(i) an investor who seeks to establish, develop, administer or provide advice or essential technical services to the operation of an enterprise in the territory of the former Contracting Party to which the investor has committed, or is in the process of committing, a substantial amount of capital, or

(ii) an employee employed by an enterprise referred to in (i) above, or by an investor, [who may be required to have been employed for a specified minimum period, for example one year], in a capacity of executive, manager or specialist and who is essential to the enterprise;

so long as that person continues to meet the requirements of this Article;

(b) (i) Each Contracting Party shall grant temporary entry and stay and provide any necessary confirming documentation to the spouse and minor children of a natural person who has been granted temporary entry, stay and authorisation to work in accordance with subparagraph (a) above. The spouse and minor children shall be admitted for the period of the stay of that person.

(ii) Each Contracting Party is encouraged to grant authorisation to work to the spouse of the person who has been granted temporary entry, stay and authorisation to work in accordance with subparagraph (a) above.

2.   No Contracting Party may deny entry and stay as provided for by this Article, or authorisation to work as provided for by paragraph 1(a) of this Article, for reasons relating to labour market or other economic needs tests or numerical restrictions in national laws, regulations, and procedures.

3.   For the purposes of this Article:

- Natural person of another Contracting Party means a natural person having the nationality of [or who is permanently residing in] another Contracting Party in accordance with its applicable law;

- Executive means a natural person who primarily directs the management of an enterprise or establishes goals and policies for the enterprise or a major component or function of the enterprise, exercises wide latitude in decision-making and receives only general supervision or direction from higher-level executives, the board of directors, or stockholders of the enterprise;

- Manager means a natural person who directs the management of an enterprise, or department, or subdivision of the enterprise, supervises and controls the work of other supervisory, professional or managerial employees, has the authority to hire and fire or recommend hiring, firing, or other personnel actions and exercises discretionary authority over day-to-day operations at a senior level; and

- Specialist means a natural person who possesses knowledge at an advanced level of expertise and who may be required to possess specific or proprietary knowledge of the enterprise's product, service, research equipment, techniques, or management.

NATIONALITY REQUIREMENTS FOR EXECUTIVES, MANAGERS AND MEMBERS OF BOARDS OF DIRECTORS

No Contracting Party may require that an enterprise of that Contracting Party that is an investment of an investor of another Contracting Party appoint as executives, managers and members of boards of directors individuals of any particular nationality.

EMPLOYMENT REQUIREMENTS

A Contracting Party shall permit investors of another Contracting Party and their investments to employ any natural person of the investor's or the investment's choice regardless of nationality and citizenship provided that such person is holding a valid permit of sejour and work delivered by the competent authorities of the former Contracting Party and that the employment concerned conforms to the terms, conditions and time limits of the permission granted to such person.

PERFORMANCE REQUIREMENTS

1.   A Contracting Party shall not, in connection with the establishment, acquisition, expansion, management, operation, maintenance, use, enjoyment, sale or other disposition of an investment in its territory of an investor of a Contracting Party or of a non-Contracting Party, impose,

enforce or maintain any of the following requirements, or enforce any commitment or undertaking:

(a)   to export a given level or percentage of goods or services;

(b)   to achieve a given level or percentage of domestic content;

(c)   to purchase, use or accord a preference to goods produced or services provided in its territory, or to purchase goods or services from persons in its territory;

(d)   to relate in any way the volume or value of imports to the volume or value of exports or to the amount of foreign exchange inflows associated with such investment;

(e)   to restrict sales of goods or services in its territory that such investment produces or provides by relating such sales to the volume or value of its exports or foreign exchange earnings;

(f)   to transfer technology, a production process or other proprietary knowledge to a natural or legal person in its territory, except when the requirement

–   is imposed or the commitment or undertaking is enforced by a court, administrative tribunal or competition authority to remedy an alleged violation of competition laws, or

–   concerns the transfer of intellectual property and is undertaken in a manner not inconsistent with the TRIPS Agreement;

(g)   to locate its headquarters for a specific region or the world market in the territory of that Contracting Party;

(h)   to supply one or more of the goods that it produces or the services that it provides to a specific region or the world market exclusively from the territory of that Contracting Party;

(i)   to achieve a given level or value of research and development in its territory;

(j)   to hire a given level of nationals;

(k)   to establish a joint venture with domestic participation; or

(l)   to achieve a minimum level of domestic equity participation other than nominal qualifying shares for directors or incorporators of corporations.

2.   A Contracting Party is not precluded by paragraph 1 from conditioning the receipt or continued receipt of an advantage, in connection with an investment in its territory of a Contracting Party or of a non-Contracting Party, on compliance with any of the requirements, commitments or undertakings set forth in paragraphs 1(f) through 1(l).

3.   [For the avoidance of doubt, nothing in paragraph 1(a), 1(b), 1(c), 1(d) and 1(e) shall be construed to prevent a Contracting Party from conditioning the receipt or continued receipt of an advantage, in connection with an investment in its territory of an investor of a Contracting Party or of a non-Contracting Party, on compliance with a requirement, commitment or undertaking to locate production, provide particular services, train or employ personnel, construct or expand particular facilities, or carry out research and development in its territory.]

4.   [Provided that such measures are not applied in an arbitrary or unjustifiable manner, or do not constitute a disguised restriction on investment, nothing in paragraphs 1(b) and 1(c) shall be construed to prevent any Contracting Party from adopting or maintaining measures, including environmental measures:

(a)   necessary to secure compliance with laws and regulations that are not inconsistent with the provisions of this Agreement;

(b)   necessary to protect human, animal or plant life or health;

(c)   necessary for the conservation of living or non-living exhaustible natural resources.]

5.a) Paragraphs 1(a), 1(b), and 1(c) do not apply to qualification requirements for goods or services with respect to export promotion and foreign aid programmes;

[(a bis) Paragraph 1(a), 1(b), and 1(c) do not apply to:

- [measures] [advantages] related to the production, processing and trade of agricultural and processed agricultural products;

- advantages related to trade in services;]

b) Paragraphs 1(b), 1(c), 1(f), and 1(h) do not apply to procurement by a Contracting Party or an entity that is owned or controlled by a Contracting Party;

[c) paragraphs 1(b) and 1(c) do not apply to requirements imposed by an importing Party relating to the content of goods necessary to qualify for preferential tariffs or preferential quotas.]

[c) Paragraphs 1(a), 1(b), 1(c) and 1(d) do not apply to customs duties, exemptions from such duties and preferential tariffs or to any trade measure regulating imports and exports provided that such measures are not applied in an arbitrary or unjustified manner, and do not constitute a disguised restriction on investment.]

PRIVATISATION

Paragraph 1 (Application of National Treatment/MFN)

1.   The obligation on a Contracting Party to accord National Treatment and MFN treatment as defined in Paragraph XX (NT/MFN) applies to:

a)   all kinds of privatisation, irrespective of the method of privatisation (whether by public offering, direct sale or other method); and

b)   subsequent transactions involving a privatised asset.

[Paragraph 1a (Voucher Schemes)

2.   Notwithstanding paragraph 1, arrangements under which natural persons of a Contracting Party are granted exclusive rights as regards the initial privatisation are acceptable as a method of privatisation under this Agreement provided that the exclusive right as regards the initial privatisation is limited to natural persons only and provided that there is no restriction on subsequent sales].

Paragraph 2 (Right to Privatise)

3.   Nothing in this Agreement shall be construed as imposing an obligation on a Contracting Party to privatise.

Paragraph 3 (Special Share Arrangements)

Alternative 1

4.   Contracting Parties acknowledge that special share arrangements are compatible with Paragraph 1, unless they explicitly or intentionally favour investors or investments of a Contracting Party or discriminate against investors or investments of another Contracting Party on the grounds of their nationality or permanent residency.

Alternative 2

5.   [Special share holding arrangements including, inter alia, a) the retention of "golden shares" by Contracting Parties, b) stable shareholder groups assembled by a Contracting Party, c) management/employee buyouts, and d) voucher schemes for members of the public, hold strong potential for discrimination against foreign investors and are, in fact, inconsistent with National Treatment and MFN treatment obligations in many instances.]

Alternative 3 = Footnote to Paragraph 1

6.   Special share arrangements which explicitly discriminate (i.e. de jure) against foreign investors and their investment are contrary to obligations on National Treatment/MFN Treatment. It is also understood that when, in their application, special share arrangements lead to de facto discrimination they are also contrary to National Treatment/MFN Treatment.

[Alternative 4

7.   Nothing in this Agreement shall prevent Contracting Parties from using special methods of privatisation or having special rules as regards ownership, management or control of privatised assets such as:

–   a Contracting Party or any person designated by the Contracting Party maintaining special shareholder rights to influence or veto any decision concerning such assets after the privatisation,

–   arrangements under which managers or other employees of an enterprise are granted special treatment as regards the acquisition of shares of that enterprise,

–   arrangements under which shareholders are required to maintain their share in the capital of the enterprise during a certain period of time,

–   arrangements under which locals of a certain community are granted special treatment as regards the acquisition of this community's property,

unless they explicitly or intentionally favour investors or investments of a Contracting Party or discriminate against investors or investments of another Contracting Party on the grounds of their nationality or permanent residency.]

Paragraph 4 (Transparency)

8.   For the purposes of this Article, each Contracting Party or its designated agency shall promptly publish or otherwise make publicly available the essential features and procedures for participation in each prospective privatisation.

Paragraph 5 (Definition)

9.   Privatisation means the sale by a Contracting Party, in part or in full, of its equity interests in any entity or other disposal having substantially the same effect.*

* This definition:

–   does not cover transactions between different levels or entities of the same Contracting Party;

–   excludes transactions in the normal conduct of business.

MONOPOLIES/STATE ENTERPRISES/CONCESSIONS

A. Article on Monopolies

1.   Nothing in this Agreement shall be construed to prevent a Contracting Party from maintaining, designating or eliminating a monopoly.

2.   Each Contracting Party shall [endeavour to] accord non-discriminatory treatment when designating a monopoly.

3.   Each Contracting Party shall ensure that any privately-owned monopoly that its national [or subnational] governments [maintain] or designate and any public monopoly that its national [or subnational] governments maintain or designate:

a)   provides non-discriminatory treatment to investments of investors of another Contracting Party in its supply of the monopoly good or service in the relevant market;

b)   provides non-discriminatory treatment to investments of investors of another Contracting Party in its purchase of the monopoly good or service in the relevant market. This paragraph does not apply to procurement by governmental agencies of goods or services for government purposes and not with a view to commercial resale or with a view to use in the production of goods or services for commercial sale;

c)   does not abuse its monopoly position, in a non-monopolised market in its territory, to engage, either directly or indirectly, including through its dealing with its parent company, its subsidiary or other enterprise with common ownership, in anti-competitive practices that adversely affect [an investor or] an investment by an investor of another Contracting Party, including through the discriminatory provision of the monopoly good or service, cross-subsidisation or predatory conduct.

[d)   Except to comply with any terms of its designation that are not inconsistent with subpara-graph (a) or (b), acts solely in accordance with commercial considerations in its purchase or sale of the monopoly good or service in the relevant market, including with regard to price, quality, availability, marketability, transportation and other terms and conditions of purchase or sale.]

[Nothing in Article A shall be construed to prevent a monopoly from charging different prices in different geographic markets, where such differences are based on normal commercial consi-derations, such as taking account of supply and demand conditions in those markets.

Article A, paragraphs 3(c) and 3(d) differences in pricing between classes of customers, between affiliated and non-affiliated firms, and cross-subsidisation are not in themselves inconsistent with this provision; rather, they are subject to this subparagraph when they are used as instruments of anticompetitive behaviour by the monopoly firm.]

4.   Each Contracting Party is allowed to lodge a reservation to the Agreement concerning an activity previously monopolised at the moment of the elimination of the monopoly.]

5.   Each Contracting Party shall notify to the Parties Group any existing designated monopoly within [60] days after the entry into force of the Agreement, any newly designated monopoly within [60] days after its creation, and any elimination of a designated monopoly [and related new reservation to the Agreement] within [60] days after its elimination.

[6.   Neither investors of another Contracting Party nor their investments may have recourse to investor-state arbitration for any matter arising out of paragraph 3 of this Article.]

 [B. Article on [State Enterprises] [Entities with Which a Government Has a Specific Relationship]

i)   Zero option. [supported by a large majority of delegations]

ii)   Additional provisions

a.   Proposal by two delegations

[1.   Each Contracting Party shall ensure that any state enterprise that it maintains or establishes accords non-discriminatory treatment in the sale, in the Contracting Party's territory, of its goods or services to investors of another Contracting Party and their investments.

2.   Neither investors of another Contracting Party nor their investments may have recourse to investor-state arbitration for any matter arising out of paragraph 2 of this Article.]

b.   Proposal by one delegation

[1.   Each Contracting Party shall ensure that any entity that a national or a subnational govern-ment owns or controls through ownership interest or which a national or subnational govern-ments authority has a relationship with through any specific legislative, regulatory or adminis-trative act, any contracts, or any practices related to some of its activities acts in a manner that is not inconsistent with the Contracting Party's obligations under this Agreement in connection with these activities.]]

C. Definitions Related to Articles on Monopolies [and State Enterprises]

1.   "Delegation" means a legislative grant, and a government order, directive or other act trans-ferring to the monopoly or state enterprise, or authorising the exercise by the monopoly or state enterprise of, governmental authority.

2.   "Designate" means to establish or authorise, or to expand the scope of a monopoly.

3. "Monopoly" means any person or entity designated by a [national [or subnational] government authority] [Contracting Party] as the sole supplier or buyer of a good or service in a relevant market in the territory of a Contracting Party. It does not include a person or entity that has an exclusive intellectual property right solely by reason of such right or the exercise of such right.

4. "Relevant market" means the geographic and product market for a good or service in the territory of the Contracting Party.

5. "Non-discriminatory treatment" means the better of national treatment and most favoured nation treatment, as set out in the relevant provisions of this Agreement.

[6. "State enterprises" means, [subject to Annex .....,] an enterprise owned, or controlled through ownership interest, by a Contracting Party.]

[D. Article on Concessions

Transparency

The procedure for granting a concession must envisage, at least, one publication in a journal of official notices. The notice must contain all the relevant information about the purpose and nature of the activity subject to concession, its conditions and deadline. The publication must be made sufficiently in advance in order to enable all interested persons to submit applications or additional relevant information. The reasons for the rejection of an application will be made known to the applicant upon request.]

[Definition

1. A concession is any delegation, direct or indirect, which entails a transferring of operation of activities, carried out by a government authority, national or subnational, or any public or para-public authority[, to a distinct and independent legal entity].

2. The delegation shall be realised either by any laws, regulations, administrative rulings or established policies, or by any private or public contract. The aim of the delegation is to entrust to a distinct [and independent] legal body with the operation of public services, including the operation of networks or infrastructures, or the exploitation of natural resources and if needed with the construction of all or part of networks or infrastructures.

3. [If necessary: The legal act of delegation includes the modes of payment to the investor. These modes of payment can consist of any price paid by consumers, any royalty, tax licence, subsidy or contribution from the delegatory authority, or any combination of the modes]].

[E. Article on the Granting of Authorisations for the Prospection, Exploitation and Production of Minerals, Including Hydrocarbons

(1) For the purpose of the present Article, "authorisation" means any law, regulation, administrative or contractual provision or instrument issued thereunder by which the competent authorities of a Contracting Party entitle any investor or a group of investors to exercise, on its own behalf and on its own risk, the exclusive right to prospect or explore for or produce minerals, including hydrocarbons, in a geographical area.

(2) Consistent with the present Agreement, the Contracting Parties may establish:

(a) procedures to be followed for the granting of authorisations according to which all interested investors may submit applications pursuant to this article;

(b) criteria on the basis of which authorisations are granted;

(c) conditions and requirements, including requirement of state participation, concerning the exercise or termination of the activities of prospecting, exploring for and producing minerals, including hydrocarbons, whether contained in the authorisation or to be accepted prior to the grant of the authorisation.

(3) The Contracting Parties shall apply such procedures, criteria, conditions and requirements as referred to in paragraph (2) above in a transparent and objective manner and in a way which

ensures that there is no discrimination on grounds of nationality between investors as regards access to and exercise of the activities of prospecting, exploring for and producing minerals, including hydrocarbons.]

ENTITIES WITH DELEGATED GOVERNMENTAL AUTHORITY

Each Contracting Party shall ensure that any entity to which it has delegated a regulatory, administrative or other governmental authority acts in a manner that is not inconsistent with the Contracting Party's obligations under this Agreement wherever such entity exercises that delegated authority.

INVESTMENT INCENTIVES

Provisions

Alternative 1

Several delegations believe that no additional text is necessary. They consider that the current draft articles in the MAI are sufficient to cover investment incentives at this time.

Alternative 2

Many delegations, however, would favour specific provisions on incentives in the MAI although they hold different views as to their nature and scope. Some proposed a built-in agenda for future work. Discussion of possible provisions focused on the following draft article which is regarded as a compromise text by those who would still prefer more far-reaching disciplines.

Article

1.   The Contracting Parties confirm that Article XX (on NT and MFN) and Article XX (Transparency) applies to [the granting of] investment incentives.

2.   [The Contracting Parties acknowledge that[, in certain circumstances,] even if applied on a nondiscriminatory basis, investment incentives may have distorting effects on the flow of capital and investment decisions. [Any Contracting Party which considers that its investors or their investments are adversely affected by an investment incentive adopted by another Contracting Party and having a distorting effect, may request consultations with that Contracting Party.] [The former Contracting Party may also bring the incentive before the Parties Group for its consideration.]]

3.   [In order to further avoid and minimise such distorting effects and to avoid undue competition between Contracting Parties in order to attract or retain investments, the Contracting Parties [shall] enter into negotiations with a view to establishing additional MAI disciplines [within three years] after the signature of this Agreement. These negotiations shall recognise the role of investment incentives with regard to the aims of policies, such as regional, structural, social, environmental or R&D policies of the Contracting Parties, and other work of a similar nature undertaken in other fora. These negotiations shall, in particular, address the issues of positive discrimination, [transparency], standstill and rollback.]

4.   [For the purpose of this Article, an "investment incentive" means: The grant of a specific advantage arising from public expenditure [a financial contribution] in connection with the establishment, acquisition, expansion, management, operation or conduct of an investment of a Contracting Party or a non-Contracting Party in its territory].

RECOGNITION ARRANGEMENTS

AUTHORISATION PROCEDURES

MEMBERSHIP OF SELF-REGULATORY BODIES

INTELLECTUAL PROPERTY

Intellectual property issues are being examined by intellectual property experts. The most recent status of discussions is reproduced here.

Transfers

Agreed: text on collective management charges should be added to the first sentence in paragraph 2 of the Commentary on Transfers after "purposes": ", or any authorised deduction by an entity charged with collective management of intellectual property rights."

Not agreed: whether the modified paragraph should remain in the Commentary or be placed in the text of the Agreement.

Monopolies

Agreed: the definition of "monopoly" should be amended to refine the definition's treatment of intellectual property rights: "Monopoly" means any person or entity designated by a [national [or subnational] government authority] [Contracting Party] as the sole supplier or buyer of a good or service in a relevant market in the territory of a Contracting Party, but does not include a person or entity that has an exclusive intellectual property right, concession, licence authorisation or permit solely by reason of such right or exercise of such right [nor does it include an entity charged with the collective management of intellectual property rights].

Not agreed: as indicated by the final bracketed phrase, whether entities charged with collective management of IPRs should also be excluded from the definition.

Performance Requirements

Agreed: paragraph 1(f) in the Article on Performance Requirements requires explicit reference to the transfer of IPRs.

Not agreed:

(a)   whether the current wording of paragraph 1(f) adequately covers future IPRs and moral rights; and

(b)   whether paragraphs 1(b) and (c) of the Article on Performance Requirements have an impact on IPRs.

Expropriation

Agreed: text is needed to ensure that certain IP management and legal provisions do not constitute expropriation.

Not agreed: flowing from proposed text: "The creation, limitation, revocation, annulment, statutory licensing, compulsory licensing and compulsory collective management of IPRs, the withholding of authorised deductions by an entity charged with the collective management of IPRs, and the sharing of remuneration between different holders of IPRs are not expropriation within the terms of this agreement, to the extent that they are not inconsistent with specialised IPR conventions."

(a)   whether there should be a specific IP text or reliance on a general text clarifying that expropriation does not include normal government regulatory activity;

(b)   whether and how the statement should be qualified;

(c)   whether that list of actions should be exhaustive or illustrative;

(d)   whether the current wording adequately covers future rights;

(e)   whether the question of consistency with IPR agreements should be worded positively;

(f)   whether a specific IP text should be in the text of the Agreement, in an interpretative footnote or in the Commentary; and

(g)   whether the word "creation" adequately covers the intended concept.

National Treatment and MFN Treatment and General Treatment

Agreed: MAI obligations should not extend NT/MFN obligations in existing IP agreements.

Not agreed:

(a) whether there should be a NT/MFN exception through a link to existing IP agreements;

(b) whether there should be a NT/MFN exception to MAI obligations for IPRs;

(c) whether the eventual solution should also be applied to the General Treatment articles; and

(d) the applicability of the MAI obligations with respect to future IPRs.

Definitions of "Investment" and "Investor"

Agreed: there needs to be clarification of the definition of "investment". The required clarification is tied to the resolution of the eventual substantial MAI obligations for IPRs.

Not agreed:

(a) whether the definition of "investment" should be limited to those IPRs included in the TRIPS Agreement;

(b) whether it should exclude copyrights and related rights;

(c) whether it should include future IPRs;

(d) whether it should include only the "economic aspects" of IPRs;

(e) whether it should include only those rights provided domestically; and

(f) what implications the definition of "investor" has for an IP "rightsholder".

Dispute Settlement

Agreed: IP experts wish to limit forum shopping and conflicting jurisprudence with the WTO.

Not agreed:

(a) how to achieve these goals;

(b) the desirability of applying investor-state dispute settlement to IPRs; and

(c) whether the existing MFN obligations in the TRIPS Agreement create the risk of "freeriders".

Information Transfers and Data Processing

Agreed: there are concerns that the text of the generalisation of financial services (see Information Transfer and Data Processing, below) has implications for IPRs, and may have to be amended or deleted to take these concerns into account.

Exhaustion of Rights

Not agreed: whether there needs to be any language on this issue to ensure that the MAI does not create new obligations in this area.

PUBLIC DEBT

CORPORATE PRACTICES

TECHNOLOGY R&D

NOT LOWERING STANDARDS (LABOUR AND ENVIRONMENT)

Alternative 1

[The Parties recognise that it is inappropriate to encourage investment by lowering [domestic] health, safety or environmental [standards] [measures] or relaxing [domestic] [core] labour standards. Accordingly, a Party should not waive or otherwise derogate from, or offer to waive or otherwise derogate from, such [standards] [measures] as an encouragement for the establishment, acquisition, expansion or retention in its territory of an investment of an investor. If a Party considers that another Party has offered such an encouragement, it may request consultations with the other Party and the two Parties shall consult with a view to avoiding any such encouragement.]

Alternative 2

[A Contracting Party [shall] [should] not waive or otherwise derogate from, or offer to waive or otherwise derogate from [domestic] health, safety or environmental [measures] [standards] or [domestic] [core] labour standards as an encouragement for the establishment, acquisition, expansion or retention of an investment of an investor.]

Alternative 3

[1. The Parties recognise that it is inappropriate to encourage investment by lowering domestic health, safety or environmental measures or relaxing international core labour standards.

2. A Contracting Party [shall] [should] accord to investors of another Contracting Party and their investments treatment no more favourable than it accords its own investors by waving or otherwise derogating from, or offering to waive or otherwise derogate from domestic health, safety, environmental or labour measures, with respect to the establishment, acquisition, expansion, operation, management, maintenance, use, enjoyment and sale or other disposition of an investment.

3. A Contracting Party [shall] [should] not take any measure which derogates from, or offer to derogate from, international health, safety or environmental laws or international core labour standards as an encouragement for investment on its territory.]

Alternative 4 (Environment Only)

[1. The Parties recognise that it is inappropriate to encourage investment by relaxing health, safety or environmental measures.

2. Accordingly, a Contracting Party shall accord to investors of another Contracting Party and their investments treatment no more favourable than it accords to its own investors and their investments by waving or otherwise derogating from, or offering to waive or otherwise derogate from health, safety environmental measures, with respect to the establishment, acquisition, expansion, operation, management, maintenance, use, enjoyment and sale or other disposition of investments.

3. In addition, a Contracting Party should not encourage investment by lowering its health, safety and environmental standards in general. If a Party considers that another Party has offered such an encouragement, it may request consultations with the other Party and the two Parties shall consult with a view to avoiding any such encouragement.]

IV. Investment Protection

1. GENERAL TREATMENT

1.1. Each Contracting Party shall accord to investments in its territory of investors of another Contracting Party fair and equitable treatment and full and constant protection and security. In no case shall a Contracting Party accord treatment less favourable than that required by international law.

1.2. A Contracting Party shall not impair by [unreasonable or discriminatory] [unreasonable and discriminatory] measures the operation, management, maintenance, use, enjoyment or disposal of investments in its territory of investors of another Contracting Party.

2. EXPROPRIATION AND COMPENSATION

2.1. A Contracting Party shall not expropriate or nationalise directly or indirectly an investment in its territory of an investor of another Contracting Party or take any measure or measures having equivalent effect (hereinafter referred to as "expropriation") except:

a) for a purpose which is in the public interest,

b) on a non-discriminatory basis,

c) in accordance with due process of law, and

d) accompanied by payment of prompt, adequate and effective compensation in accordance with Articles 2.2 to 2.5 below.

2.2. Compensation shall be paid without delay.

2.3. Compensation shall be equivalent to the fair market value of the expropriated investment immediately before the expropriation occurred. The fair market value shall not reflect any change in value occurring because the expropriation had become publicly known earlier.

2.4. Compensation shall be fully realisable and freely transferable.

2.5. [Compensation shall include interest at a commercial rate established on a market basis for the currency of payment from the date of expropriation until the date of actual payment.]

2.6. Due process of law includes, in particular, the right of an investor of a Contracting Party which claims to be affected by expropriation by another Contracting Party to prompt review of its case, including the valuation of its investment and the payment of compensation in accordance with the provisions of this article, by a judicial authority or another competent and independent authority of the latter Contracting Party.

3. PROTECTION FROM STRIFE

3.1. An investor of a Contracting Party which has suffered losses relating to its investment in the territory of another Contracting Party due to war or to other armed conflict, state of emergency, revolution, insurrection, civil disturbance, or any other similar event in the territory of the latter Contracting Party, shall be accorded by the latter Contracting Party, as regards restitution, indemnification, compensation or any other settlement, treatment no less favourable than that which it accords to its own investors or to investors of any third State, whichever is most favourable to the investor.

3.2. Notwithstanding Article 3.1, an investor of a Contracting Party which, in any of the situations referred to in that paragraph, suffers a loss in the territory of another Contracting Party resulting from

(a) requisitioning of its investment or part thereof by the latter's forces or authorities, or

(b) destruction of its investment or part thereof by the latter's forces or authorities, which was not required by the necessity of the situation,

shall be accorded by the latter Contracting Party restitution or compensation which in either case shall be prompt, adequate and effective and, with respect to compensation, shall be in accordance with Articles 2.1 to 2.5.

4. TRANSFERS

4.1. Each Contracting Party shall ensure that all payments relating to an investment in its territory of an investor of another Contracting Party may be freely transferred into and out of its territory without delay. Such transfers shall include, in particular, though not exclusively:

a) the initial capital and additional amounts to maintain or increase an investment;

b) returns;

c) payments made under a contract including a loan agreement;

d) proceeds from the sale or liquidation of all or any part of an investment;

e) payments of compensation under Articles 2 and 3;

f) payments arising out of the settlement of a dispute;

g) earnings and other remuneration of personnel engaged from abroad in connection with an investment.

4.2. Each Contracting Party shall further ensure that such transfers may be made in a freely convertible currency. [Freely convertible currency means a currency which is widely traded in international foreign exchange markets and widely used in international transactions.] or [Freely convertible currency means a currency which is, in fact, widely used to make payments for international transactions and is widely traded in the principal exchange markets].

4.3. Each Contracting Party shall also further ensure that such transfers may be made at the market rate of exchange prevailing on the date of transfer.

[4.4. In the absence of a market for foreign exchange, the rate to be used shall be the most recent exchange rate for conversion of currencies into Special Drawing Rights.]

4.5. Notwithstanding Article 4.1(b) above, a Contracting Party may restrict the transfer of a return in kind in circumstances where the Contracting Party is permitted under the GATT 1994 to restrict or prohibit the exportation or the sale for export of the product constituting the return in kind. Nevertheless, a Contracting Party shall ensure that transfers of returns in kind may be effected as authorised or specified in an investment agreement, investment authorisation, or other written agreement between the Contracting Party and an investor or investment of another Contracting Party.

4.6. Notwithstanding paragraphs 1 to 5 of this Article, a Contracting Party may delay or prevent a transfer through the equitable, non-discriminatory and good faith application of measures:

(a)   to protect the rights of creditors,

(b)   relating to or ensuring compliance with laws and regulations

   (i)   on the issuing, trading and dealing in securities, futures and derivatives,

   (ii)   concerning reports or records of transfers, or

(c)   in connection with criminal offences and orders or judgements in administrative and adjudicatory proceedings;

provided that such measures and their application shall not be used as a means of avoiding the Contracting Party's commitments or obligations under the Agreement.

5. Information Transfer and Data Processing

1.   No Contracting Party shall take measures that prevent transfers of information or the processing of information outside the territory of a Contracting Party, including transfers of data by electronic means, where such transfer of information or processing of information is:

a)   necessary for the conduct of the ordinary business of an enterprise located in a Contracting Party that is the investment of an investor of another Contracting Party; or

b)   in connection with the purchase or sale by an enterprise located in a Contracting Party that is the investment of an investor of another Contracting Party of:

   i)   data processing services; or

   ii)   information, including information provided to or by third parties.

2.   Nothing in paragraph 1:

a)   affects the enterprise's obligation to comply with any record keeping and reporting requirements; or

b)   restricts the right of a Contracting Party to protect privacy, including the protection of personal data, intellectual and industrial property, and the confidentiality of individual records and accounts, so long as such right is not used to circumvent the provisions of the Agreement.

6. Subrogation

If a Contracting Party or its designated agency makes a payment under an indemnity, guarantee or contract of insurance given in respect of an investment of an investor in the territory of another Contracting Party, the latter Contracting Party shall recognise the assignment of any right or claim of such investor to the former Contracting Party or its designated agency and the right of the former Contracting Party or its designated agency to exercise by virtue of subrogation any such right and claim to the same extent as its predecessor in title.

7. PROTECTING EXISTING INVESTMENTS

[This Agreement shall apply to investments made prior to its entry into force for the Contracting Parties concerned [consistent with the legislation of the Contracting Party in whose territory it was made] as well as investments made thereafter. This Agreement shall not apply to claims arising out of events which occurred, or to claims which had been settled, prior to its entry into force.] or [This Agreement shall apply to investments existing at the time of entry into force as well as to those established or acquired thereafter.]

V. Dispute Settlement

STATE-STATE PROCEDURES

A.   GENERAL PROVISIONS

1.   The rules and procedures set out in Articles A-C shall apply to the avoidance of conflicts and the resolution of disputes between Contracting Parties regarding the interpretation or application of the Agreement unless the disputing parties agree to apply other rules or procedures. However, the disputing parties may not depart from any obligation regarding notification of the Parties Group and the right of Parties to present views, under Article B, paragraphs 1.a and 4.c, and Article C, paragraphs 1.a, 4, and 6.e.

2.   Contracting Parties and other participants in proceedings shall protect any confidential or proprietary information which may be revealed in the course of proceedings under Articles B and C and which is designated as such by the Party providing the information. Contracting Parties and other participants in the proceedings may not reveal such information without written authorisation from the Party which provided it.

B.   CONSULTATION, CONCILIATION AND MEDIATION

1.   Consultations

a.   One or more Contracting Parties may request any other Contracting Party to enter into consultations regarding any dispute between them about the interpretation or application of the Agreement. The request shall be submitted in writing and shall provide sufficient information to understand the basis for the request, including identification of any actions at issue. The requested Party shall enter into consultations within thirty days of receipt of the request. The requesting Contracting Party shall provide the Parties Group with a copy of the request for consultation, at the time it submits the request to the other Contracting Party.

b.   A Contracting Party may not initiate arbitration against another Contracting Party under Article C of this Agreement unless the former Contracting Party has requested consultation and has afforded that other Contracting Party a consultation period of no less than 60 days after the date of the receipt of the request.

2.   Multilateral Consultations

a.   In the event that consultations under paragraph 1 of this Article have failed to resolve the dispute within 60 days after the date of receipt of the request for those consultations, the Contracting Parties in dispute may, by agreement, request the Parties Group to consider the matter.

b.   Such request shall be submitted in writing and shall give the reason for it, including identification of any actions at issue, and shall indicate the legal basis for the complaint.

c.   The Parties Group may make recommendations to the Contracting Parties in dispute. The Parties Group shall conclude its deliberations within 60 days after the date of receipt of the request.

3.   Mediation or Conciliation

If the Parties are unable to reach a mutually satisfactory resolution of a matter through consultations, they may have recourse to good offices or to mediation or conciliation under such rules and procedures as they may agree.

4.   Confidentiality of Proceedings, Notification of Results

a.   Proceedings involving consultations, mediation or conciliation shall be confidential.

b.   No Contracting Party may, in any binding legal proceedings, invoke or rely upon any statement made or position taken by another Contracting Party in consultations, conciliation or mediation proceedings initiated under this Agreement, with the exception of factual representations.

c.   The Parties to consultations, mediation, or conciliation under this Agreement shall inform the Parties Group of any mutually agreed solution.

C.   ARBITRATION

1.   Scope and Initiation of Proceedings

a.   Any dispute between Contracting Parties as to whether one of them has acted in contravention of this Agreement shall, at the request of any Contracting Party that is a party to the dispute and has complied with the consultations requirements of Article B, be submitted to an arbitral tribunal for decision. A request, identifying the matters in dispute, shall be delivered to the other Party through diplomatic channels, unless that Contracting Party has designated another channel for receipt of notification and so notified the Depositary, and a copy of the request shall be delivered to the Parties Group.

b.   A Contracting Party may not initiate proceedings under this Article for a dispute which its investor has submitted, or consented to submit, to arbitration under Article D, unless the other Contracting Party has failed to abide by and comply with the award rendered in that dispute or those proceedings have terminated without resolution by an arbitral tribunal of the investor's claim.

c.   If a dispute arises between Contracting Parties as to whether one of them has acted in contravention of a substantially similar obligation of that Contracting Party under this Agreement and another agreement to which both are party, the complaining Contracting Party may submit it for decision under the agreement of its choice. In doing so, it waives its right to submit the matter for decision under the agreement not chosen.

2.   Formation of the Tribunal

a.   Within 30 days after receipt of a request for arbitration, the Parties to the dispute shall appoint by agreement three members of the tribunal and designate one of them as Chairman. Except for compelling reasons, the members shall be persons proposed by the Secretary General ICSID. At the option of either party or, where there is more than one Party on the same side of the dispute, either side, two additional members may be appointed, one by each party or side.

b.   If the necessary appointments have not been made within the periods specified in subparagraph a, above, either Party or side to the dispute may, in the absence of any other agreement, invite the Secretary General of the Centre for the Settlement of Investment Disputes to make the necessary appointments. The Secretary-General shall do so, to the extent feasible, in consultations with the Parties to the dispute and within thirty days after receipt of the request.

c.   Parties and the Secretary-General should consider appointment to the tribunal of members of the roster maintained pursuant to subparagraph f, below. If arbitration of a dispute is considered by either Contracting Party to the dispute or the Secretary-General to require special expertise on the tribunal, rather than solely through expert advice under the rules governing the arbitration, the appointment of individuals possessing expertise not found on the roster should be considered.

d. Members of a particular arbitral tribunal shall be independent and impartial.

e. Any vacancies which may arise in a tribunal shall be filled by the procedure by which the original appointment had been made.

f. The Parties Group shall maintain a roster of highly qualified individuals willing and able to serve on arbitral tribunals under this Agreement. Each Contracting Party may nominate up to four persons who shall be included as members of the roster. Nominations are valid for five year terms. At the end of a term, the Contracting Party which nominated a member may renew the nomination or nominate a new member of the roster. A member shall withdraw from the roster if no longer willing or able to serve and the Contracting Party which nominated that member may nominate another member for a full term.

3. Consolidation

a. Contracting Parties in dispute with the same Contracting Party over the same matter should act together as far as practicable for purposes of dispute settlement under this Article. Where more than one Contracting Party requests the submission to an arbitral tribunal of a dispute with the same Contracting Party relating to the same question, a single arbitral tribunal should be established to consider such disputes whenever feasible.

b. To the extent feasible, if more than one arbitral tribunal is formed, the same persons shall be appointed as members of both and the timetables of the proceedings shall be harmonised.

4. Third Parties

Any Contracting Party wishing to do so shall be given an opportunity to present its views orally or in writing to the arbitral tribunal on the issues of a legal nature in dispute. Such a Contracting Party shall be given access to the documents of the proceedings, other than confidential or proprietary information designated under Article A, paragraph 2. The tribunal shall establish the deadlines for such submissions in light of the schedule of the proceedings and shall notify such deadlines, at least thirty days in advance thereof, to the Parties Group.

5. Scientific and Technical Expertise

a. On request of a disputing Contracting Party or, unless the disputing Contracting Parties disapprove, on its own initiative, the tribunal may request a written report of a scientific or technical review board, or expert, on any factual issue concerning environmental, health, safety or other scientific or technical matters raised by a disputing Contracting Party in a proceeding, subject to such terms and conditions as such Parties may agree.

b. The board, or expert, shall be selected by the tribunal from among highly qualified, independent experts in the scientific or technical matters, after consultations with the disputing Parties and the scientific or technical bodies identified by those Parties.

c. The disputing Contracting Parties shall be provided:

    i.   advance notice of, and an opportunity to provide comments to the tribunal on the proposed factual issues to be referred to the board, or expert; and

    ii. a copy of the board's, or expert's, report and an opportunity to provide comments on the report to the tribunal.

d. The tribunal shall take the report and any comments by the disputing Contracting Parties on the report into account in the preparation of its award.

6. Proceedings and Awards

a. The tribunal shall decide disputes in accordance with this Agreement, interpreted and applied in accordance with the applicable rules of international law.

b. The tribunal may, at the request of a Party, recommend provisional measures which either Party should take to avoid serious prejudice to the other pending its final award.

c. The tribunal, in its award, shall set out its findings of law and fact, together with the reasons therefore, and may, at the request of a Party, award the following forms of relief:

i. a declaration that an action of a Party is in contravention of its obligations under this Agreement;

ii. a recommendation that a Party bring its actions into conformity with its obligations under the Agreement;

iii. pecuniary compensation for any loss or damage to the requesting Party's investor or its investment; and

iv. any other form of relief to which the Party against whom the award is made consents, including restitution in kind to an investor.

d. The tribunal shall draft its award consistently with the requirement of confidentiality set out in Article A, paragraph 2. It shall issue its award in provisional form to the Parties to the dispute on a confidential basis, as a general rule within 180 days after the date of formation of the tribunal. The parties to the dispute may, within 30 days thereafter, submit written comment upon any portion of it. The tribunal shall consider such submissions, may solicit additional written comments of the parties, and shall issue its final award within 15 days after closure of the comment period.

e. The tribunal shall promptly transmit a copy of its final award to the Parties Group, which shall make it publicly available.

f. Tribunal awards shall be final and binding between the parties to the dispute, subject to paragraph 7 below.

g. Each party shall pay the cost of its representation in the proceedings. The costs of the tribunal shall be paid for equally by the Parties unless the tribunal directs that they be shared differently. Fees and expenses payable to tribunal members will be subject to schedules established by the Parties Group and in force at the time of the constitution of the tribunal.

7. Nullification

a. Either party to the dispute may request the annulment of an award, in whole or in part, on one or more of the following grounds, that:

i. the Tribunal was not properly constituted;

ii. the Tribunal has manifestly exceeded its powers;

iii. there was corruption on the part of a member of the Tribunal or on the part of a person providing decisive expertise or evidence;

iv. there has been a serious departure from a fundamental rule of procedure; or

v. the award has failed to state the reasons on which it is based.

b. The request shall be submitted for decision by a tribunal which shall be constituted and operate under the rules applicable to a dispute submitted under paragraph 1 of this article .

c. Such a request must be submitted within 120 days after the date on which the award was rendered or after the discovery of the facts relevant to nullification on the grounds of corruption, whichever is later and, in any event, within five years after the date on which the award was rendered.

d. The tribunal may nullify the award in whole or in part. If the award is nullified, the fact of nullification shall be communicated to the Parties Group. In such a case, the dispute may be submitted for decision to a new tribunal constituted under this Article or to any other available forum, notwithstanding the Contracting Parties waiver under paragraph 1.c. of this article.

8.   Default Rules

The PCA Optional Rules for Arbitrating Disputes between Two States shall apply to supplement provisions of these Articles. The Parties Group may adopt supplemental provisions to ensure the smooth functioning of these rules, in particular to clarify the inter-relationship between these rules and the PCA Optional Rules.

9.   Response to Non-Compliance

a.   If a Contracting Party fails within a reasonable period of time to comply with its obligations as determined in the award, such Contracting Party shall, at the request of any Contracting Party in whose favour the award was rendered, enter into consultations with a view to reaching a mutually acceptable solution. If no satisfactory solution has been agreed within thirty days after the date of the request for consultations, any Contracting Party in whose favour the award was rendered, shall notify the other Contracting Party and the Parties Group if it intends to [take measures in response][suspend the application to the other Contracting Party of obligations under this agreement].

b.   The effect of any such [responsive measures][suspension] must be proportionate to the effect of the other Party's non-compliance. Such measures may not include suspension of the application of Article[s _ (General Treatment) and] _ (Expropriation) [and should not include denial of other protections to established investment].

c.   At the request of any Party to the award upon conclusion of the thirty day period for consultation, the Parties Group shall consider the matter. [Until twenty days after the receipt by the Parties Group Secretariat of the request, responsive measures shall not be taken.] The Parties Group may:

   i.   make recommendations, by consensus minus the disputing Contracting Parties;

   ii.   suspend the non-complying Party's right to participate in decisions of the Parties Group, by consensus minus the non-complying Contracting Party; and

   iii. [by consensus minus the Contracting Party which had intended to take responsive measures, decide that some or all of the responsive measures shall not be taken. The Contracting Party shall comply with that decision.]

d.   Any dispute concerning the alleged failure of a Contracting Party to comply with its obligations as determined in an award or the lawfulness of any responsive measures shall, at the request of any Contracting Party that is party to the dispute, be submitted for decision to the arbitral tribunal which rendered the award or, if the original tribunal is unavailable, to a single member or three member arbitral tribunal designated by the Secretary-General. The request shall be submitted in the same fashion, and the proceedings carried out in accordance with the same rules as are applicable to a request made under paragraph 1.a of this Article, with such modifications as the tribunal deems appropriate, and the final award shall be issued no later than 60 days after the date of the request, in case of the original tribunal, or after the date of its formation, in the case of a new tribunal. [No responsive measures may be taken from the time of submission of a dispute unless authorised by the tribunal as an interim measure or found lawful.]

INVESTOR-STATE PROCEDURES

D.   DISPUTES BETWEEN AN INVESTOR AND A CONTRACTING PARTY

1.   Scope and Standing

a.   This article applies to disputes between a Contracting Party and an investor of another Contracting Party concerning an alleged breach of an obligation of the former under this Agreement which causes loss or damage to the investor or its investment.

b.   An investor of another Contracting Party may also submit to arbitration under this article any investment dispute concerning any obligation which the Contracting Party has entered into with regard to a specific investment of the investor through:

   i.   An investment authorisation granted by its competent authorities specifically to the investor or investment,

   ii. a written agreement granting rights with respect to [categories of subject matters] on which the investor has relied in establishing acquiring, or significantly expanding an investment.

2.   Means of Settlement

Such a dispute should, if possible, be settled by negotiation or consultation. If it is not so settled, the investor may choose to submit it for resolution:

a.   to any competent courts or administrative tribunals of the Contracting Party to the dispute;

b.   in accordance with any dispute settlement procedure agreed upon prior to the dispute arising; or

c.   by arbitration in accordance with this Article under:

   i.   the Convention on the Settlement of Investment Disputes between States and Nationals of other States (the "ICSID Convention"), if the ICSID Convention is available;

   ii. the Additional Facility Rules of the Centre for Settlement of Investment Disputes ("ICSID Additional Facility"), if the ICSID Additional Facility is available;

   iii. the Arbitration Rules of the United Nations Commission on International Trade Law ("UNCITRAL"); or

   iv. the Rules of Arbitration of the International Chamber of Commerce ("ICC").

3.   Contracting Party Consent

a.   Subject only to paragraph 3.b, each Contracting Party hereby gives its unconditional consent to the submission of a dispute to international arbitration in accordance with the provisions of this Article.

b.   A Contracting Party may, by notifying the Depositary upon deposit of its instrument of ratification or accession, provide that its consent given under paragraph 3.a only applies on the condition that the investor and the investment waive in writing the right to initiate any other dispute settlement procedure with respect to the same dispute and withdraw from any such procedure in progress before its conclusion. A Contracting Party may, at any time, reduce the scope of that limitation by notifying the Depositary.

4.   Time Periods and Notification

An investor may submit a dispute for resolution pursuant to paragraph 2.c of this Article after sixty days following the date on which notice of intent to do so was received by the Contracting Party in dispute, but no later than five years from the date the investor first acquired or should have acquired knowledge of the events which gave rise to the dispute. Notice of intent, a copy of which shall be delivered to the Parties Group, shall specify:

a.   the name and address of the disputing investor;

b.   the name and address, if any, of the investment;

c.   the provisions of this Agreement alleged to have been breached and any other relevant provisions;

d.   the issues and the factual basis for the claim; and

e.   the relief sought, including the approximate amount of any damages claimed.

5.   Written Agreement of the Parties

The consent given by a Contracting Party in subparagraph 3.a, together with either the written submission of the dispute to resolution by the investor pursuant to subparagraph 2.c or the investor's advance written consent to such submission, shall constitute the written consent and the written agreement of the parties to the dispute to its submission for settlement for the purposes of Chapter II of the ICSID Convention, the ICSID Additional Facility Rules, Article 1 of the UNCITRAL Arbitration Rules, the Rules of Arbitration of the ICC, and Article II of the United Nations Convention on the Recognition and Enforcement of Foreign Arbitral Awards (the "New York Convention"). Neither party may withdraw its consent unilaterally, except as provided in paragraph 9.e of this Article.

[6.   ...]

7.   Appointments to Arbitral Tribunals

a.   Unless the parties to the dispute otherwise agree, the tribunal shall comprise three arbitrators, one appointed by each of the disputing parties and the third, who shall be the presiding arbitrator, appointed by agreement of the disputing parties.

b.   If a tribunal has not been constituted within 90 days after the date that a claim is submitted to arbitration, the arbitrator or arbitrators not yet appointed shall, on the request of either disputing party, be appointed by the appointing authority. For arbitration under paragraph 2, subparagraphs c.i, c.ii and c.iii, and paragraph 9, the appointing authority shall be the Secretary-General of ICSID. For arbitration under paragraph 2, subparagraph c.iv, the appointing authority shall be the International Court of Arbitration of the ICC.

c.   The parties to a dispute submitted to arbitration under this article and the appointing authority should consider the appointment of:

    i.   members of the roster maintained by the Contracting Parties pursuant to Article C, paragraph 2.f; and

    ii.   individuals possessing expertise not found on the roster, if arbitration of a dispute requires special expertise on the Tribunal, rather than solely through expert advice under the rules governing the arbitration.

d.   The appointing authority shall, as far as possible, carry out its function in consultation with the parties to the dispute.

e.   In order to facilitate the appointment of arbitrators of the parties' nationality on three member ICSID tribunals under Article 39 of the ICSID Convention and Article 7 of Schedule C of the ICSID Additional Facility Rules, and without prejudice to each party's right independently to select an individual for appointment as arbitrator or to object to an arbitrator on grounds other than nationality:

    i.   the disputing Contracting Party agrees to the appointment of each individual member of a tribunal under paragraph 2.c.i or ii of this Article; and

    ii.   a disputing investor may initiate or continue a proceeding under paragraph 2.c.i or ii only on condition that the investor agrees in writing to the appointment of each individual member of the tribunal.

8.   Standing of the Investment

An enterprise constituted or organised under the law of a Contracting Party but which, from the time of the events giving rise to the dispute until its submission for resolution under paragraph 2.c, was an investment of an investor of another Contracting Party, shall, for purposes of disputes concerning that investment, be considered "an investor of another Contracting Party" under this article and "a national of another Contracting State" for purposes of Article 25(2)(b) of the ICSID Convention regarding a dispute not submitted for resolution by the investor which owns or controls it.

9. Consolidation of Multiple Proceedings

a. In the event that two or more disputes submitted to arbitration with a Contracting Party under paragraph 2.c have a question of law or fact in common, the Contracting Party may submit to a separate arbitral tribunal, established under this paragraph, a request for the consolidated consideration of all or part of them. The request shall stipulate:

    i.   the names and addresses of the parties to the proceedings sought to be consolidated,

    ii. the scope of the consolidation sought, and

    iii. the grounds for the request.

    The Contracting Party shall deliver the request to each investor party to the proceedings sought to be consolidated and a copy of the request to the Parties Group.

b. The request for consolidated consideration shall be submitted to arbitration under the rules chosen by agreement of the investor parties from the list contained in paragraph 2.c. The investor parties shall act as one side for the purpose of the formation of the tribunal.

c. If the investor parties have not agreed upon a means of arbitration and the nomination of an arbitrator within 30 days after the date of receipt of the request for consolidated consideration by the last investor to receive it:

    i.   the request shall be submitted to arbitration in accordance with this article under the UNCITRAL rules, and

    ii. the appointing authority shall appoint the entire arbitral tribunal, in accordance with paragraph 7.

d. The arbitral tribunal shall assume jurisdiction over all or part of the disputes and the other arbitral proceedings shall be stayed or adjourned, as appropriate if, after considering the views of the parties, it decides that to do so would best serve the interest of fair and efficient resolution of the disputes and that the disputes fall within the scope of this paragraph.

e. An investor may withdraw the dispute from arbitration under this paragraph 9 and such dispute may not be resubmitted to arbitration under paragraph 2.c. If it does so no later than 15 days after receipt of notice of consolidation, its earlier submission of the dispute to that arbitration shall be without prejudice to the investor's recourse to dispute settlement other than under paragraph 2.c.

f. At the request of the Contracting Party, the arbitral tribunal established under this paragraph may decide, on the same basis and with the same effect as under paragraph 9.d, whether to assume jurisdiction over all or part of a dispute falling with the scope of paragraph 9.a which is submitted to arbitration after the initiation of consolidation proceedings.

10. Preliminary Objections

a. Any objection to the jurisdiction of the tribunal or to the admissibility of the application shall be raised no later than in the statement of defence.

b. Upon receipt of such an objection, the tribunal may suspend the proceedings on the merits.

c. After hearing the parties, the tribunal should give its decision, by which it shall either uphold the objection or reject it, within 60 days after the date on which the objection was made.

11. Indemnification

A Contracting Party shall not assert as a defence, counter-claim, right of set-off or for any other reason, that indemnification or other compensation for all or part of the alleged damages has been received or will be received pursuant to an indemnity, guarantee or insurance contract.

12. Third Party Rights

The arbitral tribunal shall notify the Parties Group of its formation. Taking into account the views of the parties, it may give to any Contracting Party requesting it an opportunity to submit written views on the legal issues in dispute, provided that the proceedings are not unduly delayed thereby. Any Contracting Party requesting it within thirty days after receipt by the Parties Group of the notification of the tribunal's formation shall be given an opportunity to present its views on issues in dispute in which it has a legal interest.

13. Scientific and Technical Expertise

a. On request of a disputing Contracting Party or, unless the disputing Contracting Parties disapprove, on its own initiative, the tribunal may request a written report of a scientific or technical review board, or expert, on any factual issue concerning environmental, health, safety or other scientific or technical matters raised by a disputing Contracting Party in a proceeding, subject to such terms and conditions as such Parties may agree.

b. The board, or expert, shall be selected by the tribunal from among highly qualified, independent experts in the scientific or technical matters, after consultations with the disputing Parties and the scientific or technical bodies identified by those Parties.

c. The disputing Contracting Parties shall be provided:

   i.   advance notice of, and an opportunity to provide comments to the tribunal on, the proposed factual issues to be referred to the board, or expert; and

   ii. a copy of the board's, or expert's, report and an opportunity to provide comments on the report to the tribunal.

d. The tribunal shall take the report and any comments by the disputing Contracting Parties on the report into account in the preparation of its award.

14. Applicable Law

a. Issues in dispute under paragraph 1.a. of this article shall be decided in accordance with this Agreement, interpreted and applied in accordance with the applicable rules of international law.

b. Issues in dispute under paragraph 1.b. of this article shall be decided in accordance with such rules of law as may be agreed by the parties to the dispute. In the absence of such agreement, such issues shall be decided in accordance with the law of the Contracting Party to the dispute (including its rules on the conflict of laws), the law governing the authorisation or agreement and such rules of international law as may be applicable.

15. Interim Measures of Relief

a. An arbitral tribunal established under this Article may recommend an interim measure of protection to preserve the rights of a disputing Contracting Party or to ensure that the Tribunal's jurisdiction is made fully effective.

b. The seeking of interim relief not involving the payment of damages, from judicial or administrative tribunals, by a party to a dispute submitted to arbitration under this article, for the preservation of its rights and interests pending resolution of the dispute, is not deemed a submission of the dispute for resolution for purposes of a Contracting Party's limitation of consent under paragraph 3.b, and is permissible in arbitration under any of the provisions of paragraph 2.c.

16. Final Awards

a. The arbitral tribunal, in its award shall set out its findings of law and fact, together with the reasons therefor and may, at the request of a Party, provide the following forms of relief:

   i.   a declaration that the Contracting Party has failed to comply with its obligations under the this Agreement;

   ii. pecuniary compensation, which shall include interest from the time the loss or damage was incurred until time of payment;

    iii.   restitution in kind in appropriate cases, provided that the Contracting Party may pay pecuniary compensation in lieu thereof where restitution is not practicable; and

    iv.   with the Agreement of the parties to the dispute, any other form of relief.

b.   In appropriate cases where the loss or damage was incurred by an investment which remains a going concern, the tribunal may direct that the compensation or restitution be made to the investment.

c.   An arbitration award shall be final and binding between the parties to the dispute and shall be carried out without delay by the party against whom it is issued, subject to its post-award rights under the arbitral systems utilised.

d.   The award shall be drafted consistently with the requirements of paragraph 17 and shall be a publicly available document. A copy of the award shall be delivered to the Parties Group by the Secretary-General of ICSID, for an award under the ICSID Convention or the Rules of the ICSID Additional Facility; by the Secretary-General of the ICC International Court of Arbitration, for an award under its rules; and by the tribunal, for an award under the UNCITRAL rules.

17. Confidential and Proprietary Information

Parties and other participants in proceedings shall protect any confidential or proprietary information which may be revealed in the course of the proceedings and which is designated as such by the party providing the information. They shall not reveal such information without written authorisation from the party which provided it.

18. Place of Arbitration and Enforceability

Any arbitration under this article shall be held in a state that is party to the New York Convention. Claims submitted to arbitration under this article shall be considered to arise out of a commercial relationship or transaction for purposes of Article 1 of that Convention. Each Contracting Party shall provide for the enforcement of the pecuniary obligations imposed by an award rendered pursuant to this Article D.

19. Tribunal Member Fees

Fees and expenses payable to a member of an arbitral tribunal established under these Articles will be subject to schedules established by the Parties Group and in force at the time of the constitution of the tribunal.

20. Supplemental Provisions

The Parties Group may adopt supplemental provisions to ensure the smooth functioning of these rules, in particular to clarify the inter-relationship between these rules and the rules of arbitration available under paragraph 2.c of this article D.

VI. Exceptions and Safeguards

GENERAL EXCEPTIONS

1.   This Article shall not apply to Article IV, 2 and 3 (Expropriation and compensation and protection from strife).

2.   Nothing in this Agreement shall be construed:

a.   to prevent any Contracting Party from taking any action which it considers necessary for the protection of its essential security interests:

    (i)   taken in time of war, or armed conflict, or other emergency in international relations;

    (ii)   relating to the implementation of national policies or international agreements respecting the non-proliferation of weapons of mass destruction;

    (iii)   relating to the production of arms and ammunition;

b.   to require any Contracting Party to furnish or allow access to any information the disclosure of which it considers contrary to its essential security interests;

c.   to prevent any Contracting Party from taking any action in pursuance of its obligations under the United Nations Charter for the maintenance of international peace and security.

3.   Subject to the requirement that such measures are not applied in a manner which would constitute a means of arbitrary or unjustifiable discrimination between Contracting Parties, or a disguised investment restriction, nothing in this Agreement shall be construed to prevent any Contracting Party from taking any measure necessary for the maintenance of public order.

4.   Actions or measures taken pursuant to this Article shall be notified to the Parties Group.

5.   If a Contracting Party (the "requesting Party") has reason to believe that actions or measures taken by another Contracting Party (the "other Party") under this article have been taken solely for economic reasons, or that such actions or measures are not in proportion to the interest being protected, it may request consultations with that other Party in accordance with Article V, B.1 (State-State Consultation Procedures). That other Party shall provide information to the requesting Party regarding the actions or measures taken and the reasons therefor.

TRANSACTIONS IN PURSUIT OF MONETARY AND EXCHANGE RATE POLICIES

1.   Articles XX (National Treatment), YY (Most Favoured Nation Treatment) and ZZ (Transparency) do not apply to transactions carried out in pursuit of monetary or exchange rate policies by a central bank or monetary authority of a Contracting Party.

2.   Where such transactions do not conform with Articles XX (National Treatment), YY (Most Favoured Nation Treatment) and ZZ (Transparency), they shall not be used as a means of avoiding the Contracting Party's commitments or obligations under the Agreement.

TEMPORARY SAFEGUARD

1.   A Contracting Party may adopt or maintain measures inconsistent with its obligations under:

*   Article xx (Transfers);

*   Article yy, paragraph 1.1 (National Treatment) relating to cross-border capital transactions

(a) in the event of serious balance-of-payments and external financial difficulties or threat thereof; or

(b) where, in exceptional circumstances, movements of capital cause, or threaten to cause, serious difficulties for macroeconomic management, in particular monetary and exchange rate policies.

2.   Measures referred to in paragraph 1:

(a) shall be consistent with the Articles of Agreement of the International Monetary Fund;

(b) shall not exceed those necessary to deal with the circumstances described in paragraph 16;

(c) shall be temporary and shall be eliminated as soon as conditions permit.

3.a) Measures referred to in paragraph 1 shall be promptly notified to the Parties Group and to the International Monetary Fund, including any changes in such measures.

(b) Measures referred to in paragraph 1 and any changes therein shall be subject to review and approval or disapproval within six months of their adoption and every six months thereafter until their elimination.

(c) These reviews shall address the compliance of any measure with paragraph 2, in particular the elimination of measures in accordance with paragraph 2 (c).

4.   Measures referred to in paragraph 1 and any changes therein that are approved by the International Monetary Fund in the exercise of its jurisdiction shall be considered as consistent with this Article.

5.   With regard to measures referred to in paragraph 1, and any changes therein, not falling within paragraph 4:

(a)   The Parties Group shall consider the implications of the measures adopted under this Article for the obligations of the Contracting Party concerned under this Agreement.

(b)   The Parties Group shall request an assessment by the International Monetary Fund of the conditions mentioned under paragraph 1 and of the consistency of any measures with paragraph 2. Any such assessment by the International Monetary Fund shall be accepted by the Parties Group.

(c)   Unless the International Monetary Fund determines that the measure is either consistent or inconsistent with the provisions of this Article, the Parties Group may either approve or disapprove the measure. The Parties Group shall establish procedures for this purpose.

6.   The Contracting Parties shall seek agreement with the International Monetary Fund regarding the role of the International Monetary Fund in the review procedures established under this Article.

7.   Measures referred to in paragraph 1 and any changes therein that are approved by the International Monetary Fund in the exercise of its jurisdiction or determined to be consistent with this Article by the International Monetary Fund or the Parties Group cannot be subject to dispute settlement.

Additional Article

If a dispute arises under this Article or under Article ..... (obligations under the Articles of Agreement of the Fund), a Dispute Settlement Panel shall request an assessment by the International Monetary Fund of the consistency of the measures with its Articles of Agreement, of the conditions mentioned under paragraph 1 and of the consistency of any measures as applied with paragraph 2. Any such assessment by the International Monetary Fund shall be accepted by the Panel.

VII. Financial Services

PRUDENTIAL MEASURES

1.   Notwithstanding any other provisions of the Agreement, a Contracting Party shall not be prevented from taking prudential measures with respect to financial services, including measures for the protection of investors, depositors, policy holders or persons to whom a fiduciary duty is owed by an enterprise providing financial services, or to ensure the integrity and stability of its financial system.

2.   Where such measures do not conform with the provisions of the Agreement, they shall not be used as a means of avoiding the Contracting Party's commitments or obligations under the Agreement.

RECOGNITION ARRANGEMENTS

1.   A Contracting Party may recognise prudential measures of any other Contracting Party or non-Contracting Party in determining how the Contracting Party's measures relating to financial services shall be applied. Such recognition, which may be achieved through harmonisation or otherwise, may be based on an agreement or arrangement with the other Contracting Party or non-Contracting Party concerned or may be accorded autonomously.

2.   A Contracting Party that is a party to such an agreement or arrangement referred to in paragraph 1, whether future or existing, shall afford adequate opportunity for other interested Contracting Parties to negotiate their accession to such agreements or arrangements, or to negotiate comparable ones with it, under circumstances in which there would be equivalent regulation, oversight, implementation of such regulation, and, if appropriate, procedures concerning the sharing of information between the parties to the agreement or arrangement. Where

a Contracting Party accords recognition autonomously, it shall afford adequate opportunity for any other Contracting Party to demonstrate that such circumstances exist.

AUTHORISATION PROCEDURES

1.　Each Contracting Party's regulatory authorities shall make available to interested persons their requirements for completing applications relating to an investment in, or the operations of, a financial services enterprise.

2.　On the request of an applicant, the regulatory authority shall inform the applicant of the status of its application. If such authority requires additional information from the applicant, it shall notify the applicant without undue delay.

3.　A regulatory authority shall make an administrative decision on a completed application of an investor in a financial services enterprise or a financial services enterprise that is an investment of an investor of another Contracting Party within [120] [180] days, and shall promptly notify the applicant of the decision. An application shall not be considered complete until [all relevant hearings are held and] all necessary information is received. Where it is not practicable for a decision to be made within [120] [180] days, the regulatory authority shall notify the applicant without undue delay and shall endeavour to make the decision within a reasonable time thereafter.

TRANSPARENCY

Nothing in this Agreement requires a Contracting Party to furnish or allow access to:

a)　information related to the financial affairs and accounts of individual customers of financial services enterprises, or

b)　any confidential or proprietary information, the disclosure of which would impede law enforcement or otherwise be contrary to the public interest or prejudice legitimate commercial interests of particular enterprises.

INFORMATION TRANSFER AND DATA PROCESSING

1.　No Contracting Party shall take measures that prevent transfers of information or the processing of financial information outside the territory of a Contracting Party, including transfers of data by electronic means, where such transfer of information or processing of financial information is:

a)　necessary for the conduct of the ordinary business of a financial services enterprise located in a Contracting Party that is the investment of an investor of another Contracting Party; or

b)　in connection with the purchase or sale by a financial services enterprise located in a Contracting Party that is the investment of an investor of another Contracting Party of:

i)　financial data processing services; or

ii)　financial information, including information provided to or by third parties.

2.　Nothing in paragraph 1:

a)　affects the financial service enterprise's obligation to comply with any record keeping and reporting requirements; or

b)　restricts the right of a Contracting Party to protect privacy, including the protection of personal data and the confidentiality of individual records and accounts, so long as such right is not used to circumvent the provisions of the Agreement.

MEMBERSHIP OF SELF-REGULATORY BODIES AND ASSOCIATIONS

When membership or participation in, or access to, any self-regulatory body, securities or futures exchange or market, clearing agency, or any other organisation or association is required by a Contracting Party in order for investments of investors of any other Contracting Party in a financial services enterprise established in the territory of the Contracting Party to provide financial services on an equal basis with financial services enterprises of the Contracting Party, or when the Contracting Party provides directly or indirectly such entities, privileges or advantages in providing financial services, the Contracting Party shall ensure that such entities accord national treatment to such investments.

PAYMENTS AND CLEARING SYSTEMS/LENDER OF LAST RESORT

1.   Under terms and conditions that accord National Treatment, each Contracting Party shall grant to financial services enterprises that are investments of investors of any other Contracting Party established in its territory access to payment and clearing systems operated by public entities, and to official funding and refinancing facilities available in the normal course of ordinary business.

2.   The provisions of this Agreement are not intended to confer access to the Contracting Party's lender of last resort facilities.

DISPUTE SETTLEMENT

Composition of Dispute Settlement Panels in Financial Matters Disputes

"Panels for disputes on prudential issues and other financial matters shall have the necessary expertise relevant to the specific financial services under dispute."

DEFINITION OF FINANCIAL SERVICES

Financial services include all insurance and insurance-related services, and all banking and other financial services (excluding insurance). Financial services include the following activities:

Insurance and insurance-related services

(i)   Direct insurance (including co-insurance):

   (A) life

   (B) non-life

(ii)   Reinsurance and retrocession;

(iii)   Insurance intermediation, such as brokerage and agency;

(iv)   Services auxiliary to insurance, such as consultancy, actuarial, risk assessment and claim settlement services.

Banking and other financial services (excluding insurance)

(v)   Acceptance of deposits and other repayable funds from the public;

(vi)   Lending of all types, including consumer credit, mortgage credit, factoring and financing of commercial transaction;

(vii) Financial leasing;

(viii) All payment and money transmission services, including credit, charge and debit cards, travellers cheques and bankers drafts;

(ix)   Guarantees and commitments;

(x)   Trading for own account or for account of customers, whether on an exchange, in an over-the-counter market or otherwise, the following:

   (A)   money market instruments (including cheques, bills, certificates of deposits);

   (B)   foreign exchange;

   (C)   derivative products including, but not limited to, futures and options;

   (D)   exchange rate and interest rate instruments, including products such as swaps, forward rate agreements;

   (E)   transferable securities;

(F)   other negotiable instruments and financial assets, including bullion.

(xi) Participation in issues of all kinds of securities, including underwriting and placement as agent (whether publicly or privately) and provision of services related to such issues;

(xii) Money broking;

(xiii) Asset management, such as cash or portfolio management, all forms of collective investment management, pension fund management, custodial, depository and trust services;

(xiv) Settlement and clearing services for financial assets, including securities, derivative products, and other negotiable instruments;

(xv) Provision and transfer of financial information, and financial data processing and related software by suppliers of other financial services;

(xvi) Advisory, intermediation and other auxiliary financial services on all the activities listed in subparagraphs (v) through (xv), including credit reference and analysis, investment and portfolio research and advice, advice on acquisitions and on corporate restructuring and strategy.

VIII. Taxation

1.   Nothing in this Agreement shall apply to taxation measures except as expressly provided in paragraphs 2 to 5 below.

2.   Article ... (Expropriation) shall apply to taxation measures.

3.   Article ... (Transparency) shall apply to taxation measures, except that nothing in this Agreement shall require a Contracting Party to furnish or allow access to information covered by tax secrecy or any other provision or administrative practice protecting confidentiality in domestic laws or international agreements, and including information:

a)   contained in or exchanged pursuant to any agreement or arrangement relating to taxation between governments and investors;

b)   pursuant to any agreement with a foreign government concerning the application or interpretation of an international agreement relating to taxation in the case of an investor, including exchange of information between governments;

c)   concerning the identity of an investor or other information which would disclose any trade, business, industrial, commercial or professional secret or trade process;

d)   pertaining to the negotiation of tax treaties or of any other international agreement relating partly or wholly to taxation or the participation by a government in the work of international organisations; or

e)   the disclosure of which would affect the assessment or collection of, the enforcement or prosecution in respect of, or the determination of appeals in relation to, taxation, or any information the disclosure of which would aid or assist in the avoidance or evasion of taxes.

4.   The provisions of Article [C] (State to State Dispute Settlement) and Article [D] (Investor to State Dispute Settlement), [except for paragraph 1b of Article [D]], and only those provisions, shall apply to a dispute under paragraph 2 or 3 of this Article.4 5

5.   For the purposes of this Article:

a)   A Competent Tax Authority means the minister or ministry responsible for taxes or their authorised representatives.

b)   "Taxation measures" include

   i)   any provision relating to taxes of the law of the Contracting Party or of a political subdivision thereof or a local authority therein, or any administrative practices of the Contracting Party relating to taxes; and

ii)   any provision relating to taxes of any convention for the avoidance of double taxation or of any other international agreement or arrangement by which the Contracting Party is bound.

Taxes shall be taken for this purpose to include direct taxes, indirect taxes and social security contributions.

IX. Country Specific Exceptions [...]

X. Relationship to Other International Agreements

OBLIGATIONS UNDER THE ARTICLES OF AGREEMENT OF THE INTERNATIONAL MONETARY FUND

Nothing in this Agreement shall be regarded as altering the obligations undertaken by a Contracting Party as a Signatory of the Articles of Agreement of the International Monetary Fund.

THE OECD GUIDELINES FOR MULTINATIONAL ENTERPRISES

[The following draft text was developed on associating the Guidelines with the MAI:]

1.   The OECD Guidelines for Multinational Enterprises are set out in Annex (xx).

2.   The Contracting Parties at the invitation of the Organisation for Economic Co-operation and Development are encouraged to participate in the Guidelines work of the Organisation in order to promote co-operation on the application, clarification, interpretation and revision of the Guidelines and to facilitate the maintenance of consensus among the Contracting Parties and the members of the Organisation on the matters addressed in the Guidelines.

3.   The Contracting Parties [shall] [are encouraged to] set up National Contact Points for undertaking promotional activities, handling enquiries and for discussions with the parties concerned on all matters related to the Guidelines so that they can contribute to the solution of problems which may arise in this connection. The business community, employee organisations and other interested parties should be informed of the availability of such facilities.

4.   Annexation of the Guidelines shall not bear on the interpretation or application of the Agreement, including for the purpose of dispute settlement; nor change their non- binding character.

[Several delegations proposed that the following additional text be added to the list of powers given to the Parties Group under Section XI of the Consolidated Text, paragraph 2:

(e)   consider revision of the Guidelines referred to in Article (xx) of the [Agreement] [Final Act] by adoption of any revised Guidelines developed in the OECD.]

[Finally, delegations developed draft text that would be placed in an annex immediately before the Guidelines, as follows:

The following Guidelines for Multinational Enterprises are a joint recommendation by participating Governments to multinational enterprises operating in their territory. Their purpose is to help multinational enterprises ensure that their operations are in harmony with the national policies of the countries in which they operate. The Guidelines include recommendations on general policies, disclosure of information, competition, financing, taxation, employment and industrial relations, environmental protection and science and technology. The Guidelines are part of the OECD Declaration on International Investment and Multinational Enterprises of 21 June 1976 as amended. Background and official clarifications are found in the publication "The OECD Guidelines for Multinational Enterprises". [see below, pp. 309 et seq.]]

XI. Implementation and Operation

THE PREPARATORY GROUP

(Text to be included in the Final Act)

1.   The Signatories to the Final Act and the Signatories to the Agreement shall meet in a Preparatory Group. A Signatory to the Final Act shall cease to be eligible to attend these meetings if it fails to become a Signatory to the Agreement by the closing date for signature of the Agreement.

2.   In the Preparatory Group, the participating Signatories shall:

(a)   prepare for entry into force of the Agreement and the establishment of the Parties Group;

(b)   conduct discussions with non-signatories to the Final Act;

(c)   conduct negotiations with interested non-signatories to the Final Act with a view to their becoming signatories to the Agreement.

3.   The participating Signatories shall elect a Chair, who shall serve in a personal capacity. Meetings shall be held at intervals to be determined by participating Signatories under rules and procedures they shall determine.

4.   Except where otherwise provided, the Preparatory Group shall make decisions by consensus. A Signatory may abstain and express a differing view without barring consensus.

5.   Decisions under paragraph 4 may include a decision to adopt a different voting rule for a particular question or category of questions.

6.   Where a decision cannot be made by consensus, the decision shall be made by a majority comprising [three quarters] [two thirds] of the Signatories.

7.   Paragraph 6 shall not apply to the following decisions:

(a)   decisions under paragraph 5; [and]

(b)   decisions under Article ... [see section XI of the Consolidated Text on decisions by the Preparatory Group on the eligibility of non-signatories to the Final Act to become a Signatory to the Agreement], which shall be made by [consensus] [a majority comprising ...]; [and]

8.   Where the European Community exercises its right to vote, it shall have a number of votes equal to the number of its Member States which are Contracting Parties to this Agreement. The number of votes of the European Community and its Member States shall in no case exceed the number of the Member States of the European Community which are Contracting Parties to this Agreement.

THE PARTIES GROUP

1.   There shall be a Parties Group comprised of the Contracting Parties.

2.   The Parties Group shall facilitate the operation of this Agreement. To this end, it shall:

(a)   carry out the functions assigned to it under this Agreement;

(b)   [at the request of a Contracting Party, clarify [by consensus] the interpretation or application of this Agreement];

(c)   consider any matter that may affect the operation of this Agreement; and

(d)   take such other actions as it deems necessary to fulfil its mandate.

3.   In carrying out the functions specified in paragraph 2, the Parties Group may consult governmental and non-governmental organisations or persons.

4.   The Parties Group shall elect a Chair, who shall serve in a personal capacity. Meetings shall be held at intervals to be determined by the Parties Group. The Parties Group shall establish its rules and procedures.

5.   Except where otherwise provided, the Parties Group shall make decisions by consensus. A Contracting Party may abstain and express a differing view without barring consensus.

6.   Decisions under paragraph 5 may include a decision to adopt a different voting rule for a particular question or category of questions.

7.   Where a decision cannot be made by consensus, the decision shall be made by a majority comprising [three quarters] [two thirds] of the Contracting Parties.

8.   Paragraph 7 shall not apply to the following decisions:

(a)   decisions under paragraph 6;

(b)   decisions under Article ... [see section XII of the Consolidated Text on amendment], which shall be made by consensus;

(c)   decisions under Article ... [see Section XII of the Consolidated Text on accession], [which shall be made by consensus] [which shall be made, failing consensus, by a [three quarters] [two thirds] majority] [which shall be made by a [three quarters] [two thirds] majority]; and

(d)   decisions on budgetary matters, which shall be made by [consensus] [a [three quarters] [two thirds] majority] [of Contracting Parties whose assessed contributions represent, in combination, at least two thirds of the total assessed contributions].

9.   The Parties Group shall be assisted by a Secretariat.

10.   [Parties Group and Secretariat costs shall be borne by the Contracting Parties as approved and apportioned by the Parties Group.]

11.   Where the European Community exercises its right to vote, it shall have a number of votes equal to the number of its Member States which are Contracting Parties to this Agreement. The number of votes of the European Community and its Member States shall in no case exceed the number of the Member States of the European Community which are Contracting Parties to this Agreement.

XII. Final Provisions

SIGNATURE

This Agreement shall be open for signature at the Depositary, until [date], by Signatories of the Final Act and thereafter until entry into force by any State, or separate customs territory which possesses full autonomy on the matters covered by this Agreement, which is willing and able to take on its obligations on terms agreed between it and the Signatories of this Agreement.

ACCEPTANCE AND ENTRY INTO FORCE

In the Final Act

1.   The Signatories to this Final Act agree to submit the Agreement for the consideration of their respective competent authorities with a view to seeking approval of the Agreement in accordance with their procedures.

2.   The Signatories to this Final Act agree on the desirability of acceptance of the Agreement by all signatories with a view to its entry into force by [date] or as early as possible thereafter.

In the MAI

3.   Not later than [date], the Signatories to this Agreement will meet to determine the date for entry into force and related matters. Decisions shall be made by [consensus] [a [two-thirds] majority of the Signatories].

4.   This Agreement shall enter into force on the date determined by the Signatories to this Agreement in accordance with paragraph 3 for the Signatories that have accepted this Agreement as of that date. An acceptance following the entry into force of this Agreement shall enter into force on the 30th day following the deposit of its instrument of acceptance.

ACCESSION

1.   This Agreement shall be open for accession by any State, regional economic integration organisation, and any separate customs territory which possesses full autonomy in the conduct of matters covered by this agreement, which is willing and able to undertake its obligations on terms agreed between it and the Contracting Parties acting through the Parties Group.

2.   Decisions on accession shall be taken by the Parties Group.

3.   Accession shall take effect on the thirtieth day following the deposit of the instruments of accession with the Depositary.

NON-APPLICABILITY

This Agreement shall not apply as between any Contracting Party and any acceding Party if, at the time of accession, the Contracting Party does not consent to such application.

REVIEW

The Parties Group may review this Agreement as and when it determines.

AMENDMENT

Any Contracting Party may propose to the Parties Group an amendment to this Agreement. Any amendment adopted by the Parties Group shall enter into force on the deposit of an instrument of ratification by all of the Contracting Parties, or at such later date as may be specified by the Parties Group at the time of adoption of the amendment.

REVISIONS TO THE OECD GUIDELINES FOR MULTINATIONAL ENTERPRISES

For Guidelines Annex changes any Contracting Party may make a unilateral statement upon signature:

"In the event of modification of the Guidelines, Annex – will be modified accordingly with respect to (Contracting Party name) provided that it has not made a declaration to the contrary within 180 days of notification by the depositary of the adoption of the modification." or

"In the event of modification of the Guidelines, Annex – will be modified accordingly with respect to (Contracting Party name) provided that it has made a declaration to that effect to the depositary."

WITHDRAWAL

1.   At any time after five years from the date on which this Agreement has entered into force for a Contracting Party, that Contracting Party may give written notice to the Depositary of its withdrawal from this Agreement.

2.   Any such withdrawal shall take effect on the expiry of six months from the date of the receipt of the notice by the Depositary, or on such later date as may be specified in the notice of withdrawal. If a Contracting Party withdraws, the Agreement shall remain in force for the remaining Contracting Parties.

3.   The provisions of this Agreement shall continue to apply for a period of fifteen years from the date of notification of withdrawal to an investment existing at that date.

DEPOSITARY

The [...............] shall be the Depositary of this Agreement.

STATUS OF ANNEXES

The Annexes to this Agreement are [an integral part of the Agreement].

AUTHENTIC TEXTS

The English and French [and ....] texts of this Agreement are equally authentic.

Denial of Benefits

a. [Subject to prior notification to and consultation with the Contracting Party of the investor,] a Contracting Party may deny the benefits of the Agreement to an investor [as defined in 1 (ii)] and to its investments if investors of a non-Party own or control the first mentioned investor and that investor has no substantial business activities in the territory of the Contracting Party under whose law it is constituted or organised. or

b. [Subject to prior notification and consultation in accordance with Articles XXX (Transparency) and XXX (Consultations), a Contracting Party may deny the benefits of this Agreement to an investor of another Contracting Party that is an enterprise of such Contracting Party and to investments of such investors if investors of a non- Contracting Party own or control the enterprise and the enterprise has no substantial business activities in the territory of the Contracting Party under whose law it is constituted or organised.]

Annex 1
Country Specific Proposals for Draft Texts [...]

Annex 2
Article XX Maintaining the Overall Level of Liberalisation

(1) A Contracting Party intending to take or taking a nonconforming measure under Articles xy, ..., xz ["list B", all general exceptions] shall do so only consistent with the objectives of this Agreement and in accordance with the provisions of this Article. It shall ensure that the overall level of liberalisation is maintained, if necessary through compensatory adjustments.

(2) Compensatory adjustments shall be made on a most-favoured-nation basis.

(3) A Contracting Party shall notify its intent to take such a nonconforming measure to the Parties Group as soon as possible and not later than 3 months before the intended date of implementation of the nonconforming measure. The notification shall contain a description of the nonconforming measure, its likely impact on the overall level of liberalisation and envisaged compensatory adjustments.

(4) At the request of any Contracting Party the benefits of which under this Agreement may be affected by the intended nonconforming measure, the Parties Group shall take up the subject with a view to reaching agreement on any compensatory adjustments necessary to maintain the overall level of liberalisation.

(5) If such agreement is not reached within [...] months, any Contracting Party may, within a further [...] days, refer the matter to an arbitral tribunal in accordance with [Part C of State-State Dispute Settlement Procedures].

(6) The arbitral tribunal may, in its award, state that

(i) the overall level of liberalisation is maintained and no compensatory adjustments are necessary;

(ii) the overall level of liberalisation is not maintained and the compensatory adjustments proposed or implemented are adequate and sufficient; or

(iii) the overall level of liberalisation is not maintained and the compensatory adjustments proposed or implemented by the modifying Contracting Party are inadequate or insufficient.

(7) Necessary procedural rules shall be established by the Parties Group within [...] months after the entry into force of the Agreement.

Annex 3
Chairman's Proposals on Environment and Related Matters and on Labour

1.   The approach to the environment and to labour has evolved to achieve balance between MAI disciplines and other important areas of public policy of concern to MAI Parties and to avoid unintended consequences on normal regulatory practices. Details of the three anchors of preamble, text and association of the OECD Guidelines for Multinational Enterprises, are still under consideration. Annexed to this Chairman's Note is a package of proposals for text on environment and labour that in comprehensive fashion brings together the outstanding aspects of our work.

2.   Some portions of this package of proposals address more general concerns than just environmental or labour implications of the MAI, including the proposal for the national treatment and most favoured nation treatment articles and the proposal for the expropriation and general treatment articles.

ENVIRONMENT AND RELATED MATTERS

3.   The portions of this package of proposals that address environmental concerns in a specific manner are the Preamble, the affirmation of the right of Contracting Parties to regulate in a nondiscriminatory manner, the "not lowering measures" provision and the exception to the performance requirements disciplines.

4.   To respect the need for balance, the proposal for the environmental language in the Preamble seeks as concise a formulation as possible while making the key explicit references. Any additional proposals for preambular language currently before the Negotiating Group could be reconsidered in the context of a political declaration or associated with the MAI in some other way.

5.   The inclusion of "in like circumstances" in the national treatment and most favoured nation treatment provisions, plus the interpretative note, would address concerns about the practical implementation of the "de facto" discrimination principle and preserve the necessary scope for nondiscriminatory regulation.

6.   A specific affirmation that the MAI does not inhibit normal non-discriminatory government regulatory activity seems necessary in the environmental field. Combined with the other elements of this package of proposals, this represents a targeted approach. Another approach would be a general exception inspired by GATT Article XX, which would eliminate the need for some other elements of this package, notably the exception to the provisions on performance requirements.

7.   The proposal for binding "not lowering measures" language is limited to domestic measures and the circumstances of a particular investment. The interpretative note spells out the widely-shared views that governments must have the ability to adjust their overall environmental standards over time, and that investment should not be enticed by relaxing standards. Further consideration of the implications of binding language for the dispute settlement procedures may be required.

8.   The proposal for an interpretative note for the expropriation and general treatment articles responds to the agreement at the High Level Meeting that it needs to be made clear that the MAI will not inhibit the exercise of the normal regulatory powers of government and that the exercise of such powers will not amount to expropriation.

9.   The exception article for the provisions on performance requirements is needed because they go beyond non-discrimination. The exception covers those performance requirements that could affect compliance with laws and regulations, or that could affect health, safety or the environment.

10.   The package of proposals includes annexation of the OECD Guidelines to the text of the MAI, without changing their non-binding character.

LABOUR

11. The portions of this package of proposals that address labour concerns in a specific manner are the Preamble and the binding "not lowering measures" provision.

12. As with environment, the proposal sets out a concise formulation that maintains the key explicit references supported by the large majority of MAI Parties. As with environment, any additional proposals for preambular language currently before the Negotiating Group could be reconsidered in the context of a political declaration or associated with the MAI in some other way.

13. The inclusion of "in like circumstances" in the national treatment and most favoured nation treatment provisions, plus the interpretative note, would address concerns about the practical implementation of the "de facto" discrimination principle and preserve the necessary scope for nondiscriminatory regulation. This could be as true for labour concerns as for environmental concerns.

14. A specific affirmation that the MAI does not inhibit normal non-discriminatory government regulatory activity, to the extent that it addresses health and safety concerns, could cover measures that set labour standards.

15. The proposal for binding "not lowering measures" language is limited to domestic measures and the circumstances of a particular investment. "Domestic" is chosen as the main qualifier because approaches to "core" or "core international" labour standards appear to vary greatly among MAI Parties. "Measures" has been chosen for consistency with MAI drafting where there is a need to refer to the means by which governments take action (by domestic legislation, regulation, directives, policy, etc). The interpretative note spells out the widely-shared views that governments must have the ability to adjust their overall labour market policies as appropriate over time, and that investment should not be enticed by relaxing standards. Further consideration of the implications of binding language for dispute settlement may be required.

16. As stated above, the exception article for the provisions on performance requirements is needed because they go beyond the non-discrimination. The exception covers performance requirements that could affect compliance with laws and regulations, or that could affect health, safety or the environment.

17. Finally, the package of proposals includes annexation of the OECD Guidelines to the text of the MAI, without changing their non-binding character.

Annex 4

Package of Proposals for Text on Environment and Labour

1.   Preamble

"Recognising that investment, as an engine of economic growth, can play a key role in ensuring that economic growth is sustainable, when accompanied by appropriate environmental and labour policies;

"Re-affirming their commitment to the Rio Declaration on Environment and Development, and Agenda 21 and the Programme for its Further Implementation, including the principles of the polluter pays and the precautionary approach; and resolving to implement this Agreement in a manner consistent with sustainable development and with environmental protection and conservation;

"Renewing their commitment to the Copenhagen Declaration of the World Summit on Social Development and the observance of internationally recognised core labour standards, i.e., freedom of association, the right to organise and bargain collectively, prohibition of forced labour, the elimination of exploitative forms of child labour, and non-discrimination in employment, and noting that the International Labour Organisation is the competent body to set and deal with core labour standards worldwide;"

2. National Treatment and Most Favoured Nation Treatment

"1. Each Contracting Party shall accord to investors of another Contracting Party and to their investments, treatment no less favourable that the treatment it accords in like circumstances to its own investors and their investments with respect to the establishment, acquisition, expansion, operation, management, maintenance, use, enjoyment and sale or other disposition of investments.

2. Each Contracting Party shall accord to investors of another Contracting Party and to their investments, treatment no less favourable that the treatment it accords in like circumstances to investors of any other Contracting Party or of a non-Contracting Party, and to the investments of investors of any other Contracting Party or of a non- Contracting Party, with respect to the establishment, acquisition, expansion, operation, management, maintenance, use, enjoyment and sale or other disposition of investments.

3. Each Contracting Party shall accord to investors of another Contracting Party and to their investments the better of the treatment required by Articles 1.1 and 1.2, whichever is the more favourable to those investors or investments.

3. Affirmation of Right to Regulate

"A Contracting Party may adopt, maintain or enforce any measure that it considers appropriate to ensure that investment activity is undertaken in a manner sensitive to health, safety or environmental concerns, provided such measures are consistent with this agreement."

4. "Not Lowering Measures"

"A Contracting Party shall not waive or otherwise derogate from, or offer to waive or otherwise derogate from, its domestic health, safety, environmental, or labour measures, as an encouragement to the establishment, acquisition, expansion, operation, management, maintenance, use, enjoyment and sale or other disposition of an investment of an investor."

5. Expropriation and General Treatment

"1. GENERAL TREATMENT

1. Each Contracting Party shall accord to investments in its territory of investors of another Contracting Party fair and equitable treatment and full and constant protection and security. Such treatment shall also apply to the operation, management, maintenance, use, enjoyment or disposal of such investments. In no such case shall a Contracting Party accord treatment less favourable than that required by international law.

"2. EXPROPRIATION AND COMPENSATION

"1. A Contracting Party shall not expropriate or nationalise an investment in its territory of an investor of another Contracting Party or take any measure tantamount to expropriation or nationalisation except: ..."

6. Performance Requirements

"4. Provided that such measures are not applied in an arbitrary or unjustifiable manner, or do not constitute a disguised restriction on investment, nothing in paragraphs 1(b) and 1(c) shall be construed to prevent any Contracting Party from adopting or maintaining measures, including environmental measures:

(a) necessary to secure compliance with measures that are not inconsistent with the provisions of this Agreement;

(b) necessary to protect human, animal or plant life or health; or

(c) necessary for the conservation of living or non-living exhaustible natural resources."

7. OECD Guidelines for Multinational Enterprises

The OECD Guidelines for Multinational Enterprises will be annexed to the text of the MAI.

VII. Relevant International Labor Treaties and Conventions

VII.1. 1998 ILO DECLARATION ON FUNDAMENTAL PRINCIPLES AND RIGHTS AT WORK[1]

Preamble

Whereas the ILO was founded in the conviction that social justice is essential to universal and lasting peace;

Whereas economic growth is essential but not sufficient to ensure equity, social progress and the eradication of poverty, confirming the need for the ILO to promote strong social policies, justice and democratic institutions;

Whereas the ILO should, now more than ever, draw upon all its standard-setting, technical co-operation and research resources in all its areas of competence, in particular employment, vocational training and working conditions, to ensure that, in the context of a global strategy for economic and social development, economic and social policies are mutually reinforcing components in order to create broad-based sustainable development

Whereas the ILO should give special attention to the problems of persons with special social needs, particularly the unemployed and migrant workers, and mobilize and encourage international, regional and national efforts aimed at resolving their problems, and promote effective policies aimed at job creation;

Whereas, in seeking to maintain the link between social progress and economic growth, the guarantee of fundamental principles and rights at work is of particular significance in that it enables the persons concerned to claim freely and on the basis of equality of opportunity their fair share of the wealth which they have helped to generate, and to achieve fully their human potential;

Whereas the ILO is the constitutionally mandated international organization and the competent body to set and deal with international labour standards, and enjoys universal support and acknowledgement in promoting fundamental rights at work as the expression of its constitutional principles;

Whereas it is urgent, in a situation of growing economic interdependence, to reaffirm the immutable nature of the fundamental principles and rights embodied in the Constitution of the Organization and to promote their universal application;

The International Labour Conference

1. Recalls:

(a) that in freely joining the ILO, all Members have endorsed the principles and rights set out in its Constitution and in the Declaration of Philadelphia, and have undertaken to work towards attaining the overall objectives of the Organization to the best of their resources and fully in line with their specific circumstances;

(b) that these principles and rights have been expressed and developed in the form of specific rights and obligations in Conventions recognized as fundamental both inside and outside the Organization.

2. Declares that all Members, even if they have not ratified the Conventions in question, have an obligation arising from the very fact of membership in the Organization, to respect, to

---

1   See https://www.ilo.org/declaration/lang--en/index.htm.

promote and to realize, in good faith and in accordance with the Constitution, the principles concerning the fundamental rights which are the subject of those Conventions, namely:

(a)   freedom of association and the effective recognition of the right to collective bargaining;

(b)   the elimination of all forms of forced or compulsory labour;

(c)   the effective abolition of child labour; and

(d)   the elimination of discrimination in respect of employment and occupation.

3.   Recognizes the obligation on the Organization to assist its Members, in response to their established and expressed needs, in order to attain these objectives by making full use of its constitutional, operational and budgetary resources, including by the mobilization of external resources and support, as well as by encouraging other international organizations with which the ILO has established relations, pursuant to article 12 of its Constitution, to support these efforts:

(a)   by offering technical cooperation and advisory services to promote the ratification and implementation of the fundamental Conventions;

(b)   by assisting those Members not yet in a position to ratify some or all of these Conventions in their efforts to respect, to promote and to realize the principles concerning fundamental rights which are the subject of those Conventions; and

(c)   by helping the Members in their efforts to create a climate for economic and social development.

4.   Decides that, to give full effect to this Declaration, a promotional follow-up, which is meaningful and effective, shall be implemented in accordance with the measures specified in the annex hereto, which shall be considered as an integral part of this Declaration.

5.   Stresses that labour standards should not be used for protectionist trade purposes, and that nothing in this Declaration and its follow-up shall be invoked or otherwise used for such purposes; in addition, the comparative advantage of any country should in no way be called into question by this Declaration and its follow-up.

Annex: Follow-up to the Declaration

I. Overall Purpose

1.   The aim of the follow-up described below is to encourage the efforts made by the Members of the Organization to promote the fundamental principles and rights enshrined in the Constitution of the ILO and the Declaration of Philadelphia and reaffirmed in this Declaration.

2.   In line with this objective, which is of a strictly promotional nature, this follow-up will allow the identification of areas in which the assistance of the Organization through its technical cooperation activities may prove useful to its Members to help them implement these fundamental principles and rights. It is not a substitute for the established supervisory mechanisms, nor shall it impede their functioning; consequently, specific situations within the purview of those mechanisms shall not be examined or re-examined within the framework of this follow-up.

3.   The two aspects of this follow-up, described below, are based on existing procedures: the annual follow-up concerning non-ratified fundamental Conventions will entail merely some adaptation of the present modalities of application of article 19, paragraph 5(e) of the Constitution; and the Global Report on the effect given to the promotion of the fundamental principles and rights at work will serve to inform the recurrent discussion at the Conference on the needs of the Members, the ILO action undertaken, and the results achieved in the promotion of the fundamental principles and rights at work.

II. Annual Follow-up Concerning Non-Ratified Fundamental Conventions

A.   Purpose and Scope

1.   The purpose is to provide an opportunity to review each year, by means of simplified procedures, the efforts made in accordance with the Declaration by Members which have not yet ratified all the fundamental Conventions.

2.   The follow-up will cover the four areas of fundamental principles and rights specified in the Declaration.

B.   Modalities

1.   The follow-up will be based on reports requested from Members under article 19, paragraph 5(e) of the Constitution. The report forms will be drawn up so as to obtain information from governments which have not ratified one or more of the fundamental Conventions, on any changes which may have taken place in their law and practice, taking due account of article 23 of the Constitution and established practice.

2.   These reports, as compiled by the Office, will be reviewed by the Governing Body.

3.   Adjustments to the Governing Body's existing procedures should be examined to allow Members which are not represented on the Governing Body to provide, in the most appropriate way, clarifications which might prove necessary or useful during Governing Body discussions to supplement the information contained in their reports.

III. Global Report on Fundamental Principles and Rights at Work

A.   Purpose and Scope

1.   The purpose of this report is to provide a dynamic global picture relating to the four categories of fundamental principles and rights at work noted during the preceding four-year period, and to serve as a basis for assessing the effectiveness of the assistance provided by the Organization, and for determining priorities for the following period, including in the form of action plans for technical cooperation designed in particular to mobilize the internal and external resources necessary to carry them out.

B.   Modalities

1.   The report will be drawn up under the responsibility of the Director-General on the basis of official information, or information gathered and assessed in accordance with established procedures. In the case of States which have not ratified the fundamental Conventions, it will be based in particular on the findings of the aforementioned annual follow-up. In the case of Members which have ratified the Conventions concerned, the report will be based in particular on reports as dealt with pursuant to article 22 of the Constitution. It will also refer to the experience gained from technical cooperation and other relevant activities of the ILO.

2.   This report will be submitted to the Conference for a recurrent discussion on the strategic objective of fundamental principles and rights at work based on the modalities agreed by the Governing Body. It will then be for the Conference to draw conclusions from this discussion on all available ILO means of action, including the priorities and plans of action for technical cooperation to be implemented for the following period, and to guide the Governing Body and the Office in their responsibilities.

IV. It Is Understood That:

1.   The Conference shall, in due course, review the operation of this follow-up in the light of the experience acquired to assess whether it has adequately fulfilled the overall purpose articulated in Part I.

VII.2. 2008 ILO DECLARATION ON SOCIAL JUSTICE FOR A FAIR GLOBALIZATION

adopted by the International Labour Conference, Geneva, 10 June 2008[1]

The International Labour Conference, meeting in Geneva on the occasion of its Ninety-seventh Session,

Considering that the present context of globalization, characterized by the diffusion of new technologies, the flow of ideas, the exchange of goods and services, the increase in capital and financial flows, the internationalization of business and business processes and dialogue as well as the movement of persons, especially working women and men, is reshaping the world of work in profound ways:

–   on the one hand, the process of economic cooperation and integration has helped a number of countries to benefit from high rates of economic growth and employment creation, to absorb many of the rural poor into the modern urban economy, to advance their developmental goals, and to foster innovation in product development and the circulation of ideas;

–   on the other hand, global economic integration has caused many countries and sectors to face major challenges of income inequality, continuing high levels of unemployment and poverty, vulnerability of economies to external shocks, and the growth of both unprotected work and the informal economy, which impact on the employment relationship and the protections it can offer;

Recognizing that achieving an improved and fair outcome for all has become even more necessary in these circumstances to meet the universal aspiration for social justice, to reach full employment, to ensure the sustainability of open societies and the global economy, to achieve social cohesion and to combat poverty and rising inequalities;

Convinced that the International Labour Organization has a key role to play in helping to promote and achieve progress and social justice in a constantly changing environment:

–   based on the mandate contained in the ILO Constitution, including the Declaration of Philadelphia (1944), which continues to be fully relevant in the twenty-first century and should inspire the policy of its Members and which, among other aims, purposes and principles:

•   affirms that labour is not a commodity and that poverty anywhere constitutes a danger to prosperity everywhere;

•   recognizes that the ILO has the solemn obligation to further among the nations of the world programmes which will achieve the objectives of full employment and the raising of standards of living, a minimum living wage and the extension of social security measures to provide a basic income to all in need, along with all the other objectives set out in the Declaration of Philadelphia;

•   provides the ILO with the responsibility to examine and consider all international economic and financial policies in the light of the fundamental objective of social justice; and

–   drawing on and reaffirming the ILO Declaration on Fundamental Principles and Rights at Work and its Follow-up (1998) in which Members recognized, in the discharge of the Organization's mandate, the particular significance of the fundamental rights, namely:

---

1   See https://www.ilo.org/global/meetings-and-events/campaigns/voices-on-social-jus-
      tice/WCMS_099766/lang--en/index.htm

freedom of association and the effective recognition of the right to collective bargaining, the elimination of all forms of forced or compulsory labour, the effective abolition of child labour, and the elimination of discrimination in respect of employment and occupation;

Encouraged by the international community's recognition of Decent Work as an effective response to the challenges of globalization, having regard to:

- the outcomes of the 1995 World Summit for Social Development in Copenhagen;

- the wide support, repeatedly expressed at global and regional levels, for the decent work concept developed by the ILO; and

- the endorsement by Heads of State and Government at the 2005 World Summit of the United Nations of fair globalization and the goals of full and productive employment and decent work for all, as central objectives of their relevant national and international policies;

Convinced that in a world of growing interdependence and complexity and the internationalization of production:

- the fundamental values of freedom, human dignity, social justice, security and non-discrimination are essential for sustainable economic and social development and efficiency;

- social dialogue and the practice of tripartism between governments and the representative organizations of workers and employers within and across borders are now more relevant to achieving solutions and to building up social cohesion and the rule of law through, among other means, international labour standards;

- the importance of the employment relationship should be recognized as a means of providing legal protection to workers;

- productive, profitable and sustainable enterprises, together with a strong social economy and a viable public sector, are critical to sustainable economic development and employment opportunities; and

- the Tripartite Declaration of Principles concerning Multinational Enterprises and Social Policy (1977), as revised, which addresses the growing role of such actors in the realization of the Organization's objectives, has particular relevance; and

Recognizing that the present challenges call for the Organization to intensify its efforts and to mobilize all its means of action to promote its constitutional objectives, and that, to make these efforts effective and strengthen the ILO's capacity to assist its Members' efforts to reach the ILO's objectives in the context of globalization, the Organization must:

- ensure coherence and collaboration in its approach to advancing its development of a global and integrated approach, in line with the Decent Work Agenda and the four strategic objectives of the ILO, drawing upon the synergies among them;

- adapt its institutional practices and governance to improve effectiveness and efficiency while fully respecting the existing constitutional framework and procedures;

- assist constituents to meet the needs they have expressed at country level based on full tripartite discussion, through the provision of high-quality information, advice and technical programmes that help them meet those needs in the context of the ILO's constitutional objectives; and

- promote the ILO's standard-setting policy as a cornerstone of ILO activities by enhancing its relevance to the world of work, and ensure the role of standards as a useful means of achieving the constitutional objectives of the Organization;

Therefore adopts this tenth day of June of the year two thousand and eight the present Declaration.

I. Scope and Principles

The Conference recognizes and declares that:

A.   In the context of accelerating change, the commitments and efforts of Members and the Organization to implement the ILO's constitutional mandate, including through international labour standards, and to place full and productive employment and decent work at the centre of economic and social policies, should be based on the four equally important strategic objectives of the ILO, through which the Decent Work Agenda is expressed and which can be summarized as follows:

(i)   promoting employment by creating a sustainable institutional and economic environment in which:

- individuals can develop and update the necessary capacities and skills they need to enable them to be productively occupied for their personal fulfilment and the common well-being;

- all enterprises, public or private, are sustainable to enable growth and the generation of greater employment and income opportunities and prospects for all; and

- societies can achieve their goals of economic development, good living standards and social progress;

(ii) developing and enhancing measures of social protection – social security and labour protection – which are sustainable and adapted to national circumstances, including:

- the extension of social security to all, including measures to provide basic income to all in need of such protection, and adapting its scope and coverage to meet the new needs and uncertainties generated by the rapidity of technological, societal, demographic and economic changes;

- healthy and safe working conditions; and

- policies in regard to wages and earnings, hours and other conditions of work, designed to ensure a just share of the fruits of progress to all and a minimum living wage to all employed and in need of such protection;

(iii) promoting social dialogue and tripartism as the most appropriate methods for:

- adapting the implementation of the strategic objectives to the needs and circumstances of each country;

- translating economic development into social progress, and social progress into economic development;

- facilitating consensus building on relevant national and international policies that impact on employment and decent work strategies and programmes; and

- making labour law and institutions effective, including in respect of the recognition of the employment relationship, the promotion of good industrial relations and the building of effective labour inspection systems; and

(iv) respecting, promoting and realizing the fundamental principles and rights at work, which are of particular significance, as both rights and enabling conditions that are necessary for the full realization of all of the strategic objectives, noting:

- that freedom of association and the effective recognition of the right to collective bargaining are particularly important to enable the attainment of the four strategic objectives; and

- that the violation of fundamental principles and rights at work cannot be invoked or otherwise used as a legitimate comparative advantage and that labour standards should not be used for protectionist trade purposes.

B.   The four strategic objectives are inseparable, interrelated and mutually supportive. The failure to promote any one of them would harm progress towards the others. To optimize their impact, efforts to promote them should be part of an ILO global and integrated strategy for decent work. Gender equality and non-discrimination must be considered to be cross-cutting issues in the abovementioned strategic objectives.

C.   How Members achieve the strategic objectives is a question that must be determined by each Member subject to its existing international obligations and the fundamental principles and rights at work with due regard, among others, to:

(i)   the national conditions and circumstances, and needs as well as priorities expressed by representative organizations of employers and workers;

(ii) the interdependence, solidarity and cooperation among all Members of the ILO that are more pertinent than ever in the context of a global economy; and

(iii) the principles and provisions of international labour standards.

II. Method of Implementation

The Conference further recognizes that, in a globalized economy:

A.   The implementation of Part I of this Declaration requires that the ILO effectively assist its Members in their efforts. To that end, the Organization should review and adapt its institutional practices to enhance governance and capacity building in order to make the best use of its human and financial resources and of the unique advantage of its tripartite structure and standards system, with a view to:

(i)   better understanding its Members' needs, with respect to each of the strategic objectives, as well as past ILO action to meet them in the framework of a recurring item on the agenda of the Conference, so as to:

   –   determine how the ILO can more efficiently address these needs through coordinated use of all its means of action;

   –   determine the necessary resources to address these needs and, if appropriate, to attract additional resources; and

   –   guide the Governing Body and the Office in their responsibilities;

(ii) strengthening and streamlining its technical cooperation and expert advice in order to:

   –   support and assist efforts by individual Members to make progress on a tripartite basis towards all the strategic objectives, through country programmes for decent work, where appropriate, and within the framework of the United Nations system; and

   –   help, wherever necessary, the institutional capacity of member States, as well as representative organizations of employers and workers, to facilitate meaningful and coherent social policy and sustainable development;

(iii) promoting shared knowledge and understanding of the synergies between the strategic objectives through empirical analysis and tripartite discussion of concrete experiences, with the voluntary cooperation of countries concerned, and with a view to informing Members' decision-making in relation to the opportunities and challenges of globalization;

(iv) upon request, providing assistance to Members who wish to promote strategic objectives jointly within the framework of bilateral or multilateral agreements, subject to their compatibility with ILO obligations; and

(v)   developing new partnerships with non-state entities and economic actors, such as multinational enterprises and trade unions operating at the global sectoral level in order to enhance the effectiveness of ILO operational programmes and activities, enlist their support in any appropriate way, and otherwise promote the ILO strategic objectives. This will be done in consultation with representative national and international organizations of workers and employers.

B.   At the same time, Members have a key responsibility to contribute, through their social and economic policy, to the realization of a global and integrated strategy for the implementation of the strategic objectives, which encompass the Decent Work Agenda outlined in Part I of this Declaration. Implementation of the Decent Work Agenda at national level will depend on national needs and priorities and it will be for member States, in consultation with the representative organizations of workers and employers, to determine how to discharge that responsibility. To that end, they may consider, among other steps:

(i)   the adoption of a national or regional strategy for decent work, or both, targeting a set of priorities for the integrated pursuit of the strategic objectives;

(ii)   the establishment of appropriate indicators or statistics, if necessary with the assistance of the ILO, to monitor and evaluate the progress made;

(iii)   the review of their situation as regards the ratification or implementation of ILO instruments with a view to achieving a progressively increasing coverage of each of the strategic objectives, with special emphasis on the instruments classified as core labour standards as well as those regarded as most significant from the viewpoint of governance covering tripartism, employment policy and labour inspection;

(iv)   the taking of appropriate steps for an adequate coordination between positions taken on behalf of the member State concerned in relevant international forums and any steps they may take under the present Declaration;

(v)   the promotion of sustainable enterprises;

(vi)   where appropriate, sharing national and regional good practice gained from the successful implementation of national or regional initiatives with a decent work element; and

(vii) the provision on a bilateral, regional or multilateral basis, in so far as their resources permit, of appropriate support to other Members' efforts to give effect to the principles and objectives referred to in this Declaration.

C.   Other international and regional organizations with mandates in closely related fields can have an important contribution to make to the implementation of the integrated approach. The ILO should invite them to promote decent work, bearing in mind that each agency will have full control of its mandate. As trade and financial market policy both affect employment, it is the ILO's role to evaluate those employment effects to achieve its aim of placing employment at the heart of economic policies.

III. Final Provisions

A.   The Director-General of the International Labour Office will ensure that the present Declaration is communicated to all Members and, through them, to representative organizations of employers and workers, to international organizations with competence in related fields at the international and regional levels, and to such other entities as the Governing Body may identify. Governments, as well as employers' and workers' organizations at the national level, shall make the Declaration known in all relevant forums where they may participate or be represented, or otherwise disseminate it to any other entities that may be concerned.

B.   The Governing Body and the Director-General of the International Labour Office will have the responsibility for establishing appropriate modalities for the expeditious implementation of Part II of this Declaration.

C.   At such time(s) as the Governing Body may find appropriate, and in accordance with modalities to be established, the impact of the present Declaration, and in particular the steps taken to promote its implementation, will be the object of a review by the International Labour Conference with a view to assessing what action might be appropriate.

VII.3. 1977 TRIPARTITE DECLARATION OF PRINCIPLES CONCERNING MULTINATIONAL ENTERPRISES AND SOCIAL POLICY

Adopted by the Governing Body of the International Labour Office at its 204th Session

(Geneva, November 1977) and amended at its 279th (November 2000), 295th (March 2006) and 329th (March 2017) Sessions[1]

The International Labour Organization (ILO), with its unique tripartite structure, its competence, and its long-standing experience in the social field, has an essential role to play in evolving principles for the guidance of governments, employers' and workers' organizations, and multinational enterprises themselves.

The Governing Body of the International Labour Office approved the Tripartite Declaration of Principles concerning Multinational Enterprises and Social Policy at its 204th Session (November 1977) and subsequently amended it at its 279th Session (November 2000) and 295th Session (March 2006). The Governing Body decides at its 329th Session (March 2017) to further amend the Declaration taking account of developments since the previous update in 2006 within the ILO such as the ILO Declaration on Social Justice for a Fair Globalization, adopted by the International Labour Conference (ILC) in 2008, new international labour standards, the ILC Conclusions concerning the promotion of sustainable enterprises (2007) and the ILC Conclusions concerning decent work in global supply chains (2016); as well as the Guiding Principles on Business and Human Rights: Implementing the United Nations "Protect, Respect and Remedy" Framework (2011) and the goals and targets of the 2030 Agenda for Sustainable Development (2015) that are particularly relevant to the Declaration; and noting the Addis Ababa Action Agenda (2015) on financing for development, the Paris Agreement (2015) concerning climate change, and the OECD Guidelines for Multinational Enterprises (as revised in 2011). The Governing Body approves the following revised Tripartite Declaration of Principles concerning Multinational Enterprises and Social Policy, which may be cited as the MNE Declaration, and invites governments of States Members of the ILO, the employers' and workers' organizations concerned and the multinational enterprises operating in their territories to observe the principles embodied therein.

Aim and Scope

1.   Multinational enterprises play an important part in the economies of most countries and in international economic relations. This is of increasing interest to governments as well as to employers and workers and their respective organizations. Through international direct investment, trade and other means, such enterprises can bring substantial benefits to home and host countries by contributing to the more efficient utilization of capital, technology and labour. Within the framework of sustainable development policies established by governments, they can also make an important contribution to the promotion of economic and social welfare; to the improvement of living standards and the satisfaction of basic needs; to the creation of employment opportunities, both directly and indirectly; and to the enjoyment of human rights, including freedom of association, throughout the world. On the other hand, the advances made by multinational enterprises in organizing their operations beyond the national framework may lead to abuse of concentrations of economic power and to conflicts with national policy objectives and with the interest of the workers. In addition, the complexity of multinational enterprises and the difficulty of clearly perceiving their diverse structures, operations and policies sometimes give rise to concern either in the home or in the host countries, or in both.

---

1   See https://www.ilo.org/empent/areas/mne-declaration/lang--en/index.htm.

2.   The aim of this Declaration is to encourage the positive contribution which multinational enterprises can make to economic and social progress and the realization of decent work for all; and to minimize and resolve the difficulties to which their various operations may give rise.

3.   This aim will be furthered by appropriate laws and policies, measures and actions adopted by the governments, including in the fields of labour administration and public labour inspection, and by cooperation among the governments and the employers' and workers' organizations of all countries.

4.   The principles of this Declaration are intended to guide governments, employers' and workers' organizations of home and host countries and multinational enterprises in taking measures and actions and adopting social policies, including those based on the principles laid down in the Constitution and the relevant Conventions and Recommendations of the ILO, to further social progress and decent work.

5.   These principles do not aim at introducing or maintaining inequalities of treatment between multinational and national enterprises. They reflect good practice for all. Multinational and national enterprises, wherever the principles of the MNE Declaration are relevant to both, should be subject to the same expectations in respect of their conduct in general and their social practices in particular.

6.   To serve its purpose the MNE Declaration does not require a precise legal definition of multinational enterprises; this paragraph is designed to facilitate the understanding of the Declaration and not to provide such a definition. Multinational enterprises include enterprises – whether fully or partially state-owned or privately owned – which own or control production, distribution, services or other facilities outside the country in which they are based. They may be large or small; and can have their headquarters in any part of the world. The degree of autonomy of entities within multinational enterprises in relation to each other varies widely from one such enterprise to another, depending on the nature of the links between such entities and their fields of activity and having regard to the great diversity in the form of ownership, in the size, in the nature and location of the operations of the enterprises concerned. Unless otherwise specified, the term "multinational enterprise" is used in this Declaration to designate the various entities (parent companies or local entities or both or the organization as a whole) according to the distribution of responsibilities among them, in the expectation that they will cooperate and provide assistance to one another as necessary to facilitate observance of the principles laid down in this Declaration. In that regard, it also recognizes that multinational enterprises often operate through relationships with other enterprises as part of their overall production process and, as such, can contribute to further the aim of this Declaration.

7.   This Declaration sets out principles in the fields of employment, training, conditions of work and life, and industrial relations which governments, employers' and workers' organizations and multinational enterprises are recommended to observe on a voluntary basis; its principles shall not limit or otherwise affect obligations arising out of ratification of any ILO Convention.

General Policies

8.   All the parties concerned by the MNE Declaration should respect the sovereign rights of States, obey the national laws and regulations, give due consideration to local practices and respect relevant international standards. They should also honour commitments which they have freely entered into, in conformity with the national law and accepted international obligations. They should respect the Universal Declaration of Human Rights (1948) and the corresponding International Covenants (1966) adopted by the General Assembly of the United Nations as well as the Constitution of the International Labour Organisation and its principles according to which freedom of expression and association are essential to sustained progress.

9.   All parties should contribute to the realization of the ILO Declaration on Fundamental Principles and Rights at Work and its Follow-up, adopted in 1998. All Members, even if they have

not ratified the fundamental Conventions in question, have an obligation, arising from the very fact of membership in the Organization, to respect, to promote and to realize, in good faith and in accordance with the Constitution, the principles concerning the fundamental rights which are the subject of those Conventions, namely:

(a)   freedom of association and the effective recognition of the right to collective bargaining;

(b)   the elimination of all forms of forced or compulsory labour;

(c)   the effective abolition of child labour; and

(d)   the elimination of discrimination in respect of employment and occupation.

Governments of States which have not yet ratified the Conventions concerning fundamental principles and rights at work recognized in the 1998 Declaration are urged to do so. Multinational enterprises, through their operations, can contribute significantly to the attainment of its objectives.

10. The principles set out in the MNE Declaration are commended to governments, employers' and workers' organizations of home and host countries and to multinational enterprises themselves. The principles thereby reflect the fact that different actors have a specific role to play. In this regard for the purpose of this Declaration:

a.   The Guiding Principles on Business and Human Rights: Implementing the United Nations "Protect, Respect and Remedy" Framework (2011) outline the respective duties and responsibilities of States and enterprises on human rights. These principles are grounded in recognition of:

(i)   States' existing obligations to respect, protect and fulfil human rights and fundamental freedoms ("the State duty to protect human rights");

(ii)   the role of enterprises as specialized organs of society performing specialized functions, required to comply with all applicable laws and to respect human rights ("the corporate responsibility to respect human rights"); and

(iii) the need for rights and obligations to be matched to appropriate and effective remedies when breached ("Access to remedy").

b.   The Guiding Principles apply to all States and to all enterprises, both multinational and others, regardless of their size, sector, operational context, ownership and structure.

c.   The corporate responsibility to respect human rights requires that enterprises, including multinational enterprises wherever they operate:

(i)   avoid causing or contributing to adverse impacts through their own activities, and address such impacts when they occur; and

(ii)   seek to prevent or mitigate adverse human rights impacts that are directly linked to their operations, products or services by their business relationships, even if they have not contributed to those impacts.

d.   Enterprises, including multinational enterprises, should carry out due diligence to identify, prevent, mitigate and account for how they address their actual and potential adverse impacts that relate to internationally recognized human rights, understood, at a minimum, as those expressed in the International Bill of Human Rights and the principles concerning fundamental rights set out in the ILO Declaration on Fundamental Principles and Rights at Work.

e.   In order to gauge human rights risks, enterprises – including multinational enterprises – should identify and assess any actual or potential adverse human rights impacts with which they may be involved either through their own activities or as a result of their business relationships. This process should involve meaningful consultation with potentially affected groups and other relevant stakeholders including workers' organizations, as appropriate to the size of the enterprise and the nature and context of the operation. For the purpose of achieving the aim of the MNE Declaration, this process should take account of the central role of freedom of association and collective bargaining as well as industrial relations and social dialogue as an ongoing process.

11. Multinational enterprises should take fully into account established general policy objectives of the countries in which they operate. Their activities should be consistent with national law and in harmony with the development priorities and social aims and structure of the country in which they operate. To this effect, consultations should be held between multinational enterprises, the government and, wherever appropriate, the national employers' and workers' organizations concerned.

12. Governments of host countries should promote good social practice in accordance with this Declaration among multinational enterprises operating in their territories. Governments of home countries should promote good social practice in accordance with this Declaration among their multinational enterprises operating abroad, having regard to the social and labour law, regulations and practices in host countries as well as to relevant international standards. Both host and home country governments should be prepared to have consultations with each other, whenever the need arises, on the initiative of either.

Employment

Employment Promotion

13. With a view to stimulating sustainable economic growth and development, raising living standards, meeting employment requirements and overcoming unemployment and under-employment, governments should declare and pursue, as a major goal, an active policy designed to promote full, productive and freely chosen employment, and decent work.

14. This is particularly important in the case of host country governments where the problems of unemployment and underemployment are most serious, and in particular in developing areas of the world. In this connection, the Global Employment Agenda (2003), the ILC Conclusions concerning the promotion of sustainable enterprises (2007), the Global Jobs Pact (2009) and Goal 8 of the Sustainable Development Goals should be kept in mind.

15. Paragraphs 13 and 14 above establish the framework within which due attention should be paid, in both home and host countries, to the employment impact of multinational enterprises.

16. Multinational enterprises, particularly when operating in developing countries, should endeavour to increase employment opportunities and standards, taking into account the employment policies and objectives of the governments, as well as security of employment and the long-term development of the enterprise.

17. Before starting operations, multinational enterprises should, wherever appropriate, consult the competent authorities and the national employers' and workers' organizations in order to keep their employment plans, as far as practicable, in harmony with national social development policies. Such consultation, as in the case of national enterprises, should continue between the multinational enterprises and all parties concerned, including the workers' organizations.

18. Multinational enterprises should give priority to the employment, occupational develop-ment, promotion and advancement of nationals of the host country at all levels in cooperation, as appropriate, with representatives of the workers employed by them or of the organizations of these workers and governmental authorities.

19. Multinational enterprises, when investing in developing countries, should have regard to the importance of using technologies which generate employment, both directly and indirectly. To the extent permitted by the nature of the process and the conditions prevailing in the economic sector concerned, they should adapt technologies to the needs and characteristics of the host

countries. They should also, where possible, take part in the development of appropriate technology in host countries.

20. To promote employment in developing countries, in the context of an expanding world economy, multinational enterprises, wherever practicable, should give consideration to the conclusion of contracts with national enterprises for the manufacture of parts and equipment, to the use of local raw materials and to the progressive promotion of the local processing of raw materials. Such arrangements should not be used by multinational enterprises to avoid the responsibilities embodied in the principles of this Declaration.

21. Governments should develop and implement an integrated policy framework to facilitate the transition to the formal economy, recognizing that decent work deficits are most pronounced in the informal economy. Multinational and other enterprises should also contribute to this aim.

Social Security

22. Governments should establish and maintain, as applicable, social protection floors as a fundamental element of their national social security systems; and implement social protection floors within strategies for the extension of social security that progressively ensure higher levels of social security to as many people as possible, guided by ILO social security standards. Social partners could play a role in promoting these policies. Multinational and other enterprises could complement public social security systems and help to stimulate further their development, including through their own employer-sponsored programmes.

Elimination of Forced or Compulsory Labour

23. Governments should take effective measures to prevent and eliminate forced labour, to provide to victims protection and access to appropriate and effective remedies, such as compensation and rehabilitation, and to sanction the perpetrators of forced or compulsory labour. Governments should develop a national policy and plan of action, in consultation with employers' and workers' organizations. This shall involve systematic action by the competent authorities and, as appropriate, in coordination with employers' and workers' organizations, as well as with other groups concerned.

24. In order to suppress forced or compulsory labour, governments should provide guidance and support to employers and enterprises to take effective measures to identify, prevent, mitigate and account for how they address the risks of forced and compulsory labour in their operations or in products, services or operations in which they may be directly linked.

25. Multinational as well as national enterprises should take immediate and effective measures within their own competence to secure the prohibition and elimination of forced or compulsory labour in their operations.

Effective Abolition of Child Labour: Minimum Age and Worst Forms

26. Governments should develop a national policy designed to ensure the effective abolition of child labour; take immediate and effective measures to secure the prohibition and elimination of the worst forms of child labour as a matter of urgency; and progressively raise the minimum age for admission to employment or work to a level consistent with the fullest physical and mental development of young persons.

27. Multinational enterprises, as well as national enterprises, should respect the minimum age for admission to employment or work in order to secure the effective abolition of child labour in their operations and should take immediate and effective measures within their own competence to secure the prohibition and elimination of the worst forms of child labour as a matter of urgency.

Equality of Opportunity and Treatment

28. Governments should pursue policies designed to promote equality of opportunity and treatment in employment, with a view to eliminating any discrimination based on race, colour, sex, religion, political opinion, national extraction or social origin.

29. Governments should promote equal remuneration for men and women workers for work of equal value.

30. Multinational enterprises should be guided by the principle of non-discrimination throughout their operations without prejudice to the measures envisaged in paragraph 18 or to government policies designed to correct historical patterns of discrimination and thereby to extend equality of opportunity and treatment in employment. Multinational enterprises should accordingly make qualifications, skill and experience the basis for the recruitment, placement, training and advancement of their staff at all levels.

31. Governments should never require or encourage multinational enterprises to discriminate on any of the grounds mentioned in paragraph 28, and continuing guidance from governments, where appropriate, on the avoidance of such discrimination in employment is encouraged.

Security of Employment

32. Governments should carefully study the impact of multinational enterprises on employment in different industrial sectors. Governments, as well as multinational enterprises themselves, in all countries should take suitable measures to deal with the employment and labour market impacts of the operations of multinational enterprises.

33. Multinational enterprises as well as national enterprises, through active employment planning, should endeavour to provide stable employment for workers employed by each enterprise and should observe freely negotiated obligations concerning employment stability and social security. In view of the flexibility which multinational enterprises may have, they should strive to assume a leading role in promoting security of employment, particularly in countries where the discontinuation of operations is likely to accentuate long-term unemployment.

34. In considering changes in operations (including those resulting from mergers, takeovers or transfers of production) which would have major employment effects, multinational enterprises should provide reasonable notice of such changes to the appropriate government authorities and representatives of the workers in their employment and their organizations so that the implications may be examined jointly in order to mitigate adverse effects to the greatest possible extent. This is particularly important in the case of the closure of an entity involving collective lay-offs or dismissals.

35. Arbitrary dismissal procedures should be avoided.

36. Governments, in cooperation with multinational as well as national enterprises, should provide some form of income protection for workers whose employment has been terminated.

Training

37. Governments, in cooperation with all the parties concerned, should develop national policies for vocational training and guidance, closely linked with employment. This is the framework within which multinational enterprises should pursue their training policies.

38. In their operations, multinational enterprises should ensure that relevant training is provided for all levels of workers employed by them in the host country, as appropriate, to meet the needs of the enterprise as well as the development policies of the country. Such training should, to the extent possible, develop generally useful skills and promote career opportunities and lifelong learning. This responsibility should be carried out, where appropriate, in cooperation with the authorities of the country, employers' and workers' organizations and the competent local, national or international institutions.

39. Multinational enterprises operating in developing countries should participate, along with national enterprises, in programmes, including special funds, encouraged by host governments and supported by employers' and workers' organizations. These programmes should have the aim of encouraging skill formation, lifelong learning and development as well as providing vocational guidance, and should be jointly administered by the parties which support them. Wherever practicable, multinational enterprises should make the services of skilled resource personnel available to help in training programmes organized by governments as part of a contribution to national development.

40. Multinational enterprises, with the cooperation of governments and to the extent consistent with the efficient operation of the enterprise, should afford opportunities within the enterprise as a whole to broaden the experience of local management in suitable fields such as industrial relations.

Conditions of Work and Life

Wages, Benefits and Conditions of Work

41. Wages, benefits and conditions of work offered by multinational enterprises across their operations should be not less favourable to the workers than those offered by comparable employers in the host country. Where comparable employers do not exist, they should provide the best possible wages, benefits and conditions of work. The elements to be taken into consideration should include:

(a) the needs of workers and their families, taking into account the general level of wages in the country, the cost of living, social security benefits, and the relative living standards of other social groups; and

(b) economic factors, including the requirements of economic development, levels of productivity and the desirability of attaining and maintaining a high level of employment. Where the employer provides workers with basic amenities such as housing, medical care or food, these amenities should be of a good standard.

42. Governments, especially in developing countries, should endeavour to adopt suitable measures to ensure that lower income groups and less developed areas benefit as much as possible from the activities of multinational enterprises.

Safety and Health

43. Governments should ensure that both multinational and national enterprises provide adequate safety and health standards and contribute to a preventative safety and health culture in enterprises progressively achieving a safe and healthy working environment. This would include steps to combat workplace violence against women and men and attention to building safety. The relevant international labour standards, including the list of occupational diseases, and the ILO codes of practice and guidelines in the current list of ILO publications on occupational safety and health, should also be taken into account. Compensation should be provided to workers who have been victims of occupational accidents or diseases.

44. Multinational enterprises should maintain the highest standards of safety and health, in conformity with national requirements, bearing in mind their relevant experience within the enterprise as a whole, including any knowledge of special hazards. They should also make available to the representatives of the workers, and upon request, to the competent authorities and the workers' and employers' organizations in all countries in which they operate, information on the safety and health standards relevant to their local operations, which they observe in other countries. In particular, they should make known to those concerned any special hazards and related protective measures associated with new products and processes. They, like comparable domestic enterprises, should be expected to play a leading role in the examination of causes of industrial safety and health hazards and in the application of resulting improvements within the enterprise as a whole.

45. Multinational enterprises should cooperate in the work of international organizations concerned with the preparation and adoption of international safety and health standards.

46. In accordance with national practice, multinational enterprises should cooperate fully with the competent safety and health authorities, the representatives of the workers and their organizations, and established safety and health organizations. Where appropriate, matters relating to safety and health should be incorporated in agreements with the representatives of the workers and their organizations.

Industrial Relations

47. Multinational enterprises should observe standards of industrial relations throughout their operations.

Freedom of Association and the Right to Organize

48. Workers employed by multinational enterprises as well as those employed by national enterprises should, without distinction whatsoever, have the right to establish and, subject only to the rules of the organization concerned, to join organizations of their own choosing without previous authorization. They should also enjoy adequate protection against acts of anti-union discrimination in respect of their employment.

49. Organizations representing multinational enterprises or the workers in their employment should enjoy adequate protection against any acts of interference by each other or each other's agents or members in their establishment, functioning or administration.

50. Where appropriate, in the local circumstances, multinational enterprises should support representative employers' organizations.

51. Governments, where they do not already do so, are urged to apply the principles of Convention No. 87, Article 5, in view of the importance, in relation to multinational enterprises, of permitting organizations representing such enterprises or the workers in their employment to affiliate with international organizations of employers and workers of their own choosing.

52. Where governments of host countries offer special incentives to attract foreign investment, these incentives should not include any limitation of the workers' freedom of association or the right to organize and bargain collectively.

53. Representatives of the workers in multinational and national enterprises should not be hindered from meeting for consultation and exchange of views among themselves, provided that the functioning of the operations of the enterprise and the normal procedures which govern relationships with representatives of the workers and their organizations are not thereby prejudiced.

54. Governments should not restrict the entry of representatives of employers' and workers' organizations who come from other countries at the invitation of the local or national organizations concerned for the purpose of consultation on matters of mutual concern, solely on the grounds that they seek entry in that capacity.

Collective Bargaining

55. Workers employed by multinational enterprises should have the right, in accordance with national law and practice, to have representative organizations of their own choosing recognized for the purpose of collective bargaining.

56. Measures appropriate to national conditions should be taken to encourage and promote the full development and utilization of machinery for voluntary negotiation between employers or employers' organizations and workers' organizations, with a view to the regulation of terms and conditions of employment by means of collective agreements.

57. Multinational enterprises, as well as national enterprises, should provide workers' representatives with such facilities as may be necessary to assist in the development of effective collective agreements.

58. Multinational enterprises should enable duly authorized representatives of the workers in their employment in each of the countries in which they operate to conduct negotiations with representatives of management who are authorized to take decisions on the matters under negotiation.

59. Multinational enterprises, in the context of bona fide negotiations with the workers' representatives on conditions of employment, or while workers are exercising the right to organize, should not threaten to utilize a capacity to transfer the whole or part of an operating unit from the country concerned in order to influence unfairly those negotiations or to hinder the exercise of the right to organize; nor should they transfer workers from affiliates in foreign countries with a view to undermining bona fide negotiations with the workers' representatives or the workers' exercise of their right to organize.

60. Collective agreements should include provisions for the settlement of disputes arising over their interpretation and application and for ensuring mutually respected rights and responsibilities.

61. Multinational enterprises should provide workers' representatives with information required for meaningful negotiations with the entity involved and, where this accords with local law and practices, should also provide information to enable them to obtain a true and fair view of the performance of the entity or, where appropriate, of the enterprise as a whole.

62. Governments should supply to the representatives of workers' organizations on request, where law and practice so permit, information on the industries in which the enterprise operates, which would help in laying down objective criteria in the collective bargaining process. In this context, multinational as well as national enterprises should respond constructively to requests by governments for relevant information on their operations.

Consultation

63. In multinational as well as in national enterprises, systems devised by mutual agreement between employers and workers and their representatives should provide, in accordance with national law and practice, for regular consultation on matters of mutual concern. Such consultation should not be a substitute for collective bargaining.

Access to Remedy and Examination of Grievances

64. As part of their duty to protect against business-related human rights abuses, governments should take appropriate steps to ensure, through judicial, administrative, legislative or other appropriate means, that when such abuses occur within their territory and/or jurisdiction any affected worker or workers have access to effective remedy.

65. Multinational enterprises should use their leverage to encourage their business partners to provide effective means of enabling remediation for abuses of internationally recognized human rights.

66. Multinational as well as national enterprises should respect the right of the workers whom they employ to have all their grievances processed in a manner consistent with the following provision: any worker who, acting individually or jointly with other workers, considers that he or she has grounds for a grievance should have the right to submit such grievance without suffering any prejudice whatsoever as a result, and to have such grievance examined pursuant to an appropriate procedure. This is particularly important whenever the multinational enterprises operate in countries which do not abide by the principles of ILO Conventions pertaining to freedom of association, to the right to organize and bargain collectively, to discrimination, to child labour and to forced labour.

Settlement of Industrial Disputes

67. Governments should ensure that voluntary conciliation and arbitration machinery, appropriate to national conditions, is made available to assist in the prevention and settlement of industrial disputes between employers and workers. The procedure should be free of charge and expeditious.

68. Multinational as well as national enterprises jointly with the representatives and organizations of the workers whom they employ should seek to establish voluntary conciliation machinery, appropriate to national conditions, which may include provisions for voluntary arbitration, to assist in the prevention and settlement of industrial disputes between employers and workers. The voluntary conciliation machinery should include equal representation of employers and workers.

ANNEX I

List of ILO Declarations, international labour Conventions and Recommendations, codes of practice, guidelines and other guidance documents relevant to the Tripartite Declaration of Principles concerning Multinational Enterprises and Social Policy [...]

ANNEX II
Operational Tools [...]

VIII. Relevant International Environmental Treaties and Conventions

VIII.1. 1994 ENERGY CHARTER TREATY

PREAMBLE

The Contracting Parties to this Treaty,

Having regard to the Charter of Paris for a New Europe signed on 21 November 1990;

Having regard to the European Energy Charter adopted in the Concluding Document of the Hague Conference on the European Energy Charter signed at The Hague on 17 December 1991;

Recalling that all signatories to the Concluding Document of the Hague Conference undertook to pursue the objectives and principles of the European Energy Charter and implement and broaden their cooperation as soon as possible by negotiating in good faith an Energy Charter Treaty and Protocols, and desiring to place the commitments contained in that Charter on a secure and binding international legal basis;

Desiring also to establish the structural framework required to implement the principles enunciated in the European Energy Charter;

Wishing to implement the basic concept of the European Energy Charter initiative which is to catalyse economic growth by means of measures to liberalize investment and trade in energy;

Affirming that Contracting Parties attach the utmost importance to the effective implementation of full national treatment and most favoured nation treatment, and that these commitments will be applied to the Making of Investments pursuant to a supplementary treaty;

Having regard to the objective of progressive liberalization of international trade and to the principle of avoidance of discrimination in international trade as enunciated in the General Agreement on Tariffs and Trade and its Related Instruments and as otherwise provided for in this Treaty;

Determined progressively to remove technical, administrative and other barriers to trade in energy materials and products and related equipment, technologies and services;

Looking to the eventual membership in the General Agreement on Tariffs and Trade of those Contracting Parties which are not currently parties thereto and concerned to provide interim trade arrangements which will assist those Contracting Parties and not impede their preparation for such membership;

Mindful of the rights and obligations of certain Contracting Parties which are also parties to the General Agreement on Tariffs and Trade and its related instruments;

Having regard to competition rules concerning mergers, monopolies, anti-competitive practices and abuse of dominant position;

Having regard also to the Treaty on the Non-Proliferation of Nuclear Weapons, the Nuclear Suppliers Guidelines and other international nuclear non-proliferation obligations or understandings;

Recognizing the necessity for the most efficient exploration, production, conversion, storage, transport, distribution and use of energy;

Recalling the United Nations Framework Convention on Climate Change, the Convention on Longe-Range Transboundary Air Pollution and its protocols, and other international environmental agreements with energy-related aspects; and

Recognizing the increasingly urgent need for measures to protect the environment, including the decommissioning of energy installations and waste disposal, and for internationally agreed objectives and criteria for these purposes,

HAVE AGREED AS FOLLOWS:

PART I – DEFINITIONS AND PURPOSE

Article 1 Definitions

As used in this Treaty:

(1) "Charter" means the European Energy Charter adopted in the Concluding Document of the Hague Conference on the European Energy Charter signed at The Hague on 17 December 1991; signature of the Concluding Document is considered to be signature of the Charter.

(2) "Contracting Party" means a state or Regional Economic Integration Organization which has consented to be bound by this Treaty and for which the Treaty is in force.

(3) "Regional Economic Integration Organization" means an organization constituted by states to which they have transferred competence over certain matters a number of which are governed by this Treaty, including the authority to take decisions binding on them in respect of those matters.

(4) "Energy Materials and Products", based on the Harmonized System of the Customs Cooperation Council and the Combined Nomenclature of the European Communities, means the items included in Annex EM.

(5) "Economic Activity in the Energy Sector" means an economic activity concerning the exploration, extraction, refining, production, storage, land transport, transmission, distribution, trade, marketing, or sale of energy materials and products except those included in Annex NI, or concerning the distribution of heat to multiple premises.

(6) "Investment" means every kind of asset, owned or controlled directly or indirectly by an investor and includes:

(a) tangible and intangible, and movable and immovable, property, and any property rights such as leases, mortgages, liens, and pledges;

(b) a company or business enterprise, or shares, stock, or other forms of equity participation in a company or business enterprise, and bonds and other debt of a company or business enterprise;

(c) claims to money and claims to performance pursuant to contract having an economic value and associated with an Investment;

(d) intellectual property;

(e) returns;

(f) any right conferred by law or contract or by virtue of any licences and permits granted pursuant to law to undertake any economic activity in the energy sector.

A change in the form in which assets are invested does not affect their character as investments and the term "Investment" includes all investments, whether existing at or made after the later of the date of entry into force of this Treaty for the Contracting Party of the investor making the investment and that for the Contracting Party in the area of which the investment is made (hereinafter referred to as the "Effective Date") provided that the Treaty shall only apply to matters affecting such investments after the effective date.

"Investment" refers to any investment associated with an economic activity in the energy sector and to investments or classes of investments designated by a Contracting Party in its area as "Charter efficiency projects" and so notified to the Secretariat.

(7) "Investor" means:

(a) with respect to a Contracting Party:

(i)   a natural person having the citizenship or nationality of or who is permanently residing in that Contracting Party in accordance with its applicable law;

(ii)   a company or other organization organized in accordance with the law applicable in that Contracting Party;

(b)   with respect to a "third state", a natural person, company or other organization which fulfils, mutatis mutandis, the conditions specified in subparagraph (a) for a Contracting Party.

(8)   "Make Investments" or "Making of Investments" means establishing new investments, acquiring all or part of existing investments or moving into different fields of investment activity.

(9)   "Returns" means the amounts derived from or associated with an investment, irrespective of the form in which they are paid, including profits, dividends, interest, capital gains. royalty payments, management, technical assistance or other fees and payments in kind.

(10) "Area" means with respect to a state that is a Contracting Party:

(a)   the territory under its sovereignty, it being understood that territory includes land, internal waters and the territorial sea; and

(b)   subject to and in accordance with the international law of the sea: the sea, sea-bed and its subsoil with regard to which that Contracting Party exercises sovereign rights and jurisdiction.

With respect to a Regional Economic Integration Organization which is a Contracting Party, area means the areas of the member states of such Organization, under the provisions contained in the agreement establishing that Organization.

(11) (a)   "GATT" means "GATT 1947" or "GATT 1994", or both of them where both are applicable.

(b)   "GATT 1947" means the General Agreement on Tariffs and Trade, dated 30 October 1947, annexed to the Final Act Adopted at the Conclusion of the Second Session of the Preparatory Committee of the United Nations Conference on Trade and Employment, as subsequently rectified, amended or modified.

(c)   "GATT 1994" means the General Agreement on Tariffs and Trade as specified in Annex 1 A of the Agreement Establishing the World Trade Organization, as subsequently rectified, amended or modified.

A party to the Agreement Establishing the World Trade Organization is considered to be a party to GATT 1994.

(d)   "Related Instruments" means, as appropriate:

(i)   agreements, arrangements or other legal instruments, including decisions, declarations and understandings, concluded under the auspices of GATT 1947 as subsequently rectified, amended or modified; or

(ii)   the Agreement Establishing the World Trade Organization including its Annex 1 (except GATT 1994), its Annexes 2, 3 and 4, and the decisions, declarations and understandings related thereto, as subsequently rectified, amended or modified.

(12) "Intellectual Property" includes copyrights and related rights, trademarks, geographical indications, industrial designs, patents, layout designs of integrated circuits and the protection of undisclosed information.

(13) (a)   "Energy Charter Protocol" or "Protocol" means a treaty, the negotiation of which is authorized and the text of which is adopted by the Charter Conference, which is entered into by two or more Contracting Parties in order to complement, supplement, extend or amplify the provisions of this Treaty with respect to any specific sector or category of activity within the scope of this Treaty, or to areas of cooperation pursuant to Title III of the Charter.

(b)   "Energy Charter Declaration" or "Declaration" means a non-binding instrument, the negotiation of which is authorized and the text of which is approved by the Charter Conference, which is entered into by two or more Contracting Parties to complement or supplement the provisions of this Treaty.

(14) "Freely Convertible Currency" means a currency which is widely traded in international foreign exchange markets and widely used in international transactions.

Article 2 Purpose of the Treaty

This Treaty establishes a legal framework in order to promote long-term cooperation in the energy field, based on complementarities and mutual benefits, in accordance with the objectives and principles of the Charter.

PART II – COMMERCE

Article 3 International Markets

The Contracting Parties shall work to promote access to international markets on commercial terms, and generally to develop an open and competitive market, for energy materials and products.

Article 4 Non-Derogation from GATT and Related Instruments

Nothing in this Treaty shall derogate, as between particular Contracting Parties which are parties to the GATT, from the provisions of the GATT and Related Instruments as they are applied between those Contracting Parties.

Article 5 Trade-Related Investment Measures

(1) A Contracting Party shall not apply any trade-related investment measure that is inconsistent with the provisions of Article III or XI of the GATT; this shall be without prejudice to the Contracting Party's rights and obligations under the GATT and Related Instruments and Article 29.

(2) Such measures include any investment measure which is mandatory or enforceable under domestic law or under any administrative ruling, or compliance with which is necessary to obtain an advantage, and which requires:

(a) the purchase or use by an enterprise of products of domestic origin or from any domestic source, whether specified in terms of particular products, in terms of volume or value of products, or in terms of a proportion of volume or value of its local production; or

(b) that an enterprise's purchase or use of imported products be limited to an amount related to the volume or value of local products that it exports;

or which restricts:

(c) the importation by an enterprise of products used in or related to its local production, generally or to an amount related to the volume or value of local production that it exports;

(d) the importation by an enterprise of products used in or related to its local production by restricting its access to foreign exchange to an amount related to the foreign exchange inflows attributable to the enterprise; or

(e) the exportation or sale for export by an enterprise of products, whether specified in terms of particular products, in terms of volume or value of products, or in terms of a proportion of volume or value of its local production.

(3) Nothing in paragraph (1) shall be construed to prevent a Contracting Party from applying the trade-related investment measures described in subparagraphs (2)(a) and (c) as a condition of eligibility for export promotion, foreign aid, government procurement or preferential tariff or quota programmes.

(4) Notwithstanding paragraph (1), a Contracting Party may temporarily continue to maintain trade-related investment measures which were in effect more than 180 days before its signature of this Treaty, subject to the notification and phase-out provisions set out in Annex TRM.

Article 6 Competition

(1) Each Contracting Party shall work to alleviate market distortions and barriers to competition in economic activity in the energy sector.

(2) Each Contracting Party shall ensure that within its jurisdiction it has and enforces such laws as are necessary and appropriate to address unilateral and concerted anti- competitive conduct in economic activity in the energy sector.

(3) Contracting Parties with experience in applying competition rules shall give full consideration to providing, upon request and within available resources, technical assistance on the development and implementation of competition rules to other Contracting Parties.

(4) Contracting Parties may cooperate in the enforcement of their competition rules by consulting and exchanging information.

(5) If a Contracting Party considers that any specified anti-competitive conduct carried out within the Area of another Contracting Party is adversely affecting an important interest relevant to the purposes identified in this Article, the Contracting Party may notify the other Contracting Party and may request that its competition authorities initiate appropriate enforcement action. The notifying Contracting Party shall include in such notification sufficient information to permit the notified Contracting Party to identify the anti-competitive conduct that is the subject of the notification and shall include an offer of such further information and cooperation as the notifying Contracting Party is able to provide. The notified Contracting Party or, as the case may be, the relevant competition authorities may consult with the competition authorities of the notifying Contracting Party and shall accord full consideration to the request of the notifying Contracting Party in deciding whether or not to initiate enforcement action with respect to the alleged anti-competitive conduct identified in the notification. The notified Contracting Party shall inform the notifying Contracting Party of its decision or the decision of the relevant competition authorities and may if it wishes inform the notifying Contracting Party of the grounds for the decision. If enforcement action is initiated, the notified Contracting Party shall advise the notifying Contracting Party of its outcome and, to the extent possible, of any significant interim development.

(6) Nothing in this Article shall require the provision of information by a Contracting Party contrary to its laws regarding disclosure of information, confidentiality or business secrecy.

(7) The procedures set forth in paragraph (5) and Article 27(1) shall be the exclusive means within this Treaty of resolving any disputes that may arise over the implementation or interpretation of this Article.

Article 7 Transit

(1) Each Contracting Party shall take the necessary measures to facilitate the transit of energy materials and products consistent with the principle of freedom of transit and without distinction as to the origin, destination or ownership of such energy materials and products or discrimination as to pricing on the basis of such distinctions, and without imposing any unreasonable delays, restrictions or charges.

(2) Contracting Parties shall encourage relevant entities to cooperate in:

(a) modernizing energy transport facilities necessary to the transit of energy materials and products;

(b) the development and operation of Energy transport facilities serving the areas of more than one Contracting Party;

(c) measures to mitigate the effects of interruptions in the supply of energy materials and products;

(d) facilitating the interconnection of energy transport facilities.

(3) Each Contracting Party undertakes that its provisions relating to transport of energy materials and products and the use of energy transport facilities shall treat energy materials and products in transit in no less favourable a manner than its provisions treat such materials and products originating in or destined for its own area, unless an existing international agreement provides otherwise.

(4) In the event that transit of energy materials and products cannot be achieved on commercial terms by means of energy transport facilities the Contracting Parties shall not place obstacles in the way of new capacity being established, except as may be otherwise provided in applicable legislation which is consistent with paragraph (1).

(5) A Contracting Party through whose area energy materials and products may transit shall not be obliged to

(a)   permit the construction or modification of energy transport facilities; or

(b)   permit new or additional transit through existing energy transport facilities,

which it demonstrates to the other Contracting Parties concerned would endanger the security or efficiency of its energy systems, including the security of supply.

Contracting Parties shall, subject to paragraphs (6) and (7), secure established flows of energy materials and products to, from or between the areas of other Contracting Parties.

(6) A Contracting Party through whose area energy materials and products transit shall not, in the event of a dispute over any matter arising from that transit, interrupt or reduce, permit any entity subject to its control to interrupt or reduce, or require any entity subject to its jurisdiction to interrupt or reduce the existing flow of energy materials and products prior to the conclusion of the dispute resolution procedures set out in paragraph (7), except where this is specifically provided for in a contract or other agreement governing such transit or permitted in accordance with the conciliator's decision.

(7) The following provisions shall apply to a dispute described in paragraph (6), but only following the exhaustion of all relevant contractual or other dispute resolution remedies previously agreed between the Contracting Parties party to the dispute or between any entity referred to in paragraph (6) and an entity of another Contracting Party party to the dispute:

(a)   A Contracting Party party to the dispute may refer it to the Secretary-General by a notification summarizing the matters in dispute. The Secretary-General shall notify all Contracting Parties of any such referral.

(b)   Within 30 days of receipt of such a notification, the Secretary-General, in consultation with the parties to the dispute and the other Contracting Parties concerned, shall appoint a conciliator. Such a conciliator shall have experience in the matters subject to dispute and shall not be a national or citizen of or permanently resident in a party to the dispute or one of the other Contracting Parties concerned.

(c)   The conciliator shall seek the agreement of the parties to the dispute to a resolution thereof or upon a procedure to achieve such resolution. If within 90 days of his appointment he has failed to secure such agreement, he shall recommend a resolution to the dispute or a procedure to achieve such resolution and shall decide the interim tariffs and other terms and conditions to be observed for transit from a date which he shall specify until the dispute is resolved.

(d)   The Contracting Parties undertake to observe and ensure that the entities under their control or jurisdiction observe any interim decision under subparagraph (c) on tariffs, terms and conditions for 12 months following the conciliator's decision or until resolution of the dispute, whichever is earlier.

(e)   Notwithstanding subparagraph (b) the Secretary-General may elect not to appoint a conciliator if in his judgement the dispute concerns transit that is or has been the subject of the dispute resolution procedures set out in subparagraphs (a) to (d) and those proceedings have not resulted in a resolution of the dispute.

(f)   The Charter Conference shall adopt standard provisions concerning the conduct of conciliation and the compensation of conciliators.

(8)   Nothing in this Article shall derogate from a Contracting Party's rights and obligations under international law including customary international law, existing bilateral or multilateral agreements, including rules concerning submarine cables and pipelines.

(9)   This Article shall not be so interpreted as to oblige any Contracting Party which does not have a certain type of energy transport facilities used for transit to take any measure under this Article with respect to that type of energy transport facilities. Such a Contracting Party is, however, obliged to comply with paragraph (4).

(10) For the purposes of this Article:

(a)   "Transit" means

(i)   the carriage through the area of a Contracting Party, or to or from port facilities in its area for loading or unloading, of energy materials and products originating in the area of another state and destined for the area of a third state, so long as either the other state or the third state is a Contracting Party; or

(ii)   the carriage through the area of a Contracting Party of energy materials and products originating in the area of another Contracting Party and destined for the area of that other Contracting Party, unless the two Contracting Parties concerned decide otherwise and record their decision by a joint entry in Annex N. The two Contracting Parties may delete their listing in Annex N by delivering a joint written notification of their intentions to the Secretariat, which shall transmit that notification to all other Contracting Parties. The deletion shall take effect four weeks after such former notification.

(b)   "Energy Transport Facilities" consist of high-pressure gas transmission pipelines, high-voltage electricity transmission grids and lines, crude oil transmission pipelines, coal slurry pipelines, oil product pipelines, and other fixed facilities specifically for handling energy materials and products.

Article 8 Transfer of Technology

(1)   The Contracting Parties agree to promote access to and transfer of energy technology on a commercial and non-discriminatory basis to assist effective trade in energy materials and products and Investment and to implement the objectives of the Charter subject to their laws and regulations, and to the protection of intellectual property rights.

(2)   Accordingly, to the extent necessary to give effect to paragraph (1) the Contracting Parties shall eliminate existing and create no new obstacles to the transfer of technology in the field of energy materials and products and related equipment and services, subject to non-proliferation and other international obligations.

Article 9 Access to Capital

(1)   The Contracting Parties acknowledge the importance of open capital markets in encouraging the flow of capital to finance trade in energy materials and products and for the making of and assisting with regard to investments in economic activity in the energy sector in the areas of other Contracting Parties, particularly those with economies in transition. Each Contracting Party shall accordingly endeavour to promote conditions for access to its capital market by companies and nationals of other Contracting Parties, for the purpose of financing trade in energy materials and products and for the purpose of investment in economic activity in the energy sector in the areas of those other Contracting Parties, on a basis no less favourable than that which it accords in like circumstances to its own companies and nationals or companies and nationals of any other Contracting Party or any third state, whichever is the most favourable.

(2)   A Contracting Party may adopt and maintain programmes providing for access to public loans, grants, guarantees or insurance for facilitating trade or investment abroad. It shall make such facilities available, consistent with the objectives, constraints and criteria of such pro-grammes (including any objectives, constraints or criteria relating to the place of business of an applicant for any such facility or the place of delivery of goods or services supplied with the support of any such facility) for investments in the economic activity in the energy sector of other Contracting Parties or for financing trade in energy materials and products with other Con-tracting Parties.

(3)   Contracting Parties shall, in implementing programmes in economic activity in the energy sector to improve the economic stability and investment climates of the Contracting Parties, seek as appropriate to encourage the operations and take advantage of the expertise of relevant international financial institutions.

(4)   Nothing in this Article shall prevent:

(a)   financial institutions from applying their own lending or underwriting practices based on market principles and prudential considerations; or

(b)   a Contracting Party from taking measures:

(i)   for prudential reasons, including the protection of investors, consumers, depositors, policy-holders or persons to whom a fiduciary duty is owed by a financial service supplier; or

(ii)   to ensure the integrity and stability of its financial system and capital markets.

PART III – INVESTMENT PROMOTION AND PROTECTION

Article 10 Promotion, Protection and Treatment of Investments

(1)   Each Contracting Party shall, in accordance with the provisions of this Treaty, encourage and create stable, equitable, favourable and transparent conditions for investors of other Contracting Parties to make investments in its area. Such conditions shall include a commitment to accord at all times to investments of investors of other Contracting Parties fair and equitable treatment. Such investments shall also enjoy the most constant protection and security and no Contracting Party shall in any way impair by unreasonable or discriminatory measures their management, maintenance, use, enjoyment or disposal. In no case shall such investments be accorded treat-ment less favourable than that required by international law, including treaty obligations. Each Contracting Party shall observe any obligations it has entered into with an investor or an investment of an investor of any other Contracting Party.

(2)   Each Contracting Party shall endeavour to accord to investors of other Contracting Parties, as regards the making of investments in its area, the treatment described in paragraph (3).

(3)   For the purposes of this Article, "Treatment" means treatment accorded by a Contracting Party which is no less favourable than that which it accords to its own investors or to investors of any other Contracting Party or any third state, whichever is the most favourable.

(4)   A supplementary treaty shall, subject to conditions to be laid down therein, oblige each party thereto to accord to investors of other parties, as regards the making of investments in its area, the treatment described in paragraph (3). That treaty shall be open for signature by the States and Regional Economic Integration Organizations which have signed or acceded to this Treaty. Negotiations towards the supplementary treaty shall commence not later than 1 January 1995, with a view to concluding it by 1 January 1998.

(5)   Each Contracting Party shall, as regards the making of investments in its area, endeavour to:

(a)   limit to the minimum the exceptions to the treatment described in paragraph (3);

(b)   progressively remove existing restrictions affecting investors of other Contracting Parties;

(6) (a) A Contracting Party may, as regards the making of investments in its area, at any time declare voluntarily to the Charter Conference, through the Secretariat, its intention not to introduce new exceptions to the treatment described in paragraph (3).

(b) A Contracting Party may, furthermore, at any time make a voluntary commitment to accord to investors of other Contracting Parties, as regards the making of investments in some or all economic activities in the energy sector in its area, the treatment described in paragraph (3). Such commitments shall be notified to the Secretariat and listed in Annex VC and shall be binding under this Treaty.

(7) Each Contracting Party shall accord to investments in its area of investors of other Contracting Parties, and their related activities including management, maintenance, use, enjoyment or disposal, treatment no less favourable than that which it accords to investments of its own investors or of the investors of any other Contracting Party or any third state and their related activities including management, maintenance, use, enjoyment or disposal, whichever is the most favourable.

(8) The modalities of application of paragraph (7) in relation to programmes under which a Contracting Party provides grants or other financial assistance, or enters into contracts, for energy technology research and development, shall be reserved for the supplementary treaty described in paragraph (4). Each Contracting Party shall through the Secretariat keep the Charter Conference informed of the modalities it applies to the programmes described in this paragraph.

(9) Each State or Regional Economic Integration Organization which signs or accedes to this Treaty shall, on the date it signs the Treaty or deposits its instrument of accession, submit to the Secretariat a report summarizing all laws, regulations or other measures relevant to:

(a) exceptions to paragraph (2); or

(b) the programmes referred to in paragraph (8).

A Contracting Party shall keep its report up to date by promptly submitting amendments to the Secretariat. The Charter Conference shall review these reports periodically.

In respect of subparagraph (a) the report may designate parts of the energy sector in which a Contracting Party accords to investors of other Contracting Parties the treatment described in paragraph (3).

In respect of subparagraph (b) the review by the Charter Conference may consider the effects of such programmes on competition and investments.

(10) Notwithstanding any other provision of this Article, the treatment described in paragraphs (3) and (7) shall not apply to the protection of intellectual property; instead, the treatment shall be as specified in the corresponding provisions of the applicable international agreements for the protection of intellectual property rights to which the respective Contracting Parties are parties.

(11) For the purposes of Article 26, the application by a Contracting Party of a trade- related investment measure as described in Article 5(1) and (2) to an investment of an investor of another Contracting Party existing at the time of such application shall, subject to Article 5(3) and (4), be considered a breach of an obligation of the former Contracting Party under this part.

(12) Each Contracting Party shall ensure that its domestic law provides effective means for the assertion of claims and the enforcement of rights with respect to investments, investment agreements, and investment authorizations.

Article 11 Key Personnel

(1) A Contracting Party shall, subject to its laws and regulations relating to the entry, stay and work of natural persons, examine in good faith requests by investors of another Contracting Party, and key personnel who are employed by such investors or by investments of such investors, to enter and remain temporarily in its area to engage in activities connected with the

making or the development, management, maintenance, use, enjoyment or disposal of relevant investments, including the provision of advice or key technical services.

(2)   A Contracting Party shall permit investors of another Contracting Party which have investments in its area, and investments of such investors, to employ any key person of the investor's or the investment's choice regardless of nationality and citizenship provided that such key person has been permitted to enter, stay and work in the area of the former Contracting Party and that the employment concerned conforms to the terms, conditions and time limits of the permission granted to such key person.

Article 12 Compensation for Losses

(1)   Except where Article 13 applies, an investor of any Contracting Party which suffers a loss with respect to any investment in the area of another Contracting Party owing to war or other armed conflict, state of national emergency, civil disturbance, or other similar event in that area, shall be accorded by the latter Contracting Party, as regards restitution, indemnification, compensation or other settlement, treatment which is the most favourable of that which that Contracting Party accords to any other investor, whether its own investor, the investor of any other Contracting Party, or the investor of any third state.

(2)   Without prejudice to paragraph (1), an investor of a Contracting Party which, in any of the situations referred to in that paragraph, suffers a loss in the area of another Contracting Party resulting from

(a)   requisitioning of its investment or part thereof by the latter's forces or authorities; or

(b)   destruction of its investment or part thereof by the latter's forces or authorities, which was not required by the necessity of the situation,

shall be accorded restitution or compensation which in either case shall be prompt, adequate and effective.

Article 13 Expropriation

(1)   Investments of investors of a Contracting Party in the area of any other Contracting Party shall not be nationalized, expropriated or subjected to a measure or measures having effect equivalent to nationalization or expropriation (hereinafter referred to as "Expropriation") except where such expropriation is:

(a)   for a purpose which is in the public interest;

(b)   non-discriminatory;

(c)   carried out under due process of law; and

(d)   accompanied by the payment of prompt, adequate and effective compensation.

Such compensation shall amount to the fair market value of the investment expropriated at the time immediately before the expropriation or impending expropriation became known in such a way as to affect the value of the investment (hereinafter referred to as the "Valuation Date").

Such fair market value shall at the request of the investor be expressed in a freely convertible currency on the basis of the market rate of exchange existing for that currency on the valuation date. Compensation shall also include interest at a commercial rate established on a market basis from the date of expropriation until the date of payment.

(2)   The investor affected shall have a right to prompt review, under the law of the Contracting Party making the expropriation, by a judicial or other competent and independent authority of that Contracting Party, of its case, of the valuation of its investment, and of the payment of compensation, in accordance with the principles set out in paragraph (1).

(3)   For the avoidance of doubt, expropriation shall include situations where a Contracting Party expropriates the assets of a company or enterprise in its area in which an investor of any other Contracting Party has an investment, including through the ownership of shares.

Article 14 Transfers Related to Investments

(1)   Each Contracting Party shall with respect to investments in its area of investors of any other Contracting Party guarantee the freedom of transfer into and out of its area, including the transfer of:

(a)   the initial capital plus any additional capital for the maintenance and development of an investment;

(b)   returns;

(c)   payments under a contract, including amortization of principal and accrued interest payments pursuant to a loan agreement;

(d)   unspent earnings and other remuneration of personnel engaged from abroad in connection with that Investment;

(e)   proceeds from the sale or liquidation of all or any part of an investment;

(f)   payments arising out of the settlement of a dispute;

(g)   payments of compensation pursuant to Articles 12 and 13.

(2)   Transfers under paragraph (1) shall be effected without delay and (except in case of a return in kind) in a freely convertible currency.

(3)   Transfers shall be made at the market rate of exchange existing on the date of transfer with respect to spot transactions in the currency to be transferred. In the absence of a market for foreign exchange, the rate to be used will be the most recent rate applied to inward investments or the most recent exchange rate for conversion of currencies into Special Drawing Rights, whichever is more favourable to the investor.

(4)   Notwithstanding paragraphs (1) to (3), a Contracting Party may protect the rights of creditors, or ensure compliance with laws on the issuing, trading and dealing in securities and the satisfaction of judgements in civil, administrative and criminal adjudicatory proceedings, through the equitable, non-discriminatory, and good faith application of its laws and regulations.

(5)   Notwithstanding paragraph (2), Contracting Parties which are States that were constituent parts of the former Union of Soviet Socialist Republics may provide in agreements concluded between them that transfers of payments shall be made in the currencies of such Contracting Parties, provided that such agreements do not treat investments in their areas of investors of other Contracting Parties less favourably than either investments of investors of the Contracting Parties which have entered into such agreements or investments of investors of any third state.

(6)   Notwithstanding subparagraph (1)(b), a Contracting Party may restrict the transfer of a return in kind in circumstances where the Contracting Party is permitted under Article 29(2)(a) or the GATT and Related Instruments to restrict or prohibit the exportation or the sale for export of the product constituting the return in kind; provided that a Contracting Party shall permit transfers of returns in kind to be effected as authorized or specified in an investment agreement, investment authorization, or other written agreement between the Contracting Party and either an investor of another Contracting Party or its investment.

Article 15 Subrogation

(1)   If a Contracting Party or its designated agency (hereinafter referred to as the "Indemnifying Party") makes a payment under an indemnity or guarantee given in respect of an investment of an investor (hereinafter referred to as the "Party Indemnified") in the area of another Contracting Party (hereinafter referred to as the "Host Party"), the Host Party shall recognize:

(a) the assignment to the Indemnifying Party of all the rights and claims in respect of such investment; and

(b) the right of the Indemnifying Party to exercise all such rights and enforce such claims by virtue of subrogation.

(2) The Indemnifying Party shall be entitled in all circumstances to:

(a) the same treatment in respect of the rights and claims acquired by it by virtue of the assignment referred to in paragraph (1); and

(b) the same payments due pursuant to those rights and claims,

as the Party Indemnified was entitled to receive by virtue of this Treaty in respect of the investment concerned.

(3) In any proceeding under Article 26, a Contracting Party shall not assert as a defence, counterclaim, right of set-off or for any other reason, that indemnification or other compensation for all or part of the alleged damages has been received or will be received pursuant to an insurance or guarantee contract.

Article 16 Relation to Other Agreements

Where two or more Contracting Parties have entered into a prior international agreement, or enter into a subsequent international agreement, whose terms in either case concern the subject matter of Part III or V of this Treaty,

(1) nothing in Part III or V of this Treaty shall be construed to derogate from any provision of such terms of the other agreement or from any right to dispute resolution with respect thereto under that agreement; and

(2) nothing in such terms of the other agreement shall be construed to derogate from any provision of Part III or V of this Treaty or from any right to dispute resolution with respect thereto under this Treaty,

where any such provision is more favourable to the investor or investment.

Article 17 Non-Application of Part III in Certain Circumstances

Each Contracting Party reserves the right to deny the advantages of this Part to:

(1) a legal entity if citizens or nationals of a third state own or control such entity and if that entity has no substantial business activities in the area of the Contracting Party in which it is organized; or

(2) an investment, if the denying Contracting Party establishes that such investment is an investment of an investor of a third state with or as to which the denying Contracting Party:

(a) does not maintain a diplomatic relationship; or

(b) adopts or maintains measures that:

    (i) prohibit transactions with investors of that state; or

    (ii) would be violated or circumvented if the benefits of this Part were accorded to investors of that state or to their investments.

PART IV – MISCELLANEOUS PROVISIONS

Article 18 Sovereignty Over Energy Resources

(1) The Contracting Parties recognize state sovereignty and sovereign rights over energy resources. They reaffirm that these must be exercised in accordance with and subject to the rules of international law.

(2) Without affecting the objectives of promoting access to energy resources, and exploration and development thereof on a commercial basis, the Treaty shall in no way prejudice the rules in Contracting Parties governing the system of property ownership of energy resources.

(3)   Each State continues to hold in particular the rights to decide the geographical areas within its area to be made available for exploration and development of its energy resources, the optimalization of their recovery and the rate at which they may be depleted or otherwise exploited, to specify and enjoy any taxes, royalties or other financial payments payable by virtue of such exploration and exploitation, and to regulate the environmental and safety aspects of such exploration, development and reclamation within its area, and to participate in such exploration and exploitation, inter alia, through direct participation by the Government or through State enterprises.

(4) The Contracting Parties undertake to facilitate access to energy resources, inter alia, by allocating in a non-discriminatory manner on the basis of published criteria authorizations, licences, concessions and contracts to prospect and explore for or to exploit or extract energy resources.

Article 19 Environmental Aspects

(1)   In pursuit of sustainable development and taking into account its obligations under those international agreements concerning the environment to which it is party, each Contracting Party shall strive to minimize in an economically efficient manner harmful environmental impacts occurring either within or outside its area from all operations within the energy cycle in its area, taking proper account of safety. In doing so each Contracting Party shall act in a cost-effective manner. In its policies and actions each Contracting Party shall strive to take precautionary measures to prevent or minimize environmental degradation. The Contracting Parties agree that the polluter in the areas of Contracting Parties, should, in principle, bear the cost of pollution, including transboundary pollution, with due regard to the public interest and without distorting investment in the energy cycle or international trade. Contracting Parties shall accordingly:

(a)   take account of environmental considerations throughout the formulation and implementation of their energy policies;

(b)   promote market-oriented price formation and a fuller reflection of environmental costs and benefits throughout the energy cycle;

(c)   having regard to Article 34(4), encourage cooperation in the attainment of the environmental objectives of the Charter and cooperation in the field of international environmental standards for the energy cycle, taking into account differences in adverse effects and abatement costs between Contracting Parties;

(d)   have particular regard to improving energy efficiency, to developing and using renewable energy sources, to promoting the use of cleaner fuels and to employing technologies and technological means that reduce pollution;

(e)   promote the collection and sharing among Contracting Parties of information on environmentally sound and economically efficient energy policies and cost- effective practices and technologies;

(f)   promote public awareness of the environmental impacts of energy systems, of the scope for the prevention or abatement of their adverse environmental impacts, and of the costs associated with various prevention or abatement measures;

(g)   promote and cooperate in the research, development and application of energy efficient and environmentally sound technologies, practices and processes which will minimize harmful environmental impacts of all aspects of the energy cycle in an economically efficient manner;

(h)   encourage favourable conditions for the transfer and dissemination of such technologies consistent with the adequate and effective protection of intellectual property rights;

(i)   promote the transparent assessment at an early stage and prior to decision, and subsequent monitoring, of environmental impacts of environmentally significant energy investment projects;

(j)   promote international awareness and information exchange on Contracting Parties' relevant environmental programmes and standards and on the implementation of those programmes and standards;

(k)   participate, upon request, and within their available resources, in the development and implementation of appropriate environmental programmes in the Contracting Parties.

(2)   At the request of one or more Contracting Parties, disputes concerning the application or interpretation of provisions of this Article shall, to the extent that arrangements for the consideration of such disputes do not exist in other appropriate international fora, be reviewed by the Charter Conference aiming at a solution.

(3)   For the purposes of this Article:

(a)   "Energy Cycle" means the entire energy chain, including activities related to prospecting for, exploration, production, conversion, storage, transport, distribution and consumption of the various forms of energy, and the treatment and disposal of wastes, as well as the decommissioning, cessation or closure of these activities, minimizing harmful environmental impacts;

(b)   "Environmental Impact" means any effect caused by a given activity on the environment, including human health and safety, flora, fauna, soil, air, water, climate, landscape and historical monuments or other physical structures or the interactions among these factors; it also includes effects on cultural heritage or socio- economic conditions resulting from alterations to those factors;

(c)   "Improving Energy Efficiency" means acting to maintain the same unit of output (of a good or service) without reducing the quality or performance of the output, while reducing the amount of energy required to produce that output;

(d)   "Cost-Effective" means to achieve a defined objective at the lowest cost or to achieve the greatest benefit at a given cost.

Article 20 Transparency

(1)   Laws, regulations, judicial decisions and administrative rulings of general application which affect trade in energy materials and products are, in accordance with Article 29(2)(a), among the measures subject to the transparency disciplines of the GATT and relevant Related Instruments.

(2)   Laws, regulations, judicial decisions and administrative rulings of general application made effective by any Contracting Party, and agreements in force between Contracting Parties, which affect other matters covered by this Treaty shall also be published promptly in such a manner as to enable Contracting Parties and investors to become acquainted with them. The provisions of this paragraph shall not require any Contracting Party to disclose confidential information which would impede law enforcement or otherwise be contrary to the public interest or would prejudice the legitimate commercial interests of any investor.

(3)   Each Contracting Party shall designate one or more enquiry points to which requests for information about the abovementioned laws, regulations, judicial decisions and administrative rulings may be addressed and shall communicate promptly such designation to the Secretariat which shall make it available on request.

Article 21 Taxation

(1)   Except as otherwise provided in this Article, nothing in this Treaty shall create rights or impose obligations with respect to taxation measures of the Contracting Parties. In the event of any inconsistency between this Article and any other provision of the Treaty, this Article shall prevail to the extent of the inconsistency.

(2)   Article 7(3) shall apply to taxation measures other than those on income or on capital, except that such provision shall not apply to:

(a)   an advantage accorded by a Contracting Party pursuant to the tax provisions of any convention, agreement or arrangement described in subparagraph (7)(a)(ii); or

(b)   any taxation measure aimed at ensuring the effective collection of taxes,

except where the measure of a Contracting Party arbitrarily discriminates against energy
materials and products originating in, or destined for the area of another Contracting Party or
arbitrarily restricts benefits accorded under Article 7(3),

(3)   Article 10(2) and (7) shall apply to taxation measures of the Contracting Parties other than
those on income or on capital, except that such provisions shall not apply to:

(a)   impose most favoured nation obligations with respect to advantages accorded by a Contracting Party pursuant to the tax provisions of any convention, agreement or arrangement
described in subparagraph (7)(al(ii) or resulting from membership of any Regional Economic
Integration Organization; or

(b)   any taxation measure aimed at ensuring the effective collection of taxes, except where the
measure arbitrarily discriminates against an investor of another Contracting Party or
arbitrarily restricts benefits accorded under the investment provisions of this Treaty.

(4)   Article 29(2) to (6) shall apply to taxation measures other than those on income or on capital.

(5)   (a) Article 13 shall apply to taxes.

(b)   Whenever an issue arises under Article 13, to the extent it pertains to whether a tax constitutes an expropriation or whether a tax alleged to constitute an expropriation is discriminatory, the following provisions shall apply:

(i)   The investor or the Contracting Party alleging expropriation shall refer the issue of
whether the tax is an expropriation or whether the tax is discriminatory to the relevant
competent tax authority. Failing such referral by the investor or the Contracting Party,
bodies called upon to settle disputes pursuant to Article 26(2)(c) or 27(2) shall make a
referral to the relevant competent tax authorities;

(ii)   The competent tax authorities shall, within a period of six months of such referral, strive
to resolve the issues so referred. Where non-discrimination issues are concerned, the
competent tax authorities shall apply the non-discrimination provisions of the relevant
tax convention or, if there is no non-discrimination provision in the relevant tax
convention applicable to the tax or no such tax convention is in force between the
Contracting Parties concerned, they shall apply the non-discrimination principles under
the Model Tax Convention on Income and Capital of the Organisation for Economic Co-
operation and Development;

(iii) Bodies called upon to settle disputes pursuant to Article 26(2)(c) or 27(2) may take into
account any conclusions arrived at by the competent tax authorities regarding whether
the tax is an expropriation. Such bodies shall take into account any conclusions arrived
at within the six-month period prescribed in subparagraph (b)(ii) by the Competent tax
authorities regarding whether the tax is discriminatory. Such bodies may also take into
account any conclusions arrived at by the competent tax authorities after the expiry of
the six-month period;

(iv)   Under no circumstances shall involvement of the competent tax authorities, beyond the
end of the six-month period referred to in subparagraph (b) (ii), lead to a delay of
proceedings under Articles 26 and 27.

(6)   For the avoidance of doubt, Article 14 shall not limit the right of a Contracting Party to
impose or collect a tax by withholding or other means.

(7)   For the purposes of this Article:

(a)   The term "Taxation Measure" includes:

    (i)   any provision relating to taxes of the domestic law of the Contracting Party or of a political subdivision thereof or a local authority therein; and

    (ii) any provision relating to taxes of any convention for the avoidance of double taxation or of any other international agreement or arrangement by which the Contracting Party is bound.

(b)   There shall be regarded as taxes on income or on capital all taxes imposed on total income, on total capital or on elements of income or of capital, including taxes on gains from the alienation of property, taxes on estates, inheritances and gifts, or substantially similar taxes, taxes on the total amounts of wages or salaries paid by enterprises, as well as taxes on capital appreciation.

(c)   A "Competent Tax Authority" means the competent authority pursuant to a double taxation agreement in force between the Contracting Parties or, when no such agreement is in force, the minister or ministry responsible for taxes or their authorized representatives.

(d)   For the avoidance of doubt, the terms "tax provisions" and "taxes" do not include customs duties.

Article 22 State and Privileged Enterprises

(1)   Each Contracting Party shall ensure that any State enterprise which it maintains or establishes shall conduct its activities in relation to the sale or provision of goods and services in its area in a manner consistent with the Contracting Party's obligations under Part III of this Treaty.

(2)   No Contracting Party shall encourage or require such a State enterprise to conduct its activities in its area in a manner inconsistent with the Contracting Party's obligations under other provisions of this Treaty.

(3)   Each Contracting Party shall ensure that if it establishes or maintains an entity and entrusts the entity with regulatory, administrative or other governmental authority, such entity shall exercise that authority in a manner consistent with the Contracting Party's obligations under this Treaty.

(4)   No Contracting Party shall encourage or require any entity to which it grants exclusive or special privileges to conduct its activities in its area in a manner inconsistent with the Contracting Party's obligations under this Treaty.

(5)   For the purposes of this Article, "entity" includes any enterprise, agency or other organization or individual.

Article 23 Observance by Sub-National Authorities

(1)   Each Contracting Party is fully responsible under this Treaty for the observance of all provisions of the Treaty, and shall take such reasonable measures as may be available to it to ensure such observance by regional and local governments and authorities within its area.

(2)   The dispute settlement provisions in Parts II, IV and V of this Treaty may be invoked in respect of measures affecting the observance of the Treaty by a Contracting Party which have been taken by regional or local governments or authorities within the area of the Contracting Party.

Article 24 Exceptions

(1)   This Article shall not apply to Articles 12, 13 and 29.

(2)   The provisions of this Treaty other than

(a)   those referred to in paragraph (1); and

(b) with respect to subparagraph (i), Part III of the Treaty shall not preclude any Contracting Party from adopting or enforcing any measure

(i) necessary to protect human, animal or plant life or health;

(ii) essential to the acquisition or distribution of energy materials and products in conditions of short supply arising from causes outside the control of that Contracting Party, provided that any such measure shall be consistent with the principles that

(A) all other Contracting Parties are entitled to an equitable share of the international supply of such energy materials and products; and

(B) any such measure that is inconsistent with this Treaty shall be discontinued as soon as the conditions giving rise to it have ceased to exist; or

(iii) designed to benefit investors who are aboriginal people or socially or economically disadvantaged individuals or groups or their investments and notified to the Secretariat as such, provided that such measure

(A) has no significant impact on that Contracting Party's economy; and

(B) does not discriminate between investors of any other Contracting Party and investors of that Contracting Party not included among those for whom the measure is intended,

provided that no such measure shall constitute a disguised restriction on economic activity in the energy sector, or arbitrary or unjustifiable discrimination between Contracting Parties or between investors or other interested persons of Contracting Parties. Such measures shall be duly motivated and shall not nullify or impair any benefit one or more other Contracting Parties may reasonably expect under this Treaty to an extent greater than is strictly necessary to the stated end.

(3) The provisions of this Treaty other than those referred to in paragraph (1) shall not be construed to prevent any Contracting Party from taking any measure which it considers necessary:

(a) for the protection of its essential security interests including those

(i) relating to the supply of energy materials and products to a military establishment; or

(ii) taken in time of war, armed conflict or other emergency in international relations;

(b) relating to the implementation of national policies respecting the non-proliferation of nuclear weapons or other nuclear explosive devices or needed to fulfil its obligations under the Treaty on the Non-Proliferation of Nuclear Weapons, the Nuclear Suppliers Guidelines, and other international nuclear non-proliferation obligations or understandings; or

(c) for the maintenance of public order.

Such measure shall not constitute a disguised restriction on transit.

(4) The provisions of this Treaty which accord most favoured nation treatment shall not oblige any Contracting Party to extend to the investors of any other Contracting Party any preferential treatment:

(a) resulting from its membership of a free-trade area or customs union; or

(b) which is accorded by a bilateral or multilateral agreement concerning economic cooperation between states that were constituent parts of the former Union of Soviet Socialist Republics pending the establishment of their mutual economic relations on a definitive basis.

Article 26 Economic Integration Agreements

(1) The provisions of this Treaty shall not be so construed as to oblige a Contracting Party which is party to an Economic Integration Agreement (hereinafter referred to as "EIA") to extend, by means of most favoured nation treatment, to another Contracting Party which is not a party to

that EIA, any preferential treatment applicable between the parties to that EIA as a result of their being parties thereto.

(2) For the purposes of paragraph (1), "EIA" means an agreement substantially liberalizing, inter alia, trade and investment, by providing for the absence or elimination of substantially all discrimination between or among parties thereto through the elimination of existing discriminatory measures and/or the prohibition of new or more discriminatory measures, either at the entry into force of that agreement or on the basis of a reasonable time frame.

(3) This Article shall not affect the application of the GATT and Related Instruments according to Article 29.

PART V – DISPUTE SETTLEMENT

Article 26 Settlement of Disputes Between an Investor and a Contracting Party

(1) Disputes between a Contracting Party and an investor of another Contracting Party relating to an investment of the latter in the area of the former, which concern an alleged breach of an obligation of the former under Part III shall, if possible, be settled amicably.

(2) If such disputes can not be settled according to the provisions of paragraph (1) within a period of three months from the date on which either party to the dispute requested amicable settlement, the investor party to the dispute may choose to submit it for resolution:

(a) to the courts or administrative tribunals of the Contracting Party party to the dispute;

(b) in accordance with any applicable, previously agreed dispute settlement procedure; or

(c) in accordance with the following paragraphs of this Article.

(3) (a) Subject only to subparagraphs (b) and (c), each Contracting Party hereby gives its unconditional consent to the submission of a dispute to international arbitration or conciliation in accordance with the provisions of this Article.

(b) (i)   The Contracting Parties listed in Annex ID do not give such unconditional consent where the investor has previously submitted the dispute under subparagraph (2)(a) or (b).

(ii) For the sake of transparency, each Contracting Party that is listed in Annex ID shall provide a written statement of its policies, practices and conditions in this regard to the Secretariat no later than the date of the deposit of its instrument of ratification, acceptance or approval in accordance with Article 39 or the deposit of its instrument of accession in accordance with Article 41.

(c) A Contracting Party listed in Annex IA does not give such unconditional consent with respect to a dispute arising under the last sentence of Article 10(1).

(4) In the event that an investor chooses to submit the dispute for resolution under sub-paragraph (2)(c), the investor shall further provide its consent in writing for the dispute to be submitted to:

(a) (i)   The International Centre for Settlement of Investment Disputes, established pursuant to the Convention on the Settlement of Investment Disputes between States and Natio-nals of other States opened for signature at Washington, 18 March 1965 (hereinafter referred to as the "ICSID Convention"), if the Contracting Party of the Investor and the Contracting Party party to the dispute are both parties to the ICSID Convention; or

(ii) The International Centre for Settlement of Investment Disputes, established pursuant to the Convention referred to in subparagraph (a)(i), under the rules governing the Additional Facility for the Administration of Proceedings by the Secretariat of the Centre (hereinafter referred to as the "Additional Facility Rules"), if the Contracting Party of the investor or the Contracting Party party to the dispute, but not both, is a party to the ICSID Convention;

(b) a sole arbitrator or ad hoc arbitration tribunal established under the Arbitration Rules of the United Nations Commission on International Trade Law /hereinafter referred to as "UNCITRAL"); or

(c) an arbitral proceeding under the Arbitration Institute of the Stockholm Chamber of Commerce.

(5) (a) The consent given in paragraph (3) together with the written consent of the investor given pursuant to paragraph (4) shall be considered to satisfy the requirement for:

(i) written consent of the parties to a dispute for purposes of Chapter II of the ICSID Convention and for purposes of the Additional Facility Rules;

(ii) an "agreement in writing" for purposes of Article II of the United Nations Convention on the Recognition and Enforcement of Foreign Arbitral Awards, done at New York, 10 June 1958 (hereinafter referred to as the "New York Convention"); and

(iii) "the parties to a contract [to] have agreed in writing" for the purposes of Article 1 of the UNCITRAL Arbitration Rules.

(b) Any arbitration under this Article shall at the request of any party to the dispute be held in a State that is a party to the New York Convention. Claims submitted to arbitration hereunder shall be considered to arise out of a commercial relationship or transaction for the purposes of Article I of that Convention.

(6) A tribunal established under paragraph (4) shall decide the issues in dispute in accordance with this Treaty and applicable rules and principles of international law.

(7) An investor other than a natural person which has the nationality of a Contracting Party party to the dispute on the date of the consent in writing referred to in paragraph (4) and which, before a dispute between it and that Contracting Party arises, is controlled by investors of another Contracting Party, shall for the purpose of Article 25(2)(b) of the ICSID Convention be treated as a "national of another Contracting State" and shall for the purpose of Article 1 (6) of the Additional Facility Rules be treated as a "national of another State".

(8) The awards of arbitration, which may include an award of interest, shall be final and binding upon the parties to the dispute. An award of arbitration concerning a measure of a sub-national government or authority of the disputing Contracting Party shall provide that the Contracting Party may pay monetary damages in lieu of any other remedy granted. Each Contracting Party shall carry out without delay any such award and shall make provision for the effective enforcement in its area of such awards.

Article 27 Settlement of Disputes Between Contracting Parties

(1) Contracting Parties shall endeavour to settle disputes concerning the application or interpretation of this Treaty through diplomatic channels.

(2) If a dispute has not been settled in accordance with paragraph (1) within a reasonable period of time, either party thereto may, except as otherwise provided in this Treaty or agreed in writing by the Contracting Parties, and except as concerns the application or interpretation of Article 6 or Article 19 or, for Contracting Parties listed in Annex IA, the last sentence of Article 10(1), upon written notice to the other party to the dispute submit the matter to an ad hoc tribunal under this Article.

(3) Such an ad hoc arbitral tribunal shall be constituted as follows:

(a) The Contracting Party instituting the proceedings shall appoint one member of the tribunal and inform the other Contracting Party to the dispute of its appointment within 30 days of receipt of the notice referred to in paragraph (2) by the other Contracting Party;

(b) Within 60 days of the receipt of the written notice referred to in paragraph (2), the other Contracting Party party to the dispute shall appoint one member. If the appointment is not made within the time limit prescribed, the Contracting Party having instituted the proceedings may, within 90 days of the receipt of the written notice referred to in paragraph (2), request that the appointment be made in accordance with subparagraph (d);

(c) A third member, who may not be a national or citizen of a Contracting Party party to the dispute, shall be appointed by the Contracting Parties parties to the dispute. That member shall be the President of the tribunal. If, within 150 days of the receipt of the notice referred to in paragraph (2), the Contracting Parties are unable to agree on the appointment of a third member, that appointment shall be made, in accordance with subparagraph (d), at the request of either Contracting Party submitted within 180 days of the receipt of that notice;

(d) Appointments requested to be made in accordance with this paragraph shall be made by the Secretary-General of the Permanent Court of International Arbitration within 30 days of the receipt of a request to do so. If the Secretary-General is prevented from discharging this task, the appointments shall be made by the First Secretary of the Bureau. If the latter, in turn, is prevented from discharging this task, the appointments shall be made by the most senior Deputy;

(e) Appointments made in accordance with subparagraphs (a) to (d) shall be made with regard to the qualifications and experience, particularly in matters covered by this Treaty, of the members to be appointed;

(f) In the absence of an agreement to the contrary between the Contracting Parties, the Arbitration Rules of UNCITRAL shall govern, except to the extent modified by the Contracting Parties parties to the dispute or by the arbitrators. The tribunal shall take its decisions by a majority vote of its members;

(g) The tribunal shall decide the dispute in accordance with this Treaty and applicable rules and principles of international law;

(h) The arbitral award shall be final and binding upon the Contracting Parties parties to the dispute;

(i) Where, in making an award, a tribunal finds that a measure of a regional or local government or authority within the area of a Contracting Party listed in Part I of Annex Pis not in conformity with this Treaty, either party to the dispute may invoke the provisions of Part II of Annex P;

(j) The expenses of the tribunal, including the remuneration of its members, shall be borne in equal shares by the Contracting Parties parties to the dispute. The tribunal may, however, at its discretion direct that a higher proportion of the costs be paid by one of the Contracting Parties parties to the dispute;

(k) Unless the Contracting Parties parties to the dispute agree otherwise, the tribunal shall sit in The Hague, and use the premises and facilities of the Permanent Court of Arbitration;

(l) A copy of the award shall be deposited with the Secretariat which shall make it generally available.

Article 28 Non-Application of Article 27 to Certain Disputes

A dispute between Contracting Parties with respect to the application or interpretation of Article 5 or 29 shall not be settled under Article 27 unless the Contracting Parties parties to the dispute so agree.

PART VI – TRANSITIONAL PROVISIONS

Article 29 Interim Provisions on Trade-Related Matters

(1) The provisions of this Article shall apply to trade in energy materials and products while any Contracting Party is not a party to the GATT and Related Instruments.

(2) (a) Trade in energy materials and products between Contracting Parties at least one of which is not a party to the GATT or a relevant Related Instrument shall be governed, subject to subparagraphs (b) and (c) and to the exceptions and rules provided for in Annex G, by the provisions of GATT 1947 and Related Instruments, as applied on 1 March 1994 and practised with regard to energy materials and products by parties to GATT 1947 among themselves, as if all Contracting Parties were parties to GATT 1947 and Related Instruments.

(b) Such trade of a Contracting Party which is a State that was a constituent part of the former Union of Soviet Socialist Republics may instead be governed, subject to the provisions of Annex TFU, by an agreement between two or more such States, until 1 December 1999 or the admission of that Contracting Party to the GATT, whichever is the earlier.

(c) As concerns trade between any two parties to the GATT, subparagraph (a) shall not apply if either of those parties is not a party to GATT 1947.

(3) Each signatory to this Treaty, and each State or Regional Economic Integration Organization acceding to this Treaty, shall on the date of its signature or of its deposit of its instrument of accession provide to the Secretariat a list of all tariff rates and other charges levied on energy materials and products at the time of importation or exportation, notifying the level of such rates and charges applied on such date of signature or deposit. Any changes to such rates or other charges shall be notified to the Secretariat, which shall inform the Contracting Parties of such changes.

(4) Each Contracting Party shall endeavour not to increase any tariff rate or other charge levied at the time of importation or exportation:

(a) in the case of the importation of energy materials and products described in Part I of the Schedule relating to the Contracting Party referred to in Article II of the GATT, above the level set forth in that Schedule, if the Contracting Party is a party to the GATT;

(b) in the case of the exportation of energy materials and products, and that of their importation if the Contracting Party is not a party to the GATT, above the level most recently notified to the Secretariat, except as permitted by the provisions made applicable by subparagraph (2)(a).

(5) A Contracting Party may increase such tariff rate or other charge above the level referred to in paragraph (4) only if:

(a) in the case of a rate or other charge levied at the time of importation, such action is not inconsistent with the applicable provisions of the GATT other than those provisions of GATT 1947 and Related Instruments listed in Annex G and the corresponding provisions of GATT 1994 and Related Instruments; or

(b) it has, to the fullest extent practicable under its legislative procedures, notified the Secretariat of its proposal for such an increase, given other interested Contracting Parties reasonable opportunity for consultation with respect to its proposal, and accorded consideration to any representations from such Contracting Parties.

(6) Signatories undertake to commence negotiations not later than 1 January 1995 with a view to concluding by 1 January 1998, as appropriate in the light of any developments in the world trading system, a text of an amendment to this Treaty which shall, subject to conditions to be laid down therein, commit each Contracting Party not to increase such tariffs or charges beyond the level prescribed under that amendment.

(7) Annex D shall apply to disputes regarding compliance with provisions applicable to trade under this Article and, unless both Contracting Parties agree otherwise, to disputes regarding compliance with Article 5 between Contracting Parties at least one of which is not a party to the GATT, except that Annex D shall not apply to any dispute between Contracting Parties, the substance of which arises under an agreement that

(a) has been notified in accordance with and meets the other requirements of subparagraph (2)(b) and Annex TFU; or

(b) establishes a free-trade area or a customs union as described in Article XXIV of the GATT.

Article 30 Developments in International Trading Arrangements

Contracting Parties undertake that in the light of the results of the Uruguay Round of Multilateral Trade Negotiations embodied principally in the Final Act thereof done at Marrakesh, 15 April 1994, they will commence consideration not later than 1 July 1995 or the entry into force of this Treaty, whichever is the later, of appropriate amendments to this Treaty with a view to the adoption of any such amendments by the Charter Conference.

Article 31 Energy-Related Equipment

The provisional Charter Conference shall at its first meeting commence examination of the inclusion of energy-related equipment in the trade provisions of this Treaty.

Article 32 Transitional Arrangements

(1) In recognition of the need for time to adapt to the requirements of a market economy, a Contracting Party listed in Annex T may temporarily suspend full compliance with its obligations under one or more of the following provisions of this Treaty, subject to the conditions in paragraphs (3) to (6):

Article 6(2) and (5)

Article 7(4)

Article 9(1)

Article 10(7) – specific measures

Article 14(1)(d) – related only to transfer of unspent earnings

Article 20(3)

Article 22(1) and (3)

(2) Other Contracting Parties shall assist any Contracting Party which has suspended full compliance under paragraph (1) to achieve the conditions under which such suspension can be terminated. This assistance may be given in whatever form the other Contracting Parties consider most effective to respond to the needs notified under subparagraph (4)(c) including, where appropriate, through bilateral or multilateral arrangements.

(3) The applicable provisions, the stages towards full implementation of each, the measures to be taken and the date or, exceptionally, contingent event, by which each stage shall be completed and measure taken are listed in Annex T for each Contracting Party claiming transitional arrangements. Each such Contracting Party shall take the measure listed by the date indicated for the relevant provision and stage as set out in Annex T. Contracting Parties which have temporarily suspended full compliance under paragraph (1) undertake to comply fully with the relevant obligations by 1 July 2001. Should a Contracting Party find it necessary, due to exceptional circumstances, to request that the period of such temporary suspension be extended or that any further temporary suspension not previously listed in Annex T be introduced, the decision on a request to amend Annex T shall be made by the Charter Conference.

(4) A Contracting Party which has invoked transitional arrangements shall notify the Secretariat no less often than once every 12 months:

(a) of the implementation of any measures listed in its Annex T and of its general progress to full compliance;

(b) of the progress it expects to make during the next 12 months towards full compliance with its obligations, of any problem it foresees and of its proposals for dealing with that problem;

(c) of the need for technical assistance to facilitate completion of the stages set out in Annex T as necessary for the full implementation of this Treaty, or to deal with any problem notified pursuant to subparagraph (b) as well as to promote other necessary market-oriented reforms and modernization of its energy sector;

(d) of any possible need to make a request of the kind referred to in paragraph (3).

(5) The Secretariat shall:

(a) circulate to all Contracting Parties the notifications referred to in paragraph (4);

(b) circulate and actively promote, relying where appropriate on arrangements existing within other international organizations, the matching of needs for and offers of technical assistance referred to in paragraph (2) and subparagraph (4)(c);

(c) circulate to all Contracting Parties at the end of each six month period a summary of any notifications made under subparagraph (4)(a) or (d).

(6) The Charter Conference shall annually review the progress by Contracting Parties towards implementation of the provisions of this Article and the matching of needs and offers of technical assistance referred to in paragraph (2) and subparagraph (4)(c). In the course of that review it may decide to take appropriate action.

PART VII – STRUCTURE AND INSTITUTIONS

Article 33 Energy Charter Protocols and Declarations

(1) The Charter Conference may authorize the negotiation of a number of Energy Charter Protocols or Declarations in order to pursue the objectives and principles of the Charter.

(2) Any signatory to the Charter may participate in such negotiation.

(3) A State or Regional Economic Integration Organization shall not become a party to a Protocol or Declaration unless it is, or becomes at the same time, a signatory to the Charter and a Contracting Party to this Treaty.

(4) Subject to paragraph (3) and subparagraph (6){a), final provisions applying to a Protocol shall be defined in that Protocol.

(5) A Protocol shall apply only to the Contracting Parties which consent to be bound by it, and shall not derogate from the rights and obligations of those Contracting Parties not party to the Protocol.

(6) (a) A Protocol may assign duties to the Charter Conference and functions to the Secretariat, provided that no such assignment may be made by an amendment to a Protocol unless that amendment is approved by the Charter Conference, whose approval shall not be subject to any provisions of the Protocol which are authorized by subparagraph (b).

(b) A Protocol which provides for decisions thereunder to be taken by the Charter Conference may, subject to subparagraph (a), provide with respect to such decisions:

  (i) for voting rules other than those contained in Article 36;

  (ii) that only parties to the Protocol shall be considered to be Contracting Parties for the purposes of Article 36 or eligible to vote under the rules provided for in the Protocol.

Article 34 Energy Charter Conference

(1) The Contracting Parties shall meet periodically in the Energy Charter Conference [referred to herein as the "Charter Conference") at which each Contracting Party shall be entitled to have one representative. Ordinary meetings shall be held at intervals determined by the Charter Conference.

(2) Extraordinary meetings of the Charter Conference may be held at such times as may be determined by the Charter Conference, or at the written request of any Contracting Party,

provided that, within six weeks of the request being communicated to the Contracting Parties by the Secretariat, it is supported by at least one-third of the Contracting Parties.

(3)   The functions of the Charter Conference shall be to:

(a)   carry out the duties assigned to it by this Treaty and any Protocols;

(b)   keep under review and facilitate the implementation of the principles of the Charter and of the provisions of this Treaty and the Protocols;

(c)   facilitate in accordance with this Treaty and the Protocols the coordination of appropriate general measures to carry out the principles of the Charter;

(d)   consider and adopt programmes of work to be carried out by the Secretariat;

(e)   consider and approve the annual accounts and budget of the Secretariat;

(f)   consider and approve or adopt the terms of any headquarters or other agreement, including privileges and immunities considered necessary for the Charter Conference and the Secretariat;

(g)   encourage cooperative efforts aimed at facilitating and promoting market-oriented reforms and modernization of energy sectors in those countries of Central and Eastern Europe and the former Union of Soviet Socialist Republics undergoing economic transition;

(h)   authorize and approve the terms of reference for the negotiation of Protocols, and consider and adopt the texts thereof and of amendments thereto;

(i)   authorize the negotiation of Declarations, and approve their issuance;

(j)   decide on accessions to this Treaty;

(k)   authorize the negotiation of and consider and approve or adopt association agreements;

(l)   consider and adopt texts of amendments to this Treaty;

(m) consider and approve modifications of and technical changes to the Annexes to this Treaty;

(n)   appoint the Secretary-General and take all decisions necessary for the establishment and functioning of the Secretariat including the structure, staff levels and standard terms of employment of officials and employees.

(4)   In the performance of its duties, the Charter Conference, through the Secretariat, shall cooperate with and make as full a use as possible, consistently with economy and efficiency, of the services and programmes of other institutions and organizations with established competence in matters related to the objectives of this Treaty.

(5)   The Charter Conference may establish such subsidiary bodies as it considers appropriate for the performance of its duties.

(6)   The Charter Conference shall consider and adopt rules of procedure and financial rules.

(7)   In 1999 and thereafter at intervals (of not more than five years) to be determined by the Charter Conference, the Charter Conference shall thoroughly review the functions provided for in this Treaty in the light of the extent to which the provisions of the Treaty and Protocols have been implemented. At the conclusion of each review the Charter Conference may amend or abolish the functions specified in paragraph (3) and may discharge the Secretariat.

Article 35 Secretariat

(1)   In carrying out its duties, the Charter Conference shall have a Secretariat which shall be composed of a Secretary-General and such staff as are the minimum consistent with efficient performance.

(2)   The Secretary-General shall be appointed by the Charter Conference. The first such appointment shall be for a maximum period of five years.

(3) In the performance of its duties the Secretariat shall be responsible to and report to the Charter Conference.

(4) The Secretariat shall provide the Charter Conference with all necessary assistance for the performance of its duties and shall carry out the functions assigned to it in this Treaty or in any Protocol and any other functions assigned to it by the Charter Conference.

(5) The Secretariat may enter into such administrative and contractual arrangements as may be required for the effective discharge of its functions.

Article 36 Voting

(1) Unanimity of the Contracting Parties Present and Voting at the meeting of the Charter Conference where such matters fall to be decided shall be required for decisions by the Charter Conference to:

(a) adapt amendments to this Treaty other than amendments to Articles 34 and 35 and Annex T;

(b) approve accessions to this Treaty under Article 41 by States or Regional Economic Integration Organizations which were not signatories to the Charter as of 16 June 1995;

(c) authorize the negotiation of and approve or adapt the text of association agreements;

(d) approve modifications to Annexes EM, NI, G and B;

(e) approve technical changes to the Annexes to this Treaty; and

(f) approve the Secretary-General's nominations of panelists under Annex D, paragraph (7).

The Contracting Parties shall make every effort to reach agreement by consensus on any other matter requiring their decision under this Treaty. If agreement cannot be reached by consensus, paragraphs (2) to (5) shall apply.

(2) Decisions on budgetary matters referred to in Article 34(3)1e) shall be taken by a qualified majority of Contracting Parties whose assessed contributions as specified in Annex B represent, in combination, at least three-fourths of the total assessed contributions specified therein.

(3) Decisions on matters referred to in Article 34(7) shall be taken by a three-fourths majority of the Contracting Parties.

(4) Except in cases specified in subparagraphs (1)(a) to (f), paragraphs (2) and (3), and subject to paragraph (6), decisions provided for in this Treaty shall be taken by a three-fourths majority of the Contracting Parties present and voting at the meeting of the Charter Conference at which such matters fall to be decided.

(5) For purposes of this Article, "Contracting Parties Present and Voting" means Contracting Parties present and casting affirmative or negative votes, provided that the Charter Conference may decide upon rules of procedure to enable such decisions to be taken by Contracting Parties by correspondence.

(6) Except as provided in paragraph (2), no decision referred to in this Article shall be valid unless it has the support of a simple majority of the Contracting Parties.

(7) A Regional Economic Integration Organization shall, when voting, have a number of votes equal to the number of its member states which are Contracting Parties to this Treaty; provided that such an Organization shall not exercise its right to vote if its member states exercise theirs, and vice versa.

(8) In the event of persistent arrears in a Contracting Party's discharge of financial obligations under this Treaty, the Charter Conference may suspend that Contracting Party's voting rights in whole or in part.

Article 37 Funding Principles

(1) Each Contracting Party shall bear its own costs of representation at meetings of the Charter Conference and any subsidiary bodies.

(2) The cost of meetings of the Charter Conference and any subsidiary bodies shall be regarded as a cost of the Secretariat.

(3) The costs of the Secretariat shall be met by the Contracting Parties assessed according to their capacity to pay, determined as specified in Annex B, the provisions of which may be modified in accordance with Article 36(1)(d).

(4) A Protocol shall contain provisions to assure that any costs of the Secretariat arising from that Protocol are borne by the parties thereto.

(5) The Charter Conference may in addition accept voluntary contributions from one or more Contracting Parties or from other sources. Costs met from such contributions shall not be considered costs of the Secretariat for the purposes of paragraph (3).

PART VIII – FINAL PROVISIONS

Article 38 Signature

This Treaty shall be open for signature at Lisbon from 17 December 1994 to 16 June 1995 by the States and Regional Economic Integration Organizations which have signed the Charter.

Article 39 Ratification, Acceptance or Approval

This Treaty shall be subject to ratification, acceptance or approval by signatories. Instruments of ratification, acceptance or approval shall be deposited with the Depositary.

Article 40 Application to Territories

(1) Any State or Regional Economic Integration Organization may at the time of signature, ratification, acceptance, approval or accession, by a declaration deposited with the Depositary, declare that the Treaty shall be binding upon it with respect to all the territories for the international relations of which it is responsible, or to one or more of them. Such declaration shall take effect at the time the Treaty enters into force for that Contracting Party.

(2) Any Contracting Party may at a later date, by a declaration deposited with the Depositary, bind itself under this Treaty with respect to other territory specified in the declaration. In respect of such territory the Treaty shall enter into force on the ninetieth day following the receipt by the Depositary of such declaration.

(3) Any declaration made under the two preceding paragraphs may, in respect of any territory specified in such declaration, be withdrawn by a notification to the Depositary. The withdrawal shall, subject to the applicability of Article 47(3), become effective upon the expiry of one year after the date of receipt of such notification by the Depositary.

(4) The definition of "Area" in Article 1(10) shall be construed having regard to any declaration deposited under this Article.

Article 41 Accession

This Treaty shall be open for accession, from the date on which the Treaty is closed for signature, by States and Regional Economic Integration Organizations which have signed the Charter, on terms to be approved by the Charter Conference. The instruments of accession shall be deposited with the Depositary.

Article 42 Amendments

(1) Any Contracting Party may propose amendments to this Treaty.

(2)   The text of any proposed amendment to this Treaty shall be communicated to the Contracting Parties by the Secretariat at least three months before the date on which it is proposed for adoption by the Charter Conference.

(3)   Amendments to this Treaty, texts of which have been adopted by the Charter Conference, shall be communicated by the Secretariat to the Depositary which shall submit them to all Contracting Parties for ratification, acceptance or approval.

(4)   Instruments of ratification, acceptance or approval of amendments to this Treaty shall be deposited with the Depositary. Amendments shall enter into force between Contracting Parties having ratified, accepted or approved them on the ninetieth day after deposit with the Depositary of instruments of ratification, acceptance or approval by at least three-fourths of the Contracting Parties, Thereafter the amendments shall enter into force for any other Contracting Party on the ninetieth day after that Contracting Party deposits its instrument of ratification, acceptance or approval of the amendments.

Article 43 Association Agreements

(1)   The Charter Conference may authorize the negotiation of association agreements with States or Regional Economic Integration Organizations, or with international organizations, in order to pursue the objectives and principles of the Charter and the provisions of this Treaty or one or more Protocols.

(2)   The relationship established with and the rights enjoyed and obligations incurred by an associating State, Regional Economic Integration Organization, or international organization shall be appropriate to the particular circumstances of the association, and in each case shall be set out in the association agreement.

Article 44 Entry into Force

(1)   This Treaty shall enter into force on the ninetieth day after the date of deposit of the thirtieth instrument of ratification, acceptance or approval thereof, or of accession thereto, by a state or Regional Economic Integration Organization which is a signatory to the Charter as of 16 June 1995.

(2)   For each State or Regional Economic Integration Organization which ratifies, accepts or approves this Treaty or accedes thereto after the deposit of the thirtieth instrument of ratification, acceptance or approval, it shall enter into force on the ninetieth day after the date of deposit by such State or Regional Economic Integration Organization of its instrument of ratification, acceptance, approval or accession.

(3)   For the purposes of paragraph (1), any instrument deposited by a Regional Economic Integration Organization shall not be counted as additional to those deposited by member states of such Organization.

Article 45 Provisional Application

(1)   Each signatory agrees to apply this Treaty provisionally pending its entry into force for such signatory in accordance with Article 44, to the extent that such provisional application is not inconsistent with its constitution, laws or regulations.

(2)   (a) Notwithstanding paragraph (1) any signatory may, when signing, deliver to the Depositary a declaration that it is not able to accept provisional application. The obligation contained in paragraph (1) shall not apply to a signatory making such a declaration. Any such signatory may at any time withdraw that declaration by written notification to the Depositary.

(b)   Neither a signatory which makes a declaration in accordance with subparagraph (a) nor investors of that signatory may claim the benefits of provisional application under paragraph (1).

(c) Notwithstanding subparagraph (a), any signatory making a declaration referred to in sub-paragraph (a) shall apply Part VII provisionally pending the entry into force of the Treaty for such signatory in accordance with Article 44, to the extent that such provisional application is not inconsistent with its laws or regulations.

(3) (a) Any signatory may terminate its provisional application of this Treaty by written notification to the Depositary of its intention not to become a Contracting Party to the Treaty. Termination of provisional application for any signatory shall take effect upon the expiration of 60 days from the date on which such signatory's written notification is received by the Depositary.

(b) In the event that a signatory terminates provisional application under subparagraph (a), the obligation of the signatory under paragraph (1) to apply Parts III and V with respect to any investments made in its area during such provisional application by investors of other signatories shall nevertheless remain in effect with respect to those investments for twenty years following the effective date of termination, except as otherwise provided in subparagraph (c).

(c) Subparagraph (b) shall not apply to any signatory listed in Annex PA. A signatory shall be removed from the list in Annex PA effective upon delivery to the Depositary of its request therefor.

(4) Pending the entry into force of this Treaty the signatories shall meet periodically in the provisional Charter Conference, the first meeting of which shall be convened by the provisional Secretariat referred to in paragraph 15) not later than 180 days after the opening date for signature of the Treaty as specified in Article 38.

(5) The functions of the Secretariat shall be carried out on an interim basis by a provisional Secretariat until the entry into force of this Treaty pursuant to Article 44 and the establishment of a Secretariat.

(6) The signatories shall, in accordance with and subject to the provisions of paragraph (1) or subparagraph (2)(c) as appropriate, contribute to the costs of the provisional Secretariat as if the signatories were Contracting Parties under Article 37(3). Any modifications made to Annex B by the signatories shall terminate upon the entry into force of this Treaty.

(7) A State or Regional Economic Integration Organization which, prior to this Treaty's entry into force, accedes to the Treaty in accordance with Article 41 shall, pending the Treaty's entry into force, have the rights and assume the obligations of a signatory under this Article.

Article 46 Reservations

No reservations may be made to this Treaty.

Article 47 Withdrawal

(1) At any time after five years from the date on which this Treaty has entered into force for a Contracting Party, that Contracting Party may give written notification to the Depositary of its withdrawal from the Treaty.

(2) Any such withdrawal shall take effect upon the expiry of one year after the date of the receipt of the notification by the Depositary, or on such later date as may be specified in the notification of withdrawal.

(3) The provisions of this Treaty shall continue to apply to investments made in the area of a Contracting Party by investors of other Contracting Parties or in the area of other Contracting Parties by investors of that Contracting Party as of the date when that Contracting Party's withdrawal from the Treaty takes effect for a period of 20 years from such date.

(4) All Protocols to which a Contracting Party is party shall cease to be in force for that Contracting Party on the effective date of its withdrawal from this Treaty.

Article 48 Status of Annexes and Decisions

The Annexes to this Treaty and the Decisions set out in Annex 2 to the Final Act of the European Energy Charter Conference signed at Lisbon on 17 December 1994 are integral parts of the Treaty.

Article 49 Depositary

The Government of the Portuguese Republic shall be the Depositary of this Treaty.

Article 50 Authentic Texts

In witness whereof the undersigned, being duly authorized to that effect, have signed this Treaty in English, French, German, Italian, Russian and Spanish, of which every text is equally authentic, in one original, which will be deposited with the Government of the Portuguese Republic.

Done at Lisbon on the seventeenth day of December in the year one thousand nine hundred and ninety-four.

ANNEXES TO THE ENERGY CHARTER TREATY

1. Annex EM – Energy Materials and Products (in accordance with Article 1(4))
2. Annex NI – Non-Applicable Energy Materials and Products for Definition of "Economic Activity in the Energy Sector" (in accordance with Article 1 (5))
3. Annex TRM – Notification and Phase-out (TRIMs) (in accordance with Article 5(4))
4. Annex N – List of Contracting Parties Requiring at Least 3 Separate Areas to Be Involved in a Transit (in accordance with Article 7(10)(a))
5. Annex VC – List of Contracting Parties Which Have Made Voluntary Binding Commitments in Respect of Article 10(3) (in accordance with Article 10(6))
6. Annex ID – List of Contracting Parties Not Allowing an Investor to Resubmit the Same Dispute to International Arbitration at a Later Stage under Article 26 (in accordance with Article 26(3)(b)(i))
7. Annex IA – List of Contracting Parties Not Allowing an Investor or Contracting Party to Submit a Dispute Concerning the Last Sentence of Article 10(1) to International Arbitration (in accordance with Articles 26(3)(c) and 27(2))
8. Annex P – Special Sub-National Dispute Procedure (in accordance with Article 27(3)(i))
9. Annex G – Exceptions and Rules Governing the Application of the Provisions of the GATT and Related Instruments (in accordance with Article 29(2)(a))
10. Annex TFU – Provisions Regarding Trade Agreements Between States Which Were Constituent Parts of the Former Union of Soviet Socialist Republics (in accordance with Article 29(2)(b))
11. Annex D – Interim Provisions for Trade Dispute Settlement (in accordance with Article 29(7))
12. Annex B – Formula for Allocating Charter Costs (in accordance with Article 37(3))
13. Annex PA – List of Signatories Which Do Not Accept the Provisional Application Obligation of Article 45(3)(b) (in accordance with Article 45(3)(c))
14. Annex T – Contracting Parties' Transitional Measures (in accordance with Article 32(1))

VIII.2. 2015 INTERNATIONAL ENERGY CHARTER[1]

The representatives of the signatories meeting in The Hague on 20th and 21st May 2015;

Desirous to better reflect the new realities of the energy sector, especially the growing weight from developing countries, including emerging economies, and to serve the interests of the existing and potential participants of the Energy Charter constituency;

Having regard to the European Energy Charter adopted in the Concluding Document of the Hague Conference on the European Energy Charter signed at The Hague on 17 December 1991 signature of which allows States and Regional Economic Integration Organisations to accede to the Energy Charter Treaty of 1994 and which will continue to exist for this purpose;

Recalling the Decision adopted by the Energy Charter Conference in its 23rd Meeting in Warsaw in 2012 to engage in a process that could lead to the adoption of an updated version of the European Energy Charter;

Aware that the concept of the International Energy Charter aims at enhancing international cooperation in order to meet common challenges related to energy at national, regional and international levels, including the evolution of global energy architecture;

Recalling the objectives of the International Energy Charter:

- to support the Charter's policy of consolidation, expansion and outreach with the aim to facilitate the expansion of the geographical scope of the Energy Charter Treaty and Process;
- to engage in a structured dialogue with non-signatories of the European Energy Charter in order to promote the principles of the Charter and its framework for cooperation on the global scale;
- to modernise the European Energy Charter as the basic political declaration of the Energy Charter Process;
- to support active observership in the Energy Charter Conference, aiming at close political cooperation and early accession of observer countries to the Energy Charter Treaty;

Whereas the International Energy Charter is a declaration of political intention aiming at strengthening the energy cooperation between the signatories and does not bear any legally binding obligation;

Having regard to the principles of the UN Charter and to the outcome documents of various energy-related regional and international conferences and other events as well as initiatives listed in the Annex to this declaration;

Recognising the sovereignty of each State over its energy resources, and its rights to regulate energy transmission and transportation within its territory respecting all its relevant international obligations;

Recognising the global challenge posed by the trilemma between energy security, economic development and environmental protection, and efforts by all countries to achieve sustainable development;

Recognising the importance of energy security of energy producing, transit and consuming countries, regardless of their state of economic development, as well as access to modern energy services, which needs to be based on environmentally sound, socially acceptable and economically viable policies, with emphasis on mutual responsibilities and benefits;

---

1   See https://energycharter.org/fileadmin/DocumentsMedia/Legal/IEC_Certified_Adopted_Copy.pdf. This Charter evolved from and replaces the 1994 Treaty.

Anxious to give a new impulse to the desire for enhanced regional and global cooperation based on mutual respect and confidence;

Resolved to promote long-term energy cooperation at regional and global levels within the framework of a market economy and based on mutual assistance and the principle of non discrimination, being understood as most-favoured nation treatment as a minimum standard;

Aware that account must be taken of the problems of construction and restructuring faced by a considerable number of countries, and that it is desirable for the signatories to participate in joint efforts aimed at facilitating and promoting market-oriented reforms and modernisation of energy sectors in these countries;

Certain that taking advantage of the complementary features of energy sectors in the markets represented by the signatories will benefit the world economy;

Acknowledging that enhanced energy trade is a powerful catalyst for strengthening regional and international cooperation in energy security and for sustainable use of energy among all stakeholders, including energy producing, transit and consuming countries;

Persuaded that broader energy cooperation among signatories is essential for economic progress and more generally for social development, energy poverty alleviation, and a better quality of life;

Convinced of the signatories' common interest in problems of energy security, safety of industrial plants, including nuclear facilities, and environmental protection;

Willing to do more to attain the objectives of energy security and efficient management and use of resources, and to utilise fully the potential for environmental improvement, in moving towards sustainable development;

Willing to develop cooperation with regional and international organisations for sharing experience and specific examples from national practice in the area of sustainable development, access to modern energy services, energy poverty reduction, green economy, clean energy, energy efficiency, as well as development, introduction and broader use of new clean technologies;

Convinced of the essential importance of efficient energy systems in the production, conversion, transport, distribution and use of energy for energy security and for the protection of the environment;

Convinced that investing in energy efficiency and renewable energies can enhance energy security and contribute to sustainable economic growth;

Encouraging synergies among energy-related multilateral fora;

Aware of the obligations under major relevant multilateral agreements, of the wide range of international energy cooperation, and of the extensive activities by existing international organisations in the energy field and willing to take full advantage of the expertise of these organisations in furthering the objectives of this Charter;

Recognising the role of entrepreneurs, operating within a transparent and equitable legal framework, in promoting cooperation under this Charter;

Determined to promote closer, mutually beneficial commercial relations and investments in the energy field;

Affirming the importance of freedom of movement of energy products, and of developing an efficient international energy infrastructure in order to facilitate the development of stable and transparent trade in energy;

Aware of the need to promote technical and technological cooperation among signatories;

Affirming that the energy policies of signatories are linked by common interests of all countries and that they should be implemented, including by taking the consequent action and applying the principles set out below;

HAVE ADOPTED THE FOLLOWING

Title I: Objectives

The signatories are desirous of sustainable energy development, improving energy security and maximising the efficiency of production, conversion, transport, distribution and use of energy, to enhance safety in a manner which would be socially acceptable, economically viable, and environmentally sound.

Recognising the sovereignty of each State over its energy resources, and its rights to regulate energy transmission and transportation within its territory respecting all its relevant international obligations, and in a spirit of political and economic cooperation, they decide to promote the development of efficient, stable and transparent energy markets at regional and global levels based on the principle of non-discrimination and market-oriented price formation, taking into account environmental concerns and the role of energy in each country's national development.

They are determined to create a climate favourable to the operation of enterprises and to the flow of investments and technologies to achieve the above objectives.

To this end, and in line with these principles, they will take action in the following fields:

1.   Development of trade in energy consistent with major relevant multilateral agreements such as the WTO Agreement and its related instruments, where applicable, and nuclear non-proliferation obligations and undertakings, which will be achieved by means of:

*   an open and competitive market for energy products, materials, equipment and services;
*   access to energy resources, and exploration and development thereof on a commercial basis;
*   access to national, regional and international markets;
*   providing transparency for all segments of international energy markets (production/export, transit, consumption/import);
*   removal of technical, administrative and other barriers to trade in energy and associated equipment, technologies and energy-related services;
*   promoting the compatibility of national and regional energy systems and to create a common energy space;
*   promotion of the harmonisation of rules, regulations and standards in the field of energy;
*   promoting the realisation of infrastructure projects important for providing global and regional energy security;
*   modernisation, renewal and rationalisation by industry of services and installations for the production, conversion, transport, distribution and use of energy;
*   promoting the development and interconnection of energy transport infrastructure and the regional integration of energy markets;
*   promoting best possible access to capital, particularly through appropriate existing financial institutions;
*   facilitating access to transport infrastructure, for international transit purposes in line with the objectives of this Charter;
*   access on commercial terms to technologies for the exploration, development, conversion and use of energy resources;

2.   Cooperation in the energy field, which will entail:

- coordination of energy policies, as necessary for promoting the objectives of this Charter;
- exchange of information and experiences relevant for this Charter;
- enhancing capacity building of the countries involved;
- mutual access to technical and economic data, consistent with proprietary rights;
- formulation of stable and transparent legal frameworks creating conditions for the development of energy resources in the context of sustainable development;
- coordination and, where appropriate, harmonisation of safety principles and guidelines for energy products and their transport, as well as for energy installations, at a high level;
- facilitating the exchange of technology information and know-how in the energy and environment fields, including training activities;
- research, technological development, demonstration projects and their commercialisation;
- creating a favourable environment for investments, including joint venture investments, for design, construction and operation of energy installations.

3. Energy efficiency and environmental protection, which will imply:

- creating mechanisms and conditions for using energy as economically and efficiently as possible, including, as appropriate, regulatory and market based instruments;
- encouraging the clean and efficient use of fossil fuels;
- promotion of a sustainable energy mix designed to minimise negative environmental consequences in a cost-effective way through:
  - i.   market-oriented energy prices which more fully reflect environmental costs and benefits;
  - ii. efficient and coordinated policy measures related to energy;
  - iii. use of renewable energy sources and clean technologies, including clean fossil fuel technologies;
- achieving and maintaining a high level of nuclear safety and ensuring effective cooperation in this field;
- promotion of cooperation to reduce, as much as possible, gas flaring and venting;
- sharing of best practices on clean energy development and investment;
- promotion and use of low emission technologies.

Title II: Implementation

In order to attain the objectives set out above, the signatories will, without prejudice to the sovereignty of each State over its energy resources, and its rights to regulate energy transmission and transportation within its territory respecting all its relevant international obligations, take coordinated action to achieve greater coherence of energy policies, which should be based on the principle of non discrimination and on market-oriented price formation, taking due account of environmental concerns.

They underline that practical steps to define energy policies are necessary in order to intensify cooperation in this sector and further stress the importance of regular exchanges of views on action taken, taking full advantage of the experience of existing international organisations and institutions in this field.

The signatories recognise that commercial forms of cooperation may need to be complemented by intergovernmental cooperation, particularly in the area of energy policy formulation and analysis, as well as in areas which are essential and not suitable to private capital funding.

They decide to pursue the objectives of this Charter by strengthening and integrating regional energy markets and enhancing the efficient functioning of the global energy market by joint or coordinated action under this Charter in the following fields:

- access to and development of energy sources;
- access to energy markets;
- liberalisation of trade in energy;
- promotion and protection of investments in all energy sectors;
- safety principles and guidelines;
- research, technological development technology transfer, innovation and dissemination;
- energy efficiency, environmental protection and sustainable and clean energy;
- access to sustainable energy;
- education and training;
- diversification of energy sources and routes.

In implementing this joint or coordinated action, they decide to foster private initiative, to make full use of the potential of enterprises, institutions and all available financial sources, and to facilitate cooperation including through technical cooperation, between such enterprises or institutions from different countries, acting on the basis of market principles.

The signatories will ensure that the international rules on the protection of industrial, commercial and intellectual property are respected.

1.   Access to and development of energy sources

Considering that efficient development of energy resources is a sine qua non for attaining the objectives of this Charter, the signatories decide to facilitate access to and development of resources by the interested operators. To this end, they will ensure that relevant rules are publicly available and transparent in consistence with domestic legislation and international obligations; they recognise the need to formulate such rules wherever this has not yet been done, and to take all necessary measures to coordinate their actions in this area. Development of energy resources should take place in economic and environmentally sound conditions.

With a view to facilitating the development and diversification of resources, the signatories decide to avoid imposing discriminatory rules on operators, notably rules governing the ownership of resources, internal operation of companies and taxation.

2.   Access to markets

The signatories will strongly promote access to national, regional and international markets for energy products for the implementation of the objectives of this Charter. Such access to markets should take account of the need to facilitate the operation of market forces, and promote competition.

3.   Liberalisation of trade in energy

In order to develop and diversify trade in energy, the signatories decide progressively to remove the barriers to such trade with each other in energy products, equipment and services in a manner consistent with the provisions of the WTO Agreement and its related instruments, where applicable, and nuclear non-proliferation obligations and undertakings.

They will work together in view of the further development of market-oriented energy prices.

The signatories recognise that transit of energy products through their territories is essential for the liberalisation of trade in energy products. Transit should take place in economic and environmentally and commercially sound conditions.

They stress the importance of the development of international energy transmission networks and their interconnection, including cross-border oil and gas networks and power grids. They recognise the need to intensify efforts to coordinate among themselves, and to encourage cooperation among relevant entities in view of their development, the compatibility of technical specifications governing the installation, and the operation of such networks.

4.   Promotion and protection of investments

In order to promote the international flow of investments, the signatories will make every effort to remove all barriers to investment in the energy sector and provide, at national level, for a stable, transparent legal framework for foreign investments, in conformity with the relevant international laws and rules on investment and trade.

They affirm that it is important for the signatory States to enter into bilateral and/or multilateral agreements on promotion and protection of investments which ensure a high level of legal security and enable the use of investment risk guarantee schemes.

The signatories affirm the importance of full access to adequate dispute settlement mechanisms, including national mechanisms and international arbitration in accordance with national laws and regulations, including investment and arbitration laws and rules, all the relevant bilateral and multilateral treaties and international agreements.

Moreover, the signatories recognise the right to repatriate profits or other payments relating to an investment and to obtain or use the convertible currency needed.

They also recognise the importance of the avoidance of double taxation to foster private investment.

5.   Safety principles and guidelines

Consistent with relevant major multilateral agreements, the signatories will:

- cooperate to implement safety principles and guidelines, designed to achieve and/or maintain high levels of safety standards and the protection of health and the environment;

- develop such common safety principles and guidelines as are appropriate and/or concur on the mutual recognition of their safety principles and guidelines.

6.   Research, technological development technology transfer, innovation and dissemination

The signatories decide to promote exchanges of technology and cooperation on their technological development and innovation activities in the fields of energy production, conversion, transport, distribution and the efficient and clean use of energy, in a manner consistent with nuclear non-proliferation obligations and undertakings.

To this end, they will encourage cooperative efforts on:

- research and development activities;

- pilot or demonstration projects;

- the application of technological innovations;

- the dissemination and exchange of know-how and information on technologies.

7.   Energy efficiency, environmental protection and sustainable and clean energy

The signatories confirm that cooperation is necessary in the field of efficient use of energy, development of renewable energy sources and energy-related environmental protection.

This should include:

- ensuring, in a cost-effective manner, consistency between relevant energy policies and environmental agreements and conventions;

- ensuring market-oriented price formation, including a fuller reflection of environmental costs and benefits;

- the use of transparent and equitable market-based instruments designed to achieve energy objectives and reduce environmental problems;
- the creation of framework conditions for the exchange of know-how regarding environmentally sound energy technologies, renewable energy sources and efficient use of energy;
- the creation of framework conditions for profitable investment in energy efficiency and environmental friendly energy projects.

8. Access to sustainable energy

The signatories underline the importance of access to sustainable, modern, affordable, and cleaner energy, in particular in developing countries, which may contribute to energy poverty alleviation.

To this end, the signatories confirm that they will make efforts to strengthen their cooperation and to support initiatives and partnerships at international level which are conducive to these goals.

9. Education and training

The signatories, recognising industry's role in promoting vocational education and training in the energy field, decide to cooperate in such activities, including:

- professional education;
- occupational training;
- public information in the energy efficiency and renewable energy field.

10. Diversification of energy sources and supply routes

The signatories confirm that in order to enhance energy security, energy generation from a diverse set of sources and diversification of supply routes is of significant importance.

Title III: Specific Agreements

The signatories decide to pursue the objectives and principles of this Charter and implement and broaden their cooperation, including in the following areas:

- horizontal and organisational issues;
- energy efficiency, including environmental protection;
- prospecting, production, transportation and use of oil and oil products and modernisation of refineries;
- prospecting, production and use of natural gas, interconnection of gas networks and transmission via high-pressure gas pipelines;
- all aspects of the nuclear fuel cycle including improvements in safety in that sector;

1. modernisation of power stations, interconnection of power networks and transmission of electricity via high-voltage power lines;
2. development of integrated regional energy markets;
3. all aspects of the coal cycle, including clean coal technologies;
4. development of renewable energy sources;
5. access to sustainable energy;
6. transfers of technology and encouragement of innovation;
7. cooperation in dealing with the effects of major accidents, or of other events in the energy sector with transfrontier consequences.

Title IV: Final Provisions

The original of this Charter will be transmitted to the Government of the Netherlands which will retain it in its archives. Each of the signatories will receive from the government of the Netherlands a true copy of the Charter.

The signatories request the Government of the Netherlands to transmit the text of the International Energy Charter, as adopted during the High Level Conference on the 20th and 21st May in The Hague, along with a note verbal to the Secretary General of the United Nations for his/her information and circulation among all UN Member States. The text of the International Energy Charter will be officially translated in Arabic, Chinese, French, German, Italian, Russian, and Spanish languages and distributed.

Done at The Hague on the 20th of May 2015.

Annex [...]

IX. Dispute Settlement

IX.1. 1958 UNITED NATIONS CONVENTION ON THE RECOGNITION AND ENFORCEMENT OF FOREIGN ARBITRAL AWARDS ("NEW YORK CONVENTION")

(New York, 10 June 1958; 330 UNTS 38)

Article I

1.   This Convention shall apply to the recognition and enforcement of arbitral awards made in the territory of a State other than the State where the recognition and enforcement of such awards are sought, and arising out of differences between persons, whether physical or legal. It shall also apply to arbitral awards not considered as domestic awards in the State where their recognition and enforcement are sought.

2.   The term "arbitral awards" shall include not only awards made by arbitrators appointed for each case but also those made by permanent arbitral bodies to which the parties have submitted.

3.   When signing, ratifying or acceding to this Convention, or notifying extension under Article X hereof, any State may on the basis of reciprocity declare that it will apply the Convention to the recognition and enforcement of awards made only in the territory of another Contracting State. It may also declare that it will apply the Convention only to differences arising out of legal relationships, whether contractual or not, which are considered as commercial under the national law of the State making such declaration.

Article II

1.   Each Contracting State shall recognize an agreement in writing under which the parties undertake to submit to arbitration all or any differences which have arisen or which may arise between them in respect of a defined legal relationship, whether contractual or not, concerning a subject matter capable of settlement by arbitration.

2.   The term "agreement in writing" shall include an arbitral clause in a contract or an arbitration agreement, signed by the parties or contained in an exchange of letters or telegrams.

3.   The court of a Contracting State, when seized of an action in a matter in respect of which the parties have made an agreement within the meaning of this article, at the request of one of the parties, refer the parties to arbitration, unless it finds that the said agreement is null and void, inoperative or incapable of being performed.

Article III

Each Contracting State shall recognize arbitral awards as binding and enforce them in accordance with the rules of procedure of the territory where the award is relied upon, under the conditions laid down in the following articles. There shall not be imposed substantially more onerous conditions or higher fees or charges on the recognition or enforcement of arbitral awards to which this Convention applies than are imposed on the recognition or enforcement of domestic arbitral awards.

Article IV

1.   To obtain the recognition and enforcement mentioned in the preceding article, the party applying for recognition and enforcement shall, at the time of the application, supply:

(a)   The duly authenticated original award or a duly certified copy thereof;

(b)   The original agreement referred to in Article II or a duly certified copy thereof.

2.   If the said award or agreement is not made in an official language of the country in which the award is relied upon, the party applying for recognition and enforcement of the award shall

produce a translation of these documents into such language. The translation shall be certified by an official or sworn translator or by a diplomatic or consular agent.

Article V

1. Recognition and enforcement of the award may be refused, at the request of the party against whom it is invoked, only if that party furnishes to the competent authority where the recognition and enforcement is sought, proof that:

(a) The parties to the agreement referred to in Article II were, under the law applicable to them, under some incapacity, or the said agreement is not valid under the law to which the parties have subjected it or, failing any indication thereon, under the law of the country where the award was made; or

(b) The party against whom the award is invoked was not given proper notice of the appointment of the arbitrator or of the arbitration proceedings or was otherwise unable to present his case; or

(c) The award deals with a difference not contemplated by or not falling within the terms of the submission to arbitration, or it contains decisions on matters beyond the scope of the submission to arbitration, provided that, if the decisions on matters submitted to arbitration can be separated from those not so submitted, that part of the award which contains decisions on matters submitted to arbitration may be recognized and enforced; or

(d) The composition of the arbitral authority or the arbitral procedure was not in accordance with the agreement of the parties, or, failing such agreement, was not in accordance with the law of the country where the arbitration took place; or

(e) The award has not yet become binding on the parties, or has been set aside or suspended by a competent authority of the country in which, or under the law of which, that award was made.

2. Recognition and enforcement of an arbitral award may also be refused if the competent authority in the country where recognition and enforcement is sought finds that:

(a) The subject matter of the difference is not capable of settlement by arbitration under the law of that country; or

(b) The recognition or enforcement of the award would be contrary to the public policy of that country.

Article VI

If an application for the setting aside or suspension of the award has been made to a competent authority referred to in Article V (1) (e), the authority before which the award is sought to be relied upon may, if it considers it proper, adjourn the decision on the enforcement of the award and may also, on the application of the party claiming enforcement of the award, order the other party to give suitable security.

Article VII

1. The provisions of the present Convention shall not affect the validity of multilateral or bilateral agreements concerning the recognition and enforcement of arbitral awards entered into by the Contracting States nor deprive any interested party of any right he may have to avail himself of an arbitral award in the manner and to the extent allowed by the law or the treaties of the country where such award is sought to be relied upon.

2. The Geneva Protocol on Arbitration Clauses of 1923 and the Geneva Convention on the Execution of Foreign Arbitral Awards of 1927 shall cease to have effect between Contracting States on their becoming bound and to the extent that they become bound, by this Convention.

Article VIII

1.   This Convention shall be open until 31 December 1958 for signature on behalf of any Member of the United Nations and also on behalf of any other State which is or hereafter becomes a member of any specialized agency of the United Nations, or which is or hereafter becomes a party to the Statute of the International Court of Justice, or any other State to which an invitation has been addressed by the General Assembly of the United Nations.

2.   This Convention shall be ratified and the instrument of ratification shall be deposited with the Secretary-General of the United Nations.

Article IX

1.   This Convention shall be open for accession to all States referred to in Article VIII.

2.   Accession shall be effected by the deposit of an instrument of accession with the Secretary-General of the United Nations.

Article X

1.   Any State may, at the time of signature, ratification or accession, declare that this Convention shall extend to all or any of the territories for the international relations of which it is responsible. Such a declaration shall take effect when the Convention enters into force for the State concerned.

2.   At any time thereafter any such extension shall be made by notification addressed to the Secretary-General of the United Nations and shall take effect as from the ninetieth day after the day of receipt by the Secretary-General of the United Nations of this notification, or as from the date of entry into force of the Convention for the State concerned, whichever is the later.

3.   With respect to those territories to which this Convention is not extended at the time of signature, ratification or accession, each State concerned shall consider the possibility of taking the necessary steps in order to extend the application of this Convention to such territories, subject, where necessary for constitutional reasons, to the consent of the Governments of such territories.

Article XI

In the case of a federal or non-unitary State, the following provisions shall apply:

(a)   With respect to those articles of this Convention that come within the legislative jurisdiction of the federal authority, the obligations of the federal Government shall to this extent be the same as those of Contracting States which are not federal States;

(b)   With respect to those articles of this Convention that come within the legislative jurisdiction of constituent states or provinces which are not, under the constitutional system of the federation, bound to take legislative action, the federal Government shall bring such articles with a favourable recommendation to the notice of the appropriate authorities of constituent states or provinces at the earliest possible moment;

(c)   A federal State Party to this Convention shall, at the request of any other Contracting State transmitted through the Secretary-General of the United Nations, supply a statement of the law and practice of the federation and its constituent units in regard to any particular provision of this Convention, showing the extent to which effect has been given to that provision by legislative or other action.

Article XII

1.   This Convention shall come into force on the ninetieth day following the date of deposit of the third instrument of ratification or accession.

2.   For each State ratifying or acceding to this Convention after the deposit of the third instrument of ratification or accession, this Convention shall enter into force on the ninetieth day after deposit by such State of its instrument of ratification or accession.

Article XIII

1.   Any Contracting State may denounce this Convention by a written notification to the Secretary-General of the United Nations. Denunciation shall take effect one year after the date of receipt of the notification by the Secretary-General.

2.   Any State which has made a declaration or notification under Article X may, at any time thereafter, by notification to the Secretary-General of the United Nations, declare that this Convention shall cease to extend to the territory concerned one year after the date of the receipt of the notification by the Secretary-General.

3.   This Convention shall continue to be applicable to arbitral awards in respect of which recognition and enforcement proceedings have been instituted before the denunciation takes effect.

Article XIV

A Contracting State shall not be entitled to avail itself of the present Convention against other Contracting States except to the extent that it is itself bound to apply the Convention.

Article XV

The Secretary-General of the United Nations shall notify the States contemplated in Article VIII of the following:

(a)   Signatures and ratifications in accordance with Article VIII;

(b)   Accessions in accordance with Article IX;

(c)   Declarations and notifications under articles I, X and XI;

(d)   The date upon which this Convention enters into force in accordance with Article XII;

(e)   Denunciations and notifications in accordance with Article XIII.

Article XVI

1.   This Convention, of which the Chinese, English, French, Russian and Spanish texts shall be equally authentic, shall be deposited in the archives of the United Nations.

2.   The Secretary-General of the United Nations shall transmit a certified copy of this Convention to the States contemplated in Article VIII.

Entry into force: 7 June 1959

Ratification and binding effect as of September 2018: 159 countries[1]

---

1   See http://www.uncitral.org/uncitral/en/uncitral_texts/arbitration/NYConvention_status.html.

IX.2. 1965 CONVENTION ON THE SETTLEMENT OF INVESTMENT DISPUTES BETWEEN STATES AND NATIONALS OF OTHER STATES (ICSID)

Preamble

The Contracting States

Considering the need for international cooperation for economic development, and the role of private international investment therein;

Bearing in mind the possibility that from time to time disputes may arise in connection with such investment between Contracting States and nationals of other Contracting States;

Recognizing that while such disputes would usually be subject to national legal processes, international methods of settlement may be appropriate in certain cases;

Attaching particular importance to the availability of facilities for international conciliation or arbitration to which Contracting States and nationals of other Contracting States may submit such disputes if they so desire;

Desiring to establish such facilities under the auspices of the International Bank for Reconstruction and Development;

Recognizing that mutual consent by the parties to submit such disputes to conciliation or to arbitration through such facilities constitutes a binding agreement which requires in particular that due consideration be given to any recommendation of conciliators, and that any arbitral award be complied with; and

Declaring that no Contracting State shall by the mere fact of its ratification, acceptance or approval of this Convention and without its consent be deemed to be under any obligation to submit any particular dispute to conciliation or arbitration,

Have agreed as follows:

Chapter I International Centre for Settlement of Investment Disputes

Section 1 Establishment and Organization

Article 1

(1) There is hereby established the International Centre for Settlement of Investment Disputes (hereinafter called the Centre).

(2) The purpose of the Centre shall be to provide facilities for conciliation and arbitration of investment disputes between Contracting States and nationals of other Contracting States in accordance with the provisions of this Convention.

Article 2

The seat of the Centre shall be at the principal office of the International Bank for Reconstruction and Development (hereinafter called the Bank). The seat may be moved to another place by decision of the Administrative Council adopted by a majority of two-thirds of its members.

Article 3

The Centre shall have an Administrative Council and a Secretariat and shall maintain a Panel of Conciliators and a Panel of Arbitrators.

Section 2 The Administrative Council

Article 4

(1) The Administrative Council shall be composed of one representative of each Contracting State. An alternate may act as representative in case of his principal's absence from a meeting or inability to act.

(2)   In the absence of a contrary designation, each governor and alternate governor of the Bank appointed by a Contracting State shall be ex officio its representative and its alternate respectively.

Article 5

The President of the Bank shall be ex officio Chairman of the Administrative Council (hereinafter called the Chairman) but shall have no vote. During his absence or inability to act and during any vacancy in the office of President of the Bank, the person for the time being acting as President shall act as Chairman of the Administrative Council.

Article 6

(1)   Without prejudice to the powers and functions vested in it by other provisions of this Convention, the Administrative Council shall:

(a)   adopt the administrative and financial regulations of the Centre;

(b)   adopt the rules of procedure for the institution of conciliation and arbitration proceedings;

(c)   adopt the rules of procedure for conciliation and arbitration proceedings (hereinafter called the Conciliation Rules and the Arbitration Rules);

(d)   approve arrangements with the Bank for the use of the Bank's administrative facilities and services;

(e)   determine the conditions of service of the Secretary-General and of any Deputy Secretary-General;

(f)   adopt the annual budget of revenues and expenditures of the Centre;

(g)   approve the annual report on the operation of the Centre.

The decisions referred to in sub-paragraphs (a), (b), (c) and (f) above shall be adopted by a majority of two-thirds of the members of the Administrative Council.

(2)   The Administrative Council may appoint such committees as it considers necessary.

(3)   The Administrative Council shall also exercise such other powers and perform such other functions as it shall determine to be necessary for the implementation of the provisions of this Convention.

Article 7

(1)   The Administrative Council shall hold an annual meeting and such other meetings as may be determined by the Council, or convened by the Chairman, or convened by the Secretary-General at the request of not less than five members of the Council.

(2)   Each member of the Administrative Council shall have one vote and, except as otherwise herein provided, all matters before the Council shall be decided by a majority of the votes cast.

(3)   A quorum for any meeting of the Administrative Council shall be a majority of its members.

(4)   The Administrative Council may establish, by a majority of two-thirds of its members, a procedure whereby the Chairman may seek a vote of the Council without convening a meeting of the Council. The vote shall be considered valid only if the majority of the members of the Council cast their votes within the time limit fixed by the said procedure.

Article 8

Members of the Administrative Council and the Chairman shall serve without remuneration from the Centre.

Section 3 The Secretariat

Article 9

The Secretariat shall consist of a Secretary-General, one or more Deputy Secretaries-General and staff.

Article 10

(1) The Secretary-General and any Deputy Secretary-General shall be elected by the Administrative Council by a majority of two-thirds of its members upon the nomination of the Chairman for a term of service not exceeding six years and shall be eligible for re-election. After consulting the members of the Administrative Council, the Chairman shall propose one or more candidates for each such office.

(2) The offices of Secretary-General and Deputy Secretary-General shall be incompatible with the exercise of any political function. Neither the Secretary-General nor any Deputy Secretary-General may hold any other employment or engage in any other occupation except with the approval of the Administrative Council.

(3) During the Secretary-General's absence or inability to act, and during any vacancy of the office of Secretary-General, the Deputy Secretary-General shall act as Secretary-General. If there shall be more than one Deputy Secretary-General, the Administrative Council shall determine in advance the order in which they shall act as Secretary-General.

Article 11

The Secretary-General shall be the legal representative and the principal officer of the Centre and shall be responsible for its administration, including the appointment of staff, in accordance with the provisions of this Convention and the rules adopted by the Administrative Council. He shall perform the function of registrar and shall have the power to authenticate arbitral awards rendered pursuant to this Convention, and to certify copies thereof.

Section 4 The Panels

Article 12

The Panel of Conciliators and the Panel of Arbitrators shall each consist of qualified persons, designated as hereinafter provided, who are willing to serve thereon.

Article 13

(1) Each Contracting State may designate to each Panel four persons who may but need not be its nationals.

(2) The Chairman may designate ten persons to each Panel. The persons so designated to a Panel shall each have a different nationality.

Article 14

(1) Persons designated to serve on the Panels shall be persons of high moral character and recognized competence in the fields of law, commerce, industry or finance, who may be relied upon to exercise independent judgment. Competence in the field of law shall be of particular importance in the case of persons on the Panel of Arbitrators.

(2) The Chairman, in designating persons to serve on the Panels, shall in addition pay due regard to the importance of assuring representation on the Panels of the principal legal systems of the world and of the main forms of economic activity.

Article 15

(1) Panel members shall serve for renewable periods of six years.

(2) In case of death or resignation of a member of a Panel, the authority which designated the member shall have the right to designate another person to serve for the remainder of that member's term.

(3)   Panel members shall continue in office until their successors have been designated.

Article 16

(1)   A person may serve on both Panels.

(2)   If a person shall have been designated to serve on the same Panel by more than one Contracting State, or by one or more Contracting States and the Chairman, he shall be deemed to have been designated by the authority which first designated him or, if one such authority is the State of which he is a national, by that State.

(3)   All designations shall be notified to the Secretary-General and shall take effect from the date on which the notification is received.

Section 5 Financing the Centre

Article 17

If the expenditure of the Centre cannot be met out of charges for the use of its facilities, or out of other receipts, the excess shall be borne by Contracting States which are members of the Bank in proportion to their respective subscriptions to the capital stock of the Bank, and by Contracting States which are not members of the Bank in accordance with rules adopted by the Administrative Council.

Section 6 Status, Immunities and Privileges

Article 18

The Centre shall have full international legal personality. The legal capacity of the Centre shall include the capacity:

(a)   to contract;

(b)   to acquire and dispose of movable and immovable property;

(c)   to institute legal proceedings.

Article 19

To enable the Centre to fulfil its functions, it shall enjoy in the territories of each Contracting State the immunities and privileges set forth in this Section.

Article 20

The Centre, its property and assets shall enjoy immunity from all legal process, except when the Centre waives this immunity.

Article 21

The Chairman, the members of the Administrative Council, persons acting as conciliators or arbitrators or members of a Committee appointed pursuant to paragraph (3) of Article 52, and the officers and employees of the Secretariat

(a)   shall enjoy immunity from legal process with respect to acts performed by them in the exercise of their functions, except when the Centre waives this immunity;

(b)   not being local nationals, shall enjoy the same immunities from immigration restrictions, alien registration requirements and national service obligations, the same facilities as regards exchange restrictions and the same treatment in respect of travelling facilities as are accorded by Contracting States to the representatives, officials and employees of comparable rank of other Contracting States.

Article 22

The provisions of Article 21 shall apply to persons appearing in proceedings under this Convention as parties, agents, counsel, advocates, witnesses or experts; provided, however, that sub-paragraph (b) thereof shall apply only in connection with their travel to and from, and their stay at, the place where the proceedings are held.

Article 23

(1)   The archives of the Centre shall be inviolable, wherever they may be.

(2)   With regard to its official communications, the Centre shall be accorded by each Contracting State treatment not less favourable than that accorded to other international organizations.

Article 24

(1)   The Centre, its assets, property and income, and its operations and transactions authorized by this Convention shall be exempt from all taxation and customs duties. The Centre shall also be exempt from liability for the collection or payment of any taxes or customs duties.

(2)   Except in the case of local nationals, no tax shall be levied on or in respect of expense allowances paid by the Centre to the Chairman or members of the Administrative Council, or on or in respect of salaries, expense allowances or other emoluments paid by the Centre to officials or employees of the Secretariat.

(3)   No tax shall be levied on or in respect of fees or expense allowances received by persons acting as conciliators, or arbitrators, or members of a Committee appointed pursuant to paragraph (3) of Article 52, in proceedings under this Convention, if the sole jurisdictional basis for such tax is the location of the Centre or the place where such proceedings are conducted or the place where such fees or allowances are paid.

Chapter II Jurisdiction of the Centre

Article 25

(1)   The jurisdiction of the Centre shall extend to any legal dispute arising directly out of an investment, between a Contracting State (or any constituent subdivision or agency of a Contracting State designated to the Centre by that State) and a national of another Contracting State, which the parties to the dispute consent in writing to submit to the Centre. When the parties have given their consent, no party may withdraw its consent unilaterally.

(2)   "National of another Contracting State" means:

(a)   any natural person who had the nationality of a Contracting State other than the State party to the dispute on the date on which the parties consented to submit such dispute to conciliation or arbitration as well as on the date on which the request was registered pursuant to paragraph (3) of Article 28 or paragraph (3) of Article 36, but does not include any person who on either date also had the nationality of the Contracting State party to the dispute; and

(b)   any juridical person which had the nationality of a Contracting State other than the State party to the dispute on the date on which the parties consented to submit such dispute to conciliation or arbitration and any juridical person which had the nationality of the Contracting State party to the dispute on that date and which, because of foreign control, the parties have agreed should be treated as a national of another Contracting State for the purposes of this Convention.

(3)   Consent by a constituent subdivision or agency of a Contracting State shall require the approval of that State unless that State notifies the Centre that no such approval is required.

(4)   Any Contracting State may, at the time of ratification, acceptance or approval of this Convention or at any time thereafter, notify the Centre of the class or classes of disputes which it would or would not consider submitting to the jurisdiction of the Centre. The Secretary-General shall forthwith transmit such notification to all Contracting States. Such notification shall not constitute the consent required by paragraph (1).

Article 26

Consent of the parties to arbitration under this Convention shall, unless otherwise stated, be deemed consent to such arbitration to the exclusion of any other remedy. A Contracting State may require the exhaustion of local administrative or judicial remedies as a condition of its consent to arbitration under this Convention.

Article 27

(1) No Contracting State shall give diplomatic protection, or bring an international claim, in respect of a dispute which one of its nationals and another Contracting State shall have consented to submit or shall have submitted to arbitration under this Convention, unless such other Contracting State shall have failed to abide by and comply with the award rendered in such dispute.

(2) Diplomatic protection, for the purposes of paragraph (1), shall not include informal diplomatic exchanges for the sole purpose of facilitating a settlement of the dispute.

Chapter III Conciliation

Section 1 Request for Conciliation

Article 28

(1)   Any Contracting State or any national of a Contracting State wishing to institute conciliation proceedings shall address a request to that effect in writing to the Secretary-General who shall send a copy of the request to the other party.

(2)   The request shall contain information concerning the issues in dispute, the identity of the parties and their consent to conciliation in accordance with the rules of procedure for the institution of conciliation and arbitration proceedings.

(3)   The Secretary-General shall register the request unless he finds, on the basis of the information contained in the request, that the dispute is manifestly outside the jurisdiction of the Centre. He shall forthwith notify the parties of registration or refusal to register.

Section 2 Constitution of the Conciliation Commission

Article 29

(1) The Conciliation Commission (hereinafter called the Commission) shall be constituted as soon as possible after registration of a request pursuant to Article 28.

(2) (a) The Commission shall consist of a sole conciliator or any uneven number of conciliators appointed as the parties shall agree.

(b) Where the parties do not agree upon the number of conciliators and the method of their appointment, the Commission shall consist of three conciliators, one conciliator appointed by each party and the third, who shall be the president of the Commission, appointed by agreement of the parties.

Article 30

If the Commission shall not have been constituted within 90 days after notice of registration of the request has been dispatched by the Secretary-General in accordance with paragraph (3) of Article 28, or such other period as the parties may agree, the Chairman shall, at the request of either party and after consulting both parties as far as possible, appoint the conciliator or conciliators not yet appointed.

Article 31

(1) Conciliators may be appointed from outside the Panel of Conciliators, except in the case of appointments by the Chairman pursuant to Article 30.

(2) Conciliators appointed from outside the Panel of Conciliators shall possess the qualities stated in paragraph (1) of Article 14.

Section 3 Conciliation Proceedings

Article 32

(1)   The Commission shall be the judge of its own competence.

(2)   Any objection by a party to the dispute that that dispute is not within the jurisdiction of the Centre, or for other reasons is not within the competence of the Commission, shall be considered by the Commission which shall determine whether to deal with it as a preliminary question or to join it to the merits of the dispute.

Article 33

Any conciliation proceeding shall be conducted in accordance with the provisions of this Section and, except as the parties otherwise agree, in accordance with the Conciliation Rules in effect on the date on which the parties consented to conciliation. If any question of procedure arises which is not covered by this Section or the Conciliation Rules or any rules agreed by the parties, the Commission shall decide the question.

Article 34

(1)   It shall be the duty of the Commission to clarify the issues in dispute between the parties and to endeavour to bring about agreement between them upon mutually acceptable terms. To that end, the Commission may at any stage of the proceedings and from time to time recommend terms of settlement to the parties. The parties shall cooperate in good faith with the Commission in order to enable the Commission to carry out its functions, and shall give their most serious consideration to its recommendations.

(2)   If the parties reach agreement, the Commission shall draw up a report noting the issues in dispute and recording that the parties have reached agreement. If, at any stage of the proceedings, it appears to the Commission that there is no likelihood of agreement between the parties, it shall close the proceedings and shall draw up a report noting the submission of the dispute and recording the failure of the parties to reach agreement. If one party fails to appear or participate in the proceedings, the Commission shall close the proceedings and shall draw up a report noting that party's failure to appear or participate.

Article 35

Except as the parties to the dispute shall otherwise agree, neither party to a conciliation proceeding shall be entitled in any other proceeding, whether before arbitrators or in a court of law or otherwise, to invoke or rely on any views expressed or statements or admissions or offers of settlement made by the other party in the conciliation proceedings, or the report or any recommendations made by the Commission.

Chapter IV Arbitration

Section 1 Request for Arbitration

Article 36

(1)   Any Contracting State or any national of a Contracting State wishing to institute arbitration proceedings shall address a request to that effect in writing to the Secretary-General who shall send a copy of the request to the other party.

(2)   The request shall contain information concerning the issues in dispute, the identity of the parties and their consent to arbitration in accordance with the rules of procedure for the institution of conciliation and arbitration proceedings.

(3)   The Secretary-General shall register the request unless he finds, on the basis of the information contained in the request, that the dispute is manifestly outside the jurisdiction of the Centre. He shall forthwith notify the parties of registration or refusal to register.

Section 2 Constitution of the Tribunal

Article 37

(1)   The Arbitral Tribunal (hereinafter called the Tribunal) shall be constituted as soon as possible after registration of a request pursuant to Article 36.

(2)   (a) The Tribunal shall consist of a sole arbitrator or any uneven number of arbitrators appointed as the parties shall agree.

(b)   Where the parties do not agree upon the number of arbitrators and the method of their appointment, the Tribunal shall consist of three arbitrators, one arbitrator appointed by each party and the third, who shall be the president of the Tribunal, appointed by agreement of the parties.

Article 38

If the Tribunal shall not have been constituted within 90 days after notice of registration of the request has been dispatched by the Secretary-General in accordance with paragraph (3) of Article 36, or such other period as the parties may agree, the Chairman shall, at the request of either party and after consulting both parties as far as possible, appoint the arbitrator or arbitrators not yet appointed. Arbitrators appointed by the Chairman pursuant to this Article shall not be nationals of the Contracting State party to the dispute or of the Contracting State whose national is a party to the dispute.

Article 39

The majority of the arbitrators shall be nationals of States other than the Contracting State party to the dispute and the Contracting State whose national is a party to the dispute; provided, however, that the foregoing provisions of this Article shall not apply if the sole arbitrator or each individual member of the Tribunal has been appointed by agreement of the parties.

Article 40

(1)   Arbitrators may be appointed from outside the Panel of Arbitrators, except in the case of appointments by the Chairman pursuant to Article 38.

(2)   Arbitrators appointed from outside the Panel of Arbitrators shall possess the qualities stated in paragraph (1) of Article 14.

Section 3 Powers and Functions of the Tribunal

Article 41

(1)   The Tribunal shall be the judge of its own competence.

(2)   Any objection by a party to the dispute that that dispute is not within the jurisdiction of the Centre, or for other reasons is not within the competence of the Tribunal, shall be considered by the Tribunal which shall determine whether to deal with it as a preliminary question or to join it to the merits of the dispute.

Article 42

(1)   The Tribunal shall decide a dispute in accordance with such rules of law as may be agreed by the parties. In the absence of such agreement, the Tribunal shall apply the law of the Contracting State party to the dispute (including its rules on the conflict of laws) and such rules of international law as may be applicable.

(2)   The Tribunal may not bring in a finding of non liquet on the ground of silence or obscurity of the law.

(3)   The provisions of paragraphs (1) and (2) shall not prejudice the power of the Tribunal to decide a dispute ex aequo et bono if the parties so agree.

Article 43

Except as the parties otherwise agree, the Tribunal may, if it deems it necessary at any stage of the proceedings,

(a)   call upon the parties to produce documents or other evidence, and

(b)   visit the scene connected with the dispute, and conduct such inquiries there as it may deem appropriate.

Article 44

Any arbitration proceeding shall be conducted in accordance with the provisions of this Section and, except as the parties otherwise agree, in accordance with the Arbitration Rules in effect on the date on which the parties consented to arbitration. If any question of procedure arises which is not covered by this Section or the Arbitration Rules or any rules agreed by the parties, the Tribunal shall decide the question.

Article 45

(1)   Failure of a party to appear or to present his case shall not be deemed an admission of the other party's assertions.

(2)   If a party fails to appear or to present his case at any stage of the proceedings the other party may request the Tribunal to deal with the questions submitted to it and to render an award. Before rendering an award, the Tribunal shall notify, and grant a period of grace to, the party failing to appear or to present its case, unless it is satisfied that that party does not intend to do so.

Article 46

Except as the parties otherwise agree, the Tribunal shall, if requested by a party, determine any incidental or additional claims or counterclaims arising directly out of the subject-matter of the dispute provided that they are within the scope of the consent of the parties and are otherwise within the jurisdiction of the Centre.

Article 47

Except as the parties otherwise agree, the Tribunal may, if it considers that the circumstances so require, recommend any provisional measures which should be taken to preserve the respective rights of either party.

Section 4 The Award

Article 48

(1)   The Tribunal shall decide questions by a majority of the votes of all its members.

(2)   The award of the Tribunal shall be in writing and shall be signed by the members of the Tribunal who voted for it.

(3)   The award shall deal with every question submitted to the Tribunal, and shall state the reasons upon which it is based.

(4)   Any member of the Tribunal may attach his individual opinion to the award, whether he dissents from the majority or not, or a statement of his dissent.

(5)   The Centre shall not publish the award without the consent of the parties.

Article 49

(1)   The Secretary-General shall promptly dispatch certified copies of the award to the parties. The award shall be deemed to have been rendered on the date on which the certified copies were dispatched.

(2)   The Tribunal upon the request of a party made within 45 days after the date on which the award was rendered may after notice to the other party decide any question which it had

omitted to decide in the award, and shall rectify any clerical, arithmetical or similar error in the award. Its decision shall become part of the award and shall be notified to the parties in the same manner as the award. The periods of time provided for under paragraph (2) of Article 51 and paragraph (2) of Article 52 shall run from the date on which the decision was rendered.

Section 5 Interpretation, Revision and Annulment of the Award

Article 50

(1)   If any dispute shall arise between the parties as to the meaning or scope of an award, either party may request interpretation of the award by an application in writing addressed to the Secretary-General.

(2)   The request shall, if possible, be submitted to the Tribunal which rendered the award. If this shall not be possible, a new Tribunal shall be constituted in accordance with Section 2 of this Chapter. The Tribunal may, if it considers that the circumstances so require, stay enforcement of the award pending its decision.

Article 51

(1)   Either party may request revision of the award by an application in writing addressed to the Secretary-General on the ground of discovery of some fact of such a nature as decisively to affect the award, provided that when the award was rendered that fact was unknown to the Tribunal and to the applicant and that the applicant's ignorance of that fact was not due to negligence.

(2)   The application shall be made within 90 days after the discovery of such fact and in any event within three years after the date on which the award was rendered.

(3)   The request shall, if possible, be submitted to the Tribunal which rendered the award. If this shall not be possible, a new Tribunal shall be constituted in accordance with Section 2 of this Chapter.

(4)   The Tribunal may, if it considers that the circumstances so require, stay enforcement of the award pending its decision. If the applicant requests a stay of enforcement of the award in his application, enforcement shall be stayed provisionally until the Tribunal rules on such request.

Article 52

(1)   Either party may request annulment of the award by an application in writing addressed to the Secretary-General on one or more of the following grounds:

(a)   that the Tribunal was not properly constituted;

(b)   that the Tribunal has manifestly exceeded its powers;

(c)   that there was corruption on the part of a member of the Tribunal;

(d)   that there has been a serious departure from a fundamental rule of procedure; or

(e)   that the award has failed to state the reasons on which it is based.

(2)   The application shall be made within 120 days after the date on which the award was rendered except that when annulment is requested on the ground of corruption such applica-tion shall be made within 120 days after discovery of the corruption and in any event within three years after the date on which the award was rendered.

(3)   On receipt of the request the Chairman shall forthwith appoint from the Panel of Arbitrators an ad hoc Committee of three persons. None of the members of the Committee shall have been a member of the Tribunal which rendered the award, shall be of the same nationality as any such member, shall be a national of the State party to the dispute or of the State whose national is a party to the dispute, shall have been designated to the Panel of Arbitrators by either of those States, or shall have acted as a conciliator in the same dispute. The Committee shall have the authority to annul the award or any part thereof on any of the grounds set forth in paragraph (1).

(4)   The provisions of Articles 41-45, 48, 49, 53 and 54, and of Chapters VI and VII shall apply mutatis mutandis to proceedings before the Committee.

(5)   The Committee may, if it considers that the circumstances so require, stay enforcement of the award pending its decision. If the applicant requests a stay of enforcement of the award in his application, enforcement shall be stayed provisionally until the Committee rules on such request.

(6)   If the award is annulled the dispute shall, at the request of either party, be submitted to a new Tribunal constituted in accordance with Section 2 of this Chapter.

Section 6 Recognition and Enforcement of the Award

Article 53

(1)   The award shall be binding on the parties and shall not be subject to any appeal or to any other remedy except those provided for in this Convention. Each party shall abide by and comply with the terms of the award except to the extent that enforcement shall have been stayed pursuant to the relevant provisions of this Convention.

(2)   For the purposes of this Section, "award" shall include any decision interpreting, revising or annulling such award pursuant to Articles 50, 51 or 52.

Article 54

(1)   Each Contracting State shall recognize an award rendered pursuant to this Convention as binding and enforce the pecuniary obligations imposed by that award within its territories as if it were a final judgment of a court in that State. A Contracting State with a federal constitution may enforce such an award in or through its federal courts and may provide that such courts shall treat the award as if it were a final judgment of the courts of a constituent state.

(2)   A party seeking recognition or enforcement in the territories of a Contracting State shall furnish to a competent court or other authority which such State shall have designated for this purpose a copy of the award certified by the Secretary-General. Each Contracting State shall notify the Secretary-General of the designation of the competent court or other authority for this purpose and of any subsequent change in such designation.

(3)   Execution of the award shall be governed by the laws concerning the execution of judgments in force in the State in whose territories such execution is sought.

Article 55

Nothing in Article 54 shall be construed as derogating from the law in force in any Contracting State relating to immunity of that State or of any foreign State from execution.

Chapter V Replacement and Disqualification of Conciliators and Arbitrators

Article 56

(1)   After a Commission or a Tribunal has been constituted and proceedings have begun, its composition shall remain unchanged; provided, however, that if a conciliator or an arbitrator should die, become incapacitated, or resign, the resulting vacancy shall be filled in accordance with the provisions of Section 2 of Chapter III or Section 2 of Chapter IV.

(2)   A member of a Commission or Tribunal shall continue to serve in that capacity notwithstanding that he shall have ceased to be a member of the Panel.

(3)   If a conciliator or arbitrator appointed by a party shall have resigned without the consent of the Commission or Tribunal of which he was a member, the Chairman shall appoint a person from the appropriate Panel to fill the resulting vacancy.

Article 57

A party may propose to a Commission or Tribunal the disqualification of any of its members on account of any fact indicating a manifest lack of the qualities required by paragraph (1) of Article 14. A party to arbitration proceedings may, in addition, propose the disqualification of an arbitrator on the ground that he was ineligible for appointment to the Tribunal under Section 2 of Chapter IV.

Article 58

The decision on any proposal to disqualify a conciliator or arbitrator shall be taken by the other members of the Commission or Tribunal as the case may be, provided that where those members are equally divided, or in the case of a proposal to disqualify a sole conciliator or arbitrator, or a majority of the conciliators or arbitrators, the Chairman shall take that decision. If it is decided that the proposal is well-founded the conciliator or arbitrator to whom the decision relates shall be replaced in accordance with the provisions of Section 2 of Chapter III or Section 2 of Chapter IV.

Chapter VI Cost of Proceedings

Article 59

The charges payable by the parties for the use of the facilities of the Centre shall be determined by the Secretary-General in accordance with the regulations adopted by the Administrative Council.

Article 60

(1)   Each Commission and each Tribunal shall determine the fees and expenses of its members within limits established from time to time by the Administrative Council and after consultation with the Secretary-General.

(2)   Nothing in paragraph (1) of this Article shall preclude the parties from agreeing in advance with the Commission or Tribunal concerned upon the fees and expenses of its members.

Article 61

(1)   In the case of conciliation proceedings the fees and expenses of members of the Commission as well as the charges for the use of the facilities of the Centre, shall be borne equally by the parties. Each party shall bear any other expenses it incurs in connection with the proceedings.

(2)   In the case of arbitration proceedings the Tribunal shall, except as the parties otherwise agree, assess the expenses incurred by the parties in connection with the proceedings, and shall decide how and by whom those expenses, the fees and expenses of the members of the Tribunal and the charges for the use of the facilities of the Centre shall be paid. Such decision shall form part of the award.

Chapter VII Place of Proceedings

Article 62

Conciliation and arbitration proceedings shall be held at the seat of the Centre except as hereinafter provided.

Article 63

Conciliation and arbitration proceedings may be held, if the parties so agree,

(a)   at the seat of the Permanent Court of Arbitration or of any other appropriate institution, whether private or public, with which the Centre may make arrangements for that purpose; or

(b)   at any other place approved by the Commission or Tribunal after consultation with the Secretary-General.

Chapter VIII Disputes Between Contracting States

Article 64

Any dispute arising between Contracting States concerning the interpretation or application of this Convention which is not settled by negotiation shall be referred to the International Court of Justice by the application of any party to such dispute, unless the States concerned agree to another method of settlement.

Chapter IX Amendment

Article 65

Any Contracting State may propose amendment of this Convention. The text of a proposed amendment shall be communicated to the Secretary-General not less than 90 days prior to the meeting of the Administrative Council at which such amendment is to be considered and shall forthwith be transmitted by him to all the members of the Administrative Council.

Article 66

(1)   If the Administrative Council shall so decide by a majority of two-thirds of its members, the proposed amendment shall be circulated to all Contracting States for ratification, acceptance or approval. Each amendment shall enter into force 30 days after dispatch by the depositary of this Convention of a notification to Contracting States that all Contracting States have ratified, accepted or approved the amendment.

(2)   No amendment shall affect the rights and obligations under this Convention of any Contracting State or of any of its constituent subdivisions or agencies, or of any national of such State arising out of consent to the jurisdiction of the Centre given before the date of entry into force of the amendment.

Chapter X Final Provisions

Article 67

This Convention shall be open for signature on behalf of States members of the Bank. It shall also be open for signature on behalf of any other State which is a party to the Statute of the International Court of Justice and which the Administrative Council, by a vote of two-thirds of its members, shall have invited to sign the Convention.

Article 68

(1)   This Convention shall be subject to ratification, acceptance or approval by the signatory States in accordance with their respective constitutional procedures.

(2)   This Convention shall enter into force 30 days after the date of deposit of the twentieth instrument of ratification, acceptance or approval. It shall enter into force for each State which subsequently deposits its instrument of ratification, acceptance or approval 30 days after the date of such deposit.

Article 69

Each Contracting State shall take such legislative or other measures as may be necessary for making the provisions of this Convention effective in its territories.

Article 70

This Convention shall apply to all territories for whose international relations a Contracting State is responsible, except those which are excluded by such State by written notice to the depositary of this Convention either at the time of ratification, acceptance or approval or subsequently.

Article 71

Any Contracting State may denounce this Convention by written notice to the depositary of this Convention. The denunciation shall take effect six months after receipt of such notice.

Article 72

Notice by a Contracting State pursuant to Articles 70 or 71 shall not affect the rights or obligations under this Convention of that State or of any of its constituent subdivisions or agencies or of any national of that State arising out of consent to the jurisdiction of the Centre given by one of them before such notice was received by the depositary.

Article 73

Instruments of ratification, acceptance or approval of this Convention and of amendments thereto shall be deposited with the Bank which shall act as the depositary of this Convention. The depositary shall transmit certified copies of this Convention to States members of the Bank and to any other State invited to sign the Convention.

Article 74

The depositary shall register this Convention with the Secretariat of the United Nations in accordance with Article 102 of the Charter of the United Nations and the Regulations thereunder adopted by the General Assembly.

Article 75

The depositary shall notify all signatory States of the following:

(a) signatures in accordance with Article 67;

(b) deposits of instruments of ratification, acceptance and approval in accordance with Article 73;

(c) the date on which this Convention enters into force in accordance with Article 68;

(d) exclusions from territorial application pursuant to Article 70;

(e) the date on which any amendment of this Convention enters into force in accordance with Article 66; and

(f) denunciations in accordance with Article 71.

DONE at Washington, in the English, French and Spanish languages, all three texts being equally authentic, in a single copy which shall remain deposited in the archives of the International Bank for Reconstruction and Development, which has indicated by its signature below its agreement to fulfil the functions with which it is charged under this Convention.

RULES OF PROCEDURE FOR THE INSTITUTION OF CONCILIATION
AND ARBITRATION PROCEEDINGS (INSTITUTION RULES)

Rule 1 The Request

(1) Any Contracting State or any national of a Contracting State wishing to institute conciliation or arbitration proceedings under the Convention shall address a request to that effect in writing to the Secretary-General at the seat of the Centre. The request shall indicate whether it relates to a conciliation or an arbitration proceeding. It shall be drawn up in an official language of the Centre, shall be dated, and shall be signed by the requesting party or its duly authorized representative.

(2) The request may be made jointly by the parties to the dispute.

Rule 2 Contents of the Request

(1)   The request shall:

(a)   designate precisely each party to the dispute and state the address of each;

(b)   state, if one of the parties is a constituent subdivision or agency of a Contracting State, that it has been designated to the Centre by that State pursuant to Article 25(1) of the Convention;

(c)   indicate the date of consent and the instruments in which it is recorded, including, if one party is a constituent subdivision or agency of a Contracting State, similar data on the approval of such consent by that State unless it had notified the Centre that no such approval is required;

(d)   indicate with respect to the party that is a national of a Contracting State:

    (i)   its nationality on the date of consent; and

    (ii)   if the party is a natural person:

        (A)   his nationality on the date of the request; and

        (B)   that he did not have the nationality of the Contracting State party to the dispute either on the date of consent or on the date of the request; or

    (iii) if the party is a juridical person which on the date of consent had the nationality of the Contracting State party to the dispute, the agreement of the parties that it should be treated as a national of another Contracting State for the purposes of the Convention;

(e)   contain information concerning the issues in dispute indicating that there is, between the parties, a legal dispute arising directly out of an investment; and

(f)   state, if the requesting party is a juridical person, that it has taken all necessary internal actions to authorize the request.

(2)   The information required by subparagraphs (1)(c), (1)(d)(iii) and (1)(f) shall be supported by documentation.

(3)   "Date of consent" means the date on which the parties to the dispute consented in writing to submit it to the Centre; if both parties did not act on the same day, it means the date on which the second party acted.

Rule 3 Optional Information in the Request

The request may in addition set forth any provisions agreed by the parties regarding the number of conciliators or arbitrators and the method of their appointment, as well as any other provisions agreed concerning the settlement of the dispute.

Rule 4 Copies of the Request

(1)   The request shall be accompanied by five additional signed copies. The Secretary-General may require such further copies as he may deem necessary.

(2)   Any documentation submitted with the request shall conform to the requirements of Administrative and Financial Regulation 30.

Rule 5 Acknowledgement of the Request

(1)   On receiving a request the Secretary-General shall:

(a)   send an acknowledgement to the requesting party;

(b)   take no other action with respect to the request until he has received payment of the prescribed fee.

(2)   As soon as he has received the fee for lodging the request, the Secretary-General shall transmit a copy of the request and of the accompanying documentation to the other party.

Rule 6 Registration of the Request

(1)   The Secretary-General shall, subject to Rule 5(1)(b), as soon as possible, either:

(a)   register the request in the Conciliation or the Arbitration Register and on the same day notify the parties of the registration; or

(b)   if he finds, on the basis of the information contained in the request, that the dispute is manifestly outside the jurisdiction of the Centre, notify the parties of his refusal to register the request and of the reasons therefor.

(2)   A proceeding under the Convention shall be deemed to have been instituted on the date of the registration of the request.

Rule 7 Notice of Registration

The notice of registration of a request shall:

(a)   record that the request is registered and indicate the date of the registration and of the dispatch of that notice;

(b)   notify each party that all communications and notices in connection with the proceeding will be sent to the address stated in the request, unless another address is indicated to the Centre;

(c)   unless such information has already been provided, invite the parties to communicate to the Secretary-General any provisions agreed by them regarding the number and the method of appointment of the conciliators or arbitrators;

(d)   invite the parties to proceed, as soon as possible, to constitute a Conciliation Commission in accordance with Articles 29 to 31 of the Convention, or an Arbitral Tribunal in accordance with Articles 37 to 40;

(e)   remind the parties that the registration of the request is without prejudice to the powers and functions of the Conciliation Commission or Arbitral Tribunal in regard to jurisdiction, competence and the merits; and

(f)   be accompanied by a list of the members of the Panel of Conciliators or of Arbitrators of the Centre.

Rule 8 Withdrawal of the Request

The requesting party may, by written notice to the Secretary-General, withdraw the request before it has been registered. The Secretary-General shall promptly notify the other party, unless, pursuant to Rule 5(1)(b), the request had not been transmitted to it.

Rule 9 Final Provisions

(1)   The texts of these Rules in each official language of the Centre shall be equally authentic.

(2)   These Rules may be cited as the "Institution Rules" of the Centre.

RULES OF PROCEDURE FOR CONCILIATION PROCEEDINGS
(CONCILIATION RULES)
Chapter I Establishment of the Commission
Rule 1 General Obligations

(1)   Upon notification of the registration of the request for conciliation, the parties shall, with all possible dispatch, proceed to constitute a Commission, with due regard to Section 2 of Chapter III of the Convention.

(2) Unless such information is provided in the request, the parties shall communicate to the Secretary-General as soon as possible any provisions agreed by them regarding the number of conciliators and the method of their appointment.

Rule 2 Method of Constituting the Commission in the Absence of Previous Agreement

(1) If the parties, at the time of the registration of the request for conciliation, have not agreed upon the number of conciliators and the method of their appointment, they shall, unless they agree otherwise, follow the following procedure:

(a) the requesting party shall, within 10 days after the registration of the request, propose to the other party the appointment of a sole conciliator or of a specified uneven number of conciliators and specify the method proposed for their appointment;

(b) within 20 days after receipt of the proposals made by the requesting party, the other party shall:

 (i) accept such proposals; or

 (ii) make other proposals regarding the number of conciliators and the method of their appointment;

(c) within 20 days after receipt of the reply containing any such other proposals, the requesting party shall notify the other party whether it accepts or rejects such proposals.

(2) The communications provided for in paragraph (1) shall be made or promptly confirmed in writing and shall either be transmitted through the Secretary-General or directly between the parties with a copy to the Secretary-General. The parties shall promptly notify the Secretary-General of the contents of any agreement reached.

(3) At any time 60 days after the registration of the request, if no agreement on another procedure is reached, either party may inform the Secretary-General that it chooses the formula provided for in Article 29(2)(b) of the Convention. The Secretary- General shall thereupon promptly inform the other party that the Commission is to be constituted in accordance with that Article.

Rule 3 Appointment of Conciliators to a Commission Constituted
in Accordance with Convention Article 29(2)(b)

(1) If the Commission is to be constituted in accordance with Article 29(2)(b) of the Convention:

(a) either party shall, in a communication to the other party:

 (i) name two persons, identifying one of them as the conciliator appointed by it and the other as the conciliator proposed to be the President of the Commission; and

 (ii) invite the other party to concur in the appointment of the conciliator proposed to be the President of the Commission and to appoint another conciliator;

(b) promptly upon receipt of this communication the other party shall, in its reply:

 (i) name a person as the conciliator appointed by it; and

 (ii) concur in the appointment of the conciliator proposed to be the President of the Commission or name another person as the conciliator proposed to be President;

(c) promptly upon receipt of the reply containing such a proposal, the initiating party shall notify the other party whether it concurs in the appointment of the conciliator proposed by that party to be the President of the Commission.

(2) The communications provided for in this Rule shall be made or promptly confirmed in writing and shall either be transmitted through the Secretary-General or directly between the parties with a copy to the Secretary-General.

Rule 4 Appointment of Conciliators by the Chairman of the Administrative Council

(1)   If the Commission is not constituted within 90 days after the dispatch by the Secretary-General of the notice of registration, or such other period as the parties may agree, either party may, through the Secretary-General, address to the Chairman of the Administrative Council a request in writing to appoint the conciliator or conciliators not yet appointed and to designate a conciliator to be the President of the Commission.

(2)   The provision of paragraph (1) shall apply mutatis mutandis in the event that the parties have agreed that the conciliators shall elect the President of the Commission and they fail to do so.

(3)   The Secretary-General shall forthwith send a copy of the request to the other party.

(4)   The Chairman shall use his best efforts to comply with that request within 30 days after its receipt. Before he proceeds to make an appointment or designation, with due regard to Article 31(1) of the Convention, he shall consult both parties as far as possible.

(5)   The Secretary-General shall promptly notify the parties of any appointment or designation made by the Chairman.

Rule 5 Acceptance of Appointments

(1)   The party or parties concerned shall notify the Secretary-General of the appointment of each conciliator and indicate the method of his appointment.

(2)   As soon as the Secretary-General has been informed by a party or the Chairman of the Administrative Council of the appointment of a conciliator, he shall seek an acceptance from the appointee.

(3)   If a conciliator fails to accept his appointment within 15 days, the Secretary-General shall promptly notify the parties, and if appropriate the Chairman, and invite them to proceed to the appointment of another conciliator in accordance with the method followed for the previous appointment.

Rule 6 Constitution of the Commission

(1) The Commission shall be deemed to be constituted and the proceeding to have begun on the date the Secretary-General notifies the parties that all the conciliators have accepted their appointment.

(2)   Before or at the first session of the Commission, each conciliator shall sign a declaration in the following form: "To the best of my knowledge there is no reason why I should not serve on the Conciliation Commission constituted by the International Centre for Settlement of Investment Disputes with respect to a dispute between _____and _____.

"I shall keep confidential all information coming to my knowledge as a result of my participation in this proceeding, as well as the contents of any report drawn up by the Commission.

"I shall not accept any instruction or compensation with regard to the proceeding from any source except as provided in the Convention on the Settlement of Investment Disputes between States and Nationals of Other States and in the Regulations and Rules made pursuant thereto.

"A statement of my past and present professional, business and other relationships (if any) with the parties is attached hereto."

Any conciliator failing to sign such a declaration by the end of the first session of the Commission shall be deemed to have resigned.

Rule 7 Replacement of Conciliators

At any time before the Commission is constituted, each party may replace any conciliator appointed by it and the parties may by common consent agree to replace any conciliator. The procedure of such replacement shall be in accordance with Rules 1, 5 and 6.

Rule 8 Incapacity or Resignation of Conciliators

(1)   If a conciliator becomes incapacitated or unable to perform the duties of his office, the procedure in respect of the disqualification of conciliators set forth in Rule 9 shall apply.

(2)   A conciliator may resign by submitting his resignation to the other members of the Commission and the Secretary-General. If the conciliator was appointed by one of the parties, the Commission shall promptly consider the reasons for his resignation and decide whether it consents thereto. The Commission shall promptly notify the Secretary-General of its decision.

Rule 9 Disqualification of Conciliators

(1)   A party proposing the disqualification of a conciliator pursuant to Article 57 of the Convention shall promptly, and in any event before the Commission first recommends terms of settlement of the dispute to the parties or when the proceeding is closed (whichever occurs earlier), file its proposal with the Secretary-General, stating its reasons therefor.

(2)   The Secretary-General shall forthwith:

(a)   transmit the proposal to the members of the Commission and, if it relates to a sole conciliator or to a majority of the members of the Commission, to the Chairman of the Administrative Council; and

(b)   notify the other party of the proposal.

(3)   The conciliator to whom the proposal relates may, without delay, furnish explanations to the Commission or the Chairman, as the case may be.

(4)   Unless the proposal relates to a majority of the members of the Commission, the other members shall promptly consider and vote on the proposal in the absence of the conciliator concerned. If those members are equally divided, they shall, through the Secretary-General, promptly notify the Chairman of the proposal, of any explanation furnished by the conciliator concerned and of their failure to reach a decision.

(5)   Whenever the Chairman has to decide on a proposal to disqualify a conciliator, he shall use his best efforts to take that decision within 30 days after he has received the proposal.

(6)   The proceeding shall be suspended until a decision has been taken on the proposal.

Rule 10 Procedure During a Vacancy on the Commission

(1)   The Secretary-General shall forthwith notify the parties and, if necessary, the Chairman of the Administrative Council of the disqualification, death, incapacity or resignation of a conciliator and of the consent, if any, of the Commission to a resignation.

(2)   Upon the notification by the Secretary-General of a vacancy on the Commission, the proceeding shall be or remain suspended until the vacancy has been filled.

Rule 11 Filling Vacancies on the Commission

(1)   Except as provided in paragraph (2), a vacancy resulting from the disqualification, death, incapacity or resignation of a conciliator shall be promptly filled by the same method by which his appointment had been made.

(2)   In addition to filling vacancies relating to conciliators appointed by him, the Chairman of the Administrative Council shall appoint a person from the Panel of Conciliators:

(a)   to fill a vacancy caused by the resignation, without the consent of the Commission, of a conciliator appointed by a party; or

(b)   at the request of either party, to fill any other vacancy, if no new appointment is made and accepted within 45 days of the notification of the vacancy by the Secretary-General.

(3)   The procedure for filling a vacancy shall be in accordance with Rules 1, 4(4), 4(5), 5 and, mutatis mutandis, 6(2).

Rule 12 Resumption of Proceeding After Filling a Vacancy

As soon as a vacancy on the Commission has been filled, the proceeding shall continue from the point it had reached at the time the vacancy occurred. The newly appointed conciliator may, however, require that any hearings be repeated in whole or in part.

Chapter II Working of the Commission

Rule 13 Sessions of the Commission

(1)   The Commission shall hold its first session within 60 days after its constitution or such other period as the parties may agree. The dates of that session shall be fixed by the President of the Commission after consultation with its members and the Secretary-General. If upon its constitution the Commission has no President because the parties have agreed that the President shall be elected by its members, the Secretary-General shall fix the dates of that session. In both cases, the parties shall be consulted as far as possible.

(2)   The dates of subsequent sessions shall be determined by the Commission, after consultation with the Secretary-General and with the parties as far as possible.

(3)   The Commission shall meet at the seat of the Centre or at such other place as may have been agreed by the parties in accordance with Article 63 of the Convention. If the parties agree that the proceeding shall be held at a place other than the Centre or an institution with which the Centre has made the necessary arrangements, they shall consult with the Secretary-General and request the approval of the Commission. Failing such approval, the Commission shall meet at the seat of the Centre.

(4)   The Secretary-General shall notify the members of the Commission and the parties of the dates and place of the sessions of the Commission in good time.

Rule 14 Sittings of the Commission

(1)   The President of the Commission shall conduct its hearings and preside at its deliberations.

(2)   Except as the parties otherwise agree, the presence of a majority of the members of the Commission shall be required at its sittings.

(3)   The President of the Commission shall fix the date and hour of its sittings.

Rule 15 Deliberations of the Commission

(1)   The deliberations of the Commission shall take place in private and remain secret.

(2)   Only members of the Commission shall take part in its deliberations. No other person shall be admitted unless the Commission decides otherwise.

Rule 16 Decisions of the Commission

(1)   Decisions of the Commission shall be taken by a majority of the votes of all its members. Abstention shall count as a negative vote.

(2)   Except as otherwise provided by these Rules or decided by the Commission, it may take any decision by correspondence among its members, provided that all of them are consulted. Decisions so taken shall be certified by the President of the Commission.

Rule 17 Incapacity of the President

If at any time the President of the Commission should be unable to act, his functions shall be performed by one of the other members of the Commission, acting in the order in which the Secretary-General had received the notice of their acceptance of their appointment to the Commission.

Rule 18 Representation of the Parties

(1)   Each party may be represented or assisted by agents, counsel or advocates whose names and authority shall be notified by that party to the Secretary-General, who shall promptly inform the Commission and the other party.

(2)   For the purposes of these Rules, the expression "party" includes, where the context so admits, an agent, counsel or advocate authorized to represent that party.

Chapter III General Procedural Provisions

Rule 19 Procedural Orders

The Commission shall make the orders required for the conduct of the proceeding.

Rule 20 Preliminary Procedural Consultation

(1)   As early as possible after the constitution of a Commission, its President shall endeavor to ascertain the views of the parties regarding questions of procedure. For this purpose he may request the parties to meet him. He shall, in particular, seek their views on the following matters:

(a)   the number of members of the Commission required to constitute a quorum at its sittings;

(b)   the language or languages to be used in the proceeding;

(c)   the evidence, oral or written, which each party intends to produce or to request the Commission to call for, and the written statements which each party intends to file, as well as the time limits within which such evidence should be produced and such statements filed;

(d)   the number of copies desired by each party of instruments filed by the other; and

(e)   the manner in which the record of the hearings shall be kept.

(2)   In the conduct of the proceeding the Commission shall apply any agreement between the parties on procedural matters, except as otherwise provided in the Convention or the Administrative and Financial Regulations.

Rule 21 Procedural Languages

(1)   The parties may agree on the use of one or two languages to be used in the proceeding, provided that, if they agree on any language that is not an official language of the Centre, the Commission, after consultation with the Secretary-General, gives its approval. If the parties do not agree on any such procedural language, each of them may select one of the official languages (i.e., English, French and Spanish) for this purpose.

(2)   If two procedural languages are selected by the parties, any instrument may be filed in either language. Either language may be used at the hearings, subject, if the Commission so requires, to translation and interpretation. The recommendations and the report of the Commission shall be rendered and the record kept in both procedural languages, both versions being equally authentic.

Chapter IV Conciliation Procedures

Rule 22 Functions of the Commission

(1)   In order to clarify the issues in dispute between the parties, the Commission shall hear the parties and shall endeavor to obtain any information that might serve this end. The parties shall be associated with its work as closely as possible.

(2)   In order to bring about agreement between the parties, the Commission may, from time to time at any stage of the proceeding, make – orally or in writing – recommendations to the parties. It may recommend that the parties accept specific terms of settlement or that they refrain, while it seeks to bring about agreement between them, from specific acts that might aggravate the dispute; it shall point out to the parties the arguments in favor of its recom-

mendations. It may fix time limits within which each party shall inform the Commission of its decision concerning the recommendations made.

(3) The Commission, in order to obtain information that might enable it to discharge its functions, may at any stage of the proceeding:

(a) request from either party oral explanations, documents and other information;

(b) request evidence from other persons; and

(c) with the consent of the party concerned, visit any place connected with the dispute or conduct inquiries there, provided that the parties may participate in any such visits and inquiries.

Rule 23 Cooperation of the Parties

(1) The parties shall cooperate in good faith with the Commission and, in particular, at its request furnish all relevant documents, information and explanations as well as use the means at their disposal to enable the Commission to hear witnesses and experts whom it desires to call. The parties shall also facilitate visits to and inquiries at any place connected with the dispute that the Commission desires to undertake.

(2) The parties shall comply with any time limits agreed with or fixed by the Commission.

Rule 24 Transmission of the Request

As soon as the Commission is constituted, the Secretary-General shall transmit to each member a copy of the request by which the proceeding was initiated, of the supporting documentation, of the notice of registration and of any communication received from either party in response thereto.

Rule 25 Written Statements

(1) Upon the constitution of the Commission, its President shall invite each party to file, within 30 days or such longer time limit as he may fix, a written statement of its position. If, upon its constitution, the Commission has no President, such invitation shall be issued and any such longer time limit shall be fixed by the Secretary-General. At any stage of the proceeding, within such time limits as the Commission shall fix, either party may file such other written statements as it deems useful and relevant.

(2) Except as otherwise provided by the Commission after consultation with the parties and the Secretary-General, every written statement or other instrument shall be filed in the form of a signed original accompanied by additional copies whose number shall be two more than the number of members of the Commission.

Rule 26 Supporting Documentation

(1) Every written statement or other instrument filed by a party may be accompanied by supporting documentation, in such form and number of copies as required by Administrative and Financial Regulation 30.

(2) Supporting documentation shall ordinarily be filed together with the instrument to which it relates, and in any case within the time limit fixed for the filing of such instrument.

Rule 27 Hearings

(1) The hearings of the Commission shall take place in private and, except as the parties otherwise agree, shall remain secret.

(2) The Commission shall decide, with the consent of the parties, which other persons besides the parties, their agents, counsel and advocates, witnesses and experts during their testimony, and officers of the Commission may attend the hearings.

Rule 28 Witnesses and Experts

(1) Each party may, at any stage of the proceeding, request that the Commission hear the witnesses and experts whose evidence the party considers relevant. The Commission shall fix a time limit within which such hearing shall take place.

(2) Witnesses and experts shall, as a rule, be examined before the Commission by the parties under the control of its President. Questions may also be put to them by any member of the Commission.

(3) If a witness or expert is unable to appear before it, the Commission, in agreement with the parties, may make appropriate arrangements for the evidence to be given in a written deposition or to be taken by examination elsewhere. The parties may participate in any such examination.

Chapter V Termination of the Proceeding

Rule 29 Objections to Jurisdiction

(1) Any objection that the dispute is not within the jurisdiction of the Centre or, for other reasons, is not within the competence of the Commission shall be made as early as possible. A party shall file the objection with the Secretary-General no later than in its first written statement or at the first hearing if that occurs earlier, unless the facts on which the objection is based are unknown to the party at that time.

(2) The Commission may on its own initiative consider, at any stage of the proceeding, whether the dispute before it is within the jurisdiction of the Centre and within its own competence.

(3) Upon the formal raising of an objection, the proceeding on the merits shall be suspended. The Commission shall obtain the views of the parties on the objection.

(4) The Commission may deal with the objection as a preliminary question or join it to the merits of the dispute. If the Commission overrules the objection or joins it to the merits, it shall resume consideration of the latter without delay.

(5) If the Commission decides that the dispute is not within the jurisdiction of the Centre or not within its own competence, it shall close the proceeding and draw up a report to that effect, in which it shall state its reasons.

Rule 30 Closure of the Proceeding

(1) If the parties reach agreement on the issues in dispute, the Commission shall close the proceeding and draw up its report noting the issues in dispute and recording that the parties have reached agreement. At the request of the parties, the report shall record the detailed terms and conditions of their agreement.

(2) If at any stage of the proceeding it appears to the Commission that there is no likelihood of agreement between the parties, the Commission shall, after notice to the parties, close the proceeding and draw up its report noting the submission of the dispute to conciliation and recording the failure of the parties to reach agreement.

(3) If one party fails to appear or participate in the proceeding, the Commission shall, after notice to the parties, close the proceeding and draw up its report noting the submission of the dispute to conciliation and recording the failure of that party to appear or participate.

Rule 31 Preparation of the Report

The report of the Commission shall be drawn up and signed within 60 days after the closure of the proceeding.

Rule 32 The Report

(1) The report shall be in writing and shall contain, in addition to the material specified in paragraph (2) and in Rule 30:

(a) a precise designation of each party;

(b)   a statement that the Commission was established under the Convention, and a description of the method of its constitution;

(c)   the names of the members of the Commission, and an identification of the appointing authority of each;

(d)   the names of the agents, counsel and advocates of the parties;

(e)   the dates and place of the sittings of the Commission; and

(f)   a summary of the proceeding.

(2)   The report shall also record any agreement of the parties, pursuant to Article 35 of the Convention, concerning the use in other proceedings of the views expressed or statements or admissions or offers of settlement made in the proceeding before the Commission or of the report or any recommendation made by the Commission.

(3)   The report shall be signed by the members of the Commission; the date of each signature shall be indicated. The fact that a member refuses to sign the report shall be recorded therein.

Rule 33 Communication of the Report

(1)   Upon signature by the last conciliator to sign, the Secretary-General shall promptly:

(a)   authenticate the original text of the report and deposit it in the archives of the Centre; and

(b)   dispatch a certified copy to each party, indicating the date of dispatch on the original text and on all copies.

(2)   The Secretary-General shall, upon request, make available to a party additional certified copies of the report.

(3)   The Centre shall not publish the report without the consent of the parties.

Chapter VI General Provisions

Rule 34 Final Provisions

(1)   The texts of these Rules in each official language of the Centre shall be equally authentic.

(2)   These Rules may be cited as the "Conciliation Rules" of the Centre.

RULES OF PROCEDURE FOR ARBITRATION PROCEEDINGS

(ARBITRATION RULES)

Chapter I Establishment of the Tribunal

Rule 1 General Obligations

(1)   Upon notification of the registration of the request for arbitration, the parties shall, with all possible dispatch, proceed to constitute a Tribunal, with due regard to Section 2 of Chapter IV of the Convention.

(2)   Unless such information is provided in the request, the parties shall communicate to the Secretary-General as soon as possible any provisions agreed by them regarding the number of arbitrators and the method of their appointment.

(3)   The majority of the arbitrators shall be nationals of States other than the State party to the dispute and of the State whose national is a party to the dispute, unless the sole arbitrator or each individual member of the Tribunal is appointed by agreement of the parties. Where the Tribunal is to consist of three members, a national of either of these States may not be appointed as an arbitrator by a party without the agreement of the other party to the dispute. Where the Tribunal is to consist of five or more members, nationals of either of these States may not be appointed as arbitrators by a party if appointment by the other party of the same number of

arbitrators of either of these nationalities would result in a majority of arbitrators of these nationalities.

(4)   No person who had previously acted as a conciliator or arbitrator in any proceeding for the settlement of the dispute may be appointed as a member of the Tribunal.

Rule 2 Method of Constituting the Tribunal in the Absence of Previous Agreement

(1)   If the parties, at the time of the registration of the request for arbitration, have not agreed upon the number of arbitrators and the method of their appointment, they shall, unless they agree otherwise, follow the following procedure:

(a)   the requesting party shall, within 10 days after the registration of the request, propose to the other party the appointment of a sole arbitrator or of a specified uneven number of arbitrators and specify the method proposed for their appointment;

(b)   within 20 days after receipt of the proposals made by the requesting party, the other party shall:

   (i)   accept such proposals; or

   (ii)   make other proposals regarding the number of arbitrators and the method of their appointment;

(c)   within 20 days after receipt of the reply containing any such other proposals, the requesting party shall notify the other party whether it accepts or rejects such proposals.

(2)   The communications provided for in paragraph (1) shall be made or promptly confirmed in writing and shall either be transmitted through the Secretary-General or directly between the parties with a copy to the Secretary-General. The parties shall promptly notify the Secretary-General of the contents of any agreement reached.

(3)   At any time 60 days after the registration of the request, if no agreement on another procedure is reached, either party may inform the Secretary-General that it chooses the formula provided for in Article 37(2)(b) of the Convention. The Secretary-General shall thereupon promptly inform the other party that the Tribunal is to be constituted in accordance with that Article.

Rule 3 Appointment of Arbitrators to a Tribunal Constituted in Accordance with Convention Article 37(2)(b)

(1)   If the Tribunal is to be constituted in accordance with Article 37(2)(b) of the Convention:

(a)   either party shall in a communication to the other party:

   (i)   name two persons, identifying one of them, who shall not have the same nationality as nor be a national of either party, as the arbitrator appointed by it, and the other as the arbitrator proposed to be the President of the Tribunal; and

   (ii)   invite the other party to concur in the appointment of the arbitrator proposed to be the President of the Tribunal and to appoint another arbitrator;

(b)   promptly upon receipt of this communication the other party shall, in its reply:

   (i)   name a person as the arbitrator appointed by it, who shall not have the same nationality as nor be a national of either party; and

   (ii)   concur in the appointment of the arbitrator proposed to be the President of the Tribunal or name another person as the arbitrator proposed to be President;

(c)   promptly upon receipt of the reply containing such a proposal, the initiating party shall notify the other party whether it concurs in the appointment of the arbitrator proposed by that party to be the President of the Tribunal.

(2)   The communications provided for in this Rule shall be made or promptly confirmed in writing and shall either be transmitted through the Secretary-General or directly between the parties with a copy to the Secretary-General.

Rule 4 Appointment of Arbitrators by the Chairman of the Administrative Council

(1)   If the Tribunal is not constituted within 90 days after the dispatch by the Secretary-General of the notice of registration, or such other period as the parties may agree, either party may, through the Secretary-General, address to the Chairman of the Administrative Council a request in writing to appoint the arbitrator or arbitrators not yet appointed and to designate an arbitrator to be the President of the Tribunal.

(2)   The provision of paragraph (1) shall apply mutatis mutandis in the event that the parties have agreed that the arbitrators shall elect the President of the Tribunal and they fail to do so.

(3)   The Secretary-General shall forthwith send a copy of the request to the other party.

(4)   The Chairman shall use his best efforts to comply with that request within 30 days after its receipt. Before he proceeds to make an appointment or designation, with due regard to Articles 38 and 40(1) of the Convention, he shall consult both parties as far as possible.

(5)   The Secretary-General shall promptly notify the parties of any appointment or designation made by the Chairman.

Rule 5 Acceptance of Appointments

(1)   The party or parties concerned shall notify the Secretary-General of the appointment of each arbitrator and indicate the method of his appointment.

(2)   As soon as the Secretary-General has been informed by a party or the Chairman of the Administrative Council of the appointment of an arbitrator, he shall seek an acceptance from the appointee.

(3)   If an arbitrator fails to accept his appointment within 15 days, the Secretary- General shall promptly notify the parties, and if appropriate the Chairman, and invite them to proceed to the appointment of another arbitrator in accordance with the method followed for the previous appointment.

Rule 6 Constitution of the Tribunal

(1)   The Tribunal shall be deemed to be constituted and the proceeding to have begun on the date the Secretary-General notifies the parties that all the arbitrators have accepted their appointment.

(2)   Before or at the first session of the Tribunal, each arbitrator shall sign a declaration in the following form:

"To the best of my knowledge there is no reason why I should not serve on the Arbitral Tribunal constituted by the International Centre for Settlement of Investment Disputes with respect to a dispute between _____and_____.

"I shall keep confidential all information coming to my knowledge as a result of my participation in this proceeding, as well as the contents of any award made by the Tribunal.

"I shall judge fairly as between the parties, according to the applicable law, and shall not accept any instruction or compensation with regard to the proceeding from any source except as provided in the Convention on the Settlement of Investment Disputes between States and Nationals of Other States and in the Regulations and Rules made pursuant thereto.

"Attached is a statement of (a) my past and present professional, business and other relationships (if any) with the parties and (b) any other circumstance that might cause my reliability for independent judgment to be questioned by a party. I acknowledge that by signing this declaration, I assume a continuing obligation promptly to notify the Secretary-General of the Centre of any such relationship or circumstance that subsequently arises during this proceeding."

Any arbitrator failing to sign a declaration by the end of the first session of the Tribunal shall be deemed to have resigned.

Rule 7 Replacement of Arbitrators

At any time before the Tribunal is constituted, each party may replace any arbitrator appointed by it and the parties may by common consent agree to replace any arbitrator. The procedure of such replacement shall be in accordance with Rules 1, 5 and 6.

Rule 8 Incapacity or Resignation of Arbitrators

(1)   If an arbitrator becomes incapacitated or unable to perform the duties of his office, the procedure in respect of the disqualification of arbitrators set forth in Rule 9 shall apply.

(2)   An arbitrator may resign by submitting his resignation to the other members of the Tribunal and the Secretary-General. If the arbitrator was appointed by one of the parties, the Tribunal shall promptly consider the reasons for his resignation and decide whether it consents thereto. The Tribunal shall promptly notify the Secretary-General of its decision.

Rule 9 Disqualification of Arbitrators

(1)   A party proposing the disqualification of an arbitrator pursuant to Article 57 of the Convention shall promptly, and in any event before the proceeding is declared closed, file its proposal with the Secretary-General, stating its reasons therefor.

(2)   The Secretary-General shall forthwith:

(a)   transmit the proposal to the members of the Tribunal and, if it relates to a sole arbitrator or to a majority of the members of the Tribunal, to the Chairman of the Administrative Council; and

(b)   notify the other party of the proposal.

(3)   The arbitrator to whom the proposal relates may, without delay, furnish explanations to the Tribunal or the Chairman, as the case may be.

(4)   Unless the proposal relates to a majority of the members of the Tribunal, the other members shall promptly consider and vote on the proposal in the absence of the arbitrator concerned. If those members are equally divided, they shall, through the Secretary-General, promptly notify the Chairman of the proposal, of any explanation furnished by the arbitrator concerned and of their failure to reach a decision.

(5)   Whenever the Chairman has to decide on a proposal to disqualify an arbitrator, he shall use his best efforts to take that decision within 30 days after he has received the proposal.

(6) The proceeding shall be suspended until a decision has been taken on the proposal.

Rule 10 Procedure During a Vacancy on the Tribunal

(1)   The Secretary-General shall forthwith notify the parties and, if necessary, the Chairman of the Administrative Council of the disqualification, death, incapacity or resignation of an arbitrator and of the consent, if any, of the Tribunal to a resignation.

(2)   Upon the notification by the Secretary-General of a vacancy on the Tribunal, the proceeding shall be or remain suspended until the vacancy has been filled.

Rule 11 Filling Vacancies on the Tribunal

(1)   Except as provided in paragraph (2), a vacancy resulting from the disqualification, death, incapacity or resignation of an arbitrator shall be promptly filled by the same method by which his appointment had been made.

(2) In addition to filling vacancies relating to arbitrators appointed by him, the Chairman of the Administrative Council shall appoint a person from the Panel of Arbitrators:

(a)   to fill a vacancy caused by the resignation, without the consent of the Tribunal, of an arbitrator appointed by a party; or

(b)   at the request of either party, to fill any other vacancy, if no new appointment is made and accepted within 45 days of the notification of the vacancy by the Secretary-General.

(3)   The procedure for filling a vacancy shall be in accordance with Rules 1, 4(4), 4(5), 5 and, mutatis mutandis, 6(2).

Rule 12 Resumption of Proceeding After Filling a Vacancy

As soon as a vacancy on the Tribunal has been filled, the proceeding shall continue from the point it had reached at the time the vacancy occurred. The newly appointed arbitrator may, however, require that the oral procedure be recommenced, if this had already been started.

Chapter II Working of the Tribunal

Rule 13 Sessions of the Tribunal

(1)   The Tribunal shall hold its first session within 60 days after its constitution or such other period as the parties may agree. The dates of that session shall be fixed by the President of the Tribunal after consultation with its members and the Secretary- General. If upon its constitution the Tribunal has no President because the parties have agreed that the President shall be elected by its members, the Secretary- General shall fix the dates of that session. In both cases, the parties shall be consulted as far as possible.

(2)   The dates of subsequent sessions shall be determined by the Tribunal, after consultation with the Secretary-General and with the parties as far as possible.

(3)   The Tribunal shall meet at the seat of the Centre or at such other place as may have been agreed by the parties in accordance with Article 63 of the Convention. If the parties agree that the proceeding shall be held at a place other than the Centre or an institution with which the Centre has made the necessary arrangements, they shall consult with the Secretary-General and request the approval of the Tribunal. Failing such approval, the Tribunal shall meet at the seat of the Centre.

(4)   The Secretary-General shall notify the members of the Tribunal and the parties of the dates and place of the sessions of the Tribunal in good time.

Rule 14 Sittings of the Tribunal

(1)   The President of the Tribunal shall conduct its hearings and preside at its deliberations.

(2)   Except as the parties otherwise agree, the presence of a majority of the members of the Tribunal shall be required at its sittings.

(3)   The President of the Tribunal shall fix the date and hour of its sittings.

Rule 15 Deliberations of the Tribunal

(1)   The deliberations of the Tribunal shall take place in private and remain secret.

(2)   Only members of the Tribunal shall take part in its deliberations. No other person shall be admitted unless the Tribunal decides otherwise.

Rule 16 Decisions of the Tribunal

(1)   Decisions of the Tribunal shall be taken by a majority of the votes of all its members. Abstention shall count as a negative vote.

(2)   Except as otherwise provided by these Rules or decided by the Tribunal, it may take any decision by correspondence among its members, provided that all of them are consulted. Decisions so taken shall be certified by the President of the Tribunal.

Rule 17 Incapacity of the President

If at any time the President of the Tribunal should be unable to act, his functions shall be performed by one of the other members of the Tribunal, acting in the order in which the

Secretary-General had received the notice of their acceptance of their appointment to the Tribunal.

Rule 18 Representation of the Parties

(1)   Each party may be represented or assisted by agents, counsel or advocates whose names and authority shall be notified by that party to the Secretary-General, who shall promptly inform the Tribunal and the other party.

(2)   For the purposes of these Rules, the expression "party" includes, where the context so admits, an agent, counsel or advocate authorized to represent that party.

Chapter III General Procedural Provisions

Rule 19 Procedural Orders

The Tribunal shall make the orders required for the conduct of the proceeding.

Rule 20 Preliminary Procedural Consultation

(1)   As early as possible after the constitution of a Tribunal, its President shall endeavor to ascertain the views of the parties regarding questions of procedure. For this purpose he may request the parties to meet him. He shall, in particular, seek their views on the following matters:

(a)   the number of members of the Tribunal required to constitute a quorum at its sittings;

(b)   the language or languages to be used in the proceeding;

(c)   the number and sequence of the pleadings and the time limits within which they are to be filed;

(d)   the number of copies desired by each party of instruments filed by the other;

(e)   dispensing with the written or the oral procedure;

(f)   the manner in which the cost of the proceeding is to be apportioned; and

(g)   the manner in which the record of the hearings shall be kept.

(2)   In the conduct of the proceeding the Tribunal shall apply any agreement between the parties on procedural matters, except as otherwise provided in the Convention or the Administrative and Financial Regulations.

Rule 21 Pre-Hearing Conference

(1)   At the request of the Secretary-General or at the discretion of the President of the Tribunal, a pre-hearing conference between the Tribunal and the parties may be held to arrange for an exchange of information and the stipulation of uncontested facts in order to expedite the proceeding.

(2)   At the request of the parties, a pre-hearing conference between the Tribunal and the parties, duly represented by their authorized representatives, may be held to consider the issues in dispute with a view to reaching an amicable settlement.

Rule 22 Procedural Languages

(1)   The parties may agree on the use of one or two languages to be used in the proceeding, provided, that, if they agree on any language that is not an official language of the Centre, the Tribunal, after consultation with the Secretary-General, gives its approval. If the parties do not agree on any such procedural language, each of them may select one of the official languages (i.e., English, French and Spanish) for this purpose.

(2)   If two procedural languages are selected by the parties, any instrument may be filed in either language. Either language may be used at the hearings, subject, if the Tribunal so requires, to translation and interpretation. The orders and the award of the Tribunal shall be rendered and the record kept in both procedural languages, both versions being equally authentic.

Rule 23 Copies of Instruments

Except as otherwise provided by the Tribunal after consultation with the parties and the Secretary-General, every request, pleading, application, written observation, supporting documentation, if any, or other instrument shall be filed in the form of a signed original accompanied by the following number of additional copies:

(a)   before the number of members of the Tribunal has been determined: five;

(b)   after the number of members of the Tribunal has been determined: two more than the number of its members.

Rule 24 Supporting Documentation

Supporting documentation shall ordinarily be filed together with the instrument to which it relates, and in any case within the time limit fixed for the filing of such instrument.

Rule 25 Correction of Errors

An accidental error in any instrument or supporting document may, with the consent of the other party or by leave of the Tribunal, be corrected at any time before the award is rendered.

Rule 26 Time Limits

(1)   Where required, time limits shall be fixed by the Tribunal by assigning dates for the completion of the various steps in the proceeding. The Tribunal may delegate this power to its President.

(2)   The Tribunal may extend any time limit that it has fixed. If the Tribunal is not in session, this power shall be exercised by its President.

(3)   Any step taken after expiration of the applicable time limit shall be disregarded unless the Tribunal, in special circumstances and after giving the other party an opportunity of stating its views, decides otherwise.

Rule 27 Waiver

A party which knows or should have known that a provision of the Administrative and Financial Regulations, of these Rules, of any other rules or agreement applicable to the proceeding, or of an order of the Tribunal has not been complied with and which fails to state promptly its objections thereto, shall be deemed – subject to Article 45 of the Convention – to have waived its right to object.

Rule 28 Cost of Proceeding

(1)   Without prejudice to the final decision on the payment of the cost of the proceeding, the Tribunal may, unless otherwise agreed by the parties, decide:

(a)   at any stage of the proceeding, the portion which each party shall pay, pursuant to Administrative and Financial Regulation 14, of the fees and expenses of the Tribunal and the charges for the use of the facilities of the Centre;

(b)   with respect to any part of the proceeding, that the related costs (as determined by the Secretary-General) shall be borne entirely or in a particular share by one of the parties.

(2)   Promptly after the closure of the proceeding, each party shall submit to the Tribunal a statement of costs reasonably incurred or borne by it in the proceeding and the Secretary-General shall submit to the Tribunal an account of all amounts paid by each party to the Centre and of all costs incurred by the Centre for the proceeding. The Tribunal may, before the award has been rendered, request the parties and the Secretary-General to provide additional information concerning the cost of the proceeding.

Chapter IV Written and Oral Procedures

Rule 29 Normal Procedures

Except if the parties otherwise agree, the proceeding shall comprise two distinct phases: a written procedure followed by an oral one.

Rule 30 Transmission of the Request

As soon as the Tribunal is constituted, the Secretary-General shall transmit to each member a copy of the request by which the proceeding was initiated, of the supporting documentation, of the notice of registration and of any communication received from either party in response thereto.

Rule 31 The Written Procedure

(1)   In addition to the request for arbitration, the written procedure shall consist of the following pleadings, filed within time limits set by the Tribunal:

(a)   a memorial by the requesting party;

(b)   a counter-memorial by the other party; and, if the parties so agree or the Tribunal deems it necessary:

(c)   a reply by the requesting party; and

(d)   a rejoinder by the other party.

(2)   If the request was made jointly, each party shall, within the same time limit determined by the Tribunal, file its memorial and, if the parties so agree or the Tribunal deems it necessary, its reply; however, the parties may instead agree that one of them shall, for the purposes of paragraph (1), be considered as the requesting party.

(3)   A memorial shall contain: a statement of the relevant facts; a statement of law; and the submissions. A counter-memorial, reply or rejoinder shall contain an admission or denial of the facts stated in the last previous pleading; any additional facts, if necessary; observations concerning the statement of law in the last previous pleading; a statement of law in answer thereto; and the submissions.

Rule 32 The Oral Procedure

(1)   The oral procedure shall consist of the hearing by the Tribunal of the parties, their agents, counsel and advocates, and of witnesses and experts.

(2)   Unless either party objects, the Tribunal, after consultation with the Secretary-General, may allow other persons, besides the parties, their agents, counsel and advocates, witnesses and experts during their testimony, and officers of the Tribunal, to attend or observe all or part of the hearings, subject to appropriate logistical arrangements. The Tribunal shall for such cases establish procedures for the protection of proprietary or privileged information.

(3)   The members of the Tribunal may, during the hearings, put questions to the parties, their agents, counsel and advocates, and ask them for explanations.

Rule 33 Marshalling of Evidence

Without prejudice to the rules concerning the production of documents, each party shall, within time limits fixed by the Tribunal, communicate to the Secretary-General, for transmission to the Tribunal and the other party, precise information regarding the evidence which it intends to produce and that which it intends to request the Tribunal to call for, together with an indication of the points to which such evidence will be directed.

Rule 34 Evidence: General Principles

(1)   The Tribunal shall be the judge of the admissibility of any evidence adduced and of its probative value.

(2)   The Tribunal may, if it deems it necessary at any stage of the proceeding:

(a)   call upon the parties to produce documents, witnesses and experts; and

(b)   visit any place connected with the dispute or conduct inquiries there.

(3)   The parties shall cooperate with the Tribunal in the production of the evidence and in the other measures provided for in paragraph (2). The Tribunal shall take formal note of the failure of a party to comply with its obligations under this paragraph and of any reasons given for such failure.

(4)   Expenses incurred in producing evidence and in taking other measures in accordance with paragraph (2) shall be deemed to constitute part of the expenses incurred by the parties within the meaning of Article 61(2) of the Convention.

Rule 35 Examination of Witnesses and Experts

(1)   Witnesses and experts shall be examined before the Tribunal by the parties under the control of its President. Questions may also be put to them by any member of the Tribunal.

(2)   Each witness shall make the following declaration before giving his evidence:

"I solemnly declare upon my honour and conscience that I shall speak the truth, the whole truth and nothing but the truth."

(3)   Each expert shall make the following declaration before making his statement:

"I solemnly declare upon my honour and conscience that my statement will be in accordance with my sincere belief."

Rule 36 Witnesses and Experts: Special Rules

Notwithstanding Rule 35 the Tribunal may:

(a)   admit evidence given by a witness or expert in a written deposition; and

(b)   with the consent of both parties, arrange for the examination of a witness or expert otherwise than before the Tribunal itself. The Tribunal shall define the subject of the examination, the time limit, the procedure to be followed and other particulars. The parties may participate in the examination.

Rule 37 Visits and Inquiries; Submissions of Non-Disputing Parties

(1)   If the Tribunal considers it necessary to visit any place connected with the dispute or to conduct an inquiry there, it shall make an order to this effect. The order shall define the scope of the visit or the subject of the inquiry, the time limit, the procedure to be followed and other particulars. The parties may participate in any visit or inquiry.

(2)   After consulting both parties, the Tribunal may allow a person or entity that is not a party to the dispute (in this Rule called the "non-disputing party") to file a written submission with the Tribunal regarding a matter within the scope of the dispute. In determining whether to allow such a filing, the Tribunal shall consider, among other things, the extent to which:

(a)   the non-disputing party submission would assist the Tribunal in the determination of a factual or legal issue related to the proceeding by bringing a perspective, particular knowledge or insight that is different from that of the disputing parties;

(b)   the non-disputing party submission would address a matter within the scope of the dispute;

(c)   the non-disputing party has a significant interest in the proceeding.

The Tribunal shall ensure that the non-disputing party submission does not disrupt the proceeding or unduly burden or unfairly prejudice either party, and that both parties are given an opportunity to present their observations on the non-disputing party submission.

Rule 38 Closure of the Proceeding

(1)   When the presentation of the case by the parties is completed, the proceeding shall be declared closed.

(2)   Exceptionally, the Tribunal may, before the award has been rendered, reopen the proceeding on the ground that new evidence is forthcoming of such a nature as to constitute a decisive factor, or that there is a vital need for clarification on certain specific points.

Chapter V Particular Procedures

Rule 39 Provisional Measures

(1)   At any time after the institution of the proceeding, a party may request that provisional measures for the preservation of its rights be recommended by the Tribunal. The request shall specify the rights to be preserved, the measures the recommendation of which is requested, and the circumstances that require such measures.

(2)   The Tribunal shall give priority to the consideration of a request made pursuant to paragraph (1).

(3)   The Tribunal may also recommend provisional measures on its own initiative or recommend measures other than those specified in a request. It may at any time modify or revoke its recommendations.

(4)   The Tribunal shall only recommend provisional measures, or modify or revoke its recommendations, after giving each party an opportunity of presenting its observations.

(5)   If a party makes a request pursuant to paragraph (1) before the constitution of the Tribunal, the Secretary-General shall, on the application of either party, fix time limits for the parties to present observations on the request, so that the request and observations may be considered by the Tribunal promptly upon its constitution.

(6)   Nothing in this Rule shall prevent the parties, provided that they have so stipulated in the agreement recording their consent, from requesting any judicial or other authority to order provisional measures, prior to or after the institution of the proceeding, for the preservation of their respective rights and interests.

Rule 40 Ancillary Claims

(1)   Except as the parties otherwise agree, a party may present an incidental or additional claim or counter-claim arising directly out of the subject-matter of the dispute, provided that such ancillary claim is within the scope of the consent of the parties and is otherwise within the jurisdiction of the Centre.

(2)   An incidental or additional claim shall be presented not later than in the reply and a counter-claim no later than in the counter-memorial, unless the Tribunal, upon justification by the party presenting the ancillary claim and upon considering any objection of the other party, authorizes the presentation of the claim at a later stage in the proceeding.

(3)   The Tribunal shall fix a time limit within which the party against which an ancillary claim is presented may file its observations thereon.

Rule 41 Preliminary Objections

(1)   Any objection that the dispute or any ancillary claim is not within the jurisdiction of the Centre or, for other reasons, is not within the competence of the Tribunal shall be made as early as possible. A party shall file the objection with the Secretary-General no later than the expiration of the time limit fixed for the filing of the counter-memorial, or, if the objection relates to an ancillary claim, for the filing of the rejoinder – unless the facts on which the objection is based are unknown to the party at that time.

(2)   The Tribunal may on its own initiative consider, at any stage of the proceeding, whether the dispute or any ancillary claim before it is within the jurisdiction of the Centre and within its own competence.

(3)   Upon the formal raising of an objection relating to the dispute, the Tribunal may decide to suspend the proceeding on the merits. The President of the Tribunal, after consultation with its other members, shall fix a time limit within which the parties may file observations on the objection.

(4)   The Tribunal shall decide whether or not the further procedures relating to the objection made pursuant to paragraph (1) shall be oral. It may deal with the objection as a preliminary question or join it to the merits of the dispute. If the Tribunal overrules the objection or joins it to the merits, it shall once more fix time limits for the further procedures.

(5)   Unless the parties have agreed to another expedited procedure for making preliminary objections, a party may, no later than 30 days after the constitution of the Tribunal, and in any event before the first session of the Tribunal, file an objection that a claim is manifestly without legal merit. The party shall specify as precisely as possible the basis for the objection. The Tribunal, after giving the parties the opportunity to present their observations on the objection, shall, at its first session or promptly thereafter, notify the parties of its decision on the objection. The decision of the Tribunal shall be without prejudice to the right of a party to file an objection pursuant to paragraph (1) or to object, in the course of the proceeding, that a claim lacks legal merit.

(6)   If the Tribunal decides that the dispute is not within the jurisdiction of the Centre or not within its own competence, or that all claims are manifestly without legal merit, it shall render an award to that effect.

Rule 42 Default

(1)   If a party (in this Rule called the "defaulting party") fails to appear or to present its case at any stage of the proceeding, the other party may, at any time prior to the discontinuance of the proceeding, request the Tribunal to deal with the questions submitted to it and to render an award.

(2)   The Tribunal shall promptly notify the defaulting party of such a request. Unless it is satisfied that that party does not intend to appear or to present its case in the proceeding, it shall, at the same time, grant a period of grace and to this end:

(a)   if that party had failed to file a pleading or any other instrument within the time limit fixed therefor, fix a new time limit for its filing; or

(b)   if that party had failed to appear or present its case at a hearing, fix a new date for the hearing.

The period of grace shall not, without the consent of the other party, exceed 60 days.

(3)   After the expiration of the period of grace or when, in accordance with paragraph (2), no such period is granted, the Tribunal shall resume the consideration of the dispute. Failure of the defaulting party to appear or to present its case shall not be deemed an admission of the assertions made by the other party.

(4)   The Tribunal shall examine the jurisdiction of the Centre and its own competence in the dispute and, if it is satisfied, decide whether the submissions made are well- founded in fact and in law. To this end, it may, at any stage of the proceeding, call on the party appearing to file observations, produce evidence or submit oral explanations.

Rule 43 Settlement and Discontinuance

(1)   If, before the award is rendered, the parties agree on a settlement of the dispute or otherwise to discontinue the proceeding, the Tribunal, or the Secretary-General if the Tribunal

has not yet been constituted, shall, at their written request, in an order take note of the discontinuance of the proceeding.

(2)   If the parties file with the Secretary-General the full and signed text of their settlement and in writing request the Tribunal to embody such settlement in an award, the Tribunal may record the settlement in the form of its award.

Rule 44 Discontinuance at Request of a Party

If a party requests the discontinuance of the proceeding, the Tribunal, or the Secretary-General if the Tribunal has not yet been constituted, shall in an order fix a time limit within which the other party may state whether it opposes the discontinuance. If no objection is made in writing within the time limit, the other party shall be deemed to have acquiesced in the discontinuance and the Tribunal, or if appropriate the Secretary-General, shall in an order take note of the discontinuance of the proceeding. If objection is made, the proceeding shall continue.

Rule 45 Discontinuance for Failure of Parties to Act

If the parties fail to take any steps in the proceeding during six consecutive months or such period as they may agree with the approval of the Tribunal, or of the Secretary-General if the Tribunal has not yet been constituted, they shall be deemed to have discontinued the proceeding and the Tribunal, or if appropriate the Secretary- General, shall, after notice to the parties, in an order take note of the discontinuance.

Chapter VI The Award

Rule 46 Preparation of the Award

The award (including any individual or dissenting opinion) shall be drawn up and signed within 120 days after closure of the proceeding. The Tribunal may, however, extend this period by a further 60 days if it would otherwise be unable to draw up the award.

Rule 47 The Award

(1)   The award shall be in writing and shall contain:

(a)   a precise designation of each party;

(b)   a statement that the Tribunal was established under the Convention, and a description of the method of its constitution;

(c)   the name of each member of the Tribunal, and an identification of the appointing authority of each;

(d)   the names of the agents, counsel and advocates of the parties;

(e)   the dates and place of the sittings of the Tribunal;

(f)   a summary of the proceeding;

(g)   a statement of the facts as found by the Tribunal;

(h)   the submissions of the parties;

(i)   the decision of the Tribunal on every question submitted to it, together with the reasons upon which the decision is based; and

(j)   any decision of the Tribunal regarding the cost of the proceeding.

(2)   The award shall be signed by the members of the Tribunal who voted for it; the date of each signature shall be indicated.

(3)   Any member of the Tribunal may attach his individual opinion to the award, whether he dissents from the majority or not, or a statement of his dissent.

Rule 48 Rendering of the Award

(1)   Upon signature by the last arbitrator to sign, the Secretary-General shall promptly:

(a)   authenticate the original text of the award and deposit it in the archives of the Centre, together with any individual opinions and statements of dissent; and

(b)   dispatch a certified copy of the award (including individual opinions and statements of dissent) to each party, indicating the date of dispatch on the original text and on all copies.

(2)   The award shall be deemed to have been rendered on the date on which the certified copies were dispatched.

(3)   The Secretary-General shall, upon request, make available to a party additional certified copies of the award.

(4)   The Centre shall not publish the award without the consent of the parties. The Centre shall, however, promptly include in its publications excerpts of the legal reasoning of the Tribunal.

Rule 49 Supplementary Decisions and Rectification

(1)   Within 45 days after the date on which the award was rendered, either party may request, pursuant to Article 49(2) of the Convention, a supplementary decision on, or the rectification of, the award. Such a request shall be addressed in writing to the Secretary-General. The request shall:

(a)   identify the award to which it relates;

(b)   indicate the date of the request;

(c)   state in detail:

    (i)   any question which, in the opinion of the requesting party, the Tribunal omitted to decide in the award; and

    (ii)   any error in the award which the requesting party seeks to have rectified; and

(d)   be accompanied by a fee for lodging the request.

(2)   Upon receipt of the request and of the lodging fee, the Secretary-General shall forthwith:

(a)   register the request;

(b)   notify the parties of the registration;

(c)   transmit to the other party a copy of the request and of any accompanying documentation; and

(d)   transmit to each member of the Tribunal a copy of the notice of registration, together with a copy of the request and of any accompanying documentation.

(3)   The President of the Tribunal shall consult the members on whether it is necessary for the Tribunal to meet in order to consider the request. The Tribunal shall fix a time limit for the parties to file their observations on the request and shall determine the procedure for its consideration.

(4)   Rules 46-48 shall apply, mutatis mutandis, to any decision of the Tribunal pursuant to this Rule.

(5)   If a request is received by the Secretary-General more than 45 days after the award was rendered, he shall refuse to register the request and so inform forthwith the requesting party.

Chapter VII Interpretation, Revision and Annulment of the Award

Rule 50 The Application

(1)   An application for the interpretation, revision or annulment of an award shall be addressed in writing to the Secretary-General and shall:

(a)   identify the award to which it relates;

(b)   indicate the date of the application;

(c)   state in detail:

    (i)   in an application for interpretation, the precise points in dispute;

    (ii)   in an application for revision, pursuant to Article 51(1) of the Convention, the change sought in the award, the discovery of some fact of such a nature as decisively to affect the award, and evidence that when the award was rendered that fact was unknown to the Tribunal and to the applicant, and that the applicant's ignorance of that fact was not due to negligence;

    (iii)   in an application for annulment, pursuant to Article 52(1) of the Convention, the grounds on which it is based. These grounds are limited to the following:

       –   that the Tribunal was not properly constituted;

       –   that the Tribunal has manifestly exceeded its powers;

       –   that there was corruption on the part of a member of the Tribunal;

       –   that there has been a serious departure from a fundamental rule of procedure;

       –   that the award has failed to state the reasons on which it is based;

(d)   be accompanied by the payment of a fee for lodging the application.

(2)   Without prejudice to the provisions of paragraph (3), upon receiving an application and the lodging fee, the Secretary-General shall forthwith:

(a)   register the application;

(b)   notify the parties of the registration; and

(c)   transmit to the other party a copy of the application and of any accompanying documentation.

(3)   The Secretary-General shall refuse to register an application for:

(a)   revision, if, in accordance with Article 51(2) of the Convention, it is not made within 90 days after the discovery of the new fact and in any event within three years after the date on which the award was rendered (or any subsequent decision or correction);

(b)   annulment, if, in accordance with Article 52(2) of the Convention, it is not made:

    (i)   within 120 days after the date on which the award was rendered (or any subsequent decision or correction) if the application is based on any of the following grounds:

       –   the Tribunal was not properly constituted;

       –   the Tribunal has manifestly exceeded its powers;

       –   there has been a serious departure from a fundamental rule of procedure;

       –   the award has failed to state the reasons on which it is based;

    (ii)   in the case of corruption on the part of a member of the Tribunal, within 120 days after discovery thereof,

and in any event within three years after the date on which the award was rendered (or any subsequent decision or correction).

(4)   If the Secretary-General refuses to register an application for revision, or annulment, he shall forthwith notify the requesting party of his refusal.

Rule 51 Interpretation or Revision: Further Procedures

(1)   Upon registration of an application for the interpretation or revision of an award, the Secretary-General shall forthwith:

(a) transmit to each member of the original Tribunal a copy of the notice of registration, together with a copy of the application and of any accompanying documentation; and

(b) request each member of the Tribunal to inform him within a specified time limit whether that member is willing to take part in the consideration of the application.

(2) If all members of the Tribunal express their willingness to take part in the consideration of the application, the Secretary-General shall so notify the members of the Tribunal and the parties. Upon dispatch of these notices the Tribunal shall be deemed to be reconstituted.

(3) If the Tribunal cannot be reconstituted in accordance with paragraph (2), the Secretary-General shall so notify the parties and invite them to proceed, as soon as possible, to constitute a new Tribunal, including the same number of arbitrators, and appointed by the same method, as the original one.

Rule 52 Annulment: Further Procedures

(1) Upon registration of an application for the annulment of an award, the Secretary- General shall forthwith request the Chairman of the Administrative Council to appoint an ad hoc Committee in accordance with Article 52(3) of the Convention.

(2) The Committee shall be deemed to be constituted on the date the Secretary-General notifies the parties that all members have accepted their appointment. Before or at the first session of the Committee, each member shall sign a declaration conforming to that set forth in Rule 6(2).

Rule 53 Rules of Procedure

The provisions of these Rules shall apply mutatis mutandis to any procedure relating to the interpretation, revision or annulment of an award and to the decision of the Tribunal or Committee.

Rule 54 Stay of Enforcement of the Award

(1) The party applying for the interpretation, revision or annulment of an award may in its application, and either party may at any time before the final disposition of the application, request a stay in the enforcement of part or all of the award to which the application relates. The Tribunal or Committee shall give priority to the consideration of such a request.

(2) If an application for the revision or annulment of an award contains a request for a stay of its enforcement, the Secretary-General shall, together with the notice of registration, inform both parties of the provisional stay of the award. As soon as the Tribunal or Committee is constituted it shall, if either party requests, rule within 30 days on whether such stay should be continued; unless it decides to continue the stay, it shall automatically be terminated.

(3) If a stay of enforcement has been granted pursuant to paragraph (1) or continued pursuant to paragraph (2), the Tribunal or Committee may at any time modify or terminate the stay at the request of either party. All stays shall automatically terminate on the date on which a final decision is rendered on the application, except that a Committee granting the partial annulment of an award may order the temporary stay of enforcement of the unannulled portion in order to give either party an opportunity to request any new Tribunal constituted pursuant to Article 52(6) of the Convention to grant a stay pursuant to Rule 55(3).

(4) A request pursuant to paragraph (1), (2) (second sentence) or (3) shall specify the circumstances that require the stay or its modification or termination. A request shall only be granted after the Tribunal or Committee has given each party an opportunity of presenting its observations.

(5) The Secretary-General shall promptly notify both parties of the stay of enforcement of any award and of the modification or termination of such a stay, which shall become effective on the date on which he dispatches such notification.

Rule 55 Resubmission of Dispute after an Annulment

(1)   If a Committee annuls part or all of an award, either party may request the resubmission of the dispute to a new Tribunal. Such a request shall be addressed in writing to the Secretary-General and shall:

(a)   identify the award to which it relates;

(b)   indicate the date of the request;

(c)   explain in detail what aspect of the dispute is to be submitted to the Tribunal; and

(d)   be accompanied by a fee for lodging the request.

(2)   Upon receipt of the request and of the lodging fee, the Secretary-General shall forthwith:

(a)   register it in the Arbitration Register;

(b)   notify both parties of the registration;

(c)   transmit to the other party a copy of the request and of any accompanying documentation; and

(d)   invite the parties to proceed, as soon as possible, to constitute a new Tribunal, including the same number of arbitrators, and appointed by the same method, as the original one.

(3)   If the original award had only been annulled in part, the new Tribunal shall not reconsider any portion of the award not so annulled. It may, however, in accordance with the procedures set forth in Rule 54, stay or continue to stay the enforcement of the unannulled portion of the award until the date its own award is rendered.

(4)   Except as otherwise provided in paragraphs (1) – (3), these Rules shall apply to a proceeding on a resubmitted dispute in the same manner as if such dispute had been submitted pursuant to the Institution Rules.

Chapter VIII General Provisions

Rule 56 Final Provisions

(1)   The texts of these Rules in each official language of the Centre shall be equally authentic.

(2)   These Rules may be cited as the "Arbitration Rules" of the Centre.

RULES GOVERNING THE ADDITIONAL FACILITY
FOR THE ADMINISTRATION OF PROCEEDINGS
BY THE SECRETARIAT OF THE INTERNATIONAL CENTRE FOR SETTLEMENT
OF INVESTMENT DISPUTES
(ADDITIONAL FACILITY RULES)

Article 1 Definitions

(1)   "Convention" means the Convention on the Settlement of Investment Disputes between States and Nationals of Other States, submitted to Governments by the Executive Directors of the International Bank for Reconstruction and Development on March 18, 1965, which entered into force on October 14, 1966.

(2)   "Centre" means the International Centre for Settlement of Investment Disputes established pursuant to Article 1 of the Convention.

(3)   "Secretariat" means the Secretariat of the Centre.

(4)   "Contracting State" means a State for which the Convention has entered into force.

(5)   "Secretary-General" means the Secretary-General of the Centre or his deputy.

(6)   "National of another State" means a person who is not, or whom the parties to the proceeding in question have agreed not to treat as, a national of the State party to that proceeding.

Article 2 Additional Facility Rules

The Secretariat of the Centre is hereby authorized to administer, subject to and in accordance with these Rules, proceedings between a State (or a constituent subdivision or agency of a State) and a national of another State, falling within the following categories:

(a) conciliation and arbitration proceedings for the settlement of legal disputes arising directly out of an investment which are not within the jurisdiction of the Centre because either the State party to the dispute or the State whose national is a party to the dispute is not a Contracting State;

(b) conciliation and arbitration proceedings for the settlement of legal disputes which are not within the jurisdiction of the Centre because they do not arise directly out of an investment, provided that either the State party to the dispute or the State whose national is a party to the dispute is a Contracting State; and

(c) fact-finding proceedings.

The administration of proceedings authorized by these Rules is hereinafter referred to as the Additional Facility.

Article 3 Convention Not Applicable

Since the proceedings envisaged by Article 2 are outside the jurisdiction of the Centre, none of the provisions of the Convention shall be applicable to them or to recommendations, awards, or reports which may be rendered therein.

Article 4 Access to the Additional Facility in Respect of Conciliation and Arbitration Proceedings Subject to Secretary-General's Approval

(1) Any agreement providing for conciliation or arbitration proceedings under the Additional Facility in respect of existing or future disputes requires the approval of the Secretary-General. The parties may apply for such approval at any time prior to the institution of proceedings by submitting to the Secretariat a copy of the agreement concluded or proposed to be concluded between them together with other relevant documentation and such additional information as the Secretariat may reasonably request.

(2) In the case of an application based on Article 2(a), the Secretary-General shall give his approval only if (a) he is satisfied that the requirements of that provision are fulfilled at the time, and (b) both parties give their consent to the jurisdiction of the Centre under Article 25 of the Convention (in lieu of the Additional Facility) in the event that the jurisdictional requirements ratione personae of that Article shall have been met at the time when proceedings are instituted.

(3) In the case of an application based on Article 2(b), the Secretary-General shall give his approval only if he is satisfied (a) that the requirements of that provision are fulfilled, and (b) that the underlying transaction has features which distinguish it from an ordinary commercial transaction.

(4) If in the case of an application based on Article 2(b) the jurisdictional requirements ratione personae of Article 25 of the Convention shall have been met and the Secretary-General is of the opinion that it is likely that a Conciliation Commission or Arbitral Tribunal, as the case may be, will hold that the dispute arises directly out of an investment, he may make his approval of the application conditional upon consent by both parties to submit any dispute in the first instance to the jurisdiction of the Centre.

(5) The Secretary-General shall as soon as possible notify the parties whether he approves or disapproves the agreement of the parties. He may hold discussions with the parties or invite the parties to a meeting with the officials of the Secretariat either at the parties' request or at his own initiative. The Secretary-General shall, upon the request of the parties or any of them, keep confidential any or all information furnished to him by such parties or party in connection with the provisions of this Article.

(6) The Secretary-General shall record his approval of an agreement pursuant to this Article together with the names and addresses of the parties in a register to be maintained at the Secretariat for that purpose.

Article 5 Administrative and Financial Provisions

The responsibilities of the Secretariat in operating the Additional Facility and the financial provisions regarding its operation shall be as those established by the Administrative and Financial Regulations of the Centre for conciliation and arbitration proceedings under the Convention. Accordingly, Regulations 14 through 16, 22 through 30 and 34(1) of the Administrative and Financial Regulations of the Centre shall apply, mutatis mutandis, in respect of fact-finding, conciliation and arbitration proceedings under the Additional Facility.

Article 6 Schedules

Fact-finding, conciliation and arbitration proceedings under the Additional Facility shall be conducted in accordance with the respective Fact-finding (Additional Facility), Conciliation (Additional Facility) and Arbitration (Additional Facility) Rules set forth in Schedules A, B and C.

Schedule A – Fact-Finding (Additional Facility) Rules

CHAPTER I INSTITUTION OF PROCEEDINGS

Article 1 The Request

(1) Any State or national of a State wishing to institute an inquiry under the Additional Facility to examine and report on facts (hereinafter called a "fact-finding proceeding") shall send a request to that effect in writing to the Secretariat at the seat of the Centre. It shall be drawn up in an official language of the Centre, shall be dated and shall be signed by the requesting party or its duly authorized representative.

(2) The request may be made jointly by the parties to the fact-finding proceeding.

Article 2 Contents of the Request

(1) The request shall:

(a) designate precisely each party to the fact-finding proceeding and state the address of each;

(b) set forth the agreement between the parties providing for recourse to the fact- finding proceeding; and

(c) state the circumstances to be examined and reported on.

(2) The request shall in addition set forth any provisions agreed by the parties regarding the number of commissioners, their qualifications, appointment, replacement, resignation and disqualification, the extent of the powers of the Committee, the appointment of its President, and the place of its sessions, as well as the procedure to be followed in the fact-finding proceeding (hereinafter called the "Procedural Arrangement").

(3) The request shall be accompanied by five additional signed copies and by the fee prescribed pursuant to Regulation 16 of the Administrative and Financial Regulations of the Centre.

Article 3 Registration of the Request

(1) As soon as the Secretary-General has satisfied himself that the request conforms in form and substance to the provisions of Article 2 of these Rules he shall register the request in the Fact-finding (Additional Facility) Register, notify the requesting party and the other party of the registration and transmit to the other party a copy of the request and of the accompanying documentation, if any.

(2)   The notice of registration of a request shall:

(a)   record that the request is registered and indicate the date of the registration and of the dispatch of that notice;

(b)   notify each party that all communications in connection with the proceeding will be sent to the address stated in the request, unless another address is indicated to the Secretariat; and

(c)   request the other party to inform the Secretary-General in writing within 30 days after receipt of the notice whether it agrees with the request or it objects thereto.

(3)   In agreeing with the request, the other party may state additional circumstances which it wishes to be examined and reported on within the scope of the agreement between the parties for recourse to fact-finding proceedings. In that event, the Secretary-General shall request the requesting party to inform him promptly in writing whether it agrees to the inclusion of the additional facts or whether it objects thereto.

Article 4 Objections to the Request

(1)   Any objection by the other party pursuant to Article 3(2)(c) of these Rules shall be filed by it in writing with the Secretary-General and shall indicate on which of the following grounds it is based and the reasons therefor:

(a)   the other party is under no obligation to have recourse to fact-finding;

(b)   the circumstances indicated in the request as the circumstances to be examined and reported on are wholly or partly outside the scope of the agreement between the parties for recourse to fact-finding.

(2)   The provisions of paragraph (1) of this Article shall apply mutatis mutandis to an objection by the requesting party pursuant to Article 3(3) of these Rules.

Article 5 Settlement of Objections to the Request; Appointment of Special Commissioner

(1)   Promptly upon receipt of the notice of objections, the Secretary-General shall send a copy thereof to the requesting party or the other party, as the case may be, and shall invite the parties to meet with him in order to seek to resolve the objections by agreement.

(2)   Failing such agreement, he shall invite the parties to designate within 30 days a third party (hereinafter called the "Special Commissioner") to rule on the objections.

(3)   If the parties shall not have designated the Special Commissioner within the period specified in paragraph (2) of this Article, or such other period as the parties may agree, and if they or either one of them shall not be willing to request the Chairman of the Administrative Council (hereinafter called the "Chairman") or any other authority to designate the Special Commissioner, the Secretary-General shall inform the parties that the fact-finding proceeding cannot be held, recording the failure of the parties or one of them to cooperate.

(4)   The Special Commissioner shall rule on the objections only after hearing both parties and in his ruling shall decide whether or not the fact-finding proceeding is to continue, stating the reasons for his decision. If he decides that the proceeding is to continue, he shall determine the scope thereof.

Article 6 Absence of Procedural Arrangement

(1)   If, or to the extent that, the request does not set forth an agreement between the parties regarding the matters referred to in Article 2(2) of these Rules, the Secretary- General shall invite the parties to conclude in writing and furnish to the Secretariat within 30 days a Procedural Arrangement. The Procedural Arrangement may include any other matter or matters the parties may agree.

(2)   If the Procedural Arrangement cannot be concluded within the period referred to in paragraph (1) of this Article, or such other period as the parties may agree, the Procedural

Arrangement shall be drawn up by the Chairman after consulting with the parties and shall be binding upon the parties.

(3)   Unless the parties agree otherwise, the Procedural Arrangement drawn up by the Chairman shall provide for the appointment of three commissioners. Other provisions made by the Chairman relating to: (a) qualifications, appointment, replacement, resignation, and disqualification of the commissioners, filling up of the vacancies and consequential resumption of proceeding; and (b) incapacity of the President of the Committee and procedural matters, including procedural languages, shall, to the extent practicable, be similar to those applicable to conciliators and conciliation proceedings under the Conciliation (Additional Facility) Rules.

(4)   Notwithstanding the provisions of paragraph (3) of this Article, the Chairman may, whenever he is satisfied that the circumstances so warrant, include within the Procedural Arrangement provisions similar to written and oral procedures set forth in Chapter VII of the Arbitration (Additional Facility) Rules.

CHAPTER II THE COMMITTEE AND ITS WORKING

Article 7 Number of Commissioners

(1)   Except as the parties may otherwise agree, the Committee shall consist of a sole commissioner or any uneven number of commissioners.

(2)   If the Committee is to consist of three or more commissioners, one person shall be appointed the President of the Committee. References in these Rules to a Committee or a President of a Committee shall include a sole commissioner.

Article 8 Constitution of the Committee

(1)   The Committee shall be deemed to be constituted and the proceeding to have begun on the date the Secretary-General notifies the parties that all the commissioners have accepted their appointments.

(2)   Before or at the first session of the Committee, each commissioner shall sign a declaration in the following form:

"To the best of my knowledge there is no reason why I should not serve on the Fact- finding Committee constituted to examine certain facts under the Additional Facility pursuant to an agreement between _____ and _____.

"I shall keep confidential all information coming to my knowledge as a result of my participation in this proceeding, as well as the contents of any report drawn up by the Committee.

"I shall not accept any instruction or compensation with regard to the proceeding from any source except as provided in the Administrative and Financial Regulations of the Centre.

"A statement of my past and present professional, business and other relevant relationships (if any) with the parties is attached hereto."

Any commissioner failing to sign such a declaration by the end of the first session of the Committee shall be deemed to have resigned.

Article 9 Sessions of the Committee

(1)   The Committee shall meet for its first session within 60 days after its constitution or such other period as the parties may agree. The dates of the first and subsequent sessions shall be fixed by the President of the Committee after consultation with its members and the Secretary-General, and with the parties as far as possible. If, upon its constitution, the Committee has no President, such dates shall be fixed by the Secretary-General after consultation with the members of the Committee, and with the parties as far as possible.

(2)   The President of the Committee shall: (a) convene its subsequent sessions within time limits determined by the Committee; (b) conduct its hearings and preside at its deliberations; and (c) fix the date and hour of its sittings.

(3)   The Secretary-General shall notify the members of the Committee and the parties of the dates and place of the sessions of the Committee in good time.

(4)   The sessions of the Committee shall not be public.

Article 10 Conduct of Investigations and Examinations

Each investigation, and each examination of a locality, must be made in the presence of agents and counsel of the parties or after they have been duly notified.

Article 11 Decisions of the Committee

(1)   Except as the parties shall otherwise agree, all decisions of the Committee shall be taken by a majority of the votes of all its members.

(2)   Abstention by any member of the Committee shall count as a negative vote.

Article 12 Notices to Be Served by the Committee

The Secretary-General shall, to the extent possible, make necessary arrangements for the serving of notices by the Committee.

Article 13 Determinations of Questions of Procedure

Subject to the provisions of this Chapter, the constitution of the Committee and its procedure shall be governed by the Procedural Arrangement. Any matters not provided for in these Rules or in the Procedural Arrangement shall be determined by agreement of the parties or, failing such agreement, by the Committee.

CHAPTER III TERMINATION OF THE PROCEEDINGS

Article 14 Closure of the Proceeding

(1)   After the parties have presented all the explanations and evidence, and the witnesses (if any) have all been heard, the President of the Committee shall declare the fact-finding proceeding closed, and the Committee shall adjourn to deliberate and draw up its report (hereinafter called the "Report").

(2)   If one party fails to appear or participate in the proceeding or cooperate with the Committee at any stage, and the Committee determines that as a result thereof it is unable to carry out its task, it shall, after notice to the parties, close the proceeding and draw up its Report, noting the reference to fact-finding under the Additional Facility and recording the failure of that party to appear, participate or cooperate.

Article 15 The Report

(1)   The Report of the Committee shall be adopted by a majority of all the commissioners.

(2)   The Report shall be signed by all the commissioners. The refusal by a commissioner to sign the Report shall not invalidate the Report. The fact of such refusal shall be recorded.

(3)   If a commissioner dissents from the Report that fact will be noted in the Report. The commissioner may in addition attach a statement to the Report explaining the reasons for his dissent.

(4)   The Report shall be limited to findings of fact. The Report shall not contain any recommendations to the parties nor shall it have the character of an award.

Article 16 Effect to Be Given to the Report

The parties shall be entirely free as to the effect to be given to the Report.

CHAPTER IV MISCELLANEOUS

Article 17 Cooperation with the Committee

The parties undertake to facilitate the work of the Committee and to supply it with all means and facilities necessary to enable it to become fully acquainted with, and to accurately understand, the facts in question. Without prejudice to the generality of the foregoing, the parties in particular undertake to supply the Committee to the greatest possible extent with all relevant documents and information, as well as to use the means at their disposal to allow the Committee to visit the localities in question and to summon and hear witnesses or experts.

Article 18 Cost of the Proceeding

The fees and expenses of the members of the Committee and of any Special Commissioner, as well as the charges for the use of the facilities of the Centre, shall be borne equally by the parties. Each party shall bear any other expenses it incurs in connection with the proceeding.

Article 19 Final Provision

The text of these Rules in each official language of the Centre shall be equally authentic.

Schedule B – Conciliation (Additional Facility) Rules

CHAPTER I INTRODUCTION

Article 1 Scope of Application

Where the parties to a dispute have agreed that it shall be referred to conciliation under the Conciliation (Additional Facility) Rules, the dispute shall be settled in accordance with these Rules.

CHAPTER II INSTITUTION OF PROCEEDINGS

Article 2 The Request

(1)   Any State or any national of a State wishing to institute conciliation proceedings under the Additional Facility shall send a request to that effect in writing to the Secretariat at the seat of the Centre. It shall be drawn up in an official language of the Centre, shall be dated and shall be signed by the requesting party or its duly authorized representative.

(2)   The request may be made jointly by the parties to the dispute.

Article 3 Contents of the Request

(1)   The request shall:

(a)   designate precisely each party to the dispute and state the address of each;

(b)   set forth the relevant provisions embodying the agreement of the parties to refer the dispute to conciliation;

(c)   contain information concerning the issues in dispute;

(d)   indicate the date of approval by the Secretary-General pursuant to Article 4 of the Additional Facility Rules of the agreement of the parties providing for access to the Additional Facility; and

(e)   state, if the requesting party is a juridical person, that it has taken all necessary internal actions to authorize the request.

(2)   The request may in addition set forth any provisions agreed by the parties regarding the number of conciliators and the method of their appointment, as well as any other provisions agreed concerning the settlement of the dispute.

(3)   The request shall be accompanied by five additional signed copies, and by the fee prescribed pursuant to Regulation 16 of the Administrative and Financial Regulations of the Centre.

Article 4 Registration of the Request

As soon as the Secretary-General shall have satisfied himself that the request conforms in form and substance to the provisions of Article 3 of these Rules, he shall register the request in the Conciliation (Additional Facility) Register and on the same day dispatch to the parties a notice of registration. He shall also transmit a copy of the request and of the accompanying documentation (if any) to the other party to the dispute.

Article 5 Notice of Registration

The notice of registration of a request shall:

(a)   record that the request is registered and indicate the date of the registration and of the dispatch of the notice;

(b)   notify each party that all communications in connection with the proceeding will be sent to the address stated in the request, unless another address is indicated to the Secretariat;

(c)   unless such information has already been provided, invite the parties to communicate to the Secretary-General any provisions agreed by them regarding the number and the method of appointment of the conciliators;

(d)   remind the parties that the registration of the request is without prejudice to the powers and functions of the Conciliation Commission in regard to competence and the merits; and

(e)   invite the parties to proceed, as soon as possible, to constitute a Conciliation Commission in accordance with Chapter III of these Rules.

CHAPTER III THE COMMISSION

Article 6 General Provisions

(1)   Upon the dispatch of the notice of registration of the request for conciliation, the parties shall promptly proceed to constitute a Conciliation Commission.

(2)   The Commission shall consist of a sole conciliator or any uneven number of conciliators appointed as the parties shall agree.

(3)   In the absence of agreement between the parties regarding the number of conciliators and the method of their appointment, the Commission shall consist of three conciliators, one conciliator appointed by each party and the third, who shall be the President of the Commission, appointed by agreement of the parties.

(4)   If the Commission shall not have been constituted within 90 days after the notice of registration of the request for conciliation has been dispatched by the Secretary- General, or such other period as the parties may agree, the Chairman of the Administrative Council (hereinafter called the "Chairman") shall, at the request in writing of either party transmitted through the Secretary-General, appoint the conciliator or conciliators not yet appointed and, unless the President shall already have been designated or is to be designated later, designate a conciliator to be President of the Commission.

Article 7 Qualifications of Conciliators

Conciliators shall be persons of high moral character and recognized competence in the fields of law, commerce, industry or finance, who may be relied upon to exercise independent judgment.

Article 8 Method of Constituting the Commission
in the Absence of Previous Agreement between the Parties

(1)   If the parties, at the time of the registration of the request for conciliation, have not agreed upon the number of conciliators and the method of their appointment, they shall, unless they agree otherwise, follow the following procedures:

(a)   the requesting party shall, within 10 days after the registration of the request, propose to the other party the appointment of a sole conciliator or of a specified uneven number of conciliators and specify the method proposed for their appointment;

(b)   within 20 days after receipt of the proposals made by the requesting party, the other party shall:

   (i)   accept such proposals; or

   (ii) make other proposals regarding the number of conciliators and the method of their appointment; and

(c)   within 20 days after receipt of the reply containing any such proposals, the requesting party shall notify the other party whether it accepts or rejects such proposals.

(2)   The communications provided for in paragraph (1) of this Article shall be made or promptly confirmed in writing and shall either be transmitted through the Secretary- General or directly between the parties with a copy to the Secretary-General. The parties shall promptly notify the Secretary-General of the contents of any agreement reached.

(3)   At any time 60 days after the registration of the request, if no agreement on another procedure is reached, either party may inform the Secretary-General that it chooses the formula provided for in Article 6(3) of these Rules. The Secretary-General shall thereupon promptly inform the parties that the Commission is to be constituted in accordance with that provision.

*Article 9 Appointment of Conciliators to Commission Constituted
in Accordance with Article 6(3) of These Rules*

(1)   If the Commission is to be constituted in accordance with Article 6(3) of these Rules:

(a)   either party shall, in a communication to the other party:

   (i)   name two persons, identifying one of them as the conciliator appointed by it and the other as the conciliator proposed to be the President of the Commission; and

   (ii) invite the other party to concur in the appointment of the conciliator proposed to be the President of the Commission and to appoint another conciliator;

(b)   promptly upon receipt of this communication the other party shall, in its reply:

   (i)   name a person as the conciliator appointed by it; and

   (ii) concur in the appointment of the conciliator proposed to be the President of the Commission or name another person as the conciliator proposed to be the President; and

(c)   promptly upon receipt of the reply containing such a proposal, the initiating party shall notify the other party whether it concurs in the appointment of the conciliator proposed by that party to be the President of the Commission.

(2)   The communications provided for in this Article shall be made or promptly confirmed in writing and shall either be transmitted through the Secretary-General or directly between the parties with a copy to the Secretary-General.

*Article 10 Appointment of Conciliators and Designation of President of the Commission
by the Chairman*

(1)   Promptly upon receipt of a request by a party to the Chairman to make an appointment or designation pursuant to Article 6(4) of these Rules, the Secretary-General shall send a copy thereof to the other party.

(2)   The Chairman shall use his best efforts to comply with that request within 30 days after its receipt. Before he proceeds to make appointments or a designation, he shall consult both parties as far as possible.

(3) The Secretary-General shall promptly notify the parties of any appointment or designation made by the Chairman.

Article 11 Acceptance of Appointments

(1) The party or parties concerned shall notify the Secretary-General of the appointment of each conciliator and indicate the method of his appointment.

(2) As soon as the Secretary-General has been informed by a party or the Chairman of the appointment of a conciliator, he shall seek an acceptance from the appointee.

(3) If a conciliator fails to accept his appointment within 15 days, the Secretary-General shall promptly notify the parties, and if appropriate the Chairman, and invite them to proceed to the appointment of another conciliator in accordance with the method followed for the previous appointment.

Article 12 Replacement of Conciliators Prior to Constitution of the Commission

At any time before the Commission is constituted, each party may replace any conciliator appointed by it and the parties may by common consent agree to replace any conciliator.

Article 13 Constitution of the Commission

(1) The Commission shall be deemed to be constituted and the proceeding to have begun on the date the Secretary-General notifies the parties that all the conciliators have accepted their appointment.

(2) Before or at the first session of the Commission, each conciliator shall sign a declaration in the following form:

"To the best of my knowledge there is no reason why I should not serve on the Conciliation Commission constituted with respect to a dispute between _____ and _____.

"I shall keep confidential all information coming to my knowledge as a result of my participation in this proceeding, as well as the contents of any report drawn up by the Commission.

"I shall not accept any instruction or compensation with regard to the proceeding from any source except as provided in the Administrative and Financial Regulations of the Centre.

"A statement of my past and present professional, business and other relevant relationships (if any) with the parties is attached hereto."

Any conciliator failing to sign such a declaration by the end of the first session of the Tribunal shall be deemed to have resigned.

Article 14 Replacement of Conciliators After Constitution of the Commission

(1) After a Commission has been constituted and proceedings have begun, its composition shall remain unchanged; provided, however, that if a conciliator should die, become incapacitated, resign or be disqualified, the resulting vacancy shall be filled as provided in this Article and Article 17 of these Rules.

(2) If a conciliator becomes incapacitated or unable to perform the duties of his office, the procedure in respect of the disqualification of conciliators set forth in Article 15 shall apply.

(3) A conciliator may resign by submitting his resignation to the other members of the Commission and the Secretary-General. If the conciliator was appointed by one of the parties, the Commission shall promptly consider the reasons for his resignation and decide whether it consents thereto. The Commission shall promptly notify the Secretary-General of its decision.

Article 15 Disqualification of Conciliators

(1) A party may propose to a Commission the disqualification of any of its members on account of any fact indicating a manifest lack of the qualities required by Article 7 of these Rules.

(2)   A party proposing the disqualification of a conciliator shall promptly, and in any event before the proceeding is declared closed, file its proposal with the Secretary- General, stating its reasons therefor.

(3)   The Secretary-General shall forthwith:

(a)   transmit the proposal to the members of the Commission and, if it relates to a sole con-ciliator or to a majority of the members of the Commission, to the Chairman; and

(b)   notify the other party of the proposal.

(4)   The conciliator to whom the proposal relates may, without delay, furnish explanations to the Commission or the Chairman, as the case may be.

(5)   The decision on any proposal to disqualify a conciliator shall be taken by the other members of the Commission except that where those members are equally divided, or in the case of a proposal to disqualify a sole conciliator, or a majority of the conciliators, the Chairman shall take that decision.

(6)   Whenever the Chairman has to decide on a proposal to disqualify a conciliator, he shall use his best efforts to take that decision within 30 days after he has received the proposal.

(7)   The proceeding shall be suspended until a decision has been taken on the proposal.

Article 16 Procedure During a Vacancy on the Commission

(1)   The Secretary-General shall forthwith notify the parties and, if necessary, the Chairman of the disqualification, death, incapacity or resignation of a conciliator and of the consent, if any, of the Commission to a resignation.

(2)   Upon the notification by the Secretary-General of a vacancy on the Commission, the pro-ceeding shall be or remain suspended until the vacancy has been filled.

Article 17 Filling Vacancies on the Commission

(1)   Except as provided in paragraph (2) of this Article, a vacancy resulting from the disqualifi-cation, death, incapacity or resignation of a conciliator shall be promptly filled by the same method by which his appointment has been made.

(2)   In addition to filling vacancies relating to conciliators appointed by him, the Chairman shall:

(a)   fill a vacancy caused by the resignation, without the consent of the Commission, of a conciliator appointed by a party; or

(b)   at the request of either party, fill any other vacancy, if no new appointment is made and accepted within 45 days of the notification of the vacancy by the Secretary-General.

(3)   In filling a vacancy the party or the Chairman, as the case may be, shall observe the pro-visions of these Rules with respect to the appointment of conciliators. Article 13(2) of these Rules shall apply mutatis mutandis to the newly appointed conciliator.

Article 18 Resumption of Proceeding After Filling a Vacancy

As soon as a vacancy on the Commission has been filled, the proceeding shall continue from the point it had reached at the time the vacancy occurred. The newly appointed conciliator may, however, require that the oral procedure be recommenced, if this had already been started.

CHAPTER IV PLACE OF PROCEEDINGS

Article 19 Determination of Place of Conciliation Proceeding

Unless the parties have agreed upon the place where the conciliation proceeding is to be held, such place shall be determined by the Secretary-General in consultation with the President of the Commission, or if there is no President, with the single conciliator, having regard to the circumstances of the proceeding and the convenience of the parties.

CHAPTER V WORKING OF THE COMMISSION

Article 20 Sessions of the Commission

(1)   The Commission shall meet for its first session within 60 days after its constitution or such other period as the parties may agree. The dates of that session shall be fixed by the President of the Commission after consultation with its members and the Secretariat, and with the parties as far as possible. If, upon its constitution, the Commission has no President, such dates shall be fixed by the Secretary-General after consultation with the members of the Commission, and with the parties as far as possible.

(2)   Subsequent sessions shall be convened by the President within time limits determined by the Commission. The dates of such sessions shall be fixed by the President of the Commission after consultation with its members and the Secretariat, and with the parties as far as possible.

(3)   The Secretary-General shall notify the members of the Commission and the parties of the dates and place of the sessions of the Commission in good time.

Article 21 Sittings of the Commission

(1)   The President of the Commission shall conduct its hearings and preside at its deliberations.

(2)   Except as the parties otherwise agree, the presence of a majority of the members of the Commission shall be required at its sittings.

(3)   The President of the Commission shall fix the date and hour of its sittings.

Article 22 Deliberations of the Commission

(1)   The deliberations of the Commission shall take place in private and remain secret.

(2)   Only members of the Commission shall take part in its deliberations. No other person shall be admitted unless the Commission decides otherwise.

Article 23 Decisions of the Commission

(1)   The decisions of the Commission shall be taken by a majority of the votes of all its members. Abstention by any member of the Commission shall count as a negative vote.

(2)   Except as otherwise provided by these Rules or decided by the Commission, it may take any decision by correspondence among its members, provided that all of them are consulted. Decisions so taken shall be certified by the President of the Commission.

Article 24 Incapacity of the President

If at any time the President of the Commission should be unable to act, his functions shall be performed by one of the other members of the Commission, acting in the order in which the Secretariat had received the notice of their acceptance of their appointment to the Commission.

Article 25 Representation of the Parties

(1)   Each party may be represented or assisted by agents, counsel or advocates whose names and authority shall be notified by that party to the Secretariat, which shall promptly inform the Commission and the other party.

(2)   For the purposes of these Rules, the expression "party" includes, where the context so admits, an agent, counsel or advocate authorized to represent that party.

CHAPTER VI GENERAL PROCEDURAL PROVISIONS

Article 26 Procedural Orders

The Commission shall make the orders required for the conduct of the proceeding.

Article 27 Preliminary Procedural Consultation

(1)   As early as possible after the constitution of a Commission, its President shall endeavor to ascertain the views of the parties regarding questions of procedure. For this purpose he may request the parties to meet him. He shall, in particular, seek their views on the following matters:

(a)   the number of members of the Commission required to constitute a quorum at its sittings;

(b)   the language or languages to be used in the proceeding;

(c)   the evidence, oral or written, which each party intends to produce or to request the Commission to call for, and the written statements which each party intends to file, as well as the time limits within which such evidence should be produced and such statements filed;

(d)   the number of copies desired by each party of instruments filed by the other; and

(e)   the manner in which the record of the hearings shall be kept.

(2)   In the conduct of the proceeding the Commission shall apply any agreement between the parties on procedural matters, which is not inconsistent with any provisions of the Additional Facility Rules and the Administrative and Financial Regulations of the Centre.

Article 28 Procedural Languages

(1)   The parties may agree on the use of one or two languages to be used in the proceeding, provided that, if they agree on any language that is not an official language of the Centre, the Commission, after consultation with the Secretary-General, gives its approval. If the parties do not agree on any such procedural language, each of them may select one of the official languages (i.e., English, French and Spanish) for this purpose. Notwithstanding the foregoing, one of the official languages of the Centre shall be used for all communications to and from the Secretariat.

(2)   If two procedural languages are selected by the parties, any instrument may be filed in either language. Either language may be used at the hearings, subject, if the Commission so requires, to translation and interpretation. The recommendations and the report of the Commission shall be rendered and the record kept in both procedural languages, both versions being equally authentic.

Article 29 Supporting Documentation

Supporting documentation shall ordinarily be filed together with the instrument to which it relates, and in any case within the time limit for the filing of such instrument.

CHAPTER VII CONCILIATION PROCEDURES

Article 30 Functions of the Commission

(1)   It shall be the duty of the Commission to clarify the issues in dispute between the parties and to endeavour to bring about agreement between them upon mutually acceptable terms.

(2)   In order to clarify the issues in dispute between the parties, the Commission shall hear the parties and shall endeavour to obtain any information that might serve this end. The parties shall be associated with its work as closely as possible.

(3)   In order to bring about agreement between the parties, the Commission may, from time to time at any stage of the proceeding, make recommendations to the parties, together with arguments in favor thereof, including recommendations to the effect that the parties accept specific terms of settlement or that they refrain, while it seeks to bring about agreement between them, from specific acts that might aggravate the dispute. It may fix time limits within which each party shall inform the Commission of its decision concerning the recommendations made. The parties shall give their most serious consideration to such recommendations.

(4)   The Commission, in order to obtain information that might enable it to discharge its functions, may at any stage of the proceeding:

(a)   request from either party oral explanations, documents and other information;

(b) request evidence from other persons; and

(c) with the consent ofthe party concerned, visit any place connected with the dispute or conduct inquiries there, provided that the parties may participate in any such visits and inquiries.

Article 31 Cooperation of the Parties

The parties shall cooperate in good faith with the Commission in order to enable the Commission to carry out its functions, and shall give their most serious consideration to its recommendations. Without prejudice to the generality of the foregoing, the parties shall: (a) at the request of the Commission, furnish all relevant documents, information and explanations as well as use the means at their disposal to enable the Commission to hear witnesses and experts whom it desires to call; (b) facilitate visits to and inquiries at any place connected with the dispute that the Commission desires to undertake; and (c) comply with any time limits agreed with or fixed by the Commission.

Article 32 Transmission of the Request

As soon as the Commission is constituted, the Secretary-General shall transmit to each member of the Commission a copy each of:

(a) the request by which the proceeding was commenced;

(b) the supporting documentation;

(c) the notice of registration of the request; and

(d) any communication received from either party in response thereto.

Article 33 Written Statements

(1) Upon the constitution of the Commission, its President shall invite each party to file, within 30 days or such longer time as the President may fix, a written statement of its position. If, upon its constitution, the Commission has no President, such invitation shall be issued and any such longer time limit shall be fixed by the Secretary-General. At any stage of the proceeding, within such time limits as the Commission shall fix, either party may file such other written statements as it deems useful and relevant.

(2) Except as otherwise provided by the Commission after consultation with the parties and the Secretary-General, every written statement or other instrument shall be filed in the form of a signed original accompanied by additional copies whose number shall be two more than the number of members of the Commission.

Article 34 Hearings

(1) The hearings of the Commission shall take place in private and, except as the parties otherwise agree, shall remain secret.

(2) The Commission shall decide, with the consent of the parties, which other persons besides the parties, their agents, counsel and advocates, witnesses and experts during their testimony, and officers of the Commission may attend the hearings.

Article 35 Witnesses and Experts

(1) Each party may, at any stage of the proceeding, request that the Commission hear the witnesses and experts whose evidence the party considers relevant. The Commission shall fix a time limit within which such hearing shall take place.

(2) Witnesses and experts shall, as a rule, be examined before the Commission by the parties under the control of its President. Questions may also be put to them by any member of the Commission.

(3) If a witness or expert is unable to appear before it, the Commission, in agreement with the parties, may make appropriate arrangements for the evidence to be given in a written deposition or to be taken by examination elsewhere. The parties may participate in any such examination.

CHAPTER VIII TERMINATION OF THE PROCEEDING

Article 36 Objections to Competence

(1)   The Commission shall have the power to rule on its competence.

(2)   Any objection that the dispute is not within the competence of the Commission, shall be filed by a party with the Secretary-General as soon as possible after the constitution of the Commission and in any event no later than in its first written statement or at the first hearing if that occurs earlier, unless the facts on which the objection is based are unknown to the party at that time.

(3)   The Commission may on its own initiative consider, at any stage of the proceeding, whether the dispute before it is within its competence.

(4)   Upon the formal raising of an objection, the proceeding on the merits shall be suspended. The Commission may deal with the objection as a preliminary question or join it to the merits of the dispute. If the Commission overrules the objection or joins it to the merits, the proceedings on the merits shall be resumed. If the Commission decides that the dispute is not within its competence, it shall close the proceeding and draw up a report to that effect, in which it shall state its reasons.

Article 37 Closure of the Proceeding

(1)   If one party fails to appear or participate in the proceeding, the Commission shall, after notice to the parties, close the proceeding and draw up its report noting the reference of the dispute to conciliation and recording the failure of that party to appear or participate.

(2)   If at any stage of the proceeding it appears to the Commission that there is no likelihood of settlement between the parties, the Commission shall, after notice to the parties, close the proceeding and draw up its report noting the reference of the dispute to conciliation and recording the failure of the parties to reach a settlement.

(3)   If the parties reach agreement on the issues in dispute, the Commission shall close the proceeding and draw up its report noting the issues in dispute and recording that the parties have reached agreement. At the request of the parties, the report shall record the detailed terms and conditions of their agreement.

(4)   Except as the parties otherwise agree, neither party to a conciliation proceeding may in any other proceeding before arbitrators, courts or otherwise invoke or rely on any views expressed or statements or admissions or offers of settlement made by the other party in the conciliation proceeding, or the report or any recommendations made by the Commission.

Article 38 The Report

(1)   The report of the Commission shall be drawn up and signed as soon as possible after the closure of the proceeding. It shall contain, in addition to the material specified in Article 37 of these Rules, as appropriate:

(a)   a precise designation of each party;

(b)   a description of the method of constitution of the Commission;

(c)   the names of the members of the Commission, and an identification of the appointing authority of each;

(d)   the names of the agents, counsel and advocates of the parties;

(e)   the dates and place of the sittings of the Commission; and

(f)   a summary of the proceeding.

(2)   The report shall also record any agreement of the parties, referred to in Article 37(4) of these Rules.

(3)   The report shall be signed by the members of the Commission; the date of each signature shall be indicated. The fact that a member refuses to sign the report shall be recorded therein.

Article 39 Communication of the Report

(1) Upon signature of the last conciliator to sign, the Secretary-General shall promptly:

(a) authenticate the original text of the report and deposit it in the archives of the Secretariat; and

(b) dispatch a certified copy of the report to each party, indicating the date of dispatch on the original text and on all copies.

(2) The Secretary-General shall, upon request, make available to a party additional certified copies of the report.

CHAPTER IX COSTS

Article 40 Cost of Proceeding

The fees and expenses of the members of the Commission, as well as the charge for the use of facilities of the Centre, shall be borne equally by the parties. Each party shall bear any other expenses it incurs with the proceeding. The Secretariat shall provide the Commission and the parties all information in its possession to facilitate the division of the costs.

CHAPTER X GENERAL PROVISIONS

Article 41 Final Provision

The text of these Rules in each official language of the Centre shall be equally authentic.

Schedule C Arbitration (Additional Facility) Rules

CHAPTER I INTRODUCTION

Article 1 Scope of Application

Where the parties to a dispute have agreed that it shall be referred to arbitration under the Arbitration (Additional Facility) Rules, the dispute shall be settled in accordance with these Rules, save that if any of these Rules is in conflict with a provision of the law applicable to the arbitration from which the parties cannot derogate, that provision shall prevail.

CHAPTER II INSTITUTION OF PROCEEDINGS

Article 2 The Request

(1) Any State or any national of a State wishing to institute arbitration proceedings shall send a request to that effect in writing to the Secretariat at the seat of the Centre. It shall be drawn up in an official language of the Centre, shall be dated and shall be signed by the requesting party or its duly authorized representative.

(2) The request may be made jointly by the parties to the dispute.

Article 3 Contents of the Request

(1) The request shall:

(a) designate precisely each party to the dispute and state the address of each;

(b) set forth the relevant provisions embodying the agreement of the parties to refer the dispute to arbitration;

(c) indicate the date of approval by the Secretary-General pursuant to Article 4 of the Additional Facility Rules of the agreement of the parties providing for access to the Additional Facility;

(d) contain information concerning the issues in dispute and an indication of the amount involved, if any; and

(e) state, if the requesting party is a juridical person, that it has taken all necessary internal actions to authorize the request.

(2)   The request may in addition set forth any provisions agreed by the parties regarding the number of arbitrators and the method of their appointment, as well as any other provisions agreed concerning the settlement of the dispute.

(3)   The request shall be accompanied by five additional signed copies and by the fee prescribed pursuant to Regulation 16 of the Administrative and Financial Regulation of the Centre.

Article 4 Registration of the Request

As soon as the Secretary-General shall have satisfied himself that the request conforms in form and substance to the provisions of Article 3 of these Rules, he shall register the request in the Arbitration (Additional Facility) Register and on the same day dispatch to the parties a notice of registration. He shall also transmit a copy of the request and of the accompanying documentation (if any) to the other party to the dispute.

Article 5 Notice of Registration

The notice of registration of a request shall:

(a)   record that the request is registered and indicate the date of the registration and of the dispatch of the notice;

(b)   notify each party that all communications in connection with the proceeding will be sent to the address stated in the request, unless another address is indicated to the Secretariat;

(c)   unless such information has already been provided, invite the parties to communicate to the Secretary-General any provisions agreed by them regarding the number and the method of appointment of the arbitrators;

(d)   remind the parties that the registration of the request is without prejudice to the powers and functions of the Arbitral Tribunal in regard to competence and the merits; and

(e)   invite the parties to proceed, as soon as possible, to constitute an Arbitral Tribunal in accordance with Chapter III of these Rules.

CHAPTER III THE TRIBUNAL

Article 6 General Provisions

(1)   In the absence of agreement between the parties regarding the number of arbitrators and the method of their appointment, the Tribunal shall consist of three arbitrators, one arbitrator appointed by each party and the third, who shall be the President of the Tribunal, appointed by agreement of the parties, all in accordance with Article 9 of these Rules.

(2)   Upon the dispatch of the notice of registration of the request for arbitration, the parties shall promptly proceed to constitute a Tribunal.

(3)   The Tribunal shall consist of a sole arbitrator or any uneven number of arbitrators appointed as the parties shall agree.

(4)   If the Tribunal shall not have been constituted within 90 days after the notice of registration of the request for arbitration has been dispatched by the Secretary-General, or such other period as the parties may agree, the Chairman of the Administrative Council (hereinafter called the "Chairman") shall, at the request in writing of either party transmitted through the Secretary-General, appoint the arbitrator or arbitrators not yet appointed and, unless the President shall already have been designated or is to be designated later, designate an arbitrator to be President of the Tribunal.

(5)   Except as the parties shall otherwise agree, no person who had previously acted as a conciliator or arbitrator in any proceeding for the settlement of the dispute or as a member of any fact-finding committee relating thereto may be appointed as a member of the Tribunal.

Article 7 Nationality of Arbitrators

(1)   The majority of the arbitrators shall be nationals of States other than the State party to the dispute and of the State whose national is a party to the dispute, unless the sole arbitrator or each individual member of the Tribunal is appointed by agreement of the parties. Where the Tribunal is to consist of three members, a national of either of these States may not be appointed as an arbitrator by a party without the agreement of the other party to the dispute. Where the Tribunal is to consist of five or more members, nationals of either of these States may not be appointed as arbitrators by a party if appointment by the other party of the same number of arbitrators of either of these nationalities would result in a majority of arbitrators of these nationalities.

(2)   Arbitrators appointed by the Chairman shall not be nationals of the State party to the dispute or of the State whose national is a party to the dispute.

Article 8 Qualifications of Arbitrators

Arbitrators shall be persons of high moral character and recognized competence in the fields of law, commerce, industry or finance, who may be relied upon to exercise independent judgment.

Article 9 Method of Constituting the Tribunal in the Absence of Agreement Between the Parties

(1)   If the parties have not agreed upon the number of arbitrators and the method of their appointment within 60 days after the registration of the request, the Secretary-General shall, upon the request of either party promptly inform the parties that the Tribunal is to be consti-tuted in accordance with the following procedure:

(a)   either party shall, in a communication to the other party:

   (i)   name two persons, identifying one of them, who shall not have the same nationality as nor be a national of either party, as the arbitrator appointed by it, and the other as the arbitrator proposed to be the President of the Tribunal; and

   (ii)   invite the other party to concur in the appointment of the arbitrator proposed to be the President of the Tribunal and to appoint another arbitrator;

(b)   promptly upon receipt of this communication the other party shall, in its reply:

   (i)   name a person as the arbitrator appointed by it, who shall not have the same nationality as nor be a national of either party; and

   (ii)   concur in the appointment of the arbitrator proposed to be the President of the Tribunal or name another person as the arbitrator proposed to be President; and

(c)   promptly upon receipt of the reply containing such a proposal, the initiating party shall notify the other party whether it concurs in the appointment of the arbitrator proposed by that party to be the President of the Tribunal.

(2)   The communications provided for in paragraph (1) of this Article shall be made or promptly confirmed in writing and shall either be transmitted through the Secretary- General or directly between the parties with a copy to the Secretary-General.

Article 10 Appointment of Arbitrators and Designation of President of Tribunal
by the Chairman of the Administrative Council

(1)   Promptly upon receipt of a request by a party to the Chairman to make an appointment or designation pursuant to Article 6(4) of these Rules, the Secretary-General shall send a copy thereof to the other party.

(2)   The Chairman shall use his best efforts to comply with that request within 30 days after its receipt. Before he proceeds to make appointments or a designation, he shall consult both parties as far as possible.

(3)   The Secretary-General shall promptly notify the parties of any appointment or designation made by the Chairman.

Article 11 Acceptance of Appointments

(1)   The party or parties concerned shall notify the Secretary-General of the appointment of each arbitrator and indicate the method of his appointment.

(2)   As soon as the Secretary-General has been informed by a party or the Chairman of the appointment of an arbitrator, he shall seek an acceptance from the appointee.

(3)   If an arbitrator fails to accept his appointment within 15 days, the Secretary-General shall promptly notify the parties, and if appropriate the Chairman, and invite them to proceed to the appointment of another arbitrator in accordance with the method followed for the previous appointment.

Article 12 Replacement of Arbitrators Prior to Constitution of the Tribunal

At any time before the Tribunal is constituted, each party may replace any arbitrator appointed by it and the parties may by common consent agree to replace any arbitrator.

Article 13 Constitution of the Tribunal

(1)   The Tribunal shall be deemed to be constituted and the proceeding to have begun on the date the Secretary-General notifies the parties that all the arbitrators have accepted their appointment.

(2)   Before or at the first session of the Tribunal, each arbitrator shall sign a declaration in the following form:

"To the best of my knowledge there is no reason why I should not serve on the Arbitral Tribunal constituted with respect to a dispute between _____ and _____.

"I shall keep confidential all information coming to my knowledge as a result of my participation in this proceeding, as well as the contents of any award made by the Tribunal.

"I shall judge fairly as between the parties and shall not accept any instruction or compensation with regard to the proceeding from any source except as provided in the Administrative and Financial Regulations of the Centre.

"Attached is a statement of (a) my past and present professional, business and other relationships (if any) with the parties and (b) any other circumstance that might cause my reliability for independent judgment to be questioned by a party. I acknowledge that by signing this declaration, I assume a continuing obligation promptly to notify the Secretary-General of the Centre of any such relationship or circumstance that subsequently arises during this proceeding."

Any arbitrator failing to sign such a declaration by the end of the first session of the Tribunal shall be deemed to have resigned.

Article 14 Replacement of Arbitrators After Constitution of the Tribunal

(1)   After a Tribunal has been constituted and proceedings have begun, its composition shall remain unchanged; provided, however, that if an arbitrator should die, become incapacitated, resign or be disqualified, the resulting vacancy shall be filled as provided in this Article and Article 17 of these Rules.

(2)   If an arbitrator becomes incapacitated or unable to perform the duties of his office, the procedure in respect of the disqualification of arbitrators set forth in Article 15 shall apply.

(3)   An arbitrator may resign by submitting his resignation to the other members of the Tribunal and the Secretary-General. If the arbitrator was appointed by one of the parties, the Tribunal shall promptly consider the reasons for his resignation and decide whether it consents thereto. The Tribunal shall promptly notify the Secretary-General of its decision.

Article 15 Disqualification of Arbitrators

(1)   A party may propose to a Tribunal the disqualification of any of its members on account of any fact indicating a manifest lack of the qualities required by Article 8 of these Rules, or on the ground that he was ineligible for appointment to the Tribunal under Article 7 of these Rules.

(2)   A party proposing the disqualification of an arbitrator shall promptly, and in any event before the proceeding is declared closed, file its proposal with the Secretary-General, stating its reasons therefor.

(3)   The Secretary-General shall forthwith:

(a)   transmit the proposal to the members of the Tribunal and, if it relates to a sole arbitrator or to a majority of the members of the Tribunal, to the Chairman; and

(b)   notify the other party of the proposal.

(4)   The arbitrator to whom the proposal relates may, without delay, furnish explanations to the Tribunal or the Chairman, as the case may be.

(5)   The decision on any proposal to disqualify an arbitrator shall be taken by the other members of the Tribunal except that where those members are equally divided, or in the case of a proposal to disqualify a sole arbitrator, or a majority of the arbitrators, the Chairman shall take that decision.

(6)   Whenever the Chairman has to decide on a proposal to disqualify an arbitrator, he shall use his best efforts to take that decision within 30 days after he has received the proposal.

(7)   The proceeding shall be suspended until a decision has been taken on the proposal.

Article 16 Procedure During a Vacancy on the Tribunal

(1)   The Secretary-General shall forthwith notify the parties and, if necessary, the Chairman of the disqualification, death, incapacity or resignation of an arbitrator and of the consent, if any, of the Tribunal to a resignation.

(2)   Upon the notification by the Secretary-General of a vacancy on the Tribunal, the proceeding shall be or remain suspended until the vacancy has been filled.

Article 17 Filling Vacancies on the Tribunal

(1)   Except as provided in paragraph (2) of this Article, a vacancy resulting from the disqualification, death, incapacity or resignation of an arbitrator shall be promptly filled by the same method by which his appointment had been made.

(2)   In addition to filling vacancies relating to arbitrators appointed by him, the Chairman shall:

(a)   fill a vacancy caused by the resignation, without the consent of the Tribunal, of an arbitrator appointed by a party; or

(b)   at the request of either party, fill any other vacancy, if no new appointment is made and accepted within 45 days of the notification of the vacancy by the Secretary-General.

(3)   In filling a vacancy the party or the Chairman, as the case may be, shall observe the provisions of these Rules with respect to the appointment of arbitrators. Article 13(2) of these Rules shall apply mutatis mutandis to the newly appointed arbitrator.

Article 18 Resumption of Proceeding After Filling a Vacancy

As soon as a vacancy on the Tribunal has been filled, the proceeding shall continue from the point it had reached at the time the vacancy occurred. The newly appointed arbitrator may, however, require that the oral procedure be recommenced, if this had already been started.

CHAPTER IV PLACE OF ARBITRATION

Article 19 Limitation on Choice of Forum

Arbitration proceedings shall be held only in States that are parties to the 1958 UN Convention on the Recognition and Enforcement of Foreign Arbitral Awards.

Article 20 Determination of Place of Arbitration

(1)   Subject to Article 19 of these Rules the place of arbitration shall be determined by the Arbitral Tribunal after consultation with the parties and the Secretariat.

(2)   The Arbitral Tribunal may meet at any place it deems appropriate for the inspection of goods, other property or documents. It may also visit any place connected with the dispute or conduct inquiries there. The parties shall be given sufficient notice to enable them to be present at such inspection or visit.

(3)   The award shall be made at the place of arbitration.

CHAPTER V WORKING OF THE TRIBUNAL

Article 21 Sessions of the Tribunal

(1)   The Tribunal shall meet for its first session within 60 days after its constitution or such other period as the parties may agree. The dates of that session shall be fixed by the President of the Tribunal after consultation with its members and the Secretariat, and with the parties as far as possible. If, upon its constitution, the Tribunal has no President, such dates shall be fixed by the Secretary-General after consultation with the members of the Tribunal, and with the parties as far as possible.

(2)   Subsequent sessions shall be convened by the President within time limits determined by the Tribunal. The dates of such sessions shall be fixed by the President of the Tribunal after consultation with its members and the Secretariat, and with the parties as far as possible.

(3)   The Secretary-General shall notify the members of the Tribunal and the parties of the dates and place of the sessions of the Tribunal in good time.

Article 22 Sittings of the Tribunal

(1)   The President of the Tribunal shall conduct its hearings and preside at its deliberations.

(2)   Except as the parties otherwise agree, the presence of a majority of the members of the Tribunal shall be required at its sittings.

(3)   The President of the Tribunal shall fix the date and hour of its sittings.

Article 23 Deliberations of the Tribunal

(1)   The deliberations of the Tribunal shall take place in private and remain secret.

(2)   Only members of the Tribunal shall take part in its deliberations. No other person shall be admitted unless the Tribunal decides otherwise.

Article 24 Decisions of the Tribunal

(1)   Any award or other decision of the Tribunal shall be made by a majority of the votes of all its members. Abstention by any member of the Tribunal shall count as a negative vote.

(2)   Except as otherwise provided by these Rules or decided by the Tribunal, it may take any decisions by correspondence among its members, provided that all of them are consulted. Decisions so taken shall be certified by the President of the Tribunal.

Article 25 Incapacity of the President

If at any time the President of the Tribunal should be unable to act, his functions shall be performed by one of the other members of the Tribunal, acting in the order in which the Secretariat had received the notice of their acceptance of their appointment to the Tribunal.

Article 26 Representation of the Parties

(1)   Each party may be represented or assisted by agents, counsel or advocates whose names and authority shall be notified by that party to the Secretariat, which shall promptly inform the Tribunal and the other party.

(2)   For the purposes of these Rules, the expression "party" includes, where the context so admits, an agent, counsel or advocate authorized to represent that party.

CHAPTER VI GENERAL PROCEDURAL PROVISIONS

Article 27 Procedural Orders

The Tribunal shall make the orders required for the conduct of the proceeding.

Article 28 Preliminary Procedural Consultation

(1)   As early as possible after the constitution of a Tribunal, its President shall endeavor to ascertain the views of the parties regarding questions of procedure. For this purpose he may request the parties to meet him. He shall, in particular, seek their views on the following matters:

(a)   the number of members of the Tribunal required to constitute a quorum at its sittings;

(b)   the language or languages to be used in the proceeding;

(c)   the number and sequence of the pleadings and the time limits within which they are to be filed;

(d)   the number of copies desired by each party of instruments filed by the other;

(e)   dispensing with the written or oral procedure;

(f)   the manner in which the cost of the proceeding is to be apportioned; and

(g)   the manner in which the record of the hearings shall be kept.

(2)   In the conduct of the proceeding the Tribunal shall apply any agreement between the parties on procedural matters, which is not inconsistent with any provisions of the Additional Facility Rules and the Administrative and Financial Regulations of the Centre.

Article 29 Pre-Hearing Conference

(1)   At the request of the Secretary-General or at the discretion of the President of the Tribunal, a pre-hearing conference between the Tribunal and the parties may be held to arrange for an exchange of information and the stipulation of uncontested facts in order to expedite the proceeding.

(2)   At the request of the parties, a pre-hearing conference between the Tribunal and the parties, duly represented by their authorized representatives, may be held to consider the issues in dispute with a view to reaching an amicable settlement.

Article 30 Procedural Languages

(1)   The parties may agree on the use of one or two languages to be used in the proceeding, provided that if they agree on any language that is not an official language of the Centre, the Tribunal, after consultation with the Secretary-General, gives its approval. If the parties do not agree on any such procedural language, each of them may select one of the official languages (i.e., English, French and Spanish) for this purpose. Notwithstanding the foregoing, one of the official languages of the Centre shall be used for all communications to and from the Secretariat.

(2)   If two procedural languages are selected by the parties, any instrument may be filed in either language. Either language may be used at the hearing subject, if the Tribunal so requires, to translation and interpretation. The orders and the award of the Tribunal shall be rendered and the record kept in both procedural languages, both versions being equally authentic.

Article 31 Copies of Instruments

Except as otherwise provided by the Tribunal after consultation with the parties and the Secretariat, every request, pleading, application, written observation or other instrument shall be filed in the form of a signed original accompanied by the following number of additional copies:

(a)   before the number of members of the Tribunal has been determined: five; and

(b)   after the number of members of the Tribunal has been determined: two more than the number of its members.

Article 32 Supporting Documentation

Supporting documentation shall ordinarily be filed together with the instrument to which it relates, and in any case within the time limit fixed for the filing of such instrument.

Article 33 Time Limits

(1)   Where required, time limits shall be fixed by the Tribunal by assigning dates for the completion of the various steps in the proceeding. The Tribunal may delegate this power to its President.

(2)   The Tribunal may extend any time limit that it has fixed. If the Tribunal is not in session, this power shall be exercised by its President.

(3)   Any step taken after expiration of the applicable time limit shall be disregarded unless the Tribunal, in special circumstances and after giving the other party an opportunity of stating its views, decides otherwise.

Article 34 Waiver

A party which knows or ought to have known that a provision of these Rules, of any other rules or agreement applicable to the proceeding, or of an order of the Tribunal has not been complied with and which fails to state promptly its objections thereto, shall be deemed to have waived the right to object.

Article 35 Filling of Gaps

If any question of procedure arises which is not covered by these Rules or any rules agreed by the parties, the Tribunal shall decide the question.

CHAPTER VII WRITTEN AND ORAL PROCEDURES

Article 36 Normal Procedures

Except if the parties otherwise agree, the proceeding shall comprise two distinct phases: a written procedure followed by an oral one.

Article 37 Transmission of the Request

As soon as the Tribunal is constituted, the Secretary-General shall transmit to each member of the Tribunal a copy of the request by which the proceeding was commenced, of the supporting documentation, of the notice of registration of the request and of any communication received from either party in response thereto.

Article 38 The Written Procedure

(1)   In addition to the request for arbitration, the written procedure shall consist of the following pleadings, filed within time limits set by the Tribunal:

(a)   a memorial by the requesting party;

(b)   a counter-memorial by the other party;

and, if the parties so agree or the Tribunal deems it necessary:

(c)   a reply by the requesting party; and

(d)   a rejoinder by the other party.

(2)   If the request was made jointly, each party shall, within the same time limit determined by the Tribunal, file its memorial. However, the parties may instead agree that one of them shall, for the purposes of paragraph (1) of this Article, be considered as the requesting party.

(3)   A memorial shall contain: a statement of the relevant facts; a statement of law; and the submissions. A counter-memorial, reply or rejoinder shall contain an admission or denial of the facts stated in the last previous pleading; any additional facts, if necessary; observations concerning the statement of law in the last previous pleading; a statement of law in answer thereto; and the submissions.

Article 39 The Oral Procedure

(1)   The oral procedure shall consist of the hearing by the Tribunal of the parties, their agents, counsel and advocates, and of witnesses and experts.

(2)   Unless either party objects, the Tribunal, after consultation with the Secretary-General, may allow other persons, besides the parties, their agents, counsel and advocates, witnesses and experts during their testimony, and officers of the Tribunal, to attend or observe all or part of the hearings, subject to appropriate logistical arrangements. The Tribunal shall for such cases establish procedures for the protection of proprietary or privileged information.

(3)   The members of the Tribunal may, during the hearings, put questions to the parties, their agents, counsel and advocates, and ask them for explanations.

Article 40 Marshalling of Evidence

Without prejudice to the rules concerning the production of documents, each party shall, within time limits fixed by the Tribunal, communicate to the Secretary-General, for transmission to the Tribunal and the other party, precise information regarding the evidence which it intends to produce and that which it intends to request the Tribunal to call for, together with an indication of the points to which such evidence will be directed.

Article 41 Evidence: General Principles

(1)   The Tribunal shall be the judge of the admissibility of any evidence adduced and of its probative value.

(2)   The Tribunal may, if it deems it necessary at any stage of the proceeding, call upon the parties to produce documents, witnesses and experts.

(3)   After consulting both parties, the Tribunal may allow a person or entity that is not a party to the dispute (in this Article called the "non-disputing party") to file a written submission with the Tribunal regarding a matter within the scope of the dispute. In determining whether to allow such a filing, the Tribunal shall consider, among other things, the extent to which:

(a)   the non-disputing party submission would assist the Tribunal in the determination of a factual or legal issue related to the proceeding by bringing a perspective, particular knowledge or insight that is different from that of the disputing parties;

(b)   the non-disputing party submission would address a matter within the scope of the dispute;

(c)   the non-disputing party has a significant interest in the proceeding.

The Tribunal shall ensure that the non-disputing party submission does not disrupt the proceeding or unduly burden or unfairly prejudice either party, and that both parties are given an opportunity to present their observations on the non-disputing party submission.

Article 42 Examination of Witnesses and Experts

Witnesses and experts shall be examined before the Tribunal by the parties under the control of its President. Questions may also be put to them by any member of the Tribunal.

Article 43 Witnesses and Experts: Special Rules

The Tribunal may:

(a)   admit evidence given by a witness or expert in a written deposition;

(b)   with the consent of both parties, arrange for the examination of a witness or expert otherwise than before the Tribunal itself. The Tribunal shall define the procedure to be followed. The parties may participate in the examination; and

(c)   appoint one or more experts, define their terms of reference, examine their reports and hear from them in person.

Article 44 Closure of the Proceeding

(1)   When the presentation of the case by the parties is completed, the proceeding shall be declared closed.

(2)   Exceptionally, the Tribunal may, before the award has been rendered, reopen the proceeding on the ground that new evidence is forthcoming of such a nature as to constitute a decisive factor, or that there is a vital need for clarification on certain specific points.

CHAPTER VIII PARTICULAR PROCEDURES

Article 45 Preliminary Objections

(1)   The Tribunal shall have the power to rule on its competence. For the purposes of this Article, an agreement providing for arbitration under the Additional Facility shall be separable from the other terms of the contract in which it may have been included.

(2)   Any objection that the dispute is not within the competence of the Tribunal shall be filed with the Secretary-General as soon as possible after the constitution of the Tribunal and in any event no later than the expiration of the time limit fixed for the filing of the counter-memorial or, if the objection relates to an ancillary claim, for the filing of the rejoinder – unless the facts on which the objection is based are unknown to the party at that time.

(3)   The Tribunal may on its own initiative consider, at any stage of the proceeding, whether the dispute before it is within its competence.

(4)   Upon the formal raising of an objection relating to the dispute, the Tribunal may decide to suspend the proceeding on the merits. The President of the Tribunal, after consultation with its other members, shall fix a time limit within which the parties may file observations on the objection.

(5)   The Tribunal shall decide whether or not the further procedures relating to the objection made pursuant to paragraph (2) shall be oral. It may deal with the objection as a preliminary question or join it to the merits of the dispute. If the Tribunal overrules the objection or joins it to the merits, it shall once more fix time limits for the further procedures.

(6)   Unless the parties have agreed to another expedited procedure for making preliminary objections, a party may, no later than 30 days after the constitution of the Tribunal, and in any event before the first session of the Tribunal, file an objection that a claim is manifestly without legal merit. The party shall specify as precisely as possible the basis for the objection. The Tribunal, after giving the parties the opportunity to present their observations on the objection, shall, at its first session or promptly thereafter, notify the parties of its decision on the objection. The decision of the Tribunal shall be without prejudice to the right of a party to file an objection pursuant to paragraph (2) or to object, in the course of the proceeding, that a claim lacks legal merit.

(7)   If the Tribunal decides that the dispute is not within its competence or that all claims are manifestly without legal merit, it shall issue an award to that effect.

Article 46 Provisional Measures of Protection

(1)   Unless the arbitration agreement otherwise provides, either party may at any time during the proceeding request that provisional measures for the preservation of its rights be ordered by the Tribunal. The Tribunal shall give priority to the consideration of such a request.

(2)   The Tribunal may also recommend provisional measures on its own initiative or recommend measures other than those specified in a request. It may at any time modify or revoke its recommendations.

(3)   The Tribunal shall order or recommend provisional measures, or any modification or revocation thereof, only after giving each party an opportunity of presenting its observations.

(4)   The parties may apply to any competent judicial authority for interim or conservatory measures. By doing so they shall not be held to infringe the agreement to arbitrate or to affect the powers of the Tribunal.

Article 47 Ancillary Claims

(1)   Except as the parties otherwise agree, a party may present an incidental or additional claim or counter-claim, provided that such ancillary claim is within the scope of the arbitration agreement of the parties.

(2)   An incidental or additional claim shall be presented not later than in the reply and a counter-claim no later than in the counter-memorial, unless the Tribunal, upon justification by the party presenting the ancillary claim and upon considering any objection of the other party, authorizes the presentation of the claim at a later stage in the proceeding.

Article 48 Default

(1)   If a party fails to appear or to present its case at any stage of the proceeding, the other party may request the Tribunal to deal with the questions submitted to it and to render an award.

(2)   Whenever such a request is made by a party the Tribunal shall promptly notify the defaulting party thereof. Unless the Tribunal is satisfied that that party does not intend to appear or to present its case in the proceeding, it shall, at the same time, grant a period of grace and to this end:

(a)   if that party had failed to file a pleading or any other instrument within the time limit fixed therefor, fix a new time limit for its filing; or

(b)   if that party had failed to appear or present its case at a hearing, fix a new date for the hearing.

The period of grace shall not, without the consent of the other party, exceed 60 days.

(3)   After the expiration of the period of grace or when, in accordance with paragraph (2) of this Article, no such period is granted, the Tribunal shall examine whether the dispute is within its jurisdiction and, if it is satisfied as to its jurisdiction, decide whether the submissions made are well-founded in fact and in law. To this end, it may, at any stage of the proceeding, call on the party appearing to file observations, produce evidence or submit oral explanations.

Article 49 Settlement and Discontinuance

(1)   If, before the award is rendered, the parties agree on a settlement of the dispute or otherwise to discontinue the proceeding, the Tribunal, or the Secretary-General if the Tribunal has not yet been constituted, or has not yet met, shall, at their written request, in an order take note of the discontinuance of the proceeding.

(2)   If requested by both parties and accepted by the Tribunal, the Tribunal shall record the settlement in the form of an award. The Tribunal shall not be obliged to give reasons for such an award. The parties will accompany their request with the full and signed text of their settlement.

Article 50 Discontinuance at Request of a Party

If a party requests the discontinuance of the proceeding, the Tribunal, or the Secretary-General if the Tribunal has not yet been constituted, shall in an order fix a time limit within which the other party may state whether it opposes the discontinuance. If no objection is made in writing within the time limit, the Tribunal, or if appropriate the Secretary-General, shall in an order take note of the discontinuance of the proceeding. If objection is made, the proceeding shall continue.

Article 51 Discontinuance for Failure of Parties to Act

If the parties fail to take any steps in the proceeding during six consecutive months or such period as they may agree with the approval of the Tribunal, or of the Secretary- General if the Tribunal has not yet been constituted, they shall be deemed to have discontinued the procee- ding and the Tribunal, or if appropriate the Secretary-General, shall, after notice to the parties, in an order take note of the discontinuance.

CHAPTER IX THE AWARD

Article 52 The Award

(1) The award shall be made in writing and shall contain:

(a) a precise designation of each party;

(b) a statement that the Tribunal was established under these Rules, and a description of the method of its constitution;

(c) the name of each member of the Tribunal, and an identification of the appointing authority of each;

(d) the names of the agents, counsel and advocates of the parties;

(e) the dates and place of the sittings of the Tribunal;

(f) a summary of the proceeding;

(g) a statement of the facts as found by the Tribunal;

(h) the submissions of the parties;

(i) the decision of the Tribunal on every question submitted to it, together with the reasons upon which the decision is based; and

(j) any decision of the Tribunal regarding the cost of the proceeding.

(2) The award shall be signed by the members of the Tribunal who voted for it; the date of each signature shall be indicated. Any member of the Tribunal may attach his individual opinion to the award, whether he dissents from the majority or not, or a statement of his dissent.

(3) If the arbitration law of the country where the award is made requires that it be filed or registered by the Tribunal, the Tribunal shall comply with this requirement within the period of time required by law.

(4) The award shall be final and binding on the parties. The parties waive any time limits for the rendering of the award which may be provided for by the law of the country where the award is made.

Article 53 Authentication of the Award; Certified Copies; Date

(1) Upon signature by the last arbitrator to sign, the Secretary-General shall promptly:

(a) authenticate the original text of the award and deposit it in the archives of the Secretariat, together with any individual opinions and statements of dissent; and

(b) dispatch a certified copy of the award (including individual opinions and statements of dissent) to each party, indicating the date of dispatch on the original text and on all copies;

provided, however, that if the original text of the award must be filed or registered as contem- plated by Article 52(3) of these Rules the Secretary-General shall do so on behalf of the Tribunal or return the award to the Tribunal for this purpose.

(2)   The award shall be deemed to have been rendered on the date on which the certified copies were dispatched.

(3)   Except to the extent required for any registration or filing of the award by the Secretary-General under paragraph (1) of this Article, the Secretariat shall not publish the award without the consent of the parties. The Secretariat shall, however, promptly include in the publications of the Centre excerpts of the legal reasoning of the Tribunal.

Article 54 Applicable Law

(1)   The Tribunal shall apply the rules of law designated by the parties as applicable to the substance of the dispute. Failing such designation by the parties, the Tribunal shall apply (a) the law determined by the conflict of laws rules which it considers applicable and (b) such rules of international law as the Tribunal considers applicable.

(2)   The Tribunal may decide ex aequo et bono if the parties have expressly authorized it to do so and if the law applicable to the arbitration so permits.

Article 55 Interpretation of the Award

(1)   Within 45 days after the date of the award either party, with notice to the other party, may request that the Secretary-General obtain from the Tribunal an interpretation of the award.

(2)   The Tribunal shall determine the procedure to be followed.

(3)   The interpretation shall form part of the award, and the provisions of Articles 52 and 53 of these Rules shall apply.

Article 56 Correction of the Award

(1)   Within 45 days after the date of the award either party, with notice to the other party, may request the Secretary-General to obtain from the Tribunal a correction in the award of any clerical, arithmetical or similar errors. The Tribunal may within the same period make such corrections on its own initiative.

(2)   The provisions of Articles 52 and 53 of these Rules shall apply to such corrections.

Article 57 Supplementary Decisions

(1)   Within 45 days after the date of the award either party, with notice to the other party may request the Tribunal, through the Secretary-General, to decide any question which it had omitted to decide in the award.

(2)   The Tribunal shall determine the procedure to be followed.

(3)   The decision of the Tribunal shall become part of the award and the provisions of Articles 52 and 53 of these Rules shall apply thereto.

CHAPTER X COSTS

Article 58 Cost of Proceeding

(1)   Unless the parties otherwise agree, the Tribunal shall decide how and by whom the fees and expenses of the members of the Tribunal, the expenses and charges of the Secretariat and the expenses incurred by the parties in connection with the proceeding shall be borne. The Tribunal may, to that end, call on the Secretariat and the parties to provide it with the information it needs in order to formulate the division of the cost of the proceeding between the parties.

(2)   The decision of the Tribunal pursuant to paragraph (1) of this Article shall form part of the award.

CHAPTER XI GENERAL PROVISIONS

Article 59 Final Provision

The text of these Rules in each official language of the Centre shall be equally authentic.

IX.4. 2013 UNCITRAL RULES ON TRANSPARENCY
IN TREATY-BASED INVESTOR-STATE ARBITRATION[1]

Resolution adopted by the General Assembly on 16 December 2013 [on the report of the Sixth Committee (A/68/462)]

68/109. United Nations Commission on International Trade Law Rules on Transparency in Treaty-based Investor-State Arbitration and Arbitration Rules (as revised in 2010, with new article 1, paragraph 4, as adopted in 2013)

The General Assembly,

Recalling its resolution 2205 (XXI) of 17 December 1966, by which it established the United Nations Commission on International Trade Law with a mandate to further the progressive harmonization and unification of the law of international trade and in that respect to bear in mind the interests of all peoples, in particular those of developing countries, in the extensive development of international trade,

Recognizing the value of arbitration as a method of settling disputes that may arise in the context of international relations and the wide use of arbitration for the settlement of treaty-based investor-State disputes,

Recalling its resolutions 31/98 of 15 December 1976 and 65/22 of 6 December 2010, in which it recommended the use of the Arbitration Rules of the United Nations Commission on International Trade Law,

Bearing in mind that the Arbitration Rules are widely used for the settlement of treaty-based investor-State disputes,

Recognizing the need for provisions on transparency in the settlement of such treaty-based investor-State disputes to take account of the public interest involved in such arbitrations,

Believing that rules on transparency in treaty-based investor-State arbitration would contribute significantly to the establishment of a harmonized legal framework for a fair and efficient settlement of international investment disputes, increase transparency and accountability and promote good governance,

Noting that the Commission, at its forty-sixth session, adopted the Rules on Transparency in Treaty-based Investor-State Arbitration and amended the Arbitration Rules as revised in 2010 to include, in a new article 1, paragraph 4, a reference to the Rules on Transparency,

Noting also that the Rules on Transparency are available for use in investor-State arbitrations initiated under rules other than the Arbitration Rules or in ad hoc proceedings,

Noting further that the preparation of the Rules on Transparency was the subject of due deliberation in the Commission and that they benefitted from consultations with Governments and interested intergovernmental and international non-governmental organizations,

1.   *Expresses its appreciation* to the United Nations Commission on International Trade Law for having prepared and adopted the Rules on Transparency in Treaty-based Investor-State Arbitration and the Arbitration Rules (as revised in 2010, with new article 1, paragraph 4, as adopted in 2013), as annexed to the report of the Commission on the work of its forty-sixth session;

---

1   See http://www.uncitral.org/uncitral/en/uncitral_texts/arbitration/2014Transparency.html.

2.   *Requests* the Secretary-General to publish, including electronically, and disseminate broadly the text of the Rules on Transparency, both together with the Arbitration Rules (as revised in 2010, with new article 1, paragraph 4, as adopted in 2013) and as a stand-alone text, and to transmit them to Governments and organizations interested in the field of dispute settlement;

3.   *Recommends* the use of the Rules on Transparency in relation to the settlement of investment disputes within the scope of their application as defined in article 1 of the Rules, and invites Member States that have chosen to include the Rules in their treaties to inform the Commission accordingly;

4.   *Also recommends* that, subject to any provision in relevant treaties that may require a higher degree of transparency than that provided in the Rules on Transparency, the Rules be applied through appropriate mechanisms to investor-State arbitration initiated pursuant to treaties providing for the protection of investors or investments concluded before the date of coming into effect of the Rules, to the extent that such application is consistent with those treaties.

68th plenary meeting
16 December 2013

Article 1. Scope of Application

Applicability of the Rules

1.   The UNCITRAL Rules on Transparency in Treaty-based Investor-State Arbitration ("Rules on Transparency") shall apply to investor-State arbitration initiated under the UNCITRAL Arbitration Rules pursuant to a treaty providing for the protection of investments or investors ("treaty")[1] concluded on or after 1 April 2014 unless the Parties to the treaty[2] have agreed otherwise.

2.   In investor-State arbitrations initiated under the UNCITRAL Arbitration Rules pursuant to a treaty concluded before 1 April 2014, these Rules shall apply only when:

(a)   The parties to an arbitration (the "disputing parties") agree to their application in respect of that arbitration; or

(b)   The Parties to the treaty or, in the case of a multilateral treaty, the State of the claimant and the respondent State, have agreed after 1 April 2014 to their application.

Application of the Rules

3.   In any arbitration in which the Rules on Transparency apply pursuant to a treaty or to an agreement by the Parties to that treaty:

(a)   The disputing parties may not derogate from these Rules, by agreement or otherwise, unless permitted to do so by the treaty;

(b)   The arbitral tribunal shall have the power, besides its discretionary authority under certain provisions of these Rules, to adapt the requirements of any specific provision of these Rules to the particular circumstances of the case, after consultation with the disputing parties, if such adaptation is necessary to conduct the arbitration in a practical manner and is consistent with the transparency objective of these Rules.

---

1   For the purposes of the Rules on Transparency, a "treaty" shall be understood broadly as encompassing any bilateral or multilateral treaty that contains provisions on the protection of investments or investors and a right for investors to resort to arbitration against Parties to the treaty, including any treaty commonly referred to as a free trade agreement, economic integration agreement, trade and investment framework or cooperation agreement, or bilateral investment treaty.

2   For the purposes of the Rules on Transparency, any reference to a "Party to the treaty" or a "State" includes, for example, a regional economic integration organization where it is a Party to the treaty.

Discretion and Authority of the Arbitral Tribunal

4.   Where the Rules on Transparency provide for the arbitral tribunal to exercise discretion, the arbitral tribunal in exercising such discretion shall take into account:

(a) The public interest in transparency in treaty-based investor-State arbitration and in the particular arbitral proceedings; and

(b) The disputing parties' interest in a fair and efficient resolution of their dispute.

5.   These Rules shall not affect any authority that the arbitral tribunal may otherwise have under the UNCITRAL Arbitration Rules to conduct the arbitration in such a manner as to promote transparency, for example by accepting submissions from third persons.

6.   In the presence of any conduct, measure or other action having the effect of wholly undermining the transparency objectives of these Rules, the arbitral tribunal shall ensure that those objectives prevail.

Applicable Instrument in Case of Conflict

7.   Where the Rules on Transparency apply, they shall supplement any applicable arbitration rules. Where there is a conflict between the Rules on Transparency and the applicable arbitration rules, the Rules on Transparency shall prevail. Notwithstanding any provision in these Rules, where there is a conflict between the Rules on Transparency and the treaty, the provisions of the treaty shall prevail.

8.   Where any of these Rules is in conflict with a provision of the law applicable to the arbitration from which the disputing parties cannot derogate, that provision shall prevail.

Application in Non-UNCITRAL Arbitrations

9.   These Rules are available for use in investor-State arbitrations initiated under rules other than the UNCITRAL Arbitration Rules or in ad hoc proceedings.

Article 2. Publication of Information at the Commencement of Arbitral Proceedings

Once the notice of arbitration has been received by the respondent, each of the disputing parties shall promptly communicate a copy of the notice of arbitration to the repository referred to under article 8. Upon receipt of the notice of arbitration from the respondent, or upon receipt of the notice of arbitration and a record of its transmission to the respondent, the repository shall promptly make available to the public information regarding the name of the disputing parties, the economic sector involved and the treaty under which the claim is being made.

Article 3. Publication of Documents

1.   Subject to article 7, the following documents shall be made available to the public: the notice of arbitration, the response to the notice of arbitration, the statement of claim, the statement of defence and any further written statements or written submissions by any disputing party; a table listing all exhibits to the aforesaid documents and to expert reports and witness statements, if such table has been prepared for the proceedings, but not the exhibits themselves; any written submissions by the non- disputing Party (or Parties) to the treaty and by third persons, transcripts of hearings, where available; and orders, decisions and awards of the arbitral tribunal.

2.   Subject to article 7, expert reports and witness statements, exclusive of the exhibits thereto, shall be made available to the public, upon request by any person to the arbitral tribunal.

3.   Subject to article 7, the arbitral tribunal may decide, on its own initiative or upon request from any person, and after consultation with the disputing parties, whether and how to make available exhibits and any other documents provided to, or issued by, the arbitral tribunal not falling within paragraphs 1 or 2 above. This may include, for example, making such documents available at a specified site.

4.   The documents to be made available to the public pursuant to paragraphs 1 and 2 shall be communicated by the arbitral tribunal to the repository referred to under article 8 as soon as possible, subject to any relevant arrangements or time limits for the protection of confidential or protected information prescribed under article 7. The documents to be made available pursuant to paragraph 3 may be communicated by the arbitral tribunal to the repository referred to under article 8 as they become available and, if applicable, in a redacted form in accordance with article 7. The repository shall make all documents available in a timely manner, in the form and in the language in which it receives them.

5.   A person granted access to documents under paragraph 3 shall bear any administrative costs of making those documents available to that person, such as the costs of photocopying or shipping documents to that person, but not the costs of making those documents available to the public through the repository.

Article 4. Submission by a Third Person

1.   After consultation with the disputing parties, the arbitral tribunal may allow a person that is not a disputing party, and not a non-disputing Party to the treaty ("third person(s)"), to file a written submission with the arbitral tribunal regarding a matter within the scope of the dispute.

2.   A third person wishing to make a submission shall apply to the arbitral tribunal, and shall, in a concise written statement, which is in a language of the arbitration and complies with any page limits set by the arbitral tribunal:

(a)   Describe the third person, including, where relevant, its membership and legal status (e.g., trade association or other non-governmental organization), its general objectives, the nature of its activities and any parent organization (including any organization that directly or indirectly controls the third person);

(b)   Disclose any connection, direct or indirect, which the third person has with any disputing party;

(c)   Provide information on any government, person or organization that has provided to the third person (i) any financial or other assistance in preparing the submission; or (ii) substantial assistance in either of the two years preceding the application by the third person under this article (e.g. funding around 20 per cent of its overall operations annually);

(d)   Describe the nature of the interest that the third person has in the arbitration; and

(e)   Identify the specific issues of fact or law in the arbitration that the third person wishes to address in its written submission.

3.   In determining whether to allow such a submission, the arbitral tribunal shall take into consideration, among other factors it determines to be relevant:

(a)   Whether the third person has a significant interest in the arbitral proceedings; and

(b)   The extent to which the submission would assist the arbitral tribunal in the determination of a factual or legal issue related to the arbitral proceedings by bringing a perspective, particular knowledge or insight that is different from that of the disputing parties.

4.   The submission filed by the third person shall:

(a)   Be dated and signed by the person filing the submission on behalf of the third person;

(b)   Be concise, and in no case longer than as authorized by the arbitral tribunal;

(c)   Set out a precise statement of the third person's position on issues; and

(d)   Address only matters within the scope of the dispute.

5.   The arbitral tribunal shall ensure that any submission does not disrupt or unduly burden the arbitral proceedings, or unfairly prejudice any disputing party.

6.   The arbitral tribunal shall ensure that the disputing parties are given a reasonable opportunity to present their observations on any submission by the third person.

Article 5. Submission by a Non-Disputing Party to the Treaty

1.   The arbitral tribunal shall, subject to paragraph 4, allow, or, after consultation with the disputing parties, may invite, submissions on issues of treaty interpretation from a non-disputing
Party to the treaty.

2.   The arbitral tribunal, after consultation with the disputing parties, may allow submissions on
further matters within the scope of the dispute from a non-disputing Party to the treaty. In
determining whether to allow such submissions, the arbitral tribunal shall take into consideration, among other factors it determines to be relevant, the factors referred to in article 4,
paragraph 3, and, for greater certainty, the need to avoid submissions which would support the
claim of the investor in a manner tantamount to diplomatic protection.

3.   The arbitral tribunal shall not draw any inference from the absence of any submission or
response to any invitation pursuant to paragraphs 1 or 2.

4.   The arbitral tribunal shall ensure that any submission does not disrupt or unduly burden the
arbitral proceedings, or unfairly prejudice any disputing party.

5.   The arbitral tribunal shall ensure that the disputing parties are given a reasonable opportunity to present their observations on any submission by a non-disputing Party to the treaty.

Article 6. Hearings

1.   Subject to article 6, paragraphs 2 and 3, hearings for the presentation of evidence or for oral
argument ("hearings") shall be public.

2.   Where there is a need to protect confidential information or the integrity of the arbitral
process pursuant to article 7, the arbitral tribunal shall make arrangements to hold in private that
part of the hearing requiring such protection.

3.   The arbitral tribunal shall make logistical arrangements to facilitate the public access to
hearings (including where appropriate by organizing attendance through video links or such
other means as it deems appropriate). However, the arbitral tribunal may, after consultation with
the disputing parties, decide to hold all or part of the hearings in private where this becomes
necessary for logistical reasons, such as when the circumstances render any original arrangement
for public access to a hearing infeasible.

Article 7. Exceptions to Transparency

Confidential or Protected Information

1.   Confidential or protected information, as defined in paragraph 2 and as identified pursuant
to the arrangements referred to in paragraphs 3 and 4, shall not be made available to the public
pursuant to articles 2 to 6.

2.   Confidential or protected information consists of:

(a)   Confidential business information;

(b)   Information that is protected against being made available to the public under the treaty;

(c)   Information that is protected against being made available to the public, in the case of the
      information of the respondent State, under the law of the respondent State, and in the case
      of other information, under any law or rules determined by the arbitral tribunal to be
      applicable to the disclosure of such information; or

(d)   Information the disclosure of which would impede law enforcement.

3.   The arbitral tribunal, after consultation with the disputing parties, shall make arrangements
to prevent any confidential or protected information from being made available to the public,
including by putting in place, as appropriate:

(a) Time limits in which a disputing party, non-disputing Party to the treaty or third person shall give notice that it seeks protection for such information in documents;

(b) Procedures for the prompt designation and redaction of the particular confidential or protected information in such documents; and

(c) Procedures for holding hearings in private to the extent required by article 6, paragraph 2.

Any determination as to whether information is confidential or protected shall be made by the arbitral tribunal after consultation with the disputing parties.

4. Where the arbitral tribunal determines that information should not be redacted from a document, or that a document should not be prevented from being made available to the public, any disputing party, non-disputing Party to the treaty or third person that voluntarily introduced the document into the record shall be permitted to withdraw all or part of the document from the record of the arbitral proceedings.

5. Nothing in these Rules requires a respondent State to make available to the public information the disclosure of which it considers to be contrary to its essential security interests.

Integrity of the Arbitral Process

6. Information shall not be made available to the public pursuant to articles 2 to 6 where the information, if made available to the public, would jeopardize the integrity of the arbitral process as determined pursuant to paragraph 7.

7. The arbitral tribunal may, on its own initiative or upon the application of a disputing party, after consultation with the disputing parties where practicable, take appropriate measures to restrain or delay the publication of information where such publication would jeopardize the integrity of the arbitral process because it could hamper the collection or production of evidence, lead to the intimidation of witnesses, lawyers acting for disputing parties or members of the arbitral tribunal, or in comparably exceptional circumstances.

Article 8. Repository of Published Information

The repository of published information under the Rules on Transparency shall be the Secretary-General of the United Nations or an institution named by UNCITRAL.

X. Other Relevant National and International Rules and Guidelines

X.1. 1976 OECD GUIDELINES FOR MULTINATIONAL ENTERPRISES[1]

Preface

1.   The OECD Guidelines for Multinational Enterprises (the Guidelines) are recommendations addressed by governments to multinational enterprises. They provide voluntary principles and standards for responsible business conduct consistent with applicable laws. The Guidelines aim to ensure that the operations of these enterprises are in harmony with government policies, to strengthen the basis of mutual confidence between enterprises and the societies in which they operate, to help improve the foreign investment climate and to enhance the contribution to sustainable development made by multinational enterprises. The Guidelines are part of the OECD Declaration on International Investment and Multinational Enterprises the other elements of which relate to national treatment, conflicting requirements on enterprises, and international investment incentives and disincentives.

2.   International business has experienced far-reaching structural change and the Guidelines themselves have evolved to reflect these changes. With the rise of service and knowledge-intensive industries, service and technology enterprises have entered the international market-place. Large enterprises still account for a major share of international investment, and there is a trend toward large-scale international mergers. At the same time, foreign investment by small- and medium-sized enterprises has also increased and these enterprises now play a significant role on the international scene. Multinational enterprises, like their domestic counterparts, have evolved to encompass a broader range of business arrangements and organisational forms. Strategic alliances and closer relations with suppliers and contractors tend to blur the boundaries of the enterprise.

3.   The rapid evolution in the structure of multinational enterprises is also reflected in their operations in the developing world, where foreign direct investment has grown rapidly. In developing countries, multinational enterprises have diversified beyond primary production and extractive industries into manufacturing, assembly, domestic market development and services.

4.   The activities of multinational enterprises, through international trade and investment, have strengthened and deepened the ties that join OECD economies to each other and to the rest of the world. These activities bring substantial benefits to home and host countries. These benefits accrue when multinational enterprises supply the products and services that consumers want to buy at competitive prices and when they provide fair returns to suppliers of capital. Their trade and investment activities contribute to the efficient use of capital, technology and human and natural resources. They facilitate the transfer of technology among the regions of the world and the development of technologies that reflect local conditions. Through both formal training and on-the-job learning enterprises also promote the development of human capital in host countries.

5.   The nature, scope and speed of economic changes have presented new strategic challenges for enterprises and their stakeholders. Multinational enterprises have the opportunity to imple-ment best practice policies for sustainable development that seek to ensure coherence between social, economic and environmental objectives. The ability of multinational enterprises to promote sustainable development is greatly enhanced when trade and investment are con-ducted in a context of open, competitive and appropriately regulated markets.

---

1   As last amended in 2008, see https://www.oecd.org/corporate/mne/1922428.pdf.

6.   Many multinational enterprises have demonstrated that respect for high standards of business conduct can enhance growth. Today's competitive forces are intense and multinational enterprises face a variety of legal, social and regulatory settings. In this context, some enterprises may be tempted to neglect appropriate standards and principles of conduct in an attempt to gain undue competitive advantage. Such practices by the few may call into question the reputation of the many and may give rise to public concerns.

7.   Many enterprises have responded to these public concerns by developing internal programmes, guidance and management systems that underpin their commitment to good corporate citizenship, good practices and good business and employee conduct. Some of them have called upon consulting, auditing and certification services, contributing to the accumulation of expertise in these areas. These efforts have also promoted social dialogue on what constitutes good business conduct. The Guidelines clarify the shared expectations for business conduct of the governments adhering to them and provide a point of reference for enterprises. Thus, the Guidelines both complement and reinforce private efforts to define and implement responsible business conduct.

8.   Governments are co-operating with each other and with other actors to strengthen the international legal and policy framework in which business is conducted. The post-war period has seen the development of this framework, starting with the adoption in 1948 of the Universal Declaration of Human Rights. Recent instruments include the ILO Declaration on Fundamental Principles and Rights at Work, the Rio Declaration on Environment and Development and Agenda 21 and the Copenhagen Declaration for Social Development.

9.   The OECD has also been contributing to the international policy framework. Recent developments include the adoption of the Convention on Combating Bribery of Foreign Public Officials in International Business Transactions and of the OECD Principles of Corporate Governance, the OECD Guidelines for Consumer Protection in the Context of Electronic Commerce, and ongoing work on the OECD Guidelines on Transfer Pricing for Multinational Enterprises and Tax Administrations.

10. The common aim of the governments adhering to the Guidelines is to encourage the positive contributions that multinational enterprises can make to economic, environmental and social progress and to minimise the difficulties to which their various operations may give rise. In working towards this goal, governments find themselves in partnership with the many businesses, trade unions and other non-governmental organisations that are working in their own ways toward the same end. Governments can help by providing effective domestic policy frameworks that include stable macroeconomic policy, non-discriminatory treatment of firms, appropriate regulation and prudential supervision, an impartial system of courts and law enforcement and efficient and honest public administration. Governments can also help by maintaining and promoting appropriate standards and policies in support of sustainable development and by engaging in ongoing reforms to ensure that public sector activity is efficient and effective. Governments adhering to the Guidelines are committed to continual improvement of both domestic and international policies with a view to improving the welfare and living standards of all people.

I. Concepts and Principles

1.   The Guidelines are recommendations jointly addressed by governments to multinational enterprises. They provide principles and standards of good practice consistent with applicable laws. Observance of the Guidelines by enterprises is voluntary and not legally enforceable.

2.   Since the operations of multinational enterprises extend throughout the world, international co-operation in this field should extend to all countries. Governments adhering to the Guidelines encourage the enterprises operating on their territories to observe the Guidelines wherever they operate, while taking into account the particular circumstances of each host country.

3.   A precise definition of multinational enterprises is not required for the purposes of the Guidelines. These usually comprise companies or other entities established in more than one country and so linked that they may co-ordinate their operations in various ways. While one or more of these entities may be able to exercise a significant influence over the activities of others, their degree of autonomy within the enterprise may vary widely from one multinational enterprise to another. Ownership may be private, state or mixed. The Guidelines are addressed to all the entities within the multinational enterprise (parent companies and/or local entities). According to the actual distribution of responsibilities among them, the different entities are expected to co-operate and to assist one another to facilitate observance of the Guidelines.

4.   The Guidelines are not aimed at introducing differences of treatment between multinational and domestic enterprises; they reflect good practice for all. Accordingly, multinational and domestic enterprises are subject to the same expectations in respect of their conduct wherever the Guidelines are relevant to both.

5.   Governments wish to encourage the widest possible observance of the Guidelines. While it is acknowledged that small- and medium-sized enterprises may not have the same capacities as larger enterprises, governments adhering to the Guidelines nevertheless encourage them to observe the Guidelines recommendations to the fullest extent possible.

6.   Governments adhering to the Guidelines should not use them for protectionist purposes nor use them in a way that calls into question the comparative advantage of any country where multinational enterprises invest.

7.   Governments have the right to prescribe the conditions under which multinational enterprises operate within their jurisdictions, subject to international law. The entities of a multinational enterprise located in various countries are subject to the laws applicable in these countries. When multinational enterprises are subject to conflicting requirements by adhering countries, the governments concerned will co-operate in good faith with a view to resolving problems that may arise.

8.   Governments adhering to the Guidelines set them forth with the understanding that they will fulfil their responsibilities to treat enterprises equitably and in accordance with international law and with their contractual obligations.

9.   The use of appropriate international dispute settlement mechanisms, including arbitration, is encouraged as a means of facilitating the resolution of legal problems arising between enterprises and host country governments.

10. Governments adhering to the Guidelines will promote them and encourage their use. They will establish National Contact Points that promote the Guidelines and act as a forum for discussion of all matters relating to the Guidelines. The adhering Governments will also participate in appropriate review and consultation procedures to address issues concerning interpretation of the Guidelines in a changing world.

II. General Policies

Enterprises should take fully into account established policies in the countries in which they operate, and consider the views of other stakeholders. In this regard, enterprises should:

1.   Contribute to economic, social and environmental progress with a view to achieving sustainable development.

2.   Respect the human rights of those affected by their activities consistent with the host government's international obligations and commitments.

3.   Encourage local capacity building through close co-operation with the local community, including business interests, as well as developing the enterprise's activities in domestic and foreign markets, consistent with the need for sound commercial practice.

4.   Encourage human capital formation, in particular by creating employment opportunities and facilitating training opportunities for employees.

5.   Refrain from seeking or accepting exemptions not contemplated in the statutory or regulatory framework related to environmental, health, safety, labour, taxation, financial incentives, or other issues.

6.   Support and uphold good corporate governance principles and develop and apply good corporate governance practices.

7.   Develop and apply effective self-regulatory practices and management systems that foster a relationship of confidence and mutual trust between enterprises and the societies in which they operate.

8.   Promote employee awareness of, and compliance with, company policies through appropriate dissemination of these policies, including through training programmes.

9.   Refrain from discriminatory or disciplinary action against employees who make bona fide reports to management or, as appropriate, to the competent public authorities, on practices that contravene the law, the Guidelines or the enterprise's policies.

10.   Encourage, where practicable, business partners, including suppliers and sub-contractors, to apply principles of corporate conduct compatible with the Guidelines.

11.   Abstain from any improper involvement in local political activities.

III. Disclosure

1.   Enterprises should ensure that timely, regular, reliable and relevant information is disclosed regarding their activities, structure, financial situation and performance. This information should be disclosed for the enterprise as a whole and, where appropriate, along business lines or geographic areas. Disclosure policies of enterprises should be tailored to the nature, size and location of the enterprise, with due regard taken of costs, business confidentiality and other competitive concerns.

2.   Enterprises should apply high quality standards for disclosure, accounting, and audit. Enterprises are also encouraged to apply high quality standards for non-financial information including environmental and social reporting where they exist. The standards or policies under which both financial and non-financial information are compiled and published should be reported.

3.   Enterprises should disclose basic information showing their name, location, and structure, the name, address and telephone number of the parent enterprise and its main affiliates, its percentage ownership, direct and indirect in these affiliates, including shareholdings between them.

4.   Enterprises should also disclose material information on:

a)   The financial and operating results of the company.

b)   Company objectives.

c)   Major share ownership and voting rights.

d)   Members of the board and key executives, and their remuneration.

e)   Material foreseeable risk factors.

f)   Material issues regarding employees and other stakeholders.

g)   Governance structures and policies.

5.   Enterprises are encouraged to communicate additional information that could include:

a)   Value statements or statements of business conduct intended for public disclosure including information on the social, ethical and environmental policies of the enterprise and other codes of conduct to which the company subscribes. In addition, the date of adoption, the countries and entities to which such statements apply and its performance in relation to these statements may be communicated.

b)   Information on systems for managing risks and complying with laws, and on statements or codes of business conduct.

c)   Information on relationships with employees and other stakeholders.

IV. Employment and Industrial Relations

Enterprises should, within the framework of applicable law, regulations and prevailing labour relations and employment practices:

1.   a) Respect the right of their employees to be represented by trade unions and other bona fide representatives of employees, and engage in constructive negotiations, either individually or through employers' associations, with such representatives with a view to reaching agreements on employment conditions.

b)   Contribute to the effective abolition of child labour.

c)   Contribute to the elimination of all forms of forced or compulsory labour.

d)   Not discriminate against their employees with respect to employment or occupation on such grounds as race, colour, sex, religion, political opinion, national extraction or social origin, unless selectivity concerning employee characteristics furthers established governmental policies which specifically promote greater equality of employment opportunity or relates to the inherent requirements of a job.

2.   a) Provide facilities to employee representatives as may be necessary to assist in the development of effective collective agreements.

b)   Provide information to employee representatives which is needed for meaningful negotiations on conditions of employment.

c)   Promote consultation and co-operation between employers and employees and their representatives on matters of mutual concern.

3.   Provide information to employees and their representatives which enables them to obtain a true and fair view of the performance of the entity or, where appropriate, the enterprise as a whole.

4.   a) Observe standards of employment and industrial relations not less favourable than those observed by comparable employers in the host country.

b)   Take adequate steps to ensure occupational health and safety in their operations.

5.   In their operations, to the greatest extent practicable, employ local personnel and provide training with a view to improving skill levels, in co-operation with employee representatives and, where appropriate, relevant governmental authorities.

6.   In considering changes in their operations which would have major effects upon the livelihood of their employees, in particular in the case of the closure of an entity involving collective lay-offs or dismissals, provide reasonable notice of such changes to representatives of their employees, and, where appropriate, to the relevant governmental authorities, and co-operate with the employee representatives and appropriate governmental authorities so as to mitigate to the maximum extent practicable adverse effects. In light of the specific circumstances of each case, it would be appropriate if management were able to give such notice prior to the final decision being taken. Other means may also be employed to provide meaningful cooperation to mitigate the effects of such decisions.

7.   In the context of bona fide negotiations with representatives of employees on conditions of employment, or while employees are exercising a right to organise, not threaten to transfer the whole or part of an operating unit from the country concerned nor transfer employees from the

enterprises' component entities in other countries in order to influence unfairly those negotiations or to hinder the exercise of a right to organise.

8.   Enable authorised representatives of their employees to negotiate on collective bargaining or labour-management relations issues and allow the parties to consult on matters of mutual concern with representatives of management who are authorised to take decisions on these matters.

V. Environment

Enterprises should, within the framework of laws, regulations and administrative practices in the countries in which they operate, and in consideration of relevant international agreements, principles, objectives, and standards, take due account of the need to protect the environment, public health and safety, and generally to conduct their activities in a manner contributing to the wider goal of sustainable development. In particular, enterprises should:

1.   Establish and maintain a system of environmental management appropriate to the enterprise, including:

a)   collection and evaluation of adequate and timely information regarding the environmental, health, and safety impacts of their activities;

b)   establishment of measurable objectives and, where appropriate, targets for improved environmental performance, including periodically reviewing the continuing relevance of these objectives; and

c)   regular monitoring and verification of progress toward environmental, health, and safety objectives or targets.

2.   Taking into account concerns about cost, business confidentiality, and the protection of intellectual property rights:

a)   provide the public and employees with adequate and timely information on the potential environment, health and safety impacts of the activities of the enterprise, which could include reporting on progress in improving environmental performance; and

b)   engage in adequate and timely communication and consultation with the communities directly affected by the environmental, health and safety policies of the enterprise and by their implementation.

3.   Assess, and address in decision-making, the foreseeable environmental, health, and safety-related impacts associated with the processes, goods and services of the enterprise over their full life cycle. Where these proposed activities may have significant environmental, health, or safety impacts, and where they are subject to a decision of a competent authority, prepare an appropriate environmental impact assessment.

4.   Consistent with the scientific and technical understanding of the risks, where there are threats of serious damage to the environment, taking also into account human health and safety, not use the lack of full scientific certainty as a reason for postponing cost-effective measures to prevent or minimise such damage.

5.   Maintain contingency plans for preventing, mitigating, and controlling serious environmental and health damage from their operations, including accidents and emergencies; and mechanisms for immediate reporting to the competent authorities.

6.   Continually seek to improve corporate environmental performance, by encouraging, where appropriate, such activities as:

a)   adoption of technologies and operating procedures in all parts of the enterprise that reflect standards concerning environmental performance in the best performing part of the enterprise;

b)   development and provision of products or services that have no undue environmental impacts; are safe in their intended use; are efficient in their consumption of energy and natural resources; can be reused, recycled, or disposed of safely;

c)   promoting higher levels of awareness among customers of the environmental implications of using the products and services of the enterprise; and

d)   research on ways of improving the environmental performance of the enterprise over the longer term.

7.   Provide adequate education and training to employees in environmental health and safety matters, including the handling of hazardous materials and the prevention of environmental accidents, as well as more general environmental management areas, such as environmental impact assessment procedures, public relations, and environmental technologies.

8.   Contribute to the development of environmentally meaningful and economically efficient public policy, for example, by means of partnerships or initiatives that will enhance environmental awareness and protection.

VI. Combating Bribery

Enterprises should not, directly or indirectly, offer, promise, give, or demand a bribe or other undue advantage to obtain or retain business or other improper advantage. Nor should enterprises be solicited or expected to render a bribe or other undue advantage. In particular, enterprises should:

1.   Not offer, nor give in to demands, to pay public officials or the employees of business partners any portion of a contract payment. They should not use subcontracts, purchase orders or consulting agreements as means of channelling payments to public officials, to employees of business partners or to their relatives or business associates.

2.   Ensure that remuneration of agents is appropriate and for legitimate services only. Where relevant, a list of agents employed in connection with transactions with public bodies and state-owned enterprises should be kept and made available to competent authorities.

3.   Enhance the transparency of their activities in the fight against bribery and extortion. Measures could include making public commitments against bribery and extortion and disclosing the management systems the company has adopted in order to honour these commitments. The enterprise should also foster openness and dialogue with the public so as to promote its awareness of and co-operation with the fight against bribery and extortion.

4.   Promote employee awareness of and compliance with company policies against bribery and extortion through appropriate dissemination of these policies and through training programmes and disciplinary procedures.

5.   Adopt management control systems that discourage bribery and corrupt practices, and adopt financial and tax accounting and auditing practices that prevent the establishment of "off the books" or secret accounts or the creation of documents which do not properly and fairly record the transactions to which they relate.

6.   Not make illegal contributions to candidates for public office or to political parties or to other political organisations. Contributions should fully comply with public disclosure requirements and should be reported to senior management.

VII. Consumer Interests

When dealing with consumers, enterprises should act in accordance with fair business, marketing and advertising practices and should take all reasonable steps to ensure the safety and quality of the goods or services they provide. In particular, they should:

1.   Ensure that the goods or services they provide meet all agreed or legally required standards for consumer health and safety, including health warnings and product safety and information labels.

2.   As appropriate to the goods or services, provide accurate and clear information regarding their content, safe use, maintenance, storage, and disposal sufficient to enable consumers to make informed decisions.

3.   Provide transparent and effective procedures that address consumer complaints and contribute to fair and timely resolution of consumer disputes without undue cost or burden.

4.   Not make representations or omissions, nor engage in any other practices, that are deceptive, misleading, fraudulent, or unfair.

5.   Respect consumer privacy and provide protection for personal data.

6.   Co-operate fully and in a transparent manner with public authorities in the prevention or removal of serious threats to public health and safety deriving from the consumption or use of their products.

VIII. Science and Technology

Enterprises should:

1.   Endeavour to ensure that their activities are compatible with the science and technology (S&T) policies and plans of the countries in which they operate and as appropriate contribute to the development of local and national innovative capacity.

2.   Adopt, where practicable in the course of their business activities, practices that permit the transfer and rapid diffusion of technologies and know-how, with due regard to the protection of intellectual property rights.

3.   When appropriate, perform science and technology development work in host countries to address local market needs, as well as employ host country personnel in an S&T capacity and encourage their training, taking into account commercial needs.

4.   When granting licenses for the use of intellectual property rights or when otherwise transferring technology, do so on reasonable terms and conditions and in a manner that contributes to the long term development prospects of the host country.

5.   Where relevant to commercial objectives, develop ties with local universities, public research institutions, and participate in co-operative research projects with local industry or industry associations.

IX. Competition

Enterprises should, within the framework of applicable laws and regulations, conduct their activities in a competitive manner. In particular, enterprises should:

1.   Refrain from entering into or carrying out anti-competitive agreements among competitors:

a)   to fix prices;

b)   to make rigged bids (collusive tenders);

c)   to establish output restrictions or quotas; or

d)   to share or divide markets by allocating customers, suppliers, territories or lines of commerce.

2.   Conduct all of their activities in a manner consistent with all applicable competition laws, taking into account the applicability of the competition laws of jurisdictions whose economies would be likely to be harmed by anti-competitive activity on their part.

3.   Co-operate with the competition authorities of such jurisdictions by, among other things and subject to applicable law and appropriate safeguards, providing as prompt and complete responses as practicable to requests for information.

4.   Promote employee awareness of the importance of compliance with all applicable competition laws and policies.

X. Taxation

It is important that enterprises contribute to the public finances of host countries by making timely payment of their tax liabilities. In particular, enterprises should comply with the tax laws and regulations in all countries in which they operate and should exert every effort to act in accordance with both the letter and spirit of those laws and regulations. This would include such measures as providing to the relevant authorities the information necessary for the correct determination of taxes to be assessed in connection with their operations and conforming transfer pricing practices to the arm's length principle.

X.2. 1977 U.S. FOREIGN CORRUPT PRACTICES ACT (excerpts)

15 U.S.C. §§ 78dd-1, 78dd-2, 78dd-3, 78m, 78ff
15 U.S.C. § 78dd-1 [Section 30A of the Securities Exchange Act of 1934]

Prohibited Foreign Trade Practices by Issuers

(a) Prohibition

It shall be unlawful for any issuer which has a class of securities registered pursuant to section 78l of this title or which is required to file reports under section 78o(d) of this title, or for any officer, director, employee, or agent of such issuer or any stockholder thereof acting on behalf of such issuer, to make use of the mails or any means or instrumentality of interstate commerce corruptly in furtherance of an offer, payment, promise to pay, or authorization of the payment of any money, or offer, gift, promise to give, or authorization of the giving of anything of value to—

(1) any foreign official for purposes of—

    (A) (i) influencing any act or decision of such foreign official in his official capacity,

    (ii) inducing such foreign official to do or omit to do any act in violation of the lawful duty of such official, or

    (iii) securing any improper advantage; or

    (B) inducing such foreign official to use his influence with a foreign government or instrumentality thereof to affect or influence any act or decision of such government or instrumentality,

    in order to assist such issuer in obtaining or retaining business for or with, or directing business to, any person;

(2) any foreign political party or official thereof or any candidate for foreign political office for purposes of—

    (A) (i) influencing any act or decision of such party, official, or candidate in its or his official capacity,

    (ii) inducing such party, official, or candidate to do or omit to do an act in violation of the lawful duty of such party, official, or candidate, or

    (iii) securing any improper advantage; or

    (B) inducing such party, official, or candidate to use its or his influence with a foreign government or instrumentality thereof to affect or influence any act or decision of such government or instrumentality,

    in order to assist such issuer in obtaining or retaining business for or with, or directing business to, any person; or

(3) any person, while knowing that all or a portion of such money or thing of value will be offered, given, or promised, directly or indirectly, to any foreign official, to any foreign political party or official thereof, or to any candidate for foreign political office, for purposes of—

    (A) (i) influencing any act or decision of such foreign official, political party, party official, or candidate in his or its official capacity,

    (ii) inducing such foreign official, political party, party official, or candidate to do or omit to do any act in violation of the lawful duty of such foreign official, political party, party official, or candidate, or

    (iii) securing any improper advantage; or

(B)   inducing such foreign official, political party, party official, or candidate to use his or its influence with a foreign government or instrumentality thereof to affect or influence any act or decision of such government or instrumentality,

in order to assist such issuer in obtaining or retaining business for or with, or directing business to, any person.

(b) Exception for Routine Governmental Action

Subsections (a) and (g) of this section shall not apply to any facilitating or expediting payment to a foreign official, political party, or party official the purpose of which is to expedite or to secure the performance of a routine governmental action by a foreign official, political party, or party official.

(c) Affirmative Defenses

It shall be an affirmative defense to actions under subsection (a) or (g) of this section that—

(1)   the payment, gift, offer, or promise of anything of value that was made, was lawful under the written laws and regulations of the foreign official's, political party's, party official's, or candidate's country; or

(2)   the payment, gift, offer, or promise of anything of value that was made, was a reasonable and bona fide expenditure, such as travel and lodging expenses, incurred by or on behalf of a foreign official, party, party official, or candidate and was directly related to—

(A)   the promotion, demonstration, or explanation of products or services; or

(B)   the execution or performance of a contract with a foreign government or agency thereof.

(d) Guidelines by Attorney General

Not later than one year after August 23, 1988, the Attorney General, after consultation with the Commission, the Secretary of Commerce, the United States Trade Representative, the Secretary of State, and the Secretary of the Treasury, and after obtaining the views of all interested persons through public notice and comment procedures, shall determine to what extent compliance with this section would be enhanced and the business community would be assisted by further clarification of the preceding provisions of this section and may, based on such determination and to the extent necessary and appropriate, issue—

(1)   guidelines describing specific types of conduct, associated with common types of export sales arrangements and business contracts, which for purposes of the Department of Justice's present enforcement policy, the Attorney General determines would be in conformance with the preceding provisions of this section; and

(2)   general precautionary procedures which issuers may use on a voluntary basis to conform their conduct to the Department of Justice's present enforcement policy regarding the preceding provisions of this section.

The Attorney General shall issue the guidelines and procedures referred to in the preceding sentence in accordance with the provisions of subchapter II of chapter 5 of Title 5 and those guidelines and procedures shall be subject to the provisions of chapter 7 of that title.

(e) Opinions of Attorney General

(1)   The Attorney General, after consultation with appropriate departments and agencies of the United States and after obtaining the views of all interested persons through public notice and comment procedures, shall establish a procedure to provide responses to specific inquiries by issuers concerning conformance of their conduct with the Department of Justice's present enforcement policy regarding the preceding provisions of this section. The Attorney General shall, within 30 days after receiving such a request, issue an opinion in response to that request. The opinion shall state whether or not certain specified prospective conduct would, for purposes

of the Department of Justice's present enforcement policy, violate the preceding provisions of this section. Additional requests for opinions may be filed with the Attorney General regarding other specified prospective conduct that is beyond the scope of conduct specified in previous requests. In any action brought under the applicable provisions of this section, there shall be a rebuttable presumption that conduct, which is specified in a request by an issuer and for which the Attorney General has issued an opinion that such conduct is in conformity with the Department of Justice's present enforcement policy, is in compliance with the preceding provisions of this section. Such a presumption may be rebutted by a preponderance of the evidence. In considering the presumption for purposes of this paragraph, a court shall weight all relevant factors, including but not limited to whether the information submitted to the Attorney General was accurate and complete and whether it was within the scope of the conduct specified in any request received by the Attorney General. The Attorney General shall establish the procedure required by this paragraph in accordance with the provisions of subchapter II of chapter 5 of Title 5 and that procedure shall be subject to the provisions of chapter 7 of that title.

(2) Any document or other material which is provided to, received by, or prepared in the Department of Justice or any other department or agency of the United States in connection with a request by an issuer under the procedure established under paragraph (1), shall be exempt from disclosure under section 552 of Title 5 and shall not, except with the consent of the issuer, be made publicly available, regardless of whether the Attorney General responds to such a request or the issuer withdraws such request before receiving a response.

(3) Any issuer who has made a request to the Attorney General under paragraph (1) may withdraw such request prior to the time the Attorney General issues an opinion in response to such request. Any request so withdrawn shall have no force or effect.

(4) The Attorney General shall, to the maximum extent practicable, provide timely guidance concerning the Department of Justice's present enforcement policy with respect to the preceding provisions of this section to potential exporters and small businesses that are unable to obtain specialized counsel on issues pertaining to such provisions. Such guidance shall be limited to responses to requests under paragraph (1) concerning conformity of specified prospective conduct with the Department of Justice's present enforcement policy regarding the preceding provisions of this section and general explanations of compliance responsibilities and of potential liabilities under the preceding provisions of this section.

(f) Definitions

For purposes of this section:

(1) (A) The term "foreign official" means any officer or employee of a foreign government or any department, agency, or instrumentality thereof, or of a public international organization, or any person acting in an official capacity for or on behalf of any such government or department, agency, or instrumentality, or for or on behalf of any such public international organization.

    (B) For purposes of subparagraph (A), the term "public international organization" means—

        (i) an organization that is designated by Executive Order pursuant to section 1 of the International Organizations Immunities Act (22 U.S.C. § 288); or

        (ii) any other international organization that is designated by the President by Executive order for the purposes of this section, effective as of the date of publication of such order in the Federal Register.

(2) (A) A person's state of mind is "knowing" with respect to conduct, a circumstance, or a result if—

        (i) such person is aware that such person is engaging in such conduct, that such circumstance exists, or that such result is substantially certain to occur; or

(ii) such person has a firm belief that such circumstance exists or that such result is substantially certain to occur.

(B) When knowledge of the existence of a particular circumstance is required for an offense, such knowledge is established if a person is aware of a high probability of the existence of such circumstance, unless the person actually believes that such circumstance does not exist.

(3) (A) The term "routine governmental action" means only an action which is ordinarily and commonly performed by a foreign official in—

(i) obtaining permits, licenses, or other official documents to qualify a person to do business in a foreign country;

(ii) processing governmental papers, such as visas and work orders;

(iii) providing police protection, mail pick-up and delivery, or scheduling inspections associated with contract performance or inspections related to transit of goods across country;

(iv) providing phone service, power and water supply, loading and unloading cargo, or protecting perishable products or commodities from deterioration; or

(v) actions of a similar nature.

(B) The term "routine governmental action" does not include any decision by a foreign official whether, or on what terms, to award new business to or to continue business with a particular party, or any action taken by a foreign official involved in the decision-making process to encourage a decision to award new business to or continue business with a particular party.

(g) Alternative Jurisdiction

(1) It shall also be unlawful for any issuer organized under the laws of the United States, or a State, territory, possession, or commonwealth of the United States or a political subdivision thereof and which has a class of securities registered pursuant to section 78l of this title or which is required to file reports under section 78o(d)) of this title, or for any United States person that is an officer, director, employee, or agent of such issuer or a stockholder thereof acting on behalf of such issuer, to corruptly do any act outside the United States in furtherance of an offer, payment, promise to pay, or authorization of the payment of any money, or offer, gift, promise to give, or authorization of the giving of anything of value to any of the persons or entities set forth in paragraphs (1), (2), and (3) of this subsection (a) of this section for the purposes set forth therein, irrespective of whether such issuer or such officer, director, employee, agent, or stockholder makes use of the mails or any means or instrumentality of interstate commerce in furtherance of such offer, gift, payment, promise, or authorization.

(2) As used in this subsection, the term "United States person" means a national of the United States (as defined in section 101 of the Immigration and Nationality Act (8 U.S.C. § 1101)) or any corporation, partnership, association, joint-stock company, business trust, unincorporated organization, or sole proprietorship organized under the laws of the United States or any State, territory, possession, or commonwealth of the United States, or any political subdivision thereof.

15 U.S.C. § 78dd-2

Prohibited Foreign Trade Practices by Domestic Concerns

(a) Prohibition

It shall be unlawful for any domestic concern, other than an issuer which is subject to section 78dd-1 of this title, or for any officer, director, employee, or agent of such domestic concern or any stockholder thereof acting on behalf of such domestic concern, to make use of the mails or any means or instrumentality of interstate commerce corruptly in furtherance of an offer, payment, promise to pay, or authorization of the payment of any money, or offer, gift, promise to give, or authorization of the giving of anything of value to—

(1) any foreign official for purposes of—

   (A) (i)   influencing any act or decision of such foreign official in his official capacity,

   (ii)   inducing such foreign official to do or omit to do any act in violation of the lawful duty of such official, or

   (iii)   securing any improper advantage; or

   (B) inducing such foreign official to use his influence with a foreign government or instrumentality thereof to affect or influence any act or decision of such government or instrumentality, in order to assist such domestic concern in obtaining or retaining business for or with, or directing business to, any person; or

(2) any foreign political party or official thereof or any candidate for foreign political office for purposes of—

   (A) (i)   influencing any act or decision of such party, official, or candidate in its or his official capacity,

   (ii)   inducing such party, official, or candidate to do or omit to do an act in violation of the lawful duty of such party, official, or candidate, or

   (iii)   securing any improper advantage; or

   (B) inducing such party, official, or candidate to use its or his influence with a foreign government or instrumentality thereof to affect or influence any act or decision of such government or instrumentality, in order to assist such domestic concern in obtaining or retaining business for or with, or directing business to, any person;

(3) any person, while knowing that all or a portion of such money or thing of value will be offered, given, or promised, directly or indirectly, to any foreign official, to any foreign political party or official thereof, or to any candidate for foreign political office, for purposes of—

   (A) (i)   influencing any act or decision of such foreign official, political party, party official, or candidate in his or its official capacity,

   (ii)   inducing such foreign official, political party, party official, or candidate to do or omit to do any act in violation of the lawful duty of such foreign official, political party, party official, or candidate, or

   (iii)   securing any improper advantage; or

   (B) inducing such foreign official, political party, party official, or candidate to use his or its influence with a foreign government or instrumentality thereof to affect or influence any act or decision of such government or instrumentality,

   in order to assist such domestic concern in obtaining or retaining business for or with, or directing business to, any person.

(b) Exception for Routine Governmental Action

Subsections (a) and (i) of this section shall not apply to any facilitating or expediting payment to a foreign official, political party, or party official the purpose of which is to expedite or to secure the performance of a routine governmental action by a foreign official, political party, or party official.

(c) Affirmative Defenses

It shall be an affirmative defense to actions under subsection (a) or (I) of this section that—

(1)   the payment, gift, offer, or promise of anything of value that was made, was lawful under the written laws and regulations of the foreign official's, political party's, party official's, or candidate's country; or

(2)   the payment, gift, offer, or promise of anything of value that was made, was a reasonable and bona fide expenditure, such as travel and lodging expenses, incurred by or on behalf of a foreign official, party, party official, or candidate and was directly related to—

(A)   the promotion, demonstration, or explanation of products or services; or

(B)   the execution or performance of a contract with a foreign government or agency thereof.

(d) Injunctive Relief

(1)   When it appears to the Attorney General that any domestic concern to which this section applies, or officer, director, employee, agent, or stockholder thereof, is engaged, or about to engage, in any act or practice constituting a violation of subsection (a) or (i) of this section, the Attorney General may, in his discretion, bring a civil action in an appropriate district court of the United States to enjoin such act or practice, and upon a proper showing, a permanent injunction or a temporary restraining order shall be granted without bond.

(2)   For the purpose of any civil investigation which, in the opinion of the Attorney General, is necessary and proper to enforce this section, the Attorney General or his designee are empowered to administer oaths and affirmations, subpoena witnesses, take evidence, and require the production of any books, papers, or other documents which the Attorney General deems relevant or material to such investigation. The attendance of witnesses and the production of documentary evidence may be required from any place in the United States, or any territory, possession, or commonwealth of the United States, at any designated place of hearing.

(3)   In case of contumacy by, or refusal to obey a subpoena issued to, any person, the Attorney General may invoke the aid of any court of the United States within the jurisdiction of which such investigation or proceeding is carried on, or where such person resides or carries on business, in requiring the attendance and testimony of witnesses and the production of books, papers, or other documents. Any such court may issue an order requiring such person to appear before the Attorney General or his designee, there to produce records, if so ordered, or to give testimony touching the matter under investigation. Any failure to obey such order of the court may be punished by such court as a contempt thereof. All process in any such case may be served in the judicial district in which such person resides or may be found. The Attorney General may make such rules relating to civil investigations as may be necessary or appropriate to implement the provisions of this subsection.

(e) Guidelines by Attorney General

Not later than 6 months after August 23, 1988, the Attorney General, after consultation with the Securities and Exchange Commission, the Secretary of Commerce, the United States Trade Representative, the Secretary of State, and the Secretary of the Treasury, and after obtaining the views of all interested persons through public notice and comment procedures, shall determine to what extent compliance with this section would be enhanced and the business community would be assisted by further clarification of the preceding provisions of this section and may, based on such determination and to the extent necessary and appropriate, issue—

(1) guidelines describing specific types of conduct, associated with common types of export sales arrangements and business contracts, which for purposes of the Department of Justice's present enforcement policy, the Attorney General determines would be in conformance with the preceding provisions of this section; and

(2) general precautionary procedures which domestic concerns may use on a voluntary basis to conform their conduct to the Department of Justice's present enforcement policy regarding the preceding provisions of this section.

The Attorney General shall issue the guidelines and procedures referred to in the preceding sentence in accordance with the provisions of subchapter II of chapter 5 of Title 5 and those guidelines and procedures shall be subject to the provisions of chapter 7 of that title.

(f) Opinions of Attorney General

(1) The Attorney General, after consultation with appropriate departments and agencies of the United States and after obtaining the views of all interested persons through public notice and comment procedures, shall establish a procedure to provide responses to specific inquiries by domestic concerns concerning conformance of their conduct with the Department of Justice's present enforcement policy regarding the preceding provisions of this section. The Attorney General shall, within 30 days after receiving such a request, issue an opinion in response to that request. The opinion shall state whether or not certain specified prospective conduct would, for purposes of the Department of Justice's present enforcement policy, violate the preceding provisions of this section. Additional requests for opinions may be filed with the Attorney General regarding other specified prospective conduct that is beyond the scope of conduct specified in previous requests. In any action brought under the applicable provisions of this section, there shall be a rebuttable presumption that conduct, which is specified in a request by a domestic concern and for which the Attorney General has issued an opinion that such conduct is in conformity with the Department of Justice's present enforcement policy, is in compliance with the preceding provisions of this section. Such a presumption may be rebutted by a preponderance of the evidence. In considering the presumption for purposes of this paragraph, a court shall weigh all relevant factors, including but not limited to whether the information submitted to the Attorney General was accurate and complete and whether it was within the scope of the conduct specified in any request received by the Attorney General. The Attorney General shall establish the procedure required by this paragraph in accordance with the provisions of subchapter II of chapter 5 of Title 5 and that procedure shall be subject to the provisions of chapter 7 of that title.

(2) Any document or other material which is provided to, received by, or prepared in the Department of Justice or any other department or agency of the United States in connection with a request by a domestic concern under the procedure established under paragraph (1), shall be exempt from disclosure under section 552 of Title 5 and shall not, except with the consent of the domestic concern, by made publicly available, regardless of whether the Attorney General response to such a request or the domestic concern withdraws such request before receiving a response.

(3) Any domestic concern who has made a request to the Attorney General under paragraph (1) may withdraw such request prior to the time the Attorney General issues an opinion in response to such request. Any request so withdrawn shall have no force or effect.

(4) The Attorney General shall, to the maximum extent practicable, provide timely guidance concerning the Department of Justice's present enforcement policy with respect to the preceding provisions of this section to potential exporters and small businesses that are unable to obtain specialized counsel on issues pertaining to such provisions. Such guidance shall be limited to responses to requests under paragraph (1) concerning conformity of specified prospective conduct with the Department of Justice's present enforcement policy regarding the preceding provisions of this section and general explanations of compliance responsibilities and of potential liabilities under the preceding provisions of this section.

(g) Penalties

(1) (A) Any domestic concern that is not a natural person and that violates subsection (a) or (i) of this section shall be fined not more than $2,000,000.

(B) Any domestic concern that is not a natural person and that violates subsection (a) or (i) of this section shall be subject to a civil penalty of not more than $10,000 imposed in an action brought by the Attorney General.

(2) (A) Any natural person that is an officer, director, employee, or agent of a domestic concern, or stockholder acting on behalf of such domestic concern, who willfully violates subsection (a) or (i) of this section shall be fined not more than $100,000 or imprisoned not more than 5 years, or both.

(B) Any natural person that is an officer, director, employee, or agent of a domestic concern, or stockholder acting on behalf of such domestic concern, who violates subsection (a) or (i) of this section shall be subject to a civil penalty of not more than $10,000 imposed in an action brought by the Attorney General.

(3) Whenever a fine is imposed under paragraph (2) upon any officer, director, employee, agent, or stockholder of a domestic concern, such fine may not be paid, directly or indirectly, by such domestic concern.

(h) Definitions

For purposes of this section:

(1) The term "domestic concern" means—

(A) any individual who is a citizen, national, or resident of the United States; and

(B) any corporation, partnership, association, joint-stock company, business trust, unincorporated organization, or sole proprietorship which has its principal place of business in the United States, or which is organized under the laws of a State of the United States or a territory, possession, or commonwealth of the United States.

(2) (A) The term "foreign official" means any officer or employee of a foreign government or any department, agency, or instrumentality thereof, or of a public international organization, or any person acting in an official capacity for or on behalf of any such government or department, agency, or instrumentality, or for or on behalf of any such public international organization.

(B) For purposes of subparagraph (A), the term "public international organization" means—

(i) an organization that has been designated by Executive order pursuant to Section 1 of the International Organizations Immunities Act (22 U.S.C. § 288); or

(ii) any other international organization that is designated by the President by Executive order for the purposes of this section, effective as of the date of publication of such order in the Federal Register.

(3) (A) A person's state of mind is "knowing" with respect to conduct, a circumstance, or a result if—

(i) such person is aware that such person is engaging in such conduct, that such circumstance exists, or that such result is substantially certain to occur; or

(ii) such person has a firm belief that such circumstance exists or that such result is substantially certain to occur.

(B) When knowledge of the existence of a particular circumstance is required for an offense, such knowledge is established if a person is aware of a high probability of the existence of such circumstance, unless the person actually believes that such circumstance does not exist.

(4) (A) The term "routine governmental action" means only an action which is ordinarily and commonly performed by a foreign official in—

(i)   obtaining permits, licenses, or other official documents to qualify a person to do business in a foreign country;

(ii) processing governmental papers, such as visas and work orders;

(iii) providing police protection, mail pick-up and delivery, or scheduling inspections associated with contract performance or inspections related to transit of goods across country;

(iv) providing phone service, power and water supply, loading and unloading cargo, or protecting perishable products or commodities from deterioration; or

(v) actions of a similar nature.

(B) The term "routine governmental action" does not include any decision by a foreign official whether, or on what terms, to award new business to or to continue business with a particular party, or any action taken by a foreign official involved in the decision-making process to encourage a decision to award new business to or continue business with a particular party.

(5) The term "interstate commerce" means trade, commerce, transportation, or communication among the several States, or between any foreign country and any State or between any State and any place or ship outside thereof, and such term includes the intrastate use of—

(A) a telephone or other interstate means of communication, or

(B) any other interstate instrumentality.

(i) Alternative Jurisdiction

(1) It shall also be unlawful for any United States person to corruptly do any act outside the United States in furtherance of an offer, payment, promise to pay, or authorization of the payment of any money, or offer, gift, promise to give, or authorization of the giving of anything of value to any of the persons or entities set forth in paragraphs (1), (2), and (3) of subsection (a), for the purposes set forth therein, irrespective of whether such United States person makes use of the mails or any means or instrumentality of interstate commerce in furtherance of such offer, gift, payment, promise, or authorization.

(2) As used in this subsection, a "United States person" means a national of the United States (as defined in section 101 of the Immigration and Nationality Act (8 U.S.C. § 1101)) or any corporation, partnership, association, joint-stock company, business trust, unincorporated organization, or sole proprietorship organized under the laws of the United States or any State, territory, possession, or commonwealth of the United States, or any political subdivision thereof.

15 U.S.C. § 78dd-3

Prohibited Foreign Trade Practices by Persons Other than Issuers or Domestic Concerns

(a) Prohibition

It shall be unlawful for any person other than an issuer that is subject to section 78dd-1 [Section 30A of the Exchange Act] of this title or a domestic concern, or for any officer, director, employee, or agent of such person or any stockholder thereof acting on behalf of such person, while in the territory of the United States, corruptly to make use of the mails or any means or instrumentality of interstate commerce or to do any other act in furtherance of an offer, payment, promise to pay, or authorization of the payment of any money, or offer, gift, promise to give, or authorization of the giving of anything of value to—

(1)   any foreign official for purposes of—

    (A)   (i)   influencing any act or decision of such foreign official in his official capacity,

        (ii)   inducing such foreign official to do or omit to do any act in violation of the lawful duty of such official, or

        (iii)   securing any improper advantage; or

(B)   inducing such foreign official to use his influence with a foreign government or instrumentality thereof to affect or influence any act or decision of such government or instrumentality,

in order to assist such person in obtaining or retaining business for or with, or directing business to, any person;

(2)   any foreign political party or official thereof or any candidate for foreign political office for purposes of—

    (A)   (i)   influencing any act or decision of such party, official, or candidate in its or his official capacity,

        (ii)   inducing such party, official, or candidate to do or omit to do an act in violation of the lawful duty of such party, official, or candidate, or

        (iii)   securing any improper advantage; or

(B)   inducing such party, official, or candidate to use its or his influence with a foreign government or instrumentality thereof to affect or influence any act or decision of such government or instrumentality, in order to assist such person in obtaining or retaining business for or with, or directing business to, any person; or

(3)   any person, while knowing that all or a portion of such money or thing of value will be offered, given, or promised, directly or indirectly, to any foreign official, to any foreign political party or official thereof, or to any candidate for foreign political office, for purposes of—

    (A)   (i)   influencing any act or decision of such foreign official, political party, party official, or candidate in his or its official capacity,

        (ii)   inducing such foreign official, political party, party official, or candidate to do or omit to do any act in violation of the lawful duty of such foreign official, political party, party official, or candidate, or

        (iii)   securing any improper advantage; or

(B)   inducing such foreign official, political party, party official, or candidate to use his or its influence with a foreign government or instrumentality thereof to affect or influence any act or decision of such government or instrumentality,

in order to assist such person in obtaining or retaining business for or with, or directing business to, any person.

(b) Exception for Routine Governmental Action

Subsection (a) of this section shall not apply to any facilitating or expediting payment to a foreign official, political party, or party official the purpose of which is to expedite or to secure the performance of a routine governmental action by a foreign official, political party, or party official.

(c) Affirmative Defenses

It shall be an affirmative defense to actions under subsection (a) of this section that—

(1)   the payment, gift, offer, or promise of anything of value that was made, was lawful under the written laws and regulations of the foreign official's, political party's, party official's, or candidate's country; or

(2)   the payment, gift, offer, or promise of anything of value that was made, was a reasonable and bona fide expenditure, such as travel and lodging expenses, incurred by or on behalf of a foreign official, party, party official, or candidate and was directly related to

   (A)   the promotion, demonstration, or explanation of products or services; or

   (B)   the execution or performance of a contract with a foreign government or agency thereof.

(d) Injunctive Relief

(1)   When it appears to the Attorney General that any person to which this section applies, or officer, director, employee, agent, or stockholder thereof, is engaged, or about to engage, in any act or practice constituting a violation of subsection (a) of this section, the Attorney General may, in his discretion, bring a civil action in an appropriate district court of the United States to enjoin such act or practice, and upon a proper showing, a permanent injunction or a temporary restraining order shall be granted without bond.

(2)   For the purpose of any civil investigation which, in the opinion of the Attorney General, is necessary and proper to enforce this section, the Attorney General or his designee are empowered to administer oaths and affirmations, subpoena witnesses, take evidence, and require the production of any books, papers, or other documents which the Attorney General deems relevant or material to such investigation. The attendance of witnesses and the production of documentary evidence may be required from any place in the United States, or any territory, possession, or commonwealth of the United States, at any designated place of hearing.

(3)   In case of contumacy by, or refusal to obey a subpoena issued to, any person, the Attorney General may invoke the aid of any court of the United States within the jurisdiction of which such investigation or proceeding is carried on, or where such person resides or carries on business, in requiring the attendance and testimony of witnesses and the production of books, papers, or other documents. Any such court may issue an order requiring such person to appear before the Attorney General or his designee, there to produce records, if so ordered, or to give testimony touching the matter under investigation. Any failure to obey such order of the court may be punished by such court as a contempt thereof.

(4)   All process in any such case may be served in the judicial district in which such person resides or may be found. The Attorney General may make such rules relating to civil investigations as may be necessary or appropriate to implement the provisions of this subsection.

(e) Penalties

(1)   (A)   Any juridical person that violates subsection (a) of this section shall be fined not more than $2,000,000.

   (B)   Any juridical person that violates subsection (a) of this section shall be subject to a civil penalty of not more than $10,000 imposed in an action brought by the Attorney General.

(2)   (A)   Any natural person who willfully violates subsection (a) of this section shall be fined not more than $100,000 or imprisoned not more than 5 years, or both.

(B)   Any natural person who violates subsection (a) of this section shall be subject to a civil penalty of not more than $10,000 imposed in an action brought by the Attorney General.

(3)   Whenever a fine is imposed under paragraph (2) upon any officer, director, employee, agent, or stockholder of a person, such fine may not be paid, directly or indirectly, by such person.

(f) Definitions

For purposes of this section:

(1)   The term "person," when referring to an offender, means any natural person other than a national of the United States (as defined in 8 U.S.C. § 1101) or any corporation, partnership, association, joint-stock company, business trust, unincorporated organization, or sole proprietorship organized under the law of a foreign nation or a political subdivision thereof

(2)   (A)   The term "foreign official" means any officer or employee of a foreign government or any department, agency, or instrumentality thereof, or of a public international organization, or any person acting in an official capacity for or on behalf of any such government or department, agency, or instrumentality, or for or on behalf of any such public international organization.

For purposes of subparagraph (A), the term "public international organization" means—

(i)   an organization that has been designated by Executive Order pursuant to Section 1 of the International Organizations Immunities Act (22 U.S.C. § 288); or

(ii)   any other international organization that is designated by the President by Executive order for the purposes of this section, effective as of the date of publication of such order in the Federal Register.

(3)   (A)   A person's state of mind is "knowing" with respect to conduct, a circumstance, or a result if—

(i)   such person is aware that such person is engaging in such conduct, that such circumstance exists, or that such result is substantially certain to occur; or

(ii)   such person has a firm belief that such circumstance exists or that such result is substantially certain to occur.

(B)   When knowledge of the existence of a particular circumstance is required for an offense, such knowledge is established if a person is aware of a high probability of the existence of such circumstance, unless the person actually believes that such circumstance does not exist.

(4)   (A)   The term "routine governmental action" means only an action which is ordinarily and commonly performed by a foreign official in—

(i)   obtaining permits, licenses, or other official documents to qualify a person to do business in a foreign country;

(ii)   processing governmental papers, such as visas and work orders;

(iii)   providing police protection, mail pick-up and delivery, or scheduling inspections associated with contract performance or inspections related to transit of goods across country;

(iv)   providing phone service, power and water supply, loading and unloading cargo, or protecting perishable products or commodities from deterioration; or

(v)   actions of a similar nature.

(B)   The term "routine governmental action" does not include any decision by a foreign official whether, or on what terms, to award new business to or to continue business with a particular party, or any action taken by a foreign official involved in the decision-making process to encourage a decision to award new business to or continue business with a particular party.

(5) The term "interstate commerce" means trade, commerce, transportation, or communication among the several States, or between any foreign country and any State or between any State and any place or ship outside thereof, and such term includes the intrastate use of—

(A) a telephone or other interstate means of communication, or

(B) any other interstate instrumentality.

X.3. 1999 OECD Principles of Corporate Governance[1]

About the Principles

The Principles are intended to help policy makers evaluate and improve the legal, regulatory, and institutional framework for corporate governance, with a view to support economic efficiency, sustainable growth and financial stability. This is primarily achieved by providing shareholders, board members and executives as well as financial intermediaries and service providers with the right incentives to perform their roles within a framework of checks and balances.

The Principles are intended to be concise, understandable and accessible to the international community. On the basis of the Principles, it is the role of government, semi-government or private sector initiatives to assess the quality of the corporate governance framework and develop more detailed mandatory or voluntary provisions that can take into account country-specific economic, legal, and cultural differences.

The Principles focus on publicly traded companies, both financial and nonfinancial. To the extent they are deemed applicable, they might also be a useful tool to improve corporate governance in companies whose shares are not publicly traded. While some of the Principles may be more appropriate for larger than for smaller companies, policy makers may wish to raise awareness of good corporate governance for all companies, including smaller and unlisted companies.

Corporate governance involves a set of relationships between a company's management, its board, its shareholders and other stakeholders. Corporate governance also provides the structure through which the objectives of the company are set, and the means of attaining those objectives and monitoring performance are determined.

The Principles do not intend to prejudice or second-guess the business judgment of individual market participants, board members and company officials. What works in one company or for one group of investors may not necessarily be generally applicable to all of business or of systemic economic importance.

The Principles recognise the interests of employees and other stakeholders and their important role in contributing to the long-term success and performance of the company. Other factors relevant to a company's decisionmaking processes, such as environmental, anti-corruption or ethical concerns, are considered in the Principles but are treated more explicitly in a number of other instruments including the OECD Guidelines for Multinational Enterprises, the Convention on Combating Bribery of Foreign Public Officials in International Business Transactions, the UN Guiding Principles on Business and Human Rights, and the ILO Declaration on Fundamental Principles and Rights at Work, which are referenced in the Principles.

The Principles are developed with an understanding that corporate governance policies have an important role to play in achieving broader economic objectives with respect to investor confidence, capital formation and allocation. The quality of corporate governance affects the cost for corporations to access capital for growth and the confidence with which those that provide capital – directly or indirectly – can participate and share in their value-creation on fair and equitable terms. Together, the body of corporate governance rules and practices therefore provides a framework that helps to bridge the gap between household savings and investment in the real economy. As a consequence, good corporate governance will reassure shareholders and other stakeholders that their rights are protected and make it possible for corporations to decrease the cost of capital and to facilitate their access to the capital market.

---

1   As last amended in 2015, see https://www.oecd.org/daf/ca/Corporate-Governance-Principles-ENG.pdf.

This is of significant importance in today's globalised capital markets. International flows of capital enable companies to access financing from a much larger pool of investors. If companies and countries are to reap the full benefits of the global capital market, and if they are to attract long-term "patient" capital, corporate governance arrangements must be credible, well understood across borders and adhere to internationally accepted principles. Even if corporations do not rely primarily on foreign sources of capital, a credible corporate governance framework, supported by effective supervision and enforcement mechanisms, will help improve the confidence of domestic investors, reduce the cost of capital, underpin the good functioning of financial markets, and ultimately induce more stable sources of financing.

There is no single model of good corporate governance. However, some common elements underlie good corporate governance. The Principles build on these common elements and are formulated to embrace the different models that exist. For example, they do not advocate any particular board structure and the term "board" as used in the Principles is meant to embrace the different national models of board structures. In the typical two-tier system, found in some countries, "board" as used in the Principles refers to the "supervisory board" while "key executives" refers to the "management board". In systems where the unitary board is overseen by an internal auditor's body, the principles applicable to the board are also, mutatis mutandis, applicable. As the definition of the term "key executive" may vary among jurisdictions and depending on context, for example remuneration or related party transactions, the Principles leave it to individual jurisdictions to define this term in a functional manner that meets the intended outcome of the Principles. The terms "corporation" and "company" are used interchangeably in the text.

The Principles are non-binding and do not aim at detailed prescriptions for national legislation. Rather, they seek to identify objectives and suggest various means for achieving them. The Principles aim to provide a robust but flexible reference for policy makers and market participants to develop their own frameworks for corporate governance. To remain competitive in a changing world, corporations must innovate and adapt their corporate governance practices so that they can meet new demands and grasp new opportunities. Taking into account the costs and benefits of regulation, governments have an important responsibility for shaping an effective regulatory framework that provides for sufficient flexibility to allow markets to function effectively and to respond to new expectations of shareholders and other stakeholders.

The Principles are widely used as a benchmark by individual jurisdictions around the world. They are also one of the Financial Stability Board's Key Standards for Sound Financial Systems and provide the basis for assessment of the corporate governance component of the Reports on the Observance of Standards and Codes of the World Bank.

The Principles themselves are evolutionary in nature and are reviewed in light of significant changes in circumstances in order to maintain their role as a leading instrument for policy making in the area of corporate governance.

The Principles are presented in six different chapters: I) Ensuring the basis for an effective corporate governance framework; II) The rights and equitable treatment of shareholders and key ownership functions; III) Institutional investors, stock markets, and other intermediaries; IV) The role of stakeholders; V) Disclosure and transparency; and VI) The responsibilities of the board. Each chapter is headed by a single principle that appears in bold italics and is followed by a number of supporting sub-principles. The Principles are supplemented by annotations that contain commentary on the Principles and are intended to help readers understand their rationale. The annotations may also contain descriptions of dominant or emerging trends and offer alternative implementation methods and examples that may be useful in making the Principles operational.

I. Ensuring the Basis for an Effective Corporate Governance Framework

The corporate governance framework should promote transparent and fair markets, and the efficient allocation of resources. It should be consistent with the rule of law and support effective supervision and enforcement.

Effective corporate governance requires a sound legal, regulatory and institutional framework that market participants can rely on when they establish their private contractual relations. This corporate governance framework typically comprises elements of legislation, regulation, self-regulatory arrangements, voluntary commitments and business practices that are the result of a country's specific circumstances, history and tradition. The desirable mix between legislation, regulation, self-regulation, voluntary standards, etc., will therefore vary from country to country. The legislative and regulatory elements of the corporate governance framework can usefully be complemented by soft law elements based on the "comply or explain" principle such as corporate governance codes in order to allow for flexibility and address specificities of individual companies. What works well in one company, for one investor or a particular stakeholder may not necessarily be generally applicable to corporations, investors and stakeholders that operate in another context and under different circumstances. As new experiences accrue and business circumstances change, the different provisions of the corporate governance framework should be reviewed and, when necessary, adjusted.

Countries seeking to implement the Principles should monitor their corporate governance framework, including regulatory and listing requirements and business practices, with the objective of maintaining and strengthening its contribution to market integrity and economic performance. As part of this, it is important to take into account the interactions and complementarity between different elements of the corporate governance framework and its overall ability to promote ethical, responsible and transparent corporate governance practices. Such analysis should be viewed as an important tool in the process of developing an effective corporate governance framework. To this end, effective and continuous consultation with the public is an essential element. In some jurisdictions, this may need to be complemented by initiatives to inform companies and their stakeholders about the benefits of implementing sound corporate governance practices. Moreover, in developing a corporate governance framework in each jurisdiction, national legislators and regulators should duly consider the need for, and the results from, effective international dialogue and co-operation. If these conditions are met, the corporate governance framework is more likely to avoid over-regulation, support the exercise of entrepreneurship and limit the risks of damaging conflicts of interest in both the private sector and in public institutions.

A.   The corporate governance framework should be developed with a view to its impact on overall economic performance, market integrity and the incentives it creates for market participants and the promotion of transparent and well-functioning markets.

The corporate form of organisation of economic activity is a powerful force for growth. The regulatory and legal environment within which corporations operate is therefore of key importance to overall economic outcomes. Policy makers also have a responsibility to put in place a framework that is flexible enough to meet the needs of corporations operating in widely different circumstances, facilitating their development of new opportunities to create value and to determine the most efficient deployment of resources. Where appropriate, corporate governance frameworks should therefore allow for proportionality, in particular with respect to the size of listed companies. Other factors that may call for flexibility include the company's ownership and control structure, geographical presence, sectors of activity, and the company's stage of development. Policy makers should remain focussed on ultimate economic outcomes and when considering policy options, they will need to undertake an analysis of the impact on key variables that affect the functioning of markets, for example in terms of incentive structures, the efficiency of self-regulatory systems and dealing with systemic conflicts of interest.

Transparent and well-functioning markets serve to discipline market participants and to promote accountability.

B.   The legal and regulatory requirements that affect corporate governance practices should be consistent with the rule of law, transparent and enforceable.

If new laws and regulations are needed, such as to deal with clear cases of market imperfections, they should be designed in a way that makes them possible to implement and enforce in an efficient and even handed manner covering all parties. Consultation by government and other regulatory authorities with corporations, their representative organisations and other stake-holders, is an effective way of doing this. Mechanisms should also be established for parties to protect their rights. In order to avoid over-regulation, unenforceable laws, and unintended consequences that may impede or distort business dynamics, policy measures should be designed with a view to their overall costs and benefits.

Public authorities should have effective enforcement and sanctioning powers to deter dishonest behaviour and provide for sound corporate governance practices. In addition, enforcement can also be pursued through private action, and the effective balance between public and private enforcement will vary depending upon the specific features of each jurisdiction.

Corporate governance objectives are also formulated in voluntary codes and standards that do not have the status of law or regulation. While such codes play an important role in improving corporate governance arrangements, they might leave shareholders and other stakeholders with uncertainty concerning their status and implementation. When codes and principles are used as a national standard or as a complement to legal or regulatory provisions, market credibility requires that their status in terms of coverage, implementation, compliance and sanctions is clearly specified.

C.   The division of responsibilities among different authorities should be clearly articulated and designed to serve the public interest.

Corporate governance requirements and practices are typically influenced by an array of legal domains, such as company law, securities regulation, accounting and auditing standards, insolvency law, contract law, labour law and tax law. Corporate governance practices of individual companies are also often influenced by human rights and environmental laws. Under these circumstances, there is a risk that the variety of legal influences may cause unintentional overlaps and even conflicts, which may frustrate the ability to pursue key corporate governance objectives. It is important that policy makers are aware of this risk and take measures to limit it. Effective enforcement also requires that the allocation of responsibilities for supervision, implementation and enforcement among different authorities is clearly defined so that the competencies of complementary bodies and agencies are respected and used most effectively. Potentially conflicting objectives, for example where the same institution is charged with attracting business and sanctioning violations, should be avoided or managed through clear governance provisions. Overlapping and perhaps contradictory regulations between jurisdictions is also an issue that should be monitored so that no regulatory vacuum is allowed to develop (i.e. issues slipping through in which no authority has explicit responsibility) and to minimise the cost of compliance with multiple systems by corporations. When regulatory responsibilities or oversight are delegated to non-public bodies, it is desirable to explicitly assess why, and under what circumstances, such delegation is desirable. In addition, the public authority should maintain effective safeguards to ensure that the delegated authority is applied fairly, consistently, and in accordance with the law. It is also essential that the governance structure of any such delegated institution be transparent and encompass the public interest.

D.   Stock market regulation should support effective corporate governance.

Stock markets can play a meaningful role in enhancing corporate governance by establishing and enforcing requirements that promote effective corporate governance by their listed issuers.

Also, stock markets provide facilities by which investors can express interest or disinterest in a particular issuer's governance by allowing them to buy or sell the issuer's securities, as appropriate. The quality of the stock market's rules and regulations that establish listing criteria for issuers and that govern trading on its facilities is therefore an important element of the corporate governance framework.

What traditionally were called "stock exchanges" today come in a variety of shapes and forms. Most of the large stock exchanges are now profit maximising and themselves publicly traded joint stock companies that operate in competition with other profit maximising stock exchanges and trading venues. Regardless of the particular structure of the stock market, policy makers and regulators should assess the proper role of stock exchanges and trading venues in terms of standard setting, supervision and enforcement of corporate governance rules. This requires an analysis of how the particular business models of stock exchanges affect the incentives and ability to carry out these functions.

E.   Supervisory, regulatory and enforcement authorities should have the authority, integrity and resources to fulfil their duties in a professional and objective manner. Moreover, their rulings should be timely, transparent and fully explained.

Supervisory, regulatory and enforcement responsibilities should be vested with bodies that are operationally independent and accountable in the exercise of their functions and powers, have adequate powers, proper resources, and the capacity to perform their functions and exercise their powers, including with respect to corporate governance. Many countries have addressed the issue of political independence of the securities supervisor through the creation of a formal governing body (a board, council, or commission) whose members are given fixed terms of appointment. If the appointments are staggered and made independent from the political calendar, they can further enhance independence. These bodies should be able to pursue their functions without conflicts of interest and their decisions should be subject to judicial or administrative review. When the number of corporate events and the volume of disclosures increase, the resources of supervisory, regulatory and enforcement authorities may come under strain. As a result, in order to follow developments, they will have a significant demand for fully qualified staff to provide effective oversight and investigative capacity which will need to be appropriately funded. The ability to attract staff on competitive terms will enhance the quality and independence of supervision and enforcement.

F.   Cross-border co-operation should be enhanced, including through bilateral and multilateral arrangements for exchange of information.

High levels of cross-border ownership and trading require strong international co-operation among regulators, including through bilateral and multilateral arrangements for exchange of information. International co-operation is becoming increasingly relevant for corporate governance, notably where companies are active in many jurisdictions through both listed and unlisted entities, and seek multiple stock market listings on exchanges in different jurisdictions.

II. The Rights and Equitable Treatment of Shareholders and Key Ownership Functions

The corporate governance framework should protect and facilitate the exercise of shareholders' rights and ensure the equitable treatment of all shareholders, including minority and foreign shareholders. All shareholders should have the opportunity to obtain effective redress for violation of their rights.

Equity investors have certain property rights. For example, an equity share in a publicly traded company can be bought, sold, or transferred. An equity share also entitles the investor to participate in the profits of the corporation, with liability limited to the amount of the investment. In addition, ownership of an equity share provides a right to information about the corporation and a right to influence the corporation, primarily by participation in general shareholder meetings and by voting.

As a practical matter, however, the corporation cannot be managed by shareholder referendum. The shareholding body is made up of individuals and institutions whose interests, goals, investment horizons and capabilities vary. Moreover, the corporation's management must be able to take business decisions rapidly. In light of these realities and the complexity of managing the corporation's affairs in fast moving and ever changing markets, shareholders are not expected to assume responsibility for managing corporate activities. The responsibility for corporate strategy and operations is typically placed in the hands of the board and a management team that is selected, motivated and, when necessary, replaced by the board.

Shareholders' rights to influence the corporation centre on certain fundamental issues, such as the election of board members, or other means of influencing the composition of the board, amendments to the company's organic documents, approval of extraordinary transactions, and other basic issues as specified in company law and internal company statutes. This Section can be seen as a statement of the most basic rights of shareholders, which are recognised by law in most countries. Additional rights such as the approval or election of auditors, direct nomination of board members, the ability to pledge shares, the approval of distributions of profits, shareholder ability to vote on board member and/or key executive compensation, approval of material related party transactions and others have also been established in various jurisdictions.

Investors' confidence that the capital they provide will be protected from misuse or misappropriation by corporate managers, board members or controlling shareholders is an important factor in the development and proper functioning of capital markets. Corporate boards, managers and controlling shareholders may have the opportunity to engage in activities that advance their own interests at the expense of non-controlling shareholders. In providing protection to investors, a distinction can usefully be made between ex ante and ex post shareholder rights. Ex ante rights are, for example, pre-emptive rights and qualified majorities for certain decisions. Ex post rights allow the seeking of redress once rights have been violated. In jurisdictions where the enforcement of the legal and regulatory framework is weak, it can be desirable to strengthen the ex ante rights of shareholders such as by low share ownership thresholds for placing items on the agenda of the shareholders meeting or by requiring a supermajority of shareholders for certain important decisions. The Principles support equal treatment for foreign and domestic shareholders in corporate governance. They do not address government policies to regulate foreign direct investment.

One of the ways in which shareholders can enforce their rights is to be able to initiate legal and administrative proceedings against management and board members. Experience has shown that an important determinant of the degree to which shareholder rights are protected is whether effective methods exist to obtain redress for grievances at a reasonable cost and without excessive delay. The confidence of minority investors is enhanced when the legal system provides mechanisms for minority shareholders to bring lawsuits when they have reasonable grounds to believe that their rights have been violated. The provision of such enforcement mechanisms is a key responsibility of legislators and regulators.

There is some risk that a legal system which enables any investor to challenge corporate activity in the courts can become prone to excessive litigation. Thus, many legal systems have introduced provisions to protect management and board members against litigation abuse in the form of tests for the sufficiency of shareholder complaints, so-called safe harbours for management and board member actions (such as the business judgement rule) as well as safe harbours for the disclosure of information. In the end, a balance must be struck between allowing investors to seek remedies for infringement of ownership rights and avoiding excessive litigation. Many countries have found that alternative adjudication procedures, such as administrative hearings or arbitration procedures organised by the securities regulators or other regulatory bodies, are an efficient method for dispute settlement, at least at the first instance level. Specialised court procedures can also be a practical instrument to obtain timely injunctions, and ultimately facilitate the rapid settlement of disputes.

A.   Basic shareholder rights should include the right to: 1) secure methods of ownership registration; 2) convey or transfer shares; 3) obtain relevant and material information on the corporation on a timely and regular basis; 4) participate and vote in general shareholder meetings; 5) elect and remove members of the board; and 6) share in the profits of the corporation.

B.   Shareholders should be sufficiently informed about, and have the right to approve or participate in, decisions concerning fundamental corporate changes such as: 1) amendments to the statutes, or articles of incorporation or similar governing documents of the company; 2) the authorisation of additional shares; and 3) extraordinary transactions, including the transfer of all or substantially all assets, that in effect result in the sale of the company.

The ability of companies to form partnerships and related companies and to transfer operational assets, cash flow rights and other rights and obligations to them is important for business flexibility and for delegating accountability in complex organisations. It also allows a company to divest itself of operational assets and to become only a holding company. However, without appropriate checks and balances such possibilities may also be abused.

C.   Shareholders should have the opportunity to participate effectively and vote in general shareholder meetings and should be informed of the rules, including voting procedures, that govern general shareholder meetings:

1.   Shareholders should be furnished with sufficient and timely information concerning the date, location and agenda of general meetings, as well as full and timely information regarding the issues to be decided at the meeting.

2.   Processes and procedures for general shareholder meetings should allow for equitable treatment of all shareholders. Company procedures should not make it unduly difficult or expensive to cast votes.

The right to participate in general shareholder meetings is a fundamental shareholder right. Management and controlling investors have at times sought to discourage non- controlling or foreign investors from trying to influence the direction of the company. Some companies have charged fees for voting. Other potential impediments include prohibitions on proxy voting, the requirement of personal attendance at general shareholder meetings to vote, holding the meeting in a remote location, and allowing voting by show of hands only. Still other procedures may make it practically impossible to exercise ownership rights. Voting materials may be sent too close to the time of general shareholder meetings to allow investors adequate time for reflection and consultation. Many companies are seeking to develop better channels of communication and decision-making with shareholders. Efforts by companies to remove artificial barriers to participation in general meetings are encouraged and the corporate governance framework should facilitate the use of electronic voting in absentia, including the electronic distribution of proxy materials and reliable vote confirmation systems. In jurisdictions where private enforce-ment is weak, regulators should be in a position to curb unfair voting practices.

3.   Shareholders should have the opportunity to ask questions to the board, including questions relating to the annual external audit, to place items on the agenda of general meetings, and to propose resolutions, subject to reasonable limitations.

In order to encourage shareholder participation in general meetings, many jurisdictions have improved the ability of shareholders to place items on the agenda through a simple and clear process of filing amendments and resolutions, and to submit questions in advance of the general meeting and to obtain replies from management and board members. Shareholders should also be able to ask questions relating to the external audit report. Companies are justified in assuring that abuses of such opportunities do not occur. It is reasonable, for example, to require that in order for shareholder resolutions to be placed on the agenda, they need to be supported by shareholders holding a specified market value or percentage of shares or voting rights. This thres-hold should be determined taking into account the degree of ownership concentration, in order to ensure that minority shareholders are not effectively prevented from putting any items on the agenda. Shareholder resolutions that are approved and fall within the competence of the shareholders' meeting should be addressed by the board.

4.   *Effective shareholder participation in key corporate governance decisions, such as the nomination and election of board members, should be facilitated. Shareholders should be able to make their views known, including through votes at shareholder meetings, on the remuneration of board members and/or key executives, as applicable. The equity component of compensation schemes for board members and employees should be subject to shareholder approval.*

To elect the members of the board is a basic shareholder right. For the election process to be effective, shareholders should be able to participate in the nomination of board members and vote on individual nominees or on different lists of them. To this end, shareholders have access in a number of countries to the company's voting materials which are made available to shareholders, subject to conditions to prevent abuse. With respect to nomination of candidates, boards in many companies have established nomination committees to ensure proper compliance with established nomination procedures and to facilitate and co-ordinate the search for a balanced and qualified board. It is regarded as good practice for independent board members to have a key role on this committee. To further improve the selection process, the Principles also call for full and timely disclosure of the experience and background of candidates for the board and the nomination process, which will allow an informed assessment of the abilities and suitability of each candidate. It is considered good practice to also disclose information about any other board positions that nominees hold, and in some jurisdictions also positions that they are nominated for.

The Principles call for the disclosure of remuneration of board members and key executives. In particular, it is important for shareholders to know the remuneration policy as well as the total value of compensation arrangements made pursuant to this policy. Shareholders also have an interest in how remuneration and company performance are linked when they assess the capability of the board and the qualities they should seek in nominees for the board. The different forms of say-on-pay (binding or advisory vote, ex-ante and/or ex post, board members and/or key executives covered, individual and/or aggregate compensation, compensation policy and/or actual remuneration) play an important role in conveying the strength and tone of shareholder sentiment to the board. In the case of equity-based schemes, their potential to dilute shareholders' capital and to powerfully determine managerial incentives means that they should be approved by shareholders, either for individuals or for the policy of the scheme as a whole. Shareholder approval should also be required for any material changes to existing schemes.

5.   *Shareholders should be able to vote in person or in absentia, and equal effect should be given to votes whether cast in person or in absentia.*

The objective of facilitating shareholder participation suggests that jurisdictions and/or companies promote the enlarged use of information technology in voting, including secure electronic voting in all listed companies. The Principles recommend that voting by proxy be generally accepted. Indeed, it is important to the promotion and protection of shareholder rights that investors can place reliance upon directed proxy voting. The corporate governance framework should ensure that proxies are voted in accordance with the direction of the proxy holder. In those jurisdictions where companies are allowed to obtain proxies, it is important to disclose how the Chairperson of the meeting (as the usual recipient of shareholder proxies obtained by the company) will exercise the voting rights attaching to undirected proxies. Where proxies are held by the board or management for company pension funds and for employee stock ownership plans, the directions for voting should be disclosed. It is regarded as good practice that treasury shares and shares of the company held by subsidiaries should not be allowed to vote, nor be counted for quorum purposes.

6.   Impediments to cross border voting should be eliminated.

Foreign investors often hold their shares through chains of intermediaries. Shares are typically held in accounts with securities intermediaries, that in turn hold accounts with other intermediaries and central securities depositories in other jurisdictions, while the listed company resides in a third country. Such cross-border chains cause special challenges with respect to determining the entitlement of foreign investors to use their voting rights, and the process of communicating with such investors. In combination with business practices which provide only a very short notice period, shareholders are often left with only very limited time to react to a convening notice by the company and to make informed decisions concerning items for decision. This makes cross border voting difficult. The legal and regulatory framework should clarify who is entitled to control the voting rights in cross border situations and where necessary to simplify the depository chain. Moreover, notice periods should ensure that foreign investors in effect have the same opportunities to exercise their ownership functions as domestic investors. To further facilitate voting by foreign investors, laws, regulations and corporate practices should allow participation through electronic means in a non-discriminatory way.

D.   Shareholders, including institutional shareholders, should be allowed to consult with each other on issues concerning their basic shareholder rights as defined in the Principles, subject to exceptions to prevent abuse.

It has long been recognised that in companies with dispersed ownership, individual shareholders might have too small a stake in the company to warrant the cost of taking action or for making an investment in monitoring performance. Moreover, if small shareholders did invest resources in such activities, others would also gain without having contributed (i.e. they are "free riders"). This effect, which serves to lower incentives for monitoring, is probably less of a problem for institutions, particularly financial institutions acting in a fiduciary capacity, in deciding whether to increase their ownership to a significant stake in individual companies, or to rather simply diversify. However, other costs with regard to holding a significant stake might still be high. In many instances institutional investors are prevented from doing this because it is beyond their capacity or would require investing more of their assets in one company than may be prudent. To overcome this asymmetry which favours diversification, they should be allowed, and even encouraged, to co-operate and co-ordinate their actions in nominating and electing board members, placing proposals on the agenda and holding discussions directly with a company in order to improve its corporate governance. More generally, shareholders should be allowed to communicate with each other without having to comply with the formalities of proxy solicitation.

It must be recognised, however, that co-operation among investors could also be used to manipulate markets and to obtain control over a company without being subject to any takeover or disclosure regulations. Moreover, cooperation might also be for the purposes of circumventing competition law. However, if co-operation does not involve issues of corporate control, or conflict with concerns about market efficiency and fairness, the benefits of more effective ownership may still be obtained. To provide clarity among shareholders, regulators may issue guidance on forms of co-ordination and agreements that do or do not constitute such acting in concert in the context of takeover and other rules.

E.   All shareholders of the same series of a class should be treated equally. Capital structures and arrangements that enable certain shareholders to obtain a degree of influence or control disproportionate to their equity ownership should be disclosed.

1.   Within any series of a class, all shares should carry the same rights. All investors should be able to obtain information about the rights attached to all series and classes of shares before they purchase. Any changes in economic or voting rights should be subject to approval by those classes of shares which are negatively affected.

The optimal capital structure of the firm is best decided by the management and the board, subject to the approval of the shareholders. Some companies issue preferred (or preference) shares which have a preference in respect of receipt of the profits of the firm but which normally have limited or no voting rights. Companies may also issue participation certificates or shares with limited or no voting rights, which would presumably trade at different prices than shares with full voting rights. All of these structures may be effective in distributing risk and reward in ways that are thought to be in the best interests of the company and to cost-efficient financing.

Investors can expect to be informed regarding their voting rights before they invest. Once they have invested, their rights should not be changed unless those holding voting shares have had the opportunity to participate in the decision. Proposals to change the voting rights of different series and classes of shares should be submitted for approval at general shareholders meetings by a specified (normally higher) majority of voting shares in the affected categories.

2.   *The disclosure of capital structures and control arrangements should be required.*

Some capital structures allow a shareholder to exercise a degree of control over the corporation disproportionate to the shareholders' equity ownership in the company. Pyramid structures, cross shareholdings and shares with limited or multiple voting rights can be used to diminish the capability of non-controlling shareholders to influence corporate policy.

In addition to ownership relations, other devices can affect control over the corporation. Share-holder agreements are a common means for groups of shareholders, who individually may hold relatively small shares of total equity, to act in concert so as to constitute an effective majority, or at least the largest single block of shareholders. Shareholder agreements usually give those participating in the agreements preferential rights to purchase shares if other parties to the agreement wish to sell. These agreements can also contain provisions that require those accepting the agreement not to sell their shares for a specified time. Shareholder agreements can cover issues such as how the board or the Chairman will be selected. The agreements can also oblige those in the agreement to vote as a block. Some countries have found it necessary to closely monitor such agreements and to limit their duration.

Voting caps limit the number of votes that a shareholder may cast, regardless of the number of shares the shareholder may actually possess. Voting caps therefore redistribute control and may affect the incentives for shareholder participation in shareholder meetings.

Given the capacity of these mechanisms to redistribute the influence of shareholders on company policy, the disclosure of such capital structures and arrangements should be required. Disclosure about such schemes also allows shareholders and potential investors to make better informed decisions (see Chapter V.3).

F.   *Related-party transactions should be approved and conducted in a manner that ensures proper management of conflict of interest and protects the interest of the company and its shareholders.*

1.   *Conflicts of interest inherent in related-party transactions should be addressed.*

The potential abuse of related party transactions is an important policy issue in all markets, but particularly in those where corporate ownership is concentrated and corporate groups prevail. Banning these transactions is normally not a solution as there is nothing wrong per se with entering into transactions with related parties, provided that the conflicts of interest inherent in those transactions are adequately addressed, including through proper monitoring and disclosure. This is all the more important where significant portions of income and/or costs arise from transactions with related parties.

Jurisdictions should put in place an effective framework for clearly flagging these transactions. They include broad but precise definitions of what is understood to be a related party as well as rules to disregard some of these transactions when they are not material because they do not exceed ex ante thresholds, can be regarded as recurrent and taking place at verifiable market terms or taking place with subsidiaries where no specific interest of a related party is present. Once the related party transactions have been identified, jurisdictions set procedures for approving them in a manner that minimises their negative potential. In most jurisdictions, great emphasis is placed on board approval, often with a prominent role for independent board members, or a requirement for the board to justify the interest of the transaction for the company. Shareholders may also be given a say in approving certain transactions, with interested shareholders excluded.

2.   *Members of the board and key executives should be required to disclose to the board whether they, directly, indirectly or on behalf of third parties, have a material interest in any transaction or matter directly affecting the corporation.*

Members of the board, key executives and, in some jurisdictions, controlling shareholders have an obligation to inform the board where they have a business, family or other special relationship outside of the company that could affect their judgement with respect to a particular transaction or matter affecting the company. Such special relationships include situations where executives and board members have a relationship with the company via their association with a shareholder who is in a position to exercise control. Where a material interest has been declared, it is good practice for that person not to be involved in any decision involving the transaction or matter and for the decision of the board to be specifically motivated against the presence of such interests and/or to justify the interest of the transaction for the company, notably by mentioning the terms of the transaction.

G.   *Minority shareholders should be protected from abusive actions by, or in the interest of, controlling shareholders acting either directly or indirectly, and should have effective means of redress. Abusive selfdealing should be prohibited.*

Many publicly traded companies have a large controlling shareholder. While the presence of a controlling shareholder can reduce the agency problem by closer monitoring of management, weaknesses in the legal and regulatory framework may lead to the abuse of other shareholders in the company. Abusive self-dealing occurs when persons having close relationships to the company, including controlling shareholders, exploit those relationships to the detriment of the company and investors.

The potential for abuse is marked where the legal system allows, and the market accepts, controlling shareholders to exercise a level of control which does not correspond to the level of risk that they assume as owners through exploiting legal devices to separate ownership from control, such as pyramid structures or multiple voting rights. Such abuse may be carried out in various ways, including the extraction of direct private benefits via high pay and bonuses for employed family members and associates, inappropriate related party transactions, systematic bias in business decisions and changes in the capital structure through special issuance of shares favouring the controlling shareholder.

In addition to disclosure, a key to protecting minority shareholders is a clearly articulated duty of loyalty by board members to the company and to all shareholders. Indeed, abuse of minority shareholders is most pronounced in those countries where the legal and regulatory framework is weak in this regard. A particular issue arises in some jurisdictions where groups of companies are prevalent and where the duty of loyalty of a board member might be ambiguous and even interpreted as to the group. In these cases, some countries have developed sets of rules to control negative effects, including by specifying that a transaction in favour of another group company must be offset by receiving a corresponding benefit from other companies of the group.

Other common provisions to protect minority shareholders, which have proven effective, include pre-emptive rights in relation to share issues, qualified majorities for certain shareholder decisions and the possibility to use cumulative voting in electing members of the board. Under certain circumstances, some jurisdictions require or permit controlling shareholders to buy-out the remaining shareholders at a share-price that is established through an independent appraisal. This is particularly important when controlling shareholders decide to de-list an enterprise. Other means of improving minority shareholder rights include derivative (including multiple) and class action law suits. Some regulators have established complaint facilities, and some have the possibility to support lawsuits through disclosure of relevant information and/or funding. With the common aim of improving market credibility, the choice and ultimate design of different provisions to protect minority shareholders necessarily depends on the overall regulatory framework and the national legal system.

*H.	Markets for corporate control should be allowed to function in an efficient and transparent manner.*

*1.	The rules and procedures governing the acquisition of corporate control in the capital markets, and extraordinary transactions such as mergers, and sales of substantial portions of corporate assets, should be clearly articulated and disclosed so that investors understand their rights and recourse. Transactions should occur at transparent prices and under fair conditions that protect the rights of all shareholders according to their class.*

*2.	Anti-take-over devices should not be used to shield management and the board from accountability.*

In some jurisdictions, companies employ anti-take-over devices. However, both investors and stock exchanges have expressed concern over the possibility that widespread use of anti-take-over devices may be a serious impediment to the functioning of the market for corporate control. In some instances, take-over defences can simply be devices to shield the management or the board from shareholder monitoring. In implementing any anti-takeover devices and in dealing with take-over proposals, the fiduciary duty of the board to shareholders and the company must remain paramount. Some jurisdictions provide options for exit to dissenting shareholders in case of major corporate restructurings including mergers and amalgamations.

III. Institutional Investors, Stock Markets, and Other Intermediaries

The corporate governance framework should provide sound incentives throughout the investment chain and provide for stock markets to function in a way that contributes to good corporate governance.

In order to be effective, the legal and regulatory framework for corporate governance must be developed with a view to the economic reality in which it is to be implemented. In many jurisdictions, the real world of corporate governance and ownership is no longer characterised by a straight and uncompromised relationship between the performance of the company and the income of the ultimate beneficiaries of shareholdings. In reality, the investment chain is often long and complex, with numerous intermediaries that stand between the ultimate beneficiary and the company. The presence of intermediaries acting as independent decision makers influences the incentives and the ability to engage in corporate governance.

The share of equity investments held by institutional investors such as mutual funds, pension funds, insurance companies and hedge funds has increased significantly, and many of their assets are managed by specialised asset managers. The ability and interest of institutional investors and asset managers to engage in corporate governance varies widely. For some, engagement in corporate governance, including the exercise of voting rights, is a natural part of their business model. Others may offer their beneficiaries and clients a business model and investment strategy that does not include or motivate spending resources on active shareholder engagement. If shareholder engagement is not part of the institution's business model and investment strategy, mandatory requirements to engage, for example through voting, may be ineffective and lead to a box-ticking approach.

The Principles recommend that institutional investors disclose their policies with respect to corporate governance. Voting at shareholder meetings is, however, only one channel for shareholder engagement. Direct contact and dialogue with the board and management, represent other forms of shareholder engagement that are frequently used. In recent years, some countries have begun to consider adoption of codes on shareholder engagement ("stewardship codes") that institutional investors are invited to sign up to on a voluntary basis.

A.   Institutional investors acting in a fiduciary capacity should disclose their corporate governance and voting policies with respect to their investments, including the procedures that they have in place for deciding on the use of their voting rights.

The effectiveness and credibility of the entire corporate governance framework and company oversight depend to a large extent on institutional investors' willingness and ability to make informed use of their shareholder rights and effectively exercise their ownership functions in companies in which they invest. While this principle does not require institutional investors to vote their shares, it calls for disclosure of how they exercise their ownership rights with due consideration to cost effectiveness. For institutions acting in a fiduciary capacity, such as pension funds, collective investment schemes and some activities of insurance companies, and asset managers acting on their behalf, the right to vote can be considered part of the value of the investment being undertaken on behalf of their clients. Failure to exercise the ownership rights could result in a loss to the investor who should therefore be made aware of the policy to be followed by the institutional investors.

In some countries, the demand for disclosure of corporate governance policies to the market is quite detailed and includes requirements for explicit strategies regarding the circumstances in which the institution will intervene in a company; the approach they will use for such intervention; and how they will assess the effectiveness of the strategy. Disclosure of actual voting records is regarded as good practice, especially where an institution has a declared policy to vote. Disclosure is either to their clients (only with respect to the securities of each client) or, in the case of investment advisors to registered investment companies, to the market. A complementary approach to participation in shareholders' meetings is to establish a continuing dialogue with portfolio companies. Such a dialogue between institutional investors and companies should be encouraged, although it is incumbent on the company to treat all investors equally and not to divulge information to the institutional investors which is not at the same time made available to the market. The additional information provided by a company would normally therefore include general background information about the markets in which the company is operating and further elaboration of information already available to the market.

When institutional investors have developed and disclosed a corporate governance policy, effective implementation requires that they also set aside the appropriate human and financial resources to pursue this policy in a way that their beneficiaries and portfolio companies can expect. The nature and practical implementation of an active corporate governance policy by such institutional investors, including staffing, should be transparent to clients who rely on institutional investors with active corporate governance policies.

B.   Votes should be cast by custodians or nominees in line with the directions of the beneficial owner of the shares.

Custodian institutions holding securities as nominees for customers should not be permitted to cast the votes on those securities unless they have received specific instructions to do so. In some jurisdictions, listing requirements contain broad lists of items on which custodians may not vote without instruction, while leaving this possibility open for certain routine items. Rules should require custodian institutions to provide shareholders with timely information concerning their options in the exercise of their voting rights. Shareholders may elect to vote by themselves or to delegate all voting rights to custodians. Alternatively, shareholders may choose to be informed of all upcoming shareholder votes and may decide to cast some votes while delegating some voting rights to the custodian.

Holders of depository receipts should be provided with the same ultimate rights and practical opportunities to participate in corporate governance as are accorded to holders of the under-lying shares. Where the direct holders of shares may use proxies, the depositary, trust office or equivalent body should therefore issue proxies on a timely basis to depository receipt holders. The depository receipt holders should be able to issue binding voting instructions with respect to the shares, which the depositary or trust office holds on their behalf.

It should be noted that this principle does not apply to the exercise of voting rights by trustees or other persons acting under a special legal mandate (such as, for example, bankruptcy receivers and estate executors).

C.   Institutional investors acting in a fiduciary capacity should disclose how they manage material conflicts of interest that may affect the exercise of key ownership rights regarding their investments.

The incentives for intermediary owners to vote their shares and exercise key ownership functions may, under certain circumstances, differ from those of direct owners. Such differences may sometimes be commercially sound but may also arise from conflicts of interest which are particularly acute when the fiduciary institution is a subsidiary or an affiliate of another financial institution, and especially an integrated financial group. When such conflicts arise from material business relationships, for example, through an agreement to manage the portfolio company's funds, such conflicts should be identified and disclosed.

At the same time, institutions should disclose what actions they are taking to minimise the potentially negative impact on their ability to exercise key ownership rights. Such actions may include the separation of bonuses for fund management from those related to the acquisition of new business elsewhere in the organisation. Fee structures for asset management and other intermediary services should be transparent.

D.   The corporate governance framework should require that proxy advisors, analysts, brokers, rating agencies and others that provide analysis or advice relevant to decisions by investors, disclose and minimise conflicts of interest that might compromise the integrity of their analysis or advice.

The investment chain from ultimate owners to corporations does not only involve multiple intermediary owners. It also includes a wide variety of professions that offer advice and services to intermediary owners. Proxy advisors who offer recommendations to institutional investors on how to vote and to sell services that help in the process of voting are among the most relevant from a direct corporate governance perspective. In some cases, proxy advisors also offer corporate governance related consulting services to corporations. Other service providers rate companies according to various corporate governance criteria. Analysts, brokers and rating agencies, perform similar roles and face the same potential conflicts of interest.

Considering the importance of – and sometimes dependence on – various services in corporate governance, the corporate governance framework should promote the integrity of professions such as analysts, brokers, rating agencies, and proxy advisors. When managed appropriately, these can play an important role in shaping good corporate governance practices. At the same time, conflicts of interest may arise and affect judgement, such as when the provider of advice is also seeking to provide other services to the company in question, or where the provider has a direct material interest in the company or its competitors. Many jurisdictions have adopted regulations or encouraged the implementation of self-regulatory codes designed to mitigate such conflicts of interest or other risks related to integrity, and have provided for private and/or public monitoring arrangements.

Providers of proxy advisory services should, where appropriate in each context, disclose publicly and/or to investor clients the process and methodology that underpin their recommendations, and the criteria for their voting policies relevant for their clients.

E.   Insider trading and market manipulation should be prohibited and the applicable rules enforced.

As insider trading entails manipulation of the capital markets, it is prohibited by securities regulations, company law and/or criminal law in most countries. These practices can be seen as constituting a breach of good corporate governance as they violate the principle of equitable treatment of shareholders. However, the effectiveness of such prohibition depends on vigorous enforcement action.

F.   For companies who are listed in a jurisdiction other than their jurisdiction of incorporation, the applicable corporate governance laws and regulations should be clearly disclosed. In the case of cross listings, the criteria and procedure for recognising the listing requirements of the primary listing should be transparent and documented.

It is increasingly common that companies are listed or traded at venues located in a different jurisdiction than the one where the company is incorporated. This may create uncertainty among investors about which corporate governance rules and regulations apply for that company. It may concern everything from procedures and locations for the annual shareholders meeting, to minority rights. The company should therefore clearly disclose which jurisdiction's rules are applicable. When key corporate governance provisions fall under another jurisdiction than the jurisdiction of trading, the main differences should be noted.

Another important consequence of increased internationalisation and integration of stock markets is the prevalence of secondary listings of an already listed company on another stock exchange, so called cross-listings. Companies with cross-listings are often subject to the regulations and authorities of the jurisdiction where they have their primary listing. In case of a secondary listing, exceptions from local listing rules are typically granted based on the recognition of the listing requirements and corporate governance regulations of the exchange where the company has its primary listing. Stock markets should clearly disclose the rules and procedures that apply to cross- listings and related exceptions from local corporate governance rules.

G.   Stock markets should provide fair and efficient price discovery as a means to help promote effective corporate governance.

Effective corporate governance means that shareholders should be able to monitor and assess their corporate investments by comparing market-related information with the company's information about its prospects and performance. When shareholders believe it is advantageous, they can either use their voice to influence corporate behaviour, sell their shares (or buy additional shares), or re-evaluate a company's shares in their portfolios. The quality of and access to market information including fair and efficient price discovery regarding their investments is therefore important for shareholders to exercise their rights.

IV. The Role of Stakeholders in Corporate Governance

The corporate governance framework should recognise the rights of stakeholders established by law or through mutual agreements and encourage active co-operation between corporations and stakeholders in creating wealth, jobs, and the sustainability of financially sound enterprises.

A key aspect of corporate governance is concerned with ensuring the flow of external capital to companies both in the form of equity and credit. Corporate governance is also concerned with finding ways to encourage the various stakeholders in the firm to undertake economically optimal levels of investment in firm-specific human and physical capital. The competitiveness and ultimate success of a corporation is the result of teamwork that embodies contributions from a range of different resource providers including investors, employees, creditors, customers and suppliers, and other stakeholders. Corporations should recognise that the contributions of stakeholders constitute a valuable resource for building competitive and profitable companies. It is, therefore, in the long-term interest of corporations to foster wealth-creating co-operation among stakeholders. The governance framework should recognise the interests of stakeholders and their contribution to the long-term success of the corporation.

A.   The rights of stakeholders that are established by law or through mutual agreements are to be respected.

The rights of stakeholders are often established by law (e.g. labour, business, commercial, environmental, and insolvency laws) or by contractual relations that companies must respect. Nevertheless, even in areas where stakeholder interests are not legislated, many firms make additional commitments to stakeholders, and concern over corporate reputation and corporate performance often requires the recognition of broader interests. For multinational enterprises, this may in some jurisdictions be achieved by companies using the OECD Guidelines for Multinational Enterprises for due diligence procedures that address the impact of such commitments.

B.   Where stakeholder interests are protected by law, stakeholders should have the opportunity to obtain effective redress for violation of their rights.

The legal framework and process should be transparent and not impede the ability of stakeholders to communicate and to obtain redress for the violation of rights.

C.   Mechanisms for employee participation should be permitted to develop.

The degree to which employees participate in corporate governance depends on national laws and practices, and may vary from company to company as well. In the context of corporate governance, mechanisms for participation may benefit companies directly as well as indirectly through the readiness by employees to invest in firm specific skills. Examples of mechanisms for employee participation include: employee representation on boards; and governance processes such as works councils that consider employee viewpoints in certain key decisions. International conventions and national norms also recognise the rights of employees to information, consultation and negotiation. With respect to performance enhancing mechanisms, employee stock ownership plans or other profit sharing mechanisms are to be found in many countries. Pension commitments are also often an element of the relationship between the company and its past and present employees. Where such commitments involve establishing an independent fund, its trustees should be independent of the company's management and manage the fund for all beneficiaries.

D.   Where stakeholders participate in the corporate governance process, they should have access to relevant, sufficient and reliable information on a timely and regular basis.

Where laws and practice of corporate governance frameworks provide for participation by stakeholders, it is important that stakeholders have access to information necessary to fulfil their responsibilities.

E.   Stakeholders, including individual employees and their representative bodies, should be able to freely communicate their concerns about illegal or unethical practices to the board and to the competent public authorities and their rights should not be compromised for doing this.

Unethical and illegal practices by corporate officers may not only violate the rights of stakeholders but also be to the detriment of the company and its shareholders in terms of reputation effects and an increasing risk of future financial liabilities. It is therefore to the advantage of the company and its shareholders to establish procedures and safe-harbours for complaints by employees, either personally or through their representative bodies, and others outside the company, concerning illegal and unethical behaviour. The board should be encouraged by laws and or principles to protect these individuals and representative bodies and to give them confidential direct access to someone independent on the board, often a member of an audit or an ethics committee. Some companies have established an ombudsman to deal with complaints. Several regulators have also established confidential phone and e-mail facilities to receive allegations. While in certain countries representative employee bodies undertake the tasks of conveying concerns to the company, individual employees should not be precluded from, or be less protected, when acting alone. In the absence of timely remedial action or in the face of reasonable risk of negative employment action to a complaint regarding contravention of the law, employees are encouraged to report their bona fide complaint to the competent authorities. Many countries also provide for the possibility to bring cases of violations of the OECD Guidelines for Multinational Enterprises to the National Contact Point. The company should refrain from discriminatory or disciplinary actions against such employees or bodies.

F.   *The corporate governance framework should be complemented by an effective, efficient insolvency framework and by effective enforcement of creditor rights.*

Creditors are a key stakeholder and the terms, volume and type of credit extended to firms will depend importantly on their rights and on their enforceability. Companies with a good corporate governance record are often able to borrow larger sums and on more favourable terms than those with poor records or which operate in less transparent markets. The framework for corporate insolvency varies widely across countries. In some countries, when companies are nearing insolvency, the legislative framework imposes a duty on directors to act in the interests of creditors, who might therefore play a prominent role in the governance of the company. Other countries have mechanisms which encourage the debtor to reveal timely information about the company's difficulties so that a consensual solution can be found between the debtor and its creditors.

Creditor rights also vary, ranging from secured bond holders to unsecured creditors. Insolvency procedures usually require efficient mechanisms for reconciling the interests of different classes of creditors. In many jurisdictions provision is made for special rights such as through "debtor in possession" financing which provides incentives/protection for new funds made available to the enterprise in bankruptcy.

V. Disclosure and Transparency

The corporate governance framework should ensure that timely and accurate disclosure is made on all material matters regarding the corporation, including the financial situation, performance, ownership, and governance of the company.

In most countries a large amount of information, both mandatory and voluntary, is compiled on publicly traded and large unlisted enterprises, and subsequently disseminated to a broad range of users. Public disclosure is typically required, at a minimum, on an annual basis though some countries require periodic disclosure on a semi-annual or quarterly basis, or even more frequently in the case of material developments affecting the company. Companies often make voluntary disclosure that goes beyond minimum disclosure requirements in response to market demand.

The Principles support timely disclosure of all material developments that arise between regular reports. They also support simultaneous reporting of material or required information to all shareholders in order to ensure their equitable treatment. In maintaining close relations with investors and market participants, companies must be careful not to violate this fundamental principle of equitable treatment.

Disclosure requirements are not expected to place unreasonable administrative or cost burdens on enterprises. Nor are companies expected to disclose information that may endanger their competitive position unless disclosure is necessary to fully inform the investment decision and to avoid misleading the investor. In order to determine what information should be disclosed at a minimum, many countries apply the concept of materiality. Material information can be defined as information whose omission or misstatement could influence the economic decisions taken by users of information. Material information can also be defined as information that a reasonable investor would consider important in making an investment or voting decision.

A strong disclosure regime that promotes real transparency is a pivotal feature of market-based monitoring of companies and is central to shareholders' ability to exercise their shareholder rights on an informed basis. Experience shows that disclosure can also be a powerful tool for influencing the behaviour of companies and for protecting investors. A strong disclosure regime can help to attract capital and maintain confidence in the capital markets. By contrast, weak disclosure and non-transparent practices can contribute to unethical behaviour and to a loss of market integrity at great cost, not just to the company and its shareholders but also to the economy as a whole. Shareholders and potential investors require access to regular, reliable and comparable information in sufficient detail for them to assess the stewardship of management, and make informed decisions about the valuation, ownership and voting of shares. Insufficient or unclear information may hamper the ability of the markets to function, increase the cost of capital and result in a poor allocation of resources.

Disclosure also helps improve public understanding of the structure and activities of enterprises, corporate policies and performance with respect to environmental and ethical standards, and companies' relationships with the communities in which they operate. The OECD Guidelines for Multinational Enterprises may, in many jurisdictions be relevant for multinational enterprises.

A.   *Disclosure should include, but not be limited to, material information on:*

1.   *The financial and operating results of the company.*

Audited financial statements showing the financial performance and the financial situation of the company (most typically including the balance sheet, the profit and loss statement, the cash flow statement and notes to the financial statements) are the most widely used source of information on companies. They enable appropriate monitoring to take place and also help to value securities. Management's discussion and analysis of operations is typically included in annual reports. This discussion is most useful when read in conjunction with the accompanying financial statements. Investors are particularly interested in information that may shed light on the future performance of the enterprise.

Arguably, failures of governance can often be linked to the failure to disclose the "whole picture", particularly where off-balance sheet items are used to provide guarantees or similar commitments between related companies. It is therefore important that transactions relating to an entire group of companies be disclosed in line with high quality internationally recognised standards and include information about contingent liabilities and off-balance sheet transactions, as well as special purpose entities.

2.   *Company objectives and non-financial information.*

In addition to their commercial objectives, companies are encouraged to disclose policies and performance relating to business ethics, the environment and, where material to the company, social issues, human rights and other public policy commitments. Such information may be important for certain investors and other users of information to better evaluate the relationship between companies and the communities in which they operate and the steps that companies have taken to implement their objectives.

In many countries, such disclosures are required for large companies, typically as part of their management reports, or companies disclose non-financial information voluntarily. This may include disclosure of donations for political purposes, particularly where such information is not easily available through other disclosure channels.

Some countries require additional disclosures for large companies, for example net turnover figures or payments made to governments broken down by categories of activity and country (country-by-country reporting).

3.   *Major share ownership, including beneficial owners, and voting rights.*

One of the basic rights of investors is to be informed about the ownership structure of the enterprise and their rights vis-à-vis the rights of other owners. The right to such information should also extend to information about the structure of a group of companies and intra-group relations. Such disclosures should make transparent the objectives, nature and structure of the group. Disclosure of ownership data should be provided once certain thresholds of ownership are passed. Such disclosure might include data on major shareholders and others that, directly or indirectly, significantly influence or control or may significantly influence or control the company through, for example, special voting rights, shareholder agreements, the ownership of controlling or large blocks of shares, significant cross shareholding relationships and cross guarantees. It is also good practice to disclose shareholdings of directors, including non-executives.

Particularly for enforcement purposes, and to identify potential conflicts of interest, related party transactions and insider trading, information about record ownership needs to be complemented with current information about beneficial ownership. In cases where major shareholdings are held through intermediary structures or arrangements, information about the beneficial owners should therefore be obtainable at least by regulatory and enforcement agencies and/or through the judicial process. In addition, the OECD template Options for Obtaining Beneficial Ownership and Control Information and the Financial Action Task Force's Guidance on Transparency and Beneficial Ownership can be useful in this regard.

4.   Remuneration of members of the board and key executives

Information about board and executive remuneration is also of concern to shareholders. Of particular interest is the link between remuneration and long-term company performance. Companies are generally expected to disclose information on the remuneration of board members and key executives so that investors can assess the costs and benefits of remuneration plans and the contribution of incentive schemes, such as stock option schemes, to company performance. Disclosure on an individual basis (including termination and retirement provisions) is increasingly regarded as good practice and is now mandated in many countries. In these cases, some jurisdictions call for remuneration of a certain number of the highest paid executives to be disclosed, while in others it is confined to specified positions.

5.   Information about board members, including their qualifications, the selection process, other company directorships and whether they are regarded as independent by the board.

Investors require information on individual board members and key executives in order to evaluate their experience and qualifications and assess any potential conflicts of interest that might affect their judgement. For board members, the information should include their qualifications, share ownership in the company, membership of other boards, other executive positions, and whether they are considered by the board to be an independent member. It is important to disclose membership of other boards not only because it is an indication of experience and possible time pressures facing a member of the board, but also because it may reveal potential conflicts of interest and makes transparent the degree to which there are inter-locking boards.

National principles, and in some cases laws, lay down specific duties for board members who can be regarded as independent and recommend that a significant part, in some instances a majority, of the board should be independent. It should be incumbent on the board to set out the reasons why a member of the board can be considered independent. It is then up to the shareholders, and ultimately the market, to determine if those reasons are justified. Several countries have concluded that companies should disclose the selection process and especially whether it was open to a broad field of candidates. Such information should be provided in advance of any decision by the general shareholder's meeting or on a continuing basis if the situation has changed materially.

6.   Related party transactions.

To ensure that the company is being run with due regard to the interests of all its investors, it is essential to fully disclose all material related party transactions and the terms of such transactions to the market individually. In many jurisdictions this is indeed already a legal requirement. In case the jurisdiction does not define materiality, companies should be required to also disclose the policy/criteria adopted for determining material related party transactions. Related parties should at least include entities that control or are under common control with the company, significant shareholders including members of their families and key management personnel. While the definition of related parties in internationally accepted accounting standards provides a useful reference, the corporate governance framework should ensure that all related parties are properly identified and that in cases where specific interests of related parties are present, material transactions with consolidated subsidiaries are also disclosed.

Transactions involving the major shareholders (or their close family, relations, etc.), either directly or indirectly, are potentially the most difficult type of transactions. In some jurisdictions, shareholders above a limit as low as 5 per cent shareholding are obliged to report transactions. Disclosure requirements include the nature of the relationship where control exists and the nature and amount of transactions with related parties, grouped as appropriate. Given the inherent opaqueness of many transactions, the obligation may need to be placed on the beneficiary to inform the board about the transaction, which in turn should make a disclosure to the market. This should not absolve the firm from maintaining its own monitoring, which is an important task for the board.

To make disclosure more informative, some jurisdictions distinguish related party transactions according to their materiality and conditions. Ongoing disclosure of material transactions is required, with a possible exception for recurrent transactions on "market terms", which can be disclosed only in periodic reports. To be effective, disclosure thresholds may need to be based mainly on quantitative criteria, but avoidance of disclosure through splitting of transactions with the same related party should not be permitted.

7.   *Foreseeable risk factors.*

Users of financial information and market participants need information on reasonably fore-seeable material risks that may include: risks that are specific to the industry or the geographical areas in which the company operates; dependence on commodities; financial market risks including interest rate or currency risk; risk related to derivatives and off-balance sheet trans-actions; business conduct risks; and risks related to the environment.

The Principles envision the disclosure of sufficient and comprehensive information to fully inform investors of the material and foreseeable risks of the enterprise. Disclosure of risk is most effective when it is tailored to the particular company and industry in question. Disclosure about the system for monitoring and managing risk is increasingly regarded as good practice.

8.   *Issues regarding employees and other stakeholders.*

Companies are encouraged, and in some countries even obliged, to provide information on key issues relevant to employees and other stakeholders that may materially affect the performance of the company or that may have significant impacts upon them. Disclosure may include management/employee relations, including remuneration, collective bargaining coverage, and mechanisms for employee representation, and relations with other stakeholders such as creditors, suppliers, and local communities.

Some countries require extensive disclosure of information on human resources. Human resource policies, such as programmes for human resource development and training, retention rates of employees and employee share ownership plans, can communicate important infor-mation on the competitive strengths of companies to market participants.

9.   *Governance structures and policies, including the content of any corporate governance code or policy and the process by which it is implemented.*

Companies should report their corporate governance practices, and such disclosure should be mandated as part of the regular reporting. Companies should implement corporate governance principles set, or endorsed, by the regulatory or listing authority with mandatory reporting on a "comply or explain" or similar basis. Disclosure of the governance structures and policies of the company, including, in the case of non-operating holding companies, that of significant sub-sidiaries, is important for the assessment of a company's governance and should cover the division of authority between shareholders, management and board members. Companies should clearly disclose the different roles and responsibilities of the CEO and/or Chair and, where a single person combines both roles, the rationale for this arrangement. It is also good practice to disclose the articles of association, board charters and, where applicable, committee structures and charters.

As a matter of transparency, procedures for shareholders meetings should ensure that votes are properly counted and recorded, and that a timely announcement of the outcome is made.

B.   *Information should be prepared and disclosed in accordance with high quality standards of accounting and financial and non-financial reporting.*

The application of high quality accounting and disclosure standards is expected to significantly improve the ability of investors to monitor the company by providing increased relevance, reliability and comparability of reporting, and improved insight into company performance. Most countries mandate the use of internationally recognised standards for financial reporting, which can serve to improve transparency and the comparability of financial statements and other financial reporting between countries. Such standards should be developed through open, independent, and public processes involving the private sector and other interested parties such as professional associations and independent experts. High quality domestic standards can be achieved by making them consistent with one of the internationally recognised accounting standards. In many countries, listed companies are required to use these standards.

C.   *An annual audit should be conducted by an independent, competent and qualified, auditor in accordance with high-quality auditing standards in order to provide an external and objective assurance to the board and shareholders that the financial statements fairly represent the financial position and performance of the company in all material respects.*

In addition to certifying that the financial statements represent fairly the financial position of a company, the audit statement should also include an opinion on the way in which financial statements have been prepared and presented. This should contribute to an improved control environment in the company. In some jurisdictions, the external auditors are also required to report on the company's corporate governance.

The independence of auditors and their accountability to shareholders should be required. The designation of an audit regulator independent from the profession, consistent with the Core Principles of the International Forum of Independent Audit Regulators (IFIAR), is an important factor in improving audit quality.

It is good practice for external auditors to be recommended by an independent audit committee of the board or an equivalent body and to be appointed either by that committee/body or by shareholders directly. Moreover, the IOSCO Principles of Auditor Independence and the Role of Corporate Governance in Monitoring an Auditor's Independence states that, "standards of auditor independence should establish a framework of principles, supported by a combination of prohibitions, restrictions, other policies and procedures and disclosures, that addresses at least the following threats to independence: self-interest, self-review, advocacy, familiarity and intimi-dation".

The audit committee or an equivalent body should provide oversight of the internal audit activities and should also be charged with overseeing the overall relationship with the external auditor including the nature of non-audit services provided by the auditor to the company. Provision of non-audit services by the external auditor to a company can significantly impair their independence and might involve them auditing their own work. To deal with the skewed incentives which may arise, the disclosure of payments to external auditors for non-audit services should be required. Examples of other provisions designed to promote auditor independence include, a total ban or severe limitation on the nature of non-audit work which can be undertaken by an auditor for their audit client, mandatory rotation of auditors (either partners or in some cases the audit partnership), a fixed tenure for auditors, joint audits, a temporary ban on the employment of an ex-auditor by the audited company and prohibiting auditors or their dependents from having a financial stake or management role in the companies they audit. Some countries take a more direct regulatory approach and limit the percentage of non-audit income that the auditor can receive from a particular client or limit the total percentage of auditor income that can come from one client.

An issue which has arisen in some jurisdictions concerns the pressing need to ensure the competence of the audit profession. A registration process for individuals to confirm their qualifications is considered good practice. This needs, however, to be supported by ongoing training and monitoring of work experience to ensure appropriate levels of professional competence and scepticism.

D.   *External auditors should be accountable to the shareholders and owe a duty to the company to exercise due professional care in the conduct of the audit.*

The practice that external auditors are recommended by an independent audit committee of the board or an equivalent body and that external auditors are appointed either by that committee/body or by the shareholders' meeting directly can be regarded as good practice since it clarifies that the external auditor should be accountable to the shareholders. It also underlines that the external auditor owes a duty of due professional care to the company rather than any individual or group of corporate managers that they may interact with for the purpose of their work.

E.   *Channels for disseminating information should provide for equal, timely and cost-efficient access to relevant information by users.*

Channels for the dissemination of information can be as important as the content of the information itself. While the disclosure of information is often provided for by legislation, filing and access to information can be cumbersome and costly. Filing of statutory reports has been greatly enhanced in some countries by electronic filing and data retrieval systems. Countries should move to the next stage by integrating different sources of company information, including shareholder filings. Company websites also provide the opportunity for improving information dissemination, and some countries now require companies to have a website that provides relevant and significant information about the company itself.

Provisions for ongoing disclosure which includes periodic disclosure and continuous or current disclosure which must be provided on an ad hoc basis should be required. With respect to continuous/current disclosure, good practice is to call for "immediate" disclosure of material developments, whether this means "as soon as possible" or is defined as a prescribed maximum number of specified days. The IOSCO Principles for Periodic Disclosure by Listed Entities set guidance for the periodic reports of companies that have securities listed or admitted to trading on a regulated market on which retail investors participate. The IOSCO Principles for Ongoing Disclosure and Material Development Reporting by Listed Entities set forth common principles of ongoing disclosure and material development reporting for listed companies.

VI. The Responsibilities of the Board

The corporate governance framework should ensure the strategic guidance of the company, the effective monitoring of management by the board, and the board's accountability to the company and the shareholders.

Board structures and procedures vary both within and among countries. Some countries have two-tier boards that separate the supervisory function and the management function into different bodies. Such systems typically have a "supervisory board" composed of non-executive board members and a "management board" composed entirely of executives. Other countries have "unitary" boards, which bring together executive and non-executive board members. In some countries there is also an additional statutory body for audit purposes. The Principles are intended to apply to whatever board structure is charged with the functions of governing the enterprise and monitoring management.

Together with guiding corporate strategy, the board is chiefly responsible for monitoring managerial performance and achieving an adequate return for shareholders, while preventing conflicts of interest and balancing competing demands on the corporation. In order for boards to effectively fulfil their responsibilities they must be able to exercise objective and independent judgement. Another important board responsibility is to oversee the risk management system and systems designed to ensure that the corporation obeys applicable laws, including tax, competition, labour, environmental, equal opportunity, health and safety laws. In some countries, companies have found it useful to explicitly articulate the responsibilities that the board assumes and those for which management is accountable.

The board is not only accountable to the company and its shareholders but also has a duty to act in their best interests. In addition, boards are expected to take due regard of, and deal fairly with, other stakeholder interests including those of employees, creditors, customers, suppliers and local communities. Observance of environmental and social standards is relevant in this context.

A.   Board members should act on a fully informed basis, in good faith, with due diligence and care, and in the best interest of the company and the shareholders.

In some countries, the board is legally required to act in the interest of the company, taking into account the interests of shareholders, employees, and the public good. Acting in the best interest of the company should not permit management to become entrenched.

This principle states the two key elements of the fiduciary duty of board members: the duty of care and the duty of loyalty. The duty of care requires board members to act on a fully informed basis, in good faith, with due diligence and care. In some jurisdictions there is a standard of reference which is the behaviour that a reasonably prudent person would exercise in similar circumstances. In nearly all jurisdictions, the duty of care does not extend to errors of business judgement so long as board members are not grossly negligent and a decision is made with due diligence, etc. The principle calls for board members to act on a fully informed basis. Good practice takes this to mean that they should be satisfied that key corporate information and compliance systems are fundamentally sound and underpin the key monitoring role of the board advocated by the Principles. In many jurisdictions this meaning is already considered an element of the duty of care, while in others it is required by securities regulation, accounting standards, etc. The duty of loyalty is of central importance, since it underpins effective implementation of other principles in this document relating to, for example, the equitable treatment of shareholders, monitoring of related party transactions and the establishment of remuneration policy for key executives and board members. It is also a key principle for board members who are working within the structure of a group of companies: even though a company might be controlled by another enterprise, the duty of loyalty for a board member relates to the company and all its shareholders and not to the controlling company of the group.

B.   Where board decisions may affect different shareholder groups differently, the board should treat all shareholders fairly.

In carrying out its duties, the board should not be viewed, or act, as an assembly of individual representatives for various constituencies. While specific board members may indeed be nominated or elected by certain shareholders (and sometimes contested by others) it is an important feature of the board's work that board members when they assume their responsibilities carry out their duties in an even-handed manner with respect to all shareholders.

This principle is particularly important to establish in the presence of controlling shareholders that de facto may be able to select all board members.

C.   The board should apply high ethical standards. It should take into account the interests of stakeholders.

The board has a key role in setting the ethical tone of a company, not only by its own actions, but also in appointing and overseeing key executives and consequently the management in general. High ethical standards are in the long term interests of the company as a means to make it credible and trustworthy, not only in day-to-day operations but also with respect to longer term commitments. To make the objectives of the board clear and operational, many companies have found it useful to develop company codes of conduct based on, inter alia, professional standards and sometimes broader codes of behaviour, and to communicate them throughout the organi-sation. The latter might include a voluntary commitment by the company (including its subsidiaries) to comply with the OECD Guidelines for Multinational Enterprises which reflect all four principles contained in the ILO Declaration on Fundamental Principles and Rights at Work. Similarly, jurisdictions are increasingly demanding that boards oversee the finance and tax planning strategies management is allowed to conduct, thus discouraging practices, for example the pursuit of aggressive tax avoidance, that do not contribute to the long term interests of the company and its shareholders, and can cause legal and reputational risks.

Company-wide codes serve as a standard for conduct by both the board and key executives, setting the framework for the exercise of judgement in dealing with varying and often conflicting constituencies. At a minimum, the ethical code should set clear limits on the pursuit of private interests, including dealings in the shares of the company. An overall framework for ethical conduct goes beyond compliance with the law, which should always be a fundamental requirement.

D.   The board should fulfil certain key functions, including:

1.   Reviewing and guiding corporate strategy, major plans of action, risk management policies and procedures, annual budgets and business plans; setting performance objectives; monitoring implementation and corporate performance; and overseeing major capital expenditures, acquisitions and divestitures.

An area of increasing importance for boards and which is closely related to corporate strategy is oversight of the company's risk management. Such risk management oversight will involve oversight of the accountabilities and responsibilities for managing risks, specifying the types and degree of risk that a company is willing to accept in pursuit of its goals, and how it will manage the risks it creates through its operations and relationships. It is thus a crucial guideline for management that must manage risks to meet the company's desired risk profile.

2.   Monitoring the effectiveness of the company's governance practices and making changes as needed.

Monitoring of governance by the board also includes continuous review of the internal structure of the company to ensure that there are clear lines of accountability for management throughout the organisation. In addition to requiring the monitoring and disclosure of corporate governance practices on a regular basis, many countries have moved to recommend, or indeed mandate, self-assessment by boards of their performance as well as performance reviews of individual board members and the Chair and the CEO.

3.   Selecting, compensating, monitoring and, when necessary, replacing key executives and overseeing succession planning.

In most two tier board systems the supervisory board is also responsible for appointing the management board which will normally comprise most of the key executives.

4.   Aligning key executive and board remuneration with the longer term interests of the company and its shareholders.

It is regarded as good practice for boards to develop and disclose a remuneration policy statement covering board members and key executives. Such policy statements specify the relationship between remuneration and performance, and include measurable standards that emphasise the longer run interests of the company over short term considerations. Policy statements generally tend to set conditions for payments to board members for extra-board activities, such as consulting. They also often specify terms to be observed by board members and key executives about holding and trading the stock of the company, and the procedures to be followed in granting and re-pricing of options. In some countries, policy also covers the payments to be made when hiring and/or terminating the contract of an executive.

In large companies, it is considered good practice that remuneration policy and contracts for board members and key executives be handled by a special committee of the board comprising either wholly or a majority of independent directors and excluding executives that serve on each other's remuneration committees, which could lead to conflicts of interest. The introduction of malus and claw-back provisions is considered good practice. They grant the company the right to withhold and recover compensation from executives in cases of managerial fraud and other circumstances, for example when the company is required to restate its financial statements due to material noncompliance with financial reporting requirements.

5.   Ensuring a formal and transparent board nomination and election process.

These Principles promote an active role for shareholders in the nomination and election of board members. The board has an essential role to play in ensuring that this and other aspects of the nominations and election process are respected. First, while actual procedures for nomination may differ among countries, the board or a nomination committee has a special responsibility to make sure that established procedures are transparent and respected. Second, the board has a key role in defining the general or individual profile of board members that the company may need at any given time, considering the appropriate knowledge, competencies and expertise to complement the existing skills of the board. Third, the board or nomination committee has the responsibility to identify potential candidates to meet desired profiles and propose them to shareholders, and/or consider those candidates advanced by shareholders with the right to make nominations. There are increasing calls for open search processes extending to a broad range of people.

6.   Monitoring and managing potential conflicts of interest of management, board members and shareholders, including misuse of corporate assets and abuse in related party transactions.

It is an important function of the board to oversee the internal control systems covering financial reporting and the use of corporate assets and to guard against abusive related party transactions. These functions are often assigned to the internal auditor which should maintain direct access to the board. Where other corporate officers are responsible such as the general counsel, it is important that they maintain similar reporting responsibilities as the internal auditor.

In fulfilling its control oversight responsibilities it is important for the board to encourage the reporting of unethical/unlawful behaviour without fear of retribution. The existence of a company code of ethics should aid this process which should be underpinned by legal protection for the individuals concerned. A contact point for employees who wish to report concerns about unethical or illegal behaviour that might also compromise the integrity of financial statements should be offered by the audit committee or by an ethics committee or equivalent body.

7.   Ensuring the integrity of the corporation's accounting and financial reporting systems, including the independent audit, and that appropriate systems of control are in place, in particular, systems for risk management, financial and operational control, and compliance with the law and relevant standards.

The Board should demonstrate a leadership role to ensure that an effective means of risk oversight is in place. Ensuring the integrity of the essential reporting and monitoring systems will require the board to set and enforce clear lines of responsibility and accountability throughout the organisation. The board will also need to ensure that there is appropriate oversight by senior management. Normally, this includes the establishment of an internal audit system directly reporting to the board. It is considered good practice for the internal auditors to report to an independent audit committee of the board or an equivalent body which is also responsible for managing the relationship with the external auditor, thereby allowing a co-ordinated response by the board. It should also be regarded as good practice for this committee, or equivalent body, to review and report to the board the most critical accounting policies which are the basis for financial reports. However, the board should retain final responsibility for oversight of the company's risk management system and for ensuring the integrity of the reporting systems. Some jurisdictions have provided for the chair of the board to report on the internal control process. Companies with large or complex risks (financial and non-financial), not only in the financial sector, should consider introducing similar reporting systems, including direct reporting to the board, with regard to risk management.

Companies are also well advised to establish and ensure the effectiveness of internal controls, ethics, and compliance programmes or measures to comply with applicable laws, regulations, and standards, including statutes criminalising the bribery of foreign public officials, as required under the OECD Anti-Bribery Convention, and other forms of bribery and corruption. Moreover, compliance must also relate to other laws and regulations such as those covering securities, competition and work and safety conditions. Other laws that may be applicable include those relating to taxation, human rights, the environment, fraud, and money laundering. Such compliance programmes will also underpin the company's ethical code. To be effective, the incentive structure of the business needs to be aligned with its ethical and professional standards so that adherence to these values is rewarded and breaches of law are met with dissuasive consequences or penalties. Compliance programmes should also extend to subsidiaries and where possible to third parties, such as agents and other intermediaries, consultants, representatives, distributors, contractors and suppliers, consortia, and joint venture partners.

8.   Overseeing the process of disclosure and communications.

The functions and responsibilities of the board and management with respect to disclosure and communication need to be clearly established by the board. In some jurisdictions, the appointment of an investment relations officer who reports directly to the board is considered good practice for large listed companies.

E.   The board should be able to exercise objective independent judgement on corporate affairs.

In order to exercise its duties of monitoring managerial performance, preventing conflicts of interest and balancing competing demands on the corporation, it is essential that the board is able to exercise objective judgement. In the first instance this will mean independence and objectivity with respect to management with important implications for the composition and structure of the board. Board independence in these circumstances usually requires that a sufficient number of board members will need to be independent of management.

In countries with single tier board systems, the objectivity of the board and its independence from management may be strengthened by the separation of the role of chief executive and Chair. Separation of the two posts is generally regarded as good practice, as it can help to achieve an appropriate balance of power, increase accountability and improve the board's capacity for decision making independent of management. The designation of a lead director is also regarded as a good practice alternative in some jurisdictions if that role is defined with sufficient authority to lead the board in cases where management has clear conflicts. Such mechanisms can also help to ensure high quality governance of the enterprise and the effective functioning of the board.

The Chairman or lead director may, in some countries, be supported by a company secretary. In the case of two tier board systems, consideration should be given to whether corporate governance concerns might arise if there is a tradition for the head of the lower board becoming the Chairman of the Supervisory Board on retirement.

The manner in which board objectivity might be underpinned also depends on the ownership structure of the company. A dominant shareholder has considerable powers to appoint the board and the management. However, in this case, the board still has a fiduciary responsibility to the company and to all shareholders including minority shareholders.

The variety of board structures, ownership patterns and practices in different countries will thus require different approaches to the issue of board objectivity. In many instances objectivity requires that a sufficient number of board members not be employed by the company or its affiliates and not be closely related to the company or its management through significant economic, family or other ties. This does not prevent shareholders from being board members. In others, independence from controlling shareholders or another controlling body will need to be emphasised, in particular if the ex ante rights of minority shareholders are weak and opportunities to obtain redress are limited. This has led to both codes and the law in most jurisdictions to call for some board members to be independent of dominant shareholders, independence extending to not being their representative or having close business ties with them. In other cases, parties such as particular creditors can also exercise significant influence. Where there is a party in a special position to influence the company, there should be stringent tests to ensure the objective judgement of the board.

In defining independence for members of the board, some national principles of corporate governance have specified quite detailed presumptions for non-independence which are frequently reflected in listing requirements. While establishing necessary conditions, such "negative" criteria defining when an individual is not regarded as independent can usefully be complemented by "positive" examples of qualities that will increase the probability of effective independence.

Independent board members can contribute significantly to the decision-making of the board. They can bring an objective view to the evaluation of the performance of the board and management. In addition, they can play an important role in areas where the interests of management, the company and its shareholders may diverge such as executive remuneration, succession planning, changes of corporate control, take-over defences, large acquisitions and the audit function. In order for them to play this key role, it is desirable that boards declare who they consider to be independent and the criterion for this judgement. Some jurisdictions also require separate meetings of independent directors on a periodic basis.

1.   Boards should consider assigning a sufficient number of non-executive board members capable of exercising independent judgement to tasks where there is a potential for conflict of interest. Examples of such key responsibilities are ensuring the integrity of financial and non-financial reporting, the review of related party transactions, nomination of board members and key executives, and board remuneration.

While the responsibility for financial reporting, remuneration and nomination are frequently with the board as a whole, independent non-executive board members can provide additional assurance to market participants that their interests are safeguarded. The board should consider establishing specific committees to consider questions where there is a potential for conflict of interest. These committees should require a minimum number or be composed entirely of non-executive members. In some countries, shareholders have direct responsibility for nominating and electing non-executive directors to specialised functions.

2.   Boards should consider setting up specialised committees to support the full board in performing its functions, particularly in respect to audit, and, depending upon the company's size and risk profile, also in respect to risk management and remuneration. When committees of the board are established, their mandate, composition and working procedures should be well defined and disclosed by the board.

Where justified in terms of the size of the company and its board, the use of committees may improve the work of the board. In order to evaluate the merits of board committees it is important that the market receives a full and clear picture of their purpose, duties and composition. Such information is particularly important in the many jurisdictions where boards have established independent audit committees with powers to oversee the relationship with the external auditor and to act in many cases independently. Audit committees should also be able to oversee the effectiveness and integrity of the internal control system. Other such committees include those dealing with nomination, compensation, and risk. The establishment of additional committees can sometimes help avoid audit committee overload and to allow more board time to be dedicated to those issues. Nevertheless, the accountability of the rest of the board and the board as a whole should be clear. Disclosure need not extend to committees set up to deal with, for example, confidential commercial transactions.

3.   Board members should be able to commit themselves effectively to their responsibilities.

Service on too many boards can interfere with the performance of board members. Some countries have limited the number of board positions that can be held. Specific limitations may be less important than ensuring that members of the board enjoy legitimacy and confidence in the eyes of shareholders. Disclosure about other board memberships to shareholders is therefore a key instrument to improve board nominations. Achieving legitimacy would also be facilitated by the publication of attendance records for individual board members (e.g. whether they have missed a significant number of meetings) and any other work undertaken on behalf of the board and the associated remuneration.

4.   Boards should regularly carry out evaluations to appraise their performance and assess whether they possess the right mix of background and competences.

In order to improve board practices and the performance of its members, an increasing number of jurisdictions now encourage companies to engage in board training and voluntary board evaluation that meet the needs of the individual company. Particularly in large companies, board evaluation can be supported by external facilitators to increase objectivity. Unless certain qualifications are required, such as for financial institutions, this might include that board members acquire appropriate skills upon appointment. Thereafter, board members may remain abreast of relevant new laws, regulations, and changing commercial and other risks through in-house training and external courses. In order to avoid groupthink and bring a diversity of thought to board discussion, boards should also consider if they collectively possess the right mix of background and competences.

Countries may wish to consider measures such as voluntary targets, disclosure requirements, boardroom quotas, and private initiatives that enhance gender diversity on boards and in senior management.

F.   In order to fulfil their responsibilities, board members should have access to accurate, relevant and timely information.

Board members require relevant information on a timely basis in order to support their decision-making. Non-executive board members do not typically have the same access to information as key managers within the company. The contributions of non- executive board members to the company can be enhanced by providing access to certain key managers within the company such as, for example, the company secretary, the internal auditor, and the head of risk management or chief risk officer, and recourse to independent external advice at the expense of the company. In order to fulfil their responsibilities, board members should ensure that they obtain accurate, relevant and timely information. Where companies rely on complex risk management models, board members should be made aware of the possible shortcomings of such models.

G.   *When employee representation on the board is mandated, mechanisms should be developed to facilitate access to information and training for employee representatives, so that this representation is exercised effectively and best contributes to the enhancement of board skills, information and independence.*

When employee representation on boards is mandated by the law or collective agreements, or adopted voluntarily, it should be applied in a way that maximises its contribution to the board's independence, competence and information. Employee representatives should have the same duties and responsibilities as all other board members, and should act in the best interest of the company.

Procedures should be established to facilitate access to information, training and expertise, and the independence of employee board members from the CEO and management. These procedures should also include adequate, transparent appointment procedures, rights to report to employees on a regular basis – provided that board confidentiality requirements are duly respected – training, and clear procedures for managing conflicts of interest. A positive contribution to the board's work will also require acceptance and constructive collaboration by other members of the board as well as by management.

X.4. 1999 OECD CONVENTION ON COMBATING BRIBERY OF FOREIGN PUBLIC OFFICIALS IN INTERNATIONAL BUSINESS TRANSACTIONS[1]

Preamble

The Parties,

Considering that bribery is a widespread phenomenon in international business transactions, including trade and investment, which raises serious moral and political concerns, undermines good governance and economic development, and distorts international competitive conditions;

Considering that all countries share a responsibility to combat bribery in international business transactions;

Having regard to the Revised Recommendation on Combating Bribery in International Business Transactions, adopted by the Council of the Organisation for Economic Co-operation and Development (OECD) on 23 May 1997, C(97)123/FINAL, which, inter alia, called for effective measures to deter, prevent and combat the bribery of foreign public officials in connection with international business transactions, in particular the prompt criminalisation of such bribery in an effective and co-ordinated manner and in conformity with the agreed common elements set out in that Recommendation and with the jurisdictional and other basic legal principles of each country;

Welcoming other recent developments which further advance international understanding and co-operation in combating bribery of public officials, including actions of the United Nations, the World Bank, the International Monetary Fund, the World Trade Organisation, the Organisation of American States, the Council of Europe and the European Union;

Welcoming the efforts of companies, business organisations and trade unions as well as other non-governmental organisations to combat bribery;

Recognising the role of governments in the prevention of solicitation of bribes from individuals and enterprises in international business transactions;

Recognising that achieving progress in this field requires not only efforts on a national level but also multilateral co-operation, monitoring and follow-up;

Recognising that achieving equivalence among the measures to be taken by the Parties is an essential object and purpose of the Convention, which requires that the Convention be ratified without derogations affecting this equivalence;

HAVE AGREED AS FOLLOWS:

Article 1 The Offence of Bribery of Foreign Public Officials

1.   Each Party shall take such measures as may be necessary to establish that it is a criminal offence under its law for any person intentionally to offer, promise or give any undue pecuniary or other advantage, whether directly or through intermediaries, to a foreign public official, for that official or for a third party, in order that the official act or refrain from acting in relation to the performance of official duties, in order to obtain or retain business or other improper advantage in the conduct of international business.

2.   Each Party shall take any measures necessary to establish that complicity in, including incitement, aiding and abetting, or authorisation of an act of bribery of a foreign public official shall be a criminal offence. Attempt and conspiracy to bribe a foreign public official shall be criminal offences to the same extent as attempt and conspiracy to bribe a public official of that Party.

---

1   See http://www.oecd.org/corruption/oecdantibriberyconvention.htm.

3.   The offences set out in paragraphs 1 and 2 above are hereinafter referred to as "bribery of a foreign public official".

4.   For the purpose of this Convention:

a)   "foreign public official" means any person holding a legislative, administrative or judicial office of a foreign country, whether appointed or elected; any person exercising a public function for a foreign country, including for a public agency or public enterprise; and any official or agent of a public international organisation;

b)   "foreign country" includes all levels and subdivisions of government, from national to local;

c)   "act or refrain from acting in relation to the performance of official duties" includes any use of the public official's position, whether or not within the official's authorised competence.

Article 2 Responsibility of Legal Persons

Each Party shall take such measures as may be necessary, in accordance with its legal principles, to establish the liability of legal persons for the bribery of a foreign public official.

Article 3 Sanctions

1.   The bribery of a foreign public official shall be punishable by effective, proportionate and dissuasive criminal penalties. The range of penalties shall be comparable to that applicable to the bribery of the Party's own public officials and shall, in the case of natural persons, include deprivation of liberty sufficient to enable effective mutual legal assistance and extradition.

2.   In the event that, under the legal system of a Party, criminal responsibility is not applicable to legal persons, that Party shall ensure that legal persons shall be subject to effective, proportionate and dissuasive non-criminal sanctions, including monetary sanctions, for bribery of foreign public officials.

3.   Each Party shall take such measures as may be necessary to provide that the bribe and the proceeds of the bribery of a foreign public official, or property the value of which corresponds to that of such proceeds, are subject to seizure and confiscation or that monetary sanctions of comparable effect are applicable.

4.   Each Party shall consider the imposition of additional civil or administrative sanctions upon a person subject to sanctions for the bribery of a foreign public official.

Article 4 Jurisdiction

1.   Each Party shall take such measures as may be necessary to establish its jurisdiction over the bribery of a foreign public official when the offence is committed in whole or in part in its territory.

2.   Each Party which has jurisdiction to prosecute its nationals for offences committed abroad shall take such measures as may be necessary to establish its jurisdiction to do so in respect of the bribery of a foreign public official, according to the same principles.

3.   When more than one Party has jurisdiction over an alleged offence described in this Convention, the Parties involved shall, at the request of one of them, consult with a view to determining the most appropriate jurisdiction for prosecution.

4.   Each Party shall review whether its current basis for jurisdiction is effective in the fight against the bribery of foreign public officials and, if it is not, shall take remedial steps.

Article 5 Enforcement

Investigation and prosecution of the bribery of a foreign public official shall be subject to the applicable rules and principles of each Party. They shall not be influenced by considerations of national economic interest, the potential effect upon relations with another State or the identity of the natural or legal persons involved.

Article 6 Statute of Limitations

Any statute of limitations applicable to the offence of bribery of a foreign public official shall allow an adequate period of time for the investigation and prosecution of this offence.

Article 7 Money Laundering

Each Party which has made bribery of its own public official a predicate offence for the purpose of the application of its money laundering legislation shall do so on the same terms for the bribery of a foreign public official, without regard to the place where the bribery occurred.

Article 8 Accounting

1.   In order to combat bribery of foreign public officials effectively, each Party shall take such measures as may be necessary, within the framework of its laws and regulations regarding the maintenance of books and records, financial statement disclosures, and accounting and auditing standards, to prohibit the establishment of off-the-books accounts, the making of off-the-books or inadequately identified transactions, the recording of non-existent expenditures, the entry of liabilities with incorrect identification of their object, as well as the use of false documents, by companies subject to those laws and regulations, for the purpose of bribing foreign public officials or of hiding such bribery.

2.   Each Party shall provide effective, proportionate and dissuasive civil, administrative or criminal penalties for such omissions and falsifications in respect of the books, records, accounts and financial statements of such companies.

Article 9 Mutual Legal Assistance

1.   Each Party shall, to the fullest extent possible under its laws and relevant treaties and arrangements, provide prompt and effective legal assistance to another Party for the purpose of criminal investigations and proceedings brought by a Party concerning offences within the scope of this Convention and for non-criminal proceedings within the scope of this Convention brought by a Party against a legal person. The requested Party shall inform the requesting Party, without delay, of any additional information or documents needed to support the request for assistance and, where requested, of the status and outcome of the request for assistance.

2.   Where a Party makes mutual legal assistance conditional upon the existence of dual criminality, dual criminality shall be deemed to exist if the offence for which the assistance is sought is within the scope of this Convention.

3.   A Party shall not decline to render mutual legal assistance for criminal matters within the scope of this Convention on the ground of bank secrecy.

Article 10 Extradition

1.   Bribery of a foreign public official shall be deemed to be included as an extraditable offence under the laws of the Parties and the extradition treaties between them.

2.   If a Party which makes extradition conditional on the existence of an extradition treaty receives a request for extradition from another Party with which it has no extradition treaty, it may consider this Convention to be the legal basis for extradition in respect of the offence of bribery of a foreign public official.

3.   Each Party shall take any measures necessary to assure either that it can extradite its nationals or that it can prosecute its nationals for the offence of bribery of a foreign public official.

A Party which declines a request to extradite a person for bribery of a foreign public official solely on the ground that the person is its national shall submit the case to its competent authorities for the purpose of prosecution.

4.   Extradition for bribery of a foreign public official is subject to the conditions set out in the domestic law and applicable treaties and arrangements of each Party. Where a Party makes extradition conditional upon the existence of dual criminality, that condition shall be deemed to be fulfilled if the offence for which extradition is sought is within the scope of Article 1 of this Convention.

Article 11 Responsible Authorities

For the purposes of Article 4, paragraph 3, on consultation, Article 9, on mutual legal assistance and Article 10, on extradition, each Party shall notify to the Secretary- General of the OECD an authority or authorities responsible for making and receiving requests, which shall serve as channel of communication for these matters for that Party, without prejudice to other arrange-ments between Parties.

Article 12 Monitoring and Follow-up

The Parties shall co-operate in carrying out a programme of systematic follow-up to monitor and promote the full implementation of this Convention. Unless otherwise decided by consensus of the Parties, this shall be done in the framework of the OECD Working Group on Bribery in International Business Transactions and according to its terms of reference, or within the framework and terms of reference of any successor to its functions, and Parties shall bear the costs of the programme in accordance with the rules applicable to that body.

Article 13 Signature and Accession

1.   Until its entry into force, this Convention shall be open for signature by OECD Members and by Non-Members which have been invited to become full participants in its Working Group on Bribery in International Business Transactions.

2.   Subsequent to its entry into force, this Convention shall be open to accession by any non-signatory which is a member of the OECD or has become a full participant in the Working Group on Bribery in International Business Transactions or any successor to its functions. For each such non-signatory, the Convention shall enter into force on the sixtieth day following the date of deposit of its instrument of accession.

Article 14 Ratification and Depositary

1.   This Convention is subject to acceptance, approval or ratification by the Signatories, in accor-dance with their respective laws.

2.   Instruments of acceptance, approval, ratification or accession shall be deposited with the Secretary-General of the OECD, who shall serve as Depositary of this Convention.

Article 15 Entry into Force

1.   This Convention shall enter into force on the sixtieth day following the date upon which five of the ten countries which have the ten largest export shares set out in DAFFE/IME/BR (97)18/FINAL, and which represent by themselves at least sixty per cent of the combined total exports of those ten countries, have deposited their instruments of acceptance, approval, or ratification. For each signatory depositing its instrument after such entry into force, the Con-vention shall enter into force on the sixtieth day after deposit of its instrument.

2.   If, after 31 December 1998, the Convention has not entered into force under paragraph 1 above, any signatory which has deposited its instrument of acceptance, approval or ratification may declare in writing to the Depositary its readiness to accept entry into force of this Con-vention under this paragraph 2. The Convention shall enter into force for such a signatory on the sixtieth day following the date upon which such declarations have been deposited by at least

two signatories. For each signatory depositing its declaration after such entry into force, the Convention shall enter into force on the sixtieth day following the date of deposit.

Article 16 Amendment

Any Party may propose the amendment of this Convention. A proposed amendment shall be submitted to the Depositary which shall communicate it to the other Parties at least sixty days before convening a meeting of the Parties to consider the proposed amendment. An amendment adopted by consensus of the Parties, or by such other means as the Parties may determine by consensus, shall enter into force sixty days after the deposit of an instrument of ratification, acceptance or approval by all of the Parties, or in such other circumstances as may be specified by the Parties at the time of adoption of the amendment.

Article 17 Withdrawal

A Party may withdraw from this Convention by submitting written notification to the Depositary. Such withdrawal shall be effective one year after the date of the receipt of the notification. After withdrawal, co-operation shall continue between the Parties and the Party which has withdrawn on all requests for assistance or extradition made before the effective date of withdrawal which remain pending.

X.5. 2000 UN GLOBAL COMPACT[1]

Millennium Development Goals

Human Rights

Principle 1: Businesses should support and respect the protection of internationally proclaimed human rights; and

Principle 2: make sure that they are not complicit in human rights abuses.

Labour

Principle 3: Businesses should uphold the freedom of association and the effective recognition of the right to collective bargaining;

Principle 4: the elimination of all forms of forced and compulsory labour;

Principle 5: the effective abolition of child labour; and

Principle 6: the elimination of discrimination in respect of employment and occupation.

Environment

Principle 7: Businesses should support a precautionary approach to environmental challenges;

Principle 8: undertake initiatives to promote greater environmental responsibility; and

Principle 9: encourage the development and diffusion of environmentally friendly technologies.

Anti-Corruption

Principle 10: Businesses should work against corruption in all its forms, including extortion and bribery.

Sustainable Development Goals

No Poverty

Goal 1. End poverty in all its forms everywhere

Zero Hunger

Goal 2. End hunger, achieve food security and improved nutrition and promote sustainable agriculture

Good Health and Well-Being

Goal 3. Ensure healthy lives and promote well-being for all at all ages

Quality Education

Goal 4. Ensure inclusive and equitable quality education and promote lifelong learning opportunities for all

Gender Equality

Goal 5. Achieve gender equality and empower all women and girls

Clean Water and Sanitation

Goal 6. Ensure availability and sustainable management of water and sanitation for all

Affordable and Clean Energy

Goal 7. Ensure access to affordable, reliable, sustainable and modern energy for all

---

1   See https://www.unglobalcompact.org/what-is-gc/mission/principles and
     https://www.unglobalcompact.org/sdgs.

Decent Work and Economic Growth

Goal 8. Promote sustained, inclusive and sustainable economic growth, full and productive employment and decent work for all

Industry, Innovation, and Infrastructure

Goal 9. Build resilient infrastructure, promote inclusive and sustainable industrialization and foster innovation

Reduced Inequalities

Goal 10. Reduce inequality within and among countries

Sustainable Cities and Communities

Goal 11. Make cities and human settlements inclusive, safe, resilient and sustainable

Responsible Consumption and Production

Goal 12. Ensure sustainable consumption and production patterns

Climate Action

Goal 13. Take urgent action to combat climate change and its impacts

Life Below Water

Goal 14. Conserve and sustainably use the oceans, seas and marine resources for sustainable development

Life on Land

Goal 15. Protect, restore and promote sustainable use of terrestrial ecosystems, sustainably manage forests, combat desertification, and halt and reverse land degradation and halt biodiversity loss

Peace and Justice, Strong Institutions

Goal 16. Promote peaceful and inclusive societies for sustainable development, provide access to justice for all and build effective, accountable and inclusive institutions at all levels

Partnerships for the Goals

Goal 17. Strengthen the means of implementation and revitalize the global partnership for sustainable development

X.6. 2005 UN CONVENTION AGAINST CORRUPTION[1]

Preamble

The States Parties to this Convention,

Concerned about the seriousness of problems and threats posed by corruption to the stability and security of societies, undermining the institutions and values of democracy, ethical values and justice and jeopardizing sustainable development and the rule of law,

Concerned also about the links between corruption and other forms of crime, in particular organized crime and economic crime, including money-laundering,

Concerned further about cases of corruption that involve vast quantities of assets, which may constitute a substantial proportion of the resources of States, and that threaten the political stability and sustainable development of those States,

Convinced that corruption is no longer a local matter but a transnational phenomenon that affects all societies and economies, making international cooperation to prevent and control it essential,

Convinced also that a comprehensive and multidisciplinary approach is required to prevent and combat corruption effectively,

Convinced further that the availability of technical assistance can play an important role in enhancing the ability of States, including by strengthening capacity and by institution-building, to prevent and combat corruption effectively,

Convinced that the illicit acquisition of personal wealth can be particularly damaging to democratic institutions, national economies and the rule of law,

Determined to prevent, detect and deter in a more effective manner international transfers of illicitly acquired assets and to strengthen international cooperation in asset recovery,

Acknowledging the fundamental principles of due process of law in criminal proceedings and in civil or administrative proceedings to adjudicate property rights,

Bearing in mind that the prevention and eradication of corruption is a responsibility of all States and that they must cooperate with one another, with the support and involvement of individuals and groups outside the public sector, such as civil society, non- governmental organizations and community-based organizations, if their efforts in this area are to be effective,

Bearing also in mind the principles of proper management of public affairs and public property, fairness, responsibility and equality before the law and the need to safeguard integrity and to foster a culture of rejection of corruption,

Commending the work of the Commission on Crime Prevention and Criminal Justice and the United Nations Office on Drugs and Crime in preventing and combating corruption,

Recalling the work carried out by other international and regional organizations in this field, including the activities of the African Union, the Council of Europe, the Customs Cooperation Council (also known as the World Customs Organization), the European Union, the League of Arab States, the Organisation for Economic Cooperation and Development and the Organization of American States,

---

1   See https://www.unodc.org/unodc/en/corruption/index.html?ref=menuside. As of 15 August 2018, the Convention has been ratified by 186 countries. The only exceptions are Barbados, Eritrea, North Korea, Samoa, Somalia, St. Vincent and the Grenadines, Suriname, Syria, and Tonga.

Taking note with appreciation of multilateral instruments to prevent and combat corruption, including, inter alia, the Inter-American Convention against Corruption, adopted by the Organization of American States on 29 March 1996, the Convention on the Fight against Corruption involving Officials of the European Communities or Officials of Member States of the European Union, adopted by the Council of the European Union on 26 May 1997, the Convention on Combating Bribery of Foreign Public Officials in International Business Transactions, adopted by the Organisation for Economic Cooperation and Development on 21 November 1997, the Criminal Law Convention on Corruption, adopted by the Committee of Ministers of the Council of Europe on 27 January 1999, the Civil Law Convention on Corruption, adopted by the Committee of Ministers of the Council of Europe on 4 November 1999, and the African Union Convention on Preventing and Combating Corruption, adopted by the Heads of State and Government of the African Union on 12 July 2003,

Welcoming the entry into force on 29 September 2003 of the United Nations Convention against Transnational Organized Crime,

Have agreed as follows:

Chapter I – General Provisions

Article 1. Statement of Purpose

The purposes of this Convention are:

(a) To promote and strengthen measures to prevent and combat corruption more efficiently and effectively;

(b) To promote, facilitate and support international cooperation and technical assistance in the prevention of and fight against corruption, including in asset recovery;

(c) To promote integrity, accountability and proper management of public affairs and public property.

Article 2. Use of Terms

For the purposes of this Convention:

(a) "Public official" shall mean: (i) any person holding a legislative, executive, administrative or judicial office of a State Party, whether appointed or elected, whether permanent or temporary, whether paid or unpaid, irrespective of that person's seniority; (ii) any other person who performs a public function, including for a public agency or public enterprise, or provides a public service, as defined in the domestic law of the State Party and as applied in the pertinent area of law of that State Party; (iii) any other person defined as a "public official" in the domestic law of a State Party. However, for the purpose of some specific measures contained in chapter II of this Convention, "public official" may mean any person who performs a public function or provides a public service as defined in the domestic law of the State Party and as applied in the pertinent area of law of that State Party;

(b) "Foreign public official" shall mean any person holding a legislative, executive, administrative or judicial office of a foreign country, whether appointed or elected; and any person exercising a public function for a foreign country, including for a public agency or public enterprise;

(c) "Official of a public international organization" shall mean an international civil servant or any person who is authorized by such an organization to act on behalf of that organization;

(d) "Property" shall mean assets of every kind, whether corporeal or incorporeal, movable or immovable, tangible or intangible, and legal documents or instruments evidencing title to or interest in such assets;

(e) "Proceeds of crime" shall mean any property derived from or obtained, directly or indirectly, through the commission of an offence;

(f) "Freezing" or "seizure" shall mean temporarily prohibiting the transfer, conversion, disposition or movement of property or temporarily assuming custody or control of property on the basis of an order issued by a court or other competent authority;

(g) "Confiscation", which includes forfeiture where applicable, shall mean the permanent deprivation of property by order of a court or other competent authority;

(h) "Predicate offence" shall mean any offence as a result of which proceeds have been generated that may become the subject of an offence as defined in article 23 of this Convention;

(i) "Controlled delivery" shall mean the technique of allowing illicit or suspect consignments to pass out of, through or into the territory of one or more States, with the knowledge and under the supervision of their competent authorities, with a view to the investigation of an offence and the identification of persons involved in the commission of the offence.

Article 3. Scope of Application

1.   This Convention shall apply, in accordance with its terms, to the prevention, investigation and prosecution of corruption and to the freezing, seizure, confiscation and return of the proceeds of offences established in accordance with this Convention.

2.   For the purposes of implementing this Convention, it shall not be necessary, except as otherwise stated herein, for the offences set forth in it to result in damage or harm to state property.

Article 4. Protection of Sovereignty

1.   States Parties shall carry out their obligations under this Convention in a manner consistent with the principles of sovereign equality and territorial integrity of States and that of non-intervention in the domestic affairs of other States.

2.   Nothing in this Convention shall entitle a State Party to undertake in the territory of another State the exercise of jurisdiction and performance of functions that are reserved exclusively for the authorities of that other State by its domestic law.

Chapter II – Preventive Measures

Article 5. Preventive Anti-Corruption Policies and Practices

1.   Each State Party shall, in accordance with the fundamental principles of its legal system, develop and implement or maintain effective, coordinated anti-corruption policies that promote the participation of society and reflect the principles of the rule of law, proper management of public affairs and public property, integrity, transparency and accountability.

2.   Each State Party shall endeavour to establish and promote effective practices aimed at the prevention of corruption.

3.   Each State Party shall endeavour to periodically evaluate relevant legal instruments and administrative measures with a view to determining their adequacy to prevent and fight corruption.

4.   States Parties shall, as appropriate and in accordance with the fundamental principles of their legal system, collaborate with each other and with relevant international and regional organizations in promoting and developing the measures referred to in this article. That collaboration may include participation in international programmes and projects aimed at the prevention of corruption.

Article 6. Preventive Anti-Corruption Body or Bodies

1.   Each State Party shall, in accordance with the fundamental principles of its legal system, ensure the existence of a body or bodies, as appropriate, that prevent corruption by such means as:

(a) Implementing the policies referred to in article 5 of this Convention and, where appropriate, overseeing and coordinating the implementation of those policies;

(b) Increasing and disseminating knowledge about the prevention of corruption.

2. Each State Party shall grant the body or bodies referred to in paragraph 1 of this article the necessary independence, in accordance with the fundamental principles of its legal system, to enable the body or bodies to carry out its or their functions effectively and free from any undue influence. The necessary material resources and specialized staff, as well as the training that such staff may require to carry out their functions, should be provided.

3. Each State Party shall inform the Secretary-General of the United Nations of the name and address of the authority or authorities that may assist other States Parties in developing and implementing specific measures for the prevention of corruption.

Article 7. Public Sector

1. Each State Party shall, where appropriate and in accordance with the fundamental principles of its legal system, endeavour to adopt, maintain and strengthen systems for the recruitment, hiring, retention, promotion and retirement of civil servants and, where appropriate, other non-elected public officials:

(a) That are based on principles of efficiency, transparency and objective criteria such as merit, equity and aptitude;

(b) That include adequate procedures for the selection and training of individuals for public positions considered especially vulnerable to corruption and the rotation, where appropriate, of such individuals to other positions;

(c) That promote adequate remuneration and equitable pay scales, taking into account the level of economic development of the State Party;

(d) That promote education and training programmes to enable them to meet the requirements for the correct, honourable and proper performance of public functions and that provide them with specialized and appropriate training to enhance their awareness of the risks of corruption inherent in the performance of their functions. Such programmes may make reference to codes or standards of conduct in applicable areas.

2. Each State Party shall also consider adopting appropriate legislative and administrative measures, consistent with the objectives of this Convention and in accordance with the fundamental principles of its domestic law, to prescribe criteria concerning candidature for and election to public office.

3. Each State Party shall also consider taking appropriate legislative and administrative measures, consistent with the objectives of this Convention and in accordance with the fundamental principles of its domestic law, to enhance transparency in the funding of candidatures for elected public office and, where applicable, the funding of political parties.

4. Each State Party shall, in accordance with the fundamental principles of its domestic law, endeavour to adopt, maintain and strengthen systems that promote transparency and prevent conflicts of interest.

Article 8. Codes of Conduct for Public Officials

1. In order to fight corruption, each State Party shall promote, inter alia, integrity, honesty and responsibility among its public officials, in accordance with the fundamental principles of its legal system.

2. In particular, each State Party shall endeavour to apply, within its own institutional and legal systems, codes or standards of conduct for the correct, honourable and proper performance of public functions.

3.   For the purposes of implementing the provisions of this article, each State Party shall, where appropriate and in accordance with the fundamental principles of its legal system, take note of the relevant initiatives of regional, interregional and multilateral organizations, such as the International Code of Conduct for Public Officials contained in the annex to General Assembly resolution 51/59 of 12 December 1996.

4.   Each State Party shall also consider, in accordance with the fundamental principles of its domestic law, establishing measures and systems to facilitate the reporting by public officials of acts of corruption to appropriate authorities, when such acts come to their notice in the performance of their functions.

5.   Each State Party shall endeavour, where appropriate and in accordance with the fundamental principles of its domestic law, to establish measures and systems requiring public officials to make declarations to appropriate authorities regarding, inter alia, their outside activities, employment, investments, assets and substantial gifts or benefits from which a conflict of interest may result with respect to their functions as public officials.

6.   Each State Party shall consider taking, in accordance with the fundamental principles of its domestic law, disciplinary or other measures against public officials who violate the codes or standards established in accordance with this article.

Article 9. Public Procurement and Management of Public Finances

1.   Each State Party shall, in accordance with the fundamental principles of its legal system, take the necessary steps to establish appropriate systems of procurement, based on transparency, competition and objective criteria in decision-making, that are effective, inter alia, in preventing corruption. Such systems, which may take into account appropriate threshold values in their application, shall address, inter alia:

(a)   The public distribution of information relating to procurement procedures and contracts, including information on invitations to tender and relevant or pertinent information on the award of contracts, allowing potential tenderers sufficient time to prepare and submit their tenders;

(b)   The establishment, in advance, of conditions for participation, including selection and award criteria and tendering rules, and their publication;

(c)   The use of objective and predetermined criteria for public procurement decisions, in order to facilitate the subsequent verification of the correct application of the rules or procedures;

(d)   An effective system of domestic review, including an effective system of appeal, to ensure legal recourse and remedies in the event that the rules or procedures established pursuant to this paragraph are not followed;

(e)   Where appropriate, measures to regulate matters regarding personnel responsible for procurement, such as declaration of interest in particular public procurements, screening procedures and training requirements.

2.   Each State Party shall, in accordance with the fundamental principles of its legal system, take appropriate measures to promote transparency and accountability in the management of public finances. Such measures shall encompass, inter alia:

(a)   Procedures for the adoption of the national budget;

(b)   Timely reporting on revenue and expenditure;

(c)   A system of accounting and auditing standards and related oversight;

(d)   Effective and efficient systems of risk management and internal control; and

(e)   Where appropriate, corrective action in the case of failure to comply with the requirements established in this paragraph.

3.   Each State Party shall take such civil and administrative measures as may be necessary, in accordance with the fundamental principles of its domestic law, to preserve the integrity of accounting books, records, financial statements or other documents related to public expenditure and revenue and to prevent the falsification of such documents.

Article 10. Public Reporting

Taking into account the need to combat corruption, each State Party shall, in accordance with the fundamental principles of its domestic law, take such measures as may be necessary to enhance transparency in its public administration, including with regard to its organization, functioning and decision-making processes, where appropriate. Such measures may include, inter alia:

(a) Adopting procedures or regulations allowing members of the general public to obtain, where appropriate, information on the organization, functioning and decision-making processes of its public administration and, with due regard for the protection of privacy and personal data, on decisions and legal acts that concern members of the public;

(b) Simplifying administrative procedures, where appropriate, in order to facilitate public access to the competent decision-making authorities; and

(c) Publishing information, which may include periodic reports on the risks of corruption in its public administration.

Article 11. Measures Relating to the Judiciary and Prosecution Services

1.   Bearing in mind the independence of the judiciary and its crucial role in combating corruption, each State Party shall, in accordance with the fundamental principles of its legal system and without prejudice to judicial independence, take measures to strengthen integrity and to prevent opportunities for corruption among members of the judiciary. Such measures may include rules with respect to the conduct of members of the judiciary.

2.   Measures to the same effect as those taken pursuant to paragraph 1 of this article may be introduced and applied within the prosecution service in those States Parties where it does not form part of the judiciary but enjoys independence similar to that of the judicial service.

Article 12. Private Sector

1.   Each State Party shall take measures, in accordance with the fundamental principles of its domestic law, to prevent corruption involving the private sector, enhance accounting and auditing standards in the private sector and, where appropriate, provide effective, proportionate and dissuasive civil, administrative or criminal penalties for failure to comply with such measures.

2.   Measures to achieve these ends may include, inter alia:

(a) Promoting cooperation between law enforcement agencies and relevant private entities;

(b) Promoting the development of standards and procedures designed to safeguard the integrity of relevant private entities, including codes of conduct for the correct, honourable and proper performance of the activities of business and all relevant professions and the prevention of conflicts of interest, and for the promotion of the use of good commercial practices among businesses and in the contractual relations of businesses with the State;

(c) Promoting transparency among private entities, including, where appropriate, measures regarding the identity of legal and natural persons involved in the establishment and management of corporate entities;

(d) Preventing the misuse of procedures regulating private entities, including procedures regarding subsidies and licences granted by public authorities for commercial activities;

(e) Preventing conflicts of interest by imposing restrictions, as appropriate and for a reasonable period of time, on the professional activities of former public officials or on the employment of public officials by the private sector after their resignation or retirement, where such activities or employment relate directly to the functions held or supervised by those public officials during their tenure;

(f) Ensuring that private enterprises, taking into account their structure and size, have sufficient internal auditing controls to assist in preventing and detecting acts of corruption and that the accounts and required financial statements of such private enterprises are subject to appropriate auditing and certification procedures.

3.   In order to prevent corruption, each State Party shall take such measures as may be necessary, in accordance with its domestic laws and regulations regarding the maintenance of books and records, financial statement disclosures and accounting and auditing standards, to prohibit the following acts carried out for the purpose of committing any of the offences established in accordance with this Convention:

(a) The establishment of off-the-books accounts;

(b) The making of off-the-books or inadequately identified transactions;

(c) The recording of non-existent expenditure;

(d) The entry of liabilities with incorrect identification of their objects;

(e) The use of false documents; and

(f) The intentional destruction of bookkeeping documents earlier than foreseen by the law.

4.   Each State Party shall disallow the tax deductibility of expenses that constitute bribes, the latter being one of the constituent elements of the offences established in accordance with articles 15 and 16 of this Convention and, where appropriate, other expenses incurred in furtherance of corrupt conduct.

Article 13. Participation of Society

1.   Each State Party shall take appropriate measures, within its means and in accordance with fundamental principles of its domestic law, to promote the active participation of individuals and groups outside the public sector, such as civil society, non-governmental organizations and community-based organizations, in the prevention of and the fight against corruption and to raise public awareness regarding the existence, causes and gravity of and the threat posed by corruption. This participation should be strengthened by such measures as:

(a) Enhancing the transparency of and promoting the contribution of the public to decision-making processes;

(b) Ensuring that the public has effective access to information;

(c) Undertaking public information activities that contribute to non-tolerance of corruption, as well as public education programmes, including school and university curricula;

(d) Respecting, promoting and protecting the freedom to seek, receive, publish and disseminate information concerning corruption. That freedom may be subject to certain restrictions, but these shall only be such as are provided for by law and are necessary:

(i)   For respect of the rights or reputations of others;

(ii) For the protection of national security or ordre public or of public health or morals.

2.   Each State Party shall take appropriate measures to ensure that the relevant anti-corruption bodies referred to in this Convention are known to the public and shall provide access to such bodies, where appropriate, for the reporting, including anonymously, of any incidents that may be considered to constitute an offence established in accordance with this Convention.

Article 14. Measures to Prevent Money-Laundering

1. Each State Party shall:

(a) Institute a comprehensive domestic regulatory and supervisory regime for banks and non-bank financial institutions, including natural or legal persons that provide formal or informal services for the transmission of money or value and, where appropriate, other bodies particularly susceptible to moneylaundering, within its competence, in order to deter and detect all forms of money-laundering, which regime shall emphasize requirements for customer and, where appropriate, beneficial owner identification, record-keeping and the reporting of suspicious transactions;

(b) Without prejudice to article 46 of this Convention, ensure that administrative, regulatory, law enforcement and other authorities dedicated to combating money- laundering (including, where appropriate under domestic law, judicial authorities) have the ability to cooperate and exchange information at the national and international levels within the conditions prescribed by its domestic law and, to that end, shall consider the establishment of a financial intelligence unit to serve as a national centre for the collection, analysis and dissemination of information regarding potential money-laundering.

2. States Parties shall consider implementing feasible measures to detect and monitor the movement of cash and appropriate negotiable instruments across their borders, subject to safe-guards to ensure proper use of information and without impeding in any way the movement of legitimate capital. Such measures may include a requirement that individuals and businesses report the cross-border transfer of substantial quantities of cash and appropriate negotiable instruments.

3. States Parties shall consider implementing appropriate and feasible measures to require financial institutions, including money remitters:

(a) To include on forms for the electronic transfer of funds and related messages accurate and meaningful information on the originator;

(b) To maintain such information throughout the payment chain; and

(c) To apply enhanced scrutiny to transfers of funds that do not contain complete information on the originator.

4. In establishing a domestic regulatory and supervisory regime under the terms of this article, and without prejudice to any other article of this Convention, States Parties are called upon to use as a guideline the relevant initiatives of regional, interregional and multilateral organizations against money-laundering.

5. States Parties shall endeavour to develop and promote global, regional, subregional and bilateral cooperation among judicial, law enforcement and financial regulatory authorities in order to combat money-laundering.

Chapter III – Criminalization and Law Enforcement

Article 15. Bribery of National Public Officials

Each State Party shall adopt such legislative and other measures as may be necessary to establish as criminal offences, when committed intentionally:

(a) The promise, offering or giving, to a public official, directly or indirectly, of an undue advantage, for the official himself or herself or another person or entity, in order that the official act or refrain from acting in the exercise of his or her official duties;

(b) The solicitation or acceptance by a public official, directly or indirectly, of an undue advantage, for the official himself or herself or another person or entity, in order that the official act or refrain from acting in the exercise of his or her official duties.

Article 16. Bribery of Foreign Public Officials and Officials of Public International Organizations

1.   Each State Party shall adopt such legislative and other measures as may be necessary to establish as a criminal offence, when committed intentionally, the promise, offering or giving to a foreign public official or an official of a public international organization, directly or indirectly, of an undue advantage, for the official himself or herself or another person or entity, in order that the official act or refrain from acting in the exercise of his or her official duties, in order to obtain or retain business or other undue advantage in relation to the conduct of international business.

2.   Each State Party shall consider adopting such legislative and other measures as may be necessary to establish as a criminal offence, when committed intentionally, the solicitation or acceptance by a foreign public official or an official of a public international organization, directly or indirectly, of an undue advantage, for the official himself or herself or another person or entity, in order that the official act or refrain from acting in the exercise of his or her official duties.

Article 17. Embezzlement, Misappropriation or Other Diversion of Property by a Public Official

Each State Party shall adopt such legislative and other measures as may be necessary to establish as criminal offences, when committed intentionally, the embezzlement, misappropriation or other diversion by a public official for his or her benefit or for the benefit of another person or entity, of any property, public or private funds or securities or any other thing of value entrusted to the public official by virtue of his or her position.

Article 18. Trading in Influence

Each State Party shall consider adopting such legislative and other measures as may be necessary to establish as criminal offences, when committed intentionally:

(a)   The promise, offering or giving to a public official or any other person, directly or indirectly, of an undue advantage in order that the public official or the person abuse his or her real or supposed influence with a view to obtaining from an administration or public authority of the State Party an undue advantage for the original instigator of the act or for any other person;

(b)   The solicitation or acceptance by a public official or any other person, directly or indirectly, of an undue advantage for himself or herself or for another person in order that the public official or the person abuse his or her real or supposed influence with a view to obtaining from an administration or public authority of the State Party an undue advantage.

Article 19. Abuse of Functions

Each State Party shall consider adopting such legislative and other measures as may be necessary to establish as a criminal offence, when committed intentionally, the abuse of functions or position, that is, the performance of or failure to perform an act, in violation of laws, by a public official in the discharge of his or her functions, for the purpose of obtaining an undue advantage for himself or herself or for another person or entity.

Article 20. Illicit Enrichment

Subject to its constitution and the fundamental principles of its legal system, each State Party shall consider adopting such legislative and other measures as may be necessary to establish as a criminal offence, when committed intentionally, illicit enrichment, that is, a significant increase in the assets of a public official that he or she cannot reasonably explain in relation to his or her lawful income.

Article 21. Bribery in the Private Sector

Each State Party shall consider adopting such legislative and other measures as may be necessary to establish as criminal offences, when committed intentionally in the course of economic, financial or commercial activities:

(a)   The promise, offering or giving, directly or indirectly, of an undue advantage to any person who directs or works, in any capacity, for a private sector entity, for the person himself or herself or for another person, in order that he or she, in breach of his or her duties, act or refrain from acting;

(b)   The solicitation or acceptance, directly or indirectly, of an undue advantage by any person who directs or works, in any capacity, for a private sector entity, for the person himself or herself or for another person, in order that he or she, in breach of his or her duties, act or refrain from acting.

Article 22. Embezzlement of Property in the Private Sector

Each State Party shall consider adopting such legislative and other measures as may be necessary to establish as a criminal offence, when committed intentionally in the course of economic, financial or commercial activities, embezzlement by a person who directs or works, in any capacity, in a private sector entity of any property, private funds or securities or any other thing of value entrusted to him or her by virtue of his or her position.

Article 23. Laundering of Proceeds of Crime

1.   Each State Party shall adopt, in accordance with fundamental principles of its domestic law, such legislative and other measures as may be necessary to establish as criminal offences, when committed intentionally:

(a)   (i)   The conversion or transfer of property, knowing that such property is the proceeds of crime, for the purpose of concealing or disguising the illicit origin of the property or of helping any person who is involved in the commission of the predicate offence to evade the legal consequences of his or her action;

      (ii)   The concealment or disguise of the true nature, source, location, disposition, movement or ownership of or rights with respect to property, knowing that such property is the proceeds of crime;

(b)   Subject to the basic concepts of its legal system:

      (i)   The acquisition, possession or use of property, knowing, at the time of receipt, that such property is the proceeds of crime;

      (ii)   Participation in, association with or conspiracy to commit, attempts to commit and aiding, abetting, facilitating and counselling the commission of any of the offences established in accordance with this article.

2.   For purposes of implementing or applying paragraph 1 of this article:

(a)   Each State Party shall seek to apply paragraph 1 of this article to the widest range of predicate offences;

(b)   Each State Party shall include as predicate offences at a minimum a comprehensive range of criminal offences established in accordance with this Convention;

(c)   For the purposes of subparagraph (b) above, predicate offences shall include offences committed both within and outside the jurisdiction of the State Party in question. However, offences committed outside the jurisdiction of a State Party shall constitute predicate offences only when the relevant conduct is a criminal offence under the domestic law of the State where it is committed and would be a criminal offence under the domestic law of the State Party implementing or applying this article had it been committed there;

(d)   Each State Party shall furnish copies of its laws that give effect to this article and of any subsequent changes to such laws or a description thereof to the Secretary-General of the United Nations;

(e)   If required by fundamental principles of the domestic law of a State Party, it may be pro-vided that the offences set forth in paragraph 1 of this article do not apply to the persons who committed the predicate offence.

Article 24. Concealment

Without prejudice to the provisions of article 23 of this Convention, each State Party shall consider adopting such legislative and other measures as may be necessary to establish as a criminal offence, when committed intentionally after the commission of any of the offences established in accordance with this Convention without having participated in such offences, the concealment or continued retention of property when the person involved knows that such property is the result of any of the offences established in accordance with this Convention.

Article 25. Obstruction of Justice

Each State Party shall adopt such legislative and other measures as may be necessary to establish as criminal offences, when committed intentionally:

(a)   The use of physical force, threats or intimidation or the promise, offering or giving of an undue advantage to induce false testimony or to interfere in the giving of testimony or the production of evidence in a proceeding in relation to the commission of offences established in accordance with this Convention;

(b)   The use of physical force, threats or intimidation to interfere with the exercise of official duties by a justice or law enforcement official in relation to the commission of offences established in accordance with this Convention. Nothing in this subparagraph shall prejudice the right of States Parties to have legislation that protects other categories of public official.

Article 26. Liability of Legal Persons

1.   Each State Party shall adopt such measures as may be necessary, consistent with its legal principles, to establish the liability of legal persons for participation in the offences established in accordance with this Convention.

2.   Subject to the legal principles of the State Party, the liability of legal persons may be criminal, civil or administrative.

3.   Such liability shall be without prejudice to the criminal liability of the natural persons who have committed the offences.

4.   Each State Party shall, in particular, ensure that legal persons held liable in accordance with this article are subject to effective, proportionate and dissuasive criminal or non-criminal sanctions, including monetary sanctions.

Article 27. Participation and Attempt

1.   Each State Party shall adopt such legislative and other measures as may be necessary to establish as a criminal offence, in accordance with its domestic law, participation in any capacity such as an accomplice, assistant or instigator in an offence established in accordance with this Convention.

2.   Each State Party may adopt such legislative and other measures as may be necessary to establish as a criminal offence, in accordance with its domestic law, any attempt to commit an offence established in accordance with this Convention.

3.   Each State Party may adopt such legislative and other measures as may be necessary to establish as a criminal offence, in accordance with its domestic law, the preparation for an offence established in accordance with this Convention.

Article 28. Knowledge, Intent and Purpose as Elements of an Offence

Knowledge, intent or purpose required as an element of an offence established in accordance with this Convention may be inferred from objective factual circumstances.

Article 29. Statute of Limitations

Each State Party shall, where appropriate, establish under its domestic law a long statute of limitations period in which to commence proceedings for any offence established in accordance with this Convention and establish a longer statute of limitations period or provide for the suspension of the statute of limitations where the alleged offender has evaded the administration of justice.

Article 30. Prosecution, Adjudication and Sanctions

1.   Each State Party shall make the commission of an offence established in accordance with this Convention liable to sanctions that take into account the gravity of that offence.

2.   Each State Party shall take such measures as may be necessary to establish or maintain, in accordance with its legal system and constitutional principles, an appropriate balance between any immunities or jurisdictional privileges accorded to its public officials for the performance of their functions and the possibility, when necessary, of effectively investigating, prosecuting and adjudicating offences established in accordance with this Convention.

3.   Each State Party shall endeavour to ensure that any discretionary legal powers under its domestic law relating to the prosecution of persons for offences established in accordance with this Convention are exercised to maximize the effectiveness of law enforcement measures in respect of those offences and with due regard to the need to deter the commission of such offences.

4.   In the case of offences established in accordance with this Convention, each State Party shall take appropriate measures, in accordance with its domestic law and with due regard to the rights of the defence, to seek to ensure that conditions imposed in connection with decisions on release pending trial or appeal take into consideration the need to ensure the presence of the defendant at subsequent criminal proceedings.

5.   Each State Party shall take into account the gravity of the offences concerned when considering the eventuality of early release or parole of persons convicted of such offences.

6.   Each State Party, to the extent consistent with the fundamental principles of its legal system, shall consider establishing procedures through which a public official accused of an offence established in accordance with this Convention may, where appropriate, be removed, suspended or reassigned by the appropriate authority, bearing in mind respect for the principle of the presumption of innocence.

7.   Where warranted by the gravity of the offence, each State Party, to the extent consistent with the fundamental principles of its legal system, shall consider establishing procedures for the disqualification, by court order or any other appropriate means, for a period of time determined by its domestic law, of persons convicted of offences established in accordance with this Convention from:

(a)   Holding public office; and

(b)   Holding office in an enterprise owned in whole or in part by the State.

8.   Paragraph 1 of this article shall be without prejudice to the exercise of disciplinary powers by the competent authorities against civil servants.

9.   Nothing contained in this Convention shall affect the principle that the description of the offences established in accordance with this Convention and of the applicable legal defences or other legal principles controlling the lawfulness of conduct is reserved to the domestic law of a State Party and that such offences shall be prosecuted and punished in accordance with that law.

10.   States Parties shall endeavour to promote the reintegration into society of persons convicted of offences established in accordance with this Convention.

Article 31. Freezing, Seizure and Confiscation

1.   Each State Party shall take, to the greatest extent possible within its domestic legal system, such measures as may be necessary to enable confiscation of:

(a) Proceeds of crime derived from offences established in accordance with this Convention or property the value of which corresponds to that of such proceeds;

(b) Property, equipment or other instrumentalities used in or destined for use in offences established in accordance with this Convention.

2.   Each State Party shall take such measures as may be necessary to enable the identification, tracing, freezing or seizure of any item referred to in paragraph 1 of this article for the purpose of eventual confiscation.

3.   Each State Party shall adopt, in accordance with its domestic law, such legislative and other measures as may be necessary to regulate the administration by the competent authorities of frozen, seized or confiscated property covered in paragraphs 1 and 2 of this article.

4.   If such proceeds of crime have been transformed or converted, in part or in full, into other property, such property shall be liable to the measures referred to in this article instead of the proceeds.

5.   If such proceeds of crime have been intermingled with property acquired from legitimate sources, such property shall, without prejudice to any powers relating to freezing or seizure, be liable to confiscation up to the assessed value of the intermingled proceeds.

6.   Income or other benefits derived from such proceeds of crime, from property into which such proceeds of crime have been transformed or converted or from property with which such proceeds of crime have been intermingled shall also be liable to the measures referred to in this article, in the same manner and to the same extent as proceeds of crime.

7.   For the purpose of this article and article 55 of this Convention, each State Party shall empower its courts or other competent authorities to order that bank, financial or commercial records be made available or seized. A State Party shall not decline to act under the provisions of this paragraph on the ground of bank secrecy.

8.   States Parties may consider the possibility of requiring that an offender demonstrate the lawful origin of such alleged proceeds of crime or other property liable to confiscation, to the extent that such a requirement is consistent with the fundamental principles of their domestic law and with the nature of judicial and other proceedings.

9.   The provisions of this article shall not be so construed as to prejudice the rights of bona fide third parties.

10. Nothing contained in this article shall affect the principle that the measures to which it refers shall be defined and implemented in accordance with and subject to the provisions of the domestic law of a State Party.

Article 32. Protection of Witnesses, Experts and Victims

1.   Each State Party shall take appropriate measures in accordance with its domestic legal system and within its means to provide effective protection from potential retaliation or intimidation for witnesses and experts who give testimony concerning offences established in accordance with this Convention and, as appropriate, for their relatives and other persons close to them.

2.   The measures envisaged in paragraph 1 of this article may include, inter alia, without prejudice to the rights of the defendant, including the right to due process:

(a) Establishing procedures for the physical protection of such persons, such as, to the extent necessary and feasible, relocating them and permitting, where appropriate, non-disclosure or limitations on the disclosure of information concerning the identity and whereabouts of such persons;

(b) Providing evidentiary rules to permit witnesses and experts to give testimony in a manner that ensures the safety of such persons, such as permitting testimony to be given through the use of communications technology such as video or other adequate means.

3. States Parties shall consider entering into agreements or arrangements with other States for the relocation of persons referred to in paragraph 1 of this article.

4. The provisions of this article shall also apply to victims insofar as they are witnesses.

5. Each State Party shall, subject to its domestic law, enable the views and concerns of victims to be presented and considered at appropriate stages of criminal proceedings against offenders in a manner not prejudicial to the rights of the defence.

Article 33. Protection of Reporting Persons

Each State Party shall consider incorporating into its domestic legal system appropriate measures to provide protection against any unjustified treatment for any person who reports in good faith and on reasonable grounds to the competent authorities any facts concerning offences established in accordance with this Convention.

Article 34. Consequences of Acts of Corruption

With due regard to the rights of third parties acquired in good faith, each State Party shall take measures, in accordance with the fundamental principles of its domestic law, to address consequences of corruption. In this context, States Parties may consider corruption a relevant factor in legal proceedings to annul or rescind a contract, withdraw a concession or other similar instrument or take any other remedial action.

Article 35. Compensation for Damage

Each State Party shall take such measures as may be necessary, in accordance with principles of its domestic law, to ensure that entities or persons who have suffered damage as a result of an act of corruption have the right to initiate legal proceedings against those responsible for that damage in order to obtain compensation.

Article 36. Specialized Authorities

Each State Party shall, in accordance with the fundamental principles of its legal system, ensure the existence of a body or bodies or persons specialized in combating corruption through law enforcement. Such body or bodies or persons shall be granted the necessary independence, in accordance with the fundamental principles of the legal system of the State Party, to be able to carry out their functions effectively and without any undue influence. Such persons or staff of such body or bodies should have the appropriate training and resources to carry out their tasks.

Article 37. Cooperation with Law Enforcement Authorities

1. Each State Party shall take appropriate measures to encourage persons who participate or who have participated in the commission of an offence established in accordance with this Convention to supply information useful to competent authorities for investigative and evidentiary purposes and to provide factual, specific help to competent authorities that may contribute to depriving offenders of the proceeds of crime and to recovering such proceeds.

2. Each State Party shall consider providing for the possibility, in appropriate cases, of mitigating punishment of an accused person who provides substantial cooperation in the investigation or prosecution of an offence established in accordance with this Convention.

3. Each State Party shall consider providing for the possibility, in accordance with fundamental principles of its domestic law, of granting immunity from prosecution to a person who provides substantial cooperation in the investigation or prosecution of an offence established in accordance with this Convention.

4. Protection of such persons shall be, mutatis mutandis, as provided for in article 32 of this Convention.

5.   Where a person referred to in paragraph 1 of this article located in one State Party can provide substantial cooperation to the competent authorities of another State Party, the States Parties concerned may consider entering into agreements or arrangements, in accordance with their domestic law, concerning the potential provision by the other State Party of the treatment set forth in paragraphs 2 and 3 of this article.

Article 38. Cooperation Between National Authorities

Each State Party shall take such measures as may be necessary to encourage, in accordance with its domestic law, cooperation between, on the one hand, its public authorities, as well as its public officials, and, on the other hand, its authorities responsible for investigating and prosecuting criminal offences. Such cooperation may include:

(a)   Informing the latter authorities, on their own initiative, where there are reasonable grounds to believe that any of the offences established in accordance with articles 15, 21 and 23 of this Convention has been committed; or

(b)   Providing, upon request, to the latter authorities all necessary information.

Article 39. Cooperation Between National Authorities and the Private Sector

1.   Each State Party shall take such measures as may be necessary to encourage, in accordance with its domestic law, cooperation between national investigating and prosecuting authorities and entities of the private sector, in particular financial institutions, relating to matters involving the commission of offences established in accordance with this Convention.

2.   Each State Party shall consider encouraging its nationals and other persons with a habitual residence in its territory to report to the national investigating and prosecuting authorities the commission of an offence established in accordance with this Convention.

Article 40. Bank Secrecy

Each State Party shall ensure that, in the case of domestic criminal investigations of offences established in accordance with this Convention, there are appropriate mechanisms available within its domestic legal system to overcome obstacles that may arise out of the application of bank secrecy laws.

Article 41. Criminal Record

Each State Party may adopt such legislative or other measures as may be necessary to take into consideration, under such terms as and for the purpose that it deems appropriate, any previous conviction in another State of an alleged offender for the purpose of using such information in criminal proceedings relating to an offence established in accordance with this Convention.

Article 42. Jurisdiction

1.   Each State Party shall adopt such measures as may be necessary to establish its jurisdiction over the offences established in accordance with this Convention when:

(a)   The offence is committed in the territory of that State Party; or

(b)   The offence is committed on board a vessel that is flying the flag of that State Party or an aircraft that is registered under the laws of that State Party at the time that the offence is committed.

2.   Subject to article 4 of this Convention, a State Party may also establish its jurisdiction over any such offence when:

(a)   The offence is committed against a national of that State Party; or

(b)   The offence is committed by a national of that State Party or a stateless person who has his or her habitual residence in its territory; or

(c)   The offence is one of those established in accordance with article 23, paragraph 1 (b) (ii), of this Convention and is committed outside its territory with a view to the commission of an offence established in accordance with article 23, paragraph 1 (a) (i) or (ii) or (b) (i), of this Convention within its territory; or

(d)   The offence is committed against the State Party.

3.   For the purposes of article 44 of this Convention, each State Party shall take such measures as may be necessary to establish its jurisdiction over the offences established in accordance with this Convention when the alleged offender is present in its territory and it does not extradite such person solely on the ground that he or she is one of its nationals.

4.   Each State Party may also take such measures as may be necessary to establish its jurisdiction over the offences established in accordance with this Convention when the alleged offender is present in its territory and it does not extradite him or her.

5.   If a State Party exercising its jurisdiction under paragraph 1 or 2 of this article has been notified, or has otherwise learned, that any other States Parties are conducting an investigation, prosecution or judicial proceeding in respect of the same conduct, the competent authorities of those States Parties shall, as appropriate, consult one another with a view to coordinating their actions.

6.   Without prejudice to norms of general international law, this Convention shall not exclude the exercise of any criminal jurisdiction established by a State Party in accordance with its domestic law.

Chapter IV – International Cooperation

Article 43. International Cooperation

1.   States Parties shall cooperate in criminal matters in accordance with articles 44 to 50 of this Convention. Where appropriate and consistent with their domestic legal system, States Parties shall consider assisting each other in investigations of and proceedings in civil and administrative matters relating to corruption.

2.   In matters of international cooperation, whenever dual criminality is considered a requirement, it shall be deemed fulfilled irrespective of whether the laws of the requested State Party place the offence within the same category of offence or denominate the offence by the same terminology as the requesting State Party, if the conduct underlying the offence for which assistance is sought is a criminal offence under the laws of both States Parties.

Article 44. Extradition

1.   This article shall apply to the offences established in accordance with this Convention where the person who is the subject of the request for extradition is present in the territory of the requested State Party, provided that the offence for which extradition is sought is punishable under the domestic law of both the requesting State Party and the requested State Party.

2.   Notwithstanding the provisions of paragraph 1 of this article, a State Party whose law so permits may grant the extradition of a person for any of the offences covered by this Convention that are not punishable under its own domestic law.

3.   If the request for extradition includes several separate offences, at least one of which is extraditable under this article and some of which are not extraditable by reason of their period of imprisonment but are related to offences established in accordance with this Convention, the requested State Party may apply this article also in respect of those offences.

4.   Each of the offences to which this article applies shall be deemed to be included as an extraditable offence in any extradition treaty existing between States Parties. States Parties undertake to include such offences as extraditable offences in every extradition treaty to be concluded between them. A State Party whose law so permits, in case it uses this Convention as the basis for extradition, shall not consider any of the offences established in accordance with this Convention to be a political offence.

5. If a State Party that makes extradition conditional on the existence of a treaty receives a request for extradition from another State Party with which it has no extradition treaty, it may consider this Convention the legal basis for extradition in respect of any offence to which this article applies.

6. A State Party that makes extradition conditional on the existence of a treaty shall:

(a) At the time of deposit of its instrument of ratification, acceptance or approval of or accession to this Convention, inform the Secretary-General of the United Nations whether it will take this Convention as the legal basis for cooperation on extradition with other States Parties to this Convention; and

(b) If it does not take this Convention as the legal basis for cooperation on extradition, seek, where appropriate, to conclude treaties on extradition with other States Parties to this Convention in order to implement this article.

7. States Parties that do not make extradition conditional on the existence of a treaty shall recognize offences to which this article applies as extraditable offences between themselves.

8. Extradition shall be subject to the conditions provided for by the domestic law of the requested State Party or by applicable extradition treaties, including, inter alia, conditions in relation to the minimum penalty requirement for extradition and the grounds upon which the requested State Party may refuse extradition.

9. States Parties shall, subject to their domestic law, endeavour to expedite extradition procedures and to simplify evidentiary requirements relating thereto in respect of any offence to which this article applies.

10. Subject to the provisions of its domestic law and its extradition treaties, the requested State Party may, upon being satisfied that the circumstances so warrant and are urgent and at the request of the requesting State Party, take a person whose extradition is sought and who is present in its territory into custody or take other appropriate measures to ensure his or her presence at extradition proceedings.

11. A State Party in whose territory an alleged offender is found, if it does not extradite such person in respect of an offence to which this article applies solely on the ground that he or she is one of its nationals, shall, at the request of the State Party seeking extradition, be obliged to submit the case without undue delay to its competent authorities for the purpose of prosecution. Those authorities shall take their decision and conduct their proceedings in the same manner as in the case of any other offence of a grave nature under the domestic law of that State Party. The States Parties concerned shall cooperate with each other, in particular on procedural and evidentiary aspects, to ensure the efficiency of such prosecution.

12. Whenever a State Party is permitted under its domestic law to extradite or otherwise surrender one of its nationals only upon the condition that the person will be returned to that State Party to serve the sentence imposed as a result of the trial or proceedings for which the extradition or surrender of the person was sought and that State Party and the State Party seeking the extradition of the person agree with this option and other terms that they may deem appropriate, such conditional extradition or surrender shall be sufficient to discharge the obligation set forth in paragraph 11 of this article.

13. If extradition, sought for purposes of enforcing a sentence, is refused because the person sought is a national of the requested State Party, the requested State Party shall, if its domestic law so permits and in conformity with the requirements of such law, upon application of the requesting State Party, consider the enforcement of the sentence imposed under the domestic law of the requesting State Party or the remainder thereof.

14. Any person regarding whom proceedings are being carried out in connection with any of the offences to which this article applies shall be guaranteed fair treatment at all stages of the

proceedings, including enjoyment of all the rights and guarantees provided by the domestic law of the State Party in the territory of which that person is present.

15. Nothing in this Convention shall be interpreted as imposing an obligation to extradite if the requested State Party has substantial grounds for believing that the request has been made for the purpose of prosecuting or punishing a person on account of that person's sex, race, religion, nationality, ethnic origin or political opinions or that compliance with the request would cause prejudice to that person's position for any one of these reasons.

16. States Parties may not refuse a request for extradition on the sole ground that the offence is also considered to involve fiscal matters.

17. Before refusing extradition, the requested State Party shall, where appropriate, consult with the requesting State Party to provide it with ample opportunity to present its opinions and to provide information relevant to its allegation.

18. States Parties shall seek to conclude bilateral and multilateral agreements or arrangements to carry out or to enhance the effectiveness of extradition.

Article 45. Transfer of Sentenced Persons

States Parties may consider entering into bilateral or multilateral agreements or arrangements on the transfer to their territory of persons sentenced to imprisonment or other forms of deprivation of liberty for offences established in accordance with this Convention in order that they may complete their sentences there.

Article 46. Mutual Legal Assistance

1. States Parties shall afford one another the widest measure of mutual legal assistance in investigations, prosecutions and judicial proceedings in relation to the offences covered by this Convention.

2. Mutual legal assistance shall be afforded to the fullest extent possible under relevant laws, treaties, agreements and arrangements of the requested State Party with respect to investigations, prosecutions and judicial proceedings in relation to the offences for which a legal person may be held liable in accordance with article 26 of this Convention in the requesting State Party.

3. Mutual legal assistance to be afforded in accordance with this article may be requested for any of the following purposes:

(a) Taking evidence or statements from persons;

(b) Effecting service of judicial documents;

(c) Executing searches and seizures, and freezing;

(d) Examining objects and sites;

(e) Providing information, evidentiary items and expert evaluations;

(f) Providing originals or certified copies of relevant documents and records, including government, bank, financial, corporate or business records;

(g) Identifying or tracing proceeds of crime, property, instrumentalities or other things for evidentiary purposes;

(h) Facilitating the voluntary appearance of persons in the requesting State Party;

(i) Any other type of assistance that is not contrary to the domestic law of the requested State Party;

(j) Identifying, freezing and tracing proceeds of crime in accordance with the provisions of chapter V of this Convention;

(k) The recovery of assets, in accordance with the provisions of chapter V of this Convention.

4.   Without prejudice to domestic law, the competent authorities of a State Party may, without prior request, transmit information relating to criminal matters to a competent authority in another State Party where they believe that such information could assist the authority in undertaking or successfully concluding inquiries and criminal proceedings or could result in a request formulated by the latter State Party pursuant to this Convention.

5.   The transmission of information pursuant to paragraph 4 of this article shall be without prejudice to inquiries and criminal proceedings in the State of the competent authorities providing the information. The competent authorities receiving the information shall comply with a request that said information remain confidential, even temporarily, or with restrictions on its use. However, this shall not prevent the receiving State Party from disclosing in its proceedings information that is exculpatory to an accused person. In such a case, the receiving State Party shall notify the transmitting State Party prior to the disclosure and, if so requested, consult with the transmitting State Party. If, in an exceptional case, advance notice is not possible, the receiving State Party shall inform the transmitting State Party of the disclosure without delay.

6.   The provisions of this article shall not affect the obligations under any other treaty, bilateral or multilateral, that governs or will govern, in whole or in part, mutual legal assistance.

7.   Paragraphs 9 to 29 of this article shall apply to requests made pursuant to this article if the States Parties in question are not bound by a treaty of mutual legal assistance. If those States Parties are bound by such a treaty, the corresponding provisions of that treaty shall apply unless the States Parties agree to apply paragraphs 9 to 29 of this article in lieu thereof. States Parties are strongly encouraged to apply those paragraphs if they facilitate cooperation.

8.   States Parties shall not decline to render mutual legal assistance pursuant to this article on the ground of bank secrecy.

9.   (a) A requested State Party, in responding to a request for assistance pursuant to this article in the absence of dual criminality, shall take into account the purposes of this Convention, as set forth in article 1;

(b)   States Parties may decline to render assistance pursuant to this article on the ground of absence of dual criminality. However, a requested State Party shall, where consistent with the basic concepts of its legal system, render assistance that does not involve coercive action. Such assistance may be refused when requests involve matters of a de minimis nature or matters for which the cooperation or assistance sought is available under other provisions of this Convention;

(c)   Each State Party may consider adopting such measures as may be necessary to enable it to provide a wider scope of assistance pursuant to this article in the absence of dual criminality.

10.   A person who is being detained or is serving a sentence in the territory of one State Party whose presence in another State Party is requested for purposes of identification, testimony or otherwise providing assistance in obtaining evidence for investigations, prosecutions or judicial proceedings in relation to offences covered by this Convention may be transferred if the following conditions are met:

(a)   The person freely gives his or her informed consent;

(b)   The competent authorities of both States Parties agree, subject to such conditions as those States Parties may deem appropriate.

11.   For the purposes of paragraph 10 of this article:

(a)   The State Party to which the person is transferred shall have the authority and obligation to keep the person transferred in custody, unless otherwise requested or authorized by the State Party from which the person was transferred;

(b)   The State Party to which the person is transferred shall without delay implement its obligation to return the person to the custody of the State Party from which the person was transferred as agreed beforehand, or as otherwise agreed, by the competent authorities of both States Parties;

(c) The State Party to which the person is transferred shall not require the State Party from which the person was transferred to initiate extradition proceedings for the return of the person;

(d) The person transferred shall receive credit for service of the sentence being served in the State from which he or she was transferred for time spent in the custody of the State Party to which he or she was transferred.

12. Unless the State Party from which a person is to be transferred in accordance with paragraphs 10 and 11 of this article so agrees, that person, whatever his or her nationality, shall not be prosecuted, detained, punished or subjected to any other restriction of his or her personal liberty in the territory of the State to which that person is transferred in respect of acts, omissions or convictions prior to his or her departure from the territory of the State from which he or she was transferred.

13. Each State Party shall designate a central authority that shall have the responsibility and power to receive requests for mutual legal assistance and either to execute them or to transmit them to the competent authorities for execution. Where a State Party has a special region or territory with a separate system of mutual legal assistance, it may designate a distinct central authority that shall have the same function for that region or territory. Central authorities shall ensure the speedy and proper execution or transmission of the requests received. Where the central authority transmits the request to a competent authority for execution, it shall encourage the speedy and proper execution of the request by the competent authority. The Secretary-General of the United Nations shall be notified of the central authority designated for this purpose at the time each State Party deposits its instrument of ratification, acceptance or approval of or accession to this Convention. Requests for mutual legal assistance and any communication related thereto shall be transmitted to the central authorities designated by the States Parties. This requirement shall be without prejudice to the right of a State Party to require that such requests and communications be addressed to it through diplomatic channels and, in urgent circumstances, where the States Parties agree, through the International Criminal Police Organization, if possible.

14. Requests shall be made in writing or, where possible, by any means capable of producing a written record, in a language acceptable to the requested State Party, under conditions allowing that State Party to establish authenticity. The Secretary-General of the United Nations shall be notified of the language or languages acceptable to each State Party at the time it deposits its instrument of ratification, acceptance or approval of or accession to this Convention. In urgent circumstances and where agreed by the States Parties, requests may be made orally but shall be confirmed in writing forthwith.

15. A request for mutual legal assistance shall contain:

(a) The identity of the authority making the request;

(b) The subject matter and nature of the investigation, prosecution or judicial proceeding to which the request relates and the name and functions of the authority conducting the investigation, prosecution or judicial proceeding;

(c) A summary of the relevant facts, except in relation to requests for the purpose of service of judicial documents;

(d) A description of the assistance sought and details of any particular procedure that the requesting State Party wishes to be followed;

(e) Where possible, the identity, location and nationality of any person concerned; and

(f) The purpose for which the evidence, information or action is sought.

16. The requested State Party may request additional information when it appears necessary for the execution of the request in accordance with its domestic law or when it can facilitate such execution.

17. A request shall be executed in accordance with the domestic law of the requested State Party and, to the extent not contrary to the domestic law of the requested State Party and where possible, in accordance with the procedures specified in the request.

18. Wherever possible and consistent with fundamental principles of domestic law, when an individual is in the territory of a State Party and has to be heard as a witness or expert by the judicial authorities of another State Party, the first State Party may, at the request of the other, permit the hearing to take place by video conference if it is not possible or desirable for the individual in question to appear in person in the territory of the requesting State Party. States Parties may agree that the hearing shall be conducted by a judicial authority of the requesting State Party and attended by a judicial authority of the requested State Party.

19. The requesting State Party shall not transmit or use information or evidence furnished by the requested State Party for investigations, prosecutions or judicial proceedings other than those stated in the request without the prior consent of the requested State Party. Nothing in this paragraph shall prevent the requesting State Party from disclosing in its proceedings information or evidence that is exculpatory to an accused person. In the latter case, the requesting State Party shall notify the requested State Party prior to the disclosure and, if so requested, consult with the requested State Party. If, in an exceptional case, advance notice is not possible, the requesting State Party shall inform the requested State Party of the disclosure without delay.

20. The requesting State Party may require that the requested State Party keep confidential the fact and substance of the request, except to the extent necessary to execute the request. If the requested State Party cannot comply with the requirement of confidentiality, it shall promptly inform the requesting State Party.

21. Mutual legal assistance may be refused:

(a) If the request is not made in conformity with the provisions of this article;

(b) If the requested State Party considers that execution of the request is likely to prejudice its sovereignty, security, ordre public or other essential interests;

(c) If the authorities of the requested State Party would be prohibited by its domestic law from carrying out the action requested with regard to any similar offence, had it been subject to investigation, prosecution or judicial proceedings under their own jurisdiction;

(d) If it would be contrary to the legal system of the requested State Party relating to mutual legal assistance for the request to be granted.

22. States Parties may not refuse a request for mutual legal assistance on the sole ground that the offence is also considered to involve fiscal matters.

23. Reasons shall be given for any refusal of mutual legal assistance.

24. The requested State Party shall execute the request for mutual legal assistance as soon as possible and shall take as full account as possible of any deadlines suggested by the requesting State Party and for which reasons are given, preferably in the request. The requesting State Party may make reasonable requests for information on the status and progress of measures taken by the requested State Party to satisfy its request. The requested State Party shall respond to reasonable requests by the requesting State Party on the status, and progress in its handling, of the request. The requesting State Party shall promptly inform the requested State Party when the assistance sought is no longer required.

25. Mutual legal assistance may be postponed by the requested State Party on the ground that it interferes with an ongoing investigation, prosecution or judicial proceeding.

26. Before refusing a request pursuant to paragraph 21 of this article or postponing its execution pursuant to paragraph 25 of this article, the requested State Party shall consult with the requesting State Party to consider whether assistance may be granted subject to such terms and conditions as it deems necessary. If the requesting State Party accepts assistance subject to those conditions, it shall comply with the conditions.

27. Without prejudice to the application of paragraph 12 of this article, a witness, expert or other person who, at the request of the requesting State Party, consents to give evidence in a proceeding or to assist in an investigation, prosecution or judicial proceeding in the territory of the requesting State Party shall not be prosecuted, detained, punished or subjected to any other restriction of his or her personal liberty in that territory in respect of acts, omissions or convictions prior to his or her departure from the territory of the requested State Party. Such safe conduct shall cease when the witness, expert or other person having had, for a period of fifteen conse-cutive days or for any period agreed upon by the States Parties from the date on which he or she has been officially informed that his or her presence is no longer required by the judicial authorities, an opportunity of leaving, has nevertheless remained voluntarily in the territory of the requesting State Party or, having left it, has returned of his or her own free will.

28. The ordinary costs of executing a request shall be borne by the requested State Party, unless otherwise agreed by the States Parties concerned. If expenses of a substantial or extraordinary nature are or will be required to fulfil the request, the States Parties shall consult to determine the terms and conditions under which the request will be executed, as well as the manner in which the costs shall be borne.

29. The requested State Party:

(a) Shall provide to the requesting State Party copies of government records, documents or information in its possession that under its domestic law are available to the general public;

(b) May, at its discretion, provide to the requesting State Party in whole, in part or subject to such conditions as it deems appropriate, copies of any government records, documents or information in its possession that under its domestic law are not available to the general public.

30. States Parties shall consider, as may be necessary, the possibility of concluding bilateral or multilateral agreements or arrangements that would serve the purposes of, give practical effect to or enhance the provisions of this article.

Article 47. Transfer of Criminal Proceedings

States Parties shall consider the possibility of transferring to one another proceedings for the prosecution of an offence established in accordance with this Convention in cases where such transfer is considered to be in the interests of the proper administration of justice, in particular in cases where several jurisdictions are involved, with a view to concentrating the prosecution.

Article 48. Law Enforcement Cooperation

1. States Parties shall cooperate closely with one another, consistent with their respective domestic legal and administrative systems, to enhance the effectiveness of law enforcement action to combat the offences covered by this Convention. States Parties shall, in particular, take effective measures:

(a) To enhance and, where necessary, to establish channels of communication between their competent authorities, agencies and services in order to facilitate the secure and rapid exchange of information concerning all aspects of the offences covered by this Convention, including, if the States Parties concerned deem it appropriate, links with other criminal activities;

(b) To cooperate with other States Parties in conducting inquiries with respect to offences covered by this Convention concerning:

(i) The identity, whereabouts and activities of persons suspected of involvement in such offences or the location of other persons concerned;

(ii) The movement of proceeds of crime or property derived from the commission of such offences;

(iii) The movement of property, equipment or other instrumentalities used or intended for use in the commission of such offences;

(c) To provide, where appropriate, necessary items or quantities of substances for analytical or investigative purposes;

(d) To exchange, where appropriate, information with other States Parties concerning specific means and methods used to commit offences covered by this Convention, including the use of false identities, forged, altered or false documents and other means of concealing activities;

(e) To facilitate effective coordination between their competent authorities, agencies and services and to promote the exchange of personnel and other experts, including, subject to bilateral agreements or arrangements between the States Parties concerned, the posting of liaison officers;

(f) To exchange information and coordinate administrative and other measures taken as appropriate for the purpose of early identification of the offences covered by this Convention.

2. With a view to giving effect to this Convention, States Parties shall consider entering into bilateral or multilateral agreements or arrangements on direct cooperation between their law enforcement agencies and, where such agreements or arrangements already exist, amending them. In the absence of such agreements or arrangements between the States Parties concerned, the States Parties may consider this Convention to be the basis for mutual law enforcement cooperation in respect of the offences covered by this Convention. Whenever appropriate, States Parties shall make full use of agreements or arrangements, including international or regional organizations, to enhance the cooperation between their law enforcement agencies.

3. States Parties shall endeavour to cooperate within their means to respond to offences covered by this Convention committed through the use of modern technology.

Article 49. Joint Investigations

States Parties shall consider concluding bilateral or multilateral agreements or arrangements whereby, in relation to matters that are the subject of investigations, prosecutions or judicial proceedings in one or more States, the competent authorities concerned may establish joint investigative bodies. In the absence of such agreements or arrangements, joint investigations may be undertaken by agreement on a case-by-case basis. The States Parties involved shall ensure that the sovereignty of the State Party in whose territory such investigation is to take place is fully respected.

Article 50. Special Investigative Techniques

1. In order to combat corruption effectively, each State Party shall, to the extent permitted by the basic principles of its domestic legal system and in accordance with the conditions prescribed by its domestic law, take such measures as may be necessary, within its means, to allow for the appropriate use by its competent authorities of controlled delivery and, where it deems appropriate, other special investigative techniques, such as electronic or other forms of surveillance and undercover operations, within its territory, and to allow for the admissibility in court of evidence derived therefrom.

2. For the purpose of investigating the offences covered by this Convention, States Parties are encouraged to conclude, when necessary, appropriate bilateral or multilateral agreements or arrangements for using such special investigative techniques in the context of cooperation at the international level. Such agreements or arrangements shall be concluded and implemented in

full compliance with the principle of sovereign equality of States and shall be carried out strictly in accordance with the terms of those agreements or arrangements.

3.   In the absence of an agreement or arrangement as set forth in paragraph 2 of this article, decisions to use such special investigative techniques at the international level shall be made on a case-by-case basis and may, when necessary, take into consideration financial arrangements and understandings with respect to the exercise of jurisdiction by the States Parties concerned.

4.   Decisions to use controlled delivery at the international level may, with the consent of the States Parties concerned, include methods such as intercepting and allowing the goods or funds to continue intact or be removed or replaced in whole or in part.

Chapter V – Asset Recovery

Article 51. General Provision

The return of assets pursuant to this chapter is a fundamental principle of this Convention, and States Parties shall afford one another the widest measure of cooperation and assistance in this regard.

Article 52. Prevention and Detection of Transfers of Proceeds of Crime

1.   Without prejudice to article 14 of this Convention, each State Party shall take such measures as may be necessary, in accordance with its domestic law, to require financial institutions within its jurisdiction to verify the identity of customers, to take reasonable steps to determine the identity of beneficial owners of funds deposited into high-value accounts and to conduct en-hanced scrutiny of accounts sought or maintained by or on behalf of individuals who are, or have been, entrusted with prominent public functions and their family members and close associates. Such enhanced scrutiny shall be reasonably designed to detect suspicious transactions for the purpose of reporting to competent authorities and should not be so construed as to discourage or prohibit financial institutions from doing business with any legitimate customer.

2.   In order to facilitate implementation of the measures provided for in paragraph 1 of this article, each State Party, in accordance with its domestic law and inspired by relevant initiatives of regional, interregional and multilateral organizations against money-laundering, shall:

(a)   Issue advisories regarding the types of natural or legal person to whose accounts financial institutions within its jurisdiction will be expected to apply enhanced scrutiny, the types of accounts and transactions to which to pay particular attention and appropriate account-opening, maintenance and record-keeping measures to take concerning such accounts; and

(b)   Where appropriate, notify financial institutions within its jurisdiction, at the request of another State Party or on its own initiative, of the identity of particular natural or legal persons to whose accounts such institutions will be expected to apply enhanced scrutiny, in addition to those whom the financial institutions may otherwise identify.

3.   In the context of paragraph 2 (a) of this article, each State Party shall implement measures to ensure that its financial institutions maintain adequate records, over an appropriate period of time, of accounts and transactions involving the persons mentioned in paragraph 1 of this article, which should, as a minimum, contain information relating to the identity of the customer as well as, as far as possible, of the beneficial owner.

4.   With the aim of preventing and detecting transfers of proceeds of offences established in accordance with this Convention, each State Party shall implement appropriate and effective measures to prevent, with the help of its regulatory and oversight bodies, the establishment of banks that have no physical presence and that are not affiliated with a regulated financial group. Moreover, States Parties may consider requiring their financial institutions to refuse to enter into or continue a correspondent banking relationship with such institutions and to guard against establishing relations with foreign financial institutions that permit their accounts to be used by banks that have no physical presence and that are not affiliated with a regulated financial group.

5.   Each State Party shall consider establishing, in accordance with its domestic law, effective financial disclosure systems for appropriate public officials and shall provide for appropriate sanctions for non-compliance. Each State Party shall also consider taking such measures as may be necessary to permit its competent authorities to share that information with the competent authorities in other States Parties when necessary to investigate, claim and recover proceeds of offences established in accordance with this Convention.

6.   Each State Party shall consider taking such measures as may be necessary, in accordance with its domestic law, to require appropriate public officials having an interest in or signature or other authority over a financial account in a foreign country to report that relationship to appropriate authorities and to maintain appropriate records related to such accounts. Such measures shall also provide for appropriate sanctions for non-compliance.

Article 53. Measures for Direct Recovery of Property

Each State Party shall, in accordance with its domestic law:

(a)   Take such measures as may be necessary to permit another State Party to initiate civil action in its courts to establish title to or ownership of property acquired through the commission of an offence established in accordance with this Convention;

(b)   Take such measures as may be necessary to permit its courts to order those who have committed offences established in accordance with this Convention to pay compensation or damages to another State Party that has been harmed by such offences; and

(c)   Take such measures as may be necessary to permit its courts or competent authorities, when having to decide on confiscation, to recognize another State Party's claim as a legitimate owner of property acquired through the commission of an offence established in accordance with this Convention.

Article 54. Mechanisms for Recovery of Property Through International Cooperation in Confiscation

1.   Each State Party, in order to provide mutual legal assistance pursuant to article 55 of this Convention with respect to property acquired through or involved in the commission of an offence established in accordance with this Convention, shall, in accordance with its domestic law:

(a)   Take such measures as may be necessary to permit its competent authorities to give effect to an order of confiscation issued by a court of another State Party;

(b)   Take such measures as may be necessary to permit its competent authorities, where they have jurisdiction, to order the confiscation of such property of foreign origin by adjudication of an offence of money-laundering or such other offence as may be within its jurisdiction or by other procedures authorized under its domestic law; and

(c)   Consider taking such measures as may be necessary to allow confiscation of such property without a criminal conviction in cases in which the offender cannot be prosecuted by reason of death, flight or absence or in other appropriate cases.

2.   Each State Party, in order to provide mutual legal assistance upon a request made pursuant to paragraph 2 of article 55 of this Convention, shall, in accordance with its domestic law:

(a)   Take such measures as may be necessary to permit its competent authorities to freeze or seize property upon a freezing or seizure order issued by a court or competent authority of a requesting State Party that provides a reasonable basis for the requested State Party to believe that there are sufficient grounds for taking such actions and that the property would eventually be subject to an order of confiscation for purposes of paragraph 1 (a) of this article;

(b)   Take such measures as may be necessary to permit its competent authorities to freeze or seize property upon a request that provides a reasonable basis for the requested State Party to believe that there are sufficient grounds for taking such actions and that the property would eventually be subject to an order of confiscation for purposes of paragraph 1 (a) of this article; and

(c) Consider taking additional measures to permit its competent authorities to preserve property for confiscation, such as on the basis of a foreign arrest or criminal charge related to the acquisition of such property.

Article 55. International Cooperation for Purposes of Confiscation

1.   A State Party that has received a request from another State Party having jurisdiction over an offence established in accordance with this Convention for confiscation of proceeds of crime, property, equipment or other instrumentalities referred to in article 31, paragraph 1, of this Convention situated in its territory shall, to the greatest extent possible within its domestic legal system:

(a) Submit the request to its competent authorities for the purpose of obtaining an order of confiscation and, if such an order is granted, give effect to it; or

(b) Submit to its competent authorities, with a view to giving effect to it to the extent requested, an order of confiscation issued by a court in the territory of the requesting State Party in accordance with articles 31, paragraph 1, and 54, paragraph 1 (a), of this Convention insofar as it relates to proceeds of crime, property, equipment or other instrumentalities referred to in article 31, paragraph 1, situated in the territory of the requested State Party.

2.   Following a request made by another State Party having jurisdiction over an offence established in accordance with this Convention, the requested State Party shall take measures to identify, trace and freeze or seize proceeds of crime, property, equipment or other instrumentalities referred to in article 31, paragraph 1, of this Convention for the purpose of eventual confiscation to be ordered either by the requesting State Party or, pursuant to a request under paragraph 1 of this article, by the requested State Party.

3.   The provisions of article 46 of this Convention are applicable, mutatis mutandis, to this article. In addition to the information specified in article 46, paragraph 15, requests made pursuant to this article shall contain:

(a) In the case of a request pertaining to paragraph 1 (a) of this article, a description of the property to be confiscated, including, to the extent possible, the location and, where relevant, the estimated value of the property and a statement of the facts relied upon by the requesting State Party sufficient to enable the requested State Party to seek the order under its domestic law;

(b) In the case of a request pertaining to paragraph 1 (b) of this article, a legally admissible copy of an order of confiscation upon which the request is based issued by the requesting State Party, a statement of the facts and information as to the extent to which execution of the order is requested, a statement specifying the measures taken by the requesting State Party to provide adequate notification to bona fide third parties and to ensure due process and a statement that the confiscation order is final;

(c) In the case of a request pertaining to paragraph 2 of this article, a statement of the facts relied upon by the requesting State Party and a description of the actions requested and, where available, a legally admissible copy of an order on which the request is based.

4.   The decisions or actions provided for in paragraphs 1 and 2 of this article shall be taken by the requested State Party in accordance with and subject to the provisions of its domestic law and its procedural rules or any bilateral or multilateral agreement or arrangement to which it may be bound in relation to the requesting State Party.

5.   Each State Party shall furnish copies of its laws and regulations that give effect to this article and of any subsequent changes to such laws and regulations or a description thereof to the Secretary-General of the United Nations.

6.   If a State Party elects to make the taking of the measures referred to in paragraphs 1 and 2 of this article conditional on the existence of a relevant treaty, that State Party shall consider this Convention the necessary and sufficient treaty basis.

7.   Cooperation under this article may also be refused or provisional measures lifted if the requested State Party does not receive sufficient and timely evidence or if the property is of a de minimis value.

8.   Before lifting any provisional measure taken pursuant to this article, the requested State Party shall, wherever possible, give the requesting State Party an opportunity to present its reasons in favour of continuing the measure.

9.   The provisions of this article shall not be construed as prejudicing the rights of bona fide third parties.

Article 56. Special Cooperation

Without prejudice to its domestic law, each State Party shall endeavour to take measures to permit it to forward, without prejudice to its own investigations, prosecutions or judicial procee-dings, information on proceeds of offences established in accordance with this Convention to another State Party without prior request, when it considers that the disclosure of such infor-mation might assist the receiving State Party in initiating or carrying out investigations, pro-secutions or judicial proceedings or might lead to a request by that State Party under this chapter of the Convention.

Article 57. Return and Disposal of Assets

1.   Property confiscated by a State Party pursuant to article 31 or 55 of this Convention shall be disposed of, including by return to its prior legitimate owners, pursuant to paragraph 3 of this article, by that State Party in accordance with the provisions of this Convention and its domestic law.

2.   Each State Party shall adopt such legislative and other measures, in accordance with the fundamental principles of its domestic law, as may be necessary to enable its competent authorities to return confiscated property, when acting on the request made by another State Party, in accordance with this Convention, taking into account the rights of bona fide third parties.

3.   In accordance with articles 46 and 55 of this Convention and paragraphs 1 and 2 of this article, the requested State Party shall:

(a) In the case of embezzlement of public funds or of laundering of embezzled public funds as referred to in articles 17 and 23 of this Convention, when confiscation was executed in accordance with article 55 and on the basis of a final judgement in the requesting State Party, a requirement that can be waived by the requested State Party, return the confiscated property to the requesting State Party;

(b) In the case of proceeds of any other offence covered by this Convention, when the con-fiscation was executed in accordance with article 55 of this Convention and on the basis of a final judgement in the requesting State Party, a requirement that can be waived by the requested State Party, return the confiscated property to the requesting State Party, when the requesting State Party reasonably establishes its prior ownership of such confiscated property to the requested State Party or when the requested State Party recognizes damage to the requesting State Party as a basis for returning the confiscated property;

(c)   In all other cases, give priority consideration to returning confiscated property to the reques-
       ting State Party, returning such property to its prior legitimate owners or compensating the
       victims of the crime.

4.   Where appropriate, unless States Parties decide otherwise, the requested State Party may
deduct reasonable expenses incurred in investigations, prosecutions or judicial proceedings
leading to the return or disposition of confiscated property pursuant to this article.

5.   Where appropriate, States Parties may also give special consideration to concluding agreements or mutually acceptable arrangements, on a case-by-case basis, for the final disposal of
confiscated property.

Article 58. Financial Intelligence Unit

States Parties shall cooperate with one another for the purpose of preventing and combating the
transfer of proceeds of offences established in accordance with this Convention and of promoting ways and means of recovering such proceeds and, to that end, shall consider establishing a
financial intelligence unit to be responsible for receiving, analysing and disseminating to the
competent authorities reports of suspicious financial transactions.

Article 59. Bilateral and Multilateral Agreements and Arrangements

States Parties shall consider concluding bilateral or multilateral agreements or arrangements to
enhance the effectiveness of international cooperation undertaken pursuant to this chapter of
the Convention.

Chapter VI – Technical Assistance and Information Exchange

Article 60. Training and Technical Assistance

1.   Each State Party shall, to the extent necessary, initiate, develop or improve specific training
programmes for its personnel responsible for preventing and combating corruption. Such
training programmes could deal, inter alia, with the following areas:

(a)   Effective measures to prevent, detect, investigate, punish and control corruption, including
       the use of evidence-gathering and investigative methods;

(b)   Building capacity in the development and planning of strategic anti-corruption policy;

(c)   Training competent authorities in the preparation of requests for mutual legal assistance
       that meet the requirements of this Convention;

(d)   Evaluation and strengthening of institutions, public service management and the manage-
       ment of public finances, including public procurement, and the private sector;

(e)   Preventing and combating the transfer of proceeds of offences established in accordance
       with this Convention and recovering such proceeds;

(f)   Detecting and freezing of the transfer of proceeds of offences established in accordance
       with this Convention;

(g)   Surveillance of the movement of proceeds of offences established in accordance with this
       Convention and of the methods used to transfer, conceal or disguise such proceeds;

(h)   Appropriate and efficient legal and administrative mechanisms and methods for facilitating
       the return of proceeds of offences established in accordance with this Convention;

(i)   Methods used in protecting victims and witnesses who cooperate with judicial authorities;
       and

(j)   Training in national and international regulations and in languages.

2.   States Parties shall, according to their capacity, consider affording one another the widest
measure of technical assistance, especially for the benefit of developing countries, in their
respective plans and programmes to combat corruption, including material support and training

in the areas referred to in paragraph 1 of this article, and training and assistance and the mutual exchange of relevant experience and specialized knowledge, which will facilitate international cooperation between States Parties in the areas of extradition and mutual legal assistance.

3.   States Parties shall strengthen, to the extent necessary, efforts to maximize operational and training activities in international and regional organizations and in the framework of relevant bilateral and multilateral agreements or arrangements.

4.   States Parties shall consider assisting one another, upon request, in conducting evaluations, studies and research relating to the types, causes, effects and costs of corruption in their respective countries, with a view to developing, with the participation of competent authorities and society, strategies and action plans to combat corruption.

5.   In order to facilitate the recovery of proceeds of offences established in accordance with this Convention, States Parties may cooperate in providing each other with the names of experts who could assist in achieving that objective.

6.   States Parties shall consider using subregional, regional and international conferences and seminars to promote cooperation and technical assistance and to stimulate discussion on problems of mutual concern, including the special problems and needs of developing countries and countries with economies in transition.

7.   States Parties shall consider establishing voluntary mechanisms with a view to contributing financially to the efforts of developing countries and countries with economies in transition to apply this Convention through technical assistance programmes and projects.

8.   Each State Party shall consider making voluntary contributions to the United Nations Office on Drugs and Crime for the purpose of fostering, through the Office, programmes and projects in developing countries with a view to implementing this Convention.

Article 61. Collection, Exchange and Analysis of Information on Corruption

1.   Each State Party shall consider analysing, in consultation with experts, trends in corruption in its territory, as well as the circumstances in which corruption offences are committed.

2.   States Parties shall consider developing and sharing with each other and through international and regional organizations statistics, analytical expertise concerning corruption and information with a view to developing, insofar as possible, common definitions, standards and methodologies, as well as information on best practices to prevent and combat corruption.

3.   Each State Party shall consider monitoring its policies and actual measures to combat corruption and making assessments of their effectiveness and efficiency.

Article 62. Other Measures: Implementation of the Convention Through Economic Development and Technical Assistance

1.   States Parties shall take measures conducive to the optimal implementation of this Convention to the extent possible, through international cooperation, taking into account the negative effects of corruption on society in general, in particular on sustainable development.

2.   States Parties shall make concrete efforts to the extent possible and in coordination with each other, as well as with international and regional organizations:

(a) To enhance their cooperation at various levels with developing countries, with a view to strengthening the capacity of the latter to prevent and combat corruption;

(b) To enhance financial and material assistance to support the efforts of developing countries to prevent and fight corruption effectively and to help them implement this Convention successfully;

(c) To provide technical assistance to developing countries and countries with economies in transition to assist them in meeting their needs for the implementation of this Convention. To that end, States Parties shall endeavour to make adequate and regular voluntary contributions to an account specifically designated for that purpose in a United Nations funding mechanism. States Parties may also give special consideration, in accordance with their domestic law and the provisions of this Convention, to contributing to that account a percentage of the money or of the corresponding value of proceeds of crime or property confiscated in accordance with the provisions of this Convention;

(d) To encourage and persuade other States and financial institutions as appropriate to join them in efforts in accordance with this article, in particular by providing more training programmes and modern equipment to developing countries in order to assist them in achieving the objectives of this Convention.

3.   To the extent possible, these measures shall be without prejudice to existing foreign assistance commitments or to other financial cooperation arrangements at the bilateral, regional or international level.

4.   States Parties may conclude bilateral or multilateral agreements or arrangements on material and logistical assistance, taking into consideration the financial arrangements necessary for the means of international cooperation provided for by this Convention to be effective and for the prevention, detection and control of corruption.

Chapter VII – Mechanisms for Implementation

Article 63. Conference of the States Parties to the Convention

1.   A Conference of the States Parties to the Convention is hereby established to improve the capacity of and cooperation between States Parties to achieve the objectives set forth in this Convention and to promote and review its implementation.

2.   The Secretary-General of the United Nations shall convene the Conference of the States Parties not later than one year following the entry into force of this Convention. Thereafter, regular meetings of the Conference of the States Parties shall be held in accordance with the rules of procedure adopted by the Conference.

3.   The Conference of the States Parties shall adopt rules of procedure and rules governing the functioning of the activities set forth in this article, including rules concerning the admission and participation of observers, and the payment of expenses incurred in carrying out those activities.

4.   The Conference of the States Parties shall agree upon activities, procedures and methods of work to achieve the objectives set forth in paragraph 1 of this article, including:

(a) Facilitating activities by States Parties under articles 60 and 62 and chapters II to V of this Convention, including by encouraging the mobilization of voluntary contributions;

(b) Facilitating the exchange of information among States Parties on patterns and trends in corruption and on successful practices for preventing and combating it and for the return of proceeds of crime, through, inter alia, the publication of relevant information as mentioned in this article;

(c) Cooperating with relevant international and regional organizations and mechanisms and non-governmental organizations;

(d) Making appropriate use of relevant information produced by other international and regional mechanisms for combating and preventing corruption in order to avoid unnecessary duplication of work;

(e) Reviewing periodically the implementation of this Convention by its States Parties;

(f) Making recommendations to improve this Convention and its implementation;

(g) Taking note of the technical assistance requirements of States Parties with regard to the implementation of this Convention and recommending any action it may deem necessary in that respect.

5.   For the purpose of paragraph 4 of this article, the Conference of the States Parties shall acquire the necessary knowledge of the measures taken by States Parties in implementing this Convention and the difficulties encountered by them in doing so through information provided by them and through such supplemental review mechanisms as may be established by the Conference of the States Parties.

6.   Each State Party shall provide the Conference of the States Parties with information on its programmes, plans and practices, as well as on legislative and administrative measures to implement this Convention, as required by the Conference of the States Parties. The Conference of the States Parties shall examine the most effective way of receiving and acting upon information, including, inter alia, information received from States Parties and from competent international organizations. Inputs received from relevant non-governmental organizations duly accredited in accordance with procedures to be decided upon by the Conference of the States Parties may also be considered.

7.   Pursuant to paragraphs 4 to 6 of this article, the Conference of the States Parties shall establish, if it deems it necessary, any appropriate mechanism or body to assist in the effective implementation of the Convention.

Article 64. Secretariat

1.   The Secretary-General of the United Nations shall provide the necessary secretariat services to the Conference of the States Parties to the Convention.

2.   The secretariat shall:

(a)   Assist the Conference of the States Parties in carrying out the activities set forth in article 63 of this Convention and make arrangements and provide the necessary services for the sessions of the Conference of the States Parties;

(b)   Upon request, assist States Parties in providing information to the Conference of the States Parties as envisaged in article 63, paragraphs 5 and 6, of this Convention; and

(c)   Ensure the necessary coordination with the secretariats of relevant international and regional organizations.

Chapter VIII – Final Provisions

Article 65. Implementation of the Convention

1.   Each State Party shall take the necessary measures, including legislative and administrative measures, in accordance with fundamental principles of its domestic law, to ensure the implementation of its obligations under this Convention.

2.   Each State Party may adopt more strict or severe measures than those provided for by this Convention for preventing and combating corruption.

Article 66. Settlement of Disputes

l.   States Parties shall endeavour to settle disputes concerning the interpretation or application of this Convention through negotiation.

2.   Any dispute between two or more States Parties concerning the interpretation or application of this Convention that cannot be settled through negotiation within a reasonable time shall, at the request of one of those States Parties, be submitted to arbitration. If, six months after the date of the request for arbitration, those States Parties are unable to agree on the organization of the arbitration, any one of those States Parties may refer the dispute to the International Court of Justice by request in accordance with the Statute of the Court.

3.   Each State Party may, at the time of signature, ratification, acceptance or approval of or accession to this Convention, declare that it does not consider itself bound by paragraph 2 of this article. The other States Parties shall not be bound by paragraph 2 of this article with respect to any State Party that has made such a reservation.

4.   Any State Party that has made a reservation in accordance with paragraph 3 of this article may at any time withdraw that reservation by notification to the Secretary- General of the United Nations.

Article 67. Signature, Ratification, Acceptance, Approval and Accession

1.   This Convention shall be open to all States for signature from 9 to 11 December 2003 in Merida, Mexico, and thereafter at United Nations Headquarters in New York until 9 December 2005.

2.   This Convention shall also be open for signature by regional economic integration organizations provided that at least one member State of such organization has signed this Convention in accordance with paragraph 1 of this article.

3.   This Convention is subject to ratification, acceptance or approval. Instruments of ratification, acceptance or approval shall be deposited with the Secretary-General of the United Nations. A regional economic integration organization may deposit its instrument of ratification, acceptance or approval if at least one of its member States has done likewise. In that instrument of ratification, acceptance or approval, such organization shall declare the extent of its competence with respect to the matters governed by this Convention. Such organization shall also inform the depositary of any relevant modification in the extent of its competence.

4.   This Convention is open for accession by any State or any regional economic integration organization of which at least one member State is a Party to this Convention. Instruments of accession shall be deposited with the Secretary-General of the United Nations. At the time of its accession, a regional economic integration organization shall declare the extent of its competence with respect to matters governed by this Convention. Such organization shall also inform the depositary of any relevant modification in the extent of its competence.

Article 68. Entry into Force

1.   This Convention shall enter into force on the ninetieth day after the date of deposit of the thirtieth instrument of ratification, acceptance, approval or accession. For the purpose of this paragraph, any instrument deposited by a regional economic integration organization shall not be counted as additional to those deposited by member States of such organization.

2.   For each State or regional economic integration organization ratifying, accepting, approving or acceding to this Convention after the deposit of the thirtieth instrument of such action, this Convention shall enter into force on the thirtieth day after the date of deposit by such State or organization of the relevant instrument or on the date this Convention enters into force pursuant to paragraph 1 of this article, whichever is later.

Article 69. Amendment

1.   After the expiry of five years from the entry into force of this Convention, a State Party may propose an amendment and transmit it to the Secretary-General of the United Nations, who shall thereupon communicate the proposed amendment to the States Parties and to the Conference of the States Parties to the Convention for the purpose of considering and deciding on the proposal. The Conference of the States Parties shall make every effort to achieve consensus on each amendment. If all efforts at consensus have been exhausted and no agreement has been reached, the amendment shall, as a last resort, require for its adoption a two-thirds majority vote of the States Parties present and voting at the meeting of the Conference of the States Parties.

2.   Regional economic integration organizations, in matters within their competence, shall exercise their right to vote under this article with a number of votes equal to the number of their member States that are Parties to this Convention. Such organizations shall not exercise their right to vote if their member States exercise theirs and vice versa.

3.   An amendment adopted in accordance with paragraph 1 of this article is subject to ratification, acceptance or approval by States Parties.

4.   An amendment adopted in accordance with paragraph 1 of this article shall enter into force in respect of a State Party ninety days after the date of the deposit with the Secretary-General of the United Nations of an instrument of ratification, acceptance or approval of such amendment.

5.   When an amendment enters into force, it shall be binding on those States Parties which have expressed their consent to be bound by it. Other States Parties shall still be bound by the provisions of this Convention and any earlier amendments that they have ratified, accepted or approved.

Article 70. Denunciation

1.   A State Party may denounce this Convention by written notification to the Secretary-General of the United Nations. Such denunciation shall become effective one year after the date of receipt of the notification by the Secretary-General.

2.   A regional economic integration organization shall cease to be a Party to this Convention when all of its member States have denounced it.

Article 71. Depositary and Languages

1.   The Secretary-General of the United Nations is designated depositary of this Convention.

2.   The original of this Convention, of which the Arabic, Chinese, English, French, Russian and Spanish texts are equally authentic, shall be deposited with the Secretary-General of the United Nations.

IN WITNESS WHEREOF, the undersigned plenipotentiaries, being duly authorized thereto by their respective Governments, have signed this Convention.

X.7. 2011 UN Guiding Principles on Business and Human Rights[1]

GENERAL PRINCIPLES

These Guiding Principles are grounded in recognition of:

(a) States' existing obligations to respect, protect and fulfil human rights and fundamental freedoms;

(b) The role of business enterprises as specialized organs of society performing specialized functions, required to comply with all applicable laws and to respect human rights;

(c) The need for rights and obligations to be matched to appropriate and effective remedies when breached.

These Guiding Principles apply to all States and to all business enterprises, both transnational and others, regardless of their size, sector, location, ownership and structure.

These Guiding Principles should be understood as a coherent whole and should be read, individually and collectively, in terms of their objective of enhancing standards and practices with regard to business and human rights so as to achieve tangible results for affected individuals and communities, and thereby also contributing to a socially sustainable globalization.

Nothing in these Guiding Principles should be read as creating new international law obligations, or as limiting or undermining any legal obligations a State may have undertaken or be subject to under international law with regard to human rights.

These Guiding Principles should be implemented in a non-discriminatory manner, with particular attention to the rights and needs of, as well as the challenges faced by, individuals from groups or populations that may be at heightened risk of becoming vulnerable or marginalized, and with due regard to the different risks that may be faced by women and men.

I. THE STATE DUTY TO PROTECT HUMAN RIGHTS

A. Foundational Principles

1.   States must protect against human rights abuse within their territory and/or jurisdiction by third parties, including business enterprises. This requires taking appropriate steps to prevent, investigate, punish and redress such abuse through effective policies, legislation, regulations and adjudication.

Commentary

States' international human rights law obligations require that they respect, protect and fulfil the human rights of individuals within their territory and/or jurisdiction. This includes the duty to protect against human rights abuse by third parties, including business enterprises.

The State duty to protect is a standard of conduct. Therefore, States are not per se responsible for human rights abuse by private actors. However, States may breach their international human rights law obligations where such abuse can be attributed to them, or where they fail to take appropriate steps to prevent, investigate, punish and redress private actors' abuse. While States generally have discretion in deciding upon these steps, they should consider the full range of permissible preventative and remedial measures, including policies, legislation, regulations and adjudication. States also have the duty to protect and promote the rule of law, including by taking measures to ensure equality before the law, fairness in its application, and by providing for adequate accountability, legal certainty, and procedural and legal transparency.

This chapter focuses on preventative measures while chapter III outlines remedial measures.

---

1   See http://www.ohchr.org/Documents/Publications/GuidingPrinciplesBusinessHR_EN.pdf.

2.   States should set out clearly the expectation that all business enterprises domiciled in their territory and/or jurisdiction respect human rights throughout their operations.

Commentary

At present States are not generally required under international human rights law to regulate the extraterritorial activities of businesses domiciled in their territory and/or jurisdiction. Nor are they generally prohibited from doing so, provided there is a recognized jurisdictional basis. Within these parameters some human rights treaty bodies recommend that home States take steps to prevent abuse abroad by business enterprises within their jurisdiction.

There are strong policy reasons for home States to set out clearly the expectation that businesses respect human rights abroad, especially where the State itself is involved in or supports those businesses. The reasons include ensuring predictability for business enterprises by providing coherent and consistent messages, and preserving the State's own reputation.

States have adopted a range of approaches in this regard. Some are domestic measures with extraterritorial implications. Examples include requirements on "parent" companies to report on the global operations of the entire enterprise; multilateral soft-law instruments such as the Guidelines for Multinational Enterprises of the Organisation for Economic Co-operation and Development; and performance standards required by institutions that support overseas investments. Other approaches amount to direct extraterritorial legislation and enforcement. This includes criminal regimes that allow for prosecutions based on the nationality of the perpetrator no matter where the offence occurs. Various factors may contribute to the perceived and actual reasonableness of States' actions, for example whether they are grounded in multilateral agreement.

B. Operational Principles

General State Regulatory and Policy Functions

3.   In meeting their duty to protect, States should:

(a)   Enforce laws that are aimed at, or have the effect of, requiring business enterprises to respect human rights, and periodically to assess the adequacy of such laws and address any gaps;

(b)   Ensure that other laws and policies governing the creation and ongoing operation of business enterprises, such as corporate law, do not constrain but enable business respect for human rights;

(c)   Provide effective guidance to business enterprises on how to respect human rights throughout their operations;

(d)   Encourage, and where appropriate require, business enterprises to communicate how they address their human rights impacts.

Commentary

States should not assume that businesses invariably prefer, or benefit from, State inaction, and they should consider a smart mix of measures – national and international, mandatory and voluntary – to foster business respect for human rights.

The failure to enforce existing laws that directly or indirectly regulate business respect for human rights is often a significant legal gap in State practice. Such laws might range from non-discrimination and labour laws to environmental, property, privacy and anti-bribery laws. Therefore, it is important for States to consider whether such laws are currently being enforced effectively, and if not, why this is the case and what measures may reasonably correct the situation.

It is equally important for States to review whether these laws provide the necessary coverage in light of evolving circumstances and whether, together with relevant policies, they provide an environment conducive to business respect for human rights. For example, greater clarity in some areas of law and policy, such as those governing access to land, including entitlements in relation to ownership or use of land, is often necessary to protect both rights-holders and business enterprises.

Laws and policies that govern the creation and ongoing operation of business enterprises, such as corporate and securities laws, directly shape business behaviour. Yet their implications for human rights remain poorly understood. For example, there is a lack of clarity in corporate and securities law regarding what companies and their officers are permitted, let alone required, to do regarding human rights. Laws and policies in this area should provide sufficient guidance to enable enterprises to respect human rights, with due regard to the role of existing governance structures such as corporate boards.

Guidance to business enterprises on respecting human rights should indicate expected outcomes and help share best practices. It should advise on appropriate methods, including human rights due diligence, and how to consider effectively issues of gender, vulnerability and/or marginalization, recognizing the specific challenges that may be faced by indigenous peoples, women, national or ethnic minorities, religious and linguistic minorities, children, persons with disabilities, and migrant workers and their families.

National human rights institutions that comply with the Paris Principles have an important role to play in helping States identify whether relevant laws are aligned with their human rights obligations and are being effectively enforced, and in providing guidance on human rights also to business enterprises and other non-State actors.

Communication by business enterprises on how they address their human rights impacts can range from informal engagement with affected stakeholders to formal public reporting. State encouragement of, or where appropriate requirements for, such communication are important in fostering respect for human rights by business enterprises. Incentives to communicate adequate information could include provisions to give weight to such self-reporting in the event of any judicial or administrative proceeding. A requirement to communicate can be particularly appropriate where the nature of business operations or operating contexts pose a significant risk to human rights. Policies or laws in this area can usefully clarify what and how businesses should communicate, helping to ensure both the accessibility and accuracy of communications.

Any stipulation of what would constitute adequate communication should take into account risks that it may pose to the safety and security of individuals and facilities; legitimate requirements of commercial confidentiality; and variations in companies' size and structures.

Financial reporting requirements should clarify that human rights impacts in some instances may be "material" or "significant" to the economic performance of the business enterprise.

The State-Business Nexus

4.   *States should take additional steps to protect against human rights abuses by business enterprises that are owned or controlled by the State, or that receive substantial support and services from State agencies such as export credit agencies and official investment insurance or guarantee agencies, including, where appropriate, by requiring human rights due diligence.*

Commentary

States individually are the primary duty-bearers under international human rights law, and collectively they are the trustees of the international human rights regime. Where a business enterprise is controlled by the State or where its acts can be attributed otherwise to the State, an abuse of human rights by the business enterprise may entail a violation of the State's own international law obligations. Moreover, the closer a business enterprise is to the State, or the more it relies on statutory authority or taxpayer support, the stronger the State's policy rationale becomes for ensuring that the enterprise respects human rights.

Where States own or control business enterprises, they have greatest means within their powers to ensure that relevant policies, legislation and regulations regarding respect for human rights are implemented. Senior management typically reports to State agencies, and associated government departments have greater scope for scrutiny and oversight, including ensuring that effective human rights due diligence is implemented. (These enterprises are also subject to the corporate responsibility to respect human rights, addressed in chapter II.)

A range of agencies linked formally or informally to the State may provide support and services to business activities. These include export credit agencies, official investment insurance or guarantee agencies, development agencies and development finance institutions. Where these agencies do not explicitly consider the actual and potential adverse impacts on human rights of beneficiary enterprises, they put themselves at risk – in reputational, financial, political and potentially legal terms – for supporting any such harm, and they may add to the human rights challenges faced by the recipient State.

Given these risks, States should encourage and, where appropriate, require human rights due diligence by the agencies themselves and by those business enterprises or projects receiving their support. A requirement for human rights due diligence is most likely to be appropriate where the nature of business operations or operating contexts pose significant risk to human rights.

5.   *States should exercise adequate oversight in order to meet their international human rights obligations when they contract with, or legislate for, business enterprises to provide services that may impact upon the enjoyment of human rights.*

Commentary

States do not relinquish their international human rights law obligations when they privatize the delivery of services that may impact upon the enjoyment of human rights. Failure by States to ensure that business enterprises performing such services operate in a manner consistent with the State's human rights obligations may entail both reputational and legal consequences for the State itself. As a necessary step, the relevant service contracts or enabling legislation should clarify the State's expectations that these enterprises respect human rights. States should ensure that they can effectively oversee the enterprises' activities, including through the provision of adequate independent monitoring and accountability mechanisms.

6.   *States should promote respect for human rights by business enterprises with which they conduct commercial transactions.*

Commentary

States conduct a variety of commercial transactions with business enterprises, not least through their procurement activities. This provides States – individually and collectively – with unique opportunities to promote awareness of and respect for human rights by those enterprises, including through the terms of contracts, with due regard to States' relevant obligations under national and international law.

Supporting Business Respect for Human Rights in Conflict-Affected Areas

7.   *Because the risk of gross human rights abuses is heightened in conflictaffected areas, States should help ensure that business enterprises operating in those contexts are not involved with such abuses, including by:*

(a)   *Engaging at the earliest stage possible with business enterprises to help them identify, prevent and mitigate the human rights-related risks of their activities and business relationships;*

(b)   *Providing adequate assistance to business enterprises to assess and address the heightened risks of abuses, paying special attention to both gender-based and sexual violence;*

(c)   *Denying access to public support and services for a business enterprise that is involved with gross human rights abuses and refuses to cooperate in addressing the situation;*

(d)   Ensuring that their current policies, legislation, regulations and enforcement measures are effective in addressing the risk of business involvement in gross human rights abuses.

Commentary

Some of the worst human rights abuses involving business occur amid conflict over the control of territory, resources or a Government itself – where the human rights regime cannot be expected to function as intended. Responsible businesses increasingly seek guidance from States about how to avoid contributing to human rights harm in these difficult contexts. Innovative and practical approaches are needed. In particular, it is important to pay attention to the risk of sexual and gender-based violence, which is especially prevalent during times of conflict.

It is important for all States to address issues early before situations on the ground deteriorate. In conflict-affected areas, the "host" State may be unable to protect human rights adequately due to a lack of effective control. Where transnational corporations are involved, their "home" States therefore have roles to play in assisting both those corporations and host States to ensure that businesses are not involved with human rights abuse, while neighboring States can provide important additional support.

To achieve greater policy coherence and assist business enterprises adequately in such situations, home States should foster closer cooperation among their development assistance agencies, foreign and trade ministries, and export finance institutions in their capitals and within their embassies, as well as between these agencies and host Government actors; develop early-warning indicators to alert government agencies and business enterprises to problems; and attach appropriate consequences to any failure by enterprises to cooperate in these contexts, including by denying or withdrawing existing public support or services, or where that is not possible, denying their future provision.

States should warn business enterprises of the heightened risk of being involved with gross abuses of human rights in conflict-affected areas. They should review whether their policies, legislation, regulations and enforcement measures effectively address this heightened risk, including through provisions for human rights due diligence by business. Where they identify gaps, States should take appropriate steps to address them. This may include exploring civil, administrative or criminal liability for enterprises domiciled or operating in their territory and/or jurisdiction that commit or contribute to gross human rights abuses. Moreover, States should consider multilateral approaches to prevent and address such acts, as well as support effective collective initiatives.

All these measures are in addition to States' obligations under international humanitarian law in situations of armed conflict, and under international criminal law.

Ensuring Policy Coherence

8.   States should ensure that governmental departments, agencies and other State-based institutions that shape business practices are aware of and observe the State's human rights obligations when fulfilling their respective mandates, including by providing them with relevant information, training and support.

Commentary

There is no inevitable tension between States' human rights obligations and the laws and policies they put in place that shape business practices. However, at times, States have to make difficult balancing decisions to reconcile different societal needs. To achieve the appropriate balance, States need to take a broad approach to managing the business and human rights agenda, aimed at ensuring both vertical and horizontal domestic policy coherence.

Vertical policy coherence entails States having the necessary policies, laws and processes to implement their international human rights law obligations. Horizontal policy coherence means supporting and equipping departments and agencies, at both the national and subnational levels, that shape business practices – including those responsible for corporate law and securities regulation, investment, export credit and insurance, trade and labour – to be informed of and act in a manner compatible with the Governments' human rights obligations.

9.   *States should maintain adequate domestic policy space to meet their human rights obligations when pursuing business-related policy objectives with other States or business enterprises, for instance through investment treaties or contracts.*

Commentary

Economic agreements concluded by States, either with other States or with business enterprises – such as bilateral investment treaties, free-trade agreements or contracts for investment projects – create economic opportunities for States. But they can also affect the domestic policy space of Governments. For example, the terms of international investment agreements may constrain States from fully implementing new human rights legislation, or put them at risk of binding international arbitration if they do so. Therefore, States should ensure that they retain adequate policy and regulatory ability to protect human rights under the terms of such agreements, while providing the necessary investor protection.

10.   *States, when acting as members of multilateral institutions that deal with business-related issues, should:*

(a)   *Seek to ensure that those institutions neither restrain the ability of their member States to meet their duty to protect nor hinder business enterprises from respecting human rights;*

(b)   *Encourage those institutions, within their respective mandates and capacities, to promote business respect for human rights and, where requested, to help States meet their duty to protect against human rights abuse by business enterprises, including through technical assistance, capacity-building and awareness-raising;*

(c)   *Draw on these Guiding Principles to promote shared understanding and advance international cooperation in the management of business and human rights challenges.*

Commentary

Greater policy coherence is also needed at the international level, including where States participate in multilateral institutions that deal with business-related issues, such as international trade and financial institutions. States retain their international human rights law obligations when they participate in such institutions.

Capacity-building and awareness-raising through such institutions can play a vital role in helping all States to fulfil their duty to protect, including by enabling the sharing of information about challenges and best practices, thus promoting more consistent approaches.

Collective action through multilateral institutions can help States level the playing field with regard to business respect for human rights, but it should do so by raising the performance of laggards. Cooperation between States, multilateral institutions and other stakeholders can also play an important role.

These Guiding Principles provide a common reference point in this regard, and could serve as a useful basis for building a cumulative positive effect that takes into account the respective roles and responsibilities of all relevant stakeholders.

II. The Corporate Responsibility to Respect Human Rights

A. Foundational Principles

11.   Business enterprises should respect human rights. This means that they should avoid infringing on the human rights of others and should address adverse human rights impacts with which they are involved.

Commentary

The responsibility to respect human rights is a global standard of expected conduct for all business enterprises wherever they operate. It exists independently of States' abilities and/or willingness to fulfil their own human rights obligations, and does not diminish those obligations. And it exists over and above compliance with national laws and regulations protecting human rights.

Addressing adverse human rights impacts requires taking adequate measures for their prevention, mitigation and, where appropriate, remediation.

Business enterprises may undertake other commitments or activities to support and promote human rights, which may contribute to the enjoyment of rights. But this does not offset a failure to respect human rights throughout their operations.

Business enterprises should not undermine States' abilities to meet their own human rights obligations, including by actions that might weaken the integrity of judicial processes.

12.   The responsibility of business enterprises to respect human rights refers to internationally recognized human rights – understood, at a minimum, as those expressed in the International Bill of Human Rights and the principles concerning fundamental rights set out in the International Labour Organization's Declaration on Fundamental Principles and Rights at Work.

Commentary

Because business enterprises can have an impact on virtually the entire spectrum of internationally recognized human rights, their responsibility to respect applies to all such rights. In practice, some human rights may be at greater risk than others in particular industries or contexts, and therefore will be the focus of heightened attention. However, situations may change, so all human rights should be the subject of periodic review.

An authoritative list of the core internationally recognized human rights is contained in the International Bill of Human Rights (consisting of the Universal Declaration of Human Rights and the main instruments through which it has been codified: the International Covenant on Civil and Political Rights and the International Covenant on Economic, Social and Cultural Rights), coupled with the principles concerning fundamental rights in the eight ILO core conventions as set out in the Declaration on Fundamental Principles and Rights at Work. These are the benchmarks against which other social actors assess the human rights impacts of business enterprises. The responsibility of business enterprises to respect human rights is distinct from issues of legal liability and enforcement, which remain defined largely by national law provisions in relevant jurisdictions.

Depending on circumstances, business enterprises may need to consider additional standards. For instance, enterprises should respect the human rights of individuals belonging to specific groups or populations that require particular attention, where they may have adverse human rights impacts on them. In this connection, United Nations instruments have elaborated further on the rights of indigenous peoples; women; national or ethnic, religious and linguistic minorities; children; persons with disabilities; and migrant workers and their families. Moreover, in situations of armed conflict enterprises should respect the standards of international humanitarian law.

13. *The responsibility to respect human rights requires that business enterprises:*

(a) *Avoid causing or contributing to adverse human rights impacts through their own activities, and address such impacts when they occur;*

(b) *Seek to prevent or mitigate adverse human rights impacts that are directly linked to their operations, products or services by their business relationships, even if they have not contributed to those impacts.*

Commentary

Business enterprises may be involved with adverse human rights impacts either through their own activities or as a result of their business relationships with other parties. Guiding Principle 19 elaborates further on the implications for how business enterprises should address these situations. For the purpose of these Guiding Principles a business enterprise's "activities" are understood to include both actions and omissions; and its "business relationships" are understood to include relationships with business partners, entities in its value chain, and any other non-State or State entity directly linked to its business operations, products or services.

14. *The responsibility of business enterprises to respect human rights applies to all enterprises regardless of their size, sector, operational context, ownership and structure. Nevertheless, the scale and complexity of the means through which enterprises meet that responsibility may vary according to these factors and with the severity of the enterprise's adverse human rights impacts.*

Commentary

The means through which a business enterprise meets its responsibility to respect human rights will be proportional to, among other factors, its size. Small and medium-sized enterprises may have less capacity as well as more informal processes and management structures than larger companies, so their respective policies and processes will take on different forms. But some small and medium-sized enterprises can have severe human rights impacts, which will require corresponding measures regardless of their size. Severity of impacts will be judged by their scale, scope and irremediable character. The means through which a business enterprise meets its responsibility to respect human rights may also vary depending on whether, and the extent to which, it conducts business through a corporate group or individually. However, the responsibility to respect human rights applies fully and equally to all business enterprises.

15. *In order to meet their responsibility to respect human rights, business enterprises should have in place policies and processes appropriate to their size and circumstances, including:*

(a) *A policy commitment to meet their responsibility to respect human rights;*

(b) *A human rights due diligence process to identify, prevent, mitigate and account for how they address their impacts on human rights;*

(c) *Processes to enable the remediation of any adverse human rights impacts they cause or to which they contribute.*

Commentary

Business enterprises need to know and show that they respect human rights. They cannot do so unless they have certain policies and processes in place. Principles 16 to 24 elaborate further on these.

B. Operational Principles

Policy Commitment

16. *As the basis for embedding their responsibility to respect human rights, business enterprises should express their commitment to meet this responsibility through a statement of policy that:*

(a) *Is approved at the most senior level of the business enterprise;*

(b)   Is informed by relevant internal and/or external expertise;

(c)   Stipulates the enterprise's human rights expectations of personnel, business partners and other parties directly linked to its operations, products or services;

(d)   Is publicly available and communicated internally and externally to all personnel, business partners and other relevant parties;

(e)   Is reflected in operational policies and procedures necessary to embed it throughout the business enterprise.

Commentary

The term "statement" is used generically, to describe whatever means an enterprise employs to set out publicly its responsibilities, commitments, and expectations.

The level of expertise required to ensure that the policy statement is adequately informed will vary according to the complexity of the business enterprise's operations. Expertise can be drawn from various sources, ranging from credible online or written resources to consultation with recognized experts.

The statement of commitment should be publicly available. It should be communicated actively to entities with which the enterprise has contractual relationships; others directly linked to its operations, which may include State security forces; investors; and, in the case of operations with significant human rights risks, to the potentially affected stakeholders.

Internal communication of the statement and of related policies and procedures should make clear what the lines and systems of accountability will be, and should be supported by any necessary training for personnel in relevant business functions.

Just as States should work towards policy coherence, so business enterprises need to strive for coherence between their responsibility to respect human rights and policies and procedures that govern their wider business activities and relationships. This should include, for example, policies and procedures that set financial and other performance incentives for personnel; procurement practices; and lobbying activities where human rights are at stake.

Through these and any other appropriate means, the policy statement should be embedded from the top of the business enterprise through all its functions, which otherwise may act without awareness or regard for human rights.

Human Rights Due Diligence

17.   In order to identify, prevent, mitigate and account for how they address their adverse human rights impacts, business enterprises should carry out human rights due diligence. The process should include assessing actual and potential human rights impacts, integrating and acting upon the findings, tracking responses, and communicating how impacts are addressed. Human rights due diligence:

(a)   Should cover adverse human rights impacts that the business enterprise may cause or contribute to through its own activities, or which may be directly linked to its operations, products or services by its business relationships;

(b)   Will vary in complexity with the size of the business enterprise, the risk of severe human rights impacts, and the nature and context of its operations;

(c)   Should be ongoing, recognizing that the human rights risks may change over time as the business enterprise's operations and operating context evolve.

Commentary

This Principle defines the parameters for human rights due diligence, while Principles 18 through 21 elaborate its essential components.

Human rights risks are understood to be the business enterprise's potential adverse human rights impacts. Potential impacts should be addressed through prevention or mitigation, while actual impacts – those that have already occurred – should be a subject for remediation (Principle 22).

Human rights due diligence can be included within broader enterprise risk-management systems, provided that it goes beyond simply identifying and managing material risks to the company itself, to include risks to rights-holders.

Human rights due diligence should be initiated as early as possible in the development of a new activity or relationship, given that human rights risks can be increased or mitigated already at the stage of structuring contracts or other agreements, and may be inherited through mergers or acquisitions.

Where business enterprises have large numbers of entities in their value chains it may be un-reasonably difficult to conduct due diligence for adverse human rights impacts across them all. If so, business enterprises should identify general areas where the risk of adverse human rights impacts is most significant, whether due to certain suppliers' or clients' operating context, the particular operations, products or services involved, or other relevant considerations, and prioritize these for human rights due diligence.

Questions of complicity may arise when a business enterprise contributes to, or is seen as contri-buting to, adverse human rights impacts caused by other parties. Complicity has both non-legal and legal meanings. As a non-legal matter, business enterprises may be perceived as being "complicit" in the acts of another party where, for example, they are seen to benefit from an abuse committed by that party.

As a legal matter, most national jurisdictions prohibit complicity in the commission of a crime, and a number allow for criminal liability of business enterprises in such cases. Typically, civil actions can also be based on an enterprise's alleged contribution to a harm, although these may not be framed in human rights terms. The weight of international criminal law jurisprudence indicates that the relevant standard for aiding and abetting is knowingly providing practical assistance or encouragement that has a substantial effect on the commission of a crime.

Conducting appropriate human rights due diligence should help business enterprises address the risk of legal claims against them by showing that they took every reasonable step to avoid involvement with an alleged human rights abuse. However, business enterprises conducting such due diligence should not assume that, by itself, this will automatically and fully absolve them from liability for causing or contributing to human rights abuses.

18.   In order to gauge human rights risks, business enterprises should identify and assess any actual or potential adverse human rights impacts with which they may be involved either through their own activities or as a result of their business relationships. This process should:

(a)   Draw on internal and/or independent external human rights expertise;

(b)   Involve meaningful consultation with potentially affected groups and other relevant stakeholders, as appropriate to the size of the business enterprise and the nature and context of the operation.

Commentary

The initial step in conducting human rights due diligence is to identify and assess the nature of the actual and potential adverse human rights impacts with which a business enterprise may be involved. The purpose is to understand the specific impacts on specific people, given a specific context of operations. Typically this includes assessing the human rights context prior to a proposed business activity, where possible; identifying who may be affected; cataloguing the relevant human rights standards and issues; and projecting how the proposed activity and associated business relationships could have adverse human rights impacts on those identified.

In this process, business enterprises should pay special attention to any particular human rights impacts on individuals from groups or populations that may be at heightened risk of vulnerability or marginalization, and bear in mind the different risks that may be faced by women and men.

While processes for assessing human rights impacts can be incorporated within other processes such as risk assessments or environmental and social impact assessments, they should include all internationally recognized human rights as a reference point, since enterprises may potentially impact virtually any of these rights.

Because human rights situations are dynamic, assessments of human rights impacts should be undertaken at regular intervals: prior to a new activity or relationship; prior to major decisions or changes in the operation (e.g. market entry, product launch, policy change, or wider changes to the business); in response to or anticipation of changes in the operating environment (e.g. rising social tensions); and periodically throughout the life of an activity or relationship.

To enable business enterprises to assess their human rights impacts accurately, they should seek to understand the concerns of potentially affected stakeholders by consulting them directly in a manner that takes into account language and other potential barriers to effective engagement. In situations where such consultation is not possible, business enterprises should consider reasonable alternatives such as consulting credible, independent expert resources, including human rights defenders and others from civil society.

The assessment of human rights impacts informs subsequent steps in the human rights due diligence process.

19. In order to prevent and mitigate adverse human rights impacts, business enterprises should integrate the findings from their impact assessments across relevant internal functions and processes, and take appropriate action.

(a) Effective integration requires that:

   (i) Responsibility for addressing such impacts is assigned to the appropriate level and function within the business enterprise;

   (ii) Internal decision-making, budget allocations and oversight processes enable effective responses to such impacts.

(b) Appropriate action will vary according to:

   (i) Whether the business enterprise causes or contributes to an adverse impact, or whether it is involved solely because the impact is directly linked to its operations, products or services by a business relationship;

   (ii) The extent of its leverage in addressing the adverse impact.

Commentary

The horizontal integration across the business enterprise of specific findings from assessing human rights impacts can only be effective if its human rights policy commitment has been embedded into all relevant business functions. This is required to ensure that the assessment findings are properly understood, given due weight, and acted upon.

In assessing human rights impacts, business enterprises will have looked for both actual and potential adverse impacts. Potential impacts should be prevented or mitigated through the horizontal integration of findings across the business enterprise, while actual impacts – those that have already occurred – should be a subject for remediation (Principle 22).

Where a business enterprise causes or may cause an adverse human rights impact, it should take the necessary steps to cease or prevent the impact.

Where a business enterprise contributes or may contribute to an adverse human rights impact, it should take the necessary steps to cease or prevent its contribution and use its leverage to mitigate any remaining impact to the greatest extent possible. Leverage is considered to exist where the enterprise has the ability to effect change in the wrongful practices of an entity that causes a harm.

Where a business enterprise has not contributed to an adverse human rights impact, but that impact is nevertheless directly linked to its operations, products or services by its business relationship with another entity, the situation is more complex. Among the factors that will enter into the determination of the appropriate action in such situations are the enterprise's leverage over the entity concerned, how crucial the relationship is to the enterprise, the severity of the abuse, and whether terminating the relationship with the entity itself would have adverse human rights consequences.

The more complex the situation and its implications for human rights, the stronger is the case for the enterprise to draw on independent expert advice in deciding how to respond.

If the business enterprise has leverage to prevent or mitigate the adverse impact, it should exercise it. And if it lacks leverage there may be ways for the enterprise to increase it. Leverage may be increased by, for example, offering capacity-building or other incentives to the related entity, or collaborating with other actors.

There are situations in which the enterprise lacks the leverage to prevent or mitigate adverse impacts and is unable to increase its leverage. Here, the enterprise should consider ending the relationship, taking into account credible assessments of potential adverse human rights impacts of doing so.

Where the relationship is "crucial" to the enterprise, ending it raises further challenges. A relationship could be deemed as crucial if it provides a product or service that is essential to the enterprise's business, and for which no reasonable alternative source exists. Here the severity of the adverse human rights impact must also be considered: the more severe the abuse, the more quickly the enterprise will need to see change before it takes a decision on whether it should end the relationship. In any case, for as long as the abuse continues and the enterprise remains in the relationship, it should be able to demonstrate its own ongoing efforts to mitigate the impact and be prepared to accept any consequences – reputational, financial or legal – of the continuing connection.

20.   In order to verify whether adverse human rights impacts are being addressed, business enterprises should track the effectiveness of their response. Tracking should:

(a)   Be based on appropriate qualitative and quantitative indicators;

(b)   Draw on feedback from both internal and external sources, including affected stakeholders.

Commentary

Tracking is necessary in order for a business enterprise to know if its human rights policies are being implemented optimally, whether it has responded effectively to the identified human rights impacts, and to drive continuous improvement.

Business enterprises should make particular efforts to track the effectiveness of their responses to impacts on individuals from groups or populations that may be at heightened risk of vulnerability or marginalization.

Tracking should be integrated into relevant internal reporting processes. Business enterprises might employ tools they already use in relation to other issues. This could include performance contracts and reviews as well as surveys and audits, using gender-disaggregated data where relevant. Operational-level grievance mechanisms can also provide important feedback on the effectiveness of the business enterprise's human rights due diligence from those directly affected (see Principle 29).

21. In order to account for how they address their human rights impacts, business enterprises should be prepared to communicate this externally, particularly when concerns are raised by or on behalf of affected stakeholders. Business enterprises whose operations or operating contexts pose risks of severe human rights impacts should report formally on how they address them. In all instances, communications should:

(a) Be of a form and frequency that reflect an enterprise's human rights impacts and that are accessible to its intended audiences;

(b) Provide information that is sufficient to evaluate the adequacy of an enterprise's response to the particular human rights impact involved;

(c) In turn not pose risks to affected stakeholders, personnel or to legitimate requirements of commercial confidentiality.

Commentary

The responsibility to respect human rights requires that business enterprises have in place policies and processes through which they can both know and show that they respect human rights in practice. Showing involves communication, providing a measure of transparency and accountability to individuals or groups who may be impacted and to other relevant stakeholders, including investors.

Communication can take a variety of forms, including in-person meetings, online dialogues, consultation with affected stakeholders, and formal public reports. Formal reporting is itself evolving, from traditional annual reports and corporate responsibility/ sustainability reports, to include online updates and integrated financial and non-financial reports.

Formal reporting by enterprises is expected where risks of severe human rights impacts exist, whether this is due to the nature of the business operations or operating contexts. The reporting should cover topics and indicators concerning how enterprises identify and address adverse impacts on human rights. Independent verification of human rights reporting can strengthen its content and credibility. Sector-specific indicators can provide helpful additional detail.

Remediation

22. Where business enterprises identify that they have caused or contributed to adverse impacts, they should provide for or cooperate in their remediation through legitimate processes.

Commentary

Even with the best policies and practices, a business enterprise may cause or contribute to an adverse human rights impact that it has not foreseen or been able to prevent.

Where a business enterprise identifies such a situation, whether through its human rights due diligence process or other means, its responsibility to respect human rights requires active engagement in remediation, by itself or in cooperation with other actors. Operational-level grievance mechanisms for those potentially impacted by the business enterprise's activities can be one effective means of enabling remediation when they meet certain core criteria, as set out in Principle 31.

Where adverse impacts have occurred that the business enterprise has not caused or contributed to, but which are directly linked to its operations, products or services by a business relationship, the responsibility to respect human rights does not require that the enterprise itself provide for remediation, though it may take a role in doing so.

Some situations, in particular where crimes are alleged, typically will require cooperation with judicial mechanisms.

Further guidance on mechanisms through which remediation may be sought, including where allegations of adverse human rights impacts are contested, is included in chapter III on access to remedy.

Issues of Context

23. *In all contexts, business enterprises should:*

(a) *Comply with all applicable laws and respect internationally recognized human rights, wherever they operate;*

(b) *Seek ways to honour the principles of internationally recognized human rights when faced with conflicting requirements;*

(c) *Treat the risk of causing or contributing to gross human rights abuses as a legal compliance issue wherever they operate.*

Commentary

Although particular country and local contexts may affect the human rights risks of an enterprise's activities and business relationships, all business enterprises have the same responsibility to respect human rights wherever they operate. Where the domestic context renders it impossible to meet this responsibility fully, business enterprises are expected to respect the principles of internationally recognized human rights to the greatest extent possible in the circumstances, and to be able to demonstrate their efforts in this regard.

Some operating environments, such as conflict-affected areas, may increase the risks of enterprises being complicit in gross human rights abuses committed by other actors (security forces, for example). Business enterprises should treat this risk as a legal compliance issue, given the expanding web of potential corporate legal liability arising from extraterritorial civil claims, and from the incorporation of the provisions of the Rome Statute of the International Criminal Court in jurisdictions that provide for corporate criminal responsibility. In addition, corporate directors, officers and employees may be subject to individual liability for acts that amount to gross human rights abuses.

In complex contexts such as these, business enterprises should ensure that they do not exacerbate the situation. In assessing how best to respond, they will often be well advised to draw on not only expertise and cross-functional consultation within the enterprise, but also to consult externally with credible, independent experts, including from Governments, civil society, national human rights institutions and relevant multi- stakeholder initiatives.

24. *Where it is necessary to prioritize actions to address actual and potential adverse human rights impacts, business enterprises should first seek to prevent and mitigate those that are most severe or where delayed response would make them irremediable.*

Commentary

While business enterprises should address all their adverse human rights impacts, it may not always be possible to address them simultaneously. In the absence of specific legal guidance, if prioritization is necessary business enterprises should begin with those human rights impacts that would be most severe, recognizing that a delayed response may affect remediability. Severity is not an absolute concept in this context, but is relative to the other human rights impacts the business enterprise has identified.

III. Access to Remedy

A. Foundational Principle

25. As part of their duty to protect against business-related human rights abuse, States must take appropriate steps to ensure, through judicial, administrative, legislative or other appropriate means, that when such abuses occur within their territory and/or jurisdiction those affected have access to effective remedy.

Commentary

Unless States take appropriate steps to investigate, punish and redress business- related human rights abuses when they do occur, the State duty to protect can be rendered weak or even meaningless.

Access to effective remedy has both procedural and substantive aspects. The remedies provided by the grievance mechanisms discussed in this section may take a range of substantive forms the aim of which, generally speaking, will be to counteract or make good any human rights harms that have occurred. Remedy may include apologies, restitution, rehabilitation, financial or non-financial compensation and punitive sanctions (whether criminal or administrative, such as fines), as well as the prevention of harm through, for example, injunctions or guarantees of non-repetition. Procedures for the provision of remedy should be impartial, protected from corruption and free from political or other attempts to influence the outcome.

For the purpose of these Guiding Principles, a grievance is understood to be a perceived injustice evoking an individual's or a group's sense of entitlement, which may be based on law, contract, explicit or implicit promises, customary practice, or general notions of fairness of aggrieved communities. The term grievance mechanism is used to indicate any routinized, State-based or non-State-based, judicial or non-judicial process through which grievances concerning business-related human rights abuse can be raised and remedy can be sought.

State-based grievance mechanisms may be administered by a branch or agency of the State, or by an independent body on a statutory or constitutional basis. They may be judicial or non-judicial. In some mechanisms, those affected are directly involved in seeking remedy; in others, an intermediary seeks remedy on their behalf. Examples include the courts (for both criminal and civil actions), labour tribunals, national human rights institutions, National Contact Points under the Guidelines for Multinational Enterprises of the Organisation for Economic Co-operation and Development, many ombudsperson offices, and Government-run complaints offices.

Ensuring access to remedy for business-related human rights abuses requires also that States facilitate public awareness and understanding of these mechanisms, how they can be accessed, and any support (financial or expert) for doing so.

State-based judicial and non-judicial grievance mechanisms should form the foundation of a wider system of remedy. Within such a system, operational-level grievance mechanisms can provide early stage recourse and resolution. State-based and operational-level mechanisms, in turn, can be supplemented or enhanced by the remedial functions of collaborative initiatives as well as those of international and regional human rights mechanisms. Further guidance with regard to these mechanisms is provided in Guiding Principles 26 to 31.

B. Operational Principles

State-Based Judicial Mechanisms

26. States should take appropriate steps to ensure the effectiveness of domestic judicial mechanisms when addressing business-related human rights abuses, including considering ways to reduce legal, practical and other relevant barriers that could lead to a denial of access to remedy.

Commentary

Effective judicial mechanisms are at the core of ensuring access to remedy. Their ability to address business-related human rights abuses depends on their impartiality, integrity and ability to accord due process.

States should ensure that they do not erect barriers to prevent legitimate cases from being brought before the courts in situations where judicial recourse is an essential part of accessing remedy or alternative sources of effective remedy are unavailable. They should also ensure that the provision of justice is not prevented by corruption of the judicial process, that courts are independent of economic or political pressures from other State agents and from business actors, and that the legitimate and peaceful activities of human rights defenders are not obstructed.

Legal barriers that can prevent legitimate cases involving business-related human rights abuse from being addressed can arise where, for example:

- The way in which legal responsibility is attributed among members of a corporate group under domestic criminal and civil laws facilitates the avoidance of appropriate accountability;
- Where claimants face a denial of justice in a host State and cannot access home State courts regardless of the merits of the claim;
- Where certain groups, such as indigenous peoples and migrants, are excluded from the same level of legal protection of their human rights that applies to the wider population.

Practical and procedural barriers to accessing judicial remedy can arise where, for example:

- The costs of bringing claims go beyond being an appropriate deterrent to unmeritorious cases and/or cannot be reduced to reasonable levels through Government support, "market-based" mechanisms (such as litigation insurance and legal fee structures), or other means;
- Claimants experience difficulty in securing legal representation, due to a lack of resources or of other incentives for lawyers to advise claimants in this area;
- There are inadequate options for aggregating claims or enabling representative proceedings (such as class actions and other collective action procedures), and this prevents effective remedy for individual claimants;
- State prosecutors lack adequate resources, expertise and support to meet the State's own obligations to investigate individual and business involvement in human rights-related crimes.

Many of these barriers are the result of, or compounded by, the frequent imbalances between the parties to business-related human rights claims, such as in their financial resources, access to information and expertise. Moreover, whether through active discrimination or as the unintended consequences of the way judicial mechanisms are designed and operate, individuals from groups or populations at heightened risk of vulnerability or marginalization often face additional cultural, social, physical and financial impediments to accessing, using and benefiting from these mechanisms. Particular attention should be given to the rights and specific needs of such groups or populations at each stage of the remedial process: access, procedures and outcome.

State-Based Non-Judicial Grievance Mechanisms

27.   States should provide effective and appropriate non-judicial grievance mechanisms, alongside judicial mechanisms, as part of a comprehensive State-based system for the remedy of business-related human rights abuse.

Commentary

Administrative, legislative and other non-judicial mechanisms play an essential role in complementing and supplementing judicial mechanisms. Even where judicial systems are effective and well-resourced, they cannot carry the burden of addressing all alleged abuses; judicial remedy is not always required; nor is it always the favoured approach for all claimants.

Gaps in the provision of remedy for business-related human rights abuses could be filled, where appropriate, by expanding the mandates of existing non-judicial mechanisms and/or by adding new mechanisms. These may be mediation-based, adjudicative or follow other culturally appropriate and rights-compatible processes – or involve some combination of these – depending on the issues concerned, any public interest involved, and the potential needs of the parties. To ensure their effectiveness, they should meet the criteria set out in Principle 31.

National human rights institutions have a particularly important role to play in this regard.

As with judicial mechanisms, States should consider ways to address any imbalances between the parties to business-related human rights claims and any additional barriers to access faced by individuals from groups or populations at heightened risk of vulnerability or marginalization.

Non-State-Based Grievance Mechanisms

28.   States should consider ways to facilitate access to effective non-State-based grievance mechanisms dealing with business-related human rights harms.

Commentary

One category of non-State-based grievance mechanisms encompasses those administered by a business enterprise alone or with stakeholders, by an industry association or a multi-stakeholder group. They are non-judicial, but may use adjudicative, dialogue-based or other culturally appropriate and rights-compatible processes. These mechanisms may offer particular benefits such as speed of access and remediation, reduced costs and/or transnational reach.

Another category comprises regional and international human rights bodies. These have dealt most often with alleged violations by States of their obligations to respect human rights. However, some have also dealt with the failure of a State to meet its duty to protect against human rights abuse by business enterprises.

States can play a helpful role in raising awareness of, or otherwise facilitating access to, such options, alongside the mechanisms provided by States themselves.

29.   To make it possible for grievances to be addressed early and remediated directly, business enterprises should establish or participate in effective operational-level grievance mechanisms for individuals and communities who may be adversely impacted.

Commentary

Operational-level grievance mechanisms are accessible directly to individuals and communities who may be adversely impacted by a business enterprise. They are typically administered by enterprises, alone or in collaboration with others, including relevant stakeholders. They may also be provided through recourse to a mutually acceptable external expert or body. They do not require that those bringing a complaint first access other means of recourse. They can engage the business enterprise directly in assessing the issues and seeking remediation of any harm.

Operational-level grievance mechanisms perform two key functions regarding the responsibility of business enterprises to respect human rights.

*   First, they support the identification of adverse human rights impacts as a part of an enterprise's ongoing human rights due diligence. They do so by providing a channel for those directly impacted by the enterprise's operations to raise concerns when they believe they are being or will be adversely impacted. By analysing trends and patterns in complaints, business enterprises can also identify systemic problems and adapt their practices accordingly;

*   Second, these mechanisms make it possible for grievances, once identified, to be addressed and for adverse impacts to be remediated early and directly by the business enterprise, thereby preventing harms from compounding and grievances from escalating.

Such mechanisms need not require that a complaint or grievance amount to an alleged human rights abuse before it can be raised, but specifically aim to identify any legitimate concerns of those who may be adversely impacted. If those concerns are not identified and addressed, they may over time escalate into more major disputes and human rights abuses.

Operational-level grievance mechanisms should reflect certain criteria to ensure their effectiveness in practice (Principle 31). These criteria can be met through many different forms of grievance mechanism according to the demands of scale, resource, sector, culture and other parameters.

Operational-level grievance mechanisms can be important complements to wider stakeholder engagement and collective bargaining processes, but cannot substitute for either. They should not be used to undermine the role of legitimate trade unions in addressing labour-related disputes, nor to preclude access to judicial or other non- judicial grievance mechanisms.

30.   Industry, multi-stakeholder and other collaborative initiatives that are based on respect for human rights-related standards should ensure that effective grievance mechanisms are available.

Commentary

Human rights-related standards are increasingly reflected in commitments undertaken by industry bodies, multi-stakeholder and other collaborative initiatives, through codes of conduct, performance standards, global framework agreements between trade unions and transnational corporations, and similar undertakings.

Such collaborative initiatives should ensure the availability of effective mechanisms through which affected parties or their legitimate representatives can raise concerns when they believe the commitments in question have not been met. The legitimacy of such initiatives may be put at risk if they do not provide for such mechanisms. The mechanisms could be at the level of individual members, of the collaborative initiative, or both. These mechanisms should provide for accountability and help enable the remediation of adverse human rights impacts.

Effectiveness Criteria for Non-Judicial Grievance Mechanisms

31.   In order to ensure their effectiveness, non-judicial grievance mechanisms, both State-based and non-State-based, should be:

(a)   Legitimate: enabling trust from the stakeholder groups for whose use they are intended, and being accountable for the fair conduct of grievance processes;

(b)   Accessible: being known to all stakeholder groups for whose use they are intended, and providing adequate assistance for those who may face particular barriers to access;

(c)   Predictable: providing a clear and known procedure with an indicative time frame for each stage, and clarity on the types of process and outcome available and means of monitoring implementation;

(d)   Equitable: seeking to ensure that aggrieved parties have reasonable access to sources of information, advice and expertise necessary to engage in a grievance process on fair, informed and respectful terms;

(e)   Transparent: keeping parties to a grievance informed about its progress, and providing sufficient information about the mechanism's performance to build confidence in its effectiveness and meet any public interest at stake;

(f)   Rights-compatible: ensuring that outcomes and remedies accord with internationally recognized human rights;

(g)   A source of continuous learning: drawing on relevant measures to identify lessons for improving the mechanism and preventing future grievances and harms;

Operational-level mechanisms should also be:

(h)   Based on engagement and dialogue: consulting the stakeholder groups for whose use they are intended on their design and performance, and focusing on dialogue as the means to address and resolve grievances.

Commentary

A grievance mechanism can only serve its purpose if the people it is intended to serve know about it, trust it and are able to use it. These criteria provide a benchmark for designing, revising or assessing a non-judicial grievance mechanism to help ensure that it is effective in practice. Poorly designed or implemented grievance mechanisms can risk compounding a sense of grievance amongst affected stakeholders by heightening their sense of disempowerment and disrespect by the process.

The first seven criteria apply to any State-based or non-State-based, adjudicative or dialogue-based mechanism. The eighth criterion is specific to operational-level mechanisms that business enterprises help administer.

The term "grievance mechanism" is used here as a term of art. The term itself may not always be appropriate or helpful when applied to a specific mechanism, but the criteria for effectiveness remain the same. Commentary on the specific criteria follows:

(a) Stakeholders for whose use a mechanism is intended must trust it if they are to choose to use it. Accountability for ensuring that the parties to a grievance process cannot interfere with its fair conduct is typically one important factor in building stakeholder trust;

(b) Barriers to access may include a lack of awareness of the mechanism, language, literacy, costs, physical location and fears of reprisal;

(c) In order for a mechanism to be trusted and used, it should provide public information about the procedure it offers. Time frames for each stage should be respected wherever possible, while allowing that flexibility may sometimes be needed;

(d) In grievances or disputes between business enterprises and affected stakeholders, the latter frequently have much less access to information and expert resources, and often lack the financial resources to pay for them. Where this imbalance is not redressed, it can reduce both the achievement and perception of a fair process and make it harder to arrive at durable solutions;

(e) Communicating regularly with parties about the progress of individual grievances can be essential to retaining confidence in the process. Providing transparency about the mechanism's performance to wider stakeholders, through statistics, case studies or more detailed information about the handling of certain cases, can be important to demonstrate its legitimacy and retain broad trust. At the same time, confidentiality of the dialogue between parties and of individuals' identities should be provided where necessary;

(f) Grievances are frequently not framed in terms of human rights and many do not initially raise human rights concerns. Regardless, where outcomes have implications for human rights, care should be taken to ensure that they are in line with internationally recognized human rights;

(g) Regular analysis of the frequency, patterns and causes of grievances can enable the institution administering the mechanism to identify and influence policies, procedures or practices that should be altered to prevent future harm;

(h) For an operational-level grievance mechanism, engaging with affected stakeholder groups about its design and performance can help to ensure that it meets their needs, that they will use it in practice, and that there is a shared interest in ensuring its success. Since a business enterprise cannot, with legitimacy, both be the subject of complaints and unilaterally determine their outcome, these mechanisms should focus on reaching agreed solutions through dialogue. Where adjudication is needed, this should be provided by a legitimate, independent third-party mechanism.

X.8. 2014 NORWEGIAN GUIDELINES FOR OBSERVATION AND EXCLUSION OF COMPANIES FROM THE GOVERNMENT PENSION FUND GLOBAL[1]

Adopted 18 December 2014 by the Ministry of Finance pursuant to the Royal Decree of 19 November 2004. Latest amendment 10 February 2017.

Section 1. Scope

(1) These guidelines apply to the work of the Council on Ethics for the Government Pension Fund Global (the Council on Ethics) and Norges Bank (the Bank) on the observation and exclusion of companies from the portfolio of the Government Pension Fund Global (the Fund) in accordance with the criteria in sections 2 and 3.

(2) The guidelines cover investments in the Fund's equity and fixed-income portfolios.

(3) The Council on Ethics makes recommendations to the Bank on the observation and exclusion of companies in the Fund's portfolio in accordance with the criteria in sections 2 and 3, and on the revocation of observation and exclusion decisions; cf. section 5(5) and section 6(6).

(4) The Bank makes decisions on the observation and exclusion of companies in the Fund's portfolio in accordance with the criteria in sections 2 and 3, and on the revocation of observation and exclusion decisions; cf. section 5(5) and section 6(6). The Bank may on its own initiative make decisions on observation and exclusion and on the revocation of such decisions; cf. section 2(2)-(4).

Section 2. Criteria for Product-Based Observation and Exclusion of Companies

(1) The Fund shall not be invested in companies which themselves or through entities they control:

a) produce weapons that violate fundamental humanitarian principles through their normal use

b) produce tobacco

c) sell weapons or military materiel to states that are subject to investment restrictions on government bonds as described in the management mandate for the Government Pension Fund Global, section 3-1(2)(c).

(2) Observation or exclusion may be decided for mining companies and power producers which themselves or through entities they control derive 30 per cent or more of their income from thermal coal or base 30 per cent or more of their operations on thermal coal.

(3) In assessments pursuant to subsection (2) above, in addition to the company's current share of income or activity from thermal coal, importance shall also be attached to forward-looking assessments, including any plans the company may have that will change the share of its business based on thermal coal and the share of its business based on renewable energy sources.

(4) Recommendations and decisions on exclusion of companies based on subsections (2) and (3) above shall not include green bonds issued by the company in question where such bonds are recognised through inclusion in specific indices for green bonds or are verified by a recognised third party.

---

1   See https://www.regjeringen.no/globalassets/upload/fin/statens-pensjonsfond/formelt-grunnlag/guide-lines-for-observation-and-exclusion-from-the-gpfg---17.2.2017.pdf.

Section 3. Criteria for Conduct-Based Observation and Exclusion of Companies

Companies may be put under observation or be excluded if there is an unacceptable risk that the company contributes to or is responsible for:

a)   serious or systematic human rights violations, such as murder, torture, deprivation of liberty, forced labour and the worst forms of child labour

b)   serious violations of the rights of individuals in situations of war or conflict

c)   severe environmental damage

d)   acts or omissions that on an aggregate company level lead to unacceptable greenhouse gas emissions

e)   gross corruption

f)   other particularly serious violations of fundamental ethical norms.

Section 4. The Council on Ethics

(1)   The Council on Ethics consists of five members appointed by the Ministry of Finance (the Ministry) after receiving a nomination from the Bank. The Ministry also appoints a chair and deputy chair after receiving a nomination from the Bank. The Bank's nomination shall be submitted to the Ministry no later than two months prior to the expiry of the appointment period.

(2)   The composition of members shall ensure that the Council on Ethics possesses the required expertise to perform its functions as defined in these guidelines.

(3)   Members of the Council on Ethics shall be appointed for a period of four years. Upon the initial appointment, the Ministry may adopt transitional provisions.

(4)   The Ministry sets the remuneration of the members of the Council on Ethics and the Council on Ethics' budget.

(5)   The Council on Ethics has its own secretariat, which administratively is under the Ministry. The Council on Ethics shall ensure that the secretariat has appropriate procedures and routines in place.

(6)   The Council on Ethics shall prepare an annual operating plan, which shall be submitted to the Ministry. The operating plan shall describe the priorities set by the Council on Ethics for its work; cf. section 5.

(7)   The Council on Ethics shall submit an annual report on its activities to the Ministry. This report shall be submitted no later than three months after the end of each calendar year.

(8)   The Council on Ethics shall evaluate its work regularly.

Section 5. The Work of the Council on Ethics on Recommendations Concerning Observation and Exclusion

(1)   The Council on Ethics shall continuously monitor the Fund's portfolio, cf. section 1(2), with the aim of identifying companies that contribute to or are responsible for production or conduct as mentioned in sections 2 and 3.

(2)   The Council on Ethics may investigate matters on its own initiative or at the request of the Bank. The Council on Ethics shall develop and publish principles for the selection of companies for closer investigation. The Bank may adopt more detailed requirements relating to these principles.

(3)   The Council on Ethics shall be free to gather the information it deems necessary, and shall ensure that each matter is thoroughly investigated before making a recommendation regarding observation, exclusion or revocation of such decisions.

(4)   A company that is being considered for observation or exclusion shall be given an opportunity to present information and opinions to the Council on Ethics at an early stage of the

process. In this context, the Council on Ethics shall clarify to the company what circumstances may form the basis for observation or exclusion. If the Council on Ethics decides to recommend observation or exclusion, its draft recommendation shall be presented to the company for comments; cf. section 7.

(5)   The Council on Ethics shall regularly assess whether the basis for observation or exclusion still exists. In light of new information, the Council on Ethics may recommend that the Bank revoke an observation or exclusion decision.

(6)   The Council on Ethics shall describe the grounds for its recommendations to the Bank; cf. sections 2 and 3. The Bank may adopt more detailed requirements relating to the form of such recommendations.

(7)   The Council on Ethics shall publish its routines for the consideration of possible revocation of an observation or exclusion decision. Excluded companies shall be informed specifically of these routines.

Section 6. Norges Bank

(1)   The Bank shall make decisions on observation and exclusion in accordance with the criteria in sections 2 and 3 and on the revocation of such decisions, after receiving recommendations from the Council on Ethics. The Bank may on its own initiative make decisions on observation and exclusion in accordance with section 2(2)-(4) and on the revocation of such decisions.

(2)   In assessing whether a company is to be excluded under section 3, the Bank may consider factors such as the probability of future norm violations, the severity and extent of the violations and the connection between the norm violation and the company in which the Fund is invested. The Bank may also consider the breadth of the company's operations and governance, including whether the company is doing what can reasonably be expected to reduce the risk of future norm violations within a reasonable time frame. Relevant factors in these assessments include the company's guidelines for, and work on, safeguarding good corporate governance, the environment and social conditions, and whether the company is making a positive contribution for those who are or have been affected by the company's conduct.

(3)   Before making a decision on observation and exclusion in accordance with section 6(1), the Bank shall consider whether other measures, including the exercise of ownership rights, may be more suited to reduce the risk of continued norm violations, or whether such alternative measures may be more appropriate for other reasons. The Bank shall consider the full range of measures at its disposal and apply the measures in a coherent manner.

(4)   Observation may be decided when there is doubt as to whether the conditions for exclusion are met or as to future developments, or where observation is deemed appropriate for other reasons.

(5)   The Bank shall ensure that sufficient information is available before making a individual observation, exclusion or revocation decision.

(6)   The Bank shall regularly assess whether the basis for observation or exclusion still exists.

Section 7. Exchange of Information and Coordination Between the Bank and the Council on Ethics

(1)   To help ensure the most coherent use of measures possible in the context of promoting responsible management, the Bank and the Council on Ethics shall meet regularly to exchange information and coordinate their work.

(2)   Communication with companies shall be coordinated and aim to be perceived as consistent. The Bank shall exercise the Fund's ownership rights. The Bank shall seek to integrate the Council on Ethics' communication with companies into its general company follow-up. The Bank shall have access to the Council on Ethics' communication with companies, and may participate in meetings between the Council on Ethics and companies.

(3) The Council on Ethics may ask the Bank for information on matters concerning individual companies, including how specific companies are dealt with in the context of the exercise of ownership rights. The Bank may request the Council on Ethics to make its assessments of individual companies available.

(4) The Bank and the Council on Ethics shall establish detailed procedures for the exchange of information and coordination to clarify responsibilities and promote productive communication and integration of the work of the Bank and the Council on Ethics.

Section 8. Publication

(1) The Bank shall publish its decisions pursuant to these guidelines. Such public disclosure shall be in accordance with the management mandate for the Fund, section 6-2(4). When the Bank publishes its decisions, the Council on Ethics shall publish its recommendations. When the Bank on its own initiative makes decisions in accordance with section 6(1), the grounds for the decision shall be included in the publication.

(2) The Bank shall maintain a public list of companies excluded from the Fund or placed under observation pursuant to these guidelines.

Section 9. Meetings with the Ministry of Finance

(1) The Ministry, the Bank and the Council on Ethics shall meet at least once a year. The information exchanged at such meetings shall be part of the basis for the reporting on responsible management included in the annual report to the Storting (the Norwegian parliament) on the management of the Fund.

(2) The Ministry and the Council on Ethics shall meet at least once a year. The following matters shall be discussed at the meetings:

a)   activities in the preceding year

b)   other matters reported by the Ministry and the Council on Ethics for further consideration.

Section 10. Power of Amendment

The Ministry may supplement or amend these guidelines.

Section 11. Entry into Force [...]

Section 12. Transitional Provisions [...]

XI. Examples of Regional Agreements

XI.1. 2003 U.S. – CHILE FREE TRADE AGREEMENT (excerpts)

Index

Preamble
Chapter One –   Initial Provisions
   Article 1.1   Establishment of a Free Trade Area
   Article 1.2   Objectives
   Article 1.3   Relation to Other Agreements
   Article 1.4   Extent of Obligations
Chapter Two –   General Definitions
Chapter Three – National Treatment and Market Access for Goods
Section A   National Treatment
Section B   Tariff Elimination
Section C   Special Regimes
Section D   Non-Tariff Measures
Section E   Other Measures
Section F   Agriculture
Section G   Textiles and Apparel
Section H   Institutional Provisions
Section I   Definitions
Chapter Four – Rules of Origin and Origin Procedures
Chapter Five – Customs Administration
Chapter Six –   Sanitary and Phytosanitary Measures
Chapter Seven – Technical Barriers to Trade
Chapter Eight – Trade Remedies
Section A   Safeguards
Section B   Antidumping and Countervailing Duties
Chapter Nine – Government Procurement
Chapter Ten –   Investment
Section A   Investment
   Article 10.1   Scope and Coverage
   Article 10.2   National Treatment
   Article 10.3   Most-Favored-Nation Treatment
   Article 10.4   Minimum Standard of Treatment
   Article 10.5   Performance Requirements
   Article 10.6   Senior Management and Boards of Directors
   Article 10.7   Non-Conforming Measures
   Article 10.8   Transfers
   Article 10.9   Expropriation and Compensation
   Article 10.10 Special Formalities and Information Requirements
   Article 10.11 Denial of Benefits
   Article 10.12 Investment and Environment
   Article 10.13 Implementation
Section B   Investor-State Dispute Settlement
   Article10.14   Consultation and Negotiation
   Article 10.15 Submission of a Claim to Arbitration
   Article 10.16 Consent of Each Party to Arbitration
   Article 10.17 Conditions and Limitations on Consent of Each Party

Article 10.18 Selection of Arbitrators
Article 10.19 Conduct of the Arbitration
Article 10.20 Transparency of Arbitral Proceedings
Article 10.21 Governing Law
Article 10.22 Interpretation of Annexes
Article 10.23 Expert Reports
Article 10.24 Consolidation
Article 10.25 Awards
Article 10.26 Service of Documents
Section C   Definitions
Article 10.27 Definitions
Annex 10-A: Customary International Law
Annex 10-B: Public Debt Chile
Annex 10-C: Special Dispute Settlement Provisions
Annex 10-D: Expropriation
Annex 10-E: Submission of a Claim to Arbitration
Annex 10-F: DL 600
Annex 10-G: Service of Documents on a Party Under Section B
Annex 10-H: Possibility of a Bilateral Appellate Body/Mechanism
Chapter Eleven – Cross-Border Trade in Services
Article 11.1   Scope and Coverage
Article 11.2   National Treatment
Article 11.3   Most-Favored-Nation Treatment
Article 11.4   Market Access
Article 11.5   Local Presence
Article 11.6   Non-conforming Measures
Article 11.7   Transparency in Development and Application of Regulations
Article 11.8   Domestic Regulation
Article 11.9   Mutual Recognition
Article 11.10 Implementation
Article 11.11 Denial of Benefits
Article 11.12 Definitions
Chapter Twelve – Financial Services
Article 12.1   Scope and Coverage
Article 12.2   National Treatment
Article 12.3   Most-Favored-Nation Treatment
Article 12.4   Market Access for Financial Institutions
Article 12.5   Cross-Border Trade
Article 12.6   New Financial Services
Article 12.7   Treatment of Certain Information
Article 12.8   Senior Management and Boards of Directors
Article 12.9   Non-Conforming Measures
Article 12.10 Exceptions
Article 12.11 Transparency
Article 12.12 Self-Regulatory Organizations
Article 12.13 Payment and Clearing Systems
Article 12.14 Expedited Availability of Insurance Services
Article 12.15 Financial Services Committee
Article 12.16 Consultations
Article 12.17 Dispute Settlement
Article 12.18 Investment Disputes in Financial Services
Article 12.19 Definitions

Chapter Thirteen– Telecommunications
Chapter Fourteen – Temporary Entry for Business Persons
    Article 14.1   General Principles
    Article 14.2   General Obligations
    Article 14.3   Grant of Temporary Entry
    Article 14.4   Provision of Information
    Article 14.5   Committee on Temporary Entry
    Article 14.6   Dispute Settlement
    Article 14.7   Relation to Other Chapters
    Article 14.8   Transparency in Development and Application of Regulations
    Article 14.9   Definitions
    Annex 14.3: Temporary Entry for Business Persons
    Appendix 14.3(A)(1): Business Visitors
    Appendix 14.3(D)(2)
    Appendix 14.3(D)(6): United States
Chapter Fifteen – Electronic Commerce
Chapter Sixteen – Competition Policy, Designated Monopolies, State Enterprises
Chapter Seventeen – Intellectual Property Rights
Chapter Eighteen – Labor
    Article 18.1   Statement of Shared Commitment
    Article 18.2   Enforcement of Labor Laws
    Article 18.3   Procedural Guarantees and Public Awareness
    Article 18.4   Labor Affairs Council
    Article 18.5   Labor Cooperation Mechanism
    Article 18.6   Cooperative Consultations
    Article 18.7   Labor Roster
    Article 18.8   Definitions
    Annex 18.5: Labor Cooperation Mechanism
Chapter Nineteen – Environment
    Article 19.1   Levels of Protection
    Article 19.2   Enforcement of Environmental Laws
    Article 19.3   Environment Affairs Council
    Article 19.4   Opportunities for Public Participation
    Article 19.5   Environmental Cooperation
    Article 19.6   Environmental Consultations
    Article 19.7   Environment Roster
    Article 19.8   Procedural Matters
    Article 19.9   Relationship to Environmental Agreements
    Article 19.10 Principles of Corporate Stewardship
    Article 19.11 Definitions
    Annex 19.3: Environmental Cooperation
Chapter Twenty – Transparency
    Article 20.1   Contact Points
    Article 20.2   Publication
    Article 20.3   Notification and Provision of Information
    Article 20.4   Administrative Proceedings
    Article 20.5   Review and Appeal
    Article 20.6   Definitions
Chapter Twenty-One – Administration of the Agreement
    Article 21.1   The Free Trade Commission
    Article 21.2   Administration of Dispute Settlement Proceedings
    Annex 21.1: Implementation of Modifications Approved by the Commission

Chapter Twenty-Two – Dispute Settlement

Article 22.1   Cooperation
Article 22.2   Scope of Application
Article 22.3   Choice of Forum
Article 22.4   Consultations
Article 22.5   Commission - Good Offices, Conciliation, and Mediation
Article 22.6   Request for an Arbitral Panel
Article 22.7   Roster
Article 22.8   Qualifications of Panelists
Article 22.9   Panel Selection
Article 22.10 Rules of Procedure
Article 22.11 Experts and Technical Advice
Article 22.12 Initial Report
Article 22.13 Final Report
Article 22.14 Implementation of Final Report
Article 22.15 Non-Implementation - Suspension of Benefits
Article 22.16 Non-Implementation in Certain Disputes
Article 22.17 Compliance Review
Article 22.18 Five-Year Review
Article 22.19 Referral of Matters from Judicial or Administrative Proceedings
Article 22.20 Private Rights
Article 22.21 Alternative Dispute Resolution
Annex 22.2:   Nullification or Impairment
Annex 22.16: Inflation Adjustment Formula for Monetary Assessments

Chapter Twenty-Three – Exceptions

Article 23.1   General Exceptions
Article 23.2   Essential Security
Article 23.3   Taxation
Article 23.4   Balance of Payments Measures on Trade in Goods
Article 23.5   Disclosure of Information
Article 23.6   Definitions
Annex 23.3:   Competent Authorities

Chapter Twenty-Four – Final Provisions

Article 24.1   Annexes, Appendices, and Footnotes
Article 24.2   Amendments
Article 24.3   Amendment of the WTO Agreement
Article 24.4   Entry into Force and Termination
Article 24.5   Authentic Texts

Annexes

[...]

Chapter Ten – Investment

Section A: Investment

Article 10.1: Scope and Coverage

1.   This Chapter applies to measures adopted or maintained by a Party relating to:

(a)   investors of the other Party;

(b)   covered investments; and

(c)   with respect to Articles 10.5 and 10.12, all investments in the territory of the Party.

2.   In the event of any inconsistency between this Chapter and another Chapter, the other Chapter shall prevail to the extent of the inconsistency.

3.   A requirement by a Party that a service provider of the other Party post a bond or other form of financial security as a condition of providing a service into its territory does not of itself make this Chapter applicable to the provision of that cross-border service. This Chapter applies to that Party's treatment of the posted bond or financial security.

4.   This Chapter does not apply to measures adopted or maintained by a Party to the extent that they are covered by Chapter Twelve (Financial Services).

Article 10.2: National Treatment

1.   Each Party shall accord to investors of the other Party treatment no less favorable than that it accords, in like circumstances, to its own investors with respect to the establishment, acquisition, expansion, management, conduct, operation, and sale or other disposition of investments in its territory.

2.   Each Party shall accord to covered investments treatment no less favorable than that it accords, in like circumstances, to investments in its territory of its own investors with respect to the establishment, acquisition, expansion, management, conduct, operation, and sale or other disposition of investments.

3.   The treatment to be accorded by a Party under paragraphs 1 and 2 means, with respect to a regional level of government, treatment no less favorable than the most favorable treatment accorded, in like circumstances, by that regional level of government to investors, and to investments of investors, of the Party of which it forms a part.

Article 10.3: Most-Favored-Nation Treatment

1.   Each Party shall accord to investors of the other Party treatment no less favorable than that it accords, in like circumstances, to investors of any non-Party with respect to the establishment, acquisition, expansion, management, conduct, operation, and sale or other disposition of investments in its territory.

2.   Each Party shall accord to covered investments treatment no less favorable than that it accords, in like circumstances, to investments in its territory of investors of any non-Party with respect to the establishment, acquisition, expansion, management, conduct, operation, and sale or other disposition of investments.

Article 10.4: Minimum Standard of Treatment

1.   Each Party shall accord to covered investments treatment in accordance with customary international law, including fair and equitable treatment and full protection and security.

2.   For greater certainty, paragraph 1 prescribes the customary international law minimum standard of treatment of aliens as the minimum standard of treatment to be afforded to covered investments. The concepts of "fair and equitable treatment" and "full protection and security" do not require treatment in addition to or beyond that which is required by that standard, and do not create additional substantive rights. The obligation in paragraph 1 to provide:

(a)   "fair and equitable treatment" includes the obligation not to deny justice in criminal, civil, or administrative adjudicatory proceedings in accordance with the principle of due process embodied in the principal legal systems of the world; and

(b)   "full protection and security" requires each Party to provide the level of police protection required under customary international law.

3.   A determination that there has been a breach of another provision of this Agreement, or of a separate international agreement, does not establish that there has been a breach of this Article.

4.   Notwithstanding Article 10.7(5)(b), each Party shall accord to investors of the other Party, and to covered investments, non-discriminatory treatment with respect to measures it adopts or maintains relating to losses suffered by investments in its territory owing to armed conflict or civil strife.

5.   Notwithstanding paragraph 4, if an investor of a Party, in the situations referred to in that paragraph, suffers a loss in the territory of the other Party resulting from:

(a)   requisitioning of its covered investment or part thereof by the latter's forces or authorities; or

(b)   destruction of its covered investment or part thereof by the latter's forces or authorities, which was not required by the necessity of the situation,

the latter Party shall provide the investor restitution or compensation, which in either case shall be prompt, adequate, and effective, and, with respect to compensation, shall be in accordance with Article 10.9(2) through (4).

6.   Paragraph 4 does not apply to existing measures relating to subsidies or grants that would be inconsistent with Article 10.2 but for Article 10.7(5)(b).

Article 10.5: Performance Requirements

Mandatory Performance Requirements

1.   Neither Party may impose or enforce any of the following requirements, or enforce any commitment or undertaking, in connection with the establishment, acquisition, expansion, management, conduct, operation, or sale or other disposition of an investment of an investor of a Party or of a non-Party in its territory:

(a)   to export a given level or percentage of goods or services;

(b)   to achieve a given level or percentage of domestic content;

(c)   to purchase, use, or accord a preference to goods produced in its territory, or to purchase goods from persons in its territory;

(d)   to relate in any way the volume or value of imports to the volume or value of exports or to the amount of foreign exchange inflows associated with such investment;

(e)   to restrict sales of goods or services in its territory that such investment produces or supplies by relating such sales in any way to the volume or value of its exports or foreign exchange earnings;

(f)   to transfer a particular technology, a production process, or other proprietary knowledge to a person in its territory; or

(g)   to supply exclusively from the territory of the Party the goods that it produces or the services that it supplies to a specific regional market or to the world market.

Advantages Subject to Performance Requirements

2.   Neither Party may condition the receipt or continued receipt of an advantage, in connection with the establishment, acquisition, expansion, management, conduct, operation, or sale or other disposition of an investment in its territory of an investor of a Party or of a non-Party, on compliance with any of the following requirements:

(a)   to achieve a given level or percentage of domestic content;

(b)   to purchase, use, or accord a preference to goods produced in its territory, or to purchase goods from persons in its territory;

(c)   to relate in any way the volume or value of imports to the volume or value of exports or to the amount of foreign exchange inflows associated with such investment; or

(d)   to restrict sales of goods or services in its territory that such investment produces or supplies by relating such sales in any way to the volume or value of its exports or foreign exchange earnings.

Exceptions and Exclusions

3.   (a) Nothing in paragraph 2 shall be construed to prevent a Party from conditioning the receipt or continued receipt of an advantage, in connection with an investment in its territory of an investor of a Party or of a non-Party, on compliance with a requirement to locate production, supply a service, train or employ workers, construct or expand particular facilities, or carry out research and development, in its territory.

(b)   Paragraph 1(f) does not apply:

(i)   when a Party authorizes use of an intellectual property right in accordance with Article 31 of the TRIPS Agreement, or to measures requiring the disclosure of proprietary information that fall within the scope of, and are consistent with, Article 39 of the TRIPS Agreement; or

(ii)   when the requirement is imposed or the commitment or undertaking is enforced by a court, administrative tribunal, or competition authority to remedy a practice determined after judicial or administrative process to be anticompetitive under the Party's competition laws.

(c)   Provided that such measures are not applied in an arbitrary or unjustifiable manner, or do not constitute a disguised restriction on international trade or investment, paragraphs 1(b), (c), and (f), and 2(a) and (b), shall not be construed to prevent a Party from adopting or maintaining measures, including environmental measures:

(i)   necessary to secure compliance with laws and regulations that are not inconsistent with this Agreement;

(ii)   necessary to protect human, animal, or plant life or health; or

(iii) related to the conservation of living or non-living exhaustible natural resources.

(d)   Paragraphs 1(a), (b), and (c), and 2(a) and (b), do not apply to qualification requirements for goods or services with respect to export promotion and foreign aid programs.

(e)   Paragraphs 1(b), (c), (f), and (g), and 2(a) and (b), do not apply to procurement.

(f)   Paragraphs 2(a) and (b) do not apply to requirements imposed by an importing Party relating to the content of goods necessary to qualify for preferential tariffs or preferential quotas.

4.   For greater certainty, paragraphs 1 and 2 do not apply to any requirement other than the requirements set out in those paragraphs.

5.   This Article does not preclude enforcement of any commitment, undertaking, or requirement between private parties, where a Party did not impose or require the commitment, undertaking, or requirement.

Article 10.6: Senior Management and Boards of Directors

1.   Neither Party may require that an enterprise of that Party that is a covered investment appoint to senior management positions individuals of any particular nationality.

2.   A Party may require that a majority of the board of directors, or any committee thereof, of an enterprise of that Party that is a covered investment, be of a particular nationality, or resident in the territory of the Party, provided that the requirement does not materially impair the ability of the investor to exercise control over its investment.

Article 10.7: Non-Conforming Measures

1.   Articles 10.2, 10.3, 10.5, and 10.6 do not apply to:

(a)   any existing non-conforming measure that is maintained by a Party at:

(i)   the central level of government, as set out by that Party in its Schedule to Annex I,

(ii)   a regional level of government, as set out by that Party in its Schedule to Annex I, or

(iii) a local level of government;

(b) the continuation or prompt renewal of any non-conforming measure referred to in sub-paragraph (a); or

(c) an amendment to any non-conforming measure referred to in subparagraph (a) to the extent that the amendment does not decrease the conformity of the measure, as it existed immediately before the amendment, with Articles 10.2, 10.3, 10.5, and 10.6.

2.   Articles 10.2, 10.3, 10.5, and 10.6 do not apply to any measure that a Party adopts or maintains with respect to sectors, subsectors, or activities, as set out in its Schedule to Annex II.

3.   Neither Party may, under any measure adopted after the date of entry into force of this Agreement and covered by its Schedule to Annex II, require an investor of the other Party, by reason of its nationality, to sell or otherwise dispose of an investment existing at the time the measure becomes effective.

4.   Articles 10.2 and 10.3 do not apply to any measure that is an exception to, or derogation from, the obligations under Article 17.1(6) (General Provisions) as specifically provided for in that Article.

5.   Articles 10.2, 10.3, and 10.6 do not apply to:

(a) procurement; or

(b) subsidies or grants provided by a Party, including government-supported loans, guarantees, and insurance.

Article 10.8: Transfers

1.   Each Party shall permit all transfers relating to a covered investment to be made freely and without delay into and out of its territory. Such transfers include:

(a) contributions to capital;

(b) profits, dividends, interest, capital gains, royalty payments, management fees, and technical assistance and other fees;

(c) proceeds from the sale of all or any part of the covered investment or from the partial or complete liquidation of the covered investment;

(d) payments made under a contract entered into by the investor, or the covered investment, including payments made pursuant to a loan agreement;

(e) payments made pursuant to Article 10.4(4) and (5) and Article 10.9; and

(f) payments arising under Section B.

2.   Each Party shall permit returns in kind relating to a covered investment to be made as authorized or specified in an investment authorization or other written agreement between the Party and a covered investment or an investor of the other Party.

3.   Each Party shall permit transfers relating to a covered investment to be made in a freely usable currency at the market rate of exchange prevailing on the date of transfer.

4.   Neither Party may require its investors to transfer, or penalize its investors that fail to transfer, the income, earnings, profits, or other amounts derived from, or attributable to, investments in the territory of the other Party.

5.   Notwithstanding paragraphs 1 through 3, a Party may prevent a transfer through the equitable, nondiscriminatory, and good faith application of its laws relating to:

(a) bankruptcy, insolvency, or the protection of the rights of creditors;

(b) issuing, trading, or dealing in securities, futures, or derivatives;

(c) criminal or penal offenses;

(d) financial reporting or record keeping of transfers when necessary to assist law enforcement or financial regulatory authorities; or

(e) ensuring compliance with orders or judgments in judicial or administrative proceedings.

6. Notwithstanding paragraph 2, a Party may restrict transfers of returns in kind in circumstances where it could otherwise restrict such transfers under this Agreement, including as set out in paragraph 5.

Article 10.9: Expropriation and Compensation

1. Neither Party may expropriate or nationalize a covered investment either directly or indirectly through measures equivalent to expropriation or nationalization ("expropriation"), except:

(a) for a public purpose;

(b) in a non-discriminatory manner;

(c) on payment of prompt, adequate, and effective compensation in accordance with paragraphs 2 through 4; and

(d) in accordance with due process of law and Article 10.4(1) through (3).

2. Compensation shall:

(a) be paid without delay;

(b) be equivalent to the fair market value of the expropriated investment immediately before the expropriation took place ("the date of expropriation");

(c) not reflect any change in value occurring because the intended expropriation had become known earlier; and

(d) be fully realizable and freely transferable.

3. If the fair market value is denominated in a freely usable currency, the compensation paid shall be no less than the fair market value on the date of expropriation, plus interest at a commercially reasonable rate for that currency, accrued from the date of expropriation until the date of payment.

4. If the fair market value is denominated in a currency that is not freely usable, the compensation paid – converted into the currency of payment at the market rate of exchange prevailing on the date of payment – shall be no less than:

(a) the fair market value on the date of expropriation, converted into a freely usable currency at the market rate of exchange prevailing on that date, plus

(b) interest, at a commercially reasonable rate for that freely usable currency, accrued from the date of expropriation until the date of payment.

5. This Article does not apply to the issuance of compulsory licenses granted in relation to intellectual property rights in accordance with the TRIPS Agreement, or to the revocation, limitation, or creation of intellectual property rights, to the extent that such revocation, limitation, or creation is consistent with Chapter Seventeen (Intellectual Property Rights).

Article 10.10: Special Formalities and Information Requirements

1. Nothing in Article 10.2 shall be construed to prevent a Party from adopting or maintaining a measure that prescribes special formalities in connection with covered investments, such as a requirement that investors be residents of the Party or that covered investments be legally constituted under the laws or regulations of the Party, provided that such formalities do not materially impair the protections afforded by a Party to investors of the other Party and covered investments pursuant to this Chapter.

2.   Notwithstanding Articles 10.2 and 10.3, a Party may require an investor of the other Party, or a covered investment, to provide information concerning that investment solely for informational or statistical purposes. The Party shall protect such information that is confidential from any disclosure that would prejudice the competitive position of the investor or the covered investment. Nothing in this paragraph shall be construed to prevent a Party from otherwise obtaining or disclosing information in connection with the equitable and good faith application of its domestic law.

Article 10.11: Denial of Benefits

1.   A Party may deny the benefits of this Chapter to an investor of the other Party that is an enterprise of such other Party and to investments of that investor if an investor of a non-Party owns or controls the enterprise and the denying Party:

(a)   does not maintain diplomatic relations with the non-Party; or

(b)   adopts or maintains measures with respect to the non-Party or an investor of the non-Party that prohibit transactions with the enterprise or that would be violated or circumvented if the benefits of this Chapter were accorded to the enterprise or to its investments.

2.   Subject to Article 22.4 (Consultations), a Party may deny the benefits of this Chapter to:

(a)   an investor of the other Party that is an enterprise of such other Party and to investments of that investor if an investor of a non-Party owns or controls the enterprise and the enterprise has no substantial business activities in the territory of the other Party; or

(b)   an investor of the other Party that is an enterprise of such other Party and to investments of that investor if an investor of the denying Party owns or controls the enterprise and the enterprise has no substantial business activities in the territory of the other Party.

Article 10.12: Investment and Environment

Nothing in this Chapter shall be construed to prevent a Party from adopting, maintaining, or enforcing any measure otherwise consistent with this Chapter that it considers appropriate to ensure that investment activity in its territory is undertaken in a manner sensitive to environmental concerns.

Article 10.13: Implementation

The Parties shall consult annually, or as otherwise agreed, to review the implementation of this Chapter and consider any investment matter of mutual interest, including consideration of the development of procedures that could contribute to greater transparency of measures described in Article 10.7(1)(c).

Section B - Investor-State Dispute Settlement Article

10.14: Consultation and Negotiation

In the event of an investment dispute, the claimant and the respondent should initially seek to resolve the dispute through consultation and negotiation, which may include the use of non-binding, third-party procedures.

Article 10.15: Submission of a Claim to Arbitration

1.   In the event that a disputing party considers that an investment dispute cannot be settled by consultation and negotiation:

(a)   the claimant, on its own behalf, may submit to arbitration under this Section a claim

   (i)   that the respondent has breached

     (A)   an obligation under Section A or Annex 10-F,

     (B)   an investment authorization, or

     (C)   an investment agreement; and

    (ii)   that the claimant has incurred loss or damage by reason of, or arising out of, that breach; and

(b)   the claimant, on behalf of an enterprise of the respondent that is a juridical person that the claimant owns or controls directly or indirectly, may submit to arbitration under this Section a claim

    (i)   that the respondent has breached

        (A) an obligation under Section A or Annex 10-F,

        (B) an investment authorization, or

        (C) an investment agreement; and

    (ii)   that the enterprise has incurred loss or damage by reason of, or arising out of, that breach.

2.   For greater certainty, a claimant may submit to arbitration under this Section a claim that the respondent has breached an obligation under Section A or Annex 10-F through the actions of a designated monopoly or a state enterprise exercising delegated government authority as described in Article 16.3(3)(a) (Designated Monopolies) and Article 16.4(2) (State Enterprises), respectively.

3.   Without prejudice to Article 12.1(2) (Scope and Coverage), no claim may be submitted under this Section that alleges a violation of any provision of this Agreement other than an obligation under Section A or Annex 10-F.

4.   At least 90 days before submitting any claim to arbitration under this Section, a claimant shall deliver to the respondent a written notice of its intention to submit the claim to arbitration ("notice of intent"). The notice shall specify:

(a)   the name and address of the claimant and, where a claim is submitted on behalf of an enterprise, the name, address, and place of incorporation of the enterprise;

(b)   for each claim, the provision of this Agreement, investment authorization, or investment agreement alleged to have been breached and any other relevant provisions;

(c)   the legal and factual basis for each claim; and

(d)   the relief sought and the approximate amount of damages claimed.

5.   Provided that six months have elapsed since the events giving rise to the claim, a claimant may submit a claim referred to in paragraph 1:

(a)   under the ICSID Convention, provided that both the non-disputing Party and the respondent are parties to the ICSID Convention;

(b)   under the ICSID Additional Facility Rules, provided that either the non-disputing Party or the respondent, but not both, is a party to the ICSID Convention;

(c)   under the UNCITRAL Arbitration Rules; or

(d)   if the disputing parties agree, to any other arbitration institution or under any other arbitration rules.

6.   A claim shall be deemed submitted to arbitration under this Section when the claimant's notice of or request for arbitration ("notice of arbitration"):

(a)   referred to in paragraph 1 of Article 36 of the ICSID Convention is received by the Secretary-General;

(b)   referred to in Article 2 of Schedule C of the ICSID Additional Facility Rules is received by the Secretary-General;

(c) referred to in Article 3 of the UNCITRAL Arbitration Rules, together with the statement of claim referred to in Article 18 of the UNCITRAL Arbitration Rules, are received by the respondent; or

(d) referred to under any other arbitral institution or arbitral rules selected under paragraph 5(d) is received by the respondent.

7. The arbitration rules applicable under paragraph 5, and in effect on the date the claim or claims were submitted to arbitration under this Section, shall govern the arbitration except to the extent modified by this Agreement.

8. The claimant shall provide with the notice of arbitration referred to in paragraph 6:

(a) the name of the arbitrator that the claimant appoints; or

(b) the claimant's written consent for the Secretary-General to appoint the claimant's arbitrator.

Article 10.16: Consent of Each Party to Arbitration

1. Each Party consents to the submission of a claim to arbitration under this Section in accordance with this Agreement.

2. The consent under paragraph 1 and the submission of a claim to arbitration under this Section shall satisfy the requirements of:

(a) Chapter II of the ICSID Convention (Jurisdiction of the Centre) and the ICSID Additional Facility Rules for written consent of the parties to the dispute;

(b) Article II of the New York Convention for an "agreement in writing;" and

(c) Article I of the Inter-American Convention for an "agreement."

Article 10.17: Conditions and Limitations on Consent of Each Party

1. No claim may be submitted to arbitration under this Section if more than three years have elapsed from the date on which the claimant first acquired, or should have first acquired, knowledge of the breach alleged under Article 10.15(1) and knowledge that the claimant (for claims brought under Article 10.15(1)(a)) or the enterprise (for claims brought under Article 10.15(1)(b)) has incurred loss or damage.

2. No claim may be submitted to arbitration under this Section unless:

(a) the claimant consents in writing to arbitration in accordance with the procedures set out in this Agreement; and

(b) the notice of arbitration referred to in Article 10.15(6) is accompanied,

   (i) for claims submitted to arbitration under Article 10.15(1)(a), by the claimant's written waiver, and

   (ii) for claims submitted to arbitration under Article 10.15(1)(b), by the claimant's and the enterprise's written waivers of any right to initiate or continue before any administrative tribunal or court under the law of either Party, or other dispute settlement procedures, any proceeding with respect to the events alleged to give rise to the claimed breach.

3. Notwithstanding paragraph 2(b), the claimant (for claims brought under Article 10.15(1)(a)) and the claimant or the enterprise (for claims brought under Article 10.15(1)(b)) may initiate or continue an action that seeks interim injunctive relief and does not involve the payment of monetary damages before a judicial or administrative tribunal of the respondent, provided that the action is brought for the sole purpose of preserving the claimant's or the enterprise's rights and interests during the pendency of the arbitration.

Article 10.18: Selection of Arbitrators

1.   Unless the disputing parties otherwise agree, the tribunal shall comprise three arbitrators, one arbitrator appointed by each of the disputing parties and the third, who shall be the presiding arbitrator, appointed by agreement of the disputing parties.

2.   The Secretary-General shall serve as appointing authority for an arbitration under this Section.

3.   If a tribunal has not been constituted within 75 days from the date that a claim is submitted to arbitration under this Section, the Secretary-General, on the request of a disputing party, shall appoint, in his or her discretion, the arbitrator or arbitrators not yet appointed.

4.   For purposes of Article 39 of the ICSID Convention and Article 7 of Schedule C to the ICSID Additional Facility Rules, and without prejudice to an objection to an arbitrator on a ground other than nationality:

(a)   the respondent agrees to the appointment of each individual member of a tribunal established under the ICSID Convention or the ICSID Additional Facility Rules;

(b)   a claimant referred to in Article 10.15(1)(a) may submit a claim to arbitration under this Section, or continue a claim, under the ICSID Convention or the ICSID Additional Facility Rules, only on condition that the claimant agrees in writing to the appointment of each individual member of the tribunal; and

(c)   a claimant referred to in Article 10.15(1)(b) may submit a claim to arbitration under this Section, or continue a claim, under the ICSID Convention or the ICSID Additional Facility Rules, only on condition that the claimant and the enterprise agree in writing to the appointment of each individual member of the tribunal.

Article 10.19: Conduct of the Arbitration

1.   The disputing parties may agree on the legal place of any arbitration under the arbitral rules applicable under Article 10.15(5)(b), (c), or (d). If the disputing parties fail to reach agreement, the tribunal shall determine the place in accordance with the applicable arbitral rules, provided that the place shall be in the territory of a State that is a party to the New York Convention.

2.   The non-disputing Party may make oral and written submissions to the tribunal regarding the interpretation of this Agreement.

3.   The tribunal shall have the authority to accept and consider amicus curiae submissions from a person or entity that is not a disputing party (the "submitter"). The submissions shall be provided in both Spanish and English, and shall identify the submitter and any Party, other government, person, or organization, other than the submitter, that has provided, or will provide, any financial or other assistance in preparing the submission.

4.   Without prejudice to a tribunal's authority to address other objections as a preliminary question, such as an objection that a dispute is not within a tribunal's competence, a tribunal shall address and decide as a preliminary question any objection by the respondent that, as a matter of law, a claim submitted is not a claim for which an award in favor of the claimant may be made under Article 10.25.

(a)   Such objection shall be submitted to the tribunal as soon as possible after the tribunal is constituted, and in no event later than the date the tribunal fixes for the respondent to submit its counter-memorial (or, in the case of an amendment to the notice of arbitration referred to in Article 10.15(6), the date the tribunal fixes for the respondent to submit its response to the amendment).

(b)   On receipt of an objection under this paragraph, the tribunal shall suspend any proceedings on the merits, establish a schedule for considering the objection consistent with any schedule it has established for considering any other preliminary question, and issue a decision or award on the objection, stating the grounds therefor.

(c) In deciding an objection under this paragraph, the tribunal shall assume to be true claimant's factual allegations in support of any claim in the notice of arbitration (or any amendment thereof) and, in disputes brought under the UNCITRAL Arbitration Rules, the statement of claim referred to in Article 18 of the UNCITRAL Arbitration Rules. The tribunal may also consider any relevant facts not in dispute.

(d) The respondent does not waive any objection as to competence or any argument on the merits merely because the respondent did or did not raise an objection under this paragraph or make use of the expedited procedure set out in the following paragraph.

5.   In the event that the respondent so requests within 45 days after the tribunal is constituted, the tribunal shall decide on an expedited basis an objection under paragraph 4 or any objection that the dispute is not within the tribunal's competence. The tribunal shall suspend any proceedings on the merits and issue a decision or award on the objection(s), stating the grounds therefor, no later than 150 days after the date of the request. However, if a disputing party requests a hearing, the tribunal may take an additional 30 days to issue the decision or award. Regardless of whether a hearing is requested, a tribunal may, on a showing of extraordinary cause, delay issuing its decision or award by an additional brief period of time, which may not exceed 30 days.

6.   When it decides a respondent's objection under paragraph 4 or 5, the tribunal may, if warranted, award to the prevailing disputing party reasonable costs and attorneys' fees incurred in submitting or opposing the objection. In determining whether such an award is warranted, the tribunal shall consider whether either the claimant's claim or the respondent's objection was frivolous, and shall provide the disputing parties a reasonable opportunity to comment.

7.   A respondent may not assert as a defense, counterclaim, right of set-off, or for any other reason that the claimant has received or will receive indemnification or other compensation for all or part of the alleged damages pursuant to an insurance or guarantee contract.

8.   A tribunal may order an interim measure of protection to preserve the rights of a disputing party, or to ensure that the tribunal's jurisdiction is made fully effective, including an order to preserve evidence in the possession or control of a disputing party or to protect the tribunal's jurisdiction. A tribunal may not order attachment or enjoin the application of a measure alleged to constitute a breach referred to in Article 10.15. For purposes of this paragraph, an order includes a recommendation.

9.   (a) At the request of a disputing party, a tribunal shall, before issuing an award on liability, transmit its proposed award to the disputing parties and to the non- disputing Party. Within 60 days after the tribunal transmits its proposed award, only the disputing parties may submit written comments to the tribunal concerning any aspect of its proposed award. The tribunal shall consider any such comments and issue its award not later than 45 days after the expiration of the 60-day comment period.

(b) Subparagraph (a) shall not apply in any arbitration for which an appeal has been made available pursuant to paragraph 10.

10. If a separate multilateral agreement enters into force as between the Parties that establishes an appellate body for purposes of reviewing awards rendered by tribunals constituted pursuant to international trade or investment agreements to hear investment disputes, the Parties shall strive to reach an agreement that would have such appellate body review awards rendered under Article 10.25 in arbitrations commenced after the appellate body's establishment.

Article 10.20: Transparency of Arbitral Proceedings

1.   Subject to paragraphs 2 and 4, the respondent shall, after receiving the following documents, promptly transmit them to the non-disputing Party and make them available to the public:

(a)   the notice of intent referred to in Article 10.15(4);

(b)   the notice of arbitration referred to in Article 10.15(6);

(c)   pleadings, memorials, and briefs submitted to the tribunal by a disputing party and any written submissions submitted pursuant to Article 10.19(2) and (3) and Article 10.24;

(d)   minutes or transcripts of hearings of the tribunal, where available; and

(e)   orders, awards, and decisions of the tribunal.

2.   The tribunal shall conduct hearings open to the public and shall determine, in consultation with the disputing parties, the appropriate logistical arrangements. However, any disputing party that intends to use information designated as confidential business information or information that is privileged or otherwise protected from disclosure under a Party's law in a hearing shall so advise the tribunal. The tribunal shall make appropriate arrangements to protect the information from disclosure.

3.   Nothing in this Section requires a respondent to disclose confidential business information or information that is privileged or otherwise protected from disclosure under a Party's law or to furnish or allow access to information that it may withhold in accordance with Article 23.2 (Essential Security) or Article 23.5 (Disclosure of Information).

4.   Confidential business information or information that is privileged or otherwise protected from disclosure under a Party's law shall, if such information is submitted to the tribunal, be protected from disclosure in accordance with the following procedures:

(a)   Subject to subparagraph (d), neither the disputing parties nor the tribunal shall disclose to the non-disputing Party or to the public any confidential business information or information that is privileged or otherwise protected from disclosure under a Party's law where the disputing party that provided the information clearly designates it in accordance with subparagraph (b);

(b)   Any disputing party claiming that certain information constitutes confidential business information or information that is privileged or otherwise protected from disclosure under a Party's law shall clearly designate the information at the time it is submitted to the tribunal;

(c)   A disputing party shall, at the same time that it submits a document containing information claimed to be confidential business information or information that is privileged or otherwise protected from disclosure under a Party's law, submit a redacted version of the document that does not contain the information. Only the redacted version shall be provided to the non-disputing Party and made public in accordance with paragraph 1; and

(d)   The tribunal shall decide any objection regarding the designation of information claimed to be confidential business information or information that is privileged or otherwise protected from disclosure under a Party's law. If the tribunal determines that such information was not properly designated, the disputing party that submitted the information may:

       (i)   withdraw all or part of its submission containing such information; or

       (ii)   agree to resubmit complete and redacted documents with corrected designations in accordance with the tribunal's determination and subparagraph (c).

In either case, the other disputing party shall, whenever necessary, resubmit complete and redacted documents which either remove the information withdrawn under subparagraph (d)(i) by the disputing party that first submitted the information or redesignate the information consistent with the designation under subparagraph (d)(ii) of the disputing party that first submitted the information.

5.   Nothing in this Section authorizes a respondent to withhold from the public information required to be disclosed by its laws.

Article 10.21: Governing Law

1.   Subject to paragraph 3, when a claim is submitted under Article 10.15(1)(a)(i)(A) or Article 10.15(1)(b)(i)(A), the tribunal shall decide the issues in dispute in accordance with this Agreement and applicable rules of international law.

2.   Subject to paragraph 3, when a claim is submitted under Article 10.15(1)(a)(i)(B) or (C), or Article 10.15(1)(b)(i)(B) or (C), the tribunal shall decide the issues in dispute in accordance with the rules of law specified in the pertinent investment agreement or investment authorization, or as the disputing parties may otherwise agree. If the rules of law have not been specified or otherwise agreed, the tribunal shall apply the law of the respondent (including its rules on the conflict of laws), the terms of the investment agreement or investment authorization, such rules of international law as may be applicable, and this Agreement.

3.   A decision of the Commission declaring its interpretation of a provision of this Agreement under Article 21.1 (Free Trade Commission) shall be binding on a tribunal established under this Section, and any award must be consistent with that decision.

Article 10.22: Interpretation of Annexes

1.   Where a respondent asserts as a defense that the measure alleged to be a breach is within the scope of a non-conforming measure set out in Annex I or Annex II, the tribunal shall, on request of the respondent, request the interpretation of the Commission on the issue. The Commission shall submit in writing any decision declaring its interpretation under Article 21.1 (Free Trade Commission) to the tribunal within 60 days of delivery of the request.

2.   A decision issued by the Commission under paragraph 1 shall be binding on the tribunal, and any award must be consistent with that decision. If the Commission fails to issue such a decision within 60 days, the tribunal shall decide the issue.

Article 10.23: Expert Reports

Without prejudice to the appointment of other kinds of experts where authorized by the applicable arbitration rules, a tribunal, at the request of a disputing party or, unless the disputing parties disapprove, on its own initiative, may appoint one or more experts to report to it in writing on any factual issue concerning environmental, health, safety, or other scientific matters raised by a disputing party in a proceeding, subject to such terms and conditions as the disputing parties may agree.

Article 10.24: Consolidation

1.   Where two or more claims have been submitted separately to arbitration under Article 10.15(1) and the claims have a question of law or fact in common and arise out of the same events or circumstances, any disputing party may seek a consolidation order in accordance with the agreement of all the disputing parties sought to be covered by the order or the terms of paragraphs 2 through 10.

2.   A disputing party that seeks a consolidation order under this Article shall deliver, in writing, a request to the Secretary-General and to all the disputing parties sought to be covered by the order and shall specify in the request:

(a)   the names and addresses of all the disputing parties sought to be covered by the order;

(b)   the nature of the order sought; and

(c)   the grounds on which the order is sought.

3.   Unless the Secretary-General finds within 30 days after receiving a request under paragraph 2 that the request is manifestly unfounded, a tribunal shall be established under this Article.

4.   Unless all the disputing parties sought to be covered by the order otherwise agree, a tribunal established under this Article shall comprise three arbitrators:

(a)   one arbitrator appointed by agreement of the claimants;

(b)   one arbitrator appointed by the respondent; and

(c)   the presiding arbitrator appointed by the Secretary-General, provided, however, that the presiding arbitrator shall not be a national of either Party.

5.   If, within 60 days after the Secretary-General receives a request made under paragraph 2, the respondent fails or the claimants fail to appoint an arbitrator in accordance with paragraph 4, the Secretary-General, on the request of any disputing party sought to be covered by the order, shall appoint the arbitrator or arbitrators not yet appointed. If the respondent fails to appoint an arbitrator, the Secretary-General shall appoint a national of the respondent, and if the claimants fail to appoint an arbitrator, the Secretary-General shall appoint a national of the non-disputing Party.

6.   Where a tribunal established under this Article is satisfied that two or more claims that have been submitted to arbitration under Article 10.15(1) have a question of law or fact in common, and arise out of the same events or circumstances, the tribunal may, in the interest of fair and efficient resolution of the claims, and after hearing the disputing parties, by order:

(a)   assume jurisdiction over, and hear and determine together, all or part of the claims;

(b)   assume jurisdiction over, and hear and determine one or more of the claims, the determination of which it believes would assist in the resolution of the others; or

(c)   instruct a tribunal previously established under Article 10.18 to assume jurisdiction over, and hear and determine together, all or part of the claims, provided that

(i)   that tribunal, at the request of any claimant not previously a disputing party before that tribunal, shall be reconstituted with its original members, except that the arbitrator for the claimants shall be appointed pursuant to paragraphs 4(a) and 5; and

(ii)   that tribunal shall decide whether any prior hearing shall be repeated.

7.   Where a tribunal has been established under this Article, a claimant that has submitted a claim to arbitration under Article 10.15(1) and that has not been named in a request made under paragraph 2 may make a written request to the tribunal that it be included in any order made under paragraph 6, and shall specify in the request:

(a)   the name and address of the claimant;

(b)   the nature of the order sought; and

(c)   the grounds on which the order is sought.

The claimant shall deliver a copy of its request to the Secretary-General.

8.   A tribunal established under this Article shall conduct its proceedings in accordance with the UNCITRAL Arbitration Rules, except as modified by this Section.

9.   A tribunal established under Article 10.18 shall not have jurisdiction to decide a claim, or a part of a claim, over which a tribunal established or instructed under this Article has assumed jurisdiction.

10.   On application of a disputing party, a tribunal established under this Article, pending its decision under paragraph 6, may order that the proceedings of a tribunal established under Article 10.18 be stayed, unless the latter tribunal has already adjourned its proceedings.

Article 10.25: Awards

1.   Where a tribunal makes a final award against a respondent, the tribunal may award, separately or in combination, only:

(a)   monetary damages and any applicable interest;

(b)   restitution of property, in which case the award shall provide that the respondent may pay monetary damages and any applicable interest in lieu of restitution. A tribunal may also award costs and attorneys' fees in accordance with this Section and the applicable arbitration rules.

2.   Subject to paragraph 1, where a claim is submitted to arbitration under Article 10.15(1)(b):

(a)   an award of restitution of property shall provide that restitution be made to the enterprise;

(b)   an award of monetary damages and any applicable interest shall provide that the sum be paid to the enterprise; and

(c)   the award shall provide that it is made without prejudice to any right that any person may have in the relief under applicable domestic law.

3.   A tribunal may not award punitive damages.

4.   An award made by a tribunal shall have no binding force except between the disputing parties and in respect of the particular case.

5.   Subject to paragraph 6 and the applicable review procedure for an interim award, a disputing party shall abide by and comply with an award without delay.

6.   A disputing party may not seek enforcement of a final award until:

(a)   in the case of a final award made under the ICSID Convention.

(i)   120 days have elapsed from the date the award was rendered and no disputing party has requested revision or annulment of the award; or

(ii)   revision or annulment proceedings have been completed; and

(b)   in the case of a final award under the ICSID Additional Facility Rules, the UNCITRAL Arbitration Rules, or the rules selected pursuant to Article 10.15(5)(d)

(i)   90 days have elapsed from the date the award was rendered and no disputing party has commenced a proceeding to revise, set aside, or annul the award, or

(ii)   a court has dismissed or allowed an application to revise, set aside, or annul the award and there is no further appeal.

7.   Each Party shall provide for the enforcement of an award in its territory.

8.   If the respondent fails to abide by or comply with a final award, on delivery of a request by the non-disputing Party, a panel shall be established under Article 22.6 (Request for an Arbitral Panel). The requesting Party may seek in such proceedings:

(a)   a determination that the failure to abide by or comply with the final award is inconsistent with the obligations of this Agreement; and

(b)   if the Parties agree, a recommendation that the respondent abide by or comply with the final award.

9.   A disputing party may seek enforcement of an arbitration award under the ICSID Convention, the New York Convention, or the Inter-American Convention regardless of whether proceedings have been taken under paragraph 8.

10.   A claim that is submitted to arbitration under this Section shall be considered to arise out of a commercial relationship or transaction for purposes of Article I of the New York Convention and Article I of the Inter-American Convention.

Article 10.26: Service of Documents

Delivery of notice and other documents on a Party shall be made to the place named for that Party in Annex 10-G.

Section C - Definitions

Article 10.27: Definitions

For purposes of this Chapter:

Centre means the International Centre for Settlement of Investment Disputes (ICSID) established by the ICSID Convention;

claimant means an investor of a Party that is a party to an investment dispute with the other Party;

disputing parties means the claimant and the respondent;

disputing party means either the claimant or the respondent;

enterprise means an "enterprise" as defined in Article 2.1 (Definitions of General Application), and a branch of an enterprise;

enterprise of a Party means an enterprise constituted or organized under the law of a Party, and a branch located in the territory of a Party and carrying out business activities there;

freely usable currency means "freely usable currency" as determined by the International Monetary Fund under its Articles of Agreement;

ICSID Additional Facility Rules means the Rules Governing the Additional Facility for the Administration of Proceedings by the Secretariat of the International Centre for Settlement of Investment Disputes;

ICSID Convention means the Convention on the Settlement of Investment Disputes between States and Nationals of other States, done at Washington, March 18, 1965;

Inter-American Convention means the Inter-American Convention on International Commercial Arbitration, done at Panama, January 30, 1975;

investment means every asset that an investor owns or controls, directly or indirectly, that has the characteristics of an investment, including such characteristics as the commitment of capital or other resources, the expectation of gain or profit, or the assumption of risk. Forms that an investment may take include:

(a) an enterprise;

(b) shares, stock, and other forms of equity participation in an enterprise;

(c) bonds, debentures, loans, and other debt instruments;

(d) futures, options, and other derivatives;

(e) rights under contract, including turnkey, construction, management, production, concession, or revenue-sharing contracts;

(f) intellectual property rights;

(g) rights conferred pursuant to domestic law, such as concessions, licenses, authorizations, and permits; and

(h) other tangible or intangible, movable or immovable property, and related property rights, such as leases, mortgages, liens, and pledges;

but investment does not mean an order or judgment entered in a judicial or administrative action;

investment agreement means a written agreement that takes effect at least two years after the date of entry into force of this Agreement between a national authority of a Party and a covered investment or an investor of the other Party:

(a) that grants rights with respect to natural resources or other assets that a national authority controls; and

(b) that the covered investment or the investor relies on in establishing or acquiring a covered investment;

investment authorization means an authorization that the foreign investment authority of a Party grants to a covered investment or an investor of the other Party;

investor of a non-Party means, with respect to a Party, an investor that attempts to make, is making, or has made an investment in the territory of that Party, that is not an investor of either Party;

investor of a Party means a Party or state enterprise thereof, or a national or an enterprise of a Party, that attempts to make, is making, or has made an investment in the territory of the other Party; provided, however, that a natural person who is a dual national shall be deemed to be exclusively a national of the State of his/her dominant and effective nationality;

monopoly means "monopoly" as defined in Article 16.9 (Definitions);

New York Convention means the United Nations Convention on the Recognition and Enforcement of Foreign Arbitral Awards, done at New York, June 10, 1958;

non-disputing Party means the Party that is not a party to an investment dispute;

respondent means the Party that is a party to an investment dispute;

Secretary-General means the Secretary-General of ICSID;

tribunal means an arbitration tribunal established under Article 10.18 or 10.24; and

UNCITRAL Arbitration Rules means the arbitration rules of the United Nations Commission on International Trade Law.

Annex 10-A Customary International Law

The Parties confirm their shared understanding that "customary international law" generally and as specifically referenced in Articles 10.4 and 10.9 results from a general and consistent practice of States that they follow from a sense of legal obligation. With regard to Article 10.4, the customary international law minimum standard of treatment of aliens refers to all customary international law principles that protect the economic rights and interests of aliens.

Annex 10-B Public Debt Chile [omitted]

Annex 10-C Special Dispute Settlement Provisions Chile

1.   Where a claimant submits a claim alleging that Chile has breached an obligation under Section A, other than Article 10.3, that arises from its imposition of restrictive measures with regard to payments and transfers, Section B shall apply except as modified below:

(a) A claimant may submit any such claim only after one year has elapsed since the events giving rise to the claim;

(b) If the claim is submitted under Article 10.15(1)(b), the claimant may, on behalf of the enterprise, only seek damages with respect to the shares of the enterprise for which the claimant has a beneficial interest;

(c) Loss or damages arising from restrictive measures on capital inflows shall be limited to the reduction in value of the transfers and shall exclude loss of profits or business and any similar consequential or incidental damages;

(d)   Paragraph 1(a) shall not apply to claims that arise from restrictions on:

  (i)   transfers of proceeds of foreign direct investment by investors of the United States, excluding external debt financing covered in subparagraph (d) (ii), and excluding investments designed with the purpose of gaining direct or indirect access to the financial market; or (ii) payments pursuant to a loan or bond issued in a foreign market, including inter- and intra-company debt financing between affiliated enterprises made exclusively for the conduct, operation, management, or expansion of such affiliated enterprises, provided that these payments are made in accordance with the maturity date agreed on in the loan or bond agreement;

(e)   Excluding restrictive measures referred to in paragraph 1(d), Chile shall incur no liability, and shall not be subject to claims, for damages arising from its imposition of restrictive measures with regard to payments and transfers that were incurred within one year from the date on which the restrictions were imposed, provided that such restrictive measures do not substantially impede transfers;

(f)   A restrictive measure of Chile with regard to payments and transfers that is consistent with this Annex shall be deemed not to contravene Article 10.2 provided that, as required under existing Chilean law, it does not discriminate among investors that enter into transactions of the same nature; and

(g)   Claims arising from Chile's imposition of restrictive measures with regard to payments and transfers shall not be subject to Article 10.24 unless Chile consents.

2.   The United States may not request the establishment of an arbitral panel under Chapter Twenty-Two (Dispute Settlement) relating to Chile's imposition of restrictive measures with regard to payments and transfers until one year has elapsed since the events giving rise to the dispute.

3.   Restrictive measures on payments and transfers related to claims under this Annex shall otherwise be subject to applicable domestic law.

Annex 10-D Expropriation

The Parties confirm their shared understanding that:

1.   Article 10.9(1) is intended to reflect customary international law concerning the obligation of States with respect to expropriation.

2.   An action or a series of actions by a Party cannot constitute an expropriation unless it interferes with a tangible or intangible property right or property interest in an investment.

3.   Article 10.9(1) addresses two situations. The first is direct expropriation, where an investment is nationalized or otherwise directly expropriated through formal transfer of title or outright seizure.

4.   The second situation addressed by Article 10.9(1) is indirect expropriation, where an action or series of actions by a Party has an effect equivalent to direct expropriation without formal transfer of title or outright seizure.

(a)   The determination of whether an action or series of actions by a Party, in a specific fact situation, constitutes an indirect expropriation, requires a case-by-case, fact-based inquiry that considers, among other factors:

  (i)   the economic impact of the government action, although the fact that an action or series of actions by a Party has an adverse effect on the economic value of an investment, standing alone, does not establish that an indirect expropriation has occurred;

  (ii) the extent to which the government action interferes with distinct, reasonable invest-ment-backed expectations; and

(iii) the character of the government action.

(b) Except in rare circumstances, nondiscriminatory regulatory actions by a Party that are designed and applied to protect legitimate public welfare objectives, such as public health, safety, and the environment, do not constitute indirect expropriations.

Annex 10-E Submission of a Claim to Arbitration – Chile

1. An investor of the United States may not submit to arbitration under Section B:

(a) a claim that Chile has breached an obligation under Section A or Annex 10-F either:

   (i) on its own behalf under Article 10.15(1)(a), or

   (ii) on behalf of an enterprise of Chile that is a juridical person that the investor owns or controls directly or indirectly under Article 10.15(1)(b),

   if the investor or the enterprise, respectively, has alleged that breach of an obligation under Section A or Annex 10-F in proceedings before a court or administrative tribunal of Chile; or

(b) a claim that Chile has breached an investment agreement or investment authorization either:

   (i) on its own behalf under Article 10.15(1)(a), or

   (ii) on behalf of an enterprise of Chile that is a juridical person that the investor owns or controls directly or indirectly under Article 10.15(1)(b),

   if the investor or the enterprise, respectively, has alleged that breach of an investment agreement or investment authorization in proceedings before a court or administrative tribunal of Chile.

2. For greater certainty, if an investor of the United States elects to submit a claim of the type described in this Annex to a court or administrative tribunal of Chile, that election shall be definitive and the investor may not thereafter submit the claim to arbitration under Section B.

Annex 10-F DL 600 – Chile

1. Without prejudice to paragraphs 3 through 7, Chile shall accord to an investor of the United States or to a covered investment that is a party to an investment contract under Estatuto de la Inversión Extranjera, Decreto Ley 600 de 1974 (DL 600) the better of the treatment required under this Agreement or the treatment under the investment contract.

2. Without prejudice to paragraphs 3 through 7, Chile shall permit an investor of the United States or a covered investment that has entered into an investment contract under DL 600 to amend the investment contract to make it consistent with Chile's obligations under this Agreement.

3. Subject to paragraph 4, when an investor of the United States or a covered investment has entered into an investment contract under DL 600, an investor, on its own behalf or on behalf of the investment, may only submit a claim against Chile under Section B with regard to the contract if the investor alleges that Chile has breached an obligation under:

(a) Section A in connection with the investment contract; or

(b) this Annex; provided, however, that such an investor may not submit any claim under Section B on the basis of the equity/debt ratio requirement of an investment contract under DL 600 except for claims that Chile has accorded the investor or its covered investment treatment less favorable than Chile accords under DL 600 to an investor of a non-Party or its investment in like circumstances.

4. When an investor of the United States or a covered investment has entered into an investment contract under DL 600, and the investor, on its own behalf or on behalf of the investment, claims that Chile has breached the tax provisions of that contract, it shall, with regard

to that claim, only have recourse to the dispute settlement provisions of the investment contract or the dispute settlement provisions of this Agreement relevant to taxation measures.

5.   For greater certainty, execution of an investment contract under DL 600 by an investor of the United States or a covered investment does not create any right on the part of the investor or covered investment to engage in particular activities in Chile.

6.   Nothing in this Agreement shall limit the right of Chile's Comite de Inversiones Extranjeras, its Vicepresidencia Ejecutiva, or their successors to decide whether to authorize an investor of the United States or a covered investment to enter into an investment contract under DL 600, or to establish conditions in such contract, provided that Chile does so in a manner that is not inconsistent with Chile's obligations under Section A.

7.   Notwithstanding any other provision in this Agreement, Chile may prohibit an investor of the United States or a covered investment from transferring from Chile proceeds of the sale of all or any part of an investment made pursuant to a contract under DL 600 for up to one year after the date that the investor or covered investment transferred funds to Chile to establish the investment.

Annex 10-G Service of Documents on a Party Under Section B [omitted]

Annex 10-H Possibility of a Bilateral Appellate Body/Mechanism

Within three years after the date of entry into force of this Agreement, the Parties shall consider whether to establish a bilateral appellate body or similar mechanism to review awards rendered under Article 10.25 in arbitrations commenced after they establish the appellate body or similar mechanism.

XI.2. 1992 NAFTA AGREEMENT (excerpts)

Table of Contents

PREAMBLE
PART ONE: GENERAL PART
    Chapter One: Objectives
    Chapter Two: General Definitions
PART TWO: TRADE IN GOODS
    Chapter Three: National Treatment and Market Access for Goods
        Annex 300-A: Trade and Investment in the Automotive Sector
        Annex 300-B: Textile and Apparel Goods
    Chapter Four: Rules of Origin
        Annex 401: Specific Rules of Origin
    Chapter Five: Customs Procedures
    Chapter Six: Energy and Basic Petrochemicals
    Chapter Seven: Agriculture and Sanitary and Phytosanitary Measures
    Chapter Eight: Emergency Action
PART THREE: TECHNICAL BARRIERS TO TRADE
    Chapter Nine: Standards-Related Measures
PART FOUR: GOVERNMENT PROCUREMENT
    Chapter Ten: Government Procurement
PART FIVE: INVESTMENT, SERVICES AND RELATED MATTERS
    Chapter Eleven: Investment
    Chapter Twelve: Cross-Border Trade in Services
    Chapter Thirteen: Telecommunications
    Chapter Fourteen: Financial Services
    Chapter Fifteen: Competition Policy, Monopolies and State Enterprises
    Chapter Sixteen: Temporary Entry for Business Persons
PART SIX: INTELLECTUAL PROPERTY
    Chapter Seventeen: Intellectual Property
PART SEVEN: ADMINISTRATIVE AND INSTITUTIONAL PROVISIONS
    Chapter Eighteen: Publication, Notification and Administration of Laws
    Chapter Nineteen: Review and Dispute Settlement in Antidumping/Countervailing Duty
        Matters
    Chapter Twenty: Institutional Arrangements and Dispute Settlement Procedures
PART EIGHT: OTHER PROVISIONS
    Chapter Twenty-One: Exceptions
    Chapter Twenty-Two: Final Provisions
NOTES
ANNEXES
    Annex I: Reservations for Existing Measures and Liberalization Commitments
    Annex II: Reservations for Future Measures
    Annex III: Activities Reserved to the State
    Annex IV: Exceptions from Most-Favored-Nation Treatment
    Annex V: Quantitative Restrictions
    Annex VI: Miscellaneous Commitments
    Annex VII: Reservations, Specific Commitments and Other Items

PART FIVE: INVESTMENT, SERVICES AND RELATED MATTERS

Chapter Eleven: Investment

Section A – Investment

Article 1101: Scope and Coverage

1.   This Chapter applies to measures adopted or maintained by a Party relating to:

(a)   investors of another Party;

(b)   investments of investors of another Party in the territory of the Party; and

(c)   with respect to Articles 1106 and 1114, all investments in the territory of the Party.

2.   A Party has the right to perform exclusively the economic activities set out in Annex III and to refuse to permit the establishment of investment in such activities.

3.   This Chapter does not apply to measures adopted or maintained by a Party to the extent that they are covered by Chapter Fourteen (Financial Services).

4.   Nothing in this Chapter shall be construed to prevent a Party from providing a service or performing a function such as law enforcement, correctional services, income security or insurance, social security or insurance, social welfare, public education, public training, health, and child care, in a manner that is not inconsistent with this Chapter.

Article 1102: National Treatment

1.   Each Party shall accord to investors of another Party treatment no less favorable than that it accords, in like circumstances, to its own investors with respect to the establishment, acquisition, expansion, management, conduct, operation, and sale or other disposition of investments.

2.   Each Party shall accord to investments of investors of another Party treatment no less favorable than that it accords, in like circumstances, to investments of its own investors with respect to the establishment, acquisition, expansion, management, conduct, operation, and sale or other disposition of investments.

3.   The treatment accorded by a Party under paragraphs 1 and 2 means, with respect to a state or province, treatment no less favorable than the most favorable treatment accorded, in like circumstances, by that state or province to investors, and to investments of investors, of the Party of which it forms a part.

4.   For greater certainty, no Party may:

(a)   impose on an investor of another Party a requirement that a minimum level of equity in an enterprise in the territory of the Party be held by its nationals, other than nominal qualifying shares for directors or incorporators of corporations; or

(b)   require an investor of another Party, by reason of its nationality, to sell or otherwise dispose of an investment in the territory of the Party.

Article 1103: Most-Favored-Nation Treatment

1.   Each Party shall accord to investors of another Party treatment no less favorable than that it accords, in like circumstances, to investors of any other Party or of a non-Party with respect to the establishment, acquisition, expansion, management, conduct, operation, and sale or other disposition of investments.

2.   Each Party shall accord to investments of investors of another Party treatment no less favorable than that it accords, in like circumstances, to investments of investors of any other Party or of a non-Party with respect to the establishment, acquisition, expansion, management, conduct, operation, and sale or other disposition of investments.

Article 1104: Standard of Treatment

Each Party shall accord to investors of another Party and to investments of investors of another Party the better of the treatment required by Articles 1102 and 1103.

Article 1105: Minimum Standard of Treatment

1.   Each Party shall accord to investments of investors of another Party treatment in accordance with international law, including fair and equitable treatment and full protection and security.

2.   Without prejudice to paragraph 1 and notwithstanding Article 1108(7)(b), each Party shall accord to investors of another Party, and to investments of investors of another Party, non-discriminatory treatment with respect to measures it adopts or maintains relating to losses suffered by investments in its territory owing to armed conflict or civil strife.

3.   Paragraph 2 does not apply to existing measures relating to subsidies or grants that would be inconsistent with Article 1102 but for Article 1108(7)(b).

Article 1106: Performance Requirements

1.   No Party may impose or enforce any of the following requirements, or enforce any commitment or undertaking, in connection with the establishment, acquisition, expansion, management, conduct or operation of an investment of an investor of a Party or of a non-Party in its territory:

(a)   to export a given level or percentage of goods or services;

(b)   to achieve a given level or percentage of domestic content;

(c)   to purchase, use or accord a preference to goods produced or services provided in its territory, or to purchase goods or services from persons in its territory;

(d)   to relate in any way the volume or value of imports to the volume or value of exports or to the amount of foreign exchange inflows associated with such investment;

(e)   to restrict sales of goods or services in its territory that such investment produces or provides by relating such sales in any way to the volume or value of its exports or foreign exchange earnings;

(f)   to transfer technology, a production process or other proprietary knowledge to a person in its territory, except when the requirement is imposed or the commitment or undertaking is enforced by a court, administrative tribunal or competition authority to remedy an alleged violation of competition laws or to act in a manner not inconsistent with other provisions of this Agreement; or

(g)   to act as the exclusive supplier of the goods it produces or services it provides to a specific region or world market.

2.   A measure that requires an investment to use a technology to meet generally applicable health, safety or environmental requirements shall not be construed to be inconsistent with paragraph 1(f). For greater certainty, Articles 1102 and 1103 apply to the measure.

3.   No Party may condition the receipt or continued receipt of an advantage, in connection with an investment in its territory of an investor of a Party or of a non-Party, on compliance with any of the following requirements:

(a)   to achieve a given level or percentage of domestic content;

(b)   to purchase, use or accord a preference to goods produced in its territory, or to purchase goods from producers in its territory;

(c)   to relate in any way the volume or value of imports to the volume or value of exports or to the amount of foreign exchange inflows associated with such investment; or

(d)   to restrict sales of goods or services in its territory that such investment produces or provides by relating such sales in any way to the volume or value of its exports or foreign exchange earnings.

4.   Nothing in paragraph 3 shall be construed to prevent a Party from conditioning the receipt or continued receipt of an advantage, in connection with an investment in its territory of an investor of a Party or of a non-Party, on compliance with a requirement to locate production, provide a service, train or employ workers, construct or expand particular facilities, or carry out research and development, in its territory.

5.   Paragraphs 1 and 3 do not apply to any requirement other than the requirements set out in those paragraphs.

6.   Provided that such measures are not applied in an arbitrary or unjustifiable manner, or do not constitute a disguised restriction on international trade or investment, nothing in paragraph 1(b) or (c) or 3(a) or (b) shall be construed to prevent any Party from adopting or maintaining measures, including environmental measures:

(a)   necessary to secure compliance with laws and regulations that are not inconsistent with the provisions of this Agreement;

(b)   necessary to protect human, animal or plant life or health; or

(c)   necessary for the conservation of living or non-living exhaustible natural resources.

Article 1107: Senior Management and Boards of Directors

1.   No Party may require that an enterprise of that Party that is an investment of an investor of another Party appoint to senior management positions individuals of any particular nationality.

2.   A Party may require that a majority of the board of directors, or any committee thereof, of an enterprise of that Party that is an investment of an investor of another Party, be of a particular nationality, or resident in the territory of the Party, provided that the requirement does not materially impair the ability of the investor to exercise control over its investment.

Article 1108: Reservations and Exceptions

1.   Articles 1102, 1103, 1106 and 1107 do not apply to:

(a)   any existing non-conforming measure that is maintained by

   (i)   a Party at the federal level, as set out in its Schedule to Annex I or III,

   (ii)   a state or province, for two years after the date of entry into force of this Agreement, and thereafter as set out by a Party in its Schedule to Annex I in accordance with paragraph 2, or

   (iii) a local government;

(b)   the continuation or prompt renewal of any non-conforming measure referred to in sub-paragraph (a); or

(c)   an amendment to any non-conforming measure referred to in subparagraph (a) to the extent that the amendment does not decrease the conformity of the measure, as it existed immediately before the amendment, with Articles 1102, 1103, 1106 and 1107.

2.   Each Party may set out in its Schedule to Annex I, within two years of the date of entry into force of this Agreement, any existing nonconforming measure maintained by a state or province, not including a local government.

3.   Articles 1102, 1103, 1106 and 1107 do not apply to any measure that a Party adopts or maintains with respect to sectors, subsectors or activities, as set out in its Schedule to Annex II.

4.   No Party may, under any measure adopted after the date of entry into force of this Agreement and covered by its Schedule to Annex II, require an investor of another Party, by reason of

its nationality, to sell or otherwise dispose of an investment existing at the time the measure becomes effective.

5.   Articles 1102 and 1103 do not apply to any measure that is an exception to, or derogation from, the obligations under Article 1703 (Intellectual Property National Treatment) as specifically provided for in that Article.

6.   Article 1103 does not apply to treatment accorded by a Party pursuant to agreements, or with respect to sectors, set out in its Schedule to Annex IV.

7.   Articles 1102, 1103 and 1107 do not apply to:

(a) procurement by a Party or a state enterprise; or

(b) subsidies or grants provided by a Party or a state enterprise, including government suppor-ted loans, guarantees and insurance.

8.   The provisions of:

(a) Article 1106(1)(a), (b) and (c), and (3)(a) and (b) do not apply to qualification requirements for goods or services with respect to export promotion and foreign aid programs;

(b) Article 1106(1)(b), (c), (f) and (g), and (3)(a) and (b) do not apply to procurement by a Party or a state enterprise; and

(c) Article 1106(3)(a) and (b) do not apply to requirements imposed by an importing Party rela-ting to the content of goods necessary to qualify for preferential tariffs or preferential quotas.

Article 1109: Transfers

1.   Each Party shall permit all transfers relating to an investment of an investor of another Party in the territory of the Party to be made freely and without delay. Such transfers include:

(a) profits, dividends, interest, capital gains, royalty payments, management fees, technical assistance and other fees, returns in kind and other amounts derived from the investment;

(b) proceeds from the sale of all or any part of the investment or from the partial or complete liquidation of the investment;

(c) payments made under a contract entered into by the investor, or its investment, including payments made pursuant to a loan agreement;

(d) payments made pursuant to Article 1110; and

(e) payments arising under Section B.

2.   Each Party shall permit transfers to be made in a freely usable currency at the market rate of exchange prevailing on the date of transfer with respect to spot transactions in the currency to be transferred.

3.   No Party may require its investors to transfer, or penalize its investors that fail to transfer, the income, earnings, profits or other amounts derived from, or attributable to, investments in the territory of another Party.

4.   Notwithstanding paragraphs 1 and 2, a Party may prevent a transfer through the equitable, non-discriminatory and good faith application of its laws relating to:

(a) bankruptcy, insolvency or the protection of the rights of creditors;

(b) issuing, trading or dealing in securities;

(c) criminal or penal offenses;

(d) reports of transfers of currency or other monetary instruments; or

(e) ensuring the satisfaction of judgments in adjudicatory proceedings.

5.   Paragraph 3 shall not be construed to prevent a Party from imposing any measure through the equitable, non-discriminatory and good faith application of its laws relating to the matters set out in subparagraphs (a) through (e) of paragraph 4.

6.   Notwithstanding paragraph 1, a Party may restrict transfers of returns in kind in circumstances where it could otherwise restrict such transfers under this Agreement, including as set out in paragraph 4.

Article 1110: Expropriation and Compensation

1.   No Party may directly or indirectly nationalize or expropriate an investment of an investor of another Party in its territory or take a measure tantamount to nationalization or expropriation of such an investment ("expropriation"), except:

(a)   for a public purpose;

(b)   on a non-discriminatory basis;

(c)   in accordance with due process of law and Article 1105(1); and

(d)   on payment of compensation in accordance with paragraphs 2 through 6.

2.   Compensation shall be equivalent to the fair market value of the expropriated investment immediately before the expropriation took place ("date of expropriation"), and shall not reflect any change in value occurring because the intended expropriation had become known earlier. Valuation criteria shall include going concern value, asset value including declared tax value of tangible property, and other criteria, as appropriate, to determine fair market value.

3.   Compensation shall be paid without delay and be fully realizable.

4.   If payment is made in a G7 currency, compensation shall include interest at a commercially reasonable rate for that currency from the date of expropriation until the date of actual payment.

5.   If a Party elects to pay in a currency other than a G7 currency, the amount paid on the date of payment, if converted into a G7 currency at the market rate of exchange prevailing on that date, shall be no less than if the amount of compensation owed on the date of expropriation had been converted into that G7 currency at the market rate of exchange prevailing on that date, and interest had accrued at a commercially reasonable rate for that G7 currency from the date of expropriation until the date of payment.

6.   On payment, compensation shall be freely transferable as provided in Article 1109.

7.   This Article does not apply to the issuance of compulsory licenses granted in relation to intellectual property rights, or to the revocation, limitation or creation of intellectual property rights, to the extent that such issuance, revocation, limitation or creation is consistent with Chapter Seventeen (Intellectual Property).

8.   For purposes of this Article and for greater certainty, a non-discriminatory measure of general application shall not be considered a measure tantamount to an expropriation of a debt security or loan covered by this Chapter solely on the ground that the measure imposes costs on the debtor that cause it to default on the debt.

Article 1111: Special Formalities and Information Requirements

1.   Nothing in Article 1102 shall be construed to prevent a Party from adopting or maintaining a measure that prescribes special formalities in connection with the establishment of investments by investors of another Party, such as a requirement that investors be residents of the Party or that investments be legally constituted under the laws or regulations of the Party, provided that such formalities do not materially impair the protections afforded by a Party to investors of another Party and investments of investors of another Party pursuant to this Chapter.

2.   Notwithstanding Articles 1102 or 1103, a Party may require an investor of another Party, or its investment in its territory, to provide routine information concerning that investment solely

for informational or statistical purposes. The Party shall protect such business information that is confidential from any disclosure that would prejudice the competitive position of the investor or the investment. Nothing in this paragraph shall be construed to prevent a Party from otherwise obtaining or disclosing information in connection with the equitable and good faith application of its law.

Article 1112: Relation to Other Chapters

1.   In the event of any inconsistency between this Chapter and another Chapter, the other Chapter shall prevail to the extent of the inconsistency.

2.   A requirement by a Party that a service provider of another Party post a bond or other form of financial security as a condition of providing a service into its territory does not of itself make this Chapter applicable to the provision of that crossborder service. This Chapter applies to that Party's treatment of the posted bond or financial security.

Article 1113: Denial of Benefits

1.   A Party may deny the benefits of this Chapter to an investor of another Party that is an enterprise of such Party and to investments of such investor if investors of a non-Party own or control the enterprise and the denying Party:

(a)   does not maintain diplomatic relations with the non-Party; or

(b)   adopts or maintains measures with respect to the non-Party that prohibit transactions with the enterprise or that would be violated or circumvented if the benefits of this Chapter were accorded to the enterprise or to its investments.

2.   Subject to prior notification and consultation in accordance with Articles 1803 (Notification and Provision of Information) and 2006 (Consultations), a Party may deny the benefits of this Chapter to an investor of another Party that is an enterprise of such Party and to investments of such investors if investors of a non-Party own or control the enterprise and the enterprise has no substantial business activities in the territory of the Party under whose law it is constituted or organized.

Article 1114: Environmental Measures

1.   Nothing in this Chapter shall be construed to prevent a Party from adopting, maintaining or enforcing any measure otherwise consistent with this Chapter that it considers appropriate to ensure that investment activity in its territory is undertaken in a manner sensitive to environmental concerns.

2.   The Parties recognize that it is inappropriate to encourage investment by relaxing domestic health, safety or environmental measures. Accordingly, a Party should not waive or otherwise derogate from, or offer to waive or otherwise derogate from, such measures as an encouragement for the establishment, acquisition, expansion or retention in its territory of an investment of an investor. If a Party considers that another Party has offered such an encouragement, it may request consultations with the other Party and the two Parties shall consult with a view to avoiding any such encouragement.

Section B – Settlement of Disputes Between a Party and an Investor of Another Party

Article 1115: Purpose

Without prejudice to the rights and obligations of the Parties under Chapter Twenty (Institutional Arrangements and Dispute Settlement Procedures), this Section establishes a mechanism for the settlement of investment disputes that assures both equal treatment among investors of the Parties in accordance with the principle of international reciprocity and due process before an impartial tribunal.

Article 1116: Claim by an Investor of a Party on Its Own Behalf

1.   An investor of a Party may submit to arbitration under this Section a claim that another Party has breached an obligation under:

(a)   Section A or Article 1503(2) (State Enterprises), or

(b)   Article 1502(3)(a) (Monopolies and State Enterprises) where the monopoly has acted in a manner inconsistent with the Party's obligations under Section A,

and that the investor has incurred loss or damage by reason of, or arising out of, that breach.

2.   An investor may not make a claim if more than three years have elapsed from the date on which the investor first acquired, or should have first acquired, knowledge of the alleged breach and knowledge that the investor has incurred loss or damage.

Article 1117: Claim by an Investor of a Party on Behalf of an Enterprise

1.   An investor of a Party, on behalf of an enterprise of another Party that is a juridical person that the investor owns or controls directly or indirectly, may submit to arbitration under this Section a claim that the other Party has breached an obligation under:

(a)   Section A or Article 1503(2) (State Enterprises), or

(b)   Article 1502(3)(a) (Monopolies and State Enterprises) where the monopoly has acted in a manner inconsistent with the Party's obligations under Section A, and that the enterprise has incurred loss or damage by reason of, or arising out of, that breach.

2.   An investor may not make a claim on behalf of an enterprise described in paragraph 1 if more than three years have elapsed from the date on which the enterprise first acquired, or should have first acquired, knowledge of the alleged breach and knowledge that the enterprise has incurred loss or damage.

3.   Where an investor makes a claim under this Article and the investor or a non-controlling investor in the enterprise makes a claim under Article 1116 arising out of the same events that gave rise to the claim under this Article, and two or more of the claims are submitted to arbitration under Article 1120, the claims should be heard together by a Tribunal established under Article 1126, unless the Tribunal finds that the interests of a disputing party would be prejudiced thereby.

4.   An investment may not make a claim under this Section.

Article 1118: Settlement of a Claim through Consultation and Negotiation

The disputing parties should first attempt to settle a claim through consultation or negotiation.

Article 1119: Notice of Intent to Submit a Claim to Arbitration

The disputing investor shall deliver to the disputing Party written notice of its intention to submit a claim to arbitration at least 90 days before the claim is submitted, which notice shall specify:

(a)   the name and address of the disputing investor and, where a claim is made under Article 1117, the name and address of the enterprise;

(b)   the provisions of this Agreement alleged to have been breached and any other relevant provisions;

(c)   the issues and the factual basis for the claim; and

(d)   the relief sought and the approximate amount of damages claimed.

Article 1120: Submission of a Claim to Arbitration

1.   Except as provided in Annex 1120.1, and provided that six months have elapsed since the events giving rise to a claim, a disputing investor may submit the claim to arbitration under:

(a) the ICSID Convention, provided that both the disputing Party and the Party of the investor are parties to the Convention;

(b) the Additional Facility Rules of ICSID, provided that either the disputing Party or the Party of the investor, but not both, is a party to the ICSID Convention; or

(c) the UNCITRAL Arbitration Rules.

2. The applicable arbitration rules shall govern the arbitration except to the extent modified by this Section.

Article 1121: Conditions Precedent to Submission of a Claim to Arbitration

1. A disputing investor may submit a claim under Article 1116 to arbitration only if:

(a) the investor consents to arbitration in accordance with the procedures set out in this Agreement; and

(b) the investor and, where the claim is for loss or damage to an interest in an enterprise of another Party that is a juridical person that the investor owns or controls directly or indirectly, the enterprise, waive their right to initiate or continue before any administrative tribunal or court under the law of any Party, or other dispute settlement procedures, any proceedings with respect to the measure of the disputing Party that is alleged to be a breach referred to in Article 1116, except for proceedings for injunctive, declaratory or other extraordinary relief, not involving the payment of damages, before an administrative tribunal or court under the law of the disputing Party.

2. A disputing investor may submit a claim under Article 1117 to arbitration only if both the investor and the enterprise:

(a) consent to arbitration in accordance with the procedures set out in this Agreement; and

(b) waive their right to initiate or continue before any administrative tribunal or court under the law of any Party, or other dispute settlement procedures, any proceedings with respect to the measure of the disputing Party that is alleged to be a breach referred to in Article 1117, except for proceedings for injunctive, declaratory or other extraordinary relief, not involving the payment of damages, before an administrative tribunal or court under the law of the disputing Party.

3. A consent and waiver required by this Article shall be in writing, shall be delivered to the disputing Party and shall be included in the submission of a claim to arbitration.

4. Only where a disputing Party has deprived a disputing investor of control of an enterprise:

(a) a waiver from the enterprise under paragraph 1(b) or 2(b) shall not be required; and

(b) Annex 1120.1(b) shall not apply.

Article 1122: Consent to Arbitration

1. Each Party consents to the submission of a claim to arbitration in accordance with the procedures set out in this Agreement.

2. The consent given by paragraph 1 and the submission by a disputing investor of a claim to arbitration shall satisfy the requirement of:

(a) Chapter II of the ICSID Convention (Jurisdiction of the Centre) and the Additional Facility Rules for written consent of the parties;

(b) Article II of the New York Convention for an agreement in writing; and

(c) Article I of the Inter-American Convention for an agreement.

Article 1123: Number of Arbitrators and Method of Appointment

Except in respect of a Tribunal established under Article 1126, and unless the disputing parties otherwise agree, the Tribunal shall comprise three arbitrators, one arbitrator appointed by each of the disputing parties and the third, who shall be the presiding arbitrator, appointed by agreement of the disputing parties.

Article 1124: Constitution of a Tribunal When a Party Fails to Appoint an Arbitrator or the Disputing Parties Are Unable to Agree on a Presiding Arbitrator

1.   The Secretary-General shall serve as appointing authority for an arbitration under this Section.

2.   If a Tribunal, other than a Tribunal established under Article 1126, has not been constituted within 90 days from the date that a claim is submitted to arbitration, the Secretary-General, on the request of either disputing party, shall appoint, in his discretion, the arbitrator or arbitrators not yet appointed, except that the presiding arbitrator shall be appointed in accordance with paragraph 3.

3.   The Secretary-General shall appoint the presiding arbitrator from the roster of presiding arbitrators referred to in paragraph 4, provided that the presiding arbitrator shall not be a national of the disputing Party or a national of the Party of the disputing investor. In the event that no such presiding arbitrator is available to serve, the Secretary-General shall appoint, from the ICSID Panel of Arbitrators, a presiding arbitrator who is not a national of any of the Parties.

4.   On the date of entry into force of this Agreement, the Parties shall establish, and thereafter maintain, a roster of 45 presiding arbitrators meeting the qualifications of the Convention and rules referred to in Article 1120 and experienced in international law and investment matters. The roster members shall be appointed by consensus and without regard to nationality.

Article 1125: Agreement to Appointment of Arbitrators

For purposes of Article 39 of the ICSID Convention and Article 7 of Schedule C to the ICSID Additional Facility Rules, and without prejudice to an objection to an arbitrator based on Article 1124(3) or on a ground other than nationality:

(a)   the disputing Party agrees to the appointment of each individual member of a Tribunal established under the ICSID Convention or the ICSID Additional Facility Rules;

(b)   a disputing investor referred to in Article 1116 may submit a claim to arbitration, or continue a claim, under the ICSID Convention or the ICSID Additional Facility Rules, only on condition that the disputing investor agrees in writing to the appointment of each individual member of the Tribunal; and

(c)   a disputing investor referred to in Article 1117(1) may submit a claim to arbitration, or continue a claim, under the ICSID Convention or the ICSID Additional Facility Rules, only on condition that the disputing investor and the enterprise agree in writing to the appointment of each individual member of the Tribunal.

Article 1126: Consolidation

1.   A Tribunal established under this Article shall be established under the UNCITRAL Arbitration Rules and shall conduct its proceedings in accordance with those Rules, except as modified by this Section.

2.   Where a Tribunal established under this Article is satisfied that claims have been submitted to arbitration under Article 1120 that have a question of law or fact in common, the Tribunal may, in the interests of fair and efficient resolution of the claims, and after hearing the disputing parties, by order:

(a)   assume jurisdiction over, and hear and determine together, all or part of the claims; or

(b)   assume jurisdiction over, and hear and determine one or more of the claims, the determination of which it believes would assist in the resolution of the others.

3.   A disputing party that seeks an order under paragraph 2 shall request the Secretary-General to establish a Tribunal and shall specify in the request:

(a)   the name of the disputing Party or disputing investors against which the order is sought;

(b)   the nature of the order sought; and

(c)   the grounds on which the order is sought.

4.   The disputing party shall deliver to the disputing Party or disputing investors against which the order is sought a copy of the request.

5.   Within 60 days of receipt of the request, the Secretary-General shall establish a Tribunal comprising three arbitrators. The Secretary-General shall appoint the presiding arbitrator from the roster referred to in Article 1124(4). In the event that no such presiding arbitrator is available to serve, the Secretary-General shall appoint, from the ICSID Panel of Arbitrators, a presiding arbitrator who is not a national of any of the Parties. The Secretary-General shall appoint the two other members from the roster referred to in Article 1124(4), and to the extent not available from that roster, from the ICSID Panel of Arbitrators, and to the extent not available from that Panel, in the discretion of the Secretary-General. One member shall be a national of the disputing Party and one member shall be a national of a Party of the disputing investors.

6.   Where a Tribunal has been established under this Article, a disputing investor that has submitted a claim to arbitration under Article 1116 or 1117 and that has not been named in a request made under paragraph 3 may make a written request to the Tribunal that it be included in an order made under paragraph 2, and shall specify in the request:

(a)   the name and address of the disputing investor;

(b)   the nature of the order sought; and

(c)   the grounds on which the order is sought.

7.   A disputing investor referred to in paragraph 6 shall deliver a copy of its request to the disputing parties named in a request made under paragraph 3.

8.   A Tribunal established under Article 1120 shall not have jurisdiction to decide a claim, or a part of a claim, over which a Tribunal established under this Article has assumed jurisdiction.

9. On application of a disputing party, a Tribunal established under this Article, pending its decision under paragraph 2, may order that the proceedings of a Tribunal established under Article 1120 be stayed, unless the latter Tribunal has already adjourned its proceedings.

10.   A disputing Party shall deliver to the Secretariat, within 15 days of receipt by the disputing Party, a copy of:

(a)   a request for arbitration made under paragraph (1) of Article 36 of the ICSID Convention;

(b)   a notice of arbitration made under Article 2 of Schedule C of the ICSID Additional Facility Rules; or

(c)   a notice of arbitration given under the UNCITRAL Arbitration Rules.

11.   A disputing Party shall deliver to the Secretariat a copy of a request made under paragraph 3:

(a)   within 15 days of receipt of the request, in the case of a request made by a disputing investor;

(b)   within 15 days of making the request, in the case of a request made by the disputing Party.

12.   A disputing Party shall deliver to the Secretariat a copy of a request made under paragraph 6 within 15 days of receipt of the request.

13.   The Secretariat shall maintain a public register of the documents referred to in paragraphs 10, 11 and 12.

Article 1127: Notice

A disputing Party shall deliver to the other Parties:

(a) written notice of a claim that has been submitted to arbitration no later than 30 days after the date that the claim is submitted; and

(b) copies of all pleadings filed in the arbitration.

Article 1128: Participation by a Party

On written notice to the disputing parties, a Party may make submissions to a Tribunal on a question of interpretation of this Agreement.

Article 1129: Documents

1. A Party shall be entitled to receive from the disputing Party, at the cost of the requesting Party a copy of:

(a) the evidence that has been tendered to the Tribunal; and

(b) the written argument of the disputing parties.

2. A Party receiving information pursuant to paragraph 1 shall treat the information as if it were a disputing Party.

Article 1130: Place of Arbitration

Unless the disputing parties agree otherwise, a Tribunal shall hold an arbitration in the territory of a Party that is a party to the New York Convention, selected in accordance with:

(a) the ICSID Additional Facility Rules if the arbitration is under those Rules or the ICSID Convention; or

(b) the UNCITRAL Arbitration Rules if the arbitration is under those Rules.

Article 1131: Governing Law

1. A Tribunal established under this Section shall decide the issues in dispute in accordance with this Agreement and applicable rules of international law.

2. An interpretation by the Commission of a provision of this Agreement shall be binding on a Tribunal established under this Section.

Article 1132: Interpretation of Annexes

1. Where a disputing Party asserts as a defense that the measure alleged to be a breach is within the scope of a reservation or exception set out in Annex I, Annex II, Annex III or Annex IV, on request of the disputing Party, the Tribunal shall request the interpretation of the Commission on the issue. The Commission, within 60 days of delivery of the request, shall submit in writing its interpretation to the Tribunal.

2. Further to Article 1131(2), a Commission interpretation submitted under paragraph 1 shall be binding on the Tribunal. If the Commission fails to submit an interpretation within 60 days, the Tribunal shall decide the issue.

Article 1133: Expert Reports

Without prejudice to the appointment of other kinds of experts where authorized by the applicable arbitration rules, a Tribunal, at the request of a disputing party or, unless the disputing parties disapprove, on its own initiative, may appoint one or more experts to report to it in writing on any factual issue concerning environmental, health, safety or other scientific matters raised by a disputing party in a proceeding, subject to such terms and conditions as the disputing parties may agree.

Article 1134: Interim Measures of Protection

A Tribunal may order an interim measure of protection to preserve the rights of a disputing party, or to ensure that the Tribunal's jurisdiction is made fully effective, including an order to preserve evidence in the possession or control of a disputing party or to protect the Tribunal's jurisdiction. A Tribunal may not order attachment or enjoin the application of the measure alleged to constitute a breach referred to in Article 1116 or 1117. For purposes of this paragraph, an order includes a recommendation.

Article 1135: Final Award

1.   Where a Tribunal makes a final award against a Party, the Tribunal may award, separately or in combination, only:

(a)   monetary damages and any applicable interest;

(b)   restitution of property, in which case the award shall provide that the disputing Party may pay monetary damages and any applicable interest in lieu of restitution.

A tribunal may also award costs in accordance with the applicable arbitration rules.

2.   Subject to paragraph 1, where a claim is made under Article 1117(1):

(a)   an award of restitution of property shall provide that restitution be made to the enterprise;

(b)   an award of monetary damages and any applicable interest shall provide that the sum be paid to the enterprise; and

(c)   the award shall provide that it is made without prejudice to any right that any person may have in the relief under applicable domestic law.

3.   A Tribunal may not order a Party to pay punitive damages.

Article 1136: Finality and Enforcement of an Award

1.   An award made by a Tribunal shall have no binding force except between the disputing parties and in respect of the particular case.

2.   Subject to paragraph 3 and the applicable review procedure for an interim award, a disputing party shall abide by and comply with an award without delay.

3.   A disputing party may not seek enforcement of a final award until:

(a)   in the case of a final award made under the ICSID Convention

(i)   120 days have elapsed from the date the award was rendered and no disputing party has requested revision or annulment of the award, or

(ii)   revision or annulment proceedings have been completed; and

(b)   in the case of a final award under the ICSID Additional Facility Rules or the UNCITRAL Arbitration Rules

(i)   three months have elapsed from the date the award was rendered and no disputing party has commenced a proceeding to revise, set aside or annul the award, or

(ii)   a court has dismissed or allowed an application to revise, set aside or annul the award and there is no further appeal.

4.   Each Party shall provide for the enforcement of an award in its territory.

5.   If a disputing Party fails to abide by or comply with a final award, the Commission, on delivery of a request by a Party whose investor was a party to the arbitration, shall establish a panel under Article 2008 (Request for an Arbitral Panel). The requesting Party may seek in such proceedings:

(a)   a determination that the failure to abide by or comply with the final award is inconsistent with the obligations of this Agreement; and

(b)   a recommendation that the Party abide by or comply with the final award.

6.   A disputing investor may seek enforcement of an arbitration award under the ICSID Convention, the New York Convention or the Inter-American Convention regardless of whether proceedings have been taken under paragraph 5.

7.   A claim that is submitted to arbitration under this Section shall be considered to arise out of a commercial relationship or transaction for purposes of Article I of the New York Convention and Article I of the Inter-American Convention.

Article 1137: General

Time when a Claim is Submitted to Arbitration

1.   A claim is submitted to arbitration under this Section when:

(a)   the request for arbitration under paragraph (1) of Article 36 of the ICSID Convention has been received by the Secretary-General;

(b)   the notice of arbitration under Article 2 of Schedule C of the ICSID Additional Facility Rules has been received by the Secretary-General; or

(c)   the notice of arbitration given under the UNCITRAL Arbitration Rules is received by the disputing Party.

Service of Documents

2.   Delivery of notice and other documents on a Party shall be made to the place named for that Party in Annex 1137.2.

Receipts under Insurance or Guarantee Contracts

3.   In an arbitration under this Section, a Party shall not assert, as a defense, counterclaim, right of setoff or otherwise, that the disputing investor has received or will receive, pursuant to an insurance or guarantee contract, indemnification or other compensation for all or part of its alleged damages.

Publication of an Award

4.   Annex 1137.4 applies to the Parties specified in that Annex with respect to publication of an award.

Article 1138: Exclusions

1.   Without prejudice to the applicability or non-applicability of the dispute settlement provisions of this Section or of Chapter Twenty (Institutional Arrangements and Dispute Settlement Procedures) to other actions taken by a Party pursuant to Article 2102 (National Security), a decision by a Party to prohibit or restrict the acquisition of an investment in its territory by an investor of another Party, or its investment, pursuant to that Article shall not be subject to such provisions.

2.   The dispute settlement provisions of this Section and of Chapter Twenty shall not apply to the matters referred to in Annex 1138.2.

Section C – Definitions

Article 1139: Definitions

For purposes of this Chapter:

disputing investor means an investor that makes a claim under Section B;

disputing parties means the disputing investor and the disputing Party;

disputing party means the disputing investor or the disputing Party;

disputing Party means a Party against which a claim is made under Section B;

enterprise means an "enterprise" as defined in Article 201 (Definitions of General Application), and a branch of an enterprise;

enterprise of a Party means an enterprise constituted or organized under the law of a Party, and a branch located in the territory of a Party and carrying out business activities there.

equity or debt securities includes voting and non-voting shares, bonds, convertible debentures, stock options and warrants;

G7 Currency means the currency of Canada, France, Germany, Italy, Japan, the United Kingdom of Great Britain and Northern Ireland or the United States;

ICSID means the International Centre for Settlement of Investment Disputes;

ICSID Convention means the Convention on the Settlement of Investment Disputes between States and Nationals of other States , done at Washington, March 18, 1965;

InterAmerican Convention means the InterAmerican Convention on International Commercial Arbitration , done at Panama, January 30, 1975;

investment means:

(a)   an enterprise;

(b)   an equity security of an enterprise;

(c)   a debt security of an enterprise

    (i)   where the enterprise is an affiliate of the investor, or

    (ii)   where the original maturity of the debt security is at least three years,

but does not include a debt security, regardless of original maturity, of a state enterprise;

(d)   a loan to an enterprise

    (i)   where the enterprise is an affiliate of the investor, or

    (ii)   where the original maturity of the loan is at least three years,

but does not include a loan, regardless of original maturity, to a state enterprise;

(e)   an interest in an enterprise that entitles the owner to share in income or profits of the enterprise;

(f)   an interest in an enterprise that entitles the owner to share in the assets of that enterprise on dissolution, other than a debt security or a loan excluded from subparagraph (c) or (d);

(g)   real estate or other property, tangible or intangible, acquired in the expectation or used for the purpose of economic benefit or other business purposes; and

(h)   interests arising from the commitment of capital or other resources in the territory of a Party to economic activity in such territory, such as under

    (i)   contracts involving the presence of an investor's property in the territory of the Party, including turnkey or construction contracts, or concessions, or

    (ii)   contracts where remuneration depends substantially on the production, revenues or profits of an enterprise;

but investment does not mean,

(i)   claims to money that arise solely from

    (i)   commercial contracts for the sale of goods or services by a national or enterprise in the territory of a Party to an enterprise in the territory of another Party, or

    (ii)   the extension of credit in connection with a commercial transaction, such as trade financing, other than a loan covered by subparagraph (d); or

(j)   any other claims to money,

that do not involve the kinds of interests set out in subparagraphs (a) through (h);

investment of an investor of a Party means an investment owned or controlled directly or indirectly by an investor of such Party;

investor of a Party means a Party or state enterprise thereof, or a national or an enterprise of such Party, that seeks to make, is making or has made an investment;

investor of a non-Party means an investor other than an investor of a Party, that seeks to make, is making or has made an investment;

New York Convention means the United Nations Convention on the Recognition and Enforcement of Foreign Arbitral Awards , done at New York, June 10, 1958;

Secretary-General means the Secretary-General of ICSID;

transfers means transfers and international payments;

Tribunal means an arbitration tribunal established under Article 1120 or 1126; and

UNCITRAL Arbitration Rules means the arbitration rules of the United Nations Commission on International Trade Law, approved by the United Nations General Assembly on December 15, 1976.

Annex 1120.1 Submission of a Claim to Arbitration – Mexico

With respect to the submission of a claim to arbitration:

(a) an investor of another Party may not allege that Mexico has breached an obligation under:

    (i) Section A or Article 1503(2) (State Enterprises), or

    (ii) Article 1502(3)(a) (Monopolies and State Enterprises) where the monopoly has acted in a manner inconsistent with the Party's obligations under Section A,

both in an arbitration under this Section and in proceedings before a Mexican court or administrative tribunal; and

(b) where an enterprise of Mexico that is a juridical person that an investor of another Party owns or controls directly or indirectly alleges in proceedings before a Mexican court or administrative tribunal that Mexico has breached an obligation under:

    (i) Section A or Article 1503(2) (State Enterprises), or

    (ii) Article 1502(3)(a) (Monopolies and State Enterprises) where the monopoly has acted in a manner inconsistent with the Party's obligations under Section A,

the investor may not allege the breach in an arbitration under this Section.

Annex 1137.2 Service of Documents on a Party Under Section B

Each Party shall set out in this Annex and publish in its official journal by January 1, 1994, the place for delivery of notice and other documents under this Section.

Annex 1137.4 Publication of an Award

Canada

Where Canada is the disputing Party, either Canada or a disputing investor that is a party to the arbitration may make an award public.

Mexico

Where Mexico is the disputing Party, the applicable arbitration rules apply to the publication of an award.

United States

Where the United States is the disputing Party, either the United States or a disputing investor that is a party to the arbitration may make an award public.

Annex 1138.2 Exclusions from Dispute Settlement

Canada

A decision by Canada following a review under the Investment Canada Act , with respect to whether or not to permit an acquisition that is subject to review, shall not be subject to the dispute settlement provisions of Section B or of Chapter Twenty (Institutional Arrangements and Dispute Settlement Procedures).

Mexico

A decision by the National Commission on Foreign Investment ("Comisión Nacional de Inversiones Extranjeras") following a review pursuant to Annex I, page IM4, with respect to whether or not to permit an acquisition that is subject to review, shall not be subject to the dispute settlement provisions of Section B or of Chapter Twenty (Institutional Arrangements and Dispute Settlement Procedures).

XI.3. 2009 ASEAN COMPREHENSIVE INVESTMENT AGREEMENT[1]

The Governments of Brunei Darussalam, the Kingdom of Cambodia, the Republic of Indonesia, the Lao People's Democratic Republic, Malaysia, the Union of Myanmar, the Republic of the Philippines, the Republic of Singapore, the Kingdom of Thailand and the Socialist Republic of Viet Nam, Member States of the Association of Southeast Asian Nations ("ASEAN"), hereinafter collectively referred to as "Member States" or singularly as "Member State";

RECALLING the decisions of the 39th ASEAN Economic Ministers ("AEM") Meeting held in Makati City, Philippines on 23 August 2007 to revise the Framework Agreement on the ASEAN Investment Area signed in Makati City, Philippines on 7 October 1998 ("AIA Agreement"), as amended, into a comprehensive investment agreement which is forward-looking, with improved features and provisions, comparable to international best practices in order to increase intra-ASEAN investments and to enhance ASEAN's competitiveness in attracting inward investments into ASEAN;

RECOGNISING the different levels of development within ASEAN especially the least developed Member States which require some flexibility including special and differential treatment as ASEAN moves towards a more integrated and interdependent future;

REAFFIRMING the need to move forward from the AIA Agreement and the ASEAN Agreement for the Promotion and Protection of Investments signed in Manila, Philippines on 15 December 1987 ("ASEAN IGA"), as amended, in order to further enhance regional integration to realise the vision of the ASEAN Economic Community ("AEC");

CONVINCED that sustained inflows of new investments and reinvestments will promote and ensure dynamic development of ASEAN economies;

RECOGNISING that a conducive investment environment will enhance freer flow of capital, goods and services, technology and human resource and overall economic and social development in ASEAN; and

DETERMINED to further intensify economic cooperation between and among Member States,

HAVE AGREED as follows:

SECTION A

Article 1 Objective

The objective of this Agreement is to create a free and open investment regime in ASEAN in order to achieve the end goal of economic integration under the AEC in accordance with the AEC Blueprint, through the following:

(a) progressive liberalisation of the investment regimes of Member States;

(b) provision of enhanced protection to investors of all Member States and their investments;

(c) improvement of transparency and predictability of investment rules, regulations and procedures conducive to increased investment among Member States;

(d) joint promotion of the region as an integrated investment area; and

(e) cooperation to create favourable conditions for investment by investors of a Member State in the territory of the other Member States.

Article 2 Guiding Principles

This Agreement shall create a liberal, facilitative, transparent and competitive investment environment in ASEAN by adhering to the following principles:

---

1   See http://www.asean.org/storage/images/2013/economic/aia/ACIA_Final_Text_26%20Feb%202009.pdf

(a) provide for investment liberalisation, protection, investment promotion and facilitation;

(b) progressive liberalisation of investment with a view towards achieving a free and open investment environment in the region;

(c) benefit investors and their investments based in ASEAN;

(d) maintain and accord preferential treatment among Member States;

(e) no back-tracking of commitments made under the AIA Agreement and the ASEAN IGA;

(f) grant special and differential treatment and other flexibilities to Member States depending on their level of development and sectoral sensitivities;

(g) reciprocal treatment in the enjoyment of concessions among Member States, where appropriate; and

(h) accommodate expansion of scope of this Agreement to cover other sectors in the future.

Article 3 Scope of Application

1.   This Agreement shall apply to measures adopted or maintained by a Member State relating to:

(a) investors of any other Member State; and

(b) investments, in its territory, of investors of any other Member State.

2.   This Agreement shall apply to existing investments as at the date of entry into force of this Agreement as well as to investments made after the entry into force of this Agreement.

3.   For the purpose of liberalisation and subject to Article 9 (Reservations), this Agreement shall apply to the following sectors:

(a) manufacturing;

(b) agriculture;

(c) fishery;

(d) forestry;

(e) mining and quarrying;

(f) services incidental to manufacturing, agriculture, fishery, forestry, mining and quarrying; and

(g) any other sectors, as may be agreed upon by all Member States.

4.   This Agreement shall not apply to:

(a) any taxation measures, except for Articles 13 (Transfers) and 14 (Expropriation and Compensation);

(b) subsidies or grants provided by a Member State;

(c) government procurement;

(d) services supplied in the exercise of governmental authority by the relevant body or authority of a Member State. For the purposes of this Agreement, a service supplied in the exercise of governmental authority means any service, which is supplied neither on a commercial basis nor in competition with one or more service suppliers; and

(e) measures adopted or maintained by a Member State affecting trade in services under the ASEAN Framework Agreement on Services signed in Bangkok, Thailand on 15 December 1995 ("AFAS").

5.   Notwithstanding sub-paragraph 4 (e), for the purpose of protection of investment with respect to the commercial presence mode of service supply, Articles 11 (Treatment of Investment), 12 (Compensation in Cases of Strife), 13 (Transfers), 14 (Expropriation and Compensation) and 15 (Subrogation) and Section B (Investment Disputes Between an Investor and a Member State), shall apply, mutatis mutandis, to any measure affecting the supply of a service by a service

supplier of a Member State through commercial presence in the territory of any other Member State but only to the extent that they relate to an investment and obligation under this Agreement regardless of whether or not such service sector is scheduled in the Member States' schedule of commitments made under AFAS.

6.   Nothing in this Agreement shall affect the rights and obligations of any Member State under any tax convention. In the event of any inconsistency between this Agreement and any such convention, that convention shall prevail to the extent of the inconsistency.

Article 4 Definitions

For the purpose of this Agreement:

(a) "covered investment" means, with respect to a Member State, an investment in its territory of an investor of any other Member State in existence as of the date of entry into force of this Agreement or established, acquired or expanded thereafter, and has been admitted according to its laws, regulations, and national policies, and where applicable, specifically approved in writing[1] by the competent authority of a Member State;

(b) "freely usable currency" means a freely usable currency as determined by the International Monetary Fund ("IMF") under its Articles of Agreement and any amendments thereto;

(c) "investment"[2] means every kind of asset, owned or controlled, by an investor, including but not limited to the following:

   (i)   movable and immovable property and other property rights such as mortgages, liens or pledges;

   (ii)   shares, stocks, bonds and debentures and any other forms of participation in a juridical person and rights or interest derived therefrom;

   (iii) intellectual property rights which are conferred pursuant to the laws and regulations of each Member State;

   (iv) claims to money or to any contractual performance related to a business and having financial value;[3]

   (v)   rights under contracts, including turnkey, construction, management, production or revenue-sharing contracts; and

   (vi) business concessions required to conduct economic activities and having financial value conferred by law or under a contract, including any concessions to search, cultivate, extract or exploit natural resources.

The term "investment" also includes amounts yielded by investments, in particular, profits, interest, capital gains, dividend, royalties and fees. Any alteration of the form in which assets are invested or reinvested shall not affect their classification as investment;

(d) "investor" means a natural person of a Member State or a juridical person of a Member State that is making, or has made an investment in the territory of any other Member State;

(e) "juridical person" means any legal entity duly constituted or otherwise organised under the applicable law of a Member State, whether for profit or otherwise, and whether privately-

---

1   For the purpose of protection, the procedures relating to specific approval in writing shall be as specified in Annex 1 (Approval in Writing).

2   Where an asset lacks the characteristics of an investment, that asset is not an investment regardless of the form it may take. The characteristics of an investment include the commitment of capital, the expectation of gain or profit, or the assumption of risk.

3   For greater certainty, investment does not mean claims to money that arise solely from:
     (a) commercial contracts for sale of goods or services; or
     (b) the extension of credit in connection with such commercial contracts.

owned or governmentally-owned, including any enterprise, corporation, trust, partnership, joint venture, sole proprietorship, association, or organisation;

(f) "measures" means any measure of a Member State, whether in the form of laws, regulations, rules, procedures, decisions, and administrative actions or practice, adopted or maintained by:

(i) central, regional or local government or authorities; or

(ii) non-governmental bodies in the exercise of powers delegated by central, regional or local governments or authorities;

(g) "natural person" means any natural person possessing the nationality or citizenship of, or right of permanent residence in the Member State in accordance with its laws, regulations and national policies;

(h) "newer ASEAN Member States" means the Kingdom of Cambodia, the Lao People's Democratic Republic, the Union of Myanmar and the Socialist Republic of Viet Nam;

(i) "WTO" means the World Trade Organization; and

(j) "WTO Agreement" means the Marrakesh Agreement Establishing the World Trade Organization, done at Marrakesh, Morocco on 15 April 1994, as may be amended.

Article 5 National Treatment

1.   Each Member State shall accord to investors of any other Member State treatment no less favourable than that it accords, in like circumstances, to its own investors with respect to the admission, establishment, acquisition, expansion, management, conduct, operation and sale or other disposition of investments in its territory.

2.   Each Member State shall accord to investments of investors of any other Member State treatment no less favourable than that it accords, in like circumstances, to investments in its territory of its own investors with respect to the admission, establishment, acquisition, expansion, management, conduct, operation and sale or other disposition of investments.

Article 6 Most-Favoured-Nation Treatment[1]

1.   Each Member State shall accord to investors of another Member State treatment no less favourable than that it accords, in like circumstances, to investors of any other Member State or a non-Member State with respect to the admission, establishment, acquisition, expansion, management, conduct, operation and sale or other disposition of investments.

2.   Each Member State shall accord to investments of investors of another Member State treatment no less favourable than that it accords, in like circumstances, to investments in its territory of investors of any other Member State or a non-Member State with respect to the admission, establishment, acquisition, expansion, management, conduct, operation and sale or other disposition of investments.

3.   Paragraphs 1 and 2 shall not be construed so as to oblige a Member State to extend to investors or investments of other Member States the benefit of any treatment, preference or privilege resulting from:

---

1   For greater certainty:
     (a) this Article shall not apply to investor-State dispute settlement procedures that are available in other agreements to which Member States are party; and
     (b) in relation to investments falling within the scope of this Agreement, any preferential treatment granted by a Member State to investors of any other Member State or a non-Member State and to their investments, under any existing or future agreements or arrangements to which a Member State is a party shall be extended on a most-favoured-nation basis to all Member States.

(a) any sub-regional arrangements between and among Member States;[1] or

(b) any existing agreement notified by Member States to the AIA Council pursuant to Article 8(3) of the AIA Agreement.[2]

Article 7 Prohibition of Performance Requirements

1. The provisions of the Agreement on Trade-Related Investment Measures in Annex 1A to the WTO Agreement (TRIMs), which are not specifically mentioned in or modified by this Agreement, shall apply, mutatis mutandis, to this Agreement.

2. Member States shall undertake joint assessment on performance requirements no later than 2 years from the date of entry into force of this Agreement. The aim of such assessment shall include reviewing existing performance requirements and considering the need for additional commitments under this Article.

3. Non-WTO Members of ASEAN shall abide by the WTO provisions in accordance with their accession commitments to the WTO.

Article 8 Senior Management and Board of Directors

1. A Member State shall not require that a juridical person of that Member State appoint to senior management positions, natural persons of any particular nationality.

2. A Member State may require that a majority of the board of directors of a juridical person of that Member State, be of a particular nationality, or resident in the territory of the Member State, provided that this requirement does not materially impair the ability of the investor to exercise control over its investment.

Article 9 Reservations

1. Articles 5 (National Treatment) and 8 (Senior Management and Board of Directors) shall not apply to:

(a) any existing measure that is maintained by a Member State at:

   (i) the central level of government, as set out by that Member State in its reservation list in the Schedule referred to in paragraph 2;

   (ii) the regional level of government, as set out by that Member State in its reservation list in the Schedule referred to in paragraph 2; and

   (iii) a local level of government;

(b) the continuation or prompt renewal of any reservations referred to sub-paragraph (a).

2. Each Member State shall submit its reservation list to the ASEAN Secretariat for the endorsement of the AIA Council within 6 months after the date of signing of this Agreement. This list shall form a Schedule to this Agreement.

3. Any amendment or modification to any reservations contained in the Schedule referred to in paragraph 2 shall be in accordance with Article 10 (Modification of Commitments).

4. Each Member State shall reduce or eliminate the reservations specified in the Schedule in accordance with the three phases of the Strategic Schedule of the AEC Blueprint and Article 46 (Amendments).

---

1 For greater certainty, sub-regional arrangements between and among Member States shall include but not be limited to Greater Mekong Sub-region ("GMS"), ASEAN Mekong Basin Development Cooperation ("AMBDC"), Indonesia-Malaysia-Thailand Growth Triangle ("IMT-GT"), Indonesia-Malaysia-Singapore Growth Triangle ("IMS-GT"), Brunei-Indonesia-Malaysia-Philippines East ASEAN Growth Area ("BIMP-EAGA").

2 This sub-paragraph refers to the Treaty of Amity and Economic Relations between the Kingdom of Thailand and the United States of America signed in Bangkok, Thailand on 29 May 1966.

5.   Articles 5 (National Treatment) and 6 (Most-Favoured-Nation Treatment) shall not apply to any measure covered by an exception to, or derogation from, the obligations under Articles 3 and 4 of the Agreement on Trade-Related Aspects of Intellectual Property Rights in Annex 1C to the WTO Agreement, as may be amended ("TRIPS Agreement"), as specifically provided in those Articles and in Article 5 of the TRIPS Agreement.

Article 10 Modification of Commitments

1.   For a period of 12 months after the date of submission of each Member State's reservation list, a Member State may adopt any measures or modify any of its reservations made in the Schedule under Article 9 (Reservations) for prospective applications to investors of any other Member States and their investments, provided that such measures or modification shall not adversely affect any existing investors and investments.

2.   After the expiration of the period referred to in paragraph 1, a Member State may, by nego-tiation and agreement with any other Member States to which it made commitments under this Agreement, adopt any measure, or modify or withdraw such commitments and reservations, provided that such measure, modification or withdrawal shall not adversely affect any existing investors or investments.[1]

3.   In any such negotiations and agreement referred to in paragraph 2, which may include provisions for compensatory adjustments with respect to other sectors, the Member States concerned shall maintain a general level of reciprocal and mutually advantageous commitments and reservations that is not less favourable to investors and investments than that provided for in this Agreement prior to such negotiations and agreements.

4.   Notwithstanding paragraphs 1 and 2, a Member State shall not, under any measure adopted pursuant to this Article after the entry into force of this Agreement, require an investor of any other Member State, by reason of that investor's nationality, to sell or otherwise dispose of an investment existing at the time the measure becomes effective, unless otherwise specified in the initial approval by the relevant authorities.

Article 11 Treatment of Investment

1.   Each Member State shall accord to covered investments of investors of any other Member State, fair and equitable treatment and full protection and security.

2.   For greater certainty:

(a)   fair and equitable treatment requires each Member State not to deny justice in any legal or administrative proceedings in accordance with the principle of due process; and

(b)   full protection and security requires each Member State to take such measures as may be reasonably necessary to ensure the protection and security of the covered investments.

3.   A determination that there has been a breach of another provision of this Agreement, or of a separate international agreement, does not establish that there has been a breach of this Article.

Article 12 Compensation in Cases of Strife

Each Member State shall accord to investors of any other Member State, in relation to their covered investments which suffered losses in its territory due to armed conflict or civil strife or state of emergency, non-discriminatory treatment with respect to restitution, compensation or other valuable consideration.

---

1   For the avoidance of doubt, Member States shall not adopt any measures or modify any of its reservation under the Schedule for a period of 6 months after the expiration of the period specified in paragraph 1.

Article 13 Transfers

1.   Each Member State shall allow all transfers relating to a covered investment to be made freely and without delay into and out of its territory. Such transfers include:

(a)   contributions to capital, including the initial contribution;

(b)   profits, capital gains, dividends, royalties, license fees, technical assistance and technical and management fees, interest and other current income accruing from any covered investment;

(c)   proceeds from the total or partial sale or liquidation of any covered investment;

(d)   payments made under a contract, including a loan agreement;

(e)   payments made pursuant to Articles 12 (Compensation in Cases of Strife) and 14 (Expropriation and Compensation);

(f)   payments arising out of the settlement of a dispute by any means including adjudication, arbitration or the agreement of the Member States to the dispute; and

(g)   earnings and other remuneration of personnel employed and allowed to work in connection with that covered investment in its territory.

2.   Each Member State shall allow transfers relating to a covered investment to be made in a freely usable currency at the market rate of exchange prevailing at the time of transfer.

3.   Notwithstanding paragraphs 1 and 2, a Member State may prevent or delay a transfer through the equitable, nondiscriminatory, and good faith application of its laws and regulations relating to:

(a)   bankruptcy, insolvency, or the protection of the rights of creditors;

(b)   issuing, trading, or dealing in securities, futures, options, or derivatives;

(c)   criminal or penal offences and the recovery of the proceeds of crime;

(d)   financial reporting or record keeping of transfers when necessary to assist law enforcement or financial regulatory authorities;

(e)   ensuring compliance with orders or judgments in judicial or administrative proceedings;

(f)   taxation;

(g)   social security, public retirement, or compulsory savings schemes;

(h)   severance entitlements of employees; and

(i)   the requirement to register and satisfy other formalities imposed by the Central Bank and other relevant authorities of a Member State.

4.   Nothing in this Agreement shall affect the rights and obligations of the Member States as members of the IMF, under the Articles of Agreement of the IMF, including the use of exchange actions which are in conformity with the Articles of Agreement of the IMF, provided that a Member State shall not impose restrictions on any capital transactions inconsistently with its specific commitments under this Agreement regarding such transactions, except:

(a)   at the request of the IMF;

(b)   under Article 16 (Measures to Safeguard the Balance-of-Payments); or

(c)   where, in exceptional circumstances, movements of capital cause, or threaten to cause, serious economic or financial disturbance in the Member State concerned.

5.   The measures taken in accordance with sub-paragraph 4(c):[1]

---

1   For greater certainty, any measures taken to ensure the stability of the exchange rate including to prevent speculative capital flows shall not be adopted or maintained for the purpose of protecting a particular sector.

(a) shall be consistent with the Articles of Agreement of the IMF;

(b) shall not exceed those necessary to deal with the circumstances described in sub-paragraph 4(c);

(c) shall be temporary and shall be eliminated as soon as conditions no longer justify their institution or maintenance;

(d) shall promptly be notified to the other Member States;

(e) shall be applied such that any one of the other Member States is treated no less favourably than any other Member State or non-Member State;

(f) shall be applied on a national treatment basis; and

(g) shall avoid unnecessary damage to investors and covered investments, and the commercial, economic and financial interests of the other Member State(s).

Article 14 Expropriation and Compensation[1]

1.   A Member State shall not expropriate or nationalise a covered investment either directly or through measures equivalent to expropriation or nationalisation ("expropriation"),[2] except:

(a) for a public purpose;

(b) in a non-discriminatory manner;

(c) on payment of prompt, adequate, and effective compensation; and

(d) in accordance with due process of law.

2.   The compensation referred to in sub-paragraph 1(c) shall:

(a) be paid without delay;[3]

(b) be equivalent to the fair market value of the expropriated investment immediately before or at the time when the expropriation was publicly announced, or when the expropriation occurred, whichever is applicable;

(c) not reflect any change in value because the intended expropriation had become known earlier; and

(d) be fully realisable and freely transferable in accordance with Article 13 (Transfers) between the territories of the Member States.

3.   In the event of delay, the compensation shall include an appropriate interest in accordance with the laws and regulations of the Member State making the expropriation. The compensation, including any accrued interest, shall be payable either in the currency in which the investment was originally made or, if requested by the investor, in a freely usable currency.

4.   If an investor requests payment in a freely useable currency, the compensation referred to in sub-paragraph 1(c), including any accrued interest, shall be converted into the currency of payment at the market rate of exchange prevailing on the date of payment.

5.   This Article does not apply to the issuance of compulsory licenses granted in relation to intellectual property rights in accordance with the TRIPS Agreement.

---

1   This Article shall be read with Annex 2 (Expropriation and Compensation).

2   For the avoidance of doubt, any measure of expropriation relating to land shall be as defined in the Member States' respective existing domestic laws and regulations and any amendments thereto, and shall be for the purposes of and upon payment of compensation in accordance with the aforesaid laws and regulations.

3   Member States understand that there may be legal and administrative processes that need to be observed before payment can be made.

Article 15 Subrogation

1.   If a Member State or an agency of a Member State makes a payment to an investor of that Member State under a guarantee, a contract of insurance or other form of indemnity it has granted on non-commercial risk in respect of an investment, the other Member State shall recognise the subrogation or transfer of any right or title in respect of such investment. The subrogated or transferred right or claim shall not be greater than the original right or claim of the investor. This, however, does not necessarily imply recognition of the latter Member State of the merits of any case or the amount of any claims arising therefrom.

2.   Where a Member State or an agency of a Member State has made a payment to an investor of that Member State and has taken over rights and claims of the investor, that investor shall not, unless authorised to act on behalf of the Member State or the agency of the Member State making the payment, pursue those rights and claims against the other Member State.

3.   In the exercise of subrogated rights or claims, a Member State or the agency of the Member State exercising such rights or claims shall disclose the coverage of the claims arrangement with its investors to the relevant Member State.

Article 16 Measures to Safeguard the Balance-of-Payments

1.   In the event of serious balance-of-payments and external financial difficulties or threat thereof, a Member State may adopt or maintain restrictions on payments or transfers related to investments. It is recognised that particular pressures on the balance-of-payments of a Member State in the process of economic development may necessitate the use of restrictions to ensure, inter alia, the maintenance of a level of financial reserves adequate for the implementation of its programme of economic development.

2.   The restrictions referred to in paragraph 1 shall:

(a)   be consistent with the Articles of Agreement of the IMF;

(b)   avoid unnecessary damage to the commercial, economic and financial interests of another Member State;

(c)   not exceed those necessary to deal with the circumstances described in paragraph 1;

(d)   be temporary and be phased out progressively as the situation specified in paragraph 1 improves;

(e)   be applied such that any one of the other Member States is treated no less favourably than any other Member State or non-Member State.

3.   Any restrictions adopted or maintained under paragraph 1, or any changes therein, shall be promptly notified to the other Member States.

4.   To the extent that it does not duplicate the process under WTO, IMF, or any other similar processes, the Member State adopting any restrictions under paragraph 1 shall commence consultations with any other Member State that requests such consultations in order to review the restrictions adopted by it.

Article 17 General Exceptions

1.   Subject to the requirement that such measures are not applied in a manner which would constitute a means of arbitrary or unjustifiable discrimination between Member States or their investors where like conditions prevail, or a disguised restriction on investors of any other Member State and their investments, nothing in this Agreement shall be construed to prevent the adoption or enforcement by any Member State of measures:

(a) necessary to protect public morals or to maintain public order;[1]

(b) necessary to protect human, animal or plant life or health;

(c) necessary to secure compliance with laws or regulations which are not inconsistent with this Agreement, including those relating to:

    (i) the prevention of deceptive and fraudulent practices to deal with the effects of a default on a contract;

    (ii) the protection of the privacy of individuals in relation to the processing and dissemination of personal data and the protection of confidentiality of individual records and accounts;

    (iii) safety;

(d) aimed at ensuring the equitable or effective[2] imposition or collection of direct taxes in respect of investments or investors of any Member State;

(e) imposed for the protection of national treasures of artistic, historic or archaeological value;

(f) relating to the conservation of exhaustible natural resources if such measures are made effective in conjunction with restrictions on domestic production or consumption.

2. Insofar as measures affecting the supply of financial services are concerned, paragraph 2 (Domestic Regulation) of the Annex on Financial Services of the General Agreement on Trade in Services in Annex 1B to the WTO Agreement ("GATS") shall be incorporated into and form an integral part of this Agreement, mutatis mutandis.

Article 18 Security Exceptions

Nothing in this Agreement shall be construed:

(a) to require any Member State to furnish any information, the disclosure of which it considers contrary to its essential security interests; or

(b) to prevent any Member State from taking any action which it considers necessary for the protection of its essential security interests, including but not limited to:

    (i) action relating to fissionable and fusionable materials or the materials from which they derived;

    (ii) action relating to the traffic in arms, ammunition and implements of war and to such traffic in other goods and materials as is carried on directly or indirectly for the purpose of supplying a military establishment;

    (iii) action taken in time of war or other emergency in domestic or international relations;

    (iv) action taken so as to protect critical public infrastructure, including communication, power and water infrastructures, from deliberate attempts intended to disable or degrade such infrastructure; or

(c) to prevent any Member State from taking any action pursuant to its obligations under the United Nations Charter for the maintenance of international peace and security.

Article 19 Denial of Benefits

1. A Member State may deny the benefits of this Agreement to:

(a) an investor of another Member State that is a juridical person of such other Member State and to investments of such investor if an investor of a non-Member State owns or controls

---

1   The public order exception may be invoked by a Member State only where a genuine and sufficiently serious threat is posed to one of the fundamental interests of society.

2   For the purpose of this sub-paragraph, footnote 6 of Article XIV of the General Agreement on Trade in Services in Annex 1B to the WTO Agreement (GATS) is incorporated into and forms an integral part of this Agreement, mutatis mutandis.

the juridical person and the juridical person has no substantive business operations in the territory of such other Member State;

(b)   an investor of another Member State that is a juridical person of such other Member State and to investments of such investor if an investor of the denying Member State owns or controls the juridical person and the juridical person has no substantive business operations in the territory of such other Member State; and

(c)   an investor of another Member State that is a juridical person of such other Member State and to an investment of such investor if investors of a non-Member State own or control the juridical person, and the denying Member State does not maintain diplomatic relations with the non-Member State.

2.   Following notification to the Member State of the investor, and without prejudice to paragraph 1, a Member State may deny the benefits of this Agreement to investors of another Member State and to investments of that investor, where it establishes that such investor has made an investment in breach of the domestic laws of the denying Member State by misrepresenting its ownership in those areas of investment which are reserved for natural or juridical persons of the denying Member State.

3.   A juridical person is:

(a)   "owned" by an investor in accordance with the laws, regulations and national policies of each Member States;

(b)   "controlled" by an investor if the investor has the power to name a majority of its directors or otherwise to legally direct its actions.

Article 20 Special Formalities and Disclosure of Information

1.   Nothing in Articles 5 (National Treatment) or 6 (Most-Favoured-Nation Treatment) shall be construed to prevent a Member State from adopting or maintaining a measure that prescribes special formalities in connection with investments, including a requirement that investments be legally constituted or assume a certain legal form under the laws or regulations of the Member State and compliance with registration requirements, provided that such formalities do not materially impair the rights afforded by a Member State to investors of another Member State and investments pursuant to this Agreement.

2.   Notwithstanding Articles 5 (National Treatment) or 6 (Most-Favoured-Nation Treatment), a Member State may require an investor of another Member State, or a covered investment, to provide information concerning that investment solely for informational or statistical purposes. The Member State shall protect any confidential information from any disclosure that would prejudice legitimate commercial interests or particular juridical persons, public or private or the competitive position of the investor or the covered investment. Nothing in this paragraph shall be construed to prevent a Member State from otherwise obtaining or disclosing information in connection with the equitable and good faith application of its law.

Article 21 Transparency

1.   In order to achieve the objectives of this Agreement, each Member State shall:

(a)   promptly and at least annually inform the AIA Council of any investment-related agreements or arrangements which it has entered into and where preferential treatment was granted;

(b)   promptly and at least annually inform the AIA Council of the introduction of any new law or of any changes to existing laws, regulations or administrative guidelines, which significantly affect investments or commitments of a Member State under this Agreement;

(c)   make publicly available, all relevant laws, regulations and administrative guidelines of general application that pertain to, or affect investments in the territory of the Member State; and

(d) establish or designate an enquiry point where, upon request of any natural person, juridical person or any other Member State, all information relating to the measures required to be published or made available under subparagraphs (b) and (c) may be promptly obtained.

2.   Nothing in this Agreement shall require a Member State to furnish or allow access to any confidential information, including information concerning particular investors or investments, the disclosure of which would impede law enforcement, or otherwise be contrary to the public interest, or which would prejudice legitimate commercial interests of particular juridical persons, public or private.

Article 22 Entry, Temporary Stay and Work of Investors and Key Personnel

Subject to its immigration and labour laws, regulations and national policies relating to the entry, temporary stay and authorisation to work, and consistent with its commitments under AFAS, each Member State shall grant entry, temporary stay and authorisation to work to investors, executives, managers and members of the board of directors of a juridical person of any other Member State, for the purpose of establishing, developing, administering or advising on the operation in the territory of the former Member State of an investment to which they, or a juridical person of the other Member States that employs such executives, managers and members of the board of directors, have committed or are in the process of committing a substantial amount of capital or other resources.

Article 23 Special and Differential Treatment for the Newer ASEAN Member States

In order to increase the benefits of this Agreement for the newer ASEAN Member States, and in accordance with the objectives and principles set out in the Preamble and Articles 1 (Objective) and 2 (Guiding Principles), Member States recognise the importance of according special and differential treatment to the newer ASEAN Member States, through:

(a) technical assistance to strengthen their capacity in relation to investment policies and promotion, including in areas such as human resource development;

(b) commitments in areas of interest to the newer ASEAN Member States; and

(c) recognising that commitments by each newer ASEAN Member State may be made in accordance with its individual stage of development.

Article 24 Promotion of Investment

Member States shall cooperate in increasing awareness of ASEAN as an integrated investment area in order to increase foreign investment into ASEAN and intra-ASEAN investments through, among others:

(a) encouraging the growth and development of ASEAN small and medium enterprises and multinational enterprises;

(b) enhancing industrial complementation and production networks among multi- national enterprises in ASEAN;

(c) organising investment missions that focus on developing regional clusters and production networks;

(d) organising and supporting the organisation of various briefings and seminars on investment opportunities and on investment laws, regulations and policies; and

(e) conducting exchanges on other issues of mutual concern relating to investment promotion.

Article 25 Facilitation of Investment

Member States shall endeavour to cooperate in the facilitation of investments into and within ASEAN through, among others:

(a) creating the necessary environment for all forms of investments;

(b) streamlining and simplifying procedures for investment applications and approvals;

(c)	promoting dissemination of investment information, including investment rules, regulations, policies and procedures;

(d)	establishing one-stop investment centres;

(e)	strengthening databases on all forms of investments for policy formulation to improve ASEAN's investment environment;

(f)	undertaking consultation with the business community on investment matters; and

(g)	providing advisory services to the business community of the other Member States.

Article 26 Enhancing ASEAN Integration

Member States recognise the importance of fostering ASEAN economic integration through various initiatives, including the Initiative for ASEAN Integration, Priority Integration Sectors, and AEC, all of which include cooperation on investment. In order to enhance ASEAN economic integration, Member States shall endeavour to, among others:

(a)	harmonise, where possible, investment policies and measures to achieve industrial complementation;

(b)	build and strengthen capacity of Member States, including human resource development, in the formulation and improvement of investment policies to attract investment;

(c)	share information on investment policies and best practices, including promoted activities and industries; and

(d)	support investment promotion efforts amongst Member States for mutual benefits.

Article 27 Disputes Between or Among Member States

The ASEAN Protocol on Enhanced Dispute Settlement Mechanism signed in Vientiane, Lao PDR on 29 November 2004, as amended, shall apply to the settlement of disputes concerning the interpretation or application of this Agreement.

SECTION B

Investment Dispute Between an Investor and a Member State

Article 28 Definitions

For the purpose of this Section:

(a)	"Appointing Authority" means:

    (i)	in the case of arbitration under Article 33(1)(b) or (c), the Secretary-General of ICSID;

    (ii)	in the case of arbitration under Article 33(1)(d), the Secretary-General of the Permanent Court of Arbitration; or

    (iii)	in the case of arbitration under Article 33(1)(e) and (f), the Secretary-General, or a person holding equivalent position, of that arbitration centre or institution;

(b)	"disputing investor" means an investor of a Member State that makes a claim on its own behalf under this Section, and where relevant, includes an investor of a Member State that makes a claim on behalf of a juridical person of the other Member State that the investor owns or controls;

(c)	"disputing Member State" means a Member State against which a claim is made under this Section;

(d)	"disputing parties" means a disputing investor and a disputing Member State;

(e)	"ICSID" means the International Centre for Settlement of Investment Disputes;

(f)	"ICSID Additional Facility Rules" means the Rules Governing the Additional Facility for the Administration of Proceedings by the Secretariat of the International Centre for Settlement of Investment Disputes;

(g) "ICSID Convention" means the Convention on the Settlement of Investment Disputes between States and National of other States, done at Washington, D.C., United States of America on 18 March 1965;

(h) "New York Convention" means the United Nations Convention on the Recognition and Enforcement of Foreign Arbitral Awards, done at New York, United States of America on 10 June 1958;

(i) "non-disputing Member State" means the Member State of the disputing investor; and

(j) "UNCITRAL Arbitration Rules" means the arbitration rules of the United Nations Commission on International Trade Law, approved by the United Nations General Assembly on 15 December 1976.

Article 29 Scope of Coverage

1.   This Section shall apply to an investment dispute between a Member State and an investor of another Member State that has incurred loss or damage by reason of an alleged breach of any rights conferred by this Agreement with respect to the investment of that investor.

2.   A natural person possessing the nationality or citizenship of a Member State shall not pursue a claim against that Member State under this Section.

3.   This Section shall not apply to claims arising out of events which occurred, or claims which have been raised prior to the entry into force of this Agreement.

4.   Nothing in this Section shall be construed so as to prevent a disputing investor from seeking administrative or judicial settlement available within the country of a disputing Member State.

Article 30 Conciliation

1.   The disputing parties may at any time agree to conciliation, which may begin at any time and be terminated at the request of the disputing investor at any time.

2.   If the disputing parties agree, procedures for conciliation may continue while procedures provided for in Article 33 (Submission of a Claim) are in progress.

3.   Proceedings involving conciliation and positions taken by the disputing parties during these proceedings shall be without prejudice to the rights of either disputing parties in any further proceedings under this Section.

Article 31 Consultations

1.   In the event of an investment dispute, the disputing parties shall initially seek to resolve the dispute through consultation and negotiation, which may include the use of non-binding, third party procedures. Such consultations shall be initiated by a written request for consultations delivered by the disputing investor to the disputing Member State.

2.   Consultations shall commence within 30 days of receipt by the disputing Member State of the request for consultations, unless the disputing parties otherwise agree.

3.   With the objective of resolving an investment dispute through consultations, a disputing investor shall make all reasonable efforts to provide the disputing Member State, prior to the commencement of consultations, with information regarding the legal and factual basis for the investment dispute.

Article 32 Claim by an Investor of a Member State

If an investment dispute has not been resolved within 180 days of the receipt by a disputing Member State of a request for consultations, the disputing investor may, subject to this Section, submit to arbitration a claim:

(a) that the disputing Member State has breached an obligation arising under Articles 5 (National Treatment), 6 (Most-Favoured-Nation Treatment), 8 (Senior Management and Board of Directors), 11 (Treatment of Investment), 12 (Compensation in Cases of Strife), 13 (Transfers) and 14 (Expropriation and Compensation) relating to the management, conduct, operation or sale or other disposition of a covered investment; and

(b)   that the disputing investor in relation to its covered investment has incurred loss or damage by reason of or arising out of that breach.

Article 33 Submission of a Claim

1.   A disputing investor may submit a claim referred to in Article 32 (Claim by an Investor of a Member State) at the choice of the disputing investor:

(a)   to the courts or administrative tribunals of the disputing Member State, provided that such courts or tribunals have jurisdiction over such claims; or

(b)   under the ICSID Convention and the ICSID Rules of Procedure for Arbitration Proceedings,[1] provided that both the disputing Member State and the non- disputing Member State are parties to the ICSID Convention; or

(c)   under the ICSID Additional Facility Rules, provided that either of the disputing Member State or the non-disputing Member State is a party to the ICSID Convention; or

(d)   under the UNCITRAL Arbitration Rules; or

(e)   to the Regional Centre for Arbitration at Kuala Lumpur or any other regional centre for arbitration in ASEAN; or

(f)   if the disputing parties agree, to any other arbitration institution, provided that resort to any arbitration rules or fora under sub-paragraphs (a) to (f) shall exclude resort to the other.

2.   A claim shall be deemed submitted to arbitration under this Section when the disputing investor's notice of or request for arbitration ("notice of arbitration") is received under the applicable arbitration rules.

3.   The arbitration rules applicable under paragraph 1, as in effect on the date the claim or claims were submitted to arbitration under this Section, shall govern the arbitration except to the extent modified by this Agreement.

4.   In relation to a specific investment dispute or class of disputes, the applicable arbitration rules may be waived, varied or modified by written agreement between the disputing parties. Such rules shall be binding on the relevant tribunal or tribunals established under this Section, and on individual arbitrators serving on such tribunals.

5.   The disputing investor shall provide with the notice of arbitration:

(a)   the name of the arbitrator that the disputing investor appoints; or

(b)   the disputing investor's written consent for the Appointing Authority to appoint that arbitrator.

Article 34 Conditions and Limitations on Submission of a Claim

1.   The dispute shall be submitted to arbitration under Article 33(1)(b) to (f) in accordance with this Section, and shall be conditional upon:

(a)   the submission of the investment dispute to such arbitration taking place within 3 years of the time at which the disputing investor became aware, or should reasonably have become aware, of a breach of an obligation under this Agreement causing loss or damage to the disputing investor or a covered investment; and

(b)   the disputing investor providing written notice, which shall be submitted at least 90 days before the claim is submitted, to the disputing Member State of its intent to submit the

---

1   In the case of the Philippines, submission of a claim to ICSID and the ICSID Rules of Procedure for Arbitration Proceedings shall be subject to a written agreement between the disputing parties in the event that an investment dispute arises.

investment dispute to such arbitration and which briefly summarises the alleged breach of the disputing Member State under this Agreement (including the provisions alleged to have been breached) and the loss or damage allegedly caused to the disputing investor or a covered investment; and

(c)   the notice of arbitration under Article 33(2) being accompanied by the disputing investor's written waiver of the disputing investor's right to initiate or continue any proceedings before the courts or administrative tribunals of the disputing Member State, or other dispute settlement procedures, of any proceeding with respect to any measure alleged to constitute a breach referred to in Article 32 (Claim by an Investor of a Member State).

2.   Notwithstanding sub-paragraph 1(c), the disputing investor shall not be prevented from initiating or continuing an action that seeks interim measures of protection for the sole purpose of preserving the disputing investor's rights and interests and does not involve the payment of damages or resolution of the substance of the matter in dispute, before the courts or administrative tribunals of the disputing Member State.

3.   A Member State shall not give diplomatic protection, or bring an international claim, in respect of a dispute which one of its investors and the other Member State have consented to submit or have submitted to arbitration under this Section, unless such other Member State has failed to abide by and comply with the award rendered in such dispute. Diplomatic protection, for the purposes of this paragraph, shall not include informal diplomatic exchanges for the sole purpose of facilitating a settlement of the dispute.

4.   A disputing Member State shall not assert, as a defence, counter-claim, right of set-off or otherwise, that the disputing investor in relation to the covered investment has received or will receive, pursuant to an insurance or guarantee contract, indemnification or other compensation for all or part of any alleged loss.

Article 35 Selection of Arbitrators

1.   Unless the disputing parties otherwise agree, the tribunal shall comprise three arbitrators:

(a)   one arbitrator appointed by each of the disputing parties; and

(b)   the third arbitrator, who shall be the presiding arbitrator, appointed by agreement of the disputing parties. The third arbitrator shall be a national of a non-Member State which has diplomatic relations with the disputing Member State and non- disputing Member State, and shall not have permanent residence in either the disputing Member State or non-disputing Member State.

2.   Any person appointed as an arbitrator shall have expertise or experience in public international law, international trade or international investment rules. An arbitrator shall be chosen strictly on the basis of objectivity, reliability, sound judgment and independence and shall conduct himself or herself on the same basis throughout the course of the arbitral proceedings.

3.   Subject to Article 36 (Conduct of the Arbitration), if a tribunal has not been constituted within 75 days from the date that a claim is submitted to arbitration under this Section, the Appointing Authority, on the request of a disputing party, shall appoint, in his or her discretion, the arbitrator or arbitrators who have not been appointed.

4.   The tribunal shall reach its decisions by a majority of votes and its decisions shall be binding.

5.   The parties to the dispute shall bear the cost of their respective arbitrators to the tribunal and share equally the cost of the presiding arbitrator and other relevant costs. In all other respects, the tribunal shall determine its own procedures.

6.   The disputing parties may establish rules relating to expenses incurred by the tribunal, including remuneration of the arbitrators.

7.   Where any arbitrator appointed as provided for in this Article resigns or becomes unable to act, a successor shall be appointed in the same manner as prescribed for the appointment of the original arbitrator and the successor shall have all the powers and duties of the original arbitrator.

Article 36 Conduct of the Arbitration

1.   Where issues relating to jurisdiction or admissibility are raised as preliminary objections, the tribunal shall decide the matter before proceeding to the merits.

2.   A disputing Member State may, no later than 30 days after the constitution of the tribunal, file an objection that a claim is manifestly without merit. A disputing Member State may also file an objection that a claim is otherwise outside the jurisdiction or competence of the tribunal. The disputing Member State shall specify as precisely as possible the basis for the objection.

3.   The tribunal shall address any such objection as a preliminary question apart from the merits of the claim. The disputing parties shall be given a reasonable opportunity to present their views and observations to the tribunal. If the tribunal decides that the claim is manifestly without merit, or is otherwise not within the jurisdiction or competence of the tribunal, it shall render an award to that effect.

4.   The tribunal may, if warranted, award the prevailing party reasonable costs and fees incurred in submitting or opposing the objection. In determining whether such an award is warranted, the tribunal shall consider whether either the claim or the objection was frivolous or manifestly without merit, and shall provide the disputing parties a reasonable opportunity to comment.

5.   Unless the disputing parties otherwise agree, the tribunal shall determine the place of arbitration in accordance with the applicable arbitration rules, provided that the place shall be in the territory of a State that is a party to the New York Convention.

6.   Where an investment dispute relate to a measure which may be a taxation measure, the disputing Member State and the non-disputing Member State, including representatives of their tax administrations, shall hold consultations to determine whether the measure in question is a taxation measure.

7.   Where a disputing investor claims that the disputing Member State has breached Article 14 (Expropriation and Compensation) by the adoption or enforcement of a taxation measure, the disputing Member State and the non-disputing Member State shall, upon request from the disputing Member State, hold consultations with a view to determining whether the taxation measure in question has an effect equivalent to expropriation or nationalisation.

8.   Any tribunal that may be established under this Section shall accord serious consideration to the decision of both Member States under paragraphs 6 and 7.

9.   If both Member States fail either to initiate such consultations referred to paragraphs 6 and 7, or to make such joint decisions, within the period of 180 days from the date of the receipt of request for consultation referred to in Article 31 (Consultations), the disputing investor shall not be prevented from submitting its claim to arbitration in accordance with this Section.

Article 37 Consolidation

Where two or more claims have been submitted separately to arbitration under Article 32 (Claim by an Investor of a Member State) and the claims have a question of law or fact in common and arise out of the same or similar events or circumstances, all concerned disputing parties may agree to consolidate those claims in any manner they deem appropriate.

Article 38 Expert Reports

Without prejudice to the appointment of other kinds of experts where authorised by the applicable arbitration rules, the tribunal, at the request of the disputing parties, may appoint one or more experts to report to it in writing on any factual issue concerning environmental, public health, safety or other scientific matters raised by a disputing party in a proceeding, subject to such terms and conditions as the disputing parties may agree.

Article 39 Transparency of Arbitral Proceedings

1.   Subject to paragraphs 2 and 3, the disputing Member State may make publicly available all awards, and decisions produced by the tribunal.

2.   Any of the disputing parties that intend to use information designated as confidential information in a hearing shall so advise the tribunal. The tribunal shall make appropriate arrangements to protect the information from disclosure.

3.   Any information specifically designated as confidential that is submitted to the tribunal or the disputing parties shall be protected from disclosure to the public.

4.   A disputing party may disclose to persons directly connected with the arbitral proceedings such confidential information as it considers necessary for the preparation of its case, but it shall require that such confidential information is protected.

5.   The tribunal shall not require a Member State to furnish or allow access to information the disclosure of which would impede law enforcement or would be contrary to the Member State's law protecting Cabinet confidences, personal privacy or the financial affairs and accounts of individual customers of financial institutions, or which it determines to be contrary to its essential security.

6.   The non-disputing Member State shall be entitled, at its cost, to receive from the disputing Member State a copy of the notice of arbitration, no later than 30 days after the date that such document has been delivered to the disputing Member State. The disputing Member State shall notify all other Member States of the receipt of the notice of arbitration within 30 days thereof.

Article 40 Governing Law

1.   Subject to paragraphs 2 and 3, when a claim is submitted under Article 33 (Submission of a Claim), the tribunal shall decide the issues in dispute in accordance with this Agreement, any other applicable agreements between the Member States, and the applicable rules of inter-national law and where applicable, any relevant domestic law of the disputing Member State.

2.   The tribunal shall, on its own account or at the request of a disputing party, request a joint interpretation of any provision of this Agreement that is in issue in a dispute. The Member States shall submit in writing any joint decision declaring their interpretation to the tribunal within 60 days of the delivery of the request. Without prejudice to paragraph 3, if the Member States fail to issue such a decision within 60 days, any interpretation submitted by a Member State shall be forwarded to the disputing parties and the tribunal, which shall decide the issue on its own account.

3.   A joint decision of the Member States, declaring their interpretation of a provision of this Agreement shall be binding on a tribunal, and any decision or award issued by a tribunal must be consistent with that joint decision.

Article 41 Awards

1.   The disputing parties may agree on a resolution of the dispute at any time before the tribunal issues its final award.

2.   Where a tribunal makes a final award against either of the disputing parties, the tribunal may award, separately or in combination, only:

(a)   monetary damages and any applicable interest; and

(b)   restitution of property, in which case the award shall provide that the disputing Member State may pay monetary damages and any applicable interest in lieu of restitution.

3.   A tribunal may also award costs and attorney's fees in accordance with this Agreement and the applicable arbitration rules.

4.   A tribunal may not award punitive damages.

5.   An award made by a tribunal shall have no binding force except between the disputing parties and in respect of the particular case.

6.   Subject to paragraph 7 and the applicable review procedure for an interim award, the disputing party shall abide by and comply with an award without delay.[1]

7.   The disputing party may not seek enforcement of a final award until:

(a)   in the case of a final award under the ICSID Convention:

   (i)   120 days has elapsed from the date the award was rendered and no disputing party has requested revision or annulment of the award; or

  (ii)   revision or annulment proceedings have been completed;

(b)   in the case of a final award under the ICSID Additional Facility Rules, the UNCITRAL Arbitration Rules, or the rules selected pursuant to Article 33(1)(e):

   (i)   90 days have elapsed from the date the award was rendered and no disputing party has commenced a proceeding to revise, set aside, or annul the award; or

  (ii)   a court has dismissed or allowed an application to revise, set aside, or annul the award and there is no further appeal.

8.   A claim that is submitted for arbitration under this Section shall be considered to arise out of a commercial relationship or transaction for purposes of Article 1 of the New York Convention.

9.   Each Member State shall provide for the enforcement of an award in its territory.

SECTION C

Article 42 Institutional Arrangements

1.   The AIA Council, as established by the AEM under the AIA Agreement, shall be responsible for the implementation of this Agreement.

2.   The ASEAN Coordinating Committee on Investment ("CCI") as established by the AIA Council and comprising senior officials responsible for investment and other senior officials from relevant government agencies, shall assist the AIA Council in the performance of its functions. The CCI shall report to the AIA Council through the Senior Economic Officials Meeting ("SEOM"). The ASEAN Secretariat shall be the secretariat for the AIA Council and the CCI.

3.   The functions of the AIA Council shall be to:

(a)   provide policy guidance on global and regional investment matters concerning promotion, facilitation, protection, and liberalisation;

(b)   oversee, coordinate and review the implementation of this Agreement;

(c)   update the AEM on the implementation and operation of this Agreement;

(d)   consider and recommend to the AEM any amendments to this Agreement;

(e)   facilitate the avoidance and settlement of disputes arising from this Agreement;

(f)   supervise and coordinate the work of the CCI;

(g)   adopt any necessary decisions; and

(h)   carry out any other functions as the AEM may agree.

---

1   The Parties understand that there may be domestic legal and administrative processes that need to be observed before an award can be complied with.

Article 43 Consultations by Member States

The Member States agree to consult each other at the request of any Member State on any matter relating to investments covered by this Agreement, or otherwise affecting the implementation of this Agreement.

Article 44 Relation to Other Agreements

Nothing in this Agreement shall derogate from the existing rights and obligations of a Member State under any other international agreements to which it is a party.

Article 45 Annexes, Schedule and Future Instruments

This Agreement shall include the Annexes, the Schedule and the contents therein, which shall form an integral part of this Agreement, and all future legal instruments agreed pursuant to this Agreement.

Article 46 Amendments

The provisions of this Agreement may be modified through amendments mutually agreed upon in writing by the Member States.

Article 47 Transitional Arrangements Relating to the ASEAN IGA
and the AIA Agreement

1.   Upon the entry into force of this Agreement, the ASEAN IGA and the AIA Agreement shall be terminated.

2.   Notwithstanding the termination of the AIA Agreement, the Temporary Exclusion List and the Sensitive List to the AIA Agreement shall apply to the liberalisation provisions of the ACIA, mutatis mutandis, until such time that the Reservation List of ACIA comes into force.

3.   With respect to investments falling within the ambit of this Agreement as well as under the ASEAN IGA, or within the ambit of this Agreement and the AIA Agreement, investors of these investments may choose to apply the provisions, but only in its entirety, of either this Agreement or the ASEAN IGA or the AIA Agreement, as the case may be, for a period of 3 years after the date of termination of the ASEAN IGA and the AIA Agreement.

Article 48 Entry into Force

1.   This Agreement shall enter into force after all Member States have notified or, where necessary, deposited instruments of ratification with the Secretary-General of ASEAN, which shall not take more than 180 days after the signing of this Agreement.

2.   The Secretary-General of ASEAN shall promptly notify all Member States of the notifications or deposit of each instrument of ratification referred to in paragraph 1.

Article 49 Depositary

This Agreement shall be deposited with the Secretary-General of ASEAN, who shall promptly furnish a certified copy thereof to each Member State.

IN WITNESS WHEREOF, the undersigned, being duly authorised by their respective Governments, have signed this ASEAN Comprehensive Investment Agreement.

DONE at Cha-am, Thailand, this 26th Day of February in the Year Two Thousand and Nine, in a single original copy in the English language.

ANNEX 1 Approval in Writing

Where specific approval in writing is required for covered investments by a Member State's domestic laws, regulations and national policies, that Member State shall:

(a) inform all the other Member States through the ASEAN Secretariat of the contact details of its competent authority responsible for granting such approval;

(b) in the case of an incomplete application, identify and notify the applicant in writing within 1 month from the date of receipt of such application of all the additional information that is required;

(c) inform the applicant in writing that the investment has been specifically approved or denied within 4 months from the date of receipt of complete application by the competent authority; and

(d) in the case an application is denied, inform the applicant in writing of the reasons for such denial. The applicant shall have the opportunity of submitting, at that applicant's discretion, a new application.

ANNEX 2 Expropriation and Compensation

1.   An action or a series of related actions by a Member State cannot constitute an expropriation unless it interferes with a tangible or intangible property right or property interest in a covered investment.

2.   Article 14(1) addresses two situations:

(a) the first situation is where an investment is nationalised or otherwise directly expropriated through formal transfer of title or outright seizure; and

(b) the second situation is where an action or series of related actions by a Member State has an effect equivalent to direct expropriation without formal transfer of title or outright seizure.

3.   The determination of whether an action or series of actions by a Member State, in a specific fact situation, constitutes an expropriation of the type referred to in subparagraph 2(b), requires a case-by-case, fact-based inquiry that considers, among other factors:

(a) the economic impact of the government action, although the fact that an action or series of actions by a Member State has an adverse effect on the economic value of an investment, standing alone, does not establish that such an expropriation has occurred;

(b) whether the government action breaches the government's prior binding written commitment to the investor whether by contract, licence or other legal document; and

(c) the character of the government action, including, its objective and whether the action is disproportionate to the public purpose referred to in Article 14(1).

4.   Non-discriminatory measures of a Member State that are designed and applied to protect legitimate public welfare objectives, such as public health, safety and the environment, do not constitute an expropriation of the type referred to in sub-paragraph 2(b).

XII. Main WTO Documents Resulting from the Uruguay Round

XII.1. MARRAKESH DECLARATION OF 15 APRIL 1994

Ministers,

Representing the 124 Governments and the European Communities participating in the Uruguay Round of Multilateral Trade Negotiations, on the occasion of the final session of the Trade Negotiations Committee at Ministerial level held at Marrakesh, Morocco from 12 to 15 April 1994,

Recalling the Ministerial Declaration adopted at Punta del Este, Uruguay on 20 September 1986 to launch the Uruguay Round of Multilateral Trade Negotiations,

Recalling the progress achieved at the Ministerial meetings held at Montreal, Canada and Brussels, Belgium in December of 1988 and 1990 respectively,

Noting that the negotiations were substantially concluded on 15 December 1993,

Determined to build upon the success of the Uruguay Round through the participation of their economies in the world trading system, based upon open, market-oriented policies and the commitments set out in the Uruguay Round Agreements and Decisions,

Have today *adopted* the following:

DECLARATION

1.   Ministers salute the historic achievement represented by the conclusion of the Round, which they believe will strengthen the world economy and lead to more trade, investment, employment and income growth throughout the world. In particular, they welcome:

— the stronger and clearer legal framework they have adopted for the conduct of international trade, including a more effective and reliable dispute settlement mechanism,

— the global reduction by 40 per cent of tariffs and wider market-opening agreements on goods, and the increased predictability and security represented by a major expansion in the scope of tariff commitments, and

— the establishment of a multilateral framework of disciplines for trade in services and for the protection of trade-related intellectual property rights, as well as the reinforced multilateral trade provisions in agriculture and in textiles and clothing.

2.   Ministers affirm that the establishment of the World Trade Organization (WTO) ushers in a new era of global economic cooperation, reflecting the widespread desire to operate in a fairer and more open multilateral trading system for the benefit and welfare of their peoples. Ministers express their determination to resist protectionist pressures of all kinds. They believe that the trade liberalization and strengthened rules achieved in the Uruguay Round will lead to a progressively more open world trading environment. Ministers undertake, with immediate effect and until the entry into force of the WTO, not to take any trade measures that would undermine or adversely affect the results of the Uruguay Round negotiations or their implementation.

3.   Ministers confirm their resolution to strive for greater global coherence of policies in the fields of trade, money and finance, including cooperation between the WTO, the IMF and the World Bank for that purpose.

4.   Ministers welcome the fact that participation in the Uruguay Round was considerably wider than in any previous multilateral trade negotiation and, in particular, that developing countries played a notably active rôle in it. This has marked a historic step towards a more balanced and integrated global trade partnership. Ministers note that during the period these negotiations were underway significant measures of economic reform and autonomous trade liberalization were implemented in many developing countries and formerly centrally planned economies.

5.   Ministers recall that the results of the negotiations embody provisions conferring differential and more favourable treatment for developing economies, including special attention to the particular situation of least-developed countries. Ministers recognize the importance of the implementation of these provisions for the least-developed countries and declare their intention to continue to assist and facilitate the expansion of their trade and investment opportunities. They agree to keep under regular review by the Ministerial Conference and the appropriate organs of the WTO the impact of the results of the Round on the least-developed countries as well as on the net food-importing developing countries, with a view to fostering positive measures to enable them to achieve their development objectives. Ministers recognize the need for strengthening the capability of the GATT and the WTO to provide increased technical assistance in their areas of competence, and in particular to substantially expand its provision to the least-developed countries.

6.   Ministers declare that their signature of the "Final Act Embodying the Results of the Uruguay Round of Multilateral Trade Negotiations" and their adoption of associated Ministerial Decisions initiates the transition from the GATT to the WTO. They have in particular established a Preparatory Committee to lay the ground for the entry into force of the WTO Agreement and commit themselves to seek to complete all steps necessary to ratify the WTO Agreement so that it can enter into force by 1 January 1995 or as early as possible thereafter. Ministers have furthermore adopted a Decision on Trade and Environment.

7.   Ministers express their sincere gratitude to His Majesty King Hassan II for his personal contribution to the success of this Ministerial Meeting, and to his Government and the people of Morocco for their warm hospitality and the excellent organization they have provided. The fact that this final Ministerial Meeting of the Uruguay Round has been held at Marrakesh is an additional manifestation of Morocco's commitment to an open world trading system and to its fullest integration to the global economy.

8.   With the adoption and signature of the Final Act and the opening for acceptance of the WTO Agreement, Ministers declare the work of the Trade Negotiations Committee to be complete and the Uruguay Round formally concluded.

XII.2. FINAL ACT EMBODYING THE RESULTS OF THE URUGUAY ROUND OF MULTILATERAL TRADE NEGOTIATIONS

1.   Having met in order to conclude the Uruguay Round of Multilateral Trade Negotiations, representatives of the governments and of the European Communities, members of the Trade Negotiations Committee, *agree* that the Agreement Establishing the World Trade Organization (referred to in this Final Act as the "WTO Agreement"), the Ministerial Declarations and Decisions, and the Understanding on Commitments in Financial Services, as annexed hereto, embody the results of their negotiations and form an integral part of this Final Act.

2.   By signing the present Final Act, the representatives *agree*

(a)   to submit, as appropriate, the WTO Agreement for the consideration of their respective competent authorities with a view to seeking approval of the Agreement in accordance with their procedures; and

(b)   to adopt the Ministerial Declarations and Decisions.

3.   The representatives *agree* on the desirability of acceptance of the WTO Agreement by all participants in the Uruguay Round of Multilateral Trade Negotiations (hereinafter referred to as "participants") with a view to its entry into force by 1 January 1995, or as early as possible thereafter. Not later than late 1994, Ministers will meet, in accordance with the final paragraph of the Punta del Este Ministerial Declaration, to decide on the international implementation of the results, including the timing of their entry into force.

4.   The representatives *agree* that the WTO Agreement shall be open for acceptance as a whole, by signature or otherwise, by all participants pursuant to Article XIV thereof. The acceptance and entry into force of a Plurilateral Trade Agreement included in Annex 4 of the WTO Agreement shall be governed by the provisions of that Plurilateral Trade Agreement.

5.   Before accepting the WTO Agreement, participants which are not contracting parties to the General Agreement on Tariffs and Trade must first have concluded negotiations for their accession to the General Agreement and become contracting parties thereto. For participants which are not contracting parties to the General Agreement as of the date of the Final Act, the Schedules are not definitive and shall be subsequently completed for the purpose of their accession to the General Agreement and acceptance of the WTO Agreement.

6.   This Final Act and the texts annexed hereto shall be deposited with the Director-General to the CONTRACTING PARTIES to the General Agreement on Tariffs and Trade who shall promptly furnish to each participant a certified copy thereof.

DONE at Marrakesh this fifteenth day of April one thousand nine hundred and ninety-four, in a single copy, in the English, French and Spanish languages, each text being authentic.

[List of signatures to be included in the treaty copy of the Final Act for signature]

XII.3. MARRAKESH AGREEMENT ESTABLISHING THE
WORLD TRADE ORGANIZATION

The *Parties* to this Agreement,

Recognizing that their relations in the field of trade and economic endeavour should be conducted with a view to raising standards of living, ensuring full employment and a large and steadily growing volume of real income and effective demand, and expanding the production of and trade in goods and services, while allowing for the optimal use of the world's resources in accordance with the objective of sustainable development, seeking both to protect and preserve the environment and to enhance the means for doing so in a manner consistent with their respective needs and concerns at different levels of economic development,

Recognizing further that there is need for positive efforts designed to ensure that developing countries, and especially the least developed among them, secure a share in the growth in international trade commensurate with the needs of their economic development,

Being desirous of contributing to these objectives by entering into reciprocal and mutually advantageous arrangements directed to the substantial reduction of tariffs and other barriers to trade and to the elimination of discriminatory treatment in international trade relations,

Resolved, therefore, to develop an integrated, more viable and durable multilateral trading system encompassing the General Agreement on Tariffs and Trade, the results of past trade liberalization efforts, and all of the results of the Uruguay Round of Multilateral Trade Negotiations,

Determined to preserve the basic principles and to further the objectives underlying this multilateral trading system,

Agree as follows:

Article I Establishment of the Organization

The World Trade Organization (hereinafter referred to as "the WTO") is hereby established.

Article II Scope of the WTO

1. The WTO shall provide the common institutional framework for the conduct of trade relations among its Members in matters related to the agreements and associated legal instruments included in the Annexes to this Agreement.

2. The agreements and associated legal instruments included in Annexes 1, 2 and 3 (hereinafter referred to as "Multilateral Trade Agreements") are integral parts of this Agreement, binding on all Members.

3. The agreements and associated legal instruments included in Annex 4 (hereinafter referred to as "Plurilateral Trade Agreements") are also part of this Agreement for those Members that have accepted them, and are binding on those Members. The Plurilateral Trade Agreements do not create either obligations or rights for Members that have not accepted them.

4. The General Agreement on Tariffs and Trade 1994 as specified in Annex 1A (hereinafter referred to as "GATT 1994") is legally distinct from the General Agreement on Tariffs and Trade, dated 30 October 1947, annexed to the Final Act Adopted at the Conclusion of the Second Session of the Preparatory Committee of the United Nations Conference on Trade and Employment, as subsequently rectified, amended or modified (hereinafter referred to as "GATT 1947").

Article III Functions of the WTO

1.   The WTO shall facilitate the implementation, administration and operation, and further the objectives, of this Agreement and of the Multilateral Trade Agreements, and shall also provide the framework for the implementation, administration and operation of the Plurilateral Trade Agreements.

2.   The WTO shall provide the forum for negotiations among its Members concerning their multilateral trade relations in matters dealt with under the agreements in the Annexes to this Agreement. The WTO may also provide a forum for further negotiations among its Members concerning their multilateral trade relations, and a framework for the implementation of the results of such negotiations, as may be decided by the Ministerial Conference.

3.   The WTO shall administer the Understanding on Rules and Procedures Governing the Settlement of Disputes (hereinafter referred to as the "Dispute Settlement Understanding" or "DSU") in Annex 2 to this Agreement.

4.   The WTO shall administer the Trade Policy Review Mechanism (hereinafter referred to as the "TPRM") provided for in Annex 3 to this Agreement.

5.   With a view to achieving greater coherence in global economic policy-making, the WTO shall cooperate, as appropriate, with the International Monetary Fund and with the International Bank for Reconstruction and Development and its affiliated agencies.

Article IV Structure of the WTO

1.   There shall be a Ministerial Conference composed of representatives of all the Members, which shall meet at least once every two years. The Ministerial Conference shall carry out the functions of the WTO and take actions necessary to this effect. The Ministerial Conference shall have the authority to take decisions on all matters under any of the Multilateral Trade Agreements, if so requested by a Member, in accordance with the specific requirements for decision-making in this Agreement and in the relevant Multilateral Trade Agreement.

2.   There shall be a General Council composed of representatives of all the Members, which shall meet as appropriate. In the intervals between meetings of the Ministerial Conference, its functions shall be conducted by the General Council. The General Council shall also carry out the functions assigned to it by this Agreement. The General Council shall establish its rules of procedure and approve the rules of procedure for the Committees provided for in paragraph 7.

3.   The General Council shall convene as appropriate to discharge the responsibilities of the Dispute Settlement Body provided for in the Dispute Settlement Understanding. The Dispute Settlement Body may have its own chairman and shall establish such rules of procedure as it deems necessary for the fulfilment of those responsibilities.

4.   The General Council shall convene as appropriate to discharge the responsibilities of the Trade Policy Review Body provided for in the TPRM. The Trade Policy Review Body may have its own chairman and shall establish such rules of procedure as it deems necessary for the fulfilment of those responsibilities.

5.   There shall be a Council for Trade in Goods, a Council for Trade in Services and a Council for Trade-Related Aspects of Intellectual Property Rights (hereinafter referred to as the "Council for TRIPS"), which shall operate under the general guidance of the General Council. The Council for Trade in Goods shall oversee the functioning of the Multilateral Trade Agreements in Annex 1A. The Council for Trade in Services shall oversee the functioning of the General Agreement on Trade in Services (hereinafter referred to as "GATS"). The Council for TRIPS shall oversee the functioning of the Agreement on Trade-Related Aspects of Intellectual Property Rights (hereinafter referred to as the "Agreement on TRIPS"). These Councils shall carry out the functions assigned to them by their respective agreements and by the General Council. They shall establish their respective rules of procedure subject to the approval of the General Council. Membership in

these Councils shall be open to representatives of all Members. These Councils shall meet as necessary to carry out their functions.

6.   The Council for Trade in Goods, the Council for Trade in Services and the Council for TRIPS shall establish subsidiary bodies as required. These subsidiary bodies shall establish their respective rules of procedure subject to the approval of their respective Councils.

7.   The Ministerial Conference shall establish a Committee on Trade and Development, a Committee on Balance-of-Payments Restrictions and a Committee on Budget, Finance and Administration, which shall carry out the functions assigned to them by this Agreement and by the Multilateral Trade Agreements, and any additional functions assigned to them by the General Council, and may establish such additional Committees with such functions as it may deem appropriate. As part of its functions, the Committee on Trade and Development shall periodically review the special provisions in the Multilateral Trade Agreements in favour of the least-developed country Members and report to the General Council for appropriate action. Membership in these Committees shall be open to representatives of all Members.

8.   The bodies provided for under the Plurilateral Trade Agreements shall carry out the functions assigned to them under those Agreements and shall operate within the institutional framework of the WTO. These bodies shall keep the General Council informed of their activities on a regular basis.

Article V Relations with Other Organizations

1.   The General Council shall make appropriate arrangements for effective cooperation with other intergovernmental organizations that have responsibilities related to those of the WTO.

2.   The General Council may make appropriate arrangements for consultation and cooperation with non-governmental organizations concerned with matters related to those of the WTO.

Article VI The Secretariat

1.   There shall be a Secretariat of the WTO (hereinafter referred to as "the Secretariat") headed by a Director-General.

2.   The Ministerial Conference shall appoint the Director-General and adopt regulations setting out the powers, duties, conditions of service and term of office of the Director-General.

3.   The Director-General shall appoint the members of the staff of the Secretariat and determine their duties and conditions of service in accordance with regulations adopted by the Ministerial Conference.

4.   The responsibilities of the Director-General and of the staff of the Secretariat shall be exclusively international in character. In the discharge of their duties, the Director-General and the staff of the Secretariat shall not seek or accept instructions from any government or any other authority external to the WTO. They shall refrain from any action which might adversely reflect on their position as international officials. The Members of the WTO shall respect the international character of the responsibilities of the Director-General and of the staff of the Secretariat and shall not seek to influence them in the discharge of their duties.

Article VII Budget and Contributions

1.   The Director-General shall present to the Committee on Budget, Finance and Administration the annual budget estimate and financial statement of the WTO. The Committee on Budget, Finance and Administration shall review the annual budget estimate and the financial statement presented by the Director-General and make recommendations thereon to the General Council. The annual budget estimate shall be subject to approval by the General Council.

2.   The Committee on Budget, Finance and Administration shall propose to the General Council financial regulations which shall include provisions setting out:

(a)   the scale of contributions apportioning the expenses of the WTO among its Members; and

(b)   the measures to be taken in respect of Members in arrears.

The financial regulations shall be based, as far as practicable, on the regulations and practices of GATT 1947.

3.   The General Council shall adopt the financial regulations and the annual budget estimate by a two-thirds majority comprising more than half of the Members of the WTO.

4.   Each Member shall promptly contribute to the WTO its share in the expenses of the WTO in accordance with the financial regulations adopted by the General Council.

Article VIII Status of the WTO

1.   The WTO shall have legal personality, and shall be accorded by each of its Members such legal capacity as may be necessary for the exercise of its functions.

2.   The WTO`shall be accorded by each of its Members such privileges and immunities as are necessary for the exercise of its functions.

3.   The officials of the WTO and the representatives of the Members shall similarly be accorded by each of its Members such privileges and immunities as are necessary for the independent exercise of their functions in connection with the WTO.

4.   The privileges and immunities to be accorded by a Member to the WTO, its officials, and the representatives of its Members shall be similar to the privileges and immunities stipulated in the Convention on the Privileges and Immunities of the Specialized Agencies, approved by the General Assembly of the United Nations on 21 November 1947.

5.   The WTO may conclude a headquarters agreement.

Article IX Decision-Making

1.   The WTO shall continue the practice of decision-making by consensus followed under GATT 1947.[1] Except as otherwise provided, where a decision cannot be arrived at by consensus, the matter at issue shall be decided by voting. At meetings of the Ministerial Conference and the General Council, each Member of the WTO shall have one vote. Where the European Communities exercise their right to vote, they shall have a number of votes equal to the number of their Member States[2] which are Members of the WTO. Decisions of the Ministerial Conference and the General Council shall be taken by a majority of the votes cast, unless otherwise provided in this Agreement or in the relevant Multilateral Trade Agreement.[3]

2.   The Ministerial Conference and the General Council shall have the exclusive authority to adopt interpretations of this Agreement and of the Multilateral Trade Agreements. In the case of an interpretation of a Multilateral Trade Agreement in Annex 1, they shall exercise their authority on the basis of a recommendation by the Council overseeing the functioning of that Agreement. The decision to adopt an interpretation shall be taken by a three-fourths majority of the Members. This paragraph shall not be used in a manner that would undermine the amendment provisions in Article X.

3.   In exceptional circumstances, the Ministerial Conference may decide to waive an obligation imposed on a Member by this Agreement or any of the Multilateral Trade Agreements, provided

---

1   The body concerned shall be deemed to have decided by consensus on a matter submitted for its consideration, if no Member, present at the meeting when the decision is taken, formally objects to the proposed decision.

2   The number of votes of the European Communities and their member States shall in no case exceed the number of the member States of the European Communities.

3   Decisions by the General Council when convened as the Dispute Settlement Body shall be taken only in accordance with the provisions of paragraph 4 of Article 2 of the Dispute Settlement Understanding.

that any such decision shall be taken by three fourths[4] of the Members unless otherwise provided for in this paragraph.

(a) A request for a waiver concerning this Agreement shall be submitted to the Ministerial Conference for consideration pursuant to the practice of decision-making by consensus. The Ministerial Conference shall establish a time-period, which shall not exceed 90 days, to consider the request. If consensus is not reached during the time-period, any decision to grant a waiver shall be taken by three fourths[5] of the Members.

(b) A request for a waiver concerning the Multilateral Trade Agreements in Annexes 1A or 1B or 1C and their annexes shall be submitted initially to the Council for Trade in Goods, the Council for Trade in Services or the Council for TRIPS, respectively, for consideration during a time-period which shall not exceed 90 days. At the end of the time-period, the relevant Council shall submit a report to the Ministerial Conference.

4. A decision by the Ministerial Conference granting a waiver shall state the exceptional circumstances justifying the decision, the terms and conditions governing the application of the waiver, and the date on which the waiver shall terminate. Any waiver granted for a period of more than one year shall be reviewed by the Ministerial Conference not later than one year after it is granted, and thereafter annually until the waiver terminates. In each review, the Ministerial Conference shall examine whether the exceptional circumstances justifying the waiver still exist and whether the terms and conditions attached to the waiver have been met. The Ministerial Conference, on the basis of the annual review, may extend, modify or terminate the waiver.

5. Decisions under a Plurilateral Trade Agreement, including any decisions on interpretations and waivers, shall be governed by the provisions of that Agreement.

Article X Amendments

1. Any Member of the WTO may initiate a proposal to amend the provisions of this Agreement or the Multilateral Trade Agreements in Annex 1 by submitting such proposal to the Ministerial Conference. The Councils listed in paragraph 5 of Article IV may also submit to the Ministerial Conference proposals to amend the provisions of the corresponding Multilateral Trade Agreements in Annex 1 the functioning of which they oversee. Unless the Ministerial Conference decides on a longer period, for a period of 90 days after the proposal has been tabled formally at the Ministerial Conference any decision by the Ministerial Conference to submit the proposed amendment to the Members for acceptance shall be taken by consensus. Unless the provisions of paragraphs 2, 5 or 6 apply, that decision shall specify whether the provisions of paragraphs 3 or 4 shall apply. If consensus is reached, the Ministerial Conference shall forthwith submit the proposed amendment to the Members for acceptance. If consensus is not reached at a meeting of the Ministerial Conference within the established period, the Ministerial Conference shall decide by a two-thirds majority of the Members whether to submit the proposed amendment to the Members for acceptance. Except as provided in paragraphs 2, 5 and 6, the provisions of paragraph 3 shall apply to the proposed amendment, unless the Ministerial Conference decides by a three-fourths majority of the Members that the provisions of paragraph 4 shall apply.

2. Amendments to the provisions of this Article and to the provisions of the following Articles shall take effect only upon acceptance by all Members:

– Article IX of this Agreement;

---

4 A decision to grant a waiver in respect of any obligation subject to a transition period or a period for staged implementation that the requesting Member has not performed by the end of the relevant period shall be taken only by consensus.

5 A decision to grant a waiver in respect of any obligation subject to a transition period or a period for staged implementation that the requesting Member has not performed by the end of the relevant period shall be taken only by consensus.

- Articles I and II of GATT 1994;
- Article II:1 of GATS;
- Article 4 of the Agreement on TRIPS.

3.   Amendments to provisions of this Agreement, or of the Multilateral Trade Agreements in Annexes 1A and 1C, other than those listed in paragraphs 2 and 6, of a nature that would alter the rights and obligations of the Members, shall take effect for the Members that have accepted them upon acceptance by two thirds of the Members and thereafter for each other Member upon acceptance by it. The Ministerial Conference may decide by a three-fourths majority of the Members that any amendment made effective under this paragraph is of such a nature that any Member which has not accepted it within a period specified by the Ministerial Conference in each case shall be free to withdraw from the WTO or to remain a Member with the consent of the Ministerial Conference.

4.   Amendments to provisions of this Agreement or of the Multilateral Trade Agreements in Annexes 1A and 1C, other than those listed in paragraphs 2 and 6, of a nature that would not alter the rights and obligations of the Members, shall take effect for all Members upon acceptance by two thirds of the Members.

5.   Except as provided in paragraph 2 above, amendments to Parts I, II and III of GATS and the respective annexes shall take effect for the Members that have accepted them upon acceptance by two thirds of the Members and thereafter for each Member upon acceptance by it. The Ministerial Conference may decide by a three-fourths majority of the Members that any amendment made effective under the preceding provision is of such a nature that any Member which has not accepted it within a period specified by the Ministerial Conference in each case shall be free to withdraw from the WTO or to remain a Member with the consent of the Ministerial Conference. Amendments to Parts IV, V and VI of GATS and the respective annexes shall take effect for all Members upon acceptance by two thirds of the Members.

6.   Notwithstanding the other provisions of this Article, amendments to the Agreement on TRIPS meeting the requirements of paragraph 2 of Article 71 thereof may be adopted by the Ministerial Conference without further formal acceptance process.

7.   Any Member accepting an amendment to this Agreement or to a Multilateral Trade Agreement in Annex 1 shall deposit an instrument of acceptance with the Director-General of the WTO within the period of acceptance specified by the Ministerial Conference.

8.   Any Member of the WTO may initiate a proposal to amend the provisions of the Multilateral Trade Agreements in Annexes 2 and 3 by submitting such proposal to the Ministerial Conference. The decision to approve amendments to the Multilateral Trade Agreement in Annex 2 shall be made by consensus and these amendments shall take effect for all Members upon approval by the Ministerial Conference. Decisions to approve amendments to the Multilateral Trade Agreement in Annex 3 shall take effect for all Members upon approval by the Ministerial Conference.

9.   The Ministerial Conference, upon the request of the Members parties to a trade agreement, may decide exclusively by consensus to add that agreement to Annex 4. The Ministerial Conference, upon the request of the Members parties to a Plurilateral Trade Agreement, may decide to delete that Agreement from Annex 4.

10.   Amendments to a Plurilateral Trade Agreement shall be governed by the provisions of that Agreement.

Article XI Original Membership

1.   The contracting parties to GATT 1947 as of the date of entry into force of this Agreement, and the European Communities, which accept this Agreement and the Multilateral Trade Agreements and for which Schedules of Concessions and Commitments are annexed to GATT 1994 and for which Schedules of Specific Commitments are annexed to GATS shall become original Members of the WTO.

2.   The least-developed countries recognized as such by the United Nations will only be required to undertake commitments and concessions to the extent consistent with their individual development, financial and trade needs or their administrative and institutional capabilities.

Article XII Accession

1.   Any State or separate customs territory possessing full autonomy in the conduct of its external commercial relations and of the other matters provided for in this Agreement and the Multilateral Trade Agreements may accede to this Agreement, on terms to be agreed between it and the WTO. Such accession shall apply to this Agreement and the Multilateral Trade Agreements annexed thereto.

2.   Decisions on accession shall be taken by the Ministerial Conference. The Ministerial Conference shall approve the agreement on the terms of accession by a two-thirds majority of the Members of the WTO.

3.   Accession to a Plurilateral Trade Agreement shall be governed by the provisions of that Agreement.

Article XIII Non-Application of Multilateral Trade Agreements
Between Particular Members

1.   This Agreement and the Multilateral Trade Agreements in Annexes 1 and 2 shall not apply as between any Member and any other Member if either of the Members, at the time either becomes a Member, does not consent to such application.

2.   Paragraph 1 may be invoked between original Members of the WTO which were contracting parties to GATT 1947 only where Article XXXV of that Agreement had been invoked earlier and was effective as between those contracting parties at the time of entry into force for them of this Agreement.

3.   Paragraph 1 shall apply between a Member and another Member which has acceded under Article XII only if the Member not consenting to the application has so notified the Ministerial Conference before the approval of the agreement on the terms of accession by the Ministerial Conference.

4.   The Ministerial Conference may review the operation of this Article in particular cases at the request of any Member and make appropriate recommendations.

5.   Non-application of a Plurilateral Trade Agreement between parties to that Agreement shall be governed by the provisions of that Agreement.

Article XIV Acceptance, Entry into Force and Deposit

1.   This Agreement shall be open for acceptance, by signature or otherwise, by contracting parties to GATT 1947, and the European Communities, which are eligible to become original Members of the WTO in accordance with Article XI of this Agreement. Such acceptance shall apply to this Agreement and the Multilateral Trade Agreements annexed hereto. This Agreement and the Multilateral Trade Agreements annexed hereto shall enter into force on the date determined by Ministers in accordance with paragraph 3 of the Final Act Embodying the Results of the Uruguay Round of Multilateral Trade Negotiations and shall remain open for acceptance for a period of two years following that date unless the Ministers decide otherwise. An

acceptance following the entry into force of this Agreement shall enter into force on the 30th day following the date of such acceptance.

2.   A Member which accepts this Agreement after its entry into force shall implement those concessions and obligations in the Multilateral Trade Agreements that are to be implemented over a period of time starting with the entry into force of this Agreement as if it had accepted this Agreement on the date of its entry into force.

3.   Until the entry into force of this Agreement, the text of this Agreement and the Multilateral Trade Agreements shall be deposited with the Director-General to the CONTRACTING PARTIES to GATT 1947. The Director-General shall promptly furnish a certified true copy of this Agreement and the Multilateral Trade Agreements, and a notification of each acceptance thereof, to each government and the European Communities having accepted this Agreement. This Agreement and the Multilateral Trade Agreements, and any amendments thereto, shall, upon the entry into force of this Agreement, be deposited with the Director-General of the WTO.

4.   The acceptance and entry into force of a Plurilateral Trade Agreement shall be governed by the provisions of that Agreement. Such Agreements shall be deposited with the Director-General to the CONTRACTING PARTIES to GATT 1947. Upon the entry into force of this Agreement, such Agreements shall be deposited with the Director-General of the WTO.

Article XV Withdrawal

1.   Any Member may withdraw from this Agreement. Such withdrawal shall apply both to this Agreement and the Multilateral Trade Agreements and shall take effect upon the expiration of six months from the date on which written notice of withdrawal is received by the Director-General of the WTO.

2.   Withdrawal from a Plurilateral Trade Agreement shall be governed by the provisions of that Agreement.

Article XVI Miscellaneous Provisions

1.   Except as otherwise provided under this Agreement or the Multilateral Trade Agreements, the WTO shall be guided by the decisions, procedures and customary practices followed by the CONTRACTING PARTIES to GATT 1947 and the bodies established in the framework of GATT 1947.

2.   To the extent practicable, the Secretariat of GATT 1947 shall become the Secretariat of the WTO, and the Director-General to the CONTRACTING PARTIES to GATT 1947, until such time as the Ministerial Conference has appointed a Director-General in accordance with paragraph 2 of Article VI of this Agreement, shall serve as Director-General of the WTO.

3.   In the event of a conflict between a provision of this Agreement and a provision of any of the Multilateral Trade Agreements, the provision of this Agreement shall prevail to the extent of the conflict.

4.   Each Member shall ensure the conformity of its laws, regulations and administrative pro-cedures with its obligations as provided in the annexed Agreements.

5.   No reservations may be made in respect of any provision of this Agreement. Reservations in respect of any of the provisions of the Multilateral Trade Agreements may only be made to the extent provided for in those Agreements. Reservations in respect of a provision of a Plurilateral Trade Agreement shall be governed by the provisions of that Agreement.

6.   This Agreement shall be registered in accordance with the provisions of Article 102 of the Charter of the United Nations.

DONE at Marrakesh this fifteenth day of April one thousand nine hundred and ninety-four, in a single copy, in the English, French and Spanish languages, each text being authentic.

Explanatory Notes

The terms "country" or "countries" as used in this Agreement and the Multilateral Trade Agreements are to be understood to include any separate customs territory Member of the WTO.

In the case of a separate customs territory Member of the WTO, where an expression in this Agreement and the Multilateral Trade Agreements is qualified by the term "national", such expression shall be read as pertaining to that customs territory, unless otherwise specified.

LIST OF ANNEXES

ANNEX 1

ANNEX 1A: Multilateral Agreements on Trade in Goods
General Agreement on Tariffs and Trade 1994
Agreement on Agriculture
Agreement on the Application of Sanitary and Phytosanitary Measures
Agreement on Textiles and Clothing
Agreement on Technical Barriers to Trade
Agreement on Trade-Related Investment Measures
Agreement on Implementation of Article VI of the General Agreement on Tariffs and Trade 1994
Agreement on Implementation of Article VII of the General Agreement on Tariffs and Trade 1994
Agreement on Preshipment Inspection
Agreement on Rules of Origin
Agreement on Import Licensing Procedures
Agreement on Subsidies and Countervailing Measures
Agreement on Safeguards

ANNEX 1B: General Agreement on Trade in Services and Annexes

ANNEX 1C: Agreement on Trade-Related Aspects of Intellectual Property Rights

ANNEX 2
Understanding on Rules and Procedures Governing the Settlement of Disputes

ANNEX 3 [omitted]
Trade Policy Review Mechanism

ANNEX 4 [omitted]
Plurilateral Trade Agreements
Agreement on Trade in Civil Aircraft
Agreement on Government Procurement
International Dairy Agreement
International Bovine Meat Agreement

XIII. Annexes

XIII.1. ANNEX 1A MULTILATERAL AGREEMENTS ON TRADE IN GOODS

General Agreement on Tariffs and Trade 1994

1. The General Agreement on Tariffs and Trade 1994 ("GATT 1994") shall consist of:

(a) the provisions in the General Agreement on Tariffs and Trade, dated 30 October 1947, annexed to the Final Act Adopted at the Conclusion of the Second Session of the Preparatory Committee of the United Nations Conference on Trade and Employment (excluding the Protocol of Provisional Application), as rectified, amended or modified by the terms of legal instruments which have entered into force before the date of entry into force of the WTO Agreement;

(b) the provisions of the legal instruments set forth below that have entered into force under the GATT 1947 before the date of entry into force of the WTO Agreement:

  (i) protocols and certifications relating to tariff concessions;

  (ii) protocols of accession (excluding the provisions (a) concerning provisional application and withdrawal of provisional application and (b) providing that Part II of GATT 1947 shall be applied provisionally to the fullest extent not inconsistent with legislation existing on the date of the Protocol);

  (iii) decisions on waivers granted under Article XXV of GATT 1947 and still in force on the date of entry into force of the WTO Agreement;[...]

  (iv) other decisions of the CONTRACTING PARTIES to GATT 1947;

(c) the Understandings set forth below:

  (i) Understanding on the Interpretation of Article II:1(b) of the General Agreement on Tariffs and Trade 1994;

  (ii) Understanding on the Interpretation of Article XVII of the General Agreement on Tariffs and Trade 1994;

  (iii) Understanding on Balance-of-Payments Provisions of the General Agreement on Tariffs and Trade 1994;

  (iv) Understanding on the Interpretation of Article XXIV of the General Agreement on Tariffs and Trade 1994;

  (v) Understanding in Respect of Waivers of Obligations under the General Agreement on Tariffs and Trade 1994;

  (vi) Understanding on the Interpretation of Article XXVIII of the General Agreement on Tariffs and Trade 1994; and

(d) the Marrakesh Protocol to GATT 1994.

2. Explanatory Notes

(a) The references to "contracting party" in the provisions of GATT 1994 shall be deemed to read "Member". The references to "less-developed contracting party" and "developed contracting party" shall be deemed to read "developing country Member" and "developed country Member". The references to "Executive Secretary" shall be deemed to read "Director-General of the WTO".

(b) The references to the CONTRACTING PARTIES acting jointly in Articles XV:1, XV:2, XV:8, XXXVIII and the Notes *Ad* Article XII and XVIII; and in the provisions on special exchange agreements in Articles XV:2, XV:3, XV:6, XV:7 and XV:9 of GATT 1994 shall be deemed to be references to the WTO. The other functions that the provisions of GATT 1994 assign to the CONTRACTING PARTIES acting jointly shall be allocated by the Ministerial Conference.

(c) (i) The text of GATT 1994 shall be authentic in English, French and Spanish. [...]

3. (a) The provisions of Part II of GATT 1994 shall not apply to measures taken by a Member under specific mandatory legislation, enacted by that Member before it became a contracting party to GATT 1947, that prohibits the use, sale or lease of foreign-built or foreign-reconstructed vessels in commercial applications between points in national waters or the waters of an exclusive economic zone. This exemption applies to: (a) the continuation or prompt renewal of a non-conforming provision of such legislation; and (b) the amendment to a non-conforming provision of such legislation to the extent that the amendment does not decrease the conformity of the provision with Part II of GATT 1947. This exemption is limited to measures taken under legislation described above that is notified and specified prior to the date of entry into force of the WTO Agreement. If such legislation is subsequently modified to decrease its conformity with Part II of GATT 1994, it will no longer qualify for coverage under this paragraph.

(b) The Ministerial Conference shall review this exemption not later than five years after the date of entry into force of the WTO Agreement and thereafter every two years for as long as the exemption is in force for the purpose of examining whether the conditions which created the need for the exemption still prevail.

(c) A Member whose measures are covered by this exemption shall annually submit a detailed statistical notification consisting of a five-year moving average of actual and expected deliveries of relevant vessels as well as additional information on the use, sale, lease or repair of relevant vessels covered by this exemption.

(d) A Member that considers that this exemption operates in such a manner as to justify a reciprocal and proportionate limitation on the use, sale, lease or repair of vessels constructed in the territory of the Member invoking the exemption shall be free to introduce such a limitation subject to prior notification to the Ministerial Conference.

(e) This exemption is without prejudice to solutions concerning specific aspects of the legislation covered by this exemption negotiated in sectoral agreements or in other fora.

The General Agreement on Tariffs and Trade (GATT 1947)

The Governments of the Commonwealth of Australia, the Kingdom of Belgium, the United States of Brazil, Burma, Canada, Ceylon, the Republic of Chile, the Republic of China, the Republic of Cuba, the Czechoslovak Republic, the French Republic, India, Lebanon, the Grand-Duchy of Luxemburg, the Kingdom of the Netherlands, New Zealand, the Kingdom of Norway, Pakistan, Southern Rhodesia, Syria, the Union of South Africa, the United Kingdom of Great Britain and Northern Ireland, and the United States of America:

Recognizing that their relations in the field of trade and economic endeavour should be conducted with a view to raising standards of living, ensuring full employment and a large and steadily growing volume of real income and effective demand, developing the full use of the resources of the world and expanding the production and exchange of goods,

Being desirous of contributing to these objectives by entering into reciprocal and mutually advantageous arrangements directed to the substantial reduction of tariffs and other barriers to trade and to the elimination of discriminatory treatment in international commerce,

Have through their Representatives agreed as follows:

PART I

Article I General Most-Favoured-Nation Treatment

1. With respect to customs duties and charges of any kind imposed on or in connection with importation or exportation or imposed on the international transfer of payments for imports or exports, and with respect to the method of levying such duties and charges, and with respect to all rules and formalities in connection with importation and exportation, and with respect to all matters referred to in paragraphs 2 and 4 of Article III, any advantage, favour, privilege or immunity granted by any contracting party to any product originating in or destined for any other country shall be accorded immediately and unconditionally to the like product originating in or destined for the territories of all other contracting parties.

2. The provisions of paragraph 1 of this Article shall not require the elimination of any preferences in respect of import duties or charges which do not exceed the levels provided for in paragraph 4 of this Article and which fall within the following descriptions:

(a) Preferences in force exclusively between two or more of the territories listed in Annex A, subject to the conditions set forth therein;

(b) Preferences in force exclusively between two or more territories which on July 1, 1939, were connected by common sovereignty or relations of protection or suzerainty and which are listed in Annexes B, C and D, subject to the conditions set forth therein;

(c) Preferences in force exclusively between the United States of America and the Republic of Cuba;

(d) Preferences in force exclusively between neighbouring countries listed in Annexes E and F.

3. The provisions of paragraph 1 shall not apply to preferences between the countries formerly a part of the Ottoman Empire and detached from it on July 24, 1923, provided such preferences are approved under paragraph 5, of Article XXV which shall be applied in this respect in the light of paragraph 1 of Article XXIX.

4. The margin of preference on any product in respect of which a preference is permitted under paragraph 2 of this Article but is not specifically set forth as a maximum margin of preference in the appropriate Schedule annexed to this Agreement shall not exceed:

(a) in respect of duties or charges on any product described in such Schedule, the difference between the most-favoured-nation and preferential rates provided for therein; if no preferential rate is provided for, the preferential rate shall for the purposes of this paragraph be taken to be that in force on April 10, 1947, and, if no most-favoured-nation rate is provided for, the margin shall not exceed the difference between the most-favoured-nation and preferential rates existing on April 10, 1947;

(b) in respect of duties or charges on any product not described in the appropriate Schedule, the difference between the most-favoured-nation and preferential rates existing on April 10, 1947.

In the case of the contracting parties named in Annex G, the date of April 10, 1947, referred to in subparagraph (a) and (b) of this paragraph shall be replaced by the respective dates set forth in that Annex.

Article II Schedules of Concessions

1. (a) Each contracting party shall accord to the commerce of the other contracting parties treatment no less favourable than that provided for in the appropriate Part of the appropriate Schedule annexed to this Agreement.

(b) The products described in Part I of the Schedule relating to any contracting party, which are the products of territories of other contracting parties, shall, on their importation into the territory to which the Schedule relates, and subject to the terms, conditions or qualifications set forth in that Schedule, be exempt from ordinary customs duties in excess of those set forth and provided therein. Such products shall also be exempt from all other duties or charges of any kind imposed on or in connection with the importation in excess of those imposed on the date of this Agreement or those directly and mandatorily required to be imposed thereafter by legislation in force in the importing territory on that date.

(c) The products described in Part II of the Schedule relating to any contracting party which are the products of territories entitled under Article I to receive preferential treatment upon importation into the territory to which the Schedule relates shall, on their importation into such territory, and subject to the terms, conditions or qualifications set forth in that Schedule, be exempt from ordinary customs duties in excess of those set forth and provided for in Part II of that Schedule. Such products shall also be exempt from all other duties or charges of any kind imposed on or in connection with importation in excess of those imposed on the date of this Agreement or those directly or mandatorily required to be imposed thereafter by legislation in force in the importing territory on that date. Nothing in this Article shall prevent any contracting party from maintaining its requirements existing on the date of this Agreement as to the eligibility of goods for entry at preferential rates of duty.

2.   Nothing in this Article shall prevent any contracting party from imposing at any time on the importation of any product:

(a) a charge equivalent to an internal tax imposed consistently with the provisions of paragraph 2 of Article III in respect of the like domestic product or in respect of an article from which the imported product has been manufactured or produced in whole or in part;

(b) any anti-dumping or countervailing duty applied consistently with the provisions of Article VI;

(c) fees or other charges commensurate with the cost of services rendered.

3.   No contracting party shall alter its method of determining dutiable value or of converting currencies so as to impair the value of any of the concessions provided for in the appropriate Schedule annexed to this Agreement.

4.   If any contracting party establishes, maintains or authorizes, formally or in effect, a monopoly of the importation of any product described in the appropriate Schedule annexed to this Agreement, such monopoly shall not, except as provided for in that Schedule or as otherwise agreed between the parties which initially negotiated the concession, operate so as to afford

protection on the average in excess of the amount of protection provided for in that Schedule. The provisions of this paragraph shall not limit the use by contracting parties of any form of assistance to domestic producers permitted by other provisions of this Agreement.

5.   If any contracting party considers that a product is not receiving from another contracting party the treatment which the first contracting party believes to have been contemplated by a concession provided for in the appropriate Schedule annexed to this Agreement, it shall bring the matter directly to the attention of the other contracting party. If the latter agrees that the treatment contemplated was that claimed by the first contracting party, but declares that such treatment cannot be accorded because a court or other proper authority has ruled to the effect that the product involved cannot be classified under the tariff laws of such contracting party so as to permit the treatment contemplated in this Agreement, the two contracting parties, together with any other contracting parties substantially interested, shall enter promptly into further negotiations with a view to a compensatory adjustment of the matter.

6.   (a) The specific duties and charges included in the Schedules relating to contracting parties members of the International Monetary Fund, and margins of preference in specific duties and charges maintained by such contracting parties, are expressed in the appropriate currency at the par value accepted or provisionally recognized by the Fund at the date of this Agreement. Accordingly, in case this par value is reduced consistently with the Articles of Agreement of the International Monetary Fund by more than twenty per centum, such specific duties and charges and margins of preference may be adjusted to take account of such reduction; *provided* that the CONTRACTING PARTIES (*i.e.*, the contracting parties acting jointly as provided for in Article XXV) concur that such adjustments will not impair the value of the concessions provided for in the appropriate Schedule or elsewhere in this Agreement, due account being taken of all factors which may influence the need for, or urgency of, such adjustments.

(b)   Similar provisions shall apply to any contracting party not a member of the Fund, as from the date on which such contracting party becomes a member of the Fund or enters into a special exchange agreement in pursuance of Article XV.

7.   The Schedules annexed to this Agreement are hereby made an integral part of Part I of this Agreement.

PART II

Article III National Treatment on Internal Taxation and Regulation

1.   The contracting parties recognize that internal taxes and other internal charges, and laws, regulations and requirements affecting the internal sale, offering for sale, purchase, transportation, distribution or use of products, and internal quantitative regulations requiring the mixture, processing or use of products in specified amounts or proportions, should not be applied to imported or domestic products so as to afford protection to domestic production.

2.   The products of the territory of any contracting party imported into the territory of any other contracting party shall not be subject, directly or indirectly, to internal taxes or other internal charges of any kind in excess of those applied, directly or indirectly, to like domestic products. Moreover, no contracting party shall otherwise apply internal taxes or other internal charges to imported or domestic products in a manner contrary to the principles set forth in paragraph 1.

3.   With respect to any existing internal tax which is inconsistent with the provisions of paragraph 2, but which is specifically authorized under a trade agreement, in force on April 10, 1947, in which the import duty on the taxed product is bound against increase, the contracting party imposing the tax shall be free to postpone the application of the provisions of paragraph 2 to such tax until such time as it can obtain release from the obligations of such trade agreement in order to permit the increase of such duty to the extent necessary to compensate for the elimination of the protective element of the tax.

4.   The products of the territory of any contracting party imported into the territory of any other contracting party shall be accorded treatment no less favourable than that accorded to like products of national origin in respect of all laws, regulations and requirements affecting their internal sale, offering for sale, purchase, transportation, distribution or use. The provisions of this paragraph shall not prevent the application of differential internal transportation charges which are based exclusively on the economic operation of the means of transport and not on the nationality of the product.

5.   No contracting party shall establish or maintain any internal quantitative regulation relating to the mixture, processing or use of products in specified amounts or proportions which requires, directly or indirectly, that any specified amount or proportion of any product which is the subject of the regulation must be supplied from domestic sources. Moreover, no contracting party shall otherwise apply internal quantitative regulations in a manner contrary to the principles set forth in paragraph 1.

6.   The provisions of paragraph 5 shall not apply to any internal quantitative regulation in force in the territory of any contracting party on July 1, 1939, April 10, 1947, or March 24, 1948, at the option of that contracting party; *provided* that any such regulation which is contrary to the provisions of paragraph 5 shall not be modified to the detriment of imports and shall be treated as a customs duty for the purpose of negotiation.

7.   No internal quantitative regulation relating to the mixture, processing or use of products in specified amounts or proportions shall be applied in such a manner as to allocate any such amount or proportion among external sources of supply.

8.   (a) The provisions of this Article shall not apply to laws, regulations or requirements governing the procurement by governmental agencies of products purchased for governmental purposes and not with a view to commercial resale or with a view to use in the production of goods for commercial sale.

(b)   The provisions of this Article shall not prevent the payment of subsidies exclusively to domestic producers, including payments to domestic producers derived from the proceeds of internal taxes or charges applied consistently with the provisions of this Article and subsidies effected through governmental purchases of domestic products.

9.   The contracting parties recognize that internal maximum price control measures, even though conforming to the other provisions of this Article, can have effects prejudicial to the interests of contracting parties supplying imported products. Accordingly, contracting parties applying such measures shall take account of the interests of exporting contracting parties with a view to avoiding to the fullest practicable extent such prejudicial effects.

10.   The provisions of this Article shall not prevent any contracting party from establishing or maintaining internal quantitative regulations relating to exposed cinematograph films and meeting the requirements of Article IV.

Article IV Special Provisions Relating to Cinematograph Films

If any contracting party establishes or maintains internal quantitative regulations relating to exposed cinematograph films, such regulations shall take the form of screen quotas which shall conform to the following requirements:

(a)   Screen quotas may require the exhibition of cinematograph films of national origin during a specified minimum proportion of the total screen time actually utilized, over a specified period of not less than one year, in the commercial exhibition of all films of whatever origin, and shall be computed on the basis of screen time per theatre per year or the equivalent thereof;

(b) With the exception of screen time reserved for films of national origin under a screen quota, screen time including that released by administrative action from screen time reserved for films of national origin, shall not be allocated formally or in effect among sources of supply;

(c) Notwithstanding the provisions of subparagraph (b) of this Article, any contracting party may maintain screen quotas conforming to the requirements of subparagraph (a) of this Article which reserve a minimum proportion of screen time for films of a specified origin other than that of the contracting party imposing such screen quotas; *provided* that no such minimum proportion of screen time shall be increased above the level in effect on April 10, 1947;

(d) Screen quotas shall be subject to negotiation for their limitation, liberalization or elimination.

Article V Freedom of Transit

1.   Goods (including baggage), and also vessels and other means of transport, shall be deemed to be in transit across the territory of a contracting party when the passage across such territory, with or without trans-shipment, warehousing, breaking bulk, or change in the mode of transport, is only a portion of a complete journey beginning and terminating beyond the frontier of the contracting party across whose territory the traffic passes. Traffic of this nature is termed in this article "traffic in transit".

2.   There shall be freedom of transit through the territory of each contracting party, via the routes most convenient for international transit, for traffic in transit to or from the territory of other contracting parties. No distinction shall be made which is based on the flag of vessels, the place of origin, departure, entry, exit or destination, or on any circumstances relating to the ownership of goods, of vessels or of other means of transport.

3.   Any contracting party may require that traffic in transit through its territory be entered at the proper custom house, but, except in cases of failure to comply with applicable customs laws and regulations, such traffic coming from or going to the territory of other contracting parties shall not be subject to any unnecessary delays or restrictions and shall be exempt from customs duties and from all transit duties or other charges imposed in respect of transit, except charges for transportation or those commensurate with administrative expenses entailed by transit or with the cost of services rendered.

4.   All charges and regulations imposed by contracting parties on traffic in transit to or from the territories of other contracting parties shall be reasonable, having regard to the conditions of the traffic.

5.   With respect to all charges, regulations and formalities in connection with transit, each contracting party shall accord to traffic in transit to or from the territory of any other contracting party treatment no less favourable than the treatment accorded to traffic in transit to or from any third country.

6.   Each contracting party shall accord to products which have been in transit through the territory of any other contracting party treatment no less favourable than that which would have been accorded to such products had they been transported from their place of origin to their destination without going through the territory of such other contracting party. Any contracting party shall, however, be free to maintain its requirements of direct consignment existing on the date of this Agreement, in respect of any goods in regard to which such direct consignment is a requisite condition of eligibility for entry of the goods at preferential rates of duty or has relation to the contracting party's prescribed method of valuation for duty purposes.

7.   The provisions of this Article shall not apply to the operation of aircraft in transit, but shall apply to air transit of goods (including baggage).

Article VI Anti-Dumping and Countervailing Duties

1.   The contracting parties recognize that dumping, by which products of one country are introduced into the commerce of another country at less than the normal value of the products, is to be condemned if it causes or threatens material injury to an established industry in the territory of a contracting party or materially retards the establishment of a domestic industry. For the purposes of this Article, a product is to be considered as being introduced into the commerce of an importing country at less than its normal value, if the price of the product exported from one country to another

(a)   is less than the comparable price, in the ordinary course of trade, for the like product when destined for consumption in the exporting country, or,

(b)   in the absence of such domestic price, is less than either

    (i)   the highest comparable price for the like product for export to any third country in the ordinary course of trade, or

    (ii)   the cost of production of the product in the country of origin plus a reasonable addition for selling cost and profit.

Due allowance shall be made in each case for differences in conditions and terms of sale, for differences in taxation, and for other differences affecting price comparability.

2.   In order to offset or prevent dumping, a contracting party may levy on any dumped product an anti-dumping duty not greater in amount than the margin of dumping in respect of such product. For the purposes of this Article, the margin of dumping is the price difference determined in accordance with the provisions of paragraph 1.

3.   No countervailing duty shall be levied on any product of the territory of any contracting party imported into the territory of another contracting party in excess of an amount equal to the estimated bounty or subsidy determined to have been granted, directly or indirectly, on the manufacture, production or export of such product in the country of origin or exportation, including any special subsidy to the transportation of a particular product. The term "countervailing duty" shall be understood to mean a special duty levied for the purpose of offsetting any bounty or subsidy bestowed, directly, or indirectly, upon the manufacture, production or export of any merchandise.

4.   No product of the territory of any contracting party imported into the territory of any other contracting party shall be subject to anti-dumping or countervailing duty by reason of the exemption of such product from duties or taxes borne by the like product when destined for consumption in the country of origin or exportation, or by reason of the refund of such duties or taxes.

5.   No product of the territory of any contracting party imported into the territory of any other contracting party shall be subject to both anti-dumping and countervailing duties to compensate for the same situation of dumping or export subsidization.

6.   (a) No contracting party shall levy any anti-dumping or countervailing duty on the importation of any product of the territory of another contracting party unless it determines that the effect of the dumping or subsidization, as the case may be, is such as to cause or threaten material injury to an established domestic industry, or is such as to retard materially the establishment of a domestic industry.

(b)   The CONTRACTING PARTIES may waive the requirement of subparagraph (a) of this paragraph so as to permit a contracting party to levy an anti-dumping or countervailing duty on the importation of any product for the purpose of offsetting dumping or subsidization which causes or threatens material injury to an industry in the territory of another contracting party exporting the product concerned to the territory of the importing contracting party. The CONTRACTING PARTIES shall waive the requirements of subparagraph (a) of this paragraph, so as to permit the levying of a countervailing duty, in cases in which they find that a subsidy is causing or threatening material injury to an industry in the territory of another contracting party exporting the product concerned to the territory of the importing contracting party.

(c) In exceptional circumstances, however, where delay might cause damage which would be difficult to repair, a contracting party may levy a countervailing duty for the purpose referred to in subparagraph (b) of this paragraph without the prior approval of the CONTRACTING PARTIES; *provided* that such action shall be reported immediately to the CONTRACTING PARTIES and that the countervailing duty shall be withdrawn promptly if the CONTRACTING PARTIES disapprove.

7. A system for the stabilization of the domestic price or of the return to domestic producers of a primary commodity, independently of the movements of export prices, which results at times in the sale of the commodity for export at a price lower than the comparable price charged for the like commodity to buyers in the domestic market, shall be presumed not to result in material injury within the meaning of paragraph 6 if it is determined by consultation among the contracting parties substantially interested in the commodity concerned that:

(a) the system has also resulted in the sale of the commodity for export at a price higher than the comparable price charged for the like commodity to buyers in the domestic market, and

(b) the system is so operated, either because of the effective regulation of production, or otherwise, as not to stimulate exports unduly or otherwise seriously prejudice the interests of other contracting parties.

Article VII Valuation for Customs Purposes

1. The contracting parties recognize the validity of the general principles of valuation set forth in the following paragraphs of this Article, and they undertake to give effect to such principles, in respect of all products subject to duties or other charges or restrictions on importation and exportation based upon or regulated in any manner by value. Moreover, they shall, upon a request by another contracting party review the operation of any of their laws or regulations relating to value for customs purposes in the light of these principles. The CONTRACTING PARTIES may request from contracting parties reports on steps taken by them in pursuance of the provisions of this Article.

2. (a) The value for customs purposes of imported merchandise should be based on the actual value of the imported merchandise on which duty is assessed, or of like merchandise, and should not be based on the value of merchandise of national origin or on arbitrary or fictitious values.

(b) "Actual value" should be the price at which, at a time and place determined by the legislation of the country of importation, such or like merchandise is sold or offered for sale in the ordinary course of trade under fully competitive conditions. To the extent to which the price of such or like merchandise is governed by the quantity in a particular transaction, the price to be considered should uniformly be related to either (i) comparable quantities, or (ii) quantities not less favourable to importers than those in which the greater volume of the merchandise is sold in the trade between the countries of exportation and importation.

(c) When the actual value is not ascertainable in accordance with subparagraph (b) of this paragraph, the value for customs purposes should be based on the nearest ascertainable equivalent of such value.

3. The value for customs purposes of any imported product should not include the amount of any internal tax, applicable within the country of origin or export, from which the imported product has been exempted or has been or will be relieved by means of refund.

4. (a) Except as otherwise provided for in this paragraph, where it is necessary for the purposes of paragraph 2 of this Article for a contracting party to convert into its own currency a price expressed in the currency of another country, the conversion rate of exchange to be used shall be based, for each currency involved, on the par value as established pursuant to the Articles of Agreement of the International Monetary Fund or on the rate of exchange recognized by the Fund, or on the par value established in accordance with a special exchange agreement entered into pursuant to Article XV of this Agreement.

(b) Where no such established par value and no such recognized rate of exchange exist, the conversion rate shall reflect effectively the current value of such currency in commercial transactions.

(c) The CONTRACTING PARTIES, in agreement with the International Monetary Fund, shall formulate rules governing the conversion by contracting parties of any foreign currency in respect of which multiple rates of exchange are maintained consistently with the Articles of Agreement of the International Monetary Fund. Any contracting party may apply such rules in respect of such foreign currencies for the purposes of paragraph 2 of this Article as an alternative to the use of par values. Until such rules are adopted by the Contracting Parties, any contracting party may employ, in respect of any such foreign currency, rules of conversion for the purposes of paragraph 2 of this Article which are designed to reflect effectively the value of such foreign currency in commercial transactions.

(d) Nothing in this paragraph shall be construed to require any contracting party to alter the method of converting currencies for customs purposes which is applicable in its territory on the date of this Agreement, if such alteration would have the effect of increasing generally the amounts of duty payable.

5. The bases and methods for determining the value of products subject to duties or other charges or restrictions based upon or regulated in any manner by value should be stable and should be given sufficient publicity to enable traders to estimate, with a reasonable degree of certainty, the value for customs purposes.

Article VIII Fees and Formalities Connected with Importation and Exportation

1. (a) All fees and charges of whatever character (other than import and export duties and other than taxes within the purview of Article III) imposed by contracting parties on or in connection with importation or exportation shall be limited in amount to the approximate cost of services rendered and shall not represent an indirect protection to domestic products or a taxation of imports or exports for fiscal purposes.

(b) The contracting parties recognize the need for reducing the number and diversity of fees and charges referred to in subparagraph (a).

(c) The contracting parties also recognize the need for minimizing the incidence and complexity of import and export formalities and for decreasing and simplifying import and export documentation requirements.

2. A contracting party shall, upon request by another contracting party or by the CONTRACTING PARTIES, review the operation of its laws and regulations in the light of the provisions of this Article.

3. No contracting party shall impose substantial penalties for minor breaches of customs regulations or procedural requirements. In particular, no penalty in respect of any omission or mistake in customs documentation which is easily rectifiable and obviously made without fraudulent intent or gross negligence shall be greater than necessary to serve merely as a warning.

4.   The provisions of this Article shall extend to fees, charges, formalities and requirements imposed by governmental authorities in connection with importation and exportation, including those relating to:

(a)   consular transactions, such as consular invoices and certificates;

(b)   quantitative restrictions;

(c)   licensing;

(d)   exchange control;

(e)   statistical services;

(f)   documents, documentation and certification;

(g)   analysis and inspection; and

(h)   quarantine, sanitation and fumigation.

Article IX Marks of Origin

1.   Each contracting party shall accord to the products of the territories of other contracting parties treatment with regard to marking requirements no less favourable than the treatment accorded to like products of any third country.

2.   The contracting parties recognize that, in adopting and enforcing laws and regulations relating to marks of origin, the difficulties and inconveniences which such measures may cause to the commerce and industry of exporting countries should be reduced to a minimum, due regard being had to the necessity of protecting consumers against fraudulent or misleading indications.

3.   Whenever it is administratively practicable to do so, contracting parties should permit required marks of origin to be affixed at the time of importation.

4.   The laws and regulations of contracting parties relating to the marking of imported products shall be such as to permit compliance without seriously damaging the products, or materially reducing their value, or unreasonably increasing their cost.

5.   As a general rule, no special duty or penalty should be imposed by any contracting party for failure to comply with marking requirements prior to importation unless corrective marking is unreasonably delayed or deceptive marks have been affixed or the required marking has been intentionally omitted.

6.   The contracting parties shall co-operate with each other with a view to preventing the use of trade names in such manner as to misrepresent the true origin of a product, to the detriment of such distinctive regional or geographical names of products of the territory of a contracting party as are protected by its legislation. Each contracting party shall accord full and sympathetic consideration to such requests or representations as may be made by any other contracting party regarding the application of the undertaking set forth in the preceding sentence to names of products which have been communicated to it by the other contracting party.

Article X Publication and Administration of Trade Regulations

1.   Laws, regulations, judicial decisions and administrative rulings of general application, made effective by any contracting party, pertaining to the classification or the valuation of products for customs purposes, or to rates of duty, taxes or other charges, or to requirements, restrictions or prohibitions on imports or exports or on the transfer of payments therefor, or affecting their sale, distribution, transportation, insurance, warehousing inspection, exhibition, processing, mixing or other use, shall be published promptly in such a manner as to enable governments and traders to become acquainted with them. Agreements affecting international trade policy which are in force between the government or a governmental agency of any contracting party and the government or governmental agency of any other contracting party shall also be published. The provisions of this paragraph shall not require any contracting party to disclose confidential information which would impede law enforcement or otherwise be contrary to the public

interest or would prejudice the legitimate commercial interests of particular enterprises, public or private.

2.   No measure of general application taken by any contracting party effecting an advance in a rate of duty or other charge on imports under an established and uniform practice, or imposing a new or more burdensome requirement, restriction or prohibition on imports, or on the transfer of payments therefor, shall be enforced before such measure has been officially published.

3.   (a) Each contracting party shall administer in a uniform, impartial and reasonable manner all its laws, regulations, decisions and rulings of the kind described in paragraph 1 of this Article.

(b) Each contracting party shall maintain, or institute as soon as practicable, judicial, arbitral or administrative tribunals or procedures for the purpose, *inter alia*, of the prompt review and correction of administrative action relating to customs matters. Such tribunals or procedures shall be independent of the agencies entrusted with administrative enforcement and their decisions shall be implemented by, and shall govern the practice of, such agencies unless an appeal is lodged with a court or tribunal of superior jurisdiction within the time prescribed for appeals to be lodged by importers; *provided* that the central administration of such agency may take steps to obtain a review of the matter in another proceeding if there is good cause to believe that the decision is inconsistent with established principles of law or the actual facts.

(c) The provisions of subparagraph (b) of this paragraph shall not require the elimination or substitution of procedures in force in the territory of a contracting party on the date of this Agreement which in fact provide for an objective and impartial review of administrative action even though such procedures are not fully or formally independent of the agencies entrusted with administrative enforcement. Any contracting party employing such procedures shall, upon request, furnish the CONTRACTING PARTIES with full information thereon in order that they may determine whether such procedures conform to the requirements of this subparagraph.

Article XI General Elimination of Quantitative Restrictions

1.   No prohibitions or restrictions other than duties, taxes or other charges, whether made effective through quotas, import or export licences or other measures, shall be instituted or maintained by any contracting party on the importation of any product of the territory of any other contracting party or on the exportation or sale for export of any product destined for the territory of any other contracting party.

2.   The provisions of paragraph 1 of this Article shall not extend to the following:

(a) Export prohibitions or restrictions temporarily applied to prevent or relieve critical shortages of foodstuffs or other products essential to the exporting contracting party;

(b) Import and export prohibitions or restrictions necessary to the application of standards or regulations for the classification, grading or marketing of commodities in international trade;

(c) Import restrictions on any agricultural or fisheries product, imported in any form, necessary to the enforcement of governmental measures which operate:

   (i)   to restrict the quantities of the like domestic product permitted to be marketed or produced, or, if there is no substantial domestic production of the like product, of a domestic product for which the imported product can be directly substituted; or

   (ii) to remove a temporary surplus of the like domestic product, or, if there is no substantial domestic production of the like product, of a domestic product for which the imported product can be directly substituted, by making the surplus available to certain groups of domestic consumers free of charge or at prices below the current market level; or

(iii) to restrict the quantities permitted to be produced of any animal product the production of which is directly dependent, wholly or mainly, on the imported commodity, if
the domestic production of that commodity is relatively negligible.

Any contracting party applying restrictions on the importation of any product pursuant to subparagraph (c) of this paragraph shall give public notice of the total quantity or value of the
product permitted to be imported during a specified future period and of any change in such
quantity or value. Moreover, any restrictions applied under (i) above shall not be such as will
reduce the total of imports relative to the total of domestic production, as compared with the
proportion which might reasonably be expected to rule between the two in the absence of
restrictions. In determining this proportion, the contracting party shall pay due regard to the
proportion prevailing during a previous representative period and to any special factors which
may have affected or may be affecting the trade in the product concerned.

Article XII Restrictions to Safeguard the Balance of Payments

1. Notwithstanding the provisions of paragraph 1 of Article XI, any contracting party, in order
to safeguard its external financial position and its balance of payments, may restrict the quantity
or value of merchandise permitted to be imported, subject to the provisions of the following
paragraphs of this Article.

2. (a) Import restrictions instituted, maintained or intensified by a contracting party under this
Article shall not exceed those necessary:

(i) to forestall the imminent threat of, or to stop, a serious decline in its monetary reserves;
or

(ii) in the case of a contracting party with very low monetary reserves, to achieve a reasonable rate of increase in its reserves.

Due regard shall be paid in either case to any special factors which may be affecting the
reserves of such contracting party or its need for reserves, including, where special external
credits or other resources are available to it, the need to provide for the appropriate use of
such credits or resources.

(b) Contracting parties applying restrictions under sub-paragraph (a) of this paragraph shall progressively relax them as such conditions improve, maintaining them only to the extent that
the conditions specified in that sub-paragraph still justify their application. They shall eliminate the restrictions when conditions would no longer justify their institution or maintenance under that subparagraph.

3. (a) Contracting parties undertake, in carrying out their domestic policies, to pay due regard
to the need for maintaining or restoring equilibrium in their balance of payments on a sound
and lasting basis and to the desirability of avoiding an uneconomic employment of productive resources. They recognize that, in order to achieve these ends, it is desirable so far as
possible to adopt measures which expand rather than contract international trade.

(b) Contracting parties applying restrictions under this Article may determine the incidence of
the restrictions on imports of different products or classes of products in such a way as to
give priority to the importation of those products which are more essential.

(c) Contracting parties applying restrictions under this Article undertake:

(i) to avoid unnecessary damage to the commercial or economic interests of any other
contracting party;

(ii) not to apply restrictions so as to prevent unreasonably the importation of any description of goods in minimum commercial quantities the exclusion of which would impair
regular channels of trade; and

(iii) not to apply restrictions which would prevent the importations of commercial samples or prevent compliance with patent, trade mark, copyright, or similar procedures.

(d) The contracting parties recognize that, as a result of domestic policies directed towards the achievement and maintenance of full and productive employment or towards the development of economic resources, a contracting party may experience a high level of demand for imports involving a threat to its monetary reserves of the sort referred to in paragraph 2 (a) of this Article. Accordingly, a contracting party otherwise complying with the provisions of this Article shall not be required to withdraw or modify restrictions on the ground that a change in those policies would render unnecessary restrictions which it is applying under this Article.

4.   (a) Any contracting party applying new restrictions or raising the general level of its existing restrictions by a substantial intensification of the measures applied under this Article shall immediately after instituting or intensifying such restrictions (or, in circumstances in which prior consultation is practicable, before doing so) consult with the CONTRACTING PARTIES as to the nature of its balance of payments difficulties, alternative corrective measures which may be available, and the possible effect of the restrictions on the economies of other contracting parties.

(b) On a date to be determined by them, the CONTRACTING PARTIES shall review all restrictions still applied under this Article on that date. Beginning one year after that date, contracting parties applying import restrictions under this Article shall enter into consultations of the type provided for in subparagraph (a) of this paragraph with the CONTRACTING PARTIES annually.

(c) (i) If, in the course of consultations with a contracting party under subparagraph (a) or (b) above, the CONTRACTING PARTIES find that the restrictions are not consistent with provisions of this Article or with those of Article XIII (subject to the provisions of Article XIV), they shall indicate the nature of the inconsistency and may advise that the restrictions be suitably modified.

     (ii) If, however, as a result of the consultations, the CONTRACTING PARTIES determine that the restrictions are being applied in a manner involving an inconsistency of a serious nature with the provisions of this Article or with those of Article XIII (subject to the provisions of Article XIV) and that damage to the trade of any contracting party is caused or threatened thereby, they shall so inform the contracting party applying the restrictions and shall make appropriate recommendations for securing conformity with such provisions within the specified period of time. If such contracting party does not comply with these recommendations within the specified period, the CONTRACTING PARTIES may release any contracting party the trade of which is adversely affected by the restrictions from such obligations under this Agreement towards the contracting party applying the restrictions as they determine to be appropriate in the circumstances.

(d) The CONTRACTING PARTIES shall invite any contracting party which is applying restrictions under this Article to enter into consultations with them at the request of any contracting party which can establish a *prima facie* case that the restrictions are inconsistent with the provisions of this Article or with those of Article XIII (subject to the provisions of Article XIV) and that its trade is adversely affected thereby. However, no such invitation shall be issued unless the CONTRACTING PARTIES have ascertained that direct discussions between the contracting parties concerned have not been successful. If, as a result of the consultations with the CONTRACTING PARTIES, no agreement is reached and they determine that the restrictions are being applied inconsistently with such provisions, and that damage to the trade of the contracting party initiating the procedure is caused or threatened thereby, they shall recommend the withdrawal or modification of the restrictions. If the restrictions are not withdrawn or modified within such time as the CONTRACTING PARTIES may prescribe, they may release the contracting party initiating the procedure from such obligations under this Agreement towards the contracting party applying the restrictions as they determine to be appropriate in the circumstances.

(e) In proceeding under this paragraph, the CONTRACTING PARTIES shall have due regard to any special external factors adversely affecting the export trade of the contracting party applying the restrictions.

(f) Determinations under this paragraph shall be rendered expeditiously and, if possible, within sixty days of the initiation of the consultations.

5.   If there is a persistent and widespread application of import restrictions under this Article, indicating the existence of a general disequilibrium which is restricting international trade, the CONTRACTING PARTIES shall initiate discussions to consider whether other measures might be taken, either by those contracting parties the balance of payments of which are under pressure or by those the balance of payments of which are tending to be exceptionally favourable, or by any appropriate intergovernmental organization, to remove the underlying causes of the disequilibrium. On the invitation of the CONTRACTING PARTIES, contracting parties shall participate in such discussions.

Article XIII Non-Discriminatory Administration of Quantitative Restrictions

1.   No prohibition or restriction shall be applied by any contracting party on the importation of any product of the territory of any other contracting party or on the exportation of any product destined for the territory of any other contracting party, unless the importation of the like product of all third countries or the exportation of the like product to all third countries is similarly prohibited or restricted.

2.   In applying import restrictions to any product, contracting parties shall aim at a distribution of trade in such product approaching as closely as possible the shares which the various contracting parties might be expected to obtain in the absence of such restrictions and to this end shall observe the following provisions:

(a) Wherever practicable, quotas representing the total amount of permitted imports (whether allocated among supplying countries or not) shall be fixed, and notice given of their amount in accordance with paragraph 3 (b) of this Article;

(b) In cases in which quotas are not practicable, the restrictions may be applied by means of import licences or permits without a quota;

(c) Contracting parties shall not, except for purposes of operating quotas allocated in accordance with subparagraph (d) of this paragraph, require that import licences or permits be utilized for the importation of the product concerned from a particular country or source;

(d) In cases in which a quota is allocated among supplying countries the contracting party applying the restrictions may seek agreement with respect to the allocation of shares in the quota with all other contracting parties having a substantial interest in supplying the product concerned. In cases in which this method is not reasonably practicable, the contracting party concerned shall allot to contracting parties having a substantial interest in supplying the product shares based upon the proportions, supplied by such contracting parties during a previous representative period, of the total quantity or value of imports of the product, due account being taken of any special factors which may have affected or may be affecting the trade in the product. No conditions or formalities shall be imposed which would prevent any contracting party from utilizing fully the share of any such total quantity or value which has been allotted to it, subject to importation being made within any prescribed period to which the quota may relate.

3.   (a) In cases in which import licences are issued in connection with import restrictions, the contracting party applying the restrictions shall provide, upon the request of any contracting

party having an interest in the trade in the product concerned, all relevant information concerning the administration of the restrictions, the import licences granted over a recent period and the distribution of such licences among supplying countries; *provided* that there shall be no obligation to supply information as to the names of importing or supplying enterprises.

(b) In the case of import restrictions involving the fixing of quotas, the contracting party applying the restrictions shall give public notice of the total quantity or value of the product or products which will be permitted to be imported during a specified future period and of any change in such quantity or value. Any supplies of the product in question which were *en route* at the time at which public notice was given shall not be excluded from entry; *provided* that they may be counted so far as practicable, against the quantity permitted to be imported in the period in question, and also, where necessary, against the quantities permitted to be imported in the next following period or periods; and *provided* further that if any contracting party customarily exempts from such restrictions products entered for consumption or withdrawn from warehouse for consumption during a period of thirty days after the day of such public notice, such practice shall be considered full compliance with this subparagraph.

(c) In the case of quotas allocated among supplying countries, the contracting party applying the restrictions shall promptly inform all other contracting parties having an interest in supplying the product concerned of the shares in the quota currently allocated, by quantity or value, to the various supplying countries and shall give public notice thereof.

4. With regard to restrictions applied in accordance with paragraph 2 (d) of this Article or under paragraph 2 (c) of Article XI, the selection of a representative period for any product and the appraisal of any special factors affecting the trade in the product shall be made initially by the contracting party applying the restriction; *provided* that such contracting party shall, upon the request of any other contracting party having a substantial interest in supplying that product or upon the request of the CONTRACTING PARTIES, consult promptly with the other contracting party or the CONTRACTING PARTIES regarding the need for an adjustment of the proportion determined or of the base period selected, or for the reappraisal of the special factors involved, or for the elimination of conditions, formalities or any other provisions established unilaterally relating to the allocation of an adequate quota or its unrestricted utilization.

5. The provisions of this Article shall apply to any tariff quota instituted or maintained by any contracting party, and, in so far as applicable, the principles of this Article shall also extend to export restrictions.

Article XIV Exceptions to the Rule of Non-Discrimination

1. A contracting party which applies restrictions under Article XII or under Section B of Article XVIII may, in the application of such restrictions, deviate from the provisions of Article XIII in a manner having equivalent effect to restrictions on payments and transfers for current international transactions which that contracting party may at that time apply under Article VIII or XIV of the Articles of Agreement of the International Monetary Fund, or under analogous provisions of a special exchange agreement entered into pursuant to paragraph 6 of Article XV.

2. A contracting party which is applying import restrictions under Article XII or under Section B of Article XVIII may, with the consent of the CONTRACTING PARTIES, temporarily deviate from the provisions of Article XIII in respect of a small part of its external trade where the benefits to the contracting party or contracting parties concerned substantially outweigh any injury which may result to the trade of other contracting parties.

3. The provisions of Article XIII shall not preclude a group of territories having a common quota in the International Monetary Fund from applying against imports from other countries, but not among themselves, restrictions in accordance with the provisions of Article XII or of Section B of

Article XVIII on condition that such restrictions are in all other respects consistent with the provisions of Article XIII.

4.   A contracting party applying import restrictions under Article XII or under Section B of Article XVIII shall not be precluded by Articles XI to XV or Section B of Article XVIII of this Agreement from applying measures to direct its exports in such a manner as to increase its earnings of currencies which it can use without deviation from the provisions of Article XIII.

5.   A contracting party shall not be precluded by Articles XI to XV, inclusive, or by Section B of Article XVIII, of this Agreement from applying quantitative restrictions:

(a)   having equivalent effect to exchange restrictions authorized under Section 3 (b) of Article VII of the Articles of Agreement of the International Monetary Fund, or

(b)   under the preferential arrangements provided for in Annex A of this Agreement, pending the outcome of the negotiations referred to therein.

Article XV Exchange Arrangements

1.   The CONTRACTING PARTIES shall seek co-operation with the International Monetary Fund to the end that the CONTRACTING PARTIES and the Fund may pursue a co-ordinated policy with regard to exchange questions within the jurisdiction of the Fund and questions of quantitative restrictions and other trade measures within the jurisdiction of the CONTRACTING PARTIES.

2.   In all cases in which the CONTRACTING PARTIES are called upon to consider or deal with problems concerning monetary reserves, balances of payments or foreign exchange arrangements, they shall consult fully with the International Monetary Fund. In such consultations, the CONTRACTING PARTIES shall accept all findings of statistical and other facts presented by the Fund relating to foreign exchange, monetary reserves and balances of payments, and shall accept the determination of the Fund as to whether action by a contracting party in exchange matters is in accordance with the Articles of Agreement of the International Monetary Fund, or with the terms of a special exchange agreement between that contracting party and the CON-TRACTING PARTIES. The CONTRACTING PARTIES in reaching their final decision in cases involving the criteria set forth in paragraph 2 (a) of Article XII or in paragraph 9 of Article XVIII, shall accept the determination of the Fund as to what constitutes a serious decline in the contracting party's monetary reserves, a very low level of its monetary reserves or a reasonable rate of increase in its monetary reserves, and as to the financial aspects of other matters covered in consultation in such cases.

3.   The CONTRACTING PARTIES shall seek agreement with the Fund regarding procedures for consultation under paragraph 2 of this Article.

4.   Contracting parties shall not, by exchange action, frustrate the intent of the provisions of this Agreement, nor, by trade action, the intent of the provisions of the Articles of Agreement of the International Monetary Fund.

5.   If the CONTRACTING PARTIES consider, at any time, that exchange restrictions on payments and transfers in connection with imports are being applied by a contracting party in a manner inconsistent with the exceptions provided for in this Agreement for quantitative restrictions, they shall report thereon to the Fund.

6.   Any contracting party which is not a member of the Fund shall, within a time to be determined by the CONTRACTING PARTIES after consultation with the Fund, become a member of the Fund, or, failing that, enter into a special exchange agreement with the CONTRACTING PARTIES. A contracting party which ceases to be a member of the Fund shall forthwith enter into a special exchange agreement with the CONTRACTING PARTIES. Any special exchange agreement entered into by a contracting party under this paragraph shall thereupon become part of its obligations under this Agreement.

7. (a) A special exchange agreement between a contracting party and the CONTRACTING PARTIES under paragraph 6 of this Article shall provide to the satisfaction of the CONTRACTING PARTIES that the objectives of this Agreement will not be frustrated as a result of action in exchange matters by the contracting party in question.

(b) The terms of any such agreement shall not impose obligations on the contracting party in exchange matters generally more restrictive than those imposed by the Articles of Agreement of the International Monetary Fund on members of the Fund.

8. A contracting party which is not a member of the Fund shall furnish such information within the general scope of section 5 of Article VIII of the Articles of Agreement of the International Monetary Fund as the CONTRACTING PARTIES may require in order to carry out their functions under this Agreement.

9. Nothing in this Agreement shall preclude:

(a) the use by a contracting party of exchange controls or exchange restrictions in accordance with the Articles of Agreement of the International Monetary Fund or with that contracting party's special exchange agreement with the CONTRACTING PARTIES, or

(b) the use by a contracting party of restrictions or controls in imports or exports, the sole effect of which, additional to the effects permitted under Articles XI, XII, XIII and XIV, is to make effective such exchange controls or exchange restrictions.

Article XVI Subsidies

Section A - Subsidies in General

1. If any contracting party grants or maintains any subsidy, including any form of income or price support, which operates directly or indirectly to increase exports of any product from, or to reduce imports of any product into, its territory, it shall notify the CONTRACTING PARTIES in writing of the extent and nature of the subsidization, of the estimated effect of the subsidization on the quantity of the affected product or products imported into or exported from its territory and of the circumstances making the subsidization necessary. In any case in which it is determined that serious prejudice to the interests of any other contracting party is caused or threatened by any such subsidization, the contracting party granting the subsidy shall, upon request, discuss with the other contracting party or parties concerned, or with the CONTRACTING PARTIES, the possibility of limiting the subsidization.

Section B - Additional Provisions on Export Subsidies

2. The contracting parties recognize that the granting by a contracting party of a subsidy on the export of any product may have harmful effects for other contracting parties, both importing and exporting, may cause undue disturbance to their normal commercial interests, and may hinder the achievement of the objectives of this Agreement.

3. Accordingly, contracting parties should seek to avoid the use of subsidies on the export of primary products. If, however, a contracting party grants directly or indirectly any form of subsidy which operates to increase the export of any primary product from its territory, such subsidy shall not be applied in a manner which results in that contracting party having more than an equitable share of world export trade in that product, account being taken of the shares of the contracting parties in such trade in the product during a previous representative period, and any special factors which may have affected or may be affecting such trade in the product.

4. Further, as from 1 January 1958 or the earliest practicable date thereafter, contracting parties shall cease to grant either directly or indirectly any form of subsidy on the export of any product other than a primary product which subsidy results in the sale of such product for export at a price lower than the comparable price charged for the like product to buyers in the domestic market. Until 31 December 1957 no contracting party shall extend the scope of any such

subsidization beyond that existing on 1 January 1955 by the introduction of new, or the extension of existing, subsidies.

5.   The CONTRACTING PARTIES shall review the operation of the provisions of this Article from time to time with a view to examining its effectiveness, in the light of actual experience, in promoting the objectives of this Agreement and avoiding subsidization seriously prejudicial to the trade or interests of contracting parties.

Article XVII State Trading Enterprises

1.   (a) Each contracting party undertakes that if it establishes or maintains a State enterprise, wherever located, or grants to any enterprise, formally or in effect, exclusive or special privileges, such enterprise shall, in its purchases or sales involving either imports or exports, act in a manner consistent with the general principles of non-discriminatory treatment prescribed in this Agreement for governmental measures affecting imports or exports by private traders.

(b)   The provisions of subparagraph (a) of this paragraph shall be understood to require that such enterprises shall, having due regard to the other provisions of this Agreement, make any such purchases or sales solely in accordance with commercial considerations, including price, quality, availability, marketability, transportation and other conditions of purchase or sale, and shall afford the enterprises of the other contracting parties adequate opportunity, in accordance with customary business practice, to compete for participation in such purchases or sales.

(c)   No contracting party shall prevent any enterprise (whether or not an enterprise described in subparagraph (a) of this paragraph) under its jurisdiction from acting in accordance with the principles of subparagraphs (a) and (b) of this paragraph.

2.   The provisions of paragraph 1 of this Article shall not apply to imports of products for immediate or ultimate consumption in governmental use and not otherwise for resale or use in the production of goods for sale. With respect to such imports, each contracting party shall accord to the trade of the other contracting parties fair and equitable treatment.

3.   The contracting parties recognize that enterprises of the kind described in paragraph 1 (a) of this Article might be operated so as to create serious obstacles to trade; thus negotiations on a reciprocal and mutually advantageous basis designed to limit or reduce such obstacles are of importance to the expansion of international trade.

4.   (a) Contracting parties shall notify the CONTRACTING PARTIES of the products which are imported into or exported from their territories by enterprises of the kind described in paragraph 1 (a) of this Article.

(b)   A contracting party establishing, maintaining or authorizing an import monopoly of a product, which is not the subject of a concession under Article II, shall, on the request of another contracting party having a substantial trade in the product concerned, inform the CONTRACTING PARTIES of the import mark-up on the product during a recent representative period, or, when it is not possible to do so, of the price charged on the resale of the product.

(c)   The CONTRACTING PARTIES may, at the request of a contracting party which has reason to believe that its interest under this Agreement are being adversely affected by the operations of an enterprise of the kind described in paragraph 1 (a), request the contracting party establishing, maintaining or authorizing such enterprise to supply information about its operations related to the carrying out of the provisions of this Agreement.

(d) The provisions of this paragraph shall not require any contracting party to disclose confidential information which would impede law enforcement or otherwise be contrary to the public interest or would prejudice the legitimate commercial interests of particular enterprises.

Article XVIII Governmental Assistance to Economic Development

1.   The contracting parties recognize that the attainment of the objectives of this Agreement will be facilitated by the progressive development of their economies, particularly of those contracting parties the economies of which can only support low standards of living and are in the early stages of development.

2.   The contracting parties recognize further that it may be necessary for those contracting parties, in order to implement programmes and policies of economic development designed to raise the general standard of living of their people, to take protective or other measures affecting imports, and that such measures are justified in so far as they facilitate the attainment of the objectives of this Agreement. They agree, therefore, that those contracting parties should enjoy additional facilities to enable them (a) to maintain sufficient flexibility in their tariff structure to be able to grant the tariff protection required for the establishment of a particular industry and (b) to apply quantitative restrictions for balance of payments purposes in a manner which takes full account of the continued high level of demand for imports likely to be generated by their programmes of economic development.

3.   The contracting parties recognize finally that, with those additional facilities which are provided for in Sections A and B of this Article, the provisions of this Agreement would normally be sufficient to enable contracting parties to meet the requirements of their economic development. They agree, however, that there may be circumstances where no measure consistent with those provisions is practicable to permit a contracting party in the process of economic development to grant the governmental assistance required to promote the establishment of particular industries with a view to raising the general standard of living of its people. Special procedures are laid down in Sections C and D of this Article to deal with those cases.

4.   (a) Consequently, a contracting party, the economy of which can only support low standards of living and is in the early stages of development, shall be free to deviate temporarily from the provisions of the other Articles of this Agreement, as provided in Sections A, B and C of this Article.

(b) A contracting party, the economy of which is in the process of development, but which does not come within the scope of subparagraph (a) above, may submit applications to the CONTRACTING PARTIES under Section D of this Article.

5.   The contracting parties recognize that the export earnings of contracting parties, the economies of which are of the type described in paragraph 4 (a) and (b) above and which depend on exports of a small number of primary commodities, may be seriously reduced by a decline in the sale of such commodities. Accordingly, when the exports of primary commodities by such a contracting party are seriously affected by measures taken by another contracting party, it may have resort to the consultation provisions of Article XXII of this Agreement.

6.   The CONTRACTING PARTIES shall review annually all measures applied pursuant to the provisions of Sections C and D of this Article.

Section A

7.   (a) If a contracting party coming within the scope of paragraph 4 (a) of this Article considers it desirable, in order to promote the establishment of a particular industry with a view to raising the general standard of living of its people, to modify or withdraw a concession included in the appropriate Schedule annexed to this Agreement, it shall notify the CONTRACTING PARTIES to this effect and enter into negotiations with any contracting party with which such concession was initially negotiated, and with any other contracting party determined by the CONTRAC-

TING PARTIES to have a substantial interest therein. If agreement is reached between such contracting parties concerned, they shall be free to modify or withdraw concessions under the appropriate Schedules to this Agreement in order to give effect to such agreement, including any compensatory adjustments involved.

(b) If agreement is not reached within sixty days after the notification provided for in subparagraph (a) above, the contracting party which proposes to modify or withdraw the concession may refer the matter to the CONTRACTING PARTIES which shall promptly examine it. If they find that the contracting party which proposes to modify or withdraw the concession has made every effort to reach an agreement and that the compensatory adjustment offered by it is adequate, that contracting party shall be free to modify or withdraw the concession if, at the same time, it gives effect to the compensatory adjustment. If the CONTRACTING PARTIES do not find that the compensation offered by a contracting party proposing to modify or withdraw the concession is adequate, but find that it has made every reasonable effort to offer adequate compensation, that contracting party shall be free to proceed with such modification or withdrawal. If such action is taken, any other contracting party referred to in subparagraph (a) above shall be free to modify or withdraw substantially equivalent concessions initially negotiated with the contracting party which has taken the action.

Section B

8.   The contracting parties recognize that contracting parties coming within the scope of paragraph 4 (a) of this Article tend, when they are in rapid process of development, to experience balance of payments difficulties arising mainly from efforts to expand their internal markets as well as from the instability in their terms of trade.

9.   In order to safeguard its external financial position and to ensure a level of reserves adequate for the implementation of its programme of economic development, a contracting party coming within the scope of paragraph 4 (a) of this Article may, subject to the provisions of paragraphs 10 to 12, control the general level of its imports by restricting the quantity or value of merchandise permitted to be imported; *provided* that the import restrictions instituted, maintained or intensified shall not exceed those necessary:

(a)   to forestall the threat of, or to stop, a serious decline in its monetary reserves, or

(b)   in the case of a contracting party with inadequate monetary reserves, to achieve a reasonable rate of increase in its reserves.

Due regard shall be paid in either case to any special factors which may be affecting the reserves of the contracting party or its need for reserves, including, where special external credits or other resources are available to it, the need to provide for the appropriate use of such credits or resources.

10. In applying these restrictions, the contracting party may determine their incidence on imports of different products or classes of products in such a way as to give priority to the importation of those products which are more essential in the light of its policy of economic development; *provided* that the restrictions are so applied as to avoid unnecessary damage to the commercial or economic interests of any other contracting party and not to prevent unreasonably the importation of any description of goods in minimum commercial quantities the exclusion of which would impair regular channels of trade; and *provided* further that the restrictions are not so applied as to prevent the importation of commercial samples or to prevent compliance with patent, trade mark, copyright or similar procedures.

11. In carrying out its domestic policies, the contracting party concerned shall pay due regard to the need for restoring equilibrium in its balance of payments on a sound and lasting basis and to the desirability of assuring an economic employment of productive resources. It shall progressively relax any restrictions applied under this Section as conditions improve, maintaining them only to the extent necessary under the terms of paragraph 9 of this Article and shall

eliminate them when conditions no longer justify such maintenance; *provided* that no contracting party shall be required to withdraw or modify restrictions on the ground that a change in its development policy would render unnecessary the restrictions which it is applying under this Section.

12. (a) Any contracting party applying new restrictions or raising the general level of its existing restrictions by a substantial intensification of the measures applied under this Section, shall immediately after instituting or intensifying such restrictions (or, in circumstances in which prior consultation is practicable, before doing so) consult with the CONTRACTING PARTIES as to the nature of its balance of payments difficulties, alternative corrective measures which may be available, and the possible effect of the restrictions on the economies of other contracting parties.

(b) On a date to be determined by them the CONTRACTING PARTIES shall review all restrictions still applied under this Section on that date. Beginning two years after that date, contracting parties applying restrictions under this Section shall enter into consultations of the type provided for in subparagraph (a) above with the CONTRACTING PARTIES at intervals of approximately, but not less than, two years according to a programme to be drawn up each year by the CONTRACTING PARTIES; *provided* that no consultation under this subparagraph shall take place within two years after the conclusion of a consultation of a general nature under any other provision of this paragraph.

(c) (i) If, in the course of consultations with a contracting party under subparagraph (a) or (b) of this paragraph, the CONTRACTING PARTIES find that the restrictions are not consistent with the provisions of this Section or with those of Article XIII (subject to the provisions of Article XIV), they shall indicate the nature of the inconsistency and may advise that the restrictions be suitably modified.

(ii) If, however, as a result of the consultations, the CONTRACTING PARTIES determine that the restrictions are being applied in a manner involving an inconsistency of a serious nature with the provisions of this Section or with those of Article XIII (subject to the provisions of Article XIV) and that damage to the trade of any contracting party is caused or threatened thereby, they shall so inform the contracting party applying the restrictions and shall make appropriate recommendations for securing conformity with such provisions within a specified period. If such contracting party does not comply with these recommendations within the specified period, the CONTRACTING PARTIES may release any contracting party the trade of which is adversely affected by the restrictions from such obligations under this Agreement towards the contracting party applying the restrictions as they determine to be appropriate in the circumstances.

(d) The CONTRACTING PARTIES shall invite any contracting party which is applying restrictions under this Section to enter into consultations with them at the request of any contracting party which can establish a *prima facie* case that the restrictions are inconsistent with the provisions of this Section or with those of Article XIII (subject to the provisions of Article XIV) and that its trade is adversely affected thereby. However, no such invitation shall be issued unless the CONTRACTING PARTIES have ascertained that direct discussions between the contracting parties concerned have not been successful. If, as a result of the consultations with the CONTRACTING PARTIES no agreement is reached and they determine that the restrictions are being applied inconsistently with such provisions, and that damage to the trade of the contracting party initiating the procedure is caused or threatened thereby, they shall recommend the withdrawal or modification of the restrictions. If the restrictions are not withdrawn or modified within such time as the CONTRACTING PARTIES may prescribe, they may release the contracting party initiating the procedure from such obligations under this Agreement towards the contracting party applying the restrictions as they determine to be appropriate in the circumstances.

(e) If a contracting party against which action has been taken in accordance with the last sentence of subparagraph (c) (ii) or (d) of this paragraph, finds that the release of obligations authorized by the CONTRACTING PARTIES adversely affects the operation of its programme and policy of economic development, it shall be free, not later than sixty days after such action is taken, to give written notice to the Executive Secretary[6] to the Contracting Parties of its intention to withdraw from this Agreement and such withdrawal shall take effect on the sixtieth day following the day on which the notice is received by him.

(f) In proceeding under this paragraph, the CONTRACTING PARTIES shall have due regard to the factors referred to in paragraph 2 of this Article. Determinations under this paragraph shall be rendered expeditiously and, if possible, within sixty days of the initiation of the consultations.

Section C

13.   If a contracting party coming within the scope of paragraph 4 (a) of this Article finds that governmental assistance is required to promote the establishment of a particular industry with a view to raising the general standard of living of its people, but that no measure consistent with the other provisions of this Agreement is practicable to achieve that objective, it may have recourse to the provisions and procedures set out in this Section.

14. The contracting party concerned shall notify the CONTRACTING PARTIES of the special difficulties which it meets in the achievement of the objective outlined in paragraph 13 of this Article and shall indicate the specific measure affecting imports which it proposes to introduce in order to remedy these difficulties. It shall not introduce that measure before the expiration of the time-limit laid down in paragraph 15 or 17, as the case may be, or if the measure affects imports of a product which is the subject of a concession included in the appropriate Schedule annexed to this Agreement, unless it has secured the concurrence of the CONTRACTING PARTIES in accordance with provisions of paragraph 18; *provided* that, if the industry receiving assistance has already started production, the contracting party may, after informing the CONTRACTING PARTIES, take such measures as may be necessary to prevent, during that period, imports of the product or products concerned from increasing substantially above a normal level.

15. If, within thirty days of the notification of the measure, the CONTRACTING PARTIES do not request the contracting party concerned to consult with them, that contracting party shall be free to deviate from the relevant provisions of the other Articles of this Agreement to the extent necessary to apply the proposed measure.

16. If it is requested by the CONTRACTING PARTIES to do so, the contracting party concerned shall consult with them as to the purpose of the proposed measure, as to alternative measures which may be available under this Agreement, and as to the possible effect of the measure proposed on the commercial and economic interests of other contracting parties. If, as a result of such consultation, the CONTRACTING PARTIES agree that there is no measure consistent with the other provisions of this Agreement which is practicable in order to achieve the objective outlined in paragraph 13 of this Article, and concur in the proposed measure, the contracting party concerned shall be released from its obligations under the relevant provisions of the other Articles of this Agreement to the extent necessary to apply that measure.

17. If, within ninety days after the date of the notification of the proposed measure under paragraph 14 of this Article, the CONTRACTING PARTIES have not concurred in such measure, the contracting party concerned may introduce the measure proposed after informing the CONTRACTING PARTIES.

---

6   By the Decision of 23 March 1965, the CONTRACTING PARTIES changed the title of the head of the GATT secretariat from "Executive Secretary" to "Director-General".

18. If the proposed measure affects a product which is the subject of a concession included in the appropriate Schedule annexed to this Agreement, the contracting party concerned shall enter into consultations with any other contracting party with which the concession was initially negotiated, and with any other contracting party determined by the CONTRACTING PARTIES to have a substantial interest therein. The CONTRACTING PARTIES shall concur in the measure if they agree that there is no measure consistent with the other provisions of this Agreement which is practicable in order to achieve the objective set forth in paragraph 13 of this Article, and if they are satisfied:

(a) that agreement has been reached with such other contracting parties as a result of the consultations referred to above, or

(b) if no such agreement has been reached within sixty days after the notification provided for in paragraph 14 has been received by the CONTRACTING PARTIES, that the contracting party having recourse to this Section has made all reasonable efforts to reach an agreement and that the interests of other contracting parties are adequately safeguarded.

The contracting party having recourse to this Section shall thereupon be released from its obligations under the relevant provisions of the other Articles of this Agreement to the extent necessary to permit it to apply the measure.

19. If a proposed measure of the type described in paragraph 13 of this Article concerns an industry the establishment of which has in the initial period been facilitated by incidental protection afforded by restrictions imposed by the contracting party concerned for balance of payments purposes under the relevant provisions of this Agreement, that contracting party may resort to the provisions and procedures of this Section; *provided* that it shall not apply the proposed measure without the concurrence of the CONTRACTING PARTIES.

20. Nothing in the preceding paragraphs of this Section shall authorize any deviation from the provisions of Articles I, II and XIII of this Agreement. The provisos to paragraph 10 of this Article shall also be applicable to any restriction under this Section.

21. At any time while a measure is being applied under paragraph 17 of this Article any contracting party substantially affected by it may suspend the application to the trade of the contracting party having recourse to this Section of such substantially equivalent concessions or other obligations under this Agreement the suspension of which the CONTRACTING PARTIES do not disapprove; *provided* that sixty days' notice of such suspension is given to the CONTRACTING PARTIES not later than six months after the measure has been introduced or changed substantially to the detriment of the contracting party affected. Any such contracting party shall afford adequate opportunity for consultation in accordance with the provisions of Article XXII of this Agreement.

Section D

22. A contracting party coming within the scope of subparagraph 4 (b) of this Article desiring, in the interest of the development of its economy, to introduce a measure of the type described in paragraph 13 of this Article in respect of the establishment of a particular industry may apply to the CONTRACTING PARTIES for approval of such measure. The CONTRACTING PARTIES shall promptly consult with such contracting party and shall, in making their decision, be guided by the considerations set out in paragraph 16. If the CONTRACTING PARTIES concur in the proposed measure the contracting party concerned shall be released from its obligations under the relevant provisions of the other Articles of this Agreement to the extent necessary to permit it to apply the measure. If the proposed measure affects a product which is the subject of a concession included in the appropriate Schedule annexed to this Agreement, the provisions of paragraph 18 shall apply.

23. Any measure applied under this Section shall comply with the provisions of paragraph 20 of this Article.

Article XIX Emergency Action on Imports of Particular Products

1. (a) If, as a result of unforeseen developments and of the effect of the obligations incurred by a contracting party under this Agreement, including tariff concessions, any product is being imported into the territory of that contracting party in such increased quantities and under such conditions as to cause or threaten serious injury to domestic producers in that territory of like or directly competitive products, the contracting party shall be free, in respect of such product, and to the extent and for such time as may be necessary to prevent or remedy such injury, to suspend the obligation in whole or in part or to withdraw or modify the concession.

(b) If any product, which is the subject of a concession with respect to a preference, is being imported into the territory of a contracting party in the circumstances set forth in subparagraph (a) of this paragraph, so as to cause or threaten serious injury to domestic producers of like or directly competitive products in the territory of a contracting party which receives or received such preference, the importing contracting party shall be free, if that other contracting party so requests, to suspend the relevant obligation in whole or in part or to withdraw or modify the concession in respect of the product, to the extent and for such time as may be necessary to prevent or remedy such injury.

2. Before any contracting party shall take action pursuant to the provisions of paragraph 1 of this Article, it shall give notice in writing to the CONTRACTING PARTIES as far in advance as may be practicable and shall afford the CONTRACTING PARTIES and those contracting parties having a substantial interest as exporters of the product concerned an opportunity to consult with it in respect of the proposed action. When such notice is given in relation to a concession with respect to a preference, the notice shall name the contracting party which has requested the action. In critical circumstances, where delay would cause damage which it would be difficult to repair, action under paragraph 1 of this Article may be taken provisionally without prior consultation, on the condition that consultation shall be effected immediately after taking such action.

3. (a) If agreement among the interested contracting parties with respect to the action is not reached, the contracting party which proposes to take or continue the action shall, nevertheless, be free to do so, and if such action is taken or continued, the affected contracting parties shall then be free, not later than ninety days after such action is taken, to suspend, upon the expiration of thirty days from the day on which written notice of such suspension is received by the CONTRACTING PARTIES, the application to the trade of the contracting party taking such action, or, in the case envisaged in paragraph 1 (b) of this Article, to the trade of the contracting party requesting such action, of such substantially equivalent concessions or other obligations under this Agreement the suspension of which the CONTRACTING PARTIES do not disapprove.

(b) Notwithstanding the provisions of subparagraph (a) of this paragraph, where action is taken under paragraph 2 of this Article without prior consultation and causes or threatens serious injury in the territory of a contracting party to the domestic producers of products affected by the action, that contracting party shall, where delay would cause damage difficult to repair, be free to suspend, upon the taking of the action and throughout the period of consultation, such concessions or other obligations as may be necessary to prevent or remedy the injury.

Article XX General Exceptions

Subject to the requirement that such measures are not applied in a manner which would cons-titute a means of arbitrary or unjustifiable discrimination between countries where the same conditions prevail, or a disguised restriction on international trade, nothing in this Agreement shall be construed to prevent the adoption or enforcement by any contracting party of measures:

(a) necessary to protect public morals;

(b) necessary to protect human, animal or plant life or health;

(c) relating to the importations or exportations of gold or silver;

(d) necessary to secure compliance with laws or regulations which are not inconsistent with the provisions of this Agreement, including those relating to customs enforcement, the enforce-ment of monopolies operated under paragraph 4 of Article II and Article XVII, the protection of patents, trade marks and copyrights, and the prevention of deceptive practices;

(e) relating to the products of prison labour;

(f) imposed for the protection of national treasures of artistic, historic or archaeological value;

(g) relating to the conservation of exhaustible natural resources if such measures are made effective in conjunction with restrictions on domestic production or consumption;

(h) undertaken in pursuance of obligations under any intergovernmental commodity agree-ment which conforms to criteria submitted to the CONTRACTING PARTIES and not dis-approved by them or which is itself so submitted and not so disapproved;

(i) involving restrictions on exports of domestic materials necessary to ensure essential quan-tities of such materials to a domestic processing industry during periods when the domestic price of such materials is held below the world price as part of a governmental stabilization plan; *provided* that such restrictions shall not operate to increase the exports of or the protection afforded to such domestic industry, and shall not depart from the provisions of this Agreement relating to non-discrimination;

(j) essential to the acquisition or distribution of products in general or local short supply; *provided* that any such measures shall be consistent with the principle that all contracting parties are entitled to an equitable share of the international supply of such products, and that any such measures, which are inconsistent with the other provisions of the Agreement shall be discontinued as soon as the conditions giving rise to them have ceased to exist. The CONTRACTING PARTIES shall review the need for this sub-paragraph not later than 30 June 1960.

Article XXI Security Exceptions

Nothing in this Agreement shall be construed

(a) to require any contracting party to furnish any information the disclosure of which it considers contrary to its essential security interests; or

(b) to prevent any contracting party from taking any action which it considers necessary for the protection of its essential security interests

    (i) relating to fissionable materials or the materials from which they are derived;

    (ii) relating to the traffic in arms, ammunition and implements of war and to such traffic in other goods and materials as is carried on directly or indirectly for the purpose of supplying a military establishment;

    (iii) taken in time of war or other emergency in international relations; or

(c) to prevent any contracting party from taking any action in pursuance of its obligations under the United Nations Charter for the maintenance of international peace and security.

Article XXII Consultation

1.   Each contracting party shall accord sympathetic consideration to, and shall afford adequate opportunity for consultation regarding, such representations as may be made by another contracting party with respect to any matter affecting the operation of this Agreement.

2.   The CONTRACTING PARTIES may, at the request of a contracting party, consult with any contracting party or parties in respect of any matter for which it has not been possible to find a satisfactory solution through consultation under paragraph 1.

Article XXIII Nullification or Impairment

1.   If any contracting party should consider that any benefit accruing to it directly or indirectly under this Agreement is being nullified or impaired or that the attainment of any objective of the Agreement is being impeded as the result of

(a)   the failure of another contracting party to carry out its obligations under this Agreement, or

(b)   the application by another contracting party of any measure, whether or not it conflicts with the provisions of this Agreement, or

(c)   the existence of any other situation,

the contracting party may, with a view to the satisfactory adjustment of the matter, make written representations or proposals to the other contracting party or parties which it considers to be concerned. Any contracting party thus approached shall give sympathetic consideration to the representations or proposals made to it.

2.   If no satisfactory adjustment is effected between the contracting parties concerned within a reasonable time, or if the difficulty is of the type described in paragraph 1 (c) of this Article, the matter may be referred to the CONTRACTING PARTIES. The CONTRACTING PARTIES shall promptly investigate any matter so referred to them and shall make appropriate recommendations to the contracting parties which they consider to be concerned, or give a ruling on the matter, as appropriate. The CONTRACTING PARTIES may consult with contracting parties, with the Economic and Social Council of the United Nations and with any appropriate intergovernmental organization in cases where they consider such consultation necessary. If the CONTRACTING PARTIES consider that the circumstances are serious enough to justify such action, they may authorize a contracting party or parties to suspend the application to any other contracting party or parties of such concessions or other obligations under this Agreement as they determine to be appropriate in the circumstances. If the application to any contracting party of any concession or other obligation is in fact suspended, that contracting party shall then be free, not later than sixty days after such action is taken, to give written notice to the Executive Secretary[7] to the Contracting Parties of its intention to withdraw from this Agreement and such withdrawal shall take effect upon the sixtieth day following the day on which such notice is received by him.

---

7   By the Decision of 23 March 1965, the CONTRACTING PARTIES changed the title of the head of the GATT secretariat from "Executive Secretary" to "Director-General".

PART III

Article XXIV Territorial Application - Frontier Traffic - Customs Unions and Free-Trade Areas

1.   The provisions of this Agreement shall apply to the metropolitan customs territories of the contracting parties and to any other customs territories in respect of which this Agreement has been accepted under Article XXVI or is being applied under Article XXXIII or pursuant to the Protocol of Provisional Application. Each such customs territory shall, exclusively for the purposes of the territorial application of this Agreement, be treated as though it were a contracting party; *provided* that the provisions of this paragraph shall not be construed to create any rights or obligations as between two or more customs territories in respect of which this Agreement has been accepted under Article XXVI or is being applied under Article XXXIII or pursuant to the Protocol of Provisional Application by a single contracting party.

2.   For the purposes of this Agreement a customs territory shall be understood to mean any territory with respect to which separate tariffs or other regulations of commerce are maintained for a substantial part of the trade of such territory with other territories.

3.   The provisions of this Agreement shall not be construed to prevent:

(a)   Advantages accorded by any contracting party to adjacent countries in order to facilitate frontier traffic;

(b)   Advantages accorded to the trade with the Free Territory of Trieste by countries contiguous to that territory, provided that such advantages are not in conflict with the Treaties of Peace arising out of the Second World War.

4.   The contracting parties recognize the desirability of increasing freedom of trade by the development, through voluntary agreements, of closer integration between the economies of the countries parties to such agreements. They also recognize that the purpose of a customs union or of a free-trade area should be to facilitate trade between the constituent territories and not to raise barriers to the trade of other contracting parties with such territories.

5.   Accordingly, the provisions of this Agreement shall not prevent, as between the territories of contracting parties, the formation of a customs union or of a free-trade area or the adoption of an interim agreement necessary for the formation of a customs union or of a free-trade area; *provided* that:

(a)   with respect to a customs union, or an interim agreement leading to a formation of a customs union, the duties and other regulations of commerce imposed at the institution of any such union or interim agreement in respect of trade with contracting parties not parties to such union or agreement shall not on the whole be higher or more restrictive than the general incidence of the duties and regulations of commerce applicable in the constituent territories prior to the formation of such union or the adoption of such interim agreement, as the case may be;

(b)   with respect to a free-trade area, or an interim agreement leading to the formation of a free-trade area, the duties and other regulations of commerce maintained in each of the constituent territories and applicable at the formation of such free- trade area or the adoption of such interim agreement to the trade of contracting parties not included in such area or not parties to such agreement shall not be higher or more restrictive than the corresponding duties and other regulations of commerce existing in the same constituent territories prior to the formation of the free-trade area, or interim agreement as the case may be; and

(c)   any interim agreement referred to in subparagraphs (a) and (b) shall include a plan and schedule for the formation of such a customs union or of such a free-trade area within a reasonable length of time.

6.   If, in fulfilling the requirements of subparagraph 5 (a), a contracting party proposes to increase any rate of duty inconsistently with the provisions of Article II, the procedure set forth in Article XXVIII shall apply. In providing for compensatory adjustment, due account shall be taken of the compensation already afforded by the reduction brought about in the corresponding duty of the other constituents of the union.

7.   (a) Any contracting party deciding to enter into a customs union or free-trade area, or an interim agreement leading to the formation of such a union or area, shall promptly notify the CONTRACTING PARTIES and shall make available to them such information regarding the proposed union or area as will enable them to make such reports and recommendations to contracting parties as they may deem appropriate.

(b)   If, after having studied the plan and schedule included in an interim agreement referred to in paragraph 5 in consultation with the parties to that agreement and taking due account of the information made available in accordance with the provisions of subparagraph (a), the CONTRACTING PARTIES find that such agreement is not likely to result in the formation of a customs union or of a free-trade area within the period contemplated by the parties to the agreement or that such period is not a reasonable one, the CONTRACTING PARTIES shall make recommendations to the parties to the agreement. The parties shall not maintain or put into force, as the case may be, such agreement if they are not prepared to modify it in accordance with these recommendations.

(c)   Any substantial change in the plan or schedule referred to in paragraph 5 (c) shall be communicated to the CONTRACTING PARTIES, which may request the contracting parties concerned to consult with them if the change seems likely to jeopardize or delay unduly the formation of the customs union or of the free-trade area.

8.   For the purposes of this Agreement:

(a)   A customs union shall be understood to mean the substitution of a single customs territory for two or more customs territories, so that

(i)   duties and other restrictive regulations of commerce (except, where necessary, those permitted under Articles XI, XII, XIII, XIV, XV and XX) are eliminated with respect to substantially all the trade between the constituent territories of the union or at least with respect to substantially all the trade in products originating in such territories, and,

(ii)   subject to the provisions of paragraph 9, substantially the same duties and other regulations of commerce are applied by each of the members of the union to the trade of territories not included in the union;

(b)   A free-trade area shall be understood to mean a group of two or more customs territories in which the duties and other restrictive regulations of commerce (except, where necessary, those permitted under Articles XI, XII, XIII, XIV, XV and XX) are eliminated on substantially all the trade between the constituent territories in products originating in such territories.

9.   The preferences referred to in paragraph 2 of Article I shall not be affected by the formation of a customs union or of a free-trade area but may be eliminated or adjusted by means of negotiations with contracting parties affected. This procedure of negotiations with affected contracting parties shall, in particular, apply to the elimination of preferences required to conform with the provisions of paragraph 8 (a)(i) and paragraph 8 (b).

10.   The CONTRACTING PARTIES may by a two-thirds majority approve proposals which do not fully comply with the requirements of paragraphs 5 to 9 inclusive, provided that such proposals lead to the formation of a customs union or a free-trade area in the sense of this Article.

11.   Taking into account the exceptional circumstances arising out of the establishment of India and Pakistan as independent States and recognizing the fact that they have long constituted an economic unit, the contracting parties agree that the provisions of this Agreement shall not

prevent the two countries from entering into special arrangements with respect to the trade between them, pending the establishment of their mutual trade relations on a definitive basis.

12. Each contracting party shall take such reasonable measures as may be available to it to ensure observance of the provisions of this Agreement by the regional and local governments and authorities within its territories.

Article XXV Joint Action by the Contracting Parties

1.   Representatives of the contracting parties shall meet from time to time for the purpose of giving effect to those provisions of this Agreement which involve joint action and, generally, with a view to facilitating the operation and furthering the objectives of this Agreement. Wherever reference is made in this Agreement to the contracting parties acting jointly they are designated as the CONTRACTING PARTIES.

2.   The Secretary-General of the United Nations is requested to convene the first meeting of the CONTRACTING PARTIES, which shall take place not later than March 1, 1948.

3.   Each contracting party shall be entitled to have one vote at all meetings of the CONTRACTING PARTIES.

4.   Except as otherwise provided for in this Agreement, decisions of the CONTRACTING PARTIES shall be taken by a majority of the votes cast.

5.   In exceptional circumstances not elsewhere provided for in this Agreement, the CONTRACTING PARTIES may waive an obligation imposed upon a contracting party by this Agreement; *Provided* that any such decision shall be approved by a two-thirds majority of the votes cast and that such majority shall comprise more than half of the contracting parties. The CONTRACTING PARTIES may also by such a vote

(i)   define certain categories of exceptional circumstances to which other voting requirements shall apply for the waiver of obligations, and

(ii) prescribe such criteria as may be necessary for the application of this paragraph.

Article XXVI Acceptance, Entry into Force and Registration

1.   The date of this Agreement shall be 30 October 1947.

2.   This Agreement shall be open for acceptance by any contracting party which, on 1 March 1955, was a contracting party or was negotiating with a view to accession to this Agreement.

3.   This Agreement, done in a single English original and a single French original, both texts authentic, shall be deposited with the Secretary-General of the United Nations, who shall furnish certified copies thereof to all interested governments.

4.   Each government accepting this Agreement shall deposit an instrument of acceptance with the Executive Secretary[8] to the Contracting Parties, who will inform all interested governments of the date of deposit of each instrument of acceptance and of the day on which this Agreement enters into force under paragraph 6 of this Article.

5.   (a)   Each government accepting this Agreement does so in respect of its metropolitan territory and of the other territories for which it has international responsibility, except such separate customs territories as it shall notify to the Executive Secretary[8] to the CONTRACTING PARTIES at the time of its own acceptance.

(b) Any government, which has so notified the Executive Secretary[8] under the exceptions in subparagraph (a) of this paragraph, may at any time give notice to the Executive Secretary[8] that its acceptance shall be effective in respect of any separate customs territory or territories

---

8   By the Decision of 23 March 1965, the CONTRACTING PARTIES changed the title of the head of the GATT secretariat from "Executive Secretary" to "Director-General".

so excepted and such notice shall take effect on the thirtieth day following the day on which it is received by the Executive Secretary.[8]

(c) If any of the customs territories, in respect of which a contracting party has accepted this Agreement, possesses or acquires full autonomy in the conduct of its external commercial relations and of the other matters provided for in this Agreement, such territory shall, upon sponsorship through a declaration by the responsible contracting party establishing the above-mentioned fact, be deemed to be a contracting party.

6.   This Agreement shall enter into force, as among the governments which have accepted it, on the thirtieth day following the day on which instruments of acceptance have been deposited with Executive Secretary[8] to the Contracting Parties on behalf of governments named in Annex H, the territories of which account for 85 per centum of the total external trade of the territories of such governments, computed in accordance with the applicable column of percentages set forth therein. The instrument of acceptance of each other government shall take effect on the thirtieth day following the day on which such instrument has been deposited.

7.   The United Nations is authorized to effect registration of this Agreement as soon as it enters into force.

Article XXVII Withholding or Withdrawal of Concessions

Any contracting party shall at any time be free to withhold or to withdraw in whole or in part any concession, provided for in the appropriate Schedule annexed to this Agreement, in respect of which such contracting party determines that it was initially negotiated with a government which has not become, or has ceased to be, a contracting party. A contracting party taking such action shall notify the CONTRACTING PARTIES and, upon request, consult with contracting parties which have a substantial interest in the product concerned.

Article XXVIII Modification of Schedules

1.   On the first day of each three-year period, the first period beginning on 1 January 1958 (or on the first day of any other period that may be specified by the CONTRACTING PARTIES by two-thirds of the votes cast) a contracting party (hereafter in this Article referred to as the "applicant contracting party") may, by negotiation and agreement with any contracting party with which such concession was initially negotiated and with any other contracting party determined by the CONTRACTING PARTIES to have a principal supplying interest (which two preceding categories of contracting parties, together with the applicant contracting party, are in this Article hereinafter referred to as the "contracting parties primarily concerned"), and subject to consultation with any other contracting party determined by the CONTRACTING PARTIES to have a substantial interest in such concession, modify or withdraw a concession included in the appropriate schedule annexed to this Agreement.

2.   In such negotiations and agreement, which may include provision for compensatory adjustment with respect to other products, the contracting parties concerned shall endeavour to maintain a general level of reciprocal and mutually advantageous concessions not less favourable to trade than that provided for in this Agreement prior to such negotiations.

3.   (a) If agreement between the contracting parties primarily concerned cannot be reached before 1 January 1958 or before the expiration of a period envisaged in paragraph 1 of this Article, the contracting party which proposes to modify or withdraw the concession shall, nevertheless, be free to do so and if such action is taken any contracting party with which such concession was initially negotiated, any contracting party determined under paragraph 1 to have a principal supplying interest and any contracting party determined under paragraph 1 to have a substantial interest shall then be free not later than six months after such action is taken, to withdraw, upon the expiration of thirty days from the day on which written notice of such withdrawal is received by the CONTRACTING PARTIES, substantially equivalent concessions initially negotiated with the applicant contracting party.

(b) If agreement between the contracting parties primarily concerned is reached but any other contracting party determined under paragraph 1 of this Article to have a substantial interest is not satisfied, such other contracting party shall be free, not later than six months after action under such agreement is taken, to withdraw, upon the expiration of thirty days from the day on which written notice of such withdrawal is received by the CONTRACTING PARTIES, substantially equivalent concessions initially negotiated with the applicant contracting party.

4.   The CONTRACTING PARTIES may, at any time, in special circumstances, authorize a contracting party to enter into negotiations for modification or withdrawal of a concession included in the appropriate Schedule annexed to this Agreement subject to the following procedures and conditions:

(a) Such negotiations and any related consultations shall be conducted in accordance with the provisions of paragraph 1 and 2 of this Article.

(b) If agreement between the contracting parties primarily concerned is reached in the negotiations, the provisions of paragraph 3 (b) of this Article shall apply.

(c) If agreement between the contracting parties primarily concerned is not reached within a period of sixty days after negotiations have been authorized, or within such longer period as the CONTRACTING PARTIES may have prescribed, the applicant contracting party may refer the matter to the CONTRACTING PARTIES.

(d) Upon such reference, the CONTRACTING PARTIES shall promptly examine the matter and submit their views to the contracting parties primarily concerned with the aim of achieving a settlement. If a settlement is reached, the provisions of paragraph 3 (b) shall apply as if agreement between the contracting parties primarily concerned had been reached. If no settlement is reached between the contracting parties primarily concerned, the applicant contracting party shall be free to modify or withdraw the concession, unless the CONTRACTING PARTIES determine that the applicant contracting party has unreasonably failed to offer adequate compensation. If such action is taken, any contracting party with which the concession was initially negotiated, any contracting party determined under paragraph 4 (a) to have a principal supplying interest and any contracting party determined under paragraph 4 (a) to have a substantial interest, shall be free, not later than six months after such action is taken, to modify or withdraw, upon the expiration of thirty days from the day on which written notice of such withdrawal is received by the CONTRACTING PARTIES, substantially equivalent concessions initially negotiated with applicant contracting party.

5.   Before 1 January 1958 and before the end of any period envisaged in paragraph 1 a contracting party may elect by notifying the CONTRACTING PARTIES to reserve the right, for the duration of the next period, to modify the appropriate Schedule in accordance with the procedures of paragraph 1 to 3. If a contracting party so elects, other contracting parties shall have the right, during the same period, to modify or withdraw, in accordance with the same procedures, concessions initially negotiated with that contracting party.

Article XXVIII bis Tariff Negotiations

1.   The contracting parties recognize that customs duties often constitute serious obstacles to trade; thus negotiations on a reciprocal and mutually advantageous basis, directed to the substantial reduction of the general level of tariffs and other charges on imports and exports and in particular to the reduction of such high tariffs as discourage the importation even of minimum quantities, and conducted with due regard to the objectives of this Agreement and the varying needs of individual contracting parties, are of great importance to the expansion of international trade. The CONTRACTING PARTIES may therefore sponsor such negotiations from time to time.

2. (a) Negotiations under this Article may be carried out on a selective product-by-product basis or by the application of such multilateral procedures as may be accepted by the contracting parties concerned. Such negotiations may be directed towards the reduction of duties, the binding of duties at then existing levels or undertakings that individual duties or the average duties on specified categories of products shall not exceed specified levels. The binding against increase of low duties or of duty-free treatment shall, in principle, be recognized as a concession equivalent in value to the reduction of high duties.

(b) The contracting parties recognize that in general the success of multilateral negotiations would depend on the participation of all contracting parties which conduct a substantial proportion of their external trade with one another.

3. Negotiations shall be conducted on a basis which affords adequate opportunity to take into account:

(a) the needs of individual contracting parties and individual industries;

(b) the needs of less-developed countries for a more flexible use of tariff protection to assist their economic development and the special needs of these countries to maintain tariffs for revenue purposes; and

(c) all other relevant circumstances, including the fiscal, developmental, strategic and other needs of the contracting parties concerned.

Article XXIX The Relation of This Agreement to the Havana Charter

1. The contracting parties undertake to observe to the fullest extent of their executive authority the general principles of Chapters I to VI inclusive and of Chapter IX of the Havana Charter pending their acceptance of it in accordance with their constitutional procedures.

2. Part II of this Agreement shall be suspended on the day on which the Havana Charter enters into force.

3. If by September 30, 1949, the Havana Charter has not entered into force, the contracting parties shall meet before December 31, 1949, to agree whether this Agreement shall be amended, supplemented or maintained.

4. If at any time the Havana Charter should cease to be in force, the CONTRACTING PARTIES shall meet as soon as practicable thereafter to agree whether this Agreement shall be supplemented, amended or maintained. Pending such agreement, Part II of this Agreement shall again enter into force; *provided* that the provisions of Part II other than Article XXIII shall be replaced, *mutatis mutandis*, in the form in which they then appeared in the Havana Charter; and *provided* further that no contracting party shall be bound by any provisions which did not bind it at the time when the Havana Charter ceased to be in force.

5. If any contracting party has not accepted the Havana Charter by the date upon which it enters into force, the CONTRACTING PARTIES shall confer to agree whether, and if so in what way, this Agreement in so far as it affects relations between such contracting party and other contracting parties, shall be supplemented or amended. Pending such agreement the provisions of Part II of this Agreement shall, notwithstanding the provisions of paragraph 2 of this Article, continue to apply as between such contracting party and other contracting parties.

6. Contracting parties which are Members of the International Trade Organization shall not invoke the provisions of this Agreement so as to prevent the operation of any provision of the Havana Charter. The application of the principle underlying this paragraph to any contracting party which is not a Member of the International Trade Organization shall be the subject of an agreement pursuant to paragraph 5 of this Article.

Article XXX Amendments

1.   Except where provision for modification is made elsewhere in this Agreement, amendments to the provisions of Part I of this Agreement or the provisions of Article XXIX or of this Article shall become effective upon acceptance by all the contracting parties, and other amendments to this Agreement shall become effective, in respect of those contracting parties which accept them, upon acceptance by two-thirds of the contracting parties and thereafter for each other contracting party upon acceptance by it.

2.   Any contracting party accepting an amendment to this Agreement shall deposit an instrument of acceptance with the Secretary-General of the United Nations within such period as the CONTRACTING PARTIES may specify. The CONTRACTING PARTIES may decide that any amendment made effective under this Article is of such a nature that any contracting party which has not accepted it within a period specified by the CONTRACTING PARTIES shall be free to withdraw from this Agreement, or to remain a contracting party with the consent of the CONTRACTING PARTIES.

Article XXXI Withdrawal

Without prejudice to the provisions of paragraph 12 of Article XVIII, of Article XXIII or of paragraph 2 of Article XXX, any contracting party may withdraw from this Agreement, or may separately withdraw on behalf of any of the separate customs territories for which it has international responsibility and which at the time possesses full autonomy in the conduct of its external commercial relations and of the other matters provided for in this Agreement. The withdrawal shall take effect upon the expiration of six months from the day on which written notice of withdrawal is received by the Secretary-General of the United Nations.

Article XXXII Contracting Parties

1.   The contracting parties to this Agreement shall be understood to mean those governments which are applying the provisions of this Agreement under Articles XXVI or XXXIII or pursuant to the Protocol of Provisional Application.

2.   At any time after the entry into force of this Agreement pursuant to paragraph 6 of Article XXVI, those contracting parties which have accepted this Agreement pursuant to paragraph 4 of Article XXVI may decide that any contracting party which has not so accepted it shall cease to be a contracting party.

Article XXXIII Accession

A government not party to this Agreement, or a government acting on behalf of a separate customs territory possessing full autonomy in the conduct of its external commercial relations and of the other matters provided for in this Agreement, may accede to this Agreement, on its own behalf or on behalf of that territory, on terms to be agreed between such government and the CONTRACTING PARTIES. Decisions of the CONTRACTING PARTIES under this paragraph shall be taken by a two-thirds majority.

Article XXXIV Annexes

The annexes to this Agreement are hereby made an integral part of this Agreement.

Article XXXV Non-Application of the Agreement Between Particular Contracting Parties

1.   This Agreement, or alternatively Article II of this Agreement, shall not apply as between any contracting party and any other contracting party if:

(a)   the two contracting parties have not entered into tariff negotiations with each other, and

(b)   either of the contracting parties, at the time either becomes a contracting party, does not consent to such application.

2.   The CONTRACTING PARTIES may review the operation of this Article in particular cases at the request of any contracting party and make appropriate recommendations.

Part IV Trade and Development

Article XXXVI Principles and Objectives

1.   The contracting parties,

(a)   recalling that the basic objectives of this Agreement include the raising of standards of living and the progressive development of the economies of all contracting parties, and considering that the attainment of these objectives is particularly urgent for less-developed contracting parties;

(b)   considering that export earnings of the less-developed contracting parties can play a vital part in their economic development and that the extent of this contribution depends on the prices paid by the less-developed contracting parties for essential imports, the volume of their exports, and the prices received for these exports;

(c)   noting, that there is a wide gap between standards of living in less-developed countries and in other countries;

(d)   recognizing that individual and joint action is essential to further the development of the economies of less-developed contracting parties and to bring about a rapid advance in the standards of living in these countries;

(e)   recognizing that international trade as a means of achieving economic and social advancement should be governed by such rules and procedures - and measures in conformity with such rules and procedures - as are consistent with the objectives set forth in this Article;

(f)   noting that the CONTRACTING PARTIES may enable less-developed contracting parties to use special measures to promote their trade and development;

agree as follows.

2.   There is need for a rapid and sustained expansion of the export earnings of the less-developed contracting parties.

3.   There is need for positive efforts designed to ensure that less-developed contracting parties secure a share in the growth in international trade commensurate with the needs of their economic development.

4.   Given the continued dependence of many less-developed contracting parties on the exportation of a limited range of primary products, there is need to provide in the largest possible measure more favourable and acceptable conditions of access to world markets for these products, and wherever appropriate to devise measures designed to stabilize and improve conditions of world markets in these products, including in particular measures designed to attain stable, equitable and remunerative prices, thus permitting an expansion of world trade and demand and a dynamic and steady growth of the real export earnings of these countries so as to provide them with expanding resources for their economic development.

5.   The rapid expansion of the economies of the less-developed contracting parties will be facilitated by a diversification of the structure of their economies and the avoidance of an excessive dependence on the export of primary products. There is, therefore, need for increased access in the largest possible measure to markets under favourable conditions for processed and manufactured products currently or potentially of particular export interest to less-developed contracting parties.

6.   Because of the chronic deficiency in the export proceeds and other foreign exchange earnings of less-developed contracting parties, there are important inter-relationships between trade and financial assistance to development. There is, therefore, need for close and continuing collaboration between the CONTRACTING PARTIES and the international lending agencies so

that they can contribute most effectively to alleviating the burdens these less-developed contracting parties assume in the interest of their economic development.

7. There is need for appropriate collaboration between the CONTRACTING PARTIES, other intergovernmental bodies and the organs and agencies of the United Nations system, whose activities relate to the trade and economic development of less-developed countries.

8. The developed contracting parties do not expect reciprocity for commitments made by them in trade negotiations to reduce or remove tariffs and other barriers to the trade of less-developed contracting parties.

9. The adoption of measures to give effect to these principles and objectives shall be a matter of conscious and purposeful effort on the part of the contracting parties both individually and jointly.

Article XXXVII Commitments

1. The developed contracting parties shall to the fullest extent possible – that is, except when compelling reasons, which may include legal reasons, make it impossible – give effect to the following provisions:

(a) accord high priority to the reduction and elimination of barriers to products currently or potentially of particular export interest to less-developed contracting parties, including customs duties and other restrictions which differentiate unreasonably between such products in their primary and in their processed forms;

(b) refrain from introducing, or increasing the incidence of, customs duties or non-tariff import barriers on products currently or potentially of particular export interest to less-developed contracting parties; and

(c) (i) refrain from imposing new fiscal measures, and

(ii) in any adjustments of fiscal policy accord high priority to the reduction and elimination of fiscal measures, which would hamper, or which hamper, significantly the growth of consumption of primary products, in raw or processed form, wholly or mainly produced in the territories of less-developed contracting parties, and which are applied specifically to those products.

2. (a) Whenever it is considered that effect is not being given to any of the provisions of sub-paragraph (a), (b) or (c) of paragraph 1, the matter shall be reported to the CONTRACTING PARTIES either by the contracting party not so giving effect to the relevant provisions or by any other interested contracting party.

(b) (i) The CONTRACTING PARTIES shall, if requested so to do by any interested contracting party, and without prejudice to any bilateral consultations that may be undertaken, consult with the contracting party concerned and all interested contracting parties with respect to the matter with a view to reaching solutions satisfactory to all contracting parties concerned in order to further the objectives set forth in Article XXXVI. In the course of these consultations, the reasons given in cases where effect was not being given to the provisions of subparagraph (a), (b) or (c) of paragraph 1 shall be examined.

(ii) As the implementation of the provisions of subparagraph (a), (b) or (c) of paragraph 1 by individual contracting parties may in some cases be more readily achieved where action is taken jointly with other developed contracting parties, such consultation might, where appropriate, be directed towards this end.

(iii) The consultations by the CONTRACTING PARTIES might also, in appropriate cases, be directed towards agreement on joint action designed to further the objectives of this Agreement as envisaged in paragraph 1 of Article XXV.

3. The developed contracting parties shall:

(a) make every effort, in cases where a government directly or indirectly determines the resale price of products wholly or mainly produced in the territories of less-developed contracting parties, to maintain trade margins at equitable levels;

(b) give active consideration to the adoption of other measures designed to provide greater scope for the development of imports from less-developed contracting parties and collaborate in appropriate international action to this end;

(c) have special regard to the trade interests of less-developed contracting parties when considering the application of other measures permitted under this Agreement to meet particular problems and explore all possibilities of constructive remedies before applying such measures where they would affect essential interests of those contracting parties.

4.   Less-developed contracting parties agree to take appropriate action in implementation of the provisions of Part IV for the benefit of the trade of other less-developed contracting parties, in so far as such action is consistent with their individual present and future development, financial and trade needs taking into account past trade developments as well as the trade interests of less-developed contracting parties as a whole.

5.   In the implementation of the commitments set forth in paragraph 1 to 4 each contracting party shall afford to any other interested contracting party or contracting parties full and prompt opportunity for consultations under the normal procedures of this Agreement with respect to any matter or difficulty which may arise.

Article XXXVIII Joint Action

1.   The contracting parties shall collaborate jointly, with the framework of this Agreement and elsewhere, as appropriate, to further the objectives set forth in Article XXXVI.

2.   In particular, the CONTRACTING PARTIES shall:

(a) where appropriate, take action, including action through international arrangements, to provide improved and acceptable conditions of access to world markets for primary products of particular interest to less-developed contracting parties and to devise measures designed to stabilize and improve conditions of world markets in these products including measures designed to attain stable, equitable and remunerative prices for exports of such products;

(b) seek appropriate collaboration in matters of trade and development policy with the United Nations and its organs and agencies, including any institutions that may be created on the basis of recommendations by the United Nations Conference on Trade and Development;

(c) collaborate in analysing the development plans and policies of individual less-developed contracting parties and in examining trade and aid relationships with a view to devising concrete measures to promote the development of export potential and to facilitate access to export markets for the products of the industries thus developed and, in this connection, seek appropriate collaboration with governments and international organizations, and in particular with organizations having competence in relation to financial assistance for economic development, in systematic studies of trade and aid relationships in individual less-developed contracting parties aimed at obtaining a clear analysis of export potential, market prospects and any further action that may be required;

(d) keep under continuous review the development of world trade with special reference to the rate of growth of the trade of less-developed contracting parties and make such recommendations to contracting parties as may, in the circumstances, be deemed appropriate;

(e) collaborate in seeking feasible methods to expand trade for the purpose of economic development, through international harmonization and adjustment of national policies and regulations, through technical and commercial standards affecting production, transportation and marketing, and through export promotion by the establishment of facilities for the increased flow of trade information and the development of market research; and

(f)   establish such institutional arrangements as may be necessary to further the objectives set forth in Article XXXVI and to give effect to the provision of this Part.

Annexes [omitted]

Agreement on Agriculture

Members,

Having decided to establish a basis for initiating a process of reform of trade in agriculture in line with the objectives of the negotiations as set out in the Punta del Este Declaration;

Recalling that their long-term objective as agreed at the Mid-Term Review of the Uruguay Round "is to establish a fair and market-oriented agricultural trading system and that a reform process should be initiated through the negotiation of commitments on support and protection and through the establishment of strengthened and more operationally effective GATT rules and disciplines";

Recalling further that "the above-mentioned long-term objective is to provide for substantial progressive reductions in agricultural support and protection sustained over an agreed period of time, resulting in correcting and preventing restrictions and distortions in world agricultural markets";

Committed to achieving specific binding commitments in each of the following areas: market access; domestic support; export competition; and to reaching an agreement on sanitary and phytosanitary issues;

Having agreed that in implementing their commitments on market access, developed country Members would take fully into account the particular needs and conditions of developing country Members by providing for a greater improvement of opportunities and terms of access for agricultural products of particular interest to these Members, including the fullest liberalization of trade in tropical agricultural products as agreed at the Mid-Term Review, and for products of particular importance to the diversification of production from the growing of illicit narcotic crops;

Noting that commitments under the reform programme should be made in an equitable way among all Members, having regard to non-trade concerns, including food security and the need to protect the environment; having regard to the agreement that special and differential treatment for developing countries is an integral element of the negotiations, and taking into account the possible negative effects of the implementation of the reform programme on least-developed and net food-importing developing countries;

Hereby *agree* as follows:

Part I

Article 1 Definition of Terms

In this Agreement, unless the context otherwise requires:

(a) "Aggregate Measurement of Support" and "AMS" mean the annual level of support, expressed in monetary terms, provided for an agricultural product in favour of the producers of the basic agricultural product or non-product-specific support provided in favour of agricultural producers in general, other than support provided under programmes that qualify as exempt from reduction under Annex 2 to this Agreement, which is:

    (i)   with respect to support provided during the base period, specified in the relevant tables of supporting material incorporated by reference in Part IV of a Member's Schedule; and

    (ii)   with respect to support provided during any year of the implementation period and thereafter, calculated in accordance with the provisions of Annex 3 of this Agreement and taking into account the constituent data and methodology used in the tables of supporting material incorporated by reference in Part IV of the Member's Schedule;

(b) "basic agricultural product" in relation to domestic support commitments is defined as the product as close as practicable to the point of first sale as specified in a Member's Schedule and in the related supporting material;

(c) "budgetary outlays" or "outlays" includes revenue foregone;

(d) "Equivalent Measurement of Support" means the annual level of support, expressed in monetary terms, provided to producers of a basic agricultural product through the application of one or more measures, the calculation of which in accordance with the AMS methodology is impracticable, other than support provided under programmes that qualify as exempt from reduction under Annex 2 to this Agreement, and which is:

    (i)   with respect to support provided during the base period, specified in the relevant tables of supporting material incorporated by reference in Part IV of a Member's Schedule; and

    (ii)   with respect to support provided during any year of the implementation period and thereafter, calculated in accordance with the provisions of Annex 4 of this Agreement and taking into account the constituent data and methodology used in the tables of supporting material incorporated by reference in Part IV of the Member's Schedule;

(e) "export subsidies" refers to subsidies contingent upon export performance, including the export subsidies listed in Article 9 of this Agreement;

(f) "implementation period" means the six-year period commencing in the year 1995, except that, for the purposes of Article 13, it means the nine-year period commencing in 1995;

(g) "market access concessions" includes all market access commitments undertaken pursuant to this Agreement;

(h) "Total Aggregate Measurement of Support" and "Total AMS" mean the sum of all domestic support provided in favour of agricultural producers, calculated as the sum of all aggregate measurements of support for basic agricultural products, all non-product-specific aggregate measurements of support and all equivalent measurements of support for agricultural products, and which is:

    (i)   with respect to support provided during the base period (i.e. the "Base Total AMS") and the maximum support permitted to be provided during any year of the implementation period or thereafter (i.e. the "Annual and Final Bound Commitment Levels"), as specified in Part IV of a Member's Schedule; and

    (ii)   with respect to the level of support actually provided during any year of the implementation period and thereafter (i.e. the "Current Total AMS"), calculated in accordance with the provisions of this Agreement, including Article 6, and with the constituent data and methodology used in the tables of supporting material incorporated by reference in Part IV of the Member's Schedule;

(i) "year" in paragraph (f) above and in relation to the specific commitments of a Member refers to the calendar, financial or marketing year specified in the Schedule relating to that Member.

Article 2 Product Coverage

This Agreement applies to the products listed in Annex 1 to this Agreement, hereinafter referred to as agricultural products.

Part II

Article 3 Incorporation of Concessions and Commitments

1.   The domestic support and export subsidy commitments in Part IV of each Member's Schedule constitute commitments limiting subsidization and are hereby made an integral part of GATT 1994.

2.   Subject to the provisions of Article 6, a Member shall not provide support in favour of domestic producers in excess of the commitment levels specified in Section I of Part IV of its Schedule.

3.   Subject to the provisions of paragraphs 2(b) and 4 of Article 9, a Member shall not provide export subsidies listed in paragraph 1 of Article 9 in respect of the agricultural products or groups of products specified in Section II of Part IV of its Schedule in excess of the budgetary outlay and quantity commitment levels specified therein and shall not provide such subsidies in respect of any agricultural product not specified in that Section of its Schedule.

Part III

Article 4 Market Access

1.   Market access concessions contained in Schedules relate to bindings and reductions of tariffs, and to other market access commitments as specified therein.

2.   Members shall not maintain, resort to, or revert to any measures of the kind which have been required to be converted into ordinary customs duties,[1] except as otherwise provided for in Article 5 and Annex 5.

Article 5 Special Safeguard Provisions

1.   Notwithstanding the provisions of paragraph 1(b) of Article II of GATT 1994, any Member may take recourse to the provisions of paragraphs 4 and 5 below in connection with the importation of an agricultural product, in respect of which measures referred to in paragraph 2 of Article 4 of this Agreement have been converted into an ordinary customs duty and which is designated in its Schedule with the symbol "SSG" as being the subject of a concession in respect of which the provisions of this Article may be invoked, if:

(a)   the volume of imports of that product entering the customs territory of the Member granting the concession during any year exceeds a trigger level which relates to the existing market access opportunity as set out in paragraph 4; or, but not concurrently:

(b)   the price at which imports of that product may enter the customs territory of the Member granting the concession, as determined on the basis of the c.i.f. import price of the shipment concerned expressed in terms of its domestic currency, falls below a trigger price equal to the average 1986 to 1988 reference price[2] for the product concerned.

2.   Imports under current and minimum access commitments established as part of a concession referred to in paragraph 1 above shall be counted for the purpose of determining the volume of imports required for invoking the provisions of subparagraph 1(a) and paragraph 4,

---

1   These measures include quantitative import restrictions, variable import levies, minimum import prices, discretionary import licensing, non-tariff measures maintained through state-trading enterprises, voluntary export restraints, and similar border measures other than ordinary customs duties, whether or not the measures are maintained under country-specific derogations from the provisions of GATT 1947, but not measures maintained under balance-of-payments provisions or under other general, non-agriculture-specific provisions of GATT 1994 or of the other Multilateral Trade Agreements in Annex 1A to the WTO Agreement.

2   The reference price used to invoke the provisions of this subparagraph shall, in general, be the average c.i.f. unit value of the product concerned, or otherwise shall be an appropriate price in terms of the quality of the product and its stage of processing. It shall, following its initial use, be publicly specified and available to the extent necessary to allow other Members to assess the additional duty that may be levied.

but imports under such commitments shall not be affected by any additional duty imposed under either subparagraph 1(a) and paragraph 4 or subparagraph 1(b) and paragraph 5 below.

3.   Any supplies of the product in question which were *en route* on the basis of a contract settled before the additional duty is imposed under subparagraph 1(a) and paragraph 4 shall be exempted from any such additional duty, provided that they may be counted in the volume of imports of the product in question during the following year for the purposes of triggering the provisions of subparagraph 1(a) in that year.

4.   Any additional duty imposed under subparagraph 1(a) shall only be maintained until the end of the year in which it has been imposed, and may only be levied at a level which shall not exceed one third of the level of the ordinary customs duty in effect in the year in which the action is taken. The trigger level shall be set according to the following schedule based on market access opportunities defined as imports as a percentage of the corresponding domestic con-sumption[3] during the three preceding years for which data are available:

(a)   where such market access opportunities for a product are less than or equal to 10 per cent, the base trigger level shall equal 125 per cent;

(b)   where such market access opportunities for a product are greater than 10 per cent but less than or equal to 30 per cent, the base trigger level shall equal 110 per cent;

(c)   where such market access opportunities for a product are greater than 30 per cent, the base trigger level shall equal 105 per cent.

In all cases the additional duty may be imposed in any year where the absolute volume of im-ports of the product concerned entering the customs territory of the Member granting the concession exceeds the sum of (x) the base trigger level set out above multiplied by the average quantity of imports during the three preceding years for which data are available and (y) the absolute volume change in domestic consumption of the product concerned in the most recent year for which data are available compared to the preceding year, provided that the trigger level shall not be less than 105 per cent of the average quantity of imports in (x) above.

5.   The additional duty imposed under subparagraph 1(b) shall be set according to the fol-lowing schedule:

(a)   if the difference between the c.i.f. import price of the shipment expressed in terms of the domestic currency (hereinafter referred to as the "import price") and the trigger price as defined under that subparagraph is less than or equal to 10 per cent of the trigger price, no additional duty shall be imposed;

(b)   if the difference between the import price and the trigger price (hereinafter referred to as the "difference") is greater than 10 per cent but less than or equal to 40 per cent of the trigger price, the additional duty shall equal 30 per cent of the amount by which the difference exceeds 10 per cent;

(c)   if the difference is greater than 40 per cent but less than or equal to 60 per cent of the trigger price, the additional duty shall equal 50 per cent of the amount by which the difference exceeds 40 per cent, plus the additional duty allowed under (b);

(d)   if the difference is greater than 60 per cent but less than or equal to 75 per cent, the additional duty shall equal 70 per cent of the amount by which the difference exceeds 60 per cent of the trigger price, plus the additional duties allowed under (b) and (c);

(e)   if the difference is greater than 75 per cent of the trigger price, the additional duty shall equal 90 per cent of the amount by which the difference exceeds 75 per cent, plus the additional duties allowed under (b), (c) and (d).

---

3   Where domestic consumption is not taken into account, the base trigger level under subparagraph 4(a) shall apply.

6.   For perishable and seasonal products, the conditions set out above shall be applied in such a manner as to take account of the specific characteristics of such products. In particular, shorter time periods under subparagraph 1(a) and paragraph 4 may be used in reference to the corresponding periods in the base period and different reference prices for different periods may be used under subparagraph 1(b).

7.   The operation of the special safeguard shall be carried out in a transparent manner. Any Member taking action under subparagraph 1(a) above shall give notice in writing, including relevant data, to the Committee on Agriculture as far in advance as may be practicable and in any event within 10 days of the implementation of such action. In cases where changes in consumption volumes must be allocated to individual tariff lines subject to action under paragraph 4, relevant data shall include the information and methods used to allocate these changes. A Member taking action under paragraph 4 shall afford any interested Members the opportunity to consult with it in respect of the conditions of application of such action. Any Member taking action under subparagraph 1(b) above shall give notice in writing, including relevant data, to the Committee on Agriculture within 10 days of the implementation of the first such action or, for perishable and seasonal products, the first action in any period. Members undertake, as far as practicable, not to take recourse to the provisions of subparagraph 1(b) where the volume of imports of the products concerned are declining. In either case a Member taking such action shall afford any interested Members the opportunity to consult with it in respect of the conditions of application of such action.

8.   Where measures are taken in conformity with paragraphs 1 through 7 above, Members undertake not to have recourse, in respect of such measures, to the provisions of paragraphs 1(a) and 3 of Article XIX of GATT 1994 or paragraph 2 of Article 8 of the Agreement on Safeguards.

9.   The provisions of this Article shall remain in force for the duration of the reform process as determined under Article 20.

Part IV

Article 6 Domestic Support Commitments

1.   The domestic support reduction commitments of each Member contained in Part IV of its Schedule shall apply to all of its domestic support measures in favour of agricultural producers with the exception of domestic measures which are not subject to reduction in terms of the criteria set out in this Article and in Annex 2 to this Agreement. The commitments are expressed in terms of Total Aggregate Measurement of Support and "Annual and Final Bound Commitment Levels".

2.   In accordance with the Mid-Term Review Agreement that government measures of assistance, whether direct or indirect, to encourage agricultural and rural development are an integral part of the development programmes of developing countries, investment subsidies which are generally available to agriculture in developing country Members and agricultural input subsidies generally available to low-income or resource-poor producers in developing country Members shall be exempt from domestic support reduction commitments that would otherwise be applicable to such measures, as shall domestic support to producers in developing country Members to encourage diversification from growing illicit narcotic crops. Domestic support meeting the criteria of this paragraph shall not be required to be included in a Member's calculation of its Current Total AMS.

3.   A Member shall be considered to be in compliance with its domestic support reduction commitments in any year in which its domestic support in favour of agricultural producers expressed in terms of Current Total AMS does not exceed the corresponding annual or final bound commitment level specified in Part IV of the Member's Schedule.

4.   (a) A Member shall not be required to include in the calculation of its Current Total AMS and shall not be required to reduce:

(i)   product-specific domestic support which would otherwise be required to be included in a Member's calculation of its Current AMS where such support does not exceed 5 per cent of that Member's total value of production of a basic agricultural product during the relevant year; and

(ii) non-product-specific domestic support which would otherwise be required to be included in a Member's calculation of its Current AMS where such support does not exceed 5 per cent of the value of that Member's total agricultural production.

(b) For developing country Members, the *de minimis* percentage under this paragraph shall be 10 per cent.

5.   (a) Direct payments under production-limiting programmes shall not be subject to the commitment to reduce domestic support if:

(i)   such payments are based on fixed area and yields; or

(ii) such payments are made on 85 per cent or less of the base level of production; or

(iii) livestock payments are made on a fixed number of head.

(b) The exemption from the reduction commitment for direct payments meeting the above criteria shall be reflected by the exclusion of the value of those direct payments in a Member's calculation of its Current Total AMS.

Article 7 General Disciplines on Domestic Support

1.   Each Member shall ensure that any domestic support measures in favour of agricultural producers which are not subject to reduction commitments because they qualify under the criteria set out in Annex 2 to this Agreement are maintained in conformity therewith.

2.   (a) Any domestic support measure in favour of agricultural producers, including any modification to such measure, and any measure that is subsequently introduced that cannot be shown to satisfy the criteria in Annex 2 to this Agreement or to be exempt from reduction by reason of any other provision of this Agreement shall be included in the Member's calculation of its Current Total AMS.

(b) Where no Total AMS commitment exists in Part IV of a Member's Schedule, the Member shall not provide support to agricultural producers in excess of the relevant *de minimis* level set out in paragraph 4 of Article 6.

Part V

Article 8 Export Competition Commitments

Each Member undertakes not to provide export subsidies otherwise than in conformity with this Agreement and with the commitments as specified in that Member's Schedule.

Article 9 Export Subsidy Commitments

1.   The following export subsidies are subject to reduction commitments under this Agreement:

(a) the provision by governments or their agencies of direct subsidies, including payments-in-kind, to a firm, to an industry, to producers of an agricultural product, to a cooperative or other association of such producers, or to a marketing board, contingent on export performance;

(b) the sale or disposal for export by governments or their agencies of non-commercial stocks of agricultural products at a price lower than the comparable price charged for the like product to buyers in the domestic market;

(c) payments on the export of an agricultural product that are financed by virtue of governmental action, whether or not a charge on the public account is involved, including payments that are financed from the proceeds of a levy imposed on the agricultural product concerned or on an agricultural product from which the exported product is derived;

(d) the provision of subsidies to reduce the costs of marketing exports of agricultural products (other than widely available export promotion and advisory services) including handling, upgrading and other processing costs, and the costs of international transport and freight;

(e) internal transport and freight charges on export shipments, provided or mandated by governments, on terms more favourable than for domestic shipments;

(f) subsidies on agricultural products contingent on their incorporation in exported products.

2.   (a) Except as provided in subparagraph (b), the export subsidy commitment levels for each year of the implementation period, as specified in a Member's Schedule, represent with respect to the export subsidies listed in paragraph 1 of this Article:

(i)   in the case of budgetary outlay reduction commitments, the maximum level of expenditure for such subsidies that may be allocated or incurred in that year in respect of the agricultural product, or group of products, concerned; and

(ii)   in the case of export quantity reduction commitments, the maximum quantity of an agricultural product, or group of products, in respect of which such export subsidies may be granted in that year.

(b) In any of the second through fifth years of the implementation period, a Member may provide export subsidies listed in paragraph 1 above in a given year in excess of the corresponding annual commitment levels in respect of the products or groups of products specified in Part IV of the Member's Schedule, provided that:

(i)   the cumulative amounts of budgetary outlays for such subsidies, from the beginning of the implementation period through the year in question, does not exceed the cumulative amounts that would have resulted from full compliance with the relevant annual outlay commitment levels specified in the Member's Schedule by more than 3 per cent of the base period level of such budgetary outlays;

(ii)   the cumulative quantities exported with the benefit of such export subsidies, from the beginning of the implementation period through the year in question, does not exceed the cumulative quantities that would have resulted from full compliance with the relevant annual quantity commitment levels specified in the Member's Schedule by more than 1.75 per cent of the base period quantities;

(iii) the total cumulative amounts of budgetary outlays for such export subsidies and the quantities benefiting from such export subsidies over the entire implementation period are no greater than the totals that would have resulted from full compliance with the relevant annual commitment levels specified in the Member's Schedule; and

(iv)   the Member's budgetary outlays for export subsidies and the quantities benefiting from such subsidies, at the conclusion of the implementation period, are no greater than 64 per cent and 79 per cent of the 1986-1990 base period levels, respectively. For developing country Members these percentages shall be 76 and 86 per cent, respectively.

3.   Commitments relating to limitations on the extension of the scope of export subsidization are as specified in Schedules.

4.   During the implementation period, developing country Members shall not be required to undertake commitments in respect of the export subsidies listed in subparagraphs (d) and (e) of paragraph 1 above, provided that these are not applied in a manner that would circumvent reduction commitments.

Article 10 Prevention of Circumvention of Export Subsidy Commitments

1.   Export subsidies not listed in paragraph 1 of Article 9 shall not be applied in a manner which results in, or which threatens to lead to, circumvention of export subsidy commitments; nor shall non-commercial transactions be used to circumvent such commitments.

2.   Members undertake to work toward the development of internationally agreed disciplines to govern the provision of export credits, export credit guarantees or insurance programmes and, after agreement on such disciplines, to provide export credits, export credit guarantees or in-surance programmes only in conformity therewith.

3.   Any Member which claims that any quantity exported in excess of a reduction commitment level is not subsidized must establish that no export subsidy, whether listed in Article 9 or not, has been granted in respect of the quantity of exports in question.

4.   Members donors of international food aid shall ensure:

(a)   that the provision of international food aid is not tied directly or indirectly to commercial exports of agricultural products to recipient countries;

(b)   that international food aid transactions, including bilateral food aid which is monetized, shall be carried out in accordance with the FAO "Principles of Surplus Disposal and Consultative Obligations", including, where appropriate, the system of Usual Marketing Requirements (UMRs); and

(c)   that such aid shall be provided to the extent possible in fully grant form or on terms no less concessional than those provided for in Article IV of the Food Aid Convention 1986.

Article 11 Incorporated Products

In no case may the per-unit subsidy paid on an incorporated agricultural primary product exceed the per-unit export subsidy that would be payable on exports of the primary product as such.

Part VI

Article 12 Disciplines on Export Prohibitions and Restrictions

1.   Where any Member institutes any new export prohibition or restriction on foodstuffs in accordance with paragraph 2(a) of Article XI of GATT 1994, the Member shall observe the following provisions:

(a)   the Member instituting the export prohibition or restriction shall give due consideration to the effects of such prohibition or restriction on importing Members' food security;

(b)   before any Member institutes an export prohibition or restriction, it shall give notice in writing, as far in advance as practicable, to the Committee on Agriculture comprising such information as the nature and the duration of such measure, and shall consult, upon request, with any other Member having a substantial interest as an importer with respect to any matter related to the measure in question. The Member instituting such export prohibition or restriction shall provide, upon request, such a Member with necessary information.

2.   The provisions of this Article shall not apply to any developing country Member, unless the measure is taken by a developing country Member which is a net-food exporter of the specific foodstuff concerned.

Part VII

Article 13 Due Restraint

During the implementation period, notwithstanding the provisions of GATT 1994 and the Agree-ment on Subsidies and Countervailing Measures (referred to in this Article as the "Subsidies Agreement"):

(a)   domestic support measures that conform fully to the provisions of Annex 2 to this Agree-ment shall be:

(i)   non-actionable subsidies for purposes of countervailing duties;[4]

(ii) exempt from actions based on Article XVI of GATT 1994 and Part III of the Subsidies Agreement; and

(iii) exempt from actions based on non-violation nullification or impairment of the benefits of tariff concessions accruing to another Member under Article II of GATT 1994, in the sense of paragraph 1(b) of Article XXIII of GATT 1994;

(b) domestic support measures that conform fully to the provisions of Article 6 of this Agreement including direct payments that conform to the requirements of paragraph 5 thereof, as reflected in each Member's Schedule, as well as domestic support within *de minimis* levels and in conformity with paragraph 2 of Article 6, shall be:

(i)   exempt from the imposition of countervailing duties unless a determination of injury or threat thereof is made in accordance with Article VI of GATT 1994 and Part V of the Subsidies Agreement, and due restraint shall be shown in initiating any countervailing duty investigations;

(ii) exempt from actions based on paragraph 1 of Article XVI of GATT 1994 or Articles 5 and 6 of the Subsidies Agreement, provided that such measures do not grant support to a specific commodity in excess of that decided during the 1992 marketing year; and

(iii) exempt from actions based on non-violation nullification or impairment of the benefits of tariff concessions accruing to another Member under Article II of GATT 1994, in the sense of paragraph 1(b) of Article XXIII of GATT 1994, provided that such measures do not grant support to a specific commodity in excess of that decided during the 1992 marketing year;

(c)   export subsidies that conform fully to the provisions of Part V of this Agreement, as reflected in each Member's Schedule, shall be:

(i)   subject to countervailing duties only upon a determination of injury or threat thereof based on volume, effect on prices, or consequent impact in accordance with Article VI of GATT 1994 and Part V of the Subsidies Agreement, and due restraint shall be shown in initiating any countervailing duty investigations; and

(ii) exempt from actions based on Article XVI of GATT 1994 or Articles 3, 5 and 6 of the Subsidies Agreement.

Part VIII

Article 14 Sanitary and Phytosanitary Measures

Members agree to give effect to the Agreement on the Application of Sanitary and Phytosanitary Measures.

Part IX

Article 15 Special and Differential Treatment

1.   In keeping with the recognition that differential and more favourable treatment for developing country Members is an integral part of the negotiation, special and differential treatment in respect of commitments shall be provided as set out in the relevant provisions of this Agreement and embodied in the Schedules of concessions and commitments.

2.   Developing country Members shall have the flexibility to implement reduction commitments over a period of up to 10 years. Least-developed country Members shall not be required to undertake reduction commitments.

---

4   "Countervailing duties" where referred to in this Article are those covered by Article VI of GATT 1994 and Part V of the Agreement on Subsidies and Countervailing Measures.

Part X

Article 16 Least-Developed and Net Food-Importing Developing Countries

1.   Developed country Members shall take such action as is provided for within the framework of the Decision on Measures Concerning the Possible Negative Effects of the Reform Programme on Least-Developed and Net Food-Importing Developing Countries.

2.   The Committee on Agriculture shall monitor, as appropriate, the follow-up to this Decision.

Part XI

Article 17 Committee on Agriculture

A Committee on Agriculture is hereby established.

Article 18 Review of the Implementation of Commitments

1.   Progress in the implementation of commitments negotiated under the Uruguay Round reform programme shall be reviewed by the Committee on Agriculture.

2.   The review process shall be undertaken on the basis of notifications submitted by Members in relation to such matters and at such intervals as shall be determined, as well as on the basis of such documentation as the Secretariat may be requested to prepare in order to facilitate the review process.

3.   In addition to the notifications to be submitted under paragraph 2, any new domestic support measure, or modification of an existing measure, for which exemption from reduction is claimed shall be notified promptly. This notification shall contain details of the new or modified measure and its conformity with the agreed criteria as set out either in Article 6 or in Annex 2.

4.   In the review process Members shall give due consideration to the influence of excessive rates of inflation on the ability of any Member to abide by its domestic support commitments.

5.   Members agree to consult annually in the Committee on Agriculture with respect to their participation in the normal growth of world trade in agricultural products within the framework of the commitments on export subsidies under this Agreement.

6.   The review process shall provide an opportunity for Members to raise any matter relevant to the implementation of commitments under the reform programme as set out in this Agreement.

7.   Any Member may bring to the attention of the Committee on Agriculture any measure which it considers ought to have been notified by another Member.

Article 19 Consultation and Dispute Settlement

The provisions of Articles XXII and XXIII of GATT 1994, as elaborated and applied by the Dispute Settlement Understanding, shall apply to consultations and the settlement of disputes under this Agreement.

Part XII

Article 20 Continuation of the Reform Process

Recognizing that the long-term objective of substantial progressive reductions in support and protection resulting in fundamental reform is an ongoing process, Members agree that negotiations for continuing the process will be initiated one year before the end of the implementation period, taking into account:

(a)   the experience to that date from implementing the reduction commitments;

(b)   the effects of the reduction commitments on world trade in agriculture;

(c)   non-trade concerns, special and differential treatment to developing country Members, and the objective to establish a fair and market-oriented agricultural trading system, and the other objectives and concerns mentioned in the preamble to this Agreement; and

(d) what further commitments are necessary to achieve the above mentioned long-term objectives.

Part XIII

Article 21 Final Provisions

1.   The provisions of GATT 1994 and of other Multilateral Trade Agreements in Annex 1A to the WTO Agreement shall apply subject to the provisions of this Agreement.

2.   The Annexes to this Agreement are hereby made an integral part of this Agreement.

ANNEXES [omitted]

Agreement on the Application of
Sanitary and Phytosanitary Measures

Members,

Reaffirming that no Member should be prevented from adopting or enforcing measures necessary to protect human, animal or plant life or health, subject to the requirement that these measures are not applied in a manner which would constitute a means of arbitrary or unjustifiable discrimination between Members where the same conditions prevail or a disguised restriction on international trade;

Desiring to improve the human health, animal health and phytosanitary situation in all Members;

Noting that sanitary and phytosanitary measures are often applied on the basis of bilateral agreements or protocols;

Desiring the establishment of a multilateral framework of rules and disciplines to guide the development, adoption and enforcement of sanitary and phytosanitary measures in order to minimize their negative effects on trade;

Recognizing the important contribution that international standards, guidelines and recommendations can make in this regard;

Desiring to further the use of harmonized sanitary and phytosanitary measures between Members, on the basis of international standards, guidelines and recommendations developed by the relevant international organizations, including the Codex Alimentarius Commission, the International Office of Epizootics, and the relevant international and regional organizations operating within the framework of the International Plant Protection Convention, without requiring Members to change their appropriate level of protection of human, animal or plant life or health;

Recognizing that developing country Members may encounter special difficulties in complying with the sanitary or phytosanitary measures of importing Members, and as a consequence in access to markets, and also in the formulation and application of sanitary or phytosanitary measures in their own territories, and desiring to assist them in their endeavours in this regard;

Desiring therefore to elaborate rules for the application of the provisions of GATT 1994 which relate to the use of sanitary or phytosanitary measures, in particular the provisions of Article XX(b);[1]

Hereby agree as follows:

Article 1 General Provisions

1.   This Agreement applies to all sanitary and phytosanitary measures which may, directly or indirectly, affect international trade. Such measures shall be developed and applied in accordance with the provisions of this Agreement.

2.   For the purposes of this Agreement, the definitions provided in Annex A shall apply.

3.   The annexes are an integral part of this Agreement.

4.   Nothing in this Agreement shall affect the rights of Members under the Agreement on Technical Barriers to Trade with respect to measures not within the scope of this Agreement.

---

1   In this Agreement, reference to Article XX(b) includes also the chapeau of that Article.

Article 2 Basic Rights and Obligations

1.   Members have the right to take sanitary and phytosanitary measures necessary for the protection of human, animal or plant life or health, provided that such measures are not inconsistent with the provisions of this Agreement.

2.   Members shall ensure that any sanitary or phytosanitary measure is applied only to the extent necessary to protect human, animal or plant life or health, is based on scientific principles and is not maintained without sufficient scientific evidence, except as provided for in paragraph 7 of Article 5.

3.   Members shall ensure that their sanitary and phytosanitary measures do not arbitrarily or unjustifiably discriminate between Members where identical or similar conditions prevail, including between their own territory and that of other Members. Sanitary and phytosanitary measures shall not be applied in a manner which would constitute a disguised restriction on international trade.

4.   Sanitary or phytosanitary measures which conform to the relevant provisions of this Agreement shall be presumed to be in accordance with the obligations of the Members under the provisions of GATT 1994 which relate to the use of sanitary or phytosanitary measures, in particular the provisions of Article XX(b).

Article 3 Harmonization

1.   To harmonize sanitary and phytosanitary measures on as wide a basis as possible, Members shall base their sanitary or phytosanitary measures on international standards, guidelines or recommendations, where they exist, except as otherwise provided for in this Agreement, and in particular in paragraph 3.

2.   Sanitary or phytosanitary measures which conform to international standards, guidelines or recommendations shall be deemed to be necessary to protect human, animal or plant life or health, and presumed to be consistent with the relevant provisions of this Agreement and of GATT 1994.

3.   Members may introduce or maintain sanitary or phytosanitary measures which result in a higher level of sanitary or phytosanitary protection than would be achieved by measures based on the relevant international standards, guidelines or recommendations, if there is a scientific justification, or as a consequence of the level of sanitary or phytosanitary protection a Member determines to be appropriate in accordance with the relevant provisions of paragraphs 1 through 8 of Article 5.[2] Notwithstanding the above, all measures which result in a level of sanitary or phytosanitary protection different from that which would be achieved by measures based on international standards, guidelines or recommendations shall not be inconsistent with any other provision of this Agreement.

4.   Members shall play a full part, within the limits of their resources, in the relevant international organizations and their subsidiary bodies, in particular the Codex Alimentarius Commission, the International Office of Epizootics, and the international and regional organizations operating within the framework of the International Plant Protection Convention, to promote within these organizations the development and periodic review of standards, guidelines and recommendations with respect to all aspects of sanitary and phytosanitary measures.

5.   The Committee on Sanitary and Phytosanitary Measures provided for in paragraphs 1 and 4 of Article 12 (referred to in this Agreement as the "Committee") shall develop a procedure to

---

2   For the purposes of paragraph 3 of Article 3, there is a scientific justification if, on the basis of an examination and evaluation of available scientific information in conformity with the relevant provisions of this Agreement, a Member determines that the relevant international standards, guidelines or recommendations are not sufficient to achieve its appropriate level of sanitary or phytosanitary protection.

monitor the process of international harmonization and coordinate efforts in this regard with the relevant international organizations.

Article 4 Equivalence

1.   Members shall accept the sanitary or phytosanitary measures of other Members as equivalent, even if these measures differ from their own or from those used by other Members trading in the same product, if the exporting Member objectively demonstrates to the importing Member that its measures achieve the importing Member's appropriate level of sanitary or phytosanitary protection. For this purpose, reasonable access shall be given, upon request, to the importing Member for inspection, testing and other relevant procedures.

2.   Members shall, upon request, enter into consultations with the aim of achieving bilateral and multilateral agreements on recognition of the equivalence of specified sanitary or phytosanitary measures.

Article 5 Assessment of Risk and Determination of the Appropriate Level of Sanitary or Phytosanitary Protection

1.   Members shall ensure that their sanitary or phytosanitary measures are based on an assessment, as appropriate to the circumstances, of the risks to human, animal or plant life or health, taking into account risk assessment techniques developed by the relevant international organizations.

2.   In the assessment of risks, Members shall take into account available scientific evidence; relevant processes and production methods; relevant inspection, sampling and testing methods; prevalence of specific diseases or pests; existence of pest- or disease-free areas; relevant ecological and environmental conditions; and quarantine or other treatment.

3.   In assessing the risk to animal or plant life or health and determining the measure to be applied for achieving the appropriate level of sanitary or phytosanitary protection from such risk, Members shall take into account as relevant economic factors: the potential damage in terms of loss of production or sales in the event of the entry, establishment or spread of a pest or disease; the costs of control or eradication in the territory of the importing Member; and the relative cost-effectiveness of alternative approaches to limiting risks.

4.   Members should, when determining the appropriate level of sanitary or phytosanitary protection, take into account the objective of minimizing negative trade effects.

5.   With the objective of achieving consistency in the application of the concept of appropriate level of sanitary or phytosanitary protection against risks to human life or health, or to animal and plant life or health, each Member shall avoid arbitrary or unjustifiable distinctions in the levels it considers to be appropriate in different situations, if such distinctions result in discrimination or a disguised restriction on international trade. Members shall cooperate in the Committee, in accordance with paragraphs 1, 2 and 3 of Article 12, to develop guidelines to further the practical implementation of this provision. In developing the guidelines, the Committee shall take into account all relevant factors, including the exceptional character of human health risks to which people voluntarily expose themselves.

6.   Without prejudice to paragraph 2 of Article 3, when establishing or maintaining sanitary or phytosanitary measures to achieve the appropriate level of sanitary or phytosanitary protection, Members shall ensure that such measures are not more trade-restrictive than required to achieve their appropriate level of sanitary or phytosanitary protection, taking into account technical and economic feasibility.[3]

---

3   For purposes of paragraph 6 of Article 5, a measure is not more trade-restrictive than required unless there is another measure, reasonably available taking into account technical and economic feasibility, that achieves the appropriate level of sanitary or phytosanitary protection and is significantly less restrictive to trade.

7.   In cases where relevant scientific evidence is insufficient, a Member may provisionally adopt sanitary or phytosanitary measures on the basis of available pertinent information, including that from the relevant international organizations as well as from sanitary or phytosanitary measures applied by other Members. In such circumstances, Members shall seek to obtain the additional information necessary for a more objective assessment of risk and review the sanitary or phytosanitary measure accordingly within a reasonable period of time.

8.   When a Member has reason to believe that a specific sanitary or phytosanitary measure introduced or maintained by another Member is constraining, or has the potential to constrain, its exports and the measure is not based on the relevant international standards, guidelines or recommendations, or such standards, guidelines or recommendations do not exist, an explana- tion of the reasons for such sanitary or phytosanitary measure may be requested and shall be provided by the Member maintaining the measure.

Article 6 Adaptation to Regional Conditions, Including Pest- or Disease-Free Areas and Areas of Low Pest or Disease Prevalence

1.   Members shall ensure that their sanitary or phytosanitary measures are adapted to the sanitary or phytosanitary characteristics of the area - whether all of a country, part of a country, or all or parts of several countries - from which the product originated and to which the product is destined. In assessing the sanitary or phytosanitary characteristics of a region, Members shall take into account, *inter alia*, the level of prevalence of specific diseases or pests, the existence of eradication or control programmes, and appropriate criteria or guidelines which may be deve- loped by the relevant international organizations.

2.   Members shall, in particular, recognize the concepts of pest- or disease-free areas and areas of low pest or disease prevalence. Determination of such areas shall be based on factors such as geography, ecosystems, epidemiological surveillance, and the effectiveness of sanitary or phyto- sanitary controls.

3.   Exporting Members claiming that areas within their territories are pest- or disease-free areas or areas of low pest or disease prevalence shall provide the necessary evidence thereof in order to objectively demonstrate to the importing Member that such areas are, and are likely to remain, pest- or disease-free areas or areas of low pest or disease prevalence, respectively. For this purpose, reasonable access shall be given, upon request, to the importing Member for inspec- tion, testing and other relevant procedures.

Article 7 Transparency

Members shall notify changes in their sanitary or phytosanitary measures and shall provide infor- mation on their sanitary or phytosanitary measures in accordance with the provisions of Annex B.

Article 8 Control, Inspection and Approval Procedures

Members shall observe the provisions of Annex C in the operation of control, inspection and approval procedures, including national systems for approving the use of additives or for establishing tolerances for contaminants in foods, beverages or feedstuffs, and otherwise ensure that their procedures are not inconsistent with the provisions of this Agreement.

Article 9 Technical Assistance

1.   Members agree to facilitate the provision of technical assistance to other Members, espe- cially developing country Members, either bilaterally or through the appropriate international organizations. Such assistance may be, *inter alia*, in the areas of processing technologies, research and infrastructure, including in the establishment of national regulatory bodies, and may take the form of advice, credits, donations and grants, including for the purpose of seeking technical expertise, training and equipment to allow such countries to adjust to, and comply with, sanitary or phytosanitary measures necessary to achieve the appropriate level of sanitary or phytosanitary protection in their export markets.

2.   Where substantial investments are required in order for an exporting developing country Member to fulfil the sanitary or phytosanitary requirements of an importing Member, the latter shall consider providing such technical assistance as will permit the developing country Member to maintain and expand its market access opportunities for the product involved.

Article 10 Special and Differential Treatment

1.   In the preparation and application of sanitary or phytosanitary measures, Members shall take account of the special needs of developing country Members, and in particular of the least-developed country Members.

2.   Where the appropriate level of sanitary or phytosanitary protection allows scope for the phased introduction of new sanitary or phytosanitary measures, longer time-frames for compliance should be accorded on products of interest to developing country Members so as to maintain opportunities for their exports.

3.   With a view to ensuring that developing country Members are able to comply with the provisions of this Agreement, the Committee is enabled to grant to such countries, upon request, specified, time-limited exceptions in whole or in part from obligations under this Agreement, taking into account their financial, trade and development needs.

4.   Members should encourage and facilitate the active participation of developing country Members in the relevant international organizations.

Article 11 Consultations and Dispute Settlement

1.   The provisions of Articles XXII and XXIII of GATT 1994 as elaborated and applied by the Dispute Settlement Understanding shall apply to consultations and the settlement of disputes under this Agreement, except as otherwise specifically provided herein.

2.   In a dispute under this Agreement involving scientific or technical issues, a panel should seek advice from experts chosen by the panel in consultation with the parties to the dispute. To this end, the panel may, when it deems it appropriate, establish an advisory technical experts group, or consult the relevant international organizations, at the request of either party to the dispute or on its own initiative.

3.   Nothing in this Agreement shall impair the rights of Members under other international agreements, including the right to resort to the good offices or dispute settlement mechanisms of other international organizations or established under any international agreement.

Article 12 Administration

1.   A Committee on Sanitary and Phytosanitary Measures is hereby established to provide a regular forum for consultations. It shall carry out the functions necessary to implement the provisions of this Agreement and the furtherance of its objectives, in particular with respect to harmonization. The Committee shall reach its decisions by consensus.

2.   The Committee shall encourage and facilitate ad hoc consultations or negotiations among Members on specific sanitary or phytosanitary issues. The Committee shall encourage the use of international standards, guidelines or recommendations by all Members and, in this regard, shall sponsor technical consultation and study with the objective of increasing coordination and integration between international and national systems and approaches for approving the use of food additives or for establishing tolerances for contaminants in foods, beverages or feedstuffs.

3.   The Committee shall maintain close contact with the relevant international organizations in the field of sanitary and phytosanitary protection, especially with the Codex Alimentarius Commission, the International Office of Epizootics, and the Secretariat of the International Plant Protection Convention, with the objective of securing the best available scientific and technical advice for the administration of this Agreement and in order to ensure that unnecessary duplication of effort is avoided.

4.   The Committee shall develop a procedure to monitor the process of international harmo-nization and the use of international standards, guidelines or recommendations. For this purpose, the Committee should, in conjunction with the relevant international organizations, establish a list of international standards, guidelines or recommendations relating to sanitary or phytosanitary measures which the Committee determines to have a major trade impact. The list should include an indication by Members of those international standards, guidelines or recommendations which they apply as conditions for import or on the basis of which imported products conforming to these standards can enjoy access to their markets. For those cases in which a Member does not apply an international standard, guideline or recommendation as a condition for import, the Member should provide an indication of the reason therefor, and, in particular, whether it considers that the standard is not stringent enough to provide the appro-priate level of sanitary or phytosanitary protection. If a Member revises its position, following its indication of the use of a standard, guideline or recommendation as a condition for import, it should provide an explanation for its change and so inform the Secretariat as well as the relevant international organizations, unless such notification and explanation is given according to the procedures of Annex B.

5.   In order to avoid unnecessary duplication, the Committee may decide, as appropriate, to use the information generated by the procedures, particularly for notification, which are in operation in the relevant international organizations.

6.   The Committee may, on the basis of an initiative from one of the Members, through appro-priate channels invite the relevant international organizations or their subsidiary bodies to examine specific matters with respect to a particular standard, guideline or recommendation, including the basis of explanations for non-use given according to paragraph 4.

7.   The Committee shall review the operation and implementation of this Agreement three years after the date of entry into force of the WTO Agreement, and thereafter as the need arises. Where appropriate, the Committee may submit to the Council for Trade in Goods proposals to amend the text of this Agreement having regard, *inter alia*, to the experience gained in its imple-mentation.

Article 13 Implementation

Members are fully responsible under this Agreement for the observance of all obligations set forth herein. Members shall formulate and implement positive measures and mechanisms in support of the observance of the provisions of this Agreement by other than central government bodies. Members shall take such reasonable measures as may be available to them to ensure that non-governmental entities within their territories, as well as regional bodies in which relevant entities within their territories are members, comply with the relevant provisions of this Agree-ment. In addition, Members shall not take measures which have the effect of, directly or indirectly, requiring or encouraging such regional or non-governmental entities, or local govern-mental bodies, to act in a manner inconsistent with the provisions of this Agreement. Members shall ensure that they rely on the services of non-governmental entities for implementing sanitary or phytosanitary measures only if these entities comply with the provisions of this Agreement.

Article 14 Final Provisions

The least-developed country Members may delay application of the provisions of this Agreement for a period of five years following the date of entry into force of the WTO Agreement with respect to their sanitary or phytosanitary measures affecting importation or imported products. Other developing country Members may delay application of the provisions of this Agreement, other than paragraph 8 of Article 5 and Article 7, for two years following the date of entry into force of the WTO Agreement with respect to their existing sanitary or phytosanitary measures affecting importation or imported products, where such application is prevented by a lack of technical expertise, technical infrastructure or resources.

ANNEX A – DEFINITIONS[4]

1. *Sanitary or phytosanitary measure* - Any measure applied:

(a) to protect animal or plant life or health within the territory of the Member from risks arising from the entry, establishment or spread of pests, diseases, disease-carrying organisms or disease-causing organisms;

(b) to protect human or animal life or health within the territory of the Member from risks arising from additives, contaminants, toxins or disease-causing organisms in foods, beverages or feedstuffs;

(c) to protect human life or health within the territory of the Member from risks arising from diseases carried by animals, plants or products thereof, or from the entry, establishment or spread of pests; or

(d) to prevent or limit other damage within the territory of the Member from the entry, establishment or spread of pests.

Sanitary or phytosanitary measures include all relevant laws, decrees, regulations, requirements and procedures including, *inter alia*, end product criteria; processes and production methods; testing, inspection, certification and approval procedures; quarantine treatments including relevant requirements associated with the transport of animals or plants, or with the materials necessary for their survival during transport; provisions on relevant statistical methods, sampling procedures and methods of risk assessment; and packaging and labelling requirements directly related to food safety.

2. *Harmonization* - The establishment, recognition and application of common sanitary and phytosanitary measures by different Members.

3. *International standards, guidelines and recommendations*

(a) for food safety, the standards, guidelines and recommendations established by the Codex Alimentarius Commission relating to food additives, veterinary drug and pesticide residues, contaminants, methods of analysis and sampling, and codes and guidelines of hygienic practice;

(b) for animal health and zoonoses, the standards, guidelines and recommendations developed under the auspices of the International Office of Epizootics;

(c) for plant health, the international standards, guidelines and recommendations developed under the auspices of the Secretariat of the International Plant Protection Convention in cooperation with regional organizations operating within the framework of the International Plant Protection Convention; and

(d) for matters not covered by the above organizations, appropriate standards, guidelines and recommendations promulgated by other relevant international organizations open for membership to all Members, as identified by the Committee.

4. *Risk assessment* - The evaluation of the likelihood of entry, establishment or spread of a pest or disease within the territory of an importing Member according to the sanitary or phytosanitary measures which might be applied, and of the associated potential biological and economic consequences; or the evaluation of the potential for adverse effects on human or animal health arising from the presence of additives, contaminants, toxins or disease-causing organisms in food, beverages or feedstuffs.

---

4   For the purpose of these definitions, "animal" includes fish and wild fauna; "plant" includes forests and wild flora; "pests" include weeds; and "contaminants" include pesticide and veterinary drug residues and extraneous matter.

5.   *Appropriate level of sanitary or phytosanitary protection* - The level of protection deemed appropriate by the Member establishing a sanitary or phytosanitary measure to protect human, animal or plant life or health within its territory.

NOTE: Many Members otherwise refer to this concept as the "acceptable level of risk".

6.   *Pest- or disease-free area* - An area, whether all of a country, part of a country, or all or parts of several countries, as identified by the competent authorities, in which a specific pest or disease does not occur.

NOTE: A pest- or disease-free area may surround, be surrounded by, or be adjacent to an area – whether within part of a country or in a geographic region which includes parts of or all of several countries – in which a specific pest or disease is known to occur but is subject to regional control measures such as the establishment of protection, surveillance and buffer zones which will confine or eradicate the pest or disease in question.

7.   *Area of low pest or disease prevalence* - An area, whether all of a country, part of a country, or all or parts of several countries, as identified by the competent authorities, in which a specific pest or disease occurs at low levels and which is subject to effective surveillance, control or eradication measures.

ANNEX B – TRANSPARENCY OF SANITARY AND PHYTOSANITARY REGULATIONS

Publication of Regulations

1.   Members shall ensure that all sanitary and phytosanitary regulations[5] which have been adopted are published promptly in such a manner as to enable interested Members to become acquainted with them.

2.   Except in urgent circumstances, Members shall allow a reasonable interval between the publication of a sanitary or phytosanitary regulation and its entry into force in order to allow time for producers in exporting Members, and particularly in developing country Members, to adapt their products and methods of production to the requirements of the importing Member.

Enquiry Points

3.   Each Member shall ensure that one enquiry point exists which is responsible for the provision of answers to all reasonable questions from interested Members as well as for the provision of relevant documents regarding:

(a)   any sanitary or phytosanitary regulations adopted or proposed within its territory;

(b)   any control and inspection procedures, production and quarantine treatment, pesticide tolerance and food additive approval procedures, which are operated within its territory;

(c)   risk assessment procedures, factors taken into consideration, as well as the determination of the appropriate level of sanitary or phytosanitary protection;

(d)   the membership and participation of the Member, or of relevant bodies within its territory, in international and regional sanitary and phytosanitary organizations and systems, as well as in bilateral and multilateral agreements and arrangements within the scope of this Agreement, and the texts of such agreements and arrangements.

4.   Members shall ensure that where copies of documents are requested by interested Members, they are supplied at the same price (if any), apart from the cost of delivery, as to the nationals[6] of the Member concerned.

---

5   Sanitary and phytosanitary measures such as laws, decrees or ordinances which are applicable generally.
6   When "nationals" are referred to in this Agreement, the term shall be deemed, in the case of a separate customs territory Member of the WTO, to mean persons, natural or legal, who are domiciled or who have a real and effective industrial or commercial establishment in that customs territory.

Notification Procedures

5.   Whenever an international standard, guideline or recommendation does not exist or the content of a proposed sanitary or phytosanitary regulation is not substantially the same as the content of an international standard, guideline or recommendation, and if the regulation may have a significant effect on trade of other Members, Members shall:

(a)   publish a notice at an early stage in such a manner as to enable interested Members to become acquainted with the proposal to introduce a particular regulation;

(b)   notify other Members, through the Secretariat, of the products to be covered by the regula-tion together with a brief indication of the objective and rationale of the proposed regula-tion. Such notifications shall take place at an early stage, when amendments can still be introduced and comments taken into account;

(c)   provide upon request to other Members copies of the proposed regulation and, whenever possible, identify the parts which in substance deviate from international standards, guide-lines or recommendations;

(d)   without discrimination, allow reasonable time for other Members to make comments in writing, discuss these comments upon request, and take the comments and the results of the discussions into account.

6.   However, where urgent problems of health protection arise or threaten to arise for a Member, that Member may omit such of the steps enumerated in paragraph 5 of this Annex as it finds necessary, provided that the Member:

(a)   immediately notifies other Members, through the Secretariat, of the particular regulation and the products covered, with a brief indication of the objective and the rationale of the regulation, including the nature of the urgent problem(s);

(b)   provides, upon request, copies of the regulation to other Members;

(c)   allows other Members to make comments in writing, discusses these comments upon request, and takes the comments and the results of the discussions into account.

7.   Notifications to the Secretariat shall be in English, French or Spanish.

8.   Developed country Members shall, if requested by other Members, provide copies of the documents or, in case of voluminous documents, summaries of the documents covered by a specific notification in English, French or Spanish.

9.   The Secretariat shall promptly circulate copies of the notification to all Members and interested international organizations and draw the attention of developing country Members to any notifications relating to products of particular interest to them.

10.   Members shall designate a single central government authority as responsible for the imple-mentation, on the national level, of the provisions concerning notification procedures according to paragraphs 5, 6, 7 and 8 of this Annex.

General Reservations

11.   Nothing in this Agreement shall be construed as requiring:

(a)   the provision of particulars or copies of drafts or the publication of texts other than in the language of the Member except as stated in paragraph 8 of this Annex; or

(b)   Members to disclose confidential information which would impede enforcement of sanitary or phytosanitary legislation or which would prejudice the legitimate commercial interests of particular enterprises.

ANNEX C – CONTROL, INSPECTION AND APPROVAL PROCEDURES[7]

1. Members shall ensure, with respect to any procedure to check and ensure the fulfilment of sanitary or phytosanitary measures, that:

(a) such procedures are undertaken and completed without undue delay and in no less favourable manner for imported products than for like domestic products;

(b) the standard processing period of each procedure is published or that the anticipated processing period is communicated to the applicant upon request; when receiving an application, the competent body promptly examines the completeness of the documentation and informs the applicant in a precise and complete manner of all deficiencies; the competent body transmits as soon as possible the results of the procedure in a precise and complete manner to the applicant so that corrective action may be taken if necessary; even when the application has deficiencies, the competent body proceeds as far as practicable with the procedure if the applicant so requests; and that upon request, the applicant is informed of the stage of the procedure, with any delay being explained;

(c) information requirements are limited to what is necessary for appropriate control, inspection and approval procedures, including for approval of the use of additives or for the establishment of tolerances for contaminants in food, beverages or feedstuffs;

(d) the confidentiality of information about imported products arising from or supplied in connection with control, inspection and approval is respected in a way no less favourable than for domestic products and in such a manner that legitimate commercial interests are protected;

(e) any requirements for control, inspection and approval of individual specimens of a product are limited to what is reasonable and necessary;

(f) any fees imposed for the procedures on imported products are equitable in relation to any fees charged on like domestic products or products originating in any other Member and should be no higher than the actual cost of the service;

(g) the same criteria should be used in the siting of facilities used in the procedures and the selection of samples of imported products as for domestic products so as to minimize the inconvenience to applicants, importers, exporters or their agents;

(h) whenever specifications of a product are changed subsequent to its control and inspection in light of the applicable regulations, the procedure for the modified product is limited to what is necessary to determine whether adequate confidence exists that the product still meets the regulations concerned; and

(i) a procedure exists to review complaints concerning the operation of such procedures and to take corrective action when a complaint is justified.

Where an importing Member operates a system for the approval of the use of food additives or for the establishment of tolerances for contaminants in food, beverages or feedstuffs which prohibits or restricts access to its domestic markets for products based on the absence of an approval, the importing Member shall consider the use of a relevant international standard as the basis for access until a final determination is made.

2. Where a sanitary or phytosanitary measure specifies control at the level of production, the Member in whose territory the production takes place shall provide the necessary assistance to facilitate such control and the work of the controlling authorities.

3. Nothing in this Agreement shall prevent Members from carrying out reasonable inspection within their own territories.

---

7   Control, inspection and approval procedures include, *inter alia*, procedures for sampling, testing and certification.

Agreement on Technical Barriers to Trade

Members,

Having regard to the Uruguay Round of Multilateral Trade Negotiations;

Desiring to further the objectives of GATT 1994;

Recognizing the important contribution that international standards and conformity assessment systems can make in this regard by improving efficiency of production and facilitating the conduct of international trade;

Desiring therefore to encourage the development of such international standards and conformity assessment systems;

Desiring however to ensure that technical regulations and standards, including packaging, marking and labelling requirements, and procedures for assessment of conformity with technical regulations and standards do not create unnecessary obstacles to international trade;

Recognizing that no country should be prevented from taking measures necessary to ensure the quality of its exports, or for the protection of human, animal or plant life or health, of the environment, or for the prevention of deceptive practices, at the levels it considers appropriate, subject to the requirement that they are not applied in a manner which would constitute a means of arbitrary or unjustifiable discrimination between countries where the same conditions prevail or a disguised restriction on international trade, and are otherwise in accordance with the provisions of this Agreement;

Recognizing that no country should be prevented from taking measures necessary for the protection of its essential security interest;

Recognizing the contribution which international standardization can make to the transfer of technology from developed to developing countries;

Recognizing that developing countries may encounter special difficulties in the formulation and application of technical regulations and standards and procedures for assessment of conformity with technical regulations and standards, and desiring to assist them in their endeavours in this regard;

Hereby *agree* as follows:

Article 1 General Provisions

1.1 General terms for standardization and procedures for assessment of conformity shall normally have the meaning given to them by definitions adopted within the United Nations system and by international standardizing bodies taking into account their context and in the light of the object and purpose of this Agreement.

1.2 However, for the purposes of this Agreement the meaning of the terms given in Annex 1 applies.

1.3 All products, including industrial and agricultural products, shall be subject to the provisions of this Agreement.

1.4 Purchasing specifications prepared by governmental bodies for production or consumption requirements of governmental bodies are not subject to the provisions of this Agreement but are addressed in the Agreement on Government Procurement, according to its coverage.

1.5 The provisions of this Agreement do not apply to sanitary and phytosanitary measures as defined in Annex A of the Agreement on the Application of Sanitary and Phytosanitary Measures.

1.6 All references in this Agreement to technical regulations, standards and conformity assessment procedures shall be construed to include any amendments thereto and any additions to the rules or the product coverage thereof, except amendments and additions of an insignificant nature.

TECHNICAL REGULATIONS AND STANDARDS
Article 2 Preparation, Adoption and Application of Technical Regulations by Central Government Bodies

With respect to their central government bodies:

2.1 Members shall ensure that in respect of technical regulations, products imported from the territory of any Member shall be accorded treatment no less favourable than that accorded to like products of national origin and to like products originating in any other country.

2.2 Members shall ensure that technical regulations are not prepared, adopted or applied with a view to or with the effect of creating unnecessary obstacles to international trade. For this purpose, technical regulations shall not be more trade-restrictive than necessary to fulfil a legitimate objective, taking account of the risks non-fulfilment would create. Such legitimate objectives are, *inter alia:* national security requirements; the prevention of deceptive practices; protection of human health or safety, animal or plant life or health, or the environment. In assessing such risks, relevant elements of consideration are, *inter alia:* available scientific and technical information, related processing technology or intended end-uses of products.

2.3 Technical regulations shall not be maintained if the circumstances or objectives giving rise to their adoption no longer exist or if the changed circumstances or objectives can be addressed in a less trade-restrictive manner.

2.4 Where technical regulations are required and relevant international standards exist or their completion is imminent, Members shall use them, or the relevant parts of them, as a basis for their technical regulations except when such international standards or relevant parts would be an ineffective or inappropriate means for the fulfilment of the legitimate objectives pursued, for instance because of fundamental climatic or geographical factors or fundamental technological problems.

2.5 A Member preparing, adopting or applying a technical regulation which may have a significant effect on trade of other Members shall, upon the request of another Member, explain the justification for that technical regulation in terms of the provisions of paragraphs 2 to 4. Whenever a technical regulation is prepared, adopted or applied for one of the legitimate objectives explicitly mentioned in paragraph 2, and is in accordance with relevant international standards, it shall be rebuttably presumed not to create an unnecessary obstacle to international trade.

2.6 With a view to harmonizing technical regulations on as wide a basis as possible, Members shall play a full part, within the limits of their resources, in the preparation by appropriate international standardizing bodies of international standards for products for which they either have adopted, or expect to adopt, technical regulations.

2.7 Members shall give positive consideration to accepting as equivalent technical regulations of other Members, even if these regulations differ from their own, provided they are satisfied that these regulations adequately fulfil the objectives of their own regulations.

2.8 Wherever appropriate, Members shall specify technical regulations based on product requirements in terms of performance rather than design or descriptive characteristics.

2.9 Whenever a relevant international standard does not exist or the technical content of a proposed technical regulation is not in accordance with the technical content of relevant international standards, and if the technical regulation may have a significant effect on trade of other Members, Members shall:

2.9.1   publish a notice in a publication at an early appropriate stage, in such a manner as to enable interested parties in other Members to become acquainted with it, that they propose to introduce a particular technical regulation;

2.9.2   notify other Members through the Secretariat of the products to be covered by the proposed technical regulation, together with a brief indication of its objective and rationale. Such notifications shall take place at an early appropriate stage, when amendments can still be introduced and comments taken into account;

2.9.3   upon request, provide to other Members particulars or copies of the proposed technical regulation and, whenever possible, identify the parts which in substance deviate from relevant international standards;

2.9.4   without discrimination, allow reasonable time for other Members to make comments in writing, discuss these comments upon request, and take these written comments and the results of these discussions into account.

2.10 Subject to the provisions in the lead-in to paragraph 9, where urgent problems of safety, health, environmental protection or national security arise or threaten to arise for a Member, that Member may omit such of the steps enumerated in paragraph 9 as it finds necessary, provided that the Member, upon adoption of a technical regulation, shall:

2.10.1   notify immediately other Members through the Secretariat of the particular technical regulation and the products covered, with a brief indication of the objective and the rationale of the technical regulation, including the nature of the urgent problems;

2.10.2   upon request, provide other Members with copies of the technical regulation;

2.10.3   without discrimination, allow other Members to present their comments in writing, discuss these comments upon request, and take these written comments and the results of these discussions into account.

2.11 Members shall ensure that all technical regulations which have been adopted are published promptly or otherwise made available in such a manner as to enable interested parties in other Members to become acquainted with them.

2.12 Except in those urgent circumstances referred to in paragraph 10, Members shall allow a reasonable interval between the publication of technical regulations and their entry into force in order to allow time for producers in exporting Members, and particularly in developing country Members, to adapt their products or methods of production to the requirements of the importing Member.

Article 3 Preparation, Adoption and Application of Technical Regulations by Local Government Bodies and Non-Governmental Bodies

With respect to their local government and non-governmental bodies within their territories:

3.1 Members shall take such reasonable measures as may be available to them to ensure compliance by such bodies with the provisions of Article 2, with the exception of the obligation to notify as referred to in paragraphs 9.2 and 10.1 of Article 2.

3.2 Members shall ensure that the technical regulations of local governments on the level directly below that of the central government in Members are notified in accordance with the provisions of paragraphs 9.2 and 10.1 of Article 2, noting that notification shall not be required for technical regulations the technical content of which is substantially the same as that of previously notified technical regulations of central government bodies of the Member concerned.

3.3 Members may require contact with other Members, including the notifications, provision of information, comments and discussions referred to in paragraphs 9 and 10 of Article 2, to take place through the central government.

3.4 Members shall not take measures which require or encourage local government bodies or non-governmental bodies within their territories to act in a manner inconsistent with the provisions of Article 2.

3.5 Members are fully responsible under this Agreement for the observance of all provisions of Article 2. Members shall formulate and implement positive measures and mechanisms in support of the observance of the provisions of Article 2 by other than central government bodies.

Article 4 Preparation, Adoption and Application of Standards

4.1 Members shall ensure that their central government standardizing bodies accept and comply with the Code of Good Practice for the Preparation, Adoption and Application of Standards in Annex 3 to this Agreement (referred to in this Agreement as the "Code of Good Practice"). They shall take such reasonable measures as may be available to them to ensure that local government and non-governmental standardizing bodies within their territories, as well as regional standardizing bodies of which they or one or more bodies within their territories are members, accept and comply with this Code of Good Practice. In addition, Members shall not take measures which have the effect of, directly or indirectly, requiring or encouraging such standardizing bodies to act in a manner inconsistent with the Code of Good Practice. The obligations of Members with respect to compliance of standardizing bodies with the provisions of the Code of Good Practice shall apply irrespective of whether or not a standardizing body has accepted the Code of Good Practice.

4.2 Standardizing bodies that have accepted and are complying with the Code of Good Practice shall be acknowledged by the Members as complying with the principles of this Agreement.

CONFORMITY WITH TECHNICAL REGULATIONS AND STANDARDS
Article 5 Procedures for Assessment of Conformity by Central Government Bodies

5.1 Members shall ensure that, in cases where a positive assurance of conformity with technical regulations or standards is required, their central government bodies apply the following provisions to products originating in the territories of other Members:

5.1.1 conformity assessment procedures are prepared, adopted and applied so as to grant access for suppliers of like products originating in the territories of other Members under conditions no less favourable than those accorded to suppliers of like products of national origin or originating in any other country, in a comparable situation; access entails suppliers' right to an assessment of conformity under the rules of the procedure, including, when foreseen by this procedure, the possibility to have conformity assessment activities undertaken at the site of facilities and to receive the mark of the system;

5.1.2 conformity assessment procedures are not prepared, adopted or applied with a view to or with the effect of creating unnecessary obstacles to international trade. This means, *inter alia*, that conformity assessment procedures shall not be more strict or be applied more strictly than is necessary to give the importing Member adequate confidence that products conform with the applicable technical regulations or standards, taking account of the risks non-conformity would create.

5.2 When implementing the provisions of paragraph 1, Members shall ensure that:

5.2.1 conformity assessment procedures are undertaken and completed as expeditiously as possible and in a no less favourable order for products originating in the territories of other Members than for like domestic products;

5.2.2 the standard processing period of each conformity assessment procedure is published or that the anticipated processing period is communicated to the applicant upon request; when receiving an application, the competent body promptly examines the completeness of the documentation and informs the applicant in a precise and complete manner of all deficiencies; the competent body transmits as soon as possible the results of the assessment in a precise and complete manner to the applicant so that corrective action may be taken if necessary; even when the application has deficiencies, the competent body proceeds as far as practicable with the conformity assessment if the applicant so requests; and that, upon request, the applicant is informed of the stage of the procedure, with any delay being explained;

5.2.3   information requirements are limited to what is necessary to assess conformity and determine fees;

5.2.4   the confidentiality of information about products originating in the territories of other Members arising from or supplied in connection with such conformity assessment procedures is respected in the same way as for domestic products and in such a manner that legitimate commercial interests are protected;

5.2.5   any fees imposed for assessing the conformity of products originating in the territories of other Members are equitable in relation to any fees chargeable for assessing the conformity of like products of national origin or originating in any other country, taking into account communication, transportation and other costs arising from differences between location of facilities of the applicant and the conformity assessment body;

5.2.6   the siting of facilities used in conformity assessment procedures and the selection of samples are not such as to cause unnecessary inconvenience to applicants or their agents;

5.2.7   whenever specifications of a product are changed subsequent to the determination of its conformity to the applicable technical regulations or standards, the conformity assessment procedure for the modified product is limited to what is necessary to determine whether adequate confidence exists that the product still meets the technical regulations or standards concerned;

5.2.8   a procedure exists to review complaints concerning the operation of a conformity assessment procedure and to take corrective action when a complaint is justified.

5.3 Nothing in paragraphs 1 and 2 shall prevent Members from carrying out reasonable spot checks within their territories.

5.4 In cases where a positive assurance is required that products conform with technical regulations or standards, and relevant guides or recommendations issued by international standardizing bodies exist or their completion is imminent, Members shall ensure that central government bodies use them, or the relevant parts of them, as a basis for their conformity assessment procedures, except where, as duly explained upon request, such guides or recommendations or relevant parts are inappropriate for the Members concerned, for, *inter alia*, such reasons as: national security requirements; the prevention of deceptive practices; protection of human health or safety, animal or plant life or health, or the environment; fundamental climatic or other geographical factors; fundamental technological or infrastructural problems.

5.5 With a view to harmonizing conformity assessment procedures on as wide a basis as possible, Members shall play a full part, within the limits of their resources, in the preparation by appropriate international standardizing bodies of guides and recommendations for conformity assessment procedures.

5.6 Whenever a relevant guide or recommendation issued by an international standardizing body does not exist or the technical content of a proposed conformity assessment procedure is not in accordance with relevant guides and recommendations issued by international standardizing bodies, and if the conformity assessment procedure may have a significant effect on trade of other Members, Members shall:

5.6.1   publish a notice in a publication at an early appropriate stage, in such a manner as to enable interested parties in other Members to become acquainted with it, that they propose to introduce a particular conformity assessment procedure;

5.6.2   notify other Members through the Secretariat of the products to be covered by the proposed conformity assessment procedure, together with a brief indication of its objective and rationale. Such notifications shall take place at an early appropriate stage, when amendments can still be introduced and comments taken into account;

5.6.3   upon request, provide to other Members particulars or copies of the proposed procedure and, whenever possible, identify the parts which in substance deviate from relevant guides or recommendations issued by international standardizing bodies;

5.6.4   without discrimination, allow reasonable time for other Members to make comments in writing, discuss these comments upon request, and take these written comments and the results of these discussions into account.

5.7 Subject to the provisions in the lead-in to paragraph 6, where urgent problems of safety, health, environmental protection or national security arise or threaten to arise for a Member, that Member may omit such of the steps enumerated in paragraph 6 as it finds necessary, provided that the Member, upon adoption of the procedure, shall:

5.7.1   notify immediately other Members through the Secretariat of the particular procedure and the products covered, with a brief indication of the objective and the rationale of the procedure, including the nature of the urgent problems;

5.7.2   upon request, provide other Members with copies of the rules of the procedure;

5.7.3   without discrimination, allow other Members to present their comments in writing, discuss these comments upon request, and take these written comments and the results of these discussions into account.

5.8 Members shall ensure that all conformity assessment procedures which have been adopted are published promptly or otherwise made available in such a manner as to enable interested parties in other Members to become acquainted with them.

5.9 Except in those urgent circumstances referred to in paragraph 7, Members shall allow a reasonable interval between the publication of requirements concerning conformity assessment procedures and their entry into force in order to allow time for producers in exporting Members, and particularly in developing country Members, to adapt their products or methods of production to the requirements of the importing Member.

Article 6 Recognition of Conformity Assessment by Central Government Bodies

With respect to their central government bodies:

6.1 Without prejudice to the provisions of paragraphs 3 and 4, Members shall ensure, whenever possible, that results of conformity assessment procedures in other Members are accepted, even when those procedures differ from their own, provided they are satisfied that those procedures offer an assurance of conformity with applicable technical regulations or standards equivalent to their own procedures. It is recognized that prior consultations may be necessary in order to arrive at a mutually satisfactory understanding regarding, in particular:

6.1.1   adequate and enduring technical competence of the relevant conformity assessment bodies in the exporting Member, so that confidence in the continued reliability of their conformity assessment results can exist; in this regard, verified compliance, for instance through accreditation, with relevant guides or recommendations issued by international standardizing bodies shall be taken into account as an indication of adequate technical competence;

6.1.2   limitation of the acceptance of conformity assessment results to those produced by designated bodies in the exporting Member.

6.2 Members shall ensure that their conformity assessment procedures permit, as far as practicable, the implementation of the provisions in paragraph 1.

6.3 Members are encouraged, at the request of other Members, to be willing to enter into negotiations for the conclusion of agreements for the mutual recognition of results of each other's conformity assessment procedures. Members may require that such agreements fulfil the criteria of paragraph 1 and give mutual satisfaction regarding their potential for facilitating trade in the products concerned.

6.4 Members are encouraged to permit participation of conformity assessment bodies located in the territories of other Members in their conformity assessment procedures under conditions no less favourable than those accorded to bodies located within their territory or the territory of any other country.

Article 7 Procedures for Assessment of Conformity by Local Government Bodies

With respect to their local government bodies within their territories:

7.1 Members shall take such reasonable measures as may be available to them to ensure compliance by such bodies with the provisions of Articles 5 and 6, with the exception of the obligation to notify as referred to in paragraphs 6.2 and 7.1 of Article 5.

7.2 Members shall ensure that the conformity assessment procedures of local governments on the level directly below that of the central government in Members are notified in accordance with the provisions of paragraphs 6.2 and 7.1 of Article 5, noting that notifications shall not be required for conformity assessment procedures the technical content of which is substantially the same as that of previously notified conformity assessment procedures of central government bodies of the Members concerned.

7.3 Members may require contact with other Members, including the notifications, provision of information, comments and discussions referred to in paragraphs 6 and 7 of Article 5, to take place through the central government.

7.4 Members shall not take measures which require or encourage local government bodies within their territories to act in a manner inconsistent with the provisions of Articles 5 and 6.

7.5 Members are fully responsible under this Agreement for the observance of all provisions of Articles 5 and 6. Members shall formulate and implement positive measures and mechanisms in support of the observance of the provisions of Articles 5 and 6 by other than central government bodies.

Article 8 Procedures for Assessment of Conformity by Non-Governmental Bodies

8.1 Members shall take such reasonable measures as may be available to them to ensure that non-governmental bodies within their territories which operate conformity assessment procedures comply with the provisions of Articles 5 and 6, with the exception of the obligation to notify proposed conformity assessment procedures. In addition, Members shall not take measures which have the effect of, directly or indirectly, requiring or encouraging such bodies to act in a manner inconsistent with the provisions of Articles 5 and 6.

8.2 Members shall ensure that their central government bodies rely on conformity assessment procedures operated by non-governmental bodies only if these latter bodies comply with the provisions of Articles 5 and 6, with the exception of the obligation to notify proposed conformity assessment procedures.

Article 9 International and Regional Systems

9.1 Where a positive assurance of conformity with a technical regulation or standard is required, Members shall, wherever practicable, formulate and adopt international systems for conformity assessment and become members thereof or participate therein.

9.2 Members shall take such reasonable measures as may be available to them to ensure that international and regional systems for conformity assessment in which relevant bodies within their territories are members or participants comply with the provisions of Articles 5 and 6. In addition, Members shall not take any measures which have the effect of, directly or indirectly, requiring or encouraging such systems to act in a manner inconsistent with any of the provisions of Articles 5 and 6.

9.3 Members shall ensure that their central government bodies rely on international or regional conformity assessment systems only to the extent that these systems comply with the provisions of Articles 5 and 6, as applicable.

INFORMATION AND ASSISTANCE
Article 10 Information About Technical Regulations, Standards and Conformity Assessment Procedures

10.1 Each Member shall ensure that an enquiry point exists which is able to answer all reasonable enquiries from other Members and interested parties in other Members as well as to provide the relevant documents regarding:

10.1.1   any technical regulations adopted or proposed within its territory by central or local government bodies, by non-governmental bodies which have legal power to enforce a technical regulation, or by regional standardizing bodies of which such bodies are members or participants;

10.1.2   any standards adopted or proposed within its territory by central or local government bodies, or by regional standardizing bodies of which such bodies are members or participants;

10.1.3   any conformity assessment procedures, or proposed conformity assessment procedures, which are operated within its territory by central or local government bodies, or by non-governmental bodies which have legal power to enforce a technical regulation, or by regional bodies of which such bodies are members or participants;

10.1.4   the membership and participation of the Member, or of relevant central or local government bodies within its territory, in international and regional standardizing bodies and conformity assessment systems, as well as in bilateral and multilateral arrangements within the scope of this Agreement; it shall also be able to provide reasonable information on the provisions of such systems and arrangements;

10.1.5   the location of notices published pursuant to this Agreement, or the provision of information as to where such information can be obtained; and

10.1.6   the location of the enquiry points mentioned in paragraph 3.

10.2 If, however, for legal or administrative reasons more than one enquiry point is established by a Member, that Member shall provide to the other Members complete and unambiguous information on the scope of responsibility of each of these enquiry points. In addition, that Member shall ensure that any enquiries addressed to an incorrect enquiry point shall promptly be conveyed to the correct enquiry point.

10.3 Each Member shall take such reasonable measures as may be available to it to ensure that one or more enquiry points exist which are able to answer all reasonable enquiries from other Members and interested parties in other Members as well as to provide the relevant documents or information as to where they can be obtained regarding:

10.3.1   any standards adopted or proposed within its territory by non-governmental standardizing bodies, or by regional standardizing bodies of which such bodies are members or participants; and

10.3.2   any conformity assessment procedures, or proposed conformity assessment procedures, which are operated within its territory by non-governmental bodies, or by regional bodies of which such bodies are members or participants;

10.3.3   the membership and participation of relevant non-governmental bodies within its territory in international and regional standardizing bodies and conformity assessment systems, as well as in bilateral and multilateral arrangements within the scope of this Agreement; they shall also be able to provide reasonable information on the provisions of such systems and arrangements.

10.4 Members shall take such reasonable measures as may be available to them to ensure that where copies of documents are requested by other Members or by interested parties in other Members, in accordance with the provisions of this Agreement, they are supplied at an equitable price (if any) which shall, apart from the real cost of delivery, be the same for the nationals[1] of the Member concerned or of any other Member.

10.5 Developed country Members shall, if requested by other Members, provide, in English, French or Spanish, translations of the documents covered by a specific notification or, in case of voluminous documents, of summaries of such documents.

10.6 The Secretariat shall, when it receives notifications in accordance with the provisions of this Agreement, circulate copies of the notifications to all Members and interested international standardizing and conformity assessment bodies, and draw the attention of developing country Members to any notifications relating to products of particular interest to them.

10.7 Whenever a Member has reached an agreement with any other country or countries on issues related to technical regulations, standards or conformity assessment procedures which may have a significant effect on trade, at least one Member party to the agreement shall notify other Members through the Secretariat of the products to be covered by the agreement and include a brief description of the agreement. Members concerned are encouraged to enter, upon request, into consultations with other Members for the purposes of concluding similar agreements or of arranging for their participation in such agreements.

10.8 Nothing in this Agreement shall be construed as requiring:

10.8.1   the publication of texts other than in the language of the Member;

10.8.2   the provision of particulars or copies of drafts other than in the language of the Member except as stated in paragraph 5; or

10.8.3   Members to furnish any information, the disclosure of which they consider contrary to their essential security interests.

10.9 Notifications to the Secretariat shall be in English, French or Spanish.

10.10 Members shall designate a single central government authority that is responsible for the implementation on the national level of the provisions concerning notification procedures under this Agreement except those included in Annex 3.

10.11 If, however, for legal or administrative reasons the responsibility for notification procedures is divided among two or more central government authorities, the Member concerned shall provide to the other Members complete and unambiguous information on the scope of responsibility of each of these authorities.

Article 11 Technical Assistance to Other Members

11.1 Members shall, if requested, advise other Members, especially the developing country Members, on the preparation of technical regulations.

11.2 Members shall, if requested, advise other Members, especially the developing country Members, and shall grant them technical assistance on mutually agreed terms and conditions regar-

---

1   "Nationals" here shall be deemed, in the case of a separate customs territory Member of the WTO, to mean persons, natural or legal, who are domiciled or who have a real and effective industrial or commercial establishment in that customs territory.

ding the establishment of national standardizing bodies, and participation in the international standardizing bodies, and shall encourage their national standardizing bodies to do likewise.

11.3 Members shall, if requested, take such reasonable measures as may be available to them to arrange for the regulatory bodies within their territories to advise other Members, especially the developing country Members, and shall grant them technical assistance on mutually agreed terms and conditions regarding:

11.3.1   the establishment of regulatory bodies, or bodies for the assessment of conformity with technical regulations; and

11.3.2   the methods by which their technical regulations can best be met.

11.4 Members shall, if requested, take such reasonable measures as may be available to them to arrange for advice to be given to other Members, especially the developing country Members, and shall grant them technical assistance on mutually agreed terms and conditions regarding the establishment of bodies for the assessment of conformity with standards adopted within the territory of the requesting Member.

11.5 Members shall, if requested, advise other Members, especially the developing country Members, and shall grant them technical assistance on mutually agreed terms and conditions regarding the steps that should be taken by their producers if they wish to have access to systems for conformity assessment operated by governmental or non-governmental bodies within the territory of the Member receiving the request.

11.6 Members which are members or participants of international or regional systems for conformity assessment shall, if requested, advise other Members, especially the developing country Members, and shall grant them technical assistance on mutually agreed terms and conditions regarding the establishment of the institutions and legal framework which would enable them to fulfil the obligations of membership or participation in such systems.

11.7 Members shall, if so requested, encourage bodies within their territories which are members or participants of international or regional systems for conformity assessment to advise other Members, especially the developing country Members, and should consider requests for technical assistance from them regarding the establishment of the institutions which would enable the relevant bodies within their territories to fulfil the obligations of membership or participation.

11.8 In providing advice and technical assistance to other Members in terms of paragraphs 1 to 7, Members shall give priority to the needs of the least-developed country Members.

Article 12 Special and Differential Treatment of Developing Country Members

12.1 Members shall provide differential and more favourable treatment to developing country Members to this Agreement, through the following provisions as well as through the relevant provisions of other Articles of this Agreement.

12.2 Members shall give particular attention to the provisions of this Agreement concerning developing country Members' rights and obligations and shall take into account the special development, financial and trade needs of developing country Members in the implementation of this Agreement, both nationally and in the operation of this Agreement's institutional arrangements.

12.3 Members shall, in the preparation and application of technical regulations, standards and conformity assessment procedures, take account of the special development, financial and trade needs of developing country Members, with a view to ensuring that such technical regulations, standards and conformity assessment procedures do not create unnecessary obstacles to exports from developing country Members.

12.4 Members recognize that, although international standards, guides or recommendations may exist, in their particular technological and socio-economic conditions, developing country

Members adopt certain technical regulations, standards or conformity assessment procedures aimed at preserving indigenous technology and production methods and processes compatible with their development needs. Members therefore recognize that developing country Members should not be expected to use international standards as a basis for their technical regulations or standards, including test methods, which are not appropriate to their development, financial and trade needs.

12.5 Members shall take such reasonable measures as may be available to them to ensure that international standardizing bodies and international systems for conformity assessment are organized and operated in a way which facilitates active and representative participation of relevant bodies in all Members, taking into account the special problems of developing country Members.

12.6 Members shall take such reasonable measures as may be available to them to ensure that international standardizing bodies, upon request of developing country Members, examine the possibility of, and, if practicable, prepare international standards concerning products of special interest to developing country Members.

12.7 Members shall, in accordance with the provisions of Article 11, provide technical assistance to developing country Members to ensure that the preparation and application of technical regulations, standards and conformity assessment procedures do not create unnecessary obstacles to the expansion and diversification of exports from developing country Members. In determining the terms and conditions of the technical assistance, account shall be taken of the stage of development of the requesting Members and in particular of the least-developed country Members.

12.8 It is recognized that developing country Members may face special problems, including institutional and infrastructural problems, in the field of preparation and application of technical regulations, standards and conformity assessment procedures. It is further recognized that the special development and trade needs of developing country Members, as well as their stage of technological development, may hinder their ability to discharge fully their obligations under this Agreement. Members, therefore, shall take this fact fully into account. Accordingly, with a view to ensuring that developing country Members are able to comply with this Agreement, the Committee on Technical Barriers to Trade provided for in Article 13 (referred to in this Agreement as the "Committee") is enabled to grant, upon request, specified, time-limited exceptions in whole or in part from obligations under this Agreement. When considering such requests the Committee shall take into account the special problems, in the field of preparation and application of technical regulations, standards and conformity assessment procedures, and the special development and trade needs of the developing country Member, as well as its stage of technological development, which may hinder its ability to discharge fully its obligations under this Agreement. The Committee shall, in particular, take into account the special problems of the least-developed country Members.

12.9 During consultations, developed country Members shall bear in mind the special difficulties experienced by developing country Members in formulating and implementing standards and technical regulations and conformity assessment procedures, and in their desire to assist developing country Members with their efforts in this direction, developed country Members shall take account of the special needs of the former in regard to financing, trade and develop-ment.

12.10   The Committee shall examine periodically the special and differential treatment, as laid down in this Agreement, granted to developing country Members on national and international levels.

INSTITUTIONS, CONSULTATION AND DISPUTE SETTLEMENT
Article 13 The Committee on Technical Barriers to Trade

13.1 A Committee on Technical Barriers to Trade is hereby established, and shall be composed of representatives from each of the Members. The Committee shall elect its own Chairman and shall meet as necessary, but no less than once a year, for the purpose of affording Members the opportunity of consulting on any matters relating to the operation of this Agreement or the furtherance of its objectives, and shall carry out such responsibilities as assigned to it under this Agreement or by the Members.

13.2 The Committee shall establish working parties or other bodies as may be appropriate, which shall carry out such responsibilities as may be assigned to them by the Committee in accordance with the relevant provisions of this Agreement.

13.3 It is understood that unnecessary duplication should be avoided between the work under this Agreement and that of governments in other technical bodies. The Committee shall examine this problem with a view to minimizing such duplication.

Article 14 Consultation and Dispute Settlement

14.1 Consultations and the settlement of disputes with respect to any matter affecting the operation of this Agreement shall take place under the auspices of the Dispute Settlement Body and shall follow, *mutatis mutandis*, the provisions of Articles XXII and XXIII of GATT 1994, as elaborated and applied by the Dispute Settlement Understanding.

14.2 At the request of a party to a dispute, or at its own initiative, a panel may establish a technical expert group to assist in questions of a technical nature, requiring detailed consideration by experts.

14.3 Technical expert groups shall be governed by the procedures of Annex 2.

14.4 The dispute settlement provisions set out above can be invoked in cases where a Member considers that another Member has not achieved satisfactory results under Articles 3, 4, 7, 8 and 9 and its trade interests are significantly affected. In this respect, such results shall be equivalent to those as if the body in question were a Member.

FINAL PROVISIONS
Article 15 Final Provisions

Reservations

15.1 Reservations may not be entered in respect of any of the provisions of this Agreement without the consent of the other Members.

Review

15.2 Each Member shall, promptly after the date on which the WTO Agreement enters into force for it, inform the Committee of measures in existence or taken to ensure the implementation and administration of this Agreement. Any changes of such measures thereafter shall also be notified to the Committee.

15.3 The Committee shall review annually the implementation and operation of this Agreement taking into account the objectives thereof.

15.4 Not later than the end of the third year from the date of entry into force of the WTO Agreement and at the end of each three-year period thereafter, the Committee shall review the operation and implementation of this Agreement, including the provisions relating to transparency, with a view to recommending an adjustment of the rights and obligations of this Agreement where necessary to ensure mutual economic advantage and balance of rights and obligations, without prejudice to the provisions of Article 12. Having regard, *inter alia,* to the experience gained in the implementation of the Agreement, the Committee shall, where appropriate, submit proposals for amendments to the text of this Agreement to the Council for Trade in Goods.

Annexes

15.5 The annexes to this Agreement constitute an integral part thereof.

ANNEX 1 TERMS AND THEIR DEFINITIONS FOR THE PURPOSE OF THIS AGREEMENT

The terms presented in the sixth edition of the ISO/IEC Guide 2: 1991, General Terms and Their Definitions Concerning Standardization and Related Activities, shall, when used in this Agreement, have the same meaning as given in the definitions in the said Guide taking into account that services are excluded from the coverage of this Agreement.

For the purpose of this Agreement, however, the following definitions shall apply:

1. *Technical regulation*

Document which lays down product characteristics or their related processes and production methods, including the applicable administrative provisions, with which compliance is mandatory. It may also include or deal exclusively with terminology, symbols, packaging, marking or labelling requirements as they apply to a product, process or production method.

Explanatory note

The definition in ISO/IEC Guide 2 is not self-contained, but based on the so-called "building block" system.

2. *Standard*

Document approved by a recognized body, that provides, for common and repeated use, rules, guidelines or characteristics for products or related processes and production methods, with which compliance is not mandatory. It may also include or deal exclusively with terminology, symbols, packaging, marking or labelling requirements as they apply to a product, process or production method.

Explanatory note

The terms as defined in ISO/IEC Guide 2 cover products, processes and services. This Agreement deals only with technical regulations, standards and conformity assessment procedures related to products or processes and production methods. Standards as defined by ISO/IEC Guide 2 may be mandatory or voluntary. For the purpose of this Agreement standards are defined as voluntary and technical regulations as mandatory documents. Standards prepared by the international standardization community are based on consensus. This Agreement covers also documents that are not based on consensus.

3. *Conformity assessment procedures*

Any procedure used, directly or indirectly, to determine that relevant requirements in technical regulations or standards are fulfilled.

Explanatory note

Conformity assessment procedures include, *inter alia*, procedures for sampling, testing and inspection; evaluation, verification and assurance of conformity; registration, accreditation and approval as well as their combinations.

4. *International body or system*

Body or system whose membership is open to the relevant bodies of at least all Members.

5. *Regional body or system*

Body or system whose membership is open to the relevant bodies of only some of the Members.

6.   *Central government body*

Central government, its ministries and departments or any body subject to the control of the central government in respect of the activity in question.

Explanatory note:

In the case of the European Communities the provisions governing central government bodies apply. However, regional bodies or conformity assessment systems may be established within the European Communities, and in such cases would be subject to the provisions of this Agreement on regional bodies or conformity assessment systems.

7.   *Local government body*

Government other than a central government (e.g. states, provinces, Länder, cantons, municipalities, etc.), its ministries or departments or any body subject to the control of such a government in respect of the activity in question.

8.   *Non-Governmental body*

Body other than a central government body or a local government body, including a nongovernmental body which has legal power to enforce a technical regulation.

ANNEX 2 TECHNICAL EXPERT GROUPS

The following procedures shall apply to technical expert groups established in accordance with the provisions of Article 14.

1.   Technical expert groups are under the panel's authority. Their terms of reference and detailed working procedures shall be decided by the panel, and they shall report to the panel.

2.   Participation in technical expert groups shall be restricted to persons of professional standing and experience in the field in question.

3.   Citizens of parties to the dispute shall not serve on a technical expert group without the joint agreement of the parties to the dispute, except in exceptional circumstances when the panel considers that the need for specialized scientific expertise cannot be fulfilled otherwise. Government officials of parties to the dispute shall not serve on a technical expert group. Members of technical expert groups shall serve in their individual capacities and not as government representatives, nor as representatives of any organization. Governments or organizations shall therefore not give them instructions with regard to matters before a technical expert group.

4.   Technical expert groups may consult and seek information and technical advice from any source they deem appropriate. Before a technical expert group seeks such information or advice from a source within the jurisdiction of a Member, it shall inform the government of that Member. Any Member shall respond promptly and fully to any request by a technical expert group for such information as the technical expert group considers necessary and appropriate.

5.   The parties to a dispute shall have access to all relevant information provided to a technical expert group, unless it is of a confidential nature. Confidential information provided to the technical expert group shall not be released without formal authorization from the government, organization or person providing the information. Where such information is requested from the technical expert group but release of such information by the technical expert group is not authorized, a non-confidential summary of the information will be provided by the government, organization or person supplying the information.

6.   The technical expert group shall submit a draft report to the Members concerned with a view to obtaining their comments, and taking them into account, as appropriate, in the final report, which shall also be circulated to the Members concerned when it is submitted to the panel.

ANNEX 3 CODE OF GOOD PRACTICE FOR THE PREPARATION, ADOPTION AND APPLICATION OF STANDARDS

General Provisions

A.   For the purposes of this Code the definitions in Annex 1 of this Agreement shall apply.

B.   This Code is open to acceptance by any standardizing body within the territory of a Member of the WTO, whether a central government body, a local government body, or a non-governmental body; to any governmental regional standardizing body one or more members of which are Members of the WTO; and to any non-governmental regional standardizing body one or more members of which are situated within the territory of a Member of the WTO (referred to in this Code collectively as "standardizing bodies" and individually as "the standardizing body").

C.   Standardizing bodies that have accepted or withdrawn from this Code shall notify this fact to the ISO/IEC Information Centre in Geneva. The notification shall include the name and address of the body concerned and the scope of its current and expected standardization activities. The notification may be sent either directly to the ISO/IEC Information Centre, or through the national member body of ISO/IEC or, preferably, through the relevant national member or international affiliate of ISONET, as appropriate.

Substantive Provisions

D.   In respect of standards, the standardizing body shall accord treatment to products originating in the territory of any other Member of the WTO no less favourable than that accorded to like products of national origin and to like products originating in any other country.

E.   The standardizing body shall ensure that standards are not prepared, adopted or applied with a view to, or with the effect of, creating unnecessary obstacles to international trade.

F.   Where international standards exist or their completion is imminent, the standardizing body shall use them, or the relevant parts of them, as a basis for the standards it develops, except where such international standards or relevant parts would be ineffective or inappropriate, for instance, because of an insufficient level of protection or fundamental climatic or geographical factors or fundamental technological problems.

G.   With a view to harmonizing standards on as wide a basis as possible, the standardizing body shall, in an appropriate way, play a full part, within the limits of its resources, in the preparation by relevant international standardizing bodies of international standards regarding subject matter for which it either has adopted, or expects to adopt, standards. For standardizing bodies within the territory of a Member, participation in a particular international standardization activity shall, whenever possible, take place through one delegation representing all standardizing bodies in the territory that have adopted, or expect to adopt, standards for the subject matter to which the international standardization activity relates.

H.   The standardizing body within the territory of a Member shall make every effort to avoid duplication of, or overlap with, the work of other standardizing bodies in the national territory or with the work of relevant international or regional standardizing bodies. They shall also make every effort to achieve a national consensus on the standards they develop. Likewise the regional standardizing body shall make every effort to avoid duplication of, or overlap with, the work of relevant international standardizing bodies.

I.   Wherever appropriate, the standardizing body shall specify standards based on product requirements in terms of performance rather than design or descriptive characteristics.

J.   At least once every six months, the standardizing body shall publish a work programme containing its name and address, the standards it is currently preparing and the standards which it has adopted in the preceding period. A standard is under preparation from the moment a decision has been taken to develop a standard until that standard has been adopted. The titles of specific draft standards shall, upon request, be provided in English, French or Spanish. A notice of the existence of the work programme shall be published in a national or, as the case may be, regional publication of standardization activities.

The work programme shall for each standard indicate, in accordance with any ISONET rules, the classification relevant to the subject matter, the stage attained in the standard's development, and the references of any international standards taken as a basis. No later than at the time of publication of its work programme, the standardizing body shall notify the existence thereof to the ISO/IEC Information Centre in Geneva.

The notification shall contain the name and address of the standardizing body, the name and issue of the publication in which the work programme is published, the period to which the work programme applies, its price (if any), and how and where it can be obtained. The notification may be sent directly to the ISO/IEC Information Centre, or, preferably, through the relevant national member or international affiliate of ISONET, as appropriate.

K.   The national member of ISO/IEC shall make every effort to become a member of ISONET or to appoint another body to become a member as well as to acquire the most advanced membership type possible for the ISONET member. Other standardizing bodies shall make every effort to associate themselves with the ISONET member.

L.   Before adopting a standard, the standardizing body shall allow a period of at least 60 days for the submission of comments on the draft standard by interested parties within the territory of a Member of the WTO. This period may, however, be shortened in cases where urgent problems of safety, health or environment arise or threaten to arise. No later than at the start of the comment period, the standardizing body shall publish a notice announcing the period for commenting in the publication referred to in paragraph J. Such notification shall include, as far as practicable, whether the draft standard deviates from relevant international standards.

M.   On the request of any interested party within the territory of a Member of the WTO, the standardizing body shall promptly provide, or arrange to provide, a copy of a draft standard which it has submitted for comments. Any fees charged for this service shall, apart from the real cost of delivery, be the same for foreign and domestic parties.

N.   The standardizing body shall take into account, in the further processing of the standard, the comments received during the period for commenting. Comments received through standardizing bodies that have accepted this Code of Good Practice shall, if so requested, be replied to as promptly as possible. The reply shall include an explanation why a deviation from relevant international standards is necessary.

O.   Once the standard has been adopted, it shall be promptly published.

P.   On the request of any interested party within the territory of a Member of the WTO, the standardizing body shall promptly provide, or arrange to provide, a copy of its most recent work programme or of a standard which it produced. Any fees charged for this service shall, apart from the real cost of delivery, be the same for foreign and domestic parties.

Q.   The standardizing body shall afford sympathetic consideration to, and adequate opportunity for, consultation regarding representations with respect to the operation of this Code presented by standardizing bodies that have accepted this Code of Good Practice. It shall make an objective effort to solve any complaints.

Agreement on Trade-Related Investment Measures (TRIMs)

Members,

Considering that Ministers agreed in the Punta del Este Declaration that "Following an examination of the operation of GATT Articles related to the trade-restrictive and distorting effects of investment measures, negotiations should elaborate, as appropriate, further provisions that may be necessary to avoid such adverse effects on trade";

Desiring to promote the expansion and progressive liberalisation of world trade and to facilitate investment across international frontiers so as to increase the economic growth of all trading partners, particularly developing country Members, while ensuring free competition;

Taking into account the particular trade, development and financial needs of developing country Members, particularly those of the least-developed country Members;

Recognizing that certain investment measures can cause trade-restrictive and distorting effects;

Hereby *agree* as follows:

Article 1 Coverage

This Agreement applies to investment measures related to trade in goods only (referred to in this Agreement as "TRIMs").

Article 2 National Treatment and Quantitative Restrictions

1.   Without prejudice to other rights and obligations under GATT 1994, no Member shall apply any TRIM that is inconsistent with the provisions of Article III or Article XI of GATT 1994.

2.   An illustrative list of TRIMs that are inconsistent with the obligation of national treatment provided for in paragraph 4 of Article III of GATT 1994 and the obligation of general elimination of quantitative restrictions provided for in paragraph 1 of Article XI of GATT 1994 is contained in the Annex to this Agreement.

Article 3 Exceptions

All exceptions under GATT 1994 shall apply, as appropriate, to the provisions of this Agreement.

Article 4 Developing Country Members

A developing country Member shall be free to deviate temporarily from the provisions of Article 2 to the extent and in such a manner as Article XVIII of GATT 1994, the Understanding on the Balance-of-Payments Provisions of GATT 1994, and the Declaration on Trade Measures Taken for Balance-of-Payments Purposes adopted on 28 November 1979 (BISD 26S/205-209) permit the Member to deviate from the provisions of Articles III and XI of GATT 1994.

Article 5 Notification and Transitional Arrangements

1.   Members, within 90 days of the date of entry into force of the WTO Agreement, shall notify the Council for Trade in Goods of all TRIMs they are applying that are not in conformity with the provisions of this Agreement. Such TRIMs of general or specific application shall be notified, along with their principal features.[1]

2.   Each Member shall eliminate all TRIMs which are notified under paragraph 1 within two years of the date of entry into force of the WTO Agreement in the case of a developed country Member, within five years in the case of a developing country Member, and within seven years in the case of a least-developed country Member.

---

1   In the case of TRIMs applied under discretionary authority, each specific application shall be notified. Information that would prejudice the legitimate commercial interests of particular enterprises need not be disclosed.

3.   On request, the Council for Trade in Goods may extend the transition period for the elimination of TRIMs notified under paragraph 1 for a developing country Member, including a least-
developed country Member, which demonstrates particular difficulties in implementing the
provisions of this Agreement. In considering such a request, the Council for Trade in Goods shall
take into account the individual development, financial and trade needs of the Member in
question.

4.   During the transition period, a Member shall not modify the terms of any TRIM which it
notifies under paragraph 1 from those prevailing at the date of entry into force of the WTO
Agreement so as to increase the degree of inconsistency with the provisions of Article 2. TRIMs
introduced less than 180 days before the date of entry into force of the WTO Agreement shall not
benefit from the transitional arrangements provided in paragraph 2.

5.   Notwithstanding the provisions of Article 2, a Member, in order not to disadvantage
established enterprises which are subject to a TRIM notified under paragraph 1, may apply
during the transition period the same TRIM to a new investment (i) where the products of such
investment are like products to those of the established enterprises, and (ii) where necessary to
avoid distorting the conditions of competition between the new investment and the established
enterprises. Any TRIM so applied to a new investment shall be notified to the Council for Trade in
Goods. The terms of such a TRIM shall be equivalent in their competitive effect to those applicable to the established enterprises, and it shall be terminated at the same time.

Article 6 Transparency

1.   Members reaffirm, with respect to TRIMs, their commitment to obligations on transparency
and notification in Article X of GATT 1994, in the undertaking on "Notification" contained in the
Understanding Regarding Notification, Consultation, Dispute Settlement and Surveillance adopted on 28 November 1979 and in the Ministerial Decision on Notification Procedures adopted on
15 April 1994.

2.   Each Member shall notify the Secretariat of the publications in which TRIMs may be found,
including those applied by regional and local governments and authorities within their territories.

3.   Each Member shall accord sympathetic consideration to requests for information, and afford
adequate opportunity for consultation, on any matter arising from this Agreement raised by
another Member. In conformity with Article X of GATT 1994 no Member is required to disclose
information the disclosure of which would impede law enforcement or otherwise be contrary to
the public interest or would prejudice the legitimate commercial interests of particular enterprises, public or private.

Article 7 Committee on Trade-Related Investment Measures

1.   A Committee on Trade-Related Investment Measures (referred to in this Agreement as the
"Committee") is hereby established, and shall be open to all Members. The Committee shall elect
its own Chairman and Vice-Chairman, and shall meet not less than once a year and otherwise at
the request of any Member.

2.   The Committee shall carry out responsibilities assigned to it by the Council for Trade in
Goods and shall afford Members the opportunity to consult on any matters relating to the
operation and implementation of this Agreement.

3.   The Committee shall monitor the operation and implementation of this Agreement and
shall report thereon annually to the Council for Trade in Goods.

Article 8 Consultation and Dispute Settlement

The provisions of Articles XXII and XXIII of GATT 1994, as elaborated and applied by the Dispute Settlement Understanding, shall apply to consultations and the settlement of disputes under this Agreement.

Article 9 Review by the Council for Trade in Goods

Not later than five years after the date of entry into force of the WTO Agreement, the Council for Trade in Goods shall review the operation of this Agreement and, as appropriate, propose to the Ministerial Conference amendments to its text. In the course of this review, the Council for Trade in Goods shall consider whether the Agreement should be complemented with provisions on investment policy and competition policy.

ANNEX

Illustrative List

1. TRIMs that are inconsistent with the obligation of national treatment provided for in paragraph 4 of Article III of GATT 1994 include those which are mandatory or enforceable under domestic law or under administrative rulings, or compliance with which is necessary to obtain an advantage, and which require:

(a) the purchase or use by an enterprise of products of domestic origin or from any domestic source, whether specified in terms of particular products, in terms of volume or value of products, or in terms of a proportion of volume or value of its local production; or

(b) that an enterprise's purchases or use of imported products be limited to an amount related to the volume or value of local products that it exports.

2. TRIMs that are inconsistent with the obligation of general elimination of quantitative restrictions provided for in paragraph 1 of Article XI of GATT 1994 include those which are mandatory or enforceable under domestic law or under administrative rulings, or compliance with which is necessary to obtain an advantage, and which restrict:

(a) the importation by an enterprise of products used in or related to its local production, generally or to an amount related to the volume or value of local production that it exports;

(b) the importation by an enterprise of products used in or related to its local production by restricting its access to foreign exchange to an amount related to the foreign exchange inflows attributable to the enterprise; or

(c) the exportation or sale for export by an enterprise of products, whether specified in terms of particular products, in terms of volume or value of products, or in terms of a proportion of volume or value of its local production.

Agreement on Implementation of Article VI
of the General Agreement on Tariffs and Trade 1994

Members hereby *agree* as follows:

PART I

Article 1 Principles

An anti-dumping measure shall be applied only under the circumstances provided for in Article VI of GATT 1994 and pursuant to investigations initiated[1] and conducted in accordance with the provisions of this Agreement. The following provisions govern the application of Article VI of GATT 1994 in so far as action is taken under anti-dumping legislation or regulations.

Article 2 Determination of Dumping

2.1 For the purpose of this Agreement, a product is to be considered as being dumped, i.e. introduced into the commerce of another country at less than its normal value, if the export price of the product exported from one country to another is less than the comparable price, in the ordinary course of trade, for the like product when destined for consumption in the exporting country.

2.2 When there are no sales of the like product in the ordinary course of trade in the domestic market of the exporting country or when, because of the particular market situation or the low volume of the sales in the domestic market of the exporting country,[2] such sales do not permit a proper comparison, the margin of dumping shall be determined by comparison with a comparable price of the like product when exported to an appropriate third country, provided that this price is representative, or with the cost of production in the country of origin plus a reasonable amount for administrative, selling and general costs and for profits.

2.2.1 Sales of the like product in the domestic market of the exporting country or sales to a third country at prices below per unit (fixed and variable) costs of production plus administrative, selling and general costs may be treated as not being in the ordinary course of trade by reason of price and may be disregarded in determining normal value only if the authorities[3] determine that such sales are made within an extended period of time[4] in substantial quantities[5] and are at prices which do not provide for the recovery of all costs within a reasonable period of time. If prices which are below per unit costs at the time of sale are above weighted average per unit costs for the period of investigation, such prices shall be considered to provide for recovery of costs within a reasonable period of time.

2.2.1.1 For the purpose of paragraph 2, costs shall normally be calculated on the basis of records kept by the exporter or producer under investigation, provided that such records are in accordance with the generally accepted accounting principles of the

---

1 The term "initiated" as used in this Agreement means the procedural action by which a Member formally commences an investigation as provided in Article 5.

2 Sales of the like product destined for consumption in the domestic market of the exporting country shall normally be considered a sufficient quantity for the determination of the normal value if such sales constitute 5 per cent or more of the sales of the product under consideration to the importing Member, provided that a lower ratio should be acceptable where the evidence demonstrates that domestic sales at such lower ratio are nonetheless of sufficient magnitude to provide for a proper comparison.

3 When in this Agreement the term "authorities" is used, it shall be interpreted as meaning authorities at an appropriate senior level.

4 The extended period of time should normally be one year but shall in no case be less than six months.

5 Sales below per unit costs are made in substantial quantities when the authorities establish that the weighted average selling price of the transactions under consideration for the determination of the normal value is below the weighted average per unit costs, or that the volume of sales below per unit costs represents not less than 20 per cent of the volume sold in transactions under consideration for the determination of the normal value.

exporting country and reasonably reflect the costs associated with the production and sale of the product under consideration. Authorities shall consider all available evidence on the proper allocation of costs, including that which is made available by the exporter or producer in the course of the investigation provided that such allocations have been historically utilized by the exporter or producer, in particular in relation to establishing appropriate amortization and depreciation periods and allowances for capital expenditures and other development costs. Unless already reflected in the cost allocations under this sub-paragraph, costs shall be adjusted appropriately for those non-recurring items of cost which benefit future and/or current production, or for circumstances in which costs during the period of investigation are affected by start-up operations.[6]

2.2.2   For the purpose of paragraph 2, the amounts for administrative, selling and general costs and for profits shall be based on actual data pertaining to production and sales in the ordinary course of trade of the like product by the exporter or producer under investigation. When such amounts cannot be determined on this basis, the amounts may be determined on the basis of:

(i)   the actual amounts incurred and realized by the exporter or producer in question in respect of production and sales in the domestic market of the country of origin of the same general category of products;

(ii)   the weighted average of the actual amounts incurred and realized by other exporters or producers subject to investigation in respect of production and sales of the like product in the domestic market of the country of origin;

(iii)   any other reasonable method, provided that the amount for profit so established shall not exceed the profit normally realized by other exporters or producers on sales of products of the same general category in the domestic market of the country of origin.

2.3 In cases where there is no export price or where it appears to the authorities concerned that the export price is unreliable because of association or a compensatory arrangement between the exporter and the importer or a third party, the export price may be constructed on the basis of the price at which the imported products are first resold to an independent buyer, or if the products are not resold to an independent buyer, or not resold in the condition as imported, on such reasonable basis as the authorities may determine.

2.4 A fair comparison shall be made between the export price and the normal value. This comparison shall be made at the same level of trade, normally at the ex-factory level, and in respect of sales made at as nearly as possible the same time. Due allowance shall be made in each case, on its merits, for differences which affect price comparability, including differences in conditions and terms of sale, taxation, levels of trade, quantities, physical characteristics, and any other differences which are also demonstrated to affect price comparability.[7] In the cases referred to in paragraph 3, allowances for costs, including duties and taxes, incurred between importation and resale, and for profits accruing, should also be made. If in these cases price comparability has been affected, the authorities shall establish the normal value at a level of trade equivalent to the level of trade of the constructed export price, or shall make due allowance as warranted under this paragraph. The authorities shall indicate to the parties in question what information is necessary to ensure a fair comparison and shall not impose an unreasonable burden of proof on those parties.

---

6   The adjustment made for start-up operations shall reflect the costs at the end of the start-up period or, if that period extends beyond the period of investigation, the most recent costs which can reasonably be taken into account by the authorities during the investigation.

7   It is understood that some of the above factors may overlap, and authorities shall ensure that they do not duplicate adjustments that have been already made under this provision.

2.4.1   When the comparison under paragraph 4 requires a conversion of currencies, such conversion should be made using the rate of exchange on the date of sale,[8] provided that when a sale of foreign currency on forward markets is directly linked to the export sale involved, the rate of exchange in the forward sale shall be used. Fluctuations in exchange rates shall be ignored and in an investigation the authorities shall allow exporters at least 60 days to have adjusted their export prices to reflect sustained movements in exchange rates during the period of investigation.

2.4.2   Subject to the provisions governing fair comparison in paragraph 4, the existence of margins of dumping during the investigation phase shall normally be established on the basis of a comparison of a weighted average normal value with a weighted average of prices of all comparable export transactions or by a comparison of normal value and export prices on a transaction-to-transaction basis. A normal value established on a weighted average basis may be compared to prices of individual export transactions if the authorities find a pattern of export prices which differ significantly among different purchasers, regions or time periods, and if an explanation is provided as to why such differences cannot be taken into account appropriately by the use of a weighted average-to-weighted average or transaction-to-transaction comparison.

2.5 In the case where products are not imported directly from the country of origin but are exported to the importing Member from an intermediate country, the price at which the products are sold from the country of export to the importing Member shall normally be compared with the comparable price in the country of export. However, comparison may be made with the price in the country of origin, if, for example, the products are merely transshipped through the country of export, or such products are not produced in the country of export, or there is no comparable price for them in the country of export.

2.6 Throughout this Agreement the term "like product" ("produit similaire") shall be interpreted to mean a product which is identical, i.e. alike in all respects to the product under consideration, or in the absence of such a product, another product which, although not alike in all respects, has characteristics closely resembling those of the product under consideration.

2.7 This Article is without prejudice to the second Supplementary Provision to paragraph 1 of Article VI in Annex I to GATT 1994.

Article 3 Determination of Injury[9]

3.1 A determination of injury for purposes of Article VI of GATT 1994 shall be based on positive evidence and involve an objective examination of both (a) the volume of the dumped imports and the effect of the dumped imports on prices in the domestic market for like products, and (b) the consequent impact of these imports on domestic producers of such products.

3.2 With regard to the volume of the dumped imports, the investigating authorities shall consider whether there has been a significant increase in dumped imports, either in absolute terms or relative to production or consumption in the importing Member. With regard to the effect of the dumped imports on prices, the investigating authorities shall consider whether there has been a significant price undercutting by the dumped imports as compared with the price of a like product of the importing Member, or whether the effect of such imports is otherwise to depress prices to a significant degree or prevent price increases, which otherwise would have occurred, to a significant degree. No one or several of these factors can necessarily give decisive guidance.

---

8   Normally, the date of sale would be the date of contract, purchase order, order confirmation, or invoice, whichever establishes the material terms of sale.

9   Under this Agreement the term "injury" shall, unless otherwise specified, be taken to mean material injury to a domestic industry, threat of material injury to a domestic industry or material retardation of the establishment of such an industry and shall be interpreted in accordance with the provisions of this Article.

3.3 Where imports of a product from more than one country are simultaneously subject to anti-dumping investigations, the investigating authorities may cumulatively assess the effects of such imports only if they determine that (a) the margin of dumping established in relation to the imports from each country is more than *de minimis* as defined in paragraph 8 of Article 5 and the volume of imports from each country is not negligible and (b) a cumulative assessment of the effects of the imports is appropriate in light of the conditions of competition between the imported products and the conditions of competition between the imported products and the like domestic product.

3.4 The examination of the impact of the dumped imports on the domestic industry concerned shall include an evaluation of all relevant economic factors and indices having a bearing on the state of the industry, including actual and potential decline in sales, profits, output, market share, productivity, return on investments, or utilization of capacity; factors affecting domestic prices; the magnitude of the margin of dumping; actual and potential negative effects on cash flow, inventories, employment, wages, growth, ability to raise capital or investments. This list is not exhaustive, nor can one or several of these factors necessarily give decisive guidance.

3.5 It must be demonstrated that the dumped imports are, through the effects of dumping, as set forth in paragraphs 2 and 4, causing injury within the meaning of this Agreement. The demonstration of a causal relationship between the dumped imports and the injury to the domestic industry shall be based on an examination of all relevant evidence before the authorities. The authorities shall also examine any known factors other than the dumped imports which at the same time are injuring the domestic industry, and the injuries caused by these other factors must not be attributed to the dumped imports. Factors which may be relevant in this respect include, *inter alia*, the volume and prices of imports not sold at dumping prices, contraction in demand or changes in the patterns of consumption, trade restrictive practices of and competition between the foreign and domestic producers, developments in technology and the export performance and productivity of the domestic industry.

3.6 The effect of the dumped imports shall be assessed in relation to the domestic production of the like product when available data permit the separate identification of that production on the basis of such criteria as the production process, producers' sales and profits. If such separate identification of that production is not possible, the effects of the dumped imports shall be assessed by the examination of the production of the narrowest group or range of products, which includes the like product, for which the necessary information can be provided.

3.7 A determination of a threat of material injury shall be based on facts and not merely on allegation, conjecture or remote possibility. The change in circumstances which would create a situation in which the dumping would cause injury must be clearly foreseen and imminent.[10] In making a determination regarding the existence of a threat of material injury, the authorities should consider, *inter alia*, such factors as:

(i)   a significant rate of increase of dumped imports into the domestic market indicating the likelihood of substantially increased importation;

(ii)   sufficient freely disposable, or an imminent, substantial increase in, capacity of the exporter indicating the likelihood of substantially increased dumped exports to the importing Member's market, taking into account the availability of other export markets to absorb any additional exports;

(iii)   whether imports are entering at prices that will have a significant depressing or suppressing effect on domestic prices, and would likely increase demand for further imports; and

(iv)   inventories of the product being investigated.

---

10   One example, though not an exclusive one, is that there is convincing reason to believe that there will be, in the near future, substantially increased importation of the product at dumped prices.

No one of these factors by itself can necessarily give decisive guidance but the totality of the factors considered must lead to the conclusion that further dumped exports are imminent and that, unless protective action is taken, material injury would occur.

3.8 With respect to cases where injury is threatened by dumped imports, the application of anti-dumping measures shall be considered and decided with special care.

Article 4 Definition of Domestic Industry

4.1 For the purposes of this Agreement, the term "domestic industry" shall be interpreted as referring to the domestic producers as a whole of the like products or to those of them whose collective output of the products constitutes a major proportion of the total domestic production of those products, except that:

(i)   when producers are related[11] to the exporters or importers or are themselves importers of the allegedly dumped product, the term "domestic industry" may be interpreted as referring to the rest of the producers;

(ii) in exceptional circumstances the territory of a Member may, for the production in question, be divided into two or more competitive markets and the producers within each market may be regarded as a separate industry if (a) the producers within such market sell all or almost all of their production of the product in question in that market, and (b) the demand in that market is not to any substantial degree supplied by producers of the product in question located elsewhere in the territory. In such circumstances, injury may be found to exist even where a major portion of the total domestic industry is not injured, provided there is a concentration of dumped imports into such an isolated market and provided further that the dumped imports are causing injury to the producers of all or almost all of the production within such market.

4.2 When the domestic industry has been interpreted as referring to the producers in a certain area, i.e. a market as defined in paragraph 1(ii), anti-dumping duties shall be levied[12] only on the products in question consigned for final consumption to that area. When the constitutional law of the importing Member does not permit the levying of anti-dumping duties on such a basis, the importing Member may levy the anti-dumping duties without limitation only if (a) the exporters shall have been given an opportunity to cease exporting at dumped prices to the area concerned or otherwise give assurances pursuant to Article 8 and adequate assurances in this regard have not been promptly given, and (b) such duties cannot be levied only on products of specific producers which supply the area in question.

4.3 Where two or more countries have reached under the provisions of paragraph 8(a) of Article XXIV of GATT 1994 such a level of integration that they have the characteristics of a single, unified market, the industry in the entire area of integration shall be taken to be the domestic industry referred to in paragraph 1.

4.4 The provisions of paragraph 6 of Article 3 shall be applicable to this Article.

---

11   For the purpose of this paragraph, producers shall be deemed to be related to exporters or importers only if (a) one of them directly or indirectly controls the other; or (b) both of them are directly or indirectly controlled by a third person; or (c) together they directly or indirectly control a third person, provided that there are grounds for believing or suspecting that the effect of the relationship is such as to cause the producer concerned to behave differently from non-related producers. For the purpose of this paragraph, one shall be deemed to control another when the former is legally or operationally in a position to exercise restraint or direction over the latter.

12   As used in this Agreement "levy" shall mean the definitive or final legal assessment or collection of a duty or tax.

Article 5 Initiation and Subsequent Investigation

5.1 Except as provided for in paragraph 6, an investigation to determine the existence, degree and effect of any alleged dumping shall be initiated upon a written application by or on behalf of the domestic industry.

5.2 An application under paragraph 1 shall include evidence of (a) dumping, (b) injury within the meaning of Article VI of GATT 1994 as interpreted by this Agreement and (c) a causal link between the dumped imports and the alleged injury. Simple assertion, unsubstantiated by relevant evidence, cannot be considered sufficient to meet the requirements of this paragraph. The application shall contain such information as is reasonably available to the applicant on the following:

(i)   the identity of the applicant and a description of the volume and value of the domestic production of the like product by the applicant. Where a written application is made on behalf of the domestic industry, the application shall identify the industry on behalf of which the application is made by a list of all known domestic producers of the like product (or associations of domestic producers of the like product) and, to the extent possible, a description of the volume and value of domestic production of the like product accounted for by such producers;

(ii)   a complete description of the allegedly dumped product, the names of the country or countries of origin or export in question, the identity of each known exporter or foreign producer and a list of known persons importing the product in question;

(iii) information on prices at which the product in question is sold when destined for consumption in the domestic markets of the country or countries of origin or export (or, where appropriate, information on the prices at which the product is sold from the country or countries of origin or export to a third country or countries, or on the constructed value of the product) and information on export prices or, where appropriate, on the prices at which the product is first resold to an independent buyer in the territory of the importing Member;

(iv)   information on the evolution of the volume of the allegedly dumped imports, the effect of these imports on prices of the like product in the domestic market and the consequent impact of the imports on the domestic industry, as demonstrated by relevant factors and indices having a bearing on the state of the domestic industry, such as those listed in paragraphs 2 and 4 of Article 3.

5.3 The authorities shall examine the accuracy and adequacy of the evidence provided in the application to determine whether there is sufficient evidence to justify the initiation of an investigation.

5.4 An investigation shall not be initiated pursuant to paragraph 1 unless the authorities have determined, on the basis of an examination of the degree of support for, or opposition to, the application expressed[13] by domestic producers of the like product, that the application has been made by or on behalf of the domestic industry.[14] The application shall be considered to have been made "by or on behalf of the domestic industry" if it is supported by those domestic producers whose collective output constitutes more than 50 per cent of the total production of the like product produced by that portion of the domestic industry expressing either support for or opposition to the application. However, no investigation shall be initiated when domestic producers expressly supporting the application account for less than 25 per cent of total production of the like product produced by the domestic industry.

---

13   In the case of fragmented industries involving an exceptionally large number of producers, authorities may determine support and opposition by using statistically valid sampling techniques.

14   Members are aware that in the territory of certain Members employees of domestic producers of the like product or representatives of those employees may make or support an application for an investigation under paragraph 1.

5.5 The authorities shall avoid, unless a decision has been made to initiate an investigation, any publicizing of the application for the initiation of an investigation. However, after receipt of a properly documented application and before proceeding to initiate an investigation, the authorities shall notify the government of the exporting Member concerned.

5.6 If, in special circumstances, the authorities concerned decide to initiate an investigation without having received a written application by or on behalf of a domestic industry for the initiation of such investigation, they shall proceed only if they have sufficient evidence of dumping, injury and a causal link, as described in paragraph 2, to justify the initiation of an investigation.

5.7 The evidence of both dumping and injury shall be considered simultaneously (a) in the decision whether or not to initiate an investigation, and (b) thereafter, during the course of the investigation, starting on a date not later than the earliest date on which in accordance with the provisions of this Agreement provisional measures may be applied.

5.8 An application under paragraph 1 shall be rejected and an investigation shall be terminated promptly as soon as the authorities concerned are satisfied that there is not sufficient evidence of either dumping or of injury to justify proceeding with the case. There shall be immediate termination in cases where the authorities determine that the margin of dumping is *de minimis*, or that the volume of dumped imports, actual or potential, or the injury, is negligible. The margin of dumping shall be considered to be *de minimis* if this margin is less than 2 per cent, expressed as a percentage of the export price. The volume of dumped imports shall normally be regarded as negligible if the volume of dumped imports from a particular country is found to account for less than 3 per cent of imports of the like product in the importing Member, unless countries which individually account for less than 3 per cent of the imports of the like product in the importing Member collectively account for more than 7 per cent of imports of the like product in the importing Member.

5.9 An anti-dumping proceeding shall not hinder the procedures of customs clearance.

5.10 Investigations shall, except in special circumstances, be concluded within one year, and in no case more than 18 months, after their initiation.

Article 6 Evidence

6.1 All interested parties in an anti-dumping investigation shall be given notice of the information which the authorities require and ample opportunity to present in writing all evidence which they consider relevant in respect of the investigation in question.

6.1.1   Exporters or foreign producers receiving questionnaires used in an anti- dumping investigation shall be given at least 30 days for reply.[15] Due consideration should be given to any request for an extension of the 30-day period and, upon cause shown, such an extension should be granted whenever practicable.

6.1.2   Subject to the requirement to protect confidential information, evidence presented in writing by one interested party shall be made available promptly to other interested parties participating in the investigation.

6.1.3   As soon as an investigation has been initiated, the authorities shall provide the full text of the written application received under paragraph 1 of Article 5 to the known

---

15   As a general rule, the time-limit for exporters shall be counted from the date of receipt of the questionnaire, which for this purpose shall be deemed to have been received one week from the date on which it was sent to the respondent or transmitted to the appropriate diplomatic representative of the exporting Member or, in the case of a separate customs territory Member of the WTO, an official representative of the exporting territory.

exporters[16] and to the authorities of the exporting Member and shall make it available, upon request, to other interested parties involved. Due regard shall be paid to the requirement for the protection of confidential information, as provided for in paragraph 5.

6.2 Throughout the anti-dumping investigation all interested parties shall have a full opportunity for the defence of their interests. To this end, the authorities shall, on request, provide opportunities for all interested parties to meet those parties with adverse interests, so that opposing views may be presented and rebuttal arguments offered. Provision of such opportunities must take account of the need to preserve confidentiality and of the convenience to the parties. There shall be no obligation on any party to attend a meeting, and failure to do so shall not be prejudicial to that party's case. Interested parties shall also have the right, on justification, to present other information orally.

6.3 Oral information provided under paragraph 2 shall be taken into account by the authorities only in so far as it is subsequently reproduced in writing and made available to other interested parties, as provided for in subparagraph 1.2.

6.4 The authorities shall whenever practicable provide timely opportunities for all interested parties to see all information that is relevant to the presentation of their cases, that is not confidential as defined in paragraph 5, and that is used by the authorities in an anti-dumping investigation, and to prepare presentations on the basis of this information.

6.5 Any information which is by nature confidential (for example, because its disclosure would be of significant competitive advantage to a competitor or because its disclosure would have a significantly adverse effect upon a person supplying the information or upon a person from whom that person acquired the information), or which is provided on a confidential basis by parties to an investigation shall, upon good cause shown, be treated as such by the authorities. Such information shall not be disclosed without specific permission of the party submitting it.[17]

6.5.1 The authorities shall require interested parties providing confidential information to furnish non-confidential summaries thereof. These summaries shall be in sufficient detail to permit a reasonable understanding of the substance of the information submitted in confidence. In exceptional circumstances, such parties may indicate that such information is not susceptible of summary. In such exceptional circumstances, a statement of the reasons why summarization is not possible must be provided.

6.5.2 If the authorities find that a request for confidentiality is not warranted and if the supplier of the information is either unwilling to make the information public or to authorize its disclosure in generalized or summary form, the authorities may disregard such information unless it can be demonstrated to their satisfaction from appropriate sources that the information is correct.[18]

6.6 Except in circumstances provided for in paragraph 8, the authorities shall during the course of an investigation satisfy themselves as to the accuracy of the information supplied by interested parties upon which their findings are based.

6.7 In order to verify information provided or to obtain further details, the authorities may carry out investigations in the territory of other Members as required, provided they obtain the agreement of the firms concerned and notify the representatives of the government of the Member in question, and unless that Member objects to the investigation. The procedures described in Annex I shall apply to investigations carried out in the territory of other Members. Subject to the

---

16   It being understood that, where the number of exporters involved is particularly high, the full text of the written application should instead be provided only to the authorities of the exporting Member or to the relevant trade association.

17   Members are aware that in the territory of certain Members disclosure pursuant to a narrowly-drawn protective order may be required.

18   Members agree that requests for confidentiality should not be arbitrarily rejected.

requirement to protect confidential information, the authorities shall make the results of any such investigations available, or shall provide disclosure thereof pursuant to paragraph 9, to the firms to which they pertain and may make such results available to the applicants.

6.8 In cases in which any interested party refuses access to, or otherwise does not provide, necessary information within a reasonable period or significantly impedes the investigation, preliminary and final determinations, affirmative or negative, may be made on the basis of the facts available. The provisions of Annex II shall be observed in the application of this paragraph.

6.9 The authorities shall, before a final determination is made, inform all interested parties of the essential facts under consideration which form the basis for the decision whether to apply definitive measures. Such disclosure should take place in sufficient time for the parties to defend their interests.

6.10 The authorities shall, as a rule, determine an individual margin of dumping for each known exporter or producer concerned of the product under investigation. In cases where the number of exporters, producers, importers or types of products involved is so large as to make such a determination impracticable, the authorities may limit their examination either to a reasonable number of interested parties or products by using samples which are statistically valid on the basis of information available to the authorities at the time of the selection, or to the largest percentage of the volume of the exports from the country in question which can reasonably be investigated.

> 6.10.1   Any selection of exporters, producers, importers or types of products made under this paragraph shall preferably be chosen in consultation with and with the consent of the exporters, producers or importers concerned.

> 6.10.2   In cases where the authorities have limited their examination, as provided for in this paragraph, they shall nevertheless determine an individual margin of dumping for any exporter or producer not initially selected who submits the necessary information in time for that information to be considered during the course of the investigation, except where the number of exporters or producers is so large that individual examinations would be unduly burdensome to the authorities and prevent the timely completion of the investigation. Voluntary responses shall not be discouraged.

6.11 For the purposes of this Agreement, "interested parties" shall include:

(i)   an exporter or foreign producer or the importer of a product subject to investigation, or a trade or business association a majority of the members of which are producers, exporters or importers of such product;

(ii)   the government of the exporting Member; and

(iii)   a producer of the like product in the importing Member or a trade and business association a majority of the members of which produce the like product in the territory of the importing Member.

This list shall not preclude Members from allowing domestic or foreign parties other than those mentioned above to be included as interested parties.

6.12 The authorities shall provide opportunities for industrial users of the product under investigation, and for representative consumer organizations in cases where the product is commonly sold at the retail level, to provide information which is relevant to the investigation regarding dumping, injury and causality.

6.13 The authorities shall take due account of any difficulties experienced by interested parties, in particular small companies, in supplying information requested, and shall provide any assistance practicable.

6.14 The procedures set out above are not intended to prevent the authorities of a Member from proceeding expeditiously with regard to initiating an investigation, reaching preliminary or final determinations, whether affirmative or negative, or from applying provisional or final measures, in accordance with relevant provisions of this Agreement.

Article 7 Provisional Measures

7.1 Provisional measures may be applied only if:

(i) an investigation has been initiated in accordance with the provisions of Article 5, a public notice has been given to that effect and interested parties have been given adequate opportunities to submit information and make comments;

(ii) a preliminary affirmative determination has been made of dumping and consequent injury to a domestic industry; and

(iii) the authorities concerned judge such measures necessary to prevent injury being caused during the investigation.

7.2 Provisional measures may take the form of a provisional duty or, preferably, a security - by cash deposit or bond - equal to the amount of the anti-dumping duty provisionally estimated, being not greater than the provisionally estimated margin of dumping. Withholding of appraisement is an appropriate provisional measure, provided that the normal duty and the estimated amount of the anti-dumping duty be indicated and as long as the withholding of appraisement is subject to the same conditions as other provisional measures.

7.3 Provisional measures shall not be applied sooner than 60 days from the date of initiation of the investigation.

7.4 The application of provisional measures shall be limited to as short a period as possible, not exceeding four months or, on decision of the authorities concerned, upon request by exporters representing a significant percentage of the trade involved, to a period not exceeding six months. When authorities, in the course of an investigation, examine whether a duty lower than the margin of dumping would be sufficient to remove injury, these periods may be six and nine months, respectively.

7.5 The relevant provisions of Article 9 shall be followed in the application of provisional measures.

Article 8 Price Undertakings

8.1 Proceedings may[19] be suspended or terminated without the imposition of provisional measures or anti-dumping duties upon receipt of satisfactory voluntary undertakings from any exporter to revise its prices or to cease exports to the area in question at dumped prices so that the authorities are satisfied that the injurious effect of the dumping is eliminated. Price increases under such undertakings shall not be higher than necessary to eliminate the margin of dumping. It is desirable that the price increases be less than the margin of dumping if such increases would be adequate to remove the injury to the domestic industry.

8.2 Price undertakings shall not be sought or accepted from exporters unless the authorities of the importing Member have made a preliminary affirmative determination of dumping and injury caused by such dumping.

8.3 Undertakings offered need not be accepted if the authorities consider their acceptance impractical, for example, if the number of actual or potential exporters is too great, or for other reasons, including reasons of general policy. Should the case arise and where practicable, the authorities shall provide to the exporter the reasons which have led them to consider acceptance of an undertaking as inappropriate, and shall, to the extent possible, give the exporter an opportunity to make comments thereon.

---

19 The word "may" shall not be interpreted to allow the simultaneous continuation of proceedings with the implementation of price undertakings except as provided in paragraph 4.

8.4 If an undertaking is accepted, the investigation of dumping and injury shall nevertheless be completed if the exporter so desires or the authorities so decide. In such a case, if a negative determination of dumping or injury is made, the undertaking shall automatically lapse, except in cases where such a determination is due in large part to the existence of a price undertaking. In such cases, the authorities may require that an undertaking be maintained for a reasonable period consistent with the provisions of this Agreement. In the event that an affirmative determination of dumping and injury is made, the undertaking shall continue consistent with its terms and the provisions of this Agreement.

8.5 Price undertakings may be suggested by the authorities of the importing Member, but no exporter shall be forced to enter into such undertakings. The fact that exporters do not offer such undertakings, or do not accept an invitation to do so, shall in no way prejudice the consideration of the case. However, the authorities are free to determine that a threat of injury is more likely to be realized if the dumped imports continue.

8.6 Authorities of an importing Member may require any exporter from whom an undertaking has been accepted to provide periodically information relevant to the fulfilment of such an undertaking and to permit verification of pertinent data. In case of violation of an undertaking, the authorities of the importing Member may take, under this Agreement in conformity with its provisions, expeditious actions which may constitute immediate application of provisional measures using the best information available. In such cases, definitive duties may be levied in accordance with this Agreement on products entered for consumption not more than 90 days before the application of such provisional measures, except that any such retroactive assessment shall not apply to imports entered before the violation of the undertaking.

Article 9 Imposition and Collection of Anti-Dumping Duties

9.1 The decision whether or not to impose an anti-dumping duty in cases where all require- ments for the imposition have been fulfilled, and the decision whether the amount of the anti-dumping duty to be imposed shall be the full margin of dumping or less, are decisions to be made by the authorities of the importing Member. It is desirable that the imposition be permissive in the territory of all Members, and that the duty be less than the margin if such lesser duty would be adequate to remove the injury to the domestic industry.

9.2 When an anti-dumping duty is imposed in respect of any product, such anti-dumping duty shall be collected in the appropriate amounts in each case, on a non-discriminatory basis on imports of such product from all sources found to be dumped and causing injury, except as to imports from those sources from which price undertakings under the terms of this Agreement have been accepted. The authorities shall name the supplier or suppliers of the product concerned. If, however, several suppliers from the same country are involved, and it is imprac- ticable to name all these suppliers, the authorities may name the supplying country concerned. If several suppliers from more than one country are involved, the authorities may name either all the suppliers involved, or, if this is impracticable, all the supplying countries involved.

9.3 The amount of the anti-dumping duty shall not exceed the margin of dumping as established under Article 2.

9.3.1   When the amount of the anti-dumping duty is assessed on a retrospective basis, the determination of the final liability for payment of anti-dumping duties shall take place as soon as possible, normally within 12 months, and in no case more than 18 months, after the date on which a request for a final assessment of the amount of the anti-dumping duty has been made.[20] Any refund shall be made promptly and normally in not more than 90 days following the determination of final liability made pursuant to this sub-paragraph. In any case, where a refund is not made within 90 days, the authorities shall provide an explanation if so requested.

---

20   It is understood that the observance of the time-limits mentioned in this subparagraph and in subparagraph 3.2 may not be possible where the product in question is subject to judicial review proceedings.

9.3.2 When the amount of the anti-dumping duty is assessed on a prospective basis, provision shall be made for a prompt refund, upon request, of any duty paid in excess of the margin of dumping. A refund of any such duty paid in excess of the actual margin of dumping shall normally take place within 12 months, and in no case more than 18 months, after the date on which a request for a refund, duly supported by evidence, has been made by an importer of the product subject to the anti-dumping duty. The refund authorized should normally be made within 90 days of the above-noted decision.

9.3.3 In determining whether and to what extent a reimbursement should be made when the export price is constructed in accordance with paragraph 3 of Article 2, authorities should take account of any change in normal value, any change in costs incurred between importation and resale, and any movement in the resale price which is duly reflected in subsequent selling prices, and should calculate the export price with no deduction for the amount of anti-dumping duties paid when conclusive evidence of the above is provided.

9.4 When the authorities have limited their examination in accordance with the second sentence of paragraph 10 of Article 6, any anti-dumping duty applied to imports from exporters or producers not included in the examination shall not exceed:

(i) the weighted average margin of dumping established with respect to the selected exporters or producers or,

(ii) where the liability for payment of anti-dumping duties is calculated on the basis of a prospective normal value, the difference between the weighted average normal value of the selected exporters or producers and the export prices of exporters or producers not individually examined,

provided that the authorities shall disregard for the purpose of this paragraph any zero and *de minimis* margins and margins established under the circumstances referred to in paragraph 8 of Article 6. The authorities shall apply individual duties or normal values to imports from any exporter or producer not included in the examination who has provided the necessary information during the course of the investigation, as provided for in subparagraph 10.2 of Article 6.

9.5 If a product is subject to anti-dumping duties in an importing Member, the authorities shall promptly carry out a review for the purpose of determining individual margins of dumping for any exporters or producers in the exporting country in question who have not exported the product to the importing Member during the period of investigation, provided that these exporters or producers can show that they are not related to any of the exporters or producers in the exporting country who are subject to the anti-dumping duties on the product. Such a review shall be initiated and carried out on an accelerated basis, compared to normal duty assessment and review proceedings in the importing Member. No anti-dumping duties shall be levied on imports from such exporters or producers while the review is being carried out. The authorities may, however, withhold appraisement and/or request guarantees to ensure that, should such a review result in a determination of dumping in respect of such producers or exporters, anti-dumping duties can be levied retroactively to the date of the initiation of the review.

Article 10 Retroactivity

10.1 Provisional measures and anti-dumping duties shall only be applied to products which enter for consumption after the time when the decision taken under paragraph 1 of Article 7 and paragraph 1 of Article 9, respectively, enters into force, subject to the exceptions set out in this Article.

10.2 Where a final determination of injury (but not of a threat thereof or of a material retardation of the establishment of an industry) is made or, in the case of a final determination of a threat of injury, where the effect of the dumped imports would, in the absence of the provisional measures, have led to a determination of injury, anti- dumping duties may be levied retroactively for the period for which provisional measures, if any, have been applied.

10.3 If the definitive anti-dumping duty is higher than the provisional duty paid or payable, or the amount estimated for the purpose of the security, the difference shall not be collected. If the definitive duty is lower than the provisional duty paid or payable, or the amount estimated for the purpose of the security, the difference shall be reimbursed or the duty recalculated, as the case may be.

10.4 Except as provided in paragraph 2, where a determination of threat of injury or material retardation is made (but no injury has yet occurred) a definitive anti- dumping duty may be imposed only from the date of the determination of threat of injury or material retardation, and any cash deposit made during the period of the application of provisional measures shall be refunded and any bonds released in an expeditious manner.

10.5 Where a final determination is negative, any cash deposit made during the period of the application of provisional measures shall be refunded and any bonds released in an expeditious manner.

10.6 A definitive anti-dumping duty may be levied on products which were entered for consumption not more than 90 days prior to the date of application of provisional measures, when the authorities determine for the dumped product in question that:

(i)   there is a history of dumping which caused injury or that the importer was, or should have been, aware that the exporter practises dumping and that such dumping would cause injury, and

(ii)   the injury is caused by massive dumped imports of a product in a relatively short time which in light of the timing and the volume of the dumped imports and other circumstances (such as a rapid build-up of inventories of the imported product) is likely to seriously undermine the remedial effect of the definitive anti-dumping duty to be applied, provided that the importers concerned have been given an opportunity to comment.

10.7 The authorities may, after initiating an investigation, take such measures as the withholding of appraisement or assessment as may be necessary to collect anti-dumping duties retroactively, as provided for in paragraph 6, once they have sufficient evidence that the conditions set forth in that paragraph are satisfied.

10.8 No duties shall be levied retroactively pursuant to paragraph 6 on products entered for consumption prior to the date of initiation of the investigation.

Article 11 Duration and Review of Anti-Dumping Duties and Price Undertakings

11.1 An anti-dumping duty shall remain in force only as long as and to the extent necessary to counteract dumping which is causing injury.

11.2 The authorities shall review the need for the continued imposition of the duty, where warranted, on their own initiative or, provided that a reasonable period of time has elapsed since the imposition of the definitive anti-dumping duty, upon request by any interested party which submits positive information substantiating the need for a review.[21] Interested parties shall have the right to request the authorities to examine whether the continued imposition of the duty is necessary to offset dumping, whether the injury would be likely to continue or recur if the duty were removed or varied, or both. If, as a result of the review under this paragraph, the authorities determine that the anti-dumping duty is no longer warranted, it shall be terminated immediately.

11.3 Notwithstanding the provisions of paragraphs 1 and 2, any definitive anti- dumping duty shall be terminated on a date not later than five years from its imposition (or from the date of the most recent review under paragraph 2 if that review has covered both dumping and injury, or under this paragraph), unless the authorities determine, in a review initiated before that date on

---

21   A determination of final liability for payment of anti-dumping duties, as provided for in paragraph 3 of Article 9, does not by itself constitute a review within the meaning of this Article.

their own initiative or upon a duly substantiated request made by or on behalf of the domestic industry within a reasonable period of time prior to that date, that the expiry of the duty would be likely to lead to continuation or recurrence of dumping and injury.[22] The duty may remain in force pending the outcome of such a review.

11.4 The provisions of Article 6 regarding evidence and procedure shall apply to any review carried out under this Article. Any such review shall be carried out expeditiously and shall normally be concluded within 12 months of the date of initiation of the review.

11.5 The provisions of this Article shall apply *mutatis mutandis* to price undertakings accepted under Article 8.

Article 12 Public Notice and Explanation of Determinations

12.1 When the authorities are satisfied that there is sufficient evidence to justify the initiation of an anti-dumping investigation pursuant to Article 5, the Member or Members the products of which are subject to such investigation and other interested parties known to the investigating authorities to have an interest therein shall be notified and a public notice shall be given.

12.1.1 A public notice of the initiation of an investigation shall contain, or otherwise make available through a separate report,[23] adequate information on the following:

(i)   the name of the exporting country or countries and the product involved;

(ii) the date of initiation of the investigation;

(iii) the basis on which dumping is alleged in the application;

(iv) a summary of the factors on which the allegation of injury is based;

(v)   the address to which representations by interested parties should be directed;

(vi) the time-limits allowed to interested parties for making their views known.

12.2 Public notice shall be given of any preliminary or final determination, whether affirmative or negative, of any decision to accept an undertaking pursuant to Article 8, of the termination of such an undertaking, and of the termination of a definitive anti- dumping duty. Each such notice shall set forth, or otherwise make available through a separate report, in sufficient detail the findings and conclusions reached on all issues of fact and law considered material by the investigating authorities. All such notices and reports shall be forwarded to the Member or Members the products of which are subject to such determination or undertaking and to other interested parties known to have an interest therein.

12.2.1 A public notice of the imposition of provisional measures shall set forth, or otherwise make available through a separate report, sufficiently detailed explanations for the preliminary determinations on dumping and injury and shall refer to the matters of fact and law which have led to arguments being accepted or rejected. Such a notice or report shall, due regard being paid to the requirement for the protection of confidential information, contain in particular:

(i)   the names of the suppliers, or when this is impracticable, the supplying countries involved;

(ii) a description of the product which is sufficient for customs purposes;

(iii) the margins of dumping established and a full explanation of the reasons for the methodology used in the establishment and comparison of the export price and the normal value under Article 2;

---

22   When the amount of the anti-dumping duty is assessed on a retrospective basis, a finding in the most recent assessment proceeding under subparagraph 3.1 of Article 9 that no duty is to be levied shall not by itself require the authorities to terminate the definitive duty.

23   Where authorities provide information and explanations under the provisions of this Article in a separate report, they shall ensure that such report is readily available to the public.

(iv) considerations relevant to the injury determination as set out in Article 3;

(v) the main reasons leading to the determination.

12.2.2   A public notice of conclusion or suspension of an investigation in the case of an affir-mative determination providing for the imposition of a definitive duty or the acceptance of a price undertaking shall contain, or otherwise make available through a separate report, all rele-vant information on the matters of fact and law and reasons which have led to the imposition of final measures or the acceptance of a price undertaking, due regard being paid to the require-ment for the protection of confidential information. In particular, the notice or report shall con-tain the information described in subparagraph 2.1, as well as the reasons for the acceptance or rejection of relevant arguments or claims made by the exporters and importers, and the basis for any decision made under subparagraph 10.2 of Article 6.

12.2.3   A public notice of the termination or suspension of an investigation following the acceptance of an undertaking pursuant to Article 8 shall include, or otherwise make avail-able through a separate report, the non-confidential part of this undertaking.

12.3 The provisions of this Article shall apply *mutatis mutandis* to the initiation and completion of reviews pursuant to Article 11 and to decisions under Article 10 to apply duties retroactively.

Article 13 Judicial Review

Each Member whose national legislation contains provisions on anti-dumping measures shall maintain judicial, arbitral or administrative tribunals or procedures for the purpose, *inter alia*, of the prompt review of administrative actions relating to final determinations and reviews of determinations within the meaning of Article 11. Such tribunals or procedures shall be indepen-dent of the authorities responsible for the determination or review in question.

Article 14 Anti-Dumping Action on Behalf of a Third Country

14.1 An application for anti-dumping action on behalf of a third country shall be made by the authorities of the third country requesting action.

14.2 Such an application shall be supported by price information to show that the imports are being dumped and by detailed information to show that the alleged dumping is causing injury to the domestic industry concerned in the third country. The government of the third country shall afford all assistance to the authorities of the importing country to obtain any further infor-mation which the latter may require.

14.3 In considering such an application, the authorities of the importing country shall consider the effects of the alleged dumping on the industry concerned as a whole in the third country; that is to say, the injury shall not be assessed in relation only to the effect of the alleged dumping on the industry's exports to the importing country or even on the industry's total exports.

14.4 The decision whether or not to proceed with a case shall rest with the importing country. If the importing country decides that it is prepared to take action, the initiation of the approach to the Council for Trade in Goods seeking its approval for such action shall rest with the importing country.

Article 15 Developing Country Members

It is recognized that special regard must be given by developed country Members to the special situation of developing country Members when considering the application of anti-dumping measures under this Agreement. Possibilities of constructive remedies provided for by this Agreement shall be explored before applying anti-dumping duties where they would affect the essential interests of developing country Members.

PART II
Article 16 Committee on Anti-Dumping Practices

16.1 There is hereby established a Committee on Anti-Dumping Practices (referred to in this Agreement as the "Committee") composed of representatives from each of the Members. The Committee shall elect its own Chairman and shall meet not less than twice a year and otherwise as envisaged by relevant provisions of this Agreement at the request of any Member. The Committee shall carry out responsibilities as assigned to it under this Agreement or by the Members and it shall afford Members the opportunity of consulting on any matters relating to the operation of the Agreement or the furtherance of its objectives. The WTO Secretariat shall act as the secretariat to the Committee.

16.2 The Committee may set up subsidiary bodies as appropriate.

16.3 In carrying out their functions, the Committee and any subsidiary bodies may consult with and seek information from any source they deem appropriate. However, before the Committee or a subsidiary body seeks such information from a source within the jurisdiction of a Member, it shall inform the Member involved. It shall obtain the consent of the Member and any firm to be consulted.

16.4 Members shall report without delay to the Committee all preliminary or final anti-dumping actions taken. Such reports shall be available in the Secretariat for inspection by other Members. Members shall also submit, on a semi-annual basis, reports of any anti-dumping actions taken within the preceding six months. The semi-annual reports shall be submitted on an agreed standard form.

16.5 Each Member shall notify the Committee (a) which of its authorities are competent to initiate and conduct investigations referred to in Article 5 and (b) its domestic procedures governing the initiation and conduct of such investigations.

Article 17 Consultation and Dispute Settlement

17.1 Except as otherwise provided herein, the Dispute Settlement Understanding is applicable to consultations and the settlement of disputes under this Agreement.

17.2 Each Member shall afford sympathetic consideration to, and shall afford adequate opportunity for consultation regarding, representations made by another Member with respect to any matter affecting the operation of this Agreement.

17.3 If any Member considers that any benefit accruing to it, directly or indirectly, under this Agreement is being nullified or impaired, or that the achievement of any objective is being impeded, by another Member or Members, it may, with a view to reaching a mutually satisfactory resolution of the matter, request in writing consultations with the Member or Members in question. Each Member shall afford sympathetic consideration to any request from another Member for consultation.

17.4 If the Member that requested consultations considers that the consultations pursuant to paragraph 3 have failed to achieve a mutually agreed solution, and if final action has been taken by the administering authorities of the importing Member to levy definitive anti-dumping duties or to accept price undertakings, it may refer the matter to the Dispute Settlement Body ("DSB"). When a provisional measure has a significant impact and the Member that requested consultations considers that the measure was taken contrary to the provisions of paragraph 1 of Article 7, that Member may also refer such matter to the DSB.

17.5 The DSB shall, at the request of the complaining party, establish a panel to examine the matter based upon:

(i) a written statement of the Member making the request indicating how a benefit accruing to it, directly or indirectly, under this Agreement has been nullified or impaired, or that the achieving of the objectives of the Agreement is being impeded, and (ii)	the facts made available in conformity with appropriate domestic procedures to the authorities of the importing Member.

17.6 In examining the matter referred to in paragraph 5:

(i)	in its assessment of the facts of the matter, the panel shall determine whether the authorities' establishment of the facts was proper and whether their evaluation of those facts was unbiased and objective. If the establishment of the facts was proper and the evaluation was unbiased and objective, even though the panel might have reached a different conclusion, the evaluation shall not be overturned;

(ii)	the panel shall interpret the relevant provisions of the Agreement in accordance with customary rules of interpretation of public international law. Where the panel finds that a relevant provision of the Agreement admits of more than one permissible interpretation, the panel shall find the authorities' measure to be in conformity with the Agreement if it rests upon one of those permissible interpretations.

17.7 Confidential information provided to the panel shall not be disclosed without formal authorization from the person, body or authority providing such information. Where such information is requested from the panel but release of such information by the panel is not authorized, a non-confidential summary of the information, authorized by the person, body or authority providing the information, shall be provided.

PART III

Article 18 Final Provisions

18.1 No specific action against dumping of exports from another Member can be taken except in accordance with the provisions of GATT 1994, as interpreted by this Agreement.[24]

18.2 Reservations may not be entered in respect of any of the provisions of this Agreement without the consent of the other Members.

18.3 Subject to subparagraphs 3.1 and 3.2, the provisions of this Agreement shall apply to investigations, and reviews of existing measures, initiated pursuant to applications which have been made on or after the date of entry into force for a Member of the WTO Agreement.

18.3.1	With respect to the calculation of margins of dumping in refund procedures under paragraph 3 of Article 9, the rules used in the most recent determination or review of dumping shall apply.

18.3.2	For the purposes of paragraph 3 of Article 11, existing anti-dumping measures shall be deemed to be imposed on a date not later than the date of entry into force for a Member of the WTO Agreement, except in cases in which the domestic legislation of a Member in force on that date already included a clause of the type provided for in that paragraph.

18.4 Each Member shall take all necessary steps, of a general or particular character, to ensure, not later than the date of entry into force of the WTO Agreement for it, the conformity of its laws, regulations and administrative procedures with the provisions of this Agreement as they may apply for the Member in question.

18.5 Each Member shall inform the Committee of any changes in its laws and regulations relevant to this Agreement and in the administration of such laws and regulations.

18.6 The Committee shall review annually the implementation and operation of this Agreement taking into account the objectives thereof. The Committee shall inform annually the Council for Trade in Goods of developments during the period covered by such reviews.

18.7 The Annexes to this Agreement constitute an integral part thereof.

24	This is not intended to preclude action under other relevant provisions of GATT 1994, as appropriate.

ANNEX I – PROCEDURES FOR ON-THE-SPOT INVESTIGATIONS PURSUANT TO PARAGRAPH 7 OF ARTICLE 6

1.   Upon initiation of an investigation, the authorities of the exporting Member and the firms known to be concerned should be informed of the intention to carry out on-the-spot investigations.

2.   If in exceptional circumstances it is intended to include non-governmental experts in the investigating team, the firms and the authorities of the exporting Member should be so informed. Such non-governmental experts should be subject to effective sanctions for breach of confidentiality requirements.

3.   It should be standard practice to obtain explicit agreement of the firms concerned in the exporting Member before the visit is finally scheduled.

4.   As soon as the agreement of the firms concerned has been obtained, the investigating authorities should notify the authorities of the exporting Member of the names and addresses of the firms to be visited and the dates agreed.

5.   Sufficient advance notice should be given to the firms in question before the visit is made.

6.   Visits to explain the questionnaire should only be made at the request of an exporting firm. Such a visit may only be made if (a) the authorities of the importing Member notify the representatives of the Member in question and (b) the latter do not object to the visit.

7.   As the main purpose of the on-the-spot investigation is to verify information provided or to obtain further details, it should be carried out after the response to the questionnaire has been received unless the firm agrees to the contrary and the government of the exporting Member is informed by the investigating authorities of the anticipated visit and does not object to it; further, it should be standard practice prior to the visit to advise the firms concerned of the general nature of the information to be verified and of any further information which needs to be provided, though this should not preclude requests to be made on the spot for further details to be provided in the light of information obtained.

8.   Enquiries or questions put by the authorities or firms of the exporting Members and essential to a successful on-the-spot investigation should, whenever possible, be answered before the visit is made.

ANNEX II – BEST INFORMATION AVAILABLE IN TERMS OF PARAGRAPH 8 OF ARTICLE 6

1.   As soon as possible after the initiation of the investigation, the investigating authorities should specify in detail the information required from any interested party, and the manner in which that information should be structured by the interested party in its response. The authorities should also ensure that the party is aware that if information is not supplied within a reasonable time, the authorities will be free to make determinations on the basis of the facts available, including those contained in the application for the initiation of the investigation by the domestic industry.

2.   The authorities may also request that an interested party provide its response in a particular medium (e.g. computer tape) or computer language. Where such a request is made, the authorities should consider the reasonable ability of the interested party to respond in the preferred medium or computer language, and should not request the party to use for its response a computer system other than that used by the party. The authority should not maintain a request for a computerized response if the interested party does not maintain computerized accounts and if presenting the response as requested would result in an unreasonable extra burden on the interested party, e.g. it would entail unreasonable additional cost and trouble. The authorities should not maintain a request for a response in a particular medium or computer language if the interested party does not maintain its computerized accounts in such medium or computer

language and if presenting the response as requested would result in an unreasonable extra burden on the interested party, e.g. it would entail unreasonable additional cost and trouble.

3.   All information which is verifiable, which is appropriately submitted so that it can be used in the investigation without undue difficulties, which is supplied in a timely fashion, and, where applicable, which is supplied in a medium or computer language requested by the authorities, should be taken into account when determinations are made. If a party does not respond in the preferred medium or computer language but the authorities find that the circumstances set out in paragraph 2 have been satisfied, the failure to respond in the preferred medium or computer language should not be considered to significantly impede the investigation.

4.   Where the authorities do not have the ability to process information if provided in a particular medium (e.g. computer tape), the information should be supplied in the form of written material or any other form acceptable to the authorities.

5.   Even though the information provided may not be ideal in all respects, this should not justify the authorities from disregarding it, provided the interested party has acted to the best of its ability.

6.   If evidence or information is not accepted, the supplying party should be informed forthwith of the reasons therefor, and should have an opportunity to provide further explanations within a reasonable period, due account being taken of the time-limits of the investigation. If the explanations are considered by the authorities as not being satisfactory, the reasons for the rejection of such evidence or information should be given in any published determinations.

7.   If the authorities have to base their findings, including those with respect to normal value, on information from a secondary source, including the information supplied in the application for the initiation of the investigation, they should do so with special circumspection. In such cases, the authorities should, where practicable, check the information from other independent sources at their disposal, such as published price lists, official import statistics and customs returns, and from the information obtained from other interested parties during the investigation. It is clear, however, that if an interested party does not cooperate and thus relevant information is being withheld from the authorities, this situation could lead to a result which is less favourable to the party than if the party did cooperate.

Agreement on Implementation of Article VII
of the General Agreement on Tariffs and Trade 1994

GENERAL INTRODUCTORY COMMENTARY

1.   The primary basis for customs value under this Agreement is "transaction value" as defined in Article 1. Article 1 is to be read together with Article 8 which provides, *inter alia*, for adjustments to the price actually paid or payable in cases where certain specific elements which are considered to form a part of the value for customs purposes are incurred by the buyer but are not included in the price actually paid or payable for the imported goods. Article 8 also provides for the inclusion in the transaction value of certain considerations which may pass from the buyer to the seller in the form of specified goods or services rather than in the form of money. Articles 2 through 7 provide methods of determining the customs value whenever it cannot be determined under the provisions of Article 1.

2.   Where the customs value cannot be determined under the provisions of Article 1 there should normally be a process of consultation between the customs administration and importer with a view to arriving at a basis of value under the provisions of Article 2 or 3. It may occur, for example, that the importer has information about the customs value of identical or similar imported goods which is not immediately available to the customs administration in the port of importation. On the other hand, the customs administration may have information about the customs value of identical or similar imported goods which is not readily available to the importer. A process of consultation between the two parties will enable information to be exchanged, subject to the requirements of commercial confidentiality, with a view to determining a proper basis of value for customs purposes.

3.   Articles 5 and 6 provide two bases for determining the customs value where it cannot be determined on the basis of the transaction value of the imported goods or of identical or similar imported goods. Under paragraph 1 of Article 5 the customs value is determined on the basis of the price at which the goods are sold in the condition as imported to an unrelated buyer in the country of importation. The importer also has the right to have goods which are further processed after importation valued under the provisions of Article 5 if the importer so requests. Under Article 6 the customs value is determined on the basis of the computed value. Both these methods present certain difficulties and because of this the importer is given the right, under the provisions of Article 4, to choose the order of application of the two methods.

4.   Article 7 sets out how to determine the customs value in cases where it cannot be determined under the provisions of any of the preceding Articles.

Members,

Having regard to the Multilateral Trade Negotiations;

Desiring to further the objectives of GATT 1994 and to secure additional benefits for the international trade of developing countries;

Recognizing the importance of the provisions of Article VII of GATT 1994 and desiring to elaborate rules for their application in order to provide greater uniformity and certainty in their implementation;

Recognizing the need for a fair, uniform and neutral system for the valuation of goods for customs purposes that precludes the use of arbitrary or fictitious customs values;

Recognizing that the basis for valuation of goods for customs purposes should, to the greatest extent possible, be the transaction value of the goods being valued;

Recognizing that customs value should be based on simple and equitable criteria consistent with commercial practices and that valuation procedures should be of general application without distinction between sources of supply;

Recognizing that valuation procedures should not be used to combat dumping;

Hereby *agree* as follows:

PART I – RULES ON CUSTOMS VALUATION

Article 1 [Transaction Value of the Actual Goods]

1.   The customs value of imported goods shall be the transaction value, that is the price actually paid or payable for the goods when sold for export to the country of importation adjusted in accordance with the provisions of Article 8, provided:

(a) that there are no restrictions as to the disposition or use of the goods by the buyer other than restrictions which:

   (i)   are imposed or required by law or by the public authorities in the country of importation;

   (ii)   limit the geographical area in which the goods may be resold; or

   (iii) do not substantially affect the value of the goods;

(b) that the sale or price is not subject to some condition or consideration for which a value cannot be determined with respect to the goods being valued;

(c) that no part of the proceeds of any subsequent resale, disposal or use of the goods by the buyer will accrue directly or indirectly to the seller, unless an appropriate adjustment can be made in accordance with the provisions of Article 8; and

(d) that the buyer and seller are not related, or where the buyer and seller are related, that the transaction value is acceptable for customs purposes under the provisions of paragraph 2.

2.   (a) In determining whether the transaction value is acceptable for the purposes of paragraph 1, the fact that the buyer and the seller are related within the meaning of Article 15 shall not in itself be grounds for regarding the transaction value as unacceptable. In such case the circumstances surrounding the sale shall be examined and the transaction value shall be accepted provided that the relationship did not influence the price. If, in the light of information provided by the importer or otherwise, the customs administration has grounds for considering that the relationship influenced the price, it shall communicate its grounds to the importer and the importer shall be given a reasonable opportunity to respond. If the importer so requests, the communication of the grounds shall be in writing.

(b) In a sale between related persons, the transaction value shall be accepted and the goods valued in accordance with the provisions of paragraph 1 whenever the importer demonstrates that such value closely approximates to one of the following occurring at or about the same time:

   (i)   the transaction value in sales to unrelated buyers of identical or similar goods for export to the same country of importation;

   (ii)   the customs value of identical or similar goods as determined under the provisions of Article 5;

   (iii) the customs value of identical or similar goods as determined under the provisions of Article 6;

In applying the foregoing tests, due account shall be taken of demonstrated differences in commercial levels, quantity levels, the elements enumerated in Article 8 and costs incurred by the seller in sales in which the seller and the buyer are not related that are not incurred by the seller in sales in which the seller and the buyer are related.

(c) The tests set forth in paragraph 2(b) are to be used at the initiative of the importer and only for comparison purposes. Substitute values may not be established under the provisions of paragraph 2(b).

Article 2 [Transaction Value of Identical Goods]

1. (a) If the customs value of the imported goods cannot be determined under the provisions of Article 1, the customs value shall be the transaction value of identical goods sold for export to the same country of importation and exported at or about the same time as the goods being valued.

(b) In applying this Article, the transaction value of identical goods in a sale at the same commercial level and in substantially the same quantity as the goods being valued shall be used to determine the customs value. Where no such sale is found, the transaction value of identical goods sold at a different commercial level and/or in different quantities, adjusted to take account of differences attributable to commercial level and/or to quantity, shall be used, provided that such adjustments can be made on the basis of demonstrated evidence which clearly establishes the reasonableness and accuracy of the adjustment, whether the adjustment leads to an increase or a decrease in the value.

2. Where the costs and charges referred to in paragraph 2 of Article 8 are included in the transaction value, an adjustment shall be made to take account of significant differences in such costs and charges between the imported goods and the identical goods in question arising from differences in distances and modes of transport.

3. If, in applying this Article, more than one transaction value of identical goods is found, the lowest such value shall be used to determine the customs value of the imported goods.

Article 3 [Transaction Value of Similar Goods]

1. (a) If the customs value of the imported goods cannot be determined under the provisions of Articles 1 and 2, the customs value shall be the transaction value of similar goods sold for export to the same country of importation and exported at or about the same time as the goods being valued.

(b) In applying this Article, the transaction value of similar goods in a sale at the same commercial level and in substantially the same quantity as the goods being valued shall be used to determine the customs value. Where no such sale is found, the transaction value of similar goods sold at a different commercial level and/or in different quantities, adjusted to take account of differences attributable to commercial level and/or to quantity, shall be used, provided that such adjustments can be made on the basis of demonstrated evidence which clearly establishes the reasonableness and accuracy of the adjustment, whether the adjustment leads to an increase or a decrease in the value.

2. Where the costs and charges referred to in paragraph 2 of Article 8 are included in the transaction value, an adjustment shall be made to take account of significant differences in such costs and charges between the imported goods and the similar goods in question arising from differences in distances and modes of transport.

3. If, in applying this Article, more than one transaction value of similar goods is found, the lowest such value shall be used to determine the customs value of the imported goods.

Article 4 [Choice Between Articles 5 and 6]

If the customs value of the imported goods cannot be determined under the provisions of Articles 1, 2 and 3, the customs value shall be determined under the provisions of Article 5 or, when the customs value cannot be determined under that Article, under the provisions of Article 6 except that, at the request of the importer, the order of application of Articles 5 and 6 shall be reversed.

Article 5 [Price Charged to First Independent Buyer]

1. (a) If the imported goods or identical or similar imported goods are sold in the country of importation in the condition as imported, the customs value of the imported goods under the provisions of this Article shall be based on the unit price at which the imported goods or identical or similar imported goods are so sold in the greatest aggregate quantity, at or about the time of the importation of the goods being valued, to persons who are not related to the persons from whom they buy such goods, subject to deductions for the following:

    (i)   either the commissions usually paid or agreed to be paid or the additions usually made for profit and general expenses in connection with sales in such country of imported goods of the same class or kind;

    (ii) the usual costs of transport and insurance and associated costs incurred within the country of importation;

    (iii) where appropriate, the costs and charges referred to in paragraph 2 of Article 8; and

    (iv) the customs duties and other national taxes payable in the country of importation by reason of the importation or sale of the goods.

    (b) If neither the imported goods nor identical nor similar imported goods are sold at or about the time of importation of the goods being valued, the customs value shall, subject otherwise to the provisions of paragraph 1(a), be based on the unit price at which the imported goods or identical or similar imported goods are sold in the country of importation in the condition as imported at the earliest date after the importation of the goods being valued but before the expiration of 90 days after such importation.

2. If neither the imported goods nor identical nor similar imported goods are sold in the country of importation in the condition as imported, then, if the importer so requests, the customs value shall be based on the unit price at which the imported goods, after further processing, are sold in the greatest aggregate quantity to persons in the country of importation who are not related to the persons from whom they buy such goods, due allowance being made for the value added by such processing and the deductions provided for in paragraph 1(a).

Article 6 [Constructed Value Based on Cost of Production]

1. The customs value of imported goods under the provisions of this Article shall be based on a computed value. Computed value shall consist of the sum of:

(a) the cost or value of materials and fabrication or other processing employed in producing the imported goods;

(b) an amount for profit and general expenses equal to that usually reflected in sales of goods of the same class or kind as the goods being valued which are made by producers in the country of exportation for export to the country of importation;

(c) the cost or value of all other expenses necessary to reflect the valuation option chosen by the Member under paragraph 2 of Article 8 .

2. No Member may require or compel any person not resident in its own territory to produce for examination, or to allow access to, any account or other record for the purposes of determining a computed value. However, information supplied by the producer of the goods for the purposes of determining the customs value under the provisions of this Article may be verified in another country by the authorities of the country of importation with the agreement of the producer and provided they give sufficient advance notice to the government of the country in question and the latter does not object to the investigation.

Article 7 [Any Reasonable Method]

1.   If the customs value of the imported goods cannot be determined under the provisions of Articles 1 through 6, inclusive, the customs value shall be determined using reasonable means consistent with the principles and general provisions of this Agreement and of Article VII of GATT 1994 and on the basis of data available in the country of importation.

2.   No customs value shall be determined under the provisions of this Article on the basis of:

(a)   the selling price in the country of importation of goods produced in such country;

(b)   a system which provides for the acceptance for customs purposes of the higher of two alternative values;

(c)   the price of goods on the domestic market of the country of exportation;

(d)   the cost of production other than computed values which have been determined for identical or similar goods in accordance with the provisions of Article 6;

(e)   the price of the goods for export to a country other than the country of importation;

(f)   minimum customs values; or

(g)   arbitrary or fictitious values.

3.   If the importer so requests, the importer shall be informed in writing of the customs value determined under the provisions of this Article and the method used to determine such value.

Article 8 [Adjustments]

1.   In determining the customs value under the provisions of Article 1, there shall be added to the price actually paid or payable for the imported goods:

(a)   the following, to the extent that they are incurred by the buyer but are not included in the price actually paid or payable for the goods:

(i)   commissions and brokerage, except buying commissions;

(ii)   the cost of containers which are treated as being one for customs purposes with the goods in question;

(iii)   the cost of packing whether for labour or materials;

(b)   the value, apportioned as appropriate, of the following goods and services where supplied directly or indirectly by the buyer free of charge or at reduced cost for use in connection with the production and sale for export of the imported goods, to the extent that such value has not been included in the price actually paid or payable:

(i)   materials, components, parts and similar items incorporated in the imported goods;

(ii)   tools, dies, moulds and similar items used in the production of the imported goods;

(iii)   materials consumed in the production of the imported goods;

(iv)   engineering, development, artwork, design work, and plans and sketches undertaken elsewhere than in the country of importation and necessary for the production of the imported goods;

(iv)   engineering, development, artwork, design work, plans and sketches, undertaken elsewhere than in the country of importation and necessary for the production of the imported goods;

(c)   royalties and licence fees related to the goods being valued that the buyer must pay, either directly or indirectly, as a condition of sale of the goods being valued, to the extent that such royalties and fees are not included in the price actually paid or payable;

(d)   the value of any part of the proceeds of any subsequent resale, disposal or use of the imported goods that accrues directly or indirectly to the seller.

2.   In framing its legislation, each Member shall provide for the inclusion in or the exclusion from the customs value, in whole or in part, of the following:

(a)   the cost of transport of the imported goods to the port or place of importation;

(b)   loading, unloading and handling charges associated with the transport of the imported goods to the port or place of importation; and

(c)   the cost of insurance.

3.   Additions to the price actually paid or payable shall be made under this Article only on the basis of objective and quantifiable data.

4.   No additions shall be made to the price actually paid or payable in determining the customs value except as provided in this Article.

Article 9 [Currency Conversion]

1.   Where the conversion of currency is necessary for the determination of the customs value, the rate of exchange to be used shall be that duly published by the competent authorities of the country of importation concerned and shall reflect as effectively as possible, in respect of the period covered by each such document of publication, the current value of such currency in commercial transactions in terms of the currency of the country of importation.

2.   The conversion rate to be used shall be that in effect at the time of exportation or the time of importation, as provided by each Member.

Article 10 [Confidentiality]

All information which is by nature confidential or which is provided on a confidential basis for the purposes of customs valuation shall be treated as strictly confidential by the authorities concerned who shall not disclose it without the specific permission of the person or government providing such information, except to the extent that it may be required to be disclosed in the context of judicial proceedings.

Article 11 [Right to Appeal]

1.   The legislation of each Member shall provide in regard to a determination of customs value for the right of appeal, without penalty, by the importer or any other person liable for the payment of the duty.

2.   An initial right of appeal without penalty may be to an authority within the customs administration or to an independent body, but the legislation of each Member shall provide for the right of appeal without penalty to a judicial authority.

3.   Notice of the decision on appeal shall be given to the appellant and the reasons for such decision shall be provided in writing. The appellant shall also be informed of any rights of further appeal.

Article 12 [Publication of National Rules]

Laws, regulations, judicial decisions and administrative rulings of general application giving effect to this Agreement shall be published in conformity with Article X of GATT 1994 by the country of importation concerned.

Article 13 [Withdrawal of Goods from Customs During Investigation]

If, in the course of determining the customs value of imported goods, it becomes necessary to delay the final determination of such customs value, the importer of the goods shall nevertheless be able to withdraw them from customs if, where so required, the importer provides sufficient guarantee in the form of a surety, a deposit or some other appropriate instrument, covering the ultimate payment of customs duties for which the goods may be liable. The legislation of each Member shall make provisions for such circumstances.

Article 14 [Annexes]

The notes at Annex I to this Agreement form an integral part of this Agreement and the Articles of this Agreement are to be read and applied in conjunction with their respective notes. Annexes II and III also form an integral part of this Agreement.

Article 15 [Definitions]

1. In this Agreement:

(a) "customs value of imported goods" means the value of goods for the purposes of levying ad valorem duties of customs on imported goods;

(b) "country of importation" means country or customs territory of importation; and

(c) "produced" includes grown, manufactured and mined.

2. In this Agreement:

(a) "identical goods" means goods which are the same in all respects, including physical characteristics, quality and reputation. Minor differences in appearance would not preclude goods otherwise conforming to the definition from being regarded as identical;

(b) "similar goods" means goods which, although not alike in all respects, have like characteristics and like component materials which enable them to perform the same functions and to be commercially interchangeable. The quality of the goods, their reputation and the existence of a trademark are among the factors to be considered in determining whether goods are similar;

(c) the terms "identical goods" and "similar goods" do not include, as the case may be, goods which incorporate or reflect engineering, development, artwork, design work, and plans and sketches for which no adjustment has been made under paragraph 1(b)(iv) of Article 8 because such elements were undertaken in the country of importation;

(d) goods shall not be regarded as "identical goods" or "similar goods" unless they were produced in the same country as the goods being valued;

(e) goods produced by a different person shall be taken into account only when there are no identical goods or similar goods, as the case may be, produced by the same person as the goods being valued.

3. In this Agreement "goods of the same class or kind" means goods which fall within a group or range of goods produced by a particular industry or industry sector, and includes identical or similar goods.

4. For the purposes of this Agreement, persons shall be deemed to be related only if:

(a) they are officers or directors of one another's businesses;

(b) they are legally recognized partners in business;

(c) they are employer and employee;

(d) any person directly or indirectly owns, controls or holds 5 per cent or more of the outstanding voting stock or shares of both of them;

(e) one of them directly or indirectly controls the other;

(f) both of them are directly or indirectly controlled by a third person;

(g) together they directly or indirectly control a third person; or

(h) they are members of the same family.

5. Persons who are associated in business with one another in that one is the sole agent, sole distributor or sole concessionaire, however described, of the other shall be deemed to be related for the purposes of this Agreement if they fall within the criteria of paragraph 4.

Article 16 [Explanations in Writing]

Upon written request, the importer shall have the right to an explanation in writing from the customs administration of the country of importation as to how the customs value of the importer's goods was determined.

Article 17 [Investigative Powers of National Authorities]

Nothing in this Agreement shall be construed as restricting or calling into question the rights of customs administrations to satisfy themselves as to the truth or accuracy of any statement, document or declaration presented for customs valuation purposes.

PART II
ADMINISTRATION, CONSULTATIONS AND DISPUTE SETTLEMENT
Article 18 Institutions

1.   There is hereby established a Committee on Customs Valuation (referred to in this Agreement as "the Committee") composed of representatives from each of the Members. The Committee shall elect its own Chairman and shall normally meet once a year, or as is otherwise envisaged by the relevant provisions of this Agreement, for the purpose of affording Members the opportunity to consult on matters relating to the administration of the customs valuation system by any Member as it might affect the operation of this Agreement or the furtherance of its objectives and carrying out such other responsibilities as may be assigned to it by the Members. The WTO Secretariat shall act as the secretariat to the Committee.

2.   There shall be established a Technical Committee on Customs Valuation (referred to in this Agreement as "the Technical Committee") under the auspices of the Customs Co-operation Council (referred to in this Agreement as "the CCC"), which shall carry out the responsibilities described in Annex II to this Agreement and shall operate in accordance with the rules of procedure contained therein.

Article 19 Consultations and Dispute Settlement

1.   Except as otherwise provided herein, the Dispute Settlement Understanding is applicable to consultations and the settlement of disputes under this Agreement.

2.   If any Member considers that any benefit accruing to it, directly or indirectly, under this Agreement is being nullified or impaired, or that the achievement of any objective of this Agreement is being impeded, as a result of the actions of another Member or of other Members, it may, with a view to reaching a mutually satisfactory solution of this matter, request consultations with the Member or Members in question. Each Member shall afford sympathetic consideration to any request from another Member for consultations.

3.   The Technical Committee shall provide, upon request, advice and assistance to Members engaged in consultations.

4.   At the request of a party to the dispute, or on its own initiative, a panel established to examine a dispute relating to the provisions of this Agreement may request the Technical Committee to carry out an examination of any questions requiring technical consideration. The panel shall determine the terms of reference of the Technical Committee for the particular dispute and set a time period for receipt of the report of the Technical Committee. The panel shall take into consideration the report of the Technical Committee. In the event that the Technical Committee is unable to reach consensus on a matter referred to it pursuant to this paragraph, the panel should afford the parties to the dispute an opportunity to present their views on the matter to the panel.

5.   Confidential information provided to the panel shall not be disclosed without formal authorization from the person, body or authority providing such information. Where such information is requested from the panel but release of such information by the panel is not

authorized, a non-confidential summary of this information, authorized by the person, body or authority providing the information, shall be provided.

PART III
SPECIAL AND DIFFERENTIAL TREATMENT
Article 20 [Delayed Application for Developing Countries]

1.   Developing country Members not party to the Agreement on Implementation of Article VII of the General Agreement on Tariffs and Trade done on 12 April 1979 may delay application of the provisions of this Agreement for a period not exceeding five years from the date of entry into force of the WTO Agreement for such Members. Developing country Members who choose to delay application of this Agreement shall notify the Director-General of the WTO accordingly.

2.   In addition to paragraph 1, developing country Members not party to the Agreement on Implementation of Article VII of the General Agreement on Tariffs and Trade done on 12 April 1979 may delay application of paragraph 2(b)(iii) of Article 1 and Article 6 for a period not exceeding three years following their application of all other provisions of this Agreement. Developing country Members that choose to delay application of the provisions specified in this paragraph shall notify the Director-General of the WTO accordingly.

3.   Developed country Members shall furnish, on mutually agreed terms, technical assistance to developing country Members that so request. On this basis developed country Members shall draw up programmes of technical assistance which may include, *inter alia*, training of personnel, assistance in preparing implementation measures, access to sources of information regarding customs valuation methodology, and advice on the application of the provisions of this Agreement.

PART IV
FINAL PROVISIONS
Article 21 Reservations

Reservations may not be entered in respect of any of the provisions of this Agreement without the consent of the other Members.

Article 22 National Legislation

1.   Each Member shall ensure, not later than the date of application of the provisions of this Agreement for it, the conformity of its laws, regulations and administrative procedures with the provisions of this Agreement.

2.   Each Member shall inform the Committee of any changes in its laws and regulations relevant to this Agreement and in the administration of such laws and regulations.

Article 23 Review

The Committee shall review annually the implementation and operation of this Agreement taking into account the objectives thereof. The Committee shall annually inform the Council for Trade in Goods of developments during the period covered by such reviews.

Article 24 Secretariat

This Agreement shall be serviced by the WTO Secretariat except in regard to those responsibilities specifically assigned to the Technical Committee, which will be serviced by the CCC Secretariat.

ANNEX I – INTERPRETATIVE NOTES

General Note – Sequential Application of Valuation Methods

1.   Articles 1 through 7 define how the customs value of imported goods is to be determined under the provisions of this Agreement. The methods of valuation are set out in a sequential order of application. The primary method for customs valuation is defined in Article 1 and imported goods are to be valued in accordance with the provisions of this Article whenever the conditions prescribed therein are fulfilled.

2.   Where the customs value cannot be determined under the provisions of Article 1, it is to be determined by proceeding sequentially through the succeeding Articles to the first such Article under which the customs value can be determined. Except as provided in Article 4, it is only when the customs value cannot be determined under the provisions of a particular Article that the provisions of the next Article in the sequence can be used.

3.   If the importer does not request that the order of Articles 5 and 6 be reversed, the normal order of the sequence is to be followed. If the importer does so request but it then proves impossible to determine the customs value under the provisions of Article 6, the customs value is to be determined under the provisions of Article 5, if it can be so determined.

4.   Where the customs value cannot be determined under the provisions of Articles 1 through 6 it is to be determined under the provisions of Article 7.

Use of Generally Accepted Accounting Principles

1.   "Generally accepted accounting principles" refers to the recognized consensus or substantial authoritative support within a country at a particular time as to which economic resources and obligations should be recorded as assets and liabilities, which changes in assets and liabilities should be recorded, how the assets and liabilities and changes in them should be measured, what information should be disclosed and how it should be disclosed, and which financial statements should be prepared. These standards may be broad guidelines of general application as well as detailed practices and procedures.

2.   For the purposes of this Agreement, the customs administration of each Member shall utilize information prepared in a manner consistent with generally accepted accounting principles in the country which is appropriate for the Article in question. For example, the determination of usual profit and general expenses under the provisions of Article 5 would be carried out utilizing information prepared in a manner consistent with generally accepted accounting principles of the country of importation. On the other hand, the determination of usual profit and general expenses under the provisions of Article 6 would be carried out utilizing information prepared in a manner consistent with generally accepted accounting principles of the country of production. As a further example, the determination of an element provided for in paragraph 1(b)(ii) of Article 8 undertaken in the country of importation would be carried out utilizing information in a manner consistent with the generally accepted accounting principles of that country.

Note to Article 1 – Price Actually Paid or Payable

1.   The price actually paid or payable is the total payment made or to be made by the buyer to or for the benefit of the seller for the imported goods. The payment need not necessarily take the form of a transfer of money. Payment may be made by way of letters of credit or negotiable instruments. Payment may be made directly or indirectly. An example of an indirect payment would be the settlement by the buyer, whether in whole or in part, of a debt owed by the seller.

2.   Activities undertaken by the buyer on the buyer's own account, other than those for which an adjustment is provided in Article 8, are not considered to be an indirect payment to the seller, even though they might be regarded as of benefit to the seller. The costs of such activities shall not, therefore, be added to the price actually paid or payable in determining the customs value.

3.   The customs value shall not include the following charges or costs, provided that they are distinguished from the price actually paid or payable for the imported goods:

(a)   charges for construction, erection, assembly, maintenance or technical assistance, under-taken after importation on imported goods such as industrial plant, machinery or equip-ment;

(b)   the cost of transport after importation;

(c)   duties and taxes of the country of importation.

4.   The price actually paid or payable refers to the price for the imported goods. Thus the flow of dividends or other payments from the buyer to the seller that do not relate to the imported goods are not part of the customs value.

Paragraph 1(a)(iii)

Among restrictions which would not render a price actually paid or payable unacceptable are restrictions which do not substantially affect the value of the goods. An example of such restrictions would be the case where a seller requires a buyer of automobiles not to sell or exhibit them prior to a fixed date which represents the beginning of a model year.

Paragraph 1(b)

1.   If the sale or price is subject to some condition or consideration for which a value cannot be determined with respect to the goods being valued, the transaction value shall not be accept-able for customs purposes. Some examples of this include:

(a)   the seller establishes the price of the imported goods on condition that the buyer will also buy other goods in specified quantities;

(b)   the price of the imported goods is dependent upon the price or prices at which the buyer of the imported goods sells other goods to the seller of the imported goods;

(c)   the price is established on the basis of a form of payment extraneous to the imported goods, such as where the imported goods are semi-finished goods which have been provided by the seller on condition that the seller will receive a specified quantity of the finished goods.

2.   However, conditions or considerations relating to the production or marketing of the impor-ted goods shall not result in rejection of the transaction value. For example, the fact that the buyer furnishes the seller with engineering and plans undertaken in the country of importation shall not result in rejection of the transaction value for the purposes of Article 1. Likewise, if the buyer undertakes on the buyer's own account, even though by agreement with the seller, activities relating to the marketing of the imported goods, the value of these activities is not part of the customs value nor shall such activities result in rejection of the transaction value.

Paragraph 2

1.   Paragraphs 2(a) and 2(b) provide different means of establishing the acceptability of a transaction value.

2.   Paragraph 2(a) provides that where the buyer and the seller are related, the circumstances surrounding the sale shall be examined and the transaction value shall be accepted as the customs value provided that the relationship did not influence the price. It is not intended that there should be an examination of the circumstances in all cases where the buyer and the seller are related. Such examination will only be required where there are doubts about the accept-ability of the price. Where the customs administration have no doubts about the acceptability of the price, it should be accepted without requesting further information from the importer. For example, the customs administration may have previously examined the relationship, or it may already have detailed information concerning the buyer and the seller, and may already be satisfied from such examination or information that the relationship did not influence the price.

3.   Where the customs administration is unable to accept the transaction value without further inquiry, it should give the importer an opportunity to supply such further detailed information as may be necessary to enable it to examine the circumstances surrounding the sale. In this context, the customs administration should be prepared to examine relevant aspects of the transaction, including the way in which the buyer and seller organize their commercial relations and the way in which the price in question was arrived at, in order to determine whether the relationship influenced the price. Where it can be shown that the buyer and seller, although related under the provisions of Article 15, buy from and sell to each other as if they were not related, this would demonstrate that the price had not been influenced by the relationship. As an example of this, if the price had been settled in a manner consistent with the normal pricing practices of the industry in question or with the way the seller settles prices for sales to buyers who are not related to the seller, this would demonstrate that the price had not been influenced by the relationship. As a further example, where it is shown that the price is adequate to ensure recovery of all costs plus a profit which is representative of the firm's overall profit realized over a representative period of time (e.g. on an annual basis) in sales of goods of the same class or kind, this would demonstrate that the price had not been influenced.

4.   Paragraph 2(b) provides an opportunity for the importer to demonstrate that the transaction value closely approximates to a "test" value previously accepted by the customs administration and is therefore acceptable under the provisions of Article 1. Where a test under paragraph 2(b) is met, it is not necessary to examine the question of influence under paragraph 2(a). If the customs administration has already sufficient information to be satisfied, without further detailed in-quiries, that one of the tests provided in paragraph 2(b) has been met, there is no reason for it to require the importer to demonstrate that the test can be met. In paragraph 2(b) the term "un-related buyers" means buyers who are not related to the seller in any particular case.

Paragraph 2(b)

A number of factors must be taken into consideration in determining whether one value "closely approximates" to another value. These factors include the nature of the imported goods, the nature of the industry itself, the season in which the goods are imported, and, whether the diffe-rence in values is commercially significant. Since these factors may vary from case to case, it would be impossible to apply a uniform standard such as a fixed percentage, in each case. For example, a small difference in value in a case involving one type of goods could be unacceptable while a large difference in a case involving another type of goods might be acceptable in deter-mining whether the transaction value closely approximates to the "test" values set forth in para-graph 2(b) of Article 1.

Note to Article 2

1.   In applying Article 2, the customs administration shall, wherever possible, use a sale of iden-tical goods at the same commercial level and in substantially the same quantities as the goods being valued. Where no such sale is found, a sale of identical goods that takes place under any one of the following three conditions may be used:

(a)   a sale at the same commercial level but in different quantities;

(b)   a sale at a different commercial level but in substantially the same quantities; or

(c)   a sale at a different commercial level and in different quantities.

2.   Having found a sale under any one of these three conditions adjustments will then be made, as the case may be, for:

(a)   quantity factors only;

(b)   commercial level factors only; or

(c)   both commercial level and quantity factors.

3.	The expression "and/or" allows the flexibility to use the sales and make the necessary adjustments in any one of the three conditions described above.

4.	For the purposes of Article 2, the transaction value of identical imported goods means a customs value, adjusted as provided for in paragraphs 1(b) and 2, which has already been accepted under Article 1.

5.	A condition for adjustment because of different commercial levels or different quantities is that such adjustment, whether it leads to an increase or a decrease in the value, be made only on the basis of demonstrated evidence that clearly establishes the reasonableness and accuracy of the adjustments, e.g. valid price lists containing prices referring to different levels or different quantities. As an example of this, if the imported goods being valued consist of a shipment of 10 units and the only identical imported goods for which a transaction value exists involved a sale of 500 units, and it is recognized that the seller grants quantity discounts, the required adjustment may be accomplished by resorting to the seller's price list and using that price applicable to a sale of 10 units. This does not require that a sale had to have been made in quantities of 10 as long as the price list has been established as being bona fide through sales at other quantities. In the absence of such an objective measure, however, the determination of a customs value under the provisions of Article 2 is not appropriate.

Note to Article 3

1.	In applying Article 3, the customs administration shall, wherever possible, use a sale of similar goods at the same commercial level and in substantially the same quantities as the goods being valued. Where no such sale is found, a sale of similar goods that takes place under any one of the following three conditions may be used:

(a)	a sale at the same commercial level but in different quantities;

(b)	a sale at a different commercial level but in substantially the same quantities; or

(c)	a sale at a different commercial level and in different quantities.

2.	Having found a sale under any one of these three conditions adjustments will then be made, as the case may be, for:

(a)	quantity factors only;

(b)	commercial level factors only; or

(c)	both commercial level and quantity factors.

3.	The expression "and/or" allows the flexibility to use the sales and make the necessary adjustments in any one of the three conditions described above.

4.	For the purpose of Article 3, the transaction value of similar imported goods means a customs value, adjusted as provided for in paragraphs 1(b) and 2, which has already been accepted under Article 1.

5.	A condition for adjustment because of different commercial levels or different quantities is that such adjustment, whether it leads to an increase or a decrease in the value, be made only on the basis of demonstrated evidence that clearly establishes the reasonableness and accuracy of the adjustment, e.g. valid price lists containing prices referring to different levels or different quantities. As an example of this, if the imported goods being valued consist of a shipment of 10 units and the only similar imported goods for which a transaction value exists involved a sale of 500 units, and it is recognized that the seller grants quantity discounts, the required adjustment may be accomplished by resorting to the seller's price list and using that price applicable to a sale of 10 units. This does not require that a sale had to have been made in quantities of 10 as long as the price list has been established as being bona fide through sales at other quantities. In the absence of such an objective measure, however, the determination of a customs value under the provisions of Article 3 is not appropriate.

Note to Article 5

1.   The term "unit price at which ... goods are sold in the greatest aggregate quantity" means the price at which the greatest number of units is sold in sales to persons who are not related to the persons from whom they buy such goods at the first commercial level after importation at which such sales take place.

2.   As an example of this, goods are sold from a price list which grants favourable unit prices for purchases made in larger quantities.

Sale quantity	Unit price	Number of sales	Total quantity sold at each price
1-10 units	100	10 sales of 5 units 5 sales of 3 units	65
11-25 units	95	5 sales of 11 units	55
over 25 units	90	1 sale of 30 units 1 sale of 50 units	80

The greatest number of units sold at a price is 80; therefore, the unit price in the greatest aggregate quantity is 90.

3.   As another example of this, two sales occur. In the first sale 500 units are sold at a price of 95 currency units each. In the second sale 400 units are sold at a price of 90 currency units each. In this example, the greatest number of units sold at a particular price is 500; therefore, the unit price in the greatest aggregate quantity is 95.

4.   A third example would be the following situation where various quantities are sold at various prices.

(a) Sales

Sale quantity	Unit price
40 units	100
30 units	90
15 units	100
50 units	95
25 units	105
35 units	90
5 units	100

(b) Totals

Total quantity sold	Unit price
65	90
50	95
60	100
25	105

In this example, the greatest number of units sold at a particular price is 65; therefore, the unit price in the greatest aggregate quantity is 90.

5.   Any sale in the importing country, as described in paragraph 1 above, to a person who supplies directly or indirectly free of charge or at reduced cost for use in connection with the

production and sale for export of the imported goods any of the elements specified in paragraph 1(b) of Article 8, should not be taken into account in establishing the unit price for the purposes of Article 5.

6.   It should be noted that "profit and general expenses" referred to in paragraph 1 of Article 5 should be taken as a whole. The figure for the purposes of this deduction should be determined on the basis of information supplied by or on behalf of the importer unless the importer's figures are inconsistent with those obtained in sales in the country of importation of imported goods of the same class or kind. Where the importer's figures are inconsistent with such figures, the amount for profit and general expenses may be based upon relevant information other than that supplied by or on behalf of the importer.

7.   The "general expenses" include the direct and indirect costs of marketing the goods in question.

8.   Local taxes payable by reason of the sale of the goods for which a deduction is not made under the provisions of paragraph 1(a)(iv) of Article 5 shall be deducted under the provisions of paragraph 1(a)(i) of Article 5.

9.   In determining either the commissions or the usual profits and general expenses under the provisions of paragraph 1 of Article 5, the question whether certain goods are "of the same class or kind" as other goods must be determined on a case-by-case basis by reference to the circumstances involved. Sales in the country of importation of the narrowest group or range of imported goods of the same class or kind, which includes the goods being valued, for which the necessary information can be provided, should be examined. For the purposes of Article 5, "goods of the same class or kind" includes goods imported from the same country as the goods being valued as well as goods imported from other countries.

10. For the purposes of paragraph 1(b) of Article 5, the "earliest date" shall be the date by which sales of the imported goods or of identical or similar imported goods are made in sufficient quantity to establish the unit price.

11. Where the method in paragraph 2 of Article 5 is used, deductions made for the value added by further processing shall be based on objective and quantifiable data relating to the cost of such work. Accepted industry formulas, recipes, methods of construction, and other industry practices would form the basis of the calculations.

12. It is recognized that the method of valuation provided for in paragraph 2 of Article 5 would normally not be applicable when, as a result of the further processing, the imported goods lose their identity. However, there can be instances where, although the identity of the imported goods is lost, the value added by the processing can be determined accurately without unreasonable difficulty. On the other hand, there can also be instances where the imported goods maintain their identity but form such a minor element in the goods sold in the country of importation that the use of this valuation method would be unjustified. In view of the above, each situation of this type must be considered on a case-by-case basis.

Note to Article 6

1.   As a general rule, customs value is determined under this Agreement on the basis of information readily available in the country of importation. In order to determine a computed value, however, it may be necessary to examine the costs of producing the goods being valued and other information which has to be obtained from outside the country of importation. Furthermore, in most cases the producer of the goods will be outside the jurisdiction of the authorities of the country of importation. The use of the computed value method will generally be limited to those cases where the buyer and seller are related, and the producer is prepared to supply to the authorities of the country of importation the necessary costings and to provide facilities for any subsequent verification which may be necessary.

2.   The "cost or value" referred to in paragraph 1(a) of Article 6 is to be determined on the basis of information relating to the production of the goods being valued supplied by or on behalf of the producer. It is to be based upon the commercial accounts of the producer, provided that such accounts are consistent with the generally accepted accounting principles applied in the country where the goods are produced.

3.   The "cost or value" shall include the cost of elements specified in paragraphs 1(a)(ii) and (iii) of Article 8. It shall also include the value, apportioned as appropriate under the provisions of the relevant note to Article 8, of any element specified in paragraph 1(b) of Article 8 which has been supplied directly or indirectly by the buyer for use in connection with the production of the imported goods. The value of the elements specified in paragraph 1(b)(iv) of Article 8 which are undertaken in the country of importation shall be included only to the extent that such elements are charged to the producer. It is to be understood that no cost or value of the elements referred to in this paragraph shall be counted twice in determining the computed value.

4.   The "amount for profit and general expenses" referred to in paragraph 1(b) of Article 6 is to be determined on the basis of information supplied by or on behalf of the producer unless the producer's figures are inconsistent with those usually reflected in sales of goods of the same class or kind as the goods being valued which are made by producers in the country of exportation for export to the country of importation.

5.   It should be noted in this context that the "amount for profit and general expenses" has to be taken as a whole. It follows that if, in any particular case, the producer's profit figure is low and the producer's general expenses are high, the producer's profit and general expenses taken together may nevertheless be consistent with that usually reflected in sales of goods of the same class or kind. Such a situation might occur, for example, if a product were being launched in the country of importation and the producer accepted a nil or low profit to offset high general expenses associated with the launch. Where the producer can demonstrate a low profit on sales of the imported goods because of particular commercial circumstances, the producer's actual profit figures should be taken into account provided that the producer has valid commercial reasons to justify them and the producer's pricing policy reflects usual pricing policies in the branch of industry concerned. Such a situation might occur, for example, where producers have been forced to lower prices temporarily because of an unforeseeable drop in demand, or where they sell goods to complement a range of goods being produced in the country of importation and accept a low profit to maintain competitivity. Where the producer's own figures for profit and general expenses are not consistent with those usually reflected in sales of goods of the same class or kind as the goods being valued which are made by producers in the country of exportation for export to the country of importation, the amount for profit and general expenses may be based upon relevant information other than that supplied by or on behalf of the producer of the goods.

6.   Where information other than that supplied by or on behalf of the producer is used for the purposes of determining a computed value, the authorities of the importing country shall inform the importer, if the latter so requests, of the source of such information, the data used and the calculations based upon such data, subject to the provisions of Article 10.

7.   The "general expenses" referred to in paragraph 1(b) of Article 6 covers the direct and indirect costs of producing and selling the goods for export which are not included under paragraph 1(a) of Article 6.

8.   Whether certain goods are "of the same class or kind" as other goods must be determined on a case-by-case basis with reference to the circumstances involved. In determining the usual profits and general expenses under the provisions of Article 6, sales for export to the country of importation of the narrowest group or range of goods, which includes the goods being valued, for which the necessary information can be provided, should be examined. For the purposes of

Article 6, "goods of the same class or kind" must be from the same country as the goods being valued.

Note to Article 7

1.   Customs values determined under the provisions of Article 7 should, to the greatest extent possible, be based on previously determined customs values.

2.   The methods of valuation to be employed under Article 7 should be those laid down in Articles 1 through 6 but a reasonable flexibility in the application of such methods would be in conformity with the aims and provisions of Article 7.

3.   Some examples of reasonable flexibility are as follows:

(a)   *Identical goods* - the requirement that the identical goods should be exported at or about the same time as the goods being valued could be flexibly interpreted; identical imported goods produced in a country other than the country of exportation of the goods being valued could be the basis for customs valuation; customs values of identical imported goods already determined under the provisions of Articles 5 and 6 could be used.

(b)   *Similar goods* - the requirement that the similar goods should be exported at or about the same time as the goods being valued could be flexibly interpreted; similar imported goods produced in a country other than the country of exportation of the goods being valued could be the basis for customs valuation; customs values of similar imported goods already determined under the provisions of Articles 5 and 6 could be used.

(c)   *Deductive method* - the requirement that the goods shall have been sold in the "condition as imported" in paragraph 1(a) of Article 5 could be flexibly interpreted; the "90 days" requirement could be administered flexibly.

Note to Article 8

Paragraph 1(a)(i)

The term "buying commissions" means fees paid by an importer to the importer's agent for the service of representing the importer abroad in the purchase of the goods being valued.

Paragraph 1(b)(ii)

1.   There are two factors involved in the apportionment of the elements specified in paragraph 1(b)(ii) of Article 8 to the imported goods - the value of the element itself and the way in which that value is to be apportioned to the imported goods. The apportionment of these elements should be made in a reasonable manner appropriate to the circumstances and in accordance with generally accepted accounting principles.

2.   Concerning the value of the element, if the importer acquires the element from a seller not related to the importer at a given cost, the value of the element is that cost. If the element was produced by the importer or by a person related to the importer, its value would be the cost of producing it. If the element had been previously used by the importer, regardless of whether it had been acquired or produced by such importer, the original cost of acquisition or production would have to be adjusted downward to reflect its use in order to arrive at the value of the element.

3.   Once a value has been determined for the element, it is necessary to apportion that value to the imported goods. Various possibilities exist. For example, the value might be apportioned to the first shipment if the importer wishes to pay duty on the entire value at one time. As another example, the importer may request that the value be apportioned over the number of units produced up to the time of the first shipment. As a further example, the importer may request that the value be apportioned over the entire anticipated production where contracts or firm

commitments exist for that production. The method of apportionment used will depend upon the documentation provided by the importer.

4.   As an illustration of the above, an importer provides the producer with a mould to be used in the production of the imported goods and contracts with the producer to buy 10,000 units. By the time of arrival of the first shipment of 1,000 units, the producer has already produced 4,000 units. The importer may request the customs administration to apportion the value of the mould over 1,000 units, 4,000 units or 10,000 units.

Paragraph 1(b)(iv)

1.   Additions for the elements specified in paragraph 1(b)(iv) of Article 8 should be based on objective and quantifiable data. In order to minimize the burden for both the importer and customs administration in determining the values to be added, data readily available in the buyer's commercial record system should be used in so far as possible.

2.   For those elements supplied by the buyer which were purchased or leased by the buyer, the addition would be the cost of the purchase or the lease. No addition shall be made for those elements available in the public domain, other than the cost of obtaining copies of them.

3.   The ease with which it may be possible to calculate the values to be added will depend on a particular firm's structure and management practice, as well as its accounting methods.

4.   For example, it is possible that a firm which imports a variety of products from several countries maintains the records of its design centre outside the country of importation in such a way as to show accurately the costs attributable to a given product. In such cases, a direct adjustment may appropriately be made under the provisions of Article 8.

5.   In another case, a firm may carry the cost of the design centre outside the country of importation as a general overhead expense without allocation to specific products. In this instance, an appropriate adjustment could be made under the provisions of Article 8 with respect to the imported goods by apportioning total design centre costs over total production benefiting from the design centre and adding such apportioned cost on a unit basis to imports.

6.   Variations in the above circumstances will, of course, require different factors to be considered in determining the proper method of allocation.

7.   In cases where the production of the element in question involves a number of countries and over a period of time, the adjustment should be limited to the value actually added to that element outside the country of importation.

Paragraph 1(c)

1.   The royalties and licence fees referred to in paragraph 1(c) of Article 8 may include, among other things, payments in respect to patents, trademarks and copyrights. However, the charges for the right to reproduce the imported goods in the country of importation shall not be added to the price actually paid or payable for the imported goods in determining the customs value.

2.   Payments made by the buyer for the right to distribute or resell the imported goods shall not be added to the price actually paid or payable for the imported goods if such payments are not a condition of the sale for export to the country of importation of the imported goods.

Paragraph 3

Where objective and quantifiable data do not exist with regard to the additions required to be made under the provisions of Article 8, the transaction value cannot be determined under the provisions of Article 1. As an illustration of this, a royalty is paid on the basis of the price in a sale in the importing country of a litre of a particular product that was imported by the kilogram and made up into a solution after importation. If the royalty is based partially on the imported goods and partially on other factors which have nothing to do with the imported goods (such as when the imported goods are mixed with domestic ingredients and are no longer separately identifiable, or when the royalty cannot be distinguished from special financial arrangements between the buyer and the seller), it would be inappropriate to attempt to make an addition for the royalty. However, if the amount of this royalty is based only on the imported goods and can be readily quantified, an addition to the price actually paid or payable can be made.

Note to Article 9

For the purposes of Article 9, "time of importation" may include the time of entry for customs purposes.

Note to Article 11

1.   Article 11 provides the importer with the right to appeal against a valuation determination made by the customs administration for the goods being valued. Appeal may first be to a higher level in the customs administration, but the importer shall have the right in the final instance to appeal to the judiciary.

2.   "Without penalty" means that the importer shall not be subject to a fine or threat of fine merely because the importer chose to exercise the right of appeal. Payment of normal court costs and lawyers' fees shall not be considered to be a fine.

3.   However, nothing in Article 11 shall prevent a Member from requiring full payment of assessed customs duties prior to an appeal.

Note to Article 15

Paragraph 4

For the purposes of Article 15, the term "persons" includes a legal person, where appropriate.

Paragraph 4(e)

For the purposes of this Agreement, one person shall be deemed to control another when the former is legally or operationally in a position to exercise restraint or direction over the latter.

ANNEX II – TECHNICAL COMMITTEE ON CUSTOMS VALUATION [omitted]

ANNEX III

1.   The five-year delay in the application of the provisions of the Agreement by developing country Members provided for in paragraph 1 of Article 20 may, in practice, be insufficient for certain developing country Members. In such cases a developing country Member may request before the end of the period referred to in paragraph 1 of Article 20 an extension of such period, it being understood that the Members will give sympathetic consideration to such a request in cases where the developing country Member in question can show good cause.

2.   Developing countries which currently value goods on the basis of officially established minimum values may wish to make a reservation to enable them to retain such values on a limited and transitional basis under such terms and conditions as may be agreed to by the Members.

3.   Developing countries which consider that the reversal of the sequential order at the request of the importer provided for in Article 4 of the Agreement may give rise to real difficulties for them may wish to make a reservation to Article 4 in the following terms:

> "The Government of .... reserves the right to provide that the relevant provision of Article 4 of the Agreement shall apply only when the customs authorities agree to the request to reverse the order of Articles 5 and 6."

If developing countries make such a reservation, the Members shall consent to it under Article 21 of the Agreement.

4.   Developing countries may wish to make a reservation with respect to paragraph 2 of Article 5 of the Agreement in the following terms:

>   "The Government of .... reserves the right to provide that paragraph 2 of Article 5 of the Agreement shall be applied in accordance with the provisions of the relevant note thereto whether or not the importer so requests."

If developing countries make such a reservation, the Members shall consent to it under Article 21 of the Agreement.

5.   Certain developing countries may have problems in the implementation of Article 1 of the Agreement insofar as it relates to importations into their countries by sole agents, sole distributors and sole concessionaires. If such problems arise in practice in developing country Members applying the Agreement, a study of this question shall be made, at the request of such Members, with a view to finding appropriate solutions.

6.   Article 17 recognizes that in applying the Agreement, customs administrations may need to make enquiries concerning the truth or accuracy of any statement, document or declaration presented to them for customs valuation purposes. The Article thus acknowledges that enquiries may be made which are, for example, aimed at verifying that the elements of value declared or presented to customs in connection with a determination of customs value are complete and correct. Members, subject to their national laws and procedures, have the right to expect the full cooperation of importers in these enquiries.

7.   The price actually paid or payable includes all payments actually made or to be made as a condition of sale of the imported goods, by the buyer to the seller, or by the buyer to a third party to satisfy an obligation of the seller.

Agreement on Preshipment Inspection

Members,

Noting that Ministers on 20 September 1986 agreed that the Uruguay Round of Multilateral Trade Negotiations shall aim to "bring about further liberalization and expansion of world trade", "strengthen the role of GATT" and "increase the responsiveness of the GATT system to the evolving international economic environment";

Noting that a number of developing country Members have recourse to preshipment inspection;

Recognizing the need of developing countries to do so for as long and in so far as it is necessary to verify the quality, quantity or price of imported goods;

Mindful that such programmes must be carried out without giving rise to unnecessary delays or unequal treatment;

Noting that this inspection is by definition carried out on the territory of exporter Members;

Recognizing the need to establish an agreed international framework of rights and obligations of both user Members and exporter Members;

Recognizing that the principles and obligations of GATT 1994 apply to those activities of preshipment inspection entities that are mandated by governments that are Members of the WTO;

Recognizing that it is desirable to provide transparency of the operation of preshipment inspection entities and of laws and regulations relating to preshipment inspection;

Desiring to provide for the speedy, effective and equitable resolution of disputes between exporters and preshipment inspection entities arising under this Agreement;

Hereby *agree* as follows:

Article 1 Coverage - Definitions

1.   This Agreement shall apply to all preshipment inspection activities carried out on the territory of Members, whether such activities are contracted or mandated by the government, or any government body, of a Member.

2.   The term "user Member" means a Member of which the government or any government body contracts for or mandates the use of preshipment inspection activities.

3.   Preshipment inspection activities are all activities relating to the verification of the quality, the quantity, the price, including currency exchange rate and financial terms, and/or the customs classification of goods to be exported to the territory of the user Member.

4.   The term "preshipment inspection entity" is any entity contracted or mandated by a Member to carry out preshipment inspection activities.[1]

Article 2 Obligations of User Members
Non-Discrimination

1.   User Members shall ensure that preshipment inspection activities are carried out in a non-discriminatory manner, and that the procedures and criteria employed in the conduct of these activities are objective and are applied on an equal basis to all exporters affected by such activities. They shall ensure uniform performance of inspection by all the inspectors of the preshipment inspection entities contracted or mandated by them.

---

[1]   It is understood that this provision does not obligate Members to allow government entities of other Members to conduct preshipment inspection activities on their territory.

Governmental Requirements

2.   User Members shall ensure that in the course of preshipment inspection activities relating to their laws, regulations and requirements, the provisions of paragraph 4 of Article III of GATT 1994 are respected to the extent that these are relevant.

Site of Inspection

3.   User Members shall ensure that all preshipment inspection activities, including the issuance of a Clean Report of Findings or a note of non-issuance, are performed in the customs territory from which the goods are exported or, if the inspection cannot be carried out in that customs territory given the complex nature of the products involved, or if both parties agree, in the customs territory in which the goods are manufactured.

Standards

4.   User Members shall ensure that quantity and quality inspections are performed in accordance with the standards defined by the seller and the buyer in the purchase agreement and that, in the absence of such standards, relevant international standards[2] apply.

Transparency

5.   User Members shall ensure that preshipment inspection activities are conducted in a transparent manner.

6.   User Members shall ensure that, when initially contacted by exporters, preshipment inspection entities provide to the exporters a list of all the information which is necessary for the exporters to comply with inspection requirements. The preshipment inspection entities shall provide the actual information when so requested by exporters. This information shall include a reference to the laws and regulations of user Members relating to preshipment inspection activities, and shall also include the procedures and criteria used for inspection and for price and currency exchange-rate verification purposes, the exporters' rights vis-à-vis the inspection entities, and the appeals procedures set up under paragraph 21. Additional procedural requirements or changes in existing procedures shall not be applied to a shipment unless the exporter concerned is informed of these changes at the time the inspection date is arranged. However, in emergency situations of the types addressed by Articles XX and XXI of GATT 1994, such additional requirements or changes may be applied to a shipment before the exporter has been informed. This assistance shall not, however, relieve exporters from their obligations in respect of compliance with the import regulations of the user Members.

7.   User Members shall ensure that the information referred to in paragraph 6 is made available to exporters in a convenient manner, and that the preshipment inspection offices maintained by preshipment inspection entities serve as information points where this information is available.

8.   User Members shall publish promptly all applicable laws and regulations relating to preshipment inspection activities in such a manner as to enable other governments and traders to become acquainted with them.

Protection of Confidential Business Information

9.   User Members shall ensure that preshipment inspection entities treat all information received in the course of the preshipment inspection as business confidential to the extent that such information is not already published, generally available to third parties, or otherwise in the public domain. User Members shall ensure that preshipment inspection entities maintain procedures to this end.

---

2   An international standard is a standard adopted by a governmental or non-governmental body whose membership is open to all Members, one of whose recognized activities is in the field of standardization.

10. User Members shall provide information to Members on request on the measures they are taking to give effect to paragraph 9. The provisions of this paragraph shall not require any Member to disclose confidential information the disclosure of which would jeopardize the effectiveness of the preshipment inspection programmes or would prejudice the legitimate commercial interest of particular enterprises, public or private.

11. User Members shall ensure that preshipment inspection entities do not divulge confidential business information to any third party, except that preshipment inspection entities may share this information with the government entities that have contracted or mandated them. User Members shall ensure that confidential business information which they receive from pre-shipment inspection entities contracted or mandated by them is adequately safeguarded. Pre-shipment inspection entities shall share confidential business information with the governments contracting or mandating them only to the extent that such information is customarily required for letters of credit or other forms of payment or for customs, import licensing or exchange control purposes.

12. User Members shall ensure that preshipment inspection entities do not request exporters to provide information regarding:

(a) manufacturing data related to patented, licensed or undisclosed processes, or to processes for which a patent is pending;

(b) unpublished technical data other than data necessary to demonstrate compliance with technical regulations or standards;

(c) internal pricing, including manufacturing costs;

(d) profit levels;

(e) the terms of contracts between exporters and their suppliers unless it is not otherwise possible for the entity to conduct the inspection in question. In such cases, the entity shall only request the information necessary for this purpose.

13. The information referred to in paragraph 12, which preshipment inspection entities shall not otherwise request, may be released voluntarily by the exporter to illustrate a specific case.

Conflicts of Interest

14. User Members shall ensure that preshipment inspection entities, bearing in mind also the provisions on protection of confidential business information in paragraphs 9 through 13, maintain procedures to avoid conflicts of interest:

(a) between preshipment inspection entities and any related entities of the preshipment inspection entities in question, including any entities in which the latter have a financial or commercial interest or any entities which have a financial interest in the preshipment inspection entities in question, and whose shipments the preshipment inspection entities are to inspect;

(b) between preshipment inspection entities and any other entities, including other entities subject to preshipment inspection, with the exception of the government entities con-tracting or mandating the inspections;

(c) with divisions of preshipment inspection entities engaged in activities other than those required to carry out the inspection process.

Delays

15. User Members shall ensure that preshipment inspection entities avoid unreasonable delays in inspection of shipments. User Members shall ensure that, once a preshipment inspection entity and an exporter agree on an inspection date, the preshipment inspection entity conducts the inspection on that date unless it is rescheduled on a mutually agreed basis between the

exporter and the preshipment inspection entity, or the preshipment inspection entity is pre-vented from doing so by the exporter or by *force majeure*.[3]

16. User Members shall ensure that, following receipt of the final documents and completion of the inspection, preshipment inspection entities, within five working days, either issue a Clean Report of Findings or provide a detailed written explanation specifying the reasons for non-issuance. User Members shall ensure that, in the latter case, preshipment inspection entities give exporters the opportunity to present their views in writing and, if exporters so request, arrange for re-inspection at the earliest mutually convenient date.

17. User Members shall ensure that, whenever so requested by the exporters, preshipment inspection entities undertake, prior to the date of physical inspection, a preliminary verification of price and, where applicable, of currency exchange rate, on the basis of the contract between exporter and importer, the *pro forma* invoice and, where applicable, the application for import authorization. User Members shall ensure that a price or currency exchange rate that has been accepted by a preshipment inspection entity on the basis of such preliminary verification is not withdrawn, providing the goods conform to the import documentation and/or import licence. They shall ensure that, after a preliminary verification has taken place, preshipment inspection entities immediately inform exporters in writing either of their acceptance or of their detailed reasons for non-acceptance of the price and/or currency exchange rate.

18. User Members shall ensure that, in order to avoid delays in payment, preshipment inspec-tion entities send to exporters or to designated representatives of the exporters a Clean Report of Findings as expeditiously as possible.

19. User Members shall ensure that, in the event of a clerical error in the Clean Report of Fin-dings, preshipment inspection entities correct the error and forward the corrected information to the appropriate parties as expeditiously as possible.

Price Verification

20. User Members shall ensure that, in order to prevent over- and under-invoicing and fraud, preshipment inspection entities conduct price verification[4] according to the following guidelines:

(a) preshipment inspection entities shall only reject a contract price agreed between an exporter and an importer if they can demonstrate that their findings of an unsatisfactory price are based on a verification process which is in conformity with the criteria set out in subparagraphs (b) through (e);

(b) the preshipment inspection entity shall base its price comparison for the verification of the export price on the price(s) of identical or similar goods offered for export from the same country of exportation at or about the same time, under competitive and comparable con-ditions of sale, in conformity with customary commercial practices and net of any applicable standard discounts. Such comparison shall be based on the following:

   (i) only prices providing a valid basis of comparison shall be used, taking into account the relevant economic factors pertaining to the country of importation and a country or countries used for price comparison;

   (ii) the preshipment inspection entity shall not rely upon the price of goods offered for export to different countries of importation to arbitrarily impose the lowest price upon the shipment;

---

3   It is understood that, for the purposes of this Agreement, *"force majeure"* shall mean "irresistible compulsion or coercion, unforeseeable course of events excusing from fulfilment of contract".

4   The obligations of user Members with respect to the services of preshipment inspection entities in connec-tion with customs valuation shall be the obligations which they have accepted in GATT 1994 and the other Multilateral Trade Agreements included in Annex 1A of the WTO Agreement.

(iii) the preshipment inspection entity shall take into account the specific elements listed in subparagraph (c);

(iv) at any stage in the process described above, the preshipment inspection entity shall provide the exporter with an opportunity to explain the price;

(c) when conducting price verification, preshipment inspection entities shall make appropriate allowances for the terms of the sales contract and generally applicable adjusting factors pertaining to the transaction; these factors shall include but not be limited to the commercial level and quantity of the sale, delivery periods and conditions, price escalation clauses, quality specifications, special design features, special shipping or packing specifications, order size, spot sales, seasonal influences, licence or other intellectual property fees, and services rendered as part of the contract if these are not customarily invoiced separately; they shall also include certain elements relating to the exporter's price, such as the contractual relationship between the exporter and importer;

(d) the verification of transportation charges shall relate only to the agreed price of the mode of transport in the country of exportation as indicated in the sales contract;

(e) the following shall not be used for price verification purposes:

(i) the selling price in the country of importation of goods produced in such country;

(ii) the price of goods for export from a country other than the country of exportation;

(iii) the cost of production;

(iv) arbitrary or fictitious prices or values.

Appeals Procedures

21. User Members shall ensure that preshipment inspection entities establish procedures to receive, consider and render decisions concerning grievances raised by exporters, and that information concerning such procedures is made available to exporters in accordance with the provisions of paragraphs 6 and 7. User Members shall ensure that the procedures are developed and maintained in accordance with the following guidelines:

(a) preshipment inspection entities shall designate one or more officials who shall be available during normal business hours in each city or port in which they maintain a preshipment inspection administrative office to receive, consider and render decisions on exporters' appeals or grievances;

(b) exporters shall provide in writing to the designated official(s) the facts concerning the specific transaction in question, the nature of the grievance and a suggested solution;

(c) the designated official(s) shall afford sympathetic consideration to exporters' grievances and shall render a decision as soon as possible after receipt of the documentation referred to in subparagraph (b).

Derogation

22. By derogation to the provisions of Article 2, user Members shall provide that, with the exception of part shipments, shipments whose value is less than a minimum value applicable to such shipments as defined by the user Member shall not be inspected, except in exceptional circumstances. This minimum value shall form part of the information furnished to exporters under the provisions of paragraph 6.

Article 3 Obligations of Exporter Members
Non-discrimination

1. Exporter Members shall ensure that their laws and regulations relating to preshipment inspection activities are applied in a non-discriminatory manner.

Transparency

2.   Exporter Members shall publish promptly all applicable laws and regulations relating to preshipment inspection activities in such a manner as to enable other governments and traders to become acquainted with them.

Technical Assistance

3.   Exporter Members shall offer to provide to user Members, if requested, technical assistance directed towards the achievement of the objectives of this Agreement on mutually agreed terms.[5]

Article 4 Independent Review Procedures

Members shall encourage preshipment inspection entities and exporters mutually to resolve their disputes. However, two working days after submission of the grievance in accordance with the provisions of paragraph 21 of Article 2, either party may refer the dispute to independent review. Members shall take such reasonable measures as may be available to them to ensure that the following procedures are established and maintained to this end:

(a)   these procedures shall be administered by an independent entity constituted jointly by an organization representing preshipment inspection entities and an organization representing exporters for the purposes of this Agreement;

(b)   the independent entity referred to in subparagraph (a) shall establish a list of experts as follows:

   (i)   a section of members nominated by an organization representing preshipment inspection entities;

   (ii)   a section of members nominated by an organization representing exporters;

   (iii) a section of independent trade experts, nominated by the independent entity referred to in subparagraph (a).

The geographical distribution of the experts on this list shall be such as to enable any disputes raised under these procedures to be dealt with expeditiously. This list shall be drawn up within two months of the entry into force of the WTO Agreement and shall be updated annually. The list shall be publicly available. It shall be notified to the Secretariat and circulated to all Members;

(c)   an exporter or preshipment inspection entity wishing to raise a dispute shall contact the independent entity referred to in subparagraph (a) and request the formation of a panel. The independent entity shall be responsible for establishing a panel. This panel shall consist of three members. The members of the panel shall be chosen so as to avoid unnecessary costs and delays. The first member shall be chosen from section (i) of the above list by the preshipment inspection entity concerned, provided that this member is not affiliated to that entity. The second member shall be chosen from section (ii) of the above list by the exporter concerned, provided that this member is not affiliated to that exporter. The third member shall be chosen from section (iii) of the above list by the independent entity referred to in subparagraph (a). No objections shall be made to any independent trade expert drawn from section (iii) of the above list;

(d)   the independent trade expert drawn from section (iii) of the above list shall serve as the chairman of the panel. The independent trade expert shall take the necessary decisions to ensure an expeditious settlement of the dispute by the panel, for instance, whether the facts of the case require the panelists to meet and, if so, where such a meeting shall take place, taking into account the site of the inspection in question;

---

5   It is understood that such technical assistance may be given on a bilateral, plurilateral or multilateral basis.

(e) if the parties to the dispute so agree, one independent trade expert could be selected from section (iii) of the above list by the independent entity referred to in subparagraph (a) to review the dispute in question. This expert shall take the necessary decisions to ensure an expeditious settlement of the dispute, for instance taking into account the site of the inspection in question;

(f) the object of the review shall be to establish whether, in the course of the inspection in dispute, the parties to the dispute have complied with the provisions of this Agreement. The procedures shall be expeditious and provide the opportunity for both parties to present their views in person or in writing;

(g) decisions by a three-member panel shall be taken by majority vote. The decision on the dispute shall be rendered within eight working days of the request for independent review and be communicated to the parties to the dispute. This time-limit could be extended upon agreement by the parties to the dispute. The panel or independent trade expert shall apportion the costs, based on the merits of the case;

(h) the decision of the panel shall be binding upon the preshipment inspection entity and the exporter which are parties to the dispute.

Article 5 Notification

Members shall submit to the Secretariat copies of the laws and regulations by which they put this Agreement into force, as well as copies of any other laws and regulations relating to preshipment inspection, when the WTO Agreement enters into force with respect to the Member concerned. No changes in the laws and regulations relating to preshipment inspection shall be enforced before such changes have been officially published. They shall be notified to the Secretariat immediately after their publication. The Secretariat shall inform the Members of the availability of this information.

Article 6 Review

At the end of the second year from the date of entry into force of the WTO Agreement and every three years thereafter, the Ministerial Conference shall review the provisions, implementation and operation of this Agreement, taking into account the objectives thereof and experience gained in its operation. As a result of such review, the Ministerial Conference may amend the provisions of the Agreement.

Article 7 Consultation

Members shall consult with other Members upon request with respect to any matter affecting the operation of this Agreement. In such cases, the provisions of Article XXII of GATT 1994, as elaborated and applied by the Dispute Settlement Understanding, are applicable to this Agreement.

Article 8 Dispute Settlement

Any disputes among Members regarding the operation of this Agreement shall be subject to the provisions of Article XXIII of GATT 1994, as elaborated and applied by the Dispute Settlement Understanding.

Article 9 Final Provisions

1.   Members shall take the necessary measures for the implementation of the present Agreement.

2.   Members shall ensure that their laws and regulations shall not be contrary to the provisions of this Agreement.

Agreement on Rules of Origin

Members,

Noting that Ministers on 20 September 1986 agreed that the Uruguay Round of Multilateral Trade Negotiations shall aim to "bring about further liberalization and expansion of world trade", "strengthen the role of GATT" and "increase the responsiveness of the GATT system to the evolving international economic environment";

Desiring to further the objectives of GATT 1994;

Recognizing that clear and predictable rules of origin and their application facilitate the flow of international trade;

Desiring to ensure that rules of origin themselves do not create unnecessary obstacles to trade;

Desiring to ensure that rules of origin do not nullify or impair the rights of Members under GATT 1994;

Recognizing that it is desirable to provide transparency of laws, regulations, and practices regarding rules of origin;

Desiring to ensure that rules of origin are prepared and applied in an impartial, transparent, predictable, consistent and neutral manner;

Recognizing the availability of a consultation mechanism and procedures for the speedy, effective and equitable resolution of disputes arising under this Agreement;

Desiring to harmonize and clarify rules of origin;

Hereby *agree* as follows:

PART I – DEFINITIONS AND COVERAGE

Article 1 Rules of Origin

1.   For the purposes of Parts I to IV of this Agreement, rules of origin shall be defined as those laws, regulations and administrative determinations of general application applied by any Member to determine the country of origin of goods provided such rules of origin are not related to contractual or autonomous trade regimes leading to the granting of tariff preferences going beyond the application of paragraph 1 of Article I of GATT 1994.

2.   Rules of origin referred to in paragraph 1 shall include all rules of origin used in non-preferential commercial policy instruments, such as in the application of: most-favoured-nation treatment under Articles I, II, III, XI and XIII of GATT 1994; anti-dumping and countervailing duties under Article VI of GATT 1994; safeguard measures under Article XIX of GATT 1994; origin marking requirements under Article IX of GATT 1994; and any discriminatory quantitative restrictions or tariff quotas. They shall also include rules of origin used for government procurement and trade statistics.[1]

PART II -- DISCIPLINES TO GOVERN THE APPLICATION OF RULES OF ORIGIN

Article 2 Disciplines During the Transition Period

Until the work programme for the harmonization of rules of origin set out in Part IV is completed, Members shall ensure that:

(a)   when they issue administrative determinations of general application, the requirements to be fulfilled are clearly defined. In particular:

---

[1]   It is understood that this provision is without prejudice to those determinations made for purposes of defining "domestic industry" or "like products of domestic industry" or similar terms wherever they apply.

(i) in cases where the criterion of change of tariff classification is applied, such a rule of origin, and any exceptions to the rule, must clearly specify the subheadings or headings within the tariff nomenclature that are addressed by the rule;

(ii) in cases where the ad valorem percentage criterion is applied, the method for calculating this percentage shall also be indicated in the rules of origin;

(iii) in cases where the criterion of manufacturing or processing operation is prescribed, the operation that confers origin on the good concerned shall be precisely specified;

(b) notwithstanding the measure or instrument of commercial policy to which they are linked, their rules of origin are not used as instruments to pursue trade objectives directly or indirectly;

(c) rules of origin shall not themselves create restrictive, distorting, or disruptive effects on international trade. They shall not pose unduly strict requirements or require the fulfilment of a certain condition not related to manufacturing or processing, as a prerequisite for the determination of the country of origin. However, costs not directly related to manufacturing or processing may be included for the purposes of the application of an ad valorem percentage criterion consistent with subparagraph (a);

(d) the rules of origin that they apply to imports and exports are not more stringent than the rules of origin they apply to determine whether or not a good is domestic and shall not discriminate between other Members, irrespective of the affiliation of the manufacturers of the good concerned;[2]

(e) their rules of origin are administered in a consistent, uniform, impartial and reasonable manner;

(f) their rules of origin are based on a positive standard. Rules of origin that state what does not confer origin (negative standard) are permissible as part of a clarification of a positive standard or in individual cases where a positive determination of origin is not necessary;

(g) their laws, regulations, judicial decisions and administrative rulings of general application relating to rules of origin are published as if they were subject to, and in accordance with, the provisions of paragraph 1 of Article X of GATT 1994;

(h) upon the request of an exporter, importer or any person with a justifiable cause, assessments of the origin they would accord to a good are issued as soon as possible but no later than 150 days[3] after a request for such an assessment provided that all necessary elements have been submitted. Requests for such assessments shall be accepted before trade in the good concerned begins and may be accepted at any later point in time. Such assessments shall remain valid for three years provided that the facts and conditions, including the rules of origin, under which they have been made remain comparable. Provided that the parties concerned are informed in advance, such assessments will no longer be valid when a decision contrary to the assessment is made in a review as referred to in subparagraph (j). Such assessments shall be made publicly available subject to the provisions of subparagraph (k);

(i) when introducing changes to their rules of origin or new rules of origin, they shall not apply such changes retroactively as defined in, and without prejudice to, their laws or regulations;

---

2   With respect to rules of origin applied for the purposes of government procurement, this provision shall not create obligations additional to those already assumed by Members under GATT 1994.

3   In respect of requests made during the first year from the date of entry into force of the WTO Agreement, Members shall only be required to issue these assessments as soon as possible.

(j)   any administrative action which they take in relation to the determination of origin is review-able promptly by judicial, arbitral or administrative tribunals or procedures, independent of the authority issuing the determination, which can effect the modification or reversal of the determination;

(k)   all information that is by nature confidential or that is provided on a confidential basis for the purpose of the application of rules of origin is treated as strictly confidential by the authorities concerned, which shall not disclose it without the specific permission of the person or government providing such information, except to the extent that it may be required to be disclosed in the context of judicial proceedings.

Article 3 Disciplines After the Transition Period

Taking into account the aim of all Members to achieve, as a result of the harmonization work programme set out in Part IV, the establishment of harmonized rules of origin, Members shall ensure, upon the implementation of the results of the harmonization work programme, that:

(a)   they apply rules of origin equally for all purposes as set out in Article 1;

(b)   under their rules of origin, the country to be determined as the origin of a particular good is either the country where the good has been wholly obtained or, when more than one country is concerned in the production of the good, the country where the last substantial transformation has been carried out;

(c)   the rules of origin that they apply to imports and exports are not more stringent than the rules of origin they apply to determine whether or not a good is domestic and shall not discriminate between other Members, irrespective of the affiliation of the manufacturers of the good concerned;

(d)   the rules of origin are administered in a consistent, uniform, impartial and reasonable manner;

(e)   their laws, regulations, judicial decisions and administrative rulings of general application relating to rules of origin are published as if they were subject to, and in accordance with, the provisions of paragraph 1 of Article X of GATT 1994;

(f)   upon the request of an exporter, importer or any person with a justifiable cause, assessments of the origin they would accord to a good are issued as soon as possible but no later than 150 days after a request for such an assessment provided that all necessary elements have been submitted. Requests for such assessments shall be accepted before trade in the good concerned begins and may be accepted at any later point in time. Such assessments shall remain valid for three years provided that the facts and conditions, including the rules of origin, under which they have been made remain comparable. Provided that the parties concerned are informed in advance, such assessments will no longer be valid when a decision contrary to the assessment is made in a review as referred to in subparagraph (h). Such assessments shall be made publicly available subject to the provisions of subparagraph (i);

(g)   when introducing changes to their rules of origin or new rules of origin, they shall not apply such changes retroactively as defined in, and without prejudice to, their laws or regulations;

(h)   any administrative action which they take in relation to the determination of origin is review-able promptly by judicial, arbitral or administrative tribunals or procedures, independent of the authority issuing the determination, which can effect the modification or reversal of the determination;

(i)   all information which is by nature confidential or which is provided on a confidential basis for the purpose of the application of rules of origin is treated as strictly confidential by the authorities concerned, which shall not disclose it without the specific permission of the person or government providing such information, except to the extent that it may be required to be disclosed in the context of judicial proceedings.

PART III – PROCEDURAL ARRANGEMENTS ON NOTIFICATION, REVIEW, CONSULTATION AND DISPUTE SETTLEMENT

Article 4 Institutions

1.   There is hereby established a Committee on Rules of Origin (referred to in this Agreement as "the Committee") composed of the representatives from each of the Members. The Committee shall elect its own Chairman and shall meet as necessary, but not less than once a year, for the purpose of affording Members the opportunity to consult on matters relating to the operation of Parts I, II, III and IV or the furtherance of the objectives set out in these Parts and to carry out such other responsibilities assigned to it under this Agreement or by the Council for Trade in Goods. Where appropriate, the Committee shall request information and advice from the Technical Committee referred to in paragraph 2 on matters related to this Agreement. The Committee may also request such other work from the Technical Committee as it considers appropriate for the furtherance of the above-mentioned objectives of this Agreement. The WTO Secretariat shall act as the secretariat to the Committee.

2.   There shall be established a Technical Committee on Rules of Origin (referred to in this Agreement as "the Technical Committee") under the auspices of the Customs Co-operation Council (CCC) as set out in Annex I. The Technical Committee shall carry out the technical work called for in Part IV and prescribed in Annex I. Where appropriate, the Technical Committee shall request information and advice from the Committee on matters related to this Agreement. The Technical Committee may also request such other work from the Committee as it considers appropriate for the furtherance of the above-mentioned objectives of the Agreement. The CCC Secretariat shall act as the secretariat to the Technical Committee.

Article 5 Information and Procedures for Modification and Introduction of New Rules of Origin

1.   Each Member shall provide to the Secretariat, within 90 days after the date of entry into force of the WTO Agreement for it, its rules of origin, judicial decisions, and administrative rulings of general application relating to rules of origin in effect on that date. If by inadvertence a rule of origin has not been provided, the Member concerned shall provide it immediately after this fact becomes known. Lists of information received and available with the Secretariat shall be circulated to the Members by the Secretariat.

2.   During the period referred to in Article 2, Members introducing modifications, other than *de minimis* modifications, to their rules of origin or introducing new rules of origin, which, for the purpose of this Article, shall include any rule of origin referred to in paragraph 1 and not provided to the Secretariat, shall publish a notice to that effect at least 60 days before the entry into force of the modified or new rule in such a manner as to enable interested parties to become acquainted with the intention to modify a rule of origin or to introduce a new rule of origin, unless exceptional circumstances arise or threaten to arise for a Member. In these exceptional cases, the Member shall publish the modified or new rule as soon as possible.

Article 6 Review

1.   The Committee shall review annually the implementation and operation of Parts II and III of this Agreement having regard to its objectives. The Committee shall annually inform the Council for Trade in Goods of developments during the period covered by such reviews.

2.   The Committee shall review the provisions of Parts I, II and III and propose amendments as necessary to reflect the results of the harmonization work programme.

3.   The Committee, in cooperation with the Technical Committee, shall set up a mechanism to consider and propose amendments to the results of the harmonization work programme, taking

into account the objectives and principles set out in Article 9. This may include instances where the rules need to be made more operational or need to be updated to take into account new production processes as affected by any technological change.

Article 7 Consultation

The provisions of Article XXII of GATT 1994, as elaborated and applied by the Dispute Settlement Understanding, are applicable to this Agreement.

Article 8 Dispute Settlement

The provisions of Article XXIII of GATT 1994, as elaborated and applied by the Dispute Settlement Understanding, are applicable to this Agreement.

PART IV – HARMONIZATION OF RULES OF ORIGIN

Article 9 Objectives and Principles

1.   With the objectives of harmonizing rules of origin and, *inter alia*, providing more certainty in the conduct of world trade, the Ministerial Conference shall undertake the work programme set out below in conjunction with the CCC, on the basis of the following principles:

(a)   rules of origin should be applied equally for all purposes as set out in Article 1;

(b)   rules of origin should provide for the country to be determined as the origin of a particular good to be either the country where the good has been wholly obtained or, when more than one country is concerned in the production of the good, the country where the last substantial transformation has been carried out;

(c)   rules of origin should be objective, understandable and predictable;

(d)   notwithstanding the measure or instrument to which they may be linked, rules of origin should not be used as instruments to pursue trade objectives directly or indirectly. They should not themselves create restrictive, distorting or disruptive effects on international trade. They should not pose unduly strict requirements or require the fulfilment of a certain condition not relating to manufacturing or processing as a prerequisite for the determination of the country of origin. However, costs not directly related to manufacturing or processing may be included for purposes of the application of an ad valorem percentage criterion;

(e)   rules of origin should be administrable in a consistent, uniform, impartial and reasonable manner;

(f)   rules of origin should be coherent;

(g)   rules of origin should be based on a positive standard. Negative standards may be used to clarify a positive standard.

Work Programme

2.   (a) The work programme shall be initiated as soon after the entry into force of the WTO Agreement as possible and will be completed within three years of initiation.

(b)   The Committee and the Technical Committee provided for in Article 4 shall be the appropriate bodies to conduct this work.

(c)   To provide for detailed input by the CCC, the Committee shall request the Technical Committee to provide its interpretations and opinions resulting from the work described below on the basis of the principles listed in paragraph 1. To ensure timely completion of the work programme for harmonization, such work shall be conducted on a product sector basis, as represented by various chapters or sections of the Harmonized System (HS) nomenclature.

(i) Wholly Obtained and Minimal Operations or Processes

The Technical Committee shall develop harmonized definitions of:

- the goods that are to be considered as being wholly obtained in one country. This work shall be as detailed as possible;

- minimal operations or processes that do not by themselves confer origin to a good.

The results of this work shall be submitted to the Committee within three months of receipt of the request from the Committee.

(ii) Substantial Transformation – Change in Tariff Classification

- The Technical Committee shall consider and elaborate upon, on the basis of the criterion of substantial transformation, the use of change in tariff subheading or heading when developing rules of origin for particular products or a product sector and, if appropriate, the minimum change within the nomenclature that meets this criterion.

- The Technical Committee shall divide the above work on a product basis taking into account the chapters or sections of the HS nomenclature, so as to submit results of its work to the Committee at least on a quarterly basis. The Technical Committee shall complete the above work within one year and three months from receipt of the request of the Committee.

(iii) Substantial Transformation – Supplementary Criteria

Upon completion of the work under subparagraph (ii) for each product sector or individual product category where the exclusive use of the HS nomenclature does not allow for the expression of substantial transformation, the Technical Committee:

- shall consider and elaborate upon, on the basis of the criterion of substantial transformation, the use, in a supplementary or exclusive manner, of other requirements, including ad valorem percentages[4] and/or manufacturing or processing operations,[5] when developing rules of origin for particular products or a product sector;

- may provide explanations for its proposals;

- shall divide the above work on a product basis taking into account the chapters or sections of the HS nomenclature, so as to submit results of its work to the Committee at least on a quarterly basis. The Technical Committee shall complete the above work within two years and three months of receipt of the request from the Committee.

Role of the Committee

3.   On the basis of the principles listed in paragraph 1:

(a)   the Committee shall consider the interpretations and opinions of the Technical Committee periodically in accordance with the time-frames provided in subparagraphs (i), (ii) and (iii) of paragraph 2(c) with a view to endorsing such interpretations and opinions. The Committee may request the Technical Committee to refine or elaborate its work and/or to develop new approaches. To assist the Technical Committee, the Committee should provide its reasons for requests for additional work and, as appropriate, suggest alternative approaches;

(b)   upon completion of all the work identified in subparagraphs (i), (ii) and (iii) of paragraph 2(c), the Committee shall consider the results in terms of their overall coherence.

---

4   If the ad valorem criterion is prescribed, the method for calculating this percentage shall also be indicated in the rules of origin.

5   If the criterion of manufacturing or processing operation is prescribed, the operation that confers origin on the product concerned shall be precisely specified.

Results of the Harmonization Work Programme and Subsequent Work

4.   The Ministerial Conference shall establish the results of the harmonization work programme in an annex as an integral part of this Agreement.[6] The Ministerial Conference shall establish a time-frame for the entry into force of this annex.

ANNEX I – TECHNICAL COMMITTEE ON RULES OF ORIGIN [omitted]

ANNEX II – COMMON DECLARATION WITH REGARD TO PREFERENTIAL RULES OF ORIGIN

1.   Recognizing that some Members apply preferential rules of origin, distinct from non-preferential rules of origin, the Members hereby *agree* as follows.

2.   For the purposes of this Common Declaration, preferential rules of origin shall be defined as those laws, regulations and administrative determinations of general application applied by any Member to determine whether goods qualify for preferential treatment under contractual or autonomous trade regimes leading to the granting of tariff preferences going beyond the application of paragraph 1 of Article I of GATT 1994.

3.   The Members *agree* to ensure that:

(a)   when they issue administrative determinations of general application, the requirements to be fulfilled are clearly defined. In particular:

   (i)   in cases where the criterion of change of tariff classification is applied, such a preferential rule of origin, and any exceptions to the rule, must clearly specify the subheadings or headings within the tariff nomenclature that are addressed by the rule;

   (ii)   in cases where the ad valorem percentage criterion is applied, the method for calculating this percentage shall also be indicated in the preferential rules of origin;

   (iii) in cases where the criterion of manufacturing or processing operation is prescribed, the operation that confers preferential origin shall be precisely specified;

(b)   their preferential rules of origin are based on a positive standard. Preferential rules of origin that state what does not confer preferential origin (negative standard) are permissible as part of a clarification of a positive standard or in individual cases where a positive determination of preferential origin is not necessary;

(c)   their laws, regulations, judicial decisions and administrative rulings of general application relating to preferential rules of origin are published as if they were subject to, and in accordance with, the provisions of paragraph 1 of Article X of GATT 1994;

(d)   upon request of an exporter, importer or any person with a justifiable cause, assessments of the preferential origin they would accord to a good are issued as soon as possible but no later than 150 days[7] after a request for such an assessment provided that all necessary elements have been submitted. Requests for such assessments shall be accepted before trade in the good concerned begins and may be accepted at any later point in time. Such assessments shall remain valid for three years provided that the facts and conditions, including the preferential rules of origin, under which they have been made remain comparable. Provided that the parties concerned are informed in advance, such assessments will no longer be valid when a decision contrary to the assessment is made in a review as referred to in subparagraph (f). Such assessments shall be made publicly available subject to the provisions of subparagraph (g);

---

6   At the same time, consideration shall be given to arrangements concerning the settlement of disputes relating to customs classification.

7   In respect of requests made during the first year from entry into force of the WTO Agreement, Members shall only be required to issue these assessments as soon as possible.

(e) when introducing changes to their preferential rules of origin or new preferential rules of origin, they shall not apply such changes retroactively as defined in, and without prejudice to, their laws or regulations;

(f) any administrative action which they take in relation to the determination of preferential origin is reviewable promptly by judicial, arbitral or administrative tribunals or procedures, independent of the authority issuing the determination, which can effect the modification or reversal of the determination;

(g) all information that is by nature confidential or that is provided on a confidential basis for the purpose of the application of preferential rules of origin is treated as strictly confidential by the authorities concerned, which shall not disclose it without the specific permission of the person or government providing such information, except to the extent that it may be required to be disclosed in the context of judicial proceedings.

4.   Members *agree* to provide to the Secretariat promptly their preferential rules of origin, including a listing of the preferential arrangements to which they apply, judicial decisions, and administrative rulings of general application relating to their preferential rules of origin in effect on the date of entry into force of the WTO Agreement for the Member concerned. Furthermore, Members agree to provide any modifications to their preferential rules of origin or new preferential rules of origin as soon as possible to the Secretariat. Lists of information received and available with the Secretariat shall be circulated to the Members by the Secretariat.

Agreement on Import Licensing Procedures

Members,

Having regard to the Multilateral Trade Negotiations;

Desiring to further the objectives of GATT 1994;

Taking into account the particular trade, development and financial needs of developing country Members;

Recognizing the usefulness of automatic import licensing for certain purposes and that such licensing should not be used to restrict trade;

Recognizing that import licensing may be employed to administer measures such as those adopted pursuant to the relevant provisions of GATT 1994;

Recognizing the provisions of GATT 1994 as they apply to import licensing procedures;

Desiring to ensure that import licensing procedures are not utilized in a manner contrary to the principles and obligations of GATT 1994;

Recognizing that the flow of international trade could be impeded by the inappropriate use of import licensing procedures;

Convinced that import licensing, particularly non-automatic import licensing, should be implemented in a transparent and predictable manner;

Recognizing that non-automatic licensing procedures should be no more administratively burdensome than absolutely necessary to administer the relevant measure;

Desiring to simplify, and bring transparency to, the administrative procedures and practices used in international trade, and to ensure the fair and equitable application and administration of such procedures and practices;

Desiring to provide for a consultative mechanism and the speedy, effective and equitable resolution of disputes arising under this Agreement;

Hereby *agree* as follows:

Article 1 General Provisions

1.   For the purpose of this Agreement, import licensing is defined as administrative procedures[1] used for the operation of import licensing regimes requiring the submission of an application or other documentation (other than that required for customs purposes) to the relevant administrative body as a prior condition for importation into the customs territory of the importing Member.

2.   Members shall ensure that the administrative procedures used to implement import licensing regimes are in conformity with the relevant provisions of GATT 1994 including its annexes and protocols, as interpreted by this Agreement, with a view to preventing trade distortions that may arise from an inappropriate operation of those procedures, taking into account the economic development purposes and financial and trade needs of developing country Members.[2]

3.   The rules for import licensing procedures shall be neutral in application and administered in a fair and equitable manner.

4.   (a) The rules and all information concerning procedures for the submission of applications, including the eligibility of persons, firms and institutions to make such applications, the

---

1   Those procedures referred to as "licensing" as well as other similar administrative procedures.

2   Nothing in this Agreement shall be taken as implying that the basis, scope or duration of a measure being implemented by a licensing procedure is subject to question under this Agreement.

administrative body(ies) to be approached, and the lists of products subject to the licensing requirement shall be published, in the sources notified to the Committee on Import Licensing provided for in Article 4 (referred to in this Agreement as "the Committee"), in such a manner as to enable governments[3] and traders to become acquainted with them. Such publication shall take place, whenever practicable, 21 days prior to the effective date of the requirement but in all events not later than such effective date. Any exception, derogations or changes in or from the rules concerning licensing procedures or the list of products subject to import licensing shall also be published in the same manner and within the same time periods as specified above. Copies of these publications shall also be made available to the Secretariat.

(b) Members which wish to make comments in writing shall be provided the opportunity to discuss these comments upon request. The concerned Member shall give due consideration to these comments and results of discussion.

5. Application forms and, where applicable, renewal forms shall be as simple as possible. Such documents and information as are considered strictly necessary for the proper functioning of the licensing regime may be required on application.

6. Application procedures and, where applicable, renewal procedures shall be as simple as possible. Applicants shall be allowed a reasonable period for the submission of licence applications. Where there is a closing date, this period should be at least 21 days with provision for extension in circumstances where insufficient applications have been received within this period. Applicants shall have to approach only one administrative body in connection with an application. Where it is strictly indispensable to approach more than one administrative body, applicants shall not need to approach more than three administrative bodies.

7. No application shall be refused for minor documentation errors which do not alter basic data contained therein. No penalty greater than necessary to serve merely as a warning shall be imposed in respect of any omission or mistake in documentation or procedures which is obviously made without fraudulent intent or gross negligence.

8. Licensed imports shall not be refused for minor variations in value, quantity or weight from the amount designated on the licence due to differences occurring during shipment, differences incidental to bulk loading and other minor differences consistent with normal commercial practice.

9. The foreign exchange necessary to pay for licensed imports shall be made available to licence holders on the same basis as to importers of goods not requiring import licences.

10. With regard to security exceptions, the provisions of Article XXI of GATT 1994 apply.

11. The provisions of this Agreement shall not require any Member to disclose confidential information which would impede law enforcement or otherwise be contrary to the public interest or would prejudice the legitimate commercial interests of particular enterprises, public or private.

---

3   For the purpose of this Agreement, the term "governments" is deemed to include the competent authorities of the European Communities.

Article 2 Automatic Import Licensing[4]

1.   Automatic import licensing is defined as import licensing where approval of the application is granted in all cases, and which is in accordance with the requirements of paragraph 2(a).

2.   The following provisions,[5] in addition to those in paragraphs 1 through 11 of Article 1 and paragraph 1 of this Article, shall apply to automatic import licensing procedures:

(a)   automatic licensing procedures shall not be administered in such a manner as to have restricting effects on imports subject to automatic licensing. Automatic licensing procedures shall be deemed to have trade-restricting effects unless, *inter alia*:

(i)   any person, firm or institution which fulfils the legal requirements of the importing Member for engaging in import operations involving products subject to automatic licensing is equally eligible to apply for and to obtain import licences;

(ii)   applications for licences may be submitted on any working day prior to the customs clearance of the goods;

(iii)   applications for licences when submitted in appropriate and complete form are approved immediately on receipt, to the extent administratively feasible, but within a maximum of 10 working days;

(b)   Members recognize that automatic import licensing may be necessary whenever other appropriate procedures are not available. Automatic import licensing may be maintained as long as the circumstances which gave rise to its introduction prevail and as long as its underlying administrative purposes cannot be achieved in a more appropriate way.

Article 3 Non-Automatic Import Licensing

1.   The following provisions, in addition to those in paragraphs 1 through 11 of Article 1, shall apply to non-automatic import licensing procedures. Non-automatic import licensing procedures are defined as import licensing not falling within the definition contained in paragraph 1 of Article 2.

2.   Non-automatic licensing shall not have trade-restrictive or -distortive effects on imports additional to those caused by the imposition of the restriction. Non-automatic licensing procedures shall correspond in scope and duration to the measure they are used to implement, and shall be no more administratively burdensome than absolutely necessary to administer the measure.

3.   In the case of licensing requirements for purposes other than the implementation of quantitative restrictions, Members shall publish sufficient information for other Members and traders to know the basis for granting and/or allocating licences.

4.   Where a Member provides the possibility for persons, firms or institutions to request exceptions or derogations from a licensing requirement, it shall include this fact in the information published under paragraph 4 of Article 1 as well as information on how to make such a request and, to the extent possible, an indication of the circumstances under which requests would be considered.

5.   (a) Members shall provide, upon the request of any Member having an interest in the trade in the product concerned, all relevant information concerning:

(i)   the administration of the restrictions;

---

4   Those import licensing procedures requiring a security which have no restrictive effects on imports are to be considered as falling within the scope of paragraphs 1 and 2.

5   A developing country Member, other than a developing country Member which was a Party to the Agreement on Import Licensing Procedures done on 12 April 1979, which has specific difficulties with the requirements of subparagraphs (a)(ii) and (a)(iii) may, upon notification to the Committee, delay the application of these subparagraphs by not more than two years from the date of entry into force of the WTO Agreement for such Member.

(ii) the import licences granted over a recent period;

(iii) the distribution of such licences among supplying countries;

(iv) where practicable, import statistics (i.e. value and/or volume) with respect to the products subject to import licensing. Developing country Members would not be expected to take additional administrative or financial burdens on this account;

(b) Members administering quotas by means of licensing shall publish the overall amount of quotas to be applied by quantity and/or value, the opening and closing dates of quotas, and any change thereof, within the time periods specified in paragraph 4 of Article 1 and in such a manner as to enable governments and traders to become acquainted with them;

(c) in the case of quotas allocated among supplying countries, the Member applying the restrictions shall promptly inform all other Members having an interest in supplying the product concerned of the shares in the quota currently allocated, by quantity or value, to the various supplying countries and shall publish this information within the time periods specified in paragraph 4 of Article 1 and in such a manner as to enable governments and traders to become acquainted with them;

(d) where situations arise which make it necessary to provide for an early opening date of quotas, the information referred to in paragraph 4 of Article 1 should be published within the time-periods specified in paragraph 4 of Article 1 and in such a manner as to enable governments and traders to become acquainted with them;

(e) any person, firm or institution which fulfils the legal and administrative requirements of the importing Member shall be equally eligible to apply and to be considered for a licence. If the licence application is not approved, the applicant shall, on request, be given the reason therefor and shall have a right of appeal or review in accordance with the domestic legislation or procedures of the importing Member;

(f) the period for processing applications shall, except when not possible for reasons outside the control of the Member, not be longer than 30 days if applications are considered as and when received, i.e. on a first-come first-served basis, and no longer than 60 days if all applications are considered simultaneously. In the latter case, the period for processing applications shall be considered to begin on the day following the closing date of the announced application period;

(g) the period of licence validity shall be of reasonable duration and not be so short as to preclude imports. The period of licence validity shall not preclude imports from distant sources, except in special cases where imports are necessary to meet unforeseen short-term requirements;

(h) when administering quotas, Members shall not prevent importation from being effected in accordance with the issued licences, and shall not discourage the full utilization of quotas;

(i) when issuing licences, Members shall take into account the desirability of issuing licences for products in economic quantities;

(j) in allocating licences, the Member should consider the import performance of the applicant. In this regard, consideration should be given as to whether licences issued to applicants in the past have been fully utilized during a recent representative period. In cases where licences have not been fully utilized, the Member shall examine the reasons for this and take these reasons into consideration when allocating new licences. Consideration shall also be given to ensuring a reasonable distribution of licences to new importers, taking into account the desirability of issuing licences for products in economic quantities. In this regard, special consideration should be given to those importers importing products originating in developing country Members and, in particular, the least-developed country Members;

(k) in the case of quotas administered through licences which are not allocated among supplying countries, licence holders[6] shall be free to choose the sources of imports. In the case of quotas allocated among supplying countries, the licence shall clearly stipulate the country or countries;

(l) in applying paragraph 8 of Article 1, compensating adjustments may be made in future licence allocations where imports exceeded a previous licence level.

Article 4 Institutions

There is hereby established a Committee on Import Licensing composed of representatives from each of the Members. The Committee shall elect its own Chairman and Vice-Chairman and shall meet as necessary for the purpose of affording Members the opportunity of consulting on any matters relating to the operation of this Agreement or the furtherance of its objectives.

Article 5 Notification

1. Members which institute licensing procedures or changes in these procedures shall notify the Committee of such within 60 days of publication.

2. Notifications of the institution of import licensing procedures shall include the following information:

(a) list of products subject to licensing procedures;

(b) contact point for information on eligibility;

(c) administrative body(ies) for submission of applications;

(d) date and name of publication where licensing procedures are published;

(e) indication of whether the licensing procedure is automatic or non-automatic according to definitions contained in Articles 2 and 3;

(f) in the case of automatic import licensing procedures, their administrative purpose;

(g) in the case of non-automatic import licensing procedures, indication of the measure being implemented through the licensing procedure; and

(h) expected duration of the licensing procedure if this can be estimated with some probability, and if not, reason why this information cannot be provided.

3. Notifications of changes in import licensing procedures shall indicate the elements mentioned above, if changes in such occur.

4. Members shall notify the Committee of the publication(s) in which the information required in paragraph 4 of Article 1 will be published.

5. Any interested Member which considers that another Member has not notified the institution of a licensing procedure or changes therein in accordance with the provisions of paragraphs 1 through 3 may bring the matter to the attention of such other Member. If notification is not made promptly thereafter, such Member may itself notify the licensing procedure or changes therein, including all relevant and available information.

Article 6 Consultation and Dispute Settlement

Consultations and the settlement of disputes with respect to any matter affecting the operation of this Agreement shall be subject to the provisions of Articles XXII and XXIII of GATT 1994, as elaborated and applied by the Dispute Settlement Understanding.

---

6   Sometimes referred to as "quota holders".

Article 7 Review

1.   The Committee shall review as necessary, but at least once every two years, the implementation and operation of this Agreement, taking into account the objectives thereof, and the rights and obligations contained therein.

2.   As a basis for the Committee review, the Secretariat shall prepare a factual report based on information provided under Article 5, responses to the annual questionnaire on import licensing procedures[7] and other relevant reliable information which is available to it. This report shall provide a synopsis of the aforementioned information, in particular indicating any changes or developments during the period under review, and including any other information as agreed by the Committee.

3.   Members undertake to complete the annual questionnaire on import licensing procedures promptly and in full.

4.   The Committee shall inform the Council for Trade in Goods of developments during the period covered by such reviews.

Article 8 Final Provisions
Reservations

1.   Reservations may not be entered in respect of any of the provisions of this Agreement without the consent of the other Members.

Domestic Legislation

2.   (a) Each Member shall ensure, not later than the date of entry into force of the WTO Agreement for it, the conformity of its laws, regulations and administrative procedures with the provisions of this Agreement.

(b)   Each Member shall inform the Committee of any changes in its laws and regulations relevant to this Agreement and in the administration of such laws and regulations.

---

7   Originally circulated as GATT 1947 document L/3515 of 23 March 1971.

Agreement on Subsidies and Countervailing Measures

Members hereby *agree* as follows:

PART I: GENERAL PROVISIONS

Article 1 Definition of a Subsidy

1.1 For the purpose of this Agreement, a subsidy shall be deemed to exist if:

(a) (1) there is a financial contribution by a government or any public body within the territory of a Member (referred to in this Agreement as "government"), i.e. where:

    (i) a government practice involves a direct transfer of funds (e.g. grants, loans, and equity infusion), potential direct transfers of funds or liabilities (e.g. loan guarantees);

    (ii) government revenue that is otherwise due is foregone or not collected (e.g. fiscal incentives such as tax credits);[1]

    (iii) a government provides goods or services other than general infrastructure, or purchases goods;

    (iv) a government makes payments to a funding mechanism, or entrusts or directs a private body to carry out one or more of the type of functions illustrated in (i) to (iii) above which would normally be vested in the government and the practice, in no real sense, differs from practices normally followed by governments;

or

(2) there is any form of income or price support in the sense of Article XVI of GATT 1994;

and

(b) a benefit is thereby conferred.

1.2 A subsidy as defined in paragraph 1 shall be subject to the provisions of Part II or shall be subject to the provisions of Part III or V only if such a subsidy is specific in accordance with the provisions of Article 2.

Article 2 Specificity

2.1 In order to determine whether a subsidy, as defined in paragraph 1 of Article 1, is specific to an enterprise or industry or group of enterprises or industries (referred to in this Agreement as "certain enterprises") within the jurisdiction of the granting authority, the following principles shall apply:

(a) Where the granting authority, or the legislation pursuant to which the granting authority operates, explicitly limits access to a subsidy to certain enterprises, such subsidy shall be specific.

(b) Where the granting authority, or the legislation pursuant to which the granting authority operates, establishes objective criteria or conditions[2] governing the eligibility for, and the amount of, a subsidy, specificity shall not exist, provided that the eligibility is automatic and that such criteria and conditions are strictly adhered to. The criteria or conditions must be

---

1   In accordance with the provisions of Article XVI of GATT 1994 (Note to Article XVI) and the provisions of Annexes I through III of this Agreement, the exemption of an exported product from duties or taxes borne by the like product when destined for domestic consumption, or the remission of such duties or taxes in amounts not in excess of those which have accrued, shall not be deemed to be a subsidy.

2   Objective criteria or conditions, as used herein, mean criteria or conditions which are neutral, which do not favour certain enterprises over others, and which are economic in nature and horizontal in application, such as number of employees or size of enterprise.

clearly spelled out in law, regulation, or other official document, so as to be capable of verification.

(c) If, notwithstanding any appearance of non-specificity resulting from the application of the principles laid down in subparagraphs (a) and (b), there are reasons to believe that the subsidy may in fact be specific, other factors may be considered. Such factors are: use of a subsidy programme by a limited number of certain enterprises, predominant use by certain enterprises, the granting of disproportionately large amounts of subsidy to certain enterprises, and the manner in which discretion has been exercised by the granting authority in the decision to grant a subsidy.[3] In applying this subparagraph, account shall be taken of the extent of diversification of economic activities within the jurisdiction of the granting authority, as well as of the length of time during which the subsidy programme has been in operation.

2.2 A subsidy which is limited to certain enterprises located within a designated geographical region within the jurisdiction of the granting authority shall be specific. It is understood that the setting or change of generally applicable tax rates by all levels of government entitled to do so shall not be deemed to be a specific subsidy for the purposes of this Agreement.

2.3 Any subsidy falling under the provisions of Article 3 shall be deemed to be specific.

2.4 Any determination of specificity under the provisions of this Article shall be clearly substantiated on the basis of positive evidence.

PART II: PROHIBITED SUBSIDIES

Article 3 Prohibition

3.1 Except as provided in the Agreement on Agriculture, the following subsidies, within the meaning of Article 1, shall be prohibited:

(a) subsidies contingent, in law or in fact,[4] whether solely or as one of several other conditions, upon export performance, including those illustrated in Annex I;[5]

(b) subsidies contingent, whether solely or as one of several other conditions, upon the use of domestic over imported goods.

3.2 A Member shall neither grant nor maintain subsidies referred to in paragraph 1.

Article 4 Remedies

4.1 Whenever a Member has reason to believe that a prohibited subsidy is being granted or maintained by another Member, such Member may request consultations with such other Member.

4.2 A request for consultations under paragraph 1 shall include a statement of available evidence with regard to the existence and nature of the subsidy in question.

4.3 Upon request for consultations under paragraph 1, the Member believed to be granting or maintaining the subsidy in question shall enter into such consultations as quickly as possible. The purpose of the consultations shall be to clarify the facts of the situation and to arrive at a mutually agreed solution.

---

3   In this regard, in particular, information on the frequency with which applications for a subsidy are refused or approved and the reasons for such decisions shall be considered.

4   This standard is met when the facts demonstrate that the granting of a subsidy, without having been made legally contingent upon export performance, is in fact tied to actual or anticipated exportation or export earnings. The mere fact that a subsidy is granted to enterprises which export shall not for that reason alone be considered to be an export subsidy within the meaning of this provision.

5   Measures referred to in Annex I as not constituting export subsidies shall not be prohibited under this or any other provision of this Agreement.

4.4 If no mutually agreed solution has been reached within 30 days[6] of the request for consultations, any Member party to such consultations may refer the matter to the Dispute Settlement Body ("DSB") for the immediate establishment of a panel, unless the DSB decides by consensus not to establish a panel.

4.5 Upon its establishment, the panel may request the assistance of the Permanent Group of Experts[7] (referred to in this Agreement as the "PGE") with regard to whether the measure in question is a prohibited subsidy. If so requested, the PGE shall immediately review the evidence with regard to the existence and nature of the measure in question and shall provide an opportunity for the Member applying or maintaining the measure to demonstrate that the measure in question is not a prohibited subsidy. The PGE shall report its conclusions to the panel within a time-limit determined by the panel. The PGE's conclusions on the issue of whether or not the measure in question is a prohibited subsidy shall be accepted by the panel without modification.

4.6 The panel shall submit its final report to the parties to the dispute. The report shall be circulated to all Members within 90 days of the date of the composition and the establishment of the panel's terms of reference.

4.7 If the measure in question is found to be a prohibited subsidy, the panel shall recommend that the subsidizing Member withdraw the subsidy without delay. In this regard, the panel shall specify in its recommendation the time-period within which the measure must be withdrawn.

4.8 Within 30 days of the issuance of the panel's report to all Members, the report shall be adopted by the DSB unless one of the parties to the dispute formally notifies the DSB of its decision to appeal or the DSB decides by consensus not to adopt the report.

4.9 Where a panel report is appealed, the Appellate Body shall issue its decision within 30 days from the date when the party to the dispute formally notifies its intention to appeal. When the Appellate Body considers that it cannot provide its report within 30 days, it shall inform the DSB in writing of the reasons for the delay together with an estimate of the period within which it will submit its report. In no case shall the proceedings exceed 60 days. The appellate report shall be adopted by the DSB and unconditionally accepted by the parties to the dispute unless the DSB decides by consensus not to adopt the appellate report within 20 days following its issuance to the Members.[8]

4.10 In the event the recommendation of the DSB is not followed within the time- period specified by the panel, which shall commence from the date of adoption of the panel's report or the Appellate Body's report, the DSB shall grant authorization to the complaining Member to take appropriate[9] countermeasures, unless the DSB decides by consensus to reject the request.

4.11 In the event a party to the dispute requests arbitration under paragraph 6 of Article 22 of the Dispute Settlement Understanding ("DSU"), the arbitrator shall determine whether the countermeasures are appropriate.[10]

4.12 For purposes of disputes conducted pursuant to this Article, except for time-periods specifically prescribed in this Article, time-periods applicable under the DSU for the conduct of such disputes shall be half the time prescribed therein.

---

6   Any time-periods mentioned in this Article may be extended by mutual agreement.
7   As established in Article 24.
8   If a meeting of the DSB is not scheduled during this period, such a meeting shall be held for this purpose.
9   This expression is not meant to allow countermeasures that are disproportionate in light of the fact that the subsidies dealt with under these provisions are prohibited.
10   This expression is not meant to allow countermeasures that are disproportionate in light of the fact that the subsidies dealt with under these provisions are prohibited.

PART III: ACTIONABLE SUBSIDIES

Article 5 Adverse Effects

No Member should cause, through the use of any subsidy referred to in paragraphs 1 and 2 of Article 1, adverse effects to the interests of other Members, i.e.:

(a) injury to the domestic industry of another Member;[11]

(b) nullification or impairment of benefits accruing directly or indirectly to other Members under GATT 1994 in particular the benefits of concessions bound under Article II of GATT 1994;[12]

(c) serious prejudice to the interests of another Member.[13]

This Article does not apply to subsidies maintained on agricultural products as provided in Article 13 of the Agreement on Agriculture.

Article 6 Serious Prejudice

6.1 Serious prejudice in the sense of paragraph (c) of Article 5 shall be deemed to exist in the case of:

(a) the total ad valorem subsidization[14] of a product exceeding 5 per cent;[15]

(b) subsidies to cover operating losses sustained by an industry;

(c) subsidies to cover operating losses sustained by an enterprise, other than one-time measures which are non-recurrent and cannot be repeated for that enterprise and which are given merely to provide time for the development of long- term solutions and to avoid acute social problems;

(d) direct forgiveness of debt, i.e. forgiveness of government-held debt, and grants to cover debt repayment.[16]

6.2 Notwithstanding the provisions of paragraph 1, serious prejudice shall not be found if the subsidizing Member demonstrates that the subsidy in question has not resulted in any of the effects enumerated in paragraph 3.

6.3 Serious prejudice in the sense of paragraph (c) of Article 5 may arise in any case where one or several of the following apply:

(a) the effect of the subsidy is to displace or impede the imports of a like product of another Member into the market of the subsidizing Member;

(b) the effect of the subsidy is to displace or impede the exports of a like product of another Member from a third country market;

(c) the effect of the subsidy is a significant price undercutting by the subsidized product as compared with the price of a like product of another Member in the same market or significant price suppression, price depression or lost sales in the same market;

---

11   The term "injury to the domestic industry" is used here in the same sense as it is used in Part V.

12   The term "nullification or impairment" is used in this Agreement in the same sense as it is used in the relevant provisions of GATT 1994, and the existence of such nullification or impairment shall be established in accordance with the practice of application of these provisions.

13   The term "serious prejudice to the interests of another Member" is used in this Agreement in the same sense as it is used in paragraph 1 of Article XVI of GATT 1994, and includes threat of serious prejudice.

14   The total ad valorem subsidization shall be calculated in accordance with the provisions of Annex IV.

15   Since it is anticipated that civil aircraft will be subject to specific multilateral rules, the threshold in this subparagraph does not apply to civil aircraft.

16   Members recognize that where royalty-based financing for a civil aircraft programme is not being fully repaid due to the level of actual sales falling below the level of forecast sales, this does not in itself constitute serious prejudice for the purposes of this subparagraph.

(d)   the effect of the subsidy is an increase in the world market share of the subsidizing Member in a particular subsidized primary product or commodity[17] as compared to the average share it had during the previous period of three years and this increase follows a consistent trend over a period when subsidies have been granted.

6.4 For the purpose of paragraph 3(b), the displacement or impeding of exports shall include any case in which, subject to the provisions of paragraph 7, it has been demonstrated that there has been a change in relative shares of the market to the disadvantage of the non-subsidized like product (over an appropriately representative period sufficient to demonstrate clear trends in the development of the market for the product concerned, which, in normal circumstances, shall be at least one year). "Change in relative shares of the market" shall include any of the following situations: (a) there is an increase in the market share of the subsidized product; (b) the market share of the subsidized product remains constant in circumstances in which, in the absence of the subsidy, it would have declined; (c) the market share of the subsidized product declines, but at a slower rate than would have been the case in the absence of the subsidy.

6.5 For the purpose of paragraph 3(c), price undercutting shall include any case in which such price undercutting has been demonstrated through a comparison of prices of the subsidized product with prices of a non-subsidized like product supplied to the same market. The comparison shall be made at the same level of trade and at comparable times, due account being taken of any other factor affecting price comparability. However, if such a direct comparison is not possible, the existence of price undercutting may be demonstrated on the basis of export unit values.

6.6 Each Member in the market of which serious prejudice is alleged to have arisen shall, subject to the provisions of paragraph 3 of Annex V, make available to the parties to a dispute arising under Article 7, and to the panel established pursuant to paragraph 4 of Article 7, all relevant information that can be obtained as to the changes in market shares of the parties to the dispute as well as concerning prices of the products involved.

6.7 Displacement or impediment resulting in serious prejudice shall not arise under paragraph 3 where any of the following circumstances exist[18] during the relevant period:

(a)   prohibition or restriction on exports of the like product from the complaining Member or on imports from the complaining Member into the third country market concerned;

(b)   decision by an importing government operating a monopoly of trade or state trading in the product concerned to shift, for non-commercial reasons, imports from the complaining Member to another country or countries;

(c)   natural disasters, strikes, transport disruptions or other *force majeure* substantially affecting production, qualities, quantities or prices of the product available for export from the complaining Member;

(d)   existence of arrangements limiting exports from the complaining Member;

(e)   voluntary decrease in the availability for export of the product concerned from the complaining Member (including, *inter alia*, a situation where firms in the complaining Member have been autonomously reallocating exports of this product to new markets);

(f)   failure to conform to standards and other regulatory requirements in the importing country.

6.8 In the absence of circumstances referred to in paragraph 7, the existence of serious prejudice should be determined on the basis of the information submitted to or obtained by the panel, including information submitted in accordance with the provisions of Annex V.

---

17   Unless other multilaterally agreed specific rules apply to the trade in the product or commodity in question.

18   The fact that certain circumstances are referred to in this paragraph does not, in itself, confer upon them any legal status in terms of either GATT 1994 or this Agreement. These circumstances must not be isolated, sporadic or otherwise insignificant.

6.9 This Article does not apply to subsidies maintained on agricultural products as provided in Article 13 of the Agreement on Agriculture.

Article 7 Remedies

7.1 Except as provided in Article 13 of the Agreement on Agriculture, whenever a Member has reason to believe that any subsidy referred to in Article 1, granted or maintained by another Member, results in injury to its domestic industry, nullification or impairment or serious prejudice, such Member may request consultations with such other Member.

7.2 A request for consultations under paragraph 1 shall include a statement of available evidence with regard to (a) the existence and nature of the subsidy in question, and (b) the injury caused to the domestic industry, or the nullification or impairment, or serious prejudice[19] caused to the interests of the Member requesting consultations.

7.3 Upon request for consultations under paragraph 1, the Member believed to be granting or maintaining the subsidy practice in question shall enter into such consultations as quickly as possible. The purpose of the consultations shall be to clarify the facts of the situation and to arrive at a mutually agreed solution.

7.4 If consultations do not result in a mutually agreed solution within 60 days,[20] any Member party to such consultations may refer the matter to the DSB for the establishment of a panel, unless the DSB decides by consensus not to establish a panel. The composition of the panel and its terms of reference shall be established within 15 days from the date when it is established.

7.5 The panel shall review the matter and shall submit its final report to the parties to the dispute. The report shall be circulated to all Members within 120 days of the date of the composition and establishment of the panel's terms of reference.

7.6 Within 30 days of the issuance of the panel's report to all Members, the report shall be adopted by the DSB[21] unless one of the parties to the dispute formally notifies the DSB of its decision to appeal or the DSB decides by consensus not to adopt the report.

7.7 Where a panel report is appealed, the Appellate Body shall issue its decision within 60 days from the date when the party to the dispute formally notifies its intention to appeal. When the Appellate Body considers that it cannot provide its report within 60 days, it shall inform the DSB in writing of the reasons for the delay together with an estimate of the period within which it will submit its report. In no case shall the proceedings exceed 90 days. The appellate report shall be adopted by the DSB and unconditionally accepted by the parties to the dispute unless the DSB decides by consensus not to adopt the appellate report within 20 days following its issuance to the Members.[22]

7.8 Where a panel report or an Appellate Body report is adopted in which it is determined that any subsidy has resulted in adverse effects to the interests of another Member within the meaning of Article 5, the Member granting or maintaining such subsidy shall take appropriate steps to remove the adverse effects or shall withdraw the subsidy.

7.9 In the event the Member has not taken appropriate steps to remove the adverse effects of the subsidy or withdraw the subsidy within six months from the date when the DSB adopts the panel report or the Appellate Body report, and in the absence of agreement on compensation, the DSB shall grant authorization to the complaining Member to take countermeasures, commensurate with the degree and nature of the adverse effects determined to exist, unless the DSB decides by consensus to reject the request.

---

19   In the event that the request relates to a subsidy deemed to result in serious prejudice in terms of paragraph 1 of Article 6, the available evidence of serious prejudice may be limited to the available evidence as to whether the conditions of paragraph 1 of Article 6 have been met or not.

20   Any time-periods mentioned in this Article may be extended by mutual agreement.

21   If a meeting of the DSB is not scheduled during this period, such a meeting shall be held for this purpose.

22   If a meeting of the DSB is not scheduled during this period, such a meeting shall be held for this purpose.

7.10 In the event that a party to the dispute requests arbitration under paragraph 6 of Article 22 of the DSU, the arbitrator shall determine whether the countermeasures are commensurate with the degree and nature of the adverse effects determined to exist.

PART IV: NON-ACTIONABLE SUBSIDIES

Article 8 Identification of Non-Actionable Subsidies

8.1   The following subsidies shall be considered as non-actionable:[23]

(a)   subsidies which are not specific within the meaning of Article 2;

(b)   subsidies which are specific within the meaning of Article 2 but which meet all of the conditions provided for in paragraphs 2(a), 2(b) or 2(c) below.

8.2   Notwithstanding the provisions of Parts III and V, the following subsidies shall be non-actionable:

(a)   assistance for research activities conducted by firms or by higher education or research establishments on a contract basis with firms if:[24],[25],[26]

the assistance covers[27] not more than 75 per cent of the costs of industrial research[28] or 50 per cent of the costs of pre-competitive development activity[29],[30];

and provided that such assistance is limited exclusively to:

(i)   costs of personnel (researchers, technicians and other supporting staff employed exclusively in the research activity);

(ii)   costs of instruments, equipment, land and buildings used exclusively and permanently (except when disposed of on a commercial basis) for the research activity;

---

23   It is recognized that government assistance for various purposes is widely provided by Members and that the mere fact that such assistance may not qualify for non-actionable treatment under the provisions of this Article does not in itself restrict the ability of Members to provide such assistance.

24   Since it is anticipated that civil aircraft will be subject to specific multilateral rules, the provisions of this subparagraph do not apply to that product.

25   Not later than 18 months after the date of entry into force of the WTO Agreement, the Committee on Subsidies and Countervailing Measures provided for in Article 24 (referred to in this Agreement as "the Committee") shall review the operation of the provisions of subparagraph 2(a) with a view to making all necessary modifications to improve the operation of these provisions. In its consideration of possible modifications, the Committee shall carefully review the definitions of the categories set forth in this subparagraph in the light of the experience of Members in the operation of research programmes and the work in other relevant international institutions.

26   The provisions of this Agreement do not apply to fundamental research activities independently conducted by higher education or research establishments. The term "fundamental research" means an enlargement of general scientific and technical knowledge not linked to industrial or commercial objectives.

27   The allowable levels of non-actionable assistance referred to in this subparagraph shall be established by reference to the total eligible costs incurred over the duration of an individual project.

28   The term "industrial research" means planned search or critical investigation aimed at discovery of new knowledge, with the objective that such knowledge may be useful in developing new products, processes or services, or in bringing about a significant improvement to existing products, processes or services.

29   The term "pre-competitive development activity" means the translation of industrial research findings into a plan, blueprint or design for new, modified or improved products, processes or services whether intended for sale or use, including the creation of a first prototype which would not be capable of commercial use. It may further include the conceptual formulation and design of products, processes or services alternatives and initial demonstration or pilot projects, provided that these same projects cannot be converted or used for industrial application or commercial exploitation. It does not include routine or periodic alterations to existing products, production lines, manufacturing processes, services, and other on-going operations even though those alterations may represent improvements.

30   In the case of programmes which span industrial research and pre-competitive development activity, the allowable level of non-actionable assistance shall not exceed the simple average of the allowable levels of non-actionable assistance applicable to the above two categories, calculated on the basis of all eligible costs as set forth in items (i) to (v) of this subparagraph.

      (iii) costs of consultancy and equivalent services used exclusively for the research activity, including bought-in research, technical knowledge, patents, etc.;

      (iv) additional overhead costs incurred directly as a result of the research activity;

      (v) other running costs (such as those of materials, supplies and the like), incurred directly as a result of the research activity.

(b) assistance to disadvantaged regions within the territory of a Member given pursuant to a general framework of regional development[31] and non-specific (within the meaning of Article 2) within eligible regions provided that:

      (i) each disadvantaged region must be a clearly designated contiguous geographical area with a definable economic and administrative identity;

      (ii) the region is considered as disadvantaged on the basis of neutral and objective criteria,[32] indicating that the region's difficulties arise out of more than temporary circumstances; such criteria must be clearly spelled out in law, regulation, or other official document, so as to be capable of verification;

      (iii) the criteria shall include a measurement of economic development which shall be based on at least one of the following factors:

         – one of either income per capita or household income per capita, or GDP per capita, which must not be above 85 per cent of the average for the territory concerned;

         – unemployment rate, which must be at least 110 per cent of the average for the territory concerned;

      as measured over a three-year period; such measurement, however, may be a composite one and may include other factors.

(c) assistance to promote adaptation of existing facilities[33] to new environmental requirements imposed by law and/or regulations which result in greater constraints and financial burden on firms, provided that the assistance:

      (i) is a one-time non-recurring measure; and

      (ii) is limited to 20 per cent of the cost of adaptation; and

      (iii) does not cover the cost of replacing and operating the assisted investment, which must be fully borne by firms; and

      (iv) is directly linked to and proportionate to a firm's planned reduction of nuisances and pollution, and does not cover any manufacturing cost savings which may be achieved; and

      (v) is available to all firms which can adopt the new equipment and/or production processes.

---

31   A "general framework of regional development" means that regional subsidy programmes are part of an internally consistent and generally applicable regional development policy and that regional development subsidies are not granted in isolated geographical points having no, or virtually no, influence on the development of a region.

32   "Neutral and objective criteria" means criteria which do not favour certain regions beyond what is appropriate for the elimination or reduction of regional disparities within the framework of the regional development policy. In this regard, regional subsidy programmes shall include ceilings on the amount of assistance which can be granted to each subsidized project. Such ceilings must be differentiated according to the different levels of development of assisted regions and must be expressed in terms of investment costs or cost of job creation. Within such ceilings, the distribution of assistance shall be sufficiently broad and even to avoid the predominant use of a subsidy by, or the granting of disproportionately large amounts of subsidy to, certain enterprises as provided for in Article 2.

33   The term "existing facilities" means facilities which have been in operation for at least two years at the time when new environmental requirements are imposed.

8.3 A subsidy programme for which the provisions of paragraph 2 are invoked shall be notified in advance of its implementation to the Committee in accordance with the provisions of Part VII. Any such notification shall be sufficiently precise to enable other Members to evaluate the consistency of the programme with the conditions and criteria provided for in the relevant provisions of paragraph 2. Members shall also provide the Committee with yearly updates of such notifications, in particular by supplying information on global expenditure for each programme, and on any modification of the programme. Other Members shall have the right to request information about individual cases of subsidization under a notified programme.[34]

8.4 Upon request of a Member, the Secretariat shall review a notification made pursuant to paragraph 3 and, where necessary, may require additional information from the subsidizing Member concerning the notified programme under review. The Secretariat shall report its findings to the Committee. The Committee shall, upon request, promptly review the findings of the Secretariat (or, if a review by the Secretariat has not been requested, the notification itself), with a view to determining whether the conditions and criteria laid down in paragraph 2 have not been met. The procedure provided for in this paragraph shall be completed at the latest at the first regular meeting of the Committee following the notification of a subsidy programme, provided that at least two months have elapsed between such notification and the regular meeting of the Committee. The review procedure described in this paragraph shall also apply, upon request, to substantial modifications of a programme notified in the yearly updates referred to in paragraph 3.

8.5 Upon the request of a Member, the determination by the Committee referred to in paragraph 4, or a failure by the Committee to make such a determination, as well as the violation, in individual cases, of the conditions set out in a notified programme, shall be submitted to binding arbitration. The arbitration body shall present its conclusions to the Members within 120 days from the date when the matter was referred to the arbitration body. Except as otherwise provided in this paragraph, the DSU shall apply to arbitrations conducted under this paragraph.

Article 9 Consultations and Authorized Remedies

9.1 If, in the course of implementation of a programme referred to in paragraph 2 of Article 8, notwithstanding the fact that the programme is consistent with the criteria laid down in that paragraph, a Member has reasons to believe that this programme has resulted in serious adverse effects to the domestic industry of that Member, such as to cause damage which would be difficult to repair, such Member may request consultations with the Member granting or maintaining the subsidy.

9.2 Upon request for consultations under paragraph 1, the Member granting or maintaining the subsidy programme in question shall enter into such consultations as quickly as possible. The purpose of the consultations shall be to clarify the facts of the situation and to arrive at a mutually acceptable solution.

9.3 If no mutually acceptable solution has been reached in consultations under paragraph 2 within 60 days of the request for such consultations, the requesting Member may refer the matter to the Committee.

9.4 Where a matter is referred to the Committee, the Committee shall immediately review the facts involved and the evidence of the effects referred to in paragraph 1. If the Committee determines that such effects exist, it may recommend to the subsidizing Member to modify this programme in such a way as to remove these effects. The Committee shall present its conclusions within 120 days from the date when the matter is referred to it under paragraph 3. In the event the recommendation is not followed within six months, the Committee shall authorize

---

34   It is recognized that nothing in this notification provision requires the provision of confidential information, including confidential business information.

the requesting Member to take appropriate countermeasures commensurate with the nature and degree of the effects determined to exist.

PART V: COUNTERVAILING MEASURES

Article 10 Application of Article VI of GATT 1994[35]

Members shall take all necessary steps to ensure that the imposition of a countervailing duty[36] on any product of the territory of any Member imported into the territory of another Member is in accordance with the provisions of Article VI of GATT 1994 and the terms of this Agreement. Countervailing duties may only be imposed pursuant to investigations initiated[37] and conducted in accordance with the provisions of this Agreement and the Agreement on Agriculture.

Article 11 Initiation and Subsequent Investigation

11.1 Except as provided in paragraph 6, an investigation to determine the existence, degree and effect of any alleged subsidy shall be initiated upon a written application by or on behalf of the domestic industry.

11.2 An application under paragraph 1 shall include sufficient evidence of the existence of (a) a subsidy and, if possible, its amount, (b) injury within the meaning of Article VI of GATT 1994 as interpreted by this Agreement, and (c) a causal link between the subsidized imports and the alleged injury. Simple assertion, unsubstantiated by relevant evidence, cannot be considered sufficient to meet the requirements of this paragraph. The application shall contain such information as is reasonably available to the applicant on the following:

(i)   the identity of the applicant and a description of the volume and value of the domestic production of the like product by the applicant. Where a written application is made on behalf of the domestic industry, the application shall identify the industry on behalf of which the application is made by a list of all known domestic producers of the like product (or associations of domestic producers of the like product) and, to the extent possible, a description of the volume and value of domestic production of the like product accounted for by such producers;

(ii)   a complete description of the allegedly subsidized product, the names of the country or countries of origin or export in question, the identity of each known exporter or foreign producer and a list of known persons importing the product in question;

(iii) evidence with regard to the existence, amount and nature of the subsidy in question;

(iv)   evidence that alleged injury to a domestic industry is caused by subsidized imports through the effects of the subsidies; this evidence includes information on the evolution of the volume of the allegedly subsidized imports, the effect of these imports on prices of the like product in the domestic market and the consequent impact of the imports on the domestic

---

35   The provisions of Part II or III may be invoked in parallel with the provisions of Part V; however, with regard to the effects of a particular subsidy in the domestic market of the importing Member, only one form of relief (either a countervailing duty, if the requirements of Part V are met, or a countermeasure under Articles 4 or 7) shall be available. The provisions of Parts III and V shall not be invoked regarding measures considered non-actionable in accordance with the provisions of Part IV. However, measures referred to in paragraph 1(a) of Article 8 may be investigated in order to determine whether or not they are specific within the meaning of Article 2. In addition, in the case of a subsidy referred to in paragraph 2 of Article 8 conferred pursuant to a programme which has not been notified in accordance with paragraph 3 of Article 8, the provisions of Part III or V may be invoked, but such subsidy shall be treated as non-actionable if it is found to conform to the standards set forth in paragraph 2 of Article 8.

36   The term "countervailing duty" shall be understood to mean a special duty levied for the purpose of offsetting any subsidy bestowed directly or indirectly upon the manufacture, production or export of any merchandise, as provided for in paragraph 3 of Article VI of GATT 1994.

37   The term "initiated" as used hereinafter means procedural action by which a Member formally commences an investigation as provided in Article 11.

industry, as demonstrated by relevant factors and indices having a bearing on the state of the domestic industry, such as those listed in paragraphs 2 and 4 of Article 15.

11.3 The authorities shall review the accuracy and adequacy of the evidence provided in the application to determine whether the evidence is sufficient to justify the initiation of an investigation.

11.4 An investigation shall not be initiated pursuant to paragraph 1 unless the authorities have determined, on the basis of an examination of the degree of support for, or opposition to, the application expressed[38] by domestic producers of the like product, that the application has been made by or on behalf of the domestic industry.[39] The application shall be considered to have been made "by or on behalf of the domestic industry" if it is supported by those domestic producers whose collective output constitutes more than 50 per cent of the total production of the like product produced by that portion of the domestic industry expressing either support for or opposition to the application. However, no investigation shall be initiated when domestic producers expressly supporting the application account for less than 25 per cent of total production of the like product produced by the domestic industry.

11.5 The authorities shall avoid, unless a decision has been made to initiate an investigation, any publicizing of the application for the initiation of an investigation.

11.6 If, in special circumstances, the authorities concerned decide to initiate an investigation without having received a written application by or on behalf of a domestic industry for the initiation of such investigation, they shall proceed only if they have sufficient evidence of the existence of a subsidy, injury and causal link, as described in paragraph 2, to justify the initiation of an investigation.

11.7 The evidence of both subsidy and injury shall be considered simultaneously (a) in the decision whether or not to initiate an investigation and (b) thereafter, during the course of the investigation, starting on a date not later than the earliest date on which in accordance with the provisions of this Agreement provisional measures may be applied.

11.8 In cases where products are not imported directly from the country of origin but are exported to the importing Member from an intermediate country, the provisions of this Agreement shall be fully applicable and the transaction or transactions shall, for the purposes of this Agreement, be regarded as having taken place between the country of origin and the importing Member.

11.9 An application under paragraph 1 shall be rejected and an investigation shall be terminated promptly as soon as the authorities concerned are satisfied that there is not sufficient evidence of either subsidization or of injury to justify proceeding with the case. There shall be immediate termination in cases where the amount of a subsidy is *de minimis*, or where the volume of subsidized imports, actual or potential, or the injury, is negligible. For the purpose of this paragraph, the amount of the subsidy shall be considered to be *de minimis* if the subsidy is less than 1 per cent ad valorem.

11.10   An investigation shall not hinder the procedures of customs clearance.

11.11   Investigations shall, except in special circumstances, be concluded within one year, and in no case more than 18 months, after their initiation.

---

38   In the case of fragmented industries involving an exceptionally large number of producers, authorities may determine support and opposition by using statistically valid sampling techniques.

39   Members are aware that in the territory of certain Members employees of domestic producers of the like product or representatives of those employees may make or support an application for an investigation under paragraph 1.

Article 12 Evidence

12.1 Interested Members and all interested parties in a countervailing duty investigation shall be given notice of the information which the authorities require and ample opportunity to present in writing all evidence which they consider relevant in respect of the investigation in question.

12.1.1   Exporters, foreign producers or interested Members receiving questionnaires used in a countervailing duty investigation shall be given at least 30 days for reply.[40] Due consideration should be given to any request for an extension of the 30-day period and, upon cause shown, such an extension should be granted whenever practicable.

12.1.2   Subject to the requirement to protect confidential information, evidence presented in writing by one interested Member or interested party shall be made available promptly to other interested Members or interested parties participating in the investigation.

12.1.3   As soon as an investigation has been initiated, the authorities shall provide the full text of the written application received under paragraph 1 of Article 11 to the known exporters[41] and to the authorities of the exporting Member and shall make it available, upon request, to other interested parties involved. Due regard shall be paid to the protection of confidential information, as provided for in paragraph 4.

12.2 Interested Members and interested parties also shall have the right, upon justification, to present information orally. Where such information is provided orally, the interested Members and interested parties subsequently shall be required to reduce such submissions to writing. Any decision of the investigating authorities can only be based on such information and arguments as were on the written record of this authority and which were available to interested Members and interested parties participating in the investigation, due account having been given to the need to protect confidential information.

12.3 The authorities shall whenever practicable provide timely opportunities for all interested Members and interested parties to see all information that is relevant to the presentation of their cases, that is not confidential as defined in paragraph 4, and that is used by the authorities in a countervailing duty investigation, and to prepare presentations on the basis of this information.

12.4 Any information which is by nature confidential (for example, because its disclosure would be of significant competitive advantage to a competitor or because its disclosure would have a significantly adverse effect upon a person supplying the information or upon a person from whom the supplier acquired the information), or which is provided on a confidential basis by parties to an investigation shall, upon good cause shown, be treated as such by the authorities. Such information shall not be disclosed without specific permission of the party submitting it.[42]

12.4.1   The authorities shall require interested Members or interested parties providing confidential information to furnish non-confidential summaries thereof. These summaries shall be in sufficient detail to permit a reasonable understanding of the substance of the information submitted in confidence. In exceptional circumstances, such Members or parties may indicate that such information is not susceptible of summary. In such exceptional circumstances, a statement of the reasons why summarization is not possible must be provided.

---

40   As a general rule, the time-limit for exporters shall be counted from the date of receipt of the questionnaire, which for this purpose shall be deemed to have been received one week from the date on which it was sent to the respondent or transmitted to the appropriate diplomatic representatives of the exporting Member or, in the case of a separate customs territory Member of the WTO, an official representative of the exporting territory.

41   It being understood that where the number of exporters involved is particularly high, the full text of the application should instead be provided only to the authorities of the exporting Member or to the relevant trade association who then should forward copies to the exporters concerned.

42   Members are aware that in the territory of certain Members disclosure pursuant to a narrowly-drawn protective order may be required.

12.4.2   If the authorities find that a request for confidentiality is not warranted and if the supplier of the information is either unwilling to make the information public or to authorize its disclosure in generalized or summary form, the authorities may disregard such information unless it can be demonstrated to their satisfaction from appropriate sources that the information is correct.[43]

12.5 Except in circumstances provided for in paragraph 7, the authorities shall during the course of an investigation satisfy themselves as to the accuracy of the information supplied by interested Members or interested parties upon which their findings are based.

12.6 The investigating authorities may carry out investigations in the territory of other Members as required, provided that they have notified in good time the Member in question and unless that Member objects to the investigation. Further, the investigating authorities may carry out investigations on the premises of a firm and may examine the records of a firm if *(a)* the firm so agrees and *(b)* the Member in question is notified and does not object. The procedures set forth in Annex VI shall apply to investigations on the premises of a firm. Subject to the requirement to protect confidential information, the authorities shall make the results of any such investigations available, or shall provide disclosure thereof pursuant to paragraph 8, to the firms to which they pertain and may make such results available to the applicants.

12.7 In cases in which any interested Member or interested party refuses access to, or otherwise does not provide, necessary information within a reasonable period or significantly impedes the investigation, preliminary and final determinations, affirmative or negative, may be made on the basis of the facts available.

12.8 The authorities shall, before a final determination is made, inform all interested Members and interested parties of the essential facts under consideration which form the basis for the decision whether to apply definitive measures. Such disclosure should take place in sufficient time for the parties to defend their interests.

12.9 For the purposes of this Agreement, "interested parties" shall include:

(i)   an exporter or foreign producer or the importer of a product subject to investigation, or a trade or business association a majority of the members of which are producers, exporters or importers of such product; and

(ii)   a producer of the like product in the importing Member or a trade and business association a majority of the members of which produce the like product in the territory of the importing Member.

This list shall not preclude Members from allowing domestic or foreign parties other than those mentioned above to be included as interested parties.

12.10   The authorities shall provide opportunities for industrial users of the product under investigation, and for representative consumer organizations in cases where the product is commonly sold at the retail level, to provide information which is relevant to the investigation regarding subsidization, injury and causality.

12.11   The authorities shall take due account of any difficulties experienced by interested parties, in particular small companies, in supplying information requested, and shall provide any assistance practicable.

12.12   The procedures set out above are not intended to prevent the authorities of a Member from proceeding expeditiously with regard to initiating an investigation, reaching preliminary or final determinations, whether affirmative or negative, or from applying provisional or final measures, in accordance with relevant provisions of this Agreement.

---

43   Members agree that requests for confidentiality should not be arbitrarily rejected. Members further agree that the investigating authority may request the waiving of confidentiality only regarding information relevant to the proceedings.

Article 13 Consultations

13.1 As soon as possible after an application under Article 11 is accepted, and in any event before the initiation of any investigation, Members the products of which may be subject to such investigation shall be invited for consultations with the aim of clarifying the situation as to the matters referred to in paragraph 2 of Article 11 and arriving at a mutually agreed solution.

13.2 Furthermore, throughout the period of investigation, Members the products of which are the subject of the investigation shall be afforded a reasonable opportunity to continue consultations, with a view to clarifying the factual situation and to arriving at a mutually agreed solution.[44]

13.3 Without prejudice to the obligation to afford reasonable opportunity for consultation, these provisions regarding consultations are not intended to prevent the authorities of a Member from proceeding expeditiously with regard to initiating the investigation, reaching preliminary or final determinations, whether affirmative or negative, or from applying provisional or final measures, in accordance with the provisions of this Agreement.

13.4 The Member which intends to initiate any investigation or is conducting such an investigation shall permit, upon request, the Member or Members the products of which are subject to such investigation access to non-confidential evidence, including the non-confidential summary of confidential data being used for initiating or conducting the investigation.

Article 14 Calculation of the Amount of a Subsidy in Terms of the Benefit to the Recipient

For the purpose of Part V, any method used by the investigating authority to calculate the benefit to the recipient conferred pursuant to paragraph 1 of Article 1 shall be provided for in the national legislation or implementing regulations of the Member concerned and its application to each particular case shall be transparent and adequately explained. Furthermore, any such method shall be consistent with the following guidelines:

(a) government provision of equity capital shall not be considered as conferring a benefit, unless the investment decision can be regarded as inconsistent with the usual investment practice (including for the provision of risk capital) of private investors in the territory of that Member;

(b) a loan by a government shall not be considered as conferring a benefit, unless there is a difference between the amount that the firm receiving the loan pays on the government loan and the amount the firm would pay on a comparable commercial loan which the firm could actually obtain on the market. In this case the benefit shall be the difference between these two amounts;

(c) a loan guarantee by a government shall not be considered as conferring a benefit, unless there is a difference between the amount that the firm receiving the guarantee pays on a loan guaranteed by the government and the amount that the firm would pay on a comparable commercial loan absent the government guarantee. In this case the benefit shall be the difference between these two amounts adjusted for any differences in fees;

(d) the provision of goods or services or purchase of goods by a government shall not be considered as conferring a benefit unless the provision is made for less than adequate remuneration, or the purchase is made for more than adequate remuneration. The adequacy of remuneration shall be determined in relation to prevailing market conditions for the good or service in question in the country of provision or purchase (including price, quality, availability, marketability, transportation and other conditions of purchase or sale).

---

44   It is particularly important, in accordance with the provisions of this paragraph, that no affirmative determination whether preliminary or final be made without reasonable opportunity for consultations having been given. Such consultations may establish the basis for proceeding under the provisions of Part II, III or X.

Article 15 Determination of Injury[45]

15.1 A determination of injury for purposes of Article VI of GATT 1994 shall be based on positive evidence and involve an objective examination of both (a) the volume of the subsidized imports and the effect of the subsidized imports on prices in the domestic market for like products[46] and (b) the consequent impact of these imports on the domestic producers of such products.

15.2 With regard to the volume of the subsidized imports, the investigating authorities shall consider whether there has been a significant increase in subsidized imports, either in absolute terms or relative to production or consumption in the importing Member. With regard to the effect of the subsidized imports on prices, the investigating authorities shall consider whether there has been a significant price undercutting by the subsidized imports as compared with the price of a like product of the importing Member, or whether the effect of such imports is otherwise to depress prices to a significant degree or to prevent price increases, which otherwise would have occurred, to a significant degree. No one or several of these factors can necessarily give decisive guidance.

15.3 Where imports of a product from more than one country are simultaneously subject to countervailing duty investigations, the investigating authorities may cumulatively assess the effects of such imports only if they determine that (a) the amount of subsidization established in relation to the imports from each country is more than *de minimis* as defined in paragraph 9 of Article 11 and the volume of imports from each country is not negligible and (b) a cumulative assessment of the effects of the imports is appropriate in light of the conditions of competition between the imported products and the conditions of competition between the imported products and the like domestic product.

15.4 The examination of the impact of the subsidized imports on the domestic industry shall include an evaluation of all relevant economic factors and indices having a bearing on the state of the industry, including actual and potential decline in output, sales, market share, profits, productivity, return on investments, or utilization of capacity; factors affecting domestic prices; actual and potential negative effects on cash flow, inventories, employment, wages, growth, ability to raise capital or investments and, in the case of agriculture, whether there has been an increased burden on government support programmes. This list is not exhaustive, nor can one or several of these factors necessarily give decisive guidance.

15.5 It must be demonstrated that the subsidized imports are, through the effects[47] of subsidies, causing injury within the meaning of this Agreement. The demonstration of a causal relationship between the subsidized imports and the injury to the domestic industry shall be based on an examination of all relevant evidence before the authorities. The authorities shall also examine any known factors other than the subsidized imports which at the same time are injuring the domestic industry, and the injuries caused by these other factors must not be attributed to the subsidized imports. Factors which may be relevant in this respect include, *inter alia*, the volumes and prices of non-subsidized imports of the product in question, contraction in demand or changes in the patterns of consumption, trade restrictive practices of and competition between the foreign and domestic producers, developments in technology and the export performance and productivity of the domestic industry.

---

45 Under this Agreement the term "injury" shall, unless otherwise specified, be taken to mean material injury to a domestic industry, threat of material injury to a domestic industry or material retardation of the establishment of such an industry and shall be interpreted in accordance with the provisions of this Article.

46 Throughout this Agreement the term "like product" ("produit similaire") shall be interpreted to mean a product which is identical, i.e. alike in all respects to the product under consideration, or in the absence of such a product, another product which, although not alike in all respects, has characteristics closely resembling those of the product under consideration.

47 As set forth in paragraphs 2 and 4.

15.6 The effect of the subsidized imports shall be assessed in relation to the domestic production of the like product when available data permit the separate identification of that production on the basis of such criteria as the production process, producers' sales and profits. If such separate identification of that production is not possible, the effects of the subsidized imports shall be assessed by the examination of the production of the narrowest group or range of products, which includes the like product, for which the necessary information can be provided.

15.7 A determination of a threat of material injury shall be based on facts and not merely on allegation, conjecture or remote possibility. The change in circumstances which would create a situation in which the subsidy would cause injury must be clearly foreseen and imminent. In making a determination regarding the existence of a threat of material injury, the investigating authorities should consider, *inter alia*, such factors as:

(i)   nature of the subsidy or subsidies in question and the trade effects likely to arise therefrom;

(ii)   a significant rate of increase of subsidized imports into the domestic market indicating the likelihood of substantially increased importation;

(iii) sufficient freely disposable, or an imminent, substantial increase in, capacity of the exporter indicating the likelihood of substantially increased subsidized exports to the importing Member's market, taking into account the availability of other export markets to absorb any additional exports;

(iv)   whether imports are entering at prices that will have a significant depressing or suppressing effect on domestic prices, and would likely increase demand for further imports; and

(v)   inventories of the product being investigated.

No one of these factors by itself can necessarily give decisive guidance but the totality of the factors considered must lead to the conclusion that further subsidized exports are imminent and that, unless protective action is taken, material injury would occur.

15.8 With respect to cases where injury is threatened by subsidized imports, the application of countervailing measures shall be considered and decided with special care.

Article 16 Definition of Domestic Industry

16.1 For the purposes of this Agreement, the term "domestic industry" shall, except as provided in paragraph 2, be interpreted as referring to the domestic producers as a whole of the like products or to those of them whose collective output of the products constitutes a major proportion of the total domestic production of those products, except that when producers are related[48] to the exporters or importers or are themselves importers of the allegedly subsidized product or a like product from other countries, the term "domestic industry" may be interpreted as referring to the rest of the producers.

16.2 In exceptional circumstances, the territory of a Member may, for the production in question, be divided into two or more competitive markets and the producers within each market may be regarded as a separate industry if (a) the producers within such market sell all or almost all of their production of the product in question in that market, and (b) the demand in that market is not to any substantial degree supplied by producers of the product in question located elsewhere in the territory. In such circumstances, injury may be found to exist even where a major portion of the total domestic industry is not injured, provided there is a concentration of sub-

---

48   For the purpose of this paragraph, producers shall be deemed to be related to exporters or importers only if (a) one of them directly or indirectly controls the other; or (b) both of them are directly or indirectly controlled by a third person; or (c) together they directly or indirectly control a third person, provided that there are grounds for believing or suspecting that the effect of the relationship is such as to cause the producer concerned to behave differently from non-related producers. For the purpose of this paragraph, one shall be deemed to control another when the former is legally or operationally in a position to exercise restraint or direction over the latter.

sidized imports into such an isolated market and provided further that the subsidized imports are causing injury to the producers of all or almost all of the production within such market.

16.3 When the domestic industry has been interpreted as referring to the producers in a certain area, i.e. a market as defined in paragraph 2, countervailing duties shall be levied only on the products in question consigned for final consumption to that area. When the constitutional law of the importing Member does not permit the levying of countervailing duties on such a basis, the importing Member may levy the countervailing duties without limitation only if (a) the exporters shall have been given an opportunity to cease exporting at subsidized prices to the area concerned or otherwise give assurances pursuant to Article 18, and adequate assurances in this regard have not been promptly given, and (b) such duties cannot be levied only on products of specific producers which supply the area in question.

16.4 Where two or more countries have reached under the provisions of paragraph 8(a) of Article XXIV of GATT 1994 such a level of integration that they have the characteristics of a single, unified market, the industry in the entire area of integration shall be taken to be the domestic industry referred to in paragraphs 1 and 2.

16.5 The provisions of paragraph 6 of Article 15 shall be applicable to this Article.

Article 17 Provisional Measures

17.1 Provisional measures may be applied only if:

(a)   an investigation has been initiated in accordance with the provisions of Article 11, a public notice has been given to that effect and interested Members and interested parties have been given adequate opportunities to submit information and make comments;

(b)   a preliminary affirmative determination has been made that a subsidy exists and that there is injury to a domestic industry caused by subsidized imports; and

(c)   the authorities concerned judge such measures necessary to prevent injury being caused during the investigation.

17.2 Provisional measures may take the form of provisional countervailing duties guaranteed by cash deposits or bonds equal to the amount of the provisionally calculated amount of subsidization.

17.3 Provisional measures shall not be applied sooner than 60 days from the date of initiation of the investigation.

17.4 The application of provisional measures shall be limited to as short a period as possible, not exceeding four months.

17.5 The relevant provisions of Article 19 shall be followed in the application of provisional measures.

Article 18 Undertakings

18.1 Proceedings may[49] be suspended or terminated without the imposition of provisional measures or countervailing duties upon receipt of satisfactory voluntary undertakings under which:

(a)   the government of the exporting Member agrees to eliminate or limit the subsidy or take other measures concerning its effects; or

(b)   the exporter agrees to revise its prices so that the investigating authorities are satisfied that the injurious effect of the subsidy is eliminated. Price increases under such undertakings shall not be higher than necessary to eliminate the amount of the subsidy. It is desirable that

---

49   The word "may" shall not be interpreted to allow the simultaneous continuation of proceedings with the implementation of undertakings, except as provided in paragraph 4.

the price increases be less than the amount of the subsidy if such increases would be adequate to remove the injury to the domestic industry.

18.2 Undertakings shall not be sought or accepted unless the authorities of the importing Member have made a preliminary affirmative determination of subsidization and injury caused by such subsidization and, in case of undertakings from exporters, have obtained the consent of the exporting Member.

18.3 Undertakings offered need not be accepted if the authorities of the importing Member consider their acceptance impractical, for example if the number of actual or potential exporters is too great, or for other reasons, including reasons of general policy. Should the case arise and where practicable, the authorities shall provide to the exporter the reasons which have led them to consider acceptance of an undertaking as inappropriate, and shall, to the extent possible, give the exporter an opportunity to make comments thereon.

18.4 If an undertaking is accepted, the investigation of subsidization and injury shall nevertheless be completed if the exporting Member so desires or the importing Member so decides. In such a case, if a negative determination of subsidization or injury is made, the undertaking shall automatically lapse, except in cases where such a determination is due in large part to the existence of an undertaking. In such cases, the authorities concerned may require that an undertaking be maintained for a reasonable period consistent with the provisions of this Agreement. In the event that an affirmative determination of subsidization and injury is made, the undertaking shall continue consistent with its terms and the provisions of this Agreement.

18.5 Price undertakings may be suggested by the authorities of the importing Member, but no exporter shall be forced to enter into such undertakings. The fact that governments or exporters do not offer such undertakings, or do not accept an invitation to do so, shall in no way prejudice the consideration of the case. However, the authorities are free to determine that a threat of injury is more likely to be realized if the subsidized imports continue.

18.6 Authorities of an importing Member may require any government or exporter from whom an undertaking has been accepted to provide periodically information relevant to the fulfilment of such an undertaking, and to permit verification of pertinent data. In case of violation of an undertaking, the authorities of the importing Member may take, under this Agreement in conformity with its provisions, expeditious actions which may constitute immediate application of provisional measures using the best information available. In such cases, definitive duties may be levied in accordance with this Agreement on products entered for consumption not more than 90 days before the application of such provisional measures, except that any such retroactive assessment shall not apply to imports entered before the violation of the undertaking.

Article 19 Imposition and Collection of Countervailing Duties

19.1 If, after reasonable efforts have been made to complete consultations, a Member makes a final determination of the existence and amount of the subsidy and that, through the effects of the subsidy, the subsidized imports are causing injury, it may impose a countervailing duty in accordance with the provisions of this Article unless the subsidy or subsidies are withdrawn.

19.2 The decision whether or not to impose a countervailing duty in cases where all requirements for the imposition have been fulfilled, and the decision whether the amount of the countervailing duty to be imposed shall be the full amount of the subsidy or less, are decisions to be made by the authorities of the importing Member. It is desirable that the imposition should be permissive in the territory of all Members, that the duty should be less than the total amount of the subsidy if such lesser duty would be adequate to remove the injury to the domestic industry, and that procedures should be established which would allow the authorities concerned to take due account of representations made by domestic interested parties[50] whose interests might be adversely affected by the imposition of a countervailing duty.

19.3 When a countervailing duty is imposed in respect of any product, such countervailing duty shall be levied, in the appropriate amounts in each case, on a non-discriminatory basis on imports of such product from all sources found to be subsidized and causing injury, except as to imports from those sources which have renounced any subsidies in question or from which undertakings under the terms of this Agreement have been accepted. Any exporter whose exports are subject to a definitive countervailing duty but who was not actually investigated for reasons other than a refusal to cooperate, shall be entitled to an expedited review in order that the investigating authorities promptly establish an individual countervailing duty rate for that exporter.

19.4 No countervailing duty shall be levied[51] on any imported product in excess of the amount of the subsidy found to exist, calculated in terms of subsidization per unit of the subsidized and exported product.

Article 20 Retroactivity

20.1 Provisional measures and countervailing duties shall only be applied to products which enter for consumption after the time when the decision under paragraph 1 of Article 17 and paragraph 1 of Article 19, respectively, enters into force, subject to the exceptions set out in this Article.

20.2 Where a final determination of injury (but not of a threat thereof or of a material retardation of the establishment of an industry) is made or, in the case of a final determination of a threat of injury, where the effect of the subsidized imports would, in the absence of the provisional measures, have led to a determination of injury, countervailing duties may be levied retroactively for the period for which provisional measures, if any, have been applied.

20.3 If the definitive countervailing duty is higher than the amount guaranteed by the cash deposit or bond, the difference shall not be collected. If the definitive duty is less than the amount guaranteed by the cash deposit or bond, the excess amount shall be reimbursed or the bond released in an expeditious manner.

20.4 Except as provided in paragraph 2, where a determination of threat of injury or material retardation is made (but no injury has yet occurred) a definitive countervailing duty may be imposed only from the date of the determination of threat of injury or material retardation, and any cash deposit made during the period of the application of provisional measures shall be refunded and any bonds released in an expeditious manner.

20.5 Where a final determination is negative, any cash deposit made during the period of the application of provisional measures shall be refunded and any bonds released in an expeditious manner.

20.6 In critical circumstances where for the subsidized product in question the authorities find that injury which is difficult to repair is caused by massive imports in a relatively short period of a product benefiting from subsidies paid or bestowed inconsistently with the provisions of GATT 1994 and of this Agreement and where it is deemed necessary, in order to preclude the recurrence of such injury, to assess countervailing duties retroactively on those imports, the definitive countervailing duties may be assessed on imports which were entered for consumption not more than 90 days prior to the date of application of provisional measures.

---

50   For the purpose of this paragraph, the term "domestic interested parties" shall include consumers and industrial users of the imported product subject to investigation.

51   As used in this Agreement "levy" shall mean the definitive or final legal assessment or collection of a duty or tax.

Article 21 Duration and Review of Countervailing Duties and Undertakings

21.1 A countervailing duty shall remain in force only as long as and to the extent necessary to counteract subsidization which is causing injury.

21.2 The authorities shall review the need for the continued imposition of the duty, where warranted, on their own initiative or, provided that a reasonable period of time has elapsed since the imposition of the definitive countervailing duty, upon request by any interested party which submits positive information substantiating the need for a review. Interested parties shall have the right to request the authorities to examine whether the continued imposition of the duty is necessary to offset subsidization, whether the injury would be likely to continue or recur if the duty were removed or varied, or both. If, as a result of the review under this paragraph, the authorities determine that the countervailing duty is no longer warranted, it shall be terminated immediately.

21.3 Notwithstanding the provisions of paragraphs 1 and 2, any definitive countervailing duty shall be terminated on a date not later than five years from its imposition (or from the date of the most recent review under paragraph 2 if that review has covered both subsidization and injury, or under this paragraph), unless the authorities determine, in a review initiated before that date on their own initiative or upon a duly substantiated request made by or on behalf of the domestic industry within a reasonable period of time prior to that date, that the expiry of the duty would be likely to lead to continuation or recurrence of subsidization and injury.[52] The duty may remain in force pending the outcome of such a review.

21.4 The provisions of Article 12 regarding evidence and procedure shall apply to any review carried out under this Article. Any such review shall be carried out expeditiously and shall normally be concluded within 12 months of the date of initiation of the review.

21.5 The provisions of this Article shall apply *mutatis mutandis* to undertakings accepted under Article 18.

Article 22 Public Notice and Explanation of Determinations

22.1 When the authorities are satisfied that there is sufficient evidence to justify the initiation of an investigation pursuant to Article 11, the Member or Members the products of which are subject to such investigation and other interested parties known to the investigating authorities to have an interest therein shall be notified and a public notice shall be given.

22.2 A public notice of the initiation of an investigation shall contain, or otherwise make available through a separate report,[53] adequate information on the following:

(i)   the name of the exporting country or countries and the product involved;

(ii)   the date of initiation of the investigation;

(iii) a description of the subsidy practice or practices to be investigated;

(iv)   a summary of the factors on which the allegation of injury is based;

(v)   the address to which representations by interested Members and interested parties should be directed; and

(vi)   the time-limits allowed to interested Members and interested parties for making their views known.

22.3 Public notice shall be given of any preliminary or final determination, whether affirmative or negative, of any decision to accept an undertaking pursuant to Article 18, of the termination of

---

52   When the amount of the countervailing duty is assessed on a retrospective basis, a finding in the most recent assessment proceeding that no duty is to be levied shall not by itself require the authorities to terminate the definitive duty.

53   Where authorities provide information and explanations under the provisions of this Article in a separate report, they shall ensure that such report is readily available to the public.

such an undertaking, and of the termination of a definitive countervailing duty. Each such notice shall set forth, or otherwise make available through a separate report, in sufficient detail the findings and conclusions reached on all issues of fact and law considered material by the investigating authorities. All such notices and reports shall be forwarded to the Member or Members the products of which are subject to such determination or undertaking and to other interested parties known to have an interest therein.

22.4 A public notice of the imposition of provisional measures shall set forth, or otherwise make available through a separate report, sufficiently detailed explanations for the preliminary determinations on the existence of a subsidy and injury and shall refer to the matters of fact and law which have led to arguments being accepted or rejected. Such a notice or report shall, due regard being paid to the requirement for the protection of confidential information, contain in particular:

(i)   the names of the suppliers or, when this is impracticable, the supplying countries involved;

(ii) a description of the product which is sufficient for customs purposes;

(iii) the amount of subsidy established and the basis on which the existence of a subsidy has been determined;

(iv) considerations relevant to the injury determination as set out in Article 15;

(v)   the main reasons leading to the determination.

22.5 A public notice of conclusion or suspension of an investigation in the case of an affirmative determination providing for the imposition of a definitive duty or the acceptance of an undertaking shall contain, or otherwise make available through a separate report, all relevant information on the matters of fact and law and reasons which have led to the imposition of final measures or the acceptance of an undertaking, due regard being paid to the requirement for the protection of confidential information. In particular, the notice or report shall contain the information described in paragraph 4, as well as the reasons for the acceptance or rejection of relevant arguments or claims made by interested Members and by the exporters and importers.

22.6 A public notice of the termination or suspension of an investigation following the acceptance of an undertaking pursuant to Article 18 shall include, or otherwise make available through a separate report, the non-confidential part of this undertaking.

22.7 The provisions of this Article shall apply *mutatis mutandis* to the initiation and completion of reviews pursuant to Article 21 and to decisions under Article 20 to apply duties retroactively.

Article 23 Judicial Review

Each Member whose national legislation contains provisions on countervailing duty measures shall maintain judicial, arbitral or administrative tribunals or procedures for the purpose, *inter alia*, of the prompt review of administrative actions relating to final determinations and reviews of determinations within the meaning of Article 21. Such tribunals or procedures shall be independent of the authorities responsible for the determination or review in question, and shall provide all interested parties who participated in the administrative proceeding and are directly and individually affected by the administrative actions with access to review.

PART VI: INSTITUTIONS

Article 24 Committee on Subsidies and Countervailing Measures and Subsidiary Bodies

24.1 There is hereby established a Committee on Subsidies and Countervailing Measures composed of representatives from each of the Members. The Committee shall elect its own Chairman and shall meet not less than twice a year and otherwise as envisaged by relevant provisions of this Agreement at the request of any Member. The Committee shall carry out responsibilities as assigned to it under this Agreement or by the Members and it shall afford Members the opportunity of consulting on any matter relating to the operation of the Agreement or the furtherance of its objectives. The WTO Secretariat shall act as the secretariat to the Committee.

24.2 The Committee may set up subsidiary bodies as appropriate.

24.3 The Committee shall establish a Permanent Group of Experts composed of five independent persons, highly qualified in the fields of subsidies and trade relations. The experts will be elected by the Committee and one of them will be replaced every year. The PGE may be requested to assist a panel, as provided for in paragraph 5 of Article 4. The Committee may also seek an advisory opinion on the existence and nature of any subsidy.

24.4 The PGE may be consulted by any Member and may give advisory opinions on the nature of any subsidy proposed to be introduced or currently maintained by that Member. Such advisory opinions will be confidential and may not be invoked in proceedings under Article 7.

24.5 In carrying out their functions, the Committee and any subsidiary bodies may consult with and seek information from any source they deem appropriate. However, before the Committee or a subsidiary body seeks such information from a source within the jurisdiction of a Member, it shall inform the Member involved.

PART VII: NOTIFICATION AND SURVEILLANCE

Article 25 Notifications

25.1 Members agree that, without prejudice to the provisions of paragraph 1 of Article XVI of GATT 1994, their notifications of subsidies shall be submitted not later than 30 June of each year and shall conform to the provisions of paragraphs 2 through 6.

25.2 Members shall notify any subsidy as defined in paragraph 1 of Article 1, which is specific within the meaning of Article 2, granted or maintained within their territories.

25.3 The content of notifications should be sufficiently specific to enable other Members to evaluate the trade effects and to understand the operation of notified subsidy programmes. In this connection, and without prejudice to the contents and form of the questionnaire on subsidies,[54] Members shall ensure that their notifications contain the following information:

(i)   form of a subsidy (i.e. grant, loan, tax concession, etc.);

(ii)   subsidy per unit or, in cases where this is not possible, the total amount or the annual amount budgeted for that subsidy (indicating, if possible, the average subsidy per unit in the previous year);

(iii)   policy objective and/or purpose of a subsidy;

(iv)   duration of a subsidy and/or any other time-limits attached to it;

(v)   statistical data permitting an assessment of the trade effects of a subsidy.

25.4 Where specific points in paragraph 3 have not been addressed in a notification, an explanation shall be provided in the notification itself.

25.5 If subsidies are granted to specific products or sectors, the notifications should be organized by product or sector.

25.6 Members which consider that there are no measures in their territories requiring notification under paragraph 1 of Article XVI of GATT 1994 and this Agreement shall so inform the Secretariat in writing.

25.7 Members recognize that notification of a measure does not prejudge either its legal status under GATT 1994 and this Agreement, the effects under this Agreement, or the nature of the measure itself.

---

54   The Committee shall establish a Working Party to review the contents and form of the questionnaire as contained in BISD 9S/193-194.

25.8 Any Member may, at any time, make a written request for information on the nature and extent of any subsidy granted or maintained by another Member (including any subsidy referred to in Part IV), or for an explanation of the reasons for which a specific measure has been considered as not subject to the requirement of notification.

25.9 Members so requested shall provide such information as quickly as possible and in a comprehensive manner, and shall be ready, upon request, to provide additional information to the requesting Member. In particular, they shall provide sufficient details to enable the other Member to assess their compliance with the terms of this Agreement. Any Member which considers that such information has not been provided may bring the matter to the attention of the Committee.

25.10   Any Member which considers that any measure of another Member having the effects of a subsidy has not been notified in accordance with the provisions of paragraph 1 of Article XVI of GATT 1994 and this Article may bring the matter to the attention of such other Member. If the alleged subsidy is not thereafter notified promptly, such Member may itself bring the alleged subsidy in question to the notice of the Committee.

25.11   Members shall report without delay to the Committee all preliminary or final actions taken with respect to countervailing duties. Such reports shall be available in the Secretariat for inspection by other Members. Members shall also submit, on a semi-annual basis, reports on any countervailing duty actions taken within the preceding six months. The semi-annual reports shall be submitted on an agreed standard form.

25.12   Each Member shall notify the Committee (a) which of its authorities are competent to initiate and conduct investigations referred to in Article 11 and (b) its domestic procedures governing the initiation and conduct of such investigations.

Article 26 Surveillance

26.1 The Committee shall examine new and full notifications submitted under paragraph 1 of Article XVI of GATT 1994 and paragraph 1 of Article 25 of this Agreement at special sessions held every third year. Notifications submitted in the intervening years (updating notifications) shall be examined at each regular meeting of the Committee.

26.2 The Committee shall examine reports submitted under paragraph 11 of Article 25 at each regular meeting of the Committee.

PART VIII: DEVELOPING COUNTRY MEMBERS

Article 27 Special and Differential Treatment of Developing Country Members

27.1 Members recognize that subsidies may play an important role in economic development programmes of developing country Members.

27.2 The prohibition of paragraph 1(a) of Article 3 shall not apply to:

(a)   developing country Members referred to in Annex VII.

(b)   other developing country Members for a period of eight years from the date of entry into force of the WTO Agreement, subject to compliance with the provisions in paragraph 4.

27.3 The prohibition of paragraph 1(b) of Article 3 shall not apply to developing country Members for a period of five years, and shall not apply to least developed country Members for a period of eight years, from the date of entry into force of the WTO Agreement.

27.4 Any developing country Member referred to in paragraph 2(b) shall phase out its export subsidies within the eight-year period, preferably in a progressive manner. However, a developing country Member shall not increase the level of its export subsidies,[55] and shall eliminate them within a period shorter than that provided for in this paragraph when the use of such

---

55   For a developing country Member not granting export subsidies as of the date of entry into force of the WTO Agreement, this paragraph shall apply on the basis of the level of export subsidies granted in 1986.

export subsidies is inconsistent with its development needs. If a developing country Member deems it necessary to apply such subsidies beyond the 8-year period, it shall not later than one year before the expiry of this period enter into consultation with the Committee, which will determine whether an extension of this period is justified, after examining all the relevant economic, financial and development needs of the developing country Member in question. If the Committee determines that the extension is justified, the developing country Member concerned shall hold annual consultations with the Committee to determine the necessity of maintaining the subsidies. If no such determination is made by the Committee, the developing country Member shall phase out the remaining export subsidies within two years from the end of the last authorized period.

27.5 A developing country Member which has reached export competitiveness in any given product shall phase out its export subsidies for such product(s) over a period of two years. However, for a developing country Member which is referred to in Annex VII and which has reached export competitiveness in one or more products, export subsidies on such products shall be gradually phased out over a period of eight years.

27.6 Export competitiveness in a product exists if a developing country Member's exports of that product have reached a share of at least 3.25 per cent in world trade of that product for two consecutive calendar years. Export competitiveness shall exist either (a) on the basis of notification by the developing country Member having reached export competitiveness, or (b) on the basis of a computation undertaken by the Secretariat at the request of any Member. For the purpose of this paragraph, a product is defined as a section heading of the Harmonized System Nomenclature. The Committee shall review the operation of this provision five years from the date of the entry into force of the WTO Agreement.

27.7 The provisions of Article 4 shall not apply to a developing country Member in the case of export subsidies which are in conformity with the provisions of paragraphs 2 through 5. The relevant provisions in such a case shall be those of Article 7.

27.8 There shall be no presumption in terms of paragraph 1 of Article 6 that a subsidy granted by a developing country Member results in serious prejudice, as defined in this Agreement. Such serious prejudice, where applicable under the terms of paragraph 9, shall be demonstrated by positive evidence, in accordance with the provisions of paragraphs 3 through 8 of Article 6.

27.9 Regarding actionable subsidies granted or maintained by a developing country Member other than those referred to in paragraph 1 of Article 6, action may not be authorized or taken under Article 7 unless nullification or impairment of tariff concessions or other obligations under GATT 1994 is found to exist as a result of such a subsidy, in such a way as to displace or impede imports of a like product of another Member into the market of the subsidizing developing country Member or unless injury to a domestic industry in the market of an importing Member occurs.

27.10   Any countervailing duty investigation of a product originating in a developing country Member shall be terminated as soon as the authorities concerned determine that:

(a) the overall level of subsidies granted upon the product in question does not exceed 2 per cent of its value calculated on a per unit basis; or

(b) the volume of the subsidized imports represents less than 4 per cent of the total imports of the like product in the importing Member, unless imports from developing country Members whose individual shares of total imports represent less than 4 per cent collectively account for more than 9 per cent of the total imports of the like product in the importing Member.

27.11   For those developing country Members within the scope of paragraph 2(b) which have eliminated export subsidies prior to the expiry of the period of eight years from the date of entry into force of the WTO Agreement, and for those developing country Members referred to in

Annex VII, the number in paragraph 10(a) shall be 3 per cent rather than 2 per cent. This provision shall apply from the date that the elimination of export subsidies is notified to the Committee, and for so long as export subsidies are not granted by the notifying developing country Member. This provision shall expire eight years from the date of entry into force of the WTO Agreement.

27.12   The provisions of paragraphs 10 and 11 shall govern any determination of *de minimis* under paragraph 3 of Article 15.

27.13   The provisions of Part III shall not apply to direct forgiveness of debts, subsidies to cover social costs, in whatever form, including relinquishment of government revenue and other transfer of liabilities when such subsidies are granted within and directly linked to a privatization programme of a developing country Member, provided that both such programme and the subsidies involved are granted for a limited period and notified to the Committee and that the programme results in eventual privatization of the enterprise concerned.

27.14   The Committee shall, upon request by an interested Member, undertake a review of a specific export subsidy practice of a developing country Member to examine whether the practice is in conformity with its development needs.

27.15   The Committee shall, upon request by an interested developing country Member, undertake a review of a specific countervailing measure to examine whether it is consistent with the provisions of paragraphs 10 and 11 as applicable to the developing country Member in question.

PART IX: TRANSITIONAL ARRANGEMENTS

Article 28 Existing Programmes

28.1 Subsidy programmes which have been established within the territory of any Member before the date on which such a Member signed the WTO Agreement and which are inconsistent with the provisions of this Agreement shall be:

(a)   notified to the Committee not later than 90 days after the date of entry into force of the WTO Agreement for such Member; and

(b)   brought into conformity with the provisions of this Agreement within three years of the date of entry into force of the WTO Agreement for such Member and until then shall not be subject to Part II.

28.2 No Member shall extend the scope of any such programme, nor shall such a programme be renewed upon its expiry.

Article 29 Transformation into a Market Economy

29.1 Members in the process of transformation from a centrally-planned into a market, free-enterprise economy may apply programmes and measures necessary for such a transformation.

29.2 For such Members, subsidy programmes falling within the scope of Article 3, and notified according to paragraph 3, shall be phased out or brought into conformity with Article 3 within a period of seven years from the date of entry into force of the WTO Agreement. In such a case, Article 4 shall not apply. In addition during the same period:

(a)   Subsidy programmes falling within the scope of paragraph 1(d) of Article 6 shall not be actionable under Article 7;

(b)   With respect to other actionable subsidies, the provisions of paragraph 9 of Article 27 shall apply.

29.3 Subsidy programmes falling within the scope of Article 3 shall be notified to the Committee by the earliest practicable date after the date of entry into force of the WTO Agreement. Further notifications of such subsidies may be made up to two years after the date of entry into force of the WTO Agreement.

29.4 In exceptional circumstances Members referred to in paragraph 1 may be given departures from their notified programmes and measures and their time-frame by the Committee if such departures are deemed necessary for the process of transformation.

PART X: DISPUTE SETTLEMENT

Article 30 [Applicability of Articles XXII and XXIII of the GATT]

The provisions of Articles XXII and XXIII of GATT 1994 as elaborated and applied by the Dispute Settlement Understanding shall apply to consultations and the settlement of disputes under this Agreement, except as otherwise specifically provided herein.

PART XI: FINAL PROVISIONS

Article 31 Provisional Application

The provisions of paragraph 1 of Article 6 and the provisions of Article 8 and Article 9 shall apply for a period of five years, beginning with the date of entry into force of the WTO Agreement. Not later than 180 days before the end of this period, the Committee shall review the operation of those provisions, with a view to determining whether to extend their application, either as presently drafted or in a modified form, for a further period.

Article 32 Other Final Provisions

32.1 No specific action against a subsidy of another Member can be taken except in accordance with the provisions of GATT 1994, as interpreted by this Agreement.[56]

32.2 Reservations may not be entered in respect of any of the provisions of this Agreement without the consent of the other Members.

32.3 Subject to paragraph 4, the provisions of this Agreement shall apply to investigations, and reviews of existing measures, initiated pursuant to applications which have been made on or after the date of entry into force for a Member of the WTO Agreement.

32.4 For the purposes of paragraph 3 of Article 21, existing countervailing measures shall be deemed to be imposed on a date not later than the date of entry into force for a Member of the WTO Agreement, except in cases in which the domestic legislation of a Member in force at that date already included a clause of the type provided for in that paragraph.

32.5 Each Member shall take all necessary steps, of a general or particular character, to ensure, not later than the date of entry into force of the WTO Agreement for it, the conformity of its laws, regulations and administrative procedures with the provisions of this Agreement as they may apply to the Member in question.

32.6 Each Member shall inform the Committee of any changes in its laws and regulations relevant to this Agreement and in the administration of such laws and regulations.

32.7 The Committee shall review annually the implementation and operation of this Agreement, taking into account the objectives thereof. The Committee shall inform annually the Council for Trade in Goods of developments during the period covered by such reviews.

32.8 The Annexes to this Agreement constitute an integral part thereof.

ANNEX I – ILLUSTRATIVE LIST OF EXPORT SUBSIDIES

(a)   The provision by governments of direct subsidies to a firm or an industry contingent upon export performance.

(b)   Currency retention schemes or any similar practices which involve a bonus on exports.

(c)   Internal transport and freight charges on export shipments, provided or mandated by governments, on terms more favourable than for domestic shipments.

---

56   This paragraph is not intended to preclude action under other relevant provisions of GATT 1994, where appropriate.

(d) The provision by governments or their agencies either directly or indirectly through government-mandated schemes, of imported or domestic products or services for use in the production of exported goods, on terms or conditions more favourable than for provision of like or directly competitive products or services for use in the production of goods for domestic consumption, if (in the case of products) such terms or conditions are more favourable than those commercially available[57] on world markets to their exporters.

(e) The full or partial exemption remission, or deferral specifically related to exports, of direct taxes[58] or social welfare charges paid or payable by industrial or commercial enterprises.[59]

(f)   The allowance of special deductions directly related to exports or export performance, over and above those granted in respect to production for domestic consumption, in the calculation of the base on which direct taxes are charged.

(g) The exemption or remission, in respect of the production and distribution of exported products, of indirect taxes[58] in excess of those levied in respect of the production and distribution of like products when sold for domestic consumption.

(h) The exemption, remission or deferral of prior-stage cumulative indirect taxes[58] on goods or services used in the production of exported products in excess of the exemption, remission or deferral of like prior-stage cumulative indirect taxes on goods or services used in the production of like products when sold for domestic consumption; provided, however, that prior-stage cumulative indirect taxes may be exempted, remitted or deferred on exported products even when not exempted, remitted or deferred on like products when sold for domestic consumption, if the prior-stage cumulative indirect taxes are levied on inputs that are consumed in the production of the exported product (making normal allowance for waste).[60] This item shall be interpreted in accordance with the guidelines on consumption of inputs in the production process contained in Annex II.

---

57   The term "commercially available" means that the choice between domestic and imported products is unrestricted and depends only on commercial considerations.

58   For the purpose of this Agreement:
The term "direct taxes" shall mean taxes on wages, profits, interests, rents, royalties, and all other forms of income, and taxes on the ownership of real property;
The term "import charges" shall mean tariffs, duties, and other fiscal charges not elsewhere enumerated in this note that are levied on imports;
The term "indirect taxes" shall mean sales, excise, turnover, value added, franchise, stamp, transfer, inventory and equipment taxes, border taxes and all taxes other than direct taxes and import charges;
"Prior-stage" indirect taxes are those levied on goods or services used directly or indirectly in making the product;
"Cumulative" indirect taxes are multi-staged taxes levied where there is no mechanism for subsequent crediting of the tax if the goods or services subject to tax at one stage of production are used in a succeeding stage of production;
"Remission" of taxes includes the refund or rebate of taxes;
"Remission or drawback" includes the full or partial exemption or deferral of import charges.

59   The Members recognize that deferral need not amount to an export subsidy where, for example, appropriate interest charges are collected. The Members reaffirm the principle that prices for goods in transactions between exporting enterprises and foreign buyers under their or under the same control should for tax purposes be the prices which would be charged between independent enterprises acting at arm's length. Any Member may draw the attention of another Member to administrative or other practices which may contravene this principle and which result in a significant saving of direct taxes in export transactions. In such circumstances the Members shall normally attempt to resolve their differences using the facilities of existing bilateral tax treaties or other specific international mechanisms, without prejudice to the rights and obligations of Members under GATT 1994, including the right of consultation created in the preceding sentence.
     Paragraph (e) is not intended to limit a Member from taking measures to avoid the double taxation of foreign-source income earned by its enterprises or the enterprises of another Member.

60   Paragraph (h) does not apply to value-added tax systems and border-tax adjustment in lieu thereof; the problem of the excessive remission of value-added taxes is exclusively covered by paragraph (g).

(i)   The remission or drawback of import charges[58] in excess of those levied on imported inputs that are consumed in the production of the exported product (making normal allowance for waste); provided, however, that in particular cases a firm may use a quantity of home market inputs equal to, and having the same quality and characteristics as, the imported inputs as a substitute for them in order to benefit from this provision if the import and the corresponding export operations both occur within a reasonable time period, not to exceed two years. This item shall be interpreted in accordance with the guidelines on consumption of inputs in the production process contained in Annex II and the guidelines in the determination of substitution drawback systems as export subsidies contained in Annex III.

(j)   The provision by governments (or special institutions controlled by governments) of export credit guarantee or insurance programmes, of insurance or guarantee programmes against increases in the cost of exported products or of exchange risk programmes, at premium rates which are inadequate to cover the long-term operating costs and losses of the programmes.

(k)   The grant by governments (or special institutions controlled by and/or acting under the authority of governments) of export credits at rates below those which they actually have to pay for the funds so employed (or would have to pay if they borrowed on international capital markets in order to obtain funds of the same maturity and other credit terms and denominated in the same currency as the export credit), or the payment by them of all or part of the costs incurred by exporters or financial institutions in obtaining credits, in so far as they are used to secure a material advantage in the field of export credit terms.

Provided, however, that if a Member is a party to an international undertaking on official export credits to which at least twelve original Members to this Agreement are parties as of 1 January 1979 (or a successor undertaking which has been adopted by those original Members), or if in practice a Member applies the interest rates provisions of the relevant undertaking, an export credit practice which is in conformity with those provisions shall not be considered an export subsidy prohibited by this Agreement.

(l)   Any other charge on the public account constituting an export subsidy in the sense of Article XVI of GATT 1994.

ANNEX II – GUIDELINES ON CONSUMPTION OF INPUTS IN THE PRODUCTION PROCESS[61]

I

1.   Indirect tax rebate schemes can allow for exemption, remission or deferral of prior-stage cumulative indirect taxes levied on inputs that are consumed in the production of the exported product (making normal allowance for waste). Similarly, drawback schemes can allow for the remission or drawback of import charges levied on inputs that are consumed in the production of the exported product (making normal allowance for waste).

2.   The Illustrative List of Export Subsidies in Annex I of this Agreement makes reference to the term "inputs that are consumed in the production of the exported product" in paragraphs (h) and (i). Pursuant to paragraph (h), indirect tax rebate schemes can constitute an export subsidy to the extent that they result in exemption, remission or deferral of prior-stage cumulative indirect taxes in excess of the amount of such taxes actually levied on inputs that are consumed in the production of the exported product. Pursuant to paragraph (i), drawback schemes can constitute an export subsidy to the extent that they result in a remission or drawback of import charges in excess of those actually levied on inputs that are consumed in the production of the exported product. Both paragraphs stipulate that normal allowance for waste must be made in findings regarding consumption of inputs in the production of the exported product. Paragraph (i) also provides for substitution, where appropriate.

---

61   Inputs consumed in the production process are inputs physically incorporated, energy, fuels and oil used in the production process and catalysts which are consumed in the course of their use to obtain the exported product.

II

In examining whether inputs are consumed in the production of the exported product, as part of a countervailing duty investigation pursuant to this Agreement, investigating authorities should proceed on the following basis:

1.   Where it is alleged that an indirect tax rebate scheme, or a drawback scheme, conveys a subsidy by reason of over-rebate or excess drawback of indirect taxes or import charges on inputs consumed in the production of the exported product, the investigating authorities should first determine whether the government of the exporting Member has in place and applies a system or procedure to confirm which inputs are consumed in the production of the exported product and in what amounts. Where such a system or procedure is determined to be applied, the investigating authorities should then examine the system or procedure to see whether it is reasonable, effective for the purpose intended, and based on generally accepted commercial practices in the country of export. The investigating authorities may deem it necessary to carry out, in accordance with paragraph 6 of Article 12, certain practical tests in order to verify information or to satisfy themselves that the system or procedure is being effectively applied.

2.   Where there is no such system or procedure, where it is not reasonable, or where it is instituted and considered reasonable but is found not to be applied or not to be applied effectively, a further examination by the exporting Member based on the actual inputs involved would need to be carried out in the context of determining whether an excess payment occurred. If the investigating authorities deemed it necessary, a further examination would be carried out in accordance with paragraph 1.

3.   Investigating authorities should treat inputs as physically incorporated if such inputs are used in the production process and are physically present in the product exported. The Members note that an input need not be present in the final product in the same form in which it entered the production process.

4.   In determining the amount of a particular input that is consumed in the production of the exported product, a "normal allowance for waste" should be taken into account, and such waste should be treated as consumed in the production of the exported product. The term "waste" refers to that portion of a given input which does not serve an independent function in the production process, is not consumed in the production of the exported product (for reasons such as inefficiencies) and is not recovered, used or sold by the same manufacturer.

5.   The investigating authority's determination of whether the claimed allowance for waste is "normal" should take into account the production process, the average experience of the industry in the country of export, and other technical factors, as appropriate. The investigating authority should bear in mind that an important question is whether the authorities in the exporting Member have reasonably calculated the amount of waste, when such an amount is intended to be included in the tax or duty rebate or remission.

ANNEX III – GUIDELINES IN THE DETERMINATION OF SUBSTITUTION DRAWBACK SYSTEMS AS EXPORT SUBSIDIES

I

Drawback systems can allow for the refund or drawback of import charges on inputs which are consumed in the production process of another product and where the export of this latter product contains domestic inputs having the same quality and characteristics as those substituted for the imported inputs. Pursuant to paragraph (i) of the Illustrative List of Export Subsidies in Annex I, substitution drawback systems can constitute an export subsidy to the extent that they result in an excess drawback of the import charges levied initially on the imported inputs for which drawback is being claimed.

II

In examining any substitution drawback system as part of a countervailing duty investigation pursuant to this Agreement, investigating authorities should proceed on the following basis:

1. Paragraph (i) of the Illustrative List stipulates that home market inputs may be substituted for imported inputs in the production of a product for export provided such inputs are equal in quantity to, and have the same quality and characteristics as, the imported inputs being substituted. The existence of a verification system or procedure is important because it enables the government of the exporting Member to ensure and demonstrate that the quantity of inputs for which drawback is claimed does not exceed the quantity of similar products exported, in whatever form, and that there is not drawback of import charges in excess of those originally levied on the imported inputs in question.

2. Where it is alleged that a substitution drawback system conveys a subsidy, the investigating authorities should first proceed to determine whether the government of the exporting Member has in place and applies a verification system or procedure. Where such a system or procedure is determined to be applied, the investigating authorities should then examine the verification pro-cedures to see whether they are reasonable, effective for the purpose intended, and based on generally accepted commercial practices in the country of export. To the extent that the procedures are determined to meet this test and are effectively applied, no subsidy should be presumed to exist. It may be deemed necessary by the investigating authorities to carry out, in accordance with paragraph 6 of Article 12, certain practical tests in order to verify information or to satisfy themselves that the verification procedures are being effectively applied.

3. Where there are no verification procedures, where they are not reasonable, or where such procedures are instituted and considered reasonable but are found not to be actually applied or not applied effectively, there may be a subsidy. In such cases a further examination by the exporting Member based on the actual transactions involved would need to be carried out to determine whether an excess payment occurred. If the investigating authorities deemed it necessary, a further examination would be carried out in accordance with paragraph 2.

4. The existence of a substitution drawback provision under which exporters are allowed to select particular import shipments on which drawback is claimed should not of itself be con-sidered to convey a subsidy.

5. An excess drawback of import charges in the sense of paragraph (i) would be deemed to exist where governments paid interest on any monies refunded under their drawback schemes, to the extent of the interest actually paid or payable.

ANNEX IV – CALCULATION OF THE TOTAL AD VALOREM SUBSIDIZATION (PARAGRAPH 1(A) OF ARTICLE 6)[62]

1. Any calculation of the amount of a subsidy for the purpose of paragraph 1(a) of Article 6 shall be done in terms of the cost to the granting government.

2. Except as provided in paragraphs 3 through 5, in determining whether the overall rate of subsidization exceeds 5 per cent of the value of the product, the value of the product shall be calculated as the total value of the recipient firm's[63] sales in the most recent 12-month period, for which sales data is available, preceding the period in which the subsidy is granted.[64]

3. Where the subsidy is tied to the production or sale of a given product, the value of the product shall be calculated as the total value of the recipient firm's sales of that product in the

---

62   An understanding among Members should be developed, as necessary, on matters which are not specified in this Annex or which need further clarification for the purposes of paragraph 1(a) of Article 6.

63   The recipient firm is a firm in the territory of the subsidizing Member.

64   In the case of tax-related subsidies the value of the product shall be calculated as the total value of the recipient firm's sales in the fiscal year in which the tax-related measure was earned.

most recent 12-month period, for which sales data is available, preceding the period in which the subsidy is granted.

4.   Where the recipient firm is in a start-up situation, serious prejudice shall be deemed to exist if the overall rate of subsidization exceeds 15 per cent of the total funds invested. For purposes of this paragraph, a start-up period will not extend beyond the first year of production.[65]

5.   Where the recipient firm is located in an inflationary economy country, the value of the product shall be calculated as the recipient firm's total sales (or sales of the relevant product, if the subsidy is tied) in the preceding calendar year indexed by the rate of inflation experienced in the 12 months preceding the month in which the subsidy is to be given.

6.   In determining the overall rate of subsidization in a given year, subsidies given under different programmes and by different authorities in the territory of a Member shall be aggregated.

7.   Subsidies granted prior to the date of entry into force of the WTO Agreement, the benefits of which are allocated to future production, shall be included in the overall rate of subsidization.

8.   Subsidies which are non-actionable under relevant provisions of this Agreement shall not be included in the calculation of the amount of a subsidy for the purpose of paragraph 1(a) of Article 6.

ANNEX V – PROCEDURES FOR DEVELOPING INFORMATION CONCERNING SERIOUS PREJUDICE

1.   Every Member shall cooperate in the development of evidence to be examined by a panel in procedures under paragraphs 4 through 6 of Article 7. The parties to the dispute and any third-country Member concerned shall notify to the DSB, as soon as the provisions of paragraph 4 of Article 7 have been invoked, the organization responsible for administration of this provision within its territory and the procedures to be used to comply with requests for information.

2.   In cases where matters are referred to the DSB under paragraph 4 of Article 7, the DSB shall, upon request, initiate the procedure to obtain such information from the government of the subsidizing Member as necessary to establish the existence and amount of subsidization, the value of total sales of the subsidized firms, as well as information necessary to analyze the adverse effects caused by the subsidized product.[66] This process may include, where appropriate, presentation of questions to the government of the subsidizing Member and of the complaining Member to collect information, as well as to clarify and obtain elaboration of information available to the parties to a dispute through the notification procedures set forth in Part VII.[67]

3.   In the case of effects in third-country markets, a party to a dispute may collect information, including through the use of questions to the government of the third-country Member, necessary to analyse adverse effects, which is not otherwise reasonably available from the complaining Member or the subsidizing Member. This requirement should be administered in such a way as not to impose an unreasonable burden on the third-country Member. In particular, such a Member is not expected to make a market or price analysis specially for that purpose. The information to be supplied is that which is already available or can be readily obtained by this Member (e.g. most recent statistics which have already been gathered by relevant statistical services but which have not yet been published, customs data concerning imports and declared values of the products concerned, etc.). However, if a party to a dispute undertakes a detailed market analysis at its own expense, the task of the person or firm conducting such an analysis shall be facilitated by the authorities of the third- country Member and such a person or firm shall

65   Start-up situations include instances where financial commitments for product development or construction of facilities to manufacture products benefiting from the subsidy have been made, even though production has not begun.

66   In cases where the existence of serious prejudice has to be demonstrated.

67   The information-gathering process by the DSB shall take into account the need to protect information which is by nature confidential or which is provided on a confidential basis by any Member involved in this process.

be given access to all information which is not normally maintained confidential by the government.

4.   The DSB shall designate a representative to serve the function of facilitating the information-gathering process. The sole purpose of the representative shall be to ensure the timely development of the information necessary to facilitate expeditious subsequent multilateral review of the dispute. In particular, the representative may suggest ways to most efficiently solicit necessary information as well as encourage the cooperation of the parties.

5.   The information-gathering process outlined in paragraphs 2 through 4 shall be completed within 60 days of the date on which the matter has been referred to the DSB under paragraph 4 of Article 7. The information obtained during this process shall be submitted to the panel established by the DSB in accordance with the provisions of Part X. This information should include, *inter alia*, data concerning the amount of the subsidy in question (and, where appropriate, the value of total sales of the subsidized firms), prices of the subsidized product, prices of the non-subsidized product, prices of other suppliers to the market, changes in the supply of the subsidized product to the market in question and changes in market shares. It should also include rebuttal evidence, as well as such supplemental information as the panel deems relevant in the course of reaching its conclusions.

6.   If the subsidizing and/or third-country Member fail to cooperate in the information-gathering process, the complaining Member will present its case of serious prejudice, based on evidence available to it, together with facts and circumstances of the non-cooperation of the subsidizing and/or third-country Member. Where information is unavailable due to non-cooperation by the subsidizing and/or third-country Member, the panel may complete the record as necessary relying on best information otherwise available.

7.   In making its determination, the panel should draw adverse inferences from instances of non-cooperation by any party involved in the information-gathering process.

8.   In making a determination to use either best information available or adverse inferences, the panel shall consider the advice of the DSB representative nominated under paragraph 4 as to the reasonableness of any requests for information and the efforts made by parties to comply with these requests in a cooperative and timely manner.

9.   Nothing in the information-gathering process shall limit the ability of the panel to seek such additional information it deems essential to a proper resolution to the dispute, and which was not adequately sought or developed during that process. However, ordinarily the panel should not request additional information to complete the record where the information would support a particular party's position and the absence of that information in the record is the result of unreasonable non-cooperation by that party in the information-gathering process.

ANNEX VI – PROCEDURES FOR ON-THE-SPOT INVESTIGATIONS
PURSUANT TO PARAGRAPH 6 OF ARTICLE 12

1.   Upon initiation of an investigation, the authorities of the exporting Member and the firms known to be concerned should be informed of the intention to carry out on-the-spot investigations.

2.   If in exceptional circumstances it is intended to include non-governmental experts in the investigating team, the firms and the authorities of the exporting Member should be so informed. Such non-governmental experts should be subject to effective sanctions for breach of confidentiality requirements.

3.   It should be standard practice to obtain explicit agreement of the firms concerned in the exporting Member before the visit is finally scheduled.

4.   As soon as the agreement of the firms concerned has been obtained, the investigating authorities should notify the authorities of the exporting Member of the names and addresses of the firms to be visited and the dates agreed.

5.   Sufficient advance notice should be given to the firms in question before the visit is made.

6.   Visits to explain the questionnaire should only be made at the request of an exporting firm. In case of such a request the investigating authorities may place themselves at the disposal of the firm; such a visit may only be made if *(a)* the authorities of the importing Member notify the representatives of the government of the Member in question and *(b)* the latter do not object to the visit.

7.   As the main purpose of the on-the-spot investigation is to verify information provided or to obtain further details, it should be carried out after the response to the questionnaire has been received unless the firm agrees to the contrary and the government of the exporting Member is informed by the investigating authorities of the anticipated visit and does not object to it; further, it should be standard practice prior to the visit to advise the firms concerned of the general nature of the information to be verified and of any further information which needs to be provided, though this should not preclude requests to be made on the spot for further details to be provided in the light of information obtained.

8.   Enquiries or questions put by the authorities or firms of the exporting Members and essential to a successful on-the-spot investigation should, whenever possible, be answered before the visit is made.

ANNEX VII – DEVELOPING COUNTRY MEMBERS REFERRED TO
IN PARAGRAPH 2(A) OF ARTICLE 27

The developing country Members not subject to the provisions of paragraph 1(a) of Article 3 under the terms of paragraph 2(a) of Article 27 are:

(a)   Least-developed countries designated as such by the United Nations which are Members of the WTO.

(b)   Each of the following developing countries which are Members of the WTO shall be subject to the provisions which are applicable to other developing country Members according to paragraph 2(b) of Article 27 when GNP per capita has reached $1,000 per annum:[68] Bolivia, Cameroon, Congo, Côte d'Ivoire, Dominican Republic, Egypt, Ghana, Guatemala, Guyana, India, Indonesia, Kenya, Morocco, Nicaragua, Nigeria, Pakistan, Philippines, Senegal, Sri Lanka and Zimbabwe.

---

68   The inclusion of developing country Members in the list in paragraph (b) is based on the most recent data from the World Bank on GNP per capita.

Agreement on Safeguards

Members,

Having in mind the overall objective of the Members to improve and strengthen the international trading system based on GATT 1994;

Recognizing the need to clarify and reinforce the disciplines of GATT 1994, and specifically those of its Article XIX (Emergency Action on Imports of Particular Products), to re-establish multilateral control over safeguards and eliminate measures that escape such control;

Recognizing the importance of structural adjustment and the need to enhance rather than limit competition in international markets; and

Recognizing further that, for these purposes, a comprehensive agreement, applicable to all Members and based on the basic principles of GATT 1994, is called for;

Hereby *agree* as follows:

Article 1 General Provision

This Agreement establishes rules for the application of safeguard measures which shall be understood to mean those measures provided for in Article XIX of GATT 1994.

Article 2 Conditions

1.   A Member[1] may apply a safeguard measure to a product only if that Member has determined, pursuant to the provisions set out below, that such product is being imported into its territory in such increased quantities, absolute or relative to domestic production, and under such conditions as to cause or threaten to cause serious injury to the domestic industry that produces like or directly competitive products.

2.   Safeguard measures shall be applied to a product being imported irrespective of its source.

Article 3 Investigation

1.   A Member may apply a safeguard measure only following an investigation by the competent authorities of that Member pursuant to procedures previously established and made public in consonance with Article X of GATT 1994. This investigation shall include reasonable public notice to all interested parties and public hearings or other appropriate means in which importers, exporters and other interested parties could present evidence and their views, including the opportunity to respond to the presentations of other parties and to submit their views, *inter alia,* as to whether or not the application of a safeguard measure would be in the public interest. The competent authorities shall publish a report setting forth their findings and reasoned conclusions reached on all pertinent issues of fact and law.

2.   Any information which is by nature confidential or which is provided on a confidential basis shall, upon cause being shown, be treated as such by the competent authorities. Such information shall not be disclosed without permission of the party submitting it. Parties providing confidential information may be requested to furnish non-confidential summaries thereof or, if such parties indicate that such information cannot be summarized, the reasons why a summary cannot be provided. However, if the competent authorities find that a request for confidentiality

---

1   A customs union may apply a safeguard measure as a single unit or on behalf of a member State. When a customs union applies a safeguard measure as a single unit, all the requirements for the determination of serious injury or threat thereof under this Agreement shall be based on the conditions existing in the customs union as a whole. When a safeguard measure is applied on behalf of a member State, all the requirements for the determination of serious injury or threat thereof shall be based on the conditions existing in that member State and the measure shall be limited to that member State. Nothing in this Agreement prejudges the interpretation of the relationship between Article XIX and paragraph 8 of Article XXIV of GATT 1994.

is not warranted and if the party concerned is either unwilling to make the information public or to authorize its disclosure in generalized or summary form, the authorities may disregard such information unless it can be demonstrated to their satisfaction from appropriate sources that the information is correct.

Article 4 Determination of Serious Injury or Threat Thereof

1. For the purposes of this Agreement:

(a) "serious injury" shall be understood to mean a significant overall impairment in the position of a domestic industry;

(b) "threat of serious injury" shall be understood to mean serious injury that is clearly imminent, in accordance with the provisions of paragraph 2. A determination of the existence of a threat of serious injury shall be based on facts and not merely on allegation, conjecture or remote possibility; and

(c) in determining injury or threat thereof, a "domestic industry" shall be understood to mean the producers as a whole of the like or directly competitive products operating within the territory of a Member, or those whose collective output of the like or directly competitive products constitutes a major proportion of the total domestic production of those products.

2. (a) In the investigation to determine whether increased imports have caused or are threatening to cause serious injury to a domestic industry under the terms of this Agreement, the competent authorities shall evaluate all relevant factors of an objective and quantifiable nature having a bearing on the situation of that industry, in particular, the rate and amount of the increase in imports of the product concerned in absolute and relative terms, the share of the domestic market taken by increased imports, changes in the level of sales, production, productivity, capacity utilization, profits and losses, and employment.

(b) The determination referred to in subparagraph (a) shall not be made unless this investigation demonstrates, on the basis of objective evidence, the existence of the causal link between increased imports of the product concerned and serious injury or threat thereof. When factors other than increased imports are causing injury to the domestic industry at the same time, such injury shall not be attributed to increased imports.

(c) The competent authorities shall publish promptly, in accordance with the provisions of Article 3, a detailed analysis of the case under investigation as well as a demonstration of the relevance of the factors examined.

Article 5 Application of Safeguard Measures

1. A Member shall apply safeguard measures only to the extent necessary to prevent or remedy serious injury and to facilitate adjustment. If a quantitative restriction is used, such a measure shall not reduce the quantity of imports below the level of a recent period which shall be the average of imports in the last three representative years for which statistics are available, unless clear justification is given that a different level is necessary to prevent or remedy serious injury. Members should choose measures most suitable for the achievement of these objectives.

2. (a) In cases in which a quota is allocated among supplying countries, the Member applying the restrictions may seek agreement with respect to the allocation of shares in the quota with all other Members having a substantial interest in supplying the product concerned. In cases in which this method is not reasonably practicable, the Member concerned shall allot to Members having a substantial interest in supplying the product shares based upon the proportions, supplied by such Members during a previous representative period, of the total quantity or value of imports of the product, due account being taken of any special factors which may have affected or may be affecting the trade in the product.

(b) A Member may depart from the provisions in subparagraph (a) provided that consultations under paragraph 3 of Article 12 are conducted under the auspices of the Committee on

Safeguards provided for in paragraph 1 of Article 13 and that clear demonstration is provided to the Committee that (*i*) imports from certain Members have increased in disproportionate percentage in relation to the total increase of imports of the product concerned in the representative period, (*ii*) the reasons for the departure from the provisions in subparagraph (a) are justified, and (*iii*) the conditions of such departure are equitable to all suppliers of the product concerned. The duration of any such measure shall not be extended beyond the initial period under paragraph 1 of Article 7. The departure referred to above shall not be permitted in the case of threat of serious injury.

Article 6 Provisional Safeguard Measures

In critical circumstances where delay would cause damage which it would be difficult to repair, a Member may take a provisional safeguard measure pursuant to a preliminary determination that there is clear evidence that increased imports have caused or are threatening to cause serious injury. The duration of the provisional measure shall not exceed 200 days, during which period the pertinent requirements of Articles 2 through 7 and 12 shall be met. Such measures should take the form of tariff increases to be promptly refunded if the subsequent investigation referred to in paragraph 2 of Article 4 does not determine that increased imports have caused or threatened to cause serious injury to a domestic industry. The duration of any such provisional measure shall be counted as a part of the initial period and any extension referred to in paragraphs 1, 2 and 3 of Article 7.

Article 7 Duration and Review of Safeguard Measures

1. A Member shall apply safeguard measures only for such period of time as may be necessary to prevent or remedy serious injury and to facilitate adjustment. The period shall not exceed four years, unless it is extended under paragraph 2.

2. The period mentioned in paragraph 1 may be extended provided that the competent authorities of the importing Member have determined, in conformity with the procedures set out in Articles 2, 3, 4 and 5, that the safeguard measure continues to be necessary to prevent or remedy serious injury and that there is evidence that the industry is adjusting, and provided that the pertinent provisions of Articles 8 and 12 are observed.

3. The total period of application of a safeguard measure including the period of application of any provisional measure, the period of initial application and any extension thereof, shall not exceed eight years.

4. In order to facilitate adjustment in a situation where the expected duration of a safeguard measure as notified under the provisions of paragraph 1 of Article 12 is over one year, the Member applying the measure shall progressively liberalize it at regular intervals during the period of application. If the duration of the measure exceeds three years, the Member applying such a measure shall review the situation not later than the mid-term of the measure and, if appropriate, withdraw it or increase the pace of liberalization. A measure extended under paragraph 2 shall not be more restrictive than it was at the end of the initial period, and should continue to be liberalized.

5. No safeguard measure shall be applied again to the import of a product which has been subject to such a measure, taken after the date of entry into force of the WTO Agreement, for a period of time equal to that during which such measure had been previously applied, provided that the period of non-application is at least two years.

6. Notwithstanding the provisions of paragraph 5, a safeguard measure with a duration of 180 days or less may be applied again to the import of a product if:

(a) at least one year has elapsed since the date of introduction of a safeguard measure on the import of that product; and

(b) such a safeguard measure has not been applied on the same product more than twice in the five-year period immediately preceding the date of introduction of the measure.

Article 8 Level of Concessions and Other Obligations

1.   A Member proposing to apply a safeguard measure or seeking an extension of a safeguard measure shall endeavour to maintain a substantially equivalent level of concessions and other obligations to that existing under GATT 1994 between it and the exporting Members which would be affected by such a measure, in accordance with the provisions of paragraph 3 of Article 12. To achieve this objective, the Members concerned may agree on any adequate means of trade compensation for the adverse effects of the measure on their trade.

2.   If no agreement is reached within 30 days in the consultations under paragraph 3 of Article 12, then the affected exporting Members shall be free, not later than 90 days after the measure is applied, to suspend, upon the expiration of 30 days from the day on which written notice of such suspension is received by the Council for Trade in Goods, the application of substantially equivalent concessions or other obligations under GATT 1994, to the trade of the Member applying the safeguard measure, the suspension of which the Council for Trade in Goods does not disapprove.

3.   The right of suspension referred to in paragraph 2 shall not be exercised for the first three years that a safeguard measure is in effect, provided that the safeguard measure has been taken as a result of an absolute increase in imports and that such a measure conforms to the provisions of this Agreement.

Article 9 Developing Country Members

1.   Safeguard measures shall not be applied against a product originating in a developing country Member as long as its share of imports of the product concerned in the importing Member does not exceed 3 per cent, provided that developing country Members with less than 3 per cent import share collectively account for not more than 9 per cent of total imports of the product concerned.[2]

2.   A developing country Member shall have the right to extend the period of application of a safeguard measure for a period of up to two years beyond the maximum period provided for in paragraph 3 of Article 7. Notwithstanding the provisions of paragraph 5 of Article 7, a developing country Member shall have the right to apply a safeguard measure again to the import of a product which has been subject to such a measure, taken after the date of entry into force of the WTO Agreement, after a period of time equal to half that during which such a measure has been previously applied, provided that the period of non-application is at least two years.

Article 10 Pre-Existing Article XIX Measures

Members shall terminate all safeguard measures taken pursuant to Article XIX of GATT 1947 that were in existence on the date of entry into force of the WTO Agreement not later than eight years after the date on which they were first applied or five years after the date of entry into force of the WTO Agreement, whichever comes later.

Article 11 Prohibition and Elimination of Certain Measures

1.   (a) A Member shall not take or seek any emergency action on imports of particular products as set forth in Article XIX of GATT 1994 unless such action conforms with the provisions of that Article applied in accordance with this Agreement.

(b) Furthermore, a Member shall not seek, take or maintain any voluntary export restraints, orderly marketing arrangements or any other similar measures on the export or the import

---

2   A Member shall immediately notify an action taken under paragraph 1 of Article 9 to the Committee on Safeguards.

side.[3],[4] These include actions taken by a single Member as well as actions under agreements, arrangements and understandings entered into by two or more Members. Any such measure in effect on the date of entry into force of the WTO Agreement shall be brought into conformity with this Agreement or phased out in accordance with paragraph 2.

(c) This Agreement does not apply to measures sought, taken or maintained by a Member pursuant to provisions of GATT 1994 other than Article XIX, and Multilateral Trade Agreements in Annex 1A other than this Agreement, or pursuant to protocols and agreements or arrangements concluded within the framework of GATT 1994.

2.   The phasing out of measures referred to in paragraph 1(b) shall be carried out according to timetables to be presented to the Committee on Safeguards by the Members concerned not later than 180 days after the date of entry into force of the WTO Agreement. These timetables shall provide for all measures referred to in paragraph 1 to be phased out or brought into conformity with this Agreement within a period not exceeding four years after the date of entry into force of the WTO Agreement, subject to not more than one specific measure per importing Member,[5] the duration of which shall not extend beyond 31 December 1999. Any such exception must be mutually agreed between the Members directly concerned and notified to the Committee on Safeguards for its review and acceptance within 90 days of the entry into force of the WTO Agreement. The Annex to this Agreement indicates a measure which has been agreed as falling under this exception.

3.   Members shall not encourage or support the adoption or maintenance by public and private enterprises of non-governmental measures equivalent to those referred to in paragraph 1.

Article 12 Notification and Consultation

1.   A Member shall immediately notify the Committee on Safeguards upon:

(a)   initiating an investigatory process relating to serious injury or threat thereof and the reasons for it;

(b)   making a finding of serious injury or threat thereof caused by increased imports; and

(c)   taking a decision to apply or extend a safeguard measure.

2.   In making the notifications referred to in paragraphs 1(b) and 1(c), the Member proposing to apply or extend a safeguard measure shall provide the Committee on Safeguards with all pertinent information, which shall include evidence of serious injury or threat thereof caused by increased imports, precise description of the product involved and the proposed measure, proposed date of introduction, expected duration and timetable for progressive liberalization. In the case of an extension of a measure, evidence that the industry concerned is adjusting shall also be provided. The Council for Trade in Goods or the Committee on Safeguards may request such additional information as they may consider necessary from the Member proposing to apply or extend the measure.

3.   A Member proposing to apply or extend a safeguard measure shall provide adequate opportunity for prior consultations with those Members having a substantial interest as exporters of the product concerned, with a view to, *inter alia*, reviewing the information provided under paragraph 2, exchanging views on the measure and reaching an understanding on ways to achieve the objective set out in paragraph 1 of Article 8.

---

3   An import quota applied as a safeguard measure in conformity with the relevant provisions of GATT 1994 and this Agreement may, by mutual agreement, be administered by the exporting Member.

4   Examples of similar measures include export moderation, export-price or import-price monitoring systems, export or import surveillance, compulsory import cartels and discretionary export or import licensing schemes, any of which afford protection.

5   The only such exception to which the European Communities is entitled is indicated in the Annex to this Agreement.

4.   A Member shall make a notification to the Committee on Safeguards before taking a pro-visional safeguard measure referred to in Article 6. Consultations shall be initiated immediately after the measure is taken.

5.   The results of the consultations referred to in this Article, as well as the results of mid-term reviews referred to in paragraph 4 of Article 7, any form of compensation referred to in paragraph 1 of Article 8, and proposed suspensions of concessions and other obligations referred to in paragraph 2 of Article 8, shall be notified immediately to the Council for Trade in Goods by the Members concerned.

6.   Members shall notify promptly the Committee on Safeguards of their laws, regulations and administrative procedures relating to safeguard measures as well as any modifications made to them.

7.   Members maintaining measures described in Article 10 and paragraph 1 of Article 11 which exist on the date of entry into force of the WTO Agreement shall notify such measures to the Committee on Safeguards not later than 60 days after the date of entry into force of the WTO Agreement.

8.   Any Member may notify the Committee on Safeguards of all laws, regulations, adminis-trative procedures and any measures or actions dealt with in this Agreement that have not been notified by other Members that are required by this Agreement to make such notifications.

9.   Any Member may notify the Committee on Safeguards of any non-governmental measures referred to in paragraph 3 of Article 11.

10.   All notifications to the Council for Trade in Goods referred to in this Agreement shall normally be made through the Committee on Safeguards.

11.   The provisions on notification in this Agreement shall not require any Member to disclose confidential information the disclosure of which would impede law enforcement or otherwise be contrary to the public interest or would prejudice the legitimate commercial interests of parti-cular enterprises, public or private.

Article 13 Surveillance

1.   A Committee on Safeguards is hereby established, under the authority of the Council for Trade in Goods, which shall be open to the participation of any Member indicating its wish to serve on it. The Committee will have the following functions:

(a)   to monitor, and report annually to the Council for Trade in Goods on, the general imple-mentation of this Agreement and make recommendations towards its improvement;

(b)   to find, upon request of an affected Member, whether or not the procedural requirements of this Agreement have been complied with in connection with a safeguard measure, and report its findings to the Council for Trade in Goods;

(c)   to assist Members, if they so request, in their consultations under the provisions of this Agreement;

(d)   to examine measures covered by Article 10 and paragraph 1 of Article 11, monitor the phase-out of such measures and report as appropriate to the Council for Trade in Goods;

(e)   to review, at the request of the Member taking a safeguard measure, whether proposals to suspend concessions or other obligations are "substantially equivalent", and report as appro-priate to the Council for Trade in Goods;

(f)   to receive and review all notifications provided for in this Agreement and report as appro-priate to the Council for Trade in Goods; and

(g)   to perform any other function connected with this Agreement that the Council for Trade in Goods may determine.

2.   To assist the Committee in carrying out its surveillance function, the Secretariat shall prepare annually a factual report on the operation of this Agreement based on notifications and other reliable information available to it.

Article 14 Dispute Settlement

The provisions of Articles XXII and XXIII of GATT 1994 as elaborated and applied by the Dispute Settlement Understanding shall apply to consultations and the settlement of disputes arising under this Agreement.

ANNEX -- EXCEPTION REFERRED TO IN PARAGRAPH 2 OF ARTICLE 11 [omitted]

XII.2. ANNEX 1B

General Agreement on Trade in Services (GATS)

PART I SCOPE AND DEFINITION
    Article I   Scope and Definition

PART II GENERAL OBLIGATIONS AND DISCIPLINES
    Article II   Most-Favoured-Nation Treatment
    Article III   Transparency
    Article III *bis*   Disclosure of Confidential Information
    Article IV   Increasing Participation of Developing Countries
    Article V   Economic Integration
    Article V *bis*   Labour Markets Integration Agreements
    Article VI   Domestic Regulation
    Article VII   Recognition
    Article VIII   Monopolies and Exclusive Service Suppliers
    Article IX   Business Practices
    Article X   Emergency Safeguard Measures
    Article XI   Payments and Transfers
    Article XII   Restrictions to Safeguard the Balance of Payments
    Article XIII   Government Procurement
    Article XIV   General Exceptions
    Article XIV *bis*   Security Exceptions
    Article XV   Subsidies

PART III SPECIFIC COMMITMENTS
    Article XVI   Market Access
    Article XVII   National Treatment
    Article XVIII   Additional Commitments

PART IV PROGRESSIVE LIBERALIZATION
    Article XIX   Negotiation of Specific Commitments
    Article XX   Schedules of Specific Commitments
    Article XXI   Modification of Schedules

PART V INSTITUTIONAL PROVISIONS
    Article XXII   Consultation
    Article XXIII   Dispute Settlement and Enforcement
    Article XXIV   Council for Trade in Services
    Article XXV   Technical Cooperation
    Article XXVI   Relationship with Other International Organizations

PART VI FINAL PROVISIONS
    Article XXVII   Denial of Benefits
    Article XXVIII   Definitions
    Article XXIX   Annexes
        Annex on Article II Exemptions
        Annex on Movement of Natural Persons Supplying Services under the Agreement
        Annex on Air Transport Services
        Annex on Financial Services
        Second Annex on Financial Services
        Annex on Negotiations on Maritime Transport Services
        Annex on Telecommunications
        Annex on Negotiations on Basic Telecommunications

General Agreement on Trade in Services (GATS)

Members,

Recognizing the growing importance of trade in services for the growth and development of the world economy;

Wishing to establish a multilateral framework of principles and rules for trade in services with a view to the expansion of such trade under conditions of transparency and progressive liberalization and as a means of promoting the economic growth of all trading partners and the development of developing countries;

Desiring the early achievement of progressively higher levels of liberalization of trade in services through successive rounds of multilateral negotiations aimed at promoting the interests of all participants on a mutually advantageous basis and at securing an overall balance of rights and obligations, while giving due respect to national policy objectives;

Recognizing the right of Members to regulate, and to introduce new regulations, on the supply of services within their territories in order to meet national policy objectives and, given asymmetries existing with respect to the degree of development of services regulations in different countries, the particular need of developing countries to exercise this right;

Desiring to facilitate the increasing participation of developing countries in trade in services and the expansion of their service exports including, *inter alia*, through the strengthening of their domestic services capacity and its efficiency and competitiveness;

Taking particular account of the serious difficulty of the least-developed countries in view of their special economic situation and their development, trade and financial needs;

Hereby *agree* as follows:

PART I – SCOPE AND DEFINITION

Article I Scope and Definition

1.   This Agreement applies to measures by Members affecting trade in services.

2.   For the purposes of this Agreement, trade in services is defined as the supply of a service:

(a)   from the territory of one Member into the territory of any other Member;

(b)   in the territory of one Member to the service consumer of any other Member;

(c)   by a service supplier of one Member, through commercial presence in the territory of any other Member;

(d)   by a service supplier of one Member, through presence of natural persons of a Member in the territory of any other Member.

3.   For the purposes of this Agreement:

(a)   "measures by Members" means measures taken by:

   (i)   central, regional or local governments and authorities; and

   (ii)   non-governmental bodies in the exercise of powers delegated by central, regional or local governments or authorities;

In fulfilling its obligations and commitments under the Agreement, each Member shall take such reasonable measures as may be available to it to ensure their observance by regional and local governments and authorities and non-governmental bodies within its territory;

(b)   "services" includes any service in any sector except services supplied in the exercise of governmental authority;

(c) "a service supplied in the exercise of governmental authority" means any service which is supplied neither on a commercial basis, nor in competition with one or more service suppliers.

PART II – GENERAL OBLIGATIONS AND DISCIPLINES

Article II Most-Favoured-Nation Treatment

1.   With respect to any measure covered by this Agreement, each Member shall accord immediately and unconditionally to services and service suppliers of any other Member treatment no less favourable than that it accords to like services and service suppliers of any other country.

2.   A Member may maintain a measure inconsistent with paragraph 1 provided that such a measure is listed in, and meets the conditions of, the Annex on Article II Exemptions.

3.   The provisions of this Agreement shall not be so construed as to prevent any Member from conferring or according advantages to adjacent countries in order to facilitate exchanges limited to contiguous frontier zones of services that are both locally produced and consumed.

Article III Transparency

1.   Each Member shall publish promptly and, except in emergency situations, at the latest by the time of their entry into force, all relevant measures of general application which pertain to or affect the operation of this Agreement. International agreements pertaining to or affecting trade in services to which a Member is a signatory shall also be published.

2.   Where publication as referred to in paragraph 1 is not practicable, such information shall be made otherwise publicly available.

3.   Each Member shall promptly and at least annually inform the Council for Trade in Services of the introduction of any new, or any changes to existing, laws, regulations or administrative guidelines which significantly affect trade in services covered by its specific commitments under this Agreement.

4.   Each Member shall respond promptly to all requests by any other Member for specific information on any of its measures of general application or international agreements within the meaning of paragraph 1. Each Member shall also establish one or more enquiry points to provide specific information to other Members, upon request, on all such matters as well as those subject to the notification requirement in paragraph 3. Such enquiry points shall be established within two years from the date of entry into force of the Agreement Establishing the WTO (referred to in this Agreement as the "WTO Agreement"). Appropriate flexibility with respect to the time-limit within which such enquiry points are to be established may be agreed upon for individual developing country Members. Enquiry points need not be depositories of laws and regulations.

5.   Any Member may notify to the Council for Trade in Services any measure, taken by any other Member, which it considers affects the operation of this Agreement.

Article III bis Disclosure of Confidential Information

Nothing in this Agreement shall require any Member to provide confidential information, the disclosure of which would impede law enforcement, or otherwise be contrary to the public interest, or which would prejudice legitimate commercial interests of particular enterprises, public or private.

Article IV Increasing Participation of Developing Countries

1.   The increasing participation of developing country Members in world trade shall be facilitated through negotiated specific commitments, by different Members pursuant to Parts III and IV of this Agreement, relating to:

(a) the strengthening of their domestic services capacity and its efficiency and competitiveness, *inter alia* through access to technology on a commercial basis;

(b) the improvement of their access to distribution channels and information networks; and

(c)   the liberalization of market access in sectors and modes of supply of export interest to them.

2.   Developed country Members, and to the extent possible other Members, shall establish contact points within two years from the date of entry into force of the WTO Agreement to facilitate the access of developing country Members' service suppliers to information, related to their respective markets, concerning:

(a)   commercial and technical aspects of the supply of services;

(b)   registration, recognition and obtaining of professional qualifications; and

(c)   the availability of services technology.

3.   Special priority shall be given to the least-developed country Members in the implementation of paragraphs 1 and 2. Particular account shall be taken of the serious difficulty of the least-developed countries in accepting negotiated specific commitments in view of their special economic situation and their development, trade and financial needs.

Article V Economic Integration

1.   This Agreement shall not prevent any of its Members from being a party to or entering into an agreement liberalizing trade in services between or among the parties to such an agreement, provided that such an agreement:

(a)   has substantial sectoral coverage,[1] and

(b)   provides for the absence or elimination of substantially all discrimination, in the sense of Article XVII, between or among the parties, in the sectors covered under subparagraph (a), through:

   (i)   elimination of existing discriminatory measures, and/or

   (ii)   prohibition of new or more discriminatory measures,

   either at the entry into force of that agreement or on the basis of a reasonable time-frame, except for measures permitted under Articles XI, XII, XIV and XIV bis.

2.   In evaluating whether the conditions under paragraph 1(b) are met, consideration may be given to the relationship of the agreement to a wider process of economic integration or trade liberalization among the countries concerned.

3.(a) Where developing countries are parties to an agreement of the type referred to in paragraph 1, flexibility shall be provided for regarding the conditions set out in paragraph 1, particularly with reference to subparagraph (b) thereof, in accordance with the level of development of the countries concerned, both overall and in individual sectors and subsectors.

(b)   Notwithstanding paragraph 6, in the case of an agreement of the type referred to in paragraph 1 involving only developing countries, more favourable treatment may be granted to juridical persons owned or controlled by natural persons of the parties to such an agreement.

4.   Any agreement referred to in paragraph 1 shall be designed to facilitate trade between the parties to the agreement and shall not in respect of any Member outside the agreement raise the overall level of barriers to trade in services within the respective sectors or subsectors compared to the level applicable prior to such an agreement.

5.   If, in the conclusion, enlargement or any significant modification of any agreement under paragraph 1, a Member intends to withdraw or modify a specific commitment inconsistently with the terms and conditions set out in its Schedule, it shall provide at least 90 days advance notice of such modification or withdrawal and the procedure set forth in paragraphs 2, 3 and 4 of Article XXI shall apply.

---

1   This condition is understood in terms of number of sectors, volume of trade affected and modes of supply. In order to meet this condition, agreements should not provide for the *a priori* exclusion of any mode of supply.

6. A service supplier of any other Member that is a juridical person constituted under the laws of a party to an agreement referred to in paragraph 1 shall be entitled to treatment granted under such agreement, provided that it engages in substantive business operations in the territory of the parties to such agreement.

7.(a) Members which are parties to any agreement referred to in paragraph 1 shall promptly notify any such agreement and any enlargement or any significant modification of that agreement to the Council for Trade in Services. They shall also make available to the Council such relevant information as may be requested by it. The Council may establish a working party to examine such an agreement or enlargement or modification of that agreement and to report to the Council on its consistency with this Article.

(b) Members which are parties to any agreement referred to in paragraph 1 which is implemented on the basis of a time-frame shall report periodically to the Council for Trade in Services on its implementation. The Council may establish a working party to examine such reports if it deems such a working party necessary.

(c) Based on the reports of the working parties referred to in subparagraphs (a) and (b), the Council may make recommendations to the parties as it deems appropriate.

8. A Member which is a party to any agreement referred to in paragraph 1 may not seek compensation for trade benefits that may accrue to any other Member from such agreement.

Article V bis Labour Markets Integration Agreements

This Agreement shall not prevent any of its Members from being a party to an agreement establishing full integration[2] of the labour markets between or among the parties to such an agreement, provided that such an agreement:

(a) exempts citizens of parties to the agreement from requirements concerning residency and work permits;

(b) is notified to the Council for Trade in Services.

Article VI Domestic Regulation

1. In sectors where specific commitments are undertaken, each Member shall ensure that all measures of general application affecting trade in services are administered in a reasonable, objective and impartial manner.

2. (a) Each Member shall maintain or institute as soon as practicable judicial, arbitral or administrative tribunals or procedures which provide, at the request of an affected service supplier, for the prompt review of, and where justified, appropriate remedies for, administrative decisions affecting trade in services. Where such procedures are not independent of the agency entrusted with the administrative decision concerned, the Member shall ensure that the procedures in fact provide for an objective and impartial review.

(b) The provisions of subparagraph (a) shall not be construed to require a Member to institute such tribunals or procedures where this would be inconsistent with its constitutional structure or the nature of its legal system.

3. Where authorization is required for the supply of a service on which a specific commitment has been made, the competent authorities of a Member shall, within a reasonable period of time after the submission of an application considered complete under domestic laws and regulations, inform the applicant of the decision concerning the application. At the request of the applicant, the competent authorities of the Member shall provide, without undue delay, information concerning the status of the application.

---

2   Typically, such integration provides citizens of the parties concerned with a right of free entry to the employment markets of the parties and includes measures concerning conditions of pay, other conditions of employment and social benefits.

4.   With a view to ensuring that measures relating to qualification requirements and procedures, technical standards and licensing requirements do not constitute unnecessary barriers to
trade in services, the Council for Trade in Services shall, through appropriate bodies it may
establish, develop any necessary disciplines. Such disciplines shall aim to ensure that such
requirements are, *inter alia*:

(a)   based on objective and transparent criteria, such as competence and the ability to supply
the service;

(b)   not more burdensome than necessary to ensure the quality of the service;

(c)   in the case of licensing procedures, not in themselves a restriction on the supply of the
service.

5.(a) In sectors in which a Member has undertaken specific commitments, pending the entry into
force of disciplines developed in these sectors pursuant to paragraph 4, the Member shall
not apply licensing and qualification requirements and technical standards that nullify or
impair such specific commitments in a manner which:

(i)   does not comply with the criteria outlined in subparagraphs 4(a), (b) or (c); and

(ii)   could not reasonably have been expected of that Member at the time the specific
commitments in those sectors were made.

(b)   In determining whether a Member is in conformity with the obligation under paragraph 5(a),
account shall be taken of international standards of relevant international organizations[3]
applied by that Member.

6.   In sectors where specific commitments regarding professional services are undertaken, each
Member shall provide for adequate procedures to verify the competence of professionals of any
other Member.

Article VII Recognition

1.   For the purposes of the fulfilment, in whole or in part, of its standards or criteria for the
authorization, licensing or certification of services suppliers, and subject to the requirements of
paragraph 3, a Member may recognize the education or experience obtained, requirements met,
or licenses or certifications granted in a particular country. Such recognition, which may be
achieved through harmonization or otherwise, may be based upon an agreement or arrangement with the country concerned or may be accorded autonomously.

2.   A Member that is a party to an agreement or arrangement of the type referred to in paragraph 1, whether existing or future, shall afford adequate opportunity for other interested
Members to negotiate their accession to such an agreement or arrangement or to negotiate
comparable ones with it. Where a Member accords recognition autonomously, it shall afford
adequate opportunity for any other Member to demonstrate that education, experience,
licenses, or certifications obtained or requirements met in that other Member's territory should
be recognized.

3.   A Member shall not accord recognition in a manner which would constitute a means of
discrimination between countries in the application of its standards or criteria for the authorization, licensing or certification of services suppliers, or a disguised restriction on trade in services.

4.   Each Member shall:

(a)   within 12 months from the date on which the WTO Agreement takes effect for it, inform the
Council for Trade in Services of its existing recognition measures and state whether such
measures are based on agreements or arrangements of the type referred to in paragraph 1;

---

3   The term "relevant international organizations" refers to international bodies whose membership is open to
the relevant bodies of at least all Members of the WTO.

(b) promptly inform the Council for Trade in Services as far in advance as possible of the opening of negotiations on an agreement or arrangement of the type referred to in paragraph 1 in order to provide adequate opportunity to any other Member to indicate their interest in participating in the negotiations before they enter a substantive phase;

(c) promptly inform the Council for Trade in Services when it adopts new recognition measures or significantly modifies existing ones and state whether the measures are based on an agreement or arrangement of the type referred to in paragraph 1.

5.   Wherever appropriate, recognition should be based on multilaterally agreed criteria. In appropriate cases, Members shall work in cooperation with relevant intergovernmental and non-governmental organizations towards the establishment and adoption of common international standards and criteria for recognition and common international standards for the practice of relevant services trades and professions.

Article VIII Monopolies and Exclusive Service Suppliers

1.   Each Member shall ensure that any monopoly supplier of a service in its territory does not, in the supply of the monopoly service in the relevant market, act in a manner inconsistent with that Member's obligations under Article II and specific commitments.

2.   Where a Member's monopoly supplier competes, either directly or through an affiliated company, in the supply of a service outside the scope of its monopoly rights and which is subject to that Member's specific commitments, the Member shall ensure that such a supplier does not abuse its monopoly position to act in its territory in a manner inconsistent with such commitments.

3.   The Council for Trade in Services may, at the request of a Member which has a reason to believe that a monopoly supplier of a service of any other Member is acting in a manner inconsistent with paragraph 1 or 2, request the Member establishing, maintaining or authorizing such supplier to provide specific information concerning the relevant operations.

4.   If, after the date of entry into force of the WTO Agreement, a Member grants monopoly rights regarding the supply of a service covered by its specific commitments, that Member shall notify the Council for Trade in Services no later than three months before the intended implementation of the grant of monopoly rights and the provisions of paragraphs 2, 3 and 4 of Article XXI shall apply.

5.   The provisions of this Article shall also apply to cases of exclusive service suppliers, where a Member, formally or in effect, (a) authorizes or establishes a small number of service suppliers and (b) substantially prevents competition among those suppliers in its territory.

Article IX Business Practices

1.   Members recognize that certain business practices of service suppliers, other than those falling under Article VIII, may restrain competition and thereby restrict trade in services.

2.   Each Member shall, at the request of any other Member, enter into consultations with a view to eliminating practices referred to in paragraph 1. The Member addressed shall accord full and sympathetic consideration to such a request and shall cooperate through the supply of publicly available non-confidential information of relevance to the matter in question. The Member addressed shall also provide other information available to the requesting Member, subject to its domestic law and to the conclusion of satisfactory agreement concerning the safeguarding of its confidentiality by the requesting Member.

Article X Emergency Safeguard Measures

1.   There shall be multilateral negotiations on the question of emergency safeguard measures based on the principle of non-discrimination. The results of such negotiations shall enter into

effect on a date not later than three years from the date of entry into force of the WTO Agreement.

2. In the period before the entry into effect of the results of the negotiations referred to in paragraph 1, any Member may, notwithstanding the provisions of paragraph 1 of Article XXI, notify the Council on Trade in Services of its intention to modify or withdraw a specific commitment after a period of one year from the date on which the commitment enters into force; provided that the Member shows cause to the Council that the modification or withdrawal cannot await the lapse of the three-year period provided for in paragraph 1 of Article XXI.

3. The provisions of paragraph 2 shall cease to apply three years after the date of entry into force of the WTO Agreement.

Article XI Payments and Transfers

1. Except under the circumstances envisaged in Article XII, a Member shall not apply restrictions on international transfers and payments for current transactions relating to its specific commitments.

2. Nothing in this Agreement shall affect the rights and obligations of the members of the International Monetary Fund under the Articles of Agreement of the Fund, including the use of exchange actions which are in conformity with the Articles of Agreement, provided that a Member shall not impose restrictions on any capital transactions inconsistently with its specific commitments regarding such transactions, except under Article XII or at the request of the Fund.

Article XII Restrictions to Safeguard the Balance of Payments

1. In the event of serious balance-of-payments and external financial difficulties or threat thereof, a Member may adopt or maintain restrictions on trade in services on which it has undertaken specific commitments, including on payments or transfers for transactions related to such commitments. It is recognized that particular pressures on the balance of payments of a Member in the process of economic development or economic transition may necessitate the use of restrictions to ensure, *inter alia*, the maintenance of a level of financial reserves adequate for the implementation of its programme of economic development or economic transition.

2. The restrictions referred to in paragraph 1:

(a) shall not discriminate among Members;

(b) shall be consistent with the Articles of Agreement of the International Monetary Fund;

(c) shall avoid unnecessary damage to the commercial, economic and financial interests of any other Member;

(d) shall not exceed those necessary to deal with the circumstances described in paragraph 1;

(e) shall be temporary and be phased out progressively as the situation specified in paragraph 1 improves.

3. In determining the incidence of such restrictions, Members may give priority to the supply of services which are more essential to their economic or development programmes. However, such restrictions shall not be adopted or maintained for the purpose of protecting a particular service sector.

4. Any restrictions adopted or maintained under paragraph 1, or any changes therein, shall be promptly notified to the General Council.

5. (a) Members applying the provisions of this Article shall consult promptly with the Committee on Balance-of-Payments Restrictions on restrictions adopted under this Article.

(b) The Ministerial Conference shall establish procedures[4] for periodic consultations with the objective of enabling such recommendations to be made to the Member concerned as it may deem appropriate.

---

4   It is understood that the procedures under paragraph 5 shall be the same as the GATT 1994 procedures.

(c) Such consultations shall assess the balance-of-payment situation of the Member concerned and the restrictions adopted or maintained under this Article, taking into account, *inter alia*, such factors as:

   (i)   the nature and extent of the balance-of-payments and the external financial difficulties;

   (ii)   the external economic and trading environment of the consulting Member;

   (iii) alternative corrective measures which may be available.

(d) The consultations shall address the compliance of any restrictions with paragraph 2, in particular the progressive phaseout of restrictions in accordance with paragraph 2(e).

(e) In such consultations, all findings of statistical and other facts presented by the International Monetary Fund relating to foreign exchange, monetary reserves and balance of payments, shall be accepted and conclusions shall be based on the assessment by the Fund of the balance-of-payments and the external financial situation of the consulting Member.

6.   If a Member which is not a member of the International Monetary Fund wishes to apply the provisions of this Article, the Ministerial Conference shall establish a review procedure and any other procedures necessary.

Article XIII Government Procurement

1.   Articles II, XVI and XVII shall not apply to laws, regulations or requirements governing the procurement by governmental agencies of services purchased for governmental purposes and not with a view to commercial resale or with a view to use in the supply of services for commercial sale.

2.   There shall be multilateral negotiations on government procurement in services under this Agreement within two years from the date of entry into force of the WTO Agreement.

Article XIV General Exceptions

Subject to the requirement that such measures are not applied in a manner which would constitute a means of arbitrary or unjustifiable discrimination between countries where like conditions prevail, or a disguised restriction on trade in services, nothing in this Agreement shall be construed to prevent the adoption or enforcement by any Member of measures:

(a) necessary to protect public morals or to maintain public order;[5]

(b) necessary to protect human, animal or plant life or health;

(c) necessary to secure compliance with laws or regulations which are not inconsistent with the provisions of this Agreement including those relating to:

   (i)   the prevention of deceptive and fraudulent practices or to deal with the effects of a default on services contracts;

   (ii)   the protection of the privacy of individuals in relation to the processing and dissemination of personal data and the protection of confidentiality of individual records and accounts;

   (iii) safety;

---

5   The public order exception may be invoked only where a genuine and sufficiently serious threat is posed to one of the fundamental interests of society.

(d) inconsistent with Article XVII, provided that the difference in treatment is aimed at ensuring the equitable or effective[6] imposition or collection of direct taxes in respect of services or service suppliers of other Members;

(e) inconsistent with Article II, provided that the difference in treatment is the result of an agreement on the avoidance of double taxation or provisions on the avoidance of double taxation in any other international agreement or arrangement by which the Member is bound.

Article XIV bis Security Exceptions

1. Nothing in this Agreement shall be construed:

(a) to require any Member to furnish any information, the disclosure of which it considers contrary to its essential security interests; or

(b) to prevent any Member from taking any action which it considers necessary for the protection of its essential security interests:

    (i) relating to the supply of services as carried out directly or indirectly for the purpose of provisioning a military establishment;

    (ii) relating to fissionable and fusionable materials or the materials from which they are derived;

    (iii) taken in time of war or other emergency in international relations; or

(c) to prevent any Member from taking any action in pursuance of its obligations under the United Nations Charter for the maintenance of international peace and security.

2. The Council for Trade in Services shall be informed to the fullest extent possible of measures taken under paragraphs 1(b) and (c) and of their termination.

Article XV Subsidies

1. Members recognize that, in certain circumstances, subsidies may have distortive effects on trade in services. Members shall enter into negotiations with a view to developing the necessary multilateral disciplines to avoid such trade-distortive effects.[7] The negotiations shall also address the appropriateness of countervailing procedures. Such negotiations shall recognize the role of subsidies in relation to the development programmes of developing countries and take into account the needs of Members, particularly developing country Members, for flexibility in this area. For the purpose of such negotiations, Members shall exchange information concerning all subsidies related to trade in services that they provide to their domestic service suppliers.

---

6   Measures that are aimed at ensuring the equitable or effective imposition or collection of direct taxes include measures taken by a Member under its taxation system which:
    (i)   apply to non-resident service suppliers in recognition of the fact that the tax obligation of non-residents is determined with respect to taxable items sourced or located in the Member's territory; or
    (ii)   apply to non-residents in order to ensure the imposition or collection of taxes in the Member's territory; or
    (iii)   apply to non-residents or residents in order to prevent the avoidance or evasion of taxes, including compliance measures; or
    (iv)   apply to consumers of services supplied in or from the territory of another Member in order to ensure the imposition or collection of taxes on such consumers derived from sources in the Member's territory; or
    (v)   distinguish service suppliers subject to tax on worldwide taxable items from other service suppliers, in recognition of the difference in the nature of the tax base between them; or
    (vi)   determine, allocate or apportion income, profit, gain, loss, deduction or credit of resident persons or branches, or between related persons or branches of the same person, in order to safeguard the Member's tax base.
    Tax terms or concepts in paragraph (d) of Article XIV and in this footnote are determined according to tax definitions and concepts, or equivalent or similar definitions and concepts, under the domestic law of the Member taking the measure.

7   A future work programme shall determine how, and in what time-frame, negotiations on such multilateral disciplines will be conducted.

2.   Any Member which considers that it is adversely affected by a subsidy of another Member may request consultations with that Member on such matters. Such requests shall be accorded sympathetic consideration.

PART III – SPECIFIC COMMITMENTS

Article XVI Market Access

1.   With respect to market access through the modes of supply identified in Article I, each Member shall accord services and service suppliers of any other Member treatment no less favourable than that provided for under the terms, limitations and conditions agreed and specified in its Schedule.[8]

2.   In sectors where market-access commitments are undertaken, the measures which a Member shall not maintain or adopt either on the basis of a regional subdivision or on the basis of its entire territory, unless otherwise specified in its Schedule, are defined as:

(a)   limitations on the number of service suppliers whether in the form of numerical quotas, monopolies, exclusive service suppliers or the requirements of an economic needs test;

(b)   limitations on the total value of service transactions or assets in the form of numerical quotas or the requirement of an economic needs test;

(c)   limitations on the total number of service operations or on the total quantity of service output expressed in terms of designated numerical units in the form of quotas or the requirement of an economic needs test;[9]

(d)   limitations on the total number of natural persons that may be employed in a particular service sector or that a service supplier may employ and who are necessary for, and directly related to, the supply of a specific service in the form of numerical quotas or the requirement of an economic needs test;

(e)   measures which restrict or require specific types of legal entity or joint venture through which a service supplier may supply a service; and

(f)   limitations on the participation of foreign capital in terms of maximum percentage limit on foreign shareholding or the total value of individual or aggregate foreign investment.

Article XVII National Treatment

1.   In the sectors inscribed in its Schedule, and subject to any conditions and qualifications set out therein, each Member shall accord to services and service suppliers of any other Member, in respect of all measures affecting the supply of services, treatment no less favourable than that it accords to its own like services and service suppliers.[10]

2.   A Member may meet the requirement of paragraph 1 by according to services and service suppliers of any other Member, either formally identical treatment or formally different treatment to that it accords to its own like services and service suppliers.

3.   Formally identical or formally different treatment shall be considered to be less favourable if it modifies the conditions of competition in favour of services or service suppliers of the Member compared to like services or service suppliers of any other Member.

---

8   If a Member undertakes a market-access commitment in relation to the supply of a service through the mode of supply referred to in subparagraph 2(a) of Article I and if the cross-border movement of capital is an essential part of the service itself, that Member is thereby committed to allow such movement of capital. If a Member undertakes a market-access commitment in relation to the supply of a service through the mode of supply referred to in subparagraph 2(c) of Article I, it is thereby committed to allow related transfers of capital into its territory.

9   Subparagraph 2(c) does not cover measures of a Member which limit inputs for the supply of services.

10   Specific commitments assumed under this Article shall not be construed to require any Member to compensate for any inherent competitive disadvantages which result from the foreign character of the relevant services or service suppliers.

Article XVIII Additional Commitments

Members may negotiate commitments with respect to measures affecting trade in services not subject to scheduling under Articles XVI or XVII, including those regarding qualifications, standards or licensing matters. Such commitments shall be inscribed in a Member's Schedule.

PART IV – PROGRESSIVE LIBERALIZATION

Article XIX Negotiation of Specific Commitments

1. In pursuance of the objectives of this Agreement, Members shall enter into successive rounds of negotiations, beginning not later than five years from the date of entry into force of the WTO Agreement and periodically thereafter, with a view to achieving a progressively higher level of liberalization. Such negotiations shall be directed to the reduction or elimination of the adverse effects on trade in services of measures as a means of providing effective market access. This process shall take place with a view to promoting the interests of all participants on a mutually advantageous basis and to securing an overall balance of rights and obligations.

2. The process of liberalization shall take place with due respect for national policy objectives and the level of development of individual Members, both overall and in individual sectors. There shall be appropriate flexibility for individual developing country Members for opening fewer sectors, liberalizing fewer types of transactions, progressively extending market access in line with their development situation and, when making access to their markets available to foreign service suppliers, attaching to such access conditions aimed at achieving the objectives referred to in Article IV.

3. For each round, negotiating guidelines and procedures shall be established. For the purposes of establishing such guidelines, the Council for Trade in Services shall carry out an assessment of trade in services in overall terms and on a sectoral basis with reference to the objectives of this Agreement, including those set out in paragraph 1 of Article IV. Negotiating guidelines shall establish modalities for the treatment of liberalization undertaken autonomously by Members since previous negotiations, as well as for the special treatment for least-developed country Members under the provisions of paragraph 3 of Article IV.

4. The process of progressive liberalization shall be advanced in each such round through bilateral, plurilateral or multilateral negotiations directed towards increasing the general level of specific commitments undertaken by Members under this Agreement.

Article XX Schedules of Specific Commitments

1. Each Member shall set out in a schedule the specific commitments it undertakes under Part III of this Agreement. With respect to sectors where such commitments are undertaken, each Schedule shall specify:

(a) terms, limitations and conditions on market access;

(b) conditions and qualifications on national treatment;

(c) undertakings relating to additional commitments;

(d) where appropriate the time-frame for implementation of such commitments; and

(e) the date of entry into force of such commitments.

2. Measures inconsistent with both Articles XVI and XVII shall be inscribed in the column relating to Article XVI. In this case the inscription will be considered to provide a condition or qualification to Article XVII as well.

3. Schedules of specific commitments shall be annexed to this Agreement and shall form an integral part thereof.

Article XXI Modification of Schedules

1. (a) A Member (referred to in this Article as the "modifying Member") may modify or withdraw any commitment in its Schedule, at any time after three years have elapsed from the date on which that commitment entered into force, in accordance with the provisions of this Article.

(b) A modifying Member shall notify its intent to modify or withdraw a commitment pursuant to this Article to the Council for Trade in Services no later than three months before the intended date of implementation of the modification or withdrawal.

2. (a) At the request of any Member the benefits of which under this Agreement may be affected (referred to in this Article as an "affected Member") by a proposed modification or withdrawal notified under subparagraph 1(b), the modifying Member shall enter into negotiations with a view to reaching agreement on any necessary compensatory adjustment. In such negotiations and agreement, the Members concerned shall endeavour to maintain a general level of mutually advantageous commitments not less favourable to trade than that provided for in Schedules of specific commitments prior to such negotiations.

(b) Compensatory adjustments shall be made on a most-favoured-nation basis.

3. (a) If agreement is not reached between the modifying Member and any affected Member before the end of the period provided for negotiations, such affected Member may refer the matter to arbitration. Any affected Member that wishes to enforce a right that it may have to compensation must participate in the arbitration.

(b) If no affected Member has requested arbitration, the modifying Member shall be free to implement the proposed modification or withdrawal.

4. (a) The modifying Member may not modify or withdraw its commitment until it has made compensatory adjustments in conformity with the findings of the arbitration.

(b) If the modifying Member implements its proposed modification or withdrawal and does not comply with the findings of the arbitration, any affected Member that participated in the arbitration may modify or withdraw substantially equivalent benefits in conformity with those findings. Notwithstanding Article II, such a modification or withdrawal may be implemented solely with respect to the modifying Member.

5. The Council for Trade in Services shall establish procedures for rectification or modification of Schedules. Any Member which has modified or withdrawn scheduled commitments under this Article shall modify its Schedule according to such procedures.

PART V – INSTITUTIONAL PROVISIONS

Article XXII Consultation

1. Each Member shall accord sympathetic consideration to, and shall afford adequate opportunity for, consultation regarding such representations as may be made by any other Member with respect to any matter affecting the operation of this Agreement. The Dispute Settlement Understanding (DSU) shall apply to such consultations.

2. The Council for Trade in Services or the Dispute Settlement Body (DSB) may, at the request of a Member, consult with any Member or Members in respect of any matter for which it has not been possible to find a satisfactory solution through consultation under paragraph 1.

3. A Member may not invoke Article XVII, either under this Article or Article XXIII, with respect to a measure of another Member that falls within the scope of an international agreement between them relating to the avoidance of double taxation. In case of disagreement between Members as to whether a measure falls within the scope of such an agreement between them, it shall be open

to either Member to bring this matter before the Council for Trade in Services.[11] The Council shall refer the matter to arbitration. The decision of the arbitrator shall be final and binding on the Members.

Article XXIII Dispute Settlement and Enforcement

1.   If any Member should consider that any other Member fails to carry out its obligations or specific commitments under this Agreement, it may with a view to reaching a mutually satis-factory resolution of the matter have recourse to the DSU.

2.   If the DSB considers that the circumstances are serious enough to justify such action, it may authorize a Member or Members to suspend the application to any other Member or Members of obligations and specific commitments in accordance with Article 22 of the DSU.

3.   If any Member considers that any benefit it could reasonably have expected to accrue to it under a specific commitment of another Member under Part III of this Agreement is being nullified or impaired as a result of the application of any measure which does not conflict with the provisions of this Agreement, it may have recourse to the DSU. If the measure is determined by the DSB to have nullified or impaired such a benefit, the Member affected shall be entitled to a mutually satisfactory adjustment on the basis of paragraph 2 of Article XXI, which may include the modification or withdrawal of the measure. In the event an agreement cannot be reached between the Members concerned, Article 22 of the DSU shall apply.

Article XXIV Council for Trade in Services

1.   The Council for Trade in Services shall carry out such functions as may be assigned to it to facilitate the operation of this Agreement and further its objectives. The Council may establish such subsidiary bodies as it considers appropriate for the effective discharge of its functions.

2.   The Council and, unless the Council decides otherwise, its subsidiary bodies shall be open to participation by representatives of all Members.

3.   The Chairman of the Council shall be elected by the Members.

Article XXV Technical Cooperation

1.   Service suppliers of Members which are in need of such assistance shall have access to the services of contact points referred to in paragraph 2 of Article IV.

2.   Technical assistance to developing countries shall be provided at the multilateral level by the Secretariat and shall be decided upon by the Council for Trade in Services.

Article XXVI Relationship with Other International Organizations

The General Council shall make appropriate arrangements for consultation and cooperation with the United Nations and its specialized agencies as well as with other intergovernmental organ-izations concerned with services.

PART VI – FINAL PROVISIONS

Article XXVII Denial of Benefits

A Member may deny the benefits of this Agreement:

(a)   to the supply of a service, if it establishes that the service is supplied from or in the territory of a non-Member or of a Member to which the denying Member does not apply the WTO Agreement;

(b)   in the case of the supply of a maritime transport service, if it establishes that the service is supplied:

---

11   With respect to agreements on the avoidance of double taxation which exist on the date of entry into force of the WTO Agreement, such a matter may be brought before the Council for Trade in Services only with the consent of both parties to such an agreement.

(i)   by a vessel registered under the laws of a non-Member or of a Member to which the denying Member does not apply the WTO Agreement, and

(ii) by a person which operates and/or uses the vessel in whole or in part but which is of a non-Member or of a Member to which the denying Member does not apply the WTO Agreement;

(c) to a service supplier that is a juridical person, if it establishes that it is not a service supplier of another Member, or that it is a service supplier of a Member to which the denying Member does not apply the WTO Agreement.

Article XXVIII Definitions

For the purpose of this Agreement:

(a) "measure" means any measure by a Member, whether in the form of a law, regulation, rule, procedure, decision, administrative action, or any other form;

(b) "supply of a service" includes the production, distribution, marketing, sale and delivery of a service;

(c) "measures by Members affecting trade in services" include measures in respect of

(i)   the purchase, payment or use of a service;

(ii) the access to and use of, in connection with the supply of a service, services which are required by those Members to be offered to the public generally;

(iii) the presence, including commercial presence, of persons of a Member for the supply of a service in the territory of another Member;

(d) "commercial presence" means any type of business or professional establishment, including through

(i)   the constitution, acquisition or maintenance of a juridical person, or

(ii) the creation or maintenance of a branch or a representative office,

within the territory of a Member for the purpose of supplying a service;

(e) "sector" of a service means,

(i)   with reference to a specific commitment, one or more, or all, subsectors of that service, as specified in a Member's Schedule,

(ii) otherwise, the whole of that service sector, including all of its subsectors;

(f) "service of another Member" means a service which is supplied,

(i)   from or in the territory of that other Member, or in the case of maritime transport, by a vessel registered under the laws of that other Member, or by a person of that other Member which supplies the service through the operation of a vessel and/or its use in whole or in part; or

(ii) in the case of the supply of a service through commercial presence or through the presence of natural persons, by a service supplier of that other Member;

(g) "service supplier" means any person that supplies a service;[12]

---

12   Where the service is not supplied directly by a juridical person but through other forms of commercial presence such as a branch or a representative office, the service supplier (i.e. the juridical person) shall, nonetheless, through such presence be accorded the treatment provided for service suppliers under the Agreement. Such treatment shall be extended to the presence through which the service is supplied and need not be extended to any other parts of the supplier located outside the territory where the service is supplied.

(h) "monopoly supplier of a service" means any person, public or private, which in the relevant market of the territory of a Member is authorized or established formally or in effect by that Member as the sole supplier of that service;

(i) "service consumer" means any person that receives or uses a service;

(j) "person" means either a natural person or a juridical person;

(k) "natural person of another Member" means a natural person who resides in the territory of that other Member or any other Member, and who under the law of that other Member:

    (i) is a national of that other Member; or

    (ii) has the right of permanent residence in that other Member, in the case of a Member which:

        1. does not have nationals; or

        2. accords substantially the same treatment to its permanent residents as it does to its nationals in respect of measures affecting trade in services, as notified in its acceptance of or accession to the WTO Agreement, provided that no Member is obligated to accord to such permanent residents treatment more favourable than would be accorded by that other Member to such permanent residents. Such notification shall include the assurance to assume, with respect to those permanent residents, in accordance with its laws and regulations, the same responsibilities that other Member bears with respect to its nationals;

(l) "juridical person" means any legal entity duly constituted or otherwise organized under applicable law, whether for profit or otherwise, and whether privately-owned or governmentally-owned, including any corporation, trust, partnership, joint venture, sole proprietorship or association;

(m) "juridical person of another Member" means a juridical person which is either:

    (i) constituted or otherwise organized under the law of that other Member, and is engaged in substantive business operations in the territory of that Member or any other Member; or

    (ii) in the case of the supply of a service through commercial presence, owned or controlled by:

        1. natural persons of that Member; or

        2. juridical persons of that other Member identified under subparagraph (i);

(n) a juridical person is:

    (i) "owned" by persons of a Member if more than 50 per cent of the equity interest in it is beneficially owned by persons of that Member;

    (ii) "controlled" by persons of a Member if such persons have the power to name a majority of its directors or otherwise to legally direct its actions;

    (iii) "affiliated" with another person when it controls, or is controlled by, that other person; or when it and the other person are both controlled by the same person;

(o) "direct taxes" comprise all taxes on total income, on total capital or on elements of income or of capital, including taxes on gains from the alienation of property, taxes on estates, inheritances and gifts, and taxes on the total amounts of wages or salaries paid by enterprises, as well as taxes on capital appreciation.

Article XXIX Annexes

The Annexes to this Agreement are an integral part of this Agreement.

ANNEX ON ARTICLE II EXEMPTIONS

Scope

1.   This Annex specifies the conditions under which a Member, at the entry into force of this Agreement, is exempted from its obligations under paragraph 1 of Article II.

2.   Any new exemptions applied for after the date of entry into force of the WTO Agreement shall be dealt with under paragraph 3 of Article IX of that Agreement.

Review

3.   The Council for Trade in Services shall review all exemptions granted for a period of more than 5 years. The first such review shall take place no more than 5 years after the entry into force of the WTO Agreement.

4.   The Council for Trade in Services in a review shall:

(a)   examine whether the conditions which created the need for the exemption still prevail; and

(b)   determine the date of any further review.

Termination

5.   The exemption of a Member from its obligations under paragraph 1 of Article II of the Agreement with respect to a particular measure terminates on the date provided for in the exemption.

6.   In principle, such exemptions should not exceed a period of 10 years. In any event, they shall be subject to negotiation in subsequent trade liberalizing rounds.

7.   A Member shall notify the Council for Trade in Services at the termination of the exemption period that the inconsistent measure has been brought into conformity with paragraph 1 of Article II of the Agreement.

Lists of Article II Exemptions

[The agreed lists of exemptions under paragraph 2 of Article II are annexed here in the full treaty copy of the WTO Agreement.]

ANNEX ON MOVEMENT OF NATURAL PERSONS
SUPPLYING SERVICES UNDER THE AGREEMENT

1.   This Annex applies to measures affecting natural persons who are service suppliers of a Member, and natural persons of a Member who are employed by a service supplier of a Member, in respect of the supply of a service.

2.   The Agreement shall not apply to measures affecting natural persons seeking access to the employment market of a Member, nor shall it apply to measures regarding citizenship, residence or employment on a permanent basis.

3.   In accordance with Parts III and IV of the Agreement, Members may negotiate specific commitments applying to the movement of all categories of natural persons supplying services under the Agreement. Natural persons covered by a specific commitment shall be allowed to supply the service in accordance with the terms of that commitment.

4.   The Agreement shall not prevent a Member from applying measures to regulate the entry of natural persons into, or their temporary stay in, its territory, including those measures necessary to protect the integrity of, and to ensure the orderly movement of natural persons across, its borders, provided that such measures are not applied in such a manner as to nullify or impair the benefits accruing to any Member under the terms of a specific commitment.[13]

---

13   The sole fact of requiring a visa for natural persons of certain Members and not for those of others shall not be regarded as nullifying or impairing benefits under a specific commitment.

ANNEX ON AIR TRANSPORT SERVICES

1.   This Annex applies to measures affecting trade in air transport services, whether scheduled or non-scheduled, and ancillary services. It is confirmed that any specific commitment or obligation assumed under this Agreement shall not reduce or affect a Member's obligations under bilateral or multilateral agreements that are in effect on the date of entry into force of the WTO Agreement.

2.   The Agreement, including its dispute settlement procedures, shall not apply to measures affecting:

(a)   traffic rights, however granted; or

(b)   services directly related to the exercise of traffic rights,

except as provided in paragraph 3 of this Annex.

3.   The Agreement shall apply to measures affecting:

(a)   aircraft repair and maintenance services;

(b)   the selling and marketing of air transport services;

(c)   computer reservation system (CRS) services.

4.   The dispute settlement procedures of the Agreement may be invoked only where obligations or specific commitments have been assumed by the concerned Members and where dispute settlement procedures in bilateral and other multilateral agreements or arrangements have been exhausted.

5.   The Council for Trade in Services shall review periodically, and at least every five years, developments in the air transport sector and the operation of this Annex with a view to considering the possible further application of the Agreement in this sector.

6.   Definitions:

(a)   "Aircraft repair and maintenance services" mean such activities when undertaken on an aircraft or a part thereof while it is withdrawn from service and do not include so-called line maintenance.

(b)   "Selling and marketing of air transport services" mean opportunities for the air carrier concerned to sell and market freely its air transport services including all aspects of marketing such as market research, advertising and distribution. These activities do not include the pricing of air transport services nor the applicable conditions.

(c)   "Computer reservation system (CRS) services" mean services provided by computerised systems that contain information about air carriers' schedules, availability, fares and fare rules, through which reservations can be made or tickets may be issued.

(d)   "Traffic rights" mean the right for scheduled and non-scheduled services to operate and/or to carry passengers, cargo and mail for remuneration or hire from, to, within, or over the territory of a Member, including points to be served, routes to be operated, types of traffic to be carried, capacity to be provided, tariffs to be charged and their conditions, and criteria for designation of airlines, including such criteria as number, ownership, and control.

ANNEX ON FINANCIAL SERVICES

1. Scope and Definition

(a)   This Annex applies to measures affecting the supply of financial services. Reference to the supply of a financial service in this Annex shall mean the supply of a service as defined in paragraph 2 of Article I of the Agreement.

(b)   For the purposes of subparagraph 3(b) of Article I of the Agreement, "services supplied in the exercise of governmental authority" means the following:

        (i)   activities conducted by a central bank or monetary authority or by any other public entity in pursuit of monetary or exchange rate policies;

        (ii) activities forming part of a statutory system of social security or public retirement plans; and

        (iii) other activities conducted by a public entity for the account or with the guarantee or using the financial resources of the Government.

(c)   For the purposes of subparagraph 3(b) of Article I of the Agreement, if a Member allows any of the activities referred to in subparagraphs (b)(ii) or (b)(iii) of this paragraph to be conducted by its financial service suppliers in competition with a public entity or a financial service supplier, "services" shall include such activities.

(d)   Subparagraph 3(c) of Article I of the Agreement shall not apply to services covered by this Annex.

2. Domestic Regulation

(a)   Notwithstanding any other provisions of the Agreement, a Member shall not be prevented from taking measures for prudential reasons, including for the protection of investors, depositors, policy holders or persons to whom a fiduciary duty is owed by a financial service supplier, or to ensure the integrity and stability of the financial system. Where such measures do not conform with the provisions of the Agreement, they shall not be used as a means of avoiding the Member's commitments or obligations under the Agreement.

(b)   Nothing in the Agreement shall be construed to require a Member to disclose information relating to the affairs and accounts of individual customers or any confidential or proprietary information in the possession of public entities.

3. Recognition

(a)   A Member may recognize prudential measures of any other country in determining how the Member's measures relating to financial services shall be applied. Such recognition, which may be achieved through harmonization or otherwise, may be based upon an agreement or arrangement with the country concerned or may be accorded autonomously.

(b)   A Member that is a party to such an agreement or arrangement referred to in subparagraph (a), whether future or existing, shall afford adequate opportunity for other interested Members to negotiate their accession to such agreements or arrangements, or to negotiate comparable ones with it, under circumstances in which there would be equivalent regulation, oversight, implementation of such regulation, and, if appropriate, procedures concerning the sharing of information between the parties to the agreement or arrangement. Where a Member accords recognition autonomously, it shall afford adequate opportunity for any other Member to demonstrate that such circumstances exist.

(c)   Where a Member is contemplating according recognition to prudential measures of any other country, paragraph 4(b) of Article VII shall not apply.

4. Dispute Settlement

Panels for disputes on prudential issues and other financial matters shall have the necessary expertise relevant to the specific financial service under dispute.

5. Definitions

For the purposes of this Annex:

(a)   A financial service is any service of a financial nature offered by a financial service supplier of a Member. Financial services include all insurance and insurance-related services, and all banking and other financial services (excluding insurance). Financial services include the following activities:

Insurance and insurance-related services

    (i)   Direct insurance (including co-insurance):

        (A) life

        (B) non-life

    (ii)   Reinsurance and retrocession;

    (iii) Insurance intermediation, such as brokerage and agency;

    (iv) Services auxiliary to insurance, such as consultancy, actuarial, risk assessment and claim settlement services.

Banking and other financial services (excluding insurance)

    (v)   Acceptance of deposits and other repayable funds from the public;

    (vi) Lending of all types, including consumer credit, mortgage credit, factoring and financing of commercial transaction;

    (vii) Financial leasing;

    (viii) All payment and money transmission services, including credit, charge and debit cards, travellers cheques and bankers drafts;

    (ix) Guarantees and commitments;

    (x)   Trading for own account or for account of customers, whether on an exchange, in an over-the-counter market or otherwise, the following:

        (A) money market instruments (including cheques, bills, certificates of deposits);

        (B) foreign exchange;

        (C) derivative products including, but not limited to, futures and options;

        (D) exchange rate and interest rate instruments, including products such as swaps, forward rate agreements;

        (E) transferable securities;

        (F) other negotiable instruments and financial assets, including bullion.

    (xi) Participation in issues of all kinds of securities, including underwriting and placement as agent (whether publicly or privately) and provision of services related to such issues;

    (xii) Money broking;

    (xiii) Asset management, such as cash or portfolio management, all forms of collective investment management, pension fund management, custodial, depository and trust services;

    (xiv) Settlement and clearing services for financial assets, including securities, derivative products, and other negotiable instruments;

    (xv) Provision and transfer of financial information, and financial data processing and related software by suppliers of other financial services;

    (xvi) Advisory, intermediation and other auxiliary financial services on all the activities listed in subparagraphs (v) through (xv), including credit reference and analysis, investment and portfolio research and advice, advice on acquisitions and on corporate restructuring and strategy.

(b) A financial service supplier means any natural or juridical person of a Member wishing to supply or supplying financial services but the term "financial service supplier" does not include a public entity.

(c)   "Public entity" means:

   (i)   a government, a central bank or a monetary authority, of a Member, or an entity owned or controlled by a Member, that is principally engaged in carrying out governmental functions or activities for governmental purposes, not including an entity principally engaged in supplying financial services on commercial terms; or

   (ii)   a private entity, performing functions normally performed by a central bank or monetary authority, when exercising those functions.

SECOND ANNEX ON FINANCIAL SERVICES

1.   Notwithstanding Article II of the Agreement and paragraphs 1 and 2 of the Annex on Article II Exemptions, a Member may, during a period of 60 days beginning four months after the date of entry into force of the WTO Agreement, list in that Annex measures relating to financial services which are inconsistent with paragraph 1 of Article II of the Agreement.

2.   Notwithstanding Article XXI of the Agreement, a Member may, during a period of 60 days beginning four months after the date of entry into force of the WTO Agreement, improve, modify or withdraw all or part of the specific commitments on financial services inscribed in its Schedule.

3.   The Council for Trade in Services shall establish any procedures necessary for the application of paragraphs 1 and 2.

ANNEX ON NEGOTIATIONS ON MARITIME TRANSPORT SERVICES

1.   Article II and the Annex on Article II Exemptions, including the requirement to list in the Annex any measure inconsistent with most-favoured-nation treatment that a Member will maintain, shall enter into force for international shipping, auxiliary services and access to and use of port facilities only on:

(a)   the implementation date to be determined under paragraph 4 of the Ministerial Decision on Negotiations on Maritime Transport Services; or,

(b)   should the negotiations not succeed, the date of the final report of the Negotiating Group on Maritime Transport Services provided for in that Decision.

2.   Paragraph 1 shall not apply to any specific commitment on maritime transport services which is inscribed in a Member's Schedule.

3.   From the conclusion of the negotiations referred to in paragraph 1, and before the implementation date, a Member may improve, modify or withdraw all or part of its specific commitments in this sector without offering compensation, notwithstanding the provisions of Article XXI.

ANNEX ON TELECOMMUNICATIONS

1. Objectives

Recognizing the specificities of the telecommunications services sector and, in particular, its dual role as a distinct sector of economic activity and as the underlying transport means for other economic activities, the Members have agreed to the following Annex with the objective of elaborating upon the provisions of the Agreement with respect to measures affecting access to and use of public telecommunications transport networks and services. Accordingly, this Annex provides notes and supplementary provisions to the Agreement.

2. Scope

(a)   This Annex shall apply to all measures of a Member that affect access to and use of public telecommunications transport networks and services.[14]

(b)   This Annex shall not apply to measures affecting the cable or broadcast distribution of radio or television programming.

(c)   Nothing in this Annex shall be construed:

(i)   to require a Member to authorize a service supplier of any other Member to establish, construct, acquire, lease, operate, or supply telecommunications transport networks or services, other than as provided for in its Schedule; or

(ii)   to require a Member (or to require a Member to oblige service suppliers under its jurisdiction) to establish, construct, acquire, lease, operate or supply telecommunications transport networks or services not offered to the public generally.

3. Definitions

For the purposes of this Annex:

(a)   "Telecommunications" means the transmission and reception of signals by any electromagnetic means.

(b)   "Public telecommunications transport service" means any telecommunications transport service required, explicitly or in effect, by a Member to be offered to the public generally. Such services may include, inter alia, telegraph, telephone, telex, and data transmission typically involving the real-time transmission of customer-supplied information between two or more points without any end-to-end change in the form or content of the customer's information.

(c)   "Public telecommunications transport network" means the public telecommunications infrastructure which permits telecommunications between and among defined network termination points.

(d)   "Intra-corporate communications" means telecommunications through which a company communicates within the company or with or among its subsidiaries, branches and, subject to a Member's domestic laws and regulations, affiliates. For these purposes, "subsidiaries", "branches" and, where applicable, "affiliates" shall be as defined by each Member. "Intra-corporate communications" in this Annex excludes commercial or non-commercial services that are supplied to companies that are not related subsidiaries, branches or affiliates, or that are offered to customers or potential customers.

(e)   Any reference to a paragraph or subparagraph of this Annex includes all subdivisions thereof.

4. Transparency

In the application of Article III of the Agreement, each Member shall ensure that relevant information on conditions affecting access to and use of public telecommunications transport networks and services is publicly available, including: tariffs and other terms and conditions of service; specifications of technical interfaces with such networks and services; information on bodies responsible for the preparation and adoption of standards affecting such access and use; conditions applying to attachment of terminal or other equipment; and notifications, registration or licensing requirements, if any.

---

14   This paragraph is understood to mean that each Member shall ensure that the obligations of this Annex are applied with respect to suppliers of public telecommunications transport networks and services by whatever measures are necessary.

5. Access to and Use of Public Telecommunications Transport Networks and Services

(a)   Each Member shall ensure that any service supplier of any other Member is accorded access to and use of public telecommunications transport networks and services on reasonable and non-discriminatory terms and conditions, for the supply of a service included in its Schedule. This obligation shall be applied, *inter alia*, through paragraphs (b) through (f).[15]

(b)   Each Member shall ensure that service suppliers of any other Member have access to and use of any public telecommunications transport network or service offered within or across the border of that Member, including private leased circuits, and to this end shall ensure, subject to paragraphs (e) and (f), that such suppliers are permitted:

   (i)   to purchase or lease and attach terminal or other equipment which interfaces with the network and which is necessary to supply a supplier's services;

   (ii)   to interconnect private leased or owned circuits with public telecommunications transport networks and services or with circuits leased or owned by another service supplier; and

   (iii) to use operating protocols of the service supplier's choice in the supply of any service, other than as necessary to ensure the availability of telecommunications transport networks and services to the public generally.

(c)   Each Member shall ensure that service suppliers of any other Member may use public telecommunications transport networks and services for the movement of information within and across borders, including for intra-corporate communications of such service suppliers, and for access to information contained in data bases or otherwise stored in machine-readable form in the territory of any Member. Any new or amended measures of a Member significantly affecting such use shall be notified and shall be subject to consultation, in accordance with relevant provisions of the Agreement.

(d)   Notwithstanding the preceding paragraph, a Member may take such measures as are necessary to ensure the security and confidentiality of messages, subject to the requirement that such measures are not applied in a manner which would constitute a means of arbitrary or unjustifiable discrimination or a disguised restriction on trade in services.

(e)   Each Member shall ensure that no condition is imposed on access to and use of public telecommunications transport networks and services other than as necessary:

   (i)   to safeguard the public service responsibilities of suppliers of public telecommunications transport networks and services, in particular their ability to make their networks or services available to the public generally;

   (ii)   to protect the technical integrity of public telecommunications transport networks or services; or

   (iii) to ensure that service suppliers of any other Member do not supply services unless permitted pursuant to commitments in the Member's Schedule.

(f)   Provided that they satisfy the criteria set out in paragraph (e), conditions for access to and use of public telecommunications transport networks and services may include:

   (i)   restrictions on resale or shared use of such services;

   (ii)   a requirement to use specified technical interfaces, including interface protocols, for inter-connection with such networks and services;

---

15   The term "non-discriminatory" is understood to refer to most-favoured-nation and national treatment as defined in the Agreement, as well as to reflect sector-specific usage of the term to mean "terms and conditions no less favourable than those accorded to any other user of like public telecommunications transport networks or services under like circumstances".

(iii) requirements, where necessary, for the inter-operability of such services and to encourage the achievement of the goals set out in paragraph 7(a);

(iv) type approval of terminal or other equipment which interfaces with the network and technical requirements relating to the attachment of such equipment to such networks;

(v) restrictions on inter-connection of private leased or owned circuits with such networks or services or with circuits leased or owned by another service supplier; or

(vi) notification, registration and licensing.

(g) Notwithstanding the preceding paragraphs of this section, a developing country Member may, consistent with its level of development, place reasonable conditions on access to and use of public telecommunications transport networks and services necessary to strengthen its domestic telecommunications infrastructure and service capacity and to increase its participation in international trade in telecommunications services. Such conditions shall be specified in the Member's Schedule.

6. Technical Cooperation

(a) Members recognize that an efficient, advanced telecommunications infrastructure in countries, particularly developing countries, is essential to the expansion of their trade in services. To this end, Members endorse and encourage the participation, to the fullest extent practicable, of developed and developing countries and their suppliers of public telecommunications transport networks and services and other entities in the development programmes of international and regional organizations, including the International Telecommunication Union, the United Nations Development Programme, and the International Bank for Reconstruction and Development.

(b) Members shall encourage and support telecommunications cooperation among developing countries at the international, regional and sub-regional levels.

(c) In cooperation with relevant international organizations, Members shall make available, where practicable, to developing countries information with respect to telecommunications services and developments in telecommunications and information technology to assist in strengthening their domestic telecommunications services sector.

(d) Members shall give special consideration to opportunities for the least-developed countries to encourage foreign suppliers of telecommunications services to assist in the transfer of technology, training and other activities that support the development of their telecommunications infrastructure and expansion of their telecommunications services trade.

7. Relation to International Organizations and Agreements

(a) Members recognize the importance of international standards for global compatibility and inter-operability of telecommunication networks and services and undertake to promote such standards through the work of relevant international bodies, including the International Telecommunication Union and the International Organization for Standardization.

(b) Members recognize the role played by intergovernmental and non-governmental organizations and agreements in ensuring the efficient operation of domestic and global telecommunications services, in particular the International Telecommunication Union. Members shall make appropriate arrangements, where relevant, for consultation with such organizations on matters arising from the implementation of this Annex.

ANNEX ON NEGOTIATIONS ON BASIC TELECOMMUNICATIONS

1.   Article II and the Annex on Article II Exemptions, including the requirement to list in the Annex any measure inconsistent with most-favoured-nation treatment that a Member will maintain, shall enter into force for basic telecommunications only on:

(a)   the implementation date to be determined under paragraph 5 of the Ministerial Decision on Negotiations on Basic Telecommunications; or,

(b)   should the negotiations not succeed, the date of the final report of the Negotiating Group on Basic Telecommunications provided for in that Decision.

2.   Paragraph 1 shall not apply to any specific commitment on basic telecommunications which is inscribed in a Member's Schedule.

XII.3. ANNEX 1c

Agreement on Trade-Related Aspects of
Intellectual Property Rights (TRIPs)

PART I   GENERAL PROVISIONS AND BASIC PRINCIPLES
PART II   STANDARDS CONCERNING THE AVAILABILITY, SCOPE AND USE OF INTELLECTUAL PROPERTY
           RIGHTS
    1.   Copyright and Related Rights
    2.   Trademarks
    3.   Geographical Indications
    4.   Industrial Designs
    5.   Patents
    6.   Layout-Designs (Topographies) of Integrated Circuits
    7.   Protection of Undisclosed Information
    8.   Control of Anti-Competitive Practices in Contractual Licences
PART III   ENFORCEMENT OF INTELLECTUAL PROPERTY RIGHTS
    1.   General Obligations
    2.   Civil and Administrative Procedures and Remedies
    3.   Provisional Measures
    4.   Special Requirements Related to Border Measures
    5.   Criminal Procedures
PART IV   ACQUISITION AND MAINTENANCE OF INTELLECTUAL PROPERTY RIGHTS AND RELATED
           INTER-PARTES PROCEDURES
PART V   DISPUTE PREVENTION AND SETTLEMENT
PART VI   TRANSITIONAL ARRANGEMENTS
PART VII   INSTITUTIONAL ARRANGEMENTS; FINAL PROVISIONS

Agreement on Trade-Related Aspects of
Intellectual Property Rights (TRIPs)

Members,

Desiring to reduce distortions and impediments to international trade, and taking into account the need to promote effective and adequate protection of intellectual property rights, and to ensure that measures and procedures to enforce intellectual property rights do not themselves become barriers to legitimate trade;

Recognizing, to this end, the need for new rules and disciplines concerning:

(a) the applicability of the basic principles of GATT 1994 and of relevant international intellectual property agreements or conventions;

(b) the provision of adequate standards and principles concerning the availability, scope and use of trade-related intellectual property rights;

(c) the provision of effective and appropriate means for the enforcement of trade-related intellectual property rights, taking into account differences in national legal systems;

(d) the provision of effective and expeditious procedures for the multilateral prevention and settlement of disputes between governments; and

(e) transitional arrangements aiming at the fullest participation in the results of the negotiations;

Recognizing the need for a multilateral framework of principles, rules and disciplines dealing with international trade in counterfeit goods;

Recognizing that intellectual property rights are private rights;

Recognizing the underlying public policy objectives of national systems for the protection of intellectual property, including developmental and technological objectives;

Recognizing also the special needs of the least-developed country Members in respect of maximum flexibility in the domestic implementation of laws and regulations in order to enable them to create a sound and viable technological base;

Emphasizing the importance of reducing tensions by reaching strengthened commitments to resolve disputes on trade-related intellectual property issues through multilateral procedures;

Desiring to establish a mutually supportive relationship between the WTO and the World Intellectual Property Organization (referred to in this Agreement as "WIPO") as well as other relevant international organizations;

Hereby agree as follows:

PART I – GENERAL PROVISIONS AND BASIC PRINCIPLES

Article 1 Nature and Scope of Obligations

1.   Members shall give effect to the provisions of this Agreement. Members may, but shall not be obliged to, implement in their law more extensive protection than is required by this Agreement, provided that such protection does not contravene the provisions of this Agreement. Members shall be free to determine the appropriate method of implementing the provisions of this Agreement within their own legal system and practice.

2.   For the purposes of this Agreement, the term "intellectual property" refers to all categories of intellectual property that are the subject of Sections 1 through 7 of Part II.

3.   Members shall accord the treatment provided for in this Agreement to the nationals of other Members.[1] In respect of the relevant intellectual property right, the nationals of other Members shall be understood as those natural or legal persons that would meet the criteria for eligibility for protection provided for in the Paris Convention (1967), the Berne Convention (1971), the Rome Convention and the Treaty on Intellectual Property in Respect of Integrated Circuits, were all Members of the WTO members of those conventions.[2] Any Member availing itself of the possibilities provided in paragraph 3 of Article 5 or paragraph 2 of Article 6 of the Rome Convention shall make a notification as foreseen in those provisions to the Council for Trade-Related Aspects of Intellectual Property Rights (the "Council for TRIPS").

Article 2 Intellectual Property Conventions

1.   In respect of Parts II, III and IV of this Agreement, Members shall comply with Articles 1 through 12, and Article 19, of the Paris Convention (1967).

2.   Nothing in Parts I to IV of this Agreement shall derogate from existing obligations that Members may have to each other under the Paris Convention, the Berne Convention, the Rome Convention and the Treaty on Intellectual Property in Respect of Integrated Circuits.

---

1   When "nationals" are referred to in this Agreement, they shall be deemed, in the case of a separate customs territory Member of the WTO, to mean persons, natural or legal, who are domiciled or who have a real and effective industrial or commercial establishment in that customs territory.

2   In this Agreement, "Paris Convention" refers to the Paris Convention for the Protection of Industrial Property; "Paris Convention (1967)" refers to the Stockholm Act of this Convention of 14 July 1967. "Berne Convention" refers to the Berne Convention for the Protection of Literary and Artistic Works; "Berne Convention (1971)" refers to the Paris Act of this Convention of 24 July 1971. "Rome Convention" refers to the International Convention for the Protection of Performers, Producers of Phonograms and Broadcasting Organizations, adopted at Rome on 26 October 1961. "Treaty on Intellectual Property in Respect of Integrated Circuits" (IPIC Treaty) refers to the Treaty on Intellectual Property in Respect of Integrated Circuits, adopted at Washington on 26 May 1989. "WTO Agreement" refers to the Agreement Establishing the WTO.

Article 3 National Treatment

1.   Each Member shall accord to the nationals of other Members treatment no less favourable than that it accords to its own nationals with regard to the protection[3] of intellectual property, subject to the exceptions already provided in, respectively, the Paris Convention (1967), the Berne Convention (1971), the Rome Convention or the Treaty on Intellectual Property in Respect of Integrated Circuits. In respect of performers, producers of phonograms and broadcasting organizations, this obligation only applies in respect of the rights provided under this Agreement. Any Member availing itself of the possibilities provided in Article 6 of the Berne Convention (1971) or paragraph 1(b) of Article 16 of the Rome Convention shall make a notification as foreseen in those provisions to the Council for TRIPS.

2.   Members may avail themselves of the exceptions permitted under paragraph 1 in relation to judicial and administrative procedures, including the designation of an address for service or the appointment of an agent within the jurisdiction of a Member, only where such exceptions are necessary to secure compliance with laws and regulations which are not inconsistent with the provisions of this Agreement and where such practices are not applied in a manner which would constitute a disguised restriction on trade.

Article 4 Most-Favoured-Nation Treatment

With regard to the protection of intellectual property, any advantage, favour, privilege or immunity granted by a Member to the nationals of any other country shall be accorded immediately and unconditionally to the nationals of all other Members. Exempted from this obligation are any advantage, favour, privilege or immunity accorded by a Member:

(a)   deriving from international agreements on judicial assistance or law enforcement of a general nature and not particularly confined to the protection of intellectual property;

(b)   granted in accordance with the provisions of the Berne Convention (1971) or the Rome Convention authorizing that the treatment accorded be a function not of national treatment but of the treatment accorded in another country;

(c)   in respect of the rights of performers, producers of phonograms and broadcasting organizations not provided under this Agreement;

(d)   deriving from international agreements related to the protection of intellectual property which entered into force prior to the entry into force of the WTO Agreement, provided that such agreements are notified to the Council for TRIPS and do not constitute an arbitrary or unjustifiable discrimination against nationals of other Members.

Article 5 Multilateral Agreements on Acquisition or Maintenance of Protection

The obligations under Articles 3 and 4 do not apply to procedures provided in multilateral agreements concluded under the auspices of WIPO relating to the acquisition or maintenance of intellectual property rights.

Article 6 Exhaustion

For the purposes of dispute settlement under this Agreement, subject to the provisions of Articles 3 and 4 nothing in this Agreement shall be used to address the issue of the exhaustion of intellectual property rights.

---

3   For the purposes of Articles 3 and 4, "protection" shall include matters affecting the availability, acquisition, scope, maintenance and enforcement of intellectual property rights as well as those matters affecting the use of intellectual property rights specifically addressed in this Agreement.

Article 7 Objectives

The protection and enforcement of intellectual property rights should contribute to the promotion of technological innovation and to the transfer and dissemination of technology, to the mutual advantage of producers and users of technological knowledge and in a manner conducive to social and economic welfare, and to a balance of rights and obligations.

Article 8 Principles

1.   Members may, in formulating or amending their laws and regulations, adopt measures necessary to protect public health and nutrition, and to promote the public interest in sectors of vital importance to their socio-economic and technological development, provided that such measures are consistent with the provisions of this Agreement.

2.   Appropriate measures, provided that they are consistent with the provisions of this Agreement, may be needed to prevent the abuse of intellectual property rights by right holders or the resort to practices which unreasonably restrain trade or adversely affect the international transfer of technology.

PART II – STANDARDS CONCERNING THE AVAILABILITY, SCOPE AND USE OF INTELLECTUAL PROPERTY RIGHTS

SECTION 1: COPYRIGHT AND RELATED RIGHTS

Article 9 Relation to the Berne Convention

1.   Members shall comply with Articles 1 through 21 of the Berne Convention (1971) and the Appendix thereto. However, Members shall not have rights or obligations under this Agreement in respect of the rights conferred under Article 6bis of that Convention or of the rights derived therefrom.

2.   Copyright protection shall extend to expressions and not to ideas, procedures, methods of operation or mathematical concepts as such.

Article 10 Computer Programs and Compilations of Data

1.   Computer programs, whether in source or object code, shall be protected as literary works under the Berne Convention (1971).

2.   Compilations of data or other material, whether in machine readable or other form, which by reason of the selection or arrangement of their contents constitute intellectual creations shall be protected as such. Such protection, which shall not extend to the data or material itself, shall be without prejudice to any copyright subsisting in the data or material itself.

Article 11 Rental Rights

In respect of at least computer programs and cinematographic works, a Member shall provide authors and their successors in title the right to authorize or to prohibit the commercial rental to the public of originals or copies of their copyright works. A Member shall be excepted from this obligation in respect of cinematographic works unless such rental has led to widespread copying of such works which is materially impairing the exclusive right of reproduction conferred in that Member on authors and their successors in title. In respect of computer programs, this obligation does not apply to rentals where the program itself is not the essential object of the rental.

Article 12 Term of Protection

Whenever the term of protection of a work, other than a photographic work or a work of applied art, is calculated on a basis other than the life of a natural person, such term shall be no less than 50 years from the end of the calendar year of authorized publication, or, failing such authorized publication within 50 years from the making of the work, 50 years from the end of the calendar year of making.

Article 13 Limitations and Exceptions

Members shall confine limitations or exceptions to exclusive rights to certain special cases which do not conflict with a normal exploitation of the work and do not unreasonably prejudice the legitimate interests of the right holder.

Article 14 Protection of Performers, Producers of Phonograms (Sound Recordings) and Broadcasting Organizations

1.   In respect of a fixation of their performance on a phonogram, performers shall have the possibility of preventing the following acts when undertaken without their authorization: the fixation of their unfixed performance and the reproduction of such fixation. Performers shall also have the possibility of preventing the following acts when undertaken without their authorization: the broadcasting by wireless means and the communication to the public of their live performance.

2.   Producers of phonograms shall enjoy the right to authorize or prohibit the direct or indirect reproduction of their phonograms.

3.   Broadcasting organizations shall have the right to prohibit the following acts when undertaken without their authorization: the fixation, the reproduction of fixations, and the rebroadcasting by wireless means of broadcasts, as well as the communication to the public of television broadcasts of the same. Where Members do not grant such rights to broadcasting organizations, they shall provide owners of copyright in the subject matter of broadcasts with the possibility of preventing the above acts, subject to the provisions of the Berne Convention (1971).

4.   The provisions of Article 11 in respect of computer programs shall apply *mutatis mutandis* to producers of phonograms and any other right holders in phonograms as determined in a Member's law. If on 15 April 1994 a Member has in force a system of equitable remuneration of right holders in respect of the rental of phonograms, it may maintain such system provided that the commercial rental of phonograms is not giving rise to the material impairment of the exclusive rights of reproduction of right holders.

5.   The term of the protection available under this Agreement to performers and producers of phonograms shall last at least until the end of a period of 50 years computed from the end of the calendar year in which the fixation was made or the performance took place. The term of protection granted pursuant to paragraph 3 shall last for at least 20 years from the end of the calendar year in which the broadcast took place.

6.   Any Member may, in relation to the rights conferred under paragraphs 1, 2 and 3, provide for conditions, limitations, exceptions and reservations to the extent permitted by the Rome Convention. However, the provisions of Article 18 of the Berne Convention (1971) shall also apply, *mutatis mutandis*, to the rights of performers and producers of phonograms in phonograms.

SECTION 2: TRADEMARKS

Article 15 Protectable Subject Matter

1.   Any sign, or any combination of signs, capable of distinguishing the goods or services of one undertaking from those of other undertakings, shall be capable of constituting a trademark. Such signs, in particular words including personal names, letters, numerals, figurative elements and combinations of colours as well as any combination of such signs, shall be eligible for registration as trademarks. Where signs are not inherently capable of distinguishing the relevant goods or services, Members may make registrability depend on distinctiveness acquired through use. Members may require, as a condition of registration, that signs be visually perceptible.

2.   Paragraph 1 shall not be understood to prevent a Member from denying registration of a trademark on other grounds, provided that they do not derogate from the provisions of the Paris Convention (1967).

3.   Members may make registrability depend on use. However, actual use of a trademark shall not be a condition for filing an application for registration. An application shall not be refused solely on the ground that intended use has not taken place before the expiry of a period of three years from the date of application.

4.   The nature of the goods or services to which a trademark is to be applied shall in no case form an obstacle to registration of the trademark.

5.   Members shall publish each trademark either before it is registered or promptly after it is registered and shall afford a reasonable opportunity for petitions to cancel the registration. In addition, Members may afford an opportunity for the registration of a trademark to be opposed.

Article 16 Rights Conferred

1.   The owner of a registered trademark shall have the exclusive right to prevent all third parties not having the owner's consent from using in the course of trade identical or similar signs for goods or services which are identical or similar to those in respect of which the trademark is registered where such use would result in a likelihood of confusion. In case of the use of an identical sign for identical goods or services, a likelihood of confusion shall be presumed. The rights described above shall not prejudice any existing prior rights, nor shall they affect the possibility of Members making rights available on the basis of use.

2.   Article 6*bis* of the Paris Convention (1967) shall apply, *mutatis mutandis*, to services. In determining whether a trademark is well-known, Members shall take account of the knowledge of the trademark in the relevant sector of the public, including knowledge in the Member concerned which has been obtained as a result of the promotion of the trademark.

3.   Article 6*bis* of the Paris Convention (1967) shall apply, *mutatis mutandis*, to goods or services which are not similar to those in respect of which a trademark is registered, provided that use of that trademark in relation to those goods or services would indicate a connection between those goods or services and the owner of the registered trademark and provided that the interests of the owner of the registered trademark are likely to be damaged by such use.

Article 17 Exceptions

Members may provide limited exceptions to the rights conferred by a trademark, such as fair use of descriptive terms, provided that such exceptions take account of the legitimate interests of the owner of the trademark and of third parties.

Article 18 Term of Protection

Initial registration, and each renewal of registration, of a trademark shall be for a term of no less than seven years. The registration of a trademark shall be renewable indefinitely.

Article 19 Requirement of Use

1.   If use is required to maintain a registration, the registration may be cancelled only after an uninterrupted period of at least three years of non-use, unless valid reasons based on the existence of obstacles to such use are shown by the trademark owner. Circumstances arising independently of the will of the owner of the trademark which constitute an obstacle to the use of the trademark, such as import restrictions on or other government requirements for goods or services protected by the trademark, shall be recognized as valid reasons for non-use.

2.   When subject to the control of its owner, use of a trademark by another person shall be recognized as use of the trademark for the purpose of maintaining the registration.

Article 20 Other Requirements

The use of a trademark in the course of trade shall not be unjustifiably encumbered by special requirements, such as use with another trademark, use in a special form or use in a manner detrimental to its capability to distinguish the goods or services of one undertaking from those of other undertakings. This will not preclude a requirement prescribing the use of the trademark identifying the undertaking producing the goods or services along with, but without linking it to, the trademark distinguishing the specific goods or services in question of that undertaking.

Article 21 Licensing and Assignment

Members may determine conditions on the licensing and assignment of trademarks, it being understood that the compulsory licensing of trademarks shall not be permitted and that the owner of a registered trademark shall have the right to assign the trademark with or without the transfer of the business to which the trademark belongs.

SECTION 3: GEOGRAPHICAL INDICATIONS

Article 22 Protection of Geographical Indications

1.   Geographical indications are, for the purposes of this Agreement, indications which identify a good as originating in the territory of a Member, or a region or locality in that territory, where a given quality, reputation or other characteristic of the good is essentially attributable to its geographical origin.

2.   In respect of geographical indications, Members shall provide the legal means for interested parties to prevent:

(a)   the use of any means in the designation or presentation of a good that indicates or suggests that the good in question originates in a geographical area other than the true place of origin in a manner which misleads the public as to the geographical origin of the good;

(b)   any use which constitutes an act of unfair competition within the meaning of Article 10*bis* of the Paris Convention (1967).

3.   A Member shall, *ex officio* if its legislation so permits or at the request of an interested party, refuse or invalidate the registration of a trademark which contains or consists of a geographical indication with respect to goods not originating in the territory indicated, if use of the indication in the trademark for such goods in that Member is of such a nature as to mislead the public as to the true place of origin.

4.   The protection under paragraphs 1, 2 and 3 shall be applicable against a geographical indication which, although literally true as to the territory, region or locality in which the goods originate, falsely represents to the public that the goods originate in another territory.

Article 23 Additional Protection for Geographical Indications for Wines and Spirits

1.   Each Member shall provide the legal means for interested parties to prevent use of a geographical indication identifying wines for wines not originating in the place indicated by the geographical indication in question or identifying spirits for spirits not originating in the place indicated by the geographical indication in question, even where the true origin of the goods is indicated or the geographical indication is used in translation or accompanied by expressions such as "kind", "type", "style", "imitation" or the like.[4]

2.   The registration of a trademark for wines which contains or consists of a geographical indication identifying wines or for spirits which contains or consists of a geographical indication identifying spirits shall be refused or invalidated, *ex officio* if a Member's legislation so permits or at the request of an interested party, with respect to such wines or spirits not having this origin.

3.   In the case of homonymous geographical indications for wines, protection shall be accorded to each indication, subject to the provisions of paragraph 4 of Article 22. Each Member shall determine the practical conditions under which the homonymous indications in question will be differentiated from each other, taking into account the need to ensure equitable treatment of the producers concerned and that consumers are not misled.

---

4   Notwithstanding the first sentence of Article 42, Members may, with respect to these obligations, instead provide for enforcement by administrative action.

4.   In order to facilitate the protection of geographical indications for wines, negotiations shall be undertaken in the Council for TRIPS concerning the establishment of a multilateral system of notification and registration of geographical indications for wines eligible for protection in those Members participating in the system.

Article 24 International Negotiations; Exceptions

1.   Members agree to enter into negotiations aimed at increasing the protection of individual geographical indications under Article 23. The provisions of paragraphs 4 through 8 below shall not be used by a Member to refuse to conduct negotiations or to conclude bilateral or multi-lateral agreements. In the context of such negotiations, Members shall be willing to consider the continued applicability of these provisions to individual geographical indications whose use was the subject of such negotiations.

2.   The Council for TRIPS shall keep under review the application of the provisions of this Section; the first such review shall take place within two years of the entry into force of the WTO Agreement. Any matter affecting the compliance with the obligations under these provisions may be drawn to the attention of the Council, which, at the request of a Member, shall consult with any Member or Members in respect of such matter in respect of which it has not been possible to find a satisfactory solution through bilateral or plurilateral consultations between the Members concerned. The Council shall take such action as may be agreed to facilitate the operation and further the objectives of this Section.

3.   In implementing this Section, a Member shall not diminish the protection of geographical indications that existed in that Member immediately prior to the date of entry into force of the WTO Agreement.

4.   Nothing in this Section shall require a Member to prevent continued and similar use of a particular geographical indication of another Member identifying wines or spirits in connection with goods or services by any of its nationals or domiciliaries who have used that geographical indication in a continuous manner with regard to the same or related goods or services in the territory of that Member either (a) for at least 10 years preceding 15 April 1994 or (b) in good faith preceding that date.

5.   Where a trademark has been applied for or registered in good faith, or where rights to a trademark have been acquired through use in good faith either:

(a)   before the date of application of these provisions in that Member as defined in Part VI; or

(b)   before the geographical indication is protected in its country of origin;

measures adopted to implement this Section shall not prejudice eligibility for or the validity of the registration of a trademark, or the right to use a trademark, on the basis that such a trade-mark is identical with, or similar to, a geographical indication.

6.   Nothing in this Section shall require a Member to apply its provisions in respect of a geographical indication of any other Member with respect to goods or services for which the relevant indication is identical with the term customary in common language as the common name for such goods or services in the territory of that Member. Nothing in this Section shall require a Member to apply its provisions in respect of a geographical indication of any other Member with respect to products of the vine for which the relevant indication is identical with the customary name of a grape variety existing in the territory of that Member as of the date of entry into force of the WTO Agreement.

7.   A Member may provide that any request made under this Section in connection with the use or registration of a trademark must be presented within five years after the adverse use of the protected indication has become generally known in that Member or after the date of regis-tration of the trademark in that Member provided that the trademark has been published by that

date, if such date is earlier than the date on which the adverse use became generally known in that Member, provided that the geographical indication is not used or registered in bad faith.

8.   The provisions of this Section shall in no way prejudice the right of any person to use, in the course of trade, that person's name or the name of that person's predecessor in business, except where such name is used in such a manner as to mislead the public.

9.   There shall be no obligation under this Agreement to protect geographical indications which are not or cease to be protected in their country of origin, or which have fallen into disuse in that country.

SECTION 4: INDUSTRIAL DESIGNS

Article 25 Requirements for Protection

1.   Members shall provide for the protection of independently created industrial designs that are new or original. Members may provide that designs are not new or original if they do not significantly differ from known designs or combinations of known design features. Members may provide that such protection shall not extend to designs dictated essentially by technical or functional considerations.

2.   Each Member shall ensure that requirements for securing protection for textile designs, in particular in regard to any cost, examination or publication, do not unreasonably impair the opportunity to seek and obtain such protection. Members shall be free to meet this obligation through industrial design law or through copyright law.

Article 26 Protection

1.   The owner of a protected industrial design shall have the right to prevent third parties not having the owner's consent from making, selling or importing articles bearing or embodying a design which is a copy, or substantially a copy, of the protected design, when such acts are undertaken for commercial purposes.

2.   Members may provide limited exceptions to the protection of industrial designs, provided that such exceptions do not unreasonably conflict with the normal exploitation of protected industrial designs and do not unreasonably prejudice the legitimate interests of the owner of the protected design, taking account of the legitimate interests of third parties.

3.   The duration of protection available shall amount to at least 10 years.

SECTION 5: PATENTS

Article 27 Patentable Subject Matter

1.   Subject to the provisions of paragraphs 2 and 3, patents shall be available for any inventions, whether products or processes, in all fields of technology, provided that they are new, involve an inventive step and are capable of industrial application.[5] Subject to paragraph 4 of Article 65, paragraph 8 of Article 70 and paragraph 3 of this Article, patents shall be available and patent rights enjoyable without discrimination as to the place of invention, the field of technology and whether products are imported or locally produced.

2.   Members may exclude from patentability inventions, the prevention within their territory of the commercial exploitation of which is necessary to protect *ordre public* or morality, including to protect human, animal or plant life or health or to avoid serious prejudice to the environment, provided that such exclusion is not made merely because the exploitation is prohibited by their law.

---

5   For the purposes of this Article, the terms "inventive step" and "capable of industrial application" may be deemed by a Member to be synonymous with the terms "non-obvious" and "useful" respectively.

3.   Members may also exclude from patentability:

(a)   diagnostic, therapeutic and surgical methods for the treatment of humans or animals;

(b)   plants and animals other than micro-organisms, and essentially biological processes for the production of plants or animals other than non-biological and microbiological processes. However, Members shall provide for the protection of plant varieties either by patents or by an effective *sui generis* system or by any combination thereof. The provisions of this sub-paragraph shall be reviewed four years after the date of entry into force of the WTO Agreement.

Article 28 Rights Conferred

1.   A patent shall confer on its owner the following exclusive rights:

(a)   where the subject matter of a patent is a product, to prevent third parties not having the owner's consent from the acts of: making, using, offering for sale, selling, or importing[6] for these purposes that product;

(b)   where the subject matter of a patent is a process, to prevent third parties not having the owner's consent from the act of using the process, and from the acts of: using, offering for sale, selling, or importing for these purposes at least the product obtained directly by that process.

2.   Patent owners shall also have the right to assign, or transfer by succession, the patent and to conclude licensing contracts.

Article 29 Conditions on Patent Applicants

1.   Members shall require that an applicant for a patent shall disclose the invention in a manner sufficiently clear and complete for the invention to be carried out by a person skilled in the art and may require the applicant to indicate the best mode for carrying out the invention known to the inventor at the filing date or, where priority is claimed, at the priority date of the application.

2.   Members may require an applicant for a patent to provide information concerning the applicant's corresponding foreign applications and grants.

Article 30 Exceptions to Rights Conferred

Members may provide limited exceptions to the exclusive rights conferred by a patent, provided that such exceptions do not unreasonably conflict with a normal exploitation of the patent and do not unreasonably prejudice the legitimate interests of the patent owner, taking account of the legitimate interests of third parties.

Article 31 Other Use Without Authorization of the Right Holder

Where the law of a Member allows for other use[7] of the subject matter of a patent without the authorization of the right holder, including use by the government or third parties authorized by the government, the following provisions shall be respected:

(a)   authorization of such use shall be considered on its individual merits;

(b)   such use may only be permitted if, prior to such use, the proposed user has made efforts to obtain authorization from the right holder on reasonable commercial terms and conditions and that such efforts have not been successful within a reasonable period of time. This requirement may be waived by a Member in the case of a national emergency or other circumstances of extreme urgency or in cases of public non-commercial use. In situations of national emergency or other circumstances of extreme urgency, the right holder shall, nevertheless, be notified as soon as reasonably practicable. In the case of public non-com-

---

6   This right, like all other rights conferred under this Agreement in respect of the use, sale, importation or other distribution of goods, is subject to the provisions of Article 6.

7   "Other use" refers to use other than that allowed under Article 30.

mercial use, where the government or contractor, without making a patent search, knows or has demonstrable grounds to know that a valid patent is or will be used by or for the government, the right holder shall be informed promptly;

(c) the scope and duration of such use shall be limited to the purpose for which it was authorized, and in the case of semi-conductor technology shall only be for public non-commercial use or to remedy a practice determined after judicial or administrative process to be anti-competitive;

(d) such use shall be non-exclusive;

(e) such use shall be non-assignable, except with that part of the enterprise or goodwill which enjoys such use;

(f) any such use shall be authorized predominantly for the supply of the domestic market of the Member authorizing such use;

(g) authorization for such use shall be liable, subject to adequate protection of the legitimate interests of the persons so authorized, to be terminated if and when the circumstances which led to it cease to exist and are unlikely to recur. The competent authority shall have the authority to review, upon motivated request, the continued existence of these circumstances;

(h) the right holder shall be paid adequate remuneration in the circumstances of each case, taking into account the economic value of the authorization;

(i) the legal validity of any decision relating to the authorization of such use shall be subject to judicial review or other independent review by a distinct higher authority in that Member;

(j) any decision relating to the remuneration provided in respect of such use shall be subject to judicial review or other independent review by a distinct higher authority in that Member;

(k) Members are not obliged to apply the conditions set forth in subparagraphs (b) and (f) where such use is permitted to remedy a practice determined after judicial or administrative process to be anti-competitive. The need to correct anti-competitive practices may be taken into account in determining the amount of remuneration in such cases. Competent authorities shall have the authority to refuse termination of authorization if and when the conditions which led to such authorization are likely to recur;

(l) where such use is authorized to permit the exploitation of a patent ("the second patent") which cannot be exploited without infringing another patent ("the first patent"), the following additional conditions shall apply:

(i) the invention claimed in the second patent shall involve an important technical advance of considerable economic significance in relation to the invention claimed in the first patent;

(ii) the owner of the first patent shall be entitled to a cross-licence on reasonable terms to use the invention claimed in the second patent; and

(iii) the use authorized in respect of the first patent shall be non-assignable except with the assignment of the second patent.

Article 32 Revocation/Forfeiture

An opportunity for judicial review of any decision to revoke or forfeit a patent shall be available.

Article 33 Term of Protection

The term of protection available shall not end before the expiration of a period of twenty years counted from the filing date.[8]

---

8   It is understood that those Members which do not have a system of original grant may provide that the term of protection shall be computed from the filing date in the system of original grant.

Article 34 Process Patents: Burden of Proof

1.   For the purposes of civil proceedings in respect of the infringement of the rights of the owner referred to in paragraph 1(b) of Article 28, if the subject matter of a patent is a process for obtaining a product, the judicial authorities shall have the authority to order the defendant to prove that the process to obtain an identical product is different from the patented process. Therefore, Members shall provide, in at least one of the following circumstances, that any identical product when produced without the consent of the patent owner shall, in the absence of proof to the contrary, be deemed to have been obtained by the patented process:

(a)   if the product obtained by the patented process is new;

(b)   if there is a substantial likelihood that the identical product was made by the process and the owner of the patent has been unable through reasonable efforts to determine the process actually used.

2.   Any Member shall be free to provide that the burden of proof indicated in paragraph 1 shall be on the alleged infringer only if the condition referred to in subparagraph (a) is fulfilled or only if the condition referred to in subparagraph (b) is fulfilled.

3.   In the adduction of proof to the contrary, the legitimate interests of defendants in protecting their manufacturing and business secrets shall be taken into account.

SECTION 6: LAYOUT-DESIGNS (TOPOGRAPHIES) OF INTEGRATED CIRCUITS

Article 35 Relation to the IPIC Treaty

Members agree to provide protection to the layout-designs (topographies) of integrated circuits (referred to in this Agreement as "layout-designs") in accordance with Articles 2 through 7 (other than paragraph 3 of Article 6), Article 12 and paragraph 3 of Article 16 of the Treaty on Intellectual Property in Respect of Integrated Circuits and, in addition, to comply with the following provisions.

Article 36 Scope of the Protection

Subject to the provisions of paragraph 1 of Article 37, Members shall consider unlawful the following acts if performed without the authorization of the right holder:[9] importing, selling, or otherwise distributing for commercial purposes a protected layout-design, an integrated circuit in which a protected layout-design is incorporated, or an article incorporating such an integrated circuit only in so far as it continues to contain an unlawfully reproduced layout-design.

Article 37 Acts Not Requiring the Authorization of the Right Holder

1.   Notwithstanding Article 36, no Member shall consider unlawful the performance of any of the acts referred to in that Article in respect of an integrated circuit incorporating an unlawfully reproduced layout-design or any article incorporating such an integrated circuit where the person performing or ordering such acts did not know and had no reasonable ground to know, when acquiring the integrated circuit or article incorporating such an integrated circuit, that it incorporated an unlawfully reproduced layout-design. Members shall provide that, after the time that such person has received sufficient notice that the layout-design was unlawfully reproduced, that person may perform any of the acts with respect to the stock on hand or ordered before such time, but shall be liable to pay to the right holder a sum equivalent to a reasonable royalty such as would be payable under a freely negotiated licence in respect of such a layout-design.

2.   The conditions set out in subparagraphs (a) through (k) of Article 31 shall apply *mutatis mutandis* in the event of any non-voluntary licensing of a layout-design or of its use by or for the government without the authorization of the right holder.

---

9   The term "right holder" in this Section shall be understood as having the same meaning as the term "holder of the right" in the IPIC Treaty.

Article 38 Term of Protection

1.   In Members requiring registration as a condition of protection, the term of protection of layout-designs shall not end before the expiration of a period of 10 years counted from the date of filing an application for registration or from the first commercial exploitation wherever in the world it occurs.

2.   In Members not requiring registration as a condition for protection, layout-designs shall be protected for a term of no less than 10 years from the date of the first commercial exploitation wherever in the world it occurs.

3.   Notwithstanding paragraphs 1 and 2, a Member may provide that protection shall lapse 15 years after the creation of the layout-design.

SECTION 7: PROTECTION OF UNDISCLOSED INFORMATION

Article 39 [Trade Secrets to Be Protected]

1.   In the course of ensuring effective protection against unfair competition as provided in Article 10bis of the Paris Convention (1967), Members shall protect undisclosed information in accordance with paragraph 2 and data submitted to governments or governmental agencies in accordance with paragraph 3.

2.   Natural and legal persons shall have the possibility of preventing information lawfully within their control from being disclosed to, acquired by, or used by others without their consent in a manner contrary to honest commercial practices[10] so long as such information:

(a)   is secret in the sense that it is not, as a body or in the precise configuration and assembly of its components, generally known among or readily accessible to persons within the circles that normally deal with the kind of information in question;

(b)   has commercial value because it is secret; and

(c)   has been subject to reasonable steps under the circumstances, by the person lawfully in control of the information, to keep it secret.

3.   Members, when requiring, as a condition of approving the marketing of pharmaceutical or of agricultural chemical products which utilize new chemical entities, the submission of un-disclosed test or other data, the origination of which involves a considerable effort, shall protect such data against unfair commercial use. In addition, Members shall protect such data against disclosure, except where necessary to protect the public, or unless steps are taken to ensure that the data are protected against unfair commercial use.

SECTION 8: CONTROL OF ANTI-COMPETITIVE PRACTICES IN CONTRACTUAL LICENCES

Article 40 [Abuse of Intellectual Property Rights for Anti-Competitive Purposes]

1.   Members agree that some licensing practices or conditions pertaining to intellectual property rights which restrain competition may have adverse effects on trade and may impede the transfer and dissemination of technology.

2.   Nothing in this Agreement shall prevent Members from specifying in their legislation licensing practices or conditions that may in particular cases constitute an abuse of intellectual property rights having an adverse effect on competition in the relevant market. As provided above, a Member may adopt, consistently with the other provisions of this Agreement, appro-priate measures to prevent or control such practices, which may include for example exclusive

---

10   For the purpose of this provision, "a manner contrary to honest commercial practices" shall mean at least practices such as breach of contract, breach of confidence and inducement to breach, and includes the acquisition of undisclosed information by third parties who knew, or were grossly negligent in failing to know, that such practices were involved in the acquisition.

grantback conditions, conditions preventing challenges to validity and coercive package licensing, in the light of the relevant laws and regulations of that Member.

3. Each Member shall enter, upon request, into consultations with any other Member which has cause to believe that an intellectual property right owner that is a national or domiciliary of the Member to which the request for consultations has been addressed is undertaking practices in violation of the requesting Member's laws and regulations on the subject matter of this Section, and which wishes to secure compliance with such legislation, without prejudice to any action under the law and to the full freedom of an ultimate decision of either Member. The Member addressed shall accord full and sympathetic consideration to, and shall afford adequate opportunity for, consultations with the requesting Member, and shall cooperate through supply of publicly available non-confidential information of relevance to the matter in question and of other information available to the Member, subject to domestic law and to the conclusion of mutually satisfactory agreements concerning the safeguarding of its confidentiality by the requesting Member.

4. A Member whose nationals or domiciliaries are subject to proceedings in another Member concerning alleged violation of that other Member's laws and regulations on the subject matter of this Section shall, upon request, be granted an opportunity for consultations by the other Member under the same conditions as those foreseen in paragraph 3.

PART III – ENFORCEMENT OF INTELLECTUAL PROPERTY RIGHTS

SECTION 1: GENERAL OBLIGATIONS

Article 41 [Effective Remedies]

1. Members shall ensure that enforcement procedures as specified in this Part are available under their law so as to permit effective action against any act of infringement of intellectual property rights covered by this Agreement, including expeditious remedies to prevent infringements and remedies which constitute a deterrent to further infringements. These procedures shall be applied in such a manner as to avoid the creation of barriers to legitimate trade and to provide for safeguards against their abuse.

2. Procedures concerning the enforcement of intellectual property rights shall be fair and equitable. They shall not be unnecessarily complicated or costly, or entail unreasonable time-limits or unwarranted delays.

3. Decisions on the merits of a case shall preferably be in writing and reasoned. They shall be made available at least to the parties to the proceeding without undue delay. Decisions on the merits of a case shall be based only on evidence in respect of which parties were offered the opportunity to be heard.

4. Parties to a proceeding shall have an opportunity for review by a judicial authority of final administrative decisions and, subject to jurisdictional provisions in a Member's law concerning the importance of a case, of at least the legal aspects of initial judicial decisions on the merits of a case. However, there shall be no obligation to provide an opportunity for review of acquittals in criminal cases.

5. It is understood that this Part does not create any obligation to put in place a judicial system for the enforcement of intellectual property rights distinct from that for the enforcement of law in general, nor does it affect the capacity of Members to enforce their law in general. Nothing in this Part creates any obligation with respect to the distribution of resources as between enforcement of intellectual property rights and the enforcement of law in general.

SECTION 2: CIVIL AND ADMINISTRATIVE PROCEDURES AND REMEDIES

Article 42 Fair and Equitable Procedures

Members shall make available to right holders[11] civil judicial procedures concerning the enforcement of any intellectual property right covered by this Agreement. Defendants shall have the right to written notice which is timely and contains sufficient detail, including the basis of the claims. Parties shall be allowed to be represented by independent legal counsel, and procedures shall not impose overly burdensome requirements concerning mandatory personal appearances. All parties to such procedures shall be duly entitled to substantiate their claims and to present all relevant evidence. The procedure shall provide a means to identify and protect confidential information, unless this would be contrary to existing constitutional requirements.

Article 43 Evidence

1.   The judicial authorities shall have the authority, where a party has presented reasonably available evidence sufficient to support its claims and has specified evidence relevant to substantiation of its claims which lies in the control of the opposing party, to order that this evidence be produced by the opposing party, subject in appropriate cases to conditions which ensure the protection of confidential information.

2.   In cases in which a party to a proceeding voluntarily and without good reason refuses access to, or otherwise does not provide necessary information within a reasonable period, or significantly impedes a procedure relating to an enforcement action, a Member may accord judicial authorities the authority to make preliminary and final determinations, affirmative or negative, on the basis of the information presented to them, including the complaint or the allegation presented by the party adversely affected by the denial of access to information, subject to providing the parties an opportunity to be heard on the allegations or evidence.

Article 44 Injunctions

1.   The judicial authorities shall have the authority to order a party to desist from an infringement, *inter alia* to prevent the entry into the channels of commerce in their jurisdiction of imported goods that involve the infringement of an intellectual property right, immediately after customs clearance of such goods. Members are not obliged to accord such authority in respect of protected subject matter acquired or ordered by a person prior to knowing or having reasonable grounds to know that dealing in such subject matter would entail the infringement of an intellectual property right.

2.   Notwithstanding the other provisions of this Part and provided that the provisions of Part II specifically addressing use by governments, or by third parties authorized by a government, without the authorization of the right holder are complied with, Members may limit the remedies available against such use to payment of remuneration in accordance with subparagraph (h) of Article 31. In other cases, the remedies under this Part shall apply or, where these remedies are inconsistent with a Member's law, declaratory judgments and adequate compensation shall be available.

Article 45 Damages

1.   The judicial authorities shall have the authority to order the infringer to pay the right holder damages adequate to compensate for the injury the right holder has suffered because of an infringement of that person's intellectual property right by an infringer who knowingly, or with reasonable grounds to know, engaged in infringing activity.

2.   The judicial authorities shall also have the authority to order the infringer to pay the right holder expenses, which may include appropriate attorney's fees. In appropriate cases, Members may authorize the judicial authorities to order recovery of profits and/or payment of pre-

---

11   For the purpose of this Part, the term "right holder" includes federations and associations having legal standing to assert such rights.

established damages even where the infringer did not knowingly, or with reasonable grounds to know, engage in infringing activity.

Article 46 Other Remedies

In order to create an effective deterrent to infringement, the judicial authorities shall have the authority to order that goods that they have found to be infringing be, without compensation of any sort, disposed of outside the channels of commerce in such a manner as to avoid any harm caused to the right holder, or, unless this would be contrary to existing constitutional requirements, destroyed. The judicial authorities shall also have the authority to order that materials and implements the predominant use of which has been in the creation of the infringing goods be, without compensation of any sort, disposed of outside the channels of commerce in such a manner as to minimize the risks of further infringements. In considering such requests, the need for proportionality between the seriousness of the infringement and the remedies ordered as well as the interests of third parties shall be taken into account. In regard to counterfeit trademark goods, the simple removal of the trademark unlawfully affixed shall not be sufficient, other than in exceptional cases, to permit release of the goods into the channels of commerce.

Article 47 Right of Information

Members may provide that the judicial authorities shall have the authority, unless this would be out of proportion to the seriousness of the infringement, to order the infringer to inform the right holder of the identity of third persons involved in the production and distribution of the infringing goods or services and of their channels of distribution.

Article 48 Indemnification of the Defendant

1.   The judicial authorities shall have the authority to order a party at whose request measures were taken and who has abused enforcement procedures to provide to a party wrongfully enjoined or restrained adequate compensation for the injury suffered because of such abuse. The judicial authorities shall also have the authority to order the applicant to pay the defendant expenses, which may include appropriate attorney's fees.

2.   In respect of the administration of any law pertaining to the protection or enforcement of intellectual property rights, Members shall only exempt both public authorities and officials from liability to appropriate remedial measures where actions are taken or intended in good faith in the course of the administration of that law.

Article 49 Administrative Procedures

To the extent that any civil remedy can be ordered as a result of administrative procedures on the merits of a case, such procedures shall conform to principles equivalent in substance to those set forth in this Section.

SECTION 3: PROVISIONAL MEASURES

Article 50 [Injunctions]

1.   The judicial authorities shall have the authority to order prompt and effective provisional measures:

(a)   to prevent an infringement of any intellectual property right from occurring, and in particular to prevent the entry into the channels of commerce in their jurisdiction of goods, including imported goods immediately after customs clearance;

(b)   to preserve relevant evidence in regard to the alleged infringement.

2.   The judicial authorities shall have the authority to adopt provisional measures *inaudita altera parte* where appropriate, in particular where any delay is likely to cause irreparable harm to the right holder, or where there is a demonstrable risk of evidence being destroyed.

3.   The judicial authorities shall have the authority to require the applicant to provide any reasonably available evidence in order to satisfy themselves with a sufficient degree of certainty that the applicant is the right holder and that the applicant's right is being infringed or that such infringement is imminent, and to order the applicant to provide a security or equivalent assurance sufficient to protect the defendant and to prevent abuse.

4.   Where provisional measures have been adopted *inaudita altera parte*, the parties affected shall be given notice, without delay after the execution of the measures at the latest. A review, including a right to be heard, shall take place upon request of the defendant with a view to deciding, within a reasonable period after the notification of the measures, whether these measures shall be modified, revoked or confirmed.

5.   The applicant may be required to supply other information necessary for the identification of the goods concerned by the authority that will execute the provisional measures.

6.   Without prejudice to paragraph 4, provisional measures taken on the basis of paragraphs 1 and 2 shall, upon request by the defendant, be revoked or otherwise cease to have effect, if proceedings leading to a decision on the merits of the case are not initiated within a reasonable period, to be determined by the judicial authority ordering the measures where a Member's law so permits or, in the absence of such a determination, not to exceed 20 working days or 31 calendar days, whichever is the longer.

7.   Where the provisional measures are revoked or where they lapse due to any act or omission by the applicant, or where it is subsequently found that there has been no infringement or threat of infringement of an intellectual property right, the judicial authorities shall have the authority to order the applicant, upon request of the defendant, to provide the defendant appropriate compensation for any injury caused by these measures.

8.   To the extent that any provisional measure can be ordered as a result of administrative procedures, such procedures shall conform to principles equivalent in substance to those set forth in this Section.

Section 4: Special Requirements Related to Border Measures[12]

Article 51 Suspension of Release by Customs Authorities

Members shall, in conformity with the provisions set out below, adopt procedures[13] to enable a right holder, who has valid grounds for suspecting that the importation of counterfeit trademark or pirated copyright goods[14] may take place, to lodge an application in writing with competent authorities, administrative or judicial, for the suspension by the customs authorities of the release into free circulation of such goods. Members may enable such an application to be made in respect of goods which involve other infringements of intellectual property rights, provided that the requirements of this Section are met. Members may also provide for corresponding procedures concerning the suspension by the customs authorities of the release of infringing goods destined for exportation from their territories.

---

12   Where a Member has dismantled substantially all controls over movement of goods across its border with another Member with which it forms part of a customs union, it shall not be required to apply the provisions of this Section at that border.

13   It is understood that there shall be no obligation to apply such procedures to imports of goods put on the market in another country by or with the consent of the right holder, or to goods in transit.

14   For the purposes of this Agreement:
(a)   "counterfeit trademark goods" shall mean any goods, including packaging, bearing without authorization a trademark which is identical to the trademark validly registered in respect of such goods, or which cannot be distinguished in its essential aspects from such a trademark, and which thereby infringes the rights of the owner of the trademark in question under the law of the country of importation;
(b)   "pirated copyright goods" shall mean any goods which are copies made without the consent of the right holder or person duly authorized by the right holder in the country of production and which are made directly or indirectly from an article where the making of that copy would have constituted an infringement of a copyright or a related right under the law of the country of importation.

Article 52 Application

Any right holder initiating the procedures under Article 51 shall be required to provide adequate evidence to satisfy the competent authorities that, under the laws of the country of importation, there is *prima facie* an infringement of the right holder's intellectual property right and to supply a sufficiently detailed description of the goods to make them readily recognizable by the customs authorities. The competent authorities shall inform the applicant within a reasonable period whether they have accepted the application and, where determined by the competent authorities, the period for which the customs authorities will take action.

Article 53 Security or Equivalent Assurance

1.   The competent authorities shall have the authority to require an applicant to provide a security or equivalent assurance sufficient to protect the defendant and the competent authorities and to prevent abuse. Such security or equivalent assurance shall not unreasonably deter recourse to these procedures.

2.   Where pursuant to an application under this Section the release of goods involving industrial designs, patents, layout-designs or undisclosed information into free circulation has been suspended by customs authorities on the basis of a decision other than by a judicial or other independent authority, and the period provided for in Article 55 has expired without the granting of provisional relief by the duly empowered authority, and provided that all other conditions for importation have been complied with, the owner, importer, or consignee of such goods shall be entitled to their release on the posting of a security in an amount sufficient to protect the right holder for any infringement. Payment of such security shall not prejudice any other remedy available to the right holder, it being understood that the security shall be released if the right holder fails to pursue the right of action within a reasonable period of time.

Article 54 Notice of Suspension

The importer and the applicant shall be promptly notified of the suspension of the release of goods according to Article 51.

Article 55 Duration of Suspension

If, within a period not exceeding 10 working days after the applicant has been served notice of the suspension, the customs authorities have not been informed that proceedings leading to a decision on the merits of the case have been initiated by a party other than the defendant, or that the duly empowered authority has taken provisional measures prolonging the suspension of the release of the goods, the goods shall be released, provided that all other conditions for importation or exportation have been complied with; in appropriate cases, this time-limit may be extended by another 10 working days. If proceedings leading to a decision on the merits of the case have been initiated, a review, including a right to be heard, shall take place upon request of the defendant with a view to deciding, within a reasonable period, whether these measures shall be modified, revoked or confirmed. Notwithstanding the above, where the suspension of the release of goods is carried out or continued in accordance with a provisional judicial measure, the provisions of paragraph 6 of Article 50 shall apply.

Article 56 Indemnification of the Importer and of the Owner of the Goods

Relevant authorities shall have the authority to order the applicant to pay the importer, the consignee and the owner of the goods appropriate compensation for any injury caused to them through the wrongful detention of goods or through the detention of goods released pursuant to Article 55.

Article 57 Right of Inspection and Information

Without prejudice to the protection of confidential information, Members shall provide the competent authorities the authority to give the right holder sufficient opportunity to have any goods detained by the customs authorities inspected in order to substantiate the right holder's claims. The competent authorities shall also have authority to give the importer an equivalent opportunity to have any such goods inspected. Where a positive determination has been made on the merits of a case, Members may provide the competent authorities the authority to inform the right holder of the names and addresses of the consignor, the importer and the consignee and of the quantity of the goods in question.

Article 58 Ex Officio Action

Where Members require competent authorities to act upon their own initiative and to suspend the release of goods in respect of which they have acquired *prima facie* evidence that an intellectual property right is being infringed:

(a) the competent authorities may at any time seek from the right holder any information that may assist them to exercise these powers;

(b) the importer and the right holder shall be promptly notified of the suspension. Where the importer has lodged an appeal against the suspension with the competent authorities, the suspension shall be subject to the conditions, *mutatis mutandis*, set out at Article 55;

(c) Members shall only exempt both public authorities and officials from liability to appropriate remedial measures where actions are taken or intended in good faith.

Article 59 Remedies

Without prejudice to other rights of action open to the right holder and subject to the right of the defendant to seek review by a judicial authority, competent authorities shall have the authority to order the destruction or disposal of infringing goods in accordance with the principles set out in Article 46. In regard to counterfeit trademark goods, the authorities shall not allow the re-exportation of the infringing goods in an unaltered state or subject them to a different customs procedure, other than in exceptional circumstances.

Article 60 De Minimis Imports

Members may exclude from the application of the above provisions small quantities of goods of a non-commercial nature contained in travellers' personal luggage or sent in small consignments.

SECTION 5: CRIMINAL PROCEDURES

Article 61 [Effective Deterrent]

Members shall provide for criminal procedures and penalties to be applied at least in cases of wilful trademark counterfeiting or copyright piracy on a commercial scale. Remedies available shall include imprisonment and/or monetary fines sufficient to provide a deterrent, consistently with the level of penalties applied for crimes of a corresponding gravity. In appropriate cases, remedies available shall also include the seizure, forfeiture and destruction of the infringing goods and of any materials and implements the predominant use of which has been in the commission of the offence. Members may provide for criminal procedures and penalties to be applied in other cases of infringement of intellectual property rights, in particular where they are committed wilfully and on a commercial scale.

PART IV – ACQUISITION AND MAINTENANCE OF INTELLECTUAL PROPERTY RIGHTS AND RELATED *INTER-PARTES* PROCEDURES

Article 62 [Prohibition of Unreasonable Procedural Requirements]

1.   Members may require, as a condition of the acquisition or maintenance of the intellectual property rights provided for under Sections 2 through 6 of Part II, compliance with reasonable procedures and formalities. Such procedures and formalities shall be consistent with the provisions of this Agreement.

2. Where the acquisition of an intellectual property right is subject to the right being granted or registered, Members shall ensure that the procedures for grant or registration, subject to compliance with the substantive conditions for acquisition of the right, permit the granting or registration of the right within a reasonable period of time so as to avoid unwarranted curtailment of the period of protection.

3. Article 4 of the Paris Convention (1967) shall apply *mutatis mutandis* to service marks.

4. Procedures concerning the acquisition or maintenance of intellectual property rights and, where a Member's law provides for such procedures, administrative revocation and *inter partes* procedures such as opposition, revocation and cancellation, shall be governed by the general principles set out in paragraphs 2 and 3 of Article 41.

5. Final administrative decisions in any of the procedures referred to under paragraph 4 shall be subject to review by a judicial or quasi-judicial authority. However, there shall be no obligation to provide an opportunity for such review of decisions in cases of unsuccessful opposition or administrative revocation, provided that the grounds for such procedures can be the subject of invalidation procedures.

PART V – DISPUTE PREVENTION AND SETTLEMENT

Article 63 Transparency

1. Laws and regulations, and final judicial decisions and administrative rulings of general application, made effective by a Member pertaining to the subject matter of this Agreement (the availability, scope, acquisition, enforcement and prevention of the abuse of intellectual property rights) shall be published, or where such publication is not practicable made publicly available, in a national language, in such a manner as to enable governments and right holders to become acquainted with them. Agreements concerning the subject matter of this Agreement which are in force between the government or a governmental agency of a Member and the government or a governmental agency of another Member shall also be published.

2. Members shall notify the laws and regulations referred to in paragraph 1 to the Council for TRIPS in order to assist that Council in its review of the operation of this Agreement. The Council shall attempt to minimize the burden on Members in carrying out this obligation and may decide to waive the obligation to notify such laws and regulations directly to the Council if consultations with WIPO on the establishment of a common register containing these laws and regulations are successful. The Council shall also consider in this connection any action required regarding notifications pursuant to the obligations under this Agreement stemming from the provisions of Article 6*ter* of the Paris Convention (1967).

3. Each Member shall be prepared to supply, in response to a written request from another Member, information of the sort referred to in paragraph 1. A Member, having reason to believe that a specific judicial decision or administrative ruling or bilateral agreement in the area of intellectual property rights affects its rights under this Agreement, may also request in writing to be given access to or be informed in sufficient detail of such specific judicial decisions or administrative rulings or bilateral agreements.

4. Nothing in paragraphs 1, 2 and 3 shall require Members to disclose confidential information which would impede law enforcement or otherwise be contrary to the public interest or would prejudice the legitimate commercial interests of particular enterprises, public or private.

Article 64 Dispute Settlement

1. The provisions of Articles XXII and XXIII of GATT 1994 as elaborated and applied by the Dispute Settlement Understanding shall apply to consultations and the settlement of disputes under this Agreement except as otherwise specifically provided herein.

2. Subparagraphs 1(b) and 1(c) of Article XXIII of GATT 1994 shall not apply to the settlement of disputes under this Agreement for a period of five years from the date of entry into force of the WTO Agreement.

3. During the time period referred to in paragraph 2, the Council for TRIPS shall examine the scope and modalities for complaints of the type provided for under subparagraphs 1(b) and 1(c) of Article XXIII of GATT 1994 made pursuant to this Agreement, and submit its recommendations to the Ministerial Conference for approval. Any decision of the Ministerial Conference to approve such recommendations or to extend the period in paragraph 2 shall be made only by consensus, and approved recommendations shall be effective for all Members without further formal acceptance process.

PART VI – TRANSITIONAL ARRANGEMENTS

Article 65 Transitional Arrangements

1. Subject to the provisions of paragraphs 2, 3 and 4, no Member shall be obliged to apply the provisions of this Agreement before the expiry of a general period of one year following the date of entry into force of the WTO Agreement.

2. A developing country Member is entitled to delay for a further period of four years the date of application, as defined in paragraph 1, of the provisions of this Agreement other than Articles 3, 4 and 5.

3. Any other Member which is in the process of transformation from a centrally-planned into a market, free-enterprise economy and which is undertaking structural reform of its intellectual property system and facing special problems in the preparation and implementation of intellectual property laws and regulations, may also benefit from a period of delay as foreseen in paragraph 2.

4. To the extent that a developing country Member is obliged by this Agreement to extend product patent protection to areas of technology not so protectable in its territory on the general date of application of this Agreement for that Member, as defined in paragraph 2, it may delay the application of the provisions on product patents of Section 5 of Part II to such areas of technology for an additional period of five years.

5. A Member availing itself of a transitional period under paragraphs 1, 2, 3 or 4 shall ensure that any changes in its laws, regulations and practice made during that period do not result in a lesser degree of consistency with the provisions of this Agreement.

Article 66 Least-Developed Country Members

1. In view of the special needs and requirements of least-developed country Members, their economic, financial and administrative constraints, and their need for flexibility to create a viable technological base, such Members shall not be required to apply the provisions of this Agreement, other than Articles 3, 4 and 5, for a period of 10 years from the date of application as defined under paragraph 1 of Article 65. The Council for TRIPS shall, upon duly motivated request by a least-developed country Member, accord extensions of this period.

2. Developed country Members shall provide incentives to enterprises and institutions in their territories for the purpose of promoting and encouraging technology transfer to least-developed country Members in order to enable them to create a sound and viable technological base.

Article 67 Technical Cooperation

In order to facilitate the implementation of this Agreement, developed country Members shall provide, on request and on mutually agreed terms and conditions, technical and financial cooperation in favour of developing and least-developed country Members. Such cooperation shall include assistance in the preparation of laws and regulations on the protection and enforcement of intellectual property rights as well as on the prevention of their abuse, and shall include support regarding the establishment or reinforcement of domestic offices and agencies relevant to these matters, including the training of personnel.

PART VII – INSTITUTIONAL ARRANGEMENTS; FINAL PROVISIONS

Article 68 Council for Trade-Related Aspects of Intellectual Property Rights

The Council for TRIPS shall monitor the operation of this Agreement and, in particular, Members' compliance with their obligations hereunder, and shall afford Members the opportunity of consulting on matters relating to the trade-related aspects of intellectual property rights. It shall carry out such other responsibilities as assigned to it by the Members, and it shall, in particular, provide any assistance requested by them in the context of dispute settlement procedures. In carrying out its functions, the Council for TRIPS may consult with and seek information from any source it deems appropriate. In consultation with WIPO, the Council shall seek to establish, within one year of its first meeting, appropriate arrangements for cooperation with bodies of that Organization.

Article 69 International Cooperation

Members agree to cooperate with each other with a view to eliminating international trade in goods infringing intellectual property rights. For this purpose, they shall establish and notify contact points in their administrations and be ready to exchange information on trade in infringing goods. They shall, in particular, promote the exchange of information and cooperation between customs authorities with regard to trade in counterfeit trademark goods and pirated copyright goods.

Article 70 Protection of Existing Subject Matter

1.   This Agreement does not give rise to obligations in respect of acts which occurred before the date of application of the Agreement for the Member in question.

2.   Except as otherwise provided for in this Agreement, this Agreement gives rise to obligations in respect of all subject matter existing at the date of application of this Agreement for the Member in question, and which is protected in that Member on the said date, or which meets or comes subsequently to meet the criteria for protection under the terms of this Agreement. In respect of this paragraph and paragraphs 3 and 4, copyright obligations with respect to existing works shall be solely determined under Article 18 of the Berne Convention (1971), and obligations with respect to the rights of producers of phonograms and performers in existing phonograms shall be determined solely under Article 18 of the Berne Convention (1971) as made applicable under paragraph 6 of Article 14 of this Agreement.

3.   There shall be no obligation to restore protection to subject matter which on the date of application of this Agreement for the Member in question has fallen into the public domain.

4.   In respect of any acts in respect of specific objects embodying protected subject matter which become infringing under the terms of legislation in conformity with this Agreement, and which were commenced, or in respect of which a significant investment was made, before the date of acceptance of the WTO Agreement by that Member, any Member may provide for a limitation of the remedies available to the right holder as to the continued performance of such acts after the date of application of this Agreement for that Member. In such cases the Member shall, however, at least provide for the payment of equitable remuneration.

5.   A Member is not obliged to apply the provisions of Article 11 and of paragraph 4 of Article 14 with respect to originals or copies purchased prior to the date of application of this Agreement for that Member.

6.   Members shall not be required to apply Article 31, or the requirement in paragraph 1 of Article 27 that patent rights shall be enjoyable without discrimination as to the field of technology, to use without the authorization of the right holder where authorization for such use was granted by the government before the date this Agreement became known.

7.   In the case of intellectual property rights for which protection is conditional upon registration, applications for protection which are pending on the date of application of this Agreement for the Member in question shall be permitted to be amended to claim any enhanced protection provided under the provisions of this Agreement. Such amendments shall not include new matter.

8.   Where a Member does not make available as of the date of entry into force of the WTO Agreement patent protection for pharmaceutical and agricultural chemical products commensurate with its obligations under Article 27, that Member shall:

(a) notwithstanding the provisions of Part VI, provide as from the date of entry into force of the WTO Agreement a means by which applications for patents for such inventions can be filed;

(b) apply to these applications, as of the date of application of this Agreement, the criteria for patentability as laid down in this Agreement as if those criteria were being applied on the date of filing in that Member or, where priority is available and claimed, the priority date of the application; and

(c) provide patent protection in accordance with this Agreement as from the grant of the patent and for the remainder of the patent term, counted from the filing date in accordance with Article 33 of this Agreement, for those of these applications that meet the criteria for protection referred to in subparagraph (b).

9.   Where a product is the subject of a patent application in a Member in accordance with paragraph 8(a), exclusive marketing rights shall be granted, notwithstanding the provisions of Part VI, for a period of five years after obtaining marketing approval in that Member or until a product patent is granted or rejected in that Member, whichever period is shorter, provided that, subsequent to the entry into force of the WTO Agreement, a patent application has been filed and a patent granted for that product in another Member and marketing approval obtained in such other Member.

Article 71 Review and Amendment

1.   The Council for TRIPS shall review the implementation of this Agreement after the expiration of the transitional period referred to in paragraph 2 of Article 65. The Council shall, having regard to the experience gained in its implementation, review it two years after that date, and at identical intervals thereafter. The Council may also undertake reviews in the light of any relevant new developments which might warrant modification or amendment of this Agreement.

2.   Amendments merely serving the purpose of adjusting to higher levels of protection of intellectual property rights achieved, and in force, in other multilateral agreements and accepted under those agreements by all Members of the WTO may be referred to the Ministerial Conference for action in accordance with paragraph 6 of Article X of the WTO Agreement on the basis of a consensus proposal from the Council for TRIPS.

Article 72 Reservations

Reservations may not be entered in respect of any of the provisions of this Agreement without the consent of the other Members.

Article 73 Security Exceptions

Nothing in this Agreement shall be construed:

(a) to require a Member to furnish any information the disclosure of which it considers contrary to its essential security interests; or

(b) to prevent a Member from taking any action which it considers necessary for the protection of its essential security interests;

   (i)   relating to fissionable materials or the materials from which they are derived;

    (ii)   relating to the traffic in arms, ammunition and implements of war and to such traffic in other goods and materials as is carried on directly or indirectly for the purpose of supplying a military establishment;

    (iii) taken in time of war or other emergency in international relations; or

(c) to prevent a Member from taking any action in pursuance of its obligations under the United Nations Charter for the maintenance of international peace and security.

XII.4. ANNEX 2

UNDERSTANDING ON RULES AND PROCEDURES
GOVERNING THE SETTLEMENT OF DISPUTES (DSU)

Members hereby *agree* as follows:

Article 1 Coverage and Application

1.   The rules and procedures of this Understanding shall apply to disputes brought pursuant to the consultation and dispute settlement provisions of the agreements listed in Appendix 1 to this Understanding (referred to in this Understanding as the "covered agreements"). The rules and procedures of this Understanding shall also apply to consultations and the settlement of disputes between Members concerning their rights and obligations under the provisions of the Agreement Establishing the World Trade Organization (referred to in this Understanding as the "WTO Agreement") and of this Understanding taken in isolation or in combination with any other covered agreement.

2.   The rules and procedures of this Understanding shall apply subject to such special or additional rules and procedures on dispute settlement contained in the covered agreements as are identified in Appendix 2 to this Understanding. To the extent that there is a difference between the rules and procedures of this Understanding and the special or additional rules and procedures set forth in Appendix 2, the special or additional rules and procedures in Appendix 2 shall prevail. In disputes involving rules and procedures under more than one covered agreement, if there is a conflict between special or additional rules and procedures of such agreements under review, and where the parties to the dispute cannot agree on rules and procedures within 20 days of the establishment of the panel, the Chairman of the Dispute Settlement Body provided for in paragraph 1 of Article 2 (referred to in this Understanding as the "DSB"), in consultation with the parties to the dispute, shall determine the rules and procedures to be followed within 10 days after a request by either Member. The Chairman shall be guided by the principle that special or additional rules and procedures should be used where possible, and the rules and procedures set out in this Understanding should be used to the extent necessary to avoid conflict.

Article 2 Administration

1.   The Dispute Settlement Body is hereby established to administer these rules and procedures and, except as otherwise provided in a covered agreement, the consultation and dispute settlement provisions of the covered agreements. Accordingly, the DSB shall have the authority to establish panels, adopt panel and Appellate Body reports, maintain surveillance of implementation of rulings and recommendations, and authorize suspension of concessions and other obligations under the covered agreements. With respect to disputes arising under a covered agreement which is a Plurilateral Trade Agreement, the term "Member" as used herein shall refer only to those Members that are parties to the relevant Plurilateral Trade Agreement. Where the DSB administers the dispute settlement provisions of a Plurilateral Trade Agreement, only those Members that are parties to that Agreement may participate in decisions or actions taken by the DSB with respect to that dispute.

2.   The DSB shall inform the relevant WTO Councils and Committees of any developments in disputes related to provisions of the respective covered agreements.

3.   The DSB shall meet as often as necessary to carry out its functions within the time-frames provided in this Understanding.

4.   Where the rules and procedures of this Understanding provide for the DSB to take a decision, it shall do so by consensus.[1]

Article 3 General Provisions

1.   Members affirm their adherence to the principles for the management of disputes heretofore applied under Articles XXII and XXIII of GATT 1947, and the rules and procedures as further elaborated and modified herein.

2.   The dispute settlement system of the WTO is a central element in providing security and predictability to the multilateral trading system. The Members recognize that it serves to preserve the rights and obligations of Members under the covered agreements, and to clarify the existing provisions of those agreements in accordance with customary rules of interpretation of public international law. Recommendations and rulings of the DSB cannot add to or diminish the rights and obligations provided in the covered agreements.

3.   The prompt settlement of situations in which a Member considers that any benefits accruing to it directly or indirectly under the covered agreements are being impaired by measures taken by another Member is essential to the effective functioning of the WTO and the maintenance of a proper balance between the rights and obligations of Members.

4.   Recommendations or rulings made by the DSB shall be aimed at achieving a satisfactory settlement of the matter in accordance with the rights and obligations under this Understanding and under the covered agreements.

5.   All solutions to matters formally raised under the consultation and dispute settlement provisions of the covered agreements, including arbitration awards, shall be consistent with those agreements and shall not nullify or impair benefits accruing to any Member under those agreements, nor impede the attainment of any objective of those agreements.

6.   Mutually agreed solutions to matters formally raised under the consultation and dispute settlement provisions of the covered agreements shall be notified to the DSB and the relevant Councils and Committees, where any Member may raise any point relating thereto.

7.   Before bringing a case, a Member shall exercise its judgement as to whether action under these procedures would be fruitful. The aim of the dispute settlement mechanism is to secure a positive solution to a dispute. A solution mutually acceptable to the parties to a dispute and consistent with the covered agreements is clearly to be preferred. In the absence of a mutually agreed solution, the first objective of the dispute settlement mechanism is usually to secure the withdrawal of the measures concerned if these are found to be inconsistent with the provisions of any of the covered agreements. The provision of compensation should be resorted to only if the immediate withdrawal of the measure is impracticable and as a temporary measure pending the withdrawal of the measure which is inconsistent with a covered agreement. The last resort which this Understanding provides to the Member invoking the dispute settlement procedures is the possibility of suspending the application of concessions or other obligations under the covered agreements on a discriminatory basis vis-à-vis the other Member, subject to authorization by the DSB of such measures.

8.   In cases where there is an infringement of the obligations assumed under a covered agreement, the action is considered *prima facie* to constitute a case of nullification or impairment. This means that there is normally a presumption that a breach of the rules has an adverse impact on other Members parties to that covered agreement, and in such cases, it shall be up to the Member against whom the complaint has been brought to rebut the charge.

---

1   The DSB shall be deemed to have decided by consensus on a matter submitted for its consideration, if no Member, present at the meeting of the DSB when the decision is taken, formally objects to the proposed decision.

9.   The provisions of this Understanding are without prejudice to the rights of Members to seek authoritative interpretation of provisions of a covered agreement through decision-making under the WTO Agreement or a covered agreement which is a Plurilateral Trade Agreement.

10. It is understood that requests for conciliation and the use of the dispute settlement procedures should not be intended or considered as contentious acts and that, if a dispute arises, all Members will engage in these procedures in good faith in an effort to resolve the dispute. It is also understood that complaints and counter-complaints in regard to distinct matters should not be linked.

11. This Understanding shall be applied only with respect to new requests for consultations under the consultation provisions of the covered agreements made on or after the date of entry into force of the WTO Agreement. With respect to disputes for which the request for consultations was made under GATT 1947 or under any other predecessor agreement to the covered agreements before the date of entry into force of the WTO Agreement, the relevant dispute settlement rules and procedures in effect immediately prior to the date of entry into force of the WTO Agreement shall continue to apply.[2]

12. Notwithstanding paragraph 11, if a complaint based on any of the covered agreements is brought by a developing country Member against a developed country Member, the complaining party shall have the right to invoke, as an alternative to the provisions contained in Articles 4, 5, 6 and 12 of this Understanding, the corresponding provisions of the Decision of 5 April 1966 (BISD 14S/18), except that where the Panel considers that the time-frame provided for in paragraph 7 of that Decision is insufficient to provide its report and with the agreement of the complaining party, that time-frame may be extended. To the extent that there is a difference between the rules and procedures of Articles 4, 5, 6 and 12 and the corresponding rules and procedures of the Decision, the latter shall prevail.

Article 4 Consultations

1.   Members affirm their resolve to strengthen and improve the effectiveness of the consultation procedures employed by Members.

2.   Each Member undertakes to accord sympathetic consideration to and afford adequate opportunity for consultation regarding any representations made by another Member concerning measures affecting the operation of any covered agreement taken within the territory of the former.[3]

3.   If a request for consultations is made pursuant to a covered agreement, the Member to which the request is made shall, unless otherwise mutually agreed, reply to the request within 10 days after the date of its receipt and shall enter into consultations in good faith within a period of no more than 30 days after the date of receipt of the request, with a view to reaching a mutually satisfactory solution. If the Member does not respond within 10 days after the date of receipt of the request, or does not enter into consultations within a period of no more than 30 days, or a period otherwise mutually agreed, after the date of receipt of the request, then the Member that requested the holding of consultations may proceed directly to request the establishment of a panel.

4.   All such requests for consultations shall be notified to the DSB and the relevant Councils and Committees by the Member which requests consultations. Any request for consultations shall be submitted in writing and shall give the reasons for the request, including identification of the measures at issue and an indication of the legal basis for the complaint.

---

2   This paragraph shall also be applied to disputes on which panel reports have not been adopted or fully implemented.

3   Where the provisions of any other covered agreement concerning measures taken by regional or local governments or authorities within the territory of a Member contain provisions different from the provisions of this paragraph, the provisions of such other covered agreement shall prevail.

5. In the course of consultations in accordance with the provisions of a covered agreement, before resorting to further action under this Understanding, Members should attempt to obtain satisfactory adjustment of the matter.

6. Consultations shall be confidential, and without prejudice to the rights of any Member in any further proceedings.

7. If the consultations fail to settle a dispute within 60 days after the date of receipt of the request for consultations, the complaining party may request the establishment of a panel. The complaining party may request a panel during the 60-day period if the consulting parties jointly consider that consultations have failed to settle the dispute.

8. In cases of urgency, including those which concern perishable goods, Members shall enter into consultations within a period of no more than 10 days after the date of receipt of the request. If the consultations have failed to settle the dispute within a period of 20 days after the date of receipt of the request, the complaining party may request the establishment of a panel.

9. In cases of urgency, including those which concern perishable goods, the parties to the dispute, panels and the Appellate Body shall make every effort to accelerate the proceedings to the greatest extent possible.

10. During consultations Members should give special attention to the particular problems and interests of developing country Members.

11. Whenever a Member other than the consulting Members considers that it has a substantial trade interest in consultations being held pursuant to paragraph 1 of Article XXII of GATT 1994, paragraph 1 of Article XXII of GATS, or the corresponding provisions in other covered agreements,[4] such Member may notify the consulting Members and the DSB, within 10 days after the date of the circulation of the request for consultations under said Article, of its desire to be joined in the consultations. Such Member shall be joined in the consultations, provided that the Member to which the request for consultations was addressed agrees that the claim of substantial interest is well-founded. In that event they shall so inform the DSB. If the request to be joined in the consultations is not accepted, the applicant Member shall be free to request consultations under paragraph 1 of Article XXII or paragraph 1 of Article XXIII of GATT 1994, paragraph 1 of Article XXII or paragraph 1 of Article XXIII of GATS, or the corresponding provisions in other covered agreements.

Article 5 Good Offices, Conciliation and Mediation

1. Good offices, conciliation and mediation are procedures that are undertaken voluntarily if the parties to the dispute so agree.

2. Proceedings involving good offices, conciliation and mediation, and in particular positions taken by the parties to the dispute during these proceedings, shall be confidential, and without prejudice to the rights of either party in any further proceedings under these procedures.

3. Good offices, conciliation or mediation may be requested at any time by any party to a dispute. They may begin at any time and be terminated at any time. Once procedures for good

---

4   The corresponding consultation provisions in the covered agreements are listed hereunder: Agreement on Agriculture, Article 19; Agreement on the Application of Sanitary and Phytosanitary Measures, paragraph 1 of Article 11; Agreement on Textiles and Clothing, paragraph 4 of Article 8; Agreement on Technical Barriers to Trade, paragraph 1 of Article 14; Agreement on Trade-Related Investment Measures, Article 8; Agreement on Implementation of Article VI of GATT 1994, paragraph 2 of Article 17; Agreement on Implementation of Article VII of GATT 1994, paragraph 2 of Article 19; Agreement on Preshipment Inspection, Article 7; Agreement on Rules of Origin, Article 7; Agreement on Import Licensing Procedures, Article 6; Agreement on Subsidies and Countervailing Measures, Article 30; Agreement on Safeguards, Article 14; Agreement on Trade-Related Aspects of Intellectual Property Rights, Article 64.1; and any corresponding consultation provisions in Plurilateral Trade Agreements as determined by the competent bodies of each Agreement and as notified to the DSB.

offices, conciliation or mediation are terminated, a complaining party may then proceed with a request for the establishment of a panel.

4.   When good offices, conciliation or mediation are entered into within 60 days after the date of receipt of a request for consultations, the complaining party must allow a period of 60 days after the date of receipt of the request for consultations before requesting the establishment of a panel. The complaining party may request the establishment of a panel during the 60-day period if the parties to the dispute jointly consider that the good offices, conciliation or mediation process has failed to settle the dispute.

5.   If the parties to a dispute agree, procedures for good offices, conciliation or mediation may continue while the panel process proceeds.

6.   The Director-General may, acting in an *ex officio* capacity, offer good offices, conciliation or mediation with the view to assisting Members to settle a dispute.

Article 6 Establishment of Panels

1.   If the complaining party so requests, a panel shall be established at the latest at the DSB meeting following that at which the request first appears as an item on the DSB's agenda, unless at that meeting the DSB decides by consensus not to establish a panel.[5]

2.   The request for the establishment of a panel shall be made in writing. It shall indicate whether consultations were held, identify the specific measures at issue and provide a brief summary of the legal basis of the complaint sufficient to present the problem clearly. In case the applicant requests the establishment of a panel with other than standard terms of reference, the written request shall include the proposed text of special terms of reference.

Article 7 Terms of Reference of Panels

1.   Panels shall have the following terms of reference unless the parties to the dispute agree otherwise within 20 days from the establishment of the panel:

"To examine, in the light of the relevant provisions in (name of the covered agreement(s) cited by the parties to the dispute), the matter referred to the DSB by (name of party) in document ... and to make such findings as will assist the DSB in making the recommendations or in giving the rulings provided for in that/those agreement(s)."

2.   Panels shall address the relevant provisions in any covered agreement or agreements cited by the parties to the dispute.

3.   In establishing a panel, the DSB may authorize its Chairman to draw up the terms of reference of the panel in consultation with the parties to the dispute, subject to the provisions of paragraph 1. The terms of reference thus drawn up shall be circulated to all Members. If other than standard terms of reference are agreed upon, any Member may raise any point relating thereto in the DSB.

Article 8 Composition of Panels

1.   Panels shall be composed of well-qualified governmental and/or non-governmental individuals, including persons who have served on or presented a case to a panel, served as a representative of a Member or of a contracting party to GATT 1947 or as a representative to the Council or Committee of any covered agreement or its predecessor agreement, or in the Secretariat, taught or published on international trade law or policy, or served as a senior trade policy official of a Member.

2.   Panel members should be selected with a view to ensuring the independence of the members, a sufficiently diverse background and a wide spectrum of experience.

---

5   If the complaining party so requests, a meeting of the DSB shall be convened for this purpose within 15 days of the request, provided that at least 10 days' advance notice of the meeting is given.

3.   Citizens of Members whose governments[6] are parties to the dispute or third parties as defined in paragraph 2 of Article 10 shall not serve on a panel concerned with that dispute, unless the parties to the dispute agree otherwise.

4.   To assist in the selection of panelists, the Secretariat shall maintain an indicative list of governmental and non-governmental individuals possessing the qualifications outlined in paragraph 1, from which panelists may be drawn as appropriate. That list shall include the roster of non-governmental panelists established on 30 November 1984 (BISD 31S/9), and other rosters and indicative lists established under any of the covered agreements, and shall retain the names of persons on those rosters and indicative lists at the time of entry into force of the WTO Agreement. Members may periodically suggest names of governmental and non-governmental individuals for inclusion on the indicative list, providing relevant information on their knowledge of international trade and of the sectors or subject matter of the covered agreements, and those names shall be added to the list upon approval by the DSB. For each of the individuals on the list, the list shall indicate specific areas of experience or expertise of the individuals in the sectors or subject matter of the covered agreements.

5.   Panels shall be composed of three panelists unless the parties to the dispute agree, within 10 days from the establishment of the panel, to a panel composed of five panelists. Members shall be informed promptly of the composition of the panel.

6.   The Secretariat shall propose nominations for the panel to the parties to the dispute. The parties to the dispute shall not oppose nominations except for compelling reasons.

7.   If there is no agreement on the panelists within 20 days after the date of the establishment of a panel, at the request of either party, the Director-General, in consultation with the Chairman of the DSB and the Chairman of the relevant Council or Committee, shall determine the composition of the panel by appointing the panelists whom the Director-General considers most appropriate in accordance with any relevant special or additional rules or procedures of the covered agreement or covered agreements which are at issue in the dispute, after consulting with the parties to the dispute. The Chairman of the DSB shall inform the Members of the composition of the panel thus formed no later than 10 days after the date the Chairman receives such a request.

8.   Members shall undertake, as a general rule, to permit their officials to serve as panelists.

9.   Panelists shall serve in their individual capacities and not as government representatives, nor as representatives of any organization. Members shall therefore not give them instructions nor seek to influence them as individuals with regard to matters before a panel.

10. When a dispute is between a developing country Member and a developed country Member the panel shall, if the developing country Member so requests, include at least one panelist from a developing country Member.

11. Panelists' expenses, including travel and subsistence allowance, shall be met from the WTO budget in accordance with criteria to be adopted by the General Council, based on recommendations of the Committee on Budget, Finance and Administration.

Article 9 Procedures for Multiple Complainants

1.   Where more than one Member requests the establishment of a panel related to the same matter, a single panel may be established to examine these complaints taking into account the rights of all Members concerned. A single panel should be established to examine such complaints whenever feasible.

2.   The single panel shall organize its examination and present its findings to the DSB in such a manner that the rights which the parties to the dispute would have enjoyed had separate panels

---

6   In the case where customs unions or common markets are parties to a dispute, this provision applies to citizens of all member countries of the customs unions or common markets.

examined the complaints are in no way impaired. If one of the parties to the dispute so requests, the panel shall submit separate reports on the dispute concerned. The written submissions by each of the complainants shall be made available to the other complainants, and each complainant shall have the right to be present when any one of the other complainants presents its views to the panel.

3.   If more than one panel is established to examine the complaints related to the same matter, to the greatest extent possible the same persons shall serve as panelists on each of the separate panels and the timetable for the panel process in such disputes shall be harmonized.

Article 10 Third Parties

1.   The interests of the parties to a dispute and those of other Members under a covered agreement at issue in the dispute shall be fully taken into account during the panel process.

2.   Any Member having a substantial interest in a matter before a panel and having notified its interest to the DSB (referred to in this Understanding as a "third party") shall have an opportunity to be heard by the panel and to make written submissions to the panel. These submissions shall also be given to the parties to the dispute and shall be reflected in the panel report.

3.   Third parties shall receive the submissions of the parties to the dispute to the first meeting of the panel.

4.   If a third party considers that a measure already the subject of a panel proceeding nullifies or impairs benefits accruing to it under any covered agreement, that Member may have recourse to normal dispute settlement procedures under this Understanding. Such a dispute shall be referred to the original panel wherever possible.

Article 11 Function of Panels

The function of panels is to assist the DSB in discharging its responsibilities under this Understanding and the covered agreements. Accordingly, a panel should make an objective assessment of the matter before it, including an objective assessment of the facts of the case and the applicability of and conformity with the relevant covered agreements, and make such other findings as will assist the DSB in making the recommendations or in giving the rulings provided for in the covered agreements. Panels should consult regularly with the parties to the dispute and give them adequate opportunity to develop a mutually satisfactory solution.

Article 12 Panel Procedures

1.   Panels shall follow the Working Procedures in Appendix 3 unless the panel decides otherwise after consulting the parties to the dispute.

2.   Panel procedures should provide sufficient flexibility so as to ensure high-quality panel reports, while not unduly delaying the panel process.

3.   After consulting the parties to the dispute, the panelists shall, as soon as practicable and whenever possible within one week after the composition and terms of reference of the panel have been agreed upon, fix the timetable for the panel process, taking into account the provisions of paragraph 9 of Article 4, if relevant.

4.   In determining the timetable for the panel process, the panel shall provide sufficient time for the parties to the dispute to prepare their submissions.

5.   Panels should set precise deadlines for written submissions by the parties and the parties should respect those deadlines.

6.   Each party to the dispute shall deposit its written submissions with the Secretariat for immediate transmission to the panel and to the other party or parties to the dispute. The complaining party shall submit its first submission in advance of the responding party's first submission unless the panel decides, in fixing the timetable referred to in paragraph 3 and after consultations with the parties to the dispute, that the parties should submit their first sub-

missions simultaneously. When there are sequential arrangements for the deposit of first sub-missions, the panel shall establish a firm time-period for receipt of the responding party's submission. Any subsequent written submissions shall be submitted simultaneously.

7.   Where the parties to the dispute have failed to develop a mutually satisfactory solution, the panel shall submit its findings in the form of a written report to the DSB. In such cases, the report of a panel shall set out the findings of fact, the applicability of relevant provisions and the basic rationale behind any findings and recommendations that it makes. Where a settlement of the matter among the parties to the dispute has been found, the report of the panel shall be con-fined to a brief description of the case and to reporting that a solution has been reached.

8.   In order to make the procedures more efficient, the period in which the panel shall conduct its examination, from the date that the composition and terms of reference of the panel have been agreed upon until the date the final report is issued to the parties to the dispute, shall, as a general rule, not exceed six months. In cases of urgency, including those relating to perishable goods, the panel shall aim to issue its report to the parties to the dispute within three months.

9.   When the panel considers that it cannot issue its report within six months, or within three months in cases of urgency, it shall inform the DSB in writing of the reasons for the delay together with an estimate of the period within which it will issue its report. In no case should the period from the establishment of the panel to the circulation of the report to the Members exceed nine months.

10.   In the context of consultations involving a measure taken by a developing country Member, the parties may agree to extend the periods established in paragraphs 7 and 8 of Article 4. If, after the relevant period has elapsed, the consulting parties cannot agree that the consultations have concluded, the Chairman of the DSB shall decide, after consultation with the parties, whether to extend the relevant period and, if so, for how long. In addition, in examining a complaint against a developing country Member, the panel shall accord sufficient time for the developing country Member to prepare and present its argumentation. The provisions of paragraph 1 of Article 20 and paragraph 4 of Article 21 are not affected by any action pursuant to this paragraph.

11.   Where one or more of the parties is a developing country Member, the panel's report shall explicitly indicate the form in which account has been taken of relevant provisions on differential and more-favourable treatment for developing country Members that form part of the covered agreements which have been raised by the developing country Member in the course of the dispute settlement procedures.

12.   The panel may suspend its work at any time at the request of the complaining party for a period not to exceed 12 months. In the event of such a suspension, the time-frames set out in paragraphs 8 and 9 of this Article, paragraph 1 of Article 20, and paragraph 4 of Article 21 shall be extended by the amount of time that the work was suspended. If the work of the panel has been suspended for more than 12 months, the authority for establishment of the panel shall lapse.

Article 13 Right to Seek Information

1.   Each panel shall have the right to seek information and technical advice from any individual or body which it deems appropriate. However, before a panel seeks such information or advice from any individual or body within the jurisdiction of a Member it shall inform the authorities of that Member. A Member should respond promptly and fully to any request by a panel for such information as the panel considers necessary and appropriate. Confidential information which is provided shall not be revealed without formal authorization from the individual, body, or autho-rities of the Member providing the information.

2.   Panels may seek information from any relevant source and may consult experts to obtain their opinion on certain aspects of the matter. With respect to a factual issue concerning a scientific or other technical matter raised by a party to a dispute, a panel may request an advisory

report in writing from an expert review group. Rules for the establishment of such a group and its procedures are set forth in Appendix 4.

Article 14 Confidentiality

1. Panel deliberations shall be confidential.

2. The reports of panels shall be drafted without the presence of the parties to the dispute in the light of the information provided and the statements made.

3. Opinions expressed in the panel report by individual panelists shall be anonymous.

Article 15 Interim Review Stage

1. Following the consideration of rebuttal submissions and oral arguments, the panel shall issue the descriptive (factual and argument) sections of its draft report to the parties to the dispute. Within a period of time set by the panel, the parties shall submit their comments in writing.

2. Following the expiration of the set period of time for receipt of comments from the parties to the dispute, the panel shall issue an interim report to the parties, including both the descriptive sections and the panel's findings and conclusions. Within a period of time set by the panel, a party may submit a written request for the panel to review precise aspects of the interim report prior to circulation of the final report to the Members. At the request of a party, the panel shall hold a further meeting with the parties on the issues identified in the written comments. If no comments are received from any party within the comment period, the interim report shall be considered the final panel report and circulated promptly to the Members.

3. The findings of the final panel report shall include a discussion of the arguments made at the interim review stage. The interim review stage shall be conducted within the time-period set out in paragraph 8 of Article 12.

Article 16 Adoption of Panel Reports

1. In order to provide sufficient time for the Members to consider panel reports, the reports shall not be considered for adoption by the DSB until 20 days after the date they have been circulated to the Members.

2. Members having objections to a panel report shall give written reasons to explain their objections for circulation at least 10 days prior to the DSB meeting at which the panel report will be considered.

3. The parties to a dispute shall have the right to participate fully in the consideration of the panel report by the DSB, and their views shall be fully recorded.

4. Within 60 days after the date of circulation of a panel report to the Members, the report shall be adopted at a DSB meeting[7] unless a party to the dispute formally notifies the DSB of its decision to appeal or the DSB decides by consensus not to adopt the report. If a party has notified its decision to appeal, the report by the panel shall not be considered for adoption by the DSB until after completion of the appeal. This adoption procedure is without prejudice to the right of Members to express their views on a panel report.

Article 17 Appellate Review

Standing Appellate Body

1. A standing Appellate Body shall be established by the DSB. The Appellate Body shall hear appeals from panel cases. It shall be composed of seven persons, three of whom shall serve on any one case. Persons serving on the Appellate Body shall serve in rotation. Such rotation shall be determined in the working procedures of the Appellate Body.

---

7   If a meeting of the DSB is not scheduled within this period at a time that enables the requirements of paragraphs 1 and 4 of Article 16 to be met, a meeting of the DSB shall be held for this purpose.

2.   The DSB shall appoint persons to serve on the Appellate Body for a four-year term, and each person may be reappointed once. However, the terms of three of the seven persons appointed immediately after the entry into force of the WTO Agreement shall expire at the end of two years, to be determined by lot. Vacancies shall be filled as they arise. A person appointed to replace a person whose term of office has not expired shall hold office for the remainder of the predecessor's term.

3.   The Appellate Body shall comprise persons of recognized authority, with demonstrated expertise in law, international trade and the subject matter of the covered agreements generally. They shall be unaffiliated with any government. The Appellate Body membership shall be broadly representative of membership in the WTO. All persons serving on the Appellate Body shall be available at all times and on short notice, and shall stay abreast of dispute settlement activities and other relevant activities of the WTO. They shall not participate in the consideration of any disputes that would create a direct or indirect conflict of interest.

4.   Only parties to the dispute, not third parties, may appeal a panel report. Third parties which have notified the DSB of a substantial interest in the matter pursuant to paragraph 2 of Article 10 may make written submissions to, and be given an opportunity to be heard by, the Appellate Body.

5.   As a general rule, the proceedings shall not exceed 60 days from the date a party to the dispute formally notifies its decision to appeal to the date the Appellate Body circulates its report. In fixing its timetable the Appellate Body shall take into account the provisions of paragraph 9 of Article 4, if relevant. When the Appellate Body considers that it cannot provide its report within 60 days, it shall inform the DSB in writing of the reasons for the delay together with an estimate of the period within which it will submit its report. In no case shall the proceedings exceed 90 days.

6.   An appeal shall be limited to issues of law covered in the panel report and legal interpretations developed by the panel.

7.   The Appellate Body shall be provided with appropriate administrative and legal support as it requires.

8.   The expenses of persons serving on the Appellate Body, including travel and subsistence allowance, shall be met from the WTO budget in accordance with criteria to be adopted by the General Council, based on recommendations of the Committee on Budget, Finance and Administration.

Procedures for Appellate Review

9.   Working procedures shall be drawn up by the Appellate Body in consultation with the Chairman of the DSB and the Director-General, and communicated to the Members for their information.

10.   The proceedings of the Appellate Body shall be confidential. The reports of the Appellate Body shall be drafted without the presence of the parties to the dispute and in the light of the information provided and the statements made.

11.   Opinions expressed in the Appellate Body report by individuals serving on the Appellate Body shall be anonymous.

12.   The Appellate Body shall address each of the issues raised in accordance with paragraph 6 during the appellate proceeding.

13.   The Appellate Body may uphold, modify or reverse the legal findings and conclusions of the panel.

Adoption of Appellate Body Reports

14.   An Appellate Body report shall be adopted by the DSB and unconditionally accepted by the parties to the dispute unless the DSB decides by consensus not to adopt the Appellate Body report within 30 days following its circulation to the Members.[8] This adoption procedure is without prejudice to the right of Members to express their views on an Appellate Body report.

Article 18 Communications with the Panel or Appellate Body

1.   There shall be no *ex parte* communications with the panel or Appellate Body concerning matters under consideration by the panel or Appellate Body.

2.   Written submissions to the panel or the Appellate Body shall be treated as confidential, but shall be made available to the parties to the dispute. Nothing in this Understanding shall preclude a party to a dispute from disclosing statements of its own positions to the public. Members shall treat as confidential information submitted by another Member to the panel or the Appellate Body which that Member has designated as confidential. A party to a dispute shall also, upon request of a Member, provide a non-confidential summary of the information contained in its written submissions that could be disclosed to the public.

Article 19 Panel and Appellate Body Recommendations

1.   Where a panel or the Appellate Body concludes that a measure is inconsistent with a covered agreement, it shall recommend that the Member concerned[9] bring the measure into conformity with that agreement.[10] In addition to its recommendations, the panel or Appellate Body may suggest ways in which the Member concerned could implement the recommendations.

2.   In accordance with paragraph 2 of Article 3, in their findings and recommendations, the panel and Appellate Body cannot add to or diminish the rights and obligations provided in the covered agreements.

Article 20 Time-Frame for DSB Decisions

Unless otherwise agreed to by the parties to the dispute, the period from the date of establishment of the panel by the DSB until the date the DSB considers the panel or appellate report for adoption shall as a general rule not exceed nine months where the panel report is not appealed or 12 months where the report is appealed. Where either the panel or the Appellate Body has acted, pursuant to paragraph 9 of Article 12 or paragraph 5 of Article 17, to extend the time for providing its report, the additional time taken shall be added to the above periods.

Article 21 Surveillance of Implementation of Recommendations and Rulings

1.   Prompt compliance with recommendations or rulings of the DSB is essential in order to ensure effective resolution of disputes to the benefit of all Members.

2.   Particular attention should be paid to matters affecting the interests of developing country Members with respect to measures which have been subject to dispute settlement.

3.   At a DSB meeting held within 30 days[11] after the date of adoption of the panel or Appellate Body report, the Member concerned shall inform the DSB of its intentions in respect of implementation of the recommendations and rulings of the DSB. If it is impracticable to comply

---

8   If a meeting of the DSB is not scheduled during this period, such a meeting of the DSB shall be held for this purpose.

9   The "Member concerned" is the party to the dispute to which the panel or Appellate Body recommendations are directed.

10   With respect to recommendations in cases not involving a violation of GATT 1994 or any other covered agreement, see Article 26.

11   If a meeting of the DSB is not scheduled during this period, such a meeting of the DSB shall be held for this purpose.

immediately with the recommendations and rulings, the Member concerned shall have a reasonable period of time in which to do so. The reasonable period of time shall be:

(a) the period of time proposed by the Member concerned, provided that such period is approved by the DSB; or, in the absence of such approval,

(b) a period of time mutually agreed by the parties to the dispute within 45 days after the date of adoption of the recommendations and rulings; or, in the absence of such agreement,

(c) a period of time determined through binding arbitration within 90 days after the date of adoption of the recommendations and rulings.[12] In such arbitration, a guideline for the arbitrator[13] should be that the reasonable period of time to implement panel or Appellate Body recommendations should not exceed 15 months from the date of adoption of a panel or Appellate Body report. However, that time may be shorter or longer, depending upon the particular circumstances.

4.   Except where the panel or the Appellate Body has extended, pursuant to paragraph 9 of Article 12 or paragraph 5 of Article 17, the time of providing its report, the period from the date of establishment of the panel by the DSB until the date of determination of the reasonable period of time shall not exceed 15 months unless the parties to the dispute agree otherwise. Where either the panel or the Appellate Body has acted to extend the time of providing its report, the additional time taken shall be added to the 15-month period; provided that unless the parties to the dispute agree that there are exceptional circumstances, the total time shall not exceed 18 months.

5.   Where there is disagreement as to the existence or consistency with a covered agreement of measures taken to comply with the recommendations and rulings such dispute shall be decided through recourse to these dispute settlement procedures, including wherever possible resort to the original panel. The panel shall circulate its report within 90 days after the date of referral of the matter to it. When the panel considers that it cannot provide its report within this time frame, it shall inform the DSB in writing of the reasons for the delay together with an estimate of the period within which it will submit its report.

6.   The DSB shall keep under surveillance the implementation of adopted recommendations or rulings. The issue of implementation of the recommendations or rulings may be raised at the DSB by any Member at any time following their adoption. Unless the DSB decides otherwise, the issue of implementation of the recommendations or rulings shall be placed on the agenda of the DSB meeting after six months following the date of establishment of the reasonable period of time pursuant to paragraph 3 and shall remain on the DSB's agenda until the issue is resolved. At least 10 days prior to each such DSB meeting, the Member concerned shall provide the DSB with a status report in writing of its progress in the implementation of the recommendations or rulings.

7.   If the matter is one which has been raised by a developing country Member, the DSB shall consider what further action it might take which would be appropriate to the circumstances.

8.   If the case is one brought by a developing country Member, in considering what appropriate action might be taken, the DSB shall take into account not only the trade coverage of measures complained of, but also their impact on the economy of developing country Members concerned.

Article 22 Compensation and the Suspension of Concessions

1.   Compensation and the suspension of concessions or other obligations are temporary measures available in the event that the recommendations and rulings are not implemented within a reasonable period of time. However, neither compensation nor the suspension of con-

---

12   If the parties cannot agree on an arbitrator within ten days after referring the matter to arbitration, the arbitrator shall be appointed by the Director-General within ten days, after consulting the parties.

13   The expression "arbitrator" shall be interpreted as referring either to an individual or a group.

cessions or other obligations is preferred to full implementation of a recommendation to bring a measure into conformity with the covered agreements. Compensation is voluntary and, if granted, shall be consistent with the covered agreements.

2. If the Member concerned fails to bring the measure found to be inconsistent with a covered agreement into compliance therewith or otherwise comply with the recommendations and rulings within the reasonable period of time determined pursuant to paragraph 3 of Article 21, such Member shall, if so requested, and no later than the expiry of the reasonable period of time, enter into negotiations with any party having invoked the dispute settlement procedures, with a view to developing mutually acceptable compensation. If no satisfactory compensation has been agreed within 20 days after the date of expiry of the reasonable period of time, any party having invoked the dispute settlement procedures may request authorization from the DSB to suspend the application to the Member concerned of concessions or other obligations under the covered agreements.

3. In considering what concessions or other obligations to suspend, the complaining party shall apply the following principles and procedures:

(a) the general principle is that the complaining party should first seek to suspend concessions or other obligations with respect to the same sector(s) as that in which the panel or Appellate Body has found a violation or other nullification or impairment;

(b) if that party considers that it is not practicable or effective to suspend concessions or other obligations with respect to the same sector(s), it may seek to suspend concessions or other obligations in other sectors under the same agreement;

(c) if that party considers that it is not practicable or effective to suspend concessions or other obligations with respect to other sectors under the same agreement, and that the circumstances are serious enough, it may seek to suspend concessions or other obligations under another covered agreement;

(d) in applying the above principles, that party shall take into account:

   (i) the trade in the sector or under the agreement under which the panel or Appellate Body has found a violation or other nullification or impairment, and the importance of such trade to that party;

   (ii) the broader economic elements related to the nullification or impairment and the broader economic consequences of the suspension of concessions or other obligations;

(e) if that party decides to request authorization to suspend concessions or other obligations pursuant to subparagraphs (b) or (c), it shall state the reasons therefor in its request. At the same time as the request is forwarded to the DSB, it also shall be forwarded to the relevant Councils and also, in the case of a request pursuant to subparagraph (b), the relevant sectoral bodies;

(f) for purposes of this paragraph, "sector" means:

   (i) with respect to goods, all goods;

   (ii) with respect to services, a principal sector as identified in the current "Services Sectoral Classification List" which identifies such sectors;[14]

   (iii) with respect to trade-related intellectual property rights, each of the categories of intellectual property rights covered in Section 1, or Section 2, or Section 3, or Section 4, or Section 5, or Section 6, or Section 7 of Part II, or the obligations under Part III, or Part IV of the Agreement on TRIPS;

---

14   The list in document MTN.GNS/W/120 identifies eleven sectors.

(g) for purposes of this paragraph, "agreement" means:

   (i)   with respect to goods, the agreements listed in Annex 1A of the WTO Agreement, taken as a whole as well as the Plurilateral Trade Agreements in so far as the relevant parties to the dispute are parties to these agreements;

   (ii) with respect to services, the GATS;

   (iii) with respect to intellectual property rights, the Agreement on TRIPS.

4.   The level of the suspension of concessions or other obligations authorized by the DSB shall be equivalent to the level of the nullification or impairment.

5.   The DSB shall not authorize suspension of concessions or other obligations if a covered agreement prohibits such suspension.

6.   When the situation described in paragraph 2 occurs, the DSB, upon request, shall grant authorization to suspend concessions or other obligations within 30 days of the expiry of the reasonable period of time unless the DSB decides by consensus to reject the request. However, if the Member concerned objects to the level of suspension proposed, or claims that the principles and procedures set forth in paragraph 3 have not been followed where a complaining party has requested authorization to suspend concessions or other obligations pursuant to paragraph 3(b) or (c), the matter shall be referred to arbitration. Such arbitration shall be carried out by the original panel, if members are available, or by an arbitrator[15] appointed by the Director-General and shall be completed within 60 days after the date of expiry of the reasonable period of time. Concessions or other obligations shall not be suspended during the course of the arbitration.

7.   The arbitrator[16] acting pursuant to paragraph 6 shall not examine the nature of the concessions or other obligations to be suspended but shall determine whether the level of such suspension is equivalent to the level of nullification or impairment. The arbitrator may also determine if the proposed suspension of concessions or other obligations is allowed under the covered agreement. However, if the matter referred to arbitration includes a claim that the principles and procedures set forth in paragraph 3 have not been followed, the arbitrator shall examine that claim. In the event the arbitrator determines that those principles and procedures have not been followed, the complaining party shall apply them consistent with paragraph 3. The parties shall accept the arbitrator's decision as final and the parties concerned shall not seek a second arbitration. The DSB shall be informed promptly of the decision of the arbitrator and shall upon request, grant authorization to suspend concessions or other obligations where the request is consistent with the decision of the arbitrator, unless the DSB decides by consensus to reject the request.

8.   The suspension of concessions or other obligations shall be temporary and shall only be applied until such time as the measure found to be inconsistent with a covered agreement has been removed, or the Member that must implement recommendations or rulings provides a solution to the nullification or impairment of benefits, or a mutually satisfactory solution is reached. In accordance with paragraph 6 of Article 21, the DSB shall continue to keep under surveillance the implementation of adopted recommendations or rulings, including those cases where compensation has been provided or concessions or other obligations have been suspended but the recommendations to bring a measure into conformity with the covered agreements have not been implemented.

9.   The dispute settlement provisions of the covered agreements may be invoked in respect of measures affecting their observance taken by regional or local governments or authorities within the territory of a Member. When the DSB has ruled that a provision of a covered agreement has not been observed, the responsible Member shall take such reasonable measures as may be

---

15   The expression "arbitrator" shall be interpreted as referring either to an individual or a group.
16   The expression "arbitrator" shall be interpreted as referring either to an individual or a group or to the members of the original panel when serving in the capacity of arbitrator.

available to it to ensure its observance. The provisions of the covered agreements and this Understanding relating to compensation and suspension of concessions or other obligations apply in cases where it has not been possible to secure such observance.[17]

Article 23 Strengthening of the Multilateral System

1. When Members seek the redress of a violation of obligations or other nullification or impairment of benefits under the covered agreements or an impediment to the attainment of any objective of the covered agreements, they shall have recourse to, and abide by, the rules and procedures of this Understanding.

2. In such cases, Members shall:

(a) not make a determination to the effect that a violation has occurred, that benefits have been nullified or impaired or that the attainment of any objective of the covered agreements has been impeded, except through recourse to dispute settlement in accordance with the rules and procedures of this Understanding, and shall make any such determination consistent with the findings contained in the panel or Appellate Body report adopted by the DSB or an arbitration award rendered under this Understanding;

(b) follow the procedures set forth in Article 21 to determine the reasonable period of time for the Member concerned to implement the recommendations and rulings; and

(c) follow the procedures set forth in Article 22 to determine the level of suspension of concessions or other obligations and obtain DSB authorization in accordance with those procedures before suspending concessions or other obligations under the covered agreements in response to the failure of the Member concerned to implement the recommendations and rulings within that reasonable period of time.

Article 24 Special Procedures Involving Least-Developed Country Members

1. At all stages of the determination of the causes of a dispute and of dispute settlement procedures involving a least-developed country Member, particular consideration shall be given to the special situation of least-developed country Members. In this regard, Members shall exercise due restraint in raising matters under these procedures involving a least-developed country Member. If nullification or impairment is found to result from a measure taken by a least-developed country Member, complaining parties shall exercise due restraint in asking for compensation or seeking authorization to suspend the application of concessions or other obligations pursuant to these procedures.

2. In dispute settlement cases involving a least-developed country Member, where a satisfactory solution has not been found in the course of consultations the Director-General or the Chairman of the DSB shall, upon request by a least-developed country Member offer their good offices, conciliation and mediation with a view to assisting the parties to settle the dispute, before a request for a panel is made. The Director-General or the Chairman of the DSB, in providing the above assistance, may consult any source which either deems appropriate.

Article 25 Arbitration

1. Expeditious arbitration within the WTO as an alternative means of dispute settlement can facilitate the solution of certain disputes that concern issues that are clearly defined by both parties.

2. Except as otherwise provided in this Understanding, resort to arbitration shall be subject to mutual agreement of the parties which shall agree on the procedures to be followed. Agreements to resort to arbitration shall be notified to all Members sufficiently in advance of the actual commencement of the arbitration process.

---

17 Where the provisions of any covered agreement concerning measures taken by regional or local governments or authorities within the territory of a Member contain provisions different from the provisions of this paragraph, the provisions of such covered agreement shall prevail.

3.   Other Members may become party to an arbitration proceeding only upon the agreement of the parties which have agreed to have recourse to arbitration. The parties to the proceeding shall agree to abide by the arbitration award. Arbitration awards shall be notified to the DSB and the Council or Committee of any relevant agreement where any Member may raise any point relating thereto.

4.   Articles 21 and 22 of this Understanding shall apply *mutatis mutandis* to arbitration awards.

Article 26
1. Non-Violation Complaints of the Type Described in Paragraph 1(b) of Article XXIII of GATT 1994

Where the provisions of paragraph 1(b) of Article XXIII of GATT 1994 are applicable to a covered agreement, a panel or the Appellate Body may only make rulings and recommendations where a party to the dispute considers that any benefit accruing to it directly or indirectly under the relevant covered agreement is being nullified or impaired or the attainment of any objective of that Agreement is being impeded as a result of the application by a Member of any measure, whether or not it conflicts with the provisions of that Agreement. Where and to the extent that such party considers and a panel or the Appellate Body determines that a case concerns a measure that does not conflict with the provisions of a covered agreement to which the provisions of paragraph 1(b) of Article XXIII of GATT 1994 are applicable, the procedures in this Understanding shall apply, subject to the following:

(a)   the complaining party shall present a detailed justification in support of any complaint relating to a measure which does not conflict with the relevant covered agreement;

(b)   where a measure has been found to nullify or impair benefits under, or impede the attainment of objectives, of the relevant covered agreement without violation thereof, there is no obligation to withdraw the measure. However, in such cases, the panel or the Appellate Body shall recommend that the Member concerned make a mutually satisfactory adjustment;

(c)   notwithstanding the provisions of Article 21, the arbitration provided for in paragraph 3 of Article 21, upon request of either party, may include a determination of the level of benefits which have been nullified or impaired, and may also suggest ways and means of reaching a mutually satisfactory adjustment; such suggestions shall not be binding upon the parties to the dispute;

(d)   notwithstanding the provisions of paragraph 1 of Article 22, compensation may be part of a mutually satisfactory adjustment as final settlement of the dispute.

2. Complaints of the Type Described in Paragraph 1(c) of Article XXIII of GATT 1994

Where the provisions of paragraph 1(c) of Article XXIII of GATT 1994 are applicable to a covered agreement, a panel may only make rulings and recommendations where a party considers that any benefit accruing to it directly or indirectly under the relevant covered agreement is being nullified or impaired or the attainment of any objective of that Agreement is being impeded as a result of the existence of any situation other than those to which the provisions of paragraphs 1(a) and 1(b) of Article XXIII of GATT 1994 are applicable. Where and to the extent that such party considers and a panel determines that the matter is covered by this paragraph, the procedures of this Understanding shall apply only up to and including the point in the proceedings where the panel report has been circulated to the Members. The dispute settlement rules and procedures contained in the Decision of 12 April 1989 (BISD 36S/61-67) shall apply to consideration for adoption, and surveillance and implementation of recommendations and rulings. The following shall also apply:

(a)   the complaining party shall present a detailed justification in support of any argument made with respect to issues covered under this paragraph;

(b)   in cases involving matters covered by this paragraph, if a panel finds that cases also involve dispute settlement matters other than those covered by this paragraph, the panel shall circulate a report to the DSB addressing any such matters and a separate report on matters falling under this paragraph.

Article 27 Responsibilities of the Secretariat

1.   The Secretariat shall have the responsibility of assisting panels, especially on the legal, historical and procedural aspects of the matters dealt with, and of providing secretarial and technical support.

2.   While the Secretariat assists Members in respect of dispute settlement at their request, there may also be a need to provide additional legal advice and assistance in respect of dispute settle-ment to developing country Members. To this end, the Secretariat shall make available a qualified legal expert from the WTO technical cooperation services to any developing country Member which so requests. This expert shall assist the developing country Member in a manner ensuring the continued impartiality of the Secretariat.

3.   The Secretariat shall conduct special training courses for interested Members concerning these dispute settlement procedures and practices so as to enable Members' experts to be better informed in this regard.

APPENDIX 1 – AGREEMENTS COVERED BY THE UNDERSTANDING

(A)   Agreement Establishing the World Trade Organization

(B)   Multilateral Trade Agreements

    Annex 1A: Multilateral Agreements on Trade in Goods

    Annex 1B: General Agreement on Trade in Services

    Annex 1C: Agreement on Trade-Related Aspects of Intellectual Property Rights

    Annex 2:   Understanding on Rules and Procedures Governing the Settlement of Disputes

(C)   Plurilateral Trade Agreements

    Annex 4:   Agreement on Trade in Civil Aircraft

             Agreement on Government Procurement

             International Dairy Agreement

             International Bovine Meat Agreement

The applicability of this Understanding to the Plurilateral Trade Agreements shall be subject to the adoption of a decision by the parties to each agreement setting out the terms for the application of the Understanding to the individual agreement, including any special or additional rules or procedures for inclusion in Appendix 2, as notified to the DSB.

APPENDIX 2 – SPECIAL OR ADDITIONAL RULES AND PROCEDURES CONTAINED IN THE COVERED AGREEMENTS

Agreement Rules and Procedures

Agreement	Rules and Procedures
Agreement on the Application of Sanitary and Phytosanitary Measures	11.2
Agreement on Textiles and Clothing	[no longer in force]
Agreement on Technical Barriers to Trade	14.2 through 14.4, Annex 2
Agreement on Implementation of Article VI of GATT 1994	17.4 through 17.7
Agreement on Implementation of Article VII of GATT 1994	19.3 through 19.5, Annex II.2(f), 3, 9, 21

Agreement on Subsidies and Countervailing Measures	4.2 through 4.12, 6.6,
	7.2 through 7.10, 8.5,
	footnote 35, 24.4, 27.7, Annex V
General Agreement on Trade in Services	XXII:3, XXIII:3
Annex on Financial Services	4
Annex on Air Transport Services	4
Decision on Certain Dispute Settlement Procedures for the GATS	1 through 5

The list of rules and procedures in this Appendix includes provisions where only a part of the provision may be relevant in this context.

Any special or additional rules or procedures in the Plurilateral Trade Agreements as determined by the competent bodies of each agreement and as notified to the DSB.

APPENDIX 3 – WORKING PROCEDURES

1.   In its proceedings the panel shall follow the relevant provisions of this Understanding. In addition, the following working procedures shall apply.

2.   The panel shall meet in closed session. The parties to the dispute, and interested parties, shall be present at the meetings only when invited by the panel to appear before it.

3.   The deliberations of the panel and the documents submitted to it shall be kept confidential. Nothing in this Understanding shall preclude a party to a dispute from disclosing statements of its own positions to the public. Members shall treat as confidential information submitted by another Member to the panel which that Member has designated as confidential. Where a party to a dispute submits a confidential version of its written submissions to the panel, it shall also, upon request of a Member, provide a non-confidential summary of the information contained in its submissions that could be disclosed to the public.

4.   Before the first substantive meeting of the panel with the parties, the parties to the dispute shall transmit to the panel written submissions in which they present the facts of the case and their arguments.

5.   At its first substantive meeting with the parties, the panel shall ask the party which has brought the complaint to present its case. Subsequently, and still at the same meeting, the party against which the complaint has been brought shall be asked to present its point of view.

6.   All third parties which have notified their interest in the dispute to the DSB shall be invited in writing to present their views during a session of the first substantive meeting of the panel set aside for that purpose. All such third parties may be present during the entirety of this session.

7.   Formal rebuttals shall be made at a second substantive meeting of the panel. The party complained against shall have the right to take the floor first to be followed by the complaining party. The parties shall submit, prior to that meeting, written rebuttals to the panel.

8.   The panel may at any time put questions to the parties and ask them for explanations either in the course of a meeting with the parties or in writing.

9.   The parties to the dispute and any third party invited to present its views in accordance with Article 10 shall make available to the panel a written version of their oral statements.

10. In the interest of full transparency, the presentations, rebuttals and statements referred to in paragraphs 5 to 9 shall be made in the presence of the parties. Moreover, each party's written submissions, including any comments on the descriptive part of the report and responses to questions put by the panel, shall be made available to the other party or parties.

11. Any additional procedures specific to the panel.

12. Proposed timetable for panel work:

(a) Receipt of first written submissions of the parties:

    (1) complaining Party: _____ 3-6 weeks

    (2) Party complained against: _____ 2-3 weeks

(b) Date, time and place of first substantive meeting with the parties; third party session: _____ 1-2 weeks

(c) Receipt of written rebuttals of the parties: _____ 2-3 weeks

(d) Date, time and place of second substantive meeting with the parties: _____ 1-2 weeks

(e) Issuance of descriptive part of the report to the parties: _____ 2-4 weeks

(f) Receipt of comments by the parties on the descriptive part of the report: _____ 2 weeks

(g) Issuance of the interim report, including the findings and conclusions, to the parties: _____ 2-4 weeks

(h) Deadline for party to request review of part(s) of report: _____ 1 week

(i) Period of review by panel, including possible additional meeting with parties: _____ 2 weeks

(j) Issuance of final report to parties to dispute: _____ 2 weeks

(k) Circulation of the final report to the Members: _____ 3 weeks

The above calendar may be changed in the light of unforeseen developments. Additional meetings with the parties shall be scheduled if required.

APPENDIX 4 – EXPERT REVIEW GROUPS

The following rules and procedures shall apply to expert review groups established in accordance with the provisions of paragraph 2 of Article 13.

1.   Expert review groups are under the panel's authority. Their terms of reference and detailed working procedures shall be decided by the panel, and they shall report to the panel.

2.   Participation in expert review groups shall be restricted to persons of professional standing and experience in the field in question.

3.   Citizens of parties to the dispute shall not serve on an expert review group without the joint agreement of the parties to the dispute, except in exceptional circumstances when the panel considers that the need for specialized scientific expertise cannot be fulfilled otherwise. Government officials of parties to the dispute shall not serve on an expert review group. Members of expert review groups shall serve in their individual capacities and not as government representatives, nor as representatives of any organization. Governments or organizations shall therefore not give them instructions with regard to matters before an expert review group.

4.   Expert review groups may consult and seek information and technical advice from any source they deem appropriate. Before an expert review group seeks such information or advice from a source within the jurisdiction of a Member, it shall inform the government of that Member. Any Member shall respond promptly and fully to any request by an expert review group for such information as the expert review group considers necessary and appropriate.

5.   The parties to a dispute shall have access to all relevant information provided to an expert review group, unless it is of a confidential nature. Confidential information provi

ded to the expert review group shall not be released without formal authorization from the government, organization or person providing the information. Where such information is requested from the expert review group but release of such information by the expert review group is not authorized, a non-confidential summary of the information will be provided by the government, organization or person supplying the information.

6.   The expert review group shall submit a draft report to the parties to the dispute with a view to obtaining their comments, and taking them into account, as appropriate, in the final report, which shall also be issued to the parties to the dispute when it is submitted to the panel. The final report of the expert review group shall be advisory only.

Publications by the Council on International Law and Politics

International Business and Trade Law:

Talia Einhorn & Frank Emmert: International Business Transactions – Documents, 2nd rev. ed., Chicago 2013, ISBN 978-0985815622

Joseph E. Miller: Changing Our Approach to Changing the World – Encouraging and Enhancing American Engagement in International Philanthropy Through Tax Law Reform, Chicago 2013, ISBN 978-0985815639

Frank Emmert (ed.): Corporate Social Responsibility in Comparative Perspective, Chicago 2014, ISBN 978-0985815646

Frank Emmert (ed.): World Trade and Investment Law – Documents, Indianapolis 2018, ISBN 978-0-9858156-7-7

Csongor István Nagy (ed.), Investment Arbitration and National Interest, Indianapolis 2019, ISBN 978-0-9858156-8-4

Islamic Law Library:

Ahmed M. El Demery: The Arab Charter of Human Rights – A Voice for Sharia in the Modern World, with a Foreword by Prof. M. Cherif Bassiouni, Chicago 2015, ISBN 978-0985815653

Ahmed A. Altawyan: International Commercial Arbitration in Saudi Arabia, Indianapolis 2018, ISBN 978-0-9858156-9-1

Rakan F. Alharbi: The Development of Saudi Women's Rights – Theory, Practice, Challenges, and Solutions – a Critical and Analytical Study of the Impact of Cultural Norms on the Recognition of Women's Rights of Employment and Freedom of Movement, Indianapolis 2019 (forthcoming)

Mohammad M. Bayoumi Ibrahim: Women's Rights Under International, American, Islamic and Egyptian Law: An Irresolvable Conflict?, Indianapolis 2019 (forthcoming)

All publications of the Council on International Law and Politics are available on Amazon and from leading booksellers. Bulk orders for more than 5 copies at discounted prices can be sent directly to the Council on International Law and Politics via its website at http://www.cilpnet.com.